CHRISTIANITY IS AT WAR: THE MANIFESTO FOR CHRISTIAN MILITANCY

The Faith begins with warfare at the Holy Cross and it will triumph through warfare with the Final Crusade at Armageddon—between Christendom, headed by our Lord Jesus Christ victorious over the revived Ottoman Empire under the Antichrist

✝

by Theodore Shoebat

Copyright © 2016 Top Executive Media

All rights reserved

No part of this book may be used or reproduced in any manner whatsoever without written permission except in the case of brief quotations embodied in critical articles or reviews.

For information, please email the author at shoebat.com

ISBN: 978-0-982567-9-4-4

1st Edition

Printed in the United States

TABLE OF CONTENTS

FOREWORD xvi
PREFACE xix
PART 1, *In Holy War, the Christian Becomes an Instrument for God's Justice* 1
    What Is Holy War? 1
    The Beginning Of Wisdom Is To Hate Evil 2
    Holy War And The Divine Union With God 2
    Theosis—The Requisite For Holy War 3
    The Warrior Fights For The Law Of God 5
    The Christian Warrior Fights For The Holy Trinity 8
PART 2, *Holy War Has Always Been an Innate Part of the Christian Faith* 11
    The Founding Of Holy War 11
    The Soldiers Of The New Testament Teach Us Holy War 12
    The Righteous Soldiers Of The New Testament Foreshadow The Armies Of Christendom 13
    St. Paul And The Righteous Centurion On The Ship—An Image Of Christendom 14
    Longinus—The Transforming Of The Pagan Armies Into Christian Armies 16
    The Centurion Of Capernaum—The Image Of The Knight Of Christ 16
    The Soldiers Who Came To John The Baptist—Symbol Of The Church's Authority Over The Military 17
    Cornelius The Centurion—The Model For The Christian
    Army, And The Foreshadower Of Gentile Soldiers 18
    The First Soldiers After The New Testament 20
    The Thundering Legion 21
    Christian Soldiers In Archaeology 21
    Ancient Christian Theologians Who Supported Righteous Killing 23
    Clement Of Rome 23
    St. Irenaeus Of Lyons 24
    Tertullian 24
    Clement Of Alexandria 27
    Julius Africanus 28
    Origen 29
    Adamantius 30
    Lactantius 31
PART 3, *Christian Warfare First Took Place Within the First Century* 33
    The First Christian King And The First Christian Battle Happened In The First Century 33
    The Armenians—Amongst The First Of Holy Warriors 35
    Christianity's First Major War 36
    The Christians Choose Life, And Die In Christ 37
    Martyrdom Is Chosen Over An Easy Life 37
    The Stubborn Christians 39
    The Earth Weeps 41
    The Heathen Tyrant's Rage 42
    The Tyrants Use False Peace 43
    Plagues And Famine 44
    The Death Of The Tyrant And The Rise Of A New One 45
    The Cross Is Carried 47
    The Second War With The Pagans 49
    Holy War Is Declared 50
    The Battle Begins 51
    Christendom Defeats The Pagan Germans 53

CHRISTIANITY IS AT WAR: THE MANIFESTO FOR CHRISTIAN MILITANCY

The Battle Of Gargano... 54
Christendom's War Against Persia—The First Christian Crusades: The Evils Of The Persian Religion...... 54
Constantine Aids The Christians Against Persian Persecution 56
The Persians Try To Invade Rome.. 57
Christendom's War With Persia... 57
Persian Persecution Of Christians 61
Armenia Becomes A Christian Nation, And An Enemy Of The Pagan Persians 62
The Slaughter And War Of The Armenians Begin 63
The Vardanians 64
The Vahanians 68
Vahan The Wolf.. 75
Heraclius And The Squashing Of Persian Heathenism 76

PART 4, *Mercy And Justice*... 80
The Modern Christian Has No Balance Between Mercy And Justice 80
Mercy And Justice In The Church 86
Holy War Destroys False Peace And Brings True Peace 91
Wars Must Have A Cause.. 93

PART 5, *The Cross And War*.. 94
The Christian Warrior Is Superior To All Warriors 94
The Forgotten Christian Samurai.. 97
To Die Is To Live 99
Holy War Is The Emulation Of Christ 100
The Christian Warrior Is Unconquerable... 100
Holy War—The Greatest Expression Of Love 101
Christian Warriors Participate In The Crucifixion Of Christ 103
The Cross Is The Image Of War 105
The Cross Dispels The Fear Of Death.. 110
Holy Combat Is Unity With Christ... 112
The Christian Soldier Is Moved By Virtue 114
The Christian Soldier Is An Enemy Of The World 115
Martyrdom Is Salvation 116
Christians Carry The Cross As A Nation, Not Just As Individuals 118
The Warriors Persevere For God And For Christendom... 119
The Selfless Warrior 119
Through Suffering We Have Liberation 121
The Soldiers Of Christendom Follow God To The Death... 122
The Christian Soldier Does Not Live By The Flesh, But By The Spirit.............................. 122
Valiancy Is A Sacrifice 123
Christ—The Ultimate Warrior And The Culmination Of All Biblical Warriors.................. 124
Christ's Thirst On The Cross: The Selfless Spirit Of The Warrior.................................... 134
The Suffering Of The Christian Militant 136
The Thief On The Cross—An Illustration Of A Warrior 139
The Beatitudes—Precepts Of The Knight... 140
The Cross Makes No Sense To Earthly Eyes.. 142

PART 6, *The Church Rules the Nations* 144
Peter Walking On Water Is A Symbol Of The Church Ruling The Nations........................ 151
The Two Swords Of St. Peter.. 152
The Sword Of St. Peter Still Lies In The Church 154
St. Peter—Fortress Of The Church.. 155
Christendom: Where The Nations Strive To Destroy Evil, Not For Secularism, But For God............... 158
The Story Of The Woman At The Well And Its Connection To Christendom 161
David And Abimelech: An Image Of The Church Giving The Sword To The State 161

TABLE OF CONTENTS

The Two Swords In The Old Testament 163
Elisha And Jehu 163
Hilkia The Priest. 163
Azariah And King Asa—Another Example Of The Church Having The State Advance The Law Of God. . . . 165
Jehu And Jehosophat. 166
Elijah And Jehoram. 167
Samuel And Saul 168
David And The Priest Abimelech 168
The Priest And The Knight: The Foundation Of All Christendom. 169
Cornelius And Peter: The Knight And The Priest. 170
The Political Authority Of The Church Comes From Israel 170
Both King David And St. Peter Are Referred To As Shepherds 172
In Christendom, The Church Conveys Morality To The Society 175
In Christianity, The Church And The State Work Together 176
The King Saves His Own Soul By Advancing Christianity 178
The State Must Obey The Church In Spiritual Matters 180
All Holy Wars Are Done For A Spiritual Good 185
The Church Can Punish Rulers For Promoting Heresy And Deviancy 186
The Church Can Cause Revolts Against Corrupt And Evil States 187
Moral Anarchy Is Due To The Absence Of The Church's Authority Over The State 188
The Church Can Overthrow Heretical Leaders, Or Rulers Who Tolerate Heresies 190
Statements From Numerous Theologians Of Christendom On The Church's Power Over The State 191
The Two Swords Of St. Peter, As Carried Out In Christendom 196
Separation Of Church And State. 203
The Church Has The Right To Rebel If The State Intrudes Upon It 207
The Church Is Not To Give The State Orders That Do Not Pertain To Spiritual Matters 207

PART 7, *Priests And War* 209
The Priests' Involvement In Wars In Ancient Israel 209
The Priests' Influence In War 212
Priests Can Lead Soldiers To Fight Tyranny 213
The Priestly Involvement In War Continued In The Church 214
Constantine And His Tabernacle 215
The Emperor Theodosius And John Of Egypt 215
The General Petronas And John The Monk 216
The Emperor Alexius I And The Priest 217
Pope Leo IV And The Armies Of Italy. 217
Pope Innocent III And The Involvement Of The Priests In The Crusades. 218
On Warrior Monks 218
The Christian Knight And The Monastic Spirit 220
Cornelius The Centurion—Patriarch Of Monastic Warriors 221
The Idea Of The Warrior Monk Began In Israel 223
Warrior Monks In Christendom's Armies 224
On Christian Militias. 226

PART 8, *Dealing With Objections Against Christian Government* 230
The Law Of Moses Is Not Tyrannical, Rather It Prevents Tyranny. 230
A Vindication For Moses' Slaughtering Of The Three-Thousand For The Worship Of The Golden Calf 231
Hatred For Holy War And Christian Militancy Came From Protestant Reformers Like Luther 236
The Hatred For Christian Holy War And For Christendom Is Gnostic 241
Christian Kings Are God's Instruments For His Wrath 241
"Christ Never Launched Wars!" 242
Turn The Other Cheek 246
"Love Your Enemies" 249

CHRISTIANITY IS AT WAR: THE MANIFESTO FOR CHRISTIAN MILITANCY

Whoever Lives By The Sword Dies By The Sword. 249
"Flee Into The Mountains". 252
The Order Of Christ Demands For Capital Punishment
Against Evil Doers, And For Christian Government 252
Christ Demands For The Financial Funding Of Wars 256
Christ Is The General Of Christian Soldiers 257
The Spiritual Teachings Of Christ Are Applied To Holy War 258
The Christian Does Not Fight For Himself, But For God. 260
Holy War Is Not Done For Gain, But For God's Law And Justice 261
Vengeance Is Mine Saith The Lord 262
"We Do Not Wrestle Against Flesh And Blood" 265
The Armor Of God. 265
The Soldiers Who Protected Paul 267
King David Used Physical Arms, But At The Same Time Had Spiritual Armor 268
Joshua Did Not Fight Against Flesh And Blood When He Slaughtered The Canaanites 277
Gideon's Spiritual Armor 280
Hezekiah's Spiritual War 280
Nehemiah's Spiritual Sword 281
Abijah's Spiritual War 281
God Led Battles In Christendom 283

PART 9, *In Defense Of Christian Supremacy And Intolerance* 284
Against Religious Liberty 287
Heresy Must Be Destroyed. 288
"You Do Not Know What Manner Of Spirit You Are Of" 294
The Wheats And The Tares 295
Christ Himself Did Not Believe In Toleration 297
The Parable Of The Great Supper 298
Jesus Christ Believed In The Destruction Of False Religion 299
It Is Better For Heretics And Other Corrupters To Drown Than To Live 300
"You Are The Salt Of The Earth". 301
Christ Will Destroy All False Religions In His Return 301
"I Don't See The Apostles Enforcing Religion" 302
St. Paul Supported The Use Of The Sword By Both State And Soldier 310
Religious Tolerance And Equality Are Enemies To The Faith 313
The Heretics Of Oreleans 319
Arnold Of Brescia 320
The Shepherds 322
Intolerance Of False Religions And Ideas Continued On Through The Church 324
The Lack Of Suppressing Paganism
The Use Of Fear To Destroy Evil Is Not Wrong 345
Persecution Against Evil Is Good 346
In Defense Of Book Burning 348
The Christian King Serves God By Uprooting Evil 350
The Apostles Did Not Want Laws Based On Paganism, But Christianity 351
The Kings Of The Old Testament Are To Be Our Models 354
In Defense Of The Christian State 356
Christianity Is For Christendom And Not Anarchy 358
True Liberty Is To Follow The Law Of God 360
Christ Demands Justice Against Evil. 361
The New Covenant Is For Salvation, The Old Covenant Is For Government 362
Law Is Not Made For Private Pleasure, But For The Public Good 363
Homosexuals Cannot Be Considered As Part Of Civilized Society 366

TABLE OF CONTENTS

How To Determine Whether Or Not A Certain Action Is Dangerous 366
Evil Should Never Be Given Freedom 367
Religious Equality And Liberty Are Unnatural 370
Jews Are Never To Be Persecuted In The Christian State 370
In Defense Of Witch Burning 371

PART 10, *The Christian Spirit And War* 382
The Warrior Nature Of God 382
True Love Is Warfare 384
To Fight Evil Is To Participate In God 388
Christ's Death Was A War Done For Love 391
To Know That Christ Lives Is What Strengthens The Warriors 394
Zeal Is The Source Of All Christian Ferocity 395
To Fight For God Is A Sacrifice To God 397
Saints And War 398
The Ark Of The Covenant Was Brought To Israel's Wars,
And Statues Of Mary Were Brought To Christendom's Wars 403

PART 11, *The War Between Christendom And Babel* 406
Babel -- The First Mecca 407
Sumerian History Believed That Not All People Lived In Shinar 411
Idolatry Originated In Arabia, And Not Babylon 415
Mesopotamia, To The Ancients, Was A Part Of Arabia 422
Allah Was Worshipped In Shinar At The Time Of The Building 423
The Idea Of Unifying Societies Under A Temple Tower Was Already In Ancient Arabia 428
That Allah Was One Of The Gods Dedicated To The Tower Of Babel 430
Jesus Christ—Triumphant King Over Babel 433
Arabian Paganism Is Inherently Hateful Of Christianity 437

PART 12, *Islam: The Greatest Of All Heresies* 440
Islam And Nestorianism 443
Islam, A Judaizing Heresy 445
Islam And The Iconoclasts A Reflection On Icons 447
Islam Is Iconoclasm 450
The Power And Tyranny Of Iconoclasm In The Byzantine Empire 451
The Tyranny Of The Iconoclast Emperor, Theophilos 453
Theophanes And Theodore—Martyrs Against Iconoclasm 455
The Slandered Versus The Harlot 458
Constantine V And His Islamic Parallels 458
The Despotism Of Leo III And The Iconoclasm Of Islam 459
Islam And Manichaeanism 460
Arabia: The Originator Of The Manichaean Heresy 461
The Heretical Teachings Of Mani 463
The Massalian Gnostics 467
The Paulician Gnostics 468
The Bogomils 471
The Cathars 475
The Cathars Strike 480
The Cathars Are Destroyed 484
Islam Was Not Founded By Muhammad, But By A Fourth Century Heretic Named Arius 493
Arianism's Founding 495
Arianism Spreads Like Wildfire 496
The Council Of Nicea 498
The Arians Strike Back 500
Constantine Attacks Arianism 502

CHRISTIANITY IS AT WAR: THE MANIFESTO FOR CHRISTIAN MILITANCY

Arianism Infiltrates The Roman Government 503
The Now Arian Government Commences Tyranny Over The Christians 504
The Arians Create Their Own Council To Destroy The Nicene Creed 506
The Arians Conspire To Murder St. Athanasius, But The
Christians Pick Up Their Swords And Fight The Heretics In Combat 507
The Pope Defends Orthodoxy And Combats The Arians 509
The Arian Tyrant Constantius Takes Over The
Whole Roman Empire And Unleashes An Unrestrained Persecution On The Christians 511
The Arians Make Heretical Councils To Destroy The Nicene Creed 513
The Arians Use The State To Oppress The Church, But The Christians Do Not Tolerate It,
And Pick Up Their Weapons And Fight Back 515
Unitarianism Leads To Cruelty 517
The Heretical Emperor Constantius Dies, But The Reign Of Terror Continues On 518
Basil And Gregory Combat The Heretics And Lay Down Their Lives For God 520
Pope Gelasius I Defies The Tyranny Of The Arians 521
St. Ambrose Defies The Tyranny Of The Arians 521
The Arians Unite With The Pagans To Slaughter And Opress The Christians 521
Arianism Spreads To Germany, And The German Arians
Are Far Worse In Cruelty And Barbarism 523
The German Goths Try To Conquer Constantinople 524
An Orthodox Christian Takes The Throne And Launches A Crusade Against The Heretics 525
Theodosius Strengthens The Church 526
The Arian Germans Rise Again And Try To Conquer Constantinople 527
The Arians Invade Rome 529
The Arians Invade Spain, Italy And Sicily 530
The Gothic Emperor Theodoric Unleashes A Reign Of Terror On The Christians 531
A Major Holy War Commences And The Christians Uproot Arianism Completely From Christendom ... 531
Arianism Continues Through Islam 531

PART 13, *Islam Versus Christendom* 535
Islam's Expansion 535
Islam Invades Armenia And The Christians War Against The Muslims 540
Christendom Executes A Crusade To Defend Armenia 540
The Muslims Resume Horrific Persecution On The Christians 541
The Muslims Impose Iconoclasm On The Christians And Destroy Christian Images 541
The Armenian Christians Revolt Against Muslim Tyranny 542
The Muslims Commence A Cruel And Bloody Persecution On The Armenian Christians 542
A Christian Breaks Through Fear And Slaughters The Muslims 543
The Islamic Conquest Of Christian Egypt And The Evils Of Tolerance 544
The Muslims Commence Horrific Violence Over Egypt 547
The Muslims Impose Brutal Taxes Over The Christian Church In Egypt 548
The Christians Revolt Against Muslim Rule 548
The Muslims Destroy Christian Images And Impose Antichrist Despotism On The Christians 549
The Muslims Destroy Tens Of Thousands Of Churches In Egypt 550
Muslim Mobs Rush The Christians With Demonic Rage 551
The Christian Crusaders Try To Defend Christianity In Egypt 552
The Islamic Conquest Of Christian Sudan 552
The Islamic Conquest Of Crete, And How A Heretical Monk Betrayed His People 553
Christendom Defends Crete And Fights The Muslims 554
How The Muslims Invaded Sicily By The Help Of A Heretical Christian 555
The Muslims Try To Conquer Rome, The Christians Respond With A Crusade 556
The Sultan Fools The French 557
The Greek Christians Take Up Their Swords To Defend The Sicilian Christians 559

TABLE OF CONTENTS

Muslims Again Try To Conquer Italy 560
The Christians Slaughter The Muslims In Cilicia 561
The Muslims Take Revenge 561
The Christians Strike The Muslims In Cyprus 562
The Muslims Attack The Tomb Of Christ, And The Wife Of The King Betrays Christendom 563
The Muslims Use Deception To Reconquer Antioch From Christendom 565
The Song Of Rome 566
Muhammad Commands His Followers To Conquer Rome 567
846 Ad—The Muslims Invade 567
The Christians Fight Back In A Holy War To Defend Rome 568
The Muslims Ravage Italy 569
A Hero Arises To Lead Christendom Into Battle 569
The Vengeance Of God Destroys The Muslims 570
St. Peter's Basilica Is Restored And Repaired 571
The Pope Strengthens His Brethren 571
The Successors Of Cornelius Prepare Their Souls For Combat 572
The Final Battle For Rome 572
The Battle Over Euripos 574
The Muslims Make A Surprise Attack On The Christians,
But One Christian General Leads An Army And Crushes The Islamic Enemy 574
The Muslims Try To Retake Sicily, But The Christians
Carry Up Their Cross And Fight Them With All Courage 575
A Savage Heretic Helps The Muslims Slaughter Innocent Christians 576
The Pope Declares A Major Crusade Against The Muslims 577
The Muslims Slaughter Christian Pilgrims Trying To Go To The Holy Land 578
The Rise Of The Turks And The Restoration Of Islamic Power 579
The Seljuks Strike 580
The Seljuks Attack Christendom 581
The Christians Fight The Turks With Valor To Defend Media 582
The Christian Warriors Fight To Defend Georgia From Islamic Invasion 583
The Muslims Massacre Christian Soldiers Because Christendom Is Filled With Corruption 584
A Turk Finds The Light Of Jesus Christ And Leaves The Darkness Of Islam 586
The Song Of Orduru 587
Moral And Spiritual Decay Within Christendom
Weakened The Christians And Empowered The Muslims 593
The Song Of Manzikert 594
The Nostalgia Of The Shepherd 594
The Battle Over Manzikert—The Beginning 595
The Arrows Cover The Sun 596
A Noble King Takes The Throne 598
The Sultan Rises Up And Unsheathes The Scimitar Against Christendom 599
The Sultan Forms His Military While Christendom's Soldiers Are Abused By Corrupt Politicians 600
The Emperor Fortifies His Army 601
The Eagles Of Christendom Soar Through Canyons 601
The Christians Charge Through Muslim Territory 602
The Final Tower 604
The Screams Of Warriors Are Ignored By Cowardly Soldiers 604
A Terrifying Night 605
Surrounded By Wolves 606
Two Spies In The Wilderness 606
Endless Fields Of Deserted Misery 607
A Ruthless Winter 608

CHRISTIANITY IS AT WAR: THE MANIFESTO FOR CHRISTIAN MILITANCY

The Turks Continue The Slaughter 609
The Warriors Carry Their Cross 609
The Sword Clashes With The Scimitar 610
The Christians Push Forward To Destroy The Enemy 611
A Battle On The Plain Of Babel 612
A Paradise In The Midst Of Hell 613
Thirst Brings Negligence 613
The Wolves Go On The Hunt For Christian Prey 614
Saved By Royalty 614
The Armenians Take Revenge 614
The Season For Battle Awakens 615
It Was A War Against Heresy 616
A Meadow Of Martyrs 616
A Horrible Memory 617
The Muslims Return To Manzikert 617
The Christian Armies Approach Manzikert 618
The Christians Assail The Walls 618
The Sheep Overpower The Wolves 618
The Muslims Urge For A Peace Treaty 619
The Merciless King 619
The Peace Of Cain 620
A Hopeless Battle 620
The Last Supper 620
Christ's Words Are Fulfilled 621
The Bloodbath Continues 622
The Cries Of Abel Were Amongst The Camp 623
The Grim Noise Of Silence Under The Moonless Light 623
The Lingering Wolves 624
The Fruits Of The Spirit Defeat The Slaves Of The Flesh 625
The Warriors That Never Came 625
An Unwanted Peace 625
The Christians Send A Daring Message 626
The Christians Pray To God While The Muslims Pray To The Devil 627
An Unexpected Attack 627
The Chase Is Called Off, Confusion And Chaos Strike 628
Alp Arslan Makes His Final Speech 628
A Small Group Of Christians Hold The Line 629
The Emperor Shows His Strength 629
The Sheep Flee 630
A General Without Soldiers 630
The Shepherd Fights The Wolves 631
A Prisoner Amongst Prisoners 631
In The Presence Of The Sultan 632
A Long Journey Back Home 633
A Hero Is Never Accepted, Not Even By The People He Fights For 633
Another War Commences, Not Between Christians And Heretics, But Between Christians 633
The Forsaken Hero 633
The Turks Unleash A Torrent Of Chaos On Christendom 635
The Ignored Pope 635

PART 14, *The Warriors Of Christendom Take Up The Cross* 638
The Blood Of The Saints Cry Out For Justice 638
The Monk Who Did And Did Not Just Talk 639

TABLE OF CONTENTS

The Pope Who Watched For The Flock And Did Not Flee From The Wolves 640
Jerusalem, The Heavenly City Worth Fighting For 642
The Christians Carry The Cross And Deny Themselves 643
The Crusades—An Image Of True Christian Faith 645
Christianity—Worthy Of Fighting, Killing, And Dying For....................................... 646
The Battle For Nicaea—Holy City Of Christendom 647
The Bishop Attacks 649
The Greeks Arrive 650
The Eastern Christians Thank Their Latin Brothers... 651
The Christians Fight With All Their Heart 651
The Turks Attack The Christian Camp 652
The Bishop Strikes And The Song Of Moses Is Sung By The Christians 652
The Battle For Antioch 654
The Muslims Kill A Christian Woman And The Christians Respond With The Sword Of Justice 655
The City Of God Versus The City Of Satan 656
The Christians Override Hunger For Valiancy Before An Army Of Thousands Of Muslims 657
The Christians Make The Sign Of The Cross Before The Slaves Of The Crescent 657
The Heads Of Martyrs Inflames The Zeal Of The Warriors....................................... 658
The Crusaders Fought Not A Carnal, But A Spiritual Battle 658
Forty Knights Versus Sixty Thousand Muslims 659
The Christians Berate The Muslims In A Meeting 659
The Peace Is Broken And Cain Kills His Brother... 660
The Saints Help A Muslim Convert To Christianity And He Assists The Crusaders 661
Firruz Helps The Christians Invade Antioch 662
The Cross Invades The City 663
The Muslims Return 663
The Monk Faces The General 664
The Crusaders Spiritually Prepare For Battle 664
The Bishop Preaches A Sermon 665
The Sons Of The Cross Collide With The Slaves Of Muhammad.................................... 666
The Armies Of Heaven Join The Militants 666
The Crusaders Send A Letter To The Pope Telling Him About Their Victory 669
The Conquest Of Jerusalem 669
The Western And Eastern Christians Join Together To Worship God 670
The Crusaders Visit Bethlehem 670
The Crusaders Visit The Land Where Joshua Defeated The Canaanites 670
The Christians Defeat The Muslims In Ramlah.. 671
12,000 Christian Enter Jerusalem And Fight 60,000 Muslims 671
The Unknown Knight... 671
The Christians Break Into The City 672
A True Christian Would Have Wanted Jerusalem Conquered 674
The Muslims Try To Retake Jerusalem 674
The Crusade Of 1101.. 676
One Knight Dedicates His Whole Life To The Holy 677
The Christians Invade Egypt 677
A Monk Helps Form The Templars 677
The Muslims Slaughter The Christians In Edessa 678
St. Bernard Calls For A Crusade.. 679
Saint Louis' Crusade *A Heretic Helps The Muslims And Betrays The Crusades* 681
The Muslims Conquer Jerusalem And Make A Diabolical Slaughter
Of Christians Thanks To The Heretic King... 683

After The Slaughter, A Righteous Christian King Takes Up
The Cross And Declares A Crusade Against The Muslims 684
St. Louise Goes To Egypt And The Heretic Conspires Against Him 685
The Christians Arrive In Egypt And Take Damietta 686
St. Francis Warns The Christians Of Their Defeat 687
St. Francis Confronts The Sultan 687
The Christians Enter A Mosque That Was Once A Church, And Cleanse It 688
A Priest Takes Up Arms And Fights The Muslims 689
The Sultan Declares War On The Christians 689
The Christians And The Muslims Fight. 689
The Battle Of Mansora 690
The Christians Of France Weep 691
St. Louise Is Taken Prisoner 692
St. Louis Is Released And The Crusaders Massacred 693
The Last Of The Crusades *A Leper Defeats The Muslim King And Retakes Jerusalem* 693
The Battle Of Kerak 694
Jerusalem Is Lost To A Forerunner Of The Antichrist 694
The Martyrdom Of Raynald De Chatillon And The Rubbish Of Hollywood Films 695
Saladin Overruns Christian Africa 695
The Christians Try To Fight In A New Crusade 695
Richard The Lionheart Arises 696
The Muslims Conquer The Holy Land And Antioch, And Slaughter 100,000 Christians ... 697
The Spirit Of The Crusade Diminishes 697
The Battle Of Acre 698
The Rise Of The Ottomans 699
Western Christendom Tries To Fight The Ottomans. 700
The Westerners Refuse To Help Their Eastern Brethren 701
St. Peter Thomas Strives To Help The Eastern Christians 702
Christendom Fights The Turkish Sultan Bayazid 702
The Crusade Of Nicopolis 703
The Turks Conquer Thessalonica And The Pope Declares A Crusade 704
The Pope Who Nobody Wanted To Listen To 705

PART 15, *The Remnant Of Holy Warriors And Their Profound Victories*............................. 709
The Birth Of The Hospitallers 709
The Hospitallers Take Rhodes From The Turks 709
The Hospitallers Move To Malta And Prepare For War, While Christendom Decays 711
The Song Of Malta 712
The Battle Begins With A Wicked Woman 713
A Council Of The Wicked 714
The Turks Board Their Ships Of War And Head For Malta 715
The Christians Are On The Watch For The Coming Enemy 715
The Enemy Lands, The Christians Stand Their Ground 716
The People Of Malta Work For The Glory Of Christendom 716
The Christians Make Charge To Battle 717
The Turks Bombard The Christians With Canon Fire 717
The Christians Defend The Fort 718
The Words Of A Friar Set Aflame The Zeal Of The Christians 719
The Successors Of St. John The Baptist 719
The Cry Of Wolves In The Night 720
A Seven Hour Battle 720
The Death Of Dragut 720
The Christians Worship God As The Muslims Attack 721

TABLE OF CONTENTS

The Infinite Mercy Of God 721
The Bloodiest Assault So Far 721
Fort St. Elmo Surrounded By Wolves But Guarded By Lions 722
Fort St. Elmo Is Assailed By The Turks 722
The Saints Are Crucified Like Christ 723
A Christian Girl Is Beheaded And The Christians Unleash Holy Vengeance 723
The Turks Will Never Take Birgu 724
A Turk Comes For His Salvation 724
The Spaniards Arrive 725
The Turks Rush Fort St. Michael 725
The Christians Attack By Night 726
Repaid With Turkish Blood 726
Holy Chants Of Monks Heard In The Night 726
The Colors Of The Antichrist 726
The Bride Of Christ Verses The Harlots Of The Devil 727
Explosions That Shook The Soul 729
The Liberation Of Slaves 729
Orlando The Parrot 729
The Absent Rescue Team 730
A Change Of Procedure 730
The Turks Meet The Christian 730
The Warrior And His Hermitage 731
Wheels Of Fire 731
The Dauntless Knight 732
Surrounded By Wolves 732
A Living Hell 733
Each Man Prayed To His God 733
The Ships Of Spain Arrive, Hope Arises 734
The Sound Of Heaven 734
The Serpent Returns, And The Successors Of St. Paul Bring It Back To The Fire ... 735
September The 11Th—The Final Battle 735
The Song Of Lepanto 737
A Sinister Smile And An Absence Of Christian Zeal 737
God Will Give Us Victory 738
The Prayers Of Priests In Pure Life 738
Colossal Demons 738
The Cross Versus The Crescent 739
The Battle Of The Cross 740
A Dual Between The Cosmos 740
Inspiration Comes To The Contemplative Man 741
The Crusader Spirit Is Put To Sleep 742
The Enlightenment—Enemy Of The Faith 744
The Crusades—The Enemy Of The Useless Christian 746

PART 16, *The Reconquista, Or The Conquest Of Spain* 749
How The Conquest Of Spain Happened 749
The Reconquista Begins 750
The Old Spaniard Versus The Modern Spaniard 751
Sancho Garces 752
The Spaniards Versus The King Of Zaragoza 753
Alfonso The Battler 754
Rodrigo Versus The Five Kings 754
The Monks Who Went Against The Islamists 755

CHRISTIANITY IS AT WAR: THE MANIFESTO FOR CHRISTIAN MILITANCY

The Tragedy Of Los Arcos 755
The Restoring Of Churches 755
Muhammad Vs St. James 757
Twenty Five Christians Face Fifteen Thousand Muslims 758
The Crushing Of The Crescent 758
El Cid's Speech Before Fighting The Moroccans 760
A Battle For The Holy Trinity 760
Christendom Vs Pagandom 761
The Battle Commences And The Bishop Kills The Heretics 762
A Muslim Realizes The Truth Of The Trinity And Rejects Islam 763
The Muslims Overrun Spain, And A Crusade Is Commenced 764
The Christians Of Granada Call For Liberation 765
"For The Honor Of All Christendom" 765
The Knights Of Calatrava 766
The Hunchback Who Defeated The Muslims 767
St. Peter Pascal, A Man Who Gave Everything, But Gained Eternity 767
Gerald The Fearless 768
The Muslims Want To Conquer Rome, And Crusades Are Called 768
The Bishop Who Saved The King 769
Five Courageous Monks 769
James The Conquerer 770
San Fernando And The Fight For Cordoba 771
Prince Sancho And His Traitorous Father 774
Sancho And His Traitorous Brother 774
Robert The Bruce And Douglas The Black Go On Crusade 775
The Christians Retake The Fortress Of Algeciras 775
Pedro The Cruel And His Help To The Muslims 776
Reconquista Is Completed 776

PART 17, *In Defense Of The Spanish Inquisition* 778
The Inquisition Was A Reaction To The Ottoman Empire And To Islamic Infiltration 779
The Taking Of Constantinople 779
The Dance Of The Dervishes 780
Between Saints And Wizards 780
A Poorly Defended City 781
Not The First Time The Muslims Tried To Conquer Constantinople 782
The Turks Overrun The City 782
The Emperor Fights 784
A Surreal Sight Of Human Suffering 784
The Abomination Of Desolation 786
The Head Of The Emperor 787
The Cruel Sodomite Sultan 788
The Martyrs In Heaven 788
Rome Responds With A Call To A Crusade 789
The Christians Fight Against The Turks For The Defense Of Belgrade 790
The Massacre Of Otranto And The Spanish Inquisition 792
The Koran Is Banned 793
Islamic Infiltration Was Done In Spain And This Warranted The Spanish Inquisition 794
The Muslims Open A Hospital And Use It To Conspire An Islamic Revolution In Spain 795
The Muslims Spark A Revolution 796
The Moroccan Government Was Supporting The Islamic Revolution 797
The Muslims Begin To Murder Spaniards 798
The Muslims Attack Churches 798

The Ottoman Infiltration Of Spain 799
The Muslims Massacre The Christians In Orce 800
Islamic Human Sacrifice In Spain 801
The War Against The Moors Begins... 801
A Conspiracy To Invade Spain Is Discovered 802
The Spanish Government Declares That The Muslims Must Be Driven Out 803
The Spanish Inquisition Punishes The Muslims 803
America Had An Inquisition Against The Native Indians 806
Islamic Violence Would Be Impossible Without Muslim Sympathizers 808
The Weakness Of The Spanish Government Before The Expulsion Of The Muslims Could Be Compared To The Hesitancy Of The Founding Fathers Before Fighting Against The Barbary Pirates 809
The Birth Of The Converso 811
The Abuses Of The Inquisition Were Combated By The Church 814
The Darkest Point Of The Inquisition, And The Catholic Church's Help Of The Jews 817
Many Spaniards Disagreed With The Persecution Of The Jews 818
The Brutality Of The Inquisition Is Overly Exaggerated 819
Reforms Of The Inquisition Purge It Of Corruption 820
The Procedures Of The Inquisition Is Proof Of Its Civility 821
Torture 824
Prisons In The Spanish Inquisition 824
Secret Trials 826
Conclusion On The Inquisition 826
Massacres Of Christians Done By Jews 828

PART 18, *The Song Of Kulikovo – The Pure Image Of Christian Militancy*............. 831
The Boy Who Could Not Read 832
The Sweet Taste Of Orthodoxy 832
The Building Of The Monastery Of The Holy Trinity 833
The Tatars Come 834
The Tatars Raze Ryazan 834
The Prince Takes Refuge In The Mother Of God 835
The Muslims Head Toward The Children Of Christ 835
The Warriors Are Assembled 836
In The Flames Of Selfless Love 837
The Prince Visits The Monastery Of The Holy Trinity 837
The Warriors Gather Before The Church 838
Hermitage 839
"An Incalculable Multitude" 839
The Arrival Of The Lithuanians 840
A Battle For Christendom And For The Holy Trinity 840
The Flesh Of Kings 841
A Pack Of Wolves And A Multitude Of Lights 841
Heaven's Fields 841
A Letter From The Monk Who Once Could Not Read 842
The Warrior Monk Who Bore The Cross Of Christ 843
The Armies Collide And The Fray Commences 844
The Might Of The Holy Spirit 844
The Saints Arise From Their Agony 845
The Day Which The Lord Has Made 846
A Pilgrimage To The Monastery 847
The Virgin Mary Promises To Always Protect Russia 847
The Reason For Andronicus 848

EPILOGUE... 849

CHRISTIANITY IS AT WAR: THE MANIFESTO FOR CHRISTIAN MILITANCY

FOREWORD BY ANDREW BIESZAD

When Theodore asked me to read his book, I was interested because of my background in history and theology. I was expecting it to be another, albeit very interesting, book about history. I was wrong—it is far more than just that.

Theodore's book is a first in a very long time to venture into the concept of theosis from a Catholic perspective. While theosis is seldom spoken of in the Western Church, it is a critical part of Catholic teaching whose importance far outweighs its obscurity. This is the doctrine that Christ descended to earth in order that through His Resurrection and Ascension, we might ascend to heaven with Him and mirror Him perfectly through His will and actions. As it has been said in the Christian east, Christ lowered himself to our humanity so that He might raise us up to His divinity. This process, sometimes called "divinization" in the East, does not mean that man becomes God in His essence, as the pagan religions teach, but he becomes so in that by his free will choice, he reflects the One Who created him in his attributes and will for all that is good and beautiful, for there is no beauty outside of God because all beauty is a reflection of the One Who created it. This is the philokalia, the love of the beautiful, that theosis brings a man into, for man working with God to become like Him in the same way that God works with men to bring new life into the world through the genitive faculty unites the soul of man to his Creator in a profoundly mystical way.

This types of mystical union has been written about by many saints, but the pursuit of holiness through self-purification as is often discussed in mystical literature is where Theodore profoundly deviates. Indeed, this is what makes up the majority of his book and what he takes at length to explain through a multiplicity of examples crossing numerous times, places, cultures, and persons. He boldly dives into a pressing matter, one which is perhaps even more controversial in our modern times, due to the global secularization and the repositioning of the Church in a world which sees her as an outdated relic that needs to be "modernized." That matter is the question of holy war.

This holy war which Theodore speaks of is not the holy war of the Muslim heretics, which places beatitude in the acquisition of power, money, and sexual favors done under the name of Allah, nor does he laud fighting for the sake of the fight. What Theodore speaks of is how the union of the divine will with the human will manifests itself, among many ways, in the fight to establish righteousness upon the earth and purge it from sinfulness and wickedness, and that it is permissible to pursue this through temporal means because the theology behind it is sound and as he notes, is supported by the Church Fathers, which he copiously references throughout the breadth of the book even though the mere idea of holy war is scoffed at or looked upon with revulsion by many people today, even those with an advanced understanding of theology. However, as Theodore argues, the concept of the just war itself in Christendom as a whole is in itself a holy act and by extension, a holy war since a war which does not accord with the teachings of Christian principle is mortally sinful.

Yet it is theosis, which Theodore reiterates, that provides the very basis for the concept of Christian warfare, for it allows man to carry out in his temporal life the directives of Heaven which Christ has given us. Not only that, but this said union between the physical and the metaphysical, the temporal and the eternal, is the very fulfillment of the part of the Paternoster where we pray Thy will be done, on Earth as it is in Heaven. Theodore keeps true to tradition, as he does not advocate that Heaven is to be found on Earth or that man can make Heaven upon Earth, but he reminds the formerly Christian west of its past glory through these words, where once upon a time in Christendom there were peoples, nations, and empires that sought to put this union into practice through their laws and regulations, as the Faith was grounded into and was a part of the people.

Since theosis is primarily discussed in eastern Christian circles, Theodore's bringing this topic into the Catholic realm through his book is particularly important given the events of today. He does not consent to the power differences which continue to place the two Churches in schism with each other. In fact, he scarcely goes into the differences but rather stays united on our common apostolicity, and the fact that as the Christian west and east suffered terribly from the separation in previous centuries, that the two Churches have long strove to combat evil. It is his view that somehow it even may be the Christians of the east that come to aid the Christians of the west in the fight against the Muslims and other apostates of the Church in the coming days.

The book, as the reader will become immediately aware of, possesses two unique characteristics seldom found among books today. First, it is very long and detailed. Second, it is written in a style reminiscent of Catholic literature pre-20th century. It is a slow read with an erudite, almost regal tone that resonates throughout the pages. It is not a quick read, nor can or should it be digested quickly because it is not meant so, as it is a worthwhile read that is meant to trigger the mind to ponder that which has not been ignored for many years.

As you prepare to embark on the pages of this book, this is more than just a simple read that you have chosen. It is a venture into the annals of Christian theology and history, an explanation as explained through the great men of old, revered by the Church among her canon of saints, for why Christianity is a militant religion, one which has come to conquer the world and transfer its people and properties from the kingdom of darkness, which we all lived in under sin, to the kingdom of light where all men within it might not perish, but have eternal life.

If I could summarize in one sentence for why this book exists, it is a reminder of the ways which God has given us for the salvation of souls and to the greater glory of God and honor of His Church, ways which like the old law were once upon a time forgotten but still remain in effects and whose potency is waiting to be realized by a man who would dare to pursue them, especially in these dark times. The one who pursues this greater good will find himself a path to righteousness different than what our modern understanding comprehends and does not possess a frame of reference for but is on the same way to life which we are all called to follow.

Now that is a journey worth embarking upon.

PREFACE BY THE AUTHOR

Christianity is warfare. The Faith begins with warfare at the Holy Cross and it will triumph through warfare with the Final Crusade at Armageddon between Christendom, headed by our Eternal General, Jesus Christ, over the revived Ottoman Empire under the Antichrist. The dilemma today is the majority of Christians reject or do not know about Christian militancy. Christendom, which was Islam's greatest foe throughout history, arose because of Christian militancy. Without Christian militancy there is no Christendom and consequently, there is no Christianity. Christendom is Christian militancy. It is the mission and goal of this book to revive Christian militancy, preserved within the Church for millennia, so that it might aid in restoring Christendom in preparation for this coming epic battle.

Christendom is in the state of abandonment, forgotten and rejected as it lies in deep slumber, but it is soon to reawaken. Enemies that we now consider allies are again reviving themselves to their old powers and empires. Turkey is working effortlessly to revive its Islamic Ottoman Empire and making its Islamist envisioning more and more conspicuous. Japan is revitalizing its military more now than ever before since the end of the Second World War. Germany is dominating the rest of Europe while working with Islamic Turkey to destabilize the continent through Muslim immigration. But the traditionally Christian nations, where is their Christendom?

Japan is reviving Shintoism, Zen Buddhism and emperor worship; Turkey is reviving Islam, specifically Sufism, as its central religion, with a political aspiration of universal empire; but Christians, they have thrown out their Faith for secularism, and envisage only secular war. But this will not be the case in the future, when the lands of Christendom are surrounded by their enemies. It is a sad reality that the spirit of zeal is truly only ignited in the midst of war. In Russia, in Serbia and Poland, the flames of Christian militancy are growing, while they are still extinguished in the Western nations. But this will soon change. For where there is war, there is a cross, and thus in the bloodiest battlefields there Christ will be.

The great majority of people in the West see Christian militancy as a product of the fabricated "dark ages," as something no different than what Muslim terrorists espouse. But when we look to the records of Christian history, what we will find is that the spirit of holy war was in the foundation of Christendom itself, that is, it is of the essence of civilization—not the dead modernist society, where spiritual anarchy reigns, which we label as "Western civilization"—but true civilization, one founded upon the blood of martyrs and warriors, thinkers and monastics.

CHRISTIANITY IS AT WAR: THE MANIFESTO FOR CHRISTIAN MILITANCY

I have been seeing this theology my whole life, hearing about how God all of a sudden changed, from being the God of war to a God of pacifism. I recall reading the Scriptures during my high school years, of how the Law of God called for the wicked to be punished, of how God commanded his people to vanquish evil doers. The American evangelical explanation to all this was that God had this warlike disposition for a time, but then changed. I wondered to myself, here are the Scriptures recounting such glorious holy wars, such just laws and teachings, and all of a sudden a radical shift in the mind of God manifests itself. I thought it truly strange how anyone could have this perception of God. It was a bipolar deity that they promoted, without balance and upholding a split personality.

This was not the god that I wanted to follow. I was searching for balance, an equilibrium between justice and mercy. I also began to grow frustrated with how much Christians were ashamed of the history of Christianity. I could not hear a conversation about the Christian Faith without someone—trying to appear objective and rational—bringing up the Crusades and the Spanish Inquisition, and the berated Christian always responding with apologies and pleas for forgiveness. It was really quite sad to see, and aggravating. But what was even more exasperating and disturbing was how aggressive and vicious many Evangelicals could become once you expressed support for the Crusades or the Inquisition. I remember one Evangelical vindictively telling me about how he would not have any problem whatsoever if the Muslims invaded all of Rome. His reasoning? Because the Catholic Church did the Crusades.

But if you were to tell such people that Moses, Joshua, Elijah, Jehu, Josiah and numerous other holy men in the Scripture conducted wars against the enemies of God, they would say that this is Old Testament and that the "new covenant" has now done away with such militant ideas. This disharmony when portraying the mind of God led me to be incredulous to this interpretation. But then one day my eyes began to be opened to the harmony that I sought. I came across a book written by our Lutheran friend, professor Alvin Schmidt, called *The Great Divide*. In this book he clearly explained the Christianity of the Crusades, and it was quite different from the dismal protests of my Evangelical contemporaries. The Crusades had medics, and these helped Christians, Muslims and Jews, without discrimination or supremacist sentiments, while at the same time these very Crusaders fought and killed Muslims in holy war. Here, in this explanation, I found the balance for which I was searching, the harmony between mercy and justice, and from there, my journey through Christian history commenced.

Some years after learning from Mr. Schmidt's books, my desire to connect with ancient and pure Christianity, free from the taint of modernity and the materialistic feel-good industry, grew stronger. My soul ached to be bridged with the Christians of antiquity, for it was they who were closest to the time of Christ, to the fountainhead of the teachings of the Apostles, and to spirituality not corrupted by the bipolar theology of modern society. I began to look up ancient Christian writers, their names and books, and started reading them. Amongst the first pieces of early Christian literature that I came across was the book, *The*

Preface

Error of the Pagan Religions by Julius Firmicus Maternus, a prolific astrologer turned Christian living in the Roman Empire in the fourth century. Firmicus was born a pagan and was a fanatic about his religion, writing the largest text in Latin about astrology that we currently possess. Firmicus received enlightenment on God, and the same radical enthusiasm that he once had for paganism, he now had for the Christian Faith. He wrote the book exposing the evils of the pagan gods, the human sacrifices and the sadistic rituals of the bloodthirsty cults that were existing within the empire. The tone and the affirmations of Firmicus were like night and day in comparison to the books coming from American Christian publishers. Firmicus read the Scriptures, he read of how Moses ordered for the destruction of the idols of tyranny that the pagans so revered, and for which they shed innocent blood to satisfy the sanguinary devils they worshipped; he read of how Pinehas slew the Hebrews who venerated Moabite gods, and he did not shy away from them. No. To Firmicus, after witnessing the sinister realities of the pagan religion, the Law of God was something to uphold, it was the way by which to triumph over the bloodthirsty despotism that the heathen religions brought. Firmicus wrote his book to give a solution to paganism, and that was to destroy it. His book was actually an exhortation to the Roman government to obliterate the pagan religions and triumph for Christianity. Here again I was introduced to the balance between mercy and justice, and to the ignored truth, that one cannot say he believes in mercy, and not believe in the destruction and uprooting of beliefs that are merciless.

To peruse the writings of the Christians of antiquity, was like drinking from a well of crisp water upon a mountain untouched by the ambitions of ravenous sophists and dry and mechanical reprobates. I would continue to read more of the writings of early Christians. The epistles of Clement of Rome, Ignatius of Antioch and Polykarp—all written within the first century and all men who knew the Apostles—infused in my mind the necessity for war against the demonic. How Clement praised the valiant Judith beheading the general Holofernes as an example of charity, was yet another image of this harmony within Christianity, between mercy and justice, ferocity and charity.

I began reading some Lactantius, the philosopher of ancient Christianity. First I began reading through his *Divine Institutes*, and immediately sensed the intellectual and spiritual unity in his words. Later I read his book, *On the Anger of God* and learned of the essential attribute of anger in God, that a god not moved to anger, is not God. I soon began reading through Tertullian's *Apologia* and learned more about the evils of paganism and false religion. From Tertullian I went to other ancient Christian scholars, such as Athenagoras, and I remember reading his letter addressed to the emperor, Marcus Aurelius, on how Christians were oppressed and persecuted by the pagans, even though they were upstanding citizens. Reading this epistle further enlightened me as to the war between light and darkness and of the intellectual vigor of Christianity. One book that really brought me to a clear perspective on the tenacity of the Christian Faith was the *Ecclesiastical History* of Eusebius. It was in this book that I learned of the foundation of Christendom, how it was built upon the blood of so many martyrs. Eusebius tells of the stories of thousands of martyrdoms that took place under the pagan sword, and then he transitions into something very beautiful: the birth of Christendom. As the eyes must behold the cold white moon before the sun awakens, as the night pervades the earth before the arms of the sun caress our beings, so a river of Christian blood had to water the soils and feed the roots of the flower of Christendom before it could bloom.

Eusebius ends his book on the victories of the first Christian emperor, Constantine, and thus on the Christianization of the Roman Empire. This led me to read another masterpiece, *The Life of Constantine the Great* by the same Eusebius. In this work I learned of how Constantine vanquished the pagan tyrant and persecutor, Maxentius; how he would later defeat the bloodthirsty and traitorous Licinius; how he declared holy war on those who killed Christians; how he protected the Christian Armenians from the Persians; how he destroyed pagan temples; how he slaughtered sodomites; how he combated heresies and fought and triumphed for Jesus Christ. The life of Constantine was the beginning of Christendom, and voraciously did I continue to read of her history, of her wars and of her tragedies. In the story of Christian empire, did I find the true Faith; in the story of Christendom did I find the continuation of divine history. The holy war that was led by Abraham, by Moses, by Joshua, the prophets and the holy kings of Israel, continued on through Constantine, through Christian emperors and dauntless warriors like Cortez and Don Juan de Austria.

In so divine a history, in the holy lives of these men now hated and forsaken, did I find civilization; in the biographies of knights and emperors, bishops and monks, did I find love; in the stories of warriors of the Cross and ardent monastics, did I find God.

Christendom never died, it only went to sleep, when we put our zeal to death through the sword of idleness and surrendered ourselves to sloth in the cosmic war against evil. In the First Crusade the warriors of Christendom, before they went out to war against the Muslims to liberate Christian lands, put the sign of the Cross on their foreheads or on their chests. They put on themselves the mark of God, for in fighting and laying down their lives, they became one with Christ. This aspiration, to become one with God, is described by the ancient and medieval monks as *Theosis*, and it was this that we have thrown out for callous and mechanical theology—such as Calvinism,—and other very dangerous ideas such as darwinism and deism. The absence of any emphasis on Theosis is the reason why Christendom is now asleep. God the Son became one with Humanity, thus Christ's war against evil becomes our war against evil as well; empires of Christendom unite themselves with Christ, and venerate Him as their King, and their lands as His lands, and their military victories as His military victories, for He is one with them. But the modern heretics have divided Christ from His Humanity, so much so that they cannot even call Mary the Mother of God, regardless of the truth that Christ is God.

The journey of man is a ceaseless war. As we walk through the fields of life we must endure through what seems to be an endless multitude of tares that strive to suffocate the wheat of our hearts, and what could be a fruitful crop, the pestilential infernal spirits of the abyss are bent on destroying. The struggle over the soul of humanity is so violent, so bloody and ruthless, that we cannot help but say with the contemplative sage, "The life of man upon earth is a warfare" (Job 7:1). The life of the soul is perpetual warfare; it is the interior conflict that surpasses everything in the cosmos, for its aspiration is beyond all things, that is, the denial of everything for He Who is All, Jesus Christ. As Duns Scotus wrote of God, "You are truly what it means to be, you are the whole of what it means to exist."[1]

Ceaselessly do I hear people differentiating between spiritual warfare and physical warfare, as though the two are radically distinct. They say that the war of the Christian must solely be spiritual and interior, and not physical and exterior. To those who espouse such an idea, let me remind you that from the beginning of history man has declared holy wars, and each one of these wars was of the spiritual. God Himself used the physical phenomena of a flood to purge the earth of the wicked, and it was for a spiritual purpose. When Abraham defeated his enemies to liberate Lot and the others captured, there was Melchizedek; when Moses annihilated the three thousand worshippers of the Golden Calf, it was after he descended the holy mountain and received the Law from the Hand of God; when Joshua conquered Jericho, it was after he stood on sacred ground, and "lifted up his eyes, and saw a man standing over against him: holding a drawn sword" (Joshua 5:13), Who was God the Son, Jesus Christ. Christ fought the devil in the desert, this was a spiritual war and an image of that interior battle for mankind's soul, and this war manifested itself on Mount Golgotha, when Christ vanquished Satan on the Cross. Was not the Cross physical? Was not the nails, the Crown of Thorns, the spear that pierced His side, the scourge that struck His divine flesh, the grueling walk through the Via Dolorosa as He carried the holy wood, are these things not physical? They are all physical, and they were all endured for victory in a spiritual war. Christ's war against the devil in the desert is the image of the interior war, the denial of self, and the Crucifixion is the exterior war, the physical.

Elijah fasted in the desert for forty days, this was a part of the spiritual war; but we cannot forget that he killed all of the prophets of Baal. The first is the interior, the second the exterior. St. Paul wrote that "our wrestling is not against flesh and blood; but against principalities and power, against the rulers of the world of this darkness, against the spirits of wickedness in the high places." (Ephesians 6:12) For years I have seen this verse be used to discount holy war, and to reduce the Christian life to solely prayer and fasting. St. Paul fasted, yes; he prayed, no doubt, and when the Jews came to kill him he did not hesitate to have the plan for his assassination reported to the Roman authorities, and he made no protest against the hundreds of soldiers who guarded him with swords and spears. This was no contradiction on St. Paul's part, rather it was a harmony to what the inspired Apostle said. The use of the soldiers was for a spiritual purpose, to protect the Church from those who sought out to destroy her, and this is the whole aspiration of holy war and the objective of Christendom: protect the Church and to see to it that the world receives her light.

The women came to the well and the shepherds drove them away, and Moses arrived and drove the thieves out, "and defending the maids, watered their sheep" (Exodus 2:17). Such

---

1   Scotus, *Treatise on God as First Principle*, 1

a short story, but it is an event that would be a microcosm for the whole purpose of Christendom: the destruction of the works of the devil, and the vanquishing of their advancers who come for no reason but "to steal, and to kill, and to destroy" (John 10:10), for the perpetuation of the holy well, so that the sheep may drink. The moderns will object, and say that warfare must only be in the context of self-defense. But such is a selfish way of thinking. Christ commands us to deny the self, and this can be applied to holy war wherein the struggle is not done for personal gain, but for victory in the cosmic war for the soul of humanity and the destiny of mankind, outside of the physical and the confines of individualism. This is that same spirit that Moses had when he drove the cruel shepherds out so that the women could draw water from the well. Writing on the virtue of Moses, St. Gregory of Nyssa wrote, "Considering the right valuable in itself, Moses punished the wrong done by the shepherds, although they had done nothing against him."[2]

Holy war is not the desires of the flesh but of the striving for union with God, for to desire nothing is to love God. Holy war revolves around that teaching of Christ: "If any man will come after me, let him deny himself, and take up his cross, and follow me." (Matthew 16:24) This teaching was actually applied to holy war in the First Crusade. It is why Pope Urban II, in the Council of Clermont in which the First Crusade against the Turks was declared, said:

> Anyone who has a mind to undertake this holy pilgrimage, and enters into that bargain with God, and devotes himself as a living sacrifice, holy and acceptable, shall wear the sign of the Cross on his forehead or his chest. And conversely anyone who seeks to turn back having taken the vow shall then place the cross on his back between his shoulders. Such men will bring back to pass through this double symbolism what God himself orders in the Gospel: 'he that taketh not his cross, and followeth after me, is not worthy of me.'[3]

The denial of the self allows the spirit to give strength to the soul, and strength gives reign to zeal, which can only emanate from love. Thus, in this, the sacred struggle against darkness, the spiritual and the physical unite as one under love, in which "perfect charity casteth out fear" (1 John 4:18), working in harmony and in unity in the war against Satan and his works, as Humanity and Divinity became one in Jesus Christ in the Virgin Mary, "that he might destroy the works of the devil." (1 John 3:8)

As St. Maximus the Confessor wrote of the holy Incarnation:

> He did not refuse to take our condemnation on himself, and indeed, the more he himself became a man by nature in his incarnation, the more he deified us by grace, so that we would not only learn naturally to care for one another, and spiritually to love others as ourselves, but also like God to be concerned for others more than for ourselves, even to the point of proving that love to others by being ready to die voluntarily and virtuously for others. For as the Lord says, *There is no greater love than this, that a man lay down his life for his friend.* (Jn 15:13)

---

2   Gregory of Nyssa, *Life of Moses*, 1. 19
3   Robert the Monk, *Historia Iherosolimitana*, trans. Sweetenham, 1.3

Now, the modernly minded Christian will argue that this verse from Christ is speaking only of being killed, and not fighting, as though one cannot lay down his life while in combat. Such a limiting of a verse is contrary to how the ancient Christians applied this teaching of Christ. The ninth century Church Father, St. Cyril, applied this teaching of Christ to physical fighting during a debate with a group of Muslims during the time when wars between Christians and Muslims were very intense. "Why do you Christians disobey Christ's commandment to love your enemies, but instead persecute and kill us?" argued the Muslims. "If, in a certain law," responded Cyril, "there are two commandments that must be fulfilled, which man shall be more righteous, he who fulfills both commandments or he who fulfills only one of them?" The Muslims answered: "He that fulfills both, of course." Then Cyril said: "As individuals we forgive our enemies, but as a community we lay down our lives for one another. For the Lord has said that there is no greater love than to lay down one's life for one's neighbor. As a community we protect one another and lay down our lives for one another. Not only is your aim to enslave us physically, you also aspire to enslave us spiritually. It is for this reason that we defend ourselves. This, therefore, is justified."[4]

In these words we find the arguments of the modernist Christians, that holy warfare should only be spiritual and never physical, and that martyrdom could never be done while fighting, utterly vanquished by the voice of Christian antiquity. There is a reason why the Christians of old times never unsheathed their swords with a thought that what they were doing was unbiblical, and there is a reason why that today the very mention of crusades and holy wars are met with indignation. We have forgotten what man is, that man himself is something sacred and worthy of fighting and dying for.

Some protestor will burn the American flag, and an older man will beat him up, and we will praise him as a good patriot. But if some Christian, zealous and angry, attacks some blasphemer for desecrating a Crucifix, or for boasting homosexuality, we will condemn him as "not being like Christ and having love." This is the great hypocrisy of the modern man, that a flag is worth more than the Holy Cross on which our Salvation crushed death and vanquished the enemy of humanity; that anti-patriotism is esteemed as worthy of death, but heresy is something that is to be tolerated, and any serious anger towards sacrilege silenced as being "against the liberty of the Gospel."

Where are you, O Christendom? The hearts of the people have grown cold, and the flames of zeal, they are extinguished by the callous and cold icebergs of modern and effeminate heresies. With this am I reminded of the words of the Disciples when they said, "Was not our heart burning within us, whilst he spoke in this way, and opened to us the scriptures?" (Luke 24:32) Their hearts burned with zeal when they were with Christ, but you Christians of modern times, your hearts are as cold as your faith. The hearts of the people must be enflamed with zeal, and only then will Christendom awaken. Christendom is not founded on constitutions written on paper, but on law written upon the hearts of people. Only when

---

4 In the *Life and Teachings of Elder Thaddeus of Vitovnica*, On Serving God and Neighbor

the fires of love and compassion have sparked, and the ice of indifference has melted, will Christendom be revived.

That is the purpose of this book, to prepare the souls of Christians for the war that is to come, between Christendom and the nations of Satan and the Antichrist, between Christians and the imperialism of delusion.

Theodore Shoebat

PART 1

This section makes the case that in holy war, the Christian becomes an instrument for God's justice (theosis) for the advancement of Christian Orthodoxy and the Holy Trinity.

WHAT IS HOLY WAR?

Holy War is a Christian bridging his soul with God through committing himself to fight for God. It is another manifestation of the divine love through taking up the cross and emulating Christ by warring with the enemies of Heaven and "laying down ones life for his friends" (John 15:13) in this sacred combat.

This is that mountain upon which Christendom is built—it is the spirit of Christianity and the spirit of the sacred militant. Moses climbed the top of the lofty mountain of Sinai, to ascend to the pinnacle of eternal truth, to bring himself into the inner temple of divine mystical truth, and upon seeing the world with spiritual eyes, he went beyond the visible to witness the invisible glory.[1] Now again does glorious Christendom behold that heavenly Mount Zion with trembling reverence, approaching "the city of the living God, the heavenly Jerusalem, and to an innumerable company of angels, to the general assembly and church of the firstborn, which are written in heaven, and to God the Judge of all, and to the spirits of just men made perfect, And to Jesus the mediator of the new covenant, and to the blood of sprinkling, that speaketh better things than that of Abel." (Hebrews 12:23–24)

It is around this holy mountain that Christendom surrounds itself, and it is the God of this holy mountain, alongside His saints and "The chariots of God" who are "twenty thousand, even thousands of angels" (Psalm 68:17) where Christendom takes refuge.

---

1   See Gregory of Nyssa, *Life of Moses*, 1.46

THE BEGINNING OF WISDOM IS TO HATE EVIL

"Let us make man in our image" (Genesis 1:26)—this is what God said before He created humanity. Therefore when man emulates His Creator, he becomes like God, the Architect of mortals. St. Gregory Nazianzus said: "'Then we shall know as we are known' (1 Cor 13:12), when we mingle our god-formed mind and divine reason to what is properly its own and the image returns to the archetype for which it now longs."[2]

The warrior becomes like God, his Creator, and as God hates evil, so he, when he fights evildoers, will emulate that same divine hatred. "The fear of the Lord is the beginning of wisdom," says Solomon (Proverbs 9:10), and to fear the Lord is to hate evil, for as the same pious king said, "The fear of the Lord is to hate evil" (Proverbs 8:13).

Since the fear of the Lord is to hate evil, the beginning of wisdom is to hate evil. St. Paul said: "But of Him you are in Christ Jesus, who became for us wisdom from God" (1 Corinthians 1:30). The beginning of being in Christ—Who is Wisdom—is to hate evil, to be like Him Who came "that He might destroy the works of the devil." (1 John 3:8) When wisdom lies within the soul of the warrior, he with his sword illustrates wisdom by executing just wrath against evil and destroying it. To kill evildoers is to trample with victorious feet upon "the evil way" and to "lead in the way of righteousness" (Proverbs 8:20). All those who do not fight evil "love death" (Proverbs 8:36).

HOLY WAR AND THE DIVINE UNION WITH GOD

King David, inspired by the Lord, "strengthened himself in the Lord his God" (1 Samuel 30:6) before he charged into battle to fight the Amalekites and save the people who they were oppressing. Truly was this a crusade, with David carrying up the cross of his suffering, denying himself, and in so doing his soul ascended towards Heaven and found strength in God Who "teaches my hands to make war, so that my arms can bend a bow of bronze." (Psalm 18:34) David found strength in the Lord because the strength of God was instilled in his heart so that he, with fiery zeal, could be directed by divine guidance to fight "the battles of the Lord" (1 Samuel 25:28). When David clashed with the Amalekites and combated against them, he was not only used by God, but more sublimely, than that he was profoundly united with God in a very profound way. He achieved what St. Peter said when he wrote in his inspired epistle:

> Grace and peace be multiplied to you in the knowledge of God and of Jesus our Lord, as His divine power has given to us all things that pertain to life and godliness, through the knowledge of Him who called us by glory and virtue, by which have been given to us exceedingly great and precious promises, that through these you may be partakers of the divine nature, having escaped the corruption that is in the world through lust. (1 Peter 1:2–4)

---

2   Nazianzus, Oration 28.17, in Gregory the Confessor, *On the Cosmic Mystery of Jesus Christ*, Ambiguum 7, 2, 1077B

By fighting against the tyrannical pagans, David was both fighting for and partaking in "all things that pertain to life and godliness," through the divine power which granted to him such virtues, and in doing so, was he amongst the "partakers of the divine nature," being the instrument of God "to execute wrath on him who practices evil." (Romans 13:4)

God works through us, using us as His instruments for His divine justice, "for it is God who works in you both to will and to do for His good pleasure." (Philippians 2:3) Undoubtedly, it is God's will for us to fight the wicked and the persecutors of His Church just as it was His will for Barak to defeat the Canaanites and end their oppressions and for Joshua to defend the Gibeonites from the pagans and keep them from being annihilated. It is likewise God's will for righteous Christian people to execute justice on Earth "for the punishment of evildoers and for the praise of those who do good." (1 Peter 2:14) When Christendom wars against the haters of God, the Christian warriors fighting the holy war become valiant and saintly weapons used by God "to execute wrath on him who practices evil" (Romans 13:4).

Pope St. Urban II declared at the Council of Clermont, in which he also commissioned the First Crusade, this very belief to the courageous knights who were about to fight the Muslims. To use his words, their combat against the enemy was "God working through you."

It was by fighting in a holy struggle that David partook of virtue and committed himself to the purest manifestation of love—"to lay down one's life for his friends." (John 15:13) In the words of St. Maximus the Confessor: "It is evident that every person who participates in virtue as a matter of habit unquestionably participates in God, the substance of the virtues."[3]

St. Justin Martyr said that God "takes pleasure in those who imitate His properties, and is displeased with those that embrace what is worthless either in word or deed."[4] The one who imitates God's nature, hating evil for the cause of love and loving righteousness for the sake of justice, is the one in whom God's delights. The soldier of God who fights for the Law of Love and for the establishment of justice imitates God in His holy wrath. The imitator of God participates in God and comes into divine union with the Holy Trinity. "If a man love me, he will keep my words: and my Father will love him, and we will come unto him, and make our abode with him." (John 14:23)

THEOSIS—THE REQUISITE FOR HOLY WAR

Theosis is the basis for holy war. Theosis is partaking in the divine nature to obtain the likeness, or union with God. Its roots go back to the early Church where it had a much more profound part within Christian spirituality than it does today. In the Western Church, theosis is called by the term divinization. This is not to say that one becomes God or divine himself, as this would be blasphemy, but that one unites with God and becomes a partaker of the divine nature (2 Peter 1:4) It is through this union that a Christian becomes an instrument

---
3 St. Maximus, *On the Cosmic Mystery of Jesus Christ*, Ambiguum 7, ii, 1081A, trans. Paul M. Blowers and Robert Louis Wilken
4 Justin Martyr, *Apology*, 2.4, ed. Ronald J. Sider

for God's justice, for when the militant fights for God, he unites with Him as "God's minister, an avenger to execute wrath on him who practices evil." (Romans 13:4)

The clearest illustration of God working through His warriors to fight against evil is from the prayer of Judas Maccabees: "Strike them down with the sword of those who love thee" (1 Maccabees 4:33). Here fighting and mysticism become one. The warrior loves God, Who is Love, and in union with Love, he destroys evildoers, who are the enemies of Love. Truly, Christian mysticism cannot be separated from Holy War.

St. Thomas tells us that the king's justice is administered by God through him, saying that the sovereign is "fired with zeal for justice when he considers that he has been appointed to exercise judgment in his kingdom in the place of God; and, on the other, he will acquire kindness and clemency, for he will look upon all those subject to his government as though they were his own members."[5]

Recalling the words of St. Athanasius and repeated through St. Thomas Aquinas, God became man so that man can become like God, and so the king, becoming a son of God through Jesus Christ, becomes a vessel for the divine rule of God over the nation,[6] who dispenses "the ordinance of God" and is established as "Gods minister, an avenger to execute wrath on him who practices evil." (Romans 13:2–4)

When the holy warrior or the righteous king punishes the wicked, he becomes one amongst the "partakers of the divine nature," (2 Peter 1:4), and in so doing, he participates in the eternal law of God. This is easily deduced from St. Thomas Aquinas' words when he says that "all things participate to some degree in the eternal law."[7] The doctors of the Church teach us that all of the goodness in human will consists in following both the will and the law of God, and that all evil consists in warring with God's will and His law.[8] Thus, the king who enacts the law of God and rules in accordance to the divine will participates in the love of God and in the nature of God.

King David fought the Lord's battle, strengthening himself in God, and for this it can be said that he attained theosis, becoming like God, emulating the Almighty in His justice and virtue. God uses both the bodies and the souls of His warriors to practice virtue, and that includes becoming His weapons and uprooting evil. In the words of St. Maximus:

> The soul becomes godlike through divinization [theosis], and because God cares for what is lower, that is the body, and has given the command to love one's neighbor, the soul prudently makes use of the body. By practicing the virtues the body gains familiarity with God and becomes a fellow servant with the soul.[9]

---

5   Aquinas, *De regimine principum*, 1.14
6   See Aquinas, *De regimen principum*, 1.15
7   Aquinas, *Summa Theologiae*, Ia IIae, 91, article 2
8   Vitoria, *On Civil Power*, question 3, article 1, 16
9   St. Maximus, *On the Cosmic Mystery of Christ*, Ambiguum 7, iii, 1088B

Notice how he says that the body, being used by God for His justice, becomes a means to loving one's neighbor. What does the law say? *Love God and love thy neighbor*. This can be applied to both Holy War and righteous laws against the wicked, for to uproot evil is a part of justice. In the words of Augustine, "justice is the love of God and our neighbor by which the other virtues are pervaded: that is, it is the common root of the entire order between one man and another."[10]

St. Paul notes this same idea on how the soul reaches God, is indwelled with His eternal virtues, and the body is used to partake in those virtues. In the words of St. Paul:

> Or do you not know that your body is the temple of the Holy Spirit who is in you, whom you have from God, and you are not your own? For you were bought at a price; therefore glorify God in your body and in your spirit, which are Gods.[11]

Likewise David strengthened himself in the Lord, his soul sublimely indwelled with the virtues of God, and filled with "zeal for the lord," (1 Kings 10:16), and his strong arm striking in the spirit of that same zeal. In such a state did David glorify God in body and in spirit. The knights and crusaders who defended glorious Christendom glorified God in both soul and body, for their souls were filled with the divine virtues and they used their bodies to fight for those very virtues. In the words of Ramon Llull, a Spanish knight who warred against the Muslims in Spain,

> So then, just as all of these aforesaid practices pertain to the knight with respect to the body, so justice, wisdom, charity, loyalty, truth, humility, fortitude, hope and prowess, and the other virtues similar to these, pertain to the knight with respect to the soul.[12]

THE WARRIOR FIGHTS FOR THE LAW OF GOD

David and all of the warriors who fought for God and His Divine Law illustrated the greatest indication of inspired virtue: perseverance. It is perseverance that is the virtue that brings him to eternity. In the words of St. Bernard:

> In truth, perseverance is a sort of likeness here to eternity hereafter. In fact it is perseverance alone on which eternity is bestowed; or rather, it is perseverance which bestows man on eternity; as the Lord says, 'He that shall preserve unto the end, the same shall be saved.'[13]

St. Bernard continues, saying that perseverance "fosters a spirit of long-suffering, and gives strength to perseverance."[14] It is for this reason that the zealous warriors of Christendom trained not only their bodies, but their souls and their minds through contemplation of God to connect with the King of Heaven and the Eternal Warrior, "satisfied as with marrow and fatness, and my mouth shall praise You with joyful lips. When I remember You

---

10 Augustine, 83 quest. 1:61, in Aquinas, Summa Theoligica, IIa IIae 58, article 8
11 1 Corinthians 6:19–20
12 Ramon Lull, 2.11, trans. Noel Fallows
13 St. Bernard, *On Consideration*, 5.31
14 St. Bernard, *On Consideration*, 5.32

on my bed, I meditate on You in the night watches." (Psalm 63:5–10) The knight of Christ shall say with David:

> Oh, how I love your law! I meditate on it all day long. Your commands are always with me and make me wiser than my enemies. (Psalm 119:97–98)

In their hearts they have the precepts of God, and in their hands a sword, to protect Orthodoxy against the heathen. As we read in the Scriptures:

> Let the saints be joyful in glory; Let them sing aloud on their beds. Let the high praises of God be in their mouth, and a two-edged sword in their hand, to execute vengeance on the nations, and punishments on the peoples; To bind their kings with chains, and their nobles with fetters of iron; To execute on them the written judgment this honor have all His saints. (Psalm 149:5–9)

All of this brings to mind one of the most valiant of the warrior saints of the Church, St. Gerald of Aurillac. He led his private army to protect poor pilgrims from raiders and tyrants in ninth century France, and he, like the Hebrew saints, continuously walked with the Law of God in both his mouth and his soul. He followed the words of Christ, to "seek first the kingdom of God and His righteousness," (Matthew 6:33) and so he utterly surrendered himself to Providence and to the divine love. As St. Odo, his biographer, wrote:

> Because he gave himself wholeheartedly to the desire of heaven, his mouth was so filled from the abundance of his heart that the law of God sounded almost continuously on his lips.[15]

The warrior walks on the spiritual path, and in so doing is his body no longer a means to a human end, but a weapon for a heavenly purpose, a destiny in which he no longer suffers from fear of death, for he has denied the self with so much exertion that his physical life is no longer held above the life that lies ahead where he is to be adorned with the crown of a martyr.

When the enemies of God go against His people, the souls of His warriors "bound in the bundle of life with the Lord thy God" (1 Samuel 25:29), as it was with the soul of David. When the holy warriors forge against the heathens, and lift up their swords and strike like an inflicting storm the pagan and the heretic who seek their end, their souls are spiritually merged with the Divine One, "strengthened with might by his Spirit in the inner man" (Ephesians 3:16), they sprint through the fields of death as their General before them suffered His strenuous Passion on the wood of the Cross, upon the battlefield of the Skull.

This spiritual bonding of the warrior with God is exhibited by David who, before he battled the Amelekites, "strengthened himself in the Lord his God." (1 Samuel 30:6) When Israel and Amelek clashed in a dual of arms, a spiritual war ensued: the Amelekites were "the enemies of the Lord;" the Hebrews struck these heathens with the edge of the blade, it was a religious war a holy war.

---

15 Odo of Cluny, *Life of St. Gerald of Aurillac*, 2.15

When the monastic knight St. Gerald of Aurillac fought against his enemies, he was so confident in God that he ordered his men to fight with the backs of their swords and with their spears reversed, and he always compelled his adversaries to surrender. This way of fighting, as we are told by St. Odo of Cluny, "would have been ridiculous to the enemy if Gerald, strengthened by divine power, had not been invincible to them. For Christ, as it is written, was at his side [Psalm 118:6], who seeing the desire of his heart, saw that for love of Him he was so well-disposed that he had no wish to assail the persons of the enemy, but only to check their audacity."[16]

Observe what St. Odo writes, that Christ was beside him when he combatted the enemy, and that he was strengthened by divine power. This is the source of the Christian warrior's tenaciousness in the battlefield—it is the zeal and strength given to him by God in Whom he dwells with pious fear and trembling, guiding His warriors as a general leads his soldiers.

In Christianity, the holy warrior is continuously walking on the path of truth, on the path of the spirit, which is the Divine Law of God. As he perseveres to defend and perpetuate the Law of God, the glimmering candlelight of the Christian spirit, he walks upon the path of justice, for "the path of the just is like the shining sun, that shines ever brighter unto the perfect day." (Proverbs 4:18) He forever declares war on the ways of deceivers, for the "way of the wicked is like darkness" (Proverbs 4:19) and it is dispelled by the path of justice. They dedicate their entire beings, with all might, soul, intellect and spirit, to defend the foundation of Christendom, and that is, the holy laws of Christ, keeping within themselves the small flame that emanates from the words of Solomon,

> 'Fear God, and keep his commandments: for this is the whole duty of man. (Ecclesiastes 12:13)

To fear God and abide by His commandments is to be as the Maccabees, and to fight for the very precepts of Heaven. This is the truest essence of Christian militancy, the purest actions of the Faith—to unite the spirit of Orthodoxy with the Sword of Christ in sacred warfare to fight for the path of truth and bring to flames the crooked road of falsehood. The warriors have "praises of God" in their mouths, "and a two edged sword in their mouths," for in their spirits lies meditations upon the Law, while their hearts charge with arms to establish and defend the eternal precepts.

The warrior's soul is permeated by the Holy Law, always observing them, so that as he fights evil, he has within his own spirit the divine precepts which evil desires to destroy and he desires to protect. For as David told Solomon before he gave up the ghost:

> I go the way of all the earth; be strong, therefore, and prove yourself a man. And keep the charge of the Lord your God: to walk in His ways, to keep His statutes, His commandments, His judgments, and His testimonies, as it is written in the Law of Moses, that you may prosper in all that you do and wherever you turn; that the Lord may fulfill His word which He spoke concerning me, saying, If your sons take heed to their way, to walk before Me in

---

16 Odo of Cluny, *Life of St. Gerald of Aurillac*, 1.8

truth with all their heart and with all their soul, He said, you shall not lack a man on the throne of Israel." (1 Kings 2:2–4)

THE CHRISTIAN WARRIOR FIGHTS FOR THE HOLY TRINITY

The Christian warrior must always fight for the Holy Trinity, for "He is antichrist who denies the Father and the Son" (1 John 2:22), and so the war against evil is to fight for the Godhead. The world is at war with the Holy Trinity, because the devil is "the ruler of this world" (John 14:30). This is the same devil that Christ warred against and triumphed over when He isolated Himself in the desert. The warriors of Christendom practice isolation, withdrawing from society and entering into hermitage, taking the quiet sound of the wilderness to contemplate God and martyrdom.

Our Warrior and General Jesus Christ practiced hermitage when "He went out to the mountain to pray, and continued all night in prayer to God." (Luke 6:12) He practiced hermitage when He "was led up by the Spirit into the wilderness to be tempted by the devil." (Luke 4:1) Christ battled the devil in hermitage, showing us how, within our humanity, we vanquish temptation in hermitage, gaining strength and perseverance. This spiritual strength gained through contemplation was what the knight Ramon Lull wrote of when he described the Christian combatant making pilgrimage to a place of hermitage "to worship, contemplate and pray to God, to whom he gave thanks and blessings for the great honour that He had paid him throughout his life in this world."[17]

Who is this God but the Holy Trinity? Not the unitarian devil of the Muslims, or the capricious and unstable demon of the modalists (such as those who call themselves "Oneness" Pentecostals), nor the diabolical and deceptive devil of the Seventh Day Adventists, who blasphemously say Christ is Michael the Archangel, nor the concupiscent Satan of the Mormons, who is absent of all virtues and eternally licentious—No! None of these hell-bound devils does the Christian knight fight for. He only raises his sword for the Holy Trinity—never for any heretical demon, not even for the mere promulgation of any satanic and antichrist heresy. When we read the fourteen articles of chivalry composed by the Spanish knight Ramon Lull, one of the requirements to being a knight was to believe in the Holy Trinity:

> To believe in one God is the first article. To believe in the Father and in the Son and in the Holy Spirit are three articles, and it is proper to believe that the Father and the Son and the Holy Spirit are one God alone in eternity, without end or beginning.[18]

The knights who defend Orthodoxy and God's Church, and walk the path of the Spirit, fight for the Holy Trinity, and such zeal is the sign of sublime conviction that can only be fostered as a result of intense contemplation on the Triune Godhead. In the words of St. Gregory:

---

17 Ramon Lull, *The Book of the Order of Chivalry*, prologue, 3
18 Ramon Lull, *The Book of the Order of Chivalry*, 4.5

They will be welcomed by the ineffable light and will contemplate the holy and majestic Trinity that shines clearly and brightly and unites itself wholly to the entire soul. [19]

The Holy Trinity unites with the souls of Christendom's warriors, for they manifest and exemplify their zeal for the Holy Trinity with the highest sacrifice, that of their own lives. "For there are three that bear witness in Heaven: the Father, the Word, and the Holy Spirit; and these three are one." (1 John 5:7) Such words are the foundation of the Holy Trinity, and they remain in the heart of every Christian warrior who defends the Creed of the Faith. With holy words inspired by the highest Heaven of the infinite, does the Apostle strike down the impiety of Muhammad, and declares that the One power Who created the universe is Three.

It is the holy warrior of Christendom who protects the teachings of the Church from its enemies. How glorious it must have been to gaze upon those Christian combatants, who with hardy bodies and tenacious spirits sacrificed their lives to fight for the Holy Trinity in that glorious Battle of the Kulikovo Field, in which Russian Orthodox warriors vanquished the Muslim Tatars. How profound it must have been to see the Grand Prince Dimitry Ivanovich, who "strengthened his heart with the name of Christ,"[20] as David "strengthened himself in the Lord his God" (1 Samuel 30:6), and declared to his mighty army:

> Brethren, better an honourable death than a life purchased by shame; and it were better not to stir against Tartars at all than, having come, achieve nothing and go back. Let us now cross the Don and there lay our lives for the holy church and the Orthodox faith, for our brotherhood, for Christendom![21]

Observe the zeal that floods his words and the reverence that illuminates his inspiration. What awe! What might! What strength! Such is the prose of the knight, the epitome of the Christian spirit and the force of the divine love. For they lay down their lives for the Holy Trinity, for orthodoxy, and for the brotherhood. They illustrate the highest form of love, to "lay down one's life for his friends." (John 15:13) With the words of the holy precept within their hearts, they display the command of St. Peter:

> Honor all people. Love the brotherhood. Fear God. Honor the king. (1 Peter 2:17)

Through their honor of all men, their love of the brotherhood, their fear of God, and their exertion of virtue for Christendom, they surely had these words of St. Peter written in their hearts. Indeed, this verse of St. Peter should be inscribed on the banners of Christendom! When we imagine the knights of old, we are seeing Christendom. Let us imagine that profound example of a Christian prince, Dimitry Ivanovich, when he proclaimed the Holy Trinity and majestic Faith before fighting against the Muslims, the supporters of Antichrist, who with their pernicious doctrine of Unitarianism hate Christ and are enemies of the Holy Trinity. The grand prince declared:

---

19 Gregory, 16.9, in St. Maximus, *On the Cosmic Mystery of Christ*, iii, 1088A, trans. Blowers and Wilkens
20 *The Tale of the Battle of The Kulikovo Field*, p. 86, trans. L. Sorokina and C. Cooke
21 *The Tale of the Battle of The Kulikovo Field*, p. 86, trans. L. Sorokina and C. Cooke

> For we are all brothers, from the least to the greatest, grandsons of Adam, one house and one tribe; one baptism is ours, one Christian faith; we have one God, our Lord Jesus Christ, glorified in the Trinity; so let us now lay down our lives for His holy name, and for the Orthodox faith, and for the holy church, and all our brotherhood, the whole Orthodox Christendom! [22]

Take notice that he proclaims Christ as being "glorified in the Trinity." Such was the arrow that pierced the soul of the Muslims, trampled their false doctrine, and banished the devils that follow them. All of the crusades fought between Christians and Muslims were over one most holy declaration: the Nicene Creed, as it defines the Trinity. The Muslims wanted to destroy it, but the Christians wanted to advance it. To this day is the war the same, with the acolytes of Antichrist warring against the saintly combatants of orthodoxy.

The Battle of the Kulikovo Field was triumphed by Russian Christendom, and in our own time Russia will lead Christendom again against the revived Ottoman Empire of the Antichrist.

But where are the nations that shall join together to form the confederacy of Christendom and fight the Muslim confederacy of Antichrist? Let these nations rise, let the Holy Church illuminate its light upon them and unite them together under "one Lord, one faith, one baptism" (Ephesians 4:5). Let them place the crown of Christendom upon the holy mountain of self-denial and impenetrable martyrs, and let them be as the saints who laid the foundation for the sword of justice, "Who through faith subdued kingdoms, wrought righteousness, obtained promises, stopped the mouths of lions, quenched the violence of fire, escaped the edge of the sword, out of weakness were made strong, waxed valiant in fight, and turned to flight the armies of the aliens." (Hebrews 13:33–34) Now these saints are "the spirits of just men made perfect" (Hebrews 12:23), and they reside as royalty in the holy and heavenly mountain of Zion, "the city of the living God" from where the warriors of orthodoxy receive their inspiration and by which their very souls are ignited by the awe-inspiring will to advance virtue and justice.

---

22 *The Tale of the Battle of The Kulikovo Field*, p. 102

PART 2

This section makes the case that holy war is not a novel creation that came centuries after the New Testament, but has always been an innate part of the Christian Faith itself, hearkening back to the militant spirit of ancient Israel and perfected in the New Testament. It will also show that holy war was taught by prominent Christian theologians as far back as the first century, well before Constantine's triumph over the pagans at the Battle of Milvian Bridge in the fourth century, which is commonly claimed to be the first example of Christian warfare.

THE FOUNDING OF HOLY WAR

Holy War has always been a part of the Church. It was taught in profound spiritual stories within the New Testament. The formation of Christendom's armies began like a seed underneath the soil. It remained small and unseen, only to soon sprout and ultimately grow into a massive tree. The tree was within the seed the entire time, but when given proper care its fullness eventually manifested. The doctrine of Holy War was always in the Faith, and its ways were taught through certain people of the Church, before any crusade was ever commenced.

It is a common misconception that the concept of Holy War did not really appear until Constantine became emperor in the fourth century. It is portrayed that the Church never supported war and that She changed only when Constantine became emperor, as though Her theologians needed to find Scriptural justification to vindicate the use of the sword. What they do not understand is that the idea of Holy War was already in Sacred Scripture, having been explicitly taught in the writings of the prophets, spiritually in the teachings of Christ, later again in the writings of the Apostles, and that this beautiful teaching developed within the Church with the passing centuries.

It was not as though later fathers of the Church rejected the passages of the New Testament, but that they expounded on them, finding numerous meanings within the never-ending sea of wisdom that Scripture holds. In the earliest days of the Church, the concept of Christian Holy War saw its infancy through moments in the time of Christ and that of the Apostles. While they may not seem to pertain to militancy at first, such becomes clear when they are viewed through a spiritual lens.

THE SOLDIERS OF THE NEW TESTAMENT TEACH US HOLY WAR

Within the New Testament we find both evil war and Holy War illustrated through the actions of numerous soldiers. One set of soldiers show the pagan armies that dominated the Roman Empire, while another set of soldiers foreshadow the Christian armies of Christendom that were to come. The first exposes an army under the rule of the devil, and the second shows what type of army was to form under Christ. In the first, you have the soldiers who persecute the Church, not having any consideration for holy things, who care not about God but remain fixated on the flesh. These are the soldiers who "took Jesus into the Praetorium and gathered the whole garrison around Him. And they stripped Him and put a scarlet robe on Him. When they had twisted a crown of thorns, they put it on His head, and a reed in His right hand. And they bowed the knee before Him and mocked Him, saying, 'Hail, King of the Jews!' Then they spat on Him, and took the reed and struck Him on the head. And when they had mocked Him, they took the robe off Him, put His own clothes on Him, and led Him away to be crucified." (Matthew 27:27–31) These are the heathen soldiers, who do not fight for justice nor law but for their own gain. They are the soldiers who plunder churches, persecute Christians, and serve the will of the devil.

These same wicked soldiers are those who were so filled with the lust of gain that after crucifying Christ, they "divided His garments, casting lots for them to determine what every man should take." (Mark 15:24) These are the soldiers who "mocked Him, coming and offering Him sour wine, and saying, "If You are the King of the Jews, save Yourself." (Luke 23:36) These are the soldiers who accepted briberies from the chief priests of the Jews to lie about our Lord's resurrection and say not that He arose from the dead but that His body was stolen, as the Scriptures witness:

> When they had assembled with the elders and consulted together, they gave a large sum of money to the soldiers, saying, 'Tell them, His disciples came at night and stole Him away while we slept. And if this comes to the governors ears, we will appease him and make you secure.' So they took the money and did as they were instructed. (Matthew 28:12–15)

All of these men are the soldiers of the devil, and they foreshadow those who persecute the Church and slaughter innocent Christians. They are further illustrated by the "four squads of soldiers" who kept St. Peter in confinement and the officers who arrested him and threw him into prison (Acts 12:4). There were the two soldiers in between whom St. Peter was "bound with two chains" and "the guards before the door" who "were keeping the prison." (Acts 12:6) The persecution of Peter was both an example and a prophetic illustration of greater persecutions of Christians. Christ identifies Himself with His Church, and therefore when these savage soldiers attacked and mocked Our Lord it was prophetic of what sufferings the Church would endure at the hands of the heathens.

PART 2

THE RIGHTEOUS SOLDIERS OF THE NEW TESTAMENT FORESHADOW THE ARMIES OF CHRISTENDOM

As the evil soldiers of the New Testament foreshadow the persecutors of the Church, the righteous soldiers of the New Testament foreshadow the holy armies of Christendom who defend the Church through arms and valor. What a beautiful, prophetic image—foreshadowing the sacred armies of Christendom, their love of justice, and their zeal for the destruction of the wicked! There is the righteous commander who, seeing a mob of Jews beating St. Paul, "immediately took soldiers and centurions, and ran down to them. And when they saw the commander and the soldiers, they stopped beating Paul." (Acts 21:32) There were the soldiers who carried away Paul "because of the violence of the mob." (Acts 21:35) The same Commander, seeing that "Paul might be pulled to pieces by" the Jews, "commanded the soldiers to go down and take him by force from among them, and bring him into the barracks." (Acts 23:10)

There was also the centurion who was determined to protect St. Paul from the Jews who wanted to kill him and reported the plot to the commander, saying,

"The Jews have agreed to ask that you bring Paul down to the council tomorrow, as though they were going to inquire more fully about him. But do not yield to them, for more than forty of them lie in wait for him, men who have bound themselves by an oath that they will neither eat nor drink till they have killed him; and now they are ready, waiting for the promise from you." (Acts 23:20–21)

It was this righteous commander who, upon hearing of the plot, called for two centurions and ordered them to "Prepare two hundred soldiers, seventy horsemen, and two hundred spearmen to go to Caesarea at the third hour of the night; and provide mounts to set Paul on, and bring him safely to Felix the governor." (Acts 23:23–24)

It was this great body of warriors who protected the Apostle and "as they were commanded, took Paul and brought him by night to Antipatris." (Acts 23:31) These same seventy horsemen brought him "to Caesarea and had delivered the letter to the governor, they also presented Paul to him." (Acts 23:33)

As St. Paul, a pillar of the early Church, took no issue in using pagan soldiers to protect himself, there is no problem for the Church to use Christian armies to protect herself. St. Paul "was permitted to dwell by himself with the soldier who guarded him" (Acts 28:16), and because this is so, there is no wrongdoing when the Church uses soldiers to protect Christians and to slay persecutors. This story of the soldiers protecting St. Paul, although they were pagans, shows the Church what she is to do in a time of crises and persecution: call armies for military defense. What is good for the pillar (St. Paul) is good for the whole fortress (the Church). St. Augustine pointed to this story and esteemed it as a model for what the Church should do in time of attack and malicious heresy:

"The Apostle Paul was not thinking of his own transitory life, but of the Church of God, when he undertook to reveal to the tribune the plot of those who had conspired to kill him, and, as a consequence, he was escorted by an armed guard to the place where he was to go, thereby escaping their ambush. He had not the least hesitation in calling on Roman law by declaring himself a Roman citizen, whom it was not lawful at that time to scourge. Likewise, he appealed to the help of Caesar to save himself from being given over to the Jews who were eager to kill him—and this was a Roman prince, not a Christian one. By this he showed clearly what the ministers of Christ were to do afterward, in times of crises for the Church, when they should find their rulers Christian."[1]

Notice how he says that by St. Paul using the soldiers to protect him he was demonstrating to the Church that it is permissible for Christians to utilize armies against evildoers and enemies. It illustrates how the Church can work with the state to execute crusades or the use of an army to physically combat the enemies of the Christians and the adversaries of orthodoxy. The profound story mystically foretells of Christendom, in which the Church and the state labor together to combat evil and violent people who strive to destroy Christianity. The Church combats with the Spiritual Sword the devil and his demons, while the state fights off the followers of the demonic with the temporal sword. The story of the soldiers protecting Paul both exemplifies and foreshadows this system of Christendom, but it begins in this small moment of history, only to later grow into the fullest armies of the holy empire.

ST. PAUL AND THE RIGHTEOUS CENTURION ON THE SHIP—AN IMAGE OF CHRISTENDOM

While St. Paul was on a ship about to be destroyed by a tempestuous storm, it was the cruel soldiers who wanted to "kill the prisoners, lest any of them should swim away and escape," but it was the righteous centurion who, "wanting to save Paul, kept them from their purpose" (Acts 27:42–43). Here again we have the two armies represented—the first, cruel and merciless, and the second, just and pious. The former desired to slaughter everyone, including Paul, but the latter, with the centurion, used his authority righteously and protected the Apostle.

There is nothing evil for the Church to be protected by noble military authority, and nor is there anything sinful about the Church using that very authority to prevent violence from happening against Her. St. Paul and all of the Christians on the ship was the Church, the ship was the world, and it was heading to its destruction. It was only because of St. Paul that the people on the boat survived, and it is because of the Church—being the means by which Christ's atonement is conveyed—that humanity has salvation. For fourteen days they did not eat, and they were near death because of starvation, but St. Paul "took bread and gave thanks to God in the presence of them all; and when he had broken it he began to eat." (Acts 27:35) By this very action, the rest "were all encouraged, and also took food themselves." (Acts 27:36) Before this St. Paul told them "I urge you to take nourishment, for this is for your survival," (Acts 27:34), and through the presentation and blessing of the bread that they were encouraged to eat and save themselves.

---

1   St. Augustine, letter 185, ch. 28

There is a mystical significance behind this moment: St. Paul (the Church), guides the people from death to life by offering the bread to God "in the presence of them all." What is this but the figure of the Eucharist? By Paul eating the bread the others were motivated to follow and be saved. So the Church, "the pillar and ground of the truth" (1 Timothy 3:15) administers the Eucharist, "the bread of life" (John 6:48), and, in the words of Christ, "If anyone eats of this bread, he will live forever; and the bread that I shall give is My flesh, which I shall give for the life of the world." (John 6:51) Paul presented the bread, and guided the people to life before the ship crashed in the same way that the Church guides humanity to the Eucharist, and thus to Christ, before the world crashes into eternal damnation.

We can say that the ship is a model of the world which the Church is in. This is what St. Chrysostom meant when he said, "Let us think that the whole world is a ship, and in this the evildoers and those who have numberless vices, some rulers, others guards, others just men, as Paul was, others prisoners, those bound by their sins."[2] While we have evil soldiers who wanted to hinder the will of God and cruelly slaughter everyone on the ship, including the Apostle, we have the righteous centurion who strived to keep to the will of God and ordered the pernicious men to cease their diabolical plan. We therefore have the wicked soldiers who use their office for evil, for these wanted to kill the Apostle of God, and the righteous soldier—the centurion—who wants to do the will of God, and in doing so, obeys the Church and protects the Church. This centurion is a foreshadowing symbol of the armies of Christendom that use military authority to protect the Church and the helpless from violence.

The Centurion believed in the God of Paul. Before the ship crashed the Apostle said, "And now I urge you to take heart, for there will be no loss of life among you, but only of the ship. For there stood by me this night an angel of the God to whom I belong and whom I serve, saying, Do not be afraid, Paul; you must be brought before Caesar; and indeed God has granted you all those who sail with you. Therefore take heart, men, for I believe God that it will be just as it was told me" (Acts 27:22–25), and it was the Centurion who believed these words of prophecy. The sailors did not have faith in the God of Paul, for they were seeking "to escape from the ship," (Acts 27:30) but the centurion did have faith, since after Paul told him "Unless these men stay in the ship, you cannot be saved" (Acts 27:31), he made the "soldiers cut away the ropes of the skiff and let it fall off." (Acts 27:32)

Here we have the righteous warrior believing and acting in accordance with the will of God as was taught to him through the Church as a prophetic image of the coming Christendom in which the Christian military is directed by the Church to use Her authority for righteousness' sake. The centurion, through his authority, saved all of the prisoners in order to save Paul. Likewise, Christian military commanders under Christendom exercise their authority to preserve the Church from destruction. It is a small image of what the Church was to do as a whole in the future state of Christendom: influence the military to be noble, and use Her position not for tyranny, but for the will of God, and the advancement of His holy laws.

---

2 St. Chrysostom, homily 53 on Acts

LONGINUS—THE TRANSFORMING OF THE PAGAN ARMIES INTO CHRISTIAN ARMIES

There is something to be wondered at, and that is how there is a shift within some soldiers who behold Christ, and these are the ones who, being born in darkness, absorb themselves into "the true Light which gives light to every man coming into the world." (John 1:9) These are the beginning of the knights of Christ, the pioneers of the sacred leagues; these are the lights that are the first to break through the night, compelling one to foresee that the whole sun of Christendom's armies are about to abrupt into their full brightness. One such was the soldier who pierced the side of Christ with his spear and beheld His divine blood mixed with water as it flowed out. His name was Longinus.

When "one of the soldiers pierced His side with a spear, and immediately blood and water came out" (John 19:33) it had eternal and prophetic significance: His blood, which is administered through His Church in the sacrament of the Eucharist, united with the nations of the world, represented by the water. With the coming together of the nations with Christ, this would include the warriors of gentile lands entering the fold of the Church and thus becoming no longer the soldiers of idols, but knights of Christ. The story of Longinus beautifully prophesied the formation of Christendom's armies, and it was illustrated, quite profoundly, through this simple moment of a noble warrior's life.

As soon as Longinus beheld the water and the blood flowing forth from the divine body of Christ, he joined His Church, being in the seas of the gentiles merging with the sacred flock. It is this centurion who, after "the sun was darkened, and the veil of the temple was torn in two" and after Christ cried out, "Father, into Your hands I commit My spirit," declared, "Certainly this was a righteous Man!" (Luke 23:45–47)

It is holy Longinus who, being blinded in pagan war, beheld the Crucified General and, thinking Him dead, pierced His divine rib to have his infirm eyes touched by holy blood and water, and his sight healed, and realizing that he stood in the presence, not of a man Who lied perished, but victorious, he declared, "Truly this Man was the Son of God!" (Mark 15:39) The blindness of Longinus signifies the blindness of the pagans. The water and blood of Christ touched his eyes and healed him. This beautifully represents the blood of Christ bringing the nations into the Church. Is it not profound that the blood and water that flowed from Christ's side touched the eyes of a warrior? Truly this moment has a specific significance: the gathering together of the warriors of the gentiles, into the Church, and having them fight not pagan battles, but battles for Christ. With blood and water Christ left the womb of Mary, and with blood and water Christ died, and the Church was born, and this Church was birthed with warriors.

THE CENTURION OF CAPERNAUM—THE IMAGE OF THE KNIGHT OF CHRIST

Amongst these earliest warriors of Christ, was the noble centurion in Capernaum who asked Christ to heal his servant. His heart was not hardened like those of the pagans, who saw their servants as mere slaves to be used and disposed, but he cared for him with compassion, urging Jesus to heal him, saying, "Lord, my servant is lying at home paralyzed, dreadfully tormented." When Christ said "I will come and heal him," the centurion expressed fully his faith in Him and his humility, saying, "Lord, I am not worthy that You should come under my roof." (Matthew 8:5–8) By declaring himself unworthy, he made himself worthy, and thus is the spirit of the Christian warrior, humble before God, yet ferocious before the devil. Notice what the centurion says afterwards: he compares Christ to a military commander, saying, "For I also am a man under authority, having soldiers under me. And I say to this one, Go, and he goes; and to another, Come, and he comes; and to my servant, Do this, and he does it." (Matthew 8:9) The authority of Christ is paralleled to that of a centurion, and to this did Christ exclaim, "Assuredly, I say to you, I have not found such great faith, not even in Israel!" (Matthew 8:10) The centurion placed his life under the will of Christ, as a soldier commits himself to the guidance of his general. This beautiful moment has a mystical and prophetic meaning: the soldiers of the gentile nations, no longer fighting for pagan gods and pagan tyrants, but combating evil countries under their Holy General Jesus Christ. So when we read the story of the centurion, it is but a sight to marvel at! For it foreshadows the armies of Holy Christendom, partaking in the spiritual war against the devil, by vanquishing nations ruled by demonic religions and diabolical despots, under the leadership of their Warrior King, Jesus Christ.

THE SOLDIERS WHO CAME TO JOHN THE BAPTIST—SYMBOL OF THE CHURCH'S AUTHORITY OVER THE MILITARY

There is then the soldiers who, wanting to "bear fruits worthy of repentance," (Luke 3:8) approached St. John the Baptist and said, "And what shall we do? And the Baptist told them, "Do not intimidate anyone or accuse falsely, and be content with your wages." (Luke 3:14) They received the river of knowledge as a seed absorbs water and grows with strength. Here in this one moment we see the soldiers and the rule they are to follow, and we witness a prophetic moment that foresees the armies of Christendom and by what precept they order themselves. Here the soldiers bear their armor without repute, and maintain their position without leaving it, and here the sacred monastic instructs them on how to conduct themselves. What an image to behold! For here the Church teaches the army, and this is but a microcosm of what was to come: Christendom, in which the Church, with its priests and monks, guides the warriors on noble action, and the warriors in turn, following Christ, protect the Church from her diabolical enemies. Do not forget that it was the Popes who declared Crusades against the Muslims and the pagans, and the soldiers—like those who adhered to the Baptist—obeyed. It is here in Christendom where the soldier does not keep his office to instill fear in innocent people, but strengthen them; here the soldier does not falsely accuse to the sake of gain or the shedding of innocent blood; here the soldier is content with his wages, neither pillaging to steal extra money, nor robbing others for their property; here the soldiers humbly approach the Church, to receive her wisdom and learn of works worthy of salvation. These are the Christian armies, obeying the precepts of the Church, and obeying dutifully. Their formation is foreshadowed by this body of soldiers who came to St. John the Baptist, desiring the knowledge of God.

CORNELIUS THE CENTURION—THE MODEL FOR THE CHRISTIAN ARMY, AND THE FORESHADOWER OF GENTILE SOLDIERS

There is the blessed Cornelius, "a centurion of what was called the Italian Regiment," (Acts 10:1), who was "a devout man and one who feared God with all his household, who gave alms generously to the people, and prayed to God always." (Acts 10:2) This warrior brought all of his household to St. Peter, the head of the Church, and with a humble spirit, said, "we are all present before God, to hear all the things commanded you by God." (Acts 10:33) What a glorious image that strikes us with awe, for its simplicity covers the profundity of what it foreshadows: The commander of many men humbly heeds to the words of the Church, and this only foretells of Christendom, in which the military received the holy teachings of the Church, and not only this, but fought for the protection of those very teachings. St. Augustine, who fully supported a Christian state and military, pointed to Cornelius when vindicating Holy War:

> Among such, also, was that Cornelius to whom the angel was sent, who said: 'Cornelius, thy prayer is heard and thy alms are accepted,' when he advised him to send to the blessed Apostle Peter, to hear from him what he ought to do. And to summon the Apostle to him he sent a religious soldier. [3]

Observe how the inspired Luke described Cornelius as "a devout soldier," and from this it can be said that since God honored one soldier because of his zeal, imagine what glories there is in majestic Christendom to have entire armies of zealous warriors.

Take notice that the Scripture says Cornelius was of the Italian Regiment. How many Christian warriors has Italy brought forth! How many of her fighters combated in the holy fray for Christ against pagans and Muslims! Look at her soldiers, how they fought for Christ in so many holy wars! The Battle of Ostia, the Battle of Malta, the Battle of Lepanto, and numerous crusades, all in which Italian men of valor fought the acolytes of the devil. The first of her people to join the Church was Cornelius, and he was a warrior. Surely did Cornelius foreshadow not only Italy's soldiers, but all the warriors of the gentile lands. What arms! What strength would the gentiles bring, to protect their brethren from the successors of the evil soldiers who mocked and tormented our Lord! When the Muslims were slaughtering the Christians of the East, who came to their defense but the Christians of the West? Who came to fight for them, and to retake the sacred lands of Christ from the pagans, but the Christians of France, of Italy, England, Scotland, Ireland, Scandinavia, Germany, Spain, and Portugal? It was through Cornelius that the gates of the gentiles were opened, and it was through this same centurion that the conversion of valiant warriors would be brought to the Ark of the Church, founded by Christ and led by St. Peter and the Apostles, of which St.

---

3   Augustine, letter 189

Jerome described as "the ark of Noah, and he who is not found in it shall perish when the flood prevails."[4] St. Maximus of Turin wrote:

> This Church, having neither spot nor wrinkle anywhere on its splendid vessel, shines with the brightness of linen. In it the first animal to be sacrificed to God from the nations is the centurion Cornelius. From this vessel of his, then, Peter feeds us. For when we see the throngs of the nations hasten to the Christian faith, we rejoice together with the apostles.[5]

Who will deny that as the nations of the gentiles entered the Holy Ark, their warriors entered in as well? There were the first warriors amongst the pagan armies to accept the Faith, and gradually did their numbers grow, and eventually did they dominate the armies, and bring them into the flock of Christendom.

Who was the first of the Gentiles to find the true path but a warrior? Who are the greatest warriors of Christendom but the Gentiles? The doors to the Church were opened to a gentile warrior, and the greatest protectors of the Church are the gentile warriors. When the Muslims were tyrannizing the Christians of the East, and were striving to destroy the churches of Syria, Egypt, Iraq, the Holy Land, Greece and Asia Minor (just as they are trying to do today) who was it but those armies who sprung from the West, who was it but the Russians, the French, the Germans, the Italians, the English, the Irish, the Scottish, who rushed to their defenses? It was the inheritors of Cornelius who took up their swords and fought for the cause of God, and for the advancement of the Divine Law.

Let us not forget that the Scripture calls Cornelius "a centurion of that which is called the Italian band" (Acts 10:1), and thus does this verse have a prophetic and mystical significance: it foreshadows the armies of Christendom that were formed in the centuries after the Apostles, and the armies that is to come. For Cornelius and the numerous other soldiers who joined the Faith in the time of Christ—like the centurion whose servant Jesus healed—and in the time of the Apostles and their successors, were the earliest warriors to join the flock of Christ. Though they were small, their numbers would grow, and by the time of the glorious Constantine, so many soldiers were walking upon the path of the Spirit, and such were willing to fight and die for the most Blessed Trinity, and the True Way that conquers the nefarious wiles of the demons. Soon did the Christians eventually dominate the armies of the empire, and in due time, they were eventually all of the armies in the era of majestic Christendom.

This formation of the armies of Christ did not begin in the Middle Ages, nor even in the time of Constantine, but with Cornelius, the centurion who Christ declared, "I have not found such great faith, not even in Israel!" (Matthew 8:10) It was those noble soldiers who, desiring to "bear fruits worthy of repentance," (Luke 3:8) approached the holy monastic John the Baptist who told them, not to leave the army, but to "not intimidate anyone or accuse falsely, and be content with your wages" (Luke 3:14). Such were the earliest of Christ's warriors; these paved

---

4 St. Jerome, letter xv, to Pope Damasus
5 St. Maximus of Turin, sermon 2.2-3, trans. Boniface Ramsey

the way for the future Christian soldiers who were to partake in Holy War against the pagans and the heretics, the Muslims and the heathens who sought out to destroy the Church.

Additionally, that Cornelius was of the Italian Division foreshadows the coming Christian armies that will destroy the Antichrist, for as we read in Daniel, the Lord will send the valiant warriors of Italy, Greece and Cyprus:

> For the ships of Chittim shall come against him: therefore he shall be grieved, and return, and have indignation against the holy covenant: so shall he do; he shall even return, and have intelligence with them that forsake the holy covenant. (Daniel 11:30)

Chittim refers to the Sea Peoples, or the Italians, Greeks, and Spaniards. The position of Cornelius as the Italian Division signifies just how instrumental Italy's military will be in the Last Crusade against the Antichrist. The Douay-Rheims translation makes this more conspicuous, since it renders the same passage of Daniel as such:

> And the galleys and the Romans shall come upon him, and he shall be struck, and shall return, and shall have indignation against the covenant of the sanctuary, and he shall succeed: and he shall return and shall devise against them that have forsaken the covenant of the sanctuary. (Daniel 11:30)

When we read such passages of holy writ, let us not forget that such an event happened in providential history, in the Battle of Lepanto, in which the fleets of Italy and Spain were guided by destiny and they strengthened in God their Lord, to destroy the navy of the Antichrist Ottomans. Such a beautiful victory left one anonymous poet to write:

> High peaks of Leucadia, watch over that final day: you who saw the Roman fleet and the people of Christ taking their vengeance, and the brutal Muhammadan fall before sword and fire. You saw the Spanish youth return with a thousand ships, proud with his banners and his vast spoils. [6]

When we read from the Muslims of how much they wish to destroy Rome, let us not turn away from a most obvious truth: that the devil wants to hinder the plan of God. He is working ever so cunningly and vigorously to make Rome Muslim, knowing what threat it poses to his plans. But most definitely he will not succeed, even though Europe has gone the way of the heathen, for "If we are faithless, He remains faithful;" (1 Timothy 2:13) we cannot think that God is so unjust that He will forsake the nations that He brought into His Church, and from the prophecy of Daniel, we are certain that Europe will come back to holiness and combat the sinister forces of the Antichrist.

THE FIRST SOLDIERS AFTER THE NEW TESTAMENT

It is a myth that circulates amongst the unlearned that it was Constantine who commenced Christian involvement in the military. The pioneers of Christian military recruitment into the knights of Christ were the warriors of the New Testament. From their commencement

---

6   Anonymous, *I will Now Sing of the Happy Deeds*, 415–419, trans. Wright, Sarah, & Lemons

the number of Christian fighters in the Roman military increased, and in the end, they dominated, and the sword would ultimately belong to the Church. Let us begin with some moments that indicate this growth of Christian soldiers within the first centuries of Christianity way before Constantine.

THE THUNDERING LEGION

Eusebius wrote of "the Melitine legion," who were all Christians under the emperorship of Marcus Aurelius (161 to 180 AD). It is reported that in the emperor's war with the Germans and the Sarmatians there was an unbearable drought, and the Christian soldiers prostrated before God in the accustomed fashion of the Church and prayed for rain. It was during this that a lightning bolt struck the earth and the enemy, who was watching from a distance. The enemy fled and rain finally came. From this time on the Melitine legion, according to Apollinaris, was given the title of "fulminea," or the "thundering legion."[7] Tertullian also wrote of this event, and he described how "the great drought in Germany was broken by rain obtained through the prayers of Christians, who, as it is chanced, were among his [the emperor's] soldiers."[8]

CHRISTIAN SOLDIERS IN ARCHAEOLOGY

There is also archeological evidence that dates from around the year 230 A.D. that shows the presence of Christian soldiers before Constantine. For example there is a prayer hall for Christians that was built right next to a military camp, in which is an inscription that says: "Gaianus, also called Porphyrius, centurion, our brother, has made the pavement at his own expense as an act of liberality. Brutius has carved out the work."

There is also another inscription thanking a certain Christian woman for lending a table for the altar for the prayer hall, on which the priest would consecrate the Eucharist so that the Christian soldiers could receive Holy Communion:

> The god-loving Akeptous [a woman] has offered the table to God Jesus Christ as a memorial.[9]

This is quite profound because after Christianity would take over the Roman Empire, soldiers would receive the Eucharist before entering into battle, and here this wonderful ritual was in the earliest years of Christianity. There are also numerous engraved memorials[10] of Christian soldiers that were carved before Constantine took power. For example, one inscription speaks of a soldier who re-enlisted in the military: "For Caelius Placidius, who re-enlisted in the army. Placida his daughter and Peculius his freedman made this for the sweetest patron."

---

7   Eusebius, *Ecclesiastical History*, 5.5
8   Tertullian, *Apology*, 5.6, trans. Glover & Rendall, brackets mine
9   Ronald J. Sider, *The Early Church on Killing*, part 4, p. 144
10 All of these inscriptions can be found in Ronald J. Sider, *The Early Church on Killing*, part 4, pp. 147–151

In another engraving it speaks of Eutyche Aurelia, "member of the Second Parthian Severan Legion, in the consulship of Favianus and Mucius (AD 201)." In another it mentions "Aurelius Barbas, veteran of the army of our Emperors, prefect of the Tenth Cohort." In one it speaks of "Publius Marcellus, a Roman knight, veteran of the army of our two Emperors." In another it speaks of "Antiagrucius the centurion." In an engraving it mentions "Leontianus the soldier from the unit of the Alecutti." In another it says:

> Here lies Solomon of great memory, who became count of the Circitorians, great domesticus [military staff assistance] and vicar of Thrace.

In no way would a pagan Roman soldier have the name of Solomon because it is a biblical name. Also, take notice that this Solomon held a very prestigious position within the military, showing what high ranks Christians possessed.

In one text it speaks of "Aelius Martinus, of the first Praetorian Cohort" and "Aelius Verinus, who re-enlisted during the reign of the Augusti (Severus and Caracalla)." In another it reads of "Aurelius Manos, soldier, cavalryman, archer, and bearer of the dragon-standard on the staff of the most outstanding general Castorius Constans." In yet another one it mentions "Gaius and Menophilus, from the armies." One text is quite detailed and is dedicated to a Christian centurion named Aurelius Gaius Jr.:

> Aurelius Gaius Jr., who enlisted in the First Legion Italica stationed in Moesia [Bulgaria], was selected [to serve] in the Eighth Legion Augusta stationed in Germany, then in the Iovia Scythica in the provinces of Scythia [Dobruja in eastern Romania] and Pannonia [Hungary]; served as tyro, apprentice cavalryman, then lancer, aide-de-camp of a centurion tirarius, aide-de-camp of a centurion ordinatus, aide-de-camp of a centurion princeps, then aide-de-camp in the mobile forces of the emperor with the First Legion Iovia Scythica.

From these text we can see that Christians way before Constantine or any of the Crusades were already in high and prestigious positions within the military. These were successors of the Christian military patriarch, Cornelius the Centurion, and it would continue on to the point that eventually the whole military of the Roman Empire would be a Christian force.

By 197 AD, there were a considerable amount of Christians in the military, for in this year Tertullian, writing to the pagans, wrote of Christian servicemen in the army: "We [the Christians] sail ships, we as well as you, and along with you; we go to the wars, to the country, to market with you."[11]

We also learn from Eusebius that by the third century, in the time of the tyrants Diocletian and Maximian, there were "Very many who were soldiers in the kingdom of Christ," who were martyred for refusing to pay worship to the gods.[12] The enforcement of paganism

---

11 Tertullian, *Apology*, ch. 42.3. St. Robert Bellarmine used this same passage to prove that Christian service in the Roman military was very ancient (*On Laymen or Secular People*, ch. 14, ed. Tutino, p. 58)
12 Euseb. Eccles. *Hist.* 8.4

within the Roman military was the main reason why numerous ancient Church authorities expressed some aversion to recruitment to the army.

ANCIENT CHRISTIAN THEOLOGIANS WHO SUPPORTED RIGHTEOUS KILLING

It is a common assertion that until Constantine, Christians were pacifists and it was only after that theologians began to articulate doctrines in favor of war. But, we can find reputable Fathers of the Church and theologians who supported righteous killing.

Pacifists today like to use certain remarks by Church Fathers and other ancient Christians to prove the common claim that before Constantine waged war against the pagans, Christianity was absent of Holy War, and then as soon as Christians took power in the empire, theologians began to change their theology to be more compatible to religious warfare. But with some careful observation, what is found is that the spirit of Christian militancy was always encompassed within the heart of Christianity, waiting to be unleashed through a legitimate state.

CLEMENT OF ROME

Clement of Rome is amongst the oldest of the Church Fathers. He lived within the first century and was a direct student of Sts. Paul, Peter and John. He is even mentioned in the New Testament, with St. Paul referring to him in his letter to the Philippians:

> And I urge you also, true companion, help these women who labored with me in the gospel, with Clement also, and the rest of my fellow workers, whose names are in the Book of Life. (Philippians 4:3)

But what nobody mentions is that this Christian Church Father, a man so close to the Apostles, also believed in the use of violence for righteous and holy causes. In his letter to the Corinthians, Clement wrote a section on charity, in which he specifies kings crushing sedition, and the biblical hero Judith beheading the pagan general Holofernes as examples of charity and love:

> To bring forward some examples from among the heathen: Many kings and princes, in times of pestilence, when they had been instructed by an oracle, have given themselves up to death, in order that by their own blood they might deliver their fellow-citizens [from destruction]. Many have gone forth from their own cities so that sedition might be brought to an end within them. We know many among ourselves who have given themselves up to bonds, in order that they might ransom others. Many, too, have surrendered themselves to slavery, that with the price which they received for themselves, they might provide food for others. Many women also, being strengthened by the grace of God, have performed numerous manly exploits. The blessed Judith, when her city was besieged, asked of the elders permission to go forth into the camp of the strangers; and, exposing herself to danger, she went out for the love which she bare to her country and people then besieged; and the Lord delivered Holofernes into the hands of a woman. Esther also, being perfect in faith, exposed herself to no less danger, in order to deliver the twelve tribes of Israel from impending destruction. For with fasting and humiliation she entreated the everlasting God,

who seeth all things; and He, perceiving the humility of her spirit, delivered the people for whose sake she had encountered peril. [13]

ST. IRENAEUS OF LYONS

St. Irenaeus of Lyons was the bishop of Lyons in France from about 177 to 202 AD and a student of St. Polycarp—who was a student of St. John the Apostle himself. He wrote in full support of the state using arms against evildoers. He said that God established laws and the state's use of the sword because human beings feared men more than they did God, and so temporal punishments needed to be enacted. He also affirmed that if a magistrate kills someone for the cause of justice, then God will not punish him at all:

> For since humanity, by departing from God, reached such a pitch of fury even to look upon his brother as his enemy, and engaged without fear in every kind of restless conduct, and murder, and avarice; God imposed upon humanity the fear of people, as they did not acknowledge the fear of God, in order that, being subjected to human authority, and kept under restraint by their laws, they might attain to some degree of justice, and exercise mutual forbearance through dread of the sword suspended full in their view, as the apostle says: 'For he beareth not the sword in vain; for he is the minister of God, the avenger for wrath upon him who does evil.' And for this reason too, magistrates themselves, having laws as a clothing of righteousness whenever they act in a just and legitimate manner, shall not be called into question for their conduct, nor be liable to punishment. [14]

TERTULLIAN

The pacifists and those who are only for secular war are in the habit of referencing Tertullian to substantiate their form of Christianity, since he said,

> For to begin with the cause of the military crown itself, I think we must first enquire whether military service generally be meet for Christians. Otherwise what availeth to treat of incidental circumstances, when there is a fault in first principles? Do we believe that a human sacrament may supersede a Divine one, and that a man may pledge his faith to another lord after Christ? And renounce father and mother and all that are nearest to him, whom the Law teacheth should be honoured and loved next to God, whom the Gospel also hath in like manner honoured, only not valuing them more than Christ? Shall it be lawful for him to deal with the sword, when the Lord declareth that he that useth the sword shall perish by the sword? And shall the son of peace act in battle, whom it will not befit even to go to law? Shall he administer bonds and imprisonment, and tortures, and punishments, who may not avenge even his own injuries? [15]

While Tertullian did say this, it was more based on Christianity's eschewing from idolatry and cruelty. This becomes clearer when viewed against his other statements in regards

---

13 Clement of Rome, Corinthians, ch. 55
14 Irenaeus, *Against Heresies*, 5.24, ed. Ronald J. Sider
15 Tertullian, *De Corona*, ch. xi

the number of Christian fighters in the Roman military increased, and in the end, they dominated, and the sword would ultimately belong to the Church. Let us begin with some moments that indicate this growth of Christian soldiers within the first centuries of Christianity way before Constantine.

THE THUNDERING LEGION

Eusebius wrote of "the Melitine legion," who were all Christians under the emperorship of Marcus Aurelius (161 to 180 AD). It is reported that in the emperor's war with the Germans and the Sarmatians there was an unbearable drought, and the Christian soldiers prostrated before God in the accustomed fashion of the Church and prayed for rain. It was during this that a lightning bolt struck the earth and the enemy, who was watching from a distance. The enemy fled and rain finally came. From this time on the Melitine legion, according to Apollinaris, was given the title of "fulminea," or the "thundering legion."[7] Tertullian also wrote of this event, and he described how "the great drought in Germany was broken by rain obtained through the prayers of Christians, who, as it is chanced, were among his [the emperor's] soldiers."[8]

CHRISTIAN SOLDIERS IN ARCHAEOLOGY

There is also archeological evidence that dates from around the year 230 A.D. that shows the presence of Christian soldiers before Constantine. For example there is a prayer hall for Christians that was built right next to a military camp, in which is an inscription that says: "Gaianus, also called Porphyrius, centurion, our brother, has made the pavement at his own expense as an act of liberality. Brutius has carved out the work."

There is also another inscription thanking a certain Christian woman for lending a table for the altar for the prayer hall, on which the priest would consecrate the Eucharist so that the Christian soldiers could receive Holy Communion:

> The god-loving Akeptous [a woman] has offered the table to God Jesus Christ as a memorial.[9]

This is quite profound because after Christianity would take over the Roman Empire, soldiers would receive the Eucharist before entering into battle, and here this wonderful ritual was in the earliest years of Christianity. There are also numerous engraved memorials[10] of Christian soldiers that were carved before Constantine took power. For example, one inscription speaks of a soldier who re-enlisted in the military: "For Caelius Placidius, who re-enlisted in the army. Placida his daughter and Peculius his freedman made this for the sweetest patron."

---

7   Eusebius, *Ecclesiastical History*, 5.5
8   Tertullian, *Apology*, 5.6, trans. Glover & Rendall, brackets mine
9   Ronald J. Sider, *The Early Church on Killing*, part 4, p. 144
10 All of these inscriptions can be found in Ronald J. Sider, *The Early Church on Killing*, part 4, pp. 147–151

CHRISTIANITY IS AT WAR: THE MANIFESTO FOR CHRISTIAN MILITANCY

In another engraving it speaks of Eutyche Aurelia, "member of the Second Parthian Severan Legion, in the consulship of Favianus and Mucius (AD 201)." In another it mentions "Aurelius Barbas, veteran of the army of our Emperors, prefect of the Tenth Cohort." In one it speaks of "Publius Marcellus, a Roman knight, veteran of the army of our two Emperors." In another it speaks of "Antiagrucius the centurion." In an engraving it mentions "Leontianus the soldier from the unit of the Alecutti." In another it says:

> Here lies Solomon of great memory, who became count of the Circitorians, great domesticus [military staff assistance] and vicar of Thrace.

In no way would a pagan Roman soldier have the name of Solomon because it is a biblical name. Also, take notice that this Solomon held a very prestigious position within the military, showing what high ranks Christians possessed.

In one text it speaks of "Aelius Martinus, of the first Praetorian Cohort" and "Aelius Verinus, who re-enlisted during the reign of the Augusti (Severus and Caracalla)." In another it reads of "Aurelius Manos, soldier, cavalryman, archer, and bearer of the dragon-standard on the staff of the most outstanding general Castorius Constans." In yet another one it mentions "Gaius and Menophilus, from the armies." One text is quite detailed and is dedicated to a Christian centurion named Aurelius Gaius Jr.:

> Aurelius Gaius Jr., who enlisted in the First Legion Italica stationed in Moesia [Bulgaria], was selected [to serve] in the Eighth Legion Augusta stationed in Germany, then in the Iovia Scythica in the provinces of Scythia [Dobruja in eastern Romania] and Pannonia [Hungary]; served as tyro, apprentice cavalryman, then lancer, aide-de-camp of a centurion tirarius, aide-de-camp of a centurion ordinatus, aide-de-camp of a centurion princeps, then aide-de-camp in the mobile forces of the emperor with the First Legion Iovia Scythica.

From these text we can see that Christians way before Constantine or any of the Crusades were already in high and prestigious positions within the military. These were successors of the Christian military patriarch, Cornelius the Centurion, and it would continue on to the point that eventually the whole military of the Roman Empire would be a Christian force.

By 197 AD, there were a considerable amount of Christians in the military, for in this year Tertullian, writing to the pagans, wrote of Christian servicemen in the army: "We [the Christians] sail ships, we as well as you, and along with you; we go to the wars, to the country, to market with you."[11]

We also learn from Eusebius that by the third century, in the time of the tyrants Diocletian and Maximian, there were "Very many who were soldiers in the kingdom of Christ," who were martyred for refusing to pay worship to the gods.[12] The enforcement of paganism

---

11 Tertullian, *Apology*, ch. 42.3. St. Robert Bellarmine used this same passage to prove that Christian service in the Roman military was very ancient (*On Laymen or Secular People*, ch. 14, ed. Tutino, p. 58)
12 Euseb. Eccles. *Hist.* 8.4

to the military and killing. Tertullian believed that it was right for Christians already in the army before baptism to remain in the service, while those who are not soldiers and already baptized not to join the military:

> Clearly if their after-conversion to the Faith findeth any preoccupied in military service, their case is a different one, as was that of those whom John admitted to baptism, as was that of those most true believers the Centurions, him whom Christ approved, and him whom Peter instructed: though notwithstanding, when the Faith hath been embraced and sealed, a man must either straightway quit the service, as hath been done by many, or must in every way demur to doing anything against God, which things are not allowed, no, not on the ground of military service; or finally he must suffer for God's sake, to which also the faith of one who is not a soldier hath pledged him. [16]

The reason for Tertullian's sentiments is that when someone joined the military, they had to be an idolater, they had to declare allegiance to the gods of the empire, and so to be a Christian and join the service meant renouncing one's Faith. But, if you were already a pagan soldier and then you enter the Church, as long as you kept your Faith and did that which was just and right, then there was no reason for you to leave the occupation. This is why Tertullian, when speaking on the dangers of military service, says, "And shall he keep guard before the temples which he has renounced? And shall he take a meal where the apostle has forbidden? And shall he diligently protect by night those whom in the day-time he has put to flight by his exorcisms, leaning and resting on the spear the while with which Christ's side was pierced?"[17]

Many Christian soldiers were slaughtered in the first three hundred years of Christianity because they refused to bow down to the idols of the empire. During the reign of the tyrants, Diocletian and Maximian, there was a Christian centurion named Marcellus. There was a joint birthday party for the two tyrants, and this pious centurion was present, and a wonderful thing happened: Marcellus, before the pagan sovereigns, threw down his soldier's belt, and declared:

> I am a solider of Jesus Christ, the eternal king. From now I cease to serve your emperors and I despise the worship of your gods of wood and stone, for they are deaf and dumb images.

Marcellus was immediately arrested. He later stood trial before the judge, Fortunatus, who asked the zealous soldier, "What was your intention in violating military discipline by taking off your belt and throwing it down with your staff."

Marcellus did not say that it was because being a soldier is evil, but that the military oath that was to be taken if one wanted to be a soldier was evil, since it was indeed pagan. Marcellus' response was thus:

> while you were celebrating the emperor's feast day, I declared clearly and publicly before the standards of this legion that I was a Christian, and said that I could not serve under this military oath, but only for Christ Jesus, the son of God the Father almighty.

---

16 Tertullian, *De Corona*, xi
17 Tertullian, *De Corona*, ch. xi

Notice how he said that he would serve under Jesus Christ. In other words, if the army was Christian, and not pagan, then he would have never made such a passionate effort to express his contempt for idolatry and throw down his belt. He was later put to the sword, a witness for the most holy fighter, Jesus Christ, and a warrior martyr.[18]

There was another profound example of a Christian warrior, named Julius the Veteran, who was martyred for his faith in the year 304. As he stood trial before the prefect, Maximus, he illustrated that he was not against being in the military by declaring how he not only re-enlisted, but how he also remained and served loyally in his position:

> I was in the army, and when I had served my term I re-enlisted as a veteran. All of this time I worshipped in fear the God who made heaven and earth, and even to this day I show him my service.

The prefect, using agreeable words, tried to convince him just to make a simple sacrifice to the gods, saying: "I see that you are a wise and serious person. You shall receive a generous bonus if you will take my advice and sacrifice to the gods."

"I will not do what you wish," said Julius, "lest I incur an eternal penalty."

"If you do not respect the imperial decrees and offer sacrifice," replied the prefect, "I am going to cut your head off. Listen to me and offer the sacrifice, lest I put you to death as promised."

"I have chosen death for now," said Julius, "that I might live with the saints forever."

He entered death, the gates of Heaven awaited for his presence.[19] The story shows that Christians were indeed in the military, and only left because they did not want to abide by paganism. To illustrate this further, in the persecution of Decius, which lasted from 250–251 AD, the slaughter of the Christians "began with the brethren in the army."[20] These Christians remained loyal as soldiers, but were given the decision between martyrdom or life, and they chose a blessed death. Dionysus, the bishop of Alexandria at that time wrote of "a great many soldiers of Christ's kingdom" who chose Christ rather than pagan sacrifice. Amongst these warrior martyrs was one Philoromus, who Dionysus described as one "who held a high office under the imperial government at Alexandria, and who administered justice every day, attended by a military guard corresponding to his rank and Roman dignity."[21] The same bishop wrote of a "band of soldiers" whose names were Ammon, Zeno, Ptolemy and Ingenes, "and with them an old man, Theophilus."[22] These stories reveal the tenacious souls of the Christian soldier: they laugh at death when they die for their Faith, be it in martyrdom for a righteous and holy war, or martyrdom in persecution, either way, they are endurable soldiers on the spiritual battlefield.

---

18 For the whole story, see The Acts of Marcellus, in Ronald J. Sider, *The Early Church on Killing*, part 4, pp. 155–156
19 For the full story, see The Martyrdom of Julius of Veteran, in Ronald J. Sider, part 4, pp. 155–156
20 Eusebius, *Church History*, 8.4, ed. Ronald J. Sider
21 Eusebius, *Church History*, 8.9, 8.11, ed. Ronald J. Sider
22 Eusebius, *Church History*, 6.42, ed. Ronald J. Sider

If Tertullian's sentiments sprung from pacifism, then why would he permit baptized soldiers to remain in the military? Notice that he specifies that soldiers "must in every way demur to doing anything against God," and this statement is a warning against what pagan practices and injustices soldiers would do in his day. Imagine if the army was Christian and just, without idols and idolatry, desire for blood and cruelty; imagine if armies were not protecting pagan temples but Christian churches. Tertullian would then have no issue with military service. This is substantiated by Tertullian himself when he condemned the blade that spills innocent blood, and praised the sword that sheds blood justly:

> As for the sword, which is drunk with the blood of the brigand's victims, who would not banish it entirely from his house, much more from his bed-room, or from his pillow, from the presumption that he would be sure to dream of nothing but the apparitions of the souls which were pursuing and disquieting him for lying down with the blade which shed their own blood? Take, however, the cup which has no reproach on it, and which deserves the credit of a faithful ministration, it will be adorned by its drinking-master with chaplets, or be honoured with a handful of flowers. The sword also which has received honourable stains in war, and has been thus engaged in a better manslaughter, will secure its own praise by consecration. [23]

Tertullian was not a fanatic pacifist[24] as some try to portray him, but one who distinguished between unjust killing and just killing. Tertullian understood that at times the taking of blood is just. Notice how he makes reference to "a better manslaughter" and explains how the sword that kills justly "will secure its own praise by consecration." This signifies a holy execution of the blade, and thus was the idea of just violence within Christianity hundreds of years before Constantine. Moreover, in his infamous *Apology*, Tertullian wrote of how Christians pray not for weak soldiers, but for strong armies and for a secured empire:

> Without ceasing, for all our emperors we offer prayer. We pray for life prolonged; for security to the empire; for protection to the imperial house; for brave armies, a faithful senate, a virtuous people, the world at rest, whatever, as man or Caesar, an emperor would wish. [25]

To pray for the army is not to condemn warfare, but to support and uphold the use of military force, for a just cause of course. If the Roman Empire in Tertullian's day was Christian, then he would be praying for strong Christian soldiers and for a strong Christian empire.

CLEMENT OF ALEXANDRIA

Clement of Alexandria, a Christian apologist who lived from 150 to 215 AD, said that the soldier in the army must obey his commander if he orders justice to be done: "Has knowledge

---

23 Tertullian, *On the Resurrection of the Flesh*, ch. xvi
24 See St. Robert Bellarmine, *On Laymen or Secular People*, ch. 14, ed. Tutino, pp. 61–62, where he explains why Tertullian was not a pacifist
25 Tertullian, *Apology*, 30, ed. Ronald J. Sider

taken hold of you while engaged in military service? Listen to the commander, who orders what is right."26

Clement also wrote that it is not proper for the soldier to be adored with gold, and that to be righteous is to be strong, restrained and just, implying that the soldier is to bear these virtues and be selfless:

> The excellence of man is righteousness, and temperance, and manliness, and godliness. The beautiful man is, then, he who is just, temperate, and in a word good, not he who is rich. But now even the soldiers wish to be decked with gold. 27

The destruction of pagan inhabitants by Moses was praised by the ancient Christian scholar, Clement of Alexandria, amongst the oldest of Christianity's defenders. He wrote:

> Furthermore, he [Moses] put to flight and slew the hostile occupants of the land, falling upon them from a desert and rugged line of march (such was the excellence of his generalship). For the taking of the land of those hostile tribes was a work of skill and strategy. 28

Clement of Alexandria also defended the Hebrews' killing of pagan Midianite women, as he writes:

> When then, did not the women of the Midianites, by their beauty, seduce from wisdom into impiety, through licentiousness, the Hebrews when making war against them? For, having seduced them from a grave mode of life, and by their beauty ensnared them in wanton delights, they made them insane upon idol sacrifices and strange women; and overcome by women and by pleasure at once, they revolted from God, and the power of the enemy through female stratagem, until, when they were in peril, fear by its admonitions pulled them back. Then the survivors, valiantly undertaking the struggle for piety, got the upper hand of their foes. 29

JULIUS AFRICANUS

Julius Africanus, a Christian writer who lived from 180 to 250 and who strived to show the superiority of Christianity to all other religions, put great importance on military weaponry and even studied past battles to acquire more knowledge on this skill:

> Among all the areas of knowledge, that of war is especially valuable. I have often asked myself what determined the outcome of military battles and why the Greeks have been conquered by the Romans, the Persians by the Greeks, and never on the other hand the Persians by the Romans. Upon reflection, I have noticed that the reason is not found in superior strategy; rather the reason lies in the system of weapons and the type of military equipment. 30

---

26 Clement of Alexandria, *Exhortation to the Greeks*, ch. 10, ed. Ronald J. Sider
27 Clement of Alexandria, *The Educator*, 2.13, ed. Ronald J. Snider
28 Clement of Alexandria, Stromata, 1.24
29 Clement of Alexandria, Stromata, 1.18
30 Julius Africanus, Kestoi 7, ed. Ronald J. Sider

The fact that such a known apologist and scholar within Christianity was writing on the importance of weapons in combat, way before Constantine or any of the Crusades, shows that the early Christians were not as pacifistic as some revisionists argue, and it also indicates an admiration for warfare within the Christian community. All of the factors necessary for Holy War were already in Christianity and the Christian people, so that when the time did come to unsheathe the sword, the hearts of the saints were ready. Julius Africanus believed in attacking enemies in combat. He also promoted biological warfare, killing the enemy camp with a cleverly concocted poison that causes the plague and wipes out the whole enemy camp, their families and their nation:

> Thus one must not only attack adversaries with an open battle; it is also necessary to combat enemies with a crowd of ruses, even the most secret. [He describes how to prepare a mysterious potion that will cause the plague. One should mix it with food.] One then gives it to the enemy in any way that he can while simulating a precipitous retreat and abandoning, in the face of the attack, one's camp filled with this kind of food. This does not produce death the next day. The one who has tasted it does not perish immediately. It is a plague which works by surprise and affects those who have not eaten the bread. It expands while acquiring companions. Its attack expand to the family, the town, the army, the nation. [31]

ORIGEN

Even Origen, one of the oldest of the ancient Christian theologians, living from 185 to 254, who is touted and constantly represented as an enthusiastic pacifist, believed in the use of killing for just purposes. For example, Origen believed that it was righteous for men to assemble and assassinate a tyrant for the cause of truth, just as it is right for Christians to rebel against the devil:

> It is not irrational, then, to form associations in opposition to existing laws, if done for the sake of truth. For as those persons would do well who should enter into a secret association in order to put to death a tyrant who had seized upon the liberties of a state, so Christians also, when tyrannized over by him who is called the devil, and by falsehood, form leagues contrary to the laws of the devil, against his power, and for the safety of those others whom they may succeed in persuading to revolt from a government which is, as it were, 'Scythian,' and despotic. [32]

When Origen observed the bees, he saw their order and organization as a potential model for soldiers in war, if, he said, a war was ever necessary:

> Perhaps also the so-called wars among the bees convey instruction as to the manner in which wars, if ever there arise a necessity for them, should be waged in a just and orderly way among men. [33]

---

31 Julius Africanus, Kestoi 7, ed. Ronald J. Sider
32 Origen, *Against Celsus*, 1.1, ed. Ronald J. Sider
33 Origen, *Against Celsus*, 4.82, ed. Ronald J. Sider

Origen even held to an imperial aspiration. He affirmed that Christianity would eventually inundate the Roman Empire, and thus destroy every false religion, that the law of God will be obeyed, and that the holy Faith would be the only faith observed amongst the people. He wrote to his pagan opponent, Celsus, that "the barbarians, when they yield obedience to the word of God, will become most obedient to the law, and most humane; and every form of worship will be destroyed except the religion of Christ, which will alone prevail. And indeed it will one day triumph, as its principles take possession of the minds of people more and more each day."[34] While Origen is nowhere in this statement supporting any form of war, he nonetheless is zealously declaring his support for Christian supremacy, the destruction of paganism, and the utter inundation of Christianity in the empire, which would include the state and influence over laws.

And surely this is the aspiration of the Church and the Holy Faith—to have the entire world become Christian, under the universal empire of Christendom, under "One Lord, one faith, one baptism" (Ephesians 4:5).

ADAMANTIUS

Adamantius was a theologian who wrote against the gnostic heretics somewhere in between 290–300 AD. It has become very common for Christians to express vitriol in applying the Old Testament when it comes to warfare, and similarly in the time of Adamantius, the gnostic heretics hated the prophets of the Old Testament and in turn expressed nothing but contempt against the holy wars of the Hebrews. Adamantius wrote against this heresy in the form of a dialogue in which he vindicated the use of war against evildoers. In one part of the dialogue he says to the gnostic: "even the Gospel recognizes the right of retaliation and the slaying of evil men. Thus it says, 'The Lord of that evil servant will come on a day when he knows not, and in an hour when he is not expecting, and will cut him in two and will assign him a place among the unbelieving' [cf Luke 12:46]. Hence it is right to wage a just war against those who go to war unjustly. In the same way it was right that those who preached peace should preach it without arms."[35]

Adamantius also stated that whether or not the act of killing itself is bad is solely determined by the circumstances and the objective. If one were to kill for a righteous purpose, then it is permissible, but if one were to kill to steal property, then it is evil. The act itself is the same, but what dictates its goodness or evilness, are circumstances. Adamantius, contrary to every modern theologian out there, even said that if one called for the death of an adulterer, he does no sin:

> Should a man desire the death of someone caught in adultery, demanding the punishment of his shameless act, he does no crime. Yet, if a man kills someone who has done nothing illegal, on a mere pretext, or for the purpose of removing his household property—that is, his

---

34 Origen, *Against Celsus*, 8.68, ed. Ronald J. Sider
35 Adamantius, *Dialogue on the True Faith*, 1.10, ed Ronald J. Sider

money or goods—he does wrong. The act is the same in both cases, but the circumstances of the act make the difference. [36]

LACTANTIUS

Lactantius, the Cicero of Christianity, thrived as a theologian before and after Constantine became emperor. He is at times confused as a person who was once a pacifist, but then turned in favor for war after Constantine became the first Christian emperor. The reason for this opinion is that before Constantine he made several statements against the wars of pagan emperors, and then after Constantine, he supported his war against the pagan tyrants. This is commonly believed to be a contradiction on the part of Lactantius, but this is a misconception. What we need to keep in mind is that the wars Lactantius spoke ill of were done by pagan tyrants, and the ones he supported were done by a Christian sovereign. Both were wars, but what determined Lactantius to condemn one and praise the other, was the cause. With the pagans the cause was evil, but with the Christian emperor the cause was just. For example, before Constantine's ascension of the throne, Lactantius had this to say about the wars of pagan caesars:

> Truly the greater number of people they have cast down, plundered, and slain, so much the more noble and distinguished do they think themselves; and ensnared by the show of empty glory they give to their crimes the names of virtue. I would rather that they should make to themselves gods from the slaughter of wild beasts, than approve of an immorality so stained with blood. [37]

This is not a condemnation of war unto itself, but the cruel and senseless wars that pagan kings would endeavor purely for the sake of conquest, and of course, for their false gods. In one place Lactantius condemns war for gain, but not war for the sake of God or a just cause:

> For how can a person be just who injures, who hates, who despoils, who puts to death? And they who strive to be serviceable to their country do all these things: for they are ignorant of what this being serviceable is, who think nothing useful, nothing advantageous, but that which can be held by the hand. Whoever, then, has gained for his country these goods—as they themselves call them—that is, who by the overthrow of cities and the destruction of nations has filled the treasury with money, has taken lands and enriched his countrymen—he is extolled with praises to heaven: in him there is said to be the greatest and perfect virtue. [38]

In another line he affirms that the violent nature of the pagans springs from their worship of violent deities:

---

36 Adamantius, *Dialogue on the True Faith*, 4.10
37 Lactantius, *Divine Institutes*, 1.18, ed. Ronald J. Sider
38 Lactantius, *Divine Institutes*, 6.6, ed. Ronald J. Sider

> Nor is it difficult to show why the worshippers of the gods cannot be good and just. For how shall they abstain from the shedding of blood who worship bloodthirsty deities, Mars and Bellona? [39]

But, when Constantine attacked the pagan tyrants, he praised his triumph over them, not because he was a hypocrite, but because he was in favor of Christian Holy War, done to destroy and defeat paganism, and establish Christendom. He praised Constantine and his victory in these words:

> Constantine, with steady courage and a mind prepared for every event, led his whole forces to the neighborhood of Rome, and encamped them opposite to the Milvian Bridge. The Supreme God did so to place their [the pagans'] necks under the sword of their foes that they seemed to have entered the field, not as combatants, but as men devoted to death. Let us therefore with exultation celebrate the triumphs of God, and oftentimes with praises make mention of His victory. [40]

Lactantius' support and upholding of Christian just war against evil, is expressed in his later book entitled, *On the Anger of God*, in which he wrote that the state has the right to punish those who injure the innocent, and that wicked people need to be punished, not for the sake of punishing those who only physically hurt others—which is the modern perspective on law—but in order to preserve morals and prevent perversity and deviancy:

> But if the law is just which awards the transgressor his due, and if the judge is called upright and good when he punishes crimes,—for he guards the safety of good people who punishes the evil,—it follows that God, when He opposes the evil, is not injurious; but he himself is injurious who either injures an innocent person, or spares an injurious person that he may injure many. Therefore we arise to take vengeance, not because we have been injured, but that discipline may be preserved, morals may be corrected, and licentiousness be suppressed. This is just anger; and as it is necessary in God, from whom an example comes to people. For as we ought to restrain those who are subject to our power, so also ought God to restrain the offenses of all. [41]

Lactantius was not against war, he was for the raising of the sword, not for selfish reasons, but for spiritual reasons. He saw God as the absolute model to emulate, and so imitating Him, one would imitate His justice and His mercy. Such is a part of Holy War, and it is only commenced not for the sake of ourselves, but for the sake of the Divine Law, and for justice.

---

39 Lactantius, *Divine Institutes*, 5.10, ed. Ronald J. Sider
40 Lactantius, *On the Death of the Persecutors*, 44, 47, 52, ellipses and brackets mine, ed. Ronald J. Sider
41 Lactantius, *On the Anger of God*, 17, ed. Ronald J. Sider

PART 3

This section makes the case that wars within Christian history did not begin with Constantine in the fourth century or in the Middle Ages, as is commonly taught in the modern realm, but that Christian warfare first took place within the first century, and that Christian crusades were being done hundreds of years before the First Crusade in 1096.

THE FIRST CHRISTIAN KING AND THE FIRST CHRISTIAN BATTLE HAPPENED IN THE FIRST CENTURY

When we read or hear of Christian wars, we usually begin with the Crusades, or at times we are told of wars that took place in the fourth century, or wars that were fought between Byzantium and its enemies in the early Middle Ages. But when speaking of the earliest Christian king, and the earliest Christian battle, done with arms and weapons, what we are never told is that the first Christian battle was not done in the Middle Ages or any time around that, but within the first century after the Resurrection of our Lord. It was done by King Abgar V, who ruled over the Syrian city of Edessa, and who was the first Christian sovereign. He left the path of the heathen and sojourned to the Light of God when Christ was on earth. According to the historian Eusebius, King Abgar was dreadfully ill and, hearing of Christ and how He healed so many countless people, he sent a letter in the year 33, asking for his infirmity to be healed. Eusebius copied the letter, which he said was taken from the public records of Edessa, as follows:

> Agars, prince of Edessa, sends greeting to Jesus the excellent Savior, who has appeared in the borders of Jerusalem. I have heard the reports respecting thee and thy cures, as performed by thee without medicines, and without the use of herbs. For as it is said, thou causes the blind to see again, the lame to walk, and thou cleanest the lepers, and thou castes out the impure spirits and demons, and thou halest those that are tormented by long disease, and thou raises the dead. And hearing all these things of thee, I concluded in my mind one of two things: either that thou art God, and having descended from heaven, does these things, or else that, thou art the son of God. Therefore, now I have written and besought thee to visit me, and to heal the disease with which I am afflicted. I have, also, heard that the Jews murmur against

thee, and are plotting to injure thee; I have, however, a very small but noble state, which is sufficient for us both. [1]

Christ is said to have written a response to the king, in a letter, said by Eusebius to be taken from Edessa's public records. It is said in tradition that the letter was sent through one Ananias who took the letter from Christ and gave it to the king. Eusebius copied the letter, and it reads:

> Blessed art thou, O Agars, who, without seeing, hast believed in me. For it is written concerning me, that who have seen me will not believe, that they who have not seen, may believe and live. But in regard to what thou hast written, that I should come to thee, it is necessary that I should fulfill all things here, for which I have been sent. And after this fulfillment, thus to be received up, I will send to thee a certain one of my disciples, that he may heal thy affliction, and give life to thee and to those who are with thee. [2]

It was said that after Christ ascended to Heaven, one of the Disciples, named Thaddeus, healed the king Abgar, and from such a miracle came the first Christian ruler. After this, it did not take long for the armies of the devil to prey after the saintly king; the Persians, pagan Zoroastrians who worshipped the false god of Ahura Mazda, soon surrounded the city of Edessa, and were already planning to conquer and seize it for their own heathen expansion. Seeing such a great horde of savage barbarians before his land, while he may have prayed for his enemies, he certainly did not surrender. He took the letter that Christ wrote to him, and in the presence of all his soldiers, he raised arms high up to Heaven, his hand gripped around the letter, and he mightily prayed to the Eternal General. "Lord Jesus," he declared, "You promised us that no enemy would enter this city. But look, at this moment the Persians are attacking us." He prayed with few words, and as his hands still stood aloft, a great darkness covered the sky and blackened the day's light.

The Persians, who were now just three miles away from the city, witnessed the darkness and how it smothered the sun's rays, and surely they were terrified. So stricken with confusion were the Persians that they could barely even set up their camp and surround the city. They did not know how to strike, nor how to penetrate the walls of Edessa, but after some time, they became so desperate to fulfill their desires for conquest and pillage that they nevertheless besieged the city and attacked it with all their frenzied exertion. For many months catapults launched their missiles, for many months did the city endure the onslaughts of the pagan, and for many months did the Christian king hold his ground, neither surrendering nor acquiescing, but protecting his people from God's enemies as a true sovereign of Christendom. Above the city there was a hill from which the people received their water, and when the Persians saw it they contrived a plan to cut the water supply off and kill the inhabitants with thirst. They diverted the water from the city, to their own camp. But when they did this all of the springs under the earth miraculously burst forth, guaranteeing the city water.

---

1 Euseb. Eccles. Hist. 1.13
2 Euseb. Eccles. 1.13

However, the water that was to be diverted to the Persians dried up. So dry was the water source that the Persians who were besieging the city did not have enough to quench their parched thirsts. Their unbearable thirsts compelled them to leave the city. And so was the Christian king, thanks to God alone, victorious. And every time the Persians tried to invade the city, the letter of Christ was brought out and read at the gate, and by the will of God, the enemy was forced to flee.

In the fourth century, several hundred years after this glorious triumph, a Spanish nun named Egeria visited the city of Edessa, and there she saw a statue of King Abgar, and the local bishop told her: "There is King Abgar, who, before seeing the Lord, believed in Him and believed that He was truly the Son of God." This bishop recounted to Egeria the beautiful story of the battle between the Christians and the pagan Persians, and she recorded all that he told her in her diary, from which we know this event.[3]

Is it not majestic and awe-inspiring, that right there, in the first century—so few years after the Resurrection—we have a Christian king partaking in battle against pagans? The king fought his enemies, and within him were the teachings of Christ; for he would have known about the eternal precepts of our Lord. Christ taught us to carry our cross; to deny ourselves; to love God with all heart, mind, soul, spirit, and strength; to love our neighbors as ourselves; to sacrifice ourselves so that we could be taken up to the timeless realms of Heaven. And here, a king, being amongst the first converts, exerted the Christian spirit through Holy War; for he took up his cross in the face of the enemy; he denied himself and was utterly surrendered to the will of God; he did not seek to save himself, but others; he loved God with all his being, and so he ceaselessly defended his nation rather than allow it to be taken by the devil and his slaves; he loved his neighbor as himself, and so he protected his people, rather than sell them to the pagans through greedy compromise; he did not save himself, but rather put his own life on the line for the sake of his people. He was a warrior mystic, fighting a spiritual war through physical arms, for the glory of God and for the downfall of the devils. And in this battle, he exerted the truest form of love, and that is, righteous action.

Let this story be a lesson, that Christians were not passive only until the fourth century or the Middle Ages, but that from the beginning, the idea of combat and warfare was already within the Church, not hiding, but waiting for the obtaining of a state through which to execute Holy War. You may argue that this is only one example, and that the Apostles did not fight, but this was a Christian king, not an apostle, and he led a war. Imagine if the whole empire became Christian in the time of the Apostles; surely in such a state they would have not prohibited it from commencing a righteous war.

THE ARMENIANS—AMONGST THE FIRST OF HOLY WARRIORS

Armenia was the first nation to become officially Christian, and, it was amongst the first of the Christian peoples to fight in Holy War against the enemies of God for the glory of the Cross. In the year 312, before Constantine took power, the pagan emperor Maximian

---

3   Egeria, *Diary*, ch. 19

commenced the bloodiest persecution against Christians in pagan Rome's history. Part of the persecution was to declare war against the first Christian nation—Armenia. The Armenian Christians did not allow themselves to be slaughtered, but stood their ground for their nation and Faith. The historian Eusebius recounts this glorious event as such:

> In addition to this the tyrant was compelled to go to war with the Armenians, who had been from ancient times friends and allies of the Romans. As they were also Christians and zealous in their piety toward the Deity, the enemy of God had attempted to compel them to sacrifice to idols and demons, and had thus made friends foes, and allies enemies. All these things suddenly took place at one and the same time, and refuted the tyrant's empty vaunt against the Deity. *For he had boasted that, because of his zeal for idols and his hostility against us, neither famine nor pestilence nor war had happened in his time.* These things, therefore, coming upon him at once and together, furnished a prelude also of his own destruction. He himself with his forces was defeated in the war with the Armenians, and the rest of the inhabitants of the cities under him were terribly afflicted with famine and pestilence. [4]

CHRISTIANITY'S FIRST MAJOR WAR

A fierce fire in the midst of a marketplace was made, and as its flames consumed the materials by which it lived, a mob of Roman soldiers scoffingly approached it with their hands clenched on some battered books. Within these lied the writ of men who, having already given away their last breaths, wrote prophecies of a maiden by whose favor with God conceived as a virgin the Child by Whose divinity and by Whose death the world sees that Light which is inconceivable to the darkness. Within her womb the eternal Word became flesh, and for this Incarnation she received the enmity from the lord of all darkness, and against the Holy One do the slaves of the darkness rage. The Roman soldiers who tossed these Scriptures into the flames, did not know that they were indeed slaves to that old serpent who one day will be cast into the flames of the abyss, and their hatred was really for that virgin and her Son Who she brought forth and Who bore the Holy Cross to defeat their master—the devil.

These soldiers were under the command of three emperors, Diocletian, Maximinus, and Galerius. They hated Christianity, for the same reason why the ancient pagans hated the Law of Moses, because it was inherently contrary and militant against tyranny. Galerius believed that he was "begotten by a God,"[5] and he wanted to destroy those who declared without apology that Christ was the only Son of God.

The persecution was instigated in part by Galerius' mother, who was addicted to the worship of "the gods of the mountains," and like Jezebel before her, she desired to see the deaths of God's people. In a dinner feast she implored Diocletian and Galerius, his son-in-law, to contrive the destruction of the saints. After some discourse on the plan, Diocletian—being less inclined to the idea—decided to ask Apollo on what should be done to the Christians.

---

4   Eusebius, *Church History*, 9.8, ed. Ronald J. Sider
5   Lactantius, *On the death of the Persecutors*, ix

They consulted with a pagan priest and he, after asking the demon, declared that the Christians should not exist. Diocletian, being more moderate, said that the driving out of Christianity could be done without shedding blood, while Galerius said that those who refused the gods should be burnt alive. So the persecution began.

On a certain morning officers broke into a certain church, seized all of the sacred Scriptures and threw them into the fire.[6]

THE CHRISTIANS CHOOSE LIFE, AND DIE IN CHRIST

Flames consumed the pages of Scripture, houses of worship were toppled and the pastors, who indeed cared for their flocks unlike the hirelings, were arrested. Christians were declared incapable of all honors and employment and lost their liberty to vote. They and their congregations were to observe the festival of Christ's Passion, but in this time of forlorn days, they were to endure a travailing passion, and to suffer as their Savior had suffered. The edict of despotism was passed, and even those who were citizens of the glorious empire were stripped of their liberties for their adherence to the Nazarene.

Imagine to yourself such a sight: in one spot there lied a man whose back was being lacerated by whips, and another whose flesh was torn by sharp blades.[7] And as our souls are struck with the melancholy of unsettling pity, Can we not help but be reminded of our Lord Who too was inflicted with such cruelties? They were told just to toss a sprinkle of incense on a small pile of steaming coals before an altar of Jupiter, and for such a small action did rather endure the most unbearable pains than lose their souls. As they accepted their persecution, one cried out, not in pain, but in abhorrence of the pagan sacrifice.[8]

MARTYRDOM IS CHOSEN OVER AN EASY LIFE

In Nicomedia the edict was presented to all the people. A Christian passing by saw it, took a hold of it, defied the wishes of the state and expressed zealotry to God, and tore it to pieces. He was swiftly arrested and with calm mind persevered through the execution until his spirit left the body.[9]

In the same city another Christian man was brought before the emperors and urged to give just a little incense to Jupiter, so that he may worship Christ in peace. He refused; he was stripped naked like our Lord, and his back viscously whipped. To make the pain all the more excruciating, they poured salt and vinegar upon the mangled parts of his body. As he bore these tortures—as our Lord bore the Cross—they began to slowly cook his body with fire. Little by little, the flames consumed his flesh; but he knew within himself that all of the fires of the earth were nothing in comparison to the indescribable flames of hell which burn forever. His skin was roasted and his entire body cooked. He died a death worthy of his

---

6   Lactantius, *On the death of the Persecutors*, xi–xii
7   Euseb. Eccles. Hist. 8.2; 8.3
8   Euseb. Eccles. Hist. 8.3; Lactantius, *On the death of the Persecutors*, xiii
9   Euseb. Eccles Hist. 8.5

name; for he was called Peter. Another saint, Anthimus, bishop of the church of Nicomedia, confessed Christ only to receive decapitation, and the others around him too were not spared.

A fire broke out in the imperial palace of Nicomedia, and as usually happens, the Christians were blamed. It was a Reichstag Fire. Entire families were put to the sword, and others were taken to the seas and thrown into the waves to be left to the mercy of the ruthless waters. A sedition occurred in Syria and in Melitina, and the Christians were again brought under suspicion. Leaders of the Church were cast into prison, and in places where murderers and thieves are confined, were deacons, bishops, presbyters, and exorcists. The prisoners were requested to offer up incense to the gods, but again they continued in their obstinacy, and many martyrs were made of them, especially in Egypt and Mauritania.[10]

In Egypt, Christians were crucified with their bodies pointed to the earth and left to starve to death. Others were slowly cut with shells until they breathed their last breath. Women were made naked, and with a rope tied on one foot, raised up to the air and exposed. Christians were bound by their arms to tree branches squeezed together into clusters, and once the branches were released to resume to their original structure, their limbs would snap off.[11]

Some Christian men and women were thrown into great pyres of fire, others were beheaded, and numerous of them tossed into the ocean. As soon as one was sentenced to death, another charged foreword to confess his Faith, and so elated were they at the very aspiration of seeing their God in eternity that some went so far as to offer up to Heaven hymns and songs of exultation. Philoromus, a man of great dignity in Alexandria, and Phileas, a bishop learned in philosophy, were both brought before a tribune, and for their fervency in the true religion, both were beheaded.[12]

This Phileas, before death, wrote an epistle to the Christians of Thmuis in Egypt:

> As all these signs, examples, and noble precepts are presented to us in Holy Scriptures, those holy martyrs with us did not hesitate, whilst they sincerely directed their mental eye to that God who rules over all, and in their minds preferred death for their religion, and firmly adhered to their vocation. They had well understood that our Lord Jesus Christ became man for us, that he might remove all sin, and furnish us with the means of entering into eternal life. For he thought it not robbery to be equal with God, but humbled himself, taking upon him the form of a servant, and being found in the fashion of man, he humbled himself unto death, even the death of the cross. [13]

Many of them were thrown into prison and were given the option of being relieved if they just touched the sacrifice to the devils of the heathen. They remained in their cells, where many endured the torment of the night's silence. But these men received their peace from an authority which surpasses all physical torments, all the pomp of government, all the pride of prestige, and all the cruelty of demagogues. With neither sword nor spear but with zeal and

---

10   Euseb. Eccles. Hist. 8.6
11   Euseb. Eccles. Hist. 8.8–9
12   Euseb. Eccles. Hist. 8.9
13   Epistle of Phileas, in Euseb. Eccles. Hist. 8.10

ardency did they vanquish the ambitions of the tyrants who sought after innocent blood in return for power. Phileas, the night before receiving death, came before them and proclaimed those Scriptures that cry out against the idolatries of the pagans: "For he that offereth sacrifice to other gods, shall be destroyed. Thou shalt have none other gods but me."[14]

The Pope at the time, Gaius, was actually of the same family as the emperor Diocletian, but this did not exempt him from persecution. He did not wish to save his life through lying, diplomacy or compromise. Nor did he pride himself in his noble blood—none of that mattered for he was a citizen of Heaven—but he defied the orders of his relative, broke the decrees of the empire, and rejected the idols. He fled into hiding, and after eight years he was martyred under Diocletian, his very relation.[15]

His successor, Pope Marcellinus, ascended to the throne of St. Peter amidst a most violent persecution. In his pontificate, Diocletian orchestrated the slaughter of seventeen thousand Christians within a span of only thirty days, and under the order of the same despot, the bodies were made to rot on the streets for twenty-six days. Marcellinus was eventually arrested and asked to sacrifice to the idols, he acquiesced and offered the abominable thing. But being inspired by penitence, he recanted and was beheaded.[16]

THE STUBBORN CHRISTIANS

Soldiers surrounded a Christian town in Phrygia in what is today Turkey, and every one of its inhabitants refused the gods of the emperors. The troops hurled down fire upon the people and all were consumed by the flames. Saved by the flames of hell, and ascended into their mansions prepared by their Savior, and bestowed upon with the crowns of glory. Adanetus, a Christian of noble Italian birth, was seized and slain as he nobly took up the cause of piety.[17] Christians in Arabia were rushed by the pagans and slaughtered with axes. In Mesopotamia, Christians were hung by their feet just a little distance above the ground and made to inhale smoke from a kindled fire just a little below them until they suffocated. In Egypt, Christians were found with their ears severed, noses cut off, and hands amputated. The chronicles of the Church still weep about those forlorn trials of the saints in Antioch who were—like animals—slowly roasted in flames. Women with their daughters, rather allowing themselves to be under the cruelty of the men, threw themselves into rivers to drown. In Pontus, torturers thrusted sharp reeds into the flesh under the fingernails, and other Christians had boiling led poured on their backs.

The stubbornness of the Christians compelled the judges of the tribunes to rethink their methods. "For," they said, "the cities should not be polluted with blood any more." They decreed that only their eyes should be ripped out, or one of their legs severed off.[18] But this

---

14 See the Epistle of Phileas, in Euseb. Eccles. Hist. 8.10
15 *Liber Pontificalis*, xxix: Gaius
16 *Liber Pontificalis*, xxx: Marcellinus
17 Euseb. Eccles. Hist. 8.11
18 Euseb. Eccles. Hist. 8.12

was not truly followed and the numbers of martyrs killed for the name of Christ multiplied. Silvanus, the bishop of Gaza, was beheaded with thirty-nine others, and the bishop of Emisa (also named Silvanus) was fed to wild beasts as an entertainment. Peleus and Nilus, both bishops in Egypt, were burnt alive.[19]

But amongst all the stories of persecution, one of the most brutal is what took place in Palestine. Two Christians, Alpheus and Zeccheus, were made to suffer agonizing torture. Their backs were lacerated with metal hooks, and their feet, for a whole day and a whole night, were stretched to their utmost limits. Then, after this sadism was fulfilled, their heads were cut off for confessing God and Christ—and not Caesar—as "the only King."[20]

Romanus, a deacon and exorcist, was strapped upon a pyre, and before they burnt him alive, he said with fearlessness: "Where then is the fire?" They brought him down to punish him for his fortitude and cut his tongue off. Though he could not speak with the voice of the tongue, he still used that voice only inherent in man, and that is the voice of the heart from which emanates sublime ideals that no tyrant can take; that have no beginning nor end, but determine man's eternal fate. He was put into chains, and when the twentieth anniversary of the emperor was at hand, the Romans observed the common custom and granted liberty to all those in prison—all those but Romanus, that is. His feet were stretched to the farthermost extent, and as he laid on the wood, his life was taken.[21] People today say that these stories were exaggerated, or even made up. But these brutalities are in our own times with the same cruelty and severity by Muslims and other heathens. Can one deny the brutalities of ISIS or the Ottoman Empire?

Edicts were issued to the governor of Palestine, Urbanus, ordering that all the inhabitants must give sacrifice and make libations to idols.[22] The reason for this was inherent to all paganism. The gods of the Romans were all found in nature: the earth, the ocean, the sky, the moon, the sun, and the planets. The emperor himself was a god, and was esteemed as the planet Jupiter in the flesh. All of these can be seen by all peoples, therefore paganism united the empire, and to keep the subjects in collectivism, honor to the gods had to be proven. It was Christianity that was opposed to this tyrannical unity; for its Founder said that not all things belong to Caesar, but that what belongs to God is His and not to be touched by the government. The very teachings of the Faith are unto themselves a threat to all governments, for it undermines any attempt of the state to exalt itself equal, or above, God.

It was for this very belief that Timotheus, a Christian in Gaza, chose to be burnt very slowly in fire rather than abide by the state and worship its demons.[23] It was for this belief that God is above man that Pagas seized the hand of the governor Urbanus as he was about to make an offering to his gods, and exhorted him that it was "not right that we should

---

19 Euseb. Eccles. Hist. 8.13
20 *The Book of Martyrs*, ch. i, trans. C.F. Cruse
21 *The Book of Martyrs*, ch. ii
22 *The Book of Martyrs*, ch. iii
23 *The Book of Martyrs*, ch. iii

desert the one only and true God, to sacrifice to idols and demons." He was immediately apprehended by the guards, whipped, and cast into prison and tortured. The sides of his body were cut with blades all the way down to his very bowels and his very bones. They covered his feet with linen and doused it with oil, and then lit his feet aflame. The flesh melted like wax. They gave him one more chance to sacrifice, he refused and was thrown into the sea where he drowned.[24]

Ulpianus was sewed into a bull's hide with a dog and a poisonous asp and thrown into the sea.[25] Maximinus, as part of the celebration for his birthday, watched Christians torn limb from limb by wild beasts with delight and pleasure. Amongst them was one Christian very robust in strength, and he—to defy the emperor—attacked the bear that was supposed to eat him. When the guards managed to get ahold of him, he was amazingly still alive and breathing heavily. They tied heavy stones around his feet and cast him into the sea to drown.[26]

Theodosia, a young virgin in Caesarea, was tortured with such malice that her breasts were mutilated before she was drowned.[27] Almost one hundred Christians were ordered by the sadistic governor Firmlianus to be punished severely. First, their eyes were cut out and then seared with red-hot irons so as to uproot them, the sinews of their left legs were seared off with the same irons, and then they were made to labor forever in the dark and dismal mines of Palestine.[28]

Another Christian woman was flogged, and placed on a rack where both sides of her torso were furrowed by blades. Another woman, gazing upon such a sight of cruelty, could no longer bear it. "And how long, then, will you cruelly torture my sister?" She was ordered to be brought before an altar to give libations to the gods, but she in complete defiance to tyranny—and complete obedience to God—kicked the altar down as Gideon brought low the altar of Baal. After enduring the greatest of tortures, she was sentenced to the flames.[29]

THE EARTH WEEPS

So many bodies of the saints laid upon the ground and so much blood was swallowed by the earth as it did for the blood of Abel in mankind's first beginning. In that horrid moment of the story of the Church—which does not cease to be but a repetition of what took place between Adam's and Eve's first two sons—birds descended to consume the rotting flesh of the bodies, and dogs came about to indulge in the gore. Throughout the city of Caesarea there was found the entrails and the bones of the slain, their severed limbs and their decaying carcasses. Such a sight did not even expose the slightest bit of sadness and lamentation in those walking by, peering upon the perished bearers of the Holy Cross. Then all of a sudden the

---

24 *The Book of Martyrs*, ch. iv
25 *The Book of Martyrs*, ch. v
26 *The Book of Martyrs*, ch. vi
27 *The Book of Martyrs*, ch. vii
28 *The Book of Martyrs*, ch. viii
29 *The Book of Martyrs*, ch. viii

heavens appeared most serene, the greater part of the city's columns emanated drips of water, and though the air was dry, the streets and the marketplaces became wet. It was as though the earth was weeping, and the blood of the saints cried out to God from the ground.[30]

In the same city there were five Christians seized who, rejecting their native pagan names, called themselves Elias, Jeremiah, Isaiah, Samuel, and Daniel. They esteemed the prophets of Israel and wished to emulate them. One of them was asked where he was from, he replied that he was from the Jerusalem above in Heaven, referring to the words St. Paul, "but the Jerusalem above is free, which is the mother of us all." He was made to endure torture and was continually asked where this Jerusalem was, and with hands tied behind his back he cried out that the city was "of the pious only, for none but these were admitted to it," and that it lies "to the very east, and the very rising sun." Such were the words of a saint before he was bestowed the crown of martyrdom.[31]

Those Christians of old did not forget the great works of the scholar John who wrote down entire books of the Scriptures, not on parchments or stone, but on the tablets of his heart. And after he was slain by the tyranny of the superstitious, he was remembered with serene memories of how he preached before congregations on those very sublime and holy writings for which he died, and by which those followers of the serpent were infuriated with the rage of unclean spirits. One Eusebius, a great historian of the Church, remembered his martyrdom and his accomplishments, and was so elated by such memories that his passions, dictated by pious intellect, compelled him to praise God.[32]

THE HEATHEN TYRANT'S RAGE

The pagan rulers of Rome had no respect for human life. Galerius greatly reflected this absence of compassion.

In a past expedition in Persia, Galerius learned of that eastern despotism found in Haman and Ahasuerus, and saw all peoples as his slaves and he their master. He subjected the magistrates and the chief citizens to "the Law of Torture," and on a whim put them to death. For his own entertainment he would have one of his personal bears consume a man right in front of him, and as limbs were torn, blood was split, and the terrifying cries of suffering were heard, he would burst out into uncontrollable laughter. He ordered Christians to be chained to poles and the soles of their feet burnt until the flesh fell off the bone. After this, torches were clamped throughout their bodies, forcing them to endure the excruciating pain without any control over their limbs. This was done very slowly, lasting for whole days. Eventually their flesh was so burnt that their vitals could be seen, and at this point they were unchained and thrown into a large heap of fire. Galerius seldom sentenced Christians to prison, exile, or to work in the mines, but on a daily basis condemned them to crucifixion, to be burnt, and fed to wild beasts. So cruel and sadistic were his ways that beheading was

---

30 *The Book of Martyrs*, ch. ix
31 *The Book of Martyrs*, ch. xi
32 Euseb. Eccles. Hist., *The Book of Martyrs*, ch. xiii

esteemed as a mercy. He enforced heavy taxation that was so brutal, that even the dead were taxed, and enacted a severe census which measured the lands and crops of all men. Children were hung before their parents, slaves made to accuse their masters, and wives their husbands. He rounded up all the beggars in ships, and in the midst of the sea drowned them all. Galerius stole women and forced them into a harem, and he would take them, tie them inside his horse stables, and stretch their bodies on a torture machine, and whip them.[33]

THE TYRANTS USE FALSE PEACE

Diocletian and Maximian, like clever serpents, realized that the stubbornness of the Christians could not be broken. Thus they decided to use a very common custom within warfare: sign a truce with the Church. The edict read:

> With a most persevering and devoted earnestness, their Majesties, our sovereigns and most august emperors, had formerly directed the minds of all men to live and conduct themselves according to the true and holy way, that even those who appeared to pursue practices foreign to the Romans, should exhibit the proper worship to the immortal gods. But the obstinacy and most unconquerable determination of some, rose to such a pitch, that they could neither be induced to recede from their own purpose by a due regard to the imperial command, nor be deterred by the impending punishment inflicted. Since, then, it has happened that many incurred danger from a practice like this, their Majesties our sovereigns, the most powerful emperors, in their peculiar and exalted piety, deeming it foreign to the purpose of their Majesties, that men should be thrust into so great danger for such a cause, have commanded (me in) my devotedness to address (you in) your wisdom, that if any of the Christians be found to observe the worship of their people, that you should abstain from molesting or endangering them, nor determine that any one should be punished on such a pretext; as it has been impossible to induce them in any manner to abandon their obstinate course. It is incumbent, therefore, on your attentive care, to write to the governors and magistrates, and to the prefects of the districts of every city, that they may know that it is not necessary for them to pay any further regard to this edict (or business). [34]

The mandate spread out and was communicated by all of the provincial governors. The world cried "peace, peace," but peace never came in the empire of Romulus. As storms and torrents rage from a calm day, the deceptive silence died and the officers of the tyrant in one moment began to round up the Christians. Entire congregations were arrested, and Christian assemblies found themselves yet again under the yoke of the heathen.

A statue of Jupiter Phlilius was erected in Antioch by the famous wizard Theotecnus who, like Haman, told the emperor Maximinus that Jupiter demanded of him "to expel the Christians as his enemies, beyond the limits of the city and the adjacent territory."[35] This order began to be issued in all the cities of the empire, and even the subjects were told to

---

33 Lactantius, *On the death of the Persecutors*, xxi–xxiii
34 In Euseb. Eccles. Hist. 9.1
35 Euseb. Eccles. Hist. 9.3

purge the land of the Christians. The priests of the pagan gods were commissioned to orchestrate the persecution. They did not hesitate to comply, for they wished to establish a universal utopia-like Babel in which all worship the gods of nature as one. The people conceded, thinking that to persecute the Church for the gods would please the emperor,[36] since he too was esteemed as a god. Jupiter demanded the blood of Christians, and therefore the killing of the saints was nothing more than human sacrifice.

A number of infamous women were taken in Phoenicia and forced to make a slanderous statement that the Christians were involved in "licentious deeds" and open blasphemy against the gods. These feigned confessions were recorded and published in every city and place.[37]

A presbyter of the church at Antioch, Lucianus, made a public defense for Christianity in Nicomedia, only to be arrested and swiftly executed. Three legates were thrown into the amphitheater to be torn and consumed by beasts. Every boy in the schools were brainwashed with anti-Christian indoctrination, and each day they proclaimed mockery toward Jesus.[38] Maximinus issued another edict—this time exposing his true enmity for the Church—in which he expressed his belief that the gods demanded the blood of Christians, and that the empire needed to be united in the worship of the same pagan gods. Here is a quote from the edict sent to Tyre:

> Now at length the feeble powers of the human mind have prevailed so far as to shake off and to scatter the mists of every error, and dissipate the clouds of delusions, which before this had beset the senses of those [the Christians] who were more miserable than profane, and enveloped them in a destructive darkness and ignorance; thus leading us to acknowledge that it is regulated and strengthened by the good providence of the immortal gods. Wherefore, that supreme and mighty Jove [Jupiter], he who presides over your most illustrious city [Tyre], who has rescued your country's gods, and wives, and children, and houses, and homes, from every destructive pest, has infused into you the happy counsel, showing and proving to you how excellent, and noble, and profitable it is to observe the worship of the sacred rites of the immortal with the becoming reverence. [39]

PLAGUES AND FAMINE

As the emperors delighted in their eminence, their supreme authority over the subjects, their despotism over the liberty of the saints, the seeming victory over the Cross, the heavens refused any rain for the destitute and dry ground. As the people miserably lived without sustenance, another travail set upon the agonized multitude: a disease which took the sight from their eyes. As all of this suffering went on, it was not forgotten that Maximinus had earlier declared with great pomp that "neither famine nor pestilence nor war had happened in his times."

---

36 Euseb. Eccles. Hist. 9.4
37 Euseb. Eccles. Hist. 9.5
38 Euseb. Eccles. Hist. 9.6–7
39 In Euseb. Eccles. Hist. 9.7, brackets and ellipses mine

So great were those dark days that many sold their most valuable possessions just to obtain a small amount of food. Others spent so much of their goods that they were reduced to the utter limits of poverty. Numerous people were seen absent of their peace, eating herbs, hay, and whatever plants they could eat. Even the most prestigious of women threw away all concepts of shame and reputation and were found in the greatest despair, lying on the roads begging with their hands outstretched in the uttermost of hopelessness. Others were seen with bodies so entrenched in starvation that they appeared as walking skeletons going aimlessly to and fro, stumbling here and there like dead shadows. They wept and wailed for the smallest morsel of bread, with only enough energy to emit the most painful cry: "Hunger!" In the streets and lanes no man could walk without witnessing with a dismal mind the multitudes of bodies. It was painful to behold what violence occurred because of the wanton cruelty of man, with dogs coming about to chew on the rotting corpses. Amidst the famine and disease nothing could be heard but lamentations and nothing could be seen but tears. Who helped such a desperate people but the Christians who all the world hated? They exemplified the deepest of compassion, that sublime sentiment which breaks all the violent nature of men. Those who had eaten the Bread of Life were seen giving out bread to those who knew not God, caring for those who had none to care for them. They labored all the day, emanating that Light that is to be seen in the thickest of darkness, and throughout the land was there heard praise for the God of the Christians.[40]

THE DEATH OF THE TYRANT AND THE RISE OF A NEW ONE

As some time passed, Diocletian was taken by a most miserable disease that left him insane, and eventually death came to him. Galerius died of a most grotesque disease in which a tumor appeared in the middle of his body and a disgusting fistula extended in the innermost parts of his bowls, which led to a mass of worms in his belly. He was very corpulent, and now with this disease his whole body looked like a mass of fat. He became a putrid, intolerable sight. The physicians trying to help him could not bear his repulsive smell, and they were put to death for their intolerance of it. He was in so much misery that he began to think about God, and that his condition was a result of the persecutions he caused. He gave praise to God, ordered that the oppression upon the Christians end, and that the Church of Nicomedia which was destroyed be rebuilt. He issued this edict:

> Among other matters which we have devised for the benefit and common advantage of our people, we have first determined to restore all things according to the ancient laws and the public institutions of the Romans. And to make provisions for this, that also the Christians, should return again to a good purpose and resolution. But though we saw the great mass still persevering in their folly, and that they neither gave the honour that was due to the immortal gods, nor heeded that of the Christians, still having a regard to our clemency and our invariable practice, according to which we are wont to grant pardon to all, we most cheerfully have resolve to extend our indulgence in this matter also: that there may be Christians again,

---

40 Euseb. Eccles. Hist. 9.9

and that they may restore their houses in which they were accustomed to assemble, so that nothing be done by them contrary to their profession. [T]hey [the Christians] are obligated to implore their God for our safety, as well as that of the people and their own. That in every place the public welfare may be preserved, and they may live unmolested in their respective homes and fire-hearths.[41]

The successor of Galerius, Daia, resumed and intensified the persecution in a type of final solution to destroy all of Christianity. He prevented the Christians from building any new meeting-houses. He commissioned the pagan priests to watch over the Christians and see to it that they make sacrifices each day to the idols, that they do not hold any meetings, nor conduct worship. He raised the pagan priesthood to a higher level of authority and adorned them with white tunics edged with gold. He ordered that "they should seize [the Christians] wherever they could find them, and either force them to offer sacrifice or deliver them to the magistrates."[42] He had women kidnapped and brought to him. They were forced to strip naked and come before Daia to be observed, and if they refused to do this, he would have them drowned.[43]

Maximian, the one who shared the throne with Diocletian earlier was put to the sword after a failed attempt to assassinate another official.[44] This official was a young man, strong in body, formidable with the sword, and destined to subdue tyrants. Maximian's successor was his son, Maxentius. However, he also refused to confer the liberty to worship God. Maxentius came to the people of Rome and falsely proclaimed the Christian Faith, and thus it was through deception that he assumed power. He separated wives from their husbands for the purpose of ravishing them, only to send them back to their loyal spouses in this miserable condition. Maxentius unleashed the ruthless and fierce praetorian guards upon the people and many within the city were slain. He thirsted for the assistance of demons, and so partook in the most execrable of rituals, tearing away babes from the wombs of their mothers, splitting their bodies open and observing their insides in search of omens. There were times that he was so desperate for the harbingers of devils that he would not lift a finger without soothsayers and oracles.[45]

Maxentius established a system of pagan tyranny in that in every province there were priests of the gods, over which was a head priest. It was as though Islam had already come with its Sharia and violent jurisdiction over Christians. He commenced a despotic system of taxation in which gold, silver, and money, was forcefully confiscated from the people. If a man was wealthy, his inheritance was stolen from him. His methods of despotism were successful over all but the Christians, for they, despising the cold hands of death, gave unto God what was His and never allowed Caesar to take that which belonged to the Almighty.

---

41   In Euseb. Eccles. Hist. 8.17; Lactantius, *On the death of the Persecutors*, xxxv
42   Lactantius, *On the death of the persecutors*, xxxvi, brackets mine
43   Lactantius, *On the death of the persecutors*, xviii
44   Euseb. Eccles. Hist. 8.13; Lactantius, *On the death of the Persecutors*, xxx
45   Euseb. Eccles. Hist. 8.14

The Church was an affront to the state, and for this the Christians were crucified, thrown into the ocean, had their eyes torn out, their flesh seared with red-hot irons, and their bodies mutilated. They were cast into the mines and forced to suffer unbearable labors, thrown into prison, and made to endure hunger. The Christian women were taken to be ravished, but instead these maidens opened themselves to death rather than defilement. There was one Christian woman, the wife of a senator, who became the target of Maxentius' sadistic lusts. The tyrant's ministers came before her home and her husband, terrified of the despot's wrath—more so than God's—bid them to take her away. She requested a little time before departing, entered her chambers, unsheathed a sword, and with the greatest love for her purity, plunged the blade into her heart.[46]

THE CROSS IS CARRIED

As all of this misery, violence, and cruel tyranny went on, there was a young man outside Rome who Maximian attempted to assassinate before his own death. The sun was descending into the hour of evening, and he wondered as to which deity he should place his trust on. As he concentrated most fervently and intensely in his prayer to God, he saw a sign appear in the midst of heaven—a pillar of light in the form of a cross. He beheld its majestic presence, and upon it was inscribed the words, "In hoc signo, vincis," "Conquer, by this." He asked those around him if they too beheld what captured his gaze, and they said that they did, and his mind was fortified by this divine apparition. It is said that as he slumbered that night, Christ appeared in a dream and directed him to make a standard of war in the shape of the cross that he saw. This young man was Constantine, and alongside his co-emperor Licinius, he had already resolved to defeat Maxentius.[47] This serene image became the standard of his army, and it had engraved on it the first two letters of the name of Christ in Greek, with the P intersecting the X. He wished to inquire on who this Christ was, and so he discussed the matter with a number of men learned in the Scriptures. They told him that Christ is God, and the only Begotten Son of the one and only God. Constantine placed his trust on the Nazarene, made these priests into his officials, and fortified by his well-grounded hopes, endeavored to extinguish the fires of tyranny for the God Who is the greatest enemy to tyranny.[48]

Surely this could be called the first crusade in the history of the Church; for it was the first cause after the Resurrection in which Christians took up the Cross as their banner and by means of arms advanced the Cross over heathenism for the protection and the preservation of the Church.

Maxentius ordered his praetorian guard to satisfy their bloody desires upon the Roman populace, and countless bodies were seen throughout the city. As Constantine was approaching the metropolis, his army upheld the symbol of the Cross, that symbol of God vanquishing the arrows of hell. We can only imagine what each man was doing. There stood

---

46   Euseb. Eccles. Hist. 8.14; *Life of Constantine*, 1.34
47   Eusebius, *Life of Constantine*. 1.22–28; Socrates, Eccles. Hist. 1.2
48   Eusebius, *Life of Constantine*, 1.28–32; Socrates, Eccles. Hist. 1.2

Constantine, his hand ready for war, to conquer for the advancement of the true Faith which divides, like a cutting blade, the world between those who bear the armor of darkness and those who wear the armor of Light. There also stood Maxentius, relying on the evil omens of idolatrous priests whose souls were as empty as sepulchers. They conducted the most diabolical rituals, tearing out children from their mothers' wombs only to open up their young bodies to observe their insides for any signs from the devils they worshipped.

Constantine, thinking upon such miseries and inhumanities, armed himself and prepared his troops to battle against tyranny. He assumed God as his patron, Christ as his preserver and aid, and set the sign of the Cross in front of his army. Maxentius refused to come out of Rome to do battle, but set ambushes upon his enemies. Constantine and his army with great efficiency crushed the ambuscades of the pagans and utterly defeated the second and third divisions of Maxentius' army. The cruel despot had a bridge across the Tiber River, and it was engineered that it would fall as soon as enough men stand upon it. The trap was made for Constantine, but in the midst of the fighting, Maxentius and his army were on the bridge and they did not retreat in time. The bridge collapsed and the tyrant and his army drowned in the waters like Pharaoh's men in the Red Sea. The enemy was vanquished,[49] and Constantine would not forget to ascribe the victory to his Father in Heaven, giving his praises to God[50] for the battle was won not solely by arms and men, but through the Holy Cross, by the power of God's divine hands directing His warriors as His destined weapons to defeat His enemies.

Constantine and his army entered Rome triumphantly. Those who were imprisoned for their Faith were released. Men who were afflicted with the tyranny of the pagan turned to joy, and those who loved liberty celebrated with jubilations in the streets. The new emperor ordered that the sign of a Cross be placed beneath the hand of a statue of himself, and the following inscription to be engraved on it:

> By virtue of this salutary sign, which is the true symbol of valor, I have preserved and liberated your city from the yoke of tyranny, I have also set at liberty the Roman senate and people, and restored them to their ancient greatness and splendor.[51]

Those who had their property confiscated had what was rightfully theirs given back to them. Those who were exiled were brought back. He gave away goods from his own possessions to the churches of God to enlarge their structures, and he enriched them with generous offerings.[52] Like the glorious ancient kings Josiah and Hezekiah who destroyed the pagan buildings where devils were worshiped, Constantine closed down or destroyed the temples of the heathens where demons were venerated and horrid rituals held.[53]

Daia, after much fighting with the armies of Licinius, Constantine's co-emperor, fled to Mount Tarsus where he drank poison. He did not die instantly, but suffered excruciating

---

49 Eusebius, *Life of Constantine*, 1.38; Socrates, Eccles. Hist. 1.2
50 Socrates, Eccles. Hist. 1.2
51 Eusebius, *Life of Constantine*, 1.39–40
52 Eusebius, *Life of Constantine*, 1.42; Socrates, Eccles. Hist. 1.2–3
53 Socrates, Eccles. Hist. 1.3

pain for four days before he turned to madness. He began to force his head into a wall with such force that his eyes started to fall away from their roots. As he lost his sight, it is said that he saw a vision of ministers all in white garments. Looking upon them in reverence, he confessed his guilt, and with many tears called upon Jesus Christ to have pity on him, and he died.[54]

When Constantine and Licinius entered Rome, they took the entire party of Daia and executed them. Amongst these was Peucetius, who was in charge of persecuting the Christians in Egypt. The entire family of Daia, like the sons of Ahab, were arrested and put to death. Let us not forget about Theotecnus, who erected the statue of Jupiter in Antioch and tried to force the Christians to worship it. He too was seized, alongside all of his companions, and they were all killed[55] like Zebah and Zalmunah, who forced the Hebrews to worship the idols of Baal.

THE SECOND WAR WITH THE PAGANS
The empire was split into two legs, with Constantine ruling over the Western part and Licinius over the Eastern. Licinius confessed Christianity, and Constantine even gave him his sister in marriage, but as soon as the prestige of royalty was given to him, he returned to paganism. It was at this moment when the sword which Christ brought formed the divide between the Church and her enemies, between the Cains and the Abels. As Cain brought his brother to the fields to trick him before satisfying his murderous desire, Licinius deceived the Christians to easily ambush them. He claimed to have respect for the leaders of the Church while cunningly searching for any reason to accuse them of crimes. But since he found nothing, his evil investigations were in vain, and thus a persecution began. He was terrified of Constantine, and because of this fear his oppressions were not done out in the open, but rather were done at a local level. When news of his despotism reached the emperor, he was most displeased with his oppressive measures. Licinius sought out his forgiveness, and Constantine forgave him, but it was nothing more than a means to deceive.

Licinius then betrayed and enacted his own edict, decreeing that Christian ministers could not communicate to each other nor visit neighboring parishes. The Church in the West was illuminated by liberty, while those of the East were overwhelmed by the tyranny of false religion. Constantine encouraged the clergy to hold discussions while Licinius, attempting to uproot the Church from existence, endeavored to prevent all harmony amongst the Christians. After evading Constantine numerous times, Licinius showed his true intentions and declared open war on the Church. Licinius threatened anyone who proclaimed Christ with death. He issued an edict forbidding Christian men to be in the company of women in the Churches. He forbade women from studying the Scriptures with the bishops, commanding that they could only be taught by other women. Christian soldiers were expelled from the military if they refused to give sacrifice to idols, and Christian people were forbidden to

---
54 Lactantius, *On the death of the persecutors*, xlix
55 Euseb. Eccles. Hist. 9.11

charitably give food to those in prisons, leaving the captives to die of hunger. Bishops were also prohibited from visiting pagans. Licinius had Christian men imprisoned and exiled and ordered their wives arrested and raped by his slaves. Churches in Pontus and Amasia were leveled to the ground and bishops were put to death. Christian men were made to endure a new form of execution: they were slowly cut, piece by piece, and then thrown into the sea to be eaten by wild fishes.[56]

HOLY WAR IS DECLARED

The truth of these events were brought to Constantine and he, troubled in his own mind, took pity on the saints. He and Licinius were now enemies. He resolved that he could not permit this cruelty and concluded that Licinius needed to be removed for "the safety of the greater part of the human race."[57] Surely this could be called the second crusade in Church history, as the Cross was taken to battle to vanquish the advancers of false religion for the protection of the saints. They took up their arms, upheld their swords, and Constantine commanded the standard of the Cross to be held up amongst his troops. Thus did the Sword of St. Peter, the one that the Apostle placed into his sheath but never disowned, was unsheathed for the subduing of an enemy that needed to be destroyed. As Abraham after his victory in battle had the priest Melchizedek pray for him, around Constantine were priests, continuously praying for him and for God to deliver him his enemies. Amongst the ranks of the adversaries of God, Licinius gathered around him sorcerers and soothsayers from Egypt who, like those of the Pharaoh who went against Moses, assured the tyrant that the gods guaranteed that he would be victorious.[58] Elated by this, he gathered his greatest of warriors and his most valued friends in a pagan grove where stood before them the idols of the most ancient gods of their ancestors. They lit candles and ignited the flames for a sacrifice, and before the bright and intense fires, which enchanted the eye and brought men to spiritual trances, and in the midst of heathen zeal and hot fervency, Licinius declared:

> Friends and fellow-soldiers! These are our country's gods, and these we honor with a worship derived from our remotest ancestors. But he who leads the army now opposed to us has proved false in the religion of his forefathers, and adopted the sentiments of those who deny the existence of the gods. And yet he is so infatuated as to honor some strange and unheard-of Deity, with whose despicable standard [of the Cross] he now disgraces his army, and confiding in whose aid he has taken up arms, and is now advancing, not so much against us as against those very gods whom he has despised. However, the present occasion shall prove which of us is mistaken in his judgement, and shall decide between our gods and those whom our adversaries profess to honor. For either it will declare the victory to be ours, and so most justly evince that our gods are the true Saviors and assistants, or else, if this God of Constantine's, who comes we know not whence, shall prove superior to our many deities (for

---

56 Eusebius, *Life of Constantine*, 1.49–55; Eccles. Hist. 10.8; Socrates, Eccles. Hist. 1.3
57 Eusebius, *Life of Constantine*, 2.3; Socrates, Eccles. Hist. 1.4
58 Eusebius, *Life of Constantine*, 2.3–4; Socrates, Eccles. Hist. 1.4

at least ours have the advantage in point of numbers), let no one henceforth doubt which god he ought to worship, but attach himself at once to the superior power, and ascribe to him the honors of victory. Suppose then this strange God, whom we now regard with contempt, should really prove victorious; then indeed we must acknowledge and give him honor, and so bid a long farewell to those for whom we light our tapers in vain. But if our own gods triumph (and of this there can be no real doubt), then, as soon as we have secured the present victory, let us prosecute the war without delay against these despisers of the gods. [59]

Such words indicate that this was indeed a religious war, between the Church and the pagans, between God and His angels and the devil and his demons. It was reminiscent to the wars fought between the heathens and the Israelites. It indicates that Constantine was known by his enemies to profess Christianity and that there was certainly a dividing line, made by the sword of Christ, between those who hate the Church and those who wish for its victory over evil.

As soon as the speech was over, the war commenced. Constantine's crusade was now about to be fulfilled. The Christian emperor chose fifty men, known for their fortitude, valor, gallantry, and physical strength, to surround and protect the standard of the Cross which was to be marched in the midst of the fighting.

THE BATTLE BEGINS

On a field in the land of Bithynia, Licinius' soldiers saw Constantine's warriors amongst them, and were struck with sudden fear and trepidation. But there was no one really there—it was a vision. Soon, the true army arrived, with Constantine commanding the charge by calling on the name, "God the Supreme Savior." The enemy soldiers of the tyrant clashed with the crusaders, and in every position where the Cross was present, the warriors for God proved themselves victorious. Arrows from every direction stormed through the air, and so terrifying was it that the holder of the Cross fled, and as he ran in fright, an arrow pierced his belly and he perished. One of the warriors saw the standard, stranded and left to the enmity of the heathens, sprinted through the field without fear of the sharp missiles, held onto the Cross, ascended it heavenward, and the battle continued on. Soon, after so much grueling warfare, the enemy troops surrendered, laid down their weapons, and prostrated before Constantine. Licinius, on the other hand fled. Constantine ordered his men not to pursue him but to let him escape, and to show mercy and not to kill the prisoners of war. Whenever he saw his men becoming overly aggressive with prisoners, he would in fact pay them just to show mercy and spare them. Surely was this a moment when the world was gradually changing to the Light of Christianity. Constantine placed Licinius in a quiet abode in Thessalonica, but such an effort of amity did not prevent the pagan from resorting to his conniving nature. Licinius again consulted with the Egyptian wizards, and he gained the confidence to prepare a second attack, hiring barbarian mercenaries and making ready for another onslaught.

---

59 In Eusebius, *Life of Constantine*, 2.5

This preparation was known to Constantine, and he immediately erected a tabernacle outside of his camp where he passed his time in holy seclusion. He then rushed outside and commanded his men to move without delay.[60] Did not Jesus command His Apostles to buy swords to protect themselves and the Church? So were Constantine's men to unsheathe their swords at the moment of battle to see to it that the pagan persecutor should lose and the Christian triumph. He retired to his tabernacle, fasted and abstained from any luxurious tastes, and implored God to give him aid, and the ability to be ready to fulfill whatever it was that He wished for him to execute. He even prayed not only for the wellbeing of his subjects, but also for the safety of his own enemies.[61]

Licinius offered Constantine terms of peace, and his submission. But this, again, was the peace of Cain. He secretly sought after other wizards—being disappointed with those from Egypt—who ministered unto new gods. He gathered an army which upheld statues of demons and the dead ancestors which they worshipped. Constantine noticed this deception, and refusing to allow the enemy to gain any advantage, ordered for the charge to be made. The struggle commenced, and Licinius was defeated, arrested, and put to death[62] just as Samuel slew Agag.

The East and the West were now united, and the rays of piety were brightened. The anguishes of persecution were remembered no more, and the saints sang songs and proclaimed their joy for the emperor who rescued them through the grace of divine providence. The crusade was a victory, and as Abraham saved Lot and liberated those who were oppressed by the tyrants of the East, so was Constantine triumphant over the tyrant who tormented God's people. As Abraham gave back the goods that were stolen by the tyrants to their rightful possessors, so did Constantine restore the properties and the churches that were confiscated to their lawful Christian owners.[63]

Abraham after his victory was joined by the priest Melchizedek, who cried out in prayer:

> Blessed be Abram of the most high God, possessor of heaven and earth: and blessed be the most high God, which hath delivered thine enemies into thy hands. (Genesis 14:19–20)

So Constantine, after his triumph over the enemies of God, was received by the Christians with hymns and praises to the Almighty as "King of Kings."[64] Once the victory was taken and tyranny crushed, the wellbeing of Christians was heavily promoted by Constantine,[65] writing a letter encouraging the clergy to embellish and repair the churches that were neglected on account of the persecutions, or damaged by the pagans, and to rebuild new ones:

---

60 Eusebius, *Life of Constantine*, 2.6–8, 13; Socrates, Eccles. Hist. 1.4
61 Eusebius, *Life of Constantine*, 2.14
62 Eusebius, *Life of Constantine*, 2.18; Socrates, Eccles. Hist. 1.4
63 Eusebius, *Life of Constantine*, 2.21
64 Eusebius, *Life of Constantine*, 2.19; Eccles. Hist. 10.9
65 Socrates, Eccles. Hist. 1.4

Since an impious purpose and tyranny have even to the present time persecuted the servants of God our Savior, I have been credibly informed and am fully persuaded, most beloved brother, that all our sacred edifices have either by neglect gone to decay, or from dread of impending danger have not been adorned with becoming dignity. But now that liberty has been restored, and that persecuting dragon Licinius has by the providence of the Most High Divine that the divine power has been made manifest to all, and at the same time that those who either through fear of unbelief fell into any sins, having acknowledged the living God, will come to the true and right course of life. Wherefore enjoin the churches over which you yourself and deacons whom you know, to be diligent about the sacred edifices, either repairing those which remain standing, or enlarging them, or by erecting new ones wherever it may be requisite. [66]

With Constantine in the throne, the state and the Church worked in harmony, not that the state was superior to the Church, but that the state protected the Faith from persecutors. The Two Swords of St. Peter—that of the Church and the other of the state—were united.

Now those very Holy Scriptures, which were sentenced to be cast into the flames, were preserved by the zealotry of a man compelled by the Cross. The slaves of the darkness again were brought low, and defeated in their war in which they exerted all of their ferocity against that Light which they could not comprehend. All of their violence against the Savior of the world Who bore that Cross which appeared to the young king before the tyrant drowned in the Tiber; and all the rage against that woman by whose Seed humanity was redeemed, and for whose destiny she received the enmity of the serpent and his slaves, was shattered. It was because of that light of Truth within the Scriptures, that such a line was made between these forces of good and evil. So deep was this divide that only the Sword of Christ could have made it. The predecessors persecute the orthodox and attempt with all their abilities to destroy the pages of the Sacred Word. But the swords of the zealous rise and bring low the acolytes of the devil. By the holy writ of the prophets, the militant words of Christ in the Gospels, the call to action in the epistles and revelations of the Apostles, does the divine blade of the heavens cut asunder the old serpent. All of these victories of the saints are just foreshadowers of the coming day, in which the seed of the Virgin shall crush the head of that slithering beast.

CHRISTENDOM DEFEATS THE PAGAN GERMANS
One of the oldest battles in Christendom's history was fought in the year 405 between Rome and the pagan Germans. It is a wonderful event of ancient Christendom in which more than a hundred thousand German pagans under the savage Gothic ruler Radagaisus approached Christian Rome in order to sack it. Not one Roman solider lost his life in the fray, and the entire army of pagans submitted to the Christian sword while Radagaisus and his sons were put to death.[67] St. Paulinus of Nola, one of the great fathers of the Church, wrote a poem on the providential battle:

---
66 Victor Constantine Maximus Augustus, to Eusebius, in Socrates, 1.9
67 Augustine, *City of God*, 5.23

The enemy and their unholy king alike are slaughtered, and the victory of the boy Augustus has restored peace; though of tender years, his courage in battle emerged triumphant through God's strength, and he has shattered human resource through Christ's victory over an impious tyrant. [68]

THE BATTLE OF GARGANO

There is a great story seldom told by the trends and modish books of historians, and that is the Battle of Mt. Gargano. It was among the earliest battles to be fought in Christian history, taking place around 493 AD.

The Italian people of Sipontus had discovered the true path of light, left paganism, and followed Christ their Holy Knight. The people of Naples and Beneventum, still ardent and fanatical about their pagan religion, declared war on the young Christians. The bishop of Sipontus urged the people to fast and pray for three days. Like righteous men having both the innocence of doves and the wisdom of serpents, they both obeyed this command and armed themselves with swords and shields, making themselves ready for the snakes that were coming their way.

On the night of the third day after the sunset, the angel Gabriel appeared before the bishop. He told him that victory will come on the fourth hour of daylight upon the lofty mountain of Gargano.

When the sun ascended and the fourth hour of day came, the two armies stood before each other. Each bore arms but only one came with the Holy Spirit. Mount Gargano was struck by bolts of lightning; the heavens roared and the earth shook, and a great battle commenced. The swords of infidels stood no match to the tenacity and zeal of the saints, and on that day six hundred pagans were slain, both by the blade of Christians and by the Heaven-sent lightning bolts.[69]

CHRISTENDOM'S WAR AGAINST PERSIA—THE FIRST
CHRISTIAN CRUSADES: THE EVILS OF THE PERSIAN RELIGION

Man, to the despotic mind of the Persian tyrant, was made to be subjected as a slave and forced to worship the pagan god Ahura Mazda. Such a belief had its origins in the teachings of the prophet Zoroaster, the Muhammad of Persia. His origins began in the land of Bactria,[70] at a time when it was ruled under the king Vistacpa. As Muhammad had isolated himself in the wilderness and in the cave of Hira, Zoroaster was said to have went into seclusion in the desert, and according to a Median tradition, in a cave of Mount Elburz.[71] According to tradition, Zoroaster was called to come to the desert by "the evil spirit" to tempt him, but he stood resilient, and while in this state of aloneness, it is said that he received messages from

---

68 Poem 21
69 Jacobus de Voragine, *The Golden Legend*, vol. ii, 145, trans. Ryan
70 See Philip Smith, Anc. Hist. b. iii, ch. xviii, p. 381, sect. 10, and n. 5; Arnob. 1.5, trans. George E. McCracken.
71 See Philip Smith, Anc. Hist. b. iii, ch. xviii, pp. 381–382, sect. 10.

the god Ahura Mazda and other spirits.[72] He had then retired back to his dwelling where he would oppose the current religious sentiments and espouse his new faith. He soon convinced the king Vistacpa of his prophethood and the authenticity of his new religion. Upon the conversion of the king, most of Bactria's inhabitants followed.[73]

Zoroaster would come to the natives of the plain of the Oxus River, claiming divine inspiration and teaching the commandments of the god Ahura Mazda. His new faith had slowly began to influence the people of "happy Bactra," "Bactra of the lofty banner," and ultimately the tribes of Persia, where it would become the religion of the state. By the middle of the sixth century B.C., its Persian followers conquered both the Assyrian and Babylonian kingdoms, and in a short time afterwards, it subjugated the land of the pharaohs.[74]

It was the god of Zoroaster, Ahura Mazda, who was believed to have bestowed the king with authority, as is evidenced by the Behistun Inscriptions on which a winged figure of the deity hovers over the Biblical King Darius, holding a ring with his left hand, the symbol of kingship and sovereignty, and with his right he beckons to the emperor.[75] Ahura Mazda's connection with astral and naturist worship and the tyranny of the power is illustrated by the tomb of Darius on which is engraved the king standing before the sacred fire under which floats the same winged figure of Ahura Mazda with the sun, the emblem of light, in the background.[76]

The Persians also worshipped Venus, who they called Anahitas, adopting the cult from Arabia, where she was venerated as Allat, the female Allah. This makes a direct connection between Zoroastrianism and Islam. And like the pre-Islamic Arabs, and the Muslims today, the Persians revered the moon.[77]

The Zoroastrian doctrine taught that the whole community of believers, for the sake of their salvation, was obligated to partake in agriculture. Whether it be by farming, or by owning land—all were enforced to "further the works of life" by helping to grow crops.[78] This obligation was no mere law to prevent hunger, but an advancement toward despotism. The prophet Zoroaster taught that all lands and their produce, monies, and gains were to be given to the priestly clan, called the Magi. "Though your good works," said Zoroaster, "exceed in number the leaves of the trees, the drops of the rain, the stars in the heaven, or the sands on the seashore, they will all be unprofitable to you unless they are accepted by the destour, or priest. To obtain the acceptation of this guide to salvation, you must faithfully pay him tithes

---

72 See Augustus William AHL, *Outline of Persian History*, ch. v, p. 76; Philip Smith, Anc. Hist. b. iii, ch. xviii, pp. 381–382, sect. 10.
73 See Philip Smith, Anc. Hist. b. iii, ch. xviii, pp. 381–382, sect. 10; Augustus William AHL, *Outline of Persian History*, ch. v, pp. 76–77.
74 See G. Rawlinson, *The Religions of the Ancient World*, ch. iii., p. 95.
75 Augustus William, AHL, *Outline of Persian History*, ch. xvi, p. 130.
76 See Augustus William AHL, *Outline of Persian History*, ch. xvi, p. 134.
77 See Chron. Theophan. 305, p. 15
78 See G. Rawlinson, *The Religions of the Ancient World*, ch. iii, p. 108; Philip Smith. Anc. Hist. b. iii, ch. xviii, p. 389, sect. 16; Chateaubriand, Genius of Christianity, 2.4, trans. Charles I. White.

of all you possess, of your goods, of your lands, and of your money. If the destour be satisfied, your soul will escape hell's tortures; you will secure praise in this world and happiness in the next. For the destours are the teachers of religion; they know all things, and they deliver all men." This edict was taught to the Persian from the days of his youth; for the priests were the authorities of education, and to them was given the minds of all children, even those of the royal family.[79]

In the third century A.D., an aspiring despot named Artaxerxes founded a New Persian Empire. Artaxerxes wished to revive the empire of King Cyrus as well as that of his successors, who had for a long time subjugated all of Egypt to the confines of Ethiopia and the entire the land of Asia Minor as far as the Aegean Sea.[80] Artaxerxes declared himself King of Kings, a title which had been assumed by his predecessors, and unite by choice or by force all the tribes of Persia under the doctrines of Zoroaster.

Like Haman and Ahasuerus before him, he sent out an edict that all worship but that of Ahura Mazda and all doctrine except that of Zoroaster were prohibited and punishable by death. Every province of Persia was visited by Artaxerxes who, with a numerous army of disciplined warriors, had reduced every rebellious tribe to submission under his throne. The idols of the deified kings of the Parthians were demolished, being now replaced by the reverence for the god of Zoroaster and his servant Artaxerxes. Yet the Christians still remained steadfast in this persecution.[81]

CONSTANTINE AIDS THE CHRISTIANS AGAINST PERSIAN PERSECUTION

In 328 A.D., the emperor Constantine, led by moral obligation, sought to protect the Christians of Persia who were being cruelly persecuted by the Sassanid Persian king Shapur, who had previously made an alliance with Rome.[82] To sway him from his despotism, Constantine sent a letter to Shapur, professing to him his love for God, disdain for paganism, and contempt for tyranny. He was undoubtedly inspired by God, for only a man instilled by the instruction of his Creator could have written such words in defiance of tyranny, to this Persian despot:

> By keeping the Divine faith, I am made a partaker of the light of truth—guided by the light of truth, I advance in the knowledge of the Divine faith. Hence it is that (as my actions themselves evince), I profess the most holy religion. And this worship I declare to be that which teaches me deeper acquaintance with the most holy God, aided by whose Divine power, beginning from the very borders of the ocean, I have aroused each nation of the world in succession to a well-grounded hope of security, so that those which, groaning in servitude

---

79 See Edward Gibbon, *The Decline and Fall of the Roman Empire*, vol. i, ch. viii, p. 129, Hans-Friedrich Mueller's abridged ed.
80 See Edward Gibbon, *The Decline and Fall of the Roman Empire*, vol. i, ch. viii, p. 131, Hans-Friedrich Mueller's abridged ed.
81 See Edward Gibbon, *The Decline and Fall of the Roman Empire*, vol. i, ch. viii, p. 130, Hans-Friedrich Mueller's abridged ed.
82 Theodoret. Eccles. Hist. 124; Eusebius, *Life of Constantine*, 4.8

to the most cruel tyrants, and yielding to the pressure of their daily sufferings, had well-nigh been utterly destroyed, have been restored through my agency to a far happier state. This God I confess that I hold in unceasing honor and remembrance. This God I delight to contemplate with pure and guileless thoughts in the height of his glory. This God I invoke with bended knees, and recoil with horror from the blood of sacrifices, from their foul and detestable odors, and from every earth-born magic fire. [83]

Near the end of the letter Constantine reminded Shapur of how he crushed former tyrants who oppressed the saints, such as Maxentius and Licinius, and how he trusted that Shapur would protect the Christian population of his nation, writing: "I commend the Christians to your care, and leave them in your protection; treat them, I beseech you, with benevolence."[84] The message was simple and gentle, but yet firm: God had toppled the persecutors of the past, and you are not immune from the punishment if you tread upon their same path.[85]

THE PERSIANS TRY TO INVADE ROME

When Rome was under the Christian emperor Theodosius, the Persian king Gororanes (known as Bahram V), a hater of Christians, surrounded the city with the intent of conquering it for the cause of Ahura Mazda. The siege proved unsuccessful, but the Persians nevertheless kept their post. During this time a Persian prince who was amongst the besiegers began to blaspheme God like Goliath did, and threatened to burn the Church of Rome down. Eunomius, the bishop of Rome, was enflamed with such zealous fire that he, like David, ordered a stone to be catapulted toward the prince. It was released, and with perfect accuracy landed on the blasphemer's head, striking him dead as David's stone killed Goliath.[86]

CHRISTENDOM'S WAR WITH PERSIA

Persia had already been persecuting Christians for some time under Gororanes' father Isdegerdes, a pattern which his son merely was too glad to follow in. He invented even better methods of killing and torment. The hands and backs of Christians were flayed off. Some even had the flesh of their faces lacerated, being teared off from the forehead to the chin. Reeds were cut in half and placed very tightly on the body from head to foot. They were then removed, pulling all of the flesh out with them. The persecutors also tied the hands and feet of their victims together and then tossed them into pits filled with starving mice which would consume them alive. But there was but a small white light, shining as a holy city illuminates from amidst the ramparts of abominable darkness. There stood holy Christendom, taking in these poor children of Abel. So unbearable was this persecution that the Persian Christians fled from their land and took refuge under the protection of the only state that cared: Roman

---

83 Letter in Eusebius, *Life of Constantine*, 4.9
84 Letter in Theodoret. Eccles. Hist. 125
85 See Peter J. Liethart, *Defending Constantine*, ch. 11, p. 247
86 Theodoret. Eccles. Hist. 5.38

Christendom. The Catholic bishop, Atticus, took them in and provided for them with much generosity.

Gororanes sent forth an embassy into the Roman land, and his ambassadors demanded that the Christians be given back to the hands of the Persian pagans. Did the Romans comply? Did they appease the Persian devils for the sake of diplomacy? For the sake of international relations? Even the thought of doing such betrayal against one's brethren was unthinkable, to men who bore their crosses and carried with them swords, armed with the blade of the Spirit and the blade that strikes for the advancement of the Spirit, and with hearts resilient enough that they would do anything for the beloved Path of Christianity, and the Sword of Christ that shines all holy light. They did not seek the false peace of Cain, but instead, renewed their war against Persia. This was a Christian crusade—one that took place before the Crusades against the Muslims. Defenders of Christendom denied themselves, took up the Cross of Christ, and drew up the Sword of St. Peter, and looking to their persecuted brethren, and determined to protect them, they obeyed the command of Christ to His beloved Apostle, "strengthen your brethren." (Luke 22:33)

The emperor of Roman Christendom sent a large body of Christian troops under the general Ardabius. The warriors of Christ charged right into the Persian province of Azazene, and with sword and pious fury they struck, pummeling the enemy with efficient blows, crushing the opposers of light and the slaves of darkness. The Cross stood with them, and it was by the sacred image that they conquered. The entire Persian region was ravaged by the tenaciousness of God's armies, who "destroyed those murderers, and burned up their city." (Matthew 22:7) The general of the Persians, Narsaeus, sent messengers to Ardabius to make arrangements for the next battle, but the Christian combatant said to the messengers: "Tell Narsaeus that the Roman emperors will not fight when it pleases him."

The emperor knew that the Persians were preparing to come upon them with the entirety of their forces, and so being vigilant, he increased the number of his armies. But he did not put his trust in armies, and as "David strengthened himself in the Lord his God" (1 Samuel 30:6) before fighting the Amelekites, so did the Christian sovereign fortify his heart and put his whole trust in God. His dedication to the King of Heaven did not go unanswered, for all of Christendom was being watched by an army of angels, "The chariots of God" (Psalm 68:17), who like a fearsome torrent soared thundering Heaven to assail the malicious devils and their rebel leader. The Christians of Bithynia were the sons of the Apostles, for these were amongst the first whom the disciples sealed with the baptism of the Church, for St. Peter sent his epistle "To the pilgrims of the Dispersion in Pontus, Galatia, Cappadocia, Asia, and Bithynia" (1 Peter 1:1). Were not all of these Christians, to whom the Apostle wrote, the patriarchs of Christendom? For it would be their descendants who took up the holy mantle within the Church and now bore the Holy Cross, the sword of truth and the blade of the gallant knight, "strengthening the souls of the disciples" (Acts 14:22) with fiery exhortations to zeal and the fierce rising and hurtling of their swords. There stood the Christians of Bithynia, gazing upon

PART 3

the vision that brought their trepidatious desires peace: a whole multitude of angels, who told them to bid the people not to be fearful or worried, but to pray to God, for the Christians were going to conquer, and that they were sent from God to defend them.

The news of the vision spread around like a flame through the dry grass, burning away the parched tares of anguish, and spreading the glimmering fires of pious inspiration within the hearts of the soldiers. The combatants of mighty Christendom pitched their camps in Mesopotamia, and knowing full well that the angels of God were with them, they surrounded the city of Nisibis with lofty towers of war by which they assailed the walls of the pagan metropolis. The terrified Persian defenders looked upwards only to see the bright rays of shining armor, the descending blades of the Christians ripping through their bodies, and a torrent of carnage, soaring cries of agony, and the howling of victory resounded in the air and permeated the city. All this time the Persian general, Narsaeus, was hearing of his men's harsh predicament.

Narsaeus decided that he would lead an army into battle himself. But he dreaded the valor of the Christians, and so he sought out vicious mercenaries of the desert. They were Arabs led by the brutal warlord Al-Mundhir, the predecessors of Muhammad, whose followers the later Christians of the Crusades would combat with holy Cross and sword. Al-Mundhir brought with him a very large number of Arabian fighters and extolled the Persian general not to worry. He said he would crush the Christians, force them under his power, and conquer the Christian city of Antioch. When the battle was about to begin, over a hundred thousand Arabians stood in battle array. But there stood something before their fierce countenances: an army of Christian warriors unexpectedly appeared in front of their eyes before the time they were supposed to arrive. Something about these troops stirred their senses into fear and the mind to terror. It was somethings the Arabs could not explain, nor did they wait for them to get any closer. They took off in the utmost dread, and leaped into the river Euphrates, where nearly one hundred thousand of them drowned. But there were no soldiers—no mortal ones at least—but these were the angels who promised the pious Christians of Greece, whose ancestors were fed the heavenly food of Apostles, that victory was to come through Heaven's warriors.

This glorious victory, done by God's warring hands through the arms of His sons of war, allowed the Christians to overtake all of Nisibis, since the Arabs were most definitely not coming to attack them. The Romans sent an ambassador to the Persians to make preliminary arrangements for peace, which the Persian king gladly received, since he saw how much his men were being defeated. But there was a body of brave men who wanted nothing of peace: these were called "the Immortals," the most elite warriors of the Persian military. They utterly rejected surrendering to the Christians and convinced the king to imprison the ambassador. Another battle was about to ensue; the sons of Cain overthrew any ideas of peace. They picked up their stones and readied themselves to spill the blood of selfless martyrs. But these Christians were not as Abel, docile and naive and one led to the slaughter—no! These were sons of Abel who knew the mistake of the innocent son of Adam and instead of expecting peace, they knew war was nigh. They arrived at the field of battle, and saw before them "the Immortals" on all sides, charging directly at them. But as the collision of swords and men were about to commence, and when it seemed that they were completely surrounded, out of nowhere a Christian army led by the valiant general Procopius flanked "the Immortals" and smashed into their troops from behind. The Persians tried to fight, but their title of "Immortal" was surely brought to naught. The Christians utterly slaughtered the pagans, and the earth spewed out their blood. When Roman archers spotted the surviving "Immortals" fleeing, they aimed their bows and fired arrows into their mortal bodies. The Persian king had no choice but to surrender to the defenders of Christ, and he said to the ambassador that he imprisoned:

> I agree to the peace, not as yielding to the Romans, but to gratify you, whom I have found to be the most prudent of all the Romans.

The battle was won, the persecuted Christians were safe, and the Sword of St. Peter, covered with the blood of tyrants, was put back into its sheath until another just cause was to come about.[87]

The Persians took over Christian Syria,[88] invading the cities of Apamea and Antioch, wherein they burned down the church of Saint Julian and led the people into slavery. The response of the Church to this persecution should be a model for the church today, which has for the most part stood idly as the saints of the East have been being imprisoned and oppressed by their Muslim rulers. In our time, when pastors are confronted by people who are trying to truly help their tyrannized brethren, most will simply say "I'll pray for you" instead of actually assisting for the cause of the Church. In antiquity Saint John the Almoner, the patriarch of the Byzantine church, and Anastasius, the Egyptian patriarch, opened the doors of Egypt to the Syrian Christians, including the patriarch of Antioch, who needed to escape from the Persian despots. Not only were they given refuge, but daily alms were provided to them by the church. When some who were in charge of distributing the provisions complained about how liberal the giving was, John declared that "if the whole world came to ask alms at Alexandria they could not exhaust the riches of God's goodness." When the food supply for the runaways was out, two of the church's ships arrived from Sicily with enormous amounts of corn; and John himself devoted a yearly sum of money to caring for the poor captives.[89] Such love for one's fellow brethren truly exemplifies Christ's command to feed those Christians who are hungry and give drink to those who are athirst. But the present day church has been plagued with 'Christian corporatism,' caring more for fame and the reverence of the world than for rescuing the modest, poor, and greatly ignored and unknown believers who now suffer in the Muslim world.

---

87 The story of this battle was learned from Socrates, 7.18–20
88 See Butcher, *The Story of the Church of Egypt*, vol. i, ch. xxx, p. 344
89 Butcher, *The Story of the Church of Egypt*, vol. i, ch. xxx, pp. 344–346

In short time though, the Persians took Alexandria and eventually the whole of Egypt submitted to them, remaining for ten years as its subject. It was later freed from the Persian yoke in the seventh century by the Byzantine emperor Heraclius.[90]

PERSIAN PERSECUTION OF CHRISTIANS

There was a man named Hormisdas who was descended from the prestigious line of the great Persian Achaemenides. But when the king found out that he was Christian, he sent for him and asked him to deny Christ for Ahura Mazda. "Whoever," responded Hormisdas, "can be easily induced to contemn and to deny the God of the universe, would be much more easily persuaded to despise kings, who are but men, and by nature subject to death. If it be a crime deserving capital punishment, O king, to deny your power, how much more deserving of punishment is he who denies the Creator of all things."

The wisdom and erudition of this saint was not appreciated by the tyrant who at that point ordered all of his possession to be seized and commanded him to care for the camels. As he labored, his skin was struck by the rays of the sun and his complexion darkened. This caught the gaze of the king who, because of Hormisdas' illustrious birth, gifted him a linen tunic to persuade him into the Persian religion. He kindly accepted it, with the king asking him: "Do you now persist in carrying on this contention, but renounce the Son of the carpenter." The saint immediately sensed his beguiling, and in return, tore the tunic in two before the tyrant's eyes. "If," said the Christian, "by this present, you thought to seduce me from religion, take back your gift." He was banished, without possession or prestigious luster, out of the Persian kingdom.

Likewise a certain deacon named Benjamin settled in Persia and began to preach the gospel to the heathen priests, called Magi. He was for this arrested and thrown into prison. Two years had passed when and a Roman ambassador arrived in Persia to call for his release. The king agreed, in the condition that the deacon must stop preaching to the Magi. The ambassador consented to this, and even promised that he would convince Benjamin to comply. When the saint heard this, he declared his utter disdain for such a request and exclaimed: "I cannot refrain from communicating the light which I have received. The punishment of which those are worthy who hide their talents is declared in the Holy Gospel." The king had no knowledge of what this meant, and the deacon was set free. As soon as his liberty was gained, he resumed bringing the Light to those lost in the darkness. This continued for a year, but he was eventually seized and asked by the king to deny God. The deacon questioned the king what the punishment was for one who left the Persian kingdom, to which he responded that anyone who did such a thing would be worthy of death, and Benjamin, in turn, told him: "Of what punishment, then, is not that man worthy, who forsakes his Creator to make a god of one of his fellow-servants, and to render to him the worship which he owes to God?" This answer was received with such violence from the king that Benjamin was punished by having pointed reeds forced up each one of his fingernails and toenails. The pain did

---

90 Butcher, *The Story of the Church of Egypt*, vol. i, ch. xxx, p. 348; ch. xxxi, p. 352

not penetrate the fortress of his soul, and the Persians resorted to thrusting sharp reeds into private parts. His agony was so great from this, but his spirit still remained obstinate, never giving up his faith. The sadists had no use for torture, and soon adopted the final weapon for them, and the avenue of salvation for the saint: they impaled him, and his soul left his body.[91]

The enmity which the Persians harbored for the Christians was so great that one of their kings, Kawad, hired the Huns to make an incursion upon Christian Romans: they slaughtered many innocent farmers, burning villages and churches.[92]

A number of Persian messengers, accompanied by military personal, entered Greater Armenia and asked the people if they wished to continue to have peace with the emperor Khosroes of Persia. When they answered that they would, the envoys gave them this message: "It will be made clear that you propose to keep the terms of the treaty if you agree to worship fire as he [the emperor] does."[93] This reminds us of how Muslims in antiquity would come into nations, and before conquering them, give the inhabitants the choice to either worship Allah or be killed. The Armenians wholly rejected the pagan offer, and their bishop made his case that the Persians were foolishly worshipping fire instead of He Who created fire:

> What is there divine about fire, that it should be worshipped? God created it for men to use. It is lighted from tinder. If you put water on it, it goes out. It burns as long as you add fuel, but if you neglect it, it loses its heat.

The Persians were so angered by this that they beat the bishop with sticks and proceeded even when his body was covered with blood. The Armenians did not remain static, but were moved to action and saved their bishop by killing all of the Persians who were present. Shortly after, the Persians overran Armenia, setting ablaze many of its churches[94] in the cause of bringing the whole world into the worship of Ahura Mazda.

ARMENIA BECOMES A CHRISTIAN NATION, AND AN ENEMY OF THE PAGAN PERSIANS

When the Armenian king Trdat saw the temple of Anahitas, an Arabian goddess no different than Allah or Allat adopted by Persia, he invited St. Gregory to join him in his idolatry. When the saint refused, the king summoned him to be tortured in twelve different ways, and then had him thrown into a dungeon where he remained imprisoned for fourteen years.[95] In 301, After this, Trdat was stricken with a severe disease, and at the advice of his sister, he called for Gregory to purge him of his illness. The saint arrived, and by great faith and by the power of God, the tyrant was cured, not only from his disease, but of his hatred for the Holy Cross. The miracle shattered his sinister prejudices, he happily converted and changed his name to Johannes. This made a significant effect, with the whole population accepting

---

91 Theodoret. Eccles. Hist. 5.39
92 Zach. Mityl. Syri. Chron. 9.6
93 Gregory of Tours, *History of the Franks*, 4.40, trans. Lewis Thorpe
94 Gregory of Tours, *History of the Franks*, 4.40; 10.24; see also n. 69 in Thorpe's translation, 10.24
95 See Johannes Advall, *History of Armenia*, vol. i, part iii, ch. xv, p. 160

Christ and being baptized by Gregory. Trdat then consecrated four hundred bishops, countless priests, had built numerous churches, convents, nunneries, hospitals and schools, and instituted religious feasts and ceremonies. True enlightenment and civilization had finally come to Armenia, making it the first nation to make Christianity its official religion,[96] and thus Armenia became the desire of tyrannical nations.

In 337, Christian hating Persian tyrant Shapur II declared war on Armenia. Constantine swiftly declared a crusade on Persia in response. But sadly, Constantine died before he could war with the bloodthirsty barbarians, and Shapur II commenced a violent persecution[97] in which many martyrs were made, amongst whom was the general St. Sarkies, St. Martirose, and fourteen other soldiers.[98]

THE SLAUGHTER AND WAR OF THE ARMENIANS BEGIN

During Armenia's struggle for survival, Shapur II enlisted the assistance of Merujan, a heretic, to invade a fortress wherein a queen of Armenia by the name of Pharanzem was hiding. After the castle's gates were opened by its people, the Persians took all of the inhabitants and had them tortured until they renounced Christianity. Those who refused to apostatize were tortured to death. In Shapur's attempt to retake all of Armenia, he gave Merujan the command of an entire army and promised him the crown of the entire nation if he prevailed in getting its people to renounce Christianity for Zoroastrianism. To assist him in this endeavor, Shapur II had numerous of the Magi accompany Merujan. He marched into Armenia, breaking through it like a raging wolf, and had all of the priests sent to Persia and Assyria where many of them were put to death defending their faith while the rest of the Christians were forced into confinement. Any books they found written in the Greek language were burnt, and a new order was thenceforth decreed: that the official writing language of Armenia was to be Persian.[99] Such an edict reminds us of how Muslims, in any country they have conquered, forced the inhabitants to use the Arabic language. The Magian priests were set all over Armenia, throughout the villages and towns, where they gave the people only two options: accept the teachings of Zoroaster and his god Ahura Mazda, or remain Christian and die.[100] This method is tantamount to that of Islamists, who have forced countless Christians to accept both Allah and his prophet Muhammad, or the sword.

When the Armenian priest St. Nierses, who was abiding in Constantinople at this time, was informed of the atrocities committed against his countrymen, he fell into deep lamentation. After much prayer he beseeched the Roman emperor Theodosius to release Pap, an Armenian prince who was imprisoned in Constantinople, to march into Armenia to oust out the Persians. Theodosius nobly accepted the saint's urgent request, ordered his general

---

96 Chamich, *History of Armenia*, vol. i, part iii, ch. xv, p. 162, trans. Johannes Avdall; Peter J. Liethart, *Defending Constantine*, ch. 11, p. 246
97 See Peter J. Liethart, *Defending Constantine*, ch. 11, pp. 246–247
98 Chamich, *History of Armenia*, vol. i, part iii, ch. xvii, p. 180
99 Chamich, *History of Armenia*, vol. i, part iii, ch. xxi, pp. 209–210
100 Chamich, *History of Armenia*, vol. i, part iii, ch. xxi, p. 210

Terentius to go with a large army into Armenia, and thus a crusade ensued. Before the great war commenced, St. Nierses ascended to the top of Mount Nepat, fell on his knees, lifted his hands to God, and prayed that victory be given to the followers of the Cross. In the heat of battle, a wind came that was so strong that the arrows of the Persians were forced back. It was a miracle, and a sign that victory was destined to those saints of Armenia, and sure enough, by Providence, they prevailed.[101]

In one battle there was a Persian of gigantic stature, and when an Armenian general took it upon himself to slay him, he took his spear and cried out: "O God! Who didst guide the stone slung by David to the eye of the proud Goliah [Goliath], direct my spear to the eye of this mighty man!" He threw the spear with all of his might, and it pierced the eye of the giant. The Armenian warriors were inspired upon seeing such a sight, and fought with more courage and valiance than before, killing many Persians and putting them to flight.[102]

THE VARDANIANS

When Persia was under king Hazkert, he set as governor over Armenia one Shapur. In a hunting expedition, Shapur was horse riding through a field of dry reeds which surprisingly were set ablaze by a Christian named Atom. As Shapur was trying to escape the flames, Atom, in order to mock the Zoroastrian worship of fire, said: "Here is nothing but your father and your god, why are you afraid?" After showing the inferiority of his idolatry, Aton soon helped the governor go free.[103] It is but an image of the path to Paradise: the worship of fire will lead to eternal flames, the worship of God to eternal life.

The worship of fire, and the rest of nature, was in no way vague to the mind of the Persian. For him, to not worship fire was deserving of death and punishment. The Persian king Hazkert II wanted to see to it that the Christian Armenians, Aluans, and Georgians, venerated fire and the sun.[104] Because the worship of the sun was inseparable from the state, it would have unified Persia's subjects under its master, since all of the earth saw the solar star. In other words, Persia aspired to have a utopia tantamount to Babel. The Persian Empire wanted to force the Christians to worship the sun "on its rise,"[105] meaning that it was to be reverenced at the dawn, paralleling the obligatory dawn prayer of Islam, the Zoroastrianism of today.

Hazkert II at first compelled the Armenian chiefs to accept the nefarious doctrine of the Magi, but to no avail; for their souls were upon that Eternal Rock of salvation, which no man can shake. He arrested the two chieftains Atom the Gnunian and Manachihr, and had both of them martyred for their holy obstinacy. Many more were skinned alive, put to death by starvation, imprisoned, and many other modes of cruel affliction. But still, this did not work,

---

101 Chamich, *History of Armenia*, vol. i, part iii, ch. xxi, pp. 210–211
102 Chamich, *History of Armenia*, vol. i, part iii, ch. xvi, p. 172, trans. Johannes Avdall
103 Chamich, *History of Armenia*, vol. i, part iii, ch. xxv, pp. 242–243
104 Chamich, *History of Armenia*, vol. i, part iv, ch. i, pp. 257; ch. ii, 260.
105 Chamich, *History of Armenia*, vol. i, part iv, ch. ii p. 261

and Hazkert II resolved to imposing heavy taxes on the people, and permitting the torture of anyone who was not able to comply with the burdensome taxation. It was horrendous to live such a life, but the Armenians still endured, refusing to give up their Faith for an easier life. Hazkert II then wrote a letter to the people of Armenia, insisting them to obey him in his request to adopt the Persian religion. St. Joseph, the pope of the Armenian Church, conveyed the nation's chiefs to conduct a meeting where they wrote a letter in response to the tyrant. Upon reading this letter of refusal to his beloved gods, Hazkert II commanded all Armenian chiefs to come to his court where he ordered them all to be exiled in chains to a distant country if they did not worship the rising sun. One of the king's eunuchs, who was a Christian, advised the chiefs to comply forewarning them that if they didn't, "Christianity will perish in Armenia; for Hazkert will send troops and Magi thither, and forcibly compel the inhabitants to embrace the Persian religion." The chiefs heeded to his words, and in the next morning, bowed down to the sun in the presence of Hazkert II. The despot was ecstatic at such a sight, and gave the chiefs abundant honors, sending them back to their homes in the accompaniment of several Magi.[106]

But the words of the eunuch were but air in a never-ending cycle of lies. When the chiefs arrived in the province of Zalcote, what they saw must have instilled them with the most wearisome feeling of guilt. The chief Magi, along with some soldiers, entered the village of Anghel and desired to destroy the church there. Such a wicked endeavor was to the rage of the village priest, St. Levond, and he and his local countrymen rose up and, with force, valiantly drove out the heathen from their land.[107] The chiefs bowed down to the idols with the intent of saving their people, but what they didn't realize was that their people were ever so willing to unsheathe their swords and crush the pagan invaders. The courageous actions of St. Levond circulated throughout the nation, with many Armenians flocking to his village. It was in this time that a lost sheep would finally meet his shepherd. Vardan, a man filled with fortitude who worked with the Persians against his own countrymen, came to St. Levond and dropped to his feet in deep remorse, his eyes filled with penitent fears, and his tongue calling for forgiveness. A great deceiver arrived, named Vasak, who was commissioned by the Persians to govern over the Armenians. He was a native of Armenia, and an apostate who renounced the true Faith for the perfidious doctrines of the Magi. He told the people to adopt a mindset of tolerance, saying with a forked tongue to "let the Magi alone for some time, and they, finding the fruitlessness of their endeavors, will of their own accord leave the country."[108]

Now imagine this: there stands a priest, a defender of his people and his Faith, and by his feet lies Vardan, a man who was once a traitor, begging for forgiveness for his past evils. Amidst all of this there is a man, Vasak, who comes in peace, gently asking his people to merely tolerate the Magi, devising the lie that they are harmless. It is a profound picture for the mind: the honest sinner who comes in confession for his sins, versus the one who

---
106 Chamich, *History of Armenia*, vol. i, part iv, ch. ii, pp. 259–261
107 Chamich, *History of Armenia*, vol. i, part iv, ch. ii, pp. 261–262
108 Chamich, *History of Armenia*, vol. i, part iv, ch. ii, p. 262

comes as a lamb, but in reality is a cloaked wolf, planning on the destruction of the saints. It is a continuous evil which has slithered to our very times: pastors who are clothed with lamb's wool but armed with the fangs of a wolf have infiltrated our churches calling for the toleration of Islam, and for building bridges with mosques, never telling their congregants that they are dealing with the greatest persecutors against Christendom today. They lead their flocks to the house of slaughter, while telling them that they are partaking in true Christianity. And those who warn against such tolerance, the Vardans and Levonds of today, are accused by these same deceivers, the Vasaks of our time, as judgmental and bigoted.

Many men were tricked by Vasak and tolerated the Magi, and various nobles even allowed the wizards to reside in their mansions. It was by this tolerance of idolatry, this evil seed the sprouts of which only latch onto men's throats and strangle them that the Magi began to preach their ideology to the people. Vardan was so disgusted by this that he left Armenia, but being implored by the chiefs to come back, he returned. A sudden incursion was then made by Vardan and the chiefs and they drove out the Magi from their homes. Vasak assembled Persian troops to launch a responsive attack, but the Armenians made a preemptive strike completely defeating him. When Vasak was seized by the victorious saints, he began to swear that he had become a Christian and was spared.[109] If he never professed Christianity, he would have surely been killed.

But while many may condemn the Armenians for making sure that Vasak was a Christian, what we must understand is that the Persian religion was not merely bowing to the sun, but an entire political system. To adopt it would mean that one would have to adhere and assist to the despotism of Persia. Zoroastrians, then, were a danger to the nation of Armenia, and fully tolerating them and their ideology would have led to the complete engulfment of the nation, and the massacre and enslavement of its Christians. Vardan, therefore, had no choice but to commence a crusade against the idolaters.

In 451 A.D., the Armenian Christians held a meeting in which they discussed how they were to deal with the Persian invaders. A number of bishops stood up and declared this message to stir up the souls of their people to action, to battle for the Holy Cross, to prevail over the religion of devils:

> We now have to choose both to forsake our religion and recover our lost kingdom, or to keep our faith and suffer martyrdom. The first it is needless to say that we never will do; if we abide by the second, it is certainly true that we shall obtain the glorious crown of martyrdom; but our country will be entirely converted by the sword to the Persian religion, and in the lapse of time the light and glory of Christianity will be lost in Armenia, and the name of our God blasphemed. There is another alternative. Let us not passively earn the crown of martyrdom. Let us give up ourselves to the Most High, and not think of personal protection. Let us fight for the honour of the holy church which Christ has made his bride.[110]

---

109 Chamich, *History of Armenia*, vol. i, part iv, ch. ii, pp. 262–263
110 Chamich, *History of Armenia*, vol. i, part iv, ch. ii, pp. 263–264

Everyone in the assembly agreed and abided with this declaration; every man was determined to bear their sword and strive to prevent the demoniacal beliefs of the Persian from seeping into the hearts of their countrymen. They swore "to shed in battle every drop of blood" in defending the Holy Cross. With the force of 100,000 warriors, the Armenians stormed into the villages and cities where the Magi resided and put them to death. Any pagan temple they found they destroyed, and any church they found they purified. They marched into Duin, the capital of Armenia, and after slaying their enemies, erected a church made entirely of wood and dedicated it to St. Gregory the Illuminator.

As they went about purging their land from the invaders, they received word from the Christian Aluans that the Magi and a multitude of Persian troops were coming to their land to induce them to turn away from Christ. The Armenians sent a message to the Roman emperor Theodosius, but before he could come to their assistance, he died. His successor, Marcianus, chose not to interfere. The Armenians, left to themselves, put their trust in God—that His will be done—took upon their swords, divided their troops, and continued on. After a number of battles, the Armenians entered the country of the weary Aluans, utterly destroyed the Magi and Persian troops, and ridded the land from their altars, successfully delivering the allies from their tormentors,[111] as Joshua rescued the Hivites from the violent hands of Adonizedek. They then advanced to the gate of Chorah where they put to death every Persian in the neighborhood, and obliterated the temple of Hazkert II. Meanwhile, the conniving Vasak renounced again the Christian faith, preached the worship of fire to the Armenians, had many churches demolished, priests tortured, and villages destroyed. An agreement was then made by Hazkert and his liaisons that the entire nation of Armenia must turn to the worship of fire. Vardan and his men made a swift incursion through Armenia, invading the province which Vasak governed, taking prisoners. They sent a Persian hostage to Hazkert II, asking for peace if they would just grant them their liberty to worship God. The monarch consented to this, but deceitfully, making only a false peace[112] akin to an Islamic hudna.

A meeting was finally conveyed between Vardan and Hazkert. Picture to yourself such a moment: one saint stands before a tyrant; an individual living for freedom, versus a monarch who lives by tyranny and rules over slaves. Instead of speaking flattery and vain adulations, Vardan spoke the truth and declared the evils of the traitorous Vasak and the Persian kingdom. Diplomacy was now out of the question. The two separated, and Vardan grew his army to 66,000 men. They gathered together in the city of Artashat, and devoted themselves to martyrdom for the Holy Cross, the glory of Christ and for His Church, and met the Persians for battle near the village of Avarayr. Vardan passed among the ranks of his men with St. Levond, calling upon them to persevere in the fight against the army of evil. The sun had descended, they took the sacraments as righteous warrior saints, remained in the darkness of night with their hearts inflamed with the love of Christ and Armenia, and

---

111 Chamich, *History of Armenia*, vol. i, part iv, pp. 264–267
112 Chamich, *History of Armenia*, vol. i, part iv, ch. ii, pp. 267–269

with such high spirits did their strength arise above their natural capacity. The light of dawn cracked the darkness of the evening, they arose from their slumber eager for the intensity of war and to contend with the slaves of idols, and on that day, May 26th, 451 A.D., a great battle commenced.

The two sides collided, with the swords of the Armenians slashing through the Persian ranks, moving forward victoriously. They continued to advance crushing the Persian warriors before them; but as victory was being predicted, treachery stepped in. Five thousand men, who previously made a pact with Persia, separated themselves from the Armenians. The sudden shock and piercing pain to the hearts of the saintly warriors clouded their senses, and they soon were routed by the enemy. And on that field of battle, Vardan, and nine other chiefs, after illustrating their Christian valor and love of country, were slain. 1,036 Armenians lost their lives on that day, but the Persian victory was nothing to be proud of; for they lost 3,544. The surviving Armenians took refuge into a fortress. Vasak, the traitor, convinced them to come out, and when they did, he cruelly put them all to death; priests, such as St. Joseph, Mushey, Samuel, Abraham, St. Levond, Arshen, and the bishop Isaac, were chained by the order of the same Vasak, and sent to Persia as prisoners. He then went to battle with Himayak, the brother of Vardan, defeating and making him into a martyr. After such a loss, the Persians divided themselves and proceeded to further persecute the saints. The Armenians grew so weary of such atrocities that they rose up, pulled out their weapons and crushed the persecutors. They then marched into Persia, killing many inhabitants and burning down a great number of their villages and towns.[113]

The fate of Vasak was the king having him arrested under the suspicion that he was untrustworthy and thrown into prison where he died. His son was put in his place, but he was taken by an evil spirit and soon strangled himself to death.[114] Hazkert II, sometime after, declared war against the Huns, only to be beaten. He consulted his Magi who affirmed to him that his loss was due to the existence of priests in the kingdom, and that the only way to gain victory was to appease the gods with the blood of the saints. "Hence," they said, "the wrath of our gods is kindled against you." Upon hearing this, the king took the priests Abraham and Samuel and had them tortured to death. On July 25th, 454 A.D., all of the priests who were taken captive, including St. Levond, the commencer of the great war against Persia, were brought to a distant land and made martyrs.[115]

THE VAHANIANS

In the year 478, an Armenian Christian named Vahan, a nephew of Vardan, traveled to the royal Persian court and professed the faith of Zoroaster. The new king of Persia, Phiroz, being much pleased with his decision, granted him with many honors. But, such flattery was not to the satisfaction of his soul; in time Vahan was taken by despair and guilt, and wished for him-

---

113 Chamich, *History of Armenia*, vol. i, part iv, ch. iii, pp. 271–275
114 Chamich, *History of Armenia*, vol. i, part iv, ch. iv, p. 277
115 Chamich, *History of Armenia*, vol. i, part iv, ch. iv, pp. 278–279

self only death. He turned his eyes to Heaven and gave himself up to Providence. "All things," he said "are possible to thee, my God. I throw myself upon thee, do thou help me, and shew me the way in which I should go. Grant me a time of repentance, and of confession, that I may glorify thee." He expressed this desire to the chiefs of Armenia who besought him to cleanse the darkness that pervaded his desperate soul. At about this time, in 481, Phiroz declared war on the Christian Aluans, ordering the governor of Armenia, Atirwishnasp, to assemble the Armenians and their chiefs to assist him in this endeavor. Half of the troops recruited were Armenians who renounced Christianity, and these proved to be a menace, continuously harassing the believing warriors and accusing them of being traitors. The chieftains became so disgusted by the apostasy of their countrymen, that in a secret meeting[116] they exclaimed:

> Now is the time for a bold effort to deliver our country from the hand of the Persians and the apostates. Let us join with Valthank, the king of Georgia, or with the Huns, or Greeks, and attack them. The Almighty, seeing the purity of the motives that inspire us, will smile upon our exertions: for we do not engage in this enterprise for personal aggrandizement, but for the purpose of saving our holy church from falling under the power of the worshippers of fire. [117]

They reported their aspirations to Vahan, and he, having been struck by zeal, was filled with happiness upon hearing their desire. "Your wishes exactly agree with mine," he said, "but I scarcely dare join with you, because I have observed how often enterprises of this nature are backed by treason. Let us not apply to strangers for aid, for they may betray us. Let us place all our trust in God, for he alone disposes of events." The chieftains then responded with the words of solid believers: "We place no confidence in ourselves, nor in others; but in the power of God alone; for which we pray to St. Gregory and the blessed martyrs to intercede for us; for we prefer instant death to the pain we feel in observing the daily disgraces put on our church."

Vahan heard the call to martyrdom and became fervently ready to join allegiance in the fight. Inspiration uplifted his heart, fortified his mind, and a great determination was lodged within him to let his blood be shed in defense of Christ and Christendom. They all agreed to their mission, prayed fervently for the aid of the Almighty, and called for a priest named Athik to come to their camp and administer to them an oath of the Holy Testament, that they would forever more remain upon the path of righteous doctrine, and fight and die for it. They were now an order of warrior saints, called the Vahanians. But a treacherous chieftain leaked their plan to the governor, Atirwishnasp, who at once began his retreat from the warring Christians. When the Vahanians heard that their enemy was falling back, they rushed them, capturing a few stragglers. With the governor now gone, the Vahanians elected

---
116 Chamich, *History of Armenia*, vol. i, part iv, ch. v, pp. 286–288
117 Chamich, *History of Armenia*, vol. i, part iv, ch. v, p. 288

a new prefect named Isaac the Bagratian, in the Armenian capital of Duin where they began to prepare for war.[118]

Atirwishnasp gathered an army of seven thousand men and marched to Armenia where the Vahanians, with only four hundred warriors, were ready to fight. The faithful Armenians entered the church of Duin and devoted themselves to Christ, they then set out for the village of Varazkert where they sent Vasak, the brother of Vahan, to spy on the Persians. Vasak, to trick the Persians, sent numerous messages to them requesting peace, and when he was visited by enemy troops to receive his word, he told them: "The messages I have sent to your master were only meant to ridicule him. I had no communication to deliver; my only object was to see what kind of people you are; and I have found you a foolish and worthless set, and I predict that much evil will befall you." He made his statement, and then rode off to his brother where they awaited the coming of the Persian horde. The Armenians pitched their camp at the foot of Mount Ararat and looking to Heaven they made their pious prayers to God. When dawn had come the next day, the Armenians made ready to fight. The Persians arrived with their multitude declaring, "Surely these Armenians have abandoned their senses, and are come in quest to death!" The armies collided, and immediately traitors began to act, with one hundred Armenians going to the Persian side, leaving the saints with only three hundred.[119] This strikes us with the image of Gideon in his war with the Midianites, in which only three hundred Hebrews prevailed victoriously. "By the three hundred men that lapped will I save you," proclaimed God to Gideon, "and deliver the Midianites into thine hand: and let all the other people go every man unto his place." (Judges 7:7) It was a battle between three hundred and seven thousand one hundred; between the few and the many, the individual and the herd. The saints were victorious, losing one of their own and killing or putting to flight all of their enemies. And when the pope of Armenia heard the good news, the people gathered together in the church and offered their praise to the Almighty. Arastom, an Armenian who fought in the battle, exclaimed: "The power of the holy cross has conquered, and will ever conquer!"[120]

Another monumental event was the battle of the Vahanians versus the renowned Persian general Artirnerseh. The Armenians were on the verge of losing, mass confusion was everywhere, and despair plagued the saints. The Armenian Viren then told Vahan in the midst of all this chaos: "Do not confide in me in an hour like this." Vahan upon that moment sealed himself with the sign of the Cross and charged the Persian ranks with pure boldness and voracity. He was joined with two other distinct warriors, and together they struck disorder into the Persian lines with an implacable force, cutting down the enemy troops one after the other without stopping. They moved into the left wing of the Persian ranks where their foes fell like dry weeds before a rushing fire. They advanced victoriously over the Persians, and it

---

118 Chamich, *History of Armenia*, vol. i, part iv, ch. v–vi, pp. 288–290
119 Chamich, *History of Armenia*, vol. i, part iv, ch. vi, pp. 291–294
120 Chamich, *History of Armenia*, vol. i, part iv, ch. vi, pp. 294–295

was on that moment that Vahan realized that God had forgiven him for his past apostasy. A short time later, Vasak his brother was given the crown of martyrdom for the cause of God.[121]

A letter was received by the Armenians from Valthank, king of Georgia, asking for help from an invading force of Persians. Vahan and his men loyally arrived but they were deceived, for when they had come and waited several days, they found themselves surrounded by a vast Persian army consisting of elephants, chariots, and cavalry from various nations. The Vahanians perceived the intimidating number and fled across the river Cur. The next day came and the courage of the Armenians resumed; they re-crossed the river and a great battle ensued between the two forces with many Persians being slain. Isaac, the prefect who Vahan and the chiefs elected, one who was wholly devoted to Christ, fell by the Persian sword and died a martyr. Several Armenians who were treacherously involved with the Persians retreated, and the loyal Vahanians were thus forced to lose the battle. As Vahan was leaving the scene, he spotted one of his comrades, Babken, laying on the field amongst dead bodies and desperately wounded. Vahan rushed to him with his horse, picked him up from off the ground and saved his life. The Persians pursued and many Armenians were slaughtered. Amongst the captive Armenians was Hazd, who was brought before the Persian general Mihran who urged him to rid himself from the teachings of the Nazarene for those of Zoroaster. Hazd refused, and like many of those martyrs of old, was beheaded.[122]

By 483 A.D., Vahan was posted beyond the frontiers of Armenia with only one hundred men. They moved into the capital Duin, and when the spring season arrived, an immense army of Persians under the general Zarmihr allied themselves with apostate Armenian chiefs, and invaded Armenia. They surrounded Duin and commenced a siege upon the city. The Vahanians began to repair and strengthen Duin's fortifications, and then after putting themselves under the protection of the Almighty, ripped through the Persian forces around the city. The enemy was confounded and unable to come up with a plan, only believing that their god was enraged against them. The Persians charged the Armenian Pope Johan, but they were hindered by the gallant warriors Ordie and Cajaj, who were eventually killed. The pope rode his horse in attempt to escape, only to be surrounded by the enemy. A blade struck him; he was wounded and fell off his horse into a pile of slain bodies. The Persians thought him dead and so left him, but by Providence he was still alive and he arose and recovered himself. Vahan soon found himself in a difficult predicament, leaving him no choice but to take refuge in the fortress of Varairvar.[123] The Persians controlled the region and commenced a persecution of the Christians.

To compel the Armenians to convert to Zoroastrianism, the Persian general Shapuh kidnapped the wives of the Armenians Nerseh and Hirahat, and sent a message to them to forsake the mission of Vahan.[124] The two saints being not stricken with fear or anxiety, but

---
121 Chamich, *History of Armenia*, vol. i, part iv, ch. vi, pp. 299–301
122 Chamich, *History of Armenia*, vol. i, part iv, ch. viii, pp. 301–307
123 Chamich, *History of Armenia*, vol. i, part iv, ch. ix, pp. 307–310
124 Chamich, *History of Armenia*, vol. i, part iv, ch. x, pp. 311–312

filled with unconquerable faith, sent this response in defiance to the general and his empire of evil:

> Our actions and our labours are not directed to the attainment of worldly good, but to the establishment of the truth of our holy religion. In competition with this, our dearest object, we regard wives and children but in a very inferior view. We place our trust in the Almighty, that he will continue to preserve our wives in purity and chastity, and that he will, of his goodness, permit us again to embrace them, either in this world or in that which is to come! [125]

The spirit of Christian zeal had latched onto the hearts of these men so strongly, that not even spousal love could hinder them in their pursuit for justice and fight to shatter the foundations of tyranny. The words of these men was to the agitation and rage of Shapuh that he marched a great army into the country of the Arshamunians where the Vahanians were residing. Vahan set up some peasants armed with swords and shields; Shapuh pursued these thinking them to be Vahan's men. As they engaged, Vahan and his forces attacked Shapuh from the rear. Confusion struck the Persians, and the Armenians killed six hundred of them with the remaining three thousand scurrying away in retreat. Though they had ran away, Vahan knew that they would return, and prepared his one hundred men for the coming fight. The horde of Persians returned with thousands of men; it was a sight so intimidating that many of Vahan's troops left, leaving him only with about thirty warriors.[126] The colossal army was now before such a small number of Armenians; this was the ultimate showing of God's reasoning: that it is not about numbers, but the conviction of the heart; not about popularity, but the truth to which so few follow. The spirit of Vahan did not weaken; for truth is stronger when it is pursued by a small number, and a lie appears clearer when it is followed by the crowd.

Shapuh, at the head of his extensive army, began to mock the infinitesimal group of saints: "Support me, for I am overpowered by the novelty of this spectacle. These, our opponents, either foolishly wish to sacrifice themselves, or are protected by an invisible power. But if I am not deceived, they have given themselves up to despair, and desire to die. We shall now catch them one by one and bind them with chains!"[127] With this said, the Persians began to charge. Vahan marked himself with the symbol of the Cross and cried out with a loud voice: "Do not bid me beware, for I do not confide in man for aid, but place all my reliance on the blessed cross of our Redeemer." He declared these words, and as the hawk sharply descends with its majestic wings to strike its prey, he darted directly into the ranks of the Persian army. The chieftains with him followed, and together they slaughtered the enemy troops all around them, shedding torrents of blood. A trail of gore was made as their swords cut through the Persians with an indefatigable force. The few instilled terror into the hearts of the many.

---

[125] Chamich, *History of Armenia*, vol. i, part iv, ch. x, p. 312
[126] Chamich, *History of Armenia*, vol. i, part iv, ch. xi, pp. 312–313
[127] Chamich, *History of Armenia*, vol. i, part iv, ch. xi, p. 314

The Armenian crusaders continued to push through and advance. Four of them stood their ground forming a defensive circle of cutting daggers. A Persian horseman came upon the four warriors, but one amongst them thrust his spear into him and he fell headlong from his horse to his death. The four saints persisted in their grueling fighting like true masters of the sword. Persian after Persian fell before them regardless of how surrounded they were. After exemplifying the strongest fortitude in both body and spirit, this tetrad of warring saints fell. But the twenty six remaining did not stop nor waiver in the race to victory. Their faces were covered in sweat and blood, their bodies fatigued and wearisome, their blades bearing the signs of relentless fighting, and their eyes pierced by the shining sun and inflicted by war and its unbearable sights. But their souls remained unaffected. A small amount of weapons were gripped by men armed with the Holy Cross, the Breastplate of Righteousness, the Sword of the Spirit, the Shield of Faith, the Helmet of Salvation,[128] never wavering nor ceasing, but holding their ground and rooting themselves upon the most unbreakable of foundations. They were but few lights extinguishing an abyss of darkness from the earth, and with only twenty-six Vahanians, they prevailed and the foes of Heaven fled.[129]

King Phiroz perished shortly afterwards, and his successor Valarsh was willing to come to terms of peace.[130] Vahan sent his demands and conditions to the new monarch, whose prudence surpassed the cruelty of his predecessor, and they read as follows:

> We can come to no agreement with you by means of letters and messengers; we must have a personal interview with the king, and obtain from him his assent to three conditions, which we now purpose; if Nikhor [the Persian governor of Armenia] will execute these under the hand and seal of the Persian monarch, we will in all cases prove obedient to the Persians; if not, we cannot submit. Now the first condition we purpose, is, that we are allowed to openly profess the Christian religion, wherever we choose; and that you do not attempt the conversion of any Armenian to the doctrine of the Magi. The second is, that you favor not, nor exalt them because they profess the worship of fire. The third and last is, that the king on all occasions hear both sides, and not hasten to judgement on the information of one party against another, without hearing the latter's defense.[131]

Valarsh read this declaration, and with the nobleness of Darius when he allowed the Hebrews to build their temple agreed to its terms, ratified it by his hand, and decreed that it was to be honored by all Persian successors. Vahan was soon made governor of Armenia,[132] and following the Law of Moses, purged his country from Persian idols. Every Zoroastrian temple, those monuments of tyranny, found in his sight, was razed to the ground, and in their place he built churches, houses of civility. But when Valarsh passed away and Cavat succeeded him, the persecutions were revived and the decree was despised. An enforcement

---

128 See Ephesians 6:14–17
129 See Chamich, *History of Armenia*, vol. i, part iv, ch. x, pp. 314–316
130 Chamich, *History of Armenia*, vol. i, part iv, ch. x, p. 315
131 Chamich, *History of Armenia*, vol. i, part iv, ch. xi, pp. 317–318, brackets mine
132 Chamich, *History of Armenia*, vol. i, part iv, ch. xi, pp. 321–22

of the Persian religion was instigated by the conniving Magi, and a great number of them were sent with a new governor by the king to forcefully enter Armenia and build temples of fire. Many of the fickle inhabitants of Armenia were allured to embrace this heathenism, while most of the populace openly expressed their disgust with this idolatrous expansion. As confusion and misery struck the people, Vahan resorted to his only option of reestablishing peace: he alongside some chiefs attacked the Persians, killing the governor and all of his troops. Cavat, enraged by this incursion, desired to attack the Armenians but was prevented on account of his war with the Greeks. It was the last attack Vahan committed against the Persians. For being one of the greatest fighters for truth, justice, liberty, and Christendom, and one of the greatest enemies of tyranny, oppression, and the despotism of wizardry, Vahan breathed his last breath in the year 510.[133] He fought a good fight, finished his course, kept the Faith, and laid up for him was a crown of righteousness.

But soon the oath that was made between Persia and Armenia was broken. In the time when Persia was under king Khosrove, a Persian governor named Denshapuh began a persecution against the Christians of Armenia. Fire temples were erected and martyrs made, all by the tyrannical methods of the Magi. The pope of Armenia, Moses, implored Khosrove to remember the oath which was made between Vahak and king Valarsh. The king acknowledged this, and called off the slaughter of the Christians. The violent instigations against the Christians were resumed by the governor Suren. By his decree, believers were forced to worship the sun and fire. On account of this, every day an atrocity was committed in Armenia.

A man of heroism soon arose: Vardan II. His brother was killed under the sword of Suren, and so filled with dread was he by this, that he and other chiefs sent a letter to the Roman emperor Justinian requesting his assistance in toppling the Persian yoke. The emperor agreed, and by this Vardan II became so emboldened that with only a few companions he killed Suren, his Magi agent Vert, and all of Persian troops around them. An immense army was prepared by the king, and the Persians and the Armenians met on the plains of Khaghamakh. At dawn, the Armenians made the first strike upon the enemy side. The Persians became chaotic, their elephants were unmanageable, and many of them were cut down by the Armenians. Deren, the Persian general, the knot of desperation taking his heart, charged the Armenians with much valor. He killed many of them and made high the spirits of his men. This came before the eyes of Vardan II, and he rushed to the rear of the Persian troops and commenced such a violent onslaught that the Persians were again confounded. Fear and terror was all the Persians responded with, and as they fled, another Armenian force collided into the front of the Persian ranks, forcing the enemy to scatter on all sides.[134]

Vardan II then travelled to Constantinople and spoke with Justinian on their prior agreement. The emperor fulfilled his promise, and sent the Armenian with a vast army consisting of Greeks, Egerians, Apkhazes, and Alans. This was a crusade. The Greek troops entered Inner Armenia and crushed the Persians, killing 1,200 of them. The Persian monarch now

---

133 Chamich, *History of Armenia*, vol. i, part iv, ch. xii, pp. 326–323
134 Chamich, *History of Armenia*, vol. i, part iv, ch. xiv, pp. 335–338

wanted to end this engagement and to guarantee his victory he hastily assembled 100,000 infantry and 40,000 cavalry. Battles were fought with such a great force against the Greeks, and after much valor, a peace was settled which made Armenia remain a subject of Persia.[135]

VAHAN THE WOLF

In 604 A.D., king Khosroes of Persia sent ten thousand of his warriors under his general Mihran to attack the Armenian leader Mushel, and ultimately to enforce Zoroastrianism. Being weakened by old age, Mushel sent a letter to his son, Vahan the Wolf (or simply, Wolf), which read: "My son, I am now grown old and have no heir; I will give unto thee the whole of my possessions, and thou shalt combat with the enemies of the faith, who are now coming against us!" Wolf sought to immediately trample Mihran, not with sword and shield, but with pure wit and stratagem. He first sent a letter to Mihran requesting that he leave Armenia, to which the general responded: "Deliver Mushel into my hands, and I will quit the country!" Wolf promised that he would fulfill this, on condition that the land of Taron be held by him. They agreed and Mihran gave Wolf four thousand Persian troops to carry the plot. When they arrived in the city of Oz, the Persian troops made their rest, only to be silently strangled by determined Armenians loyal to Wolf. Reinforcements were urgently requested by Wolf and Mihran did not hesitate to comply, giving him two thousand men. Wolf had his Armenian companions dress as Persian soldiers, and when the two thousand arrived, every one of them was massacred by the Christians. He assembled eight hundred valiant men and posted them near the river Meltey, and when another two thousand Persians arrived, these ambushed them, killing all but one Persian. Wolf then sent a message to Mihran informing him that Mushel his father was finally captured and the mission complete. Wolf, attended by one hundred men, met with Mihran and promised him that Mushel will be in his hands the next day. As Mihran slumbered, Wolf thrusted his body with a javelin, preventing the misery he planned on causing for Armenia.[136]

Wolf then called for the general's secretary and made him write a letter to the Persian governor Varshin, as though he was Mihran, requesting for him and three thousand men. When these arrived, Varshin saluted Wolf who then shocked him with these words: "so you imagined to force the Armenians to embrace the Persian religion!" Wolf slew the governor, a battle ensued, and the Armenians destroyed them all with the exception of forty Persians. The band of saints withdrew to Armenia where Wolf made ready an army of twenty eight thousand warriors. The Persian general Valthank speedily marched into Armenia with his troops, and upon his arrival received a message from Wolf: "I am surprised, that after hearing of the tragic fate of Mihran, you have the rashness to come against us; perhaps you seek a wife amongst the daughters of Armenia. Come then to us, and you will find in the midst of our troops that will soon cool your amorous fire!" Two times did the Persians fight with Wolf,

---

135 Chamich, *History of Armenia*, vol. i, part iv, ch. xiv, pp. 339–340
136 Chamich, *History of Armenia*, vol. i, part iv, ch. xvi, pp. 347–350

and two times did they lose. He soon after died, but his son, Sumbat, resumed the cause. He warred with Valthank, and after a great engagement, slew the tyrannical Zoroastrian.[137]

These stories from Armenia, they are so filled with the actions of true Christians, but are so forgotten and neglected for the frivolous babbling of modern mediocrity. The ears of the masses are tickled by fluff, while those minds of pure saints yearn to see the true essence of Christianity: the rising and prevailing over evil. The few today who seek zealotry, have severed themselves from the majority who desire lies, and thirst to read of those men of old, who cared not for the wants of the herd, nor ever concerned themselves with the opinions of moderates, but like Christ, rose up as individuals, and knowing full well that they may die for their beliefs, ardently fought bearing the creed of righteousness against pure evil, never swerving but remaining rooted; never undecided, but fully convinced that the Holy Cross of Light will triumph over darkness. Many martyrs have become of these only to be disregarded by the careless; but fame does not determine success. It is the will to do good, without the care of praise or great reception that really matters. It is a reminder to us of what Wisdom profoundly tells on the death of the righteous:

> They leave us, but it is not a disaster. In fact, the righteous are at peace. It might appear that they have suffered punishment, but they have the confident hope of immortality. Their sufferings were minor compared with the blessings they will receive. God has tested them, like gold in a furnace, and found them worthy to be with him. He has accepted them, just as he accepts the sacrifices which his worshippers burn on the altar. When God comes to reward the righteous, they will blaze out against the wicked like fire in dry straw. They will rule over nations and peoples, and the Lord will be their king forever. (Wisdom 3:3–8)

There lies a story of a profound nature; one that illustrates the superiority of God over Satan; evil over good; saintliness over the demonic. The mother of the Persian king Kawad Khosru, had her soul taken by a demon. The monarch called for the Magi and the sorcerers to liberate her; but freedom never came, only further bondage from more evil spirits. Then, a monk arrived, named Moses, and he, by the power of God who gave this gift to all the saints, exorcised her of the demons, freeing her from the yoke of Satan. It was victory for the Holy Cross, over those chimeras espoused by sinister priests. One would think that the monk would remain in Persia to gain prestige; but no, he returned to his monastery near Dara,[138] triumphant not in himself, but in Christ Whose grace shatters all the works of the Devil, conquers hell, and purifies our sinful souls from the filth in which we live.

HERACLIUS AND THE SQUASHING OF PERSIAN HEATHENISM

The goal to replace Christendom with a Zoroastrian world empire was desired by Khosroes II, who hoped to take over the whole Christian Roman Empire. He mustered a large force against the Romans and their general Germanos, and defeated them. At the battle of Arx-

---

137 Chamich, *History of Armenia*, vol. i, part iv, ch. xvi, pp. 351–353
138 Zach. Mityl. Syri. Chron. 9.6

amoun, Khosroes fought the Romans using elephants, crushed them, and then took many captives and put them to death. In short time, Khosroes expanded Persian power, taking all of Mesopotamia and Syria. When the Romans attempted to defend the Syrian cities Apamea and Edessa, their entire army was wiped out, save only a few men. The Persians would soon enter Asia Minor where they took Galatia and Paphlagonia; they advanced all the way to Chalcedon, and even reached Constantinople which they assaulted greatly, but did not conquer. The Muslims also wanted to conquer Constantinople; they failed in the first attempt, but succeeded in 1453. Constantinople is on the eye of the devil, he desires to take it for in its midst lies the Hagia Sophia, one of the holiest sites in Christendom. They invaded the Cappadocian city of Caesarea in Asia Minor where they captured prisoners by the tens of thousands. The worshippers of Ahura Mazda went right into Damascus, captured the city, and began a full out massacre. When the emperor Heraclius sent messengers to Khosroes to offer a tribute for peace, the tyrant sent them back, not being interested in money but in totally conquering the Roman Empire.[139] The Muslims, not too long after Muhammad, seized Jerusalem and oppressed greatly the Christians there; the same was done by the Zoroastrian conquerors in the early seventh century. After invading Jordan, they captured the Holy City of Jerusalem where, with the help of the Jewish population, killed many Christians, taking, as some say, ninety thousand lives.[140] According to French scholar Bruno Bonnet-Eymard, Muhammad, before founding Islam, gathered a force and joined with the Persians and Jews in this savage siege of Jerusalem.[141] This may just explain why the Muslims want Jerusalem so much: they want to continue on what the Zoroastrians started.

As Khosroes was in Jerusalem, it is said that he stole the Holy Cross which Helena gave to her son Constantine.[142] After the conquest over the Holy Land, the Persians marched into North Africa, vanquishing and taking into their dominion all of Egypt, Ethiopia, and Libya. These takeovers were for strictly religious purposes, since when Heraclius sent ambassadors to Khosroes for peace, the Persian oppressor stated: "I will have no mercy on you until you renounce him who was crucified and worship the sun."[143] The persistent bloodshed and pillaging from the Persians sufficed for Heraclius' anger; he had no other choice but to declare a Holy War on Persia. His rage toward the persecutions and continuous violence against Christians by the Persians is found in the speech he made before his army:

---

139 Chron. Theophan. pp. 1–4, 6, 9–11, trans. & ed. Harry Turtledove; Theophilus of Edessa's *Chronicle*, section 1, from MSyr, p. 68, trans. Robert G. Hoyland, Liverpool University Press, brackets mine
140 Chron. Theophan. 301, p. 11; Theophilus of Edessa's *Chronicle*, section 1, from MSyr, pp. 64–5, trans. Robert G. Hoyland, Liverpool University Press, brackets mine Belloc, *The Great Heresies*, The Great and Enduring Heresy of Muhammad, p. 43
141 See Moczar, *Islam at the Gates*, prologue, p. 7
142 Chron. Theophan. Annus Mundi 6196; Jacobus de Voragine, *The Golden Legend*, 137
143 Chron. Theophan. 301, pp. 11–12

> Brothers and children, you see that God's enemies have overrun our land, laid waste our cities, burned our altars, and filled the tables of bloodless sacrifice with bloody murders. They take great pleasure in defiling our churches, which should not suffer.[144]

The Persians sent a force into Armenia, but once they found out that the Romans were in Persia, they withdrew the army to come and defend the homeland. After some fighting took place, Khosroes fled to the city Thebarmais where a lofty Zoroastrian temple stood. Heraclius pursued him, and the tyrant resumed his retreat, and when the Roman king arrived, he burned the pagan temple,[145] a great action against idolatrous oppression. Heraclius even showed mercy to the fifty thousand Persian prisoners that he had taken, letting them all go free, taking care of them, and permitting them to rest. They were stirred with such compassion that they, in tears, exclaimed Heraclius as "the savior of Persia, who would kill Khosroes, the universal destroyer."[146] Such an event shows the enormous difference between Christian justice and pagan subjugation. The struggle continued, and it wasn't getting any easier, but Heraclius kept up the spirits of his men. "Brothers," he said, "do not be troubled by your enemies' numbers for, God willing, one will chase thousands. Let us sacrifice ourselves to God for the salvation of our brothers. Let us take the martyrs' crown so the future will applaud us and God will give us our reward."[147] This statement clearly shows how these ancient Christians viewed martyrdom, that the crown of glory can be obtained by being killed in persecution, or dying in Holy War.

The Byzantines showed an impenetrable spirit when combating the heathen soldiers. Money was drained from the Persians, and so Khosroes forced the churches under his empire to give away all of their valuables and treasures.[148] When the Byzantines were in Persia fighting the pagans, their Khazar allies left them, leaving the Christian warriors by themselves. Though this must have been shocking at first, Heraclius spoke to his men of how God works not through numbers, but through those who truly believe; that "salvation does not lie in masses of men or arms. Rather He [God] sends down His aid to those who believe in His mercy."[149] It was a profound statement that shows the wonders which so few individuals can do against an army of slaves.

On a major battle in a flat valley, Heraclius illustrated his tenacity and vigor when he sprinted ahead of his army and slew a Persian officer. Another Persian came at him—the emperor killed him; and another confident enemy officer struck him on the lip with a spear, but Heraclius neutralized him as well. Trumpets roared from both side; the Christian forces made their charge upon the Persian soldiers. Almost the entire Persian army was annihilated, while fifty Romans lost their lives. The Romans pressed on and over-

---

144 Chron. Theophan. 304, p. 14
145 Chron. Theophan. 307–308, pp. 16–17
146 Chron. Theophan. 308, p. 17
147 Chron. Theophan. 311, p. 19
148 Chron. Theophan. 315, p. 21
149 Chron. Theophan. 317, p. 23

whelmed the Persians the next day, obtaining another victory. They advanced forward, searching for Khosroes. They discovered the mansions and statues of their enemy king, and to avenge the destruction of so many Christian cities and buildings by the Persians, Heraclius razed these to the ground. The emperor sent a letter to Khosroes, imploring again for peace:

> I am pursuing and chasing peace. For I do not willingly burn Persia; rather, you force me to do so. Let us now, therefore, throw down our arms and welcome peace. Let us quench this fire, before it consumes everything. [150]

> Heraclius was an emulator of Christ in His Second Coming, when He shall proclaim before His battle: "I am for peace: but when I speak, they are for war." (Psalm 120:7)

Khosroes would eventually be found in a lofty idolatrous tower that he built. It was very paralleled to the Tower of Babel: it was dedicated to the sun, moon, and stars. In an inner room of the tower, Khosroes sat on a middle seat and called himself God; on his right stood the cross he stole from Jerusalem, which he called "the Son," and on his left he placed a cock, which he referred to as "the Holy Spirit." He mockingly placed himself as part of his own trinity.[151] The intent of this tower was the same as the one in Shinar, and the Kaaba in Mecca: to be worshipped by all the earth, under astral religion. This monument of oppression needed to be destroyed. Heraclius entered the tower and beheaded Khosroes, thus ending the tyranny of Zoroastrianism, and crushing the dominion of the Persian.[152] Heraclius then retook the stolen cross, returned to Jerusalem, and placed it back in the Church of the Holy Sepulcher.[153]

---

150 Chron. Theophan. Annus Mundi 6118
151 Jacobus de Voragine, *The Golden Legend*, 137; De Croce, *Refutation of the Koran*, ch. xiii
152 Jacobus de Voragine, *The Golden Legend*, 137; De Croce, *Refutation of the Koran*, ch. xiii
153 Jacobus de Voragine, *The Golden Legend*, 137; Chron. Theophan. Annus Mundi 6120

PART 4 – MERCY AND JUSTICE

This section makes the case that within Christianity there is a balance between mercy and justice, unlike in modern times where Christianity is viewed with a radical fixation on just mercy without justice. It will also show that Christ's teaching on "turning the other cheek" and "love your enemies" were not taught to somehow counter the Old Testament, as is so commonly believed, but that these precepts were already in the Old Testament, and that Christ taught them in order to bring in a balance between mercy and justice.

THE MODERN CHRISTIAN HAS NO BALANCE BETWEEN MERCY AND JUSTICE

In Christianity there is a balance between mercy and justice; for in the holy Faith, mercy and justice are one. People talk as though the Old Testament is nothing but violence, and that the New Testament brought in a new teaching of love. But this is far from the truth. When Christ said, "love your enemies," this could be paralleled to what Solomon said, "If your enemy is hungry, give him bread to eat; and if he is thirsty, give him water to drink" (Proverbs 25:21). David had an opportunity to kill Saul, his enemy, but he instead showed mercy and gentleness; Jeremiah was cast into a pit, but expressed no malice against his enemies.[1] Christ taught us to turn the other cheek, and this was simply the same teaching that God taught through the prophet Jeremiah when he wrote: "Let him give his cheek to the one who strikes him, and be full of reproach." (Lamentations 3:30)

Yet none of these holy men ever rejected the use of arms, or condemned war. We love to quote the passages of Christ where He said, "love your enemies" and "pray for your enemies," as if this is the only actions we must do in the face of evil. All of the commands of mercy in the New Testament are taught in the Old Testament. Christ was restoring these teachings of peace and mercy to a people who only wanted violence. Christ was promoting a balance between mercy and justice, since the Jews were utterly unbalanced, only indulging in a cruel perception of justice absent of any mercy. Modern Christians have now fell into this imbalance, but this time to the opposite extreme, where all they want is mercy but no justice. In Christ there is both gentleness and ferocity, and this balance is seen where Christ says, "Love

---

1   See Adamantius, *Dialogue on the True Faith*, 1.12, ed. Ronald J. Sider

your enemies," and in another He says of the enemies of the Faith, "cast the unprofitable servant into the outer darkness." (Matthew 25:30)[2]

This balance is also found in the Father, for He said, "I kill and I make alive; I wound and I heal" (Deuteronomy 32:39). And so we, icons of God, strike injustice, correct those who advance tyranny, and show mercy when violence is not the only option.

King Solomon showed mercy to Adonijah because there was no wickedness found in him. But Solomon also said that death would come upon him "if wickedness is found in him," thus illustrating both mercy and justice, being merciful to those who deserve mercy, and fierce against those who deserve punishment:

> Now Adonijah was afraid of Solomon; so he arose, and went and took hold of the horns of the altar. And it was told Solomon, saying, 'Indeed Adonijah is afraid of King Solomon; for look, he has taken hold of the horns of the altar, saying, Let King Solomon swear to me today that he will not put his servant to death with the sword.' Then Solomon said, 'If he proves himself a worthy man, not one hair of him shall fall to the earth; but if wickedness is found in him, he shall die.' So King Solomon sent them to bring him down from the altar. And he came and fell down before King Solomon; and Solomon said to him, 'Go to your house.' (1 Kings 1:50–53)

Within Christendom, there is a balance between mercy and justice, fairness and ferocious retribution. David says of the judicious order of God:

> Righteousness and justice are the foundation of Your throne; Mercy and truth go before Your face. (Psalm 89:14)

Because God has "righteousness and justice," "mercy and truth," then these things are to be in the spirit of Christendom, and it is to these virtues that Christendom pursues. God, in some occasions, kills those who are evil enough to deserve it, and shows mercy on those who are corrupt, but not entirely depraved, and gives them chances for repentance. It is this balance that human justice should strive to emulate, for as Aquinas articulates:

> According to the order of His wisdom, God sometimes slays sinners at once, in order to deliver the good, and sometimes grants them time for repentance, according as He knows what is expedient for His elect. And this also human justice initiates as far as it can; for it slays those who are dangerous to others, while it reserves for repentance those who sin without grievously harming others.[3]

The wicked are punished by a wise king, or in the words of Solomon, "A wise king sifts out the wicked, and brings the threshing wheel over them." (Proverbs 20:26) But the same king is to show mercy, and not to be governing merely through sheer brutality:

> Mercy and truth preserve the king, and by lovingkindness he upholds his throne. (Proverbs 20:28)

---

2 See Adamantius, *Dialogue on the True Faith*, 1.14
3 *Summa Theologiae*, IIa IIae 64, article 2

The Christian king is to forsake all evil and perpetuate justice, and in so doing, he is to punish the evildoers, for they are enemies of justice and bringers of oppression. Look at the words of God, of what He proclaimed to rulers:

> Wash yourselves, make yourselves clean; Put away the evil of your doings from before My eyes. Cease to do evil, Learn to do good; Seek justice, Rebuke the oppressor; Defend the fatherless, Plead for the widow. (Isaiah 1:16–17)

The king is to dispense justice; he is to eschew evil and cling onto God, and in emulating God, he does goodness; he is to defend the orphans and intercede for the widow. All of these actions are within the admirable balance between mercy and justice. The king must be just, or in the words of Solomon, "When the righteous are in authority, the people rejoice; But when a wicked man rules, the people groan." (Proverbs 29:2)

And what is a righteous king, but one who "does not bear the sword in vain" and who unleashes "wrath on him who practices evil" (Romans 13:4–5)? A righteous government is there "for the punishment of evildoers and for the praise of those who do good." (1 Peter 2:14) This balance between mercy and justice is well illustrated by Ecclesiastes when Solomon says:

> A time to kill,
>   And a time to heal;
> A time to break down,
>   And a time to build up;
> …A time to love,
>   And a time to hate;
> A time of war,
>   And a time of peace. (Ecclesiastes 3:3, 8, ellipsis mine)

King David advanced mercy when he ordered Solomon to kill Joab for unjustly slaughtering his two commanders in a time of peace, for he broke the law of mercy:

> Moreover you know also what Joab the son of Zeruiah did to me, and what he did to the two commanders of the armies of Israel, to Abner the son of Ner and Amasa the son of Jether, whom he killed. And he shed the blood of war in peacetime, and put the blood of war on his belt that was around his waist, and on his sandals that were on his feet. (1 Kings 2:5)

While he ordered the just killing of Joab, he commanded Solomon to show mercy to the sons of Barzillai, since they helped him when he fled Absalom, for such would be the just thing to do:

> Therefore do according to your wisdom, and do not let his gray hair go down to the grave in peace. But show kindness to the sons of Barzillai the Gileadite, and let them be among those who eat at your table, for so they came to me when I fled from Absalom your brother. (1 Kings 2:6–7)

This shows a balance between mercy and just retribution against those who are deserving of punishment. This balance is illustrated by David when he writes in one verse of God's "marvelous lovingkindness" (Psalm 17:7), and in the same Psalm urges the Lord to "Deliver my life from the wicked with Your sword" (Psalm 17:13). Loving kindness and the sword go hand in hand, since mercy for the wicked, is hatred for their victims.

God smote the children of Israel and then showed mercy and compassion. In the Psalms we read of how God "slew them," and then once "they sought him: and they returned and enquired early after God," He, being full of compassion, "forgave their iniquity, and destroyed them not: yea, many a time turned he his anger away, and did not stir up all his wrath. For he remembered that they were but flesh; a wind that passeth away, and cometh not again." (Psalm 78:30–39)

Saul exerted ferocity against the Amelekites and the Amorites, but he showed mercy to the Kenites:

> And Saul said unto the Kenites, Go, depart, get you down from among the Amalekites, lest I destroy you with them: for ye shewed kindness to all the children of Israel, when they came up out of Egypt. So the Kenites departed from among the Amalekites. (I Samuel 15:6)

Imbalance in the Faith is what pushes people to either cruelty or indiscriminate toleration. It is balance that exhorts the destruction of evil, and at the same time, compassion for those in need of God and of His laws. Do not assume that I am saying that only Christians are humans and the rest animals. Do not think that I do not know that endless are the multitudes of those who put upon themselves the title of Christian, and are more savage and depraved than any heathen. I fight more against those who call themselves Christians, than anyone else.

There are Muslims, Hindus and Buddhists more righteous than many so-called Christians out there. We have had Muslims in Pakistan help us protect Christians from Islamic persecution, in our rescue mission; and when we have brought persecuted Christians from Pakistan into Thailand, we have had Buddhists help house them, and supposed Christians refuse to help us. When we brought Christians from Pakistan into Sri Lanka, Buddhist lawyers helped the Christians to get residency in the country. I will tell you this now, that these nonbelievers are closer to God than the "born again Bible believing Christian" who sees his brethren being persecuted and callously does nothing. To them can we say with Christ, "That the publicans and the harlots go into the kingdom of God before you." (Matthew 21:32)

The Samaritans rejected all of the books of the Bible except for the Five Books of Moses,[4] they as well did not consider the Temple to be the legitimate sanctuary of God. They made an evil alliance with Antiochus Epiphanies when he tyrannized Israel and desecrated the Temple; they changed the Tenth Commandment to be about the sanctity of Mount Gerizim. In other words, they were heretics, and were not orthodox in their theology.

So much anger did the Jews have for them, that we read in the Gospel that the Samaritan woman told Christ, "the Jews have no dealings with the Samaritans." (John 4:9) And despite

---

4 See St. John of Damascus, *On Heresies*, 9

all of the corruptions of their theology, Christ uses a Samaritan in His parable on who is and who is not our brothers, after a sophistical lawyer asks Christ, "And who is my neighbour?" (Luke 10:29)

A man is beaten, almost to his death, and left on the side of the road. A priest comes, sees the anguishing man, and keeps walking. A Levite comes by, and callously continues on. But then a Samaritan passes by, and what made him different from the first two? In the words of Christ, "he had compassion on him" (Luke 10:33), and this compassion was evidenced through action. The Samaritan "went to him, and bound up his wounds, pouring in oil and wine, and set him on his own beast, and brought him to an inn, and took care of him. And on the morrow when he departed, he took out two pence, and gave them to the host, and said unto him, Take care of him; and whatsoever thou spendest more, when I come again, I will repay thee." (Luke 10:34–35)

What distinguishes the sons of God from the sons of Belial, is what distinguished the Samaritan from the two priests: love, for "He who does not love does not know God, for God is love." (1 John 4:8) There are many examples of good samaritans in our own modern times. During the Armenian Genocide, when the Muslim Ottoman Empire was slaughtering millions of Christians, there were cases in which Arab Muslims righteously rescued Armenian Christians from death. One Armenian family was brutally butchered by Ottomans, and there was only one survivor, a boy named Khatchik, who was rescued by Arab Bedouins and lived with them for nine years before he left and joined a relief center for Armenians. As one scholar notes, "Some Armenians were rescued by Bedouins and other Arabs who sympathized with the Armenian situation. Sympathetic Turkish families also risked their own lives to help their Armenian neighbors escape."

Such righteous people were good samaritans. They follow God without knowing it, for they emulate God to the best of their ability. They do not prove that Islam is peaceful, but that the compassion that kindled within their souls transcended the evil teachings of Islam, and flamed so hot with the flames of love, that they burned away whatever corruptions Islam could have brought. They were righteous deeds, and such noble acts were done by God through the hands of these people.

This is why I do not like the vague talk that I hear sometimes, such as, "Lets get guns and shoot Muslims at random." Or "Lets kill the Muslims and pour pig's blood on them." Such talk is devoid of intelligence, and the intentions behind them are neither said for Christianity, but for some dry system of conservatism. What about these Muslims who rescued Christians, kill them too? Saddam protected the Christians, and when America killed him the conservatives were acting as though they won some sort of a crusade. Gaddafi was a Muslim who protected Christians, and America brought him to the slaughter. Mubarak was Muslim, and protected Christians, and look how America encouraged a mob to overthrow him, thus enabling the Muslims to kill Copts. Assad is a Muslim who is protecting the Christians, and look how the Western forces are working to get rid of him!

Even when the Israelites came to Canaan to massacre the Canaanites, they spared Rahab because she was righteous, and they spared the Hivites because they desired peace with Israel. Secular conservatism is of a diabolical nature; it tries to portray a facade of some Christian morality, but it is filled with a very callous view of humanity.

Christianity is now identified with GOP politics and materialism. I remember in one argument I saw about illegal immigration. My father and I were in a car with a woman, who is very much into this way of thinking, and her husband. We saw a Mexican man selling ice cream, and she pointed her finger at him saying, "You see this guy here, he is probably illegal!" My father asked her: "A Muslim comes into America to conspire and support terrorism, but he is legal; another, a Mexican man selling ice cream on the streets, lives in America but he is illegal, but has no ill will. Which one do you prefer?" She coldly said, "The Muslim, he is legal." She said this even though she could not stand Muslims.

Another horrifying story creeps into my memory. A boat filled with Christians and Muslims was traveling from Africa to Italy, and the Muslims seized twelve of the Christians, threw them off the boat, and laughed as they watched them drown to death. The Italian government was compassionate enough to accept the rest of the Christians and arrest the Islamic perpetrators. I remember seeing conservatives in America say that the Christians deserved to drown, that there should be no sympathy for them, and that the Italians should have never accepted them, because they were "illegal immigrants." Such people who express themselves this way, do not know God, but worship a false, mechanical, callous, cold and deistical god, who runs like a ticking clock, only functioning like a machine, without a single drop of compassion.

All of the tears of the world could not stir this god to sympathy, for it is a devil. The God of Christianity, however, has passion, emotions, anger, jealously, and love, and He honors the nonbeliever who has love, over the "conservative" who could not shed tears for martyred Christians. Such is the purpose of the parable of the Good Samaritan: to show the callousness of self-esteemed people who think they are righteous because they mechanically follow some set of rules set up by societal tradition, and accepted as "conservative." These supposed "conservatives" will show more love towards "gay people" and politicians who lie to their faces, than they would suffering Christians because they are "illegal," or even righteous Muslims just because they are "rag heads."

Human beings are born with sinful nature, and thus any good that man does is done by God through him. As the Italian mystic, Lorenzo Scupoli, said:

> There is nothing He [God] loves and desires to see in us more than a sincere consciousness of our nothingness and a firm and deep-felt conviction that any good we may have in our nature and our life comes from Him alone, since He is the source of all good, and that nothing truly good can ever come from ourselves, whether a good thought or a good action.[5]

---

5   *The Unseen Warfare*, ch. 2, trans. E. Kadloubovsky & G.E.H. Palmer

Thus when man does good, that goodness comes from God, and he is only the instrument by which the righteous act is accomplished. It is quite ineffably beautiful, and truly something of wonder: man, with all passion and enthusiasm, does good, but it is God that is working through him, and he is but the paintbrush of this immaculate painting of Providence.

We must destroy Islam, but this does not mean we destroy all Muslims. We fight Islam by declaring Christianity as superior to Islam, and through the Christianization of society (which at times require the use of force), we bring the Muslim world into the fold of Christendom. The power of Islam in the Islamic world must be destroyed through military force, and once the authority of Islam is broken and tendered, then that is when the preachers of the Gospel are sent, to bring the Muslims into the Church. This is what the Conquistadors did when they invaded Mexico.

This would be love, for it is done—not to mock and cruelly kill people—but to bring man into enlightenment. It is done in union with God, and by God, with man simply being the instrument of divine justice. The warrior is filled with love, because he has God, and through him, the enemies of light are crushed. "God has broken through my enemies by my hand like a breakthrough of water." (1 Chronicles 14:11)

MERCY AND JUSTICE IN THE CHURCH

This balance between mercy and justice continued on in the Church. Two soldiers approached St. John the Baptist, and asked him, "And what shall we do?" To this the Baptist replied, "Do not intimidate anyone or accuse falsely, and be content with your wages. (Luke 3:14)

Here lies the entire law of holy Christendom's armies. Here are the words that restrain the impulses of the soldiers, and instill temperance within their hearts. Here lies the words that bring Christendom away from the desires of gain, and guide her to strive for justice and for the defense of the Church. Here lies the Rule of St. John the Baptist[6] for Holy War. In the King James Version of this passage, the Baptist says, "Do violence to no man," meaning do not be brutal nor kill innocent peasants. When he commands the soldiers not to "accuse falsely," he means the calumny and false accusations against people to either rob them or kill them. When he says, "be content with your wages," he says so to prevent plundering and extortion, for to be satisfied with your pay is to not covet the goods of others with violent desires.[7]

Moreover, St. Robert concludes from this Rule of St. John the Baptist, that there are certain people who must be treated with mercy. Firstly, civilians who do not belong to the commonwealth or province of the enemy, and so when soldiers are passing by a land that does not pertain to the fray, they are not to oppress any locals. Secondly, any Christian clergy or farmers must never be attacked, be they within enemy territory or outside. This is in accordance to the tract of peace, called *Innovamus de Tregua et Pace*, which reads:

---

6 St. Robert called this passage "the rule of John the Baptist" (*On Laymen or Secular People*, ch. 15, ed. Tutino, p. 73)

7 St. Robert interprets St. John's rule this way (On Laymen of Secular People, ch. 15, ed. Tutino, pp. 72–73)

We decree that priests, monks, those who live in convents, pilgrims, merchants, peasants who come or go to work in the fields, and the beasts by which they plow or bring seeds to the field, should enjoy a fitting security. [8]

In this document when it mentions "merchants," it is not talking about the ones who live amongst the enemy, but traveling merchants who are going to the market and are not part of the territory of the adversary.[9] Thirdly, there are women, children, and elderly, who should not be intentionally attacked, but there are certain instances in which it is permissible to slay these. For example, if an army attacks a city knowing that women and children will die, but it is beyond their control, then this is permissible. This is why St. Robert says, "Thus when a soldier shoots into a battalion of enemies and by chance kills a child or a woman or even a priest, he does not sin, but when he kills them intentionally and has the means, if he wishes, to avoid killing them, then he sins."[10]

Today, it is very common, when progressives and modernists denounce war, to use pictures of dead women and children as a means to propaganda. But what they never care to bring up is that many of these deaths are done unintentionally and are, sadly, impossible to avoid if the enemy is to be attacked. When confronted with the deaths of civilians, we should always ask whether or not they were done deliberately.

Francisco Vitoria, considered by some to be the father of international law, who wrote much on the rules of war, said that if a war is unjust and done for the purpose of tyranny, then the Christian soldier is obligated not to take part in it. He said that "if the war seems patently unjust to the subject, he must not fight, even if he is ordered to do so by the prince. This is obvious, since one may not lawfully kill an innocent man on any authority, and in the case we are speaking of the enemy must be innocent."[11]

But if the war is just, then the soldier can take part in it, even if it is launched by a pagan king, as Augustine said: "If ordered to do so, a just man may righteously go to war, even under a sacrilegious king, so long as he is either certain the order is not against God's precept, or uncertain whether it is."[12]

The Crusaders carried out the balance between mercy and justice, between loving one's enemy and fighting the enemies of God. They did this by building hospitals in which they would tend to all peoples, Christians, Muslims and Jews, not forsaking them to let them die, but helping them with the purest love of the Christian Faith. In one medieval text we read:

> This holy house [of the Hospital], knowing that the Lord, who calls all to salvation, does not want anyone to perish, mercifully admits men of the Pagan faith [that is Muslims] and Jews because the Lord prayed for those afflicting him, saying: 'Father, forgive them for they know not what they do.' In this blessed house is powerfully fulfilled the heavenly doctrine: 'love

---

8   Quoted by St. Robert Bellarmine, *On Laymen or Secular People*, ch. 15, ed. Tutino, p. 73
9   St Robert Bellarmine, *On Laymen or Secular People*, ch. 15, ed. Tutino, p. 73
10 St. Robert Bellarmine, *On Laymen or Secular People*, ch. 15, ed. Tutino, p. 73
11 Vitoria, *On the Law of War*, question 2, article 2, 22
12 Augustine, *Contra Faustum*, 22.75, in Vitoria, *On the Law of War*, question 2, article 4, 31

your enemies and do good to those who hate you; and elsewhere: 'Friends should be loved in God and enemies on account of God'. [13]

These beautiful words alone truly eliminate all of the complaints of the haters of the Crusades, that they were anti-Semitic or anti-Jewish. How could they be anti-Jewish if they were so willing to treat them as brothers, tending to their wounds in hospitals, abiding by Christ's teaching of forgiving one's enemies?

One could say that the Crusaders fought their enemies with both sword and charity: destroying Islam by both force and by depleting its numbers by bringing Muslims into the Faith by the love of Christ.

There are other examples of this balance in Christian history. After the Christian Byzantine emperor Botoneiates defeated the rebel general Bryennios, he showed great mercy and compassion to Bryennios, sparing his life, and all those who followed him. As we learn from the ancient historian Atteleiates,

> all those who rebelled with Bryennios, who were moaning and trembling because of the laws against conspirators and the harsh vengeance that awaited those who committed that sin, he deemed worthy of total amnesty. Out of ineffable compassion he did not deprive them of their property either, though he made an exception for three or four of them, whom it would not have been safe to leave in possession of their property, but even in their case he gave them others in exchange, making his benefactions equal to what they had lost. [14]

St. Paul wrote, "If it is possible, as much as depends on you, live peaceably with all men." (Romans 12:18) Notice that he says, "if it is possible," signifying that there are times when it is not possible to have peace, when men are so wicked that they must be punished in order for peace to resume itself. Moses declares that "When you go near a city to fight against it, then proclaim an offer of peace to it." (Deuteronomy 20:10) This is because peace must always be the first step to be pursued; but when all else fails, then arms must be utilized. St. Gregory of Nazianzus, expressed this when he said that while fighting is in accordance to God's justice and law and is necessary at times, peace needs to be always the preferred choice:

> Both [the time of war and the time of peace] require some consideration, for even though it is actually possible in some cases to fight war in accordance with God's law and authority, nevertheless for as long as we can we should incline rather to peace as the more divine and sublime course. [15]

This is why war must always be for justice and the wellbeing and security of the people and the Church, not cruelty. St. Augustine condemns war for the sake of cruelty and gain when he writes, "Lust for harming, cruelty in seeking revenge, an unpacified and implacable spirit, brutality in rebelling, lust for power, and similar things are rightly condemned

---

13 Jonathan Riley-Smith, *The Crusades*, ch. 3, p. 77
14 Attaleiates, *History*, 34.10
15 St. Gregory of Nazianzus, *Oratio de Pace*, in St. Robert Bellarmine, *On Laymen or Secular People*, ch. 14, ed. Tutino, p. 58

in war."[16] Peace must be the intention of every war; it must be within the heart of the warrior, even when he takes life. "The will must want peace," says St. Augustine, "only necessity should bring war."[17]

When the Christian Roman Empire was at war with the pagan Scythians, a military leader named Synesios demanded that all the prisoners be executed. When the emperor Alexius Komnenus heard this he immediately commanded mercy, since the Scythians were human beings too. "Scyths they may be," he said, "but human beings all the same; enemies, but worthy of pity." He then ordered the prisoners to be disarmed and guarded.[18] When an assassin tried to kill him but was caught in the process, instead of having him executed, he forgave him and prevented his guards from tearing him to pieces.[19] Anna Komnenus, Alexius' daughter, described the emperor as a man who not only was a fierce warrior, but one who cared for the orphans and the widows and one who deeply read and contemplated on the Scriptures:

> In time of peace as of war he was a first-class administrator, judging the cause of the orphans, dispensing justice to the widowed and regarding with the utmost rigour every case of wrongdoing. For most of the day he laboured hard. He would relax too, but only his relaxation was itself a second labour—the reading of books and their study, the diligent observance of the command to 'search the Scriptures' [John 5:39].[20]

When he and his men were marching to battle, anytime a woman was about to give birth Alexius would order a trumpet to be sounded and the men to be stopped. Once the child was born, he gave the order to advance. If a man was on the point of death, Alexius again would have the trumpet blasted and he would visit the dying man and the priests were summoned to sing hymns and provide the necessary sacraments. The emperor would invite all the men and the women who were infirm with sickness and old-age, to sit with him at his table and eat. He would also encourage those with him to be charitable and giving. He had men help guide the blind, caring for women and infants, he made sure that orphans were cared for, and he had his hard working servants serve the impoverished.[21] Ramon Llull, a man who was both knight and theologian, wrote:

> It is the office of the knight to support widows, orphans and the helpless, for just as it is customary and right that the mighty help to defend the weak, and the weak take refuge with the mighty, so it is customary in the Order of Chivalry that because it is great, honourable and powerful it comes to the succour and aid of those who are inferior to it in honour and strength.[22]

---

16 St. Augustine, Against Faustus, 22.74, in St. Robert Bellarmine, *On Laymen or Secular People*, ch. 15, ed. Tutino, p. 70
17 St. Augustine, letter 189, as quoted by St. Robert Bellarmine, *On Laymen or Secular People*, ed. Tutino, p. 71
18 Ann Komnenus, 8.6
19 Anna Komnenus, 9.7
20 Anna Komnenus, *Alexiad*, 14.7
21 Anna Komnenus, *Alexiad*, 15.7
22 Ramon Lull, *Chivalry*, 2.19

St. Gregory VII stood for justice when he zealously called for the king to launch holy war and a crusade against the Muslim Turks; and he was for mercy when he exhorted the rulers of Sweden to:

> Strive to maintain unbroken concord and affection between yourselves, to show honor to the churches, compassion to the poor and afflicted, reverence and obedience to priests, especially to bishops, as to your fathers, to pay tithes for their use, and for the churches and for the poor, and enjoin upon your whole kingdom to do the same. [23]

St. Gerald of Aurillac was a knight who fiercely fought against the malicious oppressors who raided and pillaged poor villages in France, and while he imposed justice on the wicked, he showed much tenderness to the impoverished. As we learn from St. Odo, Gerald would set apart a ninth of the vegetables of his fields for the poor, and even provided shoes and clothes for them. It is said that "No one was ever turned away from his door without alms being given."[24] St. Odo also tells us that the "poor and the wronged always had free access to him,"[25] and this is because he was at all times willing to defend them. Moreover, while Gerald "had much care for the poor," he "was never slow in punishing the guilty."[26] One day while he was walking alongside the road, he saw a woman plowing a field, and he asked her why she was doing the work of a man. She replied that her husband was too ill to work. Taking pity on her, St. Gerald ordered that the women be given enough money so that she could hire a laborer to plow the field for as much days that were left for sowing.[27]

St. Bernard of Clairvaux, a French monk of the 13th century and one of the great cultivators of the monastic way, tells us that the Christian must be compassionate toward those who are in despair, and moved to the flames of zeal against the wicked:

> You sadly lack humanity if you are not drawn towards a man whose heart is full of grief through the wrong which has been done him, the toilsome journey, and the expenses which he has incurred. But there is no less sad lack of spirit if you are roused against him who is partly the direct, partly the indirect, cause of so many calamities. Rouse thee, man of God, when these things happen; let both your pity and your indignation be stirred. The one you owe to the injured, the other to him who inflicts the injury. Let the former be consoled for his loses, by satisfaction for his wrongs, by putting a stop to the malicious charges; let the latter be so handled that he may be sorry for having done what he was not afraid to do, and may not laugh at the punishment of the innocent. [28]

This harmony between justice and mercy is a reflection of the divine nature of God glimmering within the heart of the faithful warrior. St. Paulinus of Nola wrote of this profound character:

---

23 Gregory VII, book 9, 14, p. 592
24 Odo of Cluny, *Life of St. Gerald of Aurillac*, 1.14
25 Odo of Cluny, *Life of St. Gerald of Aurillac*, 1.17
26 Odo of Cluny, *Life of St. Gerald of Aurillac*, 1.8
27 Odo of Cluny, *Life of St. Gerald of Aurillac*, 1.21
28 St. Bernard, *On Consideration*, 3.2

So great is the love of our highest Father that even His anger springs from mercy, and He punishes to spare. [29]

HOLY WAR DESTROYS FALSE PEACE AND BRINGS TRUE PEACE

David in one verse says to pursue peace, but in a subsequent verse says that God will cut off the evil-doers from remembrance:

> Depart from evil and do good; Seek peace and pursue it. The eyes of the Lord are on the righteous, And His ears are open to their cry. The face of the Lord is against those who do evil, To cut off the remembrance of them from the earth. (Psalm 34:14–16)

The modern mind says, "How is this peace?" It is peace because it destroys those who are enemies of peace. Holy War unleashes the sword, destroys false peace and brings true peace. The true spirit of Christianity is that of war, war against the world, war against the flesh, war against evil and the guiles of Satan. Our weapons are both spiritual and temporal, armed with both "the sword of the Spirit" (Ephesians 6:17), and "the stroke of the sword" (Esther 9:5), "The sword of the Lord, and of Gideon." (Judges 7:18) One strikes the demons while the other strikes the slaves of demons who attempt to persecute the children of God. The Sword of Christ is the sword that destroys the false peace to advance the true peace. The Holy One said, "Blessed are the peacemakers: for they shall be called the children of God." (Matthew 5:9) And who will deny that in many occasions peace is established through combat? Augustine declared that just war is done for the cause of peace, and hence the soldiers who partake in it are peacemakers: "We do not seek peace in order to wage war; rather, we wage war in order to achieve peace. Be peaceful, therefore, in making war, so that, in vanquishing those against whom you fight, you may lead them to the benefit of peace."[30] Therefore, those righteous soldiers who bring peace by using force and arms against a tyrannical and persecuting enemy, "shall be called children of God." They shall be children of God because they shall be God-like, possessing a divine characteristic; they shall have theosis or that unsurpassable unity with Christ.[31] St. Augustine said:

> Among true worshippers of God, those wars which are waged not out of greed or cruelty, but with the object of securing peace by coercing the wicked and helping the good, are regarded as peaceful. [32]

Vitoria wrote: "the purpose of war is peace, and therefore those who wage just war may do everything necessary for security and peace."[33]

The Christian soldier wars against the enemies of God, and through arms destroys false peace and establishes true peace. In the Scriptures it reads: "The Lord is a warrior who ends

---

29 St. Paulinus of Nola, letter 29.8
30 Augustine, letter 189, in Aquinas, *Summa Theologiae*, IIa IIae 40, article 1
31 See Fulton Sheen, *The Cross and the Beatitudes*, ch.6, p. 76
32 Augustine, in Aquinas, *Summa Theologiae*, IIa IIae 40, article 1
33 Vitoria, *On the Law of War*, question 1, article 4, 18

CHRISTIANITY IS AT WAR: THE MANIFESTO FOR CHRISTIAN MILITANCY

war." (Judith 16:3) So the knight of Christ, being an image of God, is a warrior who uses the sword to put an end to war, cuts off the voice that says, "'Peace, peace!' When there is no peace" (Jeremiah 6:14) and advances authentic peace, not the superficial peace of the world. "Peace I leave with you," said Christ, "My peace I give to you; not as the world gives do I give to you. Let not your heart be troubled, neither let it be afraid." (John 14:27) This is the true peace, the peace that Christ brought when He brought the sword. It is the false peace—the peace of Cain—that Christ came to destroy with His sword. "Think not that I am come to send peace on earth: I came not to send peace, but a sword." (Matthew 10:34)

It is this false peace that David spoke of when he wrote:

> Let them not rejoice over me who are wrongfully my enemies; Nor let them wink with the eye who hate me without a cause. For they do not speak peace, but they devise deceitful matters against the quiet ones in the land. (Psalm 35:19–20)

There is the mercy of the just, and there is the mercy of the deceptive, who desire mercy on wicked people who deserve none. In one passage David urges God to show no mercy to evil transgressors:

> You therefore, O Lord God of hosts, the God of Israel, Awake to punish all the nations; Do not be merciful to any wicked transgressors. (Psalm 59:5)

When Christ returns He will distribute justice and be the salvation to the oppressed, but He will provide no mercy or leniency to the tyrants of the earth. For as David wrote:

> He will bring justice to the poor of the people; He will save the children of the needy, and will break in pieces the oppressor. (Psalm 72:4)

People forget that Christ is eternal, and so they limit His nature to only what is written in the Gospels, ignoring that He is both the Warrior of Justice and the Prince of Peace, just and merciful. While He is merciful, "He shall cut off the Spirit of Princes: He is terrible to the kings of the earth." (Psalm 76:12)

Christ shows mercy to the poor and to the needy, but He is ruthless to the deceivers, and to the wolves who cunningly prey upon the weak. He showed mercy to the harlot when He told her, "Neither do I condemn you; go and sin no more." (John 8:11) But He exemplified His ruthlessness when He, with force and a sharp whip, compelled the merchants in the Temple to flee.

Christ ends war through war, as the Psalms declare:

> He makes wars cease to the end of the earth; He breaks the bow and cuts the spear in two; He burns the chariot in the fire. Be still, and know that I am God; I will be exalted among the nations, I will be exalted in the earth! The Lord of hosts is with us; The God of Jacob is our refuge. Selah (Psalm 46:6–11)

WARS MUST HAVE A CAUSE

The Christian king must always be just, shining as light dissipating the darkness, as God told David:

> For all His judgments were before me; And as for His statutes, I did not depart from them. And he shall be like the light of the morning when the sun rises, a morning without clouds, like the tender grass springing out of the earth, by clear shining after rain. (2 Samuel 22:3–4)

David was just, and in exemplifying justice, he killed the heathens. When the righteous kill the wicked, their swords are not covered with blood shed with injustice, but for noble retribution. It was a sacred thing for Israel to combat the Philistines, even when it was led by Saul—his enemy—and Jonathan, of whom David chanted:

> From the blood of the slain, from the fat of the mighty, the bow of Jonathan did not turn back, and the sword of Saul did not return empty. (2 Samuel 1:22)

The "blood of the slain" belonged to the wicked ones deserving death, that is in this case the pagan Philistines. Then there is killing done without a holy cause of the spirit, but a gain of the flesh. In the Scripture, Abigail mentioned "blood causeless" (1 Samuel 25:21), that is killing done without a righteous reason. Thus, holy war must always be done in accordance to its title: it must be holy. The sword is only righteously used if it bears the blood of the wicked, for as Tertullian wrote:

> As for the sword which is drunk with the blood of the brigand's victims, who would not banish it entirely from his house, much more from his bedroom, or from his pillow, from the presumption that he would be sure to dream of nothing but the apparitions of the souls which were pursuing and disquieting him for lying down with the blade which shed their own blood? ...The sword also which has received honourable stains in war, and has been thus engaged in a better manslaughter, will secure its own praise by consecration. [34]

Christian wars must always have a holy cause, aspiring for justice and the squashing of despotism, for as David says, "Let them be ashamed which transgress without cause" (Psalm 25:3). The wars of David had a cause: the cause of God to advance the Kingdom of Heaven. Every holy war must have a cause, and not be reckless. When Christ suffered and died on the Cross, He did not endure such torment for nothing, but for a holy cause—nay—a Holy War: "For this purpose the Son of God was manifested, that He might destroy the works of the devil." (1 John 3:8)

---

34 Tertullian, *On the Resurrection of the Flesh*, ch. xvi, ellipses mine

PART 5 – THE CROSS AND WAR

"Precious in the sight of the Lord is the death of His saints." (Psalm 116:15)

THE CHRISTIAN WARRIOR IS SUPERIOR TO ALL WARRIORS

The Christian warrior is superior to all fighters; for he surpasses all temporal desires, he breaks through all the material world, and strives with every effort to reach the eternal realm of pure light, where passions and earthly attachments are absent, and all that is reached is the most supreme of love: divine union with God.

The Muslim fighters and all other pagan fighters, on the other hand, are inferior to the Christian warrior. When they fight, they do so with a hope that does not surpass the temporal, but that remains within the earthly desires.

The Muslim fighter hopes for martyrdom with the desire for infinite sexual gratification, debauchery, pederasty and drunkenness, and so when he fights, his mind is still in the temporal—nay—it is imprisoned within the fetters of the impulses. He can never surpass the earthly and break into the heavenly. He never reaches selflessness, because his goal pertains only to the pleasing of the self, and not to the sacrifice of it.

Such a fleshly disposition is utterly contrary to the Christian spirit.

The transcendence of the material into the eternal, is what brings the Christian warrior to burn with all zeal. It is the light of God, of which David said: "Lord, lift up the light of Your countenance upon us" (Psalm 4:6), that fans the flames of holy desire to partake in the good fight, and "endure hardship as a good soldier of Jesus Christ." (2 Timothy 2:3)

It is the light of God that brings into the Christian warrior (and to use the words of St. Gregory Palamas) "the fire of love for God which burns in him."[1]

---

1   St. Gregory Palamas, *The Triads*, 1. iii. 23

This zeal that burns within the warrior is as the zeal of Christ, when He took up a whip and with His own divine hands drove the thieves from His Temple, fulfilling the prophetic word: "Zeal for Your house has eaten Me up." (John 2:17)

We must ask ourselves when observing this event: why didn't the Temple guards at least try to apprehend or attack Christ? It is not as though He just came in and quickly struck some people with His whip and then left, He in fact remained in the Temple laying hands on any merchants who came inside, for Mark tells us that He "would not allow anyone to carry wares through the temple." (Mark 11:6) He remained in the Temple using physical force to protect it from the salesmen, and not only this, but He even said a sermon, saying: "My house shall be called a house of prayer for all nations. But you have made it a den of thieves." (Mark 11:17) It wasn't until "evening had come," that "He went out of the city." (Mark 11:19) He remained in the Temple for a considerable amount of time, attacking merchants and making declarations against the corruptions of the clergy. Why didn't the guards arrest Him or attack Him then? Because He was so intimidating, so aggressive, so tenacious and explosive, that not one of them would dare challenge Him. And not only this, but the multitudes were so fanatic about Him and His teachings, that the authorities "feared Him, because all the people were astonished at His teaching." (Mark 11:18) The first followers of Christ put fear into the authorities, and Christ never chided them for this. Why? Because as Christ is zealous, so are His people to be zealous, and so great must be their zeal that it should put fear into the enemies of God. It is the same zeal of Jehu when he led the crusade against the pagans, and said: "Come with me, and see my zeal for the Lord." (2 Kings 10:16)

In doing this they abide by the first commandment: "you shall love the Lord your God with all your heart, with all your soul, with all your mind, and with all your strength." (Mark 12:30) That strength is mentioned shows a physical involvement in loving God. For in this verse we have the strength of the heart, the strength of the soul and the strength of the mind. In addition, we have sheer strength which cannot be other than physical strength which Jesus displayed with the whip. Christ said: "Is not the life more than meat, and the body more than raiment?" (Matthew 7:25) The body goes beyond the material and the aesthetic, for it is to be used for that which is ineffable and completely transcends the corporeal, that immaculate place that "Eye has not seen, nor ear heard" (1 Corinthians 2:9), and that is Heaven.

This is the highest state of the spiritual ladder that the Christians can reach, to where they offer as their "bodies a living sacrifice, holy, acceptable to God, which is your reasonable service." (Romans 12:1) They crucify themselves, and say with St. Paul: "I have been crucified with Christ" (Galatians 2:20) and "have crucified the flesh with its passions and desires." (Galatians 5:24)

They with the Apostle boldly proclaim by both word and action, "I bear in my body the marks of the Lord Jesus." (Galatians 6:17) They are like Simon of Cyrene, trembling with all labor alongside Christ, carrying the Cross with Him.

✝ CHRISTIANITY IS AT WAR: THE MANIFESTO FOR CHRISTIAN MILITANCY

The willingness to die for the Faith is the greatest point for the Christian to reach in his spiritual path, for it is here where he fulfills what the Apostle wrote: "glorify God in your body and in your spirit, which are God's." (1 Corinthians 6:20)

St. Stephen glorified God in both body and spirit when he was martyred; for he gave up his body as a sacrifice, emulating the Christ and bearing the wounds of his Master, our Crucified Savior; and when he on that point, between transience and eternity, declared, "Lord Jesus, receive my spirit" (Acts 7:9), no doubt the Lord received his spirit, because he glorified God in spirit.

He proved himself a worthy soldier of the holy combat, and through the divine love of self-sacrifice, obtained divine union with the holy and blessed Trinity. St. Paulinus spoke of this tenacious will to endure suffering when he wrote: "A will prepared to suffer is sufficient, for it is the best evidence of deserving aspiration."[2] A glorious death for the cause of the Divine Truth is so great to the eyes of Heaven that David wrote:

> Precious in the sight of the Lord is the death of His saints. (Psalm 116:15)

The goal of martyrdom is not an infinite gratification of the flesh, but an ineffable crown of glory in eternal paradise, where the treasures of righteous labors which are done on earth, are enjoyed in everlasting life in union with God.

When the warrior fights, he does so with eternity in mind, and so in his effort, the mind, spirit, soul, and body, work as one for a divine aspiration. With both the bodily and spiritual faculties working in unity, all earthly passions are eclipsed, and all that is desired is the eternal reward of a blessed death. Divine union with God cultivates the virtue of hope within the soul, and so powerful is this hope that the warrior confronts the wicked adversaries with a greater fortitude and vigor. Ramon Llull spoke of this profound hope coming from union with God when he wrote that the warrior "must come so close to God through hope that with hope and with God he may fight against his enemies and those who are contrary to Chivalry."[3] The hopeful warrior fights alongside God, and that is because he is with the Creator, being used by Him as an instrument for divine justice. Through hope does the warrior surpass every travail and hardship of the body; in hope in Christ he forgoes hunger and still pursues victory; he endures fatigue and still fights without rest. In the words of Ramon Llull, "hope makes them endure hunger and thirst in the castles and cities that they defend when they are besieged."[4] In this sublime hope does the warrior say with St. Paul:

> Everywhere and in all things I have learned both to be full and to be hungry, both to abound and to suffer need. I can do all things through Christ who strengthens me. (Philippians 4:12–13)

---

2 Paulinus of Nola, poem 14, 12
3 Ramon Llull, *Chivalry*, 4.10
4 Ramon Llull, *Chivalry*, 6.5

The command of Christ, "If any man will come after me, let him deny himself, and take up his cross, and follow me" (Matthew 16:24), brings the fighter to the divine union with Christ, and enables him to ignore all fear of death. To rid oneself of the ego, leads to limitlessness in one's will to commit noble actions; for in this point one can say with St. Paul, "it is no longer I who live, but Christ lives in me" (Galatians 2:20). As St. Maximus the Confessor said,

> For he [Christ] put off the principalities and powers at the moment of his death on the cross, when he remained impervious to his sufferings and, what is more, manifested the (natural human) fear of death, thereby driving from our nature the passion associated with pain. [5]

THE FORGOTTEN CHRISTIAN SAMURAI

This spirit of the Christian warrior was fully exemplified by some of the most unheard of, obscured and ignored warriors in history: the Christian Samurai, the Samurai that the world has forgotten.

These were Samurai who picked up their cross but never dropped their swords. They picked up the cross to partake in the cosmic battle against the forces of evil.

Christianity first came to Japan in 1549, when St. Francis Xavier arrived at the shores of Kagoshima. With the spreading of the Gospel came converts, and amongst these converts would be many warriors.

What is quite amazing is that even though these Samurai became Christian, they never rejected their warrior prowess, but instead used it for a different objective: the advancement of Christianity.

The reason for this is that the missionaries who introduced to them the Faith were Catholics who held onto to the same theology as the crusaders, the warriors of God who with the sword fought for God and the Divine Law against Muslims and pagans.

The theology of Holy War is deep within the Orthodox Christian Faith, and as it was zealously maintained amongst the crusaders, it would come to the Samurai, a people most enthusiastic to battle and who would have never rejected sacred combat.

They did not accept compromise with the false religions of Japan, but honored the words of the scribe when he told Christ: "there is one God, and there is no other but He." (Mark 12:32) They maintained the exclusivity of the Christian spirit, and because of this, sparked a civil war within Japan between the Christians and the Buddhists, carrying out what Christ once declared: "Do not think that I came to bring peace on earth. I did not come to bring peace but a sword." (Matthew 10:34)

With their zeal for Christ, they divided themselves from the heathens, and with their own swords did they advance the sword of Christ. They rejected the Buddha, and forever dedicated their bodies and their souls to fighting for Christ and His holy Law.

---

5   Maximus the Confessor, *The Cosmic Mystery of Jesus Christ*, Ad Thalassium 21, On Christs Conquest of the Human Passions, trans. Blowers & Wilken

CHRISTIANITY IS AT WAR: THE MANIFESTO FOR CHRISTIAN MILITANCY

In 1567, an anonymous Christian Samurai executed one of the greatest acts of holy war in Christian history: he burned down the emperor Shomu's Buddhist Todaiji temple in Nara, where a disgusting idol of the Buddha sat.

In 1578, the Samurai leader Otomo Sorin converted to Christianity and received baptism. Like the righteous kings of Christendom, he declared that his subjects "would all have to become Christians and live with each other in brotherly love and concord."

To fulfill this noble goal, he enacted a policy of Christian unity for his people, and so ordered that the false religions of Japan—Shintoism and Buddhism—would be outlawed in his lands, and ordered that their temples be destroyed and their idols shattered.

Antonio Koteda, another Christian Samurai who was of the land of Ikisuki, is said to have "had no greater pleasure in the world than to see them pull down idols out of the temples and houses, and burn them and throw them in to the sea."

Another Christian Samurai, Omura Sumitada, was a lord who also partook in the destruction of pagan idols in Japan.

According to Luis Frois, a Catholic missionary who evangelized in Japan at this time period:

> As Dom Barthlomeo had gone off to the wars, it so happened that he passed on the way of the idol called Marishiten, which is their god of battles. When they pass it, they bow and pay reverence to it, and the pagans who are on horseback dismount as a sign of respect. Now the idol had above it a cockerel. As the tono [lord, Omura Sumitada] came there with his squadron he had his men stopped and ordered them to take the idol and burn it together with the whole temple; and he took the cockerel and gave it a blow with the sword, saying to it, 'Oh, how many times have you betrayed me!' And after everything had been burnt down, he had a very beautiful cross erected on the same spot, and after he and his men had paid very deep reverence to it, they continued on their ways to the wars.

There was one Christian Samurai named Hosokawa Akiuji, who himself destroyed several pagan temples by setting them on fire.[6]

Let us never forget these Samurai. The world wants us to solely focus on the pagan Samurai, but never the ones who realized the errors of their people, and fought to destroy paganism.

It is of every Christian to hate all that is against God. Solomon said, "The fear of the Lord is to hate evil" (Proverbs 8:13), and David beautifully wrote:

> Do I not hate those who hate you, O Lord; am I not disgusted with your enemies? (Psalm 139:21)

David also wrote: "Be angry, and do not sin." (Psalm 4:4) What this means is that when we hate evil, we prevent ourselves from falling into sin. It is when we make humor out of evil,

---

[6] All of this information on Christian samurai can be found in Stephen Turnbull, *The Samurai and the Sacred*, pp. 91–96

when we laugh at it and see it as just a choice or a silly thing that we fall into the very vice that we make fun of. "To do evil is like sport to a fool," wrote the wise Solomon, "But a man of understanding has wisdom." (Proverbs 10:23)

Never once in the Gospels do we ever read of Christ having fun. He never smiles nor laughs; He weeps and bitterly cries; His body drips with blood; He goes to war and into combat; He is a warrior and a monastic. It is in the somber presence of His Passion where we receive our strength and the zeal to pick up a whip and drive the thieves from His Church. As St. Catherine of Sienna once beautifully wrote:

> Let our hearts, our minds, and desires be lifted up with this Company of Bitterness, and let us go to the Temple of our soul, and there we shall know ourselves. Then the soul, recognizing itself not to be, will recognize the goodness of God towards it, who is He who is. Then the will shall be uplifted with zeal, and shall love what God loves and hates what God hates. [7]

Who then will enter into the somber presence of the Christian spirit, where earthly desires are cast aside, where the fires of the passions are extinguished, where the Sword of Christ declares war against the hordes of the devil, and where the armies of God are always vigilant and preparing for holy combat and martyrdom?

Who but the Christian is the warrior superior to all warriors?

TO DIE IS TO LIVE

The purpose of life is not to live. Whoever says that the purpose of life is to live is preaching the devil's lie that we should "live for the moment." The purpose of life is to die unto the self and to liberate the self from the cares of this earth, to prepare the self for the Beatific Vision. "For whosoever will save his life shall lose it: and whosoever will lose his life for my sake shall find it." (Matthew 16:25)

Life is not an end unto itself. It is a means to an end, and that end is eternity. The farmer sows the seeds, but the beauties of their fruit do not appear until the seeds themselves die. So it is with us: the glory of eternity is not experienced until the self is denied, the cross is carried, the Master is followed, and the fruits of holy labor grow from the vines in the spring of repentance, and a worthy martyrdom brings us to Paradise. As the Apostle tells us, "what you sow is not made alive unless it dies." (1 Corinthians 15:31) Martyrdom is the most sublime form of worship; it is a declaration of gratefulness to the sacrifice of Christ. As St. Paulinus said:

> The death of holy men can rightly be called their praise; for it is a precious repayment to the Lord God. [8]

---

7   Catherine of Siena, letter to Monna Colomba of Lucca
8   Paulinus of Nola, Poem 21

CHRISTIANITY IS AT WAR: THE MANIFESTO FOR CHRISTIAN MILITANCY

HOLY WAR IS THE EMULATION OF CHRIST

Man is made in the image of God, and so he takes upon himself the wounds of Christ, "the image of the invisible God." (1 Colossians 1:15) God, in the flesh, was crucified upon the Cross, and it is this very moment that we emulate; it is His spirit that we embrace; it is this very Crucifixion that we partake in, when we are inflicted with the wounds of holy combat against the devil and his followers, willing to suffer death, as He faced death with all endurance and courage.

If we follow the devil we no longer bear the image of God, for "friendship with the world is enmity with God" (James 4:4). But, when we are inflicted as Christ was inflicted, then do we bear the image of God, and we can say with St. Paul, "I bear in my body the marks of the Lord Jesus." (Galatians 6:17) The Cross is not some symbol, or some abstract picture that we are supposed to just imagine; the Holy Cross is a holy icon that we are to embrace with all of our beings. In combat, and in martyrdom, the Cross takes over our entire identities; we become the Cross, and the Cross becomes us. We enter the Cross, and we become like Christ, and through His humanity, we partake in His divinity; through His humanity, we enter eternity. In Christ we do not fear death, but fight for the Way, the Truth, and the Life; in Christ the warrior plunges through sacred combat with all self-denial and sacrificial love, and he declares with St. Paul: "I have been crucified with Christ; it is no longer I who live, but Christ lives in me; and the life which I now live in the flesh I live by faith in the Son of God, who loved me and gave Himself for me." (Galatians 2:20)

No human can enter the divinity of God by himself, and so we go to the Father through the Son, Who is both human and divine. "No one comes to the Father except through Me." (John 14:6) We enter the divine by first passing through the door of Christ's humanity. And how do we do this except by emulating His humanity? We imitate the humanity of Christ by submitting our entire will to the Father, following Jesus when He said: "I can of Myself do nothing. As I hear, I judge; and My judgment is righteous, because I do not seek My own will but the will of the Father who sent Me." (John 5:30) Our wills are utterly subsumed into the will of God; we sacrifice our will as an offering, and in turn give up ourselves for the battle, and in the holy warfare do we say the words of the Son, when He was in combat against the forces of darkness: "not as I will, but as You will." (Matthew 26:39) In the denial of the self, "it is no longer I who live," but Christ living within us, and we, participating in Christ, partake in His Warfare against the devil and his followers. To participate in Holy War against the diabolical heightens the zeal of the spirit, for in such a state does one partake in God, following the command of St. Peter: "rejoice to the extent that you partake of Christ's sufferings, that when His glory is revealed, you may also be glad with exceeding joy." (1 Peter 4:13)

THE CHRISTIAN WARRIOR IS UNCONQUERABLE

Christ is very Man and very God, as the holy fathers teach us. God became man so that we, being made in the image of God, could become like God. Our humanity is corrupt, and so a perfect humanity, free from the stain of original sin, is what we need in order to come into union with God. This is why it is through Christ's perfect humanity that sinful humans become "partakers of the divine nature" (2 Peter 1:4). We stand on earth in the taint of sin, and across from our existence there lies the spaceless plain of eternity. Eternity is beyond our reach but the humanity of Christ is the path by which we humans reach it. St. Paulinus of Nola explained how Christ's humanity is truly what connects us to everlasting life, and thus to the unconquerable path of triumph over death:

> For over the boundless space which separates things mortal and divine He has established His mediation like a bridge to connect the two, so that by this path the earthly may be joined with the heavenly, once the celestial incorruption has permeated our corrupt nature, once immortality, in the words of Scripture, has swallowed up our mortality, and our life, victorious in Christ and from Christ, has conquered and absorbed death. [9]

When Christ died He conquered while at the same time remaining unconquered. So the Christian warriors, taking up the Cross and partaking in the nature of Christ, are never conquered, even when they are slain. As St. Bernard once wrote concerning the martyrs: "Those indefatigable warriors fell on the field of battle, but they fell unconquered: even in death they triumphed."[10] St. Maximus of Turin described the Church as an army that vanquishes the enemy, but is never defeated:

> What troops of kings, what mob of soldiers has carried off such a victory as to cut down the foe while from among themselves no one falls? This is the true, this the bloodless victory, when the adversary is conquered in such a way that none of the conquerors is hurt. [11]

In the Holy Trinity there is Father, Son, and Holy Spirit; the Father and the Holy Spirit are both purely divine, while Christ is very Man and very God. There is thus a human element within the Trinity, and it is by this humanity that we partake in divinity; it is by this humanity that we participate as good soldiers in the wars of God.

HOLY WAR—THE GREATEST EXPRESSION OF LOVE

When Christ was on the Cross, what looked like an execution to earthly eyes was a holy war to spiritual eyes. St. John said: "He who says he abides in Him ought himself also to walk just as He walked." (1 John 2:6) To emulate Christ—the highest of warriors—is to be a warrior. In the sacred combat of the Cross, we war against the devil and his demons, and in turn, partake in the fray against their mortal followers. Christ Himself did not refrain from warfare when He struggled and fought against evil men, and because He is the incarnation of Love, to participate in His Holy War is to partake in love. When the Christian warrior fights against the enemies of God he is doing so in the highest form of love, because he carries his cross for the sake of the well beings of his brethren, emulating Christ when He died for us, and thus does he enter the Cross of Christ. As St. John tells us, "By this we know love, because He laid down

---

9 Paulinus, letter 13, 26
10 Bernard, *On Consideration*, 3.1
11 Maximus of Turin, sermon 83.4

His life for us. And we also ought to lay down our lives for the brethren." (1 John 3:16) It is by self-sacrifice that one knows love, and so the warrior has within himself the knowledge of love, not in a way that it is intellectual, but in a mystical union with Christ.

Notice what St. John says in another place, "He who loves his brother abides in the light" (1 John 2:10). This is not speaking of brothers by blood, but by spirit, the Christian brethren, and to love the brethren is to be willing to die for him in holy combat, and by this is one in the light that is, unified with Christ, "the true Light which gives light to every man coming into the world." (John 1:9) The Emperor Constantine, who did not hesitate to enter battle against the pagans and lay down his life in combat to protect the Church, wrote of this union with the light of God: "By keeping the Divine faith, I am made a partaker of the light of truth—guided by the light of truth, I advance in the knowledge of the Divine faith." The divine love, as being proven through the sacrifice of the self in warfare, was expressed by the knight Ramon Llull, when he wrote:

> And if you sacrifice your life upholding Chivalry in such a way that you can love, serve and profess in the most, for Chivalry resides in no other place as agreeably as in nobility of courage, and no man can love, honour or profess Chivalry more than he who gives his life for the honour and the Order of Chivalry. [12]

When the Christian fights for the protection of his brethren with the prospect of his own death, he drinks the chalice of Christ, and fulfills the greatest of all love: laying down his own life for his friends. As the monk Peter the Venerable addressed the crusaders who fought the Muslims: "For your brothers you have exposed your souls to life, your bodies to death; you have already shed blood never before shed, which in battles you daily offer to God to be shed if necessary. You are truly sharers in that lofty, special love of which the Savior said, 'Greater love hath no man than this, that a man lay down his life for his friends [John 15:13].'"[13]

He takes up the cup and drinks it, as Christ did in the Last Supper before His death, and thus by this emulation, he participates in Christ, in Whom "we live and move and have our being" (Acts 17:28). As the Latin Rule of 1129, an instructional for Templar knights, reads, the knight "should remain in his profession so that he may be able to equal the wisest of the prophets in this: 'I will take the chalice of salvation' [Psalm 116:13], i.e. death, meaning that by my death I will imitate the death of the Lord, since just as Christ laid down his life for me so I am prepared to lay down my life for my brothers."[14] The Christian warrior abides in love, for he abides in God Who is Love, and so strong is this unity, that he can say with St. Paul:

> Who shall separate us from the love of Christ? Shall tribulation, or distress, or persecution, or famine, or nakedness, or peril, or sword? As it is written: 'For Your sake we are killed all day long; We are accounted as sheep for the slaughter.' Yet in all these things we are more than conquerors through Him who loved us. For I am persuaded that neither death nor life,

---

12 Ramon Llull, *Chivalry*, 2.17
13 Peter the Venerable to Everard of Les Barres, in Barter and Bate, *Templars*.
14 Latin Rule of 1129, 5, in Barber and Bate, *Templars*

nor angels nor principalities nor powers, nor things present nor things to come, nor height nor depth, nor any other created thing, shall be able to separate us from the love of God which is in Christ Jesus our Lord. (Romans 8:35–39)

St. John also said, "But whoever has this world's goods, and sees his brother in need, and shuts up his heart from him, how does the love of God abide in him?" (1 John 3:17) In the Crusades and in all of the holy wars of Christendom, Christian warriors took up their swords, and their crosses, to liberate the brethren who were being persecuted by pagans. Surely this was love, surely did these men of valor have within them the love of God, and surely did they abide in the Light of Christ. Both the crusader and the persecuted are martyrs, and when they are slain or are wounded, they are entering into a mystical union with Christ, coming into His Cross, participating in His Passion, and obeying what St. Peter said: "rejoice to the extent that you partake of Christ's sufferings, that when His glory is revealed, you may also be glad with exceeding joy." (1 Peter 4:13)

CHRISTIAN WARRIORS PARTICIPATE IN THE CRUCIFIXION OF CHRIST

How could one say they have love or say that they "carry the cross" if they do not defend their neighbor or protect the persecuted, or are not persecuted themselves? When we defend our neighbor, when we protect the persecuted, when we are persecuted, we are not only carrying our cross, but participating in the very Crucifixion of Christ, and can say with St. Paul: "I have been crucified with Christ" (Galatians 2:20).

In this spiritual war with darkness, we partake in the Passion of our Lord, and alas this is what is to be learned from the story of Simon of Cyrene, the man who the Roman guards "compelled to bear His cross." (Matthew 27:32) Christ could have carried the cross Himself, for with Him nothing is impossible. But by Providence it was destined that Simon would help Christ carry up the cross in order to show us that God wants us to partake in the Holy Passion of His Son. It was on Simon that "they laid the cross that he might bear it after Jesus." (Luke 23:26) And so do we, the soldiers of Christ, relive what Simon underwent, suffering the travails of this great and cosmic battle against evil and the demonic, "bearing His cross," (John 19:17) that we may partake in the holy Crucifixion, for Christ loves us so much that He wishes for us to take part in His most perfect Passion, and fill up in our flesh "what is lacking in the afflictions of Christ" (Colossians 1:24).

We pick up our cross and follow Christ, and in emulating Him do we emulate His Passion. This is why Christ told St. Paul, "Saul, Saul, why are you persecuting Me?" (Acts 9:4) When the Church is persecuted, Christ is persecuted. When we defend the persecuted, we help Christ carry His Cross. To die for the Church is to die for Christ. It is to carry the Cross of Christ that one dies for the people with whom Christ identifies Himself. To persecute the Church is to persecute Christ, and so to fight and die for the Church is to fight and die for Christ, and at the same time, to emulate Christ Who is the Good Shepherd of His sheep, not running away from the wolves, but placing His life on the line for them.

When martyrdom comes, we are gloried as He was gloried through His death. "And what of the Holy of Holies?" asks St. Paulinus, "Did He not conquer when condemned, and by falling into death rise unto glory?"[15] When Christians are inflicted, they are picking up their crosses and following Christ, and thus participating in the travails He suffered on the Holy Wood. St. John said, "Beloved, do not imitate what is evil, but what is good." (3 John 1:11) And if we are to imitate what is good, who else should be our model but Christ? In being emulators of the divine Savior, we share in His suffering on the Cross, in the eternal war against evil. When we see Christians beheaded, beaten and tortured, scoffed and mocked, butchered and slaughtered, slain in combat as they fight with the soldiers of the devil, we see Christ. As Christ Himself said, regarding those who suffer for His sake, "I was hungry and you gave Me food; I was thirsty and you gave Me drink; I was a stranger and you took Me in; I was naked and you clothed Me; I was sick and you visited Me; I was in prison and you came to Me." (Matthew 25:35-36)

When one is persecuted, he is participating in holy combat against the devil, either in affronting the wicked ways of demonic people and diabolical governments, or as a warrior in the heat of holy war, fighting not only in spirit but also fighting with arms the enemies of the Church, and being wounded or gaining martyrdom by getting slain. In both situations, one carries his cross and bears the wounds of Christ in warring against the persecutors, and the end for both combatants is eternal life. For as Christ said, "Blessed are they which are persecuted for righteousness' sake: for theirs is the kingdom of heaven." (Matthew 5:10)

The French crusader Thibaut de Champagne, wrote that those who fought against the Muslims in the Crusades would be judged as righteous, for they, like Simon of Cyrene, carried the Cross with Christ, while those who did nothing will be cast into hell:

> God let himself suffer on the cross for us,
> And he will tell us on that day, when all men gather,
> 'You, who helped me carry my cross,
> Will go where my angels are;
> There you will see me and my mother, Mary.
> And you from whom I never received,
> Will all descend into the depths of hell.'

In the crusades, the great leader of the holy wars against the pagans and the heretics Pope Innocent III called for a crusade in the Fourth Lateran Council, and declared that the one who suffers for the cause of our Savior in Holy War, carries the Cross with Christ, and for this great labor, will reign with Christ after His blessed death:

> Indeed *Pasch* in Hebrew in *phase*, which is a 'pass(ing) over,' and in Greek is *paschein*, which is 'to suffer,' because it is through suffering we must pass over the glory, as Truth himself said, 'It was necessary for the Christ to suffer so as to enter into his glory.' [Luke 24:26] For that reason if we wish to co-reign [with him], it is necessary that we also co-suffer [with him],

---

15 Paulinus, letter 14, 2

although 'the sufferings of this time are not wholly worthy of the future glory that will be revealed in us.' [Romans 8:18] [16]

The fact that Innocent III said this in his declaration of war against Muslims and Cathars, shows that the carrying of the cross can be applied to Holy War and the suffering that one endures in the sacred combat.

We are but single notes in the song of God, in this constant symphony of life, with harmony and dissonance ceaselessly warring against each other. God is the composer, guiding constancy to flow, and allowing chaos to make its attack, bringing both together into a single oeuvre. Disarray is witnessed and love is beheld upon the sight of the Passion of Humanity's Hope, and so life is but a symmetry of this bittersweet icon. The pores of God dripped with blood in the somber garden, and an angel brought Him comfort. God Himself was enduring immense sorrow, and in a moment the ascension of harmony overtakes our hearts with consolation as we hear this great opus of the Eternal Composer. As God's head was pierced with thorns, and blood divine dripped upon the soils of the path of dolor, a certain man, Simeon of Cyrene, bore the burden of Love Incarnate, and such is the way of the eternal symphony, that flows through the finite universe and makes the mind aware of the mysterious wonders. Here the delirium of agony makes its noise, and there the harmony of beauty's sound is brought before the soul's eyes, for the sublime melody of selfless Compassion flowed through the temporal music of human existence, and a light shined through the teardrop of humanity's despair. For now God became Man, so that mere mortals, plunged in hopelessness, can bear the pains of Hope Incarnate; plunged in abandonment, they can endure the gloom of the One Who experienced the fullness of abandonment; plunged into death, they can resurrect as He ascended from the ruins of death. As the river flows from serene movement to violent rapids, so the symphony of life moves in a euphony, from anguish to resurrection. I am but a note amongst notes in the song of God, and with all of us together in a single harmony, we bring to the world the symphony of Heaven.

THE CROSS IS THE IMAGE OF WAR

The Holy Cross is the greatest icon of Holy War, for it is in the Cross that Christ was victorious over the devil, and it is in the Cross that we throw off the fear of death and face the enemies of God with dauntless will and with the spirits of martyrs.

Christian warfare with all of its precepts can be summed up in two passages of Christ: "Whoever desires to come after Me, let him deny himself, and take up his cross, and follow Me." (Mark 8:34) And "Greater love hath no man than this that a man lay down his life for his friends." (John 15:13) Before one sacrifices himself for his brethren, he denies himself and carries his cross, and fighting in a war against evil he, as Christ did in His war against the devil, gives up all his being for the cause of righteousness and the eternal law of Heaven.

---

16 Pope Innocent III, sermon 6: Fourth General Council of the Lateran

He goes into the holy fray with the fullest conviction that "if we died with Christ, we believe that we shall also live with Him, knowing that Christ, having been raised from the dead, dies no more." (Romans 6:8–9) The warrior does not deny Christ in the face of the enemy, but denies himself in the travails of combat. When he carries his cross, he does so in his heart, having within himself the will to sacrifice his life for the perpetuation of the Faith and of the lives of the brethren.

In the Final Crusade of the cosmic war of humanity, the armies of Christendom will be headed by our King, Jesus Christ, and on their foreheads will they bear the Holy Cross. It will be between those who have "the seal on the foreheads of the servants of our God" (Revelation 7:3) and the enemy who will have on them "the mark, either the name of the beast or the number of his name." (Revelation 13:17)

When the crusaders fought the Muslims, they had the cross engraved onto their chests and their shields so as to signify the mystical lifting of their crosses within the heart and the spirit, and the burning flame of love which they held up in their souls.

As Pope Innocent II wrote once to the knights who fought the Muslims in Jerusalem: "as proof that you are to be specially counted in the army of Christ, you always bear on your chest the sign of the life-giving cross. It has come to this that, like true Israelites and the most disciplined fighters of the divine battle, kindled by the flame of true charity, by your deeds you fulfill the words of the Gospel which says: 'Greater love hath no man than this, that a man lay down his life for his friends.'"[17]

This is also why Christian armies would hold up the Cross as their banner in warfare. In the Russian Primary Chronicle, which is amongst the oldest of records for the Russian Church, it reads: "By the Cross are vanquished the powers of the devil. The Cross helps our princes in combat, and the faithful who are protected by the Cross conquer in battle the foes who oppose them. For the Cross speedily frees from danger those who invoke it with faith, for devils fear nothing as much as the Cross."[18] Spiritual war, in which the Cross conquers, transitions into a temporal war in which the darkness is combated through arms.

When the holy Moses kept his arms stretched out while holding the sacred wooden staff for the victory of the Hebrew warriors against the pagan Amelekites, he was as Christ, Whose divine body was held to a Cross, and Whose sacred limbs were outstretched for the valiant conquest over our enemy the devil. In the words of St. Gregory of Nysa, "the outstretched hands of the lawgiver became the cause of victory foreshadowing the mystery of the cross."[19] And such is the life of the warrior, picking up his cross and following Christ, denying himself and no longer clinging onto the things of the world, breaking the chains of the flesh and liberating himself in the Spirit, he becomes an instrument for the divine justice through his own crucifixion, fighting even until the death.

---

17 Innocent II, *Omne Datum Optimum*, in Barber and Bate, *Templars*
18 *Russian Primary Chronicle*, Laurentian Text, 172, trans. Cross & Sherbowitz-Wetzor
19 St. Gregory of Nysa, *Life of Moses*, 2.153

The most Holy Cross, the Glorious Wood of our victory, our light, our hope, truly is it the emblem of the pious crusader and the knights of Christ! Let the Holy Cross be our banner! Let it be our sword against the devil when the gallant fighters of God strike with the blade and spill the blood of infidels! Let the Majestic Cross repel the demons! Let it repulse Satan, for by this most profound sign shall the saints conquer! In Christ, there is no death, there is only life. As St. Paulinus wrote: "Let us be cast down for the sake of Him, for if we fall it means resurrection. Let us die with Him in whom is life."[20] St. Maximus of Turin declared the Cross our sign of victory, and called for it to be placed on the forehead of every Christian, and connected the Holy Cross with warfare by referencing it to the slaughter of the heretics in the time of Ezekiel who did not bear the mark of God on their foreheads:

> The Son of God had no need to be born and to be baptized, for He had not committed any sin that needed to be forgiven Him to be baptized, for He had not committed any sin that needed to be forgiven Him in baptism, but His humiliation is our exaltation, His cross our victory, and His gibbet our triumph. With joy let us take this sign on our shoulders, let us bear the banners of victory, let us bear such an imperial banner, indeed, on our foreheads! When the devil sees this sign on our doorposts he trembles. Those who are not afraid of gilded temples are afraid of the cross, and those who disdain regal scepters and the purple and the banquets of the Caesars stand in fear of the meanness and the fasts of the Christian. In Ezekiel the prophet, when the angel who had been sent had slain everyone and the slaughter had begun at the holy places, only they remained unharmed who he had signed with the letter tau—that is, with the mark of the cross. Let us rejoice, then, dearest brethren, and let us lift holy hands to heaven in the form of the cross! When the demons see us thus armed they will be cast down. When Moses' hands were lifted up Amalek was conquered; when they came down a little he grew strong.[21]

In the eighth chapter of Ezekiel, we have the closest parallel to Islam in the Scriptures, describing pagans as bowing to the East with their backs toward Jerusalem, just as Muslim men do when they pray toward Mecca with their backs mockingly facing the Dome of the Rock. When the Temple of God was being tainted and corrupted by the presence of pagans and heathen rites, in which "women were sitting there weeping for Tammuz" (Ezekiel 8:14), "men with their backs toward the temple of the Lord and their faces toward the east," worshipped "the sun toward the east" (Ezekiel 8:16), and "filled the land with violence" (Ezekiel 8:17), the Lord turned to "the man clothed with linen, who had the writer's inkhorn at his side" (Ezekiel 8:3) and commanded him:

> Go through the midst of the city, through the midst of Jerusalem, and put a mark on the foreheads of the men who sigh and cry over all the abominations that are done within it. (Ezekiel 9:4)

---

20 St. Paulinus of Nola, letter 23.42
21 St. Maximus of Turin, sermon 45.2–3

What is this mark? It is, as we learn from St. Maximus of Turin, the Hebrew Tau, which is in the shape of a cross, and it was the holy mark which the saints put upon their foreheads.

| Early | Middle | Late | Modern |
2,000 BC	1,000 BC	400 BC	Today
+	×	ת	ת

The saints who weep and suffer for the evils of the world, are as Christ Who wept for Jerusalem; they are the ones who bear this mark, they are the soldiers of God who ceaselessly exert themselves in the intense combat against the devil, who "have crucified the flesh with its passions and desires" (Galatians 5:24), and who deny themselves, bear their cross and strive for victory. Those who bear the Tau, the Cross, on their foreheads, this is the spirit that they hold up. And those who did not bear the Tau on their foreheads, they were the enemies of God, for God declared to the six warriors who were armed with battle-axes,

> Go after him through the city and kill; do not let your eye spare, nor have any pity. Utterly slay old and young men, maidens and little children and women; but do not come near anyone on whom is the mark; and begin at My sanctuary. (Ezekiel 9:5–6)

So shall it be in the end, with the last and final Crusade: the children of God will have upon their foreheads the sign of the Cross, and—to use the words of St. Paulinus when he wrote of the last days—"those who do not bear the sign of salvation on their heads will flaunt before them the mark of impending death."[22] In another place the same saint wrote:

> God revealed in the persons of the few—as clear truth of the great mystery—that at the end of the world there will be a division among the tribes and a separation among all mankind, when the avenging angel will leave unscathed those whose faces are marked with the banner of the cross. [23]

In the Cross, the Son of God undergoes the greatest of suffering, to only eventually pass into glory. And so this is the mark the warriors place on themselves, when they undergo suffering for the cause of Christ, become martyrs and gain the crown of glory. They fight for the advancement of truth, the obliteration of the darkness through the light that never hides itself, when they slay and defeat the acolytes of Satan. In Pope Innocent III's sermon in which he called for the crusaders to combat the Muslims and the Cathar heretics, he told the warriors who bore the Cross to kill the heretics who did not have the Cross, and by this, bring back life to Christendom:

> Those marked [with the Tau] are not to be harmed, just as it is said elsewhere, 'Do not harm the earth, nor the sea, nor the trees until we mark the servants of our God on their foreheads [Revelation 7:3].' As to the others, however, it is said, 'Let your eye spare no one,' so that there

---

22 St. Paulinus of Nola, poem 7, 23
23 Paulinus, poem 24

will be no partiality toward any person among you. May you henceforth similarly carry it out: so strike, that you heal; slay, that you may give life, by the example of him who said, 'I will kill and I will give life; I will strike, and I will heal.' [Deuteronomy 32:39]

The crusader who kills the wicked for the cause of the Cross, heals the Church by cutting off the disease of the diabolical like a cancer.

The Holy Cross drives the devils out and compels them to tremble. As St. Maximus of Turin wrote: "But where the sign of the cross is erected the wickedness of the devil is immediately repelled and the stormy wind is calmed."[24] When the pagan tyrant Diocletian was slaying animals as sacrifices to the demons, some of those around him, who were Christians, "put the immortal sign on their foreheads. At this the demons were chased away and the holy rites interrupted."[25] The sign was the Holy Cross and it struck the demons with terror that they fled, and soon after this event would the Christian warriors go to battle against the heathens with the Cross as their banner in the Battle of Milvian Bridge. For when Constantine, who led the battle, went into war against Diocletian and his pagan army, he held the Cross aloft and had all of his soldiers engrave the cross onto their shields. When the Crusaders warred with the Muslims, they too ascended the Cross with vigor and valiancy, and when Cortez led his army of righteous conquistadors, he hoisted a flag on which were embroidered the words: "Friends, let us follow the Cross, and with faith in this symbol we shall conquer."[26] When John of Austria led the Spanish and Italian warriors to combat the Muslim Ottomans, his ships were in the formation of the Cross, and the golden versed poet, Juan Latino, praised the glorious Battle of Lepanto by declaring that it was Christ Who led the men into victory:

> Christ, head bowed, rallies the troops. Nailed to the wooden cross, he led the fleet to face the enemy.[27]

And so shall it be in the Final Crusade, wherein the armies of Christ will hold up the Holy Cross when vanquishing the forces of the Antichrist and their Islamic idol, the crescent.

The Cross was the image upheld by the warriors of old, so let us as well bear its image upon our foreheads! Look to the saints of Egypt, of Syria, of Iraq, of Russia, of Serbia, Bulgaria, Croatia, and yes, of the Roman Church, and you will see how they place the Cross on their foreheads. They bear the Cross on their foreheads; they bow down to the Cross; they kiss the Cross, both with their lips and their eyes. The fourth century pilgrim, St. Egeria, wrote:

> All the people pass through one by one; all of them bow down, touching the cross and the inscription, first with their foreheads, then with their eyes; and, after kissing the cross, they move on.[28]

---

24 Maximus of Turin, sermon 38.2
25 Lactantius, *On the Death of the Persecutors*, 10, ed. Ronald J. Sider
26 Gomara, *Cortes*, 8
27 Juan Latino, *The Song of John of Austria*
28 Egeria, *Diary*, ch. 37

✝ CHRISTIANITY IS AT WAR: THE MANIFESTO FOR CHRISTIAN MILITANCY

The Cross is the emblem of Holy War, and not only do we bear its image, we as well crucify our flesh to live by the Spirit, becoming "partakers of the divine nature" (2 Peter 1:4), and thus being soldiers of God in this great struggle and fray against the wicked and the forces of darkness. In this very action does one deny himself and carry his cross. War is the very essence of the Cross. In the Greek language, the letter T, which is a cross, represents the number 300, the same amount of soldiers Abraham led in history's first Holy War when he slew the pagans to liberate Lot.[29] And let us not forget that Gideon led three hundred soldiers to defeat the Midianites. When the Christian soldiers carry up the Holy Cross as their banner, they are carrying the very symbol of Abraham's army—they are carrying the very number of war.

When Christ was on the Cross, He was at war, and His objective was to "destroy the works of the devil." (1 John 3:8) Because Christ struggled and vanquished the devil on the Cross, Christian warriors not only carry up the Cross as their banner of victory, but are armed with swords shaped in the form of the Cross to slay the advancers of Satan. This connection, between the Cross and the sword and war against the forces of darkness, was articulated by the Spanish knight Ramon Llull:

> Unto the knight is given a sword which is made in the shape of a cross to signify that just as our Lord Jesus Christ vanquished on the Cross the death into which we had fallen because of the sin of our father Adam, so the knight must vanquish and destroy the enemies of the Cross with the sword. [30]

St. Odo wrote that those who carry their cross do so "by resisting vice, or who glorify God by doing good."[31] To resist vice is not only to fight against one's own sinful nature, but to contend against the promoters of vice; and to do good most definitely would include combating evildoers, the enemies of good. This is made more evident by St. Odo when he continues on to beautifully say: "The athlete of the heavenly hosts long struggling in the arena of this earthly life fought manfully against the forces of evil."[32] The Christian warrior enters the battlefield, in which the knights of Christ fight against the devil, with long-suffering and endurance, and with the longing for the heat of warfare.

THE CROSS DISPELS THE FEAR OF DEATH

Let us carry this holy and most ancient rite of the Cross, for it is the rite of warriors, the rite of Crusaders, the rite of the Knights of Christ! It is through the Cross that we are victorious, and it is through the Cross that we throw off all fears of death. As St. Maximus the Confessor says of Christ and the Cross:

---

29 See Paulinus, letter 24, 23
30 Ramon Llull, *Chivalry*, 4.2
31 Odo of Cluny, *Life of St. Gerald of Aurillac*, 2, preface
32 Odo of Cluny, *Life of St. Gerald of Aurillac*, 2.1

For he put off the principalities and powers at the moment of his death on the cross, when he remained impervious to his sufferings and, what is more, manifested the (natural human) fear of death, thereby driving from our nature the passion associated with pain. [33]

By contemplating on the Cross, we liberate ourselves from the fear of death. For it is in the Cross that you "Take no thought for your life," (Matthew 6:25) it is in the Cross that we cast aside the earthly cares for this life, and fixate ourselves upon the eternal, striving to be victorious in the cosmic war against evil.

"Is not the life more than meat, and the body more than raiment?" (Matthew 7:25) This is what our Lord asks, and within the sublime question there is an eternal answer. Life is more than food, because life is not a goal unto itself; life is a test of our endurance in this spiritual war in which we "must endure hardship as a good soldier of Jesus Christ." (1 Timothy 2:3) There is more to life than money, more to life than sensual pleasures, more to life than fleshly gratification, there is more to life than life itself.

Our goal of victory should override our fear of pain and hardship, or as Ramon Llull wrote of the Christian knight: "shame must cause greater suffering to his courage than hunger, thirst, heat, cold or any other suffering or hardship to his body."[34] Food is only a means to an end, to keep the body alive so that it can continue to partake in the great Holy War against the devil. Life itself should not be our intent, but a weapon unto itself for the cause of victory. Our ultimate aspiration must be triumph over the forces of darkness, for the cause of the Light, for all souls, all nations, all governments and principalities. Our spiritual eyes are fixated upon eternal victory, and for this reason do we forsake the concerns of our earthly eyes.

"No one engaged in warfare entangles himself with the affairs of this life, that he may please him who enlisted him as a soldier." (1 Timothy 2:4) The body is more than clothing, for the body is not just a figure, but an image of God that is to be used as a sacrifice for the cause of God. The warrior contemplates on martyrdom, not in agony, but in joy over the life after his own passion, thus preparing the soul for its separation from the body. In this contemplation he casts aside his own will, allows himself to be directed by the will of the Father, and accepts whatever glorious Heaven has in store for his life. Christ contemplated on His own martyrdom when He withdrew from His Disciples, knelt down and said to His Father: "Father, if it is Your will, take this cup away from Me; nevertheless not My will, but Yours, be done." (Luke 22:42)

Just as Christ subjected Himself to the will of the Father when He took the victory upon Golgotha, so the holy warrior, taking up his cross, does the will of God in battle. St. Maximus the Confessor wrote: "That which is in our power, our free will, through which the power of

---

33 Maximus the Confessor, *The Cosmic Mystery of Jesus Christ*, Ad Thalassium 21, On Christ's Conquest of the Human Passions, trans. Blowers & Wilken
34 Ramon Llull, *Chivalry*, 3.14

corruption entered into us, will surrender voluntarily to God and will have mastery of itself because it had been taught to refrain from willing anything other than what God wills."[35]

We saw such surrender of the will to God in the Crusades, in which the warriors, when they fought in battle, cried out "Deus vult!" "God wills it!" This is the submission of the will to the will of God, and this is the eternal virtue upon which the knight sets his mind, placing himself to the hands of his God to be used as a living weapon for the sacred war. The French knight, Geoffroi de Charny, wrote of this complete submission of the will that, the soldier in combat must "have the true and certain hope that comes from God that He will help you, not relying just on your strength nor your intelligence nor your power but on God alone."[36]

In the Cross there is the invigorating image of perseverance that rouses and galvanizes the spirit so that our very beings may continue on through the sacred battlefield, into the eternal realm of holy martyrs. One can even say that noble perseverance is the closest likeness to eternity in our earthly lives; for it is in the Cross that we find eternity, and it is perseverance that leads us to the consecrated hill of Golgotha. "But he who endures to the end shall be saved." (Matthew 24:13) The old warriors of Christendom had perseverance, in their dedication were they carrying their crosses, and they fought and died, journeying into eternity.

The internal strength of the crusaders rested on their hope in Heaven. "For it is no small pleasure for believers mentally to anticipate in sweet reflection the blessings promised to the faithful," says St. Paulinus, "and to walk already in imagination the paths of paradise."[37] It was this hope that gave them perseverance in their combat against the enemies of God, in the use of the sword and in endurance; and it was this hope in obtaining the crown of salvation, that drove them to fight against evil, to reach the road to Paradise. It is perseverance that fulfills the words of the Apostle: "forgetting those things which are behind and reaching forward to those things which are ahead, I press toward the goal for the prize of the upward call of God in Christ Jesus." (Philippians 3:13–14) This forgetting of things behind for the things promised, as St. Bernard tells us, "is meditation on eternity, for the things promised are eternal, it fosters a spirit of long-suffering, and gives strength to perseverance."[38] The Spanish knight, Ramon Llull, who fought the Muslims in the Reconquista, wrote of this contemplation on death and everlasting life when he described the ideal knight as such:

> And so the knight pondered death, reflecting upon the passage from this world to the next, and he understood the everlasting sentence he would have to face. [39]

HOLY COMBAT IS UNITY WITH CHRIST

The warrior, impetuous to the fear of death, endures the suffering of the saint by fighting evil through the labors of battle. The stirring of the spirit that moves him to continue in the

---

35 Maximus the Confessor, *On the Cosmic Mystery of Jesus Christ*, Ambiguum 7, 1076B, trans. Blowers & Wilken
36 Geoffroi de Charny, *A Knight's Own Book of Chivalry*, 23, trans. Elspeth Kennedy
37 Paulinus, letter 13, 24
38 Bernard, *On Consideration*, 5.14
39 Ramon Lull, *The Book of the Order of Chivalry*, prologue, 2

combat against Satan comes from a mystical relationship with Christ, having in himself to suffer and fight as his Master suffered and fought in His most holy Passion. In Christ, suffering is no longer suffering, but nearness to freedom from the shackles of the flesh; death is no longer death, but liberation. Death no longer becomes an end but a means to an eternal end. This eternal end is the fulfillment of the mystical relationship the Christian has with Christ on earth, and that is the ultimate mystical union with Christ in Heaven. As St. Maximus the Confessor wrote:

> Such will ensue if indeed the saints, for the sake of truth and righteousness, have virtuously finished the course of this life with many sufferings, liberating their nature within themselves from death as a condemnation of sin and, like Christ, the captain of our salvation (Heb. 2:10), turned death from a weapon to destroy human nature into a weapon to destroy sin. [40]

To fight for Christ is to endure the sufferings of combat in the cosmic war against evil, and thus to emulate the Savior in His agony. To suffer the travails of Christ, in fighting for Him, is to break through the prison of the flesh's enslavement, and enter the liberation of eternal peace. Christ fought against wicked men, and was martyred under their hands, before He rejoined His Father in Heaven, and so the crusader comes to divine bliss through the labors of the battlefield, fighting evildoers for the cause of righteousness and dying under their hands. The monk Hugh wrote to the crusaders: "The order of justice demands that he who wishes to reign should not shirk work; he who seeks the crown should not avoid the fight. Christ himself, whom you ought to follow, toiled and fought on earth with the wicked and evil men before ascending to Heaven to sit in peace at the right hand of the Father."[41]

Fearlessness of death was exhibited by the crusaders, who most devoutly venerated the Cross, for they held that to be inflicted for Christ was not something to be afraid of, but glorified. As St. Bernard tells us of the knights of his day:

> Indeed the soldiers of Christ confidently fight the battles of their Lord, and have no fear of sinning when killing the enemies, and no fear of incurring the danger of being killed, seeing that death suffered or inflicted for Christ is not a crime but deserves a great glory. [42]

Surely it is of the spirit of the Christian to endure suffering, to emulate Christ by emulating His perseverance, by enduring as He endured. Let us say the prayer of St. Paulinus of Nola:

> May I feel no pain in mind or body. May all my limbs perform their functions peacefully, and no experience of being crippled lament the loss of any faculty. May I enjoy peace and live untroubled, counting as nothing the marvelous things on earth. When the last hour of my day comes, may I be conscious of a life well spent, and neither fear nor desire death. [43]

---

40 Maximus the Confessor, *On the Cosmic Mystery of Jesus Christ*, Ad Thalassium 61, 100
41 Hugh 'Peccator' to the Templars in the East, in Barber and Bate, *Templars*
42 St. Bernard, in St. Robert Bellarmine, *On Laymen or Secular People*, ch. 14, ed. Tutino, p. 60
43 St. Paulinus of Nola, poem 5, 70–73, trans. P.G. Walsh

CHRISTIANITY IS AT WAR: THE MANIFESTO FOR CHRISTIAN MILITANCY

By being as Christ, we fight as He fought; we undergo combat as He underwent combat; we attack evil as He attacked the father of evil; we consume death as He took upon Himself the most hope giving death. Through suffering, in the taking up of the Cross, do we enter eternal life, as Christ bore His Passion, and transcended death into the timeless Kingdom. The Scripture says: "by his wounds you have been healed." (1 Peter 2:24) St. Paul said, "I bear in my body the marks of the Lord Jesus." (Galatians 6:17) We take upon the wounds of Christ, and by doing so are we ourselves crucified and made worthy of eternal life. To use the beautiful words of Lactantius:

> We must be on the watch, must post guards, must undertake military expeditions, must shed our blood to the uttermost; in short, we must patiently submit to all things which are unpleasant and grievous, and the more readily because God our commander has appointed for us eternal rewards for our labors.

THE CHRISTIAN SOLDIER IS MOVED BY VIRTUE

True enlightenment is obtained through virtue and this action happens when the body and spirit cease to war with each other, and instead work together for the advancement of goodness and the downfall of evil. "The spirit indeed is willing, but the flesh is weak." (Mark 14:38) But imagine when the body is subservient to the spirit, what great acts of virtue that person can do in such a state! The spirit strives for righteousness, and stirs the mind with zeal, and with the body becoming a vehicle for the spirit, the person works with full effort and "rejoices like a strong man to run its race" (Psalm 19:5) so that he may say with St. Paul: "I have fought the good fight, I have finished the race, I have kept the faith." (2 Timothy 4:7)

The Christian knight must strive to cultivate within his soul the seven virtues of knighthood, which are listed by Ramon Llull as faith, hope, charity, justice, prudence, fortitude and temperance.[44] The warrior works with exertion to follow these virtues and to emulate the Holy One, and with much toil he participates in the divine nature as he fights for justice in righteous combat against the enemies of God. As St. Gregory of Nyssa wrote in regards to the soul: "Activity directed toward virtue causes its capacity to grow through exertion; this kind of activity alone does not slacken its intensity by the effort, but increases it."[45] On the battlefield of holy combat, the intensity of battle only fans the flames of fiery love for God.

The enemy strikes, and the zeal of the Christian only increases, and the blow of his sword returns upon the adversary with a force that is ten-fold. The war is not secular, but cosmic, and it purely aspires for victory in the struggle against the forces of evil, without ever acquiescing. Christ told His disciples "that He must go to Jerusalem, and suffer many things from the elders and chief priests and scribes, and be killed, and be raised the third day." (Matthew 16:21) Christ told His disciples that He had to go into battle with the devil, to destroy His works and crush the sting of death. But Peter could not bear this, and when he tried to pre-

---

44 Ramon Llull, *Chivalry*, 6.2
45 Gregory of Nyssa, *Life of Moses*, 2.226

vent Christ from fulfilling the will of His Father, Jesus turned to him and said, "Get behind Me, Satan!" (Matthew 16:23) This is the model moment by which the Christian warrior governs himself, never forsaking the call to warfare, nor fleeing from his divine recruitment, "that he may please him who enlisted him as a soldier." (2 Timothy 2:4)

The warrior who does this abides by the first commandment, "you shall love the Lord your God with all your heart, with all your soul, with all your mind, and with all your strength." (Mark 12:30) When the warrior charges into battle for the cause of good, he gives his entire body for the holy battle, and all those fighters give up their bodies as "a living sacrifice, holy, acceptable to God, which is your reasonable service." (Romans 12:1) This precept was followed by the Knights Templar who, as we read from their own book: "do not cease from offering their lives as a sacrifice pleasing to God."[46] As our Lord says, "Is not the life more than meat, and the body than raiment?" (Matthew 6:25) Yes, the body is a holy icon that is to be used for a righteous purpose, even unto death. St. Gregory the Great exhorted a Byzantine general that when he fought against the enemies of the Faith, that he do so with all body and mind:

> As the Lord hath made your Excellency to shine with the light of victories in the military wars of this life, so ought you to oppose the enemies of the Church with all activity of mind and body, to the end that from both kinds of triumph your reputation may shine forth more and more, when in forensic wars, too, you firmly resist the adversaries of the Catholic Church in behalf of the Christian people, and bravely fight ecclesiastical battles as warriors of the Lord.[47]

They say it is an admirable thing to die for one's country, but it is far more illustrious to give one's body for Christ and His Holy War, loving God with all body, mind, strength, spirit and soul. St. Gregory VII extolled the warriors who were willing to sacrifice their bodies in the holy war against the Muslims, when he wrote in one letter:

> If, as some say, it is beautiful to die for one's country, it is most beautiful and glorious indeed to give our mortal bodies for Christ, who is life eternal.[48]

THE CHRISTIAN SOLDIER IS AN ENEMY OF THE WORLD

If one has the will to die for Christ, then it means that he has Christ within Him.

St. Ignatius, who was a pupil of St. Peter, St. Paul, and St. John,[49] and who was commissioned by St. Peter to be the bishop of Antioch, wrote that there were only two coins to choose from in this world, one of God, and the other of the world, and that the Christian must be willing to die for the former in his combat against the latter:

---

46 Latin Rule of 1129, in Barber & Bate, *Templars*
47 St. Gregory the Great, epistle 74
48 Gregory VII, *Epistolae collecatae*, 11, p. 532
49 See A Relation of the Martyrdom of St. Ignatius, where it refers to Ignatius as "the disciple of St. John the apostle" (1, trans. Wake)

For there are two sorts of coins, the one of God, the other of the world; and each of these has its proper inscription engraved upon it. So also is it here. The unbelievers are of this world; but the faithful, through charity, have the character of God the Father by Jesus Christ: by whom if we are readily disposed to die, after the likeness of his passion, his life is not in us. [50]

The Scripture says, "Do you not know that friendship with the world is enmity with God? Whoever therefore wants to be a friend of the world makes himself an enemy of God." (James 4:4) So the Christian is at war with the world, and a soldier of Christ's army, and because he is willing to die, he is in union with Christ, and engraved onto his heart are written the words: "For to me to live is Christ, and to die is gain." (Philippians 1:21) To become a friend of God is to be an enemy of the world, and thus to war against evil.

MARTYRDOM IS SALVATION

For to me, to live is Christ, and to die is gain. (Philippians 1:21)

The armies of the Lord consist of both priests and knights; the priests battle the demons and the knights destroy evil by slaying those who promote the demons. As Ramon Llull said: "knights exist in order to persecute and destroy evil,"[51] and if one dies for this cause, then they are martyrs without exception. When the martyr is slain for the true path of God, he shares in the Cross of Christ; Christ's wounds are his wounds, and his death, as the Passion of Christ, does not cease life, but commences eternal life. In Holy War, death is merely the transition from this transient existence into eternal bliss. To fight for God and to die for His cause is an evidence for one's faith, and for one's love, and it is therefore a fruit worthy of salvation.

St. John the Baptist made his cry to the people, and against the corrupt leaders, he said, "bear fruits worthy of repentance," and "every tree which does not bear good fruit is cut down and thrown into the fire." (Luke 3:8–9) It was after this that some warriors, hearing his words, asked him, "And what shall we do?" (Luke 3:14) To this did the holy monastic say,

Do not intimidate anyone or accuse falsely, and be content with your wages. (Luke 3:14)

So great was the inspiration of the Baptist, that he taught the warrior how to obtain salvation as a warrior, neither trying to persuade them to leave their office nor condemning their occupation. As St. Bede says, "even the soldiers, he compelled to seek counsel of him concerning their salvation."[52] And St. Augustine says, "For if Christian discipline disapproved of all wars, the soldiers in the Gospel who were asking for advice about salvation would have been told to throw away their weapons and to remove themselves completely from the army, but in fact they were told not to do violence to any man, or accuse any falsely, and to be content with wages."[53] Notice how Augustine observes that the soldiers were "asking for advice

---

50 St. Ignatius, *Epistle to the Magnesians*, 5
51 Ramon Llull, *Chivalry*, 6.8
52 Bede, in Aquinas, *Catena Aurea*, on Luke, lectio 4
53 Augustine, letter 138, in St. Robert Bellarmine, *On Laymen or Secular People*, ch. 14, ed. Tutino, p. 59

about salvation," meaning that their question pertained to salvation, and thus being a noble and pious warrior is a fruit worthy of redemption.

To fight for the cause and protection of true religion and for the defense of the Church, is a fruit worthy of redemption. The French knight, Geoffroi de Charny, wrote: "Again, to preserve and maintain the rights of the Holy Church, one should not hold back from committing oneself to their defense by war and battle, if they cannot be maintained in any other way. And the man who acts thus wins in noble fashion personal honor and the salvation of his soul. Moreover, the man who makes war against the enemies of religion in order to support and maintain Christianity and the worship of Our Lord is engaged in a war which is righteous, holy, certain, and sure, for his earthly body will be honored in a saintly fashion and his soul will, in a short space of time, be borne in holiness and without pain into paradise."[54]

Let us not forget the words Deborah sung in which she praised the people who fought and sacrificed their lives against the Canaanites, singing: "Zebulun is a people who jeopardized their lives to the point of death, Naphtali also, on the heights of the battlefield." (Judges 5:18–19) Who will argue that such a courageous people are not worthy of salvation?

St. Augustine says in one place, "Do not think that anybody who serves in the army cannot please God,"[55] meaning that one can please God through the office of a soldier, and whatever we do to please God affects our eternal life. The warrior bears fruit worthy of salvation by being just, and fighting for the peace of society. And if he dies in this worthy cause, denying himself, bearing the greatest love for God and laying "down his life for his friends," where then will his soul be, but that place of which St. Paul says,

> Eye has not seen, nor ear heard, nor have entered into the heart of man the things which God has prepared for those who love Him. (1 Corinthians 2:9)

St. James says, "Show me your faith without your works, and I will show you my faith by my works." (James 2:18) The soldier who fights for truth shows his faith by his works. As Ramon Llull wrote:

> On account of the faith that resides in well-trained knights they cross the sea to the Holy Land on pilgrimage and take up arms against the enemies of the Cross, and they are considered martyrs if they give their lives to exalt the Holy Catholic Faith.[56]

The knight of Christ who fights for the love of God and for the love of his brethren, and places his life for the cause of His Divine Law, shows his faith by his dauntless works, and by this faith does he have salvation. To quote St. Robert, "soldiers can attain salvation if they fulfill what John commanded them."[57] This is so because they observe their duties with and for justice, and such is the evidence of faith and love burning within their hearts. St. Paul says God "'will render to each one according to his deeds': eternal life to those who by patient

---

54 Geoffroi de Charny, *A Knight's Own Book Of Chivalry*, 35
55 St. Augustine, letter 189, in St. Robert Bellarmine, *On Laymen or Secular People*, ch. 14, ed. Tutino, p. 59
56 Ramon Llull, *Chivalry*, 6.4
57 Bellarmine, *On Laymen or Secular People*, ch. 14, ed. Tutino, pp. 55–56

continuance in doing good seek for glory, honor, and immortality" (Romans 2:6–7). This is not faith that lives in a vacuum, but faith with substance, obedience, self-denial and sacrifice.

The warrior who lays down his life for the cause of good and for victory over evil, does works for glory, honor and immortality, under Christ, "of him, and through him, and to him," (Romans 11:36) and for such receives eternal life. The warrior goes forth in the midst of the battlefield, to defend the brethren and the Faith, and if his own blood is spilt in the process, then he is a martyr; he has laid down his life for his friends, fulfilled the Law of Love, and thus is given his heavenly glory. As St. Leo IV, who fought against the Muslims in the Battle of Ostia in the ninth century, said:

> if someone die for the true faith and the salvation of his country, or in defense of Christians, he will receive from God a heavenly reward. [58]

To die for the Faith, either in Holy War or in persecution, is the ultimate action of carrying one's cross. The great Christian emperor, Alexius Comnenus, expressed this selflessness when, in his battle with pagan Scythians, someone asked him, "Why lose your life, without a thought for your own safety?" and he responded by saying: "Better to die fighting bravely than win safety by doing something unworthy."[59]

CHRISTIANS CARRY THE CROSS AS A NATION, NOT JUST AS INDIVIDUALS

When holy wars are done, it is not just the ecclesiastical authorities and the government who are involved, it is the entire nation who partakes in the eternal struggle. How then does a nation become like this? The entire population is in a state of selflessness, in that each person denies himself, carries his cross and follows Christ, fulfilling within themselves those beautiful words of St. Paul:

> I have been crucified with Christ; it is no longer I who live, but Christ lives in me; and the life which I now live in the flesh I live by faith in the Son of God, who loved me and gave Himself for me. (Galatians 2:20)

The whole nation, or nations, of Christendom work in a sublime harmony in Christ, emulating Christ, and becoming an image of Christ, throwing off or eschewing the worldly lusts, casting out the fear of death, striving with all sense of self-sacrifice the words of St. Peter: "Honor all people. Love the brotherhood. Fear God. Honor the king." (1 Peter 2:17)

When Christendom fights, the people honor the king because they follow him in his call to Crusade; they love the brotherhood, because they defend the brotherhood; they fear God because they rise above the fears of the self, not fearing "those who kill the body but cannot kill the soul," but only "Him who is able to destroy both soul and body in hell." (Matthew 10:28)

They honor all people, because they do not fight with the objective of dominating people, but to fight for the holy cause that brings salvation to humankind, and to vanquish the wicked one who was a murderer from the beginning.

---

58 Leo IV, C. 23:8:9: Omni timori (CIC 1:955), in Aquinas, *Summa Theologiae*, IIa IIae 40, article 2
59 Anna Comnena, 7.3

THE WARRIORS PERSEVERE FOR GOD AND FOR CHRISTENDOM

All of the nations of Christendom are enflamed with holy indignation, willing to fight and sacrifice themselves for their brethren, and this can only happen through the denial of the self and the divine union with Christ, "for in Him we live and move and have our being," (Acts 17:28), and in Him do we have the will to combat the devil for the glory of the Cross.

It is not the protection of the self that the Christian fights for, but the defense of others, and in so doing does he pour out the infinite river of mercy, and the boundless stream of love, that flow from the Cross. The Knight of God casts away himself in Christ; he becomes the Cross, and the Cross becomes him; he becomes "a living sacrifice, holy, acceptable to God, which is your reasonable service" (Romans 12:1), emulating Christ his General, fighting the slaves of the devil for the good of the brethren "that he may please him who enlisted him as a soldier." (1 Timothy 2:4)

THE SELFLESS WARRIOR

With a perfect hatred toward evil, and with the soul always under the protecting refuge of God, the warriors of Christendom do not fear death, but abide by the words of Christ,

> And I say to you, My friends, do not be afraid of those who kill the body, and after that have no more that they can do. But I will show you whom you should fear: Fear Him who, after He has killed, has power to cast into hell; yes, I say to you, fear Him! (Luke 12:3–5)

Such a declaration is what fills the souls of the defenders of Christendom, as they "Love the brotherhood" of Christ, and "Fear God" (1 Peter 2:17), while protecting the sacred Church from the hordes of her approaching enemies—"the enemies of the cross of Christ" (Philippians 3:18), and as they prepare to unsheathe their swords, and shed the blood of heretical armies, their spirits are ready to leave their earthly abodes, and for this they fear not death and say with David:

> Be merciful to me, O God, for man would swallow me up;
> Fighting all day he oppresses me.
> My enemies would hound me all day,
> For there are many who fight against me, O Most High.
> Whenever I am afraid,
> I will trust in You.
> In God (I will praise His word),
> In God I have put my trust;
> I will not fear.
> What can flesh do to me? (Psalm 56:1–4)

These are the words of a warrior, his soul never wavering nor moving when his enemies fight against him, never fearing what physical violence they can inflict. Within the Christian warrior, the mind and the heart are interlinked, with the mind—which meditates on the truth of God, of which David said: "his truth shall be thy shield and buckler" (Psalm 91:4)—

guides the heart—which is purified by the truth, and leads the combatant outside of himself, into the timeless realm of which the holy king said: "He that dwelleth in the secret place of the most High shall abide under the shadow of the Almighty." (Psalm 91:1)

In God there is stillness, and when the good soldier contemplates on Him within his soul in deep prayer, he will find this stillness in the mind under the purified heart, and it will remain even in the most intense of battles. David, amongst the greatest of holy warriors, said: "Meditate within your heart on your bed, and be still." (Psalm 4:4) The prophet Jeremiah wrote:

> The Lord is good to those who wait for Him, to the soul who seeks Him. It is good that one should hope and wait quietly for the salvation of the Lord. It is good for a man to bear the yoke in his youth. Let him sit alone and keep silent (Lamentations 3:25:28).

To be continually aware of God in the mind, is to have stillness. As David says: "Be still, and know that I am God!" (Psalm 46:10) Do not forget that the centurion, Cornelius, "prayed to God always." (Acts 10:2) Cornelius was an elite warrior, and no doubt would have had a stillness of faith in the most intense of battles, obeying the words of the Apostle: "pray without ceasing" (1 Thessalonians 5:17)

This means that he would have been in prayer even in battle, having within his mind that stillness of faith in God which is reflected in the words of the warrior David: "He is my refuge and my fortress: my God; in him will I trust." (Psalm 91:2) He prayed to God always because he was in constant meditation, having pure mind and pure heart, and thus, stillness. "A servant of the Lord stands bodily before men," says St. John Climacus, "but mentally he is knocking at the gates of heaven with prayer."[60] This purity of mind in battle was expressed in the Latin Rule of 1129, which was written for the instruction of the monastic knights, the Templars, and in which was said:

> Our words are directed primarily at all those who reject the option to follow their own desires and are willing to fight with purity of mind for the highest and true King [Christ] so that they choose to take up the armour of obedience and a noble life, fulfilling the vow with the utmost devotion and perseverance. [61]

For one can always be in a continuous state of prayer only when he has stillness, being never shaken even by the most harrowing of situations. The stillness of the mind can only be obtained through the purification of the heart. St. Paulinus wrote of this stillness of the mind in battle as a result of a heart liberated from earthly passions: "Even the most gruesome wars can rage, but the peace of freedom must attend our minds. However many the chains weighting my neck, the enemy would not bind my mind prisoner with my captive limbs, for in the unchained heart proud devotion would tread underfoot my unhappy slavery."[62]

---

60 Climacus, *The Ladder of Divine Ascent*, step 4, p. 113, trans. Luibheid & Russell
61 Latin Rule of 1129, prologue, in Barber and Bate, *Templars*, ch. 1, 5
62 Paulinus, poem 26, ellipses mine

How could one obtain such stillness of the mind, except by the embracing of the Cross and the denial of the self? In the Cross itself, that is where selfless love resides. Ramon Llull wrote that the knight must, like Cornelius, be in a constant state of contemplation, "worshipping and praying to God, and fearing Him, and through such a habit the knight will think of death and the vileness of this world and he will beseech heavenly glory from God and fear the torments of hell, and will therefore practice the virtues and habits that pertain to the Order of Chivalry."[63] The French knight Geoffroi de Charny wrote that the warriors of knighthood "should indeed spend all their time giving thanks, praising and honoring Our Lord."[64] From constant contemplation on Heaven after death, comes the stillness of faith. For where there is fearlessness of death, there is faith. To pick up one's cross is to have that same stillness of Faith that Christ had when He said to His Father: "not My will, but Yours, be done" (Luke 22:42), and not the wavering faith of Peter when he said: "I do not know this Man of whom you speak!" (Mark 14:71) St. Gregory of Nyssa upheld the Cross as the source for stillness:

> To look to the cross means to render one's whole life dead and crucified to the world, unmoved by evil.[65]

THROUGH SUFFERING WE HAVE LIBERATION

For the warrior of holy Christendom, "The wicked is banished in his wickedness, but the righteous has a refuge in his death." (Proverbs 14:32) The righteous fighters hope in their deaths, the crown of martyrdom is bestowed upon their heads through perishing in the heat of battle for the cause of truth and the downfall of evil. In his meditation on God, fear of death is purged from his soul and he trusts in God, reminiscing on the words of David:

> Hear my voice, O God, in my meditation;
> Preserve my life from fear of the enemy.
> …The righteous shall be glad in the Lord, and trust in Him.
> And all the upright in heart shall glory. (Psalm 64:1, 10, ellipse mine)

David obtained the enlightenment of God's laws through suffering, as he himself said:

> It is good for me that I have been afflicted; that I might learn thy statutes. (Psalm 119:21)

Through suffering we not only become closer to God, but we delve into a deeper contemplation that the pleasures of the flesh are transient, and that our life is not here for temporary things, but for an eternal cause and destiny. As St. Gregory Nazianzus said: "For if life always went well, would we not become so attached to our present state, even though we know it will not last, and by deception become enslaved to pleasure? In the end we would think that

---

63 Ramon Llull, *Chivalry*, 6.18
64 Geoffroi de Charny, *A Knight's Own Book On Chivalry*, 35
65 Gregory of Nyssa, *Life of Moses*, 2.274

our present life is the best and noblest, and forget that, being made in the image of God, we are destined for higher things."[66]

THE SOLDIERS OF CHRISTENDOM FOLLOW GOD TO THE DEATH

Those who carry out the justice of God are His holy warriors, led by their heavenly King through the sovereignty of a human governor, who is "God's minister to you for good," "an avenger to execute wrath on him who practices evil." (Romans 13:4) Above the sun of heavenly teachings, that shines its rays of zeal upon the souls of upright onlookers, stands the Holy Cross on which lies the Blood that Satan hates. And it is for this Cross, upon which the suffering Savior gained victory in the most eternal of battles, that the docile onlookers, burning with the soaring rays of Paradise's orb, take up their own crosses, with arms clutched on cross shaped swords, and charge to engulf the darkness with the flames of divine light.

In the beautiful Song of Deborah, we read with awe and wonder that "the people willingly offered themselves" (Judges 5:2) in war against the heathens, just as Christ willingly offered Himself on the cross to war and defeat Satan.

In this same song of holy praise, Deborah exalts two warriors who sacrificed themselves for God in battle, exclaiming:

> But Zabulon and Nephtali offered their lives to death in the region of Merome. (Judges 5:18)

The 48th Psalm declares that God "will be our guide even to death." (Psalm 48:14) Therefore, God is to be followed unto death, this would include warring for Christ until a glorious martyrdom is obtained, or until becoming a martyr under persecution.

THE CHRISTIAN SOLDIER DOES NOT LIVE BY THE FLESH, BUT BY THE SPIRIT

The Christian warrior puts all the desires of the flesh under the servitude of the spirit. They "walk not according to the flesh, but according to the spirit" (Romans 8:4); they fulfill the words of the holy Apostle when he wrote, "you are not in the flesh, but in the spirit, if so be that the Spirit of God dwell in you" (Romans 8:9), and thus do their bodies become "the temple of the Holy Ghost," (1 Corinthians 6:19), fighting to protect their fellow Christians who, not being warriors like them, are as well temples of God, needing protection from the thieves who wish to take their lives, as Christ took up a whip and drove the thieves from His Father's house. They uphold the sword, not for plunder and temporal power, but to defeat those who persecute "him that was after the spirit" (Galatians 4:29).

In enduring the intensity and pains of holy warfare they follow Paul when he rejoiced in his suffering for the Christians, to "fill up those things that are wanting of the sufferings of Christ, in my flesh, for his body, which is the church" (Colossians 1:24), and so in striking the enemy, and being struck, and undergoing the pains of sacred combat, the warrior of Heaven

---

66 Gregory Nazianzus, Oration 14.20, in Maximus the Confessor, *On the Cosmic Mystery of Jesus Christ*, Ambiggum 7, 4, 1093B

takes part in the Passion of Christ, fighting against the devil and his soldiers, picking up his cross, sacrificing his own life for the lives of the brotherhood and for the defeat of the forces of darkness, observing, with humble piety, the command of Christ, "let him deny himself, and take up his cross, and follow me" (Mark 8:34), undertaking the greatest form of love, placing their own selves on the brink of death in the bloody struggle of Christendom's survival, and in so doing, giving their lives for their friends, truly exhibiting the sublime words of Christ, "Greater love than this no man hath, that a man lay down his life for his friends." (John 15:13)

They follow the path described by St. Paul, "denying ungodliness and worldly desires, we should live soberly, and justly" (Titus 2:12), and in living justly do they emulate the justice of God, hating evil and loving righteousness, becoming "partakers of the divine nature" (2 Peter 1:4), sacrificing themselves for God and for the lives of their brothers, as Christ died for the Church, and fighting the devil and his wiles, as Christ warred "that he might destroy the works of the devil." (1 John 3:8)

The warriors of God do not "live according to the flesh" but by the spirit, and "mortify the deeds of the flesh" (Romans 8:13); and within themselves they bring victory in that internal battle in which "the flesh lusteth against the spirit: and the spirit against the flesh" (Galatians 5:17).

They have God within them, and from God do they receive their strength to fight for His Church and for Christendom. In emulating Christ and partaking in the justice of God, do they say with holy David,

> Do not I hate them, O Lord that hate thee? And am not I grieved with those that rise up against thee? I hate them with perfect hatred: I count them mine enemies. (Psalm 139:21–22)

It is a perfect hatred, not one of envy or fleshy strife, but of holiness and righteous indignation; it is the same hatred as Christ harbored when He made a whip and drove the thieves out from His Father's Temple.

VALIANCY IS A SACRIFICE

To love the Lord with all one's might and strength, is to give such gifts and talents of endurance as a sacrifice to God, for as David exhorts:

> Give unto the Lord, O you mighty ones,
> Give unto the Lord glory and strength. (Psalm 29:1)

God did not give man strength to only fulfill the curse in toiling the field, but strength was also given to mighty men who are asked to give their strength to God. It goes back to what Christ said, to love the Lord "with all your strength." (Mark 12:30) This can signify great feats for God in warfare. As Augustine explains, the verse signifies that "By your works let the Lord be glorified and honoured."[67] The Lord can be honored by one loving Him with all

---

67 Augustine, Exposition on Psalm 29

his strength, as Josiah loved God with all his might when killing the pagans. The warriors are "mighty" when they give themselves up for God with valor, and they are urged to sacrifice their strength, that is, to partake in holy war. Therefore, combat is esteemed as a sacrifice to God, just as Christ's combat on the Cross was a sacrifice. Nay, rather, the greatest, and the fulfillment of all sacrifices, was the sacrifice of combat done upon Golgotha.

CHRIST—THE ULTIMATE WARRIOR AND THE CULMINATION OF ALL BIBLICAL WARRIORS

Ecce homo! Behold the man! There He stood with arms bound and outstretched, there He was, suspended on nails, stricken with the agonies of paternal abandonment, that no mortal lying on this distinctly created earth could experience, and no man could share in His sufferings when He cried with filial cries, "My God, my God, why hast thou forsaken me?" He abounded in the agonies of betrayal; a king over the timeless kingdom above the temporal constellations, existing in eternity before existence came into eternal thought, He now hung upon a cross as a man without a kingdom, and as a king without subjects, cast out and ousted by men who, rejecting and scoffing Him, cried out with piercing words, "Away with him, away with him, crucify him We have no king but Caesar." (John 19:15)

This Man was a great warrior, riding upon a donkey in the meek spirit of humility, and "being in the form of God, thought it not robbery to be equal with God: But made himself of no reputation, and took upon him the form of a servant, and was made in the likeness of men: And being found in fashion as a man, he humbled himself, and became obedient unto death, even the death of the cross." (Philippians 2:6–8)

There stood this valiant Fighter, enduring the passion of anguish until the end. Warrior of all warriors, crushing the most dangerous of all enemies, that is, the fallen spirits of the abyss. He was mocked and scolded, as the marvelous knight Gideon was, when the inept spectators refused his armies bread, saying, "Are the hands of Zebah and Zalmunna now in thine hand, that we should give bread unto thine army?" (Judges 8:6)

But this Warrior was with His arms bound and outstretched, and He looked upon His enemy, the greatest enemy of mankind, the prince of darkness and the most corrupt of spirits, and fought the holiest of all sacred wars, battling with the devil and his demons through suffering; vanquishing the adversary of all souls through anguish; warring with the principalities of darkness by being pierced with nails, His side speared with a lance, his flesh cut and lacerated by the sharp ends of the scourge. It was a battle, not in some vague spiritualized sense, but an actual war, the most magnificent of all wars, in which the eternal Mount Sinai quarreled with the mountain of Babel; in which the flesh was conquered, and the grueling intensity of fighting was borne by the Holy Knight, as a valiant warrior undergoes a moribund clash with the armies of tyranny. The struggle was settled, and the enemy vanquished.

The Holy Warrior, the Glorious Son of the Father in Heaven, allowed Himself to be slain in the eternal battle: the nails that went through His holy flesh, and the lance that pierced His sacred body, struck Him as arrows strike the victorious army charging into the bastions of despotism, with gallant knights falling from their galloping horses over the cold earth. The wondrous army ends the arduous struggle with a victory that happened because of men who denied themselves, and through the determination of a fortified spirit, rode into death, rode into martyrdom, and left the callous soils of grim fields, and surpassed wearisome death, only to depart from their earthly armour, and be adorned fully embellished with the crown of glory, singing sublime hymns everlastingly and standing in the midst of angelic warriors, veterans of the first battle of eternal Christendom in which the Captain St. Michael drove out Satan and his demons from the heavenly realms.

Christ, the Holy One, was the greatest exemplary of the warrior saint; His cross is the symbol of holy warfare, His death is the model of our longed for martyrdoms. In teaching us how to die, Christ taught us how to live. "For to me to live is Christ, and to die is gain." (Philippians 1:21) In the words of St. Bernard:

> Christ's life has provided a pattern for living for me, but his death, a release from death by living he taught us how to live and by dying how to die a trusting death. For he was one destined to be raised up again and to those who suffer death brought the hope of rising again. [68]

Amidst His battle with Satan, He stood arms outstretched, and allowed Himself into martyrdom, to destroy the works of the devil. Christ by His death did not negate all the patriarchs of old, but was the culmination of them all; Abraham, Moses, Joshua and Gideon. Take the holy Samson, who with arms outstretched in the form of a cross, stood in a temple of Satan, whom the pagans worshipped as Dagon, just as Christ was under the hands of the devil's servants, amidst the shadows of "the power of darkness." (Luke 22:53) Samson was devoid of his earthly eyes, and thus was he forced to see with his spiritual eyes, throwing off the bondage of the flesh, the mortal view of the world, and keeping watch through Heaven's eyes. This reminds us of the words of St. Anthony when he said, "let not the loss of your bodily eyes distress you: for you are deprived of such eyes merely as are the common possession of gnats and flies; rather rejoice that you have eyes such as angels see with, by which the Deity himself is discerned, and his light comprehended."[69] Armed with the sword of the spirit, "strengthened with might by his Spirit in the inner man" (Ephesians 3:16), Samson committed fully to the precept of the Apostle, glorifying "God in your body, and in your spirit," (1 Corinthians 6:20), he cried:

> O Lord God, remember me, I pray thee, and strengthen me, I pray thee, only this once, O God, that I may be at once avenged of the Philistines for my two eyes. (Judges 16:28)

Samson, in the words of St. Paulinus, "lost his bodily eyes but not his spiritual eyes. For Samson would not have called upon the Lord to lend aid to his strength if his inward eyes had not been sound."[70] He picked up his cross, denied himself, and as Christ, facing the laughs

---

68 St. Bernard, *In Praise of a New Knighthood*, ch. 11
69 In Socrates, 4.25
70 Paulinus, letter 23, 18

and scorns of scoffers who rejoiced to the devil, saying, "Our god hath delivered Samson our enemy into our hand" (Judges 16:23). It is here where Samson loved the Lord with all of his physical strength (Mark 12:30). "Samson took hold of the two middle pillars upon which the house stood, and on which it was borne up, of the one with his right hand, and of the other with his left. And Samson said, Let me die with the Philistines. And he bowed himself with all his might; and the house fell upon the lords, and upon all the people that were therein. So the dead which he slew at his death were more than they which he slew in his life." (Judges 16:29–30)

Just as Christ defeated the devil, and destroyed his works by allowing Himself to die on the Holy Cross, so did Samson destroy himself, standing with hands outstretched in the form of a cross, to destroy the pagans and the temple of Dagon, that is, Satan. Such is the spirit of the Christian warrior, who exerts himself through the path of adversary, fighting both the devils and their human followers, like a good athlete, enduring until the end, charging through the enemy ranks and spilling the blood of evil doers, obtaining glory, evidencing his faith, and establishing victory.

Josiah was another precursor to Christ. He killed off the heathen priests, destroyed the houses of the homosexuals, and drove out the wizards, and how does the Scripture describe his zeal? "And like unto him was there no king before him, that turned to the Lord with all his heart, and with all his soul, and with all his might, according to all the law of Moses; neither after him arose there any like him." (2 Kings 23:25) "Heart," "soul," and "might" were the very virtues Josiah committed himself to in this crusade of extirpating the wicked, following the first eternal commandment of Christ,

> And thou shalt love the Lord thy God with all thy heart, and with all thy soul, and with all thy mind, and with all thy strength: this is the first commandment. (Mark 12:30)

Did Christ then do away with the Law of Moses? God forbid. For in the same theme and virtues "heart," "soul," and "might," Christ, as in 2 Kings 23, bind these very virtues to the laws of Moses, "'You shall love the Lord your God with all your heart, with all your soul, and with all your mind.' This is the first and great commandment. And the second is like it: 'You shall love your neighbor as yourself.' On these two commandments hang all the Law and the Prophets." (Matthew 22:37–40)

King Josiah destroying paganism and homosexuality was in accordance "to all the law of Moses," and on the first commandment of Christ hangs "all the Law of the Prophets." Therefore to fulfill the whole of the Law, is to destroy evil. Josiah, thus, both followed and foreshadowed Christ when he obliterated the wickedness of Israel.

To love God "with all thy strength" consists of a physical struggle, in conjunction with the fiery and zealous tenacity of the spirit—"love the Lord thy God with all thy heart, and with all thy soul"—for the purpose of warfare, with both the temporal sword and the sword of the spirit, glorifying "God in your body and in your spirit, which are God's." (1 Corinthians 6:20) Christ fought and defeated the devil with both His humanity and His divinity. It is thus that in original Christianity, both spirituality and fighting are one, with both the physical sword and the spiritual sword working simultaneously, with one fighting the acolytes of Satan, and the other combating the powers of darkness of the devil.

Therefore, when Josiah "slew all the priests of the high places," (2 Kings 23:20), and "burned the chariots of the sun" (2 Kings 23:11), physical force and spiritual fortitude were combined, for his sword was not against human flesh for the mere sake of killing, but for the sake of destroying what spiritual darkness plagued the land. In the life Christ, physical coercion and violence was intertwined with spiritual warfare against the devil: the Messiah "made a scourge of small cords, he drove them all out of the temple, and poured out the changers' money, and overthrew the tables" (John 2:15); He compelled the devil to "leaveth him" (Matthew 4:11), and the slaves of Satan "platted a crown of thorns" (Matthew 27:29) on His head, "smote him on the head" (Matthew 27:40), forced Him "to bear his cross" (Matthew 27:32) and "crucified him" (Matthew 27:35). He struck the thieves in the temple and drove the devil away, and in turn the wicked one inflicted Him, and such was the great battle that He led against the darkness, just as Josiah had done in his fight against paganism. Christ beheld the city of Jerusalem, "and wept over it," (Luke 19:41) on account of its rejection of God, and when Josiah heard the Law of God, "he rent his clothes" (2 Kings 22:12), grieving the sins of Israel. After Christ wept, He, with all of His physical strength in His earthly body, "went into the temple and began to cast out them that sold therein, and them that bought" (Luke 19:45), and after Josiah suffered grief, he organized the cleansing of the temple and executed divine vengeance. Even the battle that Josiah had done against the corrupt priests, is connected to the war that Christ fought as He was on the Cross. Josiah was destined to be king, and to purge Israel of its idolatrous priests, and it was foretold that on the day of his birth the altar would split in two:

> Then he cried out against the altar by the word of the Lord, and said, "O altar, altar! Thus says the Lord: Behold, a child, Josiah by name, shall be born to the house of David; and on you he shall sacrifice the priests of the high places who burn incense on you, and men's bones shall be burned on you." (1 Kings 13:2)

When Christ cried out and yielded His spirit, the "curtain of the sanctuary was split in two from top to bottom; the earth quaked and the rocks were split" (Matthew 27:51), and when Josiah was born, "the altar also was rent" (1 Kings 13:5).

In both the life of Christ and Josiah, there is a physical and spiritual struggle, all happening at the same time, consisting of grief, anguish, and combat against the devil and their human followers. And all of this is being done to observe the first commandment, "you shall love the Lord your God with all your heart, with all your soul, with all your mind, and with all your strength." (Mark 12:30) Therefore, to love God with all of one's strength is illustrated by the physical might used in both the lives of Christ and Josiah. Christ drove out the thieves in the temple, and warred against the devil on the Cross, while Josiah exterminated the pagan priests. In both, the strength of the body, the fortitude of the spirit, the zeal of the heart, and the power of the intellect, are used for the glorious aspiration of crushing the devil.

Did the life of Christ make null and void the life of Nehemiah? No. Christ's life is the fulfillment of the life of Nehemiah, and with similar fashion, resorted to aggression when it came to protecting the Temple of God. When merchants sold outside the walls of the Temple during the Sabbath, Nehemiah, with holy rage, declared to them, "Why do you spend the night around the wall? If you do so again, I will lay hands on you!" (Nehemiah 13:21) And how reminded are we of Christ, when He, angrily seeing the thieves sell their merchandise within His Father's Temple, "made a whip of cords, He drove them all out of the temple, with the sheep and the oxen, and poured out the changers money and overturned the tables. And He said to those who sold doves, "Take these things away! Do not make My Father's house a house of merchandise!" (John 2:15–16)

There is a great image of Christ, and the greatest image of the Christian warrior, and that is Urijah the Hittite. How pristine is that semblance of Christ when reading the life of Urijah. He was a man without self, his body never acquiescing to the demons of concupiscence, never giving in to the weariness of the body, nor the pleasures of comfort, never trying to save his life, but always striving to lose it.

The gilded arrow[71] of insatiable lust struck the lascivious realm of mortal nature, and burnt and rent that part of the belly where the fires of desire ignite before the idol of passion, and cut asunder the bond between two hearts united by the capriciousness of human love. Such is what ensued when the archer of hell aimed his arrows, dipped in the poisons of temptation and crafted by the hands of perdition, at David the king of Israel, who then, after soiling the marriage bed, slew the selfless Urijah. Such is what occurred so that we could truly behold the endurance of the saintly warrior, sprinting through the grueling battlefield unto death, without ever knowing, nor trying to know, that he was pierced by the arrow of betrayal.

David ambled in the freedom of the royal robe and was confined within the idleness of the king's house "at the time when kings go out to battle" (1 Samuel 11:1), fettered by the roaming eyes of voracious want, which is a ceaseless abyss, a void that is never filled. He was boundless in his liberty, and yet chained by the wandering vagrancies of lofty extravagance, which rove endlessly, as the devils move from place to place searching for an empty soul to make their abode, and they are as numerous as the luminaries that were suspended from the evening sky in that moment when David gazed upon Bathsheba, and the fires of gluttonous lust set aflame within his being. No longer did his soul ascend to the heavens, but now it was entrapped within the fetters of the flesh. No longer did he walk on the path of the spirit, he now treaded upon what seemed to him a pleasant indulgence, a harsh everglade hazed by the fog that covers all light, and an ever burning fiery whirlwind that scorches with blackness the meadows of enlightenment, and refuse to be extinguished. Absorbed in the delight

---

[71] "The gilded arrow" was inspired by Michelangelo, poem 59

PART 5

of enchanting beauty, David yielded to his desires, and the flames of careless passion were gratified with the grim pitch of callous betrayal.

As cruel love seared itself in the hot coals of faithless dung, there was Urijah amongst his troops, not within the prison of royal license, but amidst the liberation of the selfless knight. He was not held back by the fires of affection, but immersed in the heat of battle through the love of God and hatred of evil. He was not yoked by the violent demands of the flesh, but always moving on the path of the spirit, never gyrating within the labyrinth of lust, but always remaining in the state of true enlightenment, breaking the chains of carnal guile, shattering the idols of the god of our bellies, never allowing that natural attachment a husband has for his wife to hinder the cause of true religion, and nor did he ever permit the heat of marital devotion to enervate the flames of zeal that burst within his heart.

There stood Urijah, fighting for the Divine Law, extirpating idolatry, and cleansing Israel from the tyranny of the heathen; and there stood David, contriving a way to deceive Urijah, because now a child was about to be birthed from his corrupt union with a disloyal wife, and he schemed to make it as though the child was of his seed.

In this are we reminded of Christ, for as He warred against the works of the devil, so that people "shall not walk in darkness, but have the light of life" (John 8:12), Judas "conferred with the chief priests and captains, how he might betray Him to them." (Luke 22:4)

Urijah was in the field of battle, depriving himself from the comforts of this world, mortifying the flesh with the harshness of combat and the test of arms, walking the road of sainthood through the suffering the warrior endures, and the weariness of the body under the stress of a holy fray. And then there came a messenger with a royal command, demanding that he report to the king. Like a good soldier, he obeyed, not knowing that he at that very moment was undergoing betrayal. And when he arrived, David did not deride him or scold him, nor did he reveal how little he cared for him, or how much contempt his wife harbored for the marriage bed, but instead he said with cunning guile:

Go down to thy house, and wash thy feet. (2 Samuel 11:8)

And as Urijah was approaching his home, there followed him an array of delicate meats from the king himself. What is happening here, but the worst of betrayals? How reminded are we by this story, of how Christ was betrayed, not with harsh words or insults, but with a kiss. When perusing on how David attempted to cover his wickedness, and his betrayal of Urijah, with kind words and delicious foods, we can almost say with Christ "Judas, are you betraying the Son of Man with a kiss?" (Luke 22:48)

Urijah spurned the succulent meats of the king's table, and there he stood, not under the roof of his home in the embraces of his wretched wife, who he did not even know had betrayed him, not on a bed on which the weary find comfort, but at the door of David's palace, not amongst governors or princes, generals or kings, but amongst servants. How this saint could have had a place in his own home, consuming the fine edibles of a king, and enjoying an already tainted marriage bed, and yet he chose to be amongst the lowliest. From such a story of endurance, our minds are reminded of the Christ. The King of all the Earth, the Son of God, Whose throne is in Heaven and Whose footstool is the earth, and for Whom the entire universe was brought into existence, chose to be in the presence of the most despised of people. It was said of Him, "many tax collectors and sinners came and sat down with Him and His disciples" (Matthew 9:10), and the high minded who saw him scolded him with slanderous words, saying, "Why does your Teacher eat with tax collectors and sinners?" (Matthew 9:11), and those who hated him, mocked him with vitriol and malice, with words such as, "Look, a glutton and a winebibber, a friend of tax collectors and sinners!" (Matthew 11:19)

The Pharisees and scribes sneered at him, saying "How is it that He eats and drinks with tax collectors and sinners?" (Mark 2:16) In His final hours, in the midst of all the enmity that surrounded Him, before the moment in which He looked into the eyes of His betrayer, when the torrent of terror overtook His humanity, and blood dripped from His divine flesh, He still continued on, regardless of all the fear, of all the horror that awaited Him, of all the heaviness that weighed upon His entire being. As He saw the sins of the earth and committed Himself to the wine of His suffering, He pressed on, even though He was being betrayed, He pursued the mission all the way, forever devoted until the end, looking up into Heaven and declaring:

> O My Father, if it is possible, let this cup pass from Me; nevertheless, not as I will, but as Your will. (Matthew 26:29)

In His majestic Passion that caused the earth to shake, that pierced the souls of the compassionate and revealed the evilness of the callous, when He hung from the Cross, when He bore the burdens of all the earth, when He was scoffed by those unworthy of Him, hated by those He loved, and persecuted by those for whom He sacrificed His blood, betrayed and denied by the ones for whom He gave His life, He, the Perfect Warrior, endured through the battle, conquering the darkness with the light of His divinity, illustrating to man the perfect example of the holy fighter through the forbearance of His humanity, and continued the goal to vanquish the lawlessness of tyranny, and establish the Law of Love, crying out to His Father,

> Father, forgive them, for they do not know what they do. (Luke 23:24)

In the state of such suffering, Christ stood between two thieves, for even in His last moments, He remained amongst the lowly. And now we look at His great servant, Urijah, and we see how closely he emulated the spirit of sacrifice that Christ taught us through His Passion, and surely we can say that he is the perfect example of the Christian warrior.

There he stood at the door amongst servants, never knowing that he was betrayed by king and wife, nor ever considering the cares of his own life, but he looked to the Ark of God, saw how it was placed under a tent, and deemed himself unworthy to repose under a strong roof. And so too does the Christian warrior live the same. Beholding how His Lord rode on a donkey, and was crowned with thorns, he sees himself unworthy to live with pomp and extravagance, and lives the life of both fighter and ascetic.

When David saw the lowly state of Urijah, he said to him,

Did you not come from a journey? Why did you not go down to your house? (2 Samuel 11:10)

And Urijah, with the humility of a monastic and a warrior committed not to flesh and blood, but to the war against the principalities of darkness, said:

> The ark and Israel and Judah are dwelling in tents, and my lord Joab and the servants of my lord are encamped in the open fields. Shall I then go to my house to eat and drink, and to lie with my wife? As you live, and as your soul lives, I will not do this thing. (2 Samuel 11:11)

Is not the tenaciousness of Urijah amidst the happenings of holy war, like the divine endurance of Christ when He fasted in the scorching desert without touching food nor drinking water? And the deception of David, is it not like the temptation that Satan brought to Christ when He stood hungry in the desert? "If You are the Son of God, command this stone to become bread." (Luke 4:3)

The holy and pious words of Urijah to David, is it not like the rebuking words of Christ to the Devil? "It is written, Man shall not live by bread alone, but by every word of God." (Luke 4:4)

When Peter foreknew in his mind that death was waiting for Christ in Holy Jerusalem, he came under the inspiration of dark powers, and said to Christ: "Far be it from You, Lord; this shall not happen to You!" (Matthew 16:22) These were the words of the devil, and do they not remind us of the deception of David, which was cloaked with words of false concern?

Uriah threw away all want of gain, eschewed the shallow praise of royalty, fled from the luxuries of any palace, and like a good athlete, and like the finest warrior, he pursued solely those things that pertained to the Holy One, sprinting through the difficult track of the spirit, throwing off the chains of the flesh, and bearing always the full armor of God. Absent of all consideration for his own existence, Urijah is the truest image of the ascetic and the monastic knight. It can be said that this man truly exemplified the words of Christ in the most immaculate fashion:

> He who loves father or mother more than Me is not worthy of Me. And he who loves son or daughter more than Me is not worthy of Me. (Matthew 10:37)

The deviousness of a king could not puncture the holy warrior, his mind untouched by flattery, his soul impervious to any moment of opulence. His earthly eyes were utterly shut for the beautiful things of loyalty and zeal that his heavenly eyes brought to his indomitable spirit. And even when he ate and drank before the king, and became inebriated through the fruit of the vine, as our first priest, Noah, had done under the tent before a wicked Ham, he still did not yield to the demands of the tyrant, but went down amongst the plebeian servants instead of choosing the affections of his disloyal wife.

With the pen of death did the king write a decree, and with the ink of innocent blood did he splatter the crimson letters to compose a callous order, that God's mighty servant be placed at the tip of the ranks, where the combat was the most heaviest and soldiers knew doom was near; where men trampled on the slain and on those near their end, where hot vapors ascended from the clots of foul blood[72] into the air where harrowing screams of perishing troops resounded; where arrows covered the sun as the empyrean canopy once covered the youthful earth, and where warriors, armed with naked swords, with faith, and with the tenacious will of their spirits, exerted their defense with shield and weapon, with the greatest resilience against the enemy hordes, as they were being pushed off the brittle edge of mortal life.

So cruel and indifferent to humanity was David that he gave the same deathly decree to Urijah. There he stood, the vintage combatant of Heaven's Kingdom, and off he went, grasping the letter that ordered his own death. He did not even recognize that he was being betrayed, as Abel did not know the thirst for blood his brother Cain harbored when he deceptively talked with him in the fields. Uriah never opened it, nor cared to even know what was written—he just went, journeying to Joab to convey to him the order that would bring his martyrdom. Can one ever imagine such loyalty? Such faith? Truly this man was the purest manifestation of the perfect warrior of Christendom, the purest image of those words of St. Peter:

> Honor all people. Love the brotherhood. Fear God. Honor the king. (1 Peter 2:17)

As we imagine him rushing to the treacherous trap, we are reminded of Christ, Who "was led as a lamb to the slaughter" (Isaiah 53:7), or in the words of Jeremiah, "like a docile lamb brought to the slaughter" (Jeremiah 11:19).

There was Christ, ignoring the weariness of His humanity when His enemies "led Him out to crucify Him" (Mark 15:20), and there stood the selfless Hittite, handing over his own death sentence to Joab, and with heartless words the letter read:

> Set Uriah in the forefront of the hottest battle, and retreat from him, that he may be struck down and die. (2 Samuel 11:15)

Uriah drunk the sweet nectar of the eastern grape before the face of a scheming despot, and now what lied before him was the cup of his suffering. He did not object to this order, nor did he ever express any suspicion of treachery, but he went forward into the depths of the highest perils of battle. With such obedience and loyalty, we are reminded of the words of Christ when traitors and connivers pursued Him, and His own disciple contrived His death: "not as I will, but as You will." (Matthew 26:39)

Uriah surpassed what travails the despair of battle brings and fixated himself not on his will, but on the will of Heaven. He could have been in his home with a deceptive wife and the empty gifts of a king, but he chose the midst of the battlefield over the embraces of a cunning woman. He was the ideal warrior of Christendom, exemplifying fully the words of Christ,

> Whoever desires to come after Me, let him deny himself, and take up his cross, and follow Me. (Mark 8:34)

---

72 "hot vapors ascended from the clots of foul blood" was inspired by Prudentius, *The Fight For Mansoul*, 2.50

In like manner, Christ could have freed Himself, He could have had His disciples "fight, so that I should not be delivered to the Jews" (John 18:36), He could have listened to those spectating scoffers, who like David offered devilish temptation, saying

If You are the Son of God, come down from the cross. (Matthew 27:40)

But no, Christ fulfilled His own command, and denied Himself, picked up His cross, and went into the fields of a glorious death.

As Christ walked the path to His holy death betrayed, Uriah lived always ready for death while being treacherously and unfaithfully dealt with by his licentious wife, and by the conniving hand of a temporal sword. Tell me, would Bathsheba have confessed to him her actions while embracing him? Would she have revealed her wicked deeds before a tainted marriage bed? Would Judas have told Jesus that his kiss was one of betrayal? Most certainly not. But the truth that lied behind their deceitful hypocrisy was revealed by the pool of blood unjustly shed, that spilt from their heroic bodies in the fields of battle, in the scorched meadows of transient love that gives an appearance of affection for but a swift glance, and in the next instance of crumbling time, a ferocious ambush of descending bombardments by heartless men sated only by cruel bloodshed.

In the midst of the battle, when sword and shield slashed, the arrows from the archers above struck the warrior saint, and as he carried his cross, the blood of this holy martyr poured forth from his sacred body, reminding us of the divine blood that dripped from Christ who, "bearing His cross, went out to a place called the Place of a Skull, which is called in Hebrew, Golgotha" (John 19:17).

And so here, we have a most clear parallel: Bathsheba, a symbol of the corrupt church, betrayed Urijah; as Judas, who also represents the corruption within the Church, betrayed Christ. David shares this with Judas when he, because of the passions of a liaison, murdered this innocent man of God. One killed a holy man because of the intimacies of a woman, and the other because of the appeal of thirty pieces of silver.

What did this king do but send him off to his death? He did not desire to get caught in his crimes, as the Jews no longer wanted to hear of their corruptions from the lips of the Son of God. How much blood was spilt because of the inducing figure and the stirring movements of a woman! How many Adams have fallen for the serpent because of deceptive Eves! Herod looked before him and marveled at Salome, as she danced the dance of the serpent, moving and swaying, frolicking and scampering with the ornaments of her shape, as the serpent slithers about, enchanting our minds with its fruit of death. A torque of the body, a glance from the charming eye, that glosses with the glow of sorrowful ambition[73] under the richly dark curls of embellished hair, in the midst of turbid noise and wild music, of hotly pounding drums and frenzied playing flutes, that simmers the blood and sparks the flaming passions of the belly, that sears the flesh and entraps the spirit within a cage of cruel wrath, Herod kneeled to the enfeebling movement of her form, he yielded to the effect of the cobra's dance,

---

73 Inspired by Prudentius, *The Fight For Mansoul*, 1.4

and bent the knee to the harlot, who drinks the blood of saints as she sleeps on the bed of kings drunk in her fornication.

As Urijah fought to advance the laws of the highest Heaven and to war against the works of the heathen, his wife broke the law of the marriage bed with David, and the king designed his death. John the Baptist contended with the works of darkness, crying out with heavy heart "To give light to those who sit in darkness and the shadow of death, To guide our feet into the way of peace" (Luke 1:79), when he rebuked Herod for his wickedness, and it was by the dance of a harlot that he demanded "The head of John the Baptist" (Mark 6:24) and through which the saint acquired the crown of martyrdom.

John the Baptist was "The voice of one crying in the wilderness" (John 1:23), and what did John the holy revelator see when he was taken away in the Spirit "into the wilderness"? "A woman sitting on a scarlet beast which was full of names of blasphemy, having seven heads and ten horns." (Revelation 17:3) It was in this wilderness where John declared to Herod, "It is not lawful for you to have your brother's wife." (Mark 16:8) The voice crying in the wilderness revealed the fornications of a harlot, only to be killed by a harlot thirsty for the blood of this saint; and John foresaw the coming Harlot that shall drink but oceans of the blood of martyrs. The harlot whom John the Revelator saw in the wilderness, drinking the blood of saints was Arabia. So John the Baptist, the most holy saint, was beheaded in Arabia to fulfill the demands of a slithering harlot. John the Baptist, in the words of Josephus, "was sent to prison, out of Herod's temper, to Macherus and was there put to death."[74] In another work Josephus locates Macherus as "upon the mountains of Arabia."[75] As it was in Arabia where the harlot killed this saint, so it is in Arabia where the ultimate harlot, the Harlot of Babylon, reclines as she slaughters the saints.

So is this prophetic massacre foreshadowed by the slaughter of Urijah, for his death sprung from the betrayal of his wife, and from the violent hands of the royal thief who "had exceedingly many flocks and herds" (2 Samuel 12:2) but "took the poor man's lamb" (2 Samuel 12:4).

CHRIST'S THIRST ON THE CROSS: THE SELFLESS SPIRIT OF THE WARRIOR

The strength of sprit, the conquering of the flesh, and the carrying of the cross, is seen most clearly in the 300 warriors who fought under the infamous knight of the Church, Gideon. They drunk their water standing up, not caving in to the weakness of the body and throwing themselves to their knees and gulping the water like thirsty dogs, but with vigilance, quenching their thirsts while keeping watch for the enemy, putting the cause of the battle over their own needs. As we read from the Scriptures:

> And when the people were come down to the waters, the Lord said to Gideon: They that shall lap the water with their tongues, as dogs are wont to lap, thou shalt set apart by themselves: but they that shall drink bowing down their knees, shall be on the other side. And the

---

[74] Joseph. Antiq. 18.5.2, ellipse mine
[75] Joseph. *Wars of the Jews*, 1.8.2

number of them that had lapped water, casting it with the hand to their mouth, was three hundred men: and all the rest of the multitude had drunk kneeling. And the Lord said to Gideon: By the three hundred men, that lapped water, I will save you, and deliver Madian into thy hand: but let all the rest of the people return to their place. (Judges 7:5–7)

The ones that were on their guards and indifferent to the desires of their bodies were the ones capable of victory, thus they denied themselves, placing the spirit over the flesh, just as Christ put the spirit over His own thirst and hunger, in His glorious and heroic passion.

Christ had no water as He fought the devil while on the Cross, not because he was forced to thirst, but because He chose to do so under the intensity of battle. As He hung on the holy wood, His divine hands and feet pierced by the enemy with sharp nails, His royal head adorned with a crown of agony, and as His soul suffered, not only from the pains of torment, but from the heavy anguish of dereliction, and the labors to bearing humanity's sins, He said, "I thirst!" (John 19:28) And after David struck the Philistines with the utmost exertion of his body, "until his hand was weary, and his hand stuck to the sword" (2 Samuel 23:10), carrying his cross to contend with the sons of Belial, he lodged in the cave of Adullam, and said,

> Oh, that someone would give me a drink of the water from the well of Bethlehem, which is by the gate! (2 Samuel 23:25)

At his command, three of his mighty warriors charged into Bethlehem, broke through the ranks of the Philistines, and drew water from the well of Bethlehem. And David, after his and his army's grueling battles with the pagan forces, chose not to drink the water, but poured it to the earth as a sacrifice to God. He offered his thirst as a sacrifice in the midst of his battle against the demonic heathens, just as Christ, amongst His many pains, sacrificed His thirst in His war against Satan. Why did not Christ nor David drink water, even though they had the power to quench their parched thirsts? Why did David not drink the water of Bethlehem when it was in hand? Because he had the Water of Life, the Christ, Who was born in that same holy city of Bethlehem. Although surely he was thirsty in the flesh, he was "strengthened with might through His Spirit in the inner man" (Ephesians 3:16), and had the fortitude to sacrifice the fatiguing pains of thirst.

Why did Christ not satisfy His thirst through a miracle, even though he could have easily done it without effort? Because He is the Water of Life, by Whom one "will never thirst." (John 4:14) Christ surpassed His human desire for water, and so when He said, "I thirst," He did not provide Himself with water, although He could have, but instead allowed that "they gave Him sour wine mingled with gall to drink. But when He had tasted it, He would not drink." (Matthew 27:34) His thirst was never quenched, but He persevered, even with the bitter taste of gull in His holy lips. Christ showed us how the human desire for comfort—in this case the comfort of a quenched thirst—can be made subservient to the spirit. "The spirit indeed is willing, but the flesh is weak." (Matthew 26:41) But Christ teaches us how the flesh can be made a servant of the spirit, by showing how He, with the strength of a warrior, gave as a sacrifice the comforts of the flesh, as David sacrificed the comforts of water. David pushed forward, even with the myriad of enemies that stood before him. His suffering was a shadow of that immense anguish that occurred on the Cross, and as he persevered with the forbearance of a soldier, the attacks of his foe was as gull to his trembling lips:

> They also gave me gall for my food,
> And for my thirst they gave me vinegar to drink. (Psalm 69:19–21)

In both stories, David and Christ are in the midst of a battle, one with the heathen and the other with the devil—the father of the heathens. In both stories there is a thirst for physical water that is overpowered by spiritual water, and in both stories the forces of darkness are conquered, and the righteous victorious.

THE SUFFERING OF THE CHRISTIAN MILITANT

The saint weeps in the deepest melancholy, begging God for His defense because his enemies surround him, just as Christ was surrounded by enemies and wept as the thick darkness of the earth's evil surrounded Him. It is so for all the saints, for Christ was encompassed on all sides by viperous wolves. As the Savior Himself said, "If the world hates you, you know that it hated Me before it hated you." (John 15:18) And thus is the life of the saint: struggling endlessly with the world, as the shepherd is forever vigilant against the wolves. When the saints are persecuted, they are engulfed by the love of God, for in their state of agony, they are being tested by the Lord Who is love. To be persecuted is to be loved by God; it is a sign that the Father desires that you be as His Son, to live as Christ lived, to suffer just as He suffered. Those who are not persecuted, who live entrenched in the fat of comfort, without enemies from amongst the wolves, and in the avoidance from the struggle that the Sword of Christ brings, are hated by God, and thus God deprives them of the honor of persecution. As David wrote in the tenth Psalm:

> The Lord tests the righteous, but the wicked and the one who loves violence His soul hates. (Psalm 11:5)

God loved Elijah, and He thus blessed him with the oppression of Jezebel; He loved Moses and bestowed upon him the mission to confront the tyrant Pharaoh—a terrifying enterprise—to endure the arduous journey through the desert, and conduct battles against the pagans who sought out his destruction. As Christ stood upon the lofty mountain, His face radiated with ineffable light as bright as the sun, and He, in all His glory, transfigured. The tall pinnacle upon which He stood, bridged Heaven and Earth, and those two persevering saints, Elijah and Moses, descended from the Eternal Realm, and spoke with their Messiah. Their sufferings, the persecutions they were inflicted with, foreshadowed the agony their Lord was to suffer, and those around Christ, Peter, John and James, were struck with awe as though the sacred presence was a two-edged sword. And St. Peter said with innocent zeal:

> Lord, it is good for us to be here; if You wish, let us make here three tabernacles: one for You, one for Moses, and one for Elijah. (Matthew 17:4)

While he was still speaking "a bright cloud overshadowed them; and suddenly a voice came out of the cloud, saying, "This is My beloved Son, in whom I am well pleased. Hear Him!" (Matthew 17:5) And in hearing Christ, we obey His command that says, "Whoever desires to come after Me, let him deny himself, and take up his cross, and follow Me." (Mark 8:34) Thus we take up our cross as Elijah and Moses, and as Christ, the fulfillment of the prophets, when they combated with the utmost of exertion the forces of darkness. The ardent warriors of Christendom, when they combat the enemies of the Church, putting their bodies and their spirits through the suffering inherent in combat, with death and deep wounds, emulate Christ in His long-suffering when He underwent His most grueling martyrdom; in fighting with zeal and force the thieves of mens' souls, they parallel Christ when He took up a whip and drove the thieves from the Temple. The Crusaders of Christendom, the Militia of Christ, seeing their brethren persecuted and abused by satanic tyrants, and executing noble wrath upon the evil doers, imitate Moses when he "defended and avenged him who was oppressed, and struck down the Egyptian." (Acts 7:24) The holy fighters of Christ, in never bowing the knee before Satan, and in slaying those who attack the churches of God, and kill His priests, emulate Elijah when he refused to bow the knee to Baal, and when he slaughtered the prophets of Baal, who oppressed with bloodshed and violence the prophets of God.

It was on that holy mountain, upon where the Transfiguration occurred, where Christ, Elijah and Moses stood, and it is in these three, where the spirit of the warrior is found. Elijah, Moses and Christ, were not friends of the world, and because of this they were forsaken by popularity. But, the worst form of loneliness and rejection was experienced by Christ. When the Savior was upon the Holy Wood, in the presence of spiteful eyes and scoffing tongues, death was nigh, and the Son of God looked up the loftiest Heaven, and with agonizing voice cried out:

My God, My God, why have You forsaken Me? (Matthew 27:46)

And we find David, the warrior who followed his heavenly General, the Son of God, crying out with the same anguishing words:

My God, My God, why have You forsaken Me? Why are You so far from helping Me, And from the words of My groaning?
O My God, I cry in the daytime, but You do not hear; And in the night season,
and am not silent.
But You are holy, Enthroned in the praises of Israel.
Our fathers trusted in You;
They trusted, and You delivered them.
They cried to You, and were delivered;
They trusted in You, and were not ashamed.
But I am a worm, and no man;
reproach of men, and despised by the people.
All those who see Me ridicule Me;

They shoot out the lip, they shake the head, saying,
"He trusted in the Lord, let Him rescue Him;
Let Him deliver Him, since He delights in Him!
But You are He who took Me out of the womb;
You made Me trust while on My mother's breasts.
I was cast upon You from birth.
From My mothers womb
You have been My God.
Be not far from Me,
For trouble is near;
For there is none to help.
Many bulls have surrounded Me;
Strong bulls of Bashan have encircled Me.
They gape at Me with their mouths,
Like a raging and roaring lion." (Psalm 22:1–13)

The words of the holy warrior David are the words of the suffering Messiah, the eternal and divine Son—the Suffering Warrior Who shed His blood in the heat of the fray, amidst soldiers and guards, swords and lances, and the blood of the Holiest Knight, and Who stained the wood upon which He vanquished His enemies. Yes, He anguishes, He weeps, He mourns, but as a soldier in battle, mourning and weeping for his troops, sacrificing himself for the sake of those he loves, for the sake of peace, for the defeat of the enemy. He is slain in the battle in one moment, and in an ever glorious moment, He is resurrected, and He conquers. And in the end,

All the ends of the world
Shall remember and turn to the Lord,
And all the families of the nations
Shall worship before You.
For the kingdom is the Lord's,
And He rules over the nations.
All the prosperous of the earth
Shall eat and worship;
All those who go down to the dust
Shall bow before Him,
Even he who cannot keep himself alive. (Psalm 22:27–29)

The warriors of Christendom share in the struggles of our Savior; He was struck and smitten by the followers of Satan, and we are struck by the same acolytes of darkness; Christ strikes the devil on the Cross, and the Church strikes with the spiritual sword—that is, doctrine—and her warriors attack with the temporal sword—the authority to crusade and execute holy wars—as we carry our cross. The soldiers of Christ partake in the anguish and the ways of Christ, surrounded by enemies and so near to death, and yet so bridged with eternity;

they express His hatred of idolatry, strive for true religion to triumph, and take comfort in their Father in Heaven.

While the warrior for Christ plunges deep into persecutions, his spirit longs for God, his eyes weep, calling for his lord, amidst his enemies who seek his death. He asks the reason as to why God forgot him, just as Christ asked, "My God, My God, why have You forsaken Me?" And even during such great suffering, his soul still desires God. Such is the spirit of the warrior; his soul, like a sword, drives out the devils who come to shatter his hope, and in the most violent of battles, he still perseveres. There is a reason why David, the suffering saint and an image of the weeping Messiah, remembered God from Mt. Hermon, a most ascending peak, for it was here where Joshua defeated the heathen Canaanites, and it is on this same mountain where David meditated on God, the One Who brings victory to His warriors. David suffers in his agony, and yet he contemplates on the God of true peace, upon a mountain where holy warriors triumphed. "I will remember You from the land of the Jordan, And from the heights of Hermon" (Psalm 42:6). On this holy mountain there is battle, there is suffering and struggle, and on this sacred peak there is victory and peace.

THE THIEF ON THE CROSS—AN ILLUSTRATION OF A WARRIOR

As Christ hung on the Holy Wood, there was a thief on his right side, suffering through the same physical anguish as Our Lord, and in all that pain, in all that agony and in all that torment, he overcame what travails overtook his body, threw off the eyes of the flesh, and with the eyes of the spirit saw not a man crucified, spat on, scourged and belittled, but the Divine King, the sinless Savior, the Master Who gives life and defeats death.[76]

When man suffers, Satan always tries to use that suffering to pull him into blasphemy, to make him think that life no longer matters. 'You are suffering, and God does not care,' is the little deception placed into the mind by the evil spirit, to convince one to curse God. The thief on the cross, at first, embraced this allurement of the flesh, and scoffed God as He was crucified. For Matthew wrote, "the robbers who were crucified with Him reviled Him" (Matthew 27:44), and Mark recorded that "those who were crucified with Him reviled Him." (Mark 15:32) One thief mocked Him saying, "If You are the Christ, save Yourself and us. (Luke 23:39) The other thief could have continued on, gratifying the flesh by fulfilling the pleasure one feels when mocking; he could have used his own suffering as an excuse to further blaspheme, and obey Job's wife, "Curse God and die!" (Job 2:9) But something happened, something truly profound: a mystical realization, in the midst of the most unbearable torment.

Regardless of the nails that pierced his hands, and beatings that he suffered, the humiliation that he was enduring, the thief transcended the desires of the flesh, embraced his suffering, and saw God. He turned away from his evils, and ceased focusing on his own suffering, and instead contemplated on the sufferings of Christ. "Do you not even fear God," he told the wicked thief, "seeing you are under the same condemnation? And we indeed justly, for we receive the due reward of our deeds; but this Man has done nothing wrong." (Luke

---

76 See Chrysostom, *Eight Sermons on the Book of Genesis*, sermon 7, pp. 124–125

23:40-42) The thief would have known about Jesus, living in such a small place like Judea where the word spreads fast; he must have known about Christ's righteousness, he would have seen His trial, and how He was so wrongly betrayed. In that moment, when he mocked and gratified the flesh, he all of a sudden turned to himself in a sublime instance of reflection. And realizing his own unworthiness to enter Heaven, and the royalty of the Divine Savior, he said, "Lord, remember me when You come into Your kingdom." (Luke 23:42) After his own confession of his sins, under the most agonizing of pains, Christ said to him, "Assuredly, I say to you, today you will be with Me in Paradise." (Luke 23:43)

The life of Christ is truly the most awe-inspiring of stories, for within it there are stories that, seeming so simple, are really the most profound. And surely this is one of them. It has been said many times, that the thief on the cross did nothing to be saved. The reality is that he did everything. He was fettered and chained by the most excruciating of pains, brought by the same punishment imposed on our Lord, and he was yoked by the desires of the flesh, which inspired him to mock instead of revere; his body was inflicted and his flesh was amplified. He could have easily acquiesced to the pain, he could have easily gratified the flesh. "For the flesh lusts against the Spirit, and the Spirit against the flesh" (Galatians 5:17). This battle was happening within himself. But he combated this concupiscence, overcame his disordered passions, he fought the evil desires, and conquered them. "No one engaged in warfare entangles himself with the affairs of this life," (2 Timothy 2:4) and so did this man throw aside what concerns he had for his life, and triumphed over his fleshy pride. He no longer cared for his pain, for when He observed Christ with spiritual eyes, he threw out all fear of death. All his focus shifted from himself, to Christ. For he denied himself, he carried his cross, and followed the Master.

Tell me this is not work! Tell me this is not action! To vanquish the body's agonies and its longing for comfort; to cast aside one's concerns for his own self, even though he was undergoing the most brutal form of execution in the Roman Empire, and to shift one's fixation on God in such a grave moment, surely is a work that requires the most determined selflessness. It is not a mere action, but an action of the strongest love, the highest of contemplations, and one worthy of redemption through Christ.

As the thief overcame the temptations of the devil to blaspheme God, and conquered the fear of death once he saw the Savior, so does the warrior triumph over his own fear of death when he faces evil and the sword of persecutors in battle.

THE BEATITUDES—PRECEPTS OF THE KNIGHT

The Knights of Christ bear the standard of the Cross within their hearts, and with ferocity and zeal make the earth tremble, with love uproot evil, with peace end wars, with meekness melt our hearts, and with poverty do they, having nothing, possess everything, for they disregard all earthly ambitions, and within their grasp is the aim of all life, and that is everlasting life. The King of Christendom and the Master of Knighthood ascended the mountain, He looked upon all the multitude, and burning with boundless compassion, commenced His ministry with these most eternal truths:

> Blessed are the poor in spirit,
> For theirs is the kingdom of heaven.
> Blessed are those who mourn,
> For they shall be comforted.
> Blessed are the meek,
> For they shall inherit the earth.
> Blessed are those who hunger and thirst for righteousness,
> For they shall be filled.
> Blessed are the merciful,
> For they shall obtain mercy.
> Blessed are the pure in heart,
> For they shall see God.
> Blessed are the peacemakers,
> For they shall be called sons of God.
> Blessed are those who are persecuted for righteousness sake,
> For theirs is the kingdom of heaven. (Matthew 5:3–10)

The Beatitudes purely encompasses the militant spirit. They beautifully illustrate the relationship between the militant and God, and the divine union between him and our Lord. Each precept begins with an action done by man, and ends with unity with God. One is poor in spirit, and he sees the Kingdom of Heaven; one mourns and he is comforted by God; one is meek and he is given the earth by the Almighty; one thirsts for justice and he is filled by God; one is pure in heart and he sees God. In all of these there is a unity between God and those who advance His beautiful justice. The Soldiers of the Cross most zealously embrace these precepts. The warriors of Christ are poor in spirit, they impoverish themselves from earthly attachment for the hardship of combat and for victory in the Kingdom of Heaven; they mourn and weep for the travails of the earth, and desire to end it; they are meek, being unconcerned for their own person, but are "burned hot" like Moses (Exodus 32:19) when God is mocked and holiness desecrated. Christ said: "Blessed are the meek, for they shall inherit the earth. (Matthew 5:5) The meek do not react with violent passion when people insult or attack their own person, but they do respond with a ferocious zeal when God and His Holy Faith and Church are attacked. Moses was meek, being "very humble, more than all men who were on the face of the earth" (Numbers 12:3), but when he saw God being mocked in the debauchery of the people, he with all zealous rage slammed the two tablets to the ground and slaughtered three thousand of the pagans.

Christ was very meek, but when He saw His Father's House being prostituted, He took up His whip and, with force, drove the thieves out and even remained in the Temple to prevent any merchants from entering. As Fulton Sheen once wrote: "Only the principles of God's righteousness arouse a meek person."[77] And so it is only for God the Blessed Trinity that Christendom fights, and thus in such a situation is the sword unsheathed to crush persecutors and defend the persecuted.

The Christian soldiers thirst for righteousness for they fight to advance righteousness; they are merciful, for they are determined to fight the merciless; they are pure in heart, for they care not for their own lives, but for the lives of others; they are peacemakers, for through war they end war; they are persecuted, because the world hates them for their zeal, but they, like Christ, fight and die to be a glimmer of goodness that dispels the darkness.

THE CROSS MAKES NO SENSE TO EARTHLY EYES

"For the message of the cross is foolishness to those who are perishing, but to us who are being saved it is the power of God."—1 Corinthians 1:18

They say that Christianity does not make any sense. "God becomes man, and then dies on a cross, how is that logical?" This is what they say.

My response to this is: The reason why I choose Christianity is because it makes no sense. All other religions try to make sense:

Buddhism says that we must focus on ourselves.

Islam says that there is only one God and that He never became man

Hinduism teaches that anything can become divine by its own right, and that divinity is everywhere, not just in the Trinity.

Theistic evolution teaches that God set evolution up because "faith must correspond with reason."

All of these religions are attempts at making sense. Christianity does no such thing, and makes no attempt at making sense.

Christ said: "I am the bread of life. Whoever comes to me will never go hungry, and whoever believes in me will never be thirsty. But as I told you, you have seen me and still you do not believe." (John 6:35–36)

The Jews said: "How can this man give us his flesh to eat?" (John 6:52)

The Jews said this because they wanted to "make sense."

But Christ continued on, not wanting to make sense, and He declared: "Very truly I tell you, unless you eat the flesh of the Son of Man and drink his blood, you have no life in you." (John 6:53)

He intensifies His language, increasingly saying things that would not be perceived as logical. Christ was never interested in "making sense."

This is why I choose Christianity because it makes no sense.

The Faith is an ark, bringing us through the floodwaters of human beings, crazily and frantically trying to make sense of this world.

---

[77] Fulton Sheen, *The Cross and the Beatitudes*, ch. 1, p. 16

It breaks us through the flood, so that we no longer focus on the storm, but instead walk upon the waters.

As soon as we focus on the tempests of human logic, we sink as fast as Peter.

But as soon as we no longer rely on mortal reason, and cry out "Lord save me!" then Christ reaches to us and brings us back up to the state of the illogical, and we walk upon the waters, that is, we walk above the world, rising above its useless questions and ascending to the stars.

It takes us to death, and says, 'you will not see death, but life.' "For to me to live is Christ, and to die is gain." (Philippians 1:21)

It shows us this life and says, 'Life never ends, but only transitions into everlasting life.'

Through the Ark of the Faith, we are born. Then the voice of "sense" comes and says: "How can a man be born when he is old?" (John 3:4)

But the voice of Christ, not interested in making sense, says: "Flesh gives birth to flesh, but the Spirit gives birth to spirit." (John 3:6)

Christ did not thank His Father for allowing His teachings to make sense, but for having them make no sense to the sophist, and understandable to the simple. "I thank You, Father Lord of heaven and earth, that You have hidden these things from the wise and prudent and have revealed them to babes." (Matthew 11:26) Christ spoke in a way, that the deceivers do not understand the simplicity of truth. When they asked Him why He spoke in parables, He did not desire to make sense, but instead said: "I speak to them in parables, because seeing they do not see, and hearing they do not hear, nor do they understand." (Matthew 13:13)

Through Christ, we break through the desire to be logical, and find peace in the illogical.

Through the Faith we do not allow the human self—which frantically desires scientific explanation—to control us, but we deny the self.

We do not swim in the waters of rationality, but sail on the boat of mystical union with the Crucified One, and freely glide pass the torrent of capriciousness.

In the Faith, we are free from the demands of logic; in Christ, we are free from the fear of death.

PART 6 – THE CHURCH RULES THE NATIONS

Individualism is one of the greatest enemies of the Church. Individualism isolates us from the universal, and hinders us from seeing the Mystery of the Divine Destiny. Individualism says that what Christianity is all about is our personal relationship with Christ that is void and detached from the plan of God for Christendom. Christendom consists of the Church, the State, and the Prophet. Throughout the history of the Church, from Israel onward, we find all these three working together in emulation of the Holy Trinity. The Son does the will of the Father, and so the State does the will of the Church, God's representative on earth, and the prophet—like the Holy Spirit—directs the nation. By the nations unifying under Christ, and becoming Christendom, it emulates the unity of the Trinity, and in becoming one with the Trinity, it brings the nations of the earth under the kingship of Christ, and into the Trinity.

What is the divine destiny of a nation? It is not the nation unto itself, but for the nation to go beyond itself, and to transcend into the eternal thought of God, to act in accordance to the mind of God, to not isolate itself with some vain secular concept of superiority, but to have identity in Christ, being in Him by Whom the pious nations are united, not for nothing, but rather for a unified Christendom.

For a nation to understand its divine destiny, is for the nation to understand its identity. If the nation's identity is in Christ, then its destiny is sealed, to be an icon of God, and thus to advance the Faith to the nations under darkness, to unite them under the Crucified King, and bring them to that identity by which humanity is brought together, not to be left like a poor deserted creature, but as an organ in the Body of Christ, working with the other members for the glory of Heaven, and the victory of God over the principalities of evil. However, if the nation finds its identity in the diabolical, then it will do the will of the devil, saying with its father, "I will ascend to the heavens" (Isaiah 14:13), and with its predecessors, "let us build ourselves a city, and a tower whose top is in the heavens; let us make a name for ourselves" (Genesis 11:4) The builders of Babel wanted to make a name for themselves, they wanted superiority that sprung from itself; they did not want to deny the self, but worship it. It is the nation that places itself on the altar of the ego, that cannot resist the devil, but it is the nation, "whose God is the Lord" (Psalm 33:12) that surrenders its will, and does not work to ascend itself to the heavens and overthrow God, but rather, strives to advance the Kingdom of Heaven and establish Christian civilization, that is carrying out the divine destiny bestowed upon it. With this can we say with Solomon:

> Righteousness exalts a nation, but sin is a reproach to any people. (Proverbs 13:34)

To build Christian civilization, and to bring the world into the Body of Christ, this is the divine destiny for Christendom. The modern heretics of our time love to reduce the Christian life to the individual, and to forsake anything to do with bringing Christianity to the national or universal level. Everything we do as Christians can never be done for the sake of the individual, but for the advancement of the Body of Christ, and thus for Christ Himself. "And if one member suffers, all the members suffer with it; or if one member is honored, all the members rejoice with it." (1 Corinthians 12:26) All of the members rejoice, because they simultaneously work for the same purpose, and that is the majesty of the Savior, and for the erection of Christendom. All of the members suffer, because them being one in Christ, means that together they are crucified with Christ, suffering as He suffered, enduring the anguish for the one sublime cause of destroying evil and triumphing for the victory of eternal light.

Is this cause of popularity? Is it one of the masses and the mob? No, it is the cause of the wandering pilgrim who stands alone.

You are truly free when you realize that you are truly alone. It is only in this state of aloneness that you come to nothingness, and from nothingness to the desire for total surrendering to the divine will, and in this, does our aloneness become identity in Christ, not in an individualistic sense, but in the universal sense, with the aim to expand eternal Christendom throughout the world.

There is no action for the sake of individualism, this obsession with the individual over the body, this fixation on isolation over the universal, is an idol that stands upon the altar of Mammon, and every day its insatiable thirst demands for the sacrifice of ego, and from this comes disunity, schism, cruelty and sadism, from this comes death. It is impossible for the denial of the self to bring about such evils, for from the sacrifice of the self comes the will to remain united under the One to Whom the self is surrendered, and that is Christ. The body is one under Christ, and thus it is absent of egoism, and so it is free from the desire to break away and start sects and cults. Schism is not the result of some divine revelation, but a consequence of being a slave to the flesh. Hence why St. Paul lists as two of the sins of the flesh, "dissensions, sects," (Galatians 5:20), for it comes from the violent urge to cut oneself from the Body of Christ, and start some novel group, to establish power and dominate others. But in the Body of Christ, the members work as one, devoid of any idea of self-superiority, with all glorying the Holy Trinity, and all being honored by God. "But God composed the body, having given greater honor to that part which lacks it, that there should be no schism in the body, but that the members should have the same care for one another." (1 Corinthians 12:24–25)

There is something quite beautiful and profound in the life of the Church, for in everything we do, we do in God, in Whom "we live and move and have our being" (Acts 17:28). There is a mystical relationship between Christ and the Church, it is cosmic and surpasses all objective and materialistic understanding: the purpose of the Church, and all of their righteous actions, is all done as an image of Christ on Earth and ultimately, as an icon of the Holy Trinity. Read the beautiful words of our Lord and you will have a closer understanding: "Holy Father, keep through Your name those whom You have given Me that they may be one as We are." (John 17:11) The Father provides the Son with His flock, and the Son prays that His servants will be one, as the Father and the Son are one. The Church, thus, is to emulate the Trinity, but not in a figurative sense, rather, in a matrimonial relationship, in which the Body of Christ enters the Trinity in a mystical immersion that is beyond our mortal comprehension. The relationship between the Church and Christ is never figurative, it is real, with all of those who live in the Holy One being immersed in Christ. So real is this relationship, so absent is it of anything figurative, that St. Peter wrote that we, through Christ, "may be partakers of the divine nature" (2 Peter 1:4). There is nothing metaphorical in this. The reason why this is so worthy of emphasis is to show you how sublime the Christian life is, and also, how this sublimity transforms us from our obsession with the individual self, to a will to bring the Holy Faith to the universal level, that is, Christendom. It is this very mysticism of Christianity—in which the Trinity and the Church come together—that surpasses egoism and stirs in us the aspiration to build Christian civilization. This divine reality is ascertained in one of the most beautiful lines of our Lord, when He prayed to the Father:

> I do not pray for these alone, but also for those who will believe in Me through their word; that they all may be one, as You, Father, are in Me, and I in You; that they also may be one in Us, that the world may believe that You sent Me. (John 17:20–21)

One of the most aesthetic aspects of Scripture, is how from one verse (or even half a verse, or even one line), one can ascertain divine truths that are deeper than any ocean. In these words, one can see the divine destiny of Christendom. The Body of Christ is one, as the Father and the Son are one, and so the Christian world emulates the Trinity, and at the same time the Church is unified in the Holy Trinity, in that it is literally in God. And from this unity, humanity believes in Christ. Thus, by imitating the unity of the Trinity, and living in the Trinity, the world is brought into the Trinity. This is the way and divine destiny of Christendom.

When we say that God became human, we should never say that He became a separate man, or a man amongst men, but that He became Man. We learn from the great father of the

Church, St. Theodore the Studite, that "Christ did not become a mere man, nor is it orthodox to say that He assumed a particular man, but rather that He assumed man in general, or the whole human nature."[1] He continues on to say that Christ "is not one of the many, but God made man." God became Man, He became Humanity, and hence the Apostle says that "in Him all things consist." (Colossians 1:17) Thus He became the absolute center in Whom all humanity is unified, and by Whom mankind becomes one.

Before Christ, in the era of paganism and darkness, the world treated human beings as not organs working together for a single body but as separate organs that only live for the pleasure of other individuals. When we read of the colosseums, and how they were used as killing fields to slaughter countless thousands, and how the crowd—in unison—screamed with insatiable bloodlust for the death of man, we do not read of true unity, but of true worship of individualism. Men were mangled and cut to pieces, not for a greater glory, but for the satisfaction of individuals enslaved to ego and self. Christianity destroyed this disarray, for the God-Man established His Church, where there are no useless organs, but only members that work in a harmony for a mission outside of themselves. Pure individualism leads to mob violence. Self-denial leads to true unity. It is the individualist who ceaselessly says, "I want more," and in wanting more they gather together, and rage against mankind. While it is those who deny the self that work as one, not striving for vain glory, but for the glory of the mystical Body of the One Who sacrificed all. The mystical union has no rivalries, for the mission is not the self—unlike in individualism—but Christ, for "there should be no schism in the body, but that the members should have the same care for one another." (1 Corinthians 12:25) It is because of Christ that we have true unity, for it is a unity that is within and in emulation of the Holy Trinity. In the Body of Christ each member is an organ with a purpose, with all working simultaneously for the eternal destiny of Heaven, for the expansion of Christendom and the destruction of the demonic.

What creates violence is the illusion that people must be treated as separate organs without a purpose to the whole. Pagans treated humans as mere tools for the fulfillment of evil desires, while Christianity treated people as a part of the whole, the instrumental players in the divine orchestra. So many times do we catch ourselves looking at the world through the eyes of ego, rather than the eyes of Spirit. Through the eyes of the ego we do not see anything, we are blinded, living in the prison of the flesh and surrounded by the cold bars of bitter desires. Through the eyes of Heaven we look to the world and see God in the simplest of things, and behold all creatures as divinely created, and especially to man, who was made "a little lower than the angels" (Psalm 8:5), and see icons of God. I was sitting outside, and the color of the sky emanated this beautifully glowing orange hue. As I beheld this I saw above me my Bengal cat upon the edge of a ledge, rolling on the hard stone. I saw it for what it was: beautiful, with no bitter thoughts, and came to a realization that once we cease to look at the

---

1   Theodore the Studite, *On the Holy Icons*, First Refutation, ch. 4, trans. Catherine P. Roth.

✝ CHRISTIANITY IS AT WAR: THE MANIFESTO FOR CHRISTIAN MILITANCY

world through the eyes of the ego, and see the creation through the eyes of the spirit, in the simplest things, we can see God.

Egoism says to the world: "I am of the superior people, you are of the inferior!" But the Holy Faith looks to the world and says, "You are humanity. God became Man so that mankind can be unified as one, and be one with Him." In this there is no superiority. As St. Paul wrote:

> For as the body is one and has many members, but all the members of that one body, being many, are one body, so also is Christ. For by one Spirit we were all baptized into one body—whether Jews or Greeks, whether slaves or free—and have all been made to drink into one Spirit. For in fact the body is not one member but many. (1 Corinthians 12:12–14)

This unity spearheads much of the superiority complexes that we see in many churches. I remember going to a Maronite church, and frequently hearing of having Lebanese identity. And we see this evil all over the world. There are some Christians who think so highly of themselves because they are Jewish (or at least think they are). We hear of Greek Orthodox Christians reducing the Faith to being Greek; Russians to being Russian; American Evangelicals to being American Evangelicals. Their identity is not on Christ, rather it is isolated to their nationality. This is what happens when religion is conjoined with nationalist egoism. There is nothing wrong or evil with being proud of one's country, of one's history and culture (in fact, this should be encouraged), but there is something dreadfully sinister about equating or reducing the majesty of the Faith to one's country. Christ never told His Disciples, "Go to this nation," but rather, "teach ye all nations; baptizing them in the name of the Father, and of the Son, and of the Holy Ghost." (Matthew 28:19) Here in this verse we find the call for the formation of Christendom, by the bringing in nations into the Holy Trinity. St. Vladmir—the king of Russia—was baptized in the name of the Father, the Son and the Holy Spirit, and he brought his whole nation of Russia, which was at that time pagan, into the fold of Christendom, and thus into the Divine Trinity. Christ declared that St. Paul was "a chosen vessel of Mine to bear My name before Gentiles, kings, and the children of Israel." (Acts 9:15) Notice that He says kings; to bring kings into the Faith, is to bring entire nations into Christendom, and thus to be one in the Holy Trinity. The purpose of the Great Commission was to the nations, not to one particular people, for the Church surpasses all nationalistic prejudices, and is divinely appointed to be universal (hence the term Catholic). The Church, thus, denies the self to the cosmic identity in Christ, and by losing the self, loses all individualism, and becomes a player in the collective symphony of the divine destiny, with the harmony of the Faith playing to all the world, stirring the souls of entire peoples to join the orchestra of Christendom.

The Father prophesied of the Son:

> I will also give You as a light to the Gentiles,
> That You should be My salvation to the ends of the earth. (Isaiah 49:6)

This passage is speaking about the Gentile nations coming to Christ, that is, the nations of Christendom. When Christ ordered His Disciples to go to all the nations, He already knew which nations will be sheep and which will be goats. Thus, Christendom was already in the mind of God, and divinely destined to be His in His army. This is what it means to be in the eternal thought of God. For in the words of the Russian theologian, Solovyov, the true identity of the nations "is nothing other than their manner of being in the eternal thought of God."[2]

Christ wanted not just individuals to be unified with Him, but entire nations. Christ came to form Christendom, to form Christian civilization. Again the Father says of Christ:

> Kings shall see and arise,
> Princes also shall worship,
> Because of the Lord who is faithful,
> The Holy One of Israel;
> And He has chosen You. (Isaiah 49:7)

Is this speaking of individuals? No. It is speaking of multiple nations and their governments; it is speaking of Christendom and its formation. Again the prophet says:

> The Gentiles shall come to your light,
> And kings to the brightness of your rising. (Isaiah 49:7)

Christ came to create Christendom, but Christendom is dead, only waiting to be awakened from its gloomy sleep. What then is the divine destiny for the lands consecrated by the Blood of Christ? Are too always remain as secular nations, forever poisoned by the taint of modernism until Kingdom Come? I tell you, in the words of Scripture there is much hope, and there is prophecy for a restoration of the bright rays of Christendom's fortresses. In the Book of Isaiah God the Son speaks of His coming to the gentile lands, the coastlands, or the people of Chittim, who live in the coasts of the Mediterranean, and who inhabit the nations of Spain, Italy, Greece, and Cyprus, to bring them from their state of weakness, and invigorate them under His authority and kingship, and their own governments:

> Keep silence before Me, O coastlands,
> And let the people renew their strength!
> Let them come near, then let them speak;
> Let us come near together for judgment.
> Who raised up one from the east?
> Who in righteousness called him to His feet?
> Who gave the nations before him,
> And made him rule over kings?
> Who gave them as the dust to his sword,
> As driven stubble to his bow?
> Who pursued them, and passed safely
> By the way that he had not gone with his feet?

---

2 Solovyov, *The Russian Idea*, ch. iv, p. 16, trans. Fr. John P. Rickert

> Who has performed and done it,
> Calling the generations from the beginning?
> 'I, the Lord, am the first;
> And with the last I am He.'
> The coastlands saw it and feared,
> The ends of the earth were afraid;
> They drew near and came.
> Everyone helped his neighbor,
> And said to his brother,
> 'Be of good courage!' (Isaiah 41:1-6)

The Christ will reinvigorate the lands of the Gentiles; He will renew the strength of the Christian people and order their leaders to keep silence and let the people speak, to speak in lands ruled by the anti-Christian censuring governments of secularism. And then, once the Christian peoples shall be under the Kingship of Christ, then shall they say amongst themselves "Be of good courage!" The nations of the Cross will be one in identity in Christ. Once Christendom is restored, the Christian nations will become icons of the Holy Trinity.

What does this look like?

It does not take the face of secularism, but rather, Christendom is governed under three principles, and guided by three branches of authority. The three principles (as we learn from Solovyov), are piety, charity, and justice. All three of these work simultaneously, with each one balancing the other. Without piety, then you have empty charity and cruel justice. Without justice, you have license, and without charity, you have cruelty and mechanical religion. One can most definitely say that the three precepts can be summarized as the Law of Love. The three principles are governed by three branches of government: the Church, the State, and the Prophet. All three work together in emulation of the Holy Trinity. The Son does the will of the Father, and so the State does the will of the Church. The Church is God's representative on earth, hence in the Scripture it speaks of the priests as such:

> Ye are gods; and all of you are children of the most High (Psalm 82:6)

The priests are called gods, not because they are divine, but because they are God's representative. So the State obeying the will of the Church is imitating the relationship between the Son and the Father. The office of the prophet in Christendom is extremely significant. Now, by prophet I do not mean these gluttonous women and these other ridiculous lunatics you see in today's churches who are so quick to call themselves prophets while spewing out their heretical drivel. I am speaking of prophets who are both prudent and Orthodox, pious and monastic. Christendom has had numerous prophets, such as John the Monk of Egypt, St. Francis of Assisi and St. Pius V. The prophet declares the will of God to the Church and the State, and keeps the nation in constant readiness to do the will of God. Without the prophet, the Church and the State become lax, and end up either in secularism or in dry and mechanical religion. The prophet is like the Holy Spirit in this image of the Trinity, for he directs and gives instruction. Once the Christian nations take up this cross, deny the self, unify under Christ, and begin to build Christian civilization, then will they enter the eternal thought of God, being under the Father, the Son and the Holy Spirit, and become an icon of the Divine Trinity, entering into the Trinity, and unifying the world and bringing the world into the Holy Trinity, that "they all may be one, as You, Father, are in Me, and I in You; that they also may be one in Us, that the world may believe that You sent Me." (John 17:20–21)

Let us break all nationalist hinderances, and let the wings of Christendom fly to that part of the world that is under the idol of the devil, and worships the demon of unitarianism—that is, the Islamic lands—and unite them with the Trinity.

This is the destiny that mighty Heaven has for Christendom, to destroy evil and bring the nations of the earth to the enlightenment of Christ! Let all of the nations of Christ, let Russia, America, Greece, Spain, Italy, and all the peoples willing to become one with the Trinity, enter the eternal thought of God, enter Christendom, and expand the glory of the Trinity to all nations. With this, I will finish with a passage from Solovyov on the true destiny of the nations:

> For each people to participate in the life of the universal Church, in the development of the great Christian civilization, and to participate according to the particular forces and capacities given to it. This is the true aim, the only true mission of every people.

PETER WALKING ON WATER IS A SYMBOL OF THE CHURCH RULING THE NATIONS

When Christ told St. Peter that he was the rock upon which He would build His Church, and that the gates of hell would not prevail against it, He was establishing His mighty fortress that was to withstand against the enemies of God. We must always remember that the foundation of the Church is Christ, and that without Christ as the foundation, the whole body will be as the fool who built his house on the sand. Peter walked on the water, but when he lost faith in Christ, out of fear of the tumultuous storm, he sunk. It is then when the Church will cry out, "Lord, save me!" that Christ will stretch out his hand and catch it up. (Matthew 14:30–31) The boat of Peter is tossed to and fro in the wild winds of the storm, and even when Christ sleeps within its stem, it does not sink into the waves, and nor is the faith of the Church supposed to submerge into the waters of faithlessness, "because even the wind and the sea obey Him!" (Mark 4:41) The Church, founded upon Christ, is the house that is unshaken, of which Christ said, "the rain descended, the floods came, and the winds blew and beat on that house; and it did not fall, for it was founded on the rock." (Matthew 7:25) And "that Rock was Christ." (1 Corinthians 10:4)[3]

But what is the eternal meaning behind this beautiful story? The water upon which Peter walked represented nations. Hence the angel tells John,

---

3 See Pope Innocent III, sermon two: *On the Consecration of the Supreme Pontiff*; St. Bernard, *On Consideration*, 2.9

The waters which thou sawest, where the whore sitteth, are peoples, and multitudes, and nations, and tongues. (Revelation 17:15)

St. Peter is the one to whom Christ declared: "you are Peter, and on this rock I will build My church, and the gates of Hades shall not prevail against it. And I will give you the keys of the kingdom of heaven, and whatever you bind on earth will be bound in heaven, and whatever you loose on earth will be loosed in heaven." (Matthew 16:18–19). Since Peter is the head of the Church, and he is walking upon water, which symbolizes nations, then the story of St. Peter walking on water is a prophetic moment that says that the Church can and should rule the nations.

But, when Peter sees the storms—that is, the rage of nations—he becomes fearful and sinks. So what does this mean? The Church, as long as it has faith, can rule the nations, but as soon as it loses faith in Christ, and allows the world (the storms) to dictate its faith, then it will sink and become ruled by the nations. Peter walked on water, because he was to walk above the nations, and rule them. All of Christendom once ruled the nations. But now that it has quivered before the storms of the world, it has sunk.

Daniel said: "Then was the iron, the clay, the brass, the silver, and the gold, broken to pieces together, and became like the chaff of the summer threshing floors; and the wind carried them away, that no place was found for them: and the stone that smote the image became a great mountain, and filled the whole earth," (Daniel 2:35). From the stone (Messiah) will come the "great mountain" which is the Kingdom of God. The mountain will fill the whole earth. In other words, the Kingdom of God will rule over all the earth. "Therefore we will not fear, though the earth give way and the mountains fall into the heart of the sea, though its waters roar and foam and the mountains quake with their surging…Nations are in uproar, kingdoms fall; he lifts his voice, the earth melts," (Psalms 46:2–3, 6). If one reads these passages replacing the word mountain with kingdom and waters or seas with peoples, tribes, and different ethnic backgrounds, then it is easy to understand the picture. In verse 6, the Bible even gives the explanation—mountains falling (v. 2) are kingdoms falling (v. 6). Christ spoke of having the faith of a mustard seed, that we can move mountains. Are these literal mountains? No. These are governments and kingdoms. Exactly what the disciples and the first Christians did. They eventually changed the Roman Empire which was all converted to the faith.[4] Let us rise above the waters of the world, and rule the nations.

THE TWO SWORDS OF ST. PETER

In Christendom there are two authorities that rule harmoniously: the spiritual and the temporal. The first is done by the Church, and the second is done by the state, and together they work for one objective: the advancement and dominance of Christianity in the society and the world. This is called the Two Swords of St. Peter. This concept is based on the story read in the Gospel of Luke, in which Christ tells His Disciples to purchase swords.

---

4   Walid Shoebat, *God's War On Terror*, p. 290

In the Last Supper, Christ forewarned His Disciples that a time of persecution was at hand, and He said to them:

> When I sent you without money bag, knapsack, and sandals, did you lack anything? (Luke 22:35)

The Disciples said, "Nothing." Christ then told them:

> But now, he who has a money bag, let him take it, and likewise a knapsack; and he who has no sword, let him sell his garment and buy one. (Luke 22:36)

It was as if Our Lord was telling them, "As long as I was with you, you were accepted; now you will be driven out; so that you must acquire for yourselves even those things which once I forbade you to have, for you will need them."[5]

Now of course such a command was said to fulfill a prophecy, that "He was numbered with the transgressors." (Luke 22:37) But nonetheless, the purchase of swords was commanded, and thus the use of the sword was vindicated, for Christ would never command anything contrary to His own nature. Now it can be argued that each disciple was not to have a sword since when St. Peter told Christ, "Lord, look, here are two swords," Christ said, "It is enough." (Luke 22:38) But, Christ's answer was said as though He was telling him, "I say this because of your need; but if each of you cannot have one, two will suffice."[6] Vitoria, certainly amongst the most influential of theologians, said that "Christ revealed that the apostles would meet opposition and that they needed some defense, they misunderstood Him and replied: 'Lord, behold, here are two swords' (Luke 22:38)."[7] It cannot be denied that when Christ gave the order to buy a sword, it was not just to Peter, but to all of the Disciples. Our Lord did not say, "Peter, buy a sword," but, "he who has no sword, let him sell his garment and buy one."[8] Some must have already had swords, and he who had no sword was to buy one. In other words, each was asked individually to purchase a sword.

The use of the sword has never been denied for the Church, and the wielding of the blade for the sake of justice has always been embraced. It will be argued by our detractors, that the Apostles never used the sword themselves, nor did they ever declare a temporal war. Yes, this cannot be denied. But the doctrines of Holy War were within the Church, developing and being expounded, and all it needed was a state by which to unsheathe the sword to advance justice. St. Augustine said, "The Lord, indeed, had told His disciples to carry a sword; but He did not tell them to use it."[9] This is true, and we will not deny this, but what we will say is that the sword was and remains in the Church, only to be unsheathed for the appropriate reasons and circumstances, not by a simple citizen, but by a Christian government who works in

---

5   Dante, *Monarchy*, 3.8, ed. Shaw
6   Dante, *Monarchy*, 3.8
7   Vitoria, *Reflection 1 On the Power of the Church*, question 6, article 1, 1
8   See Dante, *Monarchy*, 3.8
9   Augustine, Against Faustus, 22.70

harmony with the Church for the advancement of good. The sword can only be executed through Christendom.

THE SWORD OF ST. PETER STILL LIES IN THE CHURCH

When St. Peter struck off the ear of the guard, Christ commanded him to "Put up thy sword into the sheath" (John 18:11), which indicates that the sword was never discarded, but that it remained, and still remains, within the grasp of the Church. St. Peter was reprimanded by Christ, not for the use of the sword itself, but because it was not the appropriate occasion to execute his weapon, for Christ told him "the cup which my Father hath given me, shall I not drink it?" (John 18:11). Christ, then, allowed Himself to be killed and did not desire that the zeal of Peter hinder His ultimate mission. The unsheathing of the sword of St. Peter by the Church must only be used for a just and holy cause, and not a hindrance to a holy cause.

There is, therefore, an appropriate time for the Church to unsheathe the sword that St. Peter possessed. This leads us to the theology of the Two Swords of St. Peter, a doctrine long forgotten today, but strongly emphasized in the ancient Church. The concept is centrally based on Luke 22, when Jesus tells His disciples, "he that hath no sword, let him sell his garment, and buy one," and St. Peter responds, "Lord, behold, here are two swords, and Jesus says, "It is enough."

One sword represents the temporal, or political power of the Church, and the other signifies the spiritual authority of the Church. When St. Peter declared the final decision in the Council of Jerusalem, condemning obligatory circumcision, as is recorded in Acts 15, he was unsheathing his spiritual sword against the Judaizers.

When St. Peter affirmed that "We ought to obey God rather than men" (Acts 5:29), he was unsheathing the political sword, in that he commanded defiance toward the political power of the Jewish leaders when they were attempting to prevent the Christians from preaching. When St. Peter was upholding this authority, he was zealously following what Christ commanded specifically of him:

> strengthen your brethren. (Luke 22:32)

In strengthening his brethren he was fortifying them against Satan, protecting them from the dark powers through the two swords. St. Peter struck off the ear of the guard with the political sword, and yet it was not discarded but still remained in his sheath. Therefore, the political sword remains in the hands of the Church. But when Christ reprimanded St. Peter for his use of the sword, it was an indication that the Church was not designed to be a central government, or the only political authority ruling over nations and punishing evil doers. Therefore, while the Church is in possession of the political sword, she does not strike her enemies herself, but commands temporal rulers to use it against her persecutors. Thus St. Bernard writes to the Church:

Both [swords] are yours, but both must not be taken out by your hand [10]

St. Bernard furthermore declares to the Church:

The material sword has to be taken out by the hand of the soldier at the command of the emperor but subject to the nod of the supreme priest. [11]

ST. PETER—FORTRESS OF THE CHURCH

Again, when St. Peter struck off the ear of the guard with the political sword, it was not discarded, but still remained in his sheath. It is by this sword that he strengthens the Church. Therefore, through the eyes of ancient Christians, Peter is a strengthener for Christians. St. Maximus of Turin, who lived as far back as the fourth century, wrote: "If, then, Peter is the rock upon which the Church is built, rightly does he first heal feet, so that as he maintains the foundations of a person's limbs. Rightly, I say, does he first heal a Christian's feet so that he can walk upon the rock of the Church not as one who is fearful and weak but as one who is robust and strong."[12] The French knight, Geoffroi de Charny, encouraged other knights to look up to St. Peter as a model to follow, writing: "Therefore it would be a great thing for men of worth, if they could be as steadfast in the faith in Our Lord as was this holy man of worth, St. Peter, who lived in such a holy way and who is so honored for his saintly life."[13]

The enemies of the Church are all around, and it is the job of its leaders to protect the flock like good shepherds. St. Peter drew out the physical sword when he, through divine intersession and being used as the human instrument to call for God to slay the enemies of the Church, brought to death Ananias and Sapphira for lying to him and to God:

But a certain man named Ananias, with Sapphira his wife, sold a piece of land, And by fraud kept back part of the price of the land, his wife being privy thereunto: and bringing a certain part of it, laid it at the feet of the apostles. But Peter said: Ananias, why hath Satan tempted thy heart that thou shouldst lie to the Holy Ghost, and by fraud keep part of the price of the land? Whilst it remained, did it not remain to thee? And after it was sold, was it not in thy power? Why hast thou conceived this thing in thy heart? Thou hast not lied to men, but to God. And Ananias hearing these words, fell down, and gave up the ghost. And there came great fear upon all that heard it. And the young men rising up, removed him, and carrying him out, buried him.

And it was about the space of three hours after, when his wife, not knowing what had happened, came in. And Peter said to her: Tell me, woman, whether you sold the land for so much? And she said: Yea, for so much. And Peter said unto her: Why have you agreed together to tempt the Spirit of the Lord? Behold the feet of them who have buried thy husband are at the door, and they shall carry thee out. (Acts 5:1–9)

---

10 Bernard, *On Consideration*, 4.3
11 Bernard, *On Consideration*, 4.3
12 Maximus of Turin, sermon 9, 1
13 Geoffroi de Charny, *A Knight's Own Book of Chivalry*, 35

✝ CHRISTIANITY IS AT WAR: THE MANIFESTO FOR CHRISTIAN MILITANCY

It was in this moment that St. Peter was protecting the Church from deceivers, and his authority was to such a high degree that he brought the liars to death. This same authority continues on in the Church to bring low the enemies of the Faith. In the year 1074, Pope St. Gregory VII commanded that the corrupt bishop, Gerald of Sisteron, who was tyrannizing other priests, imprisoning them and stealing their property, cease his despotism and torment of the clergy, and he made reference to the deaths of Ananias and Sapphira as proof of his authority over this wicked bishop:

> Michael, a priest of the church, knowing that it is the peculiar property of St. Peter that you have seized its estates, made prisoners of its priests and clergy and compelled them by violence to swear fidelity to you contrary to law and right. Now, since you are well aware that Ananias and Sapphira were punished with death because they did not give to St. Peter what they had promised, by whose instigation if not that of the Devil did you venture upon such an invasion, inflict such an outrage and commit such a sacrilege against the chief of the Apostles? [14]

It is of Christian duty to protect the Church from theological deception, but it is equally the duty of Christendom to protect her from physical attack, and to emulate those earliest Christians who, when watching the temple guards, were about to stone them to death if they ever, for one moment, attempted to arrest Peter and the other apostles with him, with violence, for as the Scriptures tell us:

> Then went the officer with the ministers, and brought them without violence; for they feared the people, lest they should be stoned. (Acts 5:26)

Not only are the Christians supposed to protect the Church, but the Church is commissioned by Christ to strengthen the Christians to keep on fighting against the devil and his followers. This commission was commenced when Christ declared to St. Peter:

> But I have prayed for you, that your faith should not fail; and when you have returned to Me, strengthen your brethren. (Luke 22:32)

To strengthen is to empower and invigorate the brethren, and also, to protect them from harm both spiritual and physical. For when the Muslims were slaughtering the Christians of the East, Pope St. Gregory VII sited this statement of Christ when speaking of his own obligation to help lead an army of fifty thousand warriors against the Turks, to protect and liberate the Church that was so brutally persecuted. In his letter, written in 1074 and addressed to King Henry IV, Gregory wrote:

> For it is the call of our time that the word of command shall be fulfilled which our blessed Savior deigned to speak to the prince of the Apostles: 'I have prayed for thee that thy faith fail not: and when thou art converted, strengthen thy brethren.' And because our fathers, in whose footsteps we, though unworthy, desire to walk, often went to those regions for the strengthening of the Catholic faith, we also, aided by the prayers of all Christian men, are

---

14 Gregory VII, b. 1, 67, p. 96

under compulsion to go over there for the same faith and for the defense of Christians—provided that the way shall be opened with Christ as our guide—for the way of man is not in his own hand, and the steps of a man are ordered by the Lord. 15

St. Gregory VII applied the words of Christ addressed to Peter to Holy War for the cause of strengthening or protecting the brethren. It is quite profound how one verse can move entire nations, for the protection of the Church and the preservation of Orthodoxy. Christ told St. Peter, "Indeed, Satan has asked for you, that he may sift you as wheat." (Luke 22:31) This was the prediction of war, between the devil and the Church, between the sheep nations and the goat nations that are separated by the sword which Christ brought for the purpose of universal division. "Think not that I am come to send peace on earth: I came not to send peace, but a sword." (Matthew 10:34) Christ told St. Peter "I have prayed for thee, that thy faith fail not: and when thou art converted, strengthen thy brethren." (Luke 22:32). This was the duty imposed on him, to fight, and the prediction of his victory in the very war against the forces of evil. As Pope Innocent III, amongst the greatest leaders of the Crusades, said in regards to this verse:

> This is the bridegroom's voice for which I rejoice: for just as he [Christ] who predicts the fight to Simon promises the victory, so he who imposes the duty is he who provides the help. 16

When St. Peter was arrested—this most holy man—the Jewish leaders, with souls tainted by sophism and vicious lusts, "with deceitful lips, and with a double heart" (Psalm 11:3), told St. Peter and the Apostles with violent tongues to stop declaring Christ, saying:

> you should not teach in this name; and behold, you have filled Jerusalem with your doctrine, and you have a mind to bring the blood of this man upon us. (Acts 5:28)

And who of the group did the priests speak to? It was St. Peter, the fortifier of the Christian heart. He looked at these Jewish clerics and heard their words; they were not said for the sake of peace, but to, through coercion, oppress the Church, and in that moment of time, in which the holy angels watched over them, and the devils lingered around the enemies of God, St. Peter unsheathed his sacerdotal sword and fiercely wielded it against the infernal spirits, and against the despotic adversaries of the Holy Church, and declared one of the most militant verses in all of Scripture:

> We ought to obey God, rather than men. (Acts 5:29)

In this event, spiritual war was done, with the Church taking the victory, "rejoicing that they were accounted worthy to suffer reproach for the name of Jesus. And every day they ceased not in the temple, and from house to house, to teach and preach Christ Jesus." (Acts 5:41–42)

---

15 Gregory VII, b. 2, 31, p. 165
16 Pope Innocent III, sermon 3: *On the First Anniversary*, trans. Corinne J. Vause & Frank C. Gardiner

In all of the events just described, Peter fortified the flock against persecution and tyrannical deception, and in one instance the Church would have used rocks as weapons and stoned the officers if they took him and the Apostles with violence. And all these events centered around St. Peter, the Rock upon which was built the Church over which the gates of hell are unable to prevail. Peter, therefore, is innately connected with the war against evil.

CHRISTENDOM: WHERE THE NATIONS STRIVE TO DESTROY EVIL, NOT FOR SECULARISM, BUT FOR GOD

God reigns not just over individual lives, but through the political institutions of nations. God uses nations as instruments for His war against Satan. Christendom is consecrated to God, and thus its laws and political life are a means to a divine purpose in the great struggle against evil. David said:

> Let the heavens rejoice, and let the earth be glad;
> And let them say among the nations, 'The Lord reigns.' (1 Chronicles 16:31)

Christendom is consecrated to God, and it declares, "The Lord reigns," and because of this its political body is dictated by the divine precepts, and it does not tolerate evil. Though God can use any nation He wishes, there are nations that consecrate themselves to God, and willfully fight His wars. Such is Christendom. As David says,

> Blessed is the nation whose God is the Lord,
> The people He has chosen as His own inheritance. (Psalm 33:12)

The nation that consecrates itself to God is blessed, and with consecration comes the carrying out of the Divine Law within its society, and the use of holy war to fight the enemies of Christendom and the Church. Christian nations destroy evil, not for the sake of secularism, but for God and His holy laws which bring societies to light, not darkness. In a meeting between certain Christian knights of the 12th century in Jerusalem, it was said:

> We have left our lands and our friends to come here and establish and extend God's law. [17]

Secularism only forces virtue into the fetters of human capriciousness. Today we are so saturated with secularism, that all moral judgments are based on one creed: "If it does not hurt you physically, then it should not bother you." But in Christianity, if it brings the soul to darkness, to the depths of hell and to the influence of demons, then it must be gotten rid of. Christendom's military is God's military, used by the Heavenly Fountain of Divine Justice to carry out the Almighty's retribution against the enemies of the light, and the adversaries of His Church.

We find this many times in ancient Israel. David called the military of Israel, "the armies of the living God" (1 Samuel 17:26), for, while there was a measure of separation between the Church and the state, the main aspiration of the armies were to fight for God, and to advance His eternal virtues. While there is the militia of Heaven, fighting against Satan and

---

[17] Ernoul, In Barber and Bate, The Templars, ch. 1, 4

his demons, there is a human army of God fighting the Church's enemies on earth; for David's killing of Goliath was for a religious cause, because he was ignited with anger at the giant, since he "defied the armies of the living God." (1 Samuel 17:36) And this is also beautifully illustrated when Saul tells David to "fight the Lord's battles." (1 Samuel 18:17)

Within the spirit of Christianity, polity does not rely on secular politics, but religion and the divine law. When King Asa of Judea relied on the king of Syria for help in his war with apostate Israel, Hanani the Seer corrected him, and affirmed to him that he must rely on the God of Israel for victory:

> Because you have relied on the king of Syria, and have not relied on the Lord your God, therefore the army of the king of Syria has escaped from your hand. Were the Ethiopians and the Lubim not a huge army with very many chariots and horsemen? Yet, because you relied on the Lord, He delivered them into your hand. For the eyes of the Lord run to and fro throughout the whole earth, to show Himself strong on behalf of those whose heart is loyal to Him. In this you have done foolishly; therefore from now on you shall have wars. (2 Chronicles 16:7–9)

In the Scriptures we read that because Israel belonged to God, God used the nation to drive out the heathen peoples who inhabited the land:

> And who is like Your people Israel, the one nation on the earth whom God went to redeem for Himself as a people to make for Yourself a name by great and awesome deeds, by driving out nations from before Your people whom You redeemed from Egypt? For You have made Your people Israel Your very own people forever; and You, Lord, have become their God. (1 Chronicles 17:21–22)

The Lord became their God, and by doing so, He had the Israelites remove the heathen nations, and that meant driving out their false religions. The Church, being an extension or continuation of Israel, has the obligation to drive out pagan religions from the face of the earth. This requires two components: the priest and the soldier, with one bringing the Gospel, and the other defending the teaching of the Gospel from anyone who attempts to hinder it with violence and persecution.

The priest brings the spiritual sword, and goes forth to "teach all nations, baptizing in the name of the Father, and of the Son, and of the Holy Ghost" (Matthew 28:19), and the soldier protects him as he observes this great office, with the physical sword, as the Roman soldiers defended Paul, only today it would be done with modern weapons.

In Christendom, the state is strong and maintains its strength for the protection of Christianity against those who desire to destroy it. It is therefore of the Christian spirit, that if justice is to be observed, the administer of justice must be one of power, through which he can utilize efficiently and equitably his rightful position in order to repulse the enemies of the Church who strive to bring oppression upon the sheep of Christ. An example of a king that Christendom should model itself after is King Hezekiah.

✝ CHRISTIANITY IS AT WAR: THE MANIFESTO FOR CHRISTIAN MILITANCY

After so immense a number of Israelite kings abused the Temple, filling it with idolatrous and pagan rituals, casting away the sacrificial sheep, refusing to burn incense, shutting down the vestibule of the holy place, Hezekiah enabled the orthodox priests, through the authority of the temporal sword, to unsheathe the spiritual sword against the unclean things that tainted the Temple. King Hezekiah, in the first year of his reign, opened the doors of the Temple after it had been inflicted with so much tyrannical suppression, and he gathered the Levites together, and declared with righteous fury:

> Hear me, Levites! Now sanctify yourselves, sanctify the house of the Lord God of your fathers, and carry out the rubbish from the holy place. For our fathers have trespassed and done evil in the eyes of the Lord our God; they have forsaken Him, have turned their faces away from the dwelling place of the Lord, and turned their backs on Him. They have also shut up the doors of the vestibule, put out the lamps, and have not burned incense or offered burnt offerings in the holy place to the God of Israel. Therefore the wrath of the Lord fell upon Judah and Jerusalem, and He has given them up to trouble, to desolation, and to jeering, as you see with your eyes. For indeed, because of this our fathers have fallen by the sword; and our sons, our daughters, and our wives are in captivity. Now it is in my heart to make a covenant with the Lord God of Israel that His fierce wrath may turn away from us. My sons, do not be negligent now, for the Lord has chosen you to stand before Him, to serve Him, and that you should minister to Him and burn incense. (2 Chronicles 29:5–11)

Here the king wields the physical sword, that is, his authority to use power for the perpetuation of true religion against the invasions of false religion, so that the priests could restore the Church back into the center of society. The priests not only have the authority to command kings to purge the nation of evils, but to also order kings to commence holy wars or crusades against wicked nations. As St. Thomas tells us, "it pertains to clerics to dispose and lead other men to prosecute just wars."

The armies of Christendom are religious in both virtue and in their aspiration to fight for the Divine Law, to slay the wicked and protect the innocent and the defenseless, "for the punishment of evildoers, and for the praise of them that do well." (1 Peter 2:14) Hezekiah exemplified perfectly the ideal king for Christendom: he clanged to the laws of God that were taught to him by the priests, and punished the wicked; he shattered the idols, he vanquished the pagan Philistines, he kept the commandments, he remained on the path of light, to cut asunder the path of darkness. For as the Scriptures witness:

> He removed the high places and broke the sacred pillars, cut down the wooden image and broke in pieces the bronze serpent that Moses had made; for until those days the children of Israel burned incense to it, and called it Nehushtan. He trusted in the Lord God of Israel, so that after him was none like him among all the kings of Judah, nor who were before him. For he held fast to the Lord; he did not depart from following Him, but kept His commandments, which the Lord had commanded Moses. The Lord was with him; he prospered wherever he went. And he rebelled against the king of Assyria and did not serve him. He subdued the Philistines, as far as Gaza and its territory, from watchtower to fortified city. (2 Kings 18:4–8)

Christendom does not fight for human gain, but for the Church. A model to look up to for this is the monastic warrior of France, St. Gerald of Aurillac, who did not fight for himself, nor for the praise of men, but for the defense of the churches that were frequently the prey of pillagers and raiders, and for the defense of the people, "that he may break the clods of the valley, that is, the oppressors of the lowly."[18]

THE STORY OF THE WOMAN AT THE WELL AND ITS CONNECTION TO CHRISTENDOM

There is a beautiful parallel in Scripture, between the story of warriors fighting the heathen just to obtain water for David, and the Samaritan woman at the well of Jacob. Jesus says, "Give me to drink" (John 4:7), but in the story the woman never draws water out of the well, and neither is Jesus found drinking the water. Christ profoundly told the woman, "Whosoever drinketh of this water shall thirst again: but whosoever drinketh of the water that I shall give him shall never thirst" (John 4:14), and this water is of course the Gospel. David told his soldiers, "Oh that one would give me drink of the water of Bethlehem," (1 Chronicles 11:17), that is, the city of the Messiah, from where "Christ comes" (John 7:42), from where the Living Water springs forth to redeem the world.

What do the soldiers do? They "brake through the host of the Philistines, and drew water out of the well of Bethlehem" (1 Chronicles 11:18). And so the sublime and glorious story shows, in a beautifully prophetic fashion, how the Christian warriors of God strived and fought against the heathen to bring forth the Gospel "with the jeopardy of their lives" (1 Chronicles 11:19). And they did so with arms, to both protect themselves and to see to it that the water was brought to David who did not drink it for himself but offered it to God. The water—brought from the well of Bethlehem—was a sacrifice, brought forth through war, and Christ—the Living Water from Bethlehem—is our sacrifice, for Whom we fight and die for. David received the water and poured it forth to the earth as a sacrifice, and when Christ was sacrificed, and His side was pierced, water sprung forth from His ribs, mixed with blood, showing the union between the earth and the Blood of our redemption. And see from the tall mountain of history, how many Christian martyrs and warriors sacrificed themselves, to bring the Living Water—Christ—to the world. With arms are the priests protected, by warriors willing to fight for the Gospel, so that the eternal waters that eternally quench our spiritual thirsts, may be brought to the world to quench the thirst of souls.

DAVID AND ABIMELECH: AN IMAGE OF THE CHURCH GIVING THE SWORD TO THE STATE

When St. Peter put his sword back into his sheath, he never discarded it. The sword of the Church remains hidden, and can only be used by the rulers, and not the priests. The Church, then, gives the sword to the state, and commands it when to use the blade for a righteous cause.

---

18 Odo of Cluny, *Life of St. Gerald of Aurillac*, 1.8

Amongst the most beautiful images of the Church lending the sword to the state, is when David approaches the priest, Abimelech, who gives to the king the sword, with which he then arms himself for protection:

> And David said unto Ahimelech, And is there not here under thine hand spear or sword? for I have neither brought my sword nor my weapons with me, because the king's business required haste.
>
> And the priest said, The sword of Goliath the Philistine, whom thou slewest in the valley of Elah, behold, it is here wrapped in a cloth behind the ephod: if thou wilt take that, take it: for there is no other save that here. And David said, "There is none like that; give it me." (1 Samuel 21:8–9)

Such a story is symbolic of the Church giving the temporal sword to the king. It is the Church that tells the king, "take it," and it is the king who tells the Church, "give it me." The sword is in the possession of the temple, but the priest does not use it, rather David the king does. And so the sword of St. Peter remains in his sheath, but he cannot use it, rather he gives it to the king. Remember what our Lord told St. Peter: "Put your sword in its place, for all who take the sword will perish by the sword." (Matthew 26:25) Christ warned Peter that the state, which rightly uses the sword, will slay those who live by the sword, that is, those who use the sword without authority. The sword is in the possession of the sacerdotal office, that is, the Church, and from there it proceeds to the grasp of the state, who uses it in turn to defend the Church. For when Saul slaughtered the priests, David made ready his weapon and his armies to protect Abiathar from the tyrant, as the Scriptures attest,

> And Abiathar shewed David that Saul had slain the Lord's priests. And David said unto Abiathar, I knew it that day, when Doeg the Edomite was there, that he would surely tell Saul: I have occasioned the death of all the persons of thy father's house. Abide thou with me, fear not: for he that seeketh my life seeketh thy life: but with me thou shalt be in safeguard. (1 Samuel 22:21–23)

But since David was not king yet, the story also signifies that protectors of the Church do not necessarily have to be leaders of the state, but soldiers and brave warriors who, seeing the despotism of the government, raise arms to protect Christians from violence and persecution. We must not also not forget that when the pagan queen Athaliah was persecuting the orthodox of Israel, that it was the priest Jehoiada who provided the weapons to the soldiers:

> And the priest gave the captains of hundreds the spears and shields which had belonged to King David that were in the temple of the Lord. (2 Kings 11:10)

This further illustrates the Church, not using the sword, but providing the sword to the warriors.

PART 6

THE TWO SWORDS IN THE OLD TESTAMENT
In Christendom, the priest instructs the king on Orthodoxy with the spiritual sword, and the king in turn protects Orthodoxy with the temporal sword. We see this system, in which priests, such as Jehoiada and Hilkia, commanded kings to enforce and carry out divine law, being done in ancient Israel. Numerous examples of this will be presented here.

ELISHA AND JEHU
Elisha, through inspiration, told Jehu to kill the entire house of Ahab on account of his pagan practices, his collaboration with Jezebel, and his murder of the prophets of God:

> Then he arose and went into the house. And he poured the oil on his head, and said to him, "Thus says the Lord God of Israel: I have anointed you king over the people of the Lord, over Israel. You shall strike down the house of Ahab your master, that I may avenge the blood of My servants the prophets, and the blood of all the servants of the Lord, at the hand of Jezebel. For the whole house of Ahab shall perish; and I will cut off from Ahab all the males in Israel, both bond and free. So I will make the house of Ahab like the house of Jeroboam the son of Nebat, and like the house of Baasha the son of Ahijah. The dogs shall eat Jezebel on the plot of ground at Jezreel, and there shall be none to bury her. (2 Kings 9:6–10)

HILKIA THE PRIEST
It was the priest Jehoiada who instilled the divine laws into the heart of the King Jehoash, as the Scriptures say,

> Jehoash did what was right in the sight of the Lord all the days in which Jehoiada the priest instructed him. (2 Kings 12:2)

Notice that it is the priest who instructs the king. Look upon this sacred story of the priest Hilkiah and King Josiah, and you will see the heart of Christendom. Hilkiah discovered the Book of the Covenant in the House of the Lord, saying, "I have found the Book of the Law in the house of the Lord." (2 Kings 22:8) Hilkiah gave the book to the scribe, Shaphan, and he in turn read the holy words of the divine book, and when the king Josiah heard the words of sacred writing, he was moved to zeal by the divine precepts, as the Scriptures retell:

> Then Shaphan the scribe showed the king, saying 'Hilkiah the priest has given me a book. And Shaphan read it before the king. Now it happened, when the king heard the words of the Book of the Law, that he tore his clothes.' (2 Kings 22:10–11)

The noble king called for the priest Hilkiah, and other holy men, to "Go, inquire of the Lord for me, for the people and for all Judah, concerning the words of this book that has been found; for great is the wrath of the Lord that is aroused against us, because our fathers have not obeyed the words of this book, to do according to all that is written concerning us." (2 Kings 22:13)

So then Hilkiah and the others who were with him went to inquire the will of God from Huldah the prophetess in Jerusalem, and she informed them that the Lord demanded that Josiah cleanse Israel of its paganism:

> Thus says the Lord God of Israel, Tell the man who sent you to Me 'Thus says the Lord: Behold, I will bring calamity on this place and on its inhabitants all the words of the book which the king of Judah has read because they have forsaken Me and burned incense to other gods, that they might provoke Me to anger with all the works of their hands. Therefore My wrath shall be aroused against this place and shall not be quenched. But as for the king of Judah, who sent you to inquire of the Lord, in this manner you shall speak to him,' Thus says the Lord God of Israel: 'Concerning the words which you have heard because your heart was tender, and you humbled yourself before the Lord when you heard what I spoke against this place and against its inhabitants, that they would become a desolation and a curse, and you tore your clothes and wept before Me, I also have heard you, says the Lord. 'Surely, therefore, I will gather you to your fathers, and you shall be gathered to your grave in peace; and your eyes shall not see all the calamity which I will bring on this place.' (2 Kings 22:15–20)

They heard the words of God, and Hilkiah and the others went to the king and told him the will of Heaven. He read the words of the holy book, "stood by a pillar and made a covenant before the Lord, to follow the Lord and to keep His commandments and His testimonies and His statutes, with all his heart and all his soul, to perform the words of this covenant that were written in this book. And all the people took a stand for the covenant." (2 Kings 23:3)

The priest provided the spiritual sword, that is the teachings of God, and the king in turn executed the temporal sword to advance the heavenly blade of the Law, to rid those who attempted to destroy it. He killed off the pagan priests, obliterated the houses of the wretched homosexuals, abolished child sacrifice, banished the wizards, and made it known, through his holy and just actions, that the sword of truth would dominate the dagger of tyranny and the sandy hill of heresy:

> And the king commanded Hilkiah the high priest, and the priests of the second order, and the keepers of the door, to bring forth out of the temple of the Lord all the vessels that were made for Baal, and for the grove, and for all the host of heaven: and he burned them without Jerusalem in the fields of Kidron, and carried the ashes of them unto Bethel. And he put down the idolatrous priests, whom the kings of Judah had ordained to burn incense in the high places in the cities of Judah, and in the places round about Jerusalem; them also that burned incense unto Baal, to the sun, and to the moon, and to the planets, and to all the host of heaven. And he brought out the grove from the house of the Lord, without Jerusalem, unto the brook Kidron, and burned it at the brook Kidron, and stamped it small to powder, and cast the powder thereof upon the graves of the children of the people. He broke down the houses of the sodomites that were by the house of the Lord, where the women wove hangings for the grove. He brought all the priests out of the cities of Judah, and defiled the high places where the priests had burned incense, from Geba to Beersheba, and brake down the high

places of the gates that were in the entering in of the gate of Joshua the governor of the city, which were on a man's left hand at the gate of the city.

Nevertheless the priests of the high places came not up to the altar of the Lord in Jerusalem, but they did eat of the unleavened bread among their brethren. And he defiled Topheth, which is in the valley of the children of Hinnom, that no man might make his son or his daughter to pass through the fire to Moloch. And he took away the horses that the kings of Judah had given to the sun, at the entering in of the house of the Lord, by the chamber of Nathanmelech the chamberlain, which was in the suburbs, and burned the chariots of the sun with fire. And the altars that were on the top of the upper chamber of Ahaz, which the kings of Judah had made, and the altars which Manasseh had made in the two courts of the house of the Lord, did the king beat down, and brake them down from thence, and cast the dust of them into the brook Kidron. And the high places that were before Jerusalem, which were on the right hand of the mount of corruption, which Solomon the king of Israel had built for Ashtoreth the abomination of the Zidonians, and for Chemosh the abomination of the Moabites, and for Milcom the abomination of the children of Ammon, did the king defile. And he brake in pieces the images, and cut down the groves, and filled their places with the bones of men. Moreover the altar that was at Bethel, and the high place which Jeroboam the son of Nebat, who made Israel to sin, had made, both that altar and the high place he broke down, and burned the high place, and stamped it small to powder, and burned the grove. And as Josiah turned himself, he spied the sepulchers that were there in the mount, and sent, and took the bones out of the sepulchers, and burned them upon the altar, and polluted it, according to the word of the Lord which the man of God proclaimed, who proclaimed these words.

Then he said, 'What title is that that I see?' And the men of the city told him, 'It is the sepulcher of the man of God, which came from Judah, and proclaimed these things that thou hast done against the altar of Bethel.' And he said, 'Let him alone; let no man move his bones. So they let his bones alone, with the bones of the prophet that came out of Samaria.' And all the houses also of the high places that were in the cities of Samaria, which the kings of Israel had made to provoke the Lord to anger, Josiah took away, and did to them according to all the acts that he had done in Bethel. And he slew all the priests of the high places that were there upon the altars, and burned men's bones upon them, and returned to Jerusalem. Moreover the workers with familiar spirits, and the wizards, and the images, and the idols, and all the abominations that were spied in the land of Judah and in Jerusalem, did Josiah put away, that he might perform the words of the law which were written in the book that Hilkiah the priest found in the house of the Lord. (2 Kings 23:4–24, ellipse mine)

AZARIAH AND KING ASA—ANOTHER EXAMPLE OF
THE CHURCH HAVING THE STATE ADVANCE THE LAW OF GOD

The priest Azariah told the king, Asa, to enforce the Divine Law upon the people. The priest brought the spiritual sword to the sovereign, and King Asa in turn executed the physical sword, and uprooted the pagan idols and the homosexuals, and he gathered the people together and they pledged that whoever did not seek God would be put to death:

> Now the Spirit of God came upon Azariah the son of Oded. And he went out to meet Asa, and said to him: 'Hear me, Asa, and all Judah and Benjamin. The Lord is with you while you are with Him. If you seek Him, He will be found by you; but if you forsake Him, He will forsake you. For a long time Israel has been without the true God, without a teaching priest, and without law; but when in their trouble they turned to the Lord God of Israel, and sought Him, He was found by them. And in those times there was no peace to the one who went out, nor to the one who came in, but great turmoil was on all the inhabitants of the lands. So nation was destroyed by nation, and city by city, for God troubled them with every adversity. But you, be strong and do not let your hands be weak, for your work shall be rewarded!'
>
> When Asa heard these words and the prophecy of Oded the prophet, he took courage, and removed the abominable idols from all the land of Judah and Benjamin and from the cities which he had taken in the mountains of Ephraim; and he restored the altar of the Lord that was before the vestibule of the Lord. Then he gathered all Judah and Benjamin, and those who dwelt with them from Ephraim, Manasseh, and Simeon, for they came over to him in great numbers from Israel when they saw that the Lord his God was with him. So they gathered together at Jerusalem in the third month, in the fifteenth year of the reign of Asa. And they offered to the Lord at that time seven hundred bulls and seven thousand sheep from the spoil they had brought. Then they entered into a covenant to seek the Lord God of their fathers with all their heart and with all their soul; and whoever would not seek the Lord God of Israel was to be put to death, whether small or great, whether man or woman. (2 Chronicles 15:1–13)

JEHU AND JEHOSOPHAT

When the people of Judah became riotous and lawless, a secular politician did not go to the king and tell him to fix the problem, nor did they design some government system to help stop crime. Jehu, a prophet and not a man of a secular office, corrected the king, Jehosophat, declaring:

> Should you help the wicked and love those who hate the Lord? Therefore the wrath of the Lord is upon you. Nevertheless good things are found in you, in that you have removed the wooden images from the land, and have prepared your heart to seek God. (2 Chronicles 19:2–3)

The prophet unsheathed the spiritual sword, that is his religious authority, to have the king utilize the physical sword, that is his temporal authority, to preserve and advance orthodoxy in the land. The king enabled the sword of the Spirit by ordering the judges and the priests to maintain true religion and law:

> So Jehoshaphat dwelt at Jerusalem; and he went out again among the people from Beersheba to the mountains of Ephraim, and brought them back to the Lord God of their fathers.

Then he set judges in the land throughout all the fortified cities of Judah, city by city, and said to the judges, "Take heed to what you are doing, for you do not judge for man but for the Lord, who is with you in the judgment. Now therefore, let the fear of the Lord be upon you; take care and do it, for there is no iniquity with the Lord our God, no partiality, nor taking of bribes. Moreover in Jerusalem, for the judgment of the Lord and for controversies, Jehoshaphat appointed some of the Levites and priests, and some of the chief fathers of Israel, when they returned to Jerusalem. And he commanded them, saying, "Thus you shall act in the fear of the Lord, faithfully and with a loyal heart: Whatever case comes to you from your brethren who dwell in their cities, whether of bloodshed or offenses against law or commandment, against statutes or ordinances, you shall warn them, lest they trespass against the Lord and wrath come upon you and your brethren. Do this, and you will not be guilty. 11 And take notice: Amariah the chief priest is over you in all matters of the Lord; and Zebadiah the son of Ishmael, the ruler of the house of Judah, for all the kings matters; also the Levites will be officials before you. Behave courageously, and the Lord will be with the good. (2 Chronicles 19:4–11)

ELIJAH AND JEHORAM

King Jehoram refused to utilize the temporal sword on idolatry, and instead promoted it, "he made high places in the mountains of Judah, and caused the inhabitants of Jerusalem to commit harlotry, and led Judah astray." (2 Chronicles 21:11) Because of this, God unleashed the spiritual sword, and Elijah the prophet, acting as the mouthpiece of God, wrote the king a letter:

Thus says the Lord God of your father David:

Because you have not walked in the ways of Jehoshaphat your father, or in the ways of Asa king of Judah, but have walked in the way of the kings of Israel, and have made Judah and the inhabitants of Jerusalem to play the harlot like the harlotry of the house of Ahab, and also have killed your brothers, those of your fathers household, who were better than yourself, behold, the Lord will strike your people with a serious affliction, your children, your wives, and all your possessions; and you will become very sick with a disease of your intestines, until your intestines come out by reason of the sickness, day by day. (2 Chronicles 21:12–15)

Elijah did not inflict the king, God did, and it was through the mouth of the prophet that the curse was delivered. It is reminiscent to what took place in the time of the Apostles, in which St. Peter proclaimed death on Ananias and Sapphira. Although Peter did not end their lives, the proclamation of death was done through him, and he acted as the mouthpiece of God.

SAMUEL AND SAUL

One of the clearest illustrations of the Church utilizing the temporal sword through the state, is when Samuel ordered Saul to annihilate the Amelekites, declaring with divinely inspired words:

> Now go and smite Amalek, and utterly destroy all that they have, and spare them not; but slay both man and woman, infant and suckling, ox and sheep, camel and ass. (1 Samuel 15:3)

DAVID AND THE PRIEST ABIMELECH

We again find another illustration of the Church giving the temporal sword to its warriors in the story of David's rescue of the people of Ziklag from the Amelekites. When David heard that the Amelekites overtaken the land, how they "had attacked Ziklag and burned it with fire, and had taken captive the women and those who were there, from small to great" (1 Samuel 30:1–2), and how his "two wives, Ahinoam the Jezreelites, and Abigail the widow of Nabal the Carmelite, had been taken captive" (1 Samuel 30:5), he did not immediately charge into battle, but first "strengthened himself in the Lord his God" (1 Samuel 30:6) and went to the priest, Abimelech, so that he may learn from him the will of God concerning whether or not he should attack:

> Then David said to Abiathar the priest, Ahimelech's son, 'Please bring the ephod here to me.' And Abiathar brought the ephod to David. So David inquired of the Lord, saying, 'Shall I pursue this troop? Shall I overtake them?'
>
> And He answered him, 'Pursue, for you shall surely overtake them and without fail recover all.' (1 Samuel 30:7–8)

Now it may seem from reading this that David was the one who put on the ephod, and not the priest, but this was not the case, for this would have not been in accordance to the priestly function, in which the priest carried the ephod, and in this case Abimelech turned to David so that he may have seen its shining precious stones.[19] This is confirmed by Josephus, who wrote that David "desired the high priest Abiathar to put on his sacerdotal garments, and to inquire of God, and to prophecy to him, Whether God would grant, that if he pursued after the Amalekites, he should overtake them, and save their wives and their children, and avenge himself on his enemies?—and when the high priest bade him to pursue after them, he marched apace, with his four hundred men."[20]

Here we have a pristine image of the Church, through divine inspiration, urging a military leader to charge into battle, defeat the heathens and rescue the people, who were of God's flock. It has all the imagery of a perfect crusade, and indeed it was a holy war. The two swords were upheld, with the priest unsheathing the sword of retribution, lending it to

---

19 See Haydock's *Catholic Bible Commentary*, on 1 Samuel 30:7
20 Joseph. Antiq. 6.14.6

the warrior, and the warrior executing the vengeance of God. From the time when the sun's rays are scattered about and their glowing light falls upon the earth, until the night of the next day, David with the valiant force of six hundred men, bombarded the Amalekites, and slew all of them except for four hundred who fled on camels, and he rescued everybody, including his wives, as the Scriptures recount:

> Then David attacked them from twilight until the evening of the next day. Not a man of them escaped, except four hundred young men who rode on camels and fled. So David recovered all that the Amalekites had carried away, and David rescued his two wives. And nothing of theirs was lacking, either small or great, sons or daughters, spoil or anything which they had taken from them; David recovered all. (1 Samuel 30:17–19)

It could be argued that Abigail, David's bride, is an image of the Church, the Bride of Christ, and thus the battle can act as both a template, for Christian warriors going on Crusade to defend Christendom, and a prophetic image of Christ leading the Final Crusade to defeat the Antichrist and establish the eternal Christendom.

The Philistines pounced like predators behind the mask of the night, upon the people of Keliah, and what did David do, but honor the Divine Law, which declares with vivid descriptions of how justice is administered unto evil men, not through some vague and jejune talk and diplomacy, but through arms. That is what the riveting pages of sacred history conveys to our minds, as we read ourselves:

> Then they told David, saying, Behold, the Philistines fight against Keilah, and they rob the threshing floors. Therefore David enquired of the Lord, saying, Shall I go and smite these Philistines? And the Lord said unto David, Go, and smite the Philistines, and save Keilah. And David's men said unto him, Behold, we be afraid here in Judah: how much more than if we come to Keilah against the armies of the Philistines? Then David enquired of the Lord yet again. And the Lord answered him and said, Arise, go down to Keilah; for I will deliver the Philistines into thine hand. So David and his men went to Keilah, and fought with the Philistines, and brought away their cattle, and smote them with a great slaughter. So David saved the inhabitants of Keilah. (1 Samuel 23:1–5)

David, like his patriarch the warring Abraham, charged against an enemy in order to defend the people of God, therefore he was safeguarding the Church. It was a crusade unto itself; for David took up his cross, placed himself under the labors of divine combat, of spears and swords, of melees and strikes, so that the righteous may be above the heathen.

THE PRIEST AND THE KNIGHT: THE FOUNDATION OF ALL CHRISTENDOM

The foundation of all Christian civilization is the priest and the knight. Without these, you have no Christendom. The priest teaches doctrine and combats demons with the spiritual sword; the knight protects doctrine and fights against the worshippers of demons with the physical sword. In Christendom, there is no more important relationship than that between the priest and the knight. As Ramon Llull wrote:

> Many are the offices that God has bestowed upon this world in order to be served by men, but the most noble of them all, the most honourable, the two closest offices that there are in this world are the office of the cleric and the office of the knight, and therefore the greatest friendship that there can be in this world should be between cleric and knight. [21]

It is this very relationship between the Church and the state that maintains Christian unity and perpetuates Christendom. The priest and the monk, with their spiritual sword, orders the knight to unsheathe the physical sword to protect the Church and vanquish the enemies of the Faith. This authority was transferred from Israel, where the prophets commanded kings to enforce the Divine Law, to the Church, in which lies the Two Swords, that is, the spiritual sword and the temporal sword.

CORNELIUS AND PETER: THE KNIGHT AND THE PRIEST

When the Church was established, its authority could not be limited to the Middle East. Most certainly, it was from the Near Eastern lands where the Church received its theologians who were the most formidable with the pen when writing against heretics, such as Augustine, Tertullian and Athanasius. But the Church needed not only the effectiveness of the pen and the intellect, but the strength of the sword and the valiant arm. The Church needed its gallant warriors, who with zeal and prowess were excellent with the sword against the violent followers of the very heresies the Eastern Church combated. These were the gentiles of both Eastern and Western Europe, who from being ardent believers in the dead gods, would become the most zealous and fiercest fighters for Christ and His Holy Church.

The ministry to the gentiles was first commenced by St. Peter, and the one to receive his instructions in this great enterprise was Cornelius, a centurion for the Italian division. In the meeting between Cornelius and St. Peter, the centurion told the Apostle: "Now therefore, we are all present before God, to hear all the things commanded you by God." (Acts 10:33) In this moment the warrior awaits from the Church to hear the will of God, and to loyally obey. In this very story we have an image of the warrior obeying the Church, and so it was to be in Christendom, with the Church telling the warriors the will of God, that is, to partake in the Crusades, and the warrior willfully obeying.

THE POLITICAL AUTHORITY OF THE CHURCH COMES FROM ISRAEL

In the desert, for forty days and forty nights, Christ deprived Himself of all foods; and there too, in the desert, did Elijah keep himself away from the comforts of sustenance, for the same duration as the Savior; and also, in the wilderness, did holy Moses remain, his body completely absent from any nourishment, "forty days and forty nights." (Exodus 24:18) On the high mountain, Moses heard the voice of God, and received "tablets of stone, and the law and commandments which I have written" (Exodus 24:12), and as his mind, his body, his soul and his spirit, were ascended by the divine presence and the heavenly inspiration, the people down below, whose souls were in the abyss, cried out, "make us gods" and they made

---

21 Ramon Llull, Chivalry, 2.4

a golden calf their idol, and against this evil did the Lord wax hot in His wrath, and He told Moses, "Put every man his sword by his side, and go in and out from gate to gate throughout the camp, and slay every man his brother, and every man his companion, and every man his neighbour." (Exodus 32:27)

When Moses descended down from the sacred mountain, he had the holy priests unsheathe their swords and slaughter three thousand obstinate idolaters. When Elijah stood in the desert without eating or drinking "forty days and forty nights as far as Horeb, the mountain of God" (1 Kings 19:8), he lamented to the King of Heaven, "I have been very zealous for the Lord God of hosts; because the children of Israel have forsaken Your covenant, torn down Your altars, and killed Your prophets with the sword. I alone am left; and they seek to take my life." (1 Kings 19:14) The Lord told Elijah, as He told Moses, the message of the sword: "Go, return on your way to the Wilderness of Damascus; and when you arrive, anoint Hazael as king over Syria. Also you shall anoint Jehu the son of Nimshi as king over Israel. And Elisha the son of Shaphat of Abel Meholah you shall anoint as prophet in your place. It shall be that whoever escapes the sword of Hazael, Jehu will kill; and whoever escapes the sword of Jehu, Elisha will kill." (1 Kings 19:15–17)

Moses and Elijah were in the midst of a war when they mortified their bodies in the desert, and so was Christ in a holy crusade against Satan as He fasted in the wilderness. For as St. Matthew tells us, "Jesus was led up by the Spirit into the wilderness to be tempted by the devil." (Matthew 4:1) And as the devil wanted the nation of Israel to worship the golden calf and Baal, he tried to convince Christ with the splendors of this world, to bow the knee to him, saying "All these things I will give You if You will fall down and worship me." (Matthew 4:8) But as Moses and Elijah fought Satan by taking up the sword against his human followers, Christ combated the devil who inspired all of the wicked men Moses and Elijah vanquished, not with sword, but with His own divine power and authority and compelled the evil spirit to retreat, declaring:

'Away with you, Satan! For it is written, You shall worship the Lord your God, and Him only you shall serve.' Then the devil left Him, and behold, angels came and ministered to Him. (Matthew 4:10–11)

The two holy prophets foreshadowed the coming Christ, and were fellow generals under their Divine King, unsheathing the sword against the darkness. Both went up to sacred mountains to hear the voice of God command them to partake in the holy crusade against Lucifer. God told Moses on Mount Sinai, "God's holy mountain" as St. Egeria called it,[22] to command the Levites to slaughter those who bowed down to the Golden Calf; He commanded Elijah on the holy mountain of Horeb to anoint Hazael and Jehu, and Elisha, so that they could take up the sword against the pagans; and Christ—God in the flesh and the Son of the Father—"took Peter, James, and John his brother, led them up on a high mountain by themselves" (Matthew 17:1), and "behold, Moses and Elijah appeared to them, talking

---

22 Egeria, *Diary*, ch. 1, trans. Gingras

with Him." (Matthew 17:3) God Himself led Elijah and Moses up to the tops of mountains and told them to use their authority to have officers slay the heathens, and in this sublime moment, Christ—the second person of the Godhead—is leading Peter, John and James, up to a mountain to meet these same two men, to continue the authority He conferred to them, onto His disciples. As Moses and Elijah were given the authority to appoint men to slay the enemies of His holy nation, now Christ bestowed this same authority onto His Church, to raise armies to defeat and crush those who wish to uproot and persecute His Church. And even in the end shall Christ use His Church to make victory over the Antichrist, telling His soldiers, "bring here those enemies of mine, who did not want me to reign over them, and slay them before me." (Luke 19:27)

The authority of Moses, by which the golden calf worshippers were killed, was with all the later prophets when they too had the enemies of God put to the sword. And so this same authority was transferred to the Church. St. Bernard told Pope Eugene III that in authority he was Moses, and "as a judge you are Samuel,"[23] and thus did he hold the authority to have wicked heretics punished just as the prophets did.

BOTH KING DAVID AND ST. PETER ARE REFERRED TO AS SHEPHERDS

Both King David and St. Peter are referred to as shepherds, the first ruling over Israel and the second over the flock of the Church. The authority of David's kingship, therefore, continues on through the Church in the authority Christ bestowed upon it, and is carried out within the reign of Christendom.

Christ tells Peter, "Feed my sheep," and before his time the Lord told David, "Thou shalt feed my people Israel," (2 Samuel 5:2) and in this same passage the people tell their king, "you were the one who led Israel out," that is in battle. Within David's office there is the role of military leader and spiritual authority (since he wrote the Psalms). This office continues on through the Church, and so thus the roles of temporal and spiritual authorities are within Peter.

As the 14th century French theologian, Durandus of St. Pourcain, said, "Since both authorities, temporal and spiritual, are necessary, therefore (Christ) conferred both authorities on Peter."[24] Henry of Ghent, the 13th century scholastic philosopher, affirmed that both political power and spiritual authority were conferred to Peter, writing: "Peter was, after Christ, hierarchically first over the universal Church, and he handed down both keys and entrusted both swords; so that the government of the universal Church, both spiritual and in temporal matters, should pertain to him."[25] Dionysus the Carthusian, writing on the political and spiritual authorities within the Church, wrote: "In the Church of God there is one

---

23 Bernard, *On Consideration*, 2.8
24 Durandus of St. Pourcain, De origine iurisdictionum, question 3, in Bellarmine, *On the Temporal Power of the Pope*, preface, ed. Tutino, p. 132
25 Henry of Ghent, Quodlibeta 6, question 33, in Bellarmine, *On the Temporal Power of the Pope*, preface, ed. Tutino, pp. 139–140

supreme bishop, that is, the Pope, the ruler, in whom there are both authorities and the plentitude of power, and the apex, that is, of both spiritual and secular authority."[26] Both David and Peter are referred to as shepherds, summoned by God to feed His sheep, and St. Paul also referred to the leaders of the Church as shepherds,

> Therefore take heed to yourselves and to all the flock, among which the Holy Spirit has made you overseers, to shepherd the church of God which He purchased with His own blood. (Acts 20:28)

The title of shepherd bestowed to David involved fierce military leadership, and so the same title conferred to the Church did not change. Christ said, "I am the Root and the Offspring of David," (Revelation 22:16) and David's throne "shall be established before the Lord forever." (1 Kings 2:45) The authority of shepherd was continued in the Church, and that same authority to organize holy wars, as they were done by David, for the defense of Christians from persecution, and of Orthodoxy, can be legitimately conducted within Christ's Church.

Within David's office we find spiritual authority, for he wrote the Psalms, and temporal authority, for he conducted wars against the heathen, and we find both of these offices in St. Peter, signified by his two swords. Both David and the Disciples are given the title of shepherd, and so, at times, the Church must kill off the wolves to protect the sheep. As St. Robert tells us, "An authority to keep the wolves away from the sheep with every possible means is necessary to the shepherd."[27]

David likened his killing of Goliath to his killing of a lion as a shepherd for the purpose of rescuing a single sheep, as he declared with lionhearted prose:

> Thy servant kept his father's sheep, and there came a lion, and a bear, and took a lamb out of the flock: And I went out after him, and smote him, and delivered it out of his mouth: and when he arose against me, I caught him by his beard, and smote him, and slew him. Thy servant slew both the lion and the bear: and this uncircumcised Philistine shall be as one of them, seeing he hath defied the armies of the living God. (1 Samuel 17:34–36)

Here there is a most astounding connection between holy warfare and the Church's duty to defend the flock from the wolves, her mortal enemies. David is a prefiguration of Christ, and his slaying of Goliath illustrates Christ protecting His sheep, an action that is an obligation for the Church. Therefore, at times the Church must use war to go against her enemies in order to defend the flock. The warring saint David slew the lion and the bear just to save the life of one sheep, and so Christ, the Warrior of His Father Who heads all holy battles, declares "I am the good shepherd" (John 10:11). He executes His authority as shepherd to His Church, which in turn, in order to protect the sheep, uses the sword of the state, "God's minister," (Romans 13:4) to protect His most hated flock from those pernicious vagrants who come "to steal, and to kill, and to destroy" (John 10:10). Christ said, "All who ever came before

---

26 Dionysus the Carthusian, *De regimine politiae*, article 19, in Bellarmine, *On the Temporal Power of the Pope*, preface, ed. Tutino, p. 140
27 Bellarmine, *On the Temporal Power of the Pope*, ch. 26, ed. Tutino, p. 322

CHRISTIANITY IS AT WAR: THE MANIFESTO FOR CHRISTIAN MILITANCY

Me are thieves and robbers" (John 10:8). St. Gregory VII applied these words to literal thieves, who are heretics that robbed church property.[28] Since a literal interpretation can be applied to the thieves mentioned in the verse, then the same can be applied to the words of Christ when he said that the heretics come "to kill, and to destroy." For the heretics truly desire a physical destruction of the Orthodox Faith. Some may object to the idea that the Church is Christ's representative on earth. But if St. Paul calls the ruler "God's minister" on earth, then why can't the Church be called God's minister? And why can't the Church, then, use "God's minister," or the state, to protect the flock?

Righteous kings who fight for the cause of the Divine Law, are appointed by God to partake in such a holy struggle, for as the Almighty declares, "By me kings reign, and princes decree justice." (Proverbs 8:15) The king bears the physical sword of the Church, and is commissioned through divine providence, to protect the Church through physical arms. God appointed a king, Saul, to defend His people against the Philistines, as we read the words of the Lord Himself:

> To morrow about this time I will send thee a man out of the land of Benjamin, and thou shalt anoint him to be captain over my people Israel, that he may save my people out of the hand of the Philistines: for I have looked upon my people, because their cry is come unto me. (1 Samuel 9:16)

The Scripture says: "we are ambassadors for Christ" (2 Corinthians 5:20). Do not ambassadors work with the governments of other nations? Christians can be called Heaven's ambassadors to earth; so then, why not work with the nations of the earth to advance the interests of the Kingdom of Heaven? If Americans are being killed in one nation, the American ambassador to that nation is obligated to call for the assistance of American armies.

If the slaves of the devil are massacring and persecuting Heaven's citizens, then it is the objective of the Church, God's embassy on earth, to strive for the interests of Heaven and use the armies of Christian nations, who are all ambassadors for Christ, to protect the citizens of Heaven.

The leaders of the Church, through the arms of warriors and armies, are to be shepherds, emulating the valiant David when he slew the ravenous lion and the rapacious bear, just to rescue one helpless sheep, and not to be as the hireling who "seeth the wolf coming, and leaveth the sheep, and fleeth: and the wolf catcheth them, and scattereth the sheep." (John 10:12)

St. Gregory the Great told the general Gennadius that when he fought to conquer pagan lands that he had "done very many things of advantage for feeding the sheep of the blessed Peter, Prince of the apostles, so as to have restored to him no small portions of his patrimony."[29]

---

28 Gregory VII, Epistolae collectae, 40, p. 567
29 St. Gregory the Great, epistle 74

If the Church is to be a shepherd, then it at times must kill wolves, even to save one single sheep.

IN CHRISTENDOM, THE CHURCH CONVEYS MORALITY TO THE SOCIETY

The Divine Law is given to us by God through His Church, and from the mouth of the priest it is heard by the people, and obeyed. For as the prophet Malachi said:

> For the lips of a priest should keep knowledge,
> And people should seek the law from his mouth;
> For he is the messenger of the Lord of hosts. (Malachi 2:7)

And from the priest it is not only heard by the citizens, but by the kings and the rulers. In Israel the book of the law was to be taken from the priest and copied for the king, so that he could read it, and execute its precepts. As we read in Moses:

> Also it shall be, when he sits on the throne of his kingdom, that he shall write for himself a copy of this law in a book, from the one before the priests, the Levites. And it shall be with him, and he shall read it all the days of his life, that he may learn to fear the Lord his God and be careful to observe all the words of this law and these statutes, that his heart may not be lifted above his brethren, that he may not turn aside from the commandment to the right hand or to the left, and that he may prolong his days in his kingdom, he and his children in the midst of Israel. (Deuteronomy 17:18–19)

The ruler then must be instructed in the Divine Law, and not only this, but he must exert his rule to ensure that the community continuously observe their Christian identity, and that means protecting it from the taint of deviancy and perversion, heresy and dangerous ideologies, and in so doing does he keep the unity of peace.[30] All of this fashion of governing springs from the relationship between the ruler and the priest, with the priest teaching the king the Divine Law, and the king protecting the Divine Law. In Israel, when any controversy came about, it was the priest who settled it, and his decision was to be obeyed, even by the kings, and those who did not obey were to be put to death. As we read in Deuteronomy:

> If a matter arises which is too hard for you to judge, between degrees of guilt for bloodshed, between one judgment or another, or between one punishment or another, matters of controversy within your gates, then you shall arise and go up to the place which the Lord your God chooses. And you shall come to the priests, the Levites, and to the judge there in those days, and inquire of them; they shall pronounce upon you the sentence of judgment. You shall do according to the sentence which they pronounce upon you in that place which the Lord chooses. And you shall be careful to do according to all that they order you. According to the sentence of the law in which they instruct you, according to the judgment which they tell you, you shall do; you shall not turn aside to the right hand or to the left from the sentence which they pronounce upon you. Now the man who acts presumptuously and will not heed the priest who stands to minister there before the Lord your God, or the judge, that

---

[30] See Aquinas, *De regimine principum*, 1.15

man shall die. So you shall put away the evil from Israel. And all the people shall hear and fear, and no longer act presumptuously. (Deuteronomy 17:8–13)

The Scripture does not say, "When a controversy arises, go to the Scriptures," it says, "come to the priests." St. Thomas tells us that the priests did not just have spiritual authority, but imperial rule and dominion, on account of their zeal for the law and their fatherland.[31] This shows what authority the Church holds in matters of doctrine, and what authority it holds in matters of the state, for the king is to obey the priest, even when he exhorts him to go to Holy War. The Church's power presides over criminals who break or war against the Divine Law of God; it declares the verdict, and the state unsheathes the sword upon the evildoers, just as it was with Moses and his successors. St. Bernard wrote to Pope Eugene III, "Your jurisdiction, therefore, is over criminal cases, not over property."[32] And those who say that this Church doctrine can never be put into law, let them argue with St. Augustine when he said:

> The customs of the people of God and the institutions of our forefathers should be held as law. And those who despise the customs of the Church should be as much restrained as those who disobey the Divine law.[33]

IN CHRISTIANITY, THE CHURCH AND THE STATE WORK TOGETHER

Religion and politics are never mutually exclusive; all religion is political. If some seemingly pious person says that his religion is not political, then he has no religion, but an illusion. The state of Christendom is a government that works for the cause of religion, not secular ideas that are destructive. Spiritual aspirations at times need physical things to be accomplished. This is why Christ left a temporal institution, His Church, to fulfill the spiritual mission, and that is to guard and promulgate the Faith. Since Christ uses a temporal entity to protect and inculcate the Faith, then the Church can use the state to further achieve this end.[34] St. Gregory VII wrote and affirmed this concept when he wrote how the state should be used by the Church as a vehicle to protect and advance the holy Faith and orthodox doctrine:

> Among other welcome expressions therein, this seemed especially calculated to advance the glory of the imperial government and also to strengthen the power of Holy Church, namely, that the empire and the priesthood should be bound together in harmonious union. For as the human body is guided by two eyes for its physical illumination, so the body of the Church is guided and enlightened with spiritual light when these two offices work together in the cause of pure religion.[35]

---

31 See Vitoria, *On Civil Power*, question 1, article 11b, sect. 4
32 Bernard, *On Consideration*, 1.6
33 Augustine, letter 36:1; Dist 11, c. 7: in his rebus (CIC 1:25), in Aquinas, *Summa Theologiae*, Ia IIae 97, article 3
34 See Victoria, *Reflection 1 On the Power of the Church*, question 5, article 8, 12
35 Gregory VII, book 1, 19, p. 31

In Christendom, the state obeys the Church when it demands a temporal measure to protect and advance spiritual truth. St. Ambrose, when writing on the state's obligation to advance the true Faith, said:

> Which, then, is of greater importance, the show of discipline or the cause of religion? It is needful that judgement should yield to religion. [36]

Aquinas made the same observation when he wrote that "the spiritual power is to be obeyed before the secular."[37] The priest does not urge for crusades so that he may shed blood himself, "but so that this may be done by others acting on their authority."[38]

We must realize that the system of the Two Swords is only possible in Christendom, and never possible in secular nations or nations that put diversity and tolerance over the spiritual health of its people. It is only possible in Christendom, because in such a state all of its citizens belong to the Church, under "one Lord, one faith, one baptism" (Ephesians 4:5). This includes its kings and all of its magistrates. Christ's command to St. Peter, to "Feed my sheep" (John 21:7), indicates that the Church has the authority to steer governments which are under the Church, to rule for the preservation of the flock, the preservation of the Church and the security of Orthodoxy.[39]

Since spiritual things do not submit to temporal things, but temporal things to spiritual things, the king obeys the Church in his governing when it pertains to religious matters.[40] In order to feed the sheep, one must be sure to protect the sheep, and if that means pushing the state to achieve this end, then so be it. All members of the Church must conform to the ecclesiastical authority in regards to all spiritual matters, this includes the kings of Christendom, as St. Gregory VII tells us.[41]

The ruler must obey the Church when it asks him to use his temporal power to defend Orthodoxy from the deceptions of heretics, and Christians from their persecutors. This is truly the foundation of the Two Swords system. St. Robert explained this most simply when he wrote that "just as the Church has ecclesiastical and secular princes, who are almost two arms of the Church, so it has two swords, the spiritual and the material, and therefore when the right hand cannot convert the heretic with the spiritual sword, it asks the left hand to help and to convert the heretics with the sword of iron."[42]

With the Sword of the Spirit the demons are struck, and they will flee, and with the sword of the state those who are under the influence of the same devils are crushed and compelled to disperse. With the spiritual sword, life if given, and with the temporal sword,

---

36 St. Ambrose, letter 40.11
37 Aquinas, *Scripta super libros sententiarum II*, Dist. 44, quast. 3, article 4
38 Aquinas, *Summa Theologiae*, IIa IIae 64, article 4
39 Bellarmine, *On the Temporal Power of the Pope*, ch. 2, ed. Tutino, p. 162; Bernard, *On Consideration*, 2.8
40 See Vitoria, *Reflection 1 On the Power of the Church*, question 5, article 6, 10
41 Gregory VII, book 8, 21, p. 547
42 Bellarmine, *On Laymen or Secular People*, ch. 22, ed. Tutino, p. 117

the advancers of death are destroyed so that the life of liberty may be perpetuated. As St. Bernard wrote to Pope Eugene III:

> Gird on your sword, the sword of the Spirit, which is the word of God. Glorify your right hand and arm by taking vengeance upon nations, by rebuking peoples, by binding their kings with chains, and their nobles with fetters of iron. If you do these things, you honour both your ministry and yourself the minister. That is no ordinary sovereignty. In virtue of it you drive out evil beasts from your borders, so that your flocks may be safely led into their pastures. [43]

All power, spiritual and governmental, is ordered of God, and so in Christendom the commands of God are conveyed through the mouth of the Church to the state. Since these commands are ordered, then one must obey the other, with the temporal sword obeying the spiritual sword. Pope Boniface VIII, in his bull Unam sanctum, explains the doctrine of the Two Swords as such:

> And in this power (of the Roman pontiff) the Gospel taught that there are two swords, the spiritual and the temporal, when the apostles said, 'Lord, behold, here are two swords' (Luke 22:38); and also (he goes on) that 'there is no power but of God, and all powers are ordered of God' (Rom. 13:1). But they would only be 'ordered' if one sword were below the other and guided by it, like an inferior towards the higher. [44]

THE KING SAVES HIS OWN SOUL BY ADVANCING CHRISTIANITY

The actions of the king should never be separated from his eternal salvation. Many today want to argue that how a ruler governs has no relevance to his salvation, and they say that those of the Body of Christ all are equal, and that there is no distinction between sovereigns and citizens. How then do we argue this? In the Holy Scriptures there is a distinct position given to rulers, and whether or not they use their power to glorify God or serve the devil determines their eternal end. In the Book of Wisdom it gives a severe warning to kings who rule corruptly, saying:

> Give ear, you that rule the people, and that please yourselves in multitudes of nations: For power is given you by the Lord, and strength by the most High, who will examine your works, and search out your thoughts: Because being ministers of his kingdom, you have not judged rightly, nor kept the law of justice, nor walked according to the will of God. Horribly and speedily will he appear to you: for a most severe judgment shall be for them that bear rule. For to him that is little, mercy is granted: but the mighty shall be mightily tormented. (Wisdom 6:3–7)

The prophet Isaiah gives his woes to tyrants, and forewarns them that God will punish them in the Day of Judgement for their passing of unjust and evil laws:

---

43 Bernard, *On Consideration*, 2.6
44 Boniface VIII, Unam sanctam (Extravagantes communes 1.8.1, in Vitoria, *Reflection 1 On the Power of the Church*, question 5, article 5, 14

Woe to those who decree unrighteous decrees,
Who write misfortune,
Which they have prescribed
To rob the needy of justice,
And to take what is right from the poor of My people,
That widows may be their prey,
And that they may rob the fatherless.
What will you do in the day of punishment,
And in the desolation which will come from afar? (Isaiah 10:1–3)

St. Maximus of Turin said that the Christian leader who enforces laws for the advancement of Christianity will be rewarded in the afterlife:

> Good Christian princes, indeed, go so far as to promulgate laws for the sake of religion, but the administrators do not enforce them competently. Therefore, when a prince has deposed by reason of guilt the administrator remains answerable; if he executes the law precisely he is absolved of sin, because of the well-being of the many, will be endowed with an eternal reward. [45]

These are the words of the prophets and the Church, and they give a special position to kings, with their actions as determining their eternal reward or punishment. This eternal law follows in Christendom, where the king must glorify God through justice, executing what is taught to him from Scripture through the mouth of the Church. If Christians are being persecuted and slaughtered by pagans, the governor cannot just sit there and say: "Depart in peace, be warmed and filled," (James 2:16) instead the rulers are to "be doers of the word, and not hearers only," (James 1:22), and therefore they are to be "Gods minister, an avenger to execute wrath on him who practices evil." (Romans 13:4) The salvation of the ruler depends on whether or not he rules with justice, and he strives "for the punishment of evildoers, and for the praise of them that do well." (1 Peter 2:14)

So then, we know that the actions done by the ruler effect his state in the afterlife. St. Gregory VII wrote to King William of England, that his righteous actions should be used as a model to help bring other kings into salvation, writing, "May princes find salvation to the end of time by the example of your obedience."[46]

The king who upholds the Divine Law, promulgates and enacts it, through this action shall be worthy of eternal salvation. As our Lord tells us, "Whosoever therefore shall break one of these least commandments, and shall teach men so, he shall be called the least in the kingdom of heaven: but whosoever shall do and teach them, the same shall be called great in the kingdom of heaven." (Matthew 5:19) The righteous ruler does the Law, in that he enacts them and carries them out, and so for this reason he will be called great in the kingdom of Heaven.

---

45 Maximus of Turin, sermon 106.2
46 Gregory VII, book 7, 23, p. 499

Let the temporal sword of St. Peter be unsheathed, and let it be unleashed on the wicked murderers, the sodomites and the pagans who are enemies of God. Let us do away with evil concepts of tolerance, and stop giving license to the homosexuals, to the Muslims, to all the wicked people who wish to bring paganism to our lands, who desire to destroy the Church. Let their ways be extirpated so that Christendom may be formed. St. Thomas says that the king "corrects what is disordered,"[47] and are not the sodomites, the deviants and the heretics, but products of disorder? Christ gave us the true way, He brought humanity the true path, so let righteous nations destroy and vanquish those who wish to destroy the sacred path, so that it could illuminate the whole world without the hindrance of tyranny and the workers of the diabolical.

THE STATE MUST OBEY THE CHURCH IN SPIRITUAL MATTERS

Because the rulers state, within Christendom, are Christians and thus under the Church, they must obey the Church and govern for the cause of the Faith, and not mammon. If they refuse, then the Church has the right, and obligation, to punish such corrupt rulers.

Christ physically attacked, with the whip, the people in the Temple, which was a governmental establishment. Since Christ left Peter as His representative for His Church, then the Church as well can temporally go against a corrupt government that is under the Church. A Christian king in Christendom, is part of the Body of Christ, and so as the bishop can punish the citizen, he as well can punish the king, just as Christ punished the merchants in the Temple. The Dutch theologian Albert Pighius explained this concept in the following:

> All these (kings and princes, that is, the Christian ones) are like parts and members of the Church, necessarily they are also subject to the head of the ecclesiastical hierarchy, so that he may control them with the whip of his power, keep them all working together for their mutual advantage and the advantage of the whole body.[48]

We must not forget that the prophet Samuel anointed David, and Nathan corrected David when he mortally sinned; in these two instances the Church and the state are conjoined, with the former working for the spiritual fortitude of the latter. David was spiritually under the Temple, and so it was to the authority of the Temple that he submitted in matters of morality and theology.

As the English theologian Robert Halcot wrote: "Samuel anointed David as king, in the form in which the Vicar of Christ and head of the Church confers the realm and the regal authority for the advantage of the Church; hence the right and the authority to examine the person elected to be king and to promote him to sovereignty belong to the Pope."[49] Since the king in Christendom is under the spiritual authority, he as well must submit to its teachings,

---

47 Aquinas, *De regimine principum*, 1.15
48 Albert Pighus, De ecclesiastica hierarchia, book 5, ch. 2, in Bellarmine, *On the Temporal Power of the Pope*, preface, ed. Tutino, p. 140
49 Halcot, commentary on the Book of Wisdom, section 200, in Bellarmine, *On the Temporal Power of the Pope*, preface, ed. Tutino, p. 142

and not only that, but because of his significant position, he must gear the society as well toward Christianity. The ruler, like all of the other sheep, must abide to what St. Paul wrote:

> Obey those who rule over you, and be submissive, for they watch out for your souls, as those who must give account. Let them do so with joy and not with grief, for that would be unprofitable for you. (Hebrews 13:17)

If all members of the Church are to obey ecclesiastical authorities, then that means that kings are also to obey, not just as an individual walking the spiritual path, but as a ruler whose governing can gear the society towards righteousness. In one canon of the Church, called Si imperator, in the Decretum, Pope Gelasius wrote, in regards to the relationship between the Church and the state, that it is the duty of the ruler "to learn, not to teach;"[50] and so the king is obligated to hear and to fulfill the command of the Church when it pertains to punishing evil and rewarding goodness.

St. Gregory of Nazianzus, writing in the 4th century, affirmed to the temporal authorities that they are to submit to the Church as the body submits to the soul:

> Mark what I have to say: the law of Christ puts you under my jurisdiction and authority, for we too are rulers ourselves; and, I might add, our rule is of a more important and perfect nature; else the Spirit must yield to the flesh and the things of heaven to the things of earth.[51]

Pope Gelasius wrote to the emperor Anastasius on the two powers of Church and state, and said that the influence of the priests over the rulers is so great, that in the Day of Judgement the priests will have to answer to Christ on the actions of rulers:

> There are two powers, O august Emperor, by which the world is governed, the sacred authority of the priesthood and the power of kings. Of these the priestly is by so much the greater as they will have to answer for kings themselves in the day of divine judgment. Know that you are subject to their [the priests'] judgment, not that they are to be subjected to your will.[52]

St. Gregory VII wrote:

> Does anyone doubt that the priests of Christ are to be considered as fathers and masters of kings and princes and of all believers? Would it not be regarded as pitiable madness if a son should try to rule his father or a pupil his master and to bind with unjust obligations the one through whom he expects to be bound or loosed, not only on earth but also in heaven?[53]

Pope Nicholas wrote that Christ "conferred simultaneously on the blessed Peter, keybearer of eternal life, the rights over both the earthly and the heavenly kingdoms."[54]

---

50 Si imperator, Decretum D. 96. 11, in Vitoria, *Reflection 1 On the Power of the Church*, question 1, article 1, 11
51 St. Gregory of Nazianzus, Oration 17, 8
52 Gregory VII, book 8, 21, p. 547
53 Gregory VII, book 8, 21, p. 547
54 Pope Nicholas, Decretum D. 22 1, in Vitoria, *Reflection 1 On the Power of the Church*, question 5, article 6, 10

St. Gregory the Great affirmed that any king, nobleman or magistrate who disobeys an order of the Church must be excommunicated as a corrupter of Christianity:

> If then a king, nobleman, judge, or any secular person violates or contradicts the decrees of this apostolic authority and our injunction, or orders something contrary to it, no matter his office or high position, he should, as someone who perverts the Catholic faith and destroys the sacred Church of God, be deprived of his office and should be removed from the Christian community and excluded from partaking of the body and blood of Jesus Christ our Lord. [55]

David submitted to the spiritual authority of Nathan when he berated and confronted him for his adultery. This very system, of the state being under the spiritual authority, continued on in Christendom. For example, Pope Urban II excommunicated the Frankish king Philip I, because he married an adulterous woman.[56] Pope Innocent I excommunicated the emperor Arcadius because he exiled the bishop John Chrysostom. Popes Gregory II and Gregory III excommunicated the emperor Leo the Isaurian because he was an iconoclast heretic and heavily persecuted Orthodox Christians who revered the holy icons.[57]

An example of the Church punishing an evil king is what happened between Pope Gregory VII and King Philip. In the year 1073 St. Gregory VII was struggling with a grave evil that was being done by the government: simony.

The bishops of simony would oftentimes attack the Orthodox priests, even with violence. But, St. Gregory VII executed the spiritual sword against them, using both ecclesiastical and state authority. As he wrote in one letter to the bishops of southern Italy: "because they thought their first defeat was not enough, the sword of apostolic vengeance smote them so mightily from the sole of their feet to the crown of their heads that the wounds remain unhealed to this day."[58] In the year 1080 St. Gregory VII used the spiritual sword in order to have certain rulers unsheathe the temporal sword against the simoniacal heretics in Ravenna. He summoned the Duke Robert Guiscard, Jordanes the prince of Capua, and the other chiefs of the Normans, all of whom had made oaths to always protect the Church, to lead their armies into Ravenna to rescue the church there which was being persecuted and tyrannized by the party of simony. In the letter he wrote:

> Accordingly we are proposing early in September, as soon as cool weather sets in, to enter the territory of Ravenna with an armed force, to rescue that holy church from impious hands and restore it to its father, the blessed Peter, trusting beyond all doubt by God's help to deliver it. Wherefore we hold of no account the audacity of the ungodly and the devices of those who have risen against us—nay, against St. Peter—and we desire and exhort you to look down

---

55 St. Gregory the Great, book 14, epistle 32, in Bellarmine, *On the Temporal Power of the Pope*, ch. 3, ed. Tutino, p. 175
56 Bellarmine, *On the Temporal Power of the Pope*, preface, ed. Tutino, p. 145
57 See Bellarmine, *On the Temporal Power of the Pope*, ch. 9, ed. Tutino, p. 213; Gregory VII, book 8, 21, p. 541
58 Gregory VII, book 8, 5, p. 521

upon their insolence and their undertakings equally with us and to be the more certain of their destruction, the higher you see their aims to be. [59]

This same Gregory wrote a letter to Count William of Burgundy, requesting him to send troops into Italy in order to protect the Church from the tyrant Philip, who so deeply wanted to destroy the Church. He reminded William that he made an oath before God and St. Peter that he would always protect the Church:

> Nor can you in decency forget the promise which you made to God before the tomb of Peter, chief of the Apostles, in the presence of our venerable predecessor, Pope Alexander, and of an innumerable company of bishops, abbots and people of many nations, that whenever necessary your force would not be lacking if it were called for in defense of the property of St. Peter. [60]

In the same epistle, Gregory VII expressed his aspiration to launch a holy war into Constantinople to protect the Greek Christians who were being constantly hit by the onslaught of the Turks who were viciously striving to invade the sacred city. He addressed his plea, at first, to the government, with the hope that they would unsheathe the temporal sword against the Islamic enemy. He wrote this letter in 1074, decades before the infamous First Crusade of 1098, which shows that the system of the Two Swords was not something that arose at the commencement of the First Crusade. The letter read:

> We are hoping also that another advantage may come from this, namely, that when the Normans are pacified we may cross over to Constantinople in aid of the Christians, who, oppressed by frequent attacks of the Saracens, are urging us eagerly to reach out our hands to them in succor. [61]

Pope Gregory I wrote in a letter to the Emperor Maurice, that because the authority of Heaven was given to the Church, and because the Church is what helps bring man to salvation, the earthly kingdoms must seek the Heavenly kingdom:

> For power over all men has been given from heaven to the piety of my lords to this end, that they who aspire to what is good may be helped, and that the way of heaven may be more widely open, so that an earthly kingdom may wait upon the heavenly kingdom. [62]

The state is to yield to the Church, and thus when the ecclesiastical authorities request from the temporal sword the use of force to protect Christianity and Christians, the government is obliged, within Christendom, to obey. St. Thomas declared that "secular authority is subordinated to the spiritual as the body is subordinated to the soul, and therefore the judgment is not usurped if a spiritual leader interferes in a temporal affair."[63]

---

59 Gregory VII, book 8, 7, p. 525
60 Gregory VII, b. 1, 46, p. 69
61 Gregory VII, book 1, 46, p. 69
62 Gregory I, book 3, epistle 65, NPNF, vol. 12. See also Bellarmine, *On Laymen or Secular People*, ch. 18, p. 85
63 Aquinas, question 60, article 6, in Bellarmine, *On the Temporal Power of the Pope*, ed. Tutino, p. 126

The Church is superior to the State in regards to theology and morals, while the state is in charge over secular matters, and this is why Pope Gelasius wrote to the emperor Anastasius: "O my most loving son, know that even if you preside over humankind because of your excellence in earthly matters, nevertheless you lower your head devoutly in front of those who preside over divine matters and from them you await the source of your salvation, and when receiving the heavenly sacraments from those to whom this pertains, know therefore that in these matters you depend on their judgment, and they cannot be reduced to your will."[64]

But, the two offices and their roles are not completely separated, they coincide in a dynamic and perfect harmony, with the Church driving the state to advance holy laws. The state does not define Divine Law, it enforces it, while the Church is the guide in this enactment. The Church, essentially, uses the state as a vehicle for protecting and perpetuating the truths of Heaven, and enforcing the commandments of God, in the society. If there is a dangerous movement within society that endangers the spiritual well-being of the people, that is when the Church presides over the state and guides the temporal authority to extirpate the spiritual threat. Because in Christendom all of the sheep are under the Church—their shepherd—then that means that kings are also under the Church, and they in turn are to be used as means to the Christian goal: making sure that Christian identity is preserved. They work as one for this goal, for as St. Robert says,

> But on the basis of divine Scripture, Pontiffs and kings, clergymen and laymen reborn in Christ, form one commonwealth, indeed one city, indeed one household, indeed one body. And spiritual and temporal authority do not converge in the Church as two commonwealths converge in a federation, but as the spirit and the flesh converge in one man. [65]

The state must submit to the Church in spiritual issues, as the earth receives light from the sun, for if you have the opposite, then it will be Christians being forced to submit to the religious dictates of the state, and tyranny will overrun the people. Because the Church has authority over spiritual matters, this authority transcends into a temporal authority. One can even say that the spiritual and temporal authorities intertwine into one sword within Christendom. This is what Vitoria said when he wrote that "the Church is one body, and the civil and spiritual commonwealths cannot be made into two bodies, but only one."[66]

The French theologian Durandus of St. Pourcain, explained this bridging between the temporal and spiritual authorities within the power of the Church as such:

> For the temporal jurisdiction does not extend in any way to spiritual matters, of which it knows nothing at all. The spiritual jurisdiction, by contrast, extends in the first place and chiefly to spiritual matters, but in the second place and by a certain consequence it extends also to men's actions in temporal matters that are for the sake of the spiritual end. [67]

---

64 Quoted by St. Robert Bellarmine, *On Laymen or Secular People*, ch. 17, pp. 79–80
65 Bellarmine, *On the Temporal Power of the Pope*, ch. 13, ed. Tutino, p. 247
66 Vitoria, *Reflection 1 On the Power of the Church*, question 5, articled 6, 10
67 Durandus of St. Pourcain, De origine iurisdictionum, question 3, in Bellarmine, *On the Temporal Power of the Pope*, preface, ed. Tutino, p. 132

The Church must override the state in moral and spiritual issues. For, if the Church has no temporal authority, then the state could legislate measures that are wicked that would go unchecked by the spiritual authority because the Church would have no say so over it. This is what Giles of Rome warned when he articulated:

> Some might say, however, that kings and princes are subjected spiritually, and not temporally, to the Church. But those who say so do not grasp the force of the argument. For if kings and princes were subjected to the Church only spiritually, one sword would not be subject to the other, temporal matters would not be subjected to the spiritual, there would be no order in authorities, and the lowest would not be led back to the highest through the intermediate. [68]

The reason for this is because if the state begins permitting and legislating heresies and other sinister beliefs and practices, then it could jeopardize the salvation of certain citizens. The Spanish theologian, Martin de Azpilcueta Navarrus, wrote:

> It is gathered that the reason why the Pope can depose kings even if they are negligent in governing their realms is that because of such negligence the people of God, subject to those kings, are diverted from obtaining eternal life. [69]

ALL HOLY WARS ARE DONE FOR A SPIRITUAL GOOD

The highest priority in life is eternal life, and it is to this beatific vision that all ends, and all of our earthly goals, are subordinate. The Church guides all of society toward this sublime aspiration. Society is made up of people, each with their own particular gift, and they use each one—no matter what it is—for the glory of God. And so the Church guides the artists to create beautiful and immaculate Christian art; the composer to compose harmonious music that illuminates civilization; the scholar to write erudite books on heavenly matters; the poet to produce verses that deepen our joy for the divine light; the architect and the carpenter to construct beautiful churches, and ornamental homes that always remind us of what beauty truly is. And so the political establishment must also submit to this worthy goal of Heaven, governing the masses with this end in mind, and abiding by the warnings of the Church, not to promote or enforce deviancy and not to persecute the Church.[70] As St. Thomas says:

> All persons and arts and virtues to which an end pertains have to dispose of the things that exist for that end, but physical wars among the faithful people have to be referred to the spiritual divine good, of which clergymen are in charge, and therefore it pertains to the clergymen to carry on and to induce the others to fight just wars. [71]

---

68 Aquinas, De potestate ecclesiastica, part 1, ch. 4, in Bellarmine, On the Temporal Authority of the Pope, preface, ed. Tutino, p. 127
69 Navarrus, commentary on the canon "Novit," notation 3, section 41, in Bellarmine, *On the Temporal Power of the Pope*, preface, ed. Tutino, p. 139
70 See Bellarmine, On the Temporal Power of the Church, ch. 2, ed. Tutino, p. 158
71 Aquinas, 2a 2ae, question 40, article 2, in Bellarmine, *On the Temporal Power of the Pope*, ch. 14, ed. Tutino, p. 254

Since Holy War is a means to a spiritual end, then it is a spiritual good. Therefore, physical wars done for the cause of Christianity, spiritually are beneficial.[72] All rulers are in charge of temporal matters, and they must be obeyed, and since the ecclesiastical authorities are in charge of eternal ends, which are greater, then rulers must obey the priests in this circumstance. Or as St. Thomas says, "For those who are responsible for intermediate ends should be subject to one who is responsible for the ultimate end, and be directed by his command."[73] In this same process, the ruler should restrain his subjects from deviancies and other evils, through penalties and the means of law, and reward righteousness, so as to guide the people to virtue.[74] By doing this does the ruler imitate his Lord, Who punishes those who transgress the law, and rewards those who obey it. By commencing holy wars against external enemies, and preserving the society from internal enemies, does the ruler not only keep order and protect the churches, but he defends Christian civilization.

THE CHURCH CAN PUNISH RULERS FOR PROMOTING HERESY AND DEVIANCY

The Church can also combat the state if it legislates an unjust edict against Christians or Christianity, or one that promotes mortal sin. This of course cannot be abused, and as we read from Vitoria, it cannot be done "without necessary cause." He goes on to say "that the pope must first of all use his spiritual power, by ordering the law to be revoked. But if the secular prince refuses, then the pope may and ought to revoke the law by his own authority, and the law will be revoked."[75]

In another book he says, "the pope may infringe any civil laws which promote sin,"[76] and would it not be fitting to have such a system today, where we now have the state approving homosexuality, atheism and infanticide? This is in accordance with Elijah fighting and killing the priests of Baal, and appointing Jehu to slaughter the evil tyrants; for in a situation in which the king, in this case Ahab, is too corrupt to fulfill his duty and protect the spiritual well-being of the people, the Church is obligated to call other political leaders to use the sword against the maleficent magistrates.

Elijah slaughtered the priests of Baal, but he also anointed Jehu to be ruler, so that he could kill Jezebel, the entire house of Ahab, the king Jorham, and the rest of the priests of Baal. And so the Church can appoint kings and other political leaders to war against persecutors. God commanded Elijah to anoint Jehu and command him to slay the corrupt king Jehoram, and "Jehu drew his bow with full strength and shot Jehoram between his arms; and the arrow came out at his heart, and he sank down in his chariot." (2 Kings 9:24)

---

72 Bellarmine, *On the Temporal Power of the Pope*, ch. 14, ed. Tutino, p. 254
73 Aquinas, *De regimine principum*, 1.15
74 See Aquinas, *De regiine principum*, 1.15
75 Victoria, *Reflection 1 On the Power of the Church*, question 5, article 9, 13
76 Vitoria, *On the American Indians*, question 2, article 2, 31

The glorious high priest of Israel, Jehoiada, who truly was a minister who looked after his people, and combated the demonic infiltrations of the pagans, ousted out the wicked queen Athaliah, who murdered the priests of God and brought in the cult of Baal into the Holy Land, and not only this, but he ordered that she be taken and executed, and "they had slain Athaliah with the sword in the kings house." (2 Kings 11:20) After this, the high priest replaced her with king Joash.[77] Truly it can be said that this story exhibits what power the Church has in regards to coercing the state to be in accordance to Christian virtue. When pagans attack Christians, then the Church can utilize to its utmost exertion the armies of the state to defend the flock from violent onslaughts.[78]

THE CHURCH CAN CAUSE REVOLTS AGAINST CORRUPT AND EVIL STATES

A Christian people can in no way tolerate a pagan or anti-Christian king; for when error is promoted by the sovereign, the Divine Law and human law clash, and thus the Divine Law must be preserved and the edicts of man discarded. This is where the Church intervenes, by empowering the Body of Christ to reject the infidel king, and place Orthodoxy above the state.[79]

A good illustration of this is when St. Gregory VII told King Philip of France that he would order his subjects to disobey his authority if he did not cease the heresy of simony. The king was participating in the buying and selling of ecclesiastical positions, and many greedy and corrupt bishops, who were undeserving of their office, were tyrannizing the righteous of the Church. Gregory VII unsheathed the spiritual sword and promised Philip that if he did not cease his simony, he would strike so hard with the blade of St. Peter, as to order his people to disobey his authority and revolt against him. He wrote:

> If he shall refuse to do this, let him understand beyond all doubt that we will no longer suffer this ruination of the Church but will meet such obstinate persistence in disobedience with canonical severity by authority of the blessed Apostles Peter and Paul. For either the king himself, abandoning the evil merchandise of simoniacal heresy, shall allow suitable persons to be promoted to the government of the Church, or the French people, unless they desire to reject the Christian faith, shall be smitten by the sword of a general anathema and will refuse to obey him in future. [80]

Henry IV was another king who was involved in simony, and eventually St. Gregory VII declared his excommunication in the Roman Lenten Synod of 1076, in which it was said:

> Wherefore, relying upon this commission, and for the honor and defense of thy Church, in the name of Almighty God, Father, Son and Holy Spirit, through thy power and authority, I deprive King Henry, son of the emperor Henry, who has rebelled against thy Church with unheard-of audacity, of the government over the whole kingdom of Germany and Italy, and

---

77 See Bellarmine, *On the Temporal Power of the Pope*, ch. 3, ed. Tutino, p. 171
78 See Vitoria, *Reflection 1 On the Power of the Church*, question 5, article 8, 19
79 See Bellarmine, *On the Temporal Power of the Pope*, ch. 22, ed. Tutino, p. 301
80 Gregory VII, b. 1, 35, p. 56.

I release all Christian men from the allegiance which they have sworn or may swear to him, and I forbid anyone to serve him as king. For it is fitting that who seeks to diminish the glory of thy Church should lose the glory which he seems to have. [81]

Pope Gregory VII berated the Bishop of Metz because he believed that "the authority of the Holy and Apostolic See could not excommunicate King Henry and could not absolve anybody from their oath of allegiance."[82]

Stephen the bishop of Halberstadt in Germany, supported the excommunication of king Henry, saying, "Lord Henry is a heretic, excommunicated by the Apostolic See because of his abominable evils, and he can hold neither power nor any authority over us because we are Catholic."[83]

If the throne is empty, after the deposing of the wicked king, or if the ruler needs to be replaced, the Church can intervene and ascend a more righteous sovereign. Since the Church has the power to depose kings, in Christendom, they also have the authority to coerce magistrates to elect one righteous Christian ruler who will govern for the cause of the Faith and the salvation of the people. As Vitoria explained:

> I see no reason why he whose concern it is to look after the spiritual good of Christendom should not compel Christians to elect a single prince. After all, the rulers of the Church take it upon themselves to depose otherwise legitimate princes who are heretics for the good of the Faith. Why, then, should the Church not compel Christian rulers to elect a single monarch for the good of the Faith, even if some dissent from the choice, especially when the Faith is placed in danger by those very princes' own dissent. [84]

MORAL ANARCHY IS DUE TO THE ABSENCE OF THE CHURCH'S AUTHORITY OVER THE STATE

Since the Church is the shepherd of the flock, all political measures that pertain to morality must be done with the aim of maintaining and upholding Christian Orthodoxy in the land. As the Spanish theologian, Cyprianus Benetus, wrote: "The handing over of the keys [to St. Peter] includes the conferring of earthly powers for the preservation of spiritual goods."[85]

If this is not so, then legislation in favor for giving license to deplorable actions will come to pass. The reason why we have infanticide, homosexual "marriage," and other grave evils being passed, is because the state in modern society has the authority to dictate what is and what is not life, what is and what is not marriage, and other pertinent definitions,

---

81 Gregory VII, book 3, 10 (a), p. 268)
82 Gregory VII, Registrum, book 8, epistle 21, in Bellarmine, *On the Temporal Power of the Pope*, preface, ed. Tutino, p. 125
83 Marianus Scotus, Chronicon, appendix, in Bellarmine, *On the Temporal Power of the Pope*, preface, ed. Tutino, p. 139
84 Vitoria, *On Civil Power*, question 2, sect. 3
85 Benetus, De prima orbis sede, in response to the sixth point before the second part of the first conclusion, in Bellarmine, *On the Temporal Power of the Pope*, preface, ed. Tutino, p. 136

without ever being kept in check by the Church, which is "the pillar and ground of the truth" (1 Timothy 3:15), and which is the authority on earth to determine matters of morality. "Once abolish the God," wrote GK Chesterton, "and the government becomes the God." It is the duty of the Church to prevent rulers from indulging into pompousness, for such an absence of restraint will only lead to corrupt governing, since "Pride goes before destruction" (Proverbs 16:18). For this reason St. Gregory VII wrote, "It is our care with God's help to furnish emperors, kings and other princes with the weapons of humility that thus they may be strong to keep down the floods and waves of pride." And in another place he said, "Let kings and princes fear lest the higher they are raised above their fellows in this life, the deeper they may be plunged in everlasting fire."[86]

The Church is always mocked because of its history of discriminating against false religions. But the Church knew better, and in wisdom was far more superior to all of today's commentators. The Church understood that if the serpent of evil was not cut off from the beginning, then other evils would follow, such as cannibalism and infanticide, the same demonic ideas that the heretics of today are pushing via the secular state. Vitoria, writing in the sixteenth century, wrote, "there are some sins against nature which are harmful to our neighbours, such as cannibalism and euthanasia of the old and senile, and since the defense of our neighbours is the rightful concern of each of us, even for private persons and even if it is beyond doubt that any Christian prince can compel them not to do these things."[87] There are people in our own modern society who call for euthanasia, and even cannibalism, to be allowed, and God willing a righteous Christian ruler will one day seize such evil people and put them to death. But this will only be done by a government influenced by God and His Church. This is why the system of the Two Swords is so pertinent for the restoration of Christendom.

Herve de Nedellec, the master-general of the Dominicans who lived both in the 13th and 14th centuries, succinctly explained this beautiful system: "It pertains to the Pope to correct every abuse of both the ecclesiastical authority and the earthly authority within the Christian people."[88]

The Spanish canonist Alvarus Pelagius wrote that when a king begins to become dangerously impotent or oppressive towards the Church, that the Pope "deprives him of the kingdom if he is insolent or if he persecutes the Church."[89] Hugh of St. Victor, one of the leading theologians of Christendom, wrote: "The spiritual authority has the power to instruct the earthly authority to be good, and it has the power to judge it if it is not. The

---

86 Gregory VII, book 8, 21, p. 547
87 Vitoria, On the evangelization of unbelievers, 3, ellipses mine
88 Herve de Nedellec, De potestate Papae, section "Ad evidentiam secundi," in Bellarmine, *On the Temporal Power of the Pope*, preface, ed. Tutino, p. 133
89 Alvarus Pelagius, De planctu Ecclesiae, book 1, article 21, in Bellarmine, *On the Temporal Power of the Pope*, preface, ed. Tutino, p. 136

former, however, is established in the first place by God and, if it strays, can be judged only by Him."[90]

Alexander of Hales, the English Franciscan who would teach great theologians like St. Thomas and St. Bonaventure, said: "The spiritual authority has the power to instruct the earthly authority and judge if it is good: the former, by contrast, is instituted by God in the first place, and when it strays it can be judged by God alone."[91] We are flauntingly told that our society is "secular," while it takes religious establishments, such as the honor of human life and marriage, and shreds them to pieces, and forces the people to tolerate such aberrations. In the Church, human life is seen as the most sacred of creation, nothing that should ever be belittled nor experimented with. This honor and elevation has been within the Church since the beginning, and there are countless passages from the divine words of Christ, and the sublime writings of the Fathers, to illuminate the sacredness of human life. Just look to St. Paulinus of Nola who, in one of the most beautiful verses on human life, wrote: "Do not count yourself as cheap as the stones of Pyrrha or the clay of Prometheus, for the supreme Hand made you lofty in face and mind, and deigned to fashion you in His own image."[92]

But the sons of the devil want to tarnish such a transcendent teaching; they want human life to be rendered cheap, and seen as nothing but an obstacle to their diabolical ends. We are icons of God, we are holy icons, doorways into Heaven, and the wicked heretics in power wish to destroy this holy icon called Man. This is not separation of Church and state, but the subjugation of the Church to the state. There are only two choices that we have: either the state subjugates the Church, or the Church overrides the state in moral and religious issues. Truly, it can be said, that for the Church to be above the state, is the greatest form of separation between Church and state. For in such a condition, Christians are not forced to accept what is deviant and bestial, the state cannot encroach upon the Orthodox morality, and rulers are compelled to honor and protect the wonderful Faith that gave us our civilization.

THE CHURCH CAN OVERTHROW HERETICAL LEADERS, OR RULERS WHO TOLERATE HERESIES

If a king or a ruler is a heretic, or is promulgating, tolerating, or enforcing heretical beliefs, then the Church has the right to excommunicate him, and even overpower his authority. The Dominican theologian, Ulrich of Strasbourg, wrote:

> If the king was manifestly a heretic, or if, prompted by the Church, he nevertheless neglected the administration of his kingdom insofar as matters of faith are concerned, for instance, if

---

90 Hugh of St. Victor, De Sacramentis, book 2, part 2, ch. 4, in Bellarmine, *On the Temporal Power of the Pope*, preface, ed. Tutino, p. 139
91 Alexander of Hales, in Bellarmine, *On the Temporal Power of the Pope*, preface, ed. Tutino, p. 141
92 Paulinus, poem 22

he did not make an effort to eliminate the heretics, he could be deprived of his regal dignity by the Church.[93]

In Christendom, Christians are to always, and only, have Christian rulers, and never heathen or heretical sovereigns. Amongst the Hebrews, the people were to only appoint a Jewish king, "one from among your brethren you shall set as king over you; you may not set a foreigner over you, who is not your brother." (Deuteronomy 17:15)

Because this is a moral law, the same rule applies to Christendom, and so thus Christians are to only appoint Christian rulers. And if the sovereign turns to the devil, the Church has the right to depose of him.[94] And if one is going to argue that this is unbiblical, then why did St. Paul command that temporal causes be settled through Christian judges, and not heathen and pagan judges? To the Corinthians he wrote:

> Dare any of you, having a matter against another, go to law before the unrighteous, and not before the saints? Do you not know that the saints will judge the world? And if the world will be judged by you, are you unworthy to judge the smallest matters? Do you not know that we shall judge angels? How much more, things that pertain to this life? If then you have judgments concerning things pertaining to this life, do you appoint those who are least esteemed by the church to judge? I say this to your shame. Is it so, that there is not a wise man among you, not even one, who will be able to judge between his brethren? But brother goes to law against brother, and that before unbelievers! (1 Corinthians 6:1–6)

If St. Paul commanded that the Church settle disputes in temporal matters amongst Christians, then certainly the Church can be involved in affairs pertaining to the rulers, who are also Christians. Notice how he calls the pagan judges "unrighteous," for from this we know that if it is prohibited for pagan and unrighteous judges to be over Christians, then certainly it is not right for heathen sovereigns to be over a Christian nation. Also observe how the Apostle says, "Do you not know that the saints will judge the world?" He demonstrates the authority of the Church: if the Church is going to judge the world with Christ, then certainly it can judge secular matters which are so inferior to heavenly matters.[95] St. Paul is not commanding the Christians to not appear before a pagan judge when called, but that they should not appeal to a pagan judge initially or spontaneously.[96]

STATEMENTS FROM NUMEROUS THEOLOGIANS OF CHRISTENDOM ON THE CHURCH'S POWER OVER THE STATE

When Christendom was supreme, the Church was superior to the state to the point that if a ruler became anti-Christian, it had the authority to overthrow him and obligate his subjects to disobey and reject him. Many Christians may object to this and say that this is an out-

---

93 Ulrich of Strasbourg, Summa, in Bellarmine, *On the Temporal Power of the Pope*, preface, ed. Tutino, p. 140
94 Bellarmine, *On the Temporal Power of the Pope*, ch. 20, ed. Tutino, p. 287
95 See Bellarmine, *On the Temporal Power of the Pope*, ch. 21, ed. Tutino, pp. 290–291
96 See Bellarmine, *On the Temporal Power of the Pope*, ch. 21, ed. Tutino, p. 293; Aquinas, *Summa Theologiae*, IIa IIae 10, article 8

dated idea. But, these same Christians who object today would not hesitate to support the Crusades, and yet they either forget or ignore the fact that it was a Pope, using his authority over magistrates, who commenced the Crusades, and that without this so-called "archaic" system, there would be no Crusades against Islam.

The idea of the Christian people disobeying or overthrowing a ruler for being anti-Christian, was so widely accepted in Christendom, that it is worthy to quote a number of them to illustrate how much freedom Christian people once held, and how little power governments once maintained.

Pope Innocent III, in the Third Lateran Council, explained the process of excommunicating a ruler for being deliberately tolerant of heretics, and in this case, it was pertaining to Count Raymond VI tolerating the Cathar heretics:

> If then a temporal ruler, after being admonished by the Church, neglects to purge his land of the infamy of heresy, he is to be bound with the chain of excommunication by the Metropolitan bishop and the bishops of the province. And if he does not comply within a year, this will be brought to the notice of the Supreme Pontiff, who from then on may declare his vassals absolved from their loyalty toward him and may declare his land free to be occupied by Catholics who may possess it with no objection once they have exterminated the heretics, and who may keep it in the purity of faith with the right of the princely lord untouched, provided that he presents no obstruction on this and opposes no impediment. [97]

When Christendom was having to endure the onslaught done by the German king Frederick II, a heretic who believed that God created the universe with pre-existing matter, and who preferred Islam over Christianity, Pope Innocent IV conveyed the Council of Lyon, declared him a heretic and had him excommunicated. In the Council it was exclaimed: "We therefore, after careful discussion with our brothers and the holy council about his impious excess which we have before mentioned and many others, since we hold the place of Christ on earth (although unworthy) and since it has been told to us through the person of Peter, 'Whatsoever thou shalt bind on earth shall be bound in heaven,' we declare and announce that the above-mentioned prince, who has rendered himself unworthy of his sovereignty, his kingdom, and every office and dignity, and who, because of his faults, has been debased by God so that he may not rule an empire or a kingdom, is bound to his sins, and that he is debased and deprived of every office and dignity. Furthermore, we deprive him by sentence, absolving perpetually all who are bound to him by an oath of allegiance from such an oath; forbidding strictly, by the apostolic authority, anyone from obeying and devoting himself to him as to his emperor; declaring that whoever hereafter will offer him advice, help, or support as emperor or king is subject immediately to the sentence of excommunication."[98]

---

97 Innocent III, Third Lateran Council, in Bellarmine, *On the Temporal Power of the Pope*, preface, ed. Tutino, pp. 146–147
98 Council of Lyon, in Bellarmine, *On the Temporal Power of the Pope*, preface, ed. Tutino, pp. 147–148

If such stringent rules and punishments were imposed upon the politicians of today, all of the corruptions they cause, and all of the license they have to commit the evils that they do, would be wiped out.

Dionysus the Carthusian wrote that the Pope can depose rulers "if their way of life makes them worthy of being deposed and deprived of their kingdoms."[99] Now imagine if such a rule were forced upon our own rulers; they would think twice before spitting upon the Faith and doing the work of the devil.

The Spanish theologian and political philosopher Francisco de Vitoria, wrote that in regards to spiritual matters, and for the spiritual wellbeing of the people, the Pope "can do not only what the secular princes can do but can also institute new princes and remove others and divide empires."[100] Domingo de Soto, a Dominican scholar from Spain, affirmed that "Any civil authority is subject to the ecclesiastical authority in what concerns spiritual matters, so that the Pope, through his spiritual authority, as often as the concern for the faith and religion urges it, not only can move against the kings with the thunderbolts of ecclesiastical censures and punish them but also can deprive every Christian prince of his temporal goods, and even proceed to the actual deprivation of those things."[101]

Another Spanish theologian, Alfonso de Castro, expressed the same affirmation when he wrote, "And it must not surprise anybody that the Pope can depose a king from his regal office and deprive him of his kingdom because of the crime of heresy, since in matters of faith even kings are subject to the Supreme Pontiff, just like other inferiors."[102] Martin Ledesma, a very learned theologian, said: "Insofar as the spiritual end is concerned, the Pope has the most ample temporal authority over all the princes, kings, and emperors."[103]

Pierre de la Palude, the patriarch of Jerusalem in the 14th century, said that the Pope can depose kings for heresy, malice and evil, and for incompetence when dealing with dangers:

> Even if the Pope does not have the authority to confirm any king who initially acquired the kingdom with the people's consent, nevertheless he can depose any such king not only because of heresy or schism or any other intolerable crime amid his population, but also because of incompetence, that is, if he felt that an inexperienced man or a man with insufficient strength ruled the kingdom, and because of this man's incompetence the realm of the faithful was in danger.[104]

---

99 Dionysus the Carthusian, De regimine politiae, article 19, in Bellarmine, *On the Temporal Power of the Pope*, preface, ed. Tutino, p. 140
100 Vitoria, De potestate Ecclesiae, relectio 1, question 5, proposition 8, in Bellarmine, *On the Temporal Power of the Pope*, preface, ed. Tutino, p. 136
101 Soto, in his commentary on the fourth book of the Sententiae, distinction 25, question 2, article 1, conclusion 5, as quoted by Bellarmine, *On the Temporal Power of the Pope*, preface, ed. Tutino, pp. 136–137
102 Castro, De iusta haereticorum punitione, book 2, ch. 7, in Bellarmine, *On the Temporal Power of the Pope*, preface, ed. Tutino, p. 137
103 Ledesma, Secunda quartae, question 20, article 4, conclusion 8, in Bellarmine, *On the Temporal Power of the Pope*, preface, ed. Tutino, p. 137
104 Pierre de la Palude, De causa immediata ecclesiasticae potestatis, article 4, in Bellarmine, *On the Temporal Power of the Pope*, preface, ed. Tutino, p. 132

CHRISTIANITY IS AT WAR: THE MANIFESTO FOR CHRISTIAN MILITANCY

Jacques Almain, the 16th century professor of theology, specified and explained when the Pope can rightfully depose a ruler: "The Pope can depose the emperor in two cases: first, for a purely spiritual crime, such as heresy, and second, when those who are in charge of deposing him by normal proceedings are negligent in doing it."[105]

Jacobus Simancas said that if a king "issued unjust laws against religion or against morality, or if he did something of this king to the detriment of spiritual matters, the Pope could, in the right conditions, apply a suitable remedy depriving such a prince of his government and jurisdiction."[106]

The Italian scholar of the 13th century, Hostiensis, said, "Consider that the temporal sovereigns can be excommunicated and their lands can be given to Catholics to occupy, not only because of their heretical beliefs, but also if, after being admonished, they neglect to extirpate others' heretical beliefs that they have the possibility to exterminate. The same applies for a prince who might be found negligent in ruling and administering justice."[107]

Christ has the power to depose kings on earth, since He declares, "The Father had given all things into his hands." (John 13:3) And in another place He says to the Father, "as thou hast given him power over all flesh," where all "all flesh" means "all men." (John 17:2) Because His Church is His representative, then it as well has that authority to depose governors and rulers for wickedness. This is what Petrus Bertrandus, a cardinal and bishop of Autun, said when he wrote: "The spiritual authority must dominate every human creature; and as Jesus Christ when He was in this world and even from the eternal world was Lord of nature, and on the basis of natural law could have carried out any sentence of condemnation and deposition against emperors and anybody else, so also His Vicar for the same reason."[108]

Gregory VII refers to the authority of the Church to absolve people from their obligation to obey the state; this is because once the Church excommunicates a ruler, his subjects are no longer obligated to obey him. This is one of the beauties of Christendom: once a king demonstrates his corruption and heretical beliefs, the people are given the liberty, through the might of the Church and the tremendous respect and reverence given to it, to revolt against the tyranny. As John Driedo once wrote, the Pope "can exempt completely the Christian people from obedience and subjection to them in temporal matters."[109] While a king can take the throne without the Church's permission, surely the Church has the right to cast the king out from his throne if he proves himself an enemy to Christianity. As Bartolus of Sassoferrato, an Italian

---

[105] Almain, De suprema potestate ecclesiastica et temporali, second principle question, ch. 5, in Bellarmine, *On the Temporal Power of the Pope*, preface, ed. Tutino, p. 133

[106] Simanacas, De Catholicis institutionibus, title 45, n. 25, in Bellarmine, *On the Temporal Power of the Pope*, preface, ed. Tutino, p. 137

[107] Hostiensis, Summa, section "Qua poena puniantur," n. 11, in Bellarmine, *On the Temporal Power of the Pope*, preface, ed. Tutino, p. 133

[108] Bertrandus, De origine iurisdictionis, question 4, n. 5, in Bellarmine, *On the Temporal Power of the Pope*, preface, ed. Tutino, p. 133

[109] John Driedo, De libertate Christiana, book 1, ch. 14, in Bellarmine, *On the Temporal Power of the Pope*, preface, ed. Tutino, p. 140

law professor of the 14th century wrote, "The princes of Germany have the right to choose the emperor, but only you, the Pope, have the right to depose him."[110] St. Bonaventure wrote,

> Indeed priests and bishops can remove kings and depose emperors for cause, which happened oftentimes and has been seen, for instance, when their malice requires it and the need of the commonwealth demands it.[111]

Pietro Andrea Gambari, another learned theologian from Italy, said, "Only the Pope deposes the emperor and the kings if their crimes persuade him to."[112]

Blessed Agostino Trionfo upheld the Church's right to depose emperors and other rulers of their power:

> Who will go on to deny that the emperor can be deposed by the Pope? Whoever is in charge of putting him on the throne is in charge of deposing him, as those very examples demonstrate.[113]

Pietro del Monte, a bishop of Brescia in the 15th century, maintained this same view in regards to the Church's jurisdiction, writing: "The Pope has a great authority over the emperor, since he deposes him in case of a crime."[114]

St. Antonino, a bishop of Florence, said that "The authority of emperors, kings, and princes is such that it has to be instituted, regulated, and confirmed by the Pope if it is legitimate; and by the Pope it must be judged and condemned if it is not." And in another place he writes that "[the Pope] can depose kings for a reasonable cause."[115] The Dominican Isidoro from Milan, affirms, "The Pope can depose emperors and kings because of their pressing defects."[116]

Silvestro Mazzolini de Prierio, a Dominican who did much work as a theologian and canonist in the 15th century, wrote: "The Pope can excommunicate the emperor who is worthy of being excommunicated, and he can depose the emperor who is worthy of being excommunicated, and he can depose the emperor who is worthy of being deposed."[117]

---

110 Bartolus of Sassoferrato, in his commentary on the law "Si imperialis," chapter "De legibus," section 4, in Bellarmine, *On the Temporal Power of the Pope*, preface, p. 131
111 Boneventure, De ecclesiastics hierarchy, part 2, ch. 1, in Bellarmine, *On the Temporal Power of the Pope*, preface, ed. Tutino, p. 127
112 Gambari, De officio et potestate legati, book 2, title "De variis ordinariorum nominibus," section 220, in Bellarmine, *On the Temporal Power of the Pope*, preface, ed. Tutino, p. 131
113 Agostino Trionfo, De potestate Ecclesiae, question 22, article 3, in Bellarmine, *On the Temporal Power of the Pope*, preface, ed. Tutino, p. 127
114 Pietro del Monte, Monarchia, part 2, question 4, in Bellarmine, *On the Temporal Power of the Pope*, preface, ed. Tutino, p. 129
115 St. Antonino, Summa, part 3, title 22, ch. 3, section 7, in Bellarmine, *On the Temporal Power of the Pope*, preface, ed. Tutino, p. 128
116 Isidoro, De imperii militantis Ecclesiae dignitate, book 2, title 8, conclusion 3, in Bellarmine, *On the Temporal Power of the Pope*, preface, ed. Tutino, p. 128
117 Silvestro Mazzolini de Prierio, Summa Sylvestrina, entry "Pope," n. 10, in Bellarmine, *On the Temporal Power of the Pope*, preface, ed. Tutino, p. 129

Both swords, temporal and spiritual, come together within the Church, as two roles cooperatively working for the same goal that is the perpetuation of Orthodoxy. This is why Petrus de Ancharano wrote, "The Pope has both swords, and he has authority over the empire, and it is for this reason that he crowns, anoints, and sometimes deposes the emperor."[118] St. Bernard shared a very reminiscent belief when he wrote that "the Church has both swords, the spiritual and the material."[119]

St. John of Capistrano affirmed the superiority of the Church over the state, when he said, "The Pope must be superior to the princes in both spiritual and temporal affairs, so that he may be considered worthier for his preeminence and supreme in everything."[120]

THE TWO SWORDS OF ST. PETER, AS CARRIED OUT IN CHRISTENDOM

There are many who argue that the system of government in ancient Israel, in which the Temple guides the state, should be limited only to ancient Israel. But such an idea has no basis in Scripture, and is found wanting when put against the Fathers of the Church. The Church does not begin with the presence of Christ in the world, but with Abel, and continues on throughout history, and it will continue on forever into the eternal new world. Aquinas, writing on the Israelite saints, said: "the ancient Fathers, by observing the sacraments of the Law, were brought toward Christ through the same faith and love by which we are still brought toward him. For this reason the ancient Fathers [of Israel] belonged to the same Body of the Church to which we belong."[121]

Moreover, the authority of Israel is continued in the Church. The Church is called "the Israel of God" by St. Paul (Galatians 6:16); St. Thomas says that "even the Gentiles have become the Israel of God by uprightness of mind;"[122] and St. Chrysostom says that those who are under Christ "shall enjoy peace and amity, and they may properly be called by the name of 'Israel.'"[123] The Lord told Abraham, "In your seed all the nations of the earth shall be blessed," (Genesis 22:18) this would include the governments of these nations, who would then follow the laws of God. The ministry to the Gentiles was to not only be brought to mere civilians, but governments as well, for God referred to St. Paul as "a chosen vessel of Mine to bear My name before Gentiles, kings, and the children of Israel." (Acts 9:15) Governments would turn to Christianity, and in time, form Christendom. Evils that were once esteemed righteous under pagandom, would be deemed evil and worthy of punishment under Christendom; with the change of religion came the change of law.

---

118 Petrus de Ancharano, from his commentary on Gregory IX's Decretales, ch. 6, title 2, De constitutionibus, in Bellarmine, *On the Temporal Power of the Pope*, preface, ed. Tutino, p. 129
119 St. Bernard, *On Consideration*, 4.3
120 St. John of Capistrano, De potentate auctiritate Papae, second principle section, part 2, 18th argument, in Bellarmine, *On the Temporal Power of the Pope*, preface, ed. Tutino, p. 127
121 ST III, q. 8, a. 3, in Scott Carl, Verbum Domini and Complementarity of Exegesis and Theology
122 St. Thomas Aquinas, lectures on Galatians, ch. 6, lecture 5
123 St. Chrysostom, Commentary on Galatians 6:15–16

The state's involvement in physically defending the Church is first mentioned by St. Paul when he exhorts us to pray "for kings and all who are in authority, that we may lead a quiet and peaceable life in all godliness and reverence." (1 Timothy 2:2–4) Notice how he connects the authority of kings with the peace and safety of the Church, signifying that it is the state that protects the Church, through military force, from persecutions.[124] From this safety comes "a quiet and peaceable life in all godliness and reverence." Through security and protection, Christianity is more enabled to flourish and prosper. This passage of St. Paul is a building block for not just protecting the Church from heresies or local persecutions, but for crusading. It is by this verse in 1 Timothy 2:3 that the Christian state has the authority to protect the Church from outside nations that are hostile to the Church, so that her peace and security are maintained. St. John Chrysostom interpreted this passage as such:

> When therefore they [governments] make war for this end, and stand on guard for our security, were it not unreasonable that we should not offer prayers for their safety in wars and dangers? It is not therefore flattery, but agreement to the rules of justice. For if they were not preserved, and prospered in their wars, our affairs must necessarily be involved in confusion and trouble; and if they were cut off, we must either serve ourselves, or be scattered up and down as fugitives. For they are a sort of bulwarks thrown up before us, within which those who are enclosed are in peace and safety. [125]

The righteous preachers of truth strive to promulgate holiness in the society, and it is the job of the knight to protect them, so as to continue and preserve Orthodoxy amongst the people. The knight Ramon Llull wrote that the preachers of God bring the Faith to the Muslims, and since the Muslims strive to destroy Christianity, the knights fight them to protect both the ministers and the Church:

> It is the office of the knight to uphold and defend the Holy Catholic Faith, for which God the Father sent his Son to become flesh in the glorious Virgin, our Lady Saint Mary, and for honouring and preaching the faith he suffered many travails and many wrongs in this world and a cruel death. Thus, just as our Lord God has chosen the clergy to uphold the holy faith through scripture and reason, preaching the faith to the Infidels with such great charity that they are willing to sacrifice their lives for it, so the God of glory has chosen the knights to conquer and overcome by force of arms the Infidels who contrive every day to destroy the holy Church. Therefore, God grants honour in this world and the next to those knights who are the upholders and defenders of the office of God and the faith through which we shall be saved. [126]

In Christendom, the Church strives with all adroitness to protect the Christians, and if that means commencing crusades against the oppressors, to vanquish and destroy their governments, then so be it. As Pope Pius V articulated:

---

124 See St. Robert Bellarmine, *On Laymen or Secular People*, ch. 16, ed. Tutino, p. 77
125 St. John Chrysostom, Homily VI, on Timothy 2:1–4
126 Ramon Llull, Chivalry, 2.2

> He [Christ] established him [St. Peter] alone as prince over all peoples and all kingdoms, so that he may root out, pull down, destroy, throw down, and plant, and build, so that he may preserve in unity of spirit the Christian people, bound with the bond of mutual charity, and present the Christian people safe and sound to its Savior: and performing this duty we, called by God's benignity to the steering oars of this Church, do not spare any effort, etc. [127]

The ecclesiastical authority, who are shepherds over all the sheep of the Church, including the rulers of government, have every right to exhort the state to launch wars and crusades. This is affirmed by St. Robert who said:

> In like manner, also the Roman Pontiffs, who are temporal princes, with every right can and should protect with arms the peoples entrusted to them, and if the situation requires, wage war against the enemies and call other princes for help or to form a coalition in the war. [128]

St. Pope Leo the Great affirmed the emperor Leo Augustus that by him using the temporal sword against the heretical Eutychians, he was maintaining the peace of the Church:

> For since with holy and spiritual zeal you consistently maintain the Church's peace, and nothing is more conductive to the defense of the Faith than to adhere to those things which have been incontrovertibly defined under the unceasing guidance of the Holy Spirit, we shall seem to be doing our best to upset the decrees, and at the bidding of a heretic's petition to overthrow the authorities which the universal Church has adopted, and thus to remove all limits from the conflicts of Churches, and giving full rein to rebellion, to extend rather than appease contentions. [129]

St. Pope Gregory I told the Byzantine general Gennadius: "Just as the Lord of victories made your excellence shine brightly against the enemies of war in this life, so it is necessary that the same excellence is shown against the enemies of His Church with all vigor of mind and body."[130]

In Gratian's Decretum we read that while soldiers who act evilly during their service can't return to the service "unless they come back upon suggestion of their bishops to defend justice."[131] Notice how the bishops have the authority to commission soldiers to defend justice, this would include defending the Church from dangerous enemies and persecutors.

When Theodosius was emperor of the Roman Empire, the bishop of Alexandria, Theophilus, was the one who told him to order the destruction of idols and temples, and he happily fulfilled this request. He issued an order for the demolition of all the pagan temples in Alexandria. The governor and the soldiers of Alexandria assisted in destroying them. The idols were melted to make cooking pots which were then distributed to the poor.[132]

---

127 Quoted by Bellarmine, *On the Temporal Power of the Pope*, ch. 4, ed. Tutino, p. 177, brackets mine
128 Bellarmine, *On the Temporal Power of the Pope*, ch. 11, ed. Tutino, p. 234
129 St. Pope Leo the Great, letter 156, part 1
130 Pope Gregory I, epistle 74, in St. Bellarmine, *On Laymen or Secular People*, ch. 14, ed. Tutino, p. 59
131 Gratian, Decretum, cause 33, distinction 5, as issued by St. Pope Gregory VII at the Synod of Rome in 1078, quoted by St. Robert Bellarmine, *On Laymen or Secular People*, ch. 14, ed. Tutino, pp. 62–63
132 Socrates, 5.16

In early Christendom, in the year 345, the bishop of Alexandria, Athanasius, was being persecuted by the Arian heretics (those who said that Christ was not God); they forcibly removed him from his office as bishop and tried to kill him numerous times. The Arians used the power of the emperor Constantius, who ruled the Eastern parts of the empire, to punish Athanasius. The bishop Athanasius was taken under the protection of Constans, the emperor of the Western parts of the empire, under the order of the Pope, Julius. Constans unsheathed the temporal sword of St. Peter, and threatened his brother that if he did not allow Athanasius to return to his seat in Alexandria, and punish the heretics who were persecuting him, to use his own words, "that I will myself come thither, and restore them to their own sees, in spite of your opposition."[133]

St. Pope Gregory the Great utilized the spiritual sword of his authority to guide the temporal sword of the Byzantine general Gennadius to suppress and force the heretical Donatists from seeping into the Church with their perverse doctrines:

> For it is known that men heretical in religion, if they have liberty allowed them to do harm (which God forbid), rise strenuously against the catholic faith, to the end that they may transfuse, if they can, the poison of their heresy to the corrupting of the members of the Christian body. For we have learnt that they are lifting up their necks against the Catholic Church, the Lord being opposed to them, and desire to pervert the faith of the Christian profession. But let your Eminence suppress their attempts, and subdue their proud necks to the yoke of rectitude.[134]

When the pagans of the Roman Empire were trying to revive paganism within the government, St. Ambrose—the Bishop of Milan—sent letters to the emperors, Theodosius I and Valentinian II, that they as Christians could not permit toleration of the heathen religion, and that the state was obligated to always advance the Laws of God, and not pagans. As St. Ambrose recounted this in his epistle to the tyrant Eugenius, who was himself trying to revive paganism:

> I presented two petitions to the Emperors [Theodosius I and Valentinian II], in which I pointed out that a Christian man could not contribute to the cost of the [pagan] sacrifices; that I indeed had not been the cause of their being abolished, but I certainly did urge that they should not be decreed; and lastly, that he himself would seem to be giving not restoring those sums to the images. But you know that we must constantly act in the cause of God, as is often done in the cause of liberty, also not only by priests, but also by those who are in your armies, or are reckoned in the number of those who dwell in the provinces. Though the imperial power be great, yet consider, O Emperor, how great God is. He sees the hearts of all, He questions the inmost conscience, He knows all things before they happen, He knows the inmost things of your breast. You do not suffer yourselves to be deceived, and do you desire to conceal anything from God? Has not this come into your mind? For although they acted with such perseverance, was it not your duty, O Emperor, to resist with still greater

---
133 Quoted in Socrates, 2.22
134 St. Pope Gregory the Great, epistle 74

perseverance because of the reverence due to the most high and true and living God, and to refuse what was an offense against His holy law? Although you are Emperor, you ought to be all the more subject to God. How shall the ministers of Christ dispense your gifts? [135]

St. Gregory the Great used his spiritual authority to prevent certain soldiers from abusing poor civilians. The top military commander, Theodorus, and his men were persecuting the poor of the city of Turris in Sardinia by physically abusing them, imposing heavy and brutal taxes on them, and also by casting them into prison. They hence were breaking the Rule of St. John the Baptist when he told the soldiers "Do not intimidate anyone or accuse falsely, and be content with your wages," (Luke 3:14) But to uphold this holy rule was St. Pope Gregory the Great who, unsheathing the spiritual sword, commanded the Byzantine general Gennadius to use his temporal authority to order Theodorus and his men to cease their tyranny:

> Now Marinianus, our brother and fellow-bishop of the city of Turris has tearfully represented to us that the poor of his city are being vexed everywhere, and afflicted by expenses in the way of gifts or payments; and further that the religious of his church endure serious molestation from the men of Theodorus the magister militia, and suffer bodily injuries; and that this thing is breaking out to such a pitch that (shocking to say) they are thrust into prison, and that he himself also is seriously hindered by the aforesaid glorious person in causes pertaining to His Church. How opposed such things are, if indeed they are true, to the discipline of the republic you yourselves know. And, since it befits your Excellency to amend all these things, greeting your Eminence I demand of you that you suffer them to be done no more; but straightly order him to abstain from harming the Church, and that none be aggrieved by burdens laid upon them, beyond what reason allows, and that, if there should be any suits, they be determined not by the terror of power, but by the order of the law. I pray you, then, so correct all these things, the Lord inspiring you, by the menace of your injunction that the glorious Theodorus and his men may abstain from such things, if not out of regard to rectitude, yet at any rate out of fear inspired by your command [136]

St. Gregory of Tours called for the kings of France to stop fighting amongst themselves in civil wars and turn to war with the heathens, the enemies of Christendom, referencing king Clovis who defeated the Arian heretics in France years before them:

> If only you kings had occupied yourselves with wars like those in which your ancestors larded the ground with their sweat, then the other races of the earth, filled with awe at the peace which you imposed, might have been subjected to your power! Just think of all that Clovis achieved, Clovis the founder of your victorious country, who slaughtered those rulers who opposed him, conquered hostile peoples and captured their territories, thus bequeathing to you absolute and unquestioned dominion over them! At the time when he accomplished all this, he possessed neither gold nor silver such as you have in your storehouses! But you, what are you doing? What are you trying to do? You have everything you want! Your homes are full of luxuries, there are vast supplies of wine, grain and oil in your

---

135 St. Ambrose, letter 52, 2, 4, 6–7, 8, ellipses and brackets mine
136 St. Pope Gregory the Great, epistle 61

store-houses, and in your treasuries the gold and silver are piled high. Only one thing is lacking: you cannot keep peace, and therefore you do not know the grace of God. [137]

Notice how this saint specifies that while the government is flourishing with gold, it is missing God, and thus from this it is more damaging to itself than good. The state, then, must not be secular in Christendom, but Christian, with the Church exhorting it to righteousness, as St. Gregory did unto the kings of France.

Pope Leo I wrote to the emperor Leo that he, with his temporal authority, must protect the Church from Eutychians, a wicked sect in Alexandria who rejected the humanity of Christ and also murdered and cannibalized a bishop who condemned them:

> For since the Lord has enriched your clemency with such insight into His mystery, you ought unhesitatingly to consider that the kingly power has been conferred on you not for the governance of the world alone but more especially for the guardianship of the Church: that by quelling wicked attempts you may both defend that which has been rightly decreed, and restore true peace where there has been disturbance, that is to say by deposing usurpers of the rights of others and reinstating the ancient Faith of the See of Alexandria, that by your reforms God's wrath may be appeased, and so He take not vengeance for their doings on a people hitherto religious, but forgive them. Set before the eyes of your heart, venerable Emperor, the fact that all the Lord's priests which are in the world, are beseeching you on behalf of that Faith, wherein is Redemption for the whole world. [138]

Notice how St. Leo states that the king punishing the heretics would be done so that "God's wrath may be appeased," and this is in accordance to how St. Paul described the ruler as an "avenger to execute wrath on him who practices evil." (Romans 13:4) For the emperor to punish the wicked cult, meant unleashing the wrath of Heaven.

Pope Anastasius II exhorted the emperor, Anastasius, to use the temporal sword to drive back certain schismatics in Alexandria into the Catholic Church:

> I urge on Your Serenity especially this, that when the reasons of the Alexandrines reach your most pious ears, you will drive them back to the Catholic and true faith with your authority, wisdom, and sacred commands. [139]

After Vladmir became Russia's first Christian king, the bishops of the Church told him that he must punish all of the robbers in the land, for he was appointed by God to punish the wicked. As we read from the Russian Primary Chronicle:

> While Vladmir was thus dwelling in the fear of God, the number of bandits increased, and the bishops, calling to his attention the multiplication of robbers, inquired why he did not punish them. The Prince answered that he feared the sin entailed. They replied that he was appointed by God for the chastisement of malefaction and for the practice of mercy toward

---

[137] St. Gregory of Tours, 5.1, trans. Thorpe
[138] St. Pope Leo the Great, letter 156, part 3, trans. Feltoe. See also St. Robert Bellarmine, *On Laymen or Secular People*, ch. 18, ed. Tutino, p. 83
[139] Quoted by St. Robert Bellarmine, *On Laymen or Secular People*, ch. 18, ed. Tutino, pp. 83-84

the righteous, so that it was entirely fitting for him to punish a robber condignly, but only after due process of law. Vladmir accordingly abolished wergild [injury lawsuits] and set out to punish the brigands. The bishops and the elders then suggested that as wars were frequent, the wergild might be properly spent for the purchase of arms and horses, to which Vladmir assented.[140]

When the dualist heretic Priscillian, and most of his followers, were executed for heresy, his execution was done to the aid of the Church, for when such evildoers are killed, people who belief such falsehoods in fear of capital punishment will turn to the spiritual healing of the Church as opposed to remaining in their error. St. Leo the Great praised the execution of this cult:

> And this rigorous treatment was for long a help to the Church's law of gentleness which, although it relies upon the priestly judgment, and shuns the blood-stained vengeance, yet is assisted by the stern decrees of Christian princes at times when men, who dread bodily punishment, have recourse to merely spiritual correction.[141]

In the year 1073, Pope St. Gregory VII had the count, Evulus of Roucy, enter Spain and fight the Muslims out of Christian territory and retake it for Christendom. In his letter written to the barons of France, he wrote:

> He has received a grant from the Apostolic See to this effect: that he should hold in the name of St. Peter those lands from which he could drive the pagans by his own exertions and with the help of others, under the conditions of an agreement made between us.[142]

The same glorious saint wrote an epistle to King Philip I, exhorting him to protect the church in Beauvais from persecution:

> Since therefore you stand forth as the sole heir to the nobility and glory before God and men of those who were before you in the kingship, we exhort you to imitate their virtues and, fulfilling the divine justice with all your strength, to restore and maintain the churches as far as you are able, that Almighty God may protect and exalt the government of your kingdom by the right hand of his power and may grant you the crown of everlasting glory as your reward in the life to come.[143]

When Sir Lancelin of Beauvais kidnapped Fulcher of Chartres, Pope St. Gregory VII did not just stand there, but threatened the persecutor with both the authority of the Church and the temporal punishments of the state. He wrote to the clergy in France: "If he refuses to do this do you proceed against him with both secular and spiritual weapons until you have compelled him to set free this pilgrim of St. Peter and to restore or refuse to accept whatever ransom he may have received or contracted for."[144]

---

140 *Russian Primary Chronicle*, Laurentian Text, 126, brackets mine
141 Leo the Great, letter 15, ch. 1
142 Gregory, book 1, 7, p. 11
143 Gregory VII, book 1, 77, p. 109
144 Gregory VII, b. 2, 5, p. 130

In the thirteenth century, when the Church was dealing with the onslaughts of the Cathar heretics, and the persecutions of the Muslims, Pope Innocent III made it emphatic that he would go out of his way to urge governments to combat these evil people:

> I will 'pass over' to kings, and princes, and peoples, and nations—and indeed even beyond, to arouse them with a mighty cry—so they will rise up to fight the fight of the Lord and redress the injury of the Crucified One. [145]

Pope Innocent III used the authority of the spiritual sword to exhort Christian governments to unsheathe the temporal sword, so as to protect the true Faith, the Church, and Christian civilization.

SEPARATION OF CHURCH AND STATE

The heretics will argue that sin should not be punished because "that's God's job," as they say. The state, as many of them believe, should work to reform criminals by "giving them the Gospel" and not punish them. The government, in the utopia of these heretics, essentially becomes the Church, because it is now in charge of the salvation of criminals, and not the protection of the Church. In Orthodoxy, the job of the state is to protect the Church from criminals, for St. Paul commands that we pray "for kings and all who are in authority, that we may lead a quiet and peaceable life in all godliness and reverence" (1 Timothy 2:2), and it is the Church's position to guide the people to salvation. So great is the separation between Church and State within Christendom that when the state begins to attack Christian truth, the Christian is to defy such tyranny with so much zeal and exertion that he is to be willing to die for the Faith. As St. Gregory VII wrote:

> It were better for us, if need were, to pay the debt of mortality at the hands of tyrants rather than to consent in silence to the ruin of the Christian law through fear or for any advantage. [146]

But the heretics want to break this separation, and thus they take almost the opposite view, making the state all of a sudden the distributor of salvation as opposed to being the protector of the Church, who is the bringer of the Gospel. This modern Christian view of government was very much propagated in the Protestant Reformation. Melanchthon, one of the most prestigious of Protestant Reformers, said that "The prince is God's chief bishop (summus episcopus) in the Church,"[147] and said that the state should not only be protectors of Christians and Christianity, but the judges and the teachers of the Faith, to preside over ecclesiastical councils, and to appoint ministers and pastors. Today we have the state dictating the definitions of life and marriage—all theological matters—to the point that they force Christians to accept their definitions, and then the state says that this does not contradict their Faith. In other words, the state has become God. The Church and the State

---

145 Pope Innocent III, sermon 6: Fourth General Council of the Lateran
146 Gregory VII, book 4, 1, p. 289
147 Quoted in John Witte, *Law and Protestantism*, ch. 4 p. 137

need a separation, and to argue otherwise would render the Church worthless and the State supreme.

Not surprisingly, the Protestant attempt to overthrow the Pope ended up with them simply replacing the Pope with a king. While this was taught by Protestants, the Catholic saint, Robert Bellarmine, made the distinction that lies between the ruler and the Church when he wrote that "kings have the first place among Christians as Christian men, that is, citizens of the earthly city, but not as fellow citizens among the saints and servants of God, nor as members of the Church."[148] In another book he wrote, "God wanted a political government among men, and He wanted this to be distinct from the ecclesiastical."[149] Francisco de Vitoria, who combated much of the Protestant errors, wrote,

> We have the words of Matthew to the effect that the 'keys of the kingdom' of heaven belong to the Church (Matt. 16:19, 18:18). This power is therefore different from civil power, since the civil power certainly does not hold the keys of the kingdom of heaven.[150]

Christ gave the authority over the Church to St. Peter and the Apostles, and to their successors, not to the Caesar.[151] The Church already had a system of separation of Church and State, and there was no need for a new one. The separation between Church and state formulated in Christendom was clearly explained by Hosius, the bishop of Cordoba in the fourth century, when he wrote addressing the temporal lords:

> To you God entrusted the empire, and to us He committed matters of the Church; and just as whoever steals the empire from you goes against the divine order, so beware of rendering yourself guilty of a great crime by allocating for yourself what is the Church's. It is written: 'Render to Caesar the things that are Caesar's and to God the things that are God's.' Therefore it is not lawful for us to hold the empire on earth and for you, as emperor, to hold the authority of burning incense and performing sacred rites.[152]

In one canon of the Church, the Si imperator of the Decretum, we read, "If the emperor is catholic, he is a son of the church, not its head; as far as religion is concerned, it is his duty to learn, not to teach; he has the privileges of his power, which he has been given by God for the administering of civil laws."[153]

The authorities of the Church cannot be priests and emperors at the same time, and nor can the first usurp the power of the second. St. Bernard of Clairvaux, in a letter addressed to Pope Eugenius II, wrote that the pope can never be a temporal lord,

> What else did the holy Apostle leave you? 'I give you', he said, 'What I have' (Acts 3:6). And what was that? One thing I know; 'silver and gold had he none.' These, I grant, you

---

148 St. Robert Bellarmine, *On Laymen or Secular People*, ch. 17, ed. Tutino, p. 79
149 Bellarmine, *On the Temporal Power of the Pope*, ch. 5, ed. Tutino, p. 187
150 Vitoria, *Reflection 1 On the Power of the Church*, question 1, article 1, 6
151 St. Robert Bellarmine, *On Laymen or Secular People*, ch. 17, ed. Tutino, p. 80
152 Hosius, as recorded by St. Athanasius, in Bellarmine, *On the Temporal Power of the Pope*, ch. 2, ed. Tutino, pp. 155–156
153 Si imperator, Decretum D. 96. 11, in Vitoria, *Reflection 1 On the Power of the Church*, question 1, article 1, 11

may claim by any other argument you like, but not by apostolic right, for Peter could not give you what he did not have. He gave what he had, 'the care', as he said, 'of all the church' (2 Cor. 11:28). And did he not give the power of condemnation? Listen to his own words again: 'neither as being lords over God's heritage, but being ensamples to the flock' (1 Pet. 5:3). Lest you think this was said in mere modesty, not in truth, there are the words of the Lord in the Gospel: 'the princes of the Gentiles exercise dominion over them, and they that are great exercise authority upon them; but shall not be so among you' (Matt. 25–6; Luke 22:25). This clearly prohibits the apostles from exercising dominion. How, then, do you dare arrogate to yourself both the apostleship of the lords and the lordship of the apostles? You are clearly prohibited from one of the two; if you try to have both together, you will destroy each in turn. Otherwise, believe me, you will not be exempt from the number of those of whom God said 'They set up kings, but not by me; they have made princes, and I knew them not' (Hos. 8:4). The apostolic example is that domination is banned, ministry planned. [154]

In the same letter St. Bernard wrote to the Pope, "Your power is in judging sins, not possessions; it is for sins that you received the keys of the kingdom of heaven. These miserable trifles of the earth have their own judges, earthly rulers."[155] Pope Innocent III said in one of his decretals, "We do not intend to be judge of fiefs, whose judgement belongs to him (that is, the king)."[156] Instead, the purpose of the Church is to remove heretics from the sheepfold. Hence, St. Bernard says: "The prophet does not rise to reign, but to root out the weeds."[157]

This separation of Church and State was observed amongst the Hebrews. In ancient Israel the king was not allowed to burn incense, since that was the priest's commission. When King Uzziah wanted to burn incense himself, the priests defied his intrusions, not showing any sycophantic or obsequious expression of servitude but illustrating that command of St. Peter and the Apostles, "We ought to obey God rather than men" (Acts 5:29), and drove the king out once God had struck him with leprosy:

> So Azariah the priest went in after him, and with him were eighty priests of the Lord—valiant men. And they withstood King Uzziah, and said to him, 'It is not for you, Uzziah, to burn incense to the Lord, but for the priests, the sons of Aaron, who are consecrated to burn incense. Get out of the sanctuary, for you have trespassed! You shall have no honor from the Lord God.' Then Uzziah became furious, as he had a censer in his hand to burn incense. While he was angry with the priests, leprosy broke out on his forehead before the priests in the house of the Lord beside the incense altar. Azariah the chief priest and all the priests looked at him, and there, on his forehead, he was leprous; so they thrust him out of that place. Indeed he also hurried to get out, because the Lord had struck him. (2 Chronicles 26:17–20)

---

154 St. Bernard, *On Consideration*, 2.9–11, in Vitoria, *Reflection 1 on the Power of the Church*, question 5, article 1, 2
155 St. Bernard, *On Consideration*, 2.9–11, in Vitoria, *Reflection 1 On the Power of the Church*, question 5, article 3, 5
156 Pope Innocent III, Nouit (X. 2. 1. 13), in Vitoria, *Reflection 1 On the Power of the Church*, question 5, article 3, 5
157 Bernard, *On Consideration*, 2.6

Similarly, St. Ambrose forbade the emperor Theodosius from standing in the room of the priests within the church.[158] Only the priests had the authority to make burnt offerings unto God, for this was part of their office. When king Saul made a sacrifice in Samuel's absence, Samuel was so upset that he, acting as God's representative, declared that he would no longer be king:

> Then he waited seven days, according to the time set by Samuel. But Samuel did not come to Gilgal; and the people were scattered from him. So Saul said, 'Bring a burnt offering and peace offerings here to me.' And he offered the burnt offering. Now it happened, as soon as he had finished presenting the burnt offering, that Samuel came; and Saul went out to meet him, that he might greet him.
>
> And Samuel said, 'What have you done?'
>
> Saul said, 'When I saw that the people were scattered from me, and that you did not come within the days appointed, and that the Philistines gathered together at Michmash, then I said, The Philistines will now come down on me at Gilgal, and I have not made supplication to the Lord. Therefore I felt compelled, and offered a burnt offering.'
>
> And Samuel said to Saul, 'You have done foolishly. You have not kept the commandment of the Lord your God, which He commanded you. For now the Lord would have established your kingdom over Israel forever. But now your kingdom shall not continue. The Lord has sought for Himself a man after His own heart, and the Lord has commanded him to be commander over His people, because you have not kept what the Lord commanded you.' (1 Samuel 13:8–14)

That the priests had expressed and demonstrated such resilience to the king's encroachment on the priestly office, shows how severe the separation was between the Church and the State. The state cannot overrun the sacred grounds of the priests, and while the Church cannot dictate, for the most part, the office of the government, it can most definitely unsheathe the spiritual sword and command the state to utilize its authority to maintain and enforce Orthodoxy, and all things pertaining to the soul of the nation.

This is why the Church itself can reject its leader if he falls into spiritual harlotry, and this was even declared by a pope, Innocent III, who said:

> The Roman church can dismiss the Roman pontiff only because of fornication—I mean not carnal, but spiritual fornication, for the marriage is not carnal but spiritual—and this fornication is the sin of heresy.[159]

All of these examples show that the common accusation, that the Catholic Church was after sole power and domination, are false. What they also show is that the separation between the Church and the State in Christendom is so wide that it leaves the Church to do

---

158 St. Gregory VII, To Bishop Hermann of Metz, in *Defense of the Excommunication of Henry IV*, book iv, 2, p. 293
159 Pope Innocent III, sermon 3: *On the First Anniversary*

its job to the fullest without any government restraints, and it leaves the State free to conduct its purpose—not to dictate theology, but to protect the nation—and in doing so, it protects the Faith, the pillar of civilization.

THE CHURCH HAS THE RIGHT TO REBEL IF THE STATE INTRUDES UPON IT

In Christendom, the state never treads upon the functions of the ecclesiastical office, and if a tyrant ever were to do so and attempted to suppress the worship of God, the Church has every right under Heaven to rebel through the spiritual sword and through the liberties bestowed upon it by God. For when Sanballat the Horonite, Tobiah the Ammonite official, and Geshem the Arab mockingly told Nehemiah when he was organizing the rebuilding of the Temple, "What is this thing that you are doing? Will you rebel against the king?" (Nehemiah 2:19) Nehemiah declared the authority of God over man,

> The God of heaven Himself will prosper us; therefore we His servants will arise and build, but you have no heritage or right or memorial in Jerusalem. (Nehemiah 2:20)

In other words, the will of Heaven overrode the will of the State. This right never left the Church at the advent of Christ but remained. For when the Jewish leaders commanded St. Peter and the Apostles to no longer preach Jesus, the fulfilled Temple, they did not respond with servitude but with might, with these holy words: "We ought to obey God rather than men." (Acts 5:29)

This defiance against state intrusion over the Church was done in Christendom. St. Gregory VII ordered the clergy in France to confront the tyrant Philip I, and expose all of his evils right in his presence: "Address the king jointly upon the peril of the kingdom and of himself. Show him to his face how criminal are his deeds and his policies."[160]

THE CHURCH IS NOT TO GIVE THE STATE ORDERS THAT DO NOT PERTAIN TO SPIRITUAL MATTERS

Now, if the Church commands a government to fulfill a temporal command, and not a spiritual goal, then it is not to be obeyed, because in this case it is encroaching on non-spiritual matters. Vitoria articulated this scenario as such:

> were the pope to declare such a policy inexpedient to the temporal government of the commonwealth, he should not be heeded. Such judgement belongs not to him but to the prince, and even if his judgment were true it would have nothing of papal authority. So long as a thing is not incompatible with the salvation of souls and religion, the pope's office is not involved. But if the pope declares that a policy works to the detriment of spiritual salvation—for instance, because a particular statute cannot be kept without mortal sin, is against divine law, or foments sin—then the pope's judgment is the one to be relied upon, since the king has no jurisdiction in spiritual matters, as I said before.[161]

---

160 Gregory VII, b. 2, 5, p. 130
161 Vitoria, *Reflection 1 On the Power of the Church*, question 5, article 9, 14

The Catholic theologian and cardinal, Thomas Cajetan, affirmed that the state may even resist the Church authorities if they are committing certain acts of corruption, such as simony, or recklessly spending church funds, since no obedience is owed to such wicked deeds.[162] Moreover, the priests and the bishops are not exempt from law, and if they break any just laws, they have committed sin and should be punished equally before justice.[163]

---

[162] Cajetan, De comparatione auctoritatis papae et concilii 27, in Vitoria, *Reflection 1 On the Power of the Church*, question 6, article 4, 4
[163] See Vitoria, *Reflection 1 On the Power of the Church*, Question 6, article 4, 4

PART 7 – PRIESTS AND WAR

In ancient Israel there were the priests, the prophets, and the holy men who lived as hermits in the wilderness, and they were very powerful and influential in the Lord's wars. Christendom carried on this beautiful system, in which the political and religious offices, and the role of holy men, were intricate in holy war. Within Christendom, there are prophets, saints, priests, monks, and hermits, who greatly partake in holy wars against pagans and heretics, through their prayers and their intercessions, and even at times, with their own valor.

Priests were not removed but in the battles, fighting the forces of darkness with their prayers, interceding for the armies so as to obtain victory as the soldiers fought the followers of darkness with their swords. St. Bernard wrote that the priests of the Church are to be persons "who in the eyes of kings are as John [the Baptist], to the Egyptians as Moses, to fornicators as Phinees, to idolaters as Elijah, to the covetous as Elisha, to liars as Peter, to blasphemers as Paul, to traffickers as Christ."[1] No coward can be a priest. The majority of the priests today are lazy servants or wicked men who conspire like Judas with the devil to aid the enemy. The priest must be a warrior, ever willing to battle against the demons—the enemies of humankind—and enthusiastic to support and hail the destruction of the wicked.

THE PRIESTS' INVOLVEMENT IN WARS IN ANCIENT ISRAEL

The wandering holy men of the wilderness, who resided in caves and on mountain tops, amongst nature's mists, in the awe inspiring silence of solitude, and in the sacred connection seclusion from the vagueness of humanity brings to the mind, were the mouthpieces of God to bring revelation to kings weary of their impending battles.

---

1 Bernard, *On Consideration*, 4.4

The monastic who fed off coarse foods, and within the walls of a modest monastery, under the skies and encompassed by forests and meadows, and lofty hills of a faraway land, spent entire years subduing their bodies, assiduously observing the words of St. Paul, "I discipline my body and bring it into subjection" (1 Corinthians 9:27), and in doing so, they cultivated a distinct connection with God. Because their flesh was under the power of the spirit, their souls ascended to the heavenly place, being closer to God than kings and governors. Thus, it was to them that rulers flocked, to learn from them the will of God, and what Heaven desired of them.

This is illustrated by the story of David consulting with Abiathar to ask of God whether he should go to war against the Amelekites, with the words, "Shall I pursue this troop? Shall I overtake them?" (1 Samuel 30:8)

Before Ahab went to war against Syria, an unknown prophet approached him and gave him the will of God that declared that he was to lead the battle:

> Suddenly a prophet approached Ahab king of Israel, saying, 'Thus says the Lord: Have you seen all this great multitude? Behold, I will deliver it into your hand today, and you shall know that I am the Lord.'
>
> So Ahab said, 'By whom?'
>
> And he said, 'Thus says the Lord: By the young leaders of the provinces.'
>
> Then he said, 'Who will set the battle in order?'
>
> And he answered, 'You.' (1 Kings 20:13–14)

The priests would also mediate between the armies and God, praying for victory. The holy prophet Samuel declared his prayers and offered a sacrifice to be as an intercessor between the nation and God, and thus to receive victory against the pagan Philistines, as the Scriptures bear witness:

> And the children of Israel said to Samuel, Cease not to cry unto the Lord our God for us, that he will save us out of the hand of the Philistines. And Samuel took a sucking lamb, and offered it for a burnt offering wholly unto the Lord: and Samuel cried unto the Lord for Israel; and the Lord heard him. And as Samuel was offering up the burnt offering, the Philistines drew near to battle against Israel: but the Lord thundered with a great thunder on that day upon the Philistines, and discomfited them; and they were smitten before Israel. And the men of Israel went out of Mizpeh, and pursued the Philistines, and smote them, until they came under Bethcar. (I Samuel 7:8–11)

The priest acts as a mediator between God and the world, giving the king God's will for the war. As we read in another passage, an anonymous holy man, who was called "a man of God," approached Ahab and affirmed that the Lord will deliver the enemy unto his hands:

> Then a man of God came and spoke to the king of Israel, and said, "Thus says the Lord: Because the Syrians have said, "The Lord is God of the hills, but He is not God of the valleys,

therefore I will deliver all this great multitude into your hand, and you shall know that I am the Lord. And they encamped opposite each other for seven days. So it was that on the seventh day the battle was joined; and the children of Israel killed one hundred thousand foot soldiers of the Syrians in one day. But the rest fled to Aphek, into the city; then a wall fell on twenty-seven thousand of the men who were left. (1 King 20:28–30)

Before the king went to war, there was always a mediator between God and the state, to instruct the king on the divine will. The demand for the prophet in times of war was one of great urgency. When the king of Israel was to go to war against Syria, he sent for the prophet Micaiah to reveal to him the divine plan, as the Scriptures recount:

> Then he came to the king; and the king said to him, "Micaiah, shall we go to war against Ramoth Gilead, or shall we refrain?" And he answered him, "Go and prosper, for the Lord will deliver it into the hand of the king!

So the king said to him, "How many times shall I make you swear that you tell me nothing but the truth in the name of the Lord?" Then he said, "I saw all Israel scattered on the mountains, as sheep that have no shepherd. And the Lord said, 'These have no master. Let each return to his house in peace.'" And the king of Israel said to Jehoshaphat, "Did I not tell you he would not prophesy good concerning me, but evil?" Then Micaiah said, "Therefore hear the word of the Lord: I saw the Lord sitting on His throne, and all the host of heaven standing by, on His right hand and on His left. And the Lord said, Who will persuade Ahab to go up, that he may fall at Ramoth Gilead? So one spoke in this manner, and another spoke in that manner. Then a spirit came forward and stood before the Lord, and said, I will persuade him. The Lord said to him, In what way? So he said, I will go out and be a lying spirit in the mouth of all his prophets. And the Lord said, You shall persuade him, and also prevail. Go out and do so. Therefore look! The Lord has put a lying spirit in the mouth of all these prophets of yours, and the Lord has declared disaster against you." (1 Kings 22:15–23)

When Judah was about to fight Moab, Ammon, and Mount Seir, the priest Jahaziel, acting as a mediator between Heaven and earth, prophesied to the armies that they would not have to fight because God would destroy the enemy himself:

> Listen, all you of Judah and you inhabitants of Jerusalem, and you, King Jehoshaphat! Thus says the Lord to you: Do not be afraid nor dismayed because of this great multitude, for the battle is not yours, but God's. Tomorrow go down against them. They will surely come up by the Ascent of Ziz, and you will find them at the end of the brook before the Wilderness of Jeruel. You will not need to fight in this battle. Position yourselves, stand still and see the salvation of the Lord, who is with you, O Judah and Jerusalem! Do not fear or be dismayed; tomorrow go out against them, for the Lord is with you. (2 Chronicles 20:15–17)

Before the battle, God stirred the hearts of the enemy to all of a sudden be suspicious toward one another, and by the time the Hebrews came to the battlefield, all of the pagans were dead because they killed each other.

When the Moabite Mesha rebelled against Israel, it was the prophet Elisha who prognosticated to them that the victory over the pagans was theirs, saying:

> And this is a simple matter in the sight of the Lord; He will also deliver the Moabites into your hand. Also you shall attack every fortified city and every choice city, and shall cut down every good tree, and stop up every spring of water, and ruin every good piece of land with stones. (2 Kings 3:18–19)

Elisha, acting as the mouthpiece of God, prophesied to the king that he will smite the Syrians at Aphek, and that it was the will of God that he strike them until the enemy was destroyed.

> And Elisha said to him, 'Take a bow and some arrows. So he took himself a bow and some arrows. Then he said to the king of Israel,' 'Put your hand on the bow.' So he put his hand on it, and Elisha put his hands on the king's hands. And he said, 'Open the east window;' and he opened it. Then Elisha said, 'Shoot;' and he shot. And he said, 'The arrow of the Lord's deliverance and the arrow of deliverance from Syria; for you must strike the Syrians at Aphek till you have destroyed them.' (2 Kings 13:15–17)

THE PRIESTS' INFLUENCE IN WAR

After Saul resolved to go to war with the Philistines, the priest declared, "Let us draw near unto God," (1 Samuel 14:36), exhibiting the priest's spiritual authority as a mediator in matters of war.

When Israel fought in the holy war against the Ammonites, the men of Israel were ordered to go forth both to King Saul and the prophet Samuel and go with them into battle, showing most clearly how the state and the Church cooperated in war, as the sun provides light to the moon. As we read in Scriptures:

> Then the Spirit of God came upon Saul when he heard this news, and his anger was greatly aroused. So he took a yoke of oxen and cut them in pieces, and sent them throughout all the territory of Israel by the hands of messengers, saying, "Whoever does not go out with Saul and Samuel to battle, so it shall be done to his oxen. And the fear of the Lord fell on the people, and they came out with one consent. When he numbered them in Bezek, the children of Israel were three hundred thousand, and the men of Judah thirty thousand. And they said to the messengers who came, "Thus you shall say to the men of Jabesh Gilead: Tomorrow, by the time the sun is hot, you shall have help. Then the messengers came and reported it to the men of Jabesh, and they were glad. Therefore the men of Jabesh said, "Tomorrow we will come out to you, and you may do with us whatever seems good to you. So it was, on the next day, that Saul put the people in three companies; and they came into the midst of the camp in the morning watch, and killed Ammonites until the heat of the day. And it happened that those who survived were scattered, so that no two of them were left together. Then the people said to Samuel, "Who is he who said, Shall Saul reign over us? Bring the men, that we may put them to death. (1 Samuel 11:6–12)

Here we see the significant positions of both the king and the priest in war; they are not separated, and nor are wars secular, but religious, with the two offices working together to obtain victory over evil people, to crush the enemies of God and the forces of darkness.

When the armies of Jeroboam ambushed the armies of Judah, "the priests sounded the trumpets. Then the men of Judah gave a shout; and as the men of Judah shouted, it happened that God struck Jeroboam and all Israel before Abijah and Judah. And the children of Israel fled before Judah, and God delivered them into their hand." (2 Chronicles 13:14–16)

PRIESTS CAN LEAD SOLDIERS TO FIGHT TYRANNY

One of the greatest examples of the Church using warriors to fight pagan tyranny and preserve orthodoxy within the state, is that of the priest Jehoiada. In his time the entire religious authority was under the pagan despotism of Queen Athaliah and her sons, as we read in Chronicles:

> For the sons of Athaliah, that wicked woman, had broken into the house of God, and had also presented all the dedicated things of the house of the Lord to the Baals. (2 Chronicles 24:7)

Athaliah bombarded the Temple with the worship of Baal, and not only that, but she kidnapped the infant Joash, who was the rightful heir of the throne, and kept him in captivity for six years. The priest Jehoiada used the temporal sword to rescue the infant king, when he "sent and brought the captains of hundreds of the bodyguards and the escorts and brought them into the house of the Lord to him. And he made a covenant with them and took an oath from them in the house of the Lord, and showed them the king's son." (2 Kings 11:4)

It was the priest, and not some secular politician, who organized a meeting with the warriors on how they were going to rescue the king from the rapacious hands of Athaliah. Jehoiada commanded the men to guard the king, and ordered that whoever came too close, was to be immediately killed:

> But you shall surround the king on all sides, every man with his weapons in his hand; and whoever comes within range, let him be put to death. You are to be with the king as he goes out and as he comes in. (2 Kings 11:8)

It was the priest Jehoiada, and not a man of a secular office, who made such orders, and not only that, but he even provided the warriors with weapons, as the Scriptures tell us:

> And the priest gave the captains of hundreds the spears and shields which had belonged to King David that were in the temple of the Lord. (2 Kings 11:10)

The priest gives the warriors the weapons, and the order to defend the king, and we have a template for Christendom, in which the Church has the authority to use or organize military force to protect the soul of the nation from false and pernicious ideologies. When Jehoiada brought forth the infant king, all of the men clapped their hands and cried out, "Long live the king!" (2 Kings 11:12) Here lies a perfect image of that command of St. Peter,

> Honor all people. Love the brotherhood. Fear God. Honor the king. (1 Peter 2:17)

The priest and all of his men honored all people, by breaking the shackles of tyranny so that the people could have the liberty to worship God; they loved the brotherhood because they were willing to fight for the holy priesthood, and to destroy the successors of Cain who wished to obliterate the sacred altar of Abel; they feared God, for they took up arms and put their lives on the line of sacrifice in order to see to it that God's Divine Law dominated the land, and that orthodoxy triumphed over heresy. They honored the king, since they harbored the flames of zeal to protect the infant who was destined by Heaven to reign. Here lies the spirit of Christendom, and on its banners should be embroidered the command of St. Peter, for it is in Christendom that the Church, pertaining to the things of religion and the soul of the nation, holds the authority to commence holy war against the enemies of Orthodoxy, and to utilize military force to protect its flock.

After Jehoiada placed the crown on Joash's head and anointed him as king, and the queen, Athaliah cried, "Treason, Treason" (2 Kings 11:14), it was the priest, and not a government official, who ordered the warriors:

> Take her outside under guard, and slay with the sword whoever follows her. For the priest had said, 'Do not let her be killed in the house of the Lord.' (2 Kings 11:15)

And even so, the Church has the authority to not only order military troops to take the lives of tyrants and destroy their pagan religions, but the people as well. For Jehoiada made a covenant between the nation and God, and it was because of this covenant that the people of Israel shattered the idolatries of the wicked queen, slaughtered her pagan priest, and ended up killing Athaliah herself:

> Then Jehoiada made a covenant between the Lord, the king, and the people, that they should be the Lord's people, and also between the king and the people. And all the people of the land went to the temple of Baal, and tore it down. They thoroughly broke in pieces its altars and images, and killed Mattan the priest of Baal before the altars. And the priest appointed officers over the house of the Lord. Then he took the captains of hundreds, the bodyguards, the escorts, and all the people of the land; and they brought the king down from the house of the Lord, and went by way of the gate of the escorts to the king's house. Then he sat on the throne of the kings. So all the people of the land rejoiced; and the city was quiet, for they had slain Athaliah with the sword in the king's house. (2 Kings 11:17–20)

THE PRIESTLY INVOLVEMENT IN WAR CONTINUED IN THE CHURCH

The merging of the priestly office with war, continued through the Church. St. Thomas Aquinas said that priests go to the battlefield to spiritually assist the soldiers, just as the priests of the Old Testament did:

> Prelates and clerics may take part in wars by the authority of their superiors: not, however, by fighting with their hands, but by giving spiritual assistance to those who fight justly, by

exhortation and absolution and other such spiritual aids. Thus in the Old Testament the priests were commanded to sound the sacred trumpets in the midst of the battle. [2]

The priest consecrates the nation to God, and the military and the people, under the superintendence of the priesthood, purge the land of heresy, tyranny, and false religion. Such is the spirit of Christendom, wherein the Church dedicates the nation to God, and the nation in turn strives to maintain Orthodoxy, and in doing so, utilizes its armies to defend the true Faith from countries that desire to destroy Christianity, and from those who, like a fox in the hen house, work to destroy the true religion from within. Once a nation becomes under God, all the devils of hell pursue its destruction, and it becomes the obligation of that nation to be in constant defense, and vigilantly ready to protect the bastions of Christendom, just as the holy Jehoiada conveyed men of war to protect the king from the evil queen, preserve the kingdom from the invasion of paganism, and ultimately perpetuate the holiness of Israel.

There are numerous examples of priests being involved in war within Christian history as a continuation of what the prophets of Israel once did, and it is important that we observe some of them here, to comprehend the beauties of this role and how it is applied.

CONSTANTINE AND HIS TABERNACLE

When Constantine—the first Christian emperor—was about to go to battle against the pagan Persians in the fourth century, he, emulating the Israelites, erected a tabernacle so that he would have a refuge to offer prayers to God and a place where the priests could observe their divine office. The ancient Church historian Socrates recounts this event and parallels it with the rites of Israel's prophets:

> So great indeed was the emperor's devotion to Christianity, that when he was about to enter on a war with Persia, he prepared a tabernacle formed of embroidered linen on the model of a church, just as Moses had done in the wilderness; and this so constructed as to be adapted to conveyance from place to place, in order that he might have a house of prayer even in the most desert radians. [3]

THE EMPEROR THEODOSIUS AND JOHN OF EGYPT

When Magnus Maximus, a rebel and a tyrant, attempted to invade Italy and take the empire, the emperor, Theodosius, before even meeting this enemy in battle, consulted a zealous desert hermit named John of Egypt, for it was said that he had the gift of prophecy. Like the times of Israel and Judah, Theodosius was told by this anchorite that his victory was secured by divine Providence. The prophecy was fulfilled and Maximus was killed in battle and his revolt crushed. Before Theodosius went to battle with the tyrant Eugenius, who was reviving paganism in the empire, he again consulted the same monk, and he again assured him that

---

2   Aquinas, *Summa Theologiae*, IIa IIae 40, article 2
3   Socrates, 1.18

God was on his side. In the middle of the battle, all of the arrows of the enemy were repulsed by a miraculous wind, and the warriors of the pious emperor were victorious.[4]

THE GENERAL PETRONAS AND JOHN THE MONK

In the 9th century, when the Christian general of the Byzantine empire, the valorous Petronas, was about to lead his army into war against the Muslim Arabs and their Islamic emir Amr, he did not go immediately into battle, but instead he first journeyed up to Mount Latros and met with a holy monk named John, who lived the life of hermitage. Here the warrior, who was strong in body and spirit, inquired of the monk, who possessed an internal strength cultivated through asceticism, on what he was to do. The monk did not hesitate, but instead with ardent zeal, and like the prophets of Israel, said,

Go forth against the Saracens, my son. You will have God for your vanguard.[5]

Here we have a most striking semblance with the involvement the priests and holy men of ancient Israel had in war. The leader of the army was about to charge into combat, but first sought out the wisdom of one close to God, and the monk, in turn, declared that God will fight for him against the Muslim enemy. Just as the prophet Samuel "cried unto the Lord for Israel" to have victory over the Philistines, it is said that the general Petronas was "Armed with [the monk's] prayers," as he fought the battle against the Muslims.[6] The prayers were like a sword that vanquished the devils that influenced the Muslims, while the sword of the general and his armies were combated the slaves of the demons.

The general Petronas led his army into a land called Lalakaon and set up an ambush from every direction against the coming Muslim army. Once the ambuscades were established, he provoked Amr to attack him, a trap which the Muslim fell for. Amr and his Islamic troops were surrounded on all sides, like a wild beast barreled by hunters. But Amr was courageous and was not fazed by his difficult predicament. With a sturdy spirit he said:

It is inevitable that we will be turned back by the Romans. However, there must be no wavering. We must rise up and acquit ourselves courageously in tomorrow's battle.[7]

The next day, the rays of the sun burst forth from the shadows of the night and inundated the earth with its light. There stood the Christian armies, warriors who upheld the Holy Cross on their imposing banners and within their own hearts, against the onslaught of Allah's menacing troops, the armies of Antichrist, who bore the crescent on their flags of the demoniacal genies which they worshipped within their own souls. One had the scimitars of devils while the other had the Sword of Christ that divides the House of God from the house of Satan, the Sword of the Spirit that slays demons, fierce arms strengthened by God Who "teacheth my

---

4   Augustine, *City of God*, 5.25
5   Skylitzes, *Byzantine History*, 5.13, trans. John Wortley, ellipses mine
6   Skylitzes, *Byzantine History*, 5.13
7   Skylitzes, *Byzantine History*, 5.13

hands to war" (Psalm 18:34), the prayers of a hermit who, like the prophets, interceded to the King of Heaven to fight for His people.

The Muslims charged the Christians with a great shout, and with their loud voices tried to confound them with commotion. But their attack could not break the indefatigable defense of the Christian warriors. Amr was taken back, but then after mustering all of his courage he made a second and sudden charge at the defenders of Christendom. He could not break the impervious troops of God, and after a third failed attempt he was vacuous of all resolve. He looked around him in all directions, and there stood the protectors of the Christian empire. He had no other choice but to rush the enemy with his entire being, and exert every illustration of jihad. He leaped onto the nearest Christian soldiers, and fell upon them; in his self-destructive attack, he was struck with a mortal wound and died. The enemy retreated and victory was won. The general, Petronas, did not glorify himself as the sole victor, but remembered John the Monk who, with internal fortitude, interceded between God and His armies, pleading to the Lord for victory. It was through the prayers that victory was granted, and through the sword that the victory manifested. Petronas brought the monk before the emperor, and sung praises of his virtue.[8] Thus was the power of the monastic prayers, and the influence that the hermits and anchorites had in holy war.

THE EMPEROR ALEXIUS I AND THE PRIEST

Before the emperor Alexius I was about to march against the Turks, he wasn't sure on what path to take, either to go to Philomelion or to Iconium. Having remained undecided, he determined that the decision should be left up for God to decide. So he wrote his question on two pieces of paper and placed them on the holy altar in a parish. He spent the whole night, not sleeping, but singing a hymn and in appealing to God with fervent prayers. At dawn, the priest picked up one of the pieces of paper, and read aloud which path the emperor should take, and that was, Philomelion, which he invaded and took with a great victory.[9]

POPE LEO IV AND THE ARMIES OF ITALY

When the Muslims tried to invade Rome in the 9th century, it was Pope Leo IV who commanded the soldiers of Italy to go forth and fight the enemy. As Leo recounted in one of his writings: "Because adverse tidings had often come from the Saracen side, some said that the Saracens were coming secretly and furtively to the port of Rome; and for this reason we commanded our people to assemble, and ordered them to go down to the seashore."[10]

---

8 Skylitzes, 5.13
9 Anna Komnenus, *Alexiad*, 15.4
10 Leo IV, C. 23:8:7: Igitur (CIC 1:954f), in Aquinas, *Summa Theologiae*, IIa IIae 40, article 2

CHRISTIANITY IS AT WAR: THE MANIFESTO FOR CHRISTIAN MILITANCY

POPE INNOCENT III AND THE INVOLVEMENT OF THE PRIESTS IN THE CRUSADES

In the thirteenth century, when the Christians were fighting to take back the Holy Land from the Muslims, Pope Innocent III stressed heavily on the work of the priests for the victory, and he cited the example of the Maccabees, who were all priests, to illustrate this. He said, in the Fourth Lateran Council:

> Regardless of what others may do, we, the priests of the Lord, must especially take this task, aiding and supporting with personnel and goods the needs of the Holy Land. No one at all should be left who does not participate in such a great work, lest he be deprived of such a great reward. In the past in a similar case, God achieved liberation in Israel through priests, when through the Maccabees, unquestionably priests, sons of Mattathias, he freed Jerusalem and the temple from ungodly hands. [11]

ON WARRIOR MONKS

The spirit of Christian militancy comes from its monastic nature. The idea that we are constantly to be on our guards, like soldiers, always aware that the ambushes of the demonic can come at any time, that we must be ever ready for combat against evil, and that we must be "sober, be vigilant; because your adversary the devil walks about like a roaring lion, seeking whom he may devour" (1 Peter 5:8)—this is where the zeal for holy warfare comes from. The life of the Christian has always been described as that of a soldier. St. Paul described Epaphroditus as "my brother, fellow worker, and fellow soldier" (Philippians 2:25), and he refers to Archippus as "our fellow soldier" (Philemon 1:2). The Apostle said, "You therefore must endure hardship as a good soldier of Jesus Christ" (2 Timothy 2:3), and in the same epistle he wrote: "No one engaged in warfare entangles himself with the affairs of this life, that he may please him who enlisted him as a soldier." (1 Timothy 2:4) St. Bernard described the Apostles as warriors, writing: "They were brave in war, not voluptuaries robed in silk."[12]

It is in these epistles, and the earliest writings of our Faith by the hand of our most holy patriarchs, that we find the spiritual ideas of the warrior: that he is to be separated from the earthly life, always focused and always pursuing the battle against the devil and the forces of the diabolical. And it was this monastic militancy that would continue on in the hearts of God's soldiers, from the earliest days all the way to the most glorious Crusades, to the numerous battles of Byzantium and the Christians of the East. St. Clement, the bishop of Rome who was directly appointed by the Apostles, described the zeal and the hierarchy of the Christians as the tenacity and ranks of the Roman military:

> With all zeal, then, brethren, let us serve as good soldiers under his [i.e., Christ's] irreproachable command. Let us remember the discipline, obedience and submission that our government troops exhibit when they carry out orders. It is not everyone's job to lead a

---

[11] Pope Innocent III, sermon 6: Fourth General Council of the Lateran
[12] Bernard, *On Consideration*, 2.6

thousand men, or a hundred, or fifty or some such number. Each one carries out the orders of the emperor and the governors according to his own rank. Those with great responsibility cannot do without those who have less and vice-versa. Together they form a kind of whole, and therein lies the benefit. [13]

Origen, amongst the earliest of the apologists, described Christians fighting the devil to righteous men justly putting to death an evil tyrant, writing that "those persons would do well who should enter into a secret association in order to put to death a tyrant who had seized upon the liberties of a state, so Christians also, when tyrannized over by him who is called the devil, and by falsehood, form leagues contrary to the laws of the devil, against his power, and for the safety of those others whom they may succeed in persuading to revolt from a government which is, as it were, 'Scythian,' and despotic."[14]

Amazingly, the world loves to describe those who follow the devil as 'rebels," but the reality is that those who follow God, and are His soldiers, are the true rebels who revolt against the fetters of the flesh and the principalities of darkness. St. Cyprian, when expressing his elated praise for all of the Christians who offered themselves as martyrs or to endure the torment of persecution, described such sacrificial saints as warriors in combat with the devil and the demonic:

> The combat has increased, and the glory of the combatants has increased also. Nor were you kept back from the struggle by fear of tortures, but by the very tortures themselves you were more and more stimulated to the conflict; bravely and firmly you have returned with ready devotion, to contend in the most extreme contest. Of you I find that some are already crowned, while some are 'ben' now within reach of the crown of victory; but all whom the danger has shut up in a glorious company are animated to carry on the struggle with an equal and common warmth of virtue, as it behooves the soldiers of Christ in the divine camp; that no allurements may deceive the incorruptible steadfastness of your faith, no threats terrify you, no sufferings or tortures overcome you. [15]

Truly, when the saints are attacked, their zeal increases, for as holy suffering intensifies, union with God comes to pass. This divine union through suffering in holy war is the goal of the monastic warrior, and it is done efficiently by both martyr—who is killed in persecution—and warrior, who is slain in battle. As the martyr dauntlessly is killed by the persecutor, so the warrior fights with no thought of his life. In another work St. Cyprian gives a deeper significance to the spiritual battle, and conveys the glory of valor, the impenetrable spirit, and of Christian soldiery in the war that we are in:

> For you, who have become chefs and leaders in the battle of our day, have set foreword the standard of celestial warfare; you have made a beginning of the spiritual contest which God has purposed to be now waged by your valor; you, with unshaken strength and unyielding

---

13 Clement, Letter to the Corinthians, 37, ed. Ronald J. Sider, *The Early Church on Killing*
14 Origen, *Against Celsus*, 1.1, ed. Ronald J. Sider
15 Cyprian, letter 10, ed. Ronald J. Sider

firmness, have broken the first onset of the rising war. Thence have arisen happy openings of the fight; thence have begun good auspices of victory. It happened that here martyrdoms were consummated by tortures. [16]

The holy warrior who dies for the faith returns gloriously to his Father in Heaven after being victorious over Satan, just as a temporal soldier returns with all glory to his homeland, after obtaining triumph over the enemy. As St. Cyprian said: "If to soldiers of this world it is glorious to return in triumph to their country when the foe is vanquished, how much more excellent and greater is the glory when the devil is overcome, to return in triumph to paradise, and to bring back victorious trophies to that place whence Adam was ejected as a sinner."[17]

The spiritual war against Satan and all of his temptations and deceptions is described as an actual physical war, against evil. This spiritual battle against sin and demons, then, would eventually transcend into physical war against maleficent enemies who are under the control of the demonic.

THE CHRISTIAN KNIGHT AND THE MONASTIC SPIRIT

The Christian knight is charitable and ferocious; merciful and just; zealous and filled with the highest love. He is a warrior and a monastic, all in one person. In him the physical sword and the spiritual sword are united, and strive for one glorious mission: the defeat of the devil and the victory over the diabolical. This is the goal of the Christian; this is the reason for living; this is the purpose of the sword and the aspiration of the Holy Faith, for as St. John says, "For this purpose, the Son of God appeared, that he might destroy the works of the devil." (1 John 3:8)

All of the virtues of the martyr, are the virtues of the warrior. Look to the centurion, Cornelius. There is no doubt he had all the strength of spirit, the stillness of mind, the purity of heart, and the physical endurance, to suffer under the pains of torture, and the inner fortitude to look beyond the physical world and foresee eternity in the face of a blessed death. The mindset of the Christian, whose life is only that of a pilgrim ready to leave this waiting place and journey to his eternal home, transitions most perfectly into the mind of the warrior who is ever ready for death. When the warrior finds the path of truth, he picks up his cross with vigor, for he is so used to the intensity of combat. When the demon possessed hoards pursue him, he remains posted without wavering, for through experience he does not quiver before the charge of the enemy; and when his end comes, he does not runaway, for he is so conditioned to the prospect of death, and he embraces it.

This is why, within Christendom, the spiritual war of the Christian inevitably is done through physical arms in Holy War. What the Christian is expected to endure in persecution, he as well may endure in the battlefield. One Christian writer who clearly interconnected spiritual warfare with military combat was St. Paulinus of Nola, a fourth century monk from

---

16 Cyprian, letter 28, ed. Ronald J. Sider
17 Cyprian, letter 13, ed. Ronald J. Sider

Italy. He wrote a letter to Victricius, the bishop of Rouen and an experienced soldier of the Roman army, and he described how the harshness and intensity of his military service prepared both his mind and his spirit for combat against the devil, and for physical persecution:

> He [God] allowed you to fight for Caesar so that you could learn to fight for God, in order that whilst exercising your bodily vigour in the work of the army, you could strengthen yourself for spiritual battle, reinforcing your spirit to confess the faith and hardening your body for suffering.[18]

In Christendom, physical warfare and spiritual warfare become one, and both the Sword of the Spirit and the sword of combat intertwine; Christian empire is formed, and from such do we have Christian armies. In spiritual war, the Cross is raised to chase out the demons, and in Holy War, the warriors raise up the Cross as their banner, and with swords shaped as crosses they slay and repulse men who are possessed and taken by the demons.

Moses was a warrior monk; he showed us the purest monastic life, and would be an exemplary by which all future monks would strive to emulate. He ascended the holy mountain, like the monks of today who seek hermitage in such lofty summits, and "was there with the Lord forty days and forty nights; he neither ate bread nor drank water. And He wrote on the tablets the words of the covenant, the Ten Commandments." (Exodus 34:28) He lived beyond the physical and was completely absorbed in the love of God and in the divine union. He "lived in a state beyond nature," as St. Gregory of Nyssa tells us,[19] living without the demands of the body, wholly entrenched in deep meditation and prayer. It was in this state of intense connection with the eternal that Moses wrote the Ten Commandments, the Law by which the idols are shattered and the heathen subdued. Once he descended the holy mountain, at the bottom he witnessed what debauchery his people indulged themselves in, in their worship of the golden calf and other harlotries. Moses was on the top of the mountain, because in his mind and spirit he ascended up to the heights of the divine, while his people were at the bottom because they still stood at the lower depth of carnality. Moses was of a transcendent faith, and this was shown through his monastic spirit. In his same spiritual state he had the sword unsheathed and slaughtered the pagans who remained obstinate to pure virtue. In this moment the spiritual sword worked through the temporal sword, and the spiritual battle manifested in a physical slaughter.

CORNELIUS THE CENTURION—PATRIARCH OF MONASTIC WARRIORS

Let us look to the holy pioneers of the Christian armies, the first recruits of the knights of Christ, who stood in the sacred presence of our Lord and His Apostles—the most pious patriarchs and the pillars of the Faith. Let us look to Cornelius the Centurion, who was of the Italian band, and of whom the Scripture describes as "A religious man, and fearing God with all his house, giving much alms to the people, and always praying to God." (Acts 10:1–2) He

---

18 Paulinus, letter 18, 7, brackets mine
19 Gregory of Nyssa, *Life of Moses*, 1.58

was the first of the Gentiles to join with "the true Light which gives light to every man coming into the world" (John 1:9), and through Cornelius were the gates of the Church opened to the Gentiles.

The Christian soldier does not follow modern ideals, his ways were established through those earliest warriors who took up their crosses and denied themselves. The holy Cornelius was "a devout man and one who feared God with all his household, who gave alms generously to the people, and prayed to God always." (Acts 10:2) How can a man always be praying? The passage is not speaking of external prayer, with the mouth, but meditative prayer, internal prayer in which the mind is in contemplation on the beautiful things of eternity, and on God. From this contemplation comes three great virtues, as we learn from St. Bernard: "strength, in the second freedom, in the third purity."[20] Such is the ways of the Christian knight, enflamed with zeal and devotion, charitable and just, constantly in meditation, devotion and silent prayer, and living in freedom from the chains of depravity, in the true liberty of the divine precepts. A pure mind that always strives for the cause of righteousness over evil, goes on into everlasting live, "for the mind survives the limbs which fall away," says St. Paulinus, "and lives on because its birth is divine."[21] And when Cornelius met St. Peter, he told the Apostle, "I was fasting until this hour" (Acts 10:30) This one man, Cornelius, gives us the ideal image of the Christian knight: pious, valiant and always willing to subject himself to mortification, or fasting, to vanquish the flesh and serve the Spirit.

In this man named Cornelius, we have the most pristine image of the Crusader. The warrior is ferocious, for he is a centurion; he is pious, for he is charitable and always praying and fasting. The Christian warrior is a monastic, following the ways of the monk, wielding both the spiritual sword—to fight off the devils—and the temporal sword—to slay the demons' agents. Monastic piety, ferocity, mercy and justice—these are the virtues by which the knight governs himself, and this law of chivalry all began with Cornelius.

In this state do the warriors of God follow their patriarch, Cornelius the Centurion, the pioneer of the holy knight, and it is to his ways that the knights of old committed themselves. Cornelius was charitable, and so Crusader knights were charitable. For example, we read in the Latin Rule for the Order of the Knights Templars, written in the Council of Troyes in 1129, that the knights must always be willing to care for the sick:

> Care and attention are to be given as a priority to the sick; they are to be served as if they were Christ so that the Gospel message, "I was sick and you visited me," should be kept in mind. They are to be diligently and patiently treated since heavenly rewards are undoubtedly earned through them. The necessities of life should always be given to the sick. We command the intendants of infirmities to administer to them with every attention and watchful care, faithfully and diligently, as far as the capacities of the house permit, whatever is neces-

---

20 Bernard, *On Consideration*, 5.2
21 Paulinus of Nola, poem 11, 60

sary for the sustenance of people of differing infirmities, namely meat and poultry etc., until they are restored to health. 22

The mission of the crusader was Christ, and they pursued this mission when they both healed and slew. In every man there is an image of Christ, and to medicate an injured person—even if he be an enemy—is to worship Christ. By extension, then, to slay the enemies of God to protect the Church—with whom Christ identifies Himself—is to protect an image of Christ.

Cornelius prayed always to God, and so the Templars prayed with much devotion, following their rule:

> As a general rule we order that brothers should pray, standing or sitting according to the inclination of mind or body, but with the utmost reverence, simplicity and quiet so as not to disturb one's neighbor. 23

Cornelius fasted, and so did the Templars fast to sear their flesh and subdue it for the triumph of the Spirit, and to strengthen their own selves in the battle against the Muslims. As the monk Hugh 'Peccator' wrote in a letter to the Templars:

> In the second task you have trampled your adversary underfoot; in time of peace by abstinence and fasting you fight against your own flesh, and when he [Satan] temps with pride in your good deeds you resist and you defeat him; but in war you fight with arms against the enemies of peace who harm or wish to harm. 24

Such is the life of the monastic warrior, and so many were they in Christendom's battles, and as well in the battles of the Hebrew saints. To fight against temptation within our own selves, and to war with the enemy of humanity is monastic militancy, the essence of the Faith and the foundation of Christendom.

THE IDEA OF THE WARRIOR MONK BEGAN IN ISRAEL

The idea of warrior monks, or even priests, was prominent in Medieval Christendom, but it was not originally thought of in that time period, but began in ancient Israel. The Aaronites were both priests and warriors, and they were three thousand seven hundred in David's army, and so too was Zadok a priest, and he was called "a young man, a valiant warrior," (1 Chronicles 12:28), and from his father's house there were twenty-two captains in David's army, and all of these men are described as amongst the "numbers of the divisions that were equipped for war" (1 Chronicles 12:23).

Hashabah and his brethren, seventeen hundred strong, were "men of valour" "in all the business of the Lord, and in the service of the king." (1 Chronicles 26:30) This signifies that there was a holy army, crusaders really, who dedicated themselves to God and to protecting the law of God, and the king He commissioned over Israel, from evil doers. They were a

---
22 Latin Rule of 1129, 49–50, in Barber and Bate, The Templars
23 Ibid, 57
24 Hugh 'Peccator, to the Templars in the East, ibid

manifestation of what St. Peter commanded of us: "Honour all men. Love the brotherhood. Fear God. Honour the king." (1 Peter 2:17) They were not a secular army, but a religious order, completely dedicated to God and defending His nation. Christendom continued this system of monastic warrior orders, who used the temporal sword to aid the spiritual sword.

It was the Levites, who were the official order of the priesthood, under the command of the heroic priest Jehoiada, who defended King Joash when his life was sought after by the pagan Queen Athalia, with every priest holding his weapon, both ever willing and ever ready to take the life of anyone who attempted to take the life of the royal heir. They obeyed the command of Jehoiada, when he ordered:

> But let no one come into the house of the Lord except the priests and those of the Levites who serve. They may go in, for they are holy; but all the people shall keep the watch of the Lord. And the Levites shall surround the king on all sides, every man with his weapons in his hand; and whoever comes into the house, let him be put to death. You are to be with the king when he comes in and when he goes out. (2 Chronicles 23:6–7)

When Saul failed to unsheathe the sword of justice upon the tyrant Agag, king of the Amelekites, it was the prophet Samuel, who took up the temporal sword that was supposed to be executed by the state, and he took divine vengeance upon him, telling the wicked despot before killing him,

> As thy sword hath made women childless, so shall thy mother be childless among women.'
> And Samuel hewed Agag in pieces before the Lord in Gilgal. (1 Samuel 15:33)

Let us also never forget that Moses ordered the Levites, and not secular soldiers, to slaughter the worshippers of the golden calf.

WARRIOR MONKS IN CHRISTENDOM'S ARMIES

Monastic militancy continued on through the Church, for in Christendom there were so many warriors who endured the life of the monks, fighting demons and the followers of demons. The connection between monasticism and warfare was made by St. Ambrose when he described how the monastics, Elijah, Elisha, John the Baptist, and other holy men, were all involved in warfare, either physical and spiritual, or both:

> Elijah, Elisha, John the son of Elizabeth, who clothed in sheepskins, poor and needy, and afflicted with pain, wandered in deserts, in hollows and thickets of mountains, amongst pathless rocks, rough caves, pitfalls and marshes, of whom the world was not worthy. From the same, Daniel, Ananias, Azarias, and Misael, who were brought up in the royal palace, were fed meagerly as though in the desert, with coarse food, and ordinary drink. Rightfully did those royal slaves prevail over kingdoms, despise captivity, shaking off its yoke, subdue powers, conquer the elements, quench the nature of fire, dull the flames, blunt the edge of the sword, stop the mouths of lions; they were found most strong when esteemed to be most weak, and did not shrink from the mockings of men, because they looked for heavenly

rewards; they did not dread the darkness of the prison, on whom was shining the beauty of eternal light. 25

In the most glorious Battle of the Kulikovo Field, in which the brave Russian Christians defeated the Muslim Tatars, the prince of Moscow, Dimitry Ivanovich, went to the monastery of the monk, St. Sergius, and begged him for his two monastic warriors, Peresvet and Osliaba, to join him in battle. He said to the monk:

> Good father, give me two warriors of your monastic troop, two brethren, Peresvet and Osliaba. For they are universally acclaimed as mighty warriors and valorous knights, highly expert in the art and practice of warfare. 26

In the First Crusade, before the warriors went out to Jerusalem they sought help from Daimbert, the Archbishop of Pisa who was appointed patriarch of Jerusalem in 1098. He, being zealous for their holy cause, provided for them a supply of 900 naval ships and accompanied them in their journey to fight the Muslims in Syria.[27]

Pope Pius II launched a war against his enemies; Innocent IV took many victories and established dominions over several tyrants through the Spanish cardinal Albornoz who led the armies; Pope Clement IV had the most righteous and saintly king, St. Louis, oust out the tyrant Manfred from the kingdom of Naples; Pope Leo IX fought in person amongst the soldiers against the Norman pagans to recover the city of Benevento; Pope Leo IV led an army of warriors against the Muslims to recover Ostia from their pillage; Pope Julius II emulated the warriors of Israel when he led his own army, alongside the forces of several kings, and warred against certain enemies of the Church. Before you object, let us say that the idea of warrior priests was not invented by the Church, but was inherited by the Church through the Israelites. Who can forget the great Maccabees, who were all both warriors and priests? Or Moses, who was both Pontiff and priest, and who did not hesitate to fight and defeat the Amorites?[28]

There were even monks who fought heretics themselves, without a legitimate army. For example, St. Ambrose wrote of a number of monks who burned down a Valentinian temple, writing that they, "enraged by their insolence, burnt their hurriedly-built temple in some country village."[29] When St. Ambrose discovered that the government was going to punish the monks, he sent a letter to the emperor Theodosius exhorting him to not punish them, but instead, let them go since they were destroying impiety:

> How can your piety avenge them [the Valentinians], seeing it has commanded them to be excluded, and denied them permission to meet together? 30

---

25 St. Ambrose, letter 63, 67
26 *The Tale of the Battle of the Kulikovo Field*, p. 60
27 Anna Komnenus, *Alexiad*, 11.9, see also f. 44 of the translator, Sewter
28 Bellarmine provides the sources for these events, in his *On the Temporal Power of the Pope*, ch. 11, ed. Tutino, pp. 234–235
29 St. Ambrose, letter 40.16
30 St. Ambrose, letter 40.26, brackets mine

ON CHRISTIAN MILITIAS

The two things that every tyrant wants to remove from society are God and weapons. If the tyrant can remove God, then the people will worship him. By removing God, the tyrant answers to nobody. By removing weapons, then the people can no longer fight for their right to worship God, and no longer can they fight to defend Christianity. This is why the right to bear arms is such a superior right; greater than freedom of speech or freedom of the press. You can have all the freedom of expression you want, if you have no right to bear arms, your words will not prevent terrorists from slaughtering you. You can claim religious freedom all you want, but if you have no weapons, how can you defend the Church? This is where the necessity of the Christian militia comes in. But please do not get me wrong. By Christian militias I am not speaking of these lunatics who form militias in the name of some subversive, conspiratorial, jingoist or racialist cause. I am speaking of militias who truly fight for Christianity, for the defense of Christians from a real and existential threat that pursues their destruction and enslavement.

The entire concept of Christian militias is based on one single precept that was taught by St. Peter, when the Jewish authorities ordered the Christians to no longer preach Christ: "We ought to obey God rather than men." (Acts 5:29) The Christian militia is only reformed as a response to men trying to persecute the Faith. When the Jewish officers arrested St. Peter and the other Apostles, they did so without any violence, not because they were amiable, but because they were terrified of the Christians:

> Then the captain went with the officers and brought them without violence, for they feared the people, lest they should be stoned. (Acts 5:26)

The earliest followers of Christ would have stoned the temple guards if they took the disciples away with violence; which means that the Church can fight back if violence is put against her. When the Church is surrounded by pagan enemies, left to the slaughter by indifferent governors, is deprived of state troops or officers to protect it, but is in possession of arms and weapons to unsheathe against its charging adversary, Christians then form militias, and with justice and equitableness, strike the devilish foes before they oppress the vulnerable flock. St. Odo of Cluny, amongst the holiest of monks, affirmed that if the churches cannot defend themselves from persecutors, then the laymen have every right to pick up their arms to protect themselves:

> It was lawful, therefore, for a layman to carry the sword in battle that he might protect defenseless people, as the harmless flock from evening wolves according to the saying of Scripture [Acts 20:29], and that he might restrain by arms or by the law those whom ecclesiastical censure was not able to subdue. [31]

---

31 Odo of Cluny, Life of Gerald of Aurillac, 1.8

When St. Odo writes of "ecclesiastical censure" he is making reference to the Church's authority to suppress heretics. The heretics who are not restrained by such censure, and who come with violence against the priests, must then be combated by Christians, even laymen.

The idea of Christian militias fighting a tyrannical state was opposed by the Protestant reformer Melanchthon, who was against the idea of revolution even if it were against an abusive government. If the "magistrate commands anything with tyrannical caprice," he wrote in 1521, "we must bear with this magistrate because of love, where nothing can be changed without a public uprising or sedition."[32] But the Catholic position, as conveyed by St. Robert, says that "self-defense is lawful for anybody, not only for a prince, but also for a private citizen"[33] And St. Thomas says:

> Tyrannical rule is not just, because it is not directed to the common good but to the private good of the ruler. Disruption of such a government therefore does not have the character of sedition, unless perhaps the tyrant's rule is disrupted so inordinately that the community subject to it suffers greater detriment from the ensuing disorder than it did from the tyrannical government itself. Indeed it is the tyrant who is guilty of sedition, since he nourishes discord and sedition among his subjects in order to be able to dominate them more securely.[34]

Therefore, Christians can form militias to protect themselves and to defend the Church from attackers, without state approval. Christian militias are organized for several reasons: to defend the Church from oppression and attacks, protect the defenseless, and to uproot the pagan threat before it makes a great slaughter of Christians. All of the goals of the Christian militias are governed by one aspiration: justice. If any action goes against, or as has nothing to do with justice, then it must be cast aside. Every crusade, and every holy war, must be done for the advancement of justice and for the destruction of tyranny.

When the Jews were under the sovereignty of the Persians, and were working to rebuild the Temple, they were encompassed by rapacious pagans, who cried out with heathen fury, "They will neither know nor see anything, till we come into their midst and kill them and cause the work to cease." (Nehemiah 4:11) The Jews, with the greatest consternation, cried out, "From whatever place you turn, they will be upon us." (Nehemiah 4:12) What was Nehemiah to do? He could not turn to the officers of the state, nor depend upon the government for protection. He thus resolved to form a militia, not of civil troops, but of common folk. He did not think twice when he "positioned men behind the lower parts of the wall, at the openings; and I set the people according to their families, with their swords, their spears, and their bows." (Nehemiah 4:13) He did not hesitate when he declared to the people with fortitude, "Do not be afraid of them. Remember the Lord, great and awesome, and fight for your brethren, your sons, your daughters, your wives, and your houses." (Nehemiah 4:14)

---

32 Quoted by John Witte, *Law and Protestantism*, ch. 4, p. 137
33 . Bellarmine, *On Laymen or Secular People*, ch. 15, ed. Tutino, pp. 68–69
34 Aquinas, *Summa Theologiae*, IIa IIae 64, article 2

Nehemiah was not some vigilante, but a monastic prophet, abiding by the right of the Church to defend itself against conniving wolves and enemies who conspire and plan for its destruction. It was because of the weapons bore by the people, under the command of their holy prophet, and not some secular rule, that the pagans were struck with fear, and delayed their ambush. As Nehemiah wrote:

> And it happened, when our enemies heard that it was known to us, and that God had brought their plot to nothing, that all of us returned to the wall, everyone to his work. So it was, from that time on, that half of my servants worked at construction, while the other half held the spears, the shields, the bows, and wore armor; and the leaders were behind all the house of Judah. Those who built on the wall, and those who carried burdens, loaded themselves so that with one hand they worked at construction, and with the other held a weapon. Every one of the builders had his sword girded at his side as he built. And the one who sounded the trumpet was beside me. (Nehemiah 4:15–18)

The command of Nehemiah to bear a sword by one's side, is in accordance to the injunction of Christ when He told the Apostles,

> But now, he who has a money bag, let him take it, and likewise a knapsack; and he who has no sword, let him sell his garment and buy one. (Luke 22:36)

St. Thomas, a monastic, permitted Christian revolution when the sovereign becomes severely tyrannical, and he references to the coup done by Ehud against the king of Moab, in the Old Testament, to substantiate this:

> If, however, a tyranny were so extreme as to be intolerable, it has seemed to some that it would be an act consistent with virtue if the mightier men were to slay the tyrant, exposing themselves to the peril of death in order to liberate the community. For a certain Ehud slew Eglon, king of Moab, with a dagger 'fastened to his thigh', because he oppressed the people of God with a harsh bondage; and for this deed Ehud was made a judge of the people. [35]

In another place St. Thomas wrote that "sometimes the things commanded by a ruler are against God. Therefore rulers are not to be obeyed in all things."[36] St. Thomas, in one writing, declared that "he who delivers his country by slaying a tyrant is to be praised and rewarded."[37] Peter Lombard, amongst the most influential and reputable scholastics of the Middle Ages, wrote that "if the emperor commands one thing and God another, you must disregard the former and obey God."[38] St. Thomas Aquinas wrote that there are three forms of obedience: obedience sufficient for salvation, which one is obligated to do for eternal life; the second is perfect obedience, which obeys in all things lawful; and the third is indiscriminate

---

35 Aquinas, *De regimine principum*, 1.7
36 Aquinas, *Summa Theologiae*, IIa IIae, 104, article 5
37 Aquinas, Scripta super libros sententiarum, II:44:2:2, article 2
38 Lombard, Collectanea in omnes de Pauli apostoli epistolas, PL 191:1505, in Aquinas, *Summa Theologiae*, IIa IIae, 104, article 5

obedience, which recklessly obeys all things regardless of how destructive they may be.[39] The first, no government can take away; the second must always be in accordance to God's law; and the third is both volatile and dangerous because it gives the rulers absolute license to order acts contrary to God's law. This thoughtless obedience contradicts the first two, and is more fitting to the excessive obedience seen in cults, or in the Japanese and Ottoman Turks, who obeyed their emperors in their commands to plunder, rape and slaughter millions. If what a king demands is not for God, but for the devil, then, as St. Thomas instructs, "not only is one not bound to obey the ruler, but one is bound not to obey him, as in the case of the holy martyrs who suffered death rather than obey the ungodly commands of tyrants."[40]

The Christian society has the right to overthrow its rulers if they have proven themselves to be enemies, and not defenders, of the true Faith, and this can be done even if they are legitimately ruling, as St. Thomas tells us.[41] The Church can validly push for revolution against tyrannical governments. For even in the sacred Scriptures, legitimate rulers are rightfully killed by the saints. The Scriptures praise the valiant Hezekiah for rebelling against the Assyrian empire, declaring, "The Lord was with him; he prospered wherever he went. And he rebelled against the king of Assyria and did not serve him." (2 Kings 18:7) Elijah anointed Jehu to kill the king Joram, who was legitimately ruling, and even so God commended him, saying "Because you have done well in doing what is right in My sight, and have done to the house of Ahab all that was in My heart, your sons shall sit on the throne of Israel to the fourth generation." (2 Kings 10:30)

Let the pillars of Christendom be uncovered from the rubble of modern decay; soon will Christendom arise from its slumber, and with Christ as our Captain, our General, with the armies of Heaven, the glorious saints and martyrs, with the chariots of fire, with the flames of zeal, shall we with the sword unleash the divine wrath, with our Savior leading us into the most holy fray. And when this finally occurs, let us remember the first of the Christian armies, the pious Cornelius.

---

39 Aquinas, *Summa Theologiae*, IIa IIae, 104, article 5
40 Aquinas, *Scripta super libros sententiarum II*, Dist. 44, quaest. 2, article 2, trans. R.W. Dyson
41 Aquinas, *De regimine principum*, 1.8

PART 8 – DEALING WITH OBJECTIONS AGAINST CHRISTIAN GOVERNMENT

THE LAW OF MOSES IS NOT TYRANNICAL, RATHER IT PREVENTS TYRANNY

From the land of tyranny did the Hebrews journey, into a land engrossed into the depths of the inferno that was to be the majestic Holy Land, whose foundation is Heaven, in whose heart is justice, in whose heavenly mountain lies the souls of just men, warriors and martyrs, and from their exodus came the forsaken Stone in Whom is all law, and in Whose spirit is liberty. But in order for this liberty to carry on, the enemy of liberty must be driven out, just as our Lord compelled him to flee when He stood steadfast in the desert. The adversary has many deceptions, many ideologies and false religions, and each one hinders true liberty. The devil whispers into the ear of humanity, that true freedom is solely to pursue their wants, to believe in what they want to believe. Such is a cage that imprisons us. But the voice of God commands us to follow the One Who took upon Himself all tyranny, and shattered it as Moses destroyed the gold calf. Holy Writ teaches us not to be slaves to ourselves, but to deny the self. Such is true liberation. But all of the false religions teach us to rely on ourselves. Such is the origin of all miseries, the Babel that sprung from the enslaved mob who declared, "let us build us a city and a tower, whose top [may reach] unto heaven" (Gen. 11:3).

They followed their own ideas, their own twisted opinions, and the modern world would applaud them in the name of "freedom" and "tolerance," but such was anarchy and the chain that pulled them into the yoke of tyranny. The Lord descended from Heaven into this tyranny, and He drove all of the builders away, and ended the building of the tower. The Lord defeated tyranny, because He rejected the toleration of false religion, for it is only in the true Faith where true liberty is found. It is the intolerant spirit of God that shatters the bastions of despotism. One of the most attacked events of the Bible is the story of Moses slaughtering three thousand people for worshipping a golden calf. This story has been used to prove that the Bible is tyrannical. But, the reality is that the destruction of the golden calf worshippers prevented tyranny and advanced true liberty.

A VINDICATION FOR MOSES' SLAUGHTERING OF THE THREE-THOUSAND FOR THE WORSHIP OF THE GOLDEN CALF

"Up, make us gods," commanded the masses of Hebrews to Aaron, "which shall go before us; for as for this Moses, the man that brought us up out of the land of Egypt, we wot not what is become of him." (Exodus 32:1) Such are the words of a people whose lips drip with wickedness and who welcome with untiring arms the tyrant, and reject the prophet who is of their countrymen. Moses was upon Mount Sinai receiving the Laws of Heaven, while the people had their minds contriving for wickedness, and their souls rooted in Hell. They had no patience for those divine institutions which were to be instilled by Moses; and so did they wish to observe the idolatrous system of the Egyptians,[1] while at the same time they demanded for idols which were to represent, what they thought, was the divine.[2] Aaron acquiesced to the turbulent mob, and told them to break off their golden earrings, which were worn by not just wives and daughters, but even sons; their vain ornaments were then fashioned into a golden calf.[3] "These be thy gods, O Israel," declared Aaron to the riotous multitude, "which brought thee up out of the land of Egypt."[4]

Incensed was Moses by such a sight, his heart so taken by noble anger, that he cast down the tablets and shattered them. The calf was burnt, grounded to powder, thrown into the water, and the defiant people of Israel were made to drink of it. (Exodus 32:19–20) In short time, the law of God was enacted, and due punishment executed. "Who is on the Lord's side," said the prophet, "let him come unto me." (Exodus 32:26) Such words must have pierced right through their hearts. The Law of Heaven confronted them and there came regret, which moved them to shame as the shepherd herds stranding sheep back to the flock before the wolves devour them. This commandment was a chance for those who erred to commit to penitence, and for those whose hearts were hard to reveal their deep rooted wickedness, and receive their deserving affliction. Once the repentant came to Moses' side, the prophet ordered the killing of the callous pagans. "Thus said the Lord God of Israel," declared the inspired Moses to the Levites, "Put every man his sword by his side, and go in and out from gate to gate throughout the camp, and slay every man his brother, and every man his companion, every man his neighbor." (Exodus 32:27) The sons of Levi did what was commanded, and about three thousand of the idolatrous were slain in that very day.[5]

---

1 Matthew Henry, *A Commentary on the Whole Bible*, vol. i, p. 407, on Exodus 32:1–6.
2 Poole, *A Commentary on the Holy Bible*, vol. i, p. 187, on Exodus 32:1.
3 Exodus 32:2–4.
4 Exodus 32:4.
5 Exodus 32:28.

CHRISTIANITY IS AT WAR: THE MANIFESTO FOR CHRISTIAN MILITANCY

The strains of darkness were purged from the chosen race, and as Christ chased out the thieves from His temple, so did Moses rid Israel of those robbers who preyed upon fickle and contemptuous souls. "But why?" is the question of the modern, who with his mind of the present age, sees no danger in the worship of idols. This story of Moses killing three thousand people has become a means to ridicule and mock Christianity from the time of the Enlightenment onwards. It is now time to provide the most effective defense for this action of Moses of who, to use the words of Warburton, "the most celebrated champions of infidelity have cunningly, for their own purposes, labored with all their might to overthrow."[6]

It must first be stated that the heathenish religions of the Near East were political; therefore, for the Hebrews to reverence the golden calf, they were in truth betraying Israel for a foreign political system that would have been both dangerous and tyrannical. But what political system? That of the pagan Egyptians, and specifically, that of the Pharaoh, their former oppressor, since it was indeed an idol of Egypt.[7] That the calf was Egyptian, is firmly established by God through the pen of Ezekiel:

> On that day I raised My hand in an oath to them, to bring them out of the land of Egypt into a land that I had searched out for them, flowing with milk and honey, the glory of all lands. Then I said to them, 'Each of you, throw away the abominations which are before his eyes, and do not defile yourselves with the idols of Egypt. I am the Lord your God. But they rebelled against Me and would not obey Me. They did not all cast away the abominations which were before their eyes, nor did they forsake the idols of Egypt.' Then I said, 'I will pour out My fury on them and fulfill My anger against them in the midst of the land of Egypt.' (Ezekiel 20:6–8)

The Egyptian identity of the golden calf, is made further, and more specifically, by St. Stephan, who said of the Hebrews who wanted the golden calf: "in their hearts they turned back to Egypt, saying to Aaron, Make us gods to go before us; as for this Moses who brought us out of the land of Egypt, we do not know what has become of him." (Acts 9:39–40)

Observe how St. Stephen describes the Hebrews who had worshiped the golden calf as reverting back in their hearts to Egypt, indicating that they had committed themselves to the ways of Egypt, which was directly prohibited under Levitical law: "According to the doings of the land of Egypt, where you dwelt, you shall not do" (Leviticus 18:3).

Moses himself would have easily identified the golden calf as Egyptian, since he knew that the Egyptians worshipped animals (Exodus 8:26), and for the fact that he "was learned in all the wisdom of the Egyptians," as St. Stephen affirms (Acts 7:22).

If, then, the golden calf was an Egyptian idol, and a political symbol, of which deity did it represent, and how did it pertain to the government of Egypt? On the authority of Lac-

---

6   Warburton, Dedication to a new edition of books i, ii, iii, of the *Divine Legation of Moses*, in MDCCLIV.
7   Matthew Henry, *A Commentary on the Whole Bible*, vol. i, p. 407, on Exodus 32:1–6; Philo, *The Posterity and Exile of Cain*, xlvi.158; On the *Life of Moses*, xxxi.161–162, trans. C.D. Yonge Firstly.

tantius,[8] the golden calf represented the Egyptian god Apis. The calf Apis, as we are told by Plutarch, was an image of the soul of Osiris,[9] who was worshipped as a deceased king, and with whom all perished pharaohs were made equal to. The image which the Hebrews made was thus connected with the polity of Egypt. In other words, the golden calf was a symbol of the pharaohs, one of whom had tyrannized the Hebrews. The idol, then, was an image of despotism, and for the Hebrews to erect and venerate one, meant that they had exalted a symbol of the imperial cult of the Pharaoh. Therefore, if Moses had not stopped them, the children of Israel would have ultimately become a nation tantamount to those of the rest of the tyrannical peoples of the Near East. By accepting the idol, Israel would have accepted the tyranny of the Pharaoh and of the Egyptian religion that included cannibalism and human sacrifice. The Hebrews were returning back to the tyranny that Moses risked his life to liberate them from. He had every right to express his rage against him. Any man, in his position, after going through all of the troubles he had to endure, would have been enraged at such an ungrateful people.

The pharaoh was deified as a cattle animal, being called "a strong bull,"[10] which is linked with how certain Cushite tribes revere their chiefs, such as the Nilotic Lango who call the leader of their warriors "Bull of the host," and as the Ankole who praise their divine king as "the leading bull" or "the leading bull of the herd."[11] The pharaoh was given such titles because of the majestic sentiments which a bull provokes: it strikes fear into the heart, and has a dominating spirit, aspects which the ruler was expected to possess.[12]

The equating of the pharaoh with the bull, or golden calf, was a glorification of his conquests and the dominion of his empire. Depictions of Menes, the first pharaoh, and even earlier Egyptian kings, show the rulers as bulls trampling over their enemies or destroying fortresses.[13] Menes was also depicted as a goat; and Ammon, an ancient pre-pharaonic king worshipped by the Egyptians and Libyans was deified as a ram.[14] After King Unas had died he was revered as "the Bull of heaven" who destroys his enemies.[15] The queen-mother of Egypt was revered as "the cow that hath borne a bull"; and the "bull of heaven" was an idol of the sun.[16] Thus, the pharaoh was both a bull, the offspring of a deified cow, and the sun, which is yet just another reason why sun worshipped is prohibited under Mosaic Law. Hymns would be chanted in worship for the sun, extolling it as a calf: "Hail to thee! Hail to

---

8   Lact. Div. Inst. 4.10, trans. William Fletcher. See also Poole, *A Commentary on the Holy Bible*, vol. i, p. 187, on Exodus 32:4.
9   Plutarch, *Isis and Osiris*, 20, trans. Frank Cole Babbit. See also Jamieson, Commentary, vol. i, part i, p. 407, on Exodus 32:4
10 See Frankfurt, *Kingship and the gods*, book i, part iv, ch. xiv, pp. 162.
11 *Kingship and the gods*, book i, part iv, ch. xiv, pp. 166–167
12 See Frankfurt, *Kingship and the gods*, book i, part iv, ch xiv, p. 169.
13 Frankfurt, *Kingship and the gods*, book i, part iv, ch. xiv, p. 171.
14 Diod. Sic. 3.73; Arthur Young, *Historical Dissertation on Idolatrous Corruptions*, ch. v, p. 193
15 Budge, *Osiris*, vol. i, ch. iv, p. 114.
16 See Frankfurt, *Kingship and the gods*, book i, part iv, ch. xiv, pp. 162–163.

thee, thou calf, which came forth from the Ocean of Heaven."[17] The worship of the calf was then a part of the cult of the solar star, and in turn, was connected with the worship of the pharaoh who was deified as both.

A pyramid text praises the pharaoh Pepi as both a golden calf and an offspring of the sun-god Re and a cow-goddess:

> Pepi comes to thee, O father of his! Pepi comes to thee, O Re! A calf of gold, born of heaven, the soft one of gold, formed by the Hesat-cow. [18]

The worship of the bull and cow was emphatically connected with the cult of Apis,[19] and therefore if the Hebrews had continued with this idolatrous folly, going unchecked by Moses, it would have escalated to a point in which they would have configured a society reminiscent to that of the pharaoh in which the tyrants were worshipped.

The worship of the cow was significantly associated with the cult of the pharaoh, as one finds from various statues. In an image of the pharaoh Djoser, who had made the earliest columns of the cow-goddess Hathor, the worshipped tyrant is appareled with the idols of this same Hathor. The upper corners of Menes' palette contain the heads of Hathor, with her horns and ears. On the girdle of the pharaoh is ornamented the head of the deified cow.[20] Like the calf which the Hebrews erected, Hathor was also praised as being golden; and was asked by her worshippers to give life to, and unite herself with, the pharaoh: "May the Golden One (Hathor) give life to thy [the pharaoh's] nostrils. May the Lady of the Stars innate herself with thee."[21]

The last request of the necromancer further evinces the great association between the imperial cult of Egypt, and its sidereal religion; hence why the cow was at times presented with stars upon its head.[22] By the pharaoh being worshipped as Horus, the son of the cow-goddess Hathor, and by uniting him with this goddess, the despot was perceived in the fullness of his power and authority, and as an embodiment of the heaven, the stars, the moon and the sun, the clouds and the winds. So ancient is this belief, that it was observed in the reign of Menes, the first pharaoh, and the founder of the pharaonic age.[23]

This is also expressed in a hymn on king Unas, in which he is praised as the one who controls and rules over all nature and society; his godhood is described while at the same time it is declared that he is united with the cow-goddess: "It is Unas who flooded the land when it had emerged from the Lake. It is Unas who pulled up papyrus. It is Unas who reconciled the Two Lands. It is Unas who will be united with his mother, the Great Wild Cow."[24] Whether

---

17 In Frankfurt, *Kingship and the gods*, book i, part iv, ch. xiv, p. 169.
18 In Frankfurt, *Kingship and the gods*, book i, part iv, ch. xiv, p. 170.
19 See Frankfurt, *Kingship and the gods*, book i, part iv, ch. xiv, pp. 162–163.
20 Frankfurt, *Kingship and the gods*, book i, part iv, ch. xiv, p. 172.
21 In Frankfurt, *Kingship and the gods*, book i, part iv, ch. xiv, p. 172.
22 Frankfurt, *Kingship and the gods*, book i, part iv, ch. xiv, p. 172.
23 Frankfurt, *Kingship and the gods*, book i, part iv, ch. xiv, p. 173.
24 In Frankfurt, *Kingship and the gods*, book i, part iv, ch. xiv, p. 177.

the golden calf of the Hebrews was male or female, is therefore irrelevant in regards to connecting it with the imperial cult of Egypt; for it represented the deification of the pharaoh regardless of its gender. The pharaohs, as far back as the First Dynasty, were extolled as "son of Isis,"[25] a cow goddess whose horns were believed to represent the crescent moon,[26] and who was praised as the symbol of the pharaoh.[27]

The deification of tyrants as bulls, and their mothers as cows, was done also in Mesopotamia. The people of Erech had described their king Gilgamesh as "A savage wild bull,"[28] and his mother as a "Wild Cow, the goddess Ninsun!"[29] Indeed, if Moses and his successors had suffered the Hebrews to continue their worship of the golden calf, they would have gone the way of the Mesopotamian, revering their tyrants as strong bulls and their mothers as goddesses.

The punishment which Moses ordered upon the idolatrous Hebrews was most necessary for the preservation of Hebrew civilization, and ultimately, for Christian civilization which is a continuation of Israel. One must wonder how Israel would have been if Moses had tolerated the cult of the golden calf; surely they would not be under a godly government, but a tyrannical one, dictated by an imperial cult. The children of Israel would have been worshipping their leaders instead of their Creator; the plan for them to be distinct amongst nations would have been diminished, and the history of the Hebrews but a dry narrative in text books, only to be described as no more barbarous than the Canaanites.

When Christ was in the desert for forty days He paralleled the Hebrews in the wilderness for forty years. Moses crushed the golden calf, Christ defeated the devil. Satan offered Christ all the kingdoms of the earth, and so did the golden calf symbolize all of the prestigious power of the Pharaoh which the idolatrous Hebrews desired.

The Church today has become infected with this same crime, for many ministers have now tolerated heathen religions such as that of Muhammad into their congregations, and have even allowed the worshippers of Allah to speak unto their sheep. So flooded with this evil are the churches of our time that it will take but a miracle to put an end to it before we are completely engulfed by its tainted waters. As Moses had punished those who had obstinately desired for the golden calf to be worshipped alongside God, so shall Christ, upon His second coming, give what is due to those corrupt pastors who encourage and commit to spiritual harlotry in the churches, and introducing today's golden calf, Allah, to their congregations.

With this said, the killing of the three thousand was completely justified. They wanted tyranny, and Moses wanted to prevent tyranny. The destruction of the tyrannical Egyptian religion by Moses shows that God's Law was established for the destruction of despotism

---

25 Frankfurt, *Kingship and the gods*, book i, part i, ch. iii, p. 44.
26 Diod. Sic. 1.11, trans. C.H. Oldfather.
27 Frankfurt, *Kingship and the gods*, book i, part i, ch. iii, p. 44.
28 *The Epic of Gilgamesh*, tablet i, line 81, trans. Andrew George
29 *The Epic of Gilgamesh*, tablet i, line 36, trans. Andrew George

itself. Intolerance for dangerous religions is within the foundation of liberty. Civilization will have to choose intolerance towards evil if it desires to advance.

HATRED FOR HOLY WAR AND CHRISTIAN MILITANCY CAME FROM PROTESTANT REFORMERS LIKE LUTHER

After the Protestant Reformation, there was a controversy that sparked between Protestants and Catholics, and this was over the issue of the Church's relationship with the state. The Protestants rejected the idea that the Church could organize crusades with the government, while the Catholics of course maintained the Church's role in crusading and holy wars. Luther was at the forefront of the protestant sentiment, believing that the Church should completely stay away from the war against the Ottomans, and that the war needed to be secular, not religious. He expressed this view as such:

> To make war against the Turks is nothing else than to strive against God, Who is punishing our sins by means of the Turks. How shamefully the pope has this long time baited us with the war against the Turks, gotten our money, destroyed so many Christians and made so much mischief! When will we learn that the pope is the devils most dangerous cats-paw? Was it not the pope that set good King Ladislas of Hungary and Poland, with so many thousand Christians, upon the Turks, and was he not terribly beaten at Varna because he obeyed the pope, and at his bidding broke the treaty he had made with the Turk? For to teach concerning perjury, that the pope has power to break an oath, is no heresy. How can a man become a heretic if he can do anything he pleases? Again, what misery has recently come to Hungary through this same Turkish war, begun with a papal indulgence! And yet we must continue to be blind so far as the pope is concerned! Now I set up this article not meaning to say that we are not to make war against the Turk, as that holy heresy-hunter, the pope, here charges me, but to say that we should first make ourselves better and cause God to be gracious to us; not plunge in, relying on the popes indulgence, with which he has deceived Christians heretofore and still deceives them.
>
> The histories of the Old Testament, especially Joshua 7:1 and Judges 20:12, and many more passages, show us what it is to fight against an angry God and against an enemy whom we have deserved. The pope does nothing more, with his crusading indulgences and his promises of heaven, than lead Christians lives into death, and their souls in a great crowd to hell, as befits the true Antichrist. God is not concerned about crosses and indulgences and wars. He will have our lives to be good; and from goodness the pope and his followers flee more than from anything else; and yet he would devour the Turk. That is why our war against the Turk is so successful, and where he formerly had one mile he now has a hundred miles of land; but we do not see it, so completely have we been taken captive by the Roman leader of the blind.
>
> Thus, too, it is strictly forbidden in the canon law that the clergy shall carry arms and weapons, and yet no one pours out more Christian blood than the most Holy Father, the pope, who now feeds the sheep of Christ with iron, and guns, and fire, and is worse than the Turk. He embroils kings and princes, lands and cities, but that does not make him a heretic

or a murderer, or a tyrant, but he is Christ's vicar, and he grants indulgences and sends out legates and cardinals in the interest of the war against the Turk. His papists excuse their graven image and idol, saying that the pope does not go to war nor burn anybody, but sits in his holy chair at Rome and prays complains, perhaps and only commands the temporal power to fight and burn. That is just what the Jews did. They gave Christ over to Pilate and the Gentiles to crucify, but they themselves, like great saints, would not enter Pilate's house; yet St. Stephen, in Acts 7:52, called them murderers of Christ, and died for it. Thus, because I have called the pope the greatest murderer the world has borne since its foundation, who murders both body and soul, I am a heretic, God be praised! In the eyes of his holiness and his papists. [30]

At one point, Luther even firmly held that the Ottoman Empire should not be combatted at all, that the Muslim invasion was a punishment from God, and that the Christians should simply endure it. Of course Luther's opinion quickly shifted when he realized that his own life was on the line in the face of the expanding Islamic empire. Theodorus Bibliander, an early Protestant reformer who knew Arabic and actually did the first translation of the Koran from Arabic to Latin, condemned the First Crusade, which was conducted by Pope Urban II to drive out the Muslims from Catholic lands and prevent the jihadists from further persecuting Eastern Christians:

> Urban, that most cruel tornado, driven by an evil spirit to indulge in homicide, started a war to regain Judea. [31]

To the early Protestants the Church declaring war against the Muslims, in order to prevent them from slaughtering and oppressing Christians, and further conquering Christian lands, was evil. There is an effective counter to such reckless interpretations, and that is Orthodox theology in regards to war. In the post-Reformation era, there was a very learned theologian, probably the most influential of his day, named St. Robert Bellarmine. He wrote many disputations against intense Protestant opposition towards Holy War, and the reason why he wrote—and to use his own words—"whether it is lawful to fight against the Turks" was "because of Luther."[32] He replied to Luther's vitriol against the Crusades in the following response:

> However, it must be observed that Luther does not say that the war against the Turk was unlawful because he thinks that every war in general is unlawful, for in the assertion of his article he recommends war against the Pontiff who, he says, is a most Turkish Turk, and neither does he judge in this way because he thinks that Christians have no just cause, since it is evident to everybody that the Turks occupied the lands of the Christians without any right. Every day they want to occupy more land, and it is also evident that the Turks want to eliminate all religion and to see to it that men convert from Christianity to Islam.

---

30 See Luther's defense of his thirty-third and thirty-fourth articles
31 Bibliander, *Chronologia*, table 13, in St. Robert Bellarmine, *On Laymen or Secular People*, ch. 16, ed. Tutino, p. 75
32 Bellarmine, *On Laymen or Secular People*, ch. 1, ed. Tutino, p. 3

CHRISTIANITY IS AT WAR: THE MANIFESTO FOR CHRISTIAN MILITANCY

Luther does not deny any of these things, but there are three other reasons why he thought that it was not lawful to fight against the Turks. First, because the will of God seems to be that we should be punished by the Turks as by divine punishments, and it is not lawful for us to resist God's will. That this is indeed God's will he proves in the assertion of article 34, where he argues that experience shows that so far the war against the Turks has not given any benefit to the Christians. But this first reason has little value, for even if God's will is that our sin be punished through the Turks, nevertheless it is not His will that we should not resist the Turks; indeed His will is for us to resist, which is proved from the final cause. For God does not allow the Turks to rage against us so that we may die but so that we may convert, for we are led to converting when we try to resist the Turks who are assaulting us; and by resisting we suffer, and by suffering we recognize our weakness, and hence we turn to God with our whole heart and we beg Him for help. Therefore, from the final cause for which God allows the Turks to rage against us it clearly follows that God wants us to resist the Turks. Moreover, the war of the Turks is a divine punishment just like plague, famine, heresy, the flames of sin, and such, but nobody is so foolish as to think that one should not seek a remedy against the plague, or that we should not cultivate the land so as not to die by starvation, or that we should not resist heresy. [33]

St. Robert continued in his response to describe how destructive Luther's animosity against the Crusades were against Christendom, how they were the biggest hindrance to stopping the Turks from expanding the Ottoman empire, and how many Christians lost their lives on account of Protestants who refused to fight the Muslims. He wrote about how the Christian crusaders "were reconquering more and more land until contentions started to rise among the Christian princes themselves, to such an extent that the Turks now occupy a great deal of land because of the disagreements in our camp rather than because of their own military valor, and the chief cause of such disagreements was Luther himself."[34]

One example of Protestantism's destructive effects, was that when the Turks were about to invade the Hungarians, and the king of Hungary called on Germany for help, the Germans allowed the Muslim to vanquish and devastate them, because they chose to follow Luther and not partake in the Crusade. If everyone listened to Luther, the Muslims would have overtaken all of Christendom, but because there were brave Catholics who refused to listen to that glutton, and took up arms and fought for their Faith and the Church, the Turks were greatly hindered from overtaking the whole of Christian lands.[35] In other words, if the Christians of that time rejected Catholicism and abided by Lutheranism, the Muslims would have devastated the whole of Europe; tremendously more Christians would have been slaughtered, entire populations enslaved, whole multitudes of women ravished, churches transformed into mosques, and instead of the chants of Monks, one would be hearing the Call to the Prayer. Because Catholics remained Catholic, and firmly instilled in themselves the concept

---

33 St. Robert Bellarmine, *On Laymen or Secular People*, ch. 16, ed. Tutino, pp. 76–77
34 St. Robert Bellarmine, *On Laymen or Secular People*, ch. 16, pp. 76–77
35 St. Robert Bellarmine, *On Laymen or Secular People*, ch. 16

of Holy War, the Muslims were greatly impended. If it were not for Catholics, there would be no Christianity.

But this is what the heretics want, they want Christians enslaved and massacred, churches destroyed and turned into houses of heresy. The heretics are infiltrators, and as cancer cells mimic normal cells to destroy the body, heretics mimic normal Christians to obliterate Christendom from within. All Christians who live freely today and reject Christian militancy, know this—that you are comfortable because of Christian militancy. You live comfortably because the Christians of old believed in Holy War, took up arms and fought those who wanted to destroy Christian militancy. If you hate Catholicism, then you share the same vitriol with the Muslims, and this is why Luther wanted the Muslims to invade Europe, to destroy Catholicism, as St. Robert specified in his refutation of Luther:

> The third reason [why Luther did not want to fight the Turks], and the one that seems to have been the chief one, is hatred against the Pontiff, for sometimes Luther attacked the Pontiff with so much hatred that clearly he wished to see the Turks occupy all the kingdoms of Christendom, if the name of the Pontiff could at least be wiped out in this way. [36]

Luther said that that the government of the Turks was superior to that of the Christians because their law was based on the Koran while that of the latter was not based on the Scriptures:

> They say that there is no better temporal government than among the Turks, though they have no canon nor civil law, but only their Koran; we must at least own that there is no worse government than ours, with its canon and civil law, for no estate lives according to the Scriptures, or even according to natural reason. [37]

In another place he wrote:

> I beg all the pious Christians not to obey in any way, not to serve in the army and not to hold anything against the Turks, since the Turks are ten times more prudent and honest than our princes. [38]

Luther did not care for the Christians who were slaughtered by the Turk in distant lands, but he did most certainly shift in his position when the danger was approaching his corpulent hide, and so he wrote:

> Some preachers cry with temerity that we must not resist the Turks. Such speech is seditious and must neither be uttered nor permitted. The authorities are then obliged to resist the Turks, who not only want to pillage the lands and violate and kill the women and children, but also to abrogate and destroy the laws of the land, the worship of God, and every good regulation. [39]

---

36 St. Robert Bellarmine, *On Laymen or Secular People*, ch. 16, p. 77, brackets mine
37 Luther, *Address to the Nobility of the German Nation*, part 3, 25
38 Quoted by St. Robert Bellarmine, *On Laymen or Secular People*, ch. 16, ed. Tutino, p. 78
39 Quoted by St. Robert Bellarmine, *On Laymen or Secular People*, ch. 16. ed. Tutino, p. 78

Regardless of this change in Luther's thinking, many Protestants continued to share this type of view against Holy War. Many of the Protestants who opposed the Crusades, and even capital punishment, were in fact Anabaptists and Unitarians who lived in Romania, specifically Transylvania. Bellarmine described the heretical contentions of these people as such:

> Among the chief heretical beliefs of the Anabaptists and Antitrinitarians of our time there is one that says that it is not lawful for Christians to hold magistracy and that among Christians there must not be power of capital punishment, etc., in any government, tribunal, or court. The ministers in Transylvania who oppose the trinity and the incarnation and infant baptism declared in 1568 in Alba Julia the differences between the true Christ and the false Christ, and the seventh difference is that the false Christ has in His Church kings, princes, magistrates, and swords; the true Christ cannot allow anything like this in His Church. [40]

The heretics who objected to the Crusades isolated verses from the Scriptures, and even used some of the Church Fathers, to justify their anti-crusader movement. Their opinion was quite gnostic in nature; for their objections sprung from a perspective that man could not be an instrument of God's vengeance, that he could never be used as a weapon of God, but that mortals should remain on earth awaiting some sort of supernatural intervention, and not the use of any human military force.

To vindicate their opposition toward the Crusades and Holy War, they would use verses such as, "the weapons of our warfare are not carnal" (1 Corinthians 10:4), or the more frequently used passage from Ephesians, "we do not wrestle against flesh and blood, but against principalities, against powers, against the rulers of the darkness of this age, against spiritual hosts of wickedness in the heavenly places." (Ephesians 6:12) Such application of these verses are still strongly and enthusiastically being utilized in our own times in arguments against the Crusades and militancy. It would not be inadequate to say that the anti-crusader theology of the Reformation will be the greatest hindrance to the New Crusade against the Antichrist, and amongst the most active helpers of Christendom's enemies.

These heretics express their ravenous hatred for the Crusader Spirit, but to these it is asked, how many Christians have to die, how many Christian women must be raped, how many tears must be shed, and how much saintly blood must be spilt, before a Holy War is permissible to your earthly eyes? When will these heretics confront such a question? Only when the scimitar is approaching their own necks will they believe in Holy War, but the desire will only spring from their flesh and the impulse to survive, and not the Spirit or for the continuation of Christendom. And so the holy war of the heretics is carnal and its victories temporary, since their enemies will only return after a short span of comfort has lapsed. The Holy War of the Orthodox, on the other hand, is spiritual; it emanates from the love of God, and through its intense drive for justice, it uproots the enemies of Christendom, utterly annihilating them, and blots "out the remembrance of Amalek from under heaven" (Deuteronomy 25:19).

---

40 Bellarmine, *On Laymen or Secular People*, ch. 2, ed. Tutino, p. 5

THE HATRED FOR CHRISTIAN HOLY WAR AND FOR CHRISTENDOM IS GNOSTIC

People who claim Christianity, but yet reject Holy War and Christendom have a type of thinking that emanates from a gnostic view of temporal authority. They are essentially saying that the spiritual can never merge with the political, for the latter is wicked and has no place for the former. Government, in the perspective of these heretics, must remain secular. This is the origin of all totalitarianism, when the Church no longer holds any influence with the state. It is gnostic because it hates man; it sees him as evil and as impossible to be used by God to execute His vengeance against tyranny and an antichrist army; it is gnostic because it maliciously separates any human role from God's hand in victory over His enemies.

CHRISTIAN KINGS ARE GOD'S INSTRUMENTS FOR HIS WRATH

Those who oppose Holy War see any ecclesiastical partnership with the state to commence a Crusade as evil because, as they say with their feigned piety, the humble followers of Christ would never desire to obtain such a lofty position in government, or that for a priest to sit amongst kings in order to exhort them to commence a crusade, is contrary to the lowly spirit of the Christian. Christianity has no place within the government, for judgment is not in the place of a Christian, for only God judges and only He administers vengeance, be it in war or civil law. This is what these people say, and their views can be traced back to John Wycliffe, who said:

> God does not approve that anyone be judged or condemned by civil law. [41]

If only they read Jehoshaphat, when he told the judges that they administer God's justice:

> Take heed to what you are doing, for you do not judge for man but for the Lord, who is with you in the judgment. (2 Chronicles 19:6)

The judges were representatives of God on earth, and thus were the instruments of the divine wrath. Moses warned the judges of Israel that judgement belongs to God, but nonetheless they were the ones carrying out this divine judgment:

> You shall not show partiality in judgment; you shall hear the small as well as the great; you shall not be afraid in any man's presence, for the judgment is Gods. (Deuteronomy 1:17)

The judges of the state are instruments of God's wrath against the enemies of Christendom, and while God is the One judging, the execution of that very judgment is done through mortal institutions.[42] This is further shown in Isaiah when he wrote:

> For the Lord is our Judge,
> The Lord is our Lawgiver,
> The Lord is our King;
> He will save us (Isaiah 33:22)

---

41 *Council of Constance*, session 14, 44
42 See Bellarmine, *On Laymen or Secular People*, ch. 3, ed. Tutino, p. 9

✝ CHRISTIANITY IS AT WAR: THE MANIFESTO FOR CHRISTIAN MILITANCY

God is judge, lawgiver and king, and He carries out these divine offices through their temporal representatives, the judges, the lawgivers, and the kings on earth.[43]

Moreover, it was foretold by the prophets that the kings of the earth would follow Christ, the Son of God, and this implies Christian governments forming into a unified Christendom and bearing the sword to defend Orthodoxy. As David tells us:

> Now therefore, be wise, O kings;
> Be instructed, you judges of the earth.
> Serve the Lord with fear,
> And rejoice with trembling.
> Kiss the Son, lest He be angry,
> And you perish in the way,
> When His wrath is kindled but a little.
> Blessed are all those who put their trust in Him. (Psalm 2:10–13)

In another place he declares:

> Yes, all kings shall fall down before Him;
> All nations shall serve Him. (Psalm 72:11)

What is this but nations coming together in a holy confederacy? What can this mean but the governments of Christendom, both past and those to come?[44] They serve God through their governments, and that means the sword for the Church's persecutors, and liberty for the Christians.

"CHRIST NEVER LAUNCHED WARS!"

One of the most common objections to Holy War and Christendom is this: "Christ never launched wars!" Firstly, such a sentiment is anti-Trinitarian, for it says that the Eternal Son of God—Jesus Christ—was not present in all of the wars of ancient Israel, nor had any influence on the laws of God which ordered for holy wars and for the destruction of paganism. Three men approached Abraham, and he only bowed down to one. Why? Because the One to Whom he bowed was God the Son:

> Then the Lord appeared to him by the terebinth trees of Mamre, as he was sitting in the tent door in the heat of the day. So he lifted his eyes and looked, and behold, three men were standing by him; and when he saw them, he ran from the tent door to meet them, and bowed himself to the ground, and said, "My Lord, if I have now found favor in Your sight, do not pass on by Your servant. (Genesis 18:1–3)

Therefore, when "the Lord rained brimstone and fire on Sodom and Gomorrah" (Genesis 19:23), it was Jesus Christ Who destroyed the city of the sodomites.

---

43 See Bellarmine, *On Laymen or Secular People*, ch. 10, ed. Tutino, p. 36
44 See Bellarmine, *On Laymen or Secular People*, ch. 3, ed. Tutino, p.10

It was Christ Who came to Joshua before the conquest of Jericho, and led him in the invasion and the destruction of the inhabitants. As we read in Joshua:

> And it came to pass, when Joshua was by Jericho, that he lifted his eyes and looked, and behold, a Man stood opposite him with His sword drawn in His hand. And Joshua went to Him and said to Him, "Are You for us or for our adversaries?"
>
> So He said, "No, but as Commander of the army of the Lord I have now come."
>
> And Joshua fell on his face to the earth and worshiped, and said to Him, "What does my Lord say to His servant?"
>
> Then the Commander of the Lord's army said to Joshua, "Take your sandal off your foot, for the place where you stand is holy." And Joshua did so. (Joshua 5:13–15)

This person is Jesus Christ, most definitely, for Joshua was on holy ground, which means he was before God, not God the Father, but God the Son. And it was Christ Who declared to Joshua:

> See! I have given Jericho into your hand, its king, and the mighty men of valor. (Joshua 7:2)

And it was Christ Who led the Hebrews when they "utterly destroyed all that was in the city, both man and woman, young and old, ox and sheep and donkey, with the edge of the sword." (Joshua 6:21) And Christ was surely with them when "they burned the city and all that was in it with fire." (Joshua 6:24)

The Hebrews burned down their city, and to burn down a city means to kill civilians and local people. Christ used the analogy of destroying an entire city of evil-doers when He spoke of the king who sends his armies to take vengeance upon those who slaughter his servants:

> And the rest seized his servants, treated them spitefully, and killed them. But when the king heard about it, he was furious. And he sent out his armies, destroyed those murderers, and burned up their city. (Matthew 22:6–7)

His armies are of course an indication as to Christ's militant nature; therefore there is a militant obligation within the Church that is, fighting those who aspire to obliterate Christianity.

To burn a city implies the destruction of civilians, and therefore this is permissible to Christendom if it must destroy a people who are wicked, cruel, and desire the Church's destruction. The Church allows this on rare occasions. In rare occasions it is necessary to obliterate an entire people, for, in the words of St. Robert Bellarmine, "if the enemy against whom one fights is such that it benefits the common good that he is subject to another or that he is completely destroyed. Such enemies were the Amorites, whom God ordered to be eliminated completely" (Deuteronomy 20).[45]

Now to be fair to St. Robert, he does write that "children, elderly people, and women, for such people, even if they can be captured and robbed since they are part of the city, nevertheless cannot rightfully be killed, unless they are killed by chance and by accident."[46]

---

45 Bellarmine, *On Laymen or Secular People*, ch. 15, trans. Tutino
46 Ibid

St. Robert nonetheless gives us an exception, and that is when peace can only be obtained only when the enemy, like that of the Amorites who God ordered to be destroyed completely, alongside women and children are utterly obliterated, then it is permissible.

The burning of a city was commanded by Moses against those who tempted the Israelites to go after other gods, and Christ most definitely agreed with this, for He inspired the prophet to declare this:

> And you shall gather all its plunder into the middle of the street, and completely burn with fire the city and all its plunder, for the Lord your God. It shall be a heap forever; it shall not be built again. (Deuteronomy 13:16)

Christ used the illustration of a righteous king burning down a city, and therefore a Christian ruler, like Moses, has the divine right to destroy a city that is a danger to the physical and spiritual state of the Christian nation.

Moreover, when dealing with the argument of "I don't see Christ starting wars, or killing anybody!" we must always be aware of the purpose of Christ's coming. Christ did not come to declare a temporal war, but a spiritual war. He came to fight, and to be victorious, over the forces of darkness, over the devils and their wiles, over Satan and his deceptions. He came, and to use the words of St. John, "that He might destroy the works of the devil." (1 John 3:8) He did not come to judge, but be judged, for as He declares, "God did not send His Son into the world to condemn the world, but that the world through Him might be saved." (John 3:17) He came to suffer, and not to respond to His persecutors with revenge. But, while He did indeed suffer, He left the punishment of the evildoers to the authority of His Church. We have this symbol in the person of David who did not punish Shimei when he had cursed him, saying "I will not put you to death with the sword" (1 Kings 2:8), and commanded his son, Solomon, to put him to death so that his crime would be punished, declaring, "Now therefore, do not hold him guiltless, for you are a wise man and know what you ought to do to him; but bring his gray hair down to the grave with blood." (1 Kings 2:9)

Why would we need a statement from the New Testament directly exhorting righteous war, when, for one, war is so explicitly upheld in the Scriptures of the prophets, and secondly, when war is such an innate part of our natural existence? St. Paul said that "we, being many, are one body in Christ, and individually members of one another." (Romans 12:5) Why should we deny to a nation what we would never deny for our own bodies? Individuals defend their own bodies from physical attacks, and since the Church is one body, then it as well has the natural (and divine) right to defend itself from its enemies.[47]

People who object to Holy War fail to see that the time of the Apostles, and the era prior to the advent of Christendom, was when "kings of the earth set themselves, and the rulers take counsel together, against the Lord and against His Anointed, saying, 'Let us break Their bonds in pieces and cast away Their cords from us.'" (Psalm 2:1–2) They don't wish to see divinely appointed Christendom within the words of David when he wrote with inspired prose:

---

47 See Vitoria, *On Civil Power*, Question 1, article 4.2

Now therefore, be wise, O kings; be instructed, you judges of the earth. Serve the Lord with fear, and rejoice with trembling. (Psalm 2:10)

Our detractors will argue that this is wrong, and will always say that Christ abolished the precept of "An eye for an eye and a tooth for a tooth." (Matthew 5:38) Christ never abolished this law, but He instead condemns the distortions made by the Pharisees of this law. In the Book of Exodus God established a law in which the magistrate is to put to death murderers or those who premeditate murder:

> He who strikes a man so that he dies shall surely be put to death. However, if he did not lie in wait, but God delivered him into his hand, then I will appoint for you a place where he may flee. But if a man acts with premeditation against his neighbor, to kill him by treachery, you shall take him from My altar, that he may die. (Exodus 21:12–14)

We find this also in Leviticus: "Whoever kills any man shall surely be put to death." (Leviticus 24:17) The Pharisees took these verses and applied them to private lives, as opposed to governmental authority. Individuals were then given license to carry out these laws on their own, and such was only the enabling of anarchy and lawlessness. This is what Christ condemned, and nowhere does He abolish "an eye for an eye." Such a law was not brutal, but a preventer of brutality; it restrains punishment from being more severe than the crime. It was established, in the words of St. Augustine, "so that the vengeance should not exceed the injury."[48] Then they will bring up the verse, "Resist not evil," but here Christ is not prohibiting justice by a magistrate, but retaliation done in altercations between individuals, not between the state and the people, or a righteous nation and an evil nation. St. Ambrose tells us that the Gospel is for the perfection of virtue, so as to prevent men from becoming violent, and thus to prevent the state punishing them for being criminals: "This perfection consists in extirpating the roots of contention and, by supporting each other in charity, in not giving occasion for more serious evils such as wounds and killings, because of which it would be necessary for the public magistrate to take revenge on the criminals."[49] To strike for the sake of harming is wrong, but to strike with the intention of defense, and for the cause of justice, is right. To use the words of St. Robert, "it is not the defense but the revenge that is prohibited."[50]

To strike for the cause of hatred is wrong, but to strike for the cause of love is a fruit worthy of redemption. St. Gerald of Aurillac, a monastic knight of the ninth century, did not fight against the oppressors of the helpless to gratify the desire for revenge, "but by love of the poor, who were not able to protect themselves. He ordered the poor man to be saved and the needy to be freed from the hand of the sinner. Rightly, therefore, he did not allow the sinner to prevail."[51]

---

48 Augustine, *Commentary on the Sermon on the Mount*, b. 1, ch. 19.56
49 See Bellarmine, *On the Temporal Power of The Pope*, ch. 19, ed. Tutino, p. 283
50 Bellarmine, *On Laymen or Secular People*, ch. 13, ed. Tutino, p. 51
51 Odo of Cluny, *Life of St. Gerald of Aurillac*, 1.8

Vitoria went so far as to say that one may strike back not just for defense but also to prevent humiliation, just as long as vengeance is not the goal:

> In my opinion, however, a man who has been unjustly struck may strike back immediately, even if the attack would probably have gone no further. For example, to avoid disgrace and humiliation a man who has been struck in the face with the fist may immediately retaliate with his sword, not to avenge himself but (as explained above) to escape dishonour and loss of face. 52

But revenge is not an evil unto itself when it is done for adequate and just reasons and by legitimate officials, or when it is done with a righteous mission. If there is a criminal who sheds innocent blood, then he must be executed or else he will either harm or murder others. To prevent murder, or further violence, is a just cause, and thus for the state to conduct capital punishment for this cause, is both upright and meritorious.53 As St. Thomas tells us:

> And so if a man is dangerous to the community, causing its corruption because of some sin, it is praiseworthy and wholesome that he be slain in order to preserve the common good; for 'a little leaven corrupteth the whole lump' (Corinthians 5:6). 54

Such sins would include murder, but also homosexuality and violent and heretical ideologies, which seek to destroy a Christian society and bring it to moral and spiritual decay. Such are dangerous, and such are to be uprooted. If an entire society is part of the Church, they are thus under the Church, including magistrates, and it is not unlawful, therefore, for ecclesiastical authority to work with the state to uproot the leaven from corrupting the whole lump.

TURN THE OTHER CHEEK

But of course the adversaries of Holy War will bring up the usual verses to bolster secularism. They will say, "Well, Jesus told us 'whoever slaps you on your right cheek, turn the other to him also.' (Matthew 5:38)." But to take this verse as though Christ is against the Church defending itself from annihilation through arms, is a belief of a fanatic who takes verses and pulls them to the most extreme ends. To such people I would ask, "If someone is raping your wife, do you shoot the rapist or 'turn the other cheek'?" No man would say, 'turn the other cheek.' When is it then, that when pagans and heretics are ravishing the Church, a holy war assembled to slay the evildoers and protect her, is all of a sudden wrong? At times it is of no use to turn the other cheek, when the person is going to just keep striking you. One turns the other cheek with the intent that the other person will recognize his wrong, not for him to continue his abuse.55 Jesus Himself did not apply His own commandment of turning the other cheek in the way that these extremist want us to do. For when "one of the officers who stood by struck Jesus with the palm of his hand," (John 18:22) Jesus did not turn the other

---

52 Vitoria, *On the Law of War*, question 1, article 2, 5
53 See Bellarmine, *On Laymen or Secular People*, ch. 13, ed. Tutino, p. 52
54 Aquinas, Summa Theologica, IIaIIae, articles 2
55 See St. Robert Bellarmine, *On Laymen or Secular People*, ch. 14, p. 61

cheek, but instead He said, "If I have spoken evil, bear witness of the evil; but if well, why do you strike Me?" (John 18:23) It was as if to say, that if someone were truly evil then a smack to his face would be merited. But Christ is perfect, and is deserving of no abuse, and therefore did He not turn the other cheek but corrected the officer with a fair question. St. Paul, when some of the Jews wanted to strike him in the mouth, did not turn his face to make it open for a strike, but instead berated his persecutors. When "the high priest Ananias commanded those who stood by him to strike him on the mouth," St. Paul, quite similar to Christ, harshly corrected him with a question on the Law:

> God will strike you, you whitewashed wall! For you sit to judge me according to the law, and do you command me to be struck contrary to the law? (Acts 23:3)

Again, like Christ, it was as though Paul said that the strike would be warranted if he truly was a breaker of the Law. But he was not, and therefore the blow was unjustified. Notice that he never once turned his face, and docilely made himself open for the pummeling. He questions it, berates it, and resists it with sharp words. As Augustine commentates on this story:

> For when the apostle was struck, instead of turning his other side to the man, or telling him to repeat the blow, he prayed to God to pardon his assailant in the next world, but not to leave the injury unpunished at the time. [56]

How then should we apply this precept of Our Lord, if it doesn't mean pacifism? The command of Christ to turn the other cheek is speaking of an internal state of the soul, and is not to be taken to an extreme literality. It is to be understood, in the words of St. Robert, "to concern the readiness of the spirit,"[57] to forbearance and patience. As St. Augustine tells us, "these precepts pertain rather to the inward disposition of the heart than to the actions which are done in the sight of men, requiring us, in the inmost heart, to cherish patience along with benevolence, but in the outward action to do that which seems most likely to benefit those whose good we ought to seek."[58]

The intention of this expression of kindness is to overpower the adversary with charity, so that, looking at his own wicked actions, he realizes that he is a slave to darkness. It is like presenting a lighted candle to one who has never seen a glimmering flame. He comes to the reality that he is plunged into the darkness, and with this realization, he prevents himself from further enslavement to sin. Notice Christ says if someone "shall smite you on your right cheek, turn to him the other also;" the left cheek is the most likely to be hit, since it is the easier target for the right hand of the attacker. The words of Our Lord are said by St. Augustine to mean that when one is injurious to your highest possessions, then give him your inferior possessions, and to do this would be to put eternal rewards over temporal things. So therefore the internal dispossession of the person is habitually fixated on heavenly objectives, not earthly ones. But even the commandment of turning the other cheek, once it is seared

---

56 Augustine, Against Faustus, 19.79, ed. Nicene and Post-Nicene Fathers, vol. iv
57 Bellarmine, *On Laymen or Secular People*, ch. 12, ed. Tutino, p. 48
58 Augustine, letter 138, ch. 1.13, trans. J.G. Cunningham

into our hearts and souls, can be applied to Holy War. For the precept is done for the cause of justice and the prevention of injustice, and thus Holy War is done for this very reason. These precepts of Christ are for the guidance of individuals, not governments declaring war or punishing criminals. War is not connected to individual grudges and personal revenge, but the public peace. Loving one's enemy, or turning the other cheek, does not prevent a judge from sentencing an evildoer to death, as they do not prevent the soldiers and their rulers from slaying their enemies.[59] The Christian emperor, with this very internal disposition of charity, does not strike the enemies of God in joy of bloodshed, but in love for the person being punished, for he strives to see him corrected, and no longer as a slave to the devil, but as one living in the liberty of the law. Therefore, when the Christian knight strikes the pagan adversary, he does so with charity, and not hatred. St. Augustine made this very connection between the Law of Love as taught by Christ, and righteous war done by Christendom:

> These precepts concerning patience ought to be always retained in the habitual discipline of the heart, and the benevolence which prevents the recompensing of evil for evil must be always fully cherished in the disposition. At the same time, many things must be done in correcting with a certain benevolent severity, even against their own wishes, men whose welfare rather than their wishes it is our duty to consult and the Christian Scriptures have most unambiguously commended this virtue in a magistrate. For in the correction of a son, even with some sternness, there is assuredly no diminution of a father's love; yet, in the correction, that is done which is received with reluctance and pain by one whom it seems necessary to heal by pain. And on this principle, if the commonwealth observe the precepts of the Christian religion, even its wars themselves will not be carried on without the benevolent design that, after the resisting nations have been conquered, provision may be more easily made for enjoying in peace the mutual bond of piety and justice. For the person from whom is taken away the freedom which he abuses in doing wrong is vanquished with benefit to himself; since nothing is more truly a misfortune than that good fortune of offenders, by which pernicious impunity is maintained, and the evil disposition, like an enemy within the man, is strengthened.
>
> But the perverse and froward hearts of men think human affairs are prosperous when men are concerned about magnificent mansions, and indifferent to the ruin of souls; when mighty theatres are built up, and the foundations of virtue are undermined; when the madness of extravagance is highly esteemed, and works of mercy are scorned; when, out of the wealth and affluence of rich men, luxurious provision is made for actors, and the poor are grudged the necessaries of life; when that God who, by the public declarations of His doctrine, protests against public vice, is blasphemed by impious communities, which demand gods of such character that even those theatrical representations which bring disgrace to both body and soul are fitly performed in honour of them. If God permit these things to prevail, He is in that permission showing more grievous displeasure: if He leave these crimes unpunished, such impunity is a more terrible judgment. When, on the other hand, He overthrows the

---

59 See St. Robert Bellarmine, *On Laymen or Secular People*, ch. 14, ed. Tutino, p. 61

props of vice, and reduces to poverty those lusts which were nursed by plenty, He afflicts in mercy. And in mercy, also, if such a thing were possible, even wars might be waged by the good, in order that, by bringing under the yoke the unbridled lusts of men, those vices might be abolished which ought, under a just government, to be either extirpated or suppressed. [60]

"LOVE YOUR ENEMIES"

Those who disagree with Holy War will use these words of Christ to vindicate their objections, "You have heard that it was said, 'You shall love your neighbor and hate your enemy.' But I say to you, love your enemies" (Matthew 5:43–44). But, this does not somehow bring to naught the concept of Holy War, instead it corrects the misconstruing of the command, "Hate your enemy," by telling them to love their enemies. St. Paul refers to those malicious and evil sodomites who are "hated by God" (Romans 1:30),[61] and since we are to be imitators of God, we are to thus hate our enemies for the evils that are within him, and to love him for what good is in him.

This is what Augustine meant when he said, "For every wicked man should be hated as far as he is wicked; while he should be loved as a man. The vice which we rightly hate in him is to be condemned, that by its removal the human nature which we rightly love in him may be amended."[62] This can also be deduced from the words of our Lord when He declared, "you also have those who hold the doctrine of the Nicolaitans, which thing I hate." (Revelation 2:15) And again where He says, "that you hate the deeds of the Nicolaitans, which I also hate." (Revelation 2:6)

When the wicked are punished it is, then, not out of hatred for them unto themselves, but out of hatred for the evil within them. Moreover, it should be noticed that Christ never said that this is "written in the law," but that "You have heard that it was said," meaning that this was taught by your fathers and forefathers, as if to say that they did not understand the law. Therefore Christ was not combating the law itself, but correcting a corruption of the law. In the same chapter of Matthew, Christ said, "You have heard that it was said to those of old, You shall not commit adultery." (Matthew 5:27) Does this mean that Christ wanted to do away with the law against adultery? Absolutely not. What we then must conclude is that He was confronting a corruption of this law.[63]

WHOEVER LIVES BY THE SWORD DIES BY THE SWORD

But then they will protest and object, and say, "Jesus told Peter, 'Put up again thy sword into his place: for all they that take the sword shall perish with the sword.'" (Matthew 26:52) But this does not in any way reject or condemn the state's use of the sword, rather it supports it. For who kills the one who "lives by the sword"? It is the state. The words of Christ can be

---

60 Augustine, letter 138, ch. 2.14
61 This explanation and application of Romans 1:30 was done by St. Augustine (Against Faustus, 19.24)
62 Augustine, Against Faustus, 19.24
63 See Vitoria, *On Law*, ST I–II. 98, article 1, 128

rendered this way: "anybody who commits a murder must in turn be executed by the magistrate."[64] It is in accordance to the law given to Moses, "He who strikes a man so that he dies shall surely be put to death." (Exodus 21:12)

Therefore, the temporal sword is here upheld by Christ, and the use of capital punishment on evildoers continues in Christianity. Peter was not the government, and thus he did not have the temporal authority to use the sword.[65] Augustine said this when he commented on the story of St. Peter's use of the sword, "To take the sword is to use weapons against a man's life, without the sanction of the constituted authority."[66] Moreover, Jesus did not correct Peter because righteous defense is an evil unto itself, but because his violent action was done solely as vengeance for what was being done to Our Lord, and without any thought of His divine plan. This is why Christ told Peter: "Put your sword into the sheath. Shall I not drink the cup which My Father has given Me?" (John 18:11) Peter's temporal aggression had to have been prevented as not to hinder the spiritual destiny of Christ's sacrifice. Hence Augustine, commenting on the attack made my Peter on the officer, says

> Peter's deed, however, was disapproved of by the Lord, and He prevented Him from proceeding further by the words: Put up your sword into the sheath: the cup which my Father has given me, shall I not drink it? For in such a deed that disciple only sought to defend his Master, without any thought of what it was intended to signify. And he had therefore to be exhorted to the exercise of patience, and the event itself to be recorded as an exercise of understanding.[67]

St. Peter acted from the flesh, when he struck with the sword, and not with the spirit. He only thought of temporal death, and not on eternal life. Peter, to use the words of St. Cyril when he wrote on this passage, "looked only at the death on the Cross, and not at the benefits to result therefrom; Peter tried, so far as in him lay, to prevent that which had been resolved and determined for the salvation of all men."[68] St. Peter's swift reaction was not of God, but of the devil. For even though it was done with a loving intention, the slaying of the guards would not have been for an eternal benefit, but for a damning one, preventing our Redemption, and the Atonement of the whole world.

It was out of love for Our Lord that St. Peter, when hearing of the coming death of Christ, said to Our Savior, "Far be it from You, Lord; this shall not happen to You!" (Matthew 16:22) And Yet Christ responded with these words, "Get behind Me, Satan! You are an offense to Me, for you are not mindful of the things of God, but the things of men." (Matthew 16:23) And so when Peter, out of desperate love for his Lord, struck off the ear of the servant, he was not being mindful of the things of God, but of men. At that moment of passion, Peter did not care for the loss souls of men, but for his own desires. Not only was Peter's action against the

---

64   Bellarmine, *On Laymen or Secular People*, ch. 13, ed. Tutino, pp. 49–50
65   See Bellarmine, *On Laymen or Secular People*, ch. 13, ed. Tutino, p. 50
66   Augustine, Against Faustus, 22.70
67   Augustine, Tractate 112 on John, 5, trans. John Gibb
68   St. Cyril, Commentary on John, 11.12

divine plan of God, but it was unnecessary. For what use did the Son of God have of arms, when He Himself could have, without any effort, destroyed His enemies? And what good would have been weapons when Christ was not resisting the officers, but giving Himself willingly, in accordance to the plan of His Father, to the Holy Cross? To use the words of St. Cyril:

> And, to repeat once more what we said before, seeing that His capture was effected by His own Will, and did not merely result from the malice of the Jews, how could it be right to repel or thwart, in any way, and with a sword, too, the bold attack of His combined foes and the impious conspiracy of the Jews? He says, that God the Father gave unto Him the cup, that is, death, though it was prepared for Him by the obstinate hatred of the Jews; because it would never have come to pass if He had not suffered it for our sakes. [69]

St. Ambrose, commenting on the story of St. Peter's passion, says that while it is prohibited to strike with the sword out of senseless violence, it is not prohibited to strike back with the sword for the sake of self-defense:

> O Lord, why do you order me to buy a sword and prohibit me from striking? Why do you command me to get what you forbid me to bring out? Maybe to prepare me for an act of defense and not authorize an act of revenge, so that I would decide not to take revenge even if I could. The law does not in fact forbid to strike back and therefore perhaps He said to Peter, who was offering two swords, 'It is enough' as if this were lawful until the Gospel, so that in the law there might be the knowledge of justice and in the Gospel the perfection of virtue. The law does not forbid to strike: and therefore perhaps to Peter, who was offering two swords, Christ says, 'It is enough,' as if this were lawful until the Gospel, so that in the law there might be the knowledge of justice, and in the Gospel the perfection of virtue. [70]

There are other profound meanings within the story of Peter attacking with the sword. St. Peter struck off the ear of the Jewish servant, but there is a very beautiful significance behind this moment. The hearing of the Jews who were in servitude to their corrupt ways, was now removed by a disciple of Christ, and this is what St. Hilary of Poitiers said when commenting on this verse,

> The hearing of a disobedient people subject to the priesthood was cut off by Christ's disciple, and that ear which did not hear in reception of the truth was now amputated. [71]

But there is an eternal purpose behind this. The ear of the Jew is cut off, but his hearing is only retrieved through Christ. Thus, the ears of the Jews to hear the truth of God, is only brought by Jesus Christ, and so Peter's use of the sword was by God's providence, and done as part of divine destiny, not only to instruct a most profound truth, but to bring that Jewish servant to the path of light. This is how Augustine saw this majestic moment in sacred history:

---

69 St. Cyril, Commentary on John, 11.12
70 Ambrose, commentary on Luke, book 10, in Bellarmine, *On the Temporal Power of the Pope*, ch. 19, ed. Tutino, p. 283
71 St. Hilary, Commentary on Matthew 32, trans. DH Williams, ellipses mine

What, then, is signified by the ear that was cut off in the Lord's behalf, and healed by the Lord, but the renewed hearing that has been pruned of its oldness, that it may henceforth be in the newness of the spirit, and not in the oldness of the letter? [Romans 7:6] Who can doubt that he, who had such a thing done for him by Christ, was yet destined to reign with Christ? And his being found as a servant, pertains also to that oldness that genders to bondage, which is Agar. (Galatians 4:24) But when healing came, liberty also was shadowed forth.[72]

"FLEE INTO THE MOUNTAINS"

Another argument that is put into use is when Christ said, "Then let them who are in Judea flee into the mountains" (Matthew 24:16). They will quote this verse to prove that in times of persecution crusades should not be done, but instead the Christians must flee to the wilderness and hide. That Christ told His Apostles to flee when persecuted, does not indicate that we are to observe this in every situation of persecution, but only in certain circumstances when there is no hope. David, Moses, Elijah, and Gideon, all fled in certain confrontations, but when they had armies, and positions of attack, they charged against their enemies in combat. The same can be said for Christ: for He too fled when the Jews attempted to stone Him, but when His divine eyes set upon the thieves in the Temple, He took up His whip and drove out the enemies of His Father.

THE ORDER OF CHRIST DEMANDS FOR CAPITAL PUNISHMENT AGAINST EVIL DOERS, AND FOR CHRISTIAN GOVERNMENT

Do not let the heretical connivers deceive you, and say that this ended with the New Covenant, as they love to repeat. What then, should we allow criminals to run free and spill innocent blood, and then call this "grace" and "love"? This is not love, but anarchy and the enabling of evil. It is thus an evil unto itself—nay—it is the worst form of evil, for it is what gives murderers license to slay the innocent. Some will say that this is not of Christian patience. But, in the words of St. Bernard, "Patience is not good, if, when you may be free, you allow yourself to be a slave."[73]

Many do not want to realize that our existence would be no more if it were not for just and vigorous men who took up the sword and prevented evil people from harming the wicked. This was the observation of Vitoria, who said:

> The world could not exist unless some men had the power and authority to deter the wicked by force from doing harm to the good and the innocent.[74]

The use of capital of punishment was always upheld in the Church, as we read from Pope Innocent I:

---

72 St. Augustine, Tractate 112 on John's Gospel, 5
73 Bernard, *On Consideration*, 1.3
74 Vitoria, *On the Law of War*, question 1, article 4, 19

It must be remembered that power was granted by God [to the magistrates], and to avenge crime by the sword was permitted. He who carries out this vengeance is God's minister (Romans 13:1-4). Why should we condemn a practice that all hold to be permitted by God? We uphold, therefore, what has been observed until now, in order not to alter the discipline and so that we may not appear to act contrary to God's authority. [75]

The heretics will say, "Capital punishment is man's law, not God's. Nowhere in the New Testament is capital punishment given." What then do we do with murderers, rapists, and other blood thirsty people? They will say, "Put them in prison and reform them." And to this we can use their own logic against them, and simply say, "That's man's law. Where in the New Testament is such things ever done, or even ordered?" Their line of logic only shows the incoherencies of their theological decay. If they want to use the New Testament or the New Covenant, they should know that it is much harsher than their own beliefs. The heretics say that we cannot go to the Law of Moses, so then let us go to the Law that existed before Moses, the one of Noah and Melchizedek. The Church is of the priesthood of Melchizedek, since our High Priest, Jesus Christ, is of this order. Thus in the Psalms it declares of the Christ, "You are a priest forever according to the order of Melchizedek." (Psalm 110:4) And St. Paul tells us that Christ is "High Priest forever according to the order of Melchizedek." (Hebrews 6:20)

And was it not this Melchizedek who blessed Abraham, and gave him the sacrament of bread and wine, after he slaughtered the pagan kings who stole his nephew Lot from him? He was given the title of "king of Salem," which means "king of peace," (Hebrews 7:2), and this was not the peace of the heretics, but the true peace of Christ, that slaughters evil doers for the advancement of peace. If this was then the superficial "peace" of the heretics, that tolerates all sorts of evil and spits on Holy War, why then would Melchizedek, this "king of peace," come to Abraham, whose sword was stained with the blood of tyrants, and bless him? And not only this, but he praised God for delivering the heathens into his hands. As Moses recounts to us:

> Then Melchizedek king of Salem brought out bread and wine; he was the priest
> of God Most High. And he blessed him and said:
> Blessed be Abram of God Most High,
> Possessor of heaven and earth;
> And blessed be God Most High,
> Who has delivered your enemies into your hand. (Genesis 14:18–20)

Here the high priest merges the sword with religion, here he places the Holy Faith with justice and combat, here is Holy War proclaimed![76, 77] And it is of this very priesthood, that Christ is the head. In the Old Testament, this is the only story we know of him, the only account we have of him. And in this single account, Melchizedek is blessing a war. This is

---

75 Innocent 1, Epist. 6, C. 3. 8, ad Exsuperium, Episcopum Tolosanum, 20 February 405, PL 20, 495. See also Bellarmine, *On Laymen or Secular People*, ch. 13, ed. Tutino, p. 50, where he cites Innocent I support for the death penalty in his third epistle, ch. 3, sent to Exuperius

76 St. Robert Bellarmine uses the story of Melchizedek and Abraham to support Holy War

77 *On Laymen or Secular People*, ch. 14, p. 57

most significant. The Order of Melchizedek, of which Christ is head, and which is the order of the Church, is only actively and explicitly recounted in the Old Testament as being spiritually involved in a war. What then does this mean, but that the Church is centered around war against evil? The mission of the Church is Holy War, both with spiritual and physical arms. Here Abraham unsheathes the temporal sword, and Melchizedek wields the spiritual sword, administering to the warrior the sacraments, and praising God for the victory. Christ did not come to tolerate the contrivances of the devil, He did not come to make "peace" or to "love" the devil, but instead He came "that He might destroy the works of the devil." (1 John 3:8) Christ came to destroy, He came for battle, and He came for Holy War.

The law that Melchizedek followed was that given to Noah after the flood, one of which declared:

> Whoever sheds man's blood,
> By man his blood shall be shed;
> For in the image of God
> He made man. (Genesis 9:6)

Thus from here is the slaying of evildoers by the sword of the state instituted. It is by this precept that "all who take the sword will perish by the sword." (Matthew 26:52) The Chaldaic paraphrase of this law renders the passage this way:

> Whoever sheds men's blood before witnesses, by sentence of a judge his blood should be shed. [78]

This law was given to Noah and it most certainly would have continued on with Melchizedek, for Noah was "a preacher of righteousness," (2 Peter 2:5), and he would have definitely taught the law given to him, and all pious posterity after him would have upheld these teachings. Since the Church is of the order of Melchizedek, then Holy War and capital punishment against evildoers perpetuates under Christianity, and thus in Christendom. Moreover, since governments and laws were established before the Gospel, it is inadequate and illogical to think that all of a sudden they cannot continue after the Gospel.[79] Punishment for murder is not only permissible within Christendom, but also for any ardent war made against God and His most holy laws. St. John Climachus, writing on the adversaries of the Lord, says:

> His enemies are those who not only contravene and repudiate the commands of the Lord, but make stern war against all who obey him. [80]

These are the enemies of God, and these are the evildoers who cannot be tolerated within holy Christendom. The light of Christendom cannot be permitted to be dimmed and

---

78 In Bellarmine, *On Laymen or Secular People*, ch. 13, ed. Tutino, p. 49. Bellarmine is here referring to the Jewish targums (see Tutino's footnote for this passage of Bellarmine)
79 Vitoria, *On Civil Power*, question 1, article 5.2
80 St. John Climachus, *The Ladder of Divine Ascent*, Step 1: On Renunciation of Life, trans. Luibheid & Russell, p. 73

eclipsed by the darkness of these wicked men, who declare war on all things holy, who froth at the mouth against Heaven and the divine precepts, and war against God's Church, and viciously desire to persecute the saints. Hence, is deliberate impiety punished within the realms of Christendom, and this is not solely based on Mosaic Law, but the Law taught under Melchizedek's order that is now the Church. The holy prophet Job, who lived before Moses, upheld the law against paganism by the state's judges, when he said:

> If I beheld the sun when it shined, or the moon walking in brightness; and my heart hath been secretly enticed, or my mouth hath kissed my hand: this also were an iniquity to be punished by the judge: for I should have denied the God that is above. (Job 31:26–28)

Once the people of Nineveh, who were not Israelites, "believed God," (Jonah 3:5), the king of Nineveh, who was not under the Mosaic covenant nor part of Israel, decreed that all of his subjects should worship the true God and fast for Him,

> Let neither man nor beast, herd nor flock, taste any thing: let them not feed, nor drink water: But let man and beast be covered with sackcloth, and cry mightily unto God: yea, let them turn everyone from his evil way, and from the violence that is in their hands. (Jonah 3:7–8)

So then, if it was righteous for the king of Nineveh, who was not under the Law of Israel, to decree laws of piety for his people, it is not unbiblical for Christian lands, which are not under the Mosaic covenant but Christ, to make laws upholding Orthodoxy and punishing people who maliciousness attack God and His people. If Nebuchadnezzar, who was not under Mosaic Law nor an Israelite, was considered righteous when he ordered, "I make a decree, That in every dominion of my kingdom men tremble and fear before the God of Daniel" (Daniel 6:26), and make into a law, "that the people of any nation or language who say anything against the God of Shadrach, Meshach and Abednego be cut into pieces and their houses be turned into piles of rubble," (Daniel 3:29) then it is permissible for Christendom to as well establish such edicts. God blessed Nebuchadnezzar with victories over his enemies, declaring to Ezekiel, "Son of man, Nebuchadnezzar king of Babylon caused his army to labor strenuously against Tyre; every head was made bald, and every shoulder rubbed raw; yet neither he nor his army received wages from Tyre, for the labor which they expended on it. Therefore thus says the Lord God: surely I will give the land of Egypt to Nebuchadnezzar king of Babylon; he shall take away her wealth, carry off her spoil, and remove her pillage; and that will be the wages for his army." (Ezekiel 29:18–19) If pagan kings who fight against the enemies of God, are blessed by God with temporal rewards, imagine how He will bless Christian kings who fight against the Lord's adversaries![81] This argument of severing the Mosaic Law from the Church as a way to neutralize Christian government for secular government, is truly unbiblical once put against these passages. Not only is it contrary to Scripture, but dangerous, for it gives leeway for anti-Christian measures to be legislated by politicians who would otherwise not be allowed to decree their evils in Christendom.

---

81 See Aquinas, De regiminie principum, 1.9

CHRISTIANITY IS AT WAR: THE MANIFESTO FOR CHRISTIAN MILITANCY

CHRIST DEMANDS FOR THE FINANCIAL FUNDING OF WARS

Some of the heretics argue that Christ removed the precept of war. If that were true, St. John the Baptist would have told the soldiers to leave the military, but instead he told them: "Do not intimidate anyone or accuse falsely, and be content with your wages." (Luke 3:14) We ask the heretics, Why would St. John permit what Christ was soon to prohibit? It is because Christ never prohibited just war, but despotic war, and wars done for gain. In the words of St. Ambrose, "to be in the army in not a crime, but to be in the army for the sake of pillaging is a sin."[82] St. Augustine says that St. John "did not forbid them to serve in the army when he commanded them to be satisfied with their pay."[83] Moreover, Christ's support for just war is signified by the fact that he said that the tribute to Caesar must be paid: "Render to Caesar the things that are Caesar's" (Mark 12:17). And of course this tribute would have been used for the funding of the army that would have protected the commonwealth from enemies. The Apostle explains this when he writes, "you also pay taxes, for they are God's ministers attending continually to this very thing." (Romans 13:6) This money would have been used for the funding of wars and public security, for before this passage he says that the governor "is God's minister, an avenger to execute wrath on him who practices evil." (Romans 13:4)[84]

St. Augustine attests to this as well when, commenting on this passage, he says, "For tribute-money is given on purpose to pay the soldiers for war."[85] Paul says that we must do this "not only because of wrath but also for conscience sake." (Romans 13:5) In other words, because it is righteous. If it is righteous to fund the wars of pagan emperors, how more should we then support holy wars made by Christian rulers! What if the Caesar is Christian and he executes a crusade against the pagans, would these heretics condemn such a war while supporting the wars of pagans? Do not forget that while Christ said, "Give back to Caesar the things that are Caesar's," He also said, "and to God the things that are God's." If a war is done for the destruction of evil and for the protection and advancement of the Church, it is a duty to support such a cause, for not only is it done for Caesar, but for God. The Church can even impose taxes for a righteous cause, such as the Crusades, which needed all the money they could get to fund the holy war against the Muslims. As St. Thomas wrote:

> The same applies to the cause of a prince of a whole kingdom, since, in order to maintain his government, he may extend his authority over his subjects by imposing taxes, destroying cities and towns for the protection of the whole kingdom. It is much more fitting, then, to apply this to the supreme prince, that is the Pope that would do the same for the good of the whole of Christianity.[86]

---

[82] Ambrose, sermon 7, in St. Robert Bellarmine, *On Laymen or Secular People*, ch. 14, ed. Tutino, p. 59
[83] Augustine, letter 138
[84] See Bellarmine for this interpretation, in his *On Laymen or Secular People*, ch. 14, ed. Tutino, p. 56
[85] Augustine, Against Faustus, 22.74
[86] Aquinas, *De regimine principum*, book 3, ch. 19, in Bellarmine, *On the Temporal Power of the Pope*, preface, ed. Tutino, p. 126

St. John the Baptist here does not condemn the use of a military for righteousness, but injustices that may be done by a military. A holy military, a military of Christ, fighting for Christendom, is therefore the highest manifestation of what St. John ordered. St. Bernard of Clairvaux declared that not only does this teaching of St. John signify that a Christian military is biblical, but also that it mostly rightly belongs to the warriors of Christ, the defenders of the Church and Christendom:

> What then? If it is then never legitimate for a Christian to strike with a sword, why then did the Saviour's precursor bid soldiers be content with their pay, and not rather ban military serve to them? But if, as is the case, it is legitimate for all those ordained to by the Almighty—provided they have not embraced a higher calling—then to whom, I ask, may it more rightly be allowed than to those into whose hands and hearts is committed on behalf of all of us Sion, the city of our strength? So that once the transgressors of divine law have been expelled, the righteous nation that preserves the truth may enter in surety. [87]

And for those who say that Christ did away with war after John the Baptist, you should also affirm that Christ did away with taxes. For before St. John said these words to the soldiers, he told the tax collectors, "Collect no more than what is appointed for you." (Luke 3:13) Why do these heretics always attack military use, but never say we should get rid of taxes? Try, then, to get rid of the military and cast away all taxes, and see how long any nation will survive. This is the same point St. Augustine made when he wrote against people who say such wicked things:

> When he [St. John the Baptist] commanded that their own wages ought to suffice for them, he of course did not forbid them to serve in the army. Hence, let those who say that the teaching of Christ is opposed to the state give us an army of the sort that the teachings of Christ ordered soldiers to be. Let them give us such people of the provinces, such husbands, such wives, such parents, such children, such masters, such slaves, such kings, such judges, and finally such taxpayers and tax collectors as Christian teaching prescribes, and let them dare to say that this teaching is opposed to the state; in fact, let them not hesitate to admit that it would be a great boon for the state if this were observed. [88]

CHRIST IS THE GENERAL OF CHRISTIAN SOLDIERS

The centurion went to Christ and asked him to heal his ill servant, and when Christ was about to attend to the sick man in his home, the centurion said, "Lord, I am not worthy that You should come under my roof. But only speak a word, and my servant will be healed. For I also am a man under authority, having soldiers under me. And I say to this one, Go, and he goes; and to another, Come, and he comes; and to my servant, 'Do this,' and he does it." (Matthew 8:8–9) Look and observe what beautiful and profound significance can be beheld in these few words. Here stood the centurion, a warrior who led many battles and killed

---

87 St. Bernard, *In Praise of a New Knighthood*, ch. 3, 5
88 Augustine, letter 138.15, brackets mine

CHRISTIANITY IS AT WAR: THE MANIFESTO FOR CHRISTIAN MILITANCY

many men, and he is comparing Christ to a general Who with all of His authority has the power to say the order and it shall be done. And does Christ berate this man, does He object and correct him? Absolutely not! The Scriptures say that "When Jesus heard it, He marveled, and said to those who followed, 'Assuredly, I say to you, I have not found such great faith, not even in Israel!'" (Matthew 8:10) Christ never told the centurion to leave the military, because military force, when used rightfully, is holy and noble.[89]

St. John Chrysostom said concerning those who believed in pacifism, "You use the army as a pretext and say that you cannot be pious; was not the centurion a soldier, and yet his being in the army did him no harm?"[90] Nor did Christ scold the centurion, because his words were true; for Christ is our Heavenly General, leading His holy armies to fight the devil and compel him to flee as He had done when Satan tried to tempt Him in the desert. And so, as Christ is our General in Heaven, and is always with His Church "even to the end of the age" (Matthew 28:20), He appoints "God's minister," on earth, who as the Scripture says, as "an avenger to execute wrath on him who practices evil." (Romans 13:4)

THE SPIRITUAL TEACHINGS OF CHRIST ARE APPLIED TO HOLY WAR

When you look at the New Testament, the Apostles did not govern an earthly kingdom, they did everything they could within the confines of citizens and subjects: they were preaching, converting, baptizing. They were applying the teachings of Christ solely within the Church, and could not use the state for an ecclesiastical purpose. But even their actions were done to build up a kingdom, to gradually form Christendom. Right before Constantine took control of the empire, and commenced Christendom, the Roman Empire was one third Christian, enough to influence the state and cause a revolution for a Christian government. Such a large amount of people was due to the preaching of the Apostles and their successors, and it was this labor and work that would eventually give birth to Christendom.

As soon as the Roman Empire became under the control of Christian sovereigns, the laws of the Old Testament against idolatry, homosexuality, and other evils, began to be enacted. The teachings of Christ were now not just being done under the limits of the individual, or the Church, but were being applied through a governmental position, just as they were done in ancient Israel.

Christ said, "And you shall love the Lord your God with all your heart, with all your soul, with all your mind, and with all your strength." (Mark 12:30) How could this be applied? Several ways: through martyrdom, through placing your life on the line for the advancement of Christianity, through holy war against the enemies of God. But before Christendom, how could this be applied? It was illustrated by those who taught and preached the Gospel at the peril of death, seeking martyrdom and not thinking for their own lives, or in being very committed to helping the poor, the widows and the orphans, or in exorcising demons. But with

---

89 See Bellarmine, *On Laymen or Secular People*, ch. 14, p. 56
90 St. John Chrysostom, De nuptiis, quoted by St. Robert Bellarmine, On Laymen or Secular War, ch. 14, ed. Tutino, p. 59

the rise of Christendom, these were no longer the only ways of carrying out this teaching of Christ. Now, it could be applied to holy war, to the vanquishing of pagans and heretics. This is how it was applied in ancient Israel, for in the Scriptures, when king Josiah "executed all the priests of the high places" (2 Kings 23:20) "put away those who consulted mediums and spiritists, the household gods and idols, all the abominations that were seen in the land of Judah and in Jerusalem" (2 Kings 23:24), and "he broke down the houses of the sodomites," (2 Kings 23:7) it describes him as obeying the first commandment of Christ, saying that he "turned to the Lord with all his heart, with all his soul, and with all his might" (2 Kings 23:25).

Without Christendom, Christians follow the first command of Christ within the Church, or within their own lives, but through Christendom it is applied to crusading and through holy war. Actually, in the context of Christendom, Christian soldiers and officers can love God by slaying pagans and putting homosexuals to death.

Another example from Christ's spiritual teachings is when He said, "If any man will come after me, let him deny himself, and take up his cross daily, and follow me." (Luke 9:23) How is this commandment applied without Christendom? The Apostles carried it out through martyrdom; they expanded the Gospel throughout the world, without worry for their own lives, with fearlessness of death, armed with the Sword of the Spirit, crushing demons and their doctrines. How was it also applied within Christendom? Through crusading, through taking up both the Sword of the Spirit and the temporal sword, and with a selfless disposition, to fight demons and their mortal followers. The first is martyrdom through persecution, and the other is martyrdom through holy war. Both surround a spiritual war, and both require the denial of the self and the carrying of the cross. The application of the commandment of Christ to crusading was done by Christendom. During the First Crusade, one anonymous Christian warrior applied it to the fight against the Muslims:

> When now that time was at hand which the Lord Jesus daily points out to His faithful, especially in the Gospel, saying, "If any man would come after me, let him deny himself and take up his cross and follow me, a mighty agitation was carried on throughout the region of Gaul. (Its tenor was) that if anyone desired to follow the Lord zealously, with a pure heart and mind, and wished faithfully to bear the cross after him, he would no longer hesitate to take up the way of the Holy Sepulcher."[91]

The teaching of Christ to deny the self is not about some false compromising peace, but rather it is speaking of war against Satan and his evil followers. As Christ says in the profound teaching:

> Do not think that I came to bring peace on earth. I did not come to bring peace but a sword. For I have come to set a man against his father, a daughter against her mother, and a daughter-in-law against her mother-in-law and a man's enemies will be those of his own household.' He who loves father or mother more than Me is not worthy of Me. And he who loves son or daughter more than Me is not worthy of Me. And he who does not take his cross

---

91 *The Gesta*, ed. Edward Peters

and follow after Me is not worthy of Me. He who finds his life will lose it, and he who loses his life for My sake will find it. (Matthew 10:34–39)

To deny the self is to war with the world, not to compromise with it; to deny the self is to not seek self-preservation, but to combat the evils of the world, even at the expense of one's own life, not seeking to live, but to die unto the self, being crucified with Christ, and accompanying His holy mission: to destroy the works of the devil.

Christ taught the warrior spirit of ancient Israel, for the spirit of self-denial is found amongst the oldest of the holy combatants. Moses denied himself when he defended the daughters of Jethro against the shepherds, and "stood up and helped them, and watered their flock." (Exodus 2:17) The shepherds were attacking the women, but they were not attacking Moses, they were not of any threat to his self. But he surpassed his self and the desire for self-perpetuation, he went out of himself and strived for the wellbeing of other selves. For this reason Jethro saw the holiness within Moses and gave him one of his daughters. As St. Gregory of Nyssa commented on this story: "This man [Jethro] saw in one act—the attack on the shepherds—the virtue of the young man [Moses], how he fought on behalf of the right without looking for personal gain. Considering the right valuable in itself, Moses punished the wrong done by the shepherds, although they had done nothing against him."[92] Moses fought not for any personal gain, but, denying himself, he strived for justice; thus is Christian militancy. Samson denied himself and took up his cross when he ended his life to kill off the pagan Philistines, and Uriah denied himself when he sacrificed himself for the glory of Israel. Christ denied Himself when He suffered oppressions and died on the Cross to conquer the devil, for before His Passion, He told His Father, "not as I will, but as You will." (Matthew 26:39) Here are the words of self-denial, and placing oneself completely under Providence, and dedicating oneself utterly to God, in the face of a glorious battle done for the love of the Holy Trinity. It is the spirit of Christ that is within those who die for Him, either in persecution or in crusading, for in both the denial of the self is accomplished.

THE CHRISTIAN DOES NOT FIGHT FOR HIMSELF, BUT FOR GOD

The soldiers strives for the death of death, by destroying the promoters of death, and exerts himself for the advancement of peace. Thus is what our Lord means when He says:

> Blessed are the peacemakers, for they shall be called sons of God. (Matthew 5:9)

Surely the knight of Christ fights for peace and is worthy of being called a son of God. He strikes with full exertion, with the purest of divine love and mercy, with utter disregard for his own life, and with full concern for the lives of others, protecting them from the blade of the sinister. In the heart of every warrior, is the denial of the self. When Gideon overthrew the altar of Baal and repulsed the Midianites with the sword, he did not do it for his own gain, but for God; when Moses and Joshua, and all the mighty men of Israel, combated against the Amelekites, they did not do so for their own profit, but for God; when the children of Israel

---

92 Gregory of Nyssa, *Life of Moses*, 1.19

eradicated the Benjaminites because they defended a gang of sodomites, they did not do so for earthly treasures, but for treasures in Heaven; when Moses slew the Egyptian, he did not slay for his own life, but for the life of another; when Christ unsheathed a whip and struck the thieves, He did it for the House of His Father; when all of these holy men, including our Lord, committed such feats of courage and valiancy, they didn't do it for the pleasing of the self, but in the denial of the self.

In the victory of every Holy War, man is not exalted, God is exalted. At the death of the pagan, Christ is glorified. In the words of St. Bernard: "At the death of the pagan, the Christian exults because Christ is exalted."

HOLY WAR IS NOT DONE FOR GAIN, BUT FOR GOD'S LAW AND JUSTICE

War for the cause of justice and the Holy Faith is not a sin, but war for gain is. This is why St. John the Baptist told the soldiers: "Do not intimidate anyone or accuse falsely, and be content with your wages." (Luke 3:14) A Christian soldier is content with his pay and does not fight to steal, intimidate, make himself superior to others, but fights for God Who is supreme above all. The words of the Baptist are a teaching for the soldier, not of pagan warfare—which seeks only for gain—but for the Christian solider, who never wars for temporal but for spiritual interests. This is why St. Robert declares that "those kings or soldiers who undertake a war either to harm somebody, or to enlarge the empire or to show prowess in war, or for a reason other than the common good, sin gravely, even if the authority is legitimate and the cause is just."[93] And it is also why Augustine said, "The desire to do harm, the cruelty of vengeance, an unpeaceable and implacable spirit, the fever of rebellion, the lust to dominate, and similar things: these are rightly condemned in war."[94]

Killing for the sake of earthly violence, is of the devil and not of God. The monk Hugh said to the knights who fought in Jerusalem that Satan "temps you with anger and hatred when you kill, with greed when you strip your victims."[95] St. Gregory VII wrote that one taking up arms is wrong "except in defense of his own rights or those of his lord or of a friend or of the poor, or in defense of churches and with the advice of men of religion who know how to counsel wisely in view of their eternal welfare."[96] The sword cannot be struck righteously unless the mind of the one who wields it is tempered with the virtue of justice in between both prudence and fortitude. "Therefore, whatever you want men to do to you, do also to them, for this is the Law and the Prophets." (Matthew 7:12) This is the precept of the highest Justice, and therefore the execution of the sword cannot be done for anything superficial, and nor can it be refused when its necessity is so real. For every man would hate to be imposed with an undeserving punishment. This is why both prudence and fortitude

---

93 St. Robert Bellarmine, *On Laymen or Secular People*, ch. 15, p. 70
94 Augustine, *Contra Faustum*, 22:74, in Aquinas, Summa Theologica IIa IIae 40, article 1
95 Hugh, To the Templars in the East, in Barber and Bate, Templars
96 Gregory VII, book 7, 10, p. 471

are so necessary; the first prevents rash verdicts from being made, and enables mercy, while the second prevents the mercy of the fool from taking precedence.[97]

By the will of God, did the rulers who "are not a terror to good works, but to evil" executed their authority for God, and the one who "does not bear the sword in vain" wielded the blade for the cause of Christ. St. Thomas, the Doctor of the Church, says that God rewards the ruler "who gladdens a whole province with peace, restrains the violent, preserves justice, and disposes the actions of men by means of his laws and precepts."[98] Thus was Christendom, and as it once was, so soon shall it return when Christ comes again, as it was ordained throughout Christian history "to execute wrath on him who practices evil." (Romans 13:4) So it is not as though as the revisionist says, that Christ did away with the Old Testament warfare, that only Christ has the authority to execute warfare and only when 'He returns', but that Christ when He does return, He will restore what has been done throughout Christian history and thus is Christ's reformation and not this false reformation the modernists, the useless and the lazy servants love to discuss. This is chiseled in the New testament by the words of Paul pertaining to the state ultimately were written for Christendom. But there will always be those who will say that such a verse should never be connected with the Church. How could this be said when it was the Church—St. Paul, a pillar of the Church—who wrote these words? The Church wrote these words so it could be cast away from being a part of what it said? It was the Church who wrote Romans 13, and let it be the Church who dictates its application, and let it be written for the Church. St. Robert Bellarmine, commenting on Romans 13, and responding to such heretics, wrote:

> Therefore, if such evildoers are found in the Church, why may they not be punished with the sword?[99]

VENGEANCE IS MINE SAITH THE LORD

But, as we expect, there will always be objectors who say that these precepts of Christendom are wrong because the Bible says, "Vengeance is mine; I will repay, saith the Lord." (Romans 12:19) They will always quote Romans 12, but this does not all of a sudden neutralize the use of Holy War by Christendom, for in the next chapter St. Paul says that the ruler is "an avenger to execute wrath on him who practices evil." (Romans 13:4) How can you say that vengeance belongs to God and then say that the ruler who bears the sword is an avenger? Is Paul contradicting himself or is this theology corrupt and imbalanced? The truth is the latter of the two. While vengeance does belong to God, that vengeance is done through the sword of a ruler.

Moses "was very humble, more than all men who were on the face of the earth" (Numbers 12:3), and he did say, "You shall not take vengeance," (Leviticus 19:18) but when the time came to fight the wicked, the holy prophet became an instrument of God's wrath and

---

97 See St. Bernard, *On Consideration*, 1.8
98 Aquinas, *De regimine principum*
99 Bellarmine, *On Laymen or Secular People*, ch. 13, ed. Tutino, p. 50

vengeance against those who deserved it, for he did not even spare the women when he commanded the Hebrews to slaughter the Midianites, saying: "Arm some of yourselves for war, and let them go against the Midianites to take vengeance for the Lord on Midian." (Numbers 31:3) If Christendom were to be revived, why then would it be wrong for a righteous Christian nation to be such an avenger?[100]

It would not be wrong, for Christendom was created by Christ and through Christ, and for Christ. And who can deny this when the Apostle says:

> For by Him all things were created that are in heaven and that are on earth, visible and invisible, whether thrones or dominions or principalities or powers. All things were created through Him and for Him. (Colossians 1:16)

Christendom was created through Christ and for Christ to expand His Holy Faith throughout the world and to end pagan tyranny. Power was transmitted from the pagans to the Christians, and in such a state were pagans and heretics restrained from expanding their wickedness. For as Augustine tells us of the Christian Roman Empire:

> Now in the midst of Your enemies, now in this transition of ages, in this propagation and succession of human mortality, now while the torrent of time is gliding by, unto this is the rod of Your power sent out of Sion, that You may be Ruler in the midst of Your enemies. Rule Thou, rule among Pagans, Jews, heretics, false brethren. Rule Thou, rule, O Son of David, Lord of David, rule in the midst of Pagans, Jews, heretics, false brethren. Be Thou Ruler in the midst of Your enemies. [101]

One may argue and say, "Yes, the verse in Colossians says that all 'thrones or dominions or principalities or powers' are created by God, and that would include Christendom. But this does not mean that Christendom is anything special or distinct, since God created it just as He created empires that were pagan." God brought Pharaoh to power, and permitted him to enslave the Hebrews, and He brought Moses to power to defy the tyrant, to guide the people to liberation, to establish the Divine Law, and crush the lawlessness of the pagans. There is a distinct difference between the two sovereigns, one is for tyranny while the other is for God; one hates the things of eternity while the other advances the cause of Heaven. The pagan emperor Maxentius was brought to power by God, and allowed by God to slaughter countless Christians under his empire, and God allowed Constantine to defeat the tyrant to bring the Church to liberty, and commence the formation of Christendom. One persecuted Christianity, while the other upheld the true Faith, and advanced its glory throughout the empire. And who can say without arrogance that God does not see such things and know the benefits of the Christian emperor, and the devastations brought about by the pagan despot? As Moses becoming the leader of the Hebrews is a most profound action of Providence, so is the ascendency of Constantine over the pagans a distinguished event by the will of God.

---

100 See St. Robert Bellarmine, *On Laymen or Secular People*, ch. 14, p. 60
101 Augustine, Commentary on the Psalm 110, 6

The concept that we should not take vengeance was not some new novelty said after the coming of Christ, but in ancient Israel. The Lord said, through Moses, "You shall not take vengeance, nor bear any grudge against the children of your people, but you shall love your neighbor as yourself: I am the Lord." (Leviticus 19:18) One could read this and easily conclude that all use of arms is evil, just from this one verse. These words were declared through Moses, and yet it was this same Moses who slew the worshippers of the golden calf, and ordered the slaughter of the Midianites, and was wroth when the Hebrews spared the Midianite women. Moses used the sword, and yet he said, by divine inspiration, "You shall not take vengeance." Was Moses then a hypocrite, was he self-contradictory, or is the theology of these modern heretics unbalanced? The last choice is the truth, for Moses did not kill out of revenge, or to satisfy the flames of his flesh, but for justice and Holy War, being an instrument by which God unleashes His vengeance.

> O Lord God, to whom vengeance belongs
> O God, to whom vengeance belongs, shine forth! (Psalm 94:1)

These words could easily be taken to refute Christian holy war, but it would be impossible for such an argument to stand, because it is so obvious and known by anyone familiar with the Bible that David himself kill and slaughtered the enemies of God.

The vengeance of God at times is done through the sword of noble warriors, and when the righteous witness vengeance done in such a way, they do not condemn it, but rejoice, as David says:

> The righteous shall rejoice when he sees the vengeance; he shall wash his feet in the blood of the wicked (Psalm 58:10)

The righteous rejoice in the justice of God, and take part in it crushing the wicked with their feet, knowing that the vengeance of God is being done through the hands of saintly warriors. In the words of St. Bernard:

> The knight of Christ, I say, may strike with confidence and succumb more confidently. When he strikes, he does service to Christ, and to himself when he succumbs. Nor does he bear the sword in vain. He is God's minister in the punishment of evil doers and the praise of well doers. Surely, if he kills an evil doer, he is not a man-killer, but, if I may so put it, an evil killer. Clearly he is reckoned the avenger of Christ against evildoers, and the defender of Christians. Should he be killed himself, we know he has not perished, but has come safely home. The death which he inflicts is Christ's gain, and that which he suffers, his own. At the death of the pagan, the Christian exults because Christ is exalted; in the death of the Christian the King's liberality is conspicuous when the knight is ushered home and rewarded. [102]

---

[102] St. Bernard, *In Praise of a New Knighthood*, ch.2

"WE DO NOT WRESTLE AGAINST FLESH AND BLOOD"

Probably the most frequent argument of the opponents of Holy War, is the use of the verse "For we do not wrestle against flesh and blood, but against principalities, against powers, against the rulers of the darkness of this age, against spiritual hosts of wickedness in the heavenly places." (Ephesians 6:12)

Spiritual wars can be fought through physical means. Christ fought in a spiritual war against the devil on the Cross. Was the Cross not physical? The nails? The crown of thorns? The lance that pierced His holy side? All of these things were physical; the entire Crucifixion, and the Passion of our Lord, was physical. And yet, at the same time, the entire physical event was a spiritual war against the devil.

We do not fight against flesh and blood, in that our war is not against human beings—since it is with false religions—but against the demons and their false doctrines. But in the midst of such combat, part of the spiritual war is fighting against those who, following demons, persecute the Church.

The war of the Christian is spiritual, and his weapons are as well spiritual, consisting of mainly faith and prayers, and the sacraments. But this does not mean that physical war is unnecessary, for in the holy wars of the Hebrews, spiritual war was fought through physical means, that is, through weapons and armies. For as Joshua fought the Amelekites, Moses prayed; as the Maccabees fought the pagans, the prophet Jeremiah prayed "much for the people, and for all the holy city" (2 Maccabees 15:14); before king Asa and his army fought the Ethiopians, he prayed to God for victory. And who can forget the pious centurion, Cornelius, who was baptized by St. Peter himself? Who can forget how the Scriptures describe him as a soldier who "prayed to God always" (Acts 10:2)? The Christian soldier, then, fights in Holy War by combating God's enemies, and constantly praying to God as a weapon against spiritual darkness. St. Robert once wrote that the spiritual weapons of the Faith can involve physical weapons as well:

> Even if the weapons of the spiritual commonwealth, which it uses itself, are indeed spiritual, corporeal weapons are also in its power, since one sword is subject to the other, and the Church can call upon the secular arm and use through it the corporal sword. [103]

THE ARMOR OF GOD

In any debate for Holy War what is always expected from the opposition is to refer to the Armor of God, written by St. Paul in his letter to the Ephesians:

> Finally, my brethren, be strong in the Lord and in the power of His might. Put on the whole armor of God that you may be able to stand against the wiles of the devil. For we do not wrestle against flesh and blood, but against principalities, against powers, against the rulers of the darkness of this age, against spiritual hosts of wickedness in the heavenly places. Therefore take up the whole armor of God that you may be able to withstand in the evil day,

---

[103] Bellarmine, *On the Temporal Power of the Pope*, ch. 18, ed. Tutino, p. 279

CHRISTIANITY IS AT WAR: THE MANIFESTO FOR CHRISTIAN MILITANCY

> and having done all, to stand. Stand therefore, having girded your waist with truth, having put on the breastplate of righteousness, and having shod your feet with the preparation of the gospel of peace; above all, taking the shield of faith with which you will be able to quench all the fiery darts of the wicked one. And take the helmet of salvation, and the sword of the Spirit, which is the word of God; praying always with all prayer and supplication in the Spirit, being watchful to this end with all perseverance and supplication for all the saints and for me, that utterance may be given to me, that I may open my mouth boldly to make known the mystery of the gospel, for which I am an ambassador in chains; that in it I may speak boldly, as I ought to speak. (Ephesians 6:10–20)

They quote this verse with the intent to show that Christianity is not about physical war. But, Christian militancy does not argue this. Christianity is not about killing people, nor about the destruction of flesh. Holy War is not about killing life, it is about preserving life through the use of righteous force. There are regimens that destroy simply because it loves death and domination. But Holy War is not about human domination, rather it is about spiritual domination, it is for Christian supremacy, to destroy darkness and flood the world with the light of Christ. Truly the Church is engaged in a spiritual war, not a war with the aim of gratifying some transient pleasure, but for eternal aspiration.

Demons use people to advance their destructive ideologies; and so God uses people to advance the truth. Demons use human beings to inflict horrific violence to inculcate their evil ideas; in this spiritual battlefield, God uses Christians to fight against those very violent beliefs and heresies. When the soldiers of Christ use arms to combat these violent people, who are being used by demons, it is done with spiritual reasons. Therefore, even though he uses force, he uses it for spiritual reasons and to war against spiritual doctrines. Thus, Holy War is spiritual war. It does not war against flesh and blood, but spiritual darkness.

The Armor of God can be applied to wars that consist of physically battling with armies who advance spiritual darkness. Just because a battle is physical does not automatically exclude the spiritual element. For Christ fought the devil when He hung from the Cross, and such a spiritual struggle was done through nails, through a crown of thorns, through a cross, a scourge, through physical endurance and fortitude. The same spirit of forbearance that Christ exemplified on the Cross, when He defeated the devil, is the same spirit the Christian warrior bears when he, with arms and weapons, defeats the followers of Satan. St. Paul tells us to take upon "the shield of faith," and all of the warriors of Israel fought with faith on God. St. Paul, when speaking of these very fighters, does not say: 'They were wrong because they fought against flesh and blood.' But rather, he uses their valor as models of Faith:

> And what more shall I say? For the time would fail me to tell of Gideon and Barak and Samson and Jephthah, also of David and Samuel and the prophets: who through faith subdued kingdoms, worked righteousness, obtained promises, stopped the mouths of lions, quenched the violence of fire, escaped the edge of the sword, out of weakness were made strong, became valiant in battle, turned to flight the armies of the aliens. (Hebrews 11:32–34)

The warrior bears the armor of Faith when he wields the blade against the enemies of God and vanquishes adversaries of the Holy Church. And even St. Paul, who wrote that we do not war against flesh and blood, makes knowledge of this.

The error enters in not seeing the physical struggle of spiritual warfare, that the very Word of God is a double edged sword in that God Himself is participant alongside man and as well as the elements of war. No one can say that only God killed Goliath, or that only David or the smooth stone, but that all three did. In the Bible we find verses where the Psalmist declares God or His people, or both as participating in doing the Lord's will. It is therefore crucial that one does not isolate a verse without this concept in mind. The war between the Church and Satan parallels the Triune nature of God. In God there is Father, Son and Holy Spirit, and in the Son humanity and divinity come together. In the war that was fought on the Holy Cross, the human and the spiritual worked together in a beautiful harmony as the Son of God crushed the armies of death. And even in the glorious Crucifixion, there was Simon of Cyrene, a mortal, helping the God-Man carry His Cross, illuminating to our minds the human involvement in this war of the cosmos. In the war that is waged between the Church and the temple of Satan, humanity and the spiritual join together as a single force. The sword is struck, the spear thrown, the arrow fired, and yet there is the spiritual element, working within all of the soldiers, aligned with God, as they participate in the wars of Heaven.

THE SOLDIERS WHO PROTECTED PAUL

While St. Paul did say that we do not wrestle against flesh and blood, and that we must bear the armour of God, when the Jews came to kill him, he did not hesitates to allow an army of "two hundred soldiers, seventy horsemen, and two hundred spearmen" (Acts 23:23) to protect him with physical arms. The question then is: when Paul used physical weapons to protect himself, did he cast away his spiritual armor? He bore both, physical and spiritual at the same time, proving that the two can be unified in the battle against evil.

The use of the soldiers were for both physical and spiritual reasons, and it was for a just cause. The Jews desired to physically kill him in order to obliterate his spiritual fruit, and the soldiers were used, by Providence, to protect his physical person, and thus to protect the continuation of his spiritual teaching. If soldiers, who were not Christians and did not know St. Paul's spiritual mission, can protect the Church, then Christian soldiers, who are fully aware of the Faith's spiritual fruit, are all the more obligated to protect the Church in Holy War.

As Paul was being protected by the soldiers, who were armed with swords, shields, spears, breastplates and helmets, Paul was armed with "the sword of the spirit," "the shield of the faith," "the breastplate of righteousness," and the "helmet of salvation" (Ephesians 6:14–17).

The righteous soldier in Christian holy war, while not being guarded by an army as Paul was, but a part of an army of Christendom, has both. As he carries his arms and is well trained for the fray, he has within his own soul the spiritual weapons; he has girded his "waist with truth," and "put on the breastplate of righteousness" (Ephesians 6:14).

CHRISTIANITY IS AT WAR: THE MANIFESTO FOR CHRISTIAN MILITANCY

In the Christian warrior, the physical sword and the spiritual become one, with the first being used as a means to advance righteousness, and the second to keep the wielder of the blade away from violent passions. The Spanish knight Ramon Llull affirmed that the warrior cannot be a true Christian knight if all he has are bodily weapons and his soul is absent of truth and virtue:

> So then, just as all of these aforesaid practices pertain to the knight with respect to the body, so justice, wisdom, charity, loyalty, truth, humility, fortitude, hope and prowess, and the other virtues similar to these, pertain to the knight with respect to the soul. Therefore the knight who practices these things that pertain to the Order of Chivalry with respect to the body but does not practice those virtues that pertain to Chivalry with respect to the soul is not a friend of the Order of Chivalry, for if he were it would follow that the body and Chivalry together would be contrary to the soul and its virtues, and that is not true. [104]

This is what it means to be armed with the Armour of God and physical arms at the same time; this is what it means for the Armour of God and knighthood to become one. The monk Peter the Venerable once wrote to Everard of Les Barres, the leader of the Knights Templar:

> Who will not rejoice, who will not express his joy that you have gone forth to a double conflict, not just a single one, in which, according to the apostle, you fight against spiritual wickedness [Ephesians 6:12] with the virtues of the heart and against physical enemies with the strength of your bodies? [105]

KING DAVID USED PHYSICAL ARMS, BUT AT THE SAME TIME HAD SPIRITUAL ARMOR

David used physical arms while he had the Lord "my shield," and the "the horn of my salvation," "my high tower, and my refuge, my saviour" Who "savest me from violence." (2 Samuel 22:3) St. Paul took up the "helmet of salvation" as he was guarded by well armored troops who defended him from men enslaved by the devil. Spiritual war can be fought through physical means. For to take part in such a holy war is spiritual by the virtue of its very purpose, and not carnally done for plunder and the things of the flesh. It can be said that St. Paul was not a warrior, but King David was, and he used terms very similar to the Armor of God found in Ephesians. Paul speaks of the "armour of God," and David says that God is "my shield," (2 Samuel 22:3) and "my rock," (2 Samuel 22:2) while Paul calls Christ the "spiritual rock" (1 Corinthians 10:4). St. Paul applies the armour of God to spiritual warfare against the devil, while David applies it to the victories he received from God in physical battles against the pagans that were done for the spiritual purpose of advancing God over the darkness of paganism (he as well applied it to God protecting him from King Saul).

The words of Paul, that "we do not fight against flesh and blood," can be paralleled with those of David when he defied Goliath and proclaimed before his lofty enemy:

---

104 Ramon Llull, Chivalry, 2.11
105 Peter the Venerable to Everard of Les Barres, in Barber and Bate, Templars

> Thou comest to me with a sword, and with a spear, and with a shield: but I come to thee in the name of the Lord of hosts, the God of the armies of Israel, whom thou hast defied. (1 Samuel 17:45)

David said that Goliath came with weapons while he came in the name of God, and one could easily quote such a passage to promote the idea that spiritual war casts away the use of arms. But at the same time, David did indeed use a weapon—the sling—and while he said that God "saveth not with sword and spear," (1 Samuel 17:47), he did boldly declare:

> This day will the Lord deliver thee into mine hand; and I will smite thee, and take thine head from thee; and I will give the carcasses of the host of the Philistines this day unto the fowls of the air, and to the wild beasts of the earth; that all the earth may know that there is a God in Israel. (1 Samuel 17:46)

David was in a spiritual battle, and in this holy fray he proclaimed that weapons do not save, but he was armed with a sling, a most formidable weapon. Did David lie? Did he contradict himself? Certainly not. David declared that God would deliver Goliath "into mine hand," it is God Who fought the battle, and in so doing, did the Lord use the hand of David to slay His enemy. It was a spiritual battle that was done within the physical realm; demons and angels were present, with the fallen spirits of the abyss siding with the giant who defied Heaven, and with the eternal fighters of God, under the heavenly general, Michael, defending their champion David. David fired the stone, but the stone killed Goliath. The stone is an image of Christ, "the chief corner stone" (Ephesians 2:20), and David firing the stone is an illustration of the Church fighting alongside Christ. David partakes in the combat and kills Goliath with the physical stone, but in the end it is the spiritual stone, Christ, that kills the enemy. As St. Maximus of Turin once said: "when Goliath is struck by a stone, he is struck down by the power of Christ."[106] While the spiritual forces of light and darkness clash, the soldier of light utilized his whole body in firing the smooth stone into the skull of Satan's acolyte. It was a spiritual war, but it was fought through physical means.

There are a myriad of lines from David in which he expresses his reliance on God, which could be used to refute Holy War.

One could easily try to refute Holy War, or religious war, with the words of David when he expressed his trust in God and not chariots:

> Some trust in chariots, and some in horses;
> But we will remember the name of the Lord our God.
> They have bowed down and fallen;
> But we have risen and stand upright. (Psalm 20:7-8)

David affirmed that the reliance on chariots and horses alone are vain, and that God is the One he trusts. But David himself used physical arms. Therefore, the passage is not denouncing arms unto themselves, but rather the reliance on them with a disregard to God.

---

106 Maximus of Turin, sermon 85.3

Similarly, the Christian knight Ramon Llull wrote: "the nobility of courage that is suited to Chivalry is suited better to the soul than to the body."[107] This is because the Christian warrior fights for the soul, not the gratification of the flesh. This is why he relies on God, because He is fighting for Him. The objective is the pleasing of God and not lust for blood.

In another passage David explains that a king is not saved through physical strength, nor horses, but by God and His protecting armor:

> No king is saved by the multitude of an army;
> A mighty man is not delivered by great strength.
> A horse is a vain hope for safety;
> Neither shall it deliver any by its great strength.
> Behold, the eye of the Lord is on those who fear Him,
> On those who hope in His mercy,
> To deliver their soul from death,
> And to keep them alive in famine.
> Our soul waits for the Lord;
> He is our help and our shield. (Psalm 33:16–20)

But this does not mean that David rejected the use of armies and human strength. David used strength, horses, and armies in battle, but in all his great feats, he did it with God. Again, David praises God as "our shield" and is referring to spiritual armor, similarly to how St. Paul does in Ephesians. David arms himself with the armor of God, while armed with the temporal armor of war. Thus is the ideal warrior.

David put his faith in "the shield of Your salvation," and his reliance on God, and at the same time he praises the Lord for teaching his hands "to make war," so that his arms "can bend a bow of bronze." As we read the full verse:

> He makes my feet like the feet of deer,
> And sets me on my high places.
> He teaches my hands to make war,
> So that my arms can bend a bow of bronze.
> You have also given me the shield of Your salvation;
> Your right hand has held me up,
> Your gentleness has made me great. (Psalm 18:33–35)

The warrior who defends Christendom, therefore, is armed with both spiritual arms and the weapons of temporal combat. The Christian soldier receives from God the physical tenacity and valor to vanquish God's human enemies, as he bears upon himself the full spiritual armor of the King of Heaven. He bears both, and does not exclude one from the other. Rather the spiritual weapons and the physical weapons work as one, as a single mighty force against the demonic and the slaves to the demonic. His soul relies on God, and not himself. He denies himself, obeying Christ: "If anyone desires to come after Me, let him deny

---

107 Ramon Llull, Chivalry, 3.10

himself, and take up his cross, and follow Me." (Matthew 16:24) His self is denied, his trust surrendered utterly to the divine will, just as Christ surrendered His will to the Father. But, his mind and body are still active, only now they are being completely used for advancing righteousness. The case of the Christian soldier is the same: his will is surrendered and his self is denied, and thus he follows the precept of Christ: "seek first the kingdom of God and His righteousness" (Matthew 6:33). How then does the soldier seek God first in combat? He does not fight for gain, but for God. He therefore fights in Holy War, fighting not against flesh and blood, but against Satan, the enemy of the Kingdom of God.

The sword subdues the enemy, yet it is God Who is using the wielder the sword, that very weapon, as a means to victory. This is in accordance to Paul's description of the righteous ruler, "an avenger to execute wrath on him who practices evil." (Romans 13:4) The fact that St. Paul and David believed in the use of the sword against God's enemies, illustrates that those who use the passage "we do not war against flesh and blood" to refute Holy War are contradicting Scriptures. When St. Paul was being guarded by an army of soldiers, he did so knowing that those guards could have killed somebody for his sake. But, at the same time, St. Paul did not hate his enemies, his being guarded went beyond them or him. He did not guard himself, for himself, but for a greater cause, and that is the Holy Faith. Therefore, when Christian armies fight, they do so not to war against flesh and blood, but to war against the one who the enemy follows—Satan. Holy War does not kill to kill, but to destroy the satanic ideology of Christendom's enemies. This is why Holy War is spiritual war.

David, while upholding the sword, was involved in spiritual wars, but they were done through physical weapons and combat. This is attested by the fact that God fought for Israel not just against the heathen nations, but against their gods, which are demons. As the Scripture tell us:

> And who is like Your people, like Israel, the one nation on the earth whom God went to redeem for Himself as a people, to make for Himself a name and to do for Yourself great and awesome deeds for Your land before Your people whom You redeemed for Yourself from Egypt, the nations, and their gods? (2 Samuel 7:23)

Since Joshua was in a spiritual war when he slaughtered the pagan Canaanites and destroyed their idols, David was just as much in a spiritual war when he defeated the pagan Philistines, took their idols, and with "his men burned them." (2 Samuel 5:21)

David obliterating their pagan deities illustrates the cosmic forces at work in holy war, with God, His angels and His saints, and His true Faith, fighting against Satan, his demons and his slaves, and his idolatry, clashing in a spiritual war. David strikes, and God reigns victorious, and in such a victory, His holy warriors crush the idols and drive the devil out. It can never be said that David wrestled against flesh and blood, for since he fought to purge Israel of paganism, through physical means, his war was most definitely spiritual.

The wars Israel partook in against the pagan nations were temporal ones occurring in the midst of spiritual warfare, between God, the saints, and the armies of angels, and Satan, his worshippers and his demons. The Lord led His armies, fought alongside with them, and brought them to victory.

There are various verses written by David that could be used to promote pacifism. Such as the verse that says that evildoers "shall soon be cut down like the grass, and wither as the green herb" (Psalm 37:2); "Cease from anger, and forsake wrath: fret not thyself in any wise to do evil" (Psalm 37:8); or when it reads:

> For evildoers shall be cut off;
> But those who wait on the Lord,
> They shall inherit the earth. (Psalm 37:9–17)

While such passages can be used to somehow refute holy war, as though the idea that "God will defend us" all of a sudden means we must do nothing in the face of evil, such argumentation would ignore what it says in Psalm 44, in which the conquest of Canaan is completely attributed to the sword of God and not to the physical fighting of the Hebrews:

> We have heard with our ears, O God,
> Our fathers have told us,
> The deeds You did in their days,
> In days of old:
> You drove out the nations with Your hand,
> But them You planted;
> You afflicted the peoples, and cast them out.
> For they did not gain possession of the land by their own sword,
> Nor did their own arm save them;
> But it was Your right hand, Your arm, and the light of Your countenance,
> Because You favored them. (Psalm 44:1–3)

While it says that the Hebrews did not win through their own arms, the Hebrews did in fact slaughter the Canaanites through weapons and force, as is recounted by the Book of Joshua. In another Psalm, which speaks of the conquest of the pagans of Canaan, it says that the Lord "cast out the heathen also before them," (Psalm 78:55), and He did indeed do so, through the sword of His people. The verses that seem to disregard weapons are not nullifying warfare, but instead are recognizing the spiritual leadership of God in wars, how He fights with His people, how He uses them as a means to victory over satanic darkness, and how it is through His power that Israel obtains victory. In the following verses of the 44th Psalm it declares that it is through the power of God, and not one's own strength, that His people triumph over their enemies:

> You are my King, O God;
> Command victories for Jacob.
> Through You we will push down our enemies;
> Through Your name we will trample those who rise up against us.
> For I will not trust in my bow,

Nor shall my sword save me. (Psalm 44:4–6)

One could take this verse and say, "See, the sword does not save us, there is nothing good in fighting." But the sword is most definitely used, and it is unsheathed for the ultimate divine purpose, with utter reliance on God being done by the warrior. This is why the text says: "Through you we will push down our enemies." In the 135th Psalm, it says that God defeated Og, the king of Bashan, Sihon, the king of the Amorites, and all of the nations of Canaan:

> He defeated many nations
> And slew mighty kings
> Sihon king of the Amorites,
> Og king of Bashan,
> And all the kingdoms of Canaan
> And gave their land as a heritage,
> A heritage to Israel His people. (Psalm 135:10–12)

Did not Moses defeat Og and Sihon? Did not Joshua crush the Canaanites? These glorious warriors did indeed fight these pagan peoples, but it was God Who was leading them into battle as their Divine General, directing the Hebrews to kill off the heathens. God uses the arms of men to carry out His justice. So while one could take this Psalm and argue that God was the one Who took the victory, and not man, and therefore crusading is wrong, it would be very difficult for this way of reasoning to stand once put against the rest of Scripture.

It is through God that the holy warriors drive their enemies out, it is through God that victory comes to His soldiers so that their feet "may be dipped in the blood of thine enemies" (Psalm 68:23). David says that he does not rely on the bow or the sword, just as he did not rely on the sling he used to kill Goliath, but he put his trust on God. While he used the sling, he knew that God was the one giving the victory, and the Lord was doing so through his hand. While the weapon unto itself does not gain triumph, God using His warriors, and by extension their weapons, does. Even the strength of the Christian warrior' hands, by which they slay the Church's enemies, is the strength of God for the use of holy war, as David says:

> Ascribe strength to God;
> His excellence is over Israel,
> And His strength is in the clouds.
> O God, You are more awesome than Your holy places.
> The God of Israel is He who gives strength and power to His people. (Psalm 68:34–35)

Reliance on God and not weapons was expressed in Christendom, in the Holy Wars of the Church. For example, when the Christian emperor Alexius Komnenus was about to fight the pagan Turkic Cumans, he and the whole army prayed for the Lord's intervention in the battle, "for," as his daughter would later write, "his confidence was stayed neither on men nor on horses nor on machines of war, but all his faith was placed in the power of the Lord on High."[108] This faith was clearly illustrated when, in one particular battle, he organized soldiers into a formation so well structured, that the Turks would have to fire their arrows at the left side of the Roman ranks, while the Christians would fire left handed upon the right side of the Turkish forces. He essentially placed his troops at an angle, forcing his opponents to have to endure an onslaught of arrows descending upon them slantwise. Alexius, being so amazed at this strategy, did not believe that he himself thought of this idea, but that it was God inspired, "a battle-order inspired by angels."[109]

Victory is not contingent upon arms, but faith in God; for with such faith, which is like a strong fortress, does God fight one's battles. As it says in another Psalm:

> Those who trust in the Lord
> Are like Mount Zion,
> Which cannot be moved, but abides forever.
> As the mountains surround Jerusalem,
> So the Lord surrounds His people
> From this time forth and forever. (Psalm 125:1–2)

While David wrote this wonderful prose, and trusted in the Armor of God, he as well used shields, swords, and other weapons of combat. David exhorts God to "Take hold of shield and buckler, and stand up for my help. Also draw out the spear, and stop those who pursue me." (Psalm 35:1–3) While David used physical weapons, he trusted in the spiritual armor and weapons of God.

So therefore the Christian soldier, loving God in both spirit and body against spiritual darkness, is armed with both physical weapons and the armour of God, when he fights against the forces and acolytes of demonic religions and ideologies. As soldiers were used to protect Paul, and ultimately defend the Gospel, the armies of David were used to advance God and destroy heathenism, and also to deliver David from his enemies so that his spiritual knowledge, specifically, that of the Psalms, could be taught throughout the whole world. Both St. Paul and David used arms as a means to do this end, while both were being protected by the armor of God from the spiritual darkness that hunted them.

David was a warrior, fighting against spiritual darkness by killing those who advanced that very spiritual darkness. It was the Lord who strengthened his warring hand, Who imbued him with might and inexorable fortitude, Who permeated within him the gallant spirit of a holy fighter, and used him as a divine weapon by which to drive out and destroy the pagans. And as David conducted the sacred crusade for heavenly Jerusalem against the bastions of darkness with physical arms, he was protected by the spiritual Armor of God, just as when the holy knights of Christendom fought the enemies of Christ for Jerusalem, they too held both physical weapons and spiritual weapons. David said that he had the "shield of salvation" (Psalm 22:3), this is the spiritual armor; and in the same passage he says that God

---

108 Anna Comnena, 8.5
109 Anna Komnenus, *Alexiad*, 15.4

"teaches my hands to make war, that my arms can bend a bow of bronze." (Psalm 22:35) This is the spiritual strength divinely provided for the warrior in Holy War, and this again is expressed in another line of the same Psalm:

> For You have armed me with strength for the battle;
> You have subdued under me those who rose against me.
> You have also given me the necks of my enemies,
> So that I destroyed those who hated me.
> They looked, but there was none to save;
> Even to the Lord, but He did not answer them.
> Then I beat them as fine as the dust of the earth;
> I trod them like dirt in the streets,
> And I spread them out. (2 Samuel 22:33–43)

David said that he destroyed his enemies, and then next declared that God subdued them under his feet, and gave him the necks of his enemies. While David is the one who dispatches them, it is God Who ultimately delivers them into his just hands. And so we see the Spirit of God participating in and leading righteous Holy War with His courageous servants. The warrior strikes victoriously, but it is God Who defeats the enemy, by using the arms and valor of His servants, fighting side by side with them, as a means to crushing the devil. When the crusaders war against the enemies of God, the Lord and His angels are with them. For it must be remembered that all of the Church's battles are spiritual, even if they do involve physical fighting. And the purposes of these wars are not to kill, but to advance God over evil.

David "fighteth the battles of the Lord," (1 Samuel 25:28), therefore within the Church, there is the use of the temporal sword to execute the vengeance of God's physical battles that occur over spiritual conflicts with false religion. They are God's battles, but the Scripture does not say, "Leave it at that, it is not our place to fight God's battles, vengeance is His," instead, God desires that His Church participate in His battles, that together they may, as one holy army, bring victory upon the armies of the satanic. They are the Lord's battles, but the knights of Christ fight them.

It does not say that God defeats evil people through some transparent spiritualized fashion, but through the utilization of the just sword in the hands of one whose soul is found liberated by the Sword of the Spirit, and whose mind is purified by the sacred laws that emanate from the timeless light of God.

Before David unsheathed his holy sword upon the Philistines in the valley of Rephaim, the Lord commanded him to flank the enemy and not to charge against them until he heard the sound of marching in the tops of the trees, since at that moment the Lord would lead them into battle, to strike the heathen. But did David and his armies remain static, doing nothing and saying, "The Lord will fight for us, that is not our place"? Certainly not! They fought alongside the Lord, being used by God to win His battles:

> Then the Philistines went up once again and deployed themselves in the Valley of Rephaim. Therefore David inquired of the Lord, and He said, "You shall not go up; circle around behind them, and come upon them in front of the mulberry trees. And it shall be, when you hear the sound of marching in the tops of the mulberry trees, then you shall advance quickly. For then the Lord will go out before you to strike the camp of the Philistines." And David did so, as the Lord commanded him; and he drove back the Philistines from Geba as far as Gezer. (2 Samuel 5:22–25)

The Lord smites the Philistines, while at the same time David strikes them, and this most definitely exhibits the continuous involvement of God in holy wars and His working together with His soldiers. Did God execute vengeance? Yes. But it was through the instrumentality of David and his mighty men. Did David war against flesh and blood? No, but against the false religion of the enemy. David said that "God has broken through my enemies by my hand like a breakthrough of water." (1 Chronicles 14:11) God vanquished the enemy, but through the hand of enemy. God's leadership in holy war is also attested by His words to David, "I have been with you wherever you have gone, and have cut off all your enemies from before you, and have made you a name like the name of the great men who are on the earth." (1 Chronicles 17:8)

The wars against the enemies of Heaven are God's wars, and man, in a profound harmony, participates in these wars. God is always the victor, together with His soldiers. When David's armies defeated the forces of Absalom, in which Joab "took three spears in his hand and thrust them through Absalom's heart" (2 Samuel 18:14), after the victory was gained, the priest Ahimaz declared that it was God Who defeated David's enemies:

> Blessed be the Lord your God, who has delivered up the men who raised their hand against my lord the king! (2 Samuel 18:28)

These words are paralleled to the words of the priest Melchizedek, when he proclaimed to Abraham after he defeated Chedorlaomer,

> Blessed be Abram of God Most High,
> Possessor of heaven and earth;
> And blessed be God Most High,
> Who has delivered your enemies into your hand. (Genesis 14:20)

Reminiscently, when the Israelites defeated the Hagarites, the Scripture says that "many fell dead, because the war was God's." (1 Chronicles 5:22) The war belonged to God, yes, but He used the arms of men to complete the mission. It is always the Lord Who wins the battle, and it is His warriors who take part in His victory. For when the Israelites defeated the Hagarites, it was God Who delivered them, and not their own hands:

> And they were helped against them, and the Hagarites were delivered into their hand, and all who were with them, for they cried out to God in the battle. He heeded their prayer, because they put their trust in Him. (1 Chronicle 5:20)

The Hebrews defeated the Philistines in a great battle, "and the Lord saved them by a great deliverance." (1 Chronicles 11:14)

When David was about to defend Keliah from the attacking Philistines, the Lord told him, "I will deliver the Philistines into thine hand. So David and his men went to Keilah, and fought with the Philistines, and brought away their cattle, and smote them with a great slaughter. So David saved the inhabitants of Keilah." (1 Samuel 23:1-5) Did David fight the pagans, or did God fight them? The answer is both: God fought them, using David as His scourge to fulfill the spiritual mission. Was David's war against flesh and blood? No, it was against spiritual darkness, with God defeating the enemy through physical arms and combat.

The wars that God wanted His people to fight were religious, for David asked the Lord to "deliver us from the heathen that we may give thanks to thy holy name, and glory in thy praise." (1 Chronicles 16:35) The reference to the enemy as heathens denotes the religious difference between them and Israel, and thus the spiritual struggle that the wars of Israel actually were. When Jehoshaphat fought against the Moabites, Ammonites and Midianites, he cried out to God, "art not thou God in heaven? And rulest not thou over all the kingdoms of the heathen?" (2 Chronicles 20:6) He begged for God's aid, because God is the Eternal General of His holy army, and He leads them against the hordes of Satan who are guided by demons.

When the warrior moves forth into battle, and strikes the unholy enemy of Heaven, it must be remembered that it is God Who ultimately is killing the wicked foe, using his strong arm as His weapon in the spiritual war against Satan. When the Christians of the Roman Empire defeated the pagan Persians for oppressing and attacking Christians, it was described by the ancient Christian writer Socrates as "Christ having executed his vengeance upon the Persians because they had shed the blood of so many pious worshippers."[110] St. Paulinus of Nola wrote that Christ fights the devil—the ancient serpent—through His saints, and even when they are martyred, they are victorious through the Cross and sacrifice of Jesus Christ:

> Christ confronts your poison, ancient snake, in the persons of His servants, and enmeshing you in your own snares He brings you low even as His own are slaughtered, triumphing over death by the appearance of death.[111]

JOSHUA DID NOT FIGHT AGAINST FLESH AND BLOOD WHEN HE SLAUGHTERED THE CANAANITES

When Joshua conquered and slaughtered the Canaanites, he did not war against flesh and blood, but against the spiritual darkness of the Canaanites. Rahab the harlot recognized the true God and she and her family were spared. If Joshua would have killed her even after her conversion, and her good deed of hiding the Hebrew spies, then one could say that Joshua warred against flesh blood. But this was not the case. To war against flesh and blood is to hate humanity. But the holy wars of Israel were not declared against humanity, but against

---

110 Socrates, 7.20
111 Paulinus of Nola, poem 15, 158-160

the enemy of humanity: Satan. The conquest of Canaan was a war against the devil, and in that war, the advancers of satanic religion had to be destroyed. The Canaanite kings were reminiscent to the great Indian chiefs of America, such as Metacomet and Sassacus. They were bent on subjugating their neighboring kingdoms, to seize their freedom and property. The Canaanite Adonibezek, king of Jerusalem, conquered seventy other kings prior to the Israelite arrival into Canaan, and, in his own words, "having their thumbs and their great toes cut off, gathered their meat under my table: as I have done, so God hath requited me."[112]

These very savages were killed not out of hatred for humanity, but out of hatred for Satan's influence which had conveyed itself through them.

Within the spirit of Joshua there was a balance, between mercy and justice. He showed this justice when he obliterated the Canaanites in Jericho and Ai, but he showed mercy when he protected the Canaanites of Gibeon. Most Christians do not know that one of the most profound battles in the Bible was done, not to protect Hebrews, but Canaanites.

We find within the Israelites a just nature, for when they had already made their presence in Canaan, they would in time make a league with certain Hivites, a race of Canaanite, from Gibeon, which they vowed never to break. The princes of Israel made this declaration on their league with the Hivites:

> We have sworn unto them by the Lord God of Israel: now therefore we may not touch them. This we will do to them; we will even let them live, lest wrath be upon us, because of the oath which we swore unto them. [113]

The Hebrews had let them be "hewers of wood and drawers of water unto all the congregation,"[114] but this did not stop Joshua, the leader of Israel, from protecting the Hivites from the same Canaanite tyrant, Adonizedek, after he declared to the kings of Hebron, Jarmuth, Lachish, and Eglon[115] to "smite Gibeon: for it hath made peace with Joshua and with the children of Israel."[116]

The Hivites were instilled with fear by the tyrant Adonizedek and his confederacy, and called for Joshua to "Slack not thy hand from thy servants, come up to us quickly, and save us, and help us: for all the kings of the Amorites that dwell in the mountains are gathered together against us."[117] Did Joshua simply ignore the cry of the helpless Hivites, since they were but mere servants, or because they were Canaanites? Certainly not. Joshua immediately marched with his army toward Adonizedek and his league of despots, and even God sup-

---

112 Judges 1:7. See also Newton, Rev. Hist. Anc. King., ch. i, part ii, sect. 27, 407, p. 68, ed. Larry & Marion Pierce.
113 Joshua 9:19–20.
114 Joshua 9:21.
115 Joshua 10:3.
116 Joshua 10:4.
117 Joshua 10:6.

ported him, saying "Fear them not: for I have delivered them into thine hand; there shall not a man of them stand before thee."[118]

The battle commenced in Gibeon where theses Hivites lived, with Israel attaining the victory. When it was over, Joshua proclaimed before Israel, "Sun, stand thou still upon Gibeon; and thou, Moon, in the valley of Ajalon. And the sun stood still, and the moon stayed, until the people had avenged themselves upon their enemies. And there was no day like that before it or after it that the Lord hearkened unto the voice of a man: for the Lord fought for Israel."[119] It must be stated, especially to those who see the conquest of Canaan as evil, that this most memorable event happened not for Israel's own defense, but for the defense of helpless Canaanites. When Saul was king, he slaughtered numerous of the Hivites of Gibeon (or Gibeonites) in his zealotry for Israel.[120] But this zeal of Israelite superiority was not honored by God, but punished, by a famine which came in the reign of David, who after asking God for its reason, was told: "It is for Saul, and for his bloody house, because he slew the Gibeonites."[121] How profound and different this story is when compared to the despotic book the Koran, which reads that Allah "will not charge you anything for the cheating of an oath, buts its due."[122] It is so opposed to Scripture which demands that we honor oaths even if it is with pagans. The story of the Gibeonites not only shows the love of God, but His superiority over the despotic religion of the Canaanites. They worshipped the sun by sacrificing human life to it, and the moon as well, but God stopped both to illustrate His power to them. The purpose of the conquest of Canaan was not to destroy flesh and blood, but to save it by bringing a chance for repentance and salvation to the pagans. Even with the Muslims we are not to just slaughter all of them, but to bring them back to salvation.

Israel was willing to make peace with any of the Canaanites, but it was only the Hivites of Gibeon who had done so, as Scripture witnesses: "There was not a city that made peace with the children of Israel, save the Hivites the inhabitants of Gibeon: all other they took in battle."[123]

The purpose of the conquest was not to kill human life, but to destroy paganism and spiritual darkness. Swords and weapons struck the enemies of God not to "wrestle against flesh and blood, but against principalities, against powers, against the rulers of the darkness of this age, against spiritual hosts of wickedness in the heavenly places." (Ephesians 6:12) As the intent of the conquest of Canaan was not to kill, so it is with crusades, whose purpose is not to shed blood, but to Christianize. The spreading of the true faith was the aspiration of ancient Israel, as King David himself said,

---

118 Joshua 10:8.
119 Joshua 10:12–13.
120 II Samuel 21:2.
121 II Samuel 21:1.
122 Koran in Riccoldo de Monte Croce, ch. xii, p. 70.
123 Joshua 11:19.

Declare His glory among the nations, His wonders among all peoples. For the Lord is great and greatly to be praised; He is also to be feared above all gods. (1 Chronicles 16:24–25)

GIDEON'S SPIRITUAL ARMOR

We find the spiritual sword and the temporal sword in the battle cry of the Hebrews when they, under their commander Gideon, pounced upon the Midianites and cried out, "The sword of the Lord, and of Gideon" (Judges 7:18). While Gideon speaks of his own sword, that is, the temporal sword of the Church, he proclaims the spiritual sword, "the sword of God," that fights against His enemies, both the devils and their followers. Thus in holy war, it is not just a fight against evil and malicious people, but spiritual darkness. And in the case of Gideon's battle, it was a struggle between God and Baal, orthodoxy and paganism. While God fights against the devil with His sword, He uses Gideon to defeat the followers of the devil on earth. In other words, while in a spiritual battle, God fights with the temporal sword of His Church. Hence why, in the battle, "the Lord set every man's sword against his fellow" (Judges 7:22).

HEZEKIAH'S SPIRITUAL WAR

The overly spiritualized interpretation of "we do not wrestle against flesh and blood," could also be inadequately applied to the words of King Hezekiah before the battle with Sennacherib. Hezekiah described Sennacherib as coming with the "arm of flesh" (2 Chronicles 32:7), while the Hebrews were armed with "the Lord our God to help us, and to fight our battles." Sennacherib, being of the spirit of Antichrist, mocked them, saying, "Now therefore, do not let Hezekiah deceive you or persuade you like this, and do not believe him; for no god of any nation or kingdom was able to deliver his people from my hand or the hand of my fathers. How much less will your God deliver you from my hand?" (2 Chronicles 32:13–14). God then sent His angel who cut off the Assyrians:

> Then the Lord sent an angel who cut down every mighty man of valor, leader, and captain in the camp of the king of Assyria. So he returned shamefaced to his own land. And when he had gone into the temple of his god, some of his own offspring struck him down with the sword there. (2 Chronicles 32:21)

While it was God Who defeated the pagans, and not any physical army, and while Hezekiah did say, "With him is an arm of flesh; but with us is the Lord our God, to help us and to fight our battles" (2 Chronicles 32:8), nonetheless Hezekiah did not disregard the importance of a physical army in war. Before he made his speech, when the enemy was appearing, "he set military captains over the people, gathered them together to him in the open square of the city gate, and gave them encouragement, saying, "Be strong and courageous; do not be afraid nor dismayed before the king of Assyria, nor before all the multitude that is with him; for there are more with us than with him. With him is an arm of flesh; but with us is the Lord our God, to help us and to fight our battles." (2 Chronicles 32:6–8).

Notice how he assembles an army of warriors, and then declares that the Lord will fight for them. He didn't believe in not fighting, and waiting for God to do everything in some overly spiritualized abstract way, but instead gathered his forces together and made them ready to fight under the leadership of God. The use of the physical sword is combined with the eternal blade of Heaven, and the two conjoin in a holy league, with man as the warrior and God as his general, to fight the unholy alliance of the diabolical and their mortal slaves. The story demonstrates how the temporal and the spiritual work together against Satan and his followers.

NEHEMIAH'S SPIRITUAL SWORD

When the Hebrews were laboring to rebuild the Temple, they were surrounded by pagans who planned to annihilate them, and the prophet Nehemiah said, "Our God will fight for us." (Nehemiah 4:20) One could easily isolate this verse, and use it to promote the idea of divine intervention without holy war. But while Nehemiah did say this, he did not believe in just waiting for some miracle to happen, as the lazy servants, who Christ will cast out, do. Indeed, he "set the people according to their families, with their swords, their spears, and their bows." (Nehemiah 4:13) And while he did say that the Lord will fight for them, he most definitely made sure that half the workers "held the spears, the shields, the bows, and wore armor" (Nehemiah 4:16). The prophet did proclaim the protection of God, but he also said, "Remember the Lord, great and awesome, and fight for your brethren, your sons, your daughters, your wives, and your houses." (Nehemiah 4:14) Did Nehemiah lack faith, by providing weapons to men while declaring trust in God's intervention? Did he contradict himself? No. He believed in man partaking in the wars of God against the wicked one.

For after he armed the people, the enemy found out and refrained from their violence. Nehemiah wrote "that God had brought their plot to nothing, that all of us returned to the wall, everyone to his work" (Nehemiah 4:15). Which one repulsed the enemy? Was it God, or was it the weapons? It was God, using the fear brought by the willing fighters and their weapons against His enemies. It was a spiritual battle, with God driving away the demons which the pagans worshipped, by using the arms of the people against the pagans who followed the demons. Nehemiah said, "Remember the Lord, great and awesome," this is the spiritual aspect of the battle—to contemplate on God and His precepts;—and then Nehemiah said, "fight for your brethren," this is the physical nature of the spiritual war, to protect the brotherhood for the cause of God. This is one of the ways that one may abide by the words of St. Peter: "Honor all people. Love the brotherhood. Fear God." (1 Peter 2:17) By arming themselves, the people became God's warriors, participating in His holy wars, not wrestling against flesh and blood, but against demons.

ABIJAH'S SPIRITUAL WAR

When the corrupt Jeroboam, king of Israel, and Abijah, king of the tribe of Judah, fought against each other, it was a spiritual war. Israel prostituted itself to devils, while Judah stood and fought for God, and so between the two there was a spiritual struggle, and it was done through a physical war. The great cosmic struggle between Israel and Judah is greatly attested to by the profound speech of Abijah. Before the battle, when the valiant men were set in their ranks, the formations of combat were set, and the swords of justice were about to strike the soldiers of Belial, he rose up and cried out to the enemy:

> Hear me, Jeroboam and all Israel: Should you not know that the Lord God of Israel gave the dominion over Israel to David forever, to him and his sons, by a covenant of salt? Yet Jeroboam the son of Nebat, the servant of Solomon the son of David, rose up and rebelled against his lord. Then worthless rogues gathered to him, and strengthened themselves against Rehoboam the son of Solomon, when Rehoboam was young and inexperienced and could not withstand them. And now you think to withstand the kingdom of the Lord, which is in the hand of the sons of David; and you are a great multitude, and with you are the gold calves which Jeroboam made for you as gods. Have you not cast out the priests of the Lord, the sons of Aaron, and the Levites, and made for yourselves priests, like the peoples of other lands, so that whoever comes to consecrate himself with a young bull and seven rams may be a priest of things that are not gods? But as for us, the Lord is our God, and we have not forsaken Him; and the priests who minister to the Lord are the sons of Aaron, and the Levites attend to their duties. And they burn to the Lord every morning and every evening burnt sacrifices and sweet incense; they also set the showbread in order on the pure gold table, and the lampstand of gold with its lamps to burn every evening; for we keep the command of the Lord our God, but you have forsaken Him. Now look, God Himself is with us as our head, and His priests with sounding trumpets to sound the alarm against you. O children of Israel, do not fight against the Lord God of your fathers, for you shall not prosper! (2 Chronicles 13:4–12)

Notice the reverence toward the priestly order, the holy rites, the Law of God, the incense and sacred vestments, and observe the utter contempt expressed toward the idolatries of Jeroboam, his diabolical order of feigned priests, and against the persecution he conducted against the orthodox priests. The battle was done to protect the truth of God, and end heathen tyranny. This was not just a war between two governments, but between two priesthoods, and two spiritual establishments, the kingdom of the Lord against the kingdom "of the wicked one" (1 John 3:12). The battle was not done for some temporal domination, but for the advancement of the Divine Law, to defeat the sinister principalities which Jeroboam was forging. And even when the battle commenced, and the sons of Belial flanked Judah from behind, the Lord was with them, crushing the enemy as they themselves combated in the holy melee. The warriors "cried out to the Lord, and the priests sounded the trumpets. Then the men of Judah gave a shout; and as the men of Judah shouted, it happened that God struck Jeroboam and all Israel before Abijah and Judah. And the children of Israel fled before Judah, and God delivered them into their hand. Then Abijah and his people struck them with a great slaughter; so five hundred thousand choice men of Israel fell slain." (2 Chronicles 13:15–17)

Both the warrior and the priest fought, with one thrashing the enemy with his sword, and the other thrashing the devils with his prayers. And it was God Who delivered the enemy into their hands, for the war belonged to Him and not man. Notice how it says that God delivered them, and then Abijah struck the enemy, illustrating the relationship between God and His warriors in battle.

GOD LED BATTLES IN CHRISTENDOM

The belief that God leads soldiers in holy wars against Satan, continued on in Christendom. Two examples of this are the emperor Theodosius I and the Byzantine general, Gennadius. After the pious emperor Theodosius I defeated the tyrant, Eugenius, who was striving to reestablish paganism in the Christian Roman Empire, St. Ambrose praised his victory and declared that it was God Who led him to triumph over his enemies and to establish Orthodoxy over the heathen religion:

> Thanks be to our Lord God, Who responded to your faith and piety, and has restored the form of ancient sanctity, suffering us to see in our time that which we wonder at in reading the Scriptures, namely, such a presence of the divine assistance in battle, that no mountain heights delayed the course of your approach, no hostile arms were any hindrance. [124]

St. Pope Gregory I wrote to the Byzantine general Gennadius of how his victories in war were due, not to temporal measures, but to God:

> If such prosperity had not followed your excellence in warfare as a reward of your faith, and through the grace of the Christian religion, it would not be such a wonder, but since you have made provisions for future victories (God willing) not with carnal precautions, but rather with prayers, it is something wonderful that your glory stems from God, who grants it from above, not from earthly advice. [125]

---

124 St. Ambrose, letter 61, 3
125 St. Pope Gregory I, epistle 75, in St. Robert Bellarmine, *On Laymen or Secular People*, ch. 14, p. 59

PART 9 – IN DEFENSE OF CHRISTIAN SUPREMACY AND INTOLERANCE

The heathens of the earth always talk about establishing a state of their own: the Hindus cry for a Hindu state; the Muslims an Islamic state, the atheists strive for their own utopia. But rarely ever do we hear the cries of the Church for a Christian state, for a Christian empire, for the restoration of Christendom. The flower of Christendom is enclosed with its tight pedals, awaiting for the caretakers of the holy vineyard to nurture her soils with the waters of zeal, so that she could finally bloom.

All men truly want a crusade to be done for their beliefs so that it will be the most dominate creed. The victor of this cultural war which we are in, will be the ones who will bring about the strongest, most zealous, and effective crusade. Therefore, in order for Christianity to prevail, zealots must arise. It used to be that Christianity dominated the West; it was the driving force of its universities, its artists, its philosophers, its archeologists and its historians.

But now we hear constantly in today's church that it's "not about us versus them," and what is the result of such a prevailing belief? The "them" has conquered us, and now heresy reigns supreme in the modern world, with Christianity being deemed only as a mere religious preference. Philip Yancey, a true modern deceiver in every sense of the word, once wrote that "Grace dies when it becomes us versus them."[1]

Well, no, it is about us versus them, and the contrary is never found in Scripture. David killing Goliath was "us versus them"; Elijah slaying the priests of Baal was "us versus them"; Noah's Flood was "us versus them"; Jehu shooting down Jehoram, having Jezebel thrown out of a window and Ahab's sons executed, was "us versus them"; Moses putting to death the calf worshippers was "us versus them"; Christ crushing the head of the Serpent and casting out

---

[1] Philip Yancey, *What's So Amazing About Grace?*, part iii, ch. 13, p. 172, Zondervan (1997)

demons was "us versus them"; and the coming battle between Christ and His Saints and the Antichrist and his slaves will be "us versus them."

No serious believer can ever deny that Christianity demands from us our complete willpower in fighting evil. No serious expositor on the Scripture could flee from the fact that the Scripture has more condemnations against wicked religions and practices than it does guidelines on things such as marriage and finances, two subjects that today's church never stops talking about, and yet we are so filled with divorce and debt. Tolerance toward false religions is nowhere found in the Scripture, and yet today's church is filled with it. Turning away from attacking evil ideologies is never found in the Bible, but yet much of the church encourages this.

It is told to us over and over again, "Do not impose your religion on me!" But everywhere we look and turn we are being called to the altar of conformity, and urged to never speak of Christianity. How did this happen? It was not Leftism, nor was it even socialism. These are simply symptoms to the actual problem. The root cause is a weak church.

A popular jargon today is that Islam was hijacked by "extremists," but the truth is that Christianity has been hijacked by moderates. Modernistic heretics who esteem themselves as "grace filled believers," who cry out against legalism, have succeeded in portraying the Bible as a self-help book. The reality is that the Bible is not about boosting self-esteem, or making money, it is a manual on fighting evil. It is filled with examples of how God and saintly men and women have defied tyranny: God repulsing the builders of the Tower of Babel, Moses confronting the Pharaoh, Joshua vanquishing the savage Canaanites, Othniel revolting against the despotic government of king Cushan-Rishathaim, Deborah rallying her people to overthrow the oppressor Rabin, Christ stubbornly opposing the Sanhedrin and then dying for the sins of mankind—all are actions done by zealots.

They would have never made these accomplishments if they had not a burning spirit of zealotry lodged within their hearts. Americans and Europeans are plagued with socialism, and this will only be fixed by zealots who contradict them.[2] Yet, thanks to the vague viewpoints of modernly minded Christians, zealotry has been deemed as an evil by many within the present-day church.

For example, in the United States, one named John Bevere has described "mean-spirited and legalistic pastors" as "zealots" who "have reduced holiness to a backward lifestyle and taken the joy out of living."[3]

We have forgotten the fact that Christianity is supreme over all other creeds, thus we have chosen to neglect Christian supremacy (not that a Christian is superior to all other peoples, but that Christianity is superior over all other religions). We see it as bigoted or xenophobic; but here is the truth, and there is no running away from it: every nation on earth is

---

2   See Chesterton, *St. Thomas Aquinas, St. Francis of Assisi*, ed. Ignatius, p. 23
3   John Bevere, *Extraordinary*, ch. 9, p. 84, Waterboard Press (2009)

under an ideological supremacy. We have no other choice but to esteem an idea as supreme; if we don't, someone else will, and it may not be one of liberty, but utter tyranny.

In Somalia it is Islamic supremacy, in India Hindu supremacy, in Bhutan Buddhist supremacy, and in Russia it is Christian supremacy. There is no such thing as one ideology ruling equally with the rest; one creed must dominate all others, there is no either way. Christianity is the only faith that should rule over the others, for the goodness and peace of society, and the perpetuation of civilization. The Faith cannot rule co-equally with imposters. To use the words of Chrysostom, "where there is equal authority there can never be peace; neither where a house is a democracy, nor where all are rulers; but the ruling power must of necessity be one."[4] As we laude ourselves in America as not being supremacist Christians, we still wonder as to why so many "believers" runaway from controversy, trivialize the most important priorities and prioritize the most trivial issues.

As homosexuality becomes more acceptable, and the story of Sodom is seen with indifference as just a fairy tale, Pastor Louie Giglio says that homosexuality "has not been in the range of my priorities in the past 15 years."[5] Tim Tebow, who became the idol for the modern Christians for some time, chose to run away from the spiritual fray as soon as controversy arrived when he was about to speak at a church known to be against homosexuality, Islam and Mormonism.

Today's Christian asks, "Why is there so much fear?" but the man of zeal already knows the answer: Christian supremacy has been dismantled, zeal trampled, and the soft despotism of secular and tolerance supremacy has been put on the altar and praised as the nations new god. Many current Christians ask why God demands His people to be so aggressive toward heathenism in the Old Testament, and the answer to their question is right in front of us.

The entire deconstruction of the Church in America is all due to our dislike of rocking the boat and the "us versus you mindset. We have done away with our "us versus you" mentality, but the wicked have not. They have reduced the Church from a place of great influence and erudition to a clubhouse, all because we have allowed them to. This has not only empowered the enemies of the Church in the West, but abroad: the worshippers of Allah.

The rise of Islam is determined by the zeal of the Church. If the Church is weak, Islam is strong, and if the Church is supreme, Islam goes dormant and Muslims care no more on the teachings of Muhammad. When Christ is exalted then Allah is disdained; and when God is elevated above all things, that is when the Cross shall overpower the Crescent, and the wicked prevented from ever establishing tyranny.

---

4   Chrysostom, homily 20, on Ephesians 5:22–24, trans. Oxford
5   R. Albert Mohler, Jr., Tebow's Big Fumble, posted 2/22/2013 on Christianity Today

AGAINST RELIGIOUS LIBERTY

Let us walkthrough an example as to what would have happened if the Church ruled Germany in the twentieth century. Adolf Hitler joins the National Socialists as an unknown and obscure idealist. With his charisma he gains a substantial following who call themselves "Hitlerians," and in time they become a major sect. They teach that the God of the Old Testament is evil and that Jesus was an Aryan socialist who came to destroy the Jewish establishment. They are deemed as heretical by the Church, Hitler is arrested and executed, and the Hitlerians are rounded up and coerced to go back into Christianity. Fifty years later—or less—a great amount of books are published about the tyranny of the Church, in which they mention the "poor Hitlerians," who were persecuted for their beliefs, the "religious bigotry" which the Church had toward these victims, and how the Hitlerians were just innocent Christians oppressed for their difference in theology. We would talk about the punishment of the Hitlerians, but not the dangerous aspects of their ideology, and the consequences of tolerating them. It is because the Nazis were tolerated that the Holocaust occurred, and yet till now we talk of the massacres but not of the fact that they were committed as a result of religious tolerance.

It is most interesting that Pope Pius XII, who was to the enmity of Hitler, who combated the Nazi regime, and who saved at least 700,000 Jews (but probably as many as 860,000) from the Third Reich,[6] completely rejected the concept of religious liberty:

> ...that which does not correspond to truth or to the norm of morality objectively has no right to exist, to be spread or to be activated.[7]

Now, did Pius XII say this because he was tyrannical? Quite the contrary; it was because his view regarding religious liberty was the antithesis to tyranny. He rejected false religions just as he rejected Nazism. Here is an hypothetical illustration as to just how the modern perception mistakenly sees intolerance toward non-Christian religions, and does not realize how the license of all beliefs as deserving equal status results in all sorts of evils and tyranny.

The same can be said for the French Revolution: the deists (or people who believed that there is a god but he is completely separate from the world) were enabled to thrive and propagate their theology, and once these became dominant and prestigious enough in society, out came the guillotines and the Christians, or any one posed as an obstacle to their designs, were beheaded. Yet, these same heretics—while implementing totalitarianism—argued for the "rights of man." This tells us something very revealing. Tolerance is a term used by those who use freedom to their own advantage, to be enabled to gain enough power and influence in society, until they become the establishment and kill off the opposition who, in most cases, are the Christians.

In the words of Fletcher, "The greatest of persecutors have been the very men, who have the most loudly condemned persecution."[8]

---

6   See Lapide, in Rabbi David G. Dalin, *The Myth of Hitler's Pope*, ch. 1, p, 11
7   As quoted by Lefebvre, *Religious Liberty Questioned*, part 1, p. 14
8   In his notes on Maistre's first letter on the Spanish Inquisition, D

Once a society places other gods to the same level of Christ, in a pluralistic fashion, then fervency in Christianity weakens, zealotry for the truth declines, the dangerous consequences of religious tolerance comes to be, persecution toward Christians on the part of heretics gradually arises, and the tyranny of antichrist establishes itself while extinguishing the Christian infrastructure of true civilization. The early Christians in Ephesus, once they became born again, did not hesitate in gathering all of their pagan books and throwing them into the flames, as Moses burnt the golden calf:

> Many of them also which used curious arts brought their books together, and burned them before all men: and they counted the price of them, and found it fifty thousand pieces of silver.[9]

They did not believe that error has rights, and so then why does the modern church emphasize so much on religious toleration, and the equality of rights for all religions?

Truth, by its very nature, is intolerant. Tolerate all religions, and you invite every error accept the truth, and in such a state will we be stuck repeating the question of Pontius Pilate: What is the truth?

HERESY MUST BE DESTROYED

In our day and age we laugh at the Church's history of attacking heresies and heretics. To many today it is humorous, comical, and worthy of laughter; it is all but a memory of old men in superficial and hair-splitting quarrels which no one today takes seriously. One may have an interest in heresy only in his study of history and how ancient Christians used to think, but as soon as somebody studies it in order to understand a threat dangerous to our society and to the preservation of civilization, he is hardly understood, mocked, or viewed as archaic.[10] But putting all of these mockeries aside, here is the reality: if the Church continued its intolerance toward heretics and their ideologies, there would have been no Hitler—an apostate who hated the Catholic Church—there would have been no Stalin—another hater of Christianity who left the Eastern Orthodox Church. There would have been no Islam, no socialism, no Karl Marx, no legalized abortion, no mass murders done by Communist regimes. In the words of Carroll, "Tomas de Torquemada [a Spanish inquisitor] would have known how to deal—and to deal early—with Hitler and Stalin."[11]

As the Law of Moses prevents people from committing human sacrifice, so does intolerance toward heresies preclude dangerous cults, cultish violence, and mass murderers from arising. The popular view today is that opinions don't matter, and that anybody can hold whatever opinion they want, regardless of how despotic, violent, and depraved they are. Societies who are convinced of this can do so as they please, but they will have to suffer the consequences of wicked men executing massacres and other cruelties. By reading the Mosaic

---

9   Acts 19:19
10 See Belloc, *The Great Heresies*, intro, p. 4
11 Carroll, *A History of Christendom*, vol. iii, ch. xiv, p. 609, brackets mine

books, and the rest of the Old Testament, one finds that this modern view, as much as some pastors want to deny it, is not Biblical. This is why the Church believed that opinions are in fact significant, and that heresy had no permission to even exist. Tertullian, St. Augustine, and St. Thomas Aquinas, all believed in precluding heresy from thriving and spreading. Their main reason was that the corruption of the soul was more important than damage to the flesh, since life is only limited, and hell eternal.

Such is not about the Church killing heretics, but for the support of civil laws outlawing heretical cults and dangerous ideologies. The Church never believed in the idea of itself punishing heresy, but it did uphold the sentiment that the state, in order to maintain order in society, should neutralize dangerous cults.

The Bible is like a clock functioning perfectly with all of its parts in there adequate positions, connected appropriately, and collectively working as one. The heretic comes and violently pulls out one or a few of its inner parts and robs them. The clock now stops. One man comes along and notices that the mechanism is no longer ticking and its hands have both ceased to move. As he ponders as to how and why this is, the heretic comes along and says, "There is no time, time is our greatest enemy. The world is eternal and time is an illusion used by the elites to control you, to keep making you move to make money, so that they may rob you in the end. You can control your own reality once you believe that time is not in existence, and dictate your own life and not allow the elites to decide for you what to do." The man now feels empowered and he rushes away with great energy. He spots a clock in a local inn, charges inside, seizes and dashes it to the floor and crushes it under his feet. The owner runs to him in protest. "What are you doing?!" And with a pious smile, the man will say, "There is no time, time is our greatest enemy."

This belief then spreads about, and sooner or later we have an entire multitude of people who hate clocks, believe that there is no time, and that time is a conspiracy made by some elite. At first nobody feels threatened, but rather entertained, and this new sect is only seen as a mere group of lunatics. They gradually grow in numbers and suddenly books begin to be published with titles such as, "Time Does Not Exist," "Time: The Great Illusion," "Time: The Enemy," and so on and so forth.

The unmoving clock, by which the heretic used to make his first convert, still remains, and is now an idol to the new sect. It is now custom that the time-haters visit the clock once a year in a sort of pilgrimage, as a holy image that reminds humanity each day of his missing destiny. The heretic commissions a few of his followers to look after the clock and they become a new priesthood.

But still, nobody sees them as dangerous, only stupid and laughable. One day an orthodox fellow walks along and sees the clock. "It is not moving," he says. "That is because time does not exist, time is our greatest enemy," responds one of the priests, "time is an illusion, used by the elite to control your destiny. You are the own mover of your own life. We are not dictated by the clock, but by our own consciousness." "No," says the fellow, "it is not moving because it is broken." "You are broken," says the priest sharply, "broken by this world controlled by the system of time! You can set yourself free if only you place yourself in the world of the unmoving clock." The fellow walks to the back of the clock and opens it. "It's missing parts, it's broken." The priest pulls out a gun and shoots the fellow dead. Onlookers and pedestrians begin to run and scream not knowing what hit them, or without understanding as to why a clock hater would kill someone who believes in an orthodox standard of clock engineering, and within moments the police arrive, arrest the clock-hater and take him to an interrogation room. "Why did you do it?" asks the interrogator. "He was attacking the very thing that sets us free." "What you did was murder, everyone saw you do it." "I am the mover of my own destiny, not dictated by laws made by a system of men, but by my own conscious." "And you're going to be the mover of your own destiny in a cell! You're going to be in prison for a very long time." "There is no time, time is an illusion, and time is our greatest enemy."

This is how heresy works, and the only result of it (if allowed to prosper and thrive), is death. Parts of the Bible are taken and isolated, and the rest is ignored. The bible that is corrupted by the heretic is loved by his followers; while the Bible that is left in its entirety, fully functioning without a part stolen like the ticking clock, is hated and sought for its destruction by the heterodox. Those who believe in orthodoxy, just as those who only accept the working clock in the story, are violently pursued for their lives by those who believe in heterodoxy. Thus the heretic will always try to kill the orthodox.

When studying geography, no one isolates a part of a map and says, "Here is the world." We do not peer on the Mississippi and then ignore the states through which it flows. We analyze the atlas in its entirety and never solely focus on a part of the earth and deny the existence of the rest. If anyone ever did this he would not be doing geography, but fantasy, since once you deny the existence of one part of the world you deny the existence of the whole earth. A half-truth is never a whole truth. Yet we forever do this with the Bible. Every cult that has arose bases an entire theology by isolating verses. For example, a clever sophist may bring up the quote of Jesus saying "my Father is greater than I."[12] He will then say that this is evidence that the Son is inferior to the Father, and thus the Trinity is false. Now, let's say that someone reproaches this man and points out the verse from St. John when he wrote:

> For there are three that bear record in heaven, the Father, the Word, and the Holy Ghost: and these three are one. [13]

The sophist, like any heretic, would try to explain this verse out of existence, claim that St. John's quote is inferior to the words of Christ, or compose some sort of mind boggling and hair-splitting argument to prove that it doesn't mean what it really says. Either way, this is how the heretic prospers. He thrives off those who do not wish to view the Scripture in its entirety and who need one or a few verses to be convinced of the heresy. It works upon

---

12 John 14:28
13 I John 5:7

those who refuse to understand that if you take out one part of the Bible, the rest is marred and impaired.[14]

This is of the nature of heresy, since the word itself comes from the Greek *haeresis*, meaning "from choice," because heretics choose what seems to be the best interpretation of Scripture for them.[15] They do not search for other parts of Scripture to correspond with a particular section of the Bible to confirm their interpretation, nor do they see how the Church Fathers or councils of the ancient church interpreted Scripture. They see the Bible as the progressive sees law: through moral relativism. In other words, they do that which is right in their own eyes.

Amongst the oldest definitions of heresy by the Church, was written by St. Ignatius in his epistle to the Trallian Christians, in which he wrote:

> For they that are heretics confound together the doctrine of Jesus Christ with their own poison, whilst they seem worthy of belief, as men give a deadly potion mixed with sweet wine, which he who is ignorant of, does with the treacherous pleasure sweetly drinks in his own death.[16]

Notice how he describes the one who accepts heresy as having "treacherous pleasure" while doing so; those who fall into the pit of deception, always take delight in pompously expressing their doctrinal rebellions. Many a time have we heard a myriad of reprobates ostentatiously declare, "I am a deist!" "I am a Muslim!" "I am a social darwinist!" "I am a socialist!" "I am a communist!" "I am an atheist!" "I am a vegan!" "I am a Calvinist!" But few who, without shame, proclaim, "I am a Christian!"

Robert Grosseteste, bishop of Lincoln and the first chancellor of Oxford, defined heresy in the year 1200 in these words:

> Heresy is an opinion chosen by human facilities, contrary to sacred scripture, openly held, and pertinaciously defended.[17]

Heresy always begins when someone wants to create their own sect; it always starts with someone leaving the Church and forming their false church. But this all originates from the sins of the flesh, of which Paul lists as, "seditions, heresies" (Galatians 5:20). The starting of cults is all centered on the self and is done solely for the fleshy desire for power. As St. Cyprian said:

> The beginning of heresy, the faltering step towards schism, is when a man leaves the Church and sets up his profane altar outside.[18]

---

14 This analogy was inspired by Belloc, *The Great Heresies*, intro, pp. 5–6
15 St. Isidore of Seville, On heresy and schism, in Edward Peters, *Heresy and Authority in Medieval Europe*, ch. i, p. 49; Vitoria, *Reflection 1 On The Power of the Church*, intro, 7
16 St. Ignatius, Epistle to the Trallians, 6
17 In Edward Peters, *Heresy and Authority in Medieval Europe*, ch. v, p. 167
18 Cyprian, letter 2.9, in Vitoria, *Reflection 1 On the Power of the Church*, intro, 7

There are several classifications of heresy. The first is any assertion that contradicts Scripture. The second consists of those which oppose teachings taught by the successors of the apostles—or those teachers most close to the time of the Apostles—such as St. Irenaeus of Lyon (a student of St. Polycarp who was a pupil of St. John), St. Polycarp, St. Ignatius of Antioch (a student of St. Peter and St. John), St. Clement (a pupil of St. Peter and St. Paul) and other Church Fathers. The third is to deny those Councils of the Church that preserved our most important teachings, such as the Council of Nicaea (which defined the Holy Trinity), the Council of Chalcedon (which defined the human and divine nature of Christ), the Council of Ephesus (which affirmed that God came in the flesh in the womb of Mary), and the others which, being in accordance with sacred Scripture, defended and explained tenets that are the foundation of the Christian Faith. For example, if one says "I reject the Council of Nicaea," he is then rejecting the Creed of the council that upholds the divinity of Christ, and hence it is heresy.[19]

The intention of the heretic is not to have peaceful dialogue or to reason, it is to seize power. In order for him to do so, he must replace the foundation that is the influence of all Christian civilization, and that is orthodoxy. St. Paul speaks of this evil in his epistle to the Romans:

> For they being ignorant of God's righteousness, and going about to establish their own righteousness, have not submitted themselves unto the righteousness of God. [20]

Tertullian, in his work against heretics, wrote that the devisers of heresies want to shatter the already existing foundation of the Church and replace it with their own:

> Accordingly, since the very work which they purpose to themselves comes not from the building up of their own society, but from the demolition of the truth, they undermine our edifices, that they may erect their own. [21]

St. Bernard, as pertaining to this subject, wrote:

> A new gospel is being fashioned for peoples and nations, a new faith propounded, another foundation laid than that which is laid. [22]

Heretics create new foundations in order to replace the old, and they do so knowing that by becoming the new source of doctrine, they become the new authority, and with such status they seize power. This dominance does not stop within society, but eventually permeates government, and from there it extends to dictating human life, and ultimately—and this is their priority—to bring destruction upon the Church.

One must go against heresy not to simply maintain tradition for tradition's sake, but because heresy—if given the chance to grow strong—will form a life in direct attack

---

19 This explanation was inspired by the work of John of Brevicoxa, On The Church and Heresy, vii, in Edward Peters, *Heresy and Authority in Medieval Europe*, ch. x, p. 301
20 Romans 10:3
21 Tertullian, On Prescription Against Heretics, ch. 42
22 St. Bernard to Pope Innocent II: Against Abelard, 1140, in Edward Peters, Heresy and Authority, ch. ii, p. 88

against order and civilization. "Theology is irrelevant," has become a popular phrase. But, if I deny that life is sacred, and that man is not made in God's image, I have now formulated my own theology, and it would be taboo through modern eyes to call it heresy, since it is irrelevant. Now imagine to yourself an entire society—no, an entire nation—that accepts this warped theology. No sane man would want to live in such a place, and so all of a sudden theology becomes relevant. If I deny the divinity of Christ, then I deny the sacrifice that paid for the world's sins. Someone else then must replace Christ, and gradually human sacrifice becomes common custom.

A heretic can also take and isolate the parts of the Bible that talk about giving to the poor, and affirm a theology that says that absolute poverty should be the state of all men; that private ownership is evil and that communalism is the only holy way to live. If such a theology dominated us, then we would become impoverished, communist, and our entire civilization would dwindle away. Though we do not call this heresy, nor even bad theology, this is exactly what it is. Communism is as much of a heresy as Islam.

A heretic could take all of the verses on marriage in the Scripture and warp them to be completely contrary as to what marriage is. Marriage, under such erroneous scrutiny of Holy Writ, would suddenly be considered evil, a sin, and this too would be a heresy that would destroy the entire social order from within.

A heretic could take and isolate all of the verses on Christian love and do away with all of the verses on righteous anger and justice. "All people should be loved," would be a common creed. Murderers, rapists, and every other evil-doer would be accepted, prisons would be closed, capital punishment abolished, and the entire world would be forced into mob rule and anarchy. By taking away justice and noble anger, love disappears.

One can even say that an entire religion sustains America, the religion of patriotism. Remove this religion and America ceases to exist.

The old Christians who fought with every ounce of exertion over doctrine were therefore more prudent then the modern who accepts all beliefs as deserving the same status.[23]

Moreover, we are what we are today because of our Christianity, and because people in the past strived to preserve it. We also are what we are today because remnants of past heresies have still remained and continue to rot the very foundation that still keeps us from tumbling into the abyss. The entire Middle East is Muslim—with only a few Christians here and there—and that is because heresy took over where orthodoxy once was.[24]

When Heresy first arises, it is common for modern man to ignore it with the excuse that heretics are peaceful. But what is not understood is that heretics are only peaceful until they are very numerous and have the backing of powerful people.

---

23 See Belloc, *The Great Heresies*, intro, pp. 7–9
24 Belloc, *The Great Heresies*, intro, pp. 8

Heresy grow in numbers, and its evil schemes are not put into play until whatever has been suppressing it is removed, and the accumulation of error is released to only bring about a toppling menace of disaster.[25] As Belloc says:

> The modern attack will not tolerate us. It will attempt to destroy us. Nor can we tolerate it. We must attempt to destroy it as being the fully equipped and ardent enemy of the Truth by which men live. The duel is to the death. [26]

The point is clear—All anti-Christian beliefs lead to tyranny.

"YOU DO NOT KNOW WHAT MANNER OF SPIRIT YOU ARE OF"

Our opponents frequently quote the saying of Christ where He rebuked and told the Disciples when they wanted to burn the Samaritans who didn't desire to receive Jesus, "You do not know what manner of spirit you are of." (Luke 9:55) Firstly, the Samaritans, who were born believing in their religion without ever accepting Christianity, cannot be equated with heretics who accepted Christianity and turned against it to destroy the Faith. The Samaritans were never born into Christianity, and therefore they cannot be punished for practicing a religion that they, being deceived, blindly follow. This is not the same as a heretic who has seen the light, who is knowledgeable on Christianity, and makes deliberate war against the Church.

When someone is baptized, they are making a promise to reject all the works of the devil; by turning against the Church they break their agreement, and not only this, but are maliciously striving to tear down the bastions of the Orthodox Faith. Secondly, the purpose of Christ's mission at this moment needs to be recognized. The Scripture says that the Samaritans "did not receive Him, because His face was set for the journey to Jerusalem." (Luke 9:53) Their rejection of Christ was in accordance to Providence; Christ wanted to go into Jerusalem, and so for Him to enter the Samaritan village would have been contrary to the divine plan. It is similar to how when Peter sliced off the officer's ear Christ rebuked him by saying "Shall I not drink the cup which My Father has given Me?" (John 18:11) The use of force was against the divine plan, just as to force the Samaritans to receive Christ would have been against the divine plan. Fourthly, it should be said that James and John did not want to kill the Samaritans for the sake of saving souls, but for their own lust for revenge. When the knight of the Church strikes, he does so not for the gratification of his own fleshy desires, but for the cause of righteousness and guarding the true Faith. This is why St. Robert says, "The Church, indeed, persecutes heretics out of zeal for the salvation for those souls that they pervert, out of the same zeal with which Christ twice with a scourge expelled those from the temple who were selling sheep and oxen 'and overthrew the table' (John 2 and Matthew 21)."[27]

There is a difference between someone who follows error unknowingly and one who deliberately attacks the Church. Moreover, Christ honored the Samaritans in numerous

---

25 See Belloc, *How the Reformation Happened*, intro, p. 63
26 Belloc, *The Great Heresies*, The Modern Phase, p. 108
27 Bellarmine, *On Laymen or Secular People*, ch. 22, ed. Tutino, p. 114

instances. There is the story of the Good Samaritan, and the story of Christ commending the Samaritan who bows toward Him after He heals him, saying to him: "Arise, go thy way: thy faith hath made thee whole." (Luke 17:19) Even though the theology of these Samaritans was not entirely orthodox, their good actions brought them close to God, since fruits are evidence of faith. Righteous actions, therefore, speak louder than words, and profess a righteous faith, whereas the one who may sound orthodox can preach a different gospel with evil actions.

THE WHEATS AND THE TARES

The other argument the objectors frequently mention is that Christ said:

> Let both grow together until the harvest: and in the time of harvest I will say to the reapers, Gather ye together first the tares, and bind them in bundles to burn them: but gather the wheat into my barn. (Matthew 13:20)

They will contend and say, "You see, we must allow the tares, meaning heretics, to grow with the wheat." By "tares" is not only meant heretics, but all evil people, as is made plain by the explanation of Christ when He says: "The field is the world; the good seed are the children of the kingdom; but the tares are the children of the wicked one" (Matthew 13:38). When the Lord commands us to let the tares grow with the wheat, He was not saying we should never kill any evil person, but that we should not attempt to annihilate all the wicked at the expense of giving grief to, or killing the innocent. This is why Christ explains that we are not to uproot the tares, "lest while you gather up the tares you also uproot the wheat with them." (Matthew 13:29) We cannot go around killing people just because they are not Christian, for what is a tare could eventually become a wheat. What Christ is saying is a general parable, which explains that it is impossible to get rid of all evil people, and that this complete purging of the world from the wicked will never be done by man's doing, but only in the end of the world. It was as if He was saying, "With all your diligence you will never be able to accomplish separating the many wicked from the good until the Day of Judgment, for at the time I will send my angel who will separate the wicked from among the just."[28]

If one can uproot certain tares without harming or killing the righteous, then by all means it is permissible to extirpate the evildoers. St. Augustine affirmed this observation: "Here it is shown clearly enough that where there is no fear of this [i.e. of rooting up the wheat with the tares]—that is to say, where a crime is so notorious and so execrable to all men that it has no defenders, or at any rate none who might give rise to schism—the severity of discipline should not sleep."[29] But, if certain evil people cannot be extirpated, either because we do not know them enough, or because there is a chance that the innocent, and not the guilty, will be punished, or because the enemy is stronger and more on the righteous side will die than on the wicked side, then it is more prudent to refrain from the use of force. As St. Chrysostom explains: "The Lord prohibits the extirpation of the tares lest while they are

---

[28] Bellarmine, *On the Temporal Power of the Pope*, ch. 9, ed. Tutino, p. 222
[29] Augustine, Contra Parmenianum donatistam 3:2, Aquinas, *Summa Theologiae*, IIa IIae 10, article 8

✝ CHRISTIANITY IS AT WAR: THE MANIFESTO FOR CHRISTIAN MILITANCY

gathered the wheat is also uprooted up with them, for if we killed the heretics now, a cruel and unstoppable war would be caused."[30] If one wants to argue the contrary, and affirm that this parable prohibits all killing, then murderers, rapists, and other evildoers should never be put to death, and more than that, the whole police force should be done away with. But no nation would ever do this, because it is destructive. If this verse meant that we cannot oppress or punish the wicked and the impious, then David would have sorely sinned when he said: "I will early destroy all the wicked of the land." (Psalm 101:8) This is why when we are interpreting these verses, we must always be balanced, and prevent ourselves from falling either into self-destruction (through extreme pacifism) or the destruction of the innocent (through uncontrollable violence). Moreover, the parable of the wheats and the tares is most definitely not a calling for toleration of cults; for as St. Chrysostom says, commenting on this very Scripture:

> He [Christ] doth not therefore forbid our checking of heretics, and stopping their mouths, and taking away their freedom of speech, and breaking up their assemblies and confederacies, but our killing and slaying them.[31]

The separating of the wheat to expedite the uprooting of the tares, is illustrated in the story of the cleansing of the Temple in the Book of Ezekiel. The Lord commands "the man clothed with linen, who had the writers inkhorn at his side" and ordered him to "Go through the midst of the city, through the midst of Jerusalem, and put a mark on the foreheads of the men who sigh and cry over all the abominations that are done within it." (Ezekiel 9:3–4) The mark of God, which was the Tau, or the cross, distinguished the righteous from the wicked, the wheat from the tares, and would prevent them from killing the innocent when they would "Utterly slay old and young men, maidens and little children and women; but do not come near anyone on whom is the mark; and begin at My sanctuary." (Ezekiel 9:5)

When the Cathars, who were devil worshippers who spat upon the prophets and murdered Christians, overran southern France, and when the Muslims dominated the Holy Land, upon which God walked, did Pope Innocent III call for toleration of these heretics? No.

He called for the warriors of Christendom to bear the Holy Cross, upon their bodies and upon their foreheads, and looking into the sacred book of Ezekiel, referencing to the eighth and ninth chapters, he urged for the crusaders to be as the six holy men who slew all those who did not have the mark of God. In the Fourth General Council of the Lateran, Innocent III exclaimed with just and righteous words ordering the extirpation of the Cathars from France and the Muslims from the Holy Land:

> Just as 'the man dressed in linen, who had the ink-horn of a scribe in his loins, should pass through the center of the city and mark the Tau on the foreheads of the men who sigh and mourn over all the abominations that are committed within it,' so the High Priest, who has been constituted watchman over the house of Israel, should pass through the whole church

---

30 See Bellarmine, *On Laymen or Secular People*, ch. 22, ed. Tutino, pp. 115–116
31 St. Chrysostom, Homily 46 on Matthew

which is the city of the great King, the city on a mountain investigating and inquiring into the merits of individuals, to see whether 'they are saying that good is evil or evil good; lest they are judging darkness to be light or light darkness;' lest 'they are killing souls that are not dying, or giving life to souls that should not live.'[32]

CHRIST HIMSELF DID NOT BELIEVE IN TOLERATION

Even in the New Testament, Christ declares that the Church can consider as heathens those who do not obey its authority, for He says that when an offender does not listen to the one he has trespassed, "tell it unto the church: but if he neglect to hear the church, let him be unto thee as an heathen man and a publican." (Matthew 18:17) Such offenders, then, are no longer part of the Church, and thus can be apprehended by the temporal authorities and punished. In the prior passage, before the offender is taken to be heard by the Church, Christ said that he is to be taken before two or three witnesses that everything he says may be testified. Christ declares "take with thee one or two more, that in the mouth of two or three witnesses every word may be established." (Matthew 18:16) This is in accordance with the Law taught through Moses, which states, "Whoever is deserving of death shall be put to death on the testimony of two or three witnesses; he shall not be put to death on the testimony of one witness." (Deuteronomy 17:16) Moses said this in the context of executing those who have "gone and served other gods and worshiped them, either the sun or moon or any of the host of heaven" (Deuteronomy 17:3), and those who partake in such an act are to be investigated diligently, and "if it is indeed true and certain that such an abomination has been committed in Israel, then you shall bring out to your gates that man or woman who has committed that wicked thing, and shall stone to death that man or woman with stones." (Deuteronomy 17:4–5) The person who does such an evil is a heathen, and he is to be executed, and Christ says that the one who disobeys the Church, "let him be unto thee as a heathen man and a publican." (Matthew 18:17) The Church has the authority to deem someone a heathen, and that heathen can be taken by the state and punished, even by death. St. Robert read this passage and deduced this, writing that "the Church can expel, and have considered as heathens and publicans, those who do not want to obey, and therefore the Church can send them to the secular authority as men who are no longer children of the Church." He concludes by saying that "it is lawful that heretics, who in everyone's judgment are rebels against the Church and disturb the public peace, be removed from the Church and punished with death and by the secular judge."[33] Vitoria also agreed with the killing of heretics, when he wrote that "civil laws have been enacted on the burning of heretics and so on, a matter which concerns the supernatural good."[34]

---

32 Fourth General Council of the Lateran, trans. Gardiner
33 Bellarmine, *On Laymen or Secular People*, ch. 21, ed. Tutino, p. 103
34 Vitoria, *On Law*, ST I–II, article 1, 122b

THE PARABLE OF THE GREAT SUPPER

Laws against heretics are scripturally based, as we are told by Augustine in his writings against the suicidal cult of the Donatists, from Luke 14 in Christ's parable of the great supper. A certain man prepares a grand dinner and commands his servant to bring those who were invited. But these refuse to come and make excuses:

> The first said to him, 'I have bought a piece of ground, and I must go and see it. I ask you to have me excused.' And another said, 'I have bought five yoke of oxen, and I am going to test them. I ask you to have me excused.' Still another said, 'I have married a wife, and therefore I cannot come.' (Luke 14:18–20)

The master then tells his servant to bring in the outcasts of society to the supper instead:

> Go out quickly into the streets and lanes of the city, and bring in hither the poor, and the maimed, and the halt, and the blind. (Luke 14:21)

The servant obeys and does this, and afterwards the master says:

> Go out into the highways and hedges, and compel them to come in, that my house may be filled. [35]

The supper is the unity of the Body of Christ, and those who are "in the highways and hedges," are those within heresies and schisms. The command to "compel" them, means to coerce them (in this case, the Donatists) back into the Church. Augustine believed that this was the duty of a Christian government to fulfill. But these laws were not done until after the Donatists proved themselves worthy of punishment, since they were notorious for violence against Christians. The bishops of the Donatist church, then, were fined and their church property confiscated, in order to reprimand them from violently preventing their members to returning to the Christian Church. "Our idea was that if they were frightened in this manner," wrote Augustine, "and so did not dare to commit such acts, there would be freedom for the Catholic truth to be taught and embraced, so that no one would be forced to it, but any who wished might follow it without fear, and thus we should not have any false or feigned Catholics."[36] The purpose of the laws was to end and prevent oppression upon the Church, and thus to end tyranny. The laws against Donatist violence were very effective and brought about immediate conversions.

The Church is like a field with farmers, as St. Paul wrote: "For we are God's fellow workers; you are God's field, you are God's building." (1 Corinthians 3:9) Notice that the apostle says that he and the other authorities of the Church are workers, that is, they are like farmers and the laymen are like a field. It is the job of the farmer to pluck out what doesn't belong on the field, and to plant what is right for the soil. So, then, it is of the authorities to uproot heresies from the Church; to sow seeds in fertile soil, or the soul that is ready and willing to receive the seeds of the Gospel, rather than cast pearls before swine. The Lord declared to Jeremiah:

---

35 Luke 14:23
36 Augustine, *On the Treatment of the Donatists*, ch. 25; letter 88

See, I have this day set you over the nations and over the kingdoms,
To root out and to pull down,
To destroy and to throw down,
To build and to plant. (Jeremiah 1:10)

The clergy is not there to make their bellies fat, but to labor for the purging of the Church, so that it could be unspotted before the Lord, uprooting the tares and protecting the wheat. St. Bernard, commentating on the passage of Jeremiah, said:

> Learn that you need a hoe, not a scepter, to do the work of the Prophet. Indeed, he did not rise up to reign, but to root out. [37]

JESUS CHRIST BELIEVED IN THE DESTRUCTION OF FALSE RELIGION

Christ believed in intolerance towards false religions, and this is proven by the fact that Christ quoted the Shema, the very quote of Moses, said in the context of slaying evil doers.

Christ, in His summarizing of the Law to the scribe, declares the Hebrew Shema: "Hear, O Israel; the Lord our God is one Lord: and thou shalt love the Lord thy God with all thy heart, and with all thy heart, and with all thy soul, and with all thy mind, and with all thy strength: this is the first commandment." (Mark 12:29–30)

This is a quoting of Moses when he proclaimed: "Hear, O Israel: the Lord our God is one Lord: and thou shalt love the Lord thy God with all thine heart, and with all thy soul, and with all thy might."[38]

Now this declaration of faith is referenced to again by Moses in the order to punish heretics or false prophets:

> If there arise among you a prophet, or a dreamer of dreams, and giveth thee a sign or a wonder, and the sign or the wonder come to pass, whereof he spake unto thee, saying, Let us go after other gods, which thou hast not known, and let us serve them; thou shalt not hearken unto the words of that prophet, or that dreamer of dreams: for the Lord your God proveth you, to know whether ye love the Lord your God with all your heart and with all your soul. Ye shall walk after the Lord your God, and fear him, and keep his commandments, and obey his voice, and ye shall serve him, and cleave unto him. And that prophet, or that dreamer of dreams, shall be put to death; because he hath spoken to turn you away from the Lord your God, which brought you out of the land of Egypt, and redeemed you out of the house of bondage, to thrust thee out of the way which the Lord thy God commanded thee to walk in. So shalt thou put the evil away from the midst of thee. [39]

Christ's reiterating of the Shema is then referring to the Mosaic exclusivity of God, and thus also to the civil law against heresy or the promotion of pagan religions. This is further substantiated by the response of the scribe to Jesus:

---

37 St. Bernard, *On Consideration*, 2.6.9
38 Deuteronomy 6:4–5
39 Deuteronomy 13:1–5

CHRISTIANITY IS AT WAR: THE MANIFESTO FOR CHRISTIAN MILITANCY

Well, master, thou hast said the truth, for there is one God; and there is none but he; and to love him with all the heart, and with all understanding, and with all the soul, and with all the strength, and to love his neighbor as himself, is more important than all whole burnt offerings and sacrifices. [40]

His statement that "there is one God; and there is none but he," hinges with the Shema, and thus to the Mosaic Law against heresy or the promulgation of paganism. The Shema is unto itself against any form of inclusiveness or tolerance towards false religions. The injunction in Deuteronomy 13 to kill the promoters of paganism, was upheld by St. Robert Bellarmine, amongst the most authoritative theologians on Christian law, in his writing on why heretics are to be punished, and at times, even executed,

> First, this [the punishment of heretics] is proved out of Scripture. The Old Testament in Deuteronomy 13 most vigorously commands the killing without mercy of false prophets who incite the worship of other gods. [41]

Furthermore, when Christ and the scribe place the exclusivity of God as over sacrifices, they are in accordance to the statement in Deuteronomy 11, when it reads:

> And a curse, if ye will not obey the commandments of the Lord your God, but turn aside out of the way which I command you this day, to go after other gods, which ye have not known. [42]

This verse is clearly stating—according to Rashi—that to leave God for a false doctrine, is to deny the whole of the law.[43] Now, we don't need to observe sacrificial law anymore, for we have the sacrifice of Christ, but the Shema still applies to us. To say that Christians can believe in Christ, and accept a false doctrine (such as the denial of the Trinity or the rejection of the Resurrection), would be like a Hebrew worshipping Baal and conducting sacrifices on the side, or worshipping the golden calf and making burnt offerings to God. Christ exalts the Shema because He rejects religious inclusivism, and still upholds the legislation against heresy.[44] Christ does not accept religious liberty, so why should we?

IT IS BETTER FOR HERETICS AND OTHER CORRUPTERS TO DROWN THAN TO LIVE

Christ, when warning against those who would corrupt Christians with false doctrine, declared that it would be better for such a deceiver to be drowned:

> Verily I say unto you, except ye be converted, and become as little children, ye shall not enter into the kingdom of heaven. Whosoever therefore shall humble himself as this little child,

---

40 Mark 12:32–33
41 Bellarmine, *On Laymen or Secular People*, ch. 21, ed. Tutino, p. 103
42 Deuteronomy 11:28
43 See Ainsworth, *Annotations*, vol. ii, on Deut. 11.28
44 This interpretation is agreeable to what was written by ancient Christian Firmicus, *On the Error of the Pagan Religions*, 28.8

the same is greatest in the kingdom of heaven. And whoso shall receive one such little child in my name receiveth me. But whoso shall offend one of these little ones, which believe in me, it were better for that a millstone were hanged about his neck, and that he were drowned in the depth of the sea. [45]

The children He is referring to are the believers, and by "shall offend" it is meant "shall scandalize," that is, to lead one into sin through the teachings of wicked doctrines,[46] and heresy can be definitely included as amongst the means by which the elect are brought to evil. St. Clement—a pupil of St. Peter, St. Paul, and St. John—used this very statement of Christ in his condemning and rebuking of the schismatics of the church of Corinth,[47] which signifies that to "offend" can be to bring Christians into theological falsehoods. Now, this is not to say that Christians can freely roam about and drown people who they deem as heretics, but that the verse, when plainly read, implies that it is better for a false teacher to be put to death, rather than be allowed to live and pursue his evil ways.

"YOU ARE THE SALT OF THE EARTH"

The passage of Christ, "You are the salt of the earth," applies to the removal of corrupt clergy who teach false doctrine and evil teachings. Christ told the Disciples:

> You are the salt of the earth; but if the salt loses its flavor, how shall it be seasoned? It is then good for nothing but to be thrown out and trampled underfoot by men. (Matthew 5:13)

These words are addressed to the clergy, since they were declared to the Disciples, and they are referring to the need of tolerance toward corrupt and heretical prelates. They lose their flavor because they have fallen into evil, and they are good for nothing but to be driven out, that is, excommunicated, and "trampled underfoot by men," that is they are to be punished because they have sinned against their neighbor.[48]

CHRIST WILL DESTROY ALL FALSE RELIGIONS IN HIS RETURN

The victory of God over idolatry will surely occur in the final coming of Christ, in which the Savior shall utterly banish heathenism from the earth, as is foretold through the pen of Isaiah, in sublime prose:

> But the idols He shall utterly abolish.
> They shall go into the holes of the rocks,
> And into the caves of the earth,
> From the terror of the Lord
> And the glory of His majesty,
> When He arises to shake the earth mightily. (Isaiah 2:18–19)

---

45 Matthew 18:3–6
46 See Haydock's exposition on this verse, in his *Catholic Bible Commentary*, 1859 ed.
47 St. Clement, Epistle to the Corinthians, 41
48 See Pope Innocent III, sermon 4: *On the Consecration of Pontiffs*

Zephaniah prophesied that Christ will extirpate idolatry in the world, and will compel all men to worship Him:

> The Lord will be terrible unto them: for he will famish all the gods of the earth; and men shall worship him, everyone from his place, even all the isles of the heathen. [49]

Christ shall come and establish those laws which were by inspiration bestowed to Moses, who had enforced that idolatry be proscribed amongst God's people.

"I DON'T SEE THE APOSTLES ENFORCING RELIGION"

People will say that the Apostles never launched holy wars, but to such arguments St. Augustine wrote:

> Since, then, kings did not yet serve the Lord in the times of the Apostles, but were still devising vain things against Him [God] and against His Christ, so that all the predictions of the Prophets might be fulfilled, certainly they were not then able to restrain wickedness by law, but were practicing it themselves. [50]

Such people refuse to recognize circumstances, or to notice any sort of proportionality between the times of the Apostles and the time of Christendom. They are impervious to the fact that the Apostles were not kings or governors, and could not dictate or push for any laws in their position, in which paganism reigned and Christianity was in such a small minority. It is inadequate, and quite unreasonable, to equate the condition of the Apostles to the state of Christianity in the eras of Christendom. In order to launch a crusade or just war one must have, in the words of St. Robert, "legitimate authority, a just cause, a good intention, and an appropriate way of proceeding."[51] For, as he says, "Whoever wages war without authority or just cause sins not only against charity, but also against justice, and he is not so much a soldier as a robber."[52]

Some may argue that Christ or the Apostles did not believe in using the state to advance Christian virtue. But the reason for this was because there were no emperors who believed in Christ in those times, and so they would not have enacted laws in favor of the Church.

It is not the Church which executes these laws, but the state. Therefore it is not for us, as the Church, to become a mob and attack our enemies, but for the government to enact law to protect the Church. This is why the circumstance of the Apostles is important in our study: they had no state by which to punish evil and advance good. To isolate Christianity to just New Testament times, is like isolating Israel to only the times of their enslavement under Egypt.

When the Hebrews were slaves in Egypt, and were being persecuted under the Pharaoh, did they declare wars against heathens, or establish jurisprudence outlawing heresy or paganism? No, because they did not have the enabling of, nor the influence over the gov-

---

49 Zephaniah 2:11
50 Augustine, letter 185, ch. 20, brackets mine
51 Bellarmine, *On Laymen Or Secular People*, ch. 15, ed. Tutino, p. 68
52 St. Robert Bellarmine, *On Laymen or Secular People*, ch. 15, ed. Tutino, p. 71

ernment, to do so. As soon as they gained their freedom from the oppressions of Egypt, and when they had Moses as their political leader, then they began to observe the Divine Law and launch holy wars. The same can be said for Christian history; the Christians were heavily persecuted by the Roman government, and so had no state to govern. As soon as the Christians took over the empire, then they began to enact the laws of God and commence crusades and holy wars. The Church, "the pillar and ground of the truth" (1 Timothy 3:15), does not end at the New Testament, but continues on, alive and vigorous, and continuously expounding upon the holy and inspired prose of the Apostles and the Disciples.

Christians need influence over the state in order to enact Christian law, and we see illustrations of this in the Scriptures. The king of Nineveh did not compel his subjects to observe a national fast until Jonah convinced him to believe in God. Hezekiah would have never broken the idols and removed the high places if he had never believed in God, the same can be said for Josiah. The kings Asa and Jehoshaphat would have never driven out the sodomites (or homosexuals) from their kingdoms if they had not believed in God and His Law. Therefore, the Apostles could not restrain heresy and homosexuality by legislation, because they did not have the favor of the government.[53]

When the Hebrews were under the neo-Babylonian kingdom of Nebuchadnezzar, did they declare war against the pagan king, or attempt to enforce Mosaic Law on him because he subscribed to a false religion? No, but when the miracle of Shadrach, Mishach, and Abednego, surviving the great furnace, influenced him, he established this decree:

> Blessed be the God of Shadrach, Meshach, and Abednego, who hath sent his angel, and delivered his servants that trusted in him, and have changed the king's words, and yielded their bodies, that they might not serve nor worship any god, except their own God. Therefore I make a decree, that every people, nation, and language, which speak anything amiss against the God of Shadrach, and Meshach, and Abednego, shall be cut in pieces, and their houses shall be made a dunghill: because there is no other God that can deliver after this sort.[54]

Did Daniel, or any other Hebrew within the government, object or reprove the king? God did not want Sidrach, Misach, and Abednego to obey the decree of Babylon and worship the golden image, but God did not have a problem with Nebuchadnezzar issuing a law of intolerance against His enemies.[55] In fact, it was God Who inspired him to establish this legislation of intolerance toward blasphemers.

When the Hebrews were under the Persian Empire, did they organize attacks on pagans, or devise a coup against the king, to overthrow him on account of him being of a false religion? No, because they did not have the government on their side to permit them to observe the laws of God. But, when God's people were about to be massacred by the heathens who

---

53 Augustine, *On the Treatment of the Donatistss*, ch. 19
54 Daniel 3:28–29
55 Augustine, *On the Treatment of the Donatists*, ch. 8

lived in the provinces of the Persian empire, because of their Faith and the sway of the wicked Haman, Mordecai and Esther made such an effective influence on the government, that the king, because of the wits of Mordecai, and the beauties of Esther, decreed that the Jews be permitted to attack and kill those who planned on persecuting them:

> Wherein the king granted the Jews which were in every city to gather themselves together, and to stand for their life, to destroy, to slay, and to cause to perish, all the power of the people and province that would assault them, both little ones and women, and to take the spoil of them for a prey, Upon one day in all the provinces of king Ahasuerus, namely, upon the thirteenth day of the twelfth month, which is the month Adar. [56]

Did Mordecai prevent this decree from disseminating throughout the empire, or did the Jews object? No, they embraced it, followed it, and rejoiced on account of its justice:

> The copy of the writing for a commandment to be given in every province was published unto all people, and that the Jews should be ready against that day to avenge themselves on their enemies. So the posts that rode upon mules and camels went out, being hastened and pressed on by the king's commandment. And the decree was given at Shushan the palace. And Mordecai went out from the presence of the king in royal apparel of blue and white, and with a great crown of gold, and with a garment of fine linen and purple: and the city of Shushan rejoiced and was glad. The Jews had light, and gladness, and joy, and honour. And in every province, and in every city, whithersoever the king's commandment and his decree came, the Jews had joy and gladness, a feast and a good day. And many of the people of the land became Jews; for the fear of the Jews fell upon them. The Jews gathered themselves together in their cities throughout all the provinces of the king Ahasuerus, to lay hand on such as sought their hurt: and no man could withstand them; for the fear of them fell upon all people. And all the rulers of the provinces, and the lieutenants, and the deputies, and officers of the king, helped the Jews; because the fear of Mordecai fell upon them. For Mordecai was great in the king's house, and his fame went out throughout all the provinces: for this man Mordecai waxed greater and greater. Thus the Jews smote all their enemies with the stroke of the sword, and slaughter, and destruction, and did what they would unto those that hated them. And in Shushan the palace the Jews slew and destroyed five hundred men. And Parshandatha, and Dalphon, and Aspatha, And Poratha, and Adalia, and Aridatha, And Parmashta, and Arisai, and Aridai, and Vajezatha, The ten sons of Haman the son of Hammedatha, the enemy of the Jews, slew them; but on the spoil laid they not their hand. [57]

The same can be said for the Persian king Artaxerxes when he enabled the prophet Ezra to govern the land of Israel through the divine precepts, and declared that whoever did not obey the sacred Law, was to be punished by death, confiscation of property, imprisonment, or exile:

---

56 Esther 8:11–12
57 Esther 8:13–9:10

PART 9

> And I, even I, Artaxerxes the king, issue a decree to all the treasurers who are in the region beyond the River, that whatever Ezra the priest, the scribe of the Law of the God of heaven, may require of you, let it be done diligently, up to one hundred talents of silver, one hundred kors of wheat, one hundred baths of wine, one hundred baths of oil, and salt without prescribed limit. Whatever is commanded by the God of heaven, let it diligently be done for the house of the God of heaven. For why should there be wrath against the realm of the king and his sons? Also we inform you that it shall not be lawful to impose tax, tribute, or custom on any of the priests, Levites, singers, gatekeepers, Nethinim, or servants of this house of God. And you, Ezra, according to your God-given wisdom, set magistrates and judges who may judge all the people who are in the region beyond the River, all such as know the laws of your God; and teach those who do not know them. Whoever will not observe the law of your God and the law of the king, let judgment be executed speedily on him, whether it be death, or banishment, or confiscation of goods, or imprisonment. (Ezra 7:21–26)

If then, a pagan king such as Artaxerxes can allow and decree the use of temporal punishment for the breaking of God's law, why then is a Christian king or government all of a sudden deprived of this divine right? For a Christian king to enforce the Divine Law against the enemies of God and of His Church, is more glorious than for any other sovereign to do so. The Christian king has the law "written not with ink but by the Spirit of the living God, not on tablets of stone but on tablets of flesh, that is, of the heart." (2 Corinthians 3:3) He does not just know the Law by itself, but the One Who declared before white washed tombs and dead sepulchers, "Do not think that I came to destroy the Law or the Prophets. I did not come to destroy but to fulfill." (Matthew 5:17) The Christian king punishes evil through God's Law, for it "is holy, and the commandment holy and just and good." (Romans 7:12) The Christian king does not have a cold set of demands separated from the heart, but the Law of Love, that is, "the fulfillment of the law." (Romans 13:10) It is with the Law of Love, that Christian kings "are not a terror to good works, but to evil." (Romans 13:3) It is with the Law of Love, that the Christian king "is God's minister to you for good." (Romans 13:4) It is with the Law of Love that the Christian king imposes the Law for "the punishment of evildoers and for the praise of those who do good." (1 Peter 2:14)

When the Jews were under the Persians, they did not declare wars, but this alone could not be used to prove that the Hebrews did away with holy war and militancy, just as the early Church did not declare war when they were under the pagan power of the Romans cannot be utilized to substantiate Christian pacifism, or refute the doctrine of Crusading. Nehemiah, though no warrior himself, never objected to being escorted by an armed guard of soldiers commissioned by the king to protect him, as he wrote himself:

> Then I went to the governors in the region beyond the River, and gave them the king's letters. Now the king had sent captains of the army and horsemen with me. (Nehemiah 2:9)

In this case Nehemiah can be paralleled to St. Paul who, while never declaring war, never protested when a large body of Roman troops protected him.

So the same situation occurred in the Church, at its beginning the Christians were oppressed greatly under the pagan tyranny of Rome, but once the saints infiltrated the government, they soon had a hold on the state, that they enacted laws against the very pagan religion which sought their destruction, and against the heresies that desired the ruin of all Christendom.

The modern Christians will say, "I don't see the Apostles enforcing religion." Yet neither the Apostles, nor Christ, ever prohibited or ordered the killing of heretics. Therefore, a direct command of toleration cannot be deduced from this.[58]

They will quote from Paul when he said, "For there must also be factions among you, that those who are approved may be recognized among you." (1 Corinthians 11:19) They will read this and say, "See, Paul tolerated different sects and heresies." But this verse is making a simple observation of human society. It's like saying, "There must be murders," not that murders must be tolerated, but that murders will always happen, just as cults will always appear. But this does not mean that we tolerate or accept such evils. Christ said, "Woe to the world because of offenses! For offenses must come, but woe to that man by whom the offense comes!" (Matthew 18:7) Christ here says that offenses must come, but this does not mean that we tolerate them, for even Christ warns against the offenders. Offenses will always be here, just as crimes will always be here, but this does not signify that criminals be permitted to create havoc.[59] Thus, there must heresies, but this does not mean that we tolerate them. Pope Leo X wrote: "there must be heresies to test the faithful, still they must be destroyed at their very birth."[60]

Furthermore, when St. Paul wrote that "there must also be factions among you" he was writing this with the intention of stirring in the Corinthians the will to unify, come into Communion with the Church under the Lord's Supper, and cease their heresies and schisms. For in the next passage he chides them, writing that "you come together in one place, it is not to eat the Lord's Supper. For in eating, each one takes his own supper ahead of others; and one is hungry and another is drunk. What! Do you not have houses to eat and drink in? Or do you despise the church of God and shame those who have nothing? What shall I say to you? Shall I praise you in this? I do not praise you." (1 Corinthians 11:20–23) That St. Paul was exhorting the Corinthians to be under one Communion, is signified by the next passage in which he describes the Last Supper:

> For I received from the Lord that which I also delivered to you: that the Lord Jesus on the same night in which He was betrayed took bread; and when He had given thanks, He broke it and said, 'Take, eat; this is My body which is broken for you; do this in remembrance of Me.' In the same manner He also took the cup after supper, saying, 'This cup is the new covenant in My blood. This do, as often as you drink it, in remembrance of Me.' (1 Corinthians 11:23–25)

---

58 Bellarmine, *On Laymen or Secular People*, ch. 22, ed. Tutino, p. 113
59 See Bellarmine, *On Laymen or Secular People*, ch. 22, ed. Tutino, p. 114
60 Leo X, *Exsurge Domine*

St. Paul does not praise them for their factionalism, nor does he tolerate them, but he instead urges them to be unified under the one Eucharist of the Church. All the while, St. Paul observes that there will always be heresies, but this does not denote toleration, nor is it some push for the state to permit such heresies to be taught or inundate society.

Moreover, the Apostles lived in a pagan society, and the Church, "did not yet have the strength to restrain earthly princes."[61] Now, in a Christian society, in which the state and the Church work together, the people are expected to be unified under "one Lord, one faith, one baptism" (Ephesians 4:5). Freedom of religion would thus harm this union, and would be destructive to the Church and the spiritual state of the nation.[62] The peace of Christendom depends upon the peace of the Church. Thus Leo X wrote:

> Let all this holy Church of God, I say, arise, and with the blessed apostles intercede with almighty God to purge the errors of His sheep, to banish all heresies from the lands of the faithful, and be pleased to maintain the peace and unity of His holy Church.[63]

This is why the government of the Christian empire must look after the welfare of the Church, from threats both physical and heretical. St. Pope Gregory I wrote to the emperor Maurice that he is to use his authority to protect the Church from heretics within the priesthood, since the peace and harmony of the empire lies on the peace of the Church:

> Our most pious and God-appointed lord, among his other august cares and burdens, watches also in the uprightness of spiritual zeal over the preservation of peace among the priesthood. Inasmuch as he piously and truly considers that no one can govern earthly things aright unless he knows how to deal with divine things, and that the peace of the republic hangs on the peace of the universal Church. Wherefore most providently for restraining warlike movements does the most pious Lord seek the peace of the Church, and, for compacting it, deigns to bring back the hearts of its priest to concord. And this indeed is what I wish; and, as far as I am concerned, I render obedience to his most serene commands. But since it is not my cause, but God's, since the pious laws, since the venerable synods, since the very commands of our Lord Jesus Christ are disturbed by the invention of a certain proud and pompous phrase, let the most pious Lord cut the place of the sore, and bind the resisting patient in the chains of august authority. For in the blinding up these things tightly you relieve the republic; and, while you cut off such things, you provide for the lengthening of your reign.[64]

It is the emperor who cuts off the heretical sores of the body politic, at the exhortation of the Church. Where obedience to God and faith are preserved, there lies order. If we expect society to obey human law, it is best to get them to first obey divine law. To say that people should be permitted to believe and practice whatever ideas they want, is like saying a shepherd should allow his sheep to wander about wherever they wish, or for a captain of a ship to

---
61 Bellarmine
62 See Bellarmine, *On Laymen or Secular People*, ch. 18
63 Leo, *Exsurge Domine*
64 Gregory I, book 5, epistle 20

discard the steering oar and allow the ship to be carried freely by the capricious winds.⁶⁵ To say that cult leaders or promoters of dangerous beliefs should not be punished, is not only anarchical, but reckless in the governing of a society and in the preservation of societal order. Should a shepherd put down his rod and his sword, and allow the wolf to have free reign over his sheep? Christ said, "Beware of false prophets, which come to you in sheep's clothing, but inwardly they are ravening wolves," (Matthew 7:15) and wolves are rightfully and justly killed if they cannot be driven away. They will say that this is against the love of the Church, but it is not, simply for the reason that it would be against the love of the Church to allow such reprobates and vile devils to persecute and corrupt the citizens of the Church.⁶⁶

Christ also said, "He that entereth not by the door into the sheepfold, but climbeth up some other way, the same is a thief and a robber" (John 10:1). The thief and a robber is the inventor of malicious sects, and if we punish the stealers of money and property, then surely the stealers of souls must as well be punished. St. Paul warns that the message of the heretics "will spread like cancer." (2 Timothy 2:17) And no one will disagree that cancer must be cut off. The Apostles could not extirpate the heretical groups of their time, because they had no state; but in the state of Christendom, the magistrate has the authority to cut off heretical cults as a doctor cuts away cancer.⁶⁷ St. Paul said that we "are one body in Christ" (Romans 12:5), and what does the immune system do with a disease? It destroys it. And if it cannot, then what does the doctor do to the disease? He cuts it off. And so if an individual has the right to purge himself from diseases, then Christendom, the Body of Christ, has just as much a right to cut off the disease of heresy and depravity from itself. As Vitoria says, "there is no reason why the commonwealth should not have the same power to compel and coerce its members as if they were its limbs for the utility and safety of the common good."⁶⁸ Since the perversity of the modernists and the false doctrines of heretics are a danger to the Christian body, then they rightly must be uprooted.

"Cast out the bondwoman and her son: for the son of the bondwoman shall not be heir with the son of the freewoman." (Galatians 4:30) These are the words of St. Paul in his letter to the Galatians, and he is referring to Hagar—the bondwoman—and her son Ishmael, being driven out because the latter cannot be an heir with the freewoman's son—Isaac. This is symbolic of two different religions: one being true and bringing freedom, and the other being false and tyrannical. "So then, brethren," writes St. Paul, "we are not children of the bondwoman, but of the free."⁶⁹ Now, the historical context in which Paul is writing is very significant. His letter to the Galatians was dealing with the heretical Judaizers who wanted to establish circumcision as necessary for salvation, and Paul is describing them as being of the

---

65 See Bellarmine, *On Laymen or Secular People*, ch. 18, ed. Tutino, p. 86
66 See Bellarmine, *On Laymen or Secular People*, ch. 22, ed. Tutino, p. 119
67 See Bellarmine, *On Laymen or Secular People*, ch. 21, ed. Tutino, p. 104
68 Vitoria, *On Civil Power*, question 1, article 4.2; see also question 2, sect. 3
69 Galatians 4:31

bondwoman, or being after the flesh. And what is the result of this heresy? Despotism. Paul refers to these heretics as persecutors of the orthodox:

> But as then he that was born after the flesh persecuted him that was born after the Spirit, even so it is now. [70]

And what is the solution to this problem? St. Paul writes: "Nevertheless what saith the scripture? Cast out the bondwoman and her son." So then, false religion brings despotism, and thus does not deserve liberty. The truth sets us free, and thus error brings us into tyranny. Error has no rights, thus tyranny deserves no liberty. Interestingly, Paul's words in Galatians were applied by the Christians of the Middle Ages to the retaking of Jerusalem by the crusaders from the Muslims. The Christians had every right to drive out the Muslims from their rulership over the Holy City, for they were of Arabia—or Hagar—and persecuted those of the Spirit, and had to be cast out because they could not be heir with the children of the freewoman.

Pope Innocent III, one of the most significant spiritual leaders of the Crusades, called the warriors to fulfill what St. Paul wrote to the Galatians, and throw out the bondswomen—or the Muslims—from the Holy Land, for they corrupted the land where God in the Flesh was born, and where He walked, and where He redeemed the world through His death. Now, it was the calling of the Christians to sacrifice their own lives for the land where the greatest of all sacrifices was done. Innocent III also exclaimed on how the holy places of Israel, and the Holy Cross of Christ, were being tainted and desecrated by the Muslims, and thus they needed to be conquered and extirpated from the blessed land:

> [T]he holy places are all profaned, and the sepulcher of the Lord which used to be revered, is now defiled. Where Jesus Christ the only begotten Son of God was adored, Mohammed, the son of perdition is now worshipped. The alien's sons insult me, and they taunt the wood of the Cross, saying, 'You trusted in the wood, now let us see if it can help you.' O what shame, what chaos, what ignominy, that the sons of the slave woman, the unworthy Agarenes [Muslims], now hold our mother enslaved, the mother of all the faithful, of whom the Psalmist surely speaks, 'Mother Sion,' he says, 'Everyone is born in her, and the Most High himself has founded her.' It is there that God our King, before all the ages, chose to accomplish our salvation in the midst of the world. [71]

"But where is your love?" asks the modern. Those who desire not to partake in the crusade against evil for the sake of love, have no love in them. To love, is to help the oppressed and the downtrodden, and in doing so, the oppressors must be put to an end, and the yokes which bound their victims broken. This love, which is of the purest form, is declared in Isaiah:

> Is not this the fast that I have chosen? To loose the bands of wickedness, to undo the heavy burdens, and to let the oppressed go free, and that ye break every yoke? Is it not to deal thy bread to the hungry, and that thou bring the poor that are cast out to thy house? When thou seest the naked, that thou cover him; and that thou hide not thyself from thine own flesh?

---

70 Galatians 4:29
71 Pope Innocent III, sermon 6: Fourth General Council of the Lateran

Then shall thy light break forth as the morning, and thine health shall spring forth speedily: and thy righteousness shall go before thee; the glory of the Lord shall be thy reward. (Isaiah 58:6–8)

Toleration of all religions—or more correctly, toleration of error—is an idea which was never accepted by the Church, and nor shall it ever be. We may argue that this sentiment is not love, but we cannot equate the modern perception of love with the Biblical view of love.

To God love is not accepting everyone as they are, falsehoods and all, but in part, punishing those who are evil to bring them away from error. This love is explicitly found in the Proverbs:

He who spares his rod hates his son, but he who loves him disciplines him promptly. [72]

ST. PAUL SUPPORTED THE USE OF THE SWORD BY BOTH STATE AND SOLDIER

St. Paul upheld the use of the sword against evildoers by the state when he wrote:

For rulers are not a terror to good works, but to evil. Do you want to be unafraid of the authority? Do what is good, and you will have praise from the same. For he is God's minister to you for good. But if you do evil, be afraid; for he does not bear the sword in vain; for he is God's minister, an avenger to execute wrath on him who practices evil. Therefore you must be subject, not only because of wrath but also for conscience sake. (Romans 13:3–5)

Romans 13 is not solely applicable to a government punishing its citizens, but also to a righteous nation punishing a wicked nation. For the army of the state is an extension of its sword, and therefore the warriors who strikes an evil people in defense of Christians, does so in obedience to God's minister, and for this reason, are they as well executers of the divine wrath. This is why St. Bernard applied Romans 13 to the military defense of Christians by crusaders who were fighting the Muslims, when he wrote that the "knight of Christ" does not "bear the sword in vain. He is God's minister in the punishment of evil doers and the praise of well doers. Surely, if he kills an evil doer, he is not a man-killer, but, if I may put it, an evil-killer. Clearly he is reckoned the avenger of Christ against evildoers, and the defender of Christians."[73] Romans 13 was applied to warfare by Aquinas when he wrote:

And just as it is lawful for them [kings] to use the material sword in defense of the commonwealth against those who trouble it from within, when they punish evildoers, according to the Apostle (Romans 13:4), 'He beareth not the sword in vain: for he is the minister of God, a revenger to execute wrath upon him that doeth evil': so too, it pertains to them to use the sword of war to protect the commonwealth against the enemies from without. [74]

---

72 Proverbs 13:24
73 St. Bernard, *In Praise of a New Knighthood*, ch. 3, 4
74 Aquinas, *Summa Theologiae*, IIa IIae 40, article 1

Vitoria also applied Romans 13 to war, writing that "it is lawful to draw the sword and use weapons against malefactors and seditious subjects within the commonwealth; therefore it must be lawful to use the sword and take up arms against foreign enemies too."[75]

The sword of justice, and not of tyranny, is a terror solely to those who do evil. And what Christian would ever say that homosexuality, murder, or any deliberate war against God and His Holy Faith is not evil? These are most certainly evils that are to be uprooted, and their partakers compelled to give up their wickedness or be exterminated. But the conniving heretics will argue that Paul's support for the sword was written in the context of pagan Rome, and thus the use of the sword should be limited to the values of pagan Rome, and never in accordance to those of Christendom. What then should happen if the whole pagan empire turn Christian, and the idols and heathenish philosophies cast aside and forgotten? Should Paul's words as well be forgotten? The verses of Paul are not written just for pagan governments, but for all governments, including Christian. St. Paul does not say, "For pagan rulers are not a terror to good works, but to evil." And nor does he ever say, "The pagan ruler does not bear the sword in vain." The passage should never be isolated to the laws of pagan Rome. And even if a nation was pagan, that does not mean that its governors could not enact laws for the cause of the Faith, for Nebuchadnezzar was pagan and justly decreed against blasphemy. But if you wish to go to the extreme of isolating Paul's words to pagan Rome, how then would you deal with all of the evils passed by the Roman government. Rome allowed abortions, and no Christian in that time was for it, but vigorously wrote against it. In the Didache, the oldest Christian writing outside of the New Testament, it says, "do not kill a fetus by abortion, or commit infanticide."[76] And if the ancient Christians could influence the pagan government to punish such an evil action, they most certainly would have done it. For Tertullian, one of the oldest of the Christian apologists and a man who lived in pagan Rome, when he wrote his condemnation of abortion, did not fail to mention a law holy and righteous: "The law of Moses, indeed, punishes with due penalties the man who shall cause abortion."[77] And if the ancient Christians did succeed in having pagan Rome outlaw abortion, such a holy law could be esteemed as nothing but Christian, and not at all connected to the savage ways of the pagans. The Roman Empire eventually did become Christian, and such wickedness was eventually overthrown. And how did these ancient Christians succeed in overtaking the empire with the light of the Faith? They did not do so by isolating the words of St. Paul, but applying it to its fullest extent.

For while Paul's words may be applied to any government, it was written solely for the Church, and ultimately, in regards to the state, for Christendom. The ministry of Christ was not established to form a minority of Christians so that they could remain in a world dominated by darkness. The light of Christ was brought to humanity, to illuminate the whole earth, and to dissipate the black night of the devil. Christ commanded, "Teach ye all nations;

---

75 Vitoria, *On the Law of War*, question 1, article 1
76 *Didache*, 2, trans. Kleist
77 Tertullian, *On the Soul*, ch. 31, trans. Peter Holmes

baptizing them in the name of the Father, and of the Son, and of the Holy Ghost." (Matthew 28:19) The Lord is "not willing that any should perish, but that all should come to repentance." (2 Peter 3:9) So how then could the Church remain so small, and never reach to the heights of the earth and flood all nations with its beauties? It was impossible that it could do this, and only a wicked heretic would wish it to. The Church had to expand, and expand it did. And soon did the luminaries of the Orthodox Faith inundate the earth and destroy the bastions of darkness. The Roman Empire eventually became Christian, and what was it supposed to do, but change its ways for the cause of Christ? And this it most certainly did, by the will of God. St. Augustine elaborately explained that the Apostles had no power to punish sacrilege, but now that the whole empire was Christian, it was thus established to punish the haters of God and bring low the towers of heresy and the pinnacles of those who wanted to destroy Christianity and the most glorious Church:

> Since, then, kings did not yet serve the Lord in the times of the Apostles, but were still devising vain things against Him and against His Christ, so that all the predictions of the Prophets might be fulfilled, certainly they were not then able to restrain wickedness by law, but were practicing it themselves. The sequence of time was so unrolled that the Jews killed the preachers of Christ, thinking they were doing a service to God, as Christ had foretold, and the Gentiles raged against the Christians, and the patience of the martyrs won the victory. But after the prophetic words began to be fulfilled, as it is written: 'And all the kings of the earth shall adore him; all nations shall serve him [Psalm 71:11],' what serious-minded man would say to kings: 'Do not trouble to care whether the Church of your Lord is hampered or attacked by anyone in your kingdom; let it not concern you whether a man chooses to practice or to flout religion'? For it would not be possible to say to them: 'Let it not concern you whether anyone in your kingdom chooses to be virtuous or shameless.' Why, then, since free will has been divinely bestowed on man, should adultery be punished by law and sacrilege permitted? Is it a lesser matter for a soul to keep the faith with God than for a woman to keep it with her husband? Or if offenses committed, not through contempt but through ignorance of religion, are to be punished more leniently, is that any reason for overlooking them altogether?[78]

"But seek ye first the kingdom of God, and his righteousness" (Matthew 6:33), this is what our Lord tells us. In society, we must seek His Kingdom; when warring with evil we must seek His Kingdom. In the Douay-Rheims rendition of this verse, Christ says: "Seek ye therefore first the kingdom of God, and his justice, and all these things shall be added unto you." In seeking the Kingdom of Heaven first, we seek justice, and thus do we seek the destruction of evil. Remember what the scribe told Christ: "there is one God, and there is no other but He." (Mark 12:32)

There is only one God, the most holy and blessed Trinity, and He is to be supreme over our laws and our government. Remember what our Lord told the scribe after he said these words: "You are not far from the kingdom of God." (Mark 12:34)

---
78 Augustine, letter 185, ch. 20

If we are to first seek the Kingdom of Heaven, then we are to shatter the other gods, and the other religions and ideologies that have so tainted Christian society. It will be then that we will come closer to the Kingdom of God, once indifferentism is destroyed, the flames of zeal finally rekindled, and the establishments of Christianity put back into their rightful positions.

To kill and punish murderers and those sacrilegious reprobates, who froth at the mouth against God with blasphemies and based mockeries, insults, and calls to violence, is not murder, but lawfulness. As we read in St. Jerome:

> To punish murderers and impious men is not shedding blood, but applying the laws. [79]

St. Paul said, "Do you not know that a little leaven leavens the whole lump? Therefore purge out the old leaven, that you may be a new lump, since you truly are unleavened." (1 Corinthians 5:6–7) And so the wicked must be cut off, and not allowed to corrupt the whole society. St. Thomas connected this passage of St. Paul with the killing of dangerous people: "And so if some man is dangerous to the community, causing its corruption because of some sin, it is praiseworthy and wholesome that he be slain in order to preserve the common good; for 'a little leaven corrupteth the whole lump' (Corinthians 5:6)."[80]

RELIGIOUS TOLERANCE AND EQUALITY ARE ENEMIES TO THE FAITH

Religious tolerance and the idea of absolute equality are enemies of Christianity. Many people believe that society must be under a system of complete equality, such as in the utopia of Plato in which property, and even wives, children, mothers and fathers, were shared equally.[81] But, this is most pernicious for humanity; for instead of leaving man to live as an individual, it enforces him and his countrymen to live in a collective mass, existing as a herd of brutes.

As we learn from the philosopher Roger Scruton, there are only two forms of equality necessary for society: equality of opportunity, and equality before the law. Since the subject at hand is law versus tyranny, we shall focus on the latter. The laws of Moses uphold equality before the law, declaring: "Ye shall have one manner of law, as well for the stranger, as for one of your own country: for I am the Lord." (Leviticus 24:22) This system of equal laws is a requisite only for a noble constitution. The person under mosaic percepts were guaranteed the security of his property. But as soon as he broke the law, he was stripped of these rights,[82] since having equality before the law implies that all unlawfulness is punished equally, observing no regard for who the perpetuator is, of his status, or mental state, but what he did to deserve punishment. Nicodemus, the Pharisee who spoke with Jesus, spoke of this trait of the Law when he asked:

> Does our law judge a man before it hears him and knows what he is doing? [83]

---

79 St. Jerome, Commentary on Jeremiah, in Bellarmine, On Secular People or Laymen, ch. 13, ed. Tutino, p. 50
80 Aquinas, *Summa Theologiae*, IIa IIae 64, article 3
81 Lact. Div. Inst. 3.22, trans. William Fletcher.
82 Clarke, Commentary, vol. i, p. 590, on Leviticus 24:22.
83 John 7:51

The phrase to emphasis on is "any man," meaning that all persons are given the liberty to make their case before being judged, and not vice-versa.

The Law of Moses cares not for the person, but only for his actions. It cares not whether the person is poor or prestigious, but if he is virtuous or wicked. For, it reads in Leviticus: "Ye shall do no unrighteousness in judgment: thou shalt not respect the person of the poor, not honour the person of the mighty: but in righteousness shalt thou judge thy neighbour." (Leviticus 19:15) Moses later declares to the people that "Ye shall not respect persons in judgment but ye shall hear the small as well as the great; ye shall not be afraid of the face of man; for the judgment is God's: and the cause that is too hard for you, bring it unto me, and I will hear it." (Deuteronomy 1:17)

There are then those who say that the state should never be involved with religion, that it should not only tolerate, but protect all belief systems no matter how wicked or dangerous, and that it should only act when someone uses violence.

This was the error of the pagans who accepted every religious belief, except Christianity of course. The problem with ultra-tolerance is that it is maliciously self-destructive; it believes in accepting every belief, only to eventually persecute those who do not believe in accepting every belief.

When the pagans ruled Rome, they had no problem with Christians worshipping Jesus, just as long as they respected the other gods. It was because the Christians declared that the other gods must be rejected, that the pagans began their persecutions. Therefore, the root of the pagan tyranny against the early Christians, was toleration. Thus, absolute toleration is of the devil and will only lead to despotism over the Church. The main enemy of tolerance is Christianity, because the very nature of the Faith is intolerant, and declares that there is an absolute truth that is to be embraced, while everything else is false. This is why Pope Leo I, when speaking on pagan Rome, said: "When this city, while ignorant of the Author of its progress, dominated almost every people, it was a slave to every people's errors and seemed to have adopted a great religion because it did not reject any falsehood."[84]

It is because of the Holy Faith's intolerant nature that the proponents of ultra-tolerance (even if they call themselves Christian) will always war against Christianity. They will use absolute toleration to fragment Christian society through the influence of numerous sects, which eventually leads to an absolute intolerance of Christianity. This is not a novel theory, but an observation of history. St. Augustine made this same observation when writing on the dangers of religious tolerance; he specified that the pagan emperor Julian established a policy that tolerated all heretical sects, especially the Donatists, and pagan religions, deliberately for the purpose of destroying Christianity. He wrote of how "Julian, a deserter and enemy of Christ, who yielded to the petition of your [the Donatists'] sectaries, Rogation and Pontius, by giving freedom to the sect of Donatus, to their own peril, and by giving back their basilicas

---

[84] Pope Leo I, sermon 82 on Peter and Paul, in St. Robert Bellarmine, *On Laymen or Secular People*, ch. 18, ed. Tutino, p. 81

to the heretics, while he was also restoring the temples to the demons. He thought that in this way the name of Christian could be blotted out from the earth, if he should attack the unity of the Church from which he had apostatized, and should allow the accursed forces of dissension to be free of restriction."[85]

Valens, the Arian emperor, allowed for a policy of "freedom of religion" while at the same time he persecuted Orthodox Christians; Julian the Apostate legislated the same sort of measure, and he too persecuted the faithful. Not only is freedom of religion done in order to water down the Faith and engulf it in an ocean of confusion, but it also enables people of false religions to take power in the government and use temporal authority to persecute the Church.

Those who uphold error, will afflict and tyrannize those who fight and strive for the Truth. Error brings terror, and truth brings civilization. As we read in the Epistle of St. Barnabas, written at about the late first century or early second century, the persecutors of the righteous are those involved in falsehood, paganism, witchcraft, absence of compassion for the oppressed, slayers of children, and other crimes and sins:

> For it is the way of eternal death, with punishment, in which they that walk meet those things that destroy their own souls. Such are—idolatry, confidence, pride of power, hypocrisy, double-mindedness, adultery, murder, rapine, pride, transgression, deceit, malice, arrogance, witchcraft, covetousness, and the want of the fear of God. In this walk those who are the persecutors of them that are good—haters of truth, lovers of lies; who know not the reward of righteousness, nor cleave to anything that is good; who administer not righteous judgement to the widow and orphan; who watch for wickedness, and not for the fear of the Lord: from whom gentleness and patience are far off; who love vanity, and follow after rewards; having no compassion upon the poor; nor take any pains for such as are heavy laden and oppressed: ready to evil speaking, not knowing him that made him; murderers of children, corrupters of the creature of God, that turn away from the needy, oppress the afflicted; are the advocates of the rich, but unjust judges of the poor; being altogether sinners. [86]

It is no coincidence that those who are followers of false religions and evil practices, are placed in line with those who seek the blood of the righteous and the innocent, especially children.

In this world one belief must rule, and the struggle is between good and evil, with evil continuously trying to dominate, and good always striving to triumph. Once evil is given tolerance it will always work to persecute and destroy Christianity. The Church itself witnessed this when it was dealing with the Donatist heretics.

In the time of St. Augustine, the Church was dealing with a most dangerous sect of heretics called the Donatists, founded by Donatus. They were schismatics who broke away from the Catholic Church, and believed with shameless pride that the true church was to be found in Africa alone. In doing this they became very insurrectionist, and like all heretics,

---

85 Augustine, letter 105, brackets mine
86 *The Catholic Epistle of Barnabas*, 20, trans. Wake

tried to replace the Church.[87] They held a fanatic belief in martyrdom, reminiscent to that of the Muslim. They would attack pagan idols simply to be killed by the pagans; they would willfully seek death unlike true Christian martyrs who simply accepted their end when it came. They would threaten armed men with death if they did not kill them. If they could not find someone to spill their blood, they would jump off cliffs or drown or burn themselves alive. They burnt down homes, stabbed Christians with swords, beat men almost to death, and took others and tied them to millstones and afflicted them with blows. They would also throw a liquid made up of vinegar and lime into the eyes of Christians to blind them. They took a bishop and severed off his hands and tongue, burnt down churches, threw Bibles into the flames, and even massacred Catholics.[88] They sent a message to the Catholic Church which said, "Keep away from our flocks, if you do not want us to kill you."[89] A Donatist named Restitutus of Victoriana joined the Catholic Church, and this incensed the Donatists so much that they dragged him from his home, beat him and imprisoned him. He was later freed when the Donatist bishop Proculeianus intervened since he knew that it would lead to trouble for his cult.[90] Another Donatist, Marcian of Urga, joined the Catholic Faith and had to go into hiding from fear of the demonic cult. The Donatists found out where he was hiding, beat him almost to death and then stoned him. For this crime the state burned down the homes of the criminals. Maximinus, a Donatist bishop, also left the cult and joined the Catholic Church, and so angered by this were the Donatist that they sent out this message:

> If anyone remains in communion with Maximinus, his house will be burned down.[91]

Possidius, the Bishop of Calama, was attacked by the Donatists in the farm of Oliveta, and they "left him half-dead and tried to burn down the house from which we had escaped. They would have done it, too, if the tenants of that same farm had not three times put out the flames which endangered their own safety."[92]

They attacked the Bishop of Bagai in his church, beat him with clubs and stabbed him in the groin. As they dragged his body, with a trail of blood following him, some dirt clogged the wound and stopped the bleeding, sustaining him from death. They dropped his body, and the Christians tried to carry him away. But anger seized the Donatists and they grabbed him again and drove the Christians away with vicious kicks. They thought the Bishop was dead and so they tossed him from a tower. He landed on a soft surface, and was discovered in the evening by some good samaritans who rescued and brought him to a church where he was

---

87 Augustine, *On the Treatment of the Donatists*, chs. 1, 3, trans. Sister Wilfrid Parsons, *The Fathers of the Church*, vol. 30
88 Augustine, *On the Treatment of the Donatists*, chs. 12, 15, 18, 30; letter 88
89 Augustine, letter 105, trans. Parsons
90 Augustine, letter 105
91 Augustine, letter 105
92 Augustine, letter 105

revived. The Bishop then requested from the Roman emperor that laws be passed to protect the Church from these heretics.[93]

The legislation was of course a policy of intolerance towards the Donatists, and this was because, as Augustine observed, "when emperors pass laws favoring falsehood and opposing truth, staunch believers are tested [through persecution] and faithful champions are crowned [with martyrdom]; but, when they pass good laws favoring truth and opposing falsehood, the cruel extremists are constrained by fear and the intelligent are converted."[94] When the Donatists began to protest the suppression against their cult, St. Augustine, in a letter written to them, said:

> If you are angry with us because you are forced by the decrees of the emperors to rejoin us, you brought this on yourselves by stirring up violence and threats whenever we wished to preach the truth, and you tried to prevent anyone from listening to it in safety or choosing it voluntarily. [95]

From all of the violence that this cult caused, there is one thing that we can conclude: the Donatists, even though they cried out that they wanted freedom, did not themselves believe in freedom. If the Donatists were this violent as private citizens, we can only imagine how more brutal they would have been if they had controlled the whole government. From the example of the Donatists we can learn much on the nature and aspirations of dangerous cults: they aggressively strive for power until they have dominated every infrastructure of society—education, the arts, the government—and then they suffocate the whole population, until their beliefs become the generally accepted view, and the Christians are deemed worthy of death and tyranny. If the Christian Roman state had the same mindset as the moderns of today, the Donatists would have continued further in their bloodshed. But thank goodness the emperors did not possess the tolerant sentiment, and most fortunately, they listened to St. Augustine who said to the Donatists:

> If you, private citizens, so boldly and violently force men either to accept error or to remain in it, how much greater right and duty have we to resist your outrages by means of the lawfully constituted authority, which God has made subject to Christ, according to His prophecy, and so to rescue unfortunate souls from your tyranny, to free them from long-continued false teaching and let them breathe the clear air of truth! [96]

Those who preach falsehoods and heresies work arduously for Orthodox Christians to accept their evils, but error has no rights and does not deserve liberty, and so it deserves to be abolished through the force of the state.

If heretics, or the haters of Christianity, are given power, or a position of dominance, they will persecute the Christians just as Cain killed Abel.

---

93 Augustine, *On the Treatment of the Donatists*, chs. 27–8
94 Augustine, *On the Treatment of the Donatists*, ch. 8, brackets mine
95 Augustine, letter 105
96 Augustine, letter 105

Since heresy means "choice," its existence is dependent upon religious liberty, in which the freedom to choose the heresy is given. Thus heresy cannot prosper without religious liberty, and thus, the tyrannical suffocate where the Church of "one Lord, one faith, one baptism" (Ephesians 4:5) rules. The viciousness of heresy, and the vigorousness of its spreading, is the reason why the Church began to kill heretics and purge the land of their doctrines. The Church did not always deal with this problem through capital punishment; it first used excommunication, then some sanctions, then exile, and then, in the end, when all of these were not sufficient enough in ending the problem, it resorted to the death penalty. St. Robert Bellarmine explains this:

> First, is used only excommunication, then it added pecuniary sanctions, next it used exile, and, finally, it was obliged to implement the death penalty, for heretics despise excommunication, and they say it is cold lightening. If you threaten a pecuniary sanction, they neither fear God nor show reverence toward men, known that there will be no lack of fools who will believe in them and will support them. If you lock them in prison or send them into exile, they corrupt with speech those who are near them and with books those who are far. Therefore the only remedy is to send them quickly to the place where they belong. [97]

When people hear this they automatically think that countless people will be killed. This is a mistake. Only a few would be punished or (in some cases) killed, for such coercion would compel the rest to conform to Orthodoxy. As St. Robert says, "many people may be reformed through the punishment of a few,"[98] and so for the whole group to witness a few suffer punishment, brings the whole to the truth. Solomon, the wisest of men, said, "The rod and rebuke give wisdom," (Proverbs 29:15) and so the punishment of the wicked stirs in them the desire for wisdom, so as to leave the road of darkness and move to the path of Light. St. Augustine prescribed the use of punishment against the Circumcellions, a group of fanatic Donatists, because, as he said, coercion made them more inclined to search and accept Christianity:

> Oh, if I could show you, from the very ranks of the Circumcellions, how many now become active Catholics, condemn their former life and the wretched error which made them think they were doing a service to the Church of God when they thus rashly disturbed the peace! Yet they would not have been brought to this state of health if they had not been restrained, like the fever-stricken, with the shackles of those laws which are displeasing to you. [99]

Heretics always want to destroy the Church, and so tolerance of evil and destructive beliefs will only lead to death. There are three stories that show both the destructive nature of cults and the reason why the Church outlawed them: these are the stories of the heretics of Orleans, Arnold of Brescia, and the violent cult of the Middle Ages called the Shepherds.

---

97 Bellarmine, *On Laymen or Secular People*, ch. 21, ed. Tutino, p. 108
98 Bellarmine, *On Laymen or Secular People*, ch. 21, ed. Tutino, p. 108
99 Augustine, letter 93

THE HERETICS OF ORELEANS

In France, in the early eleventh century, there was an emissary named Arefast who had a clerk named Heribert. This clerk left off to the city of Orleans to study, but instead of inquiring into learning, he met two men and fell under their influence. When he returned home Heribert startled Arefast with strange words, telling him that Orleans showed "more brightly than other cities with the light of wisdom and the torch of holiness." By such terms he showed Arefast that he was taken by some unknown doctrine. Concerned, He visited a prudent clerk and asked him for council as to what to do with Heribert. The wise clerk told him to seek the help of God every morning, to go to church to pray, and to strengthen himself with Holy Communion. With this, he was then able to enter this sect which Heribert was a part of, and act as though he was one them. For much time he went to their meetings and listened to their wise men speak, listening quietly without objection.

Arefast watched with undisclosed horror at the ritual they conducted. They met on certain nights in a house wherein they would do a ritual in which each would hold a candlelight and call on the names of particular demons. They would continue to call on these names until they saw a vision of Satan before them. As soon as this happened they put out the lights and all of the men would seize on whatever woman he could grab and an orgy would ensue. The children conceived from this foul union were gathered together, a large fire was set, and the little ones were thrown into the flames. Their ashes were then collected and kept to be eaten by the members who were about to die to ensure their salvation. Once it was consumed, they said that it would lead the members into an obstinate addiction to the heresy, and an absolute deriding of Christianity.

After some time passed, they saw Arefast as an able student and ready to hear the true teachings of the cult.

When they began to reveal their real beliefs, it showed the depths of their wickedness and heresy. "Christ was not born of the Virgin Mary," they said, "he did not suffer for men, he was not really buried in the sepulcher and did not rise from the dead," they then added, "there is no cleansing of sin in baptism, nor in the sacrament of the body and blood in Christ administered by a priest. Nothing is to be gained from praying to the holy martyrs and confessors."

Arefast, upon hearing this, acted foolish and asked as to how man was to have salvation. "There is no doubt, brother," responded the wise men, "that until now you have lain with the ignorant in the Charybdis of false belief. Now you have been raised to the summit of all truths. With unimpeded mind you may begin to open your eyes to the light of the true faith. We will open the door of salvation to you. Through the laying of our hands upon you, you will be cleansed of every spot of sin. You will be replenished with the gift of the Holy Spirit, which will teach you unreservedly the underlying meaning of the scriptures, and true righteousness. When you have fed on the heavenly food and have achieved inner satisfaction you will often see angelic visions with us, and sustained by that solace you will be able to go where you will without let or hindrance, whenever you want to. You will want for nothing, for God, in whom are all the treasures of wealth and wisdom, will never fail to be your comparison in all things."

What is important to understand is that from such heretical beliefs, this cult decayed to the point that they began to murder children. It is another evidence to the point that heresy leads to violence.

Arefast soon after reported the group to the king and Queen Constance, and the entire cult was arrested, tried, and all but two (a clerk and a nun who confessed) were burnt alive.[100]

The teachings and violent actions of this cult are quite similar to another French heresy in Soissons. This group was led by a villager named Clement, and they declared that the salvation of Christ was a delusion; infant baptism was useless; that marriage was evil and propagation of children forbidden; and that the mouths of priests were "the mouths of hell." Male members lied with other men, and women with women, and the only book of the Bible they would read was Acts. They would gather together in their meetings, and once a certain woman lied down on the floor and uncovered her buttocks, they would all scream "Chaos!" and an orgy would commence. Once the babies conceived were born, the members would gather in a circle around a huge fire and pass the babies around until they died from the heat. The heretics were soon arrested and those who did not confess and renounce the heresy were thrown into a cell and kept there until the clergy could conclude a punishment. The people feared that the clergy was weak and that they would not punish them adequately, and so they rushed into the prison, seized the heretics and burnt them alive.[101] The laity knew better than those of us today, as to how to deal with heretics. But because we are so plunged into tolerance, all kinds of cults and heresies have abounded. The rushing of the prison reminds us of how the Americans of the nineteenth century charged into a prison in Illinois and killed Joseph Smith.

ARNOLD OF BRESCIA

In twelfth century Italy there was a man named Arnold of Brescia, who preached a heresy that was to lead inexorably to violence and chaos. He rallied up the simple people of Italy to believe that any clergyman who owned property, and did not live in poverty, could not be saved. All of their possessions, he taught, should be owned by the state and used only by the people. It was, in a sense, a form of liberation theology or Christian socialism. He was eventually allowed to stay in Rome, since he came in peace, and the Church believed that there was a prospect of convincing him of his wrongs. He acted with the Church, as Cain did before murdering Abel, and Bernard of Clairvaux knew this, and wrote a letter to the Church warning them on the discreet but evil intentions of this man, that tolerating him would only give him more power to execute his true violent plans, and that the only solution was to get rid of him:

---

100 This whole story is from Paul of St. Pere de Chartres: Heretics at Orleans, 1022, in Edward Peters, Heresy and Authority, ch. ii, pp. 66–71
101 Guibert of Nogent: Heretics at Soissons, 1114, in Edward Peters, Heresy and Authority, ch. ii, pp. 72–74

Arnold of Brescia is all honey and sweetness in his words, but mortally venomous in his doctrine. On his face he shows the simplicity of the dove, but he has the poisoned tail of the scorpion. His homeland [Brescia] expelled him as a man ejects his vomit; Rome had horror to host him; France was indisposed to receive him, Germany could not but abominate him, and to this date Italy refuses to receive him back. Despite all this, it has been said that you received him. Take care that you do not play his game and, with your authority, give him wings to fly in order to continue to do harm. He has both a great skill and the firm purpose to do evil. If to these two things, you add your favor, we will have the triple-braided rope that is difficult to break, and you cannot imagine the evil he is capable of doing. If it is true that you hosted him, I believe it is because either you do not know him well, or what is more probable, knowing who he is, you hope to change and convert him. I hope this will be so! God grant that you change this hard rock into a son of Abraham! What a pleasing gift you would offer to the Church if you could present to her as a vase of honor the one who until now has been a vase of ignominy! You could try to do this. However, any prudent man would be careful not to surpass the number of such attempts of conversion that the Apostle recommended when he said: "Warn a divisive person once, and then warn him a second time. After that, have nothing to do with him. You may be sure that such a man is warped and sinful; he is self-condemned." (Titus 3:10–11) On the other hand, treating him in a familiar way, admitting him to your friendship, and even seating him at your table would be a sure sign of your protection, showing that you cover the enemy with strong armor. With this, he will achieve his goal and, disguised as your close friend, he will easily convince souls [to adopt his bad position] Even if he removes his mask and publicly propagates his pernicious errors, who will dare to contradict him, since he is your friend? Once you have read everything in this letter, I expect from your uprightness and prudence that you will do that which is in the interest of the Church. [102]

The modern would read this and think that Bernard is just an intolerant, paranoid, Christian bigot, no man worthy of respect or attention. But let us see the result of tolerating Arnold, to understand the fruits of religious equality and liberty.

Arnold's following eventually became so numerous, and his preaching so vociferous, that his followers became violent toward the clergy. Homes and palaces of Roman nobles and cardinals were raided and destroyed by the mob, and several of the cardinals were severely wounded. Arnold at last fell into the hands of certain men, taken into custody, tried and burnt on a pyre.[103]

This Arnold had the spirit of Judas, which is that of a socialist. After Mary Magdalen anointed Jesus' feet with the costly ointment, Judas said, with false piety, "Why was not this ointment sold for three hundred pence, sand given to the poor?"[104] He urged this, not because he cared for the poor, but because he was a thief, and wished only to steel and to kill.

---

102 Letter 169 in *Obras completas del Doctor Melifluo*, San Bernardo, Abad de Claraval, Barcelona: Rafael Casulleras, 1929, vol. V, p. 408, in http://www.traditioninaction.org/religious/n024rp_ArnoldBrescia.htm
103 Otto of Freising: Arnold of Brescia in Rome, 1148–55, in Edward Peters, Heresy and Authority, ch. ii, pp 78–80
104 John 12:5

✝ CHRISTIANITY IS AT WAR: THE MANIFESTO FOR CHRISTIAN MILITANCY

THE SHEPHERDS

Another perfect example of how heresy leads to violence and tyranny, is the Shepherds, a cult which arose and gained much power in the Middle Ages in the mid thirteenth century.[105]

Their leader, Roger, who they called the Master, was initially a wizard learned in the magical arts. He made a compact with the Sultan of Babylon, that he would start an entire movement of youths, aged 25 or 30 or 16, under the pretense of a crusade. Once the youths would be in Egypt, the Muslims would easily slaughter them because of their lack of training, and Roger would receive four gold besants for each Christian head. After this agreement was made, Roger prophesied that the Muslims would defeat the king of France, Louis IX. The Sultan cheered at such a thought, gave Roger an immense amount of gold and silver, and kissed him on the mouth. He would now become a seemingly harmless lay preacher who would sojourn to shepherd villages in the countryside and gain the people to follow him. When he arrived to France, specifically in Picardy, he took a certain powder and tossed it into the air as a sacrifice to the devil. After this, he approached a number of youthful shepherds and, being a very deceptively uplifting talker, said: "Through you, my sweet children, will Outremer [the Kingdom of Jerusalem] be delivered from the enemies of the Christian faith."

With such flattery that satisfies itching ears, within a very short time, entire multitudes followed him. They became very popular amongst the common folk to the point that they could say whatever they pleased without worry. In less than eight days he had more than thirty-thousand followers, all fervent for his teachings. Like all heresies, the group claimed to be orthodox to deceive the naive, preaching the Cross and the salvation of Christ.

But this was all a facade. Roger, once seeing that he had such a huge following, could no longer hide his poisons, and began to preach against the Sacraments, holy water, and the Holy Cross. Some of the higher members claimed to have had visions from angels and conversed with them, and also to have had the power of healing. So bewitched were the followers that they gave away great amounts of food to the higher members and Roger, and they would even beg them to take away their homes and possessions.

They gave Roger whatever he asked. Roger, like a Muslim, grew his beard long to appear as a holy man. He even began to dissolve marriages for no reason whatsoever, and to take all of the children from families so that the number of his cult grew to sixty thousand. They attracted the lowest sort: outlaws, thieves, heretics, apostates, pagans and prostitutes. From what appeared to be a mere sect, became a gang of violent ruffians holding axes, swords, knives.

When clergymen, who had the gift of discernment, warned the people against the leader and his teachings, the multitude grew enraged and declared that the group consisted of good people, and that the clergy were just envious. Roger, being filled with hatred for the clergy, ordered his followers to attack all the priests that they encountered. They reached Paris,

---

[105] All historical information here regarding the Shepherds are learned from all the documents presented and translated by Peter Jackson, *The Seventh Crusade*, ch. 8, pp. 179–93

Roger met with the queen of France, Blanche, and deceived her with the greatest sophisms. She, as a result, thought them to be orthodox and enacted a policy of toleration for them.

She went so far as to command that no one speak against them because she believed that they were working on behalf of God. She was deceived as Eve was deceived, and as Roger beguiled her like the old serpent, he taught his men that whoever murdered a priest or cleric would receive forgiveness of sins. In other words, he promoted human sacrifice. It was because of the queen's toleration for them, that they began to grow and preach, and thrive. Because of this confidence, they began to physically attack clergymen and Catholic laymen, killing many of both. Meanwhile Roger gave the appearance that he himself was a priest, and dressed as a priest, all for the sake of appearing orthodox, just as Cain appeared peaceful before murdering his brother.

As he put on this facade, his men lurked about the city to murder Catholic scholars. When the Dominican Friars in Tours began to preach against them, they wrecked their houses, looting their property, and severally wounded four of them. They took eleven Friars and whipped them mercilessly in the middle of the city as a public spectacle. They entered a church, took the Eucharist and hurled it to the floor mockingly. They took a statue of the Virgin Mary, hacked its nose off and gouged out the eyes. They looted the churches. The shepherds in the city of Orleans broke into the major university there and slew several priests. One day when Roger was walking over the bridge over the Loire River, he passed by a random priest, and when he was close enough he pulled out his sword, hacked him to death, and then dumped the body into the water. When these heretics would linger about the city, clerics and scholars would lock their doors. Throughout France they attempted to attack and destroy towns and cities, and to butcher their inhabitants. All of this went on without much concern from the common French people, for at this time religious fervor declined, fear of heresy also was lacking; in fact the common people praised these heretics, and this is the result of such hatred for the Church and for orthodoxy. It is the consequences of such "madness of the common folk, offering the sick to be cured by men like this, namely murderers, assassins and thieves, and, when they were cured or did not even improve, preaching the virtues of [these] wretched men."[106]

The master then led his followers to attack a Jewish area in the city of Bourges. Jews were protected under the government in France, but what is there to expect from a mob of heretics? They tore up their books and looted their money and their silver. They then began to annihilate the Jews in the area completely. After this cruel blood bath they left, but not without the anger of a nearby burgess who chased after Roger and slew him. It was said that his last word before death was the name of Muhammad. Many of the other Shepherds were tracked down and, rightfully, put to death.

When the remainder tried to cross the sea to make it to Egypt and fulfill the prophecy of Roger, the leaders amongst them were arrested and thrown into prison. Under interrogation

---

[106] Annales monastery de Burton, in Peter Jackson's *Seventh Crusade*, ch. 8, document 94, p. 191

they confessed their scheme of bringing in youths to Egypt to be killed and receive money from the Muslims. After this, they were justly hung.

Aside from making money from the Muslims, the ultimate goal of the Shepherds was to eliminate the Catholic Church within France, and then next to obliterate the military might and the rich, in order to make the country completely open to Islamic attacks. Thus one medieval chronicle explains:

> It is said that their design had been first to exterminate the clergy from the country, secondly to eliminate the religious, and later on to turn against the knights and nobility, so that the land would thus be bereft of all protection and would more easily be exposed to the errors and attacks of the pagans. [107]

One of the most prestigious and reputable medieval scholastics, Roger Bacon, also wrote that Roger and the superior Shepherds were agents to the Muslims:

> It is greatly to be feared lest the Tatars and the Saracen, while remaining in their own territories, send to the Christians men through whom they may, by means of astrology, spread misfortune and provoke dissension among the princes, for the Christians' enemies make the greatest efforts to arouse war and dissension among them. This kind of thing has many times occurred, although the foolish multitude does not reflect whence it originates. The wise are in no doubt that these men were agents of the Tatars or the Saracens, and that they possessed some device whereby they mesmerized the people.

Today we have so many plants in the West who are working to break the sacred bastions of the Christian Faith, to enable the invasion of the heathens. Why is this? Because of toleration.

INTOLERANCE OF FALSE RELIGIONS AND IDEAS CONTINUED ON THROUGH THE CHURCH

The authority of ancient Israel to oppress paganism and heresy continued on through the Church. For when certain heretics of the fourth century complained that the prefect Macharius killed two of their members, the fourth century Church Father St. Optatus of Milevis responded to them with these words: "You see that Moses, Phinee, Elias, and Macharius have done a similar thing, because it is the revenge of the one God that proceeds from all of them."[108] Notice how he says that the vengeance of God is unleashed through the named authorities. This goes clearly in accordance to what St. Paul wrote, when he described how the ruler "is God's minister, an avenger to execute wrath on him who practices evil." (Romans 13:4) Also notice how he references Old Testament prophets, showing clearly how the authority of Israel continues through the Church. This application of Romans 13 to the killing of heretics was also articulated by St. Bernard when, in a sermon against the Cathar heretics, said:

---

107 Annales monastery de Burton, in Peter Jackson's *Seventh Crusade*, ch. 8, document 94, p. 191
108 Optatus of Milevis, book 3, in Bellarmine, *On Laymen or Secular People*, ch. 21, ed. Tutino, p. 107

It is better without a doubt that they be punished by the sword—the sword, that is, of him who does not bear it in vain—than to allow many people to be drawn into error. For he is the minister of God, an avenger to execute wrath upon whoever does evil. [109]

St. John said that if a heretic comes to you, "receive him not into your house" (2 John 1:10). St. Irenaeus, a pupil of St. Polycarp who was a direct student of St. John, wrote that "The apostles and their disciples had so much fear that they did not even speak with those who corrupted the truth." St. Cyprian, one of the earliest of the Church Fathers, wrote in an epistle: "O most loving brethren, you should be wary of and avoid the words and speeches of those whose discourses creep in as a cancer," and later he wrote, "No transactions, no feasts, no conversations should be exchanged with such people, and we should be separated from them as much as they are exiled from the Church." St. Athanasius wrote that the great hermit of the desert, St. Anthony, "did not even exchange friendly words with the Manichaeans and other heretics, declaring that being friendly and talking with those people was the ruin of the soul. And he detested the Arians so much that he said to everybody that one should not even come close to them." On his deathbed St. Anthony exhorted his followers: "Avoid the poison of heretics and schismatics, and follow my hatred toward them; you know that I have never had even a peaceful conversation with them."[110] St. Maximus of Turin went so far as to say that no Christian should allow his servants to conduct pagan rituals on his fields or his home: "I admonish your charity brethren, that as devout and holy people you should remove every idolatrous pollution from your possessions and wipe out the entire Gentile error from your fields, for it is not lawful for you who have Christ in your hearts to have Antichrist in your houses for your servants to worship the devil in shrines while you adore God in church."[111]

Imagine, then, an entire empire of Orthodox Christians, and which one will accept a heretic in their home? Invite them to a feast, give them a platform to preach their ideas? Not one. So then, in Christendom, a heretic is not allowed not just in a private home, but from entering the nation as a whole. When the Manichaean heretic Priscillian went about with his disciples throughout the empire, preaching against the Holy Trinity, denouncing marriage, promoting astrology and dualism, what did the government of Christendom do? Did it tolerate them? No. He and most of his disciples were seized and executed, as cancer is cut off from the body, because they knew that such a cult would subvert the holy laws of Christianity and bring nothing but chaos to society. Pope St. Leo the Great praised the killing of these heretics in a letter in which he wrote:

> Rightly then our fathers, in whose times this abominable heresy sprung up, promptly pursued it throughout the world, that the blasphemous error might everywhere be driven from the Church: for even the leaders of the world so abhorred this profane folly that they laid low its originator, with most of his disciples, by the sword of the public laws. For they saw that

---

109 St. Bernard, sermon 66 on the Songs of Songs, in Bellarmine, *On Laymen or Secular People*, ch. 21, ed. Tutino, p. 107
110 All of these quotes are compiled in Bellarmine, *On Laymen or Secular People*, ch. 20, ed. Tutino, p. 96
111 Maximus of Turin, sermon 107.1

all desire for honorable conduct was removed, all marriage-ties undone, and the Divine and the human law simultaneously undermined, if it were allowed for men of this kind to live anywhere under such a creed. [112]

They will always argue that we must tolerate every religion and ideology, just as long as their followers do not hurt anyone. Essentially, this type of governing springs from quite an old heresy that never fully flourished until the Enlightenment. It took much time for it to dominate the western world, and the reason for this is that the idea of religious toleration was seen as not absurd to the people of Christendom, but dangerous. This sentiment was expressed by St. Robert when he, writing on toleration, said:

> This error is, however, very dangerous, and without a doubt the Christian princes are obliged not to grant their subjects freedom of belief but to see to it that the faith that the Catholic bishops and especially the Supreme Pontiff teach to be the true one is preserved. [113]

The reason the Christians of Christendom were so intolerant was because they took the Scriptures very seriously. They read the words of Solomon when he wrote that "A wise king sifts out the wicked, and brings the threshing wheel over them" (Proverbs 20:26), and declared that no doubt amongst the wicked are those who introduce evil and dangerous religions and ideas.[114] They observed how in ancient Israel, when true religion reigned the Orthodox kings did not permit freedom of religion, and thus Christian kings must do the same, "for the Church must not be arranged any worse than the synagogue was."[115]

The heretics and anti-Christian acolytes should not even be allowed to speak their destructive beliefs, for they mix the truth with lies so as to deceive and gain the confidence of the credulous. Christ did not even allow the devils to speak, for when the demons came to him crying out, "Thou art Christ the Son of God," Christ "suffered them not to speak" (Luke 4:41). And when a demon came to the Apostles saying, "These men are the servants of the most high God," (Acts 16:17) Paul prohibited him from speaking any further. If demons are prohibited from speaking even the truth, how much more should the followers of the devils be prohibited![116]

Intolerance for false religions, and the use, or the desire to use, the state to prohibit dangerous beliefs, continued on from Israel through the Church.

Even in the earlier times of the Church there were desires amongst Christians to have some control over cults. This is reflected by Tertullian, one of oldest of Christian writers, who believed that heretics should not be allowed to own Bibles, and if this was ever followed, the propagation of dangerous cults—such as Islam and Mormonism—would be prevented,

---

112 Leo the Great, letter 15, ch. 1
113 St. Robert Bellarmine, *On Laymen or Secular People*, ch. 18, p. 82
114 See St. Robert Bellarmine, *On Laymen or Secular People*, ch. 18, ed. Tutino, p. 82
115 St. Robert Bellarmine, *On Laymen or Secular People*, ch. 18, p. 85
116 See Bellarmine, *On Laymen or Secular People*, ch. 20, ed. Tutino, p. 97

and many lives would have been saved from their dangerous founders and their pernicious followers:

> We are therefore come to (the gist of) our position; for at this point we were aiming, and for this we were preparing in the preamble of our address (which we have just completed) so that we may now join issue on the contention to which our adversaries challenge us. They put forward the Scriptures, and by this insolence of theirs they at once influence some. In the encounter itself, however, they weary the strong, they catch the weak, and dismiss waverers with a doubt. Accordingly, we oppose to them this step above all others, of not admitting them to any discussion of the Scriptures. If in these lie their resources, before they can use them, it ought to be clearly seen to whom belongs the possession of the Scriptures, that none may be admitted to the use thereof who has no title at all to the privilege. Thus, not being Christians, they have acquired no right to the Christian Scriptures; and it may be very fairly said to them, 'Who are you? When and whence did you come? As you are none of mine, what have you to do with that which is mine?' [117]

St. Cyprian, in 252 or 257 AD, before Christianity was legalized by Constantine and during the great pagan persecutions upon the Christians, firmly wrote in favor of the Mosaic law against paganism, and praised the actions of Mattathias (the father of Judas Maccabees) when he slew the traitorous Jew who offered sacrifice to the gods of Antiochus Epiphanies:

> That God is so wrathful against idolatry, that He hath even commanded them to be killed, who entice to offer sacrifice and serve idols. And again the Lord speaks and says, that neither must a city be spared, though one and all in it consent in idolatry in remembrance of which strict commandment Mattathias slew him who had come to the altar to sacrifice. But if before the coming of Christ these commandments were kept concerning the worship of God, and the spurning of idols, how much more are they to be kept, since Christ's coming! [118]

The first use of the state by a Christian ruler to obliterate paganism was done by Constantine the Great in the fourth century. After Christ resurrected from the dead, and the stone that covered the tomb was moved so that the divine majesty could be beheld by those with hearts of stone, the pious Christians, ceaselessly contemplating on the Holy Sacrifice of their Savior, would pilgrimage to the scared sepulcher, to meditate on the divine, and to offer their prayers, in the place where the Incarnate God slew death and triumphantly departed from the grave. The pagans, having nothing but spite for the Christians, and contempt for their joy, covered the entire tomb with earth, and upon it built a temple to the horrid demon Venus. When Constantine took the throne, and glorious Christendom was founded and commenced, this pious emperor, by the command of his mother, St. Helena, destroyed the temple of Venus and shattered its idols, and ordered that the fragments of what was obliterated be moved far away, and he even commanded that the earth from underneath the temple be dug

---

117 Tertullian, *On the Prescription Against Heretics*, chs. xv, xxxvii, ANF, vol. iii
118 Cyprian, treatise xiii, 5, trans. & ed. Oxford, ellipses mine. See St. Robert Bellarmine, *On Laymen or Secular People*, ch. 21, ed. Tutino, p. 106, where refers to this text when substantiating the punishing of heretics

out in considerable depth, and gotten rid of, for it was polluted by the pagans' hellish sacrifices. It was in this purging of the heathen temple, that the Tomb of Christ was discovered.[119]

In that sacred plain on which lies the Oak of Mamre, where holy Abraham, guided by the light of inspiration, entertained angels, and where he "built an altar there to the Lord" (Genesis 13:18), pagans came and erected their idols. St. Helena, seeing how such a sacred place was tainted, informed her son, the Emperor Constantine, and he, with divine zeal, unsheathed the Sword of St. Peter, and ordered that the unholy images be destroyed, and that a house of prayer be built upon it.[120] Constantine wrote an epistle to Eusebius of Caesarea conveying the order:

> She [St Helena] assures me, then, that the place which takes its name from the oak of Mambre, where we find that Abraham dwelt, is defiled by certain of the slaves of superstition in every possible way. She declares that idols which should be utterly destroyed have been erected on the site of that tree, that an altar is near the spot, and that impure sacrifices are continually performed. Now since it is evident that these practices are equally inconsistent with the character of our times, and unworthy the sanctity of the place itself, I wish your Gravities to be informed that the illustrious Count Acacius, our friend, has received instructions by letter from me, to the effect that every idol which shall be found in the place above-mentioned shall immediately be consigned to the flames, that the altar be utterly demolished, and that if any one, after this our mandate, shall be guilty of impiety of any kind in this place, he shall be visited with condign punishment. The place itself we have directed to be adorned with an unpolluted structure—I mean a church—in order that it may become a fitting place of assembly for holy men. Meantime, should any breach of these our commands occur, it should be made known to our clemency without the least delay by letters from you, that we may direct the person to be dealt with, as a transgressor of the law, in the severest manner. For you are not ignorant that the Supreme God first appeared to Abraham, and conversed with him, in that place. There it was that the observance of the Divine law first began: there first the Savior Himself, with the two angels, vouchsafed to Abraham a manifestation of His presence; there God first appeared to men; there He gave promise to Abraham concerning his future seed, and straightway fulfilled that promise; there he foretold that he should be the father of a multitude of nations.[121]

Notice what reverence Constantine shows to Abraham, as the father of not only Israel, but ultimately of the Christian Church; and look, at the great zeal he expresses against impiety for the sacred places, and the immense energy he exerts to see to it that Orthodoxy is protected from the enemies of Christianity. Surely, Constantine, regardless of all the slanderers who venomously sully him, was a great Christian emperor, one who fought for the Faith, and strived with unresting hands to combat the enemies of holy truth. He labored, with the temporal sword of the Church, to purge the empire of sickening practices. He saw how in Phoenicia they forced women to be temple prostitutes, how their poor children had no knowledge

---

[119] Eusebius, *Life of Constantine*, 3.24; Socrates, 1.17
[120] Socrates, 1.18
[121] Constantine's Letter to Eusebius, 3.42, brackets mine

of who their father was, and how homosexuals partook in devil worship. Scorning such evil, Constantine hastened to abolish this practice, and he had churches built over the place where these demonic orgies were done, and ordered that a bishop and a sacred clergy be put over them. He saw with contempt the diabolical temple of Venus at Aphaca, on Mount Libanus in Phoenicia, where homosexual rites and orgies were performed. In the words of Eusebius,

> Here men undeserving of the name forgot the dignity of their sex, and propitiated the demon by their effeminate conduct. Here too unlawful commerce of women and adulterous intercourse, with other horrible infamous practices, were perpetuated in this temple as in a place beyond the scope and restraint of law. [122]

Did Constantine tolerate such a place? Did he say, "live and let live" and went on with it? Did he say the usual opinion of, "well as along as they're not hurting anyone, I don't care"? Absolutely not. He was a defender of Christendom, not an impotent governor who allows his country to decay through indifferentism. He had the entire building demolished, and the depraved rituals observed within it outlawed.[123] In Cilicia there was a famous temple which was believed to house a demon that was worshipped as a holder of healing powers, and it was said that the demon would manifest itself to people while they stayed inside in the evening time. Constantine did not see their belief as within some vague notion of religious freedom, but instead he ordered that the entire temple of Satan be burned to the ground,[124] and the order was swiftly fulfilled, as Eusebius explains:

> For since it happened that many of these pretenders to wisdom were deluded votaries of the demon worshipped in Cilicia, whom thousands regarded with reverence as the possessor of saving and healing power, who sometimes appeared to those who passed the night in his temple, sometimes restored the diseased to health (though in reality he was a destroyer of souls, who drew his easily deluded worshippers from the true Savior to involve them in impious error), the emperor, consistently with his practice and desire to advance the worship of Him who is at once a jealous God and the true Savior, gave directions that this temple also should be razed to the ground. In prompt obedience to his command, a band of soldiers laid this building, the object of admiration even to noble philosophers, prostrate in the dust, rather a deceiver of souls, who had seduced mankind for so long a series of years. [125]

The laws against idolatry was a reflection of the hatred against idols harbored by the Christian people themselves. When the emperor Valens, an Arian heretic who rejected Christ's divinity, was conducting his persecution against Christians for their belief in the Trinity, he banished a group of monks out of Egypt and placed them in an island. The inhabitants of the island were all pagans, worshipped their pagan priest as a god, and revolved around an idolatrous temple. Because of the monks' presence in such a dark place, the demons who

---

122 Eusebius, *Life of Constantine*, 3.40
123 Eusebius, *Life of Constantine*, 3.40; Socrates, 1.18
124 Socrates, 1.18; Eusebius, *Life of Constantine*, 3.45
125 Eusebius, *Life of Constantine*, 3.45

inhabited the island were filled with terror, and the daughter of the priest became possessed by a devil. The girl rushed to the monks and said, "Why are ye come here to cast us out from hence also?" The monks exorcised the demon out of her, and all of the inhabitants, including the priest, converted to Christianity. When this had happened, the people no longer could tolerate their idols, and they swiftly destroyed them.[126]

One of the best examples of an ancient Christian writer calling for the state to obliterate pagan beliefs was Firmicus Maternus. He was a Roman of the senatorial class who was once so entrenched in the pagan religion that he wrote the most complete Latin book on astrology known to date. He eventually converted to Christianity and wrote a book at around the mid-400s on why paganism should be outlawed. He described the violence of paganism, with its human sacrifice, cruelty, and chaotic rituals, and then called the emperors Consantius II and Constance to then ban idolatry on the authority of the Mosaic Law. His statement shows how the Church continued the anti-pagan laws of the Torah:

> Take away, yes, calmly take away, Most Holy Emperors, the adornments of the temples. Let the fire of the mint or the blaze of the smelters melt them down, and confiscate all the votive offerings to your own use and ownership. Since the time of the destruction of the temples you have been, by God's power, advanced in greatness. Moreover, the ordinances of the sacrosanct Law declare that God commands men not to make idols. For in Exodus we find this written: 'You shall not make to yourself gods of silver nor gods of gold. And again in the same book I find the voice of God commanding: Thou shalt not make to thyself an idol nor the likeness of anything. Also our Lord Jesus Christ, safeguarding the ordinances of His Father's law, promulgates this same teaching in a worshipful commandment, for He says: Hear, O Israel: the Lord thy God is one God, and thou shalt love the Lord thy God with thy whole strength. This is the first thing. And the second is like to it: Thou shalt love thy neighbor as thyself. On these two precepts dependeth the whole of the law and the prophets.' And following this divine and worshipful precept comes the Lord's immortal and holy conclusion. For by way of pointing out more clearly the way of salvation, He adds these words: 'Now this is eternal life that they may know thee, the only true Lord, and Jesus Christ, whom thou hast sent.' [John 17:3] You know the series of the holy commandments: what you must follow and what you must shun you have learned from the worshipful and immortal voice. Hear on the other hand what destruction is in store for the scorners, and in what calamities the stringency of the worshipful law has bound them fast. For the conclusion of the worshipful law has bound them fast. For the conclusion of the worshipful commandment is gathered up in these words: 'He that sacrificeth to gods shall be destroyed root and branch, save only the Lord.' [Exodus 22:20] But on you also, Most Holy Emperors, devolves the imperative necessity to castigate and punish this evil, and the law of the Supreme Deity enjoins on you that your severity should be visited in every way on the crime of idolatry. Hear and store up in your sacred intelligence what is God's commandment regarding this crime. In Deuteronomy this law is written, for it says: 'But if thy brother, or thy son, or thy wife that is in thy

---

126 Socrates, 4.24

bosom, or thy friend who is equal to thy own soul, should ask thee, secretly saying: Let us go and worship other gods, the gods of the Gentiles; thou shalt not consent to him nor hear him, neither shall thy eye spare him, and thou shalt not conceal him. Announcing thou shalt announce about him; they hand shall be first upon him to kill him, and afterwards the hands of all the people; and they shall stone him and he shall die, because he sought to withdraw thee from thy Lord. He bids spare neither son nor brother, and thrusts the avenging sword through the body of a beloved wife. A friend too He persecutes with lofty severity, and the whole populace takes up arms to rend bodies of sacrilegious men. Even for whole cities, if they are caught in this crime, destruction is decreed; and that your providence may more plainly learn this, I shall quote the sentence of the established law. In the same book [of Deuteronomy] the Lord establishes the penalty for whole cities with the following words, for He says: 'Or if one of the cities which the Lord thy God gives thee to dwell in, thou hear men saying: Let us go and serve other gods which you know not: killing thou shalt slay all who are in the city with the death of the sword, and shalt burn the city with fire. And it shall be without habitation, nor shall it be built any more forever, that the Lord may turn from the indignation of His wrath.' ...To you, Most Holy Emperors, the Supreme Deity promises the rewards of His mercy and decrees a multiplication on the greatest scale. Therefore do what he bids; fulfill what He commands. [127]

The Theodosian Code, or the law in the Christian Roman Empire, established prohibition of pagan sacrifices and going into heathen temples (though this law was not entirely enforced):

It is our pleasure that the temples shall be immediately closed in all places and in all cities, and access to them forbidden, so as to deny to all abandoned men the opportunity to commit sin. It is also our will that all men shall abstain from [pagan] sacrifices. But if perchance any man should perpetuate any such criminality, he shall be struck down with the avenging sword. [128]

When the pagan Symmachus, who was at the head of the senate at Rome in the 4th century,[129] requested that an Altar to Victory be placed in the Senate House, St. Ambrose and other Christian leaders wanted nothing of it. The Pope at the time, Damasus, objected to the request, made clear that he gave "no such authority," did not consent "with such requests of the heathen," and did not believe that the empire should open itself to idolatry. In his letter to the emperor Valentinian II, St. Ambrose not only urged that the idol not be placed, but called for the abolishment of idolatry altogether:

For salvation is not sure unless everyone worship in truth the true God, that is the God of the Christians, under Whose sway are all things; for He alone is the true God, Who is to be worshipped from the bottom of the heart; for the gods of the heaven, as Scripture says, are

---

[127] Firmicus, *On the Error of the Pagan Religions*, 28.6–8; 29.1–2, trans. Clarence A. Forbes, ellipses and brackets mine
[128] *Theodosian Code*, bk. xvi, 10, 4, as quoted by Lefebvre, *Religious Liberty Questioned*, part 2, p. 62
[129] Socrates, 5.14

devils. Now everyone is a soldier of this true God, and he who receives and worships Him in his inmost spirit does not bring to His service dissimulation, or pretense, but earnest faith and devotion. And they [the pagans] are complaining of their losses, who never spared our blood, who destroyed very buildings of the churches. Had these things not been abolished I could prove that they ought to be done away by your authority I call upon your own feelings not to determine to answer according to this petition of the heathen, nor to attach to an answer of such a sort the sacrilege of your subscription. [130]

If St. Ambrose were alive today and witnessed all of the inclusivity and toleration occurring in the modern church, no doubt he would declare it heretical, and wanting of significant reform. In other words, he would pull a whip and drive all the spiritual pimps and prostitutes out. If St. Ambrose was with us currently, and he was informed that the Muslim congressman, Keith Ellison, was about to swear upon the Koran, he would urge that such action be prohibited, nay, outlawed. When America did permit Ellison to swear upon the Koran, and not the Bible, it was only an indication that we have thrown out true Christianity, for the heresy of indifference, which only allows the heretics to further advance over a nation. Today we have heretics promoting universalism, and in Ambrose's day the same evil doctrine was being taught. The pagan Symmachus actually called for universalism to be accepted by the empire, placing an emphasis that all roads lead to heaven. In fact, Symmachus used this very type of terminology: "What difference does it make by what pains each seeks the truth? We cannot attain so great a secret by one road; but this discussion is rather for persons at ease, we offer now prayers, not conflict."[131] Of course if Symmachus was fully appeased it would be simply a small step for a full pagan advancement over the empire which, if accomplished, would have led to the same violence which the pagan emperors inflicted upon the earliest Christians. St. Ambrose surely and prudently knew this. When writing on Symmachus' universalist belief, Ambrose propounded a strict and militant Christian exclusivity that took no prisoners: "By one road, says he, one cannot do so great a secret. What you know not, that we know by the voice of God. And what you seek by fancies, we have found out from the very Wisdom and Truth of God. Your ways, therefore, do not agree with ours."[132]

St. Ambrose further lamented that there was one thing which the Church could not endure, "that they [the pagans] should taunt us that they supplicate their gods in your [the emperors'] names, and without your commands, commit an immense sacrilege, interpreting your shutting your eyes as consent. To claim a sacrifice on this one altar, what is it but to insult the Faith? Is it to be borne that a heathen should sacrifice and a Christian be present?"[133]

Of course when the Church gained its liberty, and much influence in the Roman state, it had to take a very strict stance against any attempt to revive pagan power in the empire,

---

[130] St. Ambrose, Epistle xvii.1–11 trans. Rev. H. De Romestin, in Nicene and Post-Nice Fathers, vol. 10, ellipses mine
[131] The Memorial of Symmachus, 10
[132] Ambrose, Epistle 18, 8
[133] Ambrose, epistle 18, 22, 31, ellipses mine

because when it did not have its liberty—look at what slavery it had to endure under the idolaters. This was not paranoia, but preservation. One may sympathize with Symmachus, but when the pagans had power over the empire, they showed not one ounce of sympathy for the Christians when they slaughtered them in the most gruesome ways. One can read the most saddening letter of Athenagoras to the emperor Marcus Aurelius and his son Commodus, in which he protests ever so desperately on the injustice towards the Christians, while the other religions were tolerated by the state, to learn how evil the pagans were:

> In Egypt even cats and crocodiles, snakes, asps, serpents, and dogs are revered as gods. All these you and your laws leave unmolested, deeming it wicked and impious not to venerate gods at all and a bounden duty for each to honour as gods those whom he would, that thus a fear of the divine power may keep men from wrong-doing. Pray, do not be led astray by hearsay as happens to the man in the street: to us hatred is shown because of our name. Yet names are not deserving of hatred; it is wrongdoing that should be judged and chastised. Hence it is that the individual, marveling at your meekness and gentleness and your peaceable friendly ways with all men, lives in equality before the law; cities, according to their deserts, enjoy equality of prestige, and the whole world rejoices in a profound peace through your enlightenment. Now with us who are called Christians, so far are you from caring for people like us that you allow us to be harried, robbed, and pursued though we do no wrong and are—as this work will show in due course—of all men the most reverent and righteous in matters that concern God and your kingdom. Thus when the mob is at enmity with us for our name's sake alone, we have made so bold as to declare to you our position.[134]

They were under the cruel watch of the pagans, and just imagine to yourself living in a world where men were significantly influenced by the pagan writer Celsus, who wrote in the second century a calling for the slaughter of, and the taking of liberties from, all Christians:

> And further: those who do stand next to your little god are hardly secure! You are banished from land and sea, bound and punished for your devotion to [your Christian demon] and taken away to be crucified. Where then if your God's vengeance on his persecutors? If they [the Christians] persist in refusing to worship the various gods who preside over the day-to-day activities of life, then they should not be permitted to live until marriageable age; they should not be permitted to marry, to have children, nor to do anything else over which a god presides. You [the Christians] are really quite tedious in your claims: if those who now reign were persuaded by your doctrine, you argue, and these same were taken prisoner, you could persuade those who reign after them and those after and so on and so on, more and more reigning and being taken captive and the like, until there came finally a ruler who, being sensible and reading these events as representing the will and plan of God, would try wiping you out before you succeeded in bringing down the empire and him with it.[135]

---

134 Athenagoras, Embassy, 1
135 Celsus, *On the True Doctrine*, ch. x, trans. R. Joseph Hoffmann, Oxford University Press, 1987, ellipses and brackets mine

✝ CHRISTIANITY IS AT WAR: THE MANIFESTO FOR CHRISTIAN MILITANCY

The evils of the pagans, and of the later heretics, were the reasons why the Christians took no chances in tolerating them, but rather abolished them and their beliefs. Thomas Aquinas unequivocally believed in civil laws banning heresy, and having cult leaders and heresiarchs (not the followers of heresy, but the makers of it) put to death. Some may argue that heresies are necessary to sharpen the minds of the orthodox, but, as Aquinas argues, the true intention of the heretic is not to have theological debates. "What they really intend is the corruption of the faith," says Aquinas, "which is to inflict very great harm indeed. Consequently we should consider what they directly intend, and expel them, rather than what is beside their intention, and so tolerate them." Do we not punish people for forging fake money, why then do we not punish those who make false religions?[136] Because our pocket books are far more important to us than our God. As Bishop Fellay affirms, "When you say that the state must recognize—must give the same rights—to all religions, you ask our Lord to step down."

When you find a piece of gold you immediately rush with desperation to the nearest specialist to confirm its authenticity. But as soon as we are approached by a certain evil religion, the great bulk of us simply turns away in carelessness, with empty terms such as "your faith is your business" (as though faith is a business), or "live and let live;" and truth, without which every precious diamond and metal is insignificant, is rejected by our apathy.

This is not the mindset of the ancient clergymen. Aquinas, unlike today's ministers, did not compromise nor vacillate his affirmation on heretics, when he wrote:

> Wherefore if forgers of money and other evildoers are forthwith condemned to death by the secular authority, much more reason is there for heretics, as soon as they are convicted of heresy, to be not only excommunicated but even put to death. [137]

St. Robert, Aquinas' student, reiterated this: "forgers by everybody's judgement deserve death, and heretics are forgers of the word of God."[138]

The Theodosian Code of 483 established Christian legislation for the outlawing of teaching heresy, though it allowed for personal belief in heresy:

> All heresies are forbidden by both divine and imperial laws and shall forever cease. If any profane man by his punishable teachings should weaken the concept of God, he shall have the right to know such noxious doctrines only for himself but shall not reveal them to others to their hurt. [139]

The purpose of such laws was to make the world safer for Christians, because once heretics are in a position of power or feel very confident, they will inflict violence upon Christians. Outlaw the heretic, before he outlaws you.

---

136 Aquinas, *Whether Heretics Should Be Tolerated*, II–II Q. II Art. 3, in Edward Peters, *Heresy and Authority in Medieval Europe*, ch. v, pp. 182–3; Lefebvre, *Religious Liberty Questioned*, part 2, p. 59
137 Aquinas, St. Thomas Aquinas: *Whether Heretics Should Be Tolerated*, II–II, Q. 11, Art. 3, in Edward Peters, *Heresy and Authority in Medieval Europe*, ch. v, p. 182
138 Bellarmine, *On Laymen or Secular People*, ch. 21, ed. Tutino, p. 108
139 *Theodosian Code*, 16.5, in Edward Peters, *Heresy and Authority in Medieval Europe*, ch. i, p. 45

There is a great story to illustrate this assertion. There was a certain heretic named Hainricus from the area of Thewin, and before he was executed he proclaimed before the people in front of him:

> It is right that you should condemn us in this matter, for, if we were not a minority among you, the sentence of death which you exercise against us in this manner we would exercise against your clergy and religious and laypeople. [140]

THE LACK OF SUPPRESSING PAGANISM IN CHRISTENDOM RESULTED IN TYRANNY

The toleration of paganism leads to the intolerance of Christianity. Therefore, for tyranny to be prevented, Christianity must reign supreme.

Constantine had no tolerance for paganism. When he heard of a temple of Ashtar in Aphaca, which was built upon Mount Libanus, and how within it men took the form of women, and conducted depraved rites, he, in accordance with the Law of Moses, ordered it to be demolished. He also abolished any pagan temples in Phoenicia, alongside their grotesque rituals.[141]

Marcus, the bishop of Arethusa, was allowed under Constantine to destroy a pagan temple and replace it with a Christian church.[142] This story is another indication as to how the early Christians did not see the prohibitions against idolatry in the law of Moses as null, but as still applicable under a government which allowed them to observe it and carry it out. This was also done by one Artemius, the commander of the military in Egypt, who went about and destroyed some idols of the pagans.[143]

"How intolerant!" are the words of the modern when hearing of this; but they always neglect the evils of such religion, and the violent consequences of tolerating it. A lack of intolerance toward pagan religions resulted in tyranny taking over Christendom. Let the following story be not a forgotten lesson, but a lesson for all times, and for the restoration of Christendom.

After Constantine died, and his son, Constantius, was warring with the usurper Magnentius, there was a certain Julian who had a meeting with a wizard in a pagan temple in Greece. Julian was raised in the Christian Faith, but a dangerous intrigue stirred within his soul for the philosophies and doctrines of the pagans. He first started out under the mentoring of a Syrian pagan named Libanus the Sophist, who was driven out of Constantinople by the other teachers, and would viciously vent against them in his treatises. Because Libanus was a pagan, Julian was prohibited from being taught by him. But nevertheless, Julian would continue to read his works in private. As he grew in knowledge of, and fanaticism for the

---

140 The Passau Anonymous: On the Origins of Heresy and the Sect of the Waldensians, in Edward Peters, *Heresy and Authority in Medieval Europe*, ch. iv, p. 152
141 Eusebius, *Life of Constantine*, 3.46
142 Theodoret. Eccles. Hist. 3.7
143 Theodoret. Eccles. Hist. 3.18

pagan philosophies, he became violently anxious for the imperial throne. He presented himself as a Christian so as to prevent suspicion; he would even shave his head to make it seem as though he was living a monastic life. In public he acted like a Christian, reading the Scriptures and acting pious; but in private he pursued the pagan philosophies. He decided to consult innumerable diviners and occultists to prophesy on whether or not his aspiration will be fulfilled. The wizard conjured the demons, and when Julian began to see the dark spirits, sudden terror filled his heart, he made, with a trembling hand, the sign of the Cross on his forehead, and upon doing so the demonic attack disappeared. The wizard was angered by this, and Julian retorted that he admired the power of the Cross, and that the demons were terrified at the sight of it. "Do not take up that idea, good man," said the sorcerer, "They did not fear that which you mention, but disappeared because they abominated the action which you performed." Julian, being immensely pliable, believed the deceiver, and was after that initiated into the mysteries of the heathen. He eventually obtained the throne, and with his demonic goals and intentions against the Faith, infiltrated the empire. He concealed his religion from the Roman soldiers, because they, on account of the emperor Constantine, were taught the Scriptures and were averse to heathenism.[144]

Surely today's people would be indifferent to Julian's religion; they would say, "His faith doesn't matter," "His religion is irrelevant, what matters is that he fixes the country and the economy!" Many would exclaim, "This is the beauty of freedom of religion, peoples of all faiths have the liberty to become a part of government and society." Those of an Enlightenment persuasion would praise Julian's election as a triumph of multiculturalism and religious diversity. But, truly, the result of such a man in power, the modern does not think upon. Let us see the consequences of Julian's sovereignty, so that we may know the outcome of heretical infiltrators in our own nations.

Julian was a demonic man, and emphatically possessed by demons, for according to Gregory, he had "an eye scowling and always in motion, together with a frenzied aspect; a gait irregular and tottering, a nose breathing only contempt and insult, with ridiculous contortions of countenance expressive of the same thing; immoderate and very loud laughter, nods, as it were, of assent, and drawings back of the head as if in denial, without any visible cause; speech with hesitancy and interrupted by his breathing; disorderly and senseless questions, answers no better, all jumbled together without the least consistency or method."[145]

At the start of his reign, Julian did not just immediately express his hatred for Christianity, or declare paganism superior to the Orthodox Faith. He in fact conducted himself quite mildly toward all people, but as time went on, he did not continue to express the same friendliness equally to everyone.[146] This is the strategy of all tyrannies: they initially present themselves as advocates of equality, only to later advance equality for evil, and impose inequality against those who oppose evil. Like a Muslim, Julian hated the doctrine of the Trinity and

---

144 Theodoret. Eccles. Hist. 2.1–3; Socrates, 3.1
145 In Socrates, 3.33
146 Socrates, 3.11

the Sonship of Christ, since he, in the word of one ancient writer, "had made an attack on those books which made the man of Palestine [Christ] both God, and the Son of God."[147] Julian's ascendance to the thrown only empowered the pagans throughout the empire, since under Constantine they and their thuggish and chaotic religion was suppressed. But under a pagan king, the worship of idols became more conspicuous, their temples were opened, and their repugnant rituals were done with great confidence. Almost soon after his taking of the thrown, he had the pagan temples opened, and he himself publicly sacrificed to the goddess Fortune in a pagan temple where her image was erected. The air became filled with the smoke from their sacrifices, and the earth covered in the blood of animals they killed for their gods.[148] The pagans were ecstatic, angrily remembering how for so long their temples were closed down and suppressed, and were so anxious to see their temples reopened.[149] But the overall society of today would not be bothered by such rites, to the current man it would be their right to religious equality, worthy of praise, and not a danger at all to civilization. But, to the Christian at that time, it was the sign of a coming nightmare.

Let us hear a story of how zealous the ancient Christians were, so as to illustrate the flames of truth that kindled within their soul, and when compared to those of today, to expose the cold stones that lodge within the modern minds. After Julius ordered that the pagan temples be reopened, the governor of Phrygia, named Amachius, commanded that the pagan temple at Merum, be opened, cleaned, and its idols polished. Two Christians, Theodolus and Tatian, would have nothing of this. They were unable to endure the site of a house of the heathen being restored, nor could they stand and watch idly as the bases of the enemy of truth, and the adversaries against the Path of Light, made such an attack on Christianity. They could not uphold false and compromising peace, but instead they were stirred by the torrent of apostolic zeal, "strengthened with might through His Spirit in the inner man," (Ephesians 3:16) and in such a disposition, unleashed the spirit of Christian militancy, and unsheathed the Sword of Christ that shatters the false peace of tyrants and establishes the true peace of God. When the sun was down, and the evening came, they rushed the temple and shattered the idols, and broke the images to pieces, and each one "turned to the Lord with all his heart, and with all his soul, and with all his might, according to all the law of Moses" (2 Kings 23:25) for these Christian warriors were only continuing the Law that was brought down to the prophet on Mt. Sinai, that commanded Israel to break the images of the heathen. The pagans spotted them, and the governor planned on wiping out the entire Christian populace in the area. The two saints, not wanting to see the blood of their brothers spilt, brought themselves before the tyrant. They were ordered to make sacrifice to the devils, and with the greatest ardency they refused. They despised their threats, and even when execution imperiled them, they laughed at death—nay—they drunk death as their Savior, the mighty and eternal General of Heaven, consumed agony and anguish as though it were water. They were tortured as Christ was tor-

---

147 In Socrates, 3.23, brackets
148 Theodoret. Eccles. Hist. 2.6; Socrates, 3.1, 11
149 Socrates, 3.1

tured, emulating their Messiah, being one with Him, and in their endurance partaking in His divine nature. They then placed them on a gridiron, and as the flames cooked their body, they looked to the governor and mocked him, saying, "If you wish to eat broiled flesh, Amachius, turn us on the other side also, lest we should appear but half cooked to your taste." And with that, they gave up the ghost,[150] from time they left to the realm of timelessness.

Pagans overran the market places and assaulted Christians, and when they in return rebuked them, their anger swelled, and they attacked with more ferociousness. Julian did not stop them, nor did he attempt to maintain peace, but encouraged them in their violence. He gave access to some of the most ardent pagans to enter the military, and once they became officers, they commenced to treat Christians with every type of indignity. There was no one the Christians could turn to, for at one time when they entreated the emperor Julian for help, he did not give them justice and amity, but mockingly told them:

It is your duty to bear these afflictions patiently; for this is the command of your God. [151]

Near the time of Julian's ascendency to the throne, there was an elderly bishop of Chalcedon in Bithynia named Maris who, because of his age, was blind. But his infirmity did not stop him from personally confronting the emperor and berating him for his apostasy and idolatry. Julian was exasperated by his heroic defiance. "You blind fool," cried the tyrant, "this Galilaean God of yours will never cure you." And what did the good bishop say? "I thank God for bereaving me of my sight that I might not behold the face of one who has fallen into such awful impiety."

Although he was deeply wroth at his defiance, Julian knew that if he killed the old bishop he would become a praised martyr. So he devised another way to persecute them: he decreed that Christians could no longer study literature, "Lest," he said, "When they have sharpened their tongue, they should be able the more readily to meet the argument of the heathen."[152] What does such an edict tell us? Intelligent and erudite citizens are a terror to tyrannies, and prove most difficult for the despot to rule over.

Julian made an imperial law forbidding Christians from studying Greek literature. This did not cause the Christians to stumble in fear in some strange attachment to the philosophies and poems of pagans. They overcame the edict by their own wits. Two brothers, both named Apollinaris, got together and formed their own genre of Christian literature and poetry. The older Apollinaris rendered the books of Moses in poetic form and in a heroic verse that would describe the glorious moments of Moses and his works in a robust fashion and epic style. The younger Apollinaris expounded on the Scriptures, writing commentaries in the form of dialogues, much like Plato's dialogues. They overcame the attempts of the tyrant to suffocate Christianity, and made a beautiful and original expression of their Faith, much more majestic than anything the pagans could compose.

---

150 Socrates, 3.15
151 Socrates, 3.13
152 Socrates, 3.12

Julian also made into law that Christians could no longer be a part of government, or hold any political office, unless they rejected their Faith and sacrificed to idols. And what does such an enactment convey to our minds? The fight for the soul of the nation, is the fight over who will control the government. You cannot influence the spiritual state of a people without first influencing the laws. Every tyrant understands this, and thus this is why they are always adverse toward Christians, and Christianity, having any position or pre-eminence in the state.

The Christians who were in government did not allow the decree to bring them into trepidation, but gladly resigned their offices.[153] Julian went further in his tyranny. He utilized his temporal power to force Christians to sacrifice to idols, and those who refused were burdened with a heavy tax. From this he accumulated an enormous amount of wealth.

As time continued, so escalated the depravity of the pagans. In cities throughout the empire, especially in Athens and Alexandria, pagan priests resumed a deplorable rite that was suppressed by Constantine and his sons: human sacrifice and ritual cannibalism. They took young infants and split open their bodies, inspecting their entrails for blemishes or dents that could represent an omen, and even ate their flesh.[154] Such is the result of allowing paganism to be done freely.

The heathens of Phoenicia seized Cyril, a deacon of Heliopolis who despised idolatry, killed him, teared open his stomach and ate his liver.[155] Yet these same Phoenicians, while having such disrespect for human life, loved animals so much that according to Herodotus, they "would sooner taste the flesh of a man, than that of a cow."[156] This history parallels what the wicked amongst us aspire to do. They first influence society, then they take positions in government, and then violence ensues, even the most horrific violence, like cannibalism. Look at today, where pagans and heretics have made much influence in society, they have taken positions in the state, and now they promote and enact laws in support for cannibalism and infanticide.

Other results of Julian's pagan revival was a variety of murders: in Palestine, heathens kidnapped Christians, teared open their stomachs, filled them with barley, and left them to be eaten by pigs. In Sebaste, a city of Palestine, pagans opened the coffin of John the Baptist, burnt his bones and tossed away the ashes,[157] just as the Muslims in our own day desecrated Joseph's tomb. At Emessa, the idolaters desecrated an entire church and placed inside of it an image of Bacchus Androgynes.[158] Thus are the actions of fundamental believers in paganism, and the harsh realities of their inhumanity.

---

153 Socrates, 3.13
154 Socrates, 3.13
155 Theodoret. Eccles. Hist. 3.6–7
156 Herod. Hist. 2.11, in Arthur Young, *Historical Dissertation on Idolatrous Corruptions*, ch. v, p. 206
157 Theodoret. Eccles. Hist. 3.8
158 Theodoret. Eccles. Hist. 3.8

CHRISTIANITY IS AT WAR: THE MANIFESTO FOR CHRISTIAN MILITANCY

At Dorostolis, a city in Thrace, a Christian named Emilius was burnt alive by Capitolinus, the governor of the province. Marcus, the bishop of Arethusa who, under Constantine, destroyed a pagan temple and erected a church in its stead, was seized and his body was lacerated. He was then given over to a group of sadistic youths, who repeatedly stabbed him with their writing utensils; after this, he was covered in honey and left exposed for the bees and wasps to attack him. With his body covered in wounds from the lacerations, and gashes from the stabbings and the stings of the bees and wasps, he was suspended in the air and surrounded by pagans who demanded that he rebuild the pagan temple he destroyed.[159] The modern Christian would have been amongst that crowd, reprimanding him that he should have had "grace," and that he should have never illustrated his zeal against paganism, but should have had "love." This Christian of old, though he was not introduced to our modern enlightenment, surpassed any one of these moderns in both Faith and righteousness. He refused to rebuild the temple; they demanded money from him for the building expenses, but he still denied them. They assumed that his refusal to pay was on account of poverty, so they lowered the payment, but he proceeded his Faith over the heathen religion, which is false and deserves no rights. He ridiculed the pagans, and told them that they were crawling on the earth while he was elevated towards Heaven. They reduced their demands to an infinitesimal price, but he replied that it would be just as impious to give but a coin as to give the whole sum. They admired greatly his pugnaciousness, and respected his zealotry, and they soon converted to the Christian Faith, and Marcus, a persecutor of paganism, taught the heathens the Scriptures.[160]

In Alexandria, there was an old place where the pagans would sacrifice human beings to Mithra. Since it was vacant, the Christians decided to build a church over it, and as they dug up the land, they found a large body of human bones and skulls. These were the remains of the sacrificial victims of the pagan religion. The Christians, angry at such abominations, took up the skulls and exposed them throughout the town, parading them to show Christianity's victory over the vile pagan religion. The pagans, enraged at this, grabbed whatever weapons that they could and assailed the Christians, slaughtering many. They killed them with swords, stoned them to death with stones, crushed them with clubs, and to show their hatred for Christ, crucified some of them. The Christian who helped organize the building of the church over the pagan land, George (who was actually an Arian heretic), was taken and dragged alive by a camel, they then burned him alive alongside the poor animal.[161]

St. Athanasius, a very erudite bishop in Egypt, was decreed by Julian to be put to death, because the pagans, knowing of his great crusade against their religion, stated that if he was allowed to live, not one pagan temple would be left standing. Athanasius' followers were horrified at such a decree, but Athanasius said to them: "This commotion will quickly terminate: it is a cloud which appears and then vanishes away." When the assassins of the emperor came

---

159 Theodoret. Eccles Hist. 3.7
160 Theodoret. Eccles. Hist. 3.8
161 Socrates, 3.2

to kill him, he fled to Thebes, and when they came to slay him there, he sailed to Alexandria where he would remain for the rest of Julian's life.[162]

When Julian wanted to war against the Persians, he first consulted with a sorcerer in the temple of Apollo, so that he would know the future. The wizard said that he was unable to consult the dark powers until the bodies in the neighborhood were removed. The bodies he was referring to were those of the Christians, Babylas the martyr, and another man who were both murdered by the pagans. The bodies of the martyrs hindered the power of the sorcerer, and Julian knew this. He ordered that the Christians remove the bodies, and they did so with much joy, they placed them in a car drawn by two horses, and followed them while singing, "Let all those who adore graven images be confounded." They esteemed this moment as a victory over the demons,[163] because they comprehended the true purpose of Christianity: to destroy the works of the devil.

Angered by their joy, Julian ordered for them to be arrested. The vice-governor, Salustius, suggested to the tyrant not to kill the Christians, since they were seeking martyrdom, and that it was this which they desired. But he was unable to restrain his rage, and so ordered the arrest of a Christian young man named Theodore, who was an ardent defender of the Faith, and had his shoulders shredded with whips and the sides of his body mutilated with nails. Salustius tried to convince Julian to release Theodore, by telling him that the man was filled with fortitude, and that the violence put upon him degraded them. The argument was proficient, and mercy was granted to Theodore. Some people asked Theodore if he felt any pain while going through the tremendous torture, and he replied that at the beginning he suffered some pains, but then a man appeared in front of him, and wiped his face with a soft and cooling linen, giving him the courage to persevere. This vision so greatly impacted him, that when the torture did cease, he was not joyful, but disappointed.[164]

There were two Christians, Felix and Elpdius, who left the Faith and converted to paganism in order to win favor of the emperor. These two apostates were commissioned by Julian to seize the images and icons from the churches, and when Felix stood before some of these holy vessels, he exclaimed, "Behold, in what kind of vessels the Son of Mary is ministered unto."[165] This Felix was soon struck with some illness during which blood would drain out of his mouth and from every other part of his body, soon all of the plasma effused out, and he died. Julian, too, was inflicted with an unusual and grotesque sickness, in which his own excrement ejected out of his mouth, an ailment known today as fecal vomiting. His wife, beholding his suffering, urged him with these words:

> You ought to praise Christ the Saviour, for having, by this chastisement revealed to you his power; for you would never have known towards whom you were evincing so much hostility, had He, with His usual long-suffering, exempted you from affliction.

---

[162] Theodoret. Eccles. Hist. 3.9
[163] Theodoret. Eccles. Hist. 3.10; Socrates, 3.28
[164] Theodoret. Eccles. Hist. 3.11
[165] Theodoret. Eccles. Hist. 3.12

Such an entreaty provoked him to ponder on his own actions, and he ordered for a certain church he had stolen and given to the pagans to be restored, but sadly he passed away before this was carried out.[166]

Under Julian, at around 362 AD, there was a young man who was the son of a prestigious pagan priest, who was greatly influenced by a Christian woman in Antioch. He asked her how he could bring his father away from his superstition, she told him to flee his father, to put God before his family, to flee to a certain city, and she promised him that she would take the measures for such an affair. He replied:

From henceforth I shall come to you; and I shall commit my life into your keeping.

When the emperor made pilgrimage to the temple of Apollo in Daphne, the youth's father joined him to conduct a ritual for the tyrant, and his son followed along. When the emperor was about to eat his dinner, the young man, in accordance to custom, sprinkled water offered to idols upon the food, and then he returned to Antioch to fulfill the promise he made to the Christian woman. "I am come to you, according to my promise, do you fulfill yours, and take measures for my deliverance." She brought him to a holy man named Meletius, who concealed and hid him for a long time in his home. His father, being ever so worried because he could not find his son, ran through all of the streets of Daphne, and then he went to Antioch and conducted a most nervous and careful search, and eventually he spotted his son in the home of Melitius. He seized him and flogged his body severely, he took a pointed object, made it very hot, and burnt his hands, his feet, and his back. After this, he threw him into a room and locked him in. While in the house he, seeing all of his father's idols, was taken by a zealous indignation, and he destroyed all of them.[167] It is quite remarkable, that today's church leaders would consider this act unchristian, or they would remark that the young Christian is following the Mosaic law in regards to idols, and that this is incorrect since we are living in the "age of grace." But this story reveals that the Church, as early as the fourth century—as we can tell by its record—accepted the destroying of idols, and considered it not only as applicable and noble, but incumbent upon a Christian. The young man, knowing his father's love for his heathen images, was terrified of his return home. Being filled with fear and dread, he cried out to Jesus Christ: "These things have I done and suffered for thy sake."

All of a sudden the bolts of the door broke, and the doors burst open. He ran back to the Christian woman who, with a vehicle of Meletius, brought him to Cyril, the bishop of Jerusalem, with whom he would stay. After the death of Julian, this young man convinced his father of his errors, and led him to the Church.[168]

Julian had such hatred for the Christian Faith, that he would even cast things offered to idols into rivers and streams, and sprinkle water dedicated to pagan images on the bread and all the other types of food, so that no one could drink of them without partaking in the

---

166 Theodoret. Eccles. Hist. 3.13
167 Theodoret. Eccles. Hist. 3.13
168 Theodoret. Eccles. Hist. 3.13

unholy sacrifices. The Christians wept, but they continued to eat nonetheless, since they remembered the words of St. Paul, when he wrote: "Whatsoever is sold in the shambles, that eat, asking no question for conscience sake."[169] There were two guards of the emperor, named Juventius and Maximus, who were Christians from their youth, and they, unable to bear the abominations of the corrupt sovereign, declared at a certain party of friends, their objections to the tyranny. "You have delivered us," they said, "to a monarch who is more wicked than all the nations of the earth." Someone who was present heard these words, and reported them to the emperor who then sent for the two men to be brought to him. When they were present, Julian asked them what it was that they had said, and they, with their zeal still warm, declared:

> Having been brought up, O emperor, in the true religion, and having been accustomed to obey the admirable laws enacted by Constantine, and by his sons, we cannot but be deeply grieved at witnessing everything filled with abominations, and the very food contaminated by being mixed with the sacrifices offered to idols. We have lamented over this in our own houses, and now, in your presence, we publicly express our regret. This is the only care of sorrow which we experience under your government. [170]

The quote provokes the reader to a sudden realization, that under Constantine the idolatries of the heathen were kept under control, on account of the influence of the Church on the state, and while many may consider this Christian tyranny, or as many modern Christians would think, a contradiction to the "age of grace," these laws were suppressing the despotism of the pagans. The results of restraining Constantine's anti-idolatry laws, were the same as when the Israelites threw away Moses' precepts against paganism: tyranny, and the violent rulership of Julian suffices for evidence.

Julian, upon hearing their defiant words, had the two saints tortured to death, and ordered the story of their execution to be circulated throughout the empire.[171] The Christians rejected the decrees of the king, disobeyed the government, and did not allow Caesar to take that which was God's.

The commander of the soldiers who guarded Julian's palace, Valentinian, was one day walking with the emperor as he was entering a pagan temple, and when a heathen priest threw water dedicated to idols, some of it landed on his robe. Valentinian, angered that the pagan water touched him, struck the priest and told him that he defiled him.[172] This story reveals to us a different picture of Christianity, showing us our Faith in its earlier and purer form, that it was militant and completely adverse to the ways of the heathen. Valentinian was, for this action, exiled to the desert, but he would eventually ascend to the throne and become an emperor.[173]

---

169 I Corinthians 10:25, as quoted by Theodoret. Eccles. Hist. 3.15
170 Theodoret. Eccles. Hist. 3.15
171 Theodoret. Eccles. Hist. 3.15
172 Theodoret. Eccles. Hist. 3.16
173 Theodoret. Eccles. Hist. 3.16

Julian continued his despotism, offering free gold to the soldiers, and when they would arrive to receive the gift, they were asked to offer incense to the gods. Many fell for this trap, but others who were prudent and familiar with the wiles of Cain's successors, avoided the offer.[174] Artemius, the military commander in Egypt who, when Constantine was emperor, destroyed idols, was beheaded under the order of Julian.[175] When this man broke the images, as the Hebrews shattered the idols of the Canaanites, he was acting in accordance to the Mosaic law, and his actions were done to obliterate the very religion which ended up killing him.

There is another story which exemplifies how ancient Christianity upheld the act of defying tyranny and ruining paganism. Publia, a virtuous woman who led a group of maidens who all made oaths of perpetual virginity, wished to defy Julian, and so when he was passing by, she assembled the women and led them into song. They, with melodious and loud voices, sung the words of David, "The idols of the nations are but silver and gold, the works of men's hands." After they expressed their disdain with idolatry, they proclaimed, "Let those who made them, and all those who trust in them, become like unto them." Julian was much vexed by this, and he ordered them to be silent. But they did not listen, and instead, they sung, "Let God arise, and let his enemies be scattered." Julian, losing all patience with the stubborn Christian, order for Publia to be given a blow on each side of her face. She went back into her house, and notwithstanding the tyranny of the government, continued to harass the emperor with her intolerance toward his erroneous religion.[176]

When Julian attempted to defeat the Persians, at around 363 AD, his warlike gods did not help, he received no help from Mars, and nor was he conferred the assistance of Zeus. His army was vanquished by the Persians at a certain desert, and he was left wandering about the wilderness, his life being drained as each moment passed. He was inflicted with a detrimental wound, and it is said that before he died, he took some of his blood, threw it up towards heaven and cried, "Galilean! Thou hast conquered!"

After he died, a temple, in which Julian spent much time, was examined, and the things they discovered further justify the outlawing of the pagan religion. They found a woman suspended by her hair, her hands stretched out and her stomach ripped open.[177] In his palace there was found numerous chests all filled with human heads as a result of the diabolical rituals Julian partook in, and there were many dungeons in which there was seen dead bodies, all of whom were ritually sacrificed.[178]

It is no wonder that the people cheered at the death of this diabolical despot, and that Constantine suppressed the religion which gave rise to his evils, and that God Himself, above whom there is no human law or constitution, commanded that false religions never

---

174 Theodoret. Eccles. Hist. 3.16
175 Theodoret. Eccles. Hist. 3.18
176 Theodoret. Eccles. Hist. 3.19
177 Theodoret. Eccles. Hist. 3.26
178 Theodoret. Eccles. Hist. 3.27

be allowed to percolate a society. For, once heathenism and heresy are permitted to thrive in any civilization, they eventually infiltrate the government, as Julian did, and enact tyranny.

THE USE OF FEAR TO DESTROY EVIL IS NOT WRONG

To use fear to control a society and prevent it from committing crimes is not a sin. A Christian ruler may use fear to bring his people to order and amiability, to prevent evil sedition and revolt, and to preclude paganism and demonic ideas from influencing the society. King David used fear against his heathen enemies, as he expresses in one passage:

> The foreigners submit to me;
> As soon as they hear, they obey me.
> The foreigners fade away,
> And come frightened from their hideouts. (2 Samuel 22: 45-46)

You may say that the use of fear is against love, but in Christianity, love and fear can work together. We read in Scripture that after Peter killed Ananias, "great fear came on all them that heard these things." (Acts 5:5) St. Maximus of Turin wrote: "had Peter been able to correct Ananias' avarice, he would not have punished him, but in punishing him he corrects others. For he wished to punish the one but to instill fear in the many."[179] In instilling fear, we have correction, and such correction is done for the purpose of love. The law is love, and so to administer the law is done for the purpose love, for "the purpose of the commandment is love from a pure heart, from a good conscience, and from sincere faith" (1 Timothy 1:5) When Moses slaughtered three thousand Hebrews for worshipping the golden calf, he destroyed a part of the people to instill correction on the rest, and prevent them from falling off the cliff of goodness into the pit of evil. And this was done for the cause of God Who is love. St. Gregory of Nyssa, when commenting on this story of Moses, wrote:

> So if any time someone observes the same evil in many, but the wrath of God is vented not against everyone but only against some, it is fitting that one perceive the correction as administered through love for mankind. While not all are struck, the blows upon some chastise all to turn them from evil.[180]

Fear is a powerful tool, but it must be used for righteousness, and for the prevention of evils. The enemies of Christ were hesitant to kill Him, for they "feared Him, because all the people were astonished at His teaching." (Mark 11:8) They feared the people because they were zealous for Christ, and Christ never reprimanded them for their zeal. Why? Because it is of a true believer to be a fanatic.

When the priests and elders wished to assault Christ, they refrained since "they feared the multitude, because they took him for a prophet." (Matthew 21:46)

In another time, the religious leaders decided not to kill Christ on the feast day, "lest there be an uproar among the people." (Matthew 26:4; see also Mark 11:32) Thus the fol-

---

179 Maximus of Turin, sermon 18.1
180 Gregory of Nyssa, *Life of Moses*, 2.206

lowers of Christ did not obligate themselves to be pacifistic, but resistant, to the attacks of Christ's enemies. They instilled fear, and that fear was effective in restraining the wicked.

A similar situation took place after the Resurrection of Christ, in which when the officers came to arrest Peter and a number of the other Christian leaders, they did not do so in the presence of the early Christians because they feared that they would stone them:

> Then went the captain with the officers, and brought them without violence: for they feared the people, lest they should have been stoned. (Acts 5:26)

The zeal of the people was so great that they would have stoned officers if they ever saw them arrest St. Peter with violence. This fiery love for God's Apostles instilled fear into the hearts of the officers, and surely it was effective and not something that was ever reprimanded.

The unity of fear and love is exemplified within the knight of Christendom who, through his arms protects the helpless and instills fear in those who may attack them and keeps them from being killed. As the Spanish knight Ramon Llull wrote:

> Love and fear are joined as one against enmity and contempt, and thus the knight, because of his nobility of courage, good habits and the very high and great honour that is bestowed upon him by being chosen, and because of his horse and arms, must be loved and feared by the people. For through love, charity and learning shall be restored, and through fear, truth and justice shall be restored. [181]

PERSECUTION AGAINST EVIL IS GOOD

Those who argue for complete toleration say that if the state were to persecute certain religions, then that would constitute as persecution, and how then, they say, is this so different from persecuting Christians. This point would be valid if all religion were equal, but they are not. One of the problems with this way of thinking is that it equates all persecutions. To persecute is not evil unto itself, it is who is persecuting and who is being persecuted that determines whether it is right or wrong. The state persecutes murderers, thieves, rapists, and other evildoers, by throwing them in prison and executing them. Yet we would not consider this evil. So then, to persecute a religion that promotes evil, such as human sacrifice, cannibalism, atheism, sacrilege, sedition, abortion, and numerous other deplorable acts, is not evil. But, to persecute Christianity, the religion that birthed the greatest of civilizations, this is evil because it harms both the spiritual and temporal well-being of society.

Look to all the pagan and heathen nations that persecute Christians, and look to all the supposed Christian nations. What are they doing, but nothing, to help their brethren? We see such bloodshed, and we cannot help but cry out with the prophet: "Will you keep silent when the impious devours the righteous" (Habakkuk 1:13).

---

[181] Ramon Llull, Chivalry, 1.6

PART 9

If a pagan state decrees for the suppression of Christianity, or for the enforcement of falsehood, then Christians are obligated to resist it. But, if a Christian state enacts a law in favor of truth, and for the persecution of evil, then Christians are obligated to praise this. When Shadrach, Meshach and Abednego disobeyed the edict of the king and refused to bow down to the golden image, this disobedience pleased God and was worthy of admiration. And when this same king, Nebuchadnezzar, established a law in favor of the truth, and for the suppression of blasphemy, declaring "that any people, nation, or language which speaks anything amiss against the God of Shadrach, Meshach, and Abednego shall be cut in pieces, and their houses shall be made an ash heap" (Daniel 3:29), this act of persecution was pleasing to God and also worthy of our admiration. Not all rebellions are equal; some are worthy of condemnation, some of praise. Not all persecutions are the same, some are tyrannical, and some are necessary for the safety of the Christian society. This is exactly what St. Augustine declared when he expressed his support for the persecution of the Donatists, a most violent and insidious cult:

> If the emperors were in error—perish the thought!—in accordance with their error they would issue laws against the truth, and through these the just would be both tried and crowned by not doing what was commanded because it was forbidden by God. Thus Nebuchadnezzar had commanded his golden statue to be adored, and they who refused to do it pleased God who forbade such acts. But when the emperors hold to truth, in accordance with that truth they give commands against error, and whoever despises them brings down judgment on himself. He pays the penalty exacted by men and he has no standing before God, because he refused to do what truth itself commanded him by the 'heart of the king' [Proverbs 21:1]. Thus Nebuchadnezzar himself was afterward moved by the miracle of the preservation of the three children, and, turning against error and toward truth, he published an edict that 'Whoever should speak blasphemy against the God of Sidrach, Misach and Abednego, should be destroyed and their houses laid waste.' And do you refuse to admit that Christian emperors should give like commands against you, when they know that Christ is mocked by you in those whom you rebaptize? If the commands of a king do not extend to the preaching of religion and the prevention of sacrilege, why do you single out the edict of a king giving such commands? Do you not know that the words of a king are 'signs and wonders [which] the most high God hath wrought toward me? It hath seemed good in my sight to publish how great and mighty is his kingdom, an everlasting kingdom, and his power to all generations.' [Daniel 3:99, 100, Douay-Rheims] [182]

Augustine believed that because kings of the Old Testament enacted laws against blasphemy, then Christian kings also have this same authority. This point is pertinent since it spearheads the common objection made by the heretics: that the coming of Christ ended any permission to enforce these precepts against sacrilege. Moreover, notice how Augustine affirms that the Christian emperors act for "the prevention of sacrilege," and in this context, it was to prevent the Donatist from baptizing people already baptized in the Catholic Church.

---

[182] Augustine, letter 105, brackets mine

The pious emperors precluded heresy, and they did so rightly, knowing full well what violence and destruction heretics do when they are left without restraint.

IN DEFENSE OF BOOK BURNING

The books of heretics, or any books that promote hatred against God, or any maliciousness against the true Faith, should not be allowed to be freely published and distributed, but burned and abolished. St. Robert wrote that the books of heretics "are rightly forbidden and burned." Such a measure would be in accordance with the Church, since even before the establishment of Christendom, the Apostles had the earliest Christians burn their pagan books. As St. Luke recorded:

> Also, many of those who had practiced magic brought their books together and burned them in the sight of all. And they counted up the value of them, and it totaled fifty thousand pieces of silver. So the word of the Lord grew mightily and prevailed. (Acts 19:19)

Notice how by burning the books "the word of the Lord grew mightily and prevailed." This shows that Christianity thrives where evil teachings are uprooted, refuting the common belief amongst many Christians that "what is outlawed will only grow stronger."

This story of book burning has both a collective and governmental application, that is, both Christian societies and Christian governments have the authority to burn demonic literature. If a small society of Christians could burn down their own pagan books, then an entire Christian empire, under the Church and a Christian state, has the authority to prohibit the diabolical books.

Now, this is not to say that the books of pagans and heretics should never be read, because it is always necessary to understand the nature of evil, and so this is why the Church has always had very erudite thinkers and theologians who, reading such books, were able to combat the false and evil beliefs. We read in a letter written by Dionysus, bishop of Alexandria in the mid third century, that he received a vision in which he heard a voice that declared, "Read all that thou takest in hand, for thou art qualified to correct and prove all, and this very thing has been the cause of thy faith in Christ from the beginning."[183] There is nothing wrong in reading perfidious books for the sake of exposing them, but the majority of people, when perusing such books, do not do so for the sake of combating them, but of curiosity, and strong interest in darkness. This is where the problem lies, and thus this is why the distribution of such must be very limited, never being allowed to freely flood the laity, and only being read for the reason of exposing it, and thus, educating the people on its evils and dangers. Evil should be exposed only to be condemned, rejected, cast away and destroyed, never glorified.

Constantine decreed "that if any one shall be detected in concealing a book compiled by Arius, and shall not instantly bring it foreword and burn it, the penalty for this offense shall be death; for immediately after the conviction the criminal shall suffer capital punishment."[184]

---

183 Euseb. Eccles. Hist. 7.7
184 The Emperor's Letter, in Socrates, 1.9

PART 9

Tell me, where are the books written by Arius today? They don't exist on account of such laws. The influence of Arianism continued through Muhammad by word of mouth, and if Islam was stopped by such laws, there would be no Islamic problem to deal with today. The same can be for Mormonism and the rest of the insidious cults that exist today.

In the fourth century there was a dualist cult led by one Priscillian, who read and promoted the gnostic gospels, such as the Gospel of Thomas and Gospel of Andrew. These were false gospels that taught all sorts of gnostic doctrines, and St. Pope Leo the Great declared that such books were to be not only prohibited but burned:

> And the apocryphal scriptures, which, under the names of the Apostles, form a nursery-ground for many falsehoods, are not only to be proscribed, but also taken away altogether and burnt to ashes in the fire. For although there are certain things in them which seem to have a show of piety, yet they are never free from poison, and through the allurements of their stories they have the secret effect of first beguiling men with miraculous narratives, and then catching them in the noose of some error.[185]

After the Council of Ephesus, the books of Nestorius were ordered by the Emperor Theodosius to be set to the flames. The same emperor also decreed that astrologers were obligated by law to burn their books in front of the bishops if they contained anything against the Catholic Faith.[186] After the Council of Chalcedon, all the books written by the heretic Eutychius were condemned and a law made by the emperors Valentinian and Macian prohibited anyone from reading or owning any copies. Not only that, but the books were ordered to be assiduously searched and burned.[187]

The Byzantine Emperor Tiberius ordered one of the books of Eutychius to be set to the flames, and when the heretic Athimus was condemned for his Eutychian sympathies, the emperor Justinian established that anyone caught in the act of possessing or transcribing his books would suffer "amputation of the hands."[188]

In the Seventh Ecumenical Council, held in Nicaea in 787, the books of the iconoclast heretics were ordered to be confiscated and kept from anyone reading them, even clergy:

> The present Canon decrees that all the false writings which the iconomachists [iconoclasts] composed against the holy icons and which are flimsy as children's toys, and as crazy as the raving and insane bacchantes those women who used to dance drunken at the festival of the tutelar of intoxication Dionysus all those writings, I say, must be surrendered to the Patriarchate of Constantinople, to be put together with the other books by heretics in such a place, that is to say, that no one will ever be able to take them therefrom with a view to reading them. As for anyone who should hide them, with a view to reading them himself

---

185 Leo the Great, letter 15, ch. 1
186 Bellarmine, *On Laymen or Secular People*, ch. 20, ed. Tutino, p. 93
187 Bellarmine, *On Laymen or Secular People*, ch. 20, ed. Tutino, p. 93
188 Bellarmine, *On Laymen or Secular People*, ch. 20, p. 94

or providing them for others to read, if he be a bishop, a presbyter, or a deacon, let him be deposed from office; but if he be a layman or a monk, let him be excommunicated. [189]

Of course most people today would object to the burning of anti-Christian books, but such a policy is very effective. Ask yourself a simple question, how many books of the ancient heretics, be it from Arius, Marcion, Valentinus, Eunomius, Nestorius, or Pelagius, still thrive today? The answer is almost none of their books are existent today,[190] except for a few fragments here and there that have survived through Christian apologists quoting them to refute them. Yet, the books of Mormons, Jehovah's Witnesses, Christian Scientists, atheists and other nefarious groups, are not only existent today, but are vibrantly distributed, and have even become quite popular. The typical notion that Christians need to just refute such books, has proven to be quite ineffective by the severe inundation of such demonic books. Simply refuting the books is not enough; they need to be utterly uprooted.

Books are more dangerous than speeches; they contain all of the arguments of the heretics in a coherent form, and not only that, they preserve the dangerous beliefs, so that they can last for generations; they can be copied, and distributed to countless people. The dangers of perfidious books was articulated by St. Robert when he said:

> For an argument put in writing is better prepared and more artful than that which is used in speech. Afterward it is always at one's disposal, for while discussions and conversations are rare and the words uttered orally soon disappear, the words in books remain forever and are always with us, walk with us, and dwell with us at home. Moreover, books are spread more widely, and anybody can speak with almost the entire world at once through a book. Books invade the homes and offices of many people whom the author of the book never saw and to whom he would hardly ever be introduced. [191]

The Koran, alongside all other anti-Christian texts, must be banned and outlawed; the books must be burned and never allowed to have influence in society.

THE CHRISTIAN KING SERVES GOD BY UPROOTING EVIL

A Christian king can never serve the Lord, and kiss the demon of tolerance; and this same king can never judge the judgement of the Lord, and give license to sacrilege. A governor who claims Christianity, and permits the works of the devil, and does not strive to be as Christ, and "destroy the works of the devil" (1 John 3:8), is nothing but a thief and an aid to the devil's agents. In the words of St. Augustine:

> How, then, do kings serve the Lord with fear except by forbidding and restraining with religious severity all acts committed against the commandments of the Lord? [192]

---

189 Canon 9 of the Seventh Ecumenical Council. See also Bellarmine, *On Laymen or Secular People*, ch. 20, ed. Tutino, pp. 94–95, brackets mine
190 See Bellarmine, *On Laymen or Secular People*, ch. 20, ed. Tutino, p. 95
191 Bellarmine, *On Laymen or Secular People*, ch. 20, ed. Tutino, p. 96
192 Augustine, letter 185, ch. 19

There are those who say, "The state has no place in Christianity!" But to such a fanatical claim we are quickly posed with the question, "How then does the king serve God?" We may argue that the king as an individual worships God, but that his reverence is not associated with his stately affairs. But this means that when the king worships God, he no longer is a king, but a mere citizen. This separation between the ruler's position and his religion is the origin of modern society's destructive measures. For today, politicians pass laws accepting the murder of infants, allowing the deplorable assembly of sodomites, the establishment of sodomite 'marriage', and other evils, and when that is all done, they pray to God and then pompously assert, "I don't like to use my position to enforce my faith." Or they will say something like, "I know my faith teaches that its wrong, but it's none of my business what people do." The question still stands, "How does a king worship God, as a king, in his position of authority, and through his authority?" Does he worship God by allowing such evils to take place and turn the other way with an empty grin, and portray himself as a moderate? To use the words of St. Augustine when writing on such an issue:

> A sovereign serves God one way as man, another way as king; he serves Him as man by living according to the faith, he serves Him as king by exerting the necessary strength to sanction laws which command goodness and prohibit the opposite. [193]

The words of Augustine simply expound on what the Apostles already taught, that governors are "those who are sent by him for the punishment of evildoers and for the praise of those who do good." (1 Peter 2:14)

Since St. Peter says that the state is to punish evil and reward righteousness, what this means is that evil has no rights, no liberty, and that freedom must be only given to do good. As Vitoria interpreted this passage, you cannot use "your liberty for a cloak of maliciousness, but as the servants of God."[194]

THE APOSTLES DID NOT WANT LAWS BASED ON PAGANISM, BUT CHRISTIANITY

St. Peter and St. Paul both describe the role of the state as an institution given to us by God for the punishment of evildoers and the rewarding of the righteous. St. Peter writes that rulers are "those who are sent by him for the punishment of evildoers and for the praise of those who do good" (1 Peter 2:14), and St. Paul says that "he is God's minister, an avenger to execute wrath on him who practices evil." (Romans 13:4)

Quite disturbingly, though, there are modern theologians today who, in the attempt to cast away the spirit of Christendom, say that these passages of St. Peter and St. Paul should be isolated solely to the times of the Apostles, that is, the era of pagan Rome. This way of interpreting would leave the definitions of "evildoer" and "those who do good" to the mercy of how pagandom would have perceived evil and good. If by what the Apostles

---

[193] Augustine, letter 185, ch. 19
[194] Vitoria, *On Civil Power*, question 1, article 5.2

meant by "evil" should be defined in the context of pagan Rome, then what they meant by "good" must equally be left to the definitions of pagan Rome as well.

This is quite dangerous; for it would force the crumbling of Christendom, and reduce our laws to the despotism of pagan Rome, or to the anarchical license of secular government, and not Christian empire. When St. Paul said "do that which is good" (Romans 13:3) in regards to obeying government, or when St. Peter spoke of "those who do good" (1 Peter 2:14), if by "good" they solely meant that which was good for the pagan, or for the secularist, then that definition of "good" would have been completely contrary to the Christian Faith. Neither St. Paul nor St. Peter, being writers of eternal and not secular values, would ever perceive "good" in such a superficial way. The Christian who lives in civil life, lives a life for the good, not just to please the state, but more importantly, to please God and to obtain union with Him in eternity. "But seek ye first the kingdom of God" (Matthew 6:33). This is what our Lord commands of us: not to first seek what is good in the eyes of the kingdom of Caesar, but to first seek what is good to the Kingdom of God.[195] This is the practice of what is truly good, and this is how the Apostles would have esteemed "good."

So by "good," St. Peter and St. Paul are exhorting the Christians not to obey only what Caesar wants, but to pursue first what God wants. Hence St. Peter said, "We ought to obey God rather than men." (Acts 5:29) St. John Chrysostom wrote: "What is good? Obedience. And what is evil? Disobedience."[196] Disobedience to God is obedience to the devil. What then is good but to obey God? When the ruler does good he is doing something pleasing to God. What then should impede the Christian state to enforce more than the pagans? To punish the evil the pagans permitted, and reward the good that the pagans prohibited.

"For rulers are not a terror to good works," wrote St. Paul, "but to evil. Do you want to be unafraid of the authority? Do what is good, and you will have praise from the same. For he is God's minister to you for good. But if you do evil, be afraid; for he does not bear the sword in vain; for he is God's minister, an avenger to execute wrath on him who practices evil." (Romans 13:3–4) We cannot restrict these words to only how the Caesar would have seen good, but to how God sees good. Therefore, the sword that is not held in vain is unleashed on all the breakers of goodness, that is, what to God is goodness. So if the pagan rulers unknowingly punished those who broke God's law, and were honored for this, how much more then must Christian rulers, who know God, punish those who disobey the Divine Law! Pagan rulers enforce God's law in a limited sense, since they do not know God, and also because they enforce many edicts that are not godly. Now, in Christendom, where kings know God and His law, and "seek first the kingdom of God and His righteousness" (Matthew 6:33) they are all the more obligated to enact the Divine Law, and to see to it that their citizens "Do what is good."

In the words of St. Robert Bellarmine, "the human law directs human acts to external acts of love, that is, to the peace and preservation of the commonwealth, but the divine law

---

195 See Vitoria, *Reflection 1 On the Power of the Church*, question 1, article 1
196 Chrysostom, *Eight Sermons on the Book of Genesis*, sermon 7, p. 115

directs also to internal acts of charity."¹⁹⁷ Through such measures are the last line from St. Peter's words fulfilled, "Honour the king." (1 Peter 2:17)¹⁹⁸ The irony of many Christian professors today is that they say we must honor the government, but when Christendom comes into the discussion, they begin to vacillate their own opinions. If we are to obey pagan rulers, then we are to obey Christendom's laws. In the same epistle St. Peter says, "Submit yourselves to every ordinance of man for the Lord's sake" (1 Peter 2:13). He places obedience to the state as being done for God's sake, and thus is it done for the love of God. St. Peter said this regarding the pagan emperor and governors of his day, how much more then should we give this utmost obedience to a Christian emperor of Christendom! And since the rulers administer their authority through the command of God, those who resist them resist the ordinance of the Almighty no differently than if they broke the Divine Law.¹⁹⁹

These preachers and seminary professors insist that while it is not wrong for a Christian to be ruled by pagans, it is certainly not biblical to form Christendom, as though Christians are made to be subjects to heathens, and to never govern themselves. Not ironically, those who preach this doctrine also love to boast that they enjoy "liberty in Christ," as they express their desire for Christian servitude to pagan despots. These same heretics were saying such drivel in the time of St. Robert Bellarmine, who answered to their jargon in these words, "if it is lawful for Christians to be subject to a pagan king, why not rather to a Christian king? And if it is lawful for a Christian to be subject, why not rule? Being subject seems more against evangelical freedom than ruling."²⁰⁰ They make it as though sovereignty is an evil unto itself, while deliberately concealing the fact that while there are wicked tyrants, there are righteous rulers. In the Scriptures there is mentioned evil kings, such as Nimrod, Pharaoh, Saul, Jeroboam, and many others, and meanwhile, those same Holy Scriptures commend numerous other rulers for being righteous, such as Noah, Abraham, Moses, Joshua, and almost all of the judges of Israel and many kings of Judah.²⁰¹ To use the words of Bellarmine:

> Just as there are both good and bad kings among Catholics, but no good king can be found among heretics, so even among Catholics, so even among the kings of Judah there were many good ones and many evil ones, but among the kings of Israel not one good one was to be found. ²⁰²

What is even more ironic is that all of these seminary professors, alongside their students, who insist that we must isolate St. Paul to the context of pagan Rome, and thus never support Christendom's laws, also boast about how much they love St. Augustine, who would

---

197 Bellarmine, *On Laymen or Secular People*, ch. 11, ed. Tutino, p. 42
198 That 1 Peter 2:17 has political significance applicable to Christendom, see Bellarmine, *On Laymen or Secular People*, ch. 3, ed. Tutino, p. 11
199 See Bellarmine, *On Laymen or Secular People*, ch. 11, ed. Tutino, p. 45
200 Bellarmine, *On Laymen or Secular People*, ch. 3, ed. Tutino, p. 10
201 See Bellarmine, *On Laymen or Secular People*, ch. 4, ed. Tutino, p. 16
202 Bellarmine, *On Laymen or Secular People*, ch. 4, ed. Tutino, p. 17

no doubt reject their ideas. Why do Christian kings unsheathe the sword against the enemies of Christ? Because, and to use Augustine, "they are called Catholic Christians, not servers of idols like your Julian [the pagan emperor]; not heretics, as certain ones have been and have persecuted the Church, when true Christians have suffered the most glorious martyrdom for Catholic truth, not justly deserved penalties for heretical error."[203] Let these words be heard by the heretics who condemn Christian empire and who hate Christendom. Let them dare object to St. Augustine, and then turn around and use his work as though they are of the same Church as this learned Father. All of these sophists who tout and boast about how they 'honor' the Church Fathers,' when they ignore, or refuse to read, how ardently Augustine helped the foundation for holy Christendom, and the wonderful laws of this bloomed flower.

THE KINGS OF THE OLD TESTAMENT ARE TO BE OUR MODELS

Since the pagans cannot be Christendom's models for punishing evil-doers, who then should be our models but the righteous kings of Israel? Amazingly, the people who insist that we must isolate St. Peter's description of an ideal governor to the rulers of the pagan Roman Empire, are those who also incessantly say that we must abide by Scripture. Yet when the ancient kings of Israel are presented as models or examples of how Christendom should govern itself, these are thrown out, and pagan Rome is now pushed as something to follow, or to take precedence over the holy sovereigns of God's land. When St. Augustine illustrated how a king is to serve God, he did not list edicts in favor of pagan values, but laws for the destruction of idolatry and slanderers, and for the uplifting of holiness, giving praise to Hezekiah's shattering of the idols, Josiah's demolition of the sodomite houses, the king of Nineveh's decree for his people to fast for God, Darius feeding Daniel's enemies to the lions, and Nebuchadnezzar's decree against blasphemy of the true God:

> It was thus that Ezechias [Hezekiah] served Him [God] by destroying the groves and temples of idols and the high places which had been set up contrary to the commandments of God; thus Josias served Him by performing similar acts [see 2 Kings 23:1–25]; thus the king of the Ninevites served Him by compelling the whole city to appease the Lord; thus Darius served Him by giving Daniel power to break the idol, and by feeding his enemies to the lions; thus Nebuchadnezzar, of whom we spoke above, served Him when he restrained all his subjects from blaspheming God by a terrible penalty.[204]

Such examples from the valorous and pious kings of old were followed in Christendom, such as when the emperor Theodosius, who eradicated religious toleration and abolished pagan idolatry,[205] suppressed the Arian heretics who were persecuting the Church and ordered that all of the pagan idols be destroyed. St. Augustine praised this policy of Theodosius as a great illustration of a Christian emperor:

---

203 Augustine, letter 105, brackets mine
204 Augustine, letter 185, ch. 19, brackets mine
205 St. Robert Bellarmine, *On Laymen or Secular People*, ch. 18, p. 84

Amid all of these events, from the very commencement of his reign, he did not cease to help the troubled church against the impious by most just and merciful laws, which the heretical Valens, favouring the Arians, had vehemently inflicted. Indeed, he rejoiced more to be a member of this church than he did to be a king upon the earth. The idols of the Gentiles he everywhere ordered to be overthrown, understanding well that not even terrestrial gifts are placed in the power of demons, but in that of the true God. [206]

St. Odo also referred to the kings David, Hezekiah and Josiah as righteous warriors, and said that Christian kings who committed actions similar to theirs are following God's commandments.

"Were not king David, Ezechias, and Josias mighty and warlike? The same things have been heard in this age of those who take care to glorify Him by keeping His commandments, and whom God honors with miracles, as King Oswald of the English."[207]

If we are to gauge the level of religious liberty on the basis of Christianity, then we are to heed to Scripture, in which there is no license for false religion, but authority granted to the only true Faith. If toleration of evil doctrines is Biblical, then why do the prophets, from Moses onward, call for the end of idolatry and afflict punishments on those who observe false religions?[208]

The heretics today say that it is wrong for any government to kill for the cause of true religion. To say such a thing goes against Moses, Joshua and all of the other rulers who did justice for God. To use the words of St. Robert Bellarmine, "Moses himself and Joshua, Samuel, David, Elias, and other most holy men killed many people."[209] In another place this same father, in support of Holy War, said:

> In the Old Testament we read that Abraham, Moses, Joshua, Gideon, Samson, David, Josiah, and the Maccabees waged war with much praise. [210]

St. Odo of Cluny made reference to the warriors of Israel, such as Abraham and David, to vindicate holy war:

> Let no one be worried because a just man sometimes made use of fighting, which seems incompatible with religion. For some of the Fathers, and of these the most holy and most patient, when the cause of justice demanded, valiantly took up arms against their adversaries, as Abraham, who destroyed a great multitude of the enemy to rescue his nephew, and King David who sent his forces even against his own son. [211]

Did not Moses kill people for worshipping the golden calf? Did not Joshua slaughter the Canaanites for their idolatries and other deplorable rituals? The use of the sword

---

206 Augustine, *City of God*, 5.26
207 Odo of Cluny, *Life of St. Gerald of Aurillac*, 1.42
208 Augustine, letter 173, trans. Sister Wilfrid Parsons, *The Fathers of the Church*, vol. 30
209 Bellarmine, *On Laymen or Secular People*, ch. 13, ed. Tutino, p. 49
210 Bellarmine, *On Laymen or Secular People*, ch. 14, p. 56
211 Odo of Cluny, *Life of St. Gerald of Aurillac*, 1.8

against impious people did not end with Israel, but continued on in Christianity. As Vitoria tells us, "anything which is permitted in natural and Mosaic law is by that token permitted in evangelical law."[212] The wars waged by the Hebrews are not entirely restricted to their historical context, but rather they are models as to how wars are to be conducted by the armies of the Church, such as the great forces that were launched by the pious Constantine and also the great Christian emperor Theodosius the Great, who waged many wars.[213] God allowed some of the pagans to remain in the land to teach future generations on how to war, as we read in Judges:

> Now these are the nations which the Lord left, that He might test Israel by them, that is, all who had not known any of the wars in Canaan (this was only so that the generations of the children of Israel might be taught to know war, at least those who had not formerly known it), namely, five lords of the Philistines, all the Canaanites, the Sidonians, and the Hivites who dwelt in Mount Lebanon, from Mount Baal Hermon to the entrance of Hamath. And they were left, that He might test Israel by them, to know whether they would obey the commandments of the Lord, which He had commanded their fathers by the hand of Moses. (Judges 3:1–4)

The importance of war was instilled into the Hebrews, for God knew that they would be slaughtered without such knowledge, and so the pertinence of the militant continued in the Church, on account of all the persecutors she has faced and still faces.

IN DEFENSE OF THE CHRISTIAN STATE

Government was introduced to humanity by God, for St. Paul said that "Whosoever therefore resisteth the power, resisteth the ordinance of God." Since the state is brought to us through divine law, there is nothing wrong or evil if the state governs with divine law,[214] and not pagan edicts. St. Paul says that "all things are ordained" by God (Romans 13:1), and therefore law, that is righteous law, comes from God. And so the laws of Christendom, which were once enacted, came from God.[215] God, through Solomon, tells us:

> By me kings reign, and rulers decree justice. (Proverbs 8:15)

Notice that it does not say that all decrees come from God, but only decrees of justice. Therefore, tyrannical decrees do not come from God, but only those of righteousness. All kings are appointed by God, but this does not mean that every decree is of God—many in fact are of the devil. This is why in the Wisdom of Solomon we read:

> Give ear, you that rule the people, and that please yourselves in multitudes of nations:

> For power is given you by the Lord, and strength by the most High, who will examine your works, and search out your thoughts:

---

212 Vitoria, *On the Law of War*, question 1, article 1, 1
213 Vitoria, *On the Law of War*, question 1, article 2, 1
214 See Bellarmine, *On Laymen or Secular People*, ch. 6, ed. Tutino, p. 22
215 See Vitoria, *On Civil Power*, Question 1, article 3.1–2, ed. Pagden & Lawrance

Because being ministers of his kingdom, you have not judged rightly, nor kept the law of justice, nor walked according to the will of God.

Horribly and speedily will he appear to you: for a most severe judgment shall be for them that bear rule.

For to him that is little, mercy is granted: but the mighty shall be mightily tormented. (Wisdom 6:3–7)

A pagan may decree justice (such as Nebuchadnezzar and Darius), and that would come from God, but his edicts supporting pagan injunctions would not; while in Christendom, the Christian ruler decrees that which is in accordance to the Divine Law, and never pagan gods. Decrees based on Christianity are just, and thus come from God through the government of Christendom. When a ruler enacts a law in favor of truth and the Holy Faith, it is not he who does it, but Christ through him. "The emperors command this," said St. Augustine when writing the punishment of heretics, "and it is what Christ also commands, because, when they command what is good, Christ gives the command through them."[216] St. Gregory of Nazianzus declared that it is Christ Who gives the sword to the state, and Christ Who rules with the ruler, as he said in one homily, addressing temporal rulers,

> You rule with Christ and you govern with Christ; it is from him that you receive your sword, not to use, but to brandish. [217]

When the righteous king slays homosexuals, it is Christ Who commands him; when he extirpates heretical and evil cults, it is Christ Who commands him; when he wars against an aggressive and pagan nation, it is Christ Who commands him. Why then is it so wrong to have a Christian state, for truly it was by God that Christendom reined, and all of its just edicts came from the Almighty. There is no evil in forming Christendom again, and when it does revive, it will be by the will of Heaven.

But then there will be those who say, "All of this nonsense about law is putting trust in man and not God, and the Bible says, 'Cursed be the man that trusteth in man' (Jeremiah 17:5)." To this common objection we reply with the same answer St. Augustine gave to those who used the same argument:

> So, then, if you want to know on whom we rely, think of Him Whom the Prophet foretold, saying: 'All the kings of the earth shall adore him; all nations shall serve him.' (Psalm 71:11) That is why we make use of this power of the Church which the Lord both promised and gave to it. [218]

---

216 Augustine, letter 105
217 St. Gregory of Nazianzus, Oration 17, 9
218 St. Augustine, letter 105

✝ CHRISTIANITY IS AT WAR: THE MANIFESTO FOR CHRISTIAN MILITANCY

CHRISTIANITY IS FOR CHRISTENDOM AND NOT ANARCHY

In our own time there are various Christians who maliciously cry out against any sort of Christian influence over the government. Ironically, these same persons want to influence us to not bring the Faith into government, while saying we should have no influence over the state.

The hatred toward Christian influence over government amongst certain cults is nothing but a heretical form of anarchism, and it is such mindsets that enable tyrannies; for a government absent of Christianity, is a government filled with devil-worship. To remove Christianity from the state, is to only leave a void ever-ready to be filled by some diabolical scheme that is always contriving to tyrannize Christians. This destructive belief was enthusiastically held by both the Anabaptists and the Waldensians. They were seditious in their ideology, and believed that government law was evil because "the obligation of the laws removes Christian freedom" and that "the end of the civil laws is external peace."[219]

Many today argue that the Waldensians were people of peace, but how could that be so when they were fanatically pushing for such a revolutionary ideology, that would have overturned the government and shattered Christendom into anarchy? The Waldensians also believed that once a civil ruler was in a state of mortal sin then he has lost all right to rule.[220] Such a fanatical belief would have only led to sedition. Most people think that if the followers of a religion aren't personally hurting anyone then that is indicative to a peaceful religion. This is the modern heresy of indifferentism, and it has enabled every evil ideology and religion to thrive. The Waldensians didn't have to kill anyone to be recognized as dangerous; the fact that they believed in no government evidenced that they were indeed dangerous. If their cult was permitted to inculcate itself, then it would have eventually led to a violent revolution against the state. Those who hate government should put their beliefs against the words of the wise Solomon:

> Where there is no counsel, the people fall; but in the multitude of counselors there is safety. (Proverbs 11:14)

A society without government, is no society at all, but a dispersed and confused mob.[221] The Church has no issue with the state killing those who deserve death. For as St. John Chrysostom said:

> Do you see that ruler and sword are there for wrongdoing? In any case, listen to a still clearer statement of this: 'It brings vengeance to the wrongdoing.' He did not say, 'A ruler is not without purpose: what, then?' The sword is not carried to no purpose.[222]

What then will these heretics say, when they read of how St. Paul brought the Gospel to Sergius Paulus, the governor of Paphos? Did St. Paul command him to renounce his position?

---
219 Bellarmine, *On Laymen or Secular People*, ch. 9, ed. Tutino, pp. 34–35
220 See Vitoria, *On the American Indians*, question 1, article 2
221 See Bellarmine, *On Laymen or Secular Government*, ch. 5, ed. Tutino, p. 19
222 Chrysostom, *Eight Sermons on the Book of Genesis*, sermon 2, p. 70

A sorcerer named Bar-Jesus tried to dissuade the governor from hearing the Apostle, and Paul harshly berated the witch, saying, "O full of all deceit and all fraud, you son of the devil, you enemy of all righteousness, will you not cease perverting the straight ways of the Lord? And now, indeed, the hand of the Lord is upon you, and you shall be blind, not seeing the sun for a time." (Acts 13:10) The sorcerer was struck with blindness, and "the proconsul believed, when he saw what had been done, being astonished at the teaching of the Lord." (Acts 13:12) The man was now a Christian, and he continued being a governor.

What was happening in the time of the Apostles was not mere preaching, but infiltration of the government to have them leave paganism and become Christian. St. Paul was even appointed by God to bring the Gospel to not only citizens but governments and kings. The Lord referred to St. Paul as "a chosen vessel of Mine to bear My name before Gentiles, kings, and the children of Israel." (Acts 9:15) Paul was to preach to kings, because he was to plant the seeds that would eventually grow into the divinely destined tree of Christendom, the nations called by Heaven to soon war against the Antichrist and his empire of slaves. Here one governor joins the true path of Christ, but in a few centuries the empire would soon be Christian, and in some time after that, the full flower of Christendom would blossom.

The society of the Apostles was only the infant state of Christianity; their teachings would later be expounded through the Church Fathers and various councils, and in time, the fullest manifestation of the Faith would come to pass in the glorious Middle Ages and in the Renaissance, when Christendom flourished with all of its majesty. But of course there are the objectors who fight Christendom, and scream and holler that Christian empire is utterly unbiblical. If the objectors want Christians to be so severed from the state, will they ever say that Christians stop being citizens?[223] The heretics of today who want to keep the Faith separate from the state are no different than that witch who wanted to prevent Paul from preaching to the governor.

So then, when all of the Roman Empire's citizens became Christian, its governors, its judges, and its emperors, as well followed the Faith, and they did not say the modern drivel of "I separate my faith from my politics." Instead they glorified God with all of their lives, with their intellects and very beings, through both their individual selves and their civil authority. Christ said "You shall love the Lord your God with all your heart, with all your soul, with all your strength, and with all your mind," (Luke 10:27) and how is a ruler supposed to do this if he is using his position as a means not for the advancement of Christianity, but the policies of antichrist? When Josiah was king he did not sever his throne from his zeal, when he "slew all the priests of the high places that were there upon the altars," (2 Kings 23:20) and "brake down the houses of the sodomites" (2 Kings 23:7). And when he had exhibited such immense zeal for God, he was following the first commandment of the Divine Law, for the Scripture says that he "turned to the Lord with all his heart, and

---

223 See Bellarmine, *On Laymen and Secular People*, ch. 10, ed. Tutino, p. 36

with all his soul, and with all his might, according to all the law of Moses; neither after him arose there any like him." (2 Kings 23:25)

He abided by the Law of Christ by slaying the enemies of Heaven through his kingly office. The same can be said for Moses when he slew all of the worshippers of the golden calf. Before he unsheathed the sword he said, "Who is on the Lord's side? Let him come unto me." And then, "all the sons of Levi gathered themselves together unto him." (Exodus 32:26) The priests gathered to him, and that is, the teachers of the Law. So when Moses killed for God, he did so for the love of God, and thus for the whole of the Law, the purpose of which is love. St. Gregory of Nyssa affirmed this interpretation, for he rendered the verse as, "If anyone wishes to be the friend of God, let him be a friend of me, the Law."[224]

TRUE LIBERTY IS TO FOLLOW THE LAW OF GOD

Do not let these heretics deceive you, when they say that such governance contradicts the "liberty" that we have in Christ.[225] To these reprobates liberty is anarchy; they take the word liberty and soil it! They use it as a disguise for license to cults and violent and reckless groups. They will never tell you that by liberty is not meant liberty from righteous law, but liberty from being enslaved to sin. For Christ tells us:

> Whosoever committeth sin is the servant of sin. And the servant abideth not in the house for ever: but the Son abideth ever. If the Son therefore shall make you free, ye shall be free indeed. (John 8:34–36)

To be free is to choose good and reject evil, and therefore the law does not prevent liberty, but guides man to liberty by providing the condition to partake in this freedom. The Scriptures say, "And I will walk at liberty, For I seek Your precepts." (Psalm 119:45) This is true liberty, the one that remains within the Law of God, and from the tyranny of the absolute toleration and license given to evil. St. Paul says that "where the Spirit of the Lord is, there is liberty." (1 Corinthians 3:17) And wherever the Lord is, there is not lawlessness, but law, and therefore liberty. For this reason law should never be cast away, and secular government allowed to triumph, for even St. Paul upheld the Law of God when he said, "Do we then make void the law through faith? God forbid: yea, we establish the law." (Romans 3:31) The Law, without Christ, is useless to the Church. It is when the Law comes together with the Cross, that we follow its precepts. St. Maximus of Turin explained this in one sermon:

> For the letter of the law is bitter without the mystery of the cross; about this the Apostle says: 'The letter kills.' When the sacraments of the passion are joined to it, all its bitterness is spiritually buried, and about that the Apostle says: 'But the Spirit gives life.'[226]

---

224 St. Gregory of Nyssa, *Life of Moses*, 2.207
225 Vitoria dealt with this argument in his day, and he writes about it in his, *On Civil Power*, question 1, article 5.2
226 Maximus of Turin, sermon 67.4

CHRIST DEMANDS JUSTICE AGAINST EVIL

Christ is the greatest enemy against tyranny, because He was most hated by tyranny. But in the end He took the victory, and destroyed the works of the devil. All demonic ideologies bring tyranny, they are all the works of the devil and they hate justice, and yet they all are subdued by the Cross of Christ. This is why, all those who hate the Cross of Christ, hate justice. This is why Muslims hate the Cross of Christ.

Christ is the foundation and cause of all justice, for St. Paul wrote in the same chapter of Romans, "Now the righteousness of God apart from the law is revealed, being witnessed by the Law and the Prophets, even the righteousness of God, through faith in Jesus Christ, to all and on all who believe." (Romans 3:21-23) When we fight for Christ and His most divine laws, it will be for justice. Anything against Christ is against justice, and so the destruction and the submission of such evildoers, for whom the ruler "does not bear the sword in vain" (Romans 13:4), is not done for the cause of evil, but for Jesus Christ, Who is the incarnation of Truth and Justice.

Justice is not removed or done away with because of Jesus Christ, rather it is in fact strengthened.[227] The New Covenant does not prohibit or make null governmental law, but only law done apart from Christ. We must still do righteous works under Christ, for "of him, and through him, and to him, are all things: to whom be glory forever." (Romans 11:36)

Christ freed us from the defects of the soul, but not from the sinful nature of the flesh, hence why St. Paul says, "I see another law in my members, warring against the law of my mind, and bringing me into captivity to the law of sin which is in my members." (Romans 7:23) And so the children of God, while being free from the spiritual servitude of sin, are still under the sin of the body.[228] For this we are to obey the commandments of God. As our Lord says: "If you love Me, keep My commandments." (John 14:15)

St. Gregory of Nysa once said, "The victory of true religion is the death and destruction of idolatry." So let the victory of Christianity be established. Do not forget, that our civilization was founded upon no sodomite, no Muslim, no feminist wretch, no socialist and no atheist, our civilization was founded upon Jesus Christ, and it will be for, with, under, and in Jesus Christ and His most Holy Cross, that we will have victory.

Christ is not only the foundation of all justice, but He is the incarnation of justice. When we thirst for Christ, we thirst for the Water of Life, that is, we thirst for justice and are counted amongst those of whom Jesus said: "Blessed are they that hunger and thirst after justice: for they shall have their fill." (Matthew 5:6) And there in the Gospel we read that most beautiful and sublime moment in the Passion of our Lord, when He declared in His humanity: "I thirst." (John 19:28) Christ did not thirst for physical water, for all of the rivers of the world are His. Christ thirsted after justice when He hung from the Cross. And so was Pure Justice crucified, and in His agony, He thirsted for justice. And when He cried out from the Cross,

---

227 Aquinas, *Summa Theologiae*, IIa IIae, 104, article 6
228 Aquinas, *Summa Theologiae*, IIa IIae, 104, article 6

CHRISTIANITY IS AT WAR: THE MANIFESTO FOR CHRISTIAN MILITANCY

"It is finished!" it was not a cry of defeat, but a declaration of victory; a victory for justice over evil, for the destruction of the works of devil (1 John 3:8), which are the enemies of all justice, for they are the enemies of the Holy Cross.

Thus is the Holy Cross the image of justice, for in that moment of His suffering, did true justice fully manifest itself, combating the devils and conquering sin, vanquishing the tyranny of the diabolical, shattering the love of earthly life by crushing death, so that sacred war against the forces of evil is unleashed through Christ in Whom "Love has been perfected among us" (1 John 4:17), without the hindrance of fear, that heavenly life may be pursued in the ever flowing rivers of love that "casts out fear" (1 John 4:18).[229]

Christ said, "Seek ye therefore first the kingdom of God, and his justice, and all these things shall be added unto you." (Matthew 6:33) To seek the Kingdom of Heaven first is to then seek justice, and thus to war against the forces of evil. "The fear of the LORD is the beginning of wisdom" (Proverbs 9:10), and "The fear of the LORD is to hate evil" (Proverbs 8:13). Since the beginning of wisdom is to fear the Lord, and the possessing of that wisdom means hating evil, then to seek the Kingdom of God first, is to have this very wisdom, and to despise all of the sinister forces of darkness, and this most definitely entails striving for justice. For to strive for justice is to carry the Cross of Christ, Who is the incarnation of Justice.

To pursue justice is to have zeal within the spirit, that same zeal that Christ possessed when He drove the merchants out when they prostituted His Father's House, and fulfilled the holy prophesy, "Zeal for your house will consume me." (John 2:17)

Now that we—the Church—are all temples of the Holy Spirit (1 Corinthians 6:19), then we must have zeal for all of the Christians who are being persecuted and afflicted by thieves who come for no other reason but "to steal and kill and destroy" (John 10:10).

Christendom, headed by the General Jesus Christ, will soon arise to destroy all of the enemies of the Cross—the Muslims, the sodomites, the atheists, and all of the adversaries of the Crucified One—all such insidious people will either be converted to the true Faith or struck down by our Holy King, Who "shall execute kings in the day of His wrath. He shall judge among the nations, He shall fill the places with dead bodies, He shall execute the heads of many countries." (Psalm 110:5–6)

THE NEW COVENANT IS FOR SALVATION, THE OLD COVENANT IS FOR GOVERNMENT

So many today throw away the Old Testament and say it is completely done with, and that all we need is the New Testament. But there are those who are prudent enough to seek a balance between the Old and the New, but do not know how to fully illustrate it. This balance between the Old and New can be simply explained this way: the Old Law is for government, the New Law for salvation. In the Old Testament, the Israelites were given peace and security as a

---

[229] For an explanation on the connection between John 19:28 and Matthew 5:6, see Fulton Sheen, *The Cross and the Beatitudes*, ch. 5

result of following the Law, and this is an earthly benefit. But in the New Testament, we are given heavenly rewards, with Christ inviting us to the Kingdom of Heaven. And so Augustine says that "promises of temporal goods are contained in the Old Testament, and this is why it is called Old; but the promise of eternal life belongs to the New Testament."[230]

Peter Lombard wrote that "the old law restrains the hand, but the new law controls the mind."[231] This is why we still need law, to restrain the masses from unrestrained license, and from deviant excess and disordered passions. As St. Paul says:

> the law is not made for a righteous person, but for the lawless and insubordinate, for the ungodly and for sinners, for the unholy and profane, for murderers of fathers and murderers of mothers, for manslayers, for fornicators, for sodomites, for kidnappers, for liars, for perjurers, and if there is any other thing that is contrary to sound doctrine, according to the glorious gospel of the blessed God which was committed to my trust. (1 Timothy 1:9–11)

The law directs the citizens to good, and does not give them to an environment for wicked practices. Even in the Garden of Eden, before the Mosaic Law was established, where our first parents were free from the fetters of sin, God gave them a law that was so be enforced. For, in the words of St. Robert Bellarmine, "Adam was created free, yet a law was imposed on him not to eat from the tree of the knowledge of good and evil (Genesis 2)."[232] All law is here, not to tolerate wickedness, but punish it, and thus enable true liberty. Or to use the words of Augustine, "Every punishment, if it is just, is punishment of a sin."[233]

We have all heard the useless argument: when a sin is punished, people will be more enthusiastic to indulge in what is prohibited. What then? Should we allow murder, and expect less murders? Should we permit rape and expect less rapes? The golden tongued father of the Church, St. John Chrysostom, said:

> We all know what is wrong before doing it, but we learn it more clearly after doing it—and much more clearly after doing it—and much more clearly when we are punished. Thus, Cain also knew that murdering one's brother is wrong even beforehand, but later learned it more clearly through being punished.[234]

LAW IS NOT MADE FOR PRIVATE PLEASURE, BUT FOR THE PUBLIC GOOD

Today, many love to say that if people are indulging in what they want to do, "and as long as they are not hurting anyone and doing it in the privacy of their own homes," then they are completely fine with it, no matter how evil or deviant. This is especially true when it comes to any debate over homosexuality, or disordered beliefs. They hold that no law should be

---

230 Augustine, Contra Adimantum Manichaei disipulum 17, in Aquinas, *Summa Theologiae*, Ia IIae, 91, article 5
231 Peter Lombard, Sententiae 3:41:1 (PL 192:838), in Aquinas, *Summa Theologiae*, Ia IIae, 91, article 5
232 Bellarmine, *On Laymen or Secular People*, ch. 10, ed. Tutino, pp. 38–39
233 Augustine, Retractationes, 1.9, in Bellarmine, *On Laymen or Secular People*, ch. 11, ed. Tutino, p. 44
234 Chrysostom, *Eight Sermons on the Book of Genesis*, sermon 7, p. 117

made against the acts, even though they are a danger to society, because they consider it a private pleasure.

Many claiming Christians will express their support for the sodomites, and they many times will bring up the "love of Christ" to vindicate their support for them. Let us remind such people that nowhere in Scripture is evil tolerated simply because it does not physically or directly harm someone, or because it is private. In fact, Christianity is so much against allowing private deviancy, that it says that those who "approve of those who practice them" are "worthy of death" (Romans 1:32). This means that opinions expressed in favor for homosexuality and other deviancies (such as cannibalism), are worthy of capital punishment. This purely illustrates that Christianity is so much against the license to do evil—even if it is done in private—that it prohibits any approval of it. For those who disapprove, let them read the words of St. Isidore where he said that law "is composed of no private advantage, but for the common benefit of the citizens."[235] Let them read St. Thomas where he says that "Law must therefore attend especially to the ordering of things toward blessedness."[236]

Does homosexuality bring blessedness, does the tolerance of such a deviant act bring any blessed fruition to a people? Does it honor the sacrament of marriage from which children, "a blessing and a gift from the Lord" (Psalm 127:3), come to this world? St. Thomas also says that "every law is directed to the common good."[237] What good has ever come from the act of homosexuality? No offspring, no sacrament, nothing. St. Thomas also says that the natural affections between man and woman "is directed to a common good: namely, to the preservation of nature in the species or in the individual."[238] And later this same Doctor of the Church affirms that "sexual intercourse between men is especially said to be a vice against nature."[239]

And so the natural affections are to be upheld, protected, and honored by the state, and anything that comes against it, let it be uprooted and cut off like cancer, for such is against the common good. Let the woman who "exchanged the natural use for what is against nature" and the man who left "the natural use of the woman," (Romans 1:26–27) "be put to death." (Leviticus 20:13)

Homosexuality needs to be treated as sedition against the people. What is a people? A people, as St. Augustine defines one, is not to mean "any indiscriminate multitude, but an assembly of those united by agreement as to what is right and by a common interest." Therefore, sedition is not just against the government itself, but against the collective and common morals and precepts by which a community is united. As St. Thomas says,

---

235 Isidore, Etymologiae, 5.21, in Aquinas, *Summa Theologiae*, Ia IIae 90, article 2
236 Aquinas, *Summa Theologiae*, Ia IIae 90, article 2
237 Aquinas, *Summa Theologiae*, Ia IIae 90, article 2
238 Aquinas, *Summa Theologiae*, Ia IIae, 92, article 6
239 Aquinas, *Summa Theologiae*, Ia IIae 94, article 3

"sedition is opposed to justice and the common good."[240] Since homosexuality is against the sacrament of marriage, which is the building block of society, then it is against the common good, and the very Faith of our civilization, and thus is an enemy to the Christian people and should be treated as sedition. Let the heretics who believe in such license read where St. Paul refers to these sodomites as "deserving of death," and also those who "approve of those who practice them" (Romans 1:32), and let them dare say that homosexuality should be allowed in a Christian society. The first principle of law is that good must be rewarded and strived for, and evil punished,[241] and this is why we say with St. Peter that rulers are sent by God "for the punishment of evildoers and for the praise of those who do good." (1 Peter 2:14) It is the job of the ruler to cut off those who are a danger to the spiritual and moral health of the community,[242] and to help bring that community to good behavior. How can good behavior be expected when the state allows the people to believe and practice whatever demonic ideology they want to follow? Anarchy only leads to more anarchy; rebellion to more rebellion. So only violence, disorder and perversion can come out as a result of absolute freedom of religion. This is why we need laws against cults and other insidious organizations, and most certainly they must apply to the sodomites, the godless and all of the promoters of perversion. Vitoria, who stands amongst the most learned of theologians and one of the fathers of international law, said:

> Princes have enacted laws concerning moral goodness, such as prohibiting blasphemy, sodomy, and so on; laws must concern moral actions, or these would be invalid.[243]

To those who object to intolerance against homosexuality, or any grave evil, we repeat the words of Solomon, "He who justifies the wicked, and he who condemns the just, both of them alike are an abomination to the Lord." (Proverbs 17:15)

The inculcation of the homosexual ideology is due to the weakness of churches. In ancient Israel, when low class priests reigned, sodomites were also given leeway to conduct their evils and further degenerate society. For after Jeroboam made "of the lowest of the people priests of the high places" (13:33), "there were also sodomites in the land: and they did according to all the abominations of the nations which the Lord cast out before the children of Israel." (14:24)

This is why the sodomites must be rooted out, for such is what God commands, and failure to do so leads only to spiritual, and then ultimately, to societal anarchy. This command was obeyed by Asa who, doing right for God, rooted out the sodomites:

> And Asa did that which was right in the eyes of the Lord, as did David his father. And he took away the sodomites out of the land, and removed all the idols that his fathers had made. (1 Kings 15:11–12)

---

240 Aquinas, *Summa Theologiae*, IIa IIae 64, article 2
241 Aquinas, *Summa Theologiae*, Ia IIae, 94, article 2
242 See Aquinas, *Summa Theologiae*, IIa IIae 64, article 3
243 Vitora, *On Law*, ST I–II. 92, article 1, 122b

The societal anarchy that comes from toleration toward homosexuality is illustrated by the modern advocates of "consensual cannibalism," or the diabolical idea that says that cannibalism is permissible as long as the one getting eaten is being eaten willfully. For all of the advocates for this heathen practice are atheists, occultists, and promoters of homosexuality. In other words, if a society can accept the demonic actions of the sodomites under the pretense of "privacy" and "individual freedom," then it can just as easily permit the consumption of human flesh under the guise of "privacy" and "individual freedom." But the uprooting of the homosexuals will only happen once the Church is restored to its rightful place.

HOMOSEXUALS CANNOT BE CONSIDERED AS PART OF CIVILIZED SOCIETY

God's law should be the only acceptable system for society, because it is the only system that promotes the natural order by which a healthy civilization flourishes. Christianity teaches that marriage must be between man and woman, and anything contrary to this must be uprooted because it is a hindrance to the natural order.

Since a part (and the order of a part) stands in relation to the whole, then the order of marriage stands in relationship to the rest of civilization. Marriage's end is orderly and fruitful reproduction of humankind, without which there is no civilization. With this said, homosexuals (or sodomites) cannot be considered as a part of civilized life, because their activity is not in relation to the whole of civilization, but a willful declaration of war against it, a willful hindrance to the order that perpetuates civilization, a contumacious attempt to destroy the very means by which humankind exists. Since what is good for the part is good for the whole of civilization, sodomites cannot be esteemed as part of it, for they are not beneficial to the part nor the whole. If everyone were a sodomite, we would cease to be a civilization, but a mere aggregate that leads to a transient existence that ends in the inevitable death of itself. Men die, but because of procreation, civilization lives on. Therefore, homosexuals cannot be a part of civilization.

HOW TO DETERMINE WHETHER OR NOT A CERTAIN ACTION IS DANGEROUS

There are those who argue that homosexuality is not harmful. But, before making such a rash conclusion, we must first observe the process by which an action is determined to be dangerous or not. The way we determine if something is harmful or evil is to consider the result of it being commonly accepted or participated in by everybody. Once we make this observation, then we can determine whether an act is worthy of toleration or punishment. A dangerous act committed by even one person must be punished so as to prevent the crime from being collectively acceptable. As Vitoria articulates:

> We must instead consider what would happen if it were done commonly, by all or by many. For instance, if the export of money outside the kingdom is prohibited, then anyone who smuggles out money commits a mortal crime, because although a single infringement is

of little damage to the commonwealth, if it were to become general the kingdom would be wasted away; therefore the law obliges all on pain of death. Similarly, one case of fornication does little harm, but general fornication would do great damage, and therefore this too is a mortal crime on every occasion. [244]

The reason why homosexuality, and even infanticide, have become so dangerously common, is because we have refused to see it as a crime. "A little homosexuality here, and some abortions there, or some drug usage, will not hurt you." This is what the moderns say, and this sophist way of talking has efficiently deceived many (and we can thank the obsession with free speech for that). Notice how people frequently say that such and such a perversion is not done by everyone. They use the minority participation in a crime to somehow make the warning against it benign. A small step is a great fall, and a little leaven spoils the whole batch; if we allow such wickedness to be done in incriminates, then they will soon be done in great numbers. Crush the eggs of the baby serpents before they hatch. As Augustine once said:

> When we take away from someone the freedom to do wrong, it is beneficial for him that he should be vanquished, for nothing is more unfortunate than the happiness of sinners, when impunity nourishes guilt and an evil will arise like an enemy within. [245]

EVIL SHOULD NEVER BE GIVEN FREEDOM

All people wish to have the liberty to follow their religions, but what do these religions entail? The liberty to observe violent rituals, to spread sedition, and to corrupt the Church? To what end will this religious equality result in? It always results in the death of liberty and triumph of despotism. That is why there is no concept of religious liberty in both Holy Scripture and Church tradition.

People will object, and say that there should be no coercion in religion. But, within Christianity, the Faith can never be left freely nor rejected freely. One chooses the Faith freely, but if he leaves it, even if he is not punished by the state, he will be punished by God in the end eventually. And if someone outright rejects the Faith, even in a secular state, he too will ultimately be punished by God, regardless.[246] Therefore, while the idea of "freedom" may be maintained by a secular state, it will never be accepted in the Kingdom of God. Notwithstanding, the idea of coercing those who have left the Faith to return to the Church was upheld in Christendom, for within Orthodoxy, evil is to never be given freedom. As Augustine once wrote:

> When, then, should the Church not compel her lost sons to return if the lost sons have compelled others to be lost? Is it no part of the shepherd's care when he has found those sheep, also, which have not been rudely snatched away, but have been gently coaxed and led

---

[244] Vitoria, *On Civil Power*, question 3, article 2
[245] Augustine, letter 138:2, in Aquinas, *Summa Theologiae* IIa IIae 40, article 1
[246] See Bellarmine, *On Laymen or Secular People*, ch. 22, ed. Tutino, p. 119

astray from the flock, and have begun to be claimed by others, to call them back to the Lord's sheepfold, by threats or pain of blows if they try to resist?[247]

In the same writing Augustine writes, concerning the Donatist heretics—a suicide cult—that they are to be compelled back into the Church, just as Christ used the injury of blindness against Paul to compel him into the Church:

> As the Donatists cannot prove that what they are forced to is evil, they claim that they ought not to be forced into good. But we have shown that Paul was forced by Christ; therefore, the Church imitates her Lord in forcing them, although in her early days she did not expect to have to compel anyone to in order to fulfill the prophetic utterance.[248]

Augustine also supported the death penalty for the heretical Donatists, writing that if they were killed it would be just: "They kill the souls and are afflicted in the bodies, they cause eternal death and complain of suffering temporal death."[249] Though Augustine did say that the Church wishes no heretic to perish[250] he did affirm that at times evildoers must die if the only solution for peace is their deaths, and he used the death of Absalom as an example, since David did not want his son to die, but his death was, at that point, the only means to having sufficient peace:

> Who of us would wish them [the Donatists] to lose anything, much less that they be lost themselves? If the house of David could win peace in no other way than through the death of Absalom, David's son, in the war which he was carrying on against his father—although the latter had instructed his followers with great care to keep him safe and sound as far as it was possible for them to do so, that he might repent and receive pardon from his father's love—what was left for him but to weep over his son's loss, and find comfort for his grief in the peace granted for his kingdom?[251]

While man has free will, he should not be free to do evil, but punished for his crimes, as St. Augustine says, "Free will has been given to man, but if man has done evil, he should suffer punishment."[252]

But the heretics will interject, and say freedom of conscious, which is a fancy way of saying, "freedom to do whatever we want," must be upheld. The freedom of human will is upheld as a god in the society of these heretics; they are obsessed with "freedom," and all what this leads to is a fixation on the freedom to make others miserable. The wills of wicked people must never be made equal to the wills of the righteous, for the latter lives in true liberty, and cannot bend the knee to the former who is a slave, and who will only enslave others. If

---

247 Augustine, letter 185, ch. 23
248 Augustine, letter 185, ch. 23
249 Augustine, Contra epistolam Parmeniani, book 1, ch. 7, in Bellarmine, *On Laymen or Secular People*, ch. 21, ed. Tutino, p. 106
250 See Aquinas, *Summa Theologiae*, IIa IIae 10, article 8
251 Augustine, letter 185, ch. 32. See also Bellarmine, *On Laymen or Secular People*, ch. 21, ed. Tutino, pp. 106–107
252 Augustine, Contra Gaudentium, book 1, ch. 19, in Bellarmine, *On Laymen or Secular People*, ch. 22, ed. Tutino, p. 119

we allow society to be dictated by the capricious will of the masses, then we will have given power to chaos. They will say that this is "unloving," but in fact it is the most loving thing you can do for the reprobates, for the punishment they endure is tremendously less severe than the distorted state they are in. As we read from St. Augustine:

> But we also have to do many things, even against the will of people who need to be punished with a certain kind harshness, for we have to consider their benefit rather than their will. [253]

God liberated his people from the oppressions of Egypt, but did He then say, "Now go out, live and let live, do what you want with your liberty as long you aren't hurting anyone; go out and observe your individual desires"? No, God through the legislation of Moses, established certain laws which preserved the liberty of Israel by restraining the very ideologies which brought tyranny to the ancient Middle East. They came to liberty, but made sure that it was preserved by restraining ideas and beliefs that are enemies to liberty.

If all peoples became Christian, would that be beneficial? Of course, it would lead to self-governance under the divine law placed in our hearts, and in the common peace of man. Now, let us change the situation. If all peoples became Mormon, would that be beneficial? Any look into the history of the Latter-Day Saints tells us that if the Mormon religion—with all of its violence, depravity, occultism, and the like—were to ever triumph, society would decay and be plunged into polygamy, the human sacrificial ritual of blood atonement, and a cruel tyranny under concupiscent men. Christianity, on the other hand, neutralized these very practices and pacified the entire cult on account of the intolerance of numerous American people. Mormonism—regardless of the politeness of its followers—is not beneficial unto itself, while Christianity is.

The conferring to the people the absolute freedom to choose their rights and politicians, and their government, leads the state to fully becoming indifferent to the will and precepts of God, and dependent on the whims of the masses. Nonetheless, if it is allowed that the people plunge themselves into depravity, and become an occult, paganist, and heretical society, then the triumph of evil would be unstoppable. This is why the Church must be there; to keep in check the propagation of wicked doctrines. The failure to do so will lead, and has led, to an inevitable victory to tyranny.

There are three options that we must choose, what we decide determines one's inner conviction in fighting this great war with evil. Should evil never be tolerated? Should evil sometimes be tolerated? Or, should evil, sometimes, not be tolerated?

There are only three choices, and if one is a Christian, one must then choose the first of the three. If evil is to never be tolerated, then false religions—which are all inherently evil, being inventions of the devil—must never be permitted to exist and propagate.

---

[253] Augustine, Letter 138.14, trans. Roland Teske

RELIGIOUS EQUALITY AND LIBERTY ARE UNNATURAL

Is there not built within man a natural urge to find God? Yes. But which god? They are not all the same; thus absolute liberty can only be applied to the one objective God. The natural right to worship can be observed within the realm of venerating the true God Who created the natural order in which exists the desire to seek and to find Him. In other words, to worship the Creator is in accordance with the natural order, and thus to worship any other god is contrary to the natural order—therefore, error has no right.[254]

For any Christian to deny this would be to implicitly affirm that the identity of the true God is subjective, and left to the judgments of the wavering opinions of man, and that error has rights.

Freedom cannot be an end unto itself; it is what we do with, and how we protect, that freedom that matters. Liberty is the freedom to make a willing decision, but the object of this liberation must be righteous. The propagation of false religion is an indication of freedom, just as a disease is a proof that the body is functioning; that the immune system is working enough to send signals that it is fighting an illness. But this does not mean that we tolerate the disease, and merely complain about its symptoms, we must sever off the malady, just as we must drive away evil religion.[255]

St. Augustine, while rejecting the method of forced conversions, believed that the state had an obligation to prohibit and punish heresy as a measure to prevent the wicked ideas of heretical cults from coming into practice:

> No one is indeed to be compelled to embrace the faith against his will; but by the severity, or one might rather say, by the mercy of God, it is common for treachery to be chastised by the scourge of tribulation for no one can do well unless he has deliberately chosen, and unless he has loved what is in free will; but the fear of punishment keeps the evil desire from escaping beyond the bounds of thought. [256]

JEWS ARE NEVER TO BE PERSECUTED IN THE CHRISTIAN STATE

Those who disagree with us will say that because we want heresy suppressed, that we will want to automatically persecute Jews. This is far from the truth, because while the Jews do live in error, they are of an exceptional position. St. Paul said, "What have I to do to judge them that are without?" (1 Corinthians 5:12) In other words, it does not pertain to the Church to punish those for being in the faith that they are born into, since they were never Christian to begin with, and never broke the oath of baptism.[257] As St. Robert explains the difference between the Jews and actual heretics who wish to destroy the Faith:

> I reply, first, that the Jews never accepted the Christian faith, while the heretics did. Second, the Jews worship the religion that God established, even though temporarily,

---
254 See Lefebvre, *Religious Liberty Questioned*, part 2, pp. 45–46
255 See Lefebvre, *Religious Liberty Questioned*, part 1, pp. 5–6
256 Augustine, in Edward Peters, *Heresy and Authority in Medieval Europe*, ch. i, intro to Compelle Intrare, p. 43
257 See Aquinas, *Summa Theologiae*, IIa IIae 12, article 2

while heretics worship a religion invented by the Devil. Third, the Judaic sect is useful for the Church, for their books are prophecies of our matters, and their ceremonies prefigure our rituals: from this we prove to the pagans that we did not invent these prophecies, since they are preserved by our enemies. Finally, the Jews do not try to corrupt the Christians, in general, as heretics do. [258]

St. Thomas Aquinas had this same belief in regards to the care and protection of the Jews:

> There are some unbelievers who have never received the faith, such as the heathens and the Jews. These are in no way to be compelled into the faith, so that they may believe; for belief in an act of will. [259]

And in another place he says: "Those Jews who have not in any way received the faith, ought not to be coerced into the faith."[260] St. Gregory believed in giving the Jews absolute freedom to observe their religion, writing in one dissertation: "They should have license to observe and celebrate all their festivals, just as they and their forefathers have observed them for long ages gone by."[261] In another place Gregory wrote: "those who sincerely desire to lead those outside the Christian religion to perfect faith should be careful to use blandishments, not cruelty."[262]

Gratian, in his canon De Iudaeis, wrote: "Concerning the Jews, the holy Council laid down that no one should use force to compel belief, since God is merciful to those He wishes, and hardens the hearts of those He wishes."[263]

Most importantly it can never go unmentioned that when the Jews suffered the greatest persecution of their history—the Holocaust—it was Pope Pius XII who rescued more Jews than any other individual in history, saving over eight hundred thousand from the murderous hands of the Nazis. Yes, there have been anti-Jewish statements made throughout Christian history, but when push came to shove, and Jews were actually being killed, it was Christendom who came to their aid more than anything else. Countless Christian soldiers fought and died, and oceans of Christian blood were spilt, to save the Jews and give them the State of Israel.

IN DEFENSE OF WITCH BURNING

There is a verse in Scripture which is avoided by today's Christians and forevermore cited by the haters of the Bible, it is Exodus 22:18: "Thou shalt not suffer a witch to live."[264] The remark has no commas or semicolons, it ends with a period and gives no other explanation,

---

258 Bellarmine, *On Laymen or Secular People*, ch. 22, ed. Tutino, pp. 111–112
259 Aquinas, *Summa Theologiae*, IIa IIae 10, article 8
260 Aquinas, *Summa Theologiae*, IIa IIae 10, article 8
261 Gregory, Dist. 45m c. 3: Qui sincere (CIC 1:160), in Aquinas, *Summa Theologiae* IIa IIae 10, article 11
262 Gregory, Qui sincere (Decretum D.45. 3), in Vitoria, *On the American Indians*, question 2, article 5, 39
263 Gratian, De Iudaeis (Decretum D.45. 5), in Vitoria, *On the American Indians*, question 2, article 5, 39
264 Exodus 22:18

CHRISTIANITY IS AT WAR: THE MANIFESTO FOR CHRISTIAN MILITANCY

no vacillation, no pre-qualification, and no apology. It does not say, "Thou shalt not suffer a witch to live, unless she or he is nice," or "Thou shalt not suffer a witch to live, unless she or he worships one god and loves everybody," but "Thou shalt not suffer a witch to live." It is so emphatic in its tone, so foreign and incompatible to the modern ways of thinking, that the contemporary pastor never mentions it, and when reading the Old Testament he merely skips it; he does not vindicate nor defend it. It is not that they don't have the courage to defend it, but because they don't have the soul to do defend it. They do not want Christianity to appear as intolerant, they want to make it as a nonjudgmental movement that gives the appearance of tolerance for all. All of this leads to one thing: the swaying of the church from its true purpose: the destruction of the works of the Devil.

I have seen so many books on grace, but not one book nor chapter giving a detailed defense for this verse. It is almost as if they want to present the Bible as a book with just freedom, and no restrictions. It is like writing a law that contains only liberties and no punishments. This verse, and all of the other anti-idolatry laws of the Bible are neglected by the modern church because it would sound too over the top, and give "negative connotations" (a term so popular today)—in other words, it would be too zealous. They ignore the Old Testament so much that they might as well rip it out, and then take the New Testament, omit all of the judgmental verses from there and make a new and very marketable book called "The Nice Bible," in which only the verses that people find to uplift them and give them better self-esteem will be shown. It would be perfect for marketing, because it would only have the popular verses, isolated from the rest of Scripture and completely disconnected from its initial meanings. It would just quote "God is love" and "I can do all things through Christ," but it would never have "Thou shalt not suffer a witch to live." If I type in an online book database, the words grace, "God is love," and "I can do all things," I find a numberless amount of publications done by famous pastors. But, when I type in "Thou shalt not suffer a witch to live," I get only either leftist books condemning the Church, books written by old theologians who are all dead and whose works no one wants to read and whose subjects nobody today cares about, or Christian books who chastise the old zealots for burning witches. Simply put, the Left is advancing over society, many present day Christians care only about the Bible when it's marketed for modern minds, and that the contemporary church chooses to ignore the true purpose of Christianity: fighting evil.

I have seen so many books and lectures from Christians professing to be "Defending the Faith," but I have found none which defends that verse of Moses' second book, "Thou shalt not suffer a witch live." If we are truly going to be defenders of the Faith, then we cannot ignore this one verse, even though it has lost all popularity. Because of this neglect, I will defend this verse regardless of the fact that it does not tickle the ears of the majority, and hopefully by my commentary I will reveal and show—in the words of Eusebius—"what is passed over in silence."[265]

The theologians and ministers of old had no problem in agreeing with and defending Exodus 22:18, which is why there is such a distinct different between today's Bible teachers and those of olden times. You shall know a pastor by his library. Every time I meet a new pastor I always ask him, "What is your favorite Bible commentator?" They usually tell me numerous names, and then I always respond with, "What do you think of Matthew Henry?" Henry was a seventeenth century reverend who wrote a voluminous commentary, and the usual reply I receive to this question is, "No, he is too long," "preachy," or "I he wish he wrote less, I just want a simple answer." In other words, he is too zealous. To these people, the Bible is not a detailed book, and it is definitely not about fighting evil, but one that is supposed to make them "feel comfortable," as though Scripture was made for fickle mobs. Let us compare Matthew Henry to some of the current popular commentaries on their explanation on Exodus 22:18, the one outlawing witches. Chuck Smith almost skims right through it, only writing in regards to the verse, "Now we get a lot of little rules here again with capital punishment,"[266] as if the outlawing of witchcraft is just a "little rule." Because many Christians today see this verse as "a little rule," witchcraft is now running rampant throughout the nation, and Islam has infiltrated the church now more than ever.

Now, this is how Matthew Henry exposits Exodus 22:18:

> Witchcraft not only gives that honour to the devil which is due to God alone, but bids defiance to the divine Providence, wages war with God's government, and puts his work into the devil's hand, expecting him to do good and evil, and so making indeed the god of this world; justly therefore was it punished with death, especially among a people that were blessed with a divine revelation, and cared for by divine Providence above any people under the sun. By our [English] law, consulting covenanting with, invocating, or employing, any evil spirit, to any intent whatsoever, and exercising any enchanting, charm, or sorcery, whereby hurt shall be done to any person whatsoever, is made felony, without benefit of clergy; also pretending to tell where goods lost or stolen may be found, or the like, is an iniquity punishable by the judge, and the second offence with death. The justice of our law herein is supported by the law of God recorded here.[267]

In ancient Christendom priests in parishes throughout Europe preached with all fervency and prudence against witchcraft so that, in the words of the tenth century cleric Regino of Prum, "they may know this to be in every way false and such phantasms are imposed on the minds of infidels and not by divine but by the malignant spirit."[268]

---

[265] Eusebius, *The Proof of the Gospel*, 1, intro. trans. W.J. Ferrar
[266] Smith, Chuck. "Exodus 21–22." The Word for Today. Blue Letter Bible. 1 Jun 2005. 2013. 25 Feb 2013.
[267] Henry, Commentary on the Whole Bible, on Exodus 22:18
[268] Regino of Prum, Canon Episcopi, in Alan Charles Kors and Edward Peters, *Witchcraft in Europe*, part 2, p. 62

Witchcraft was a very real occurrence in old Europe just as it is today. The only difference between now and then was that it was not tolerated, not by the society, nor the Church nor the government. Intolerance toward witchcraft was done from the Church's earliest times.

In the time of Emperor Constantine the Great, there were laws which described occultists as "enemies of the human race," who were worthy of death.[269]

Caesarius of Arles, writing at around the year 530, says that "No one should summon charmers, for if a man does this evil he immediately loses the sacrament of baptism, becoming at once impious and pagan."[270]

At around the year 800 there was a Church synod held in the area of Freising and Salzburg which also believed in conducting investigations and punishments on those who were involved in wizardry:

> Concerning incantations, auguries, and divination, and of those things done by people who conjure up tempests and commit other similar crimes, it is pleasing to the holy council that, wherever they may be found, the archpriest of the diocese shall examine what they do and constrain them by the most careful examination and make them confess to their evils. But he should subject them to moderation in punishment so that they do not lose their lives, but should be confined in prison for their own salvation, until by the inspiration of God they spontaneously mend the ways of sinners.[271]

In the sixteenth century a woman in Spain was put into prison for some time, made to recluse in a monastery, and suffered one hundred lashes and confiscation of goods, after confessing that she "made an explicit pact" with Satan, and "separated herself from God."[272]

In the year 1080 Pope St. Gregory VII wrote a letter to King Haakon of Denmark exhorting him to utterly abolish and outlaw all sorceries and witchcraft from his kingdom:

> We therefore direct you by apostolic authority to abolish this pestilent practice absolutely from your kingdom and no longer presume to inflict such disgrace upon priests and clerics, who deserve honor and reverence, by ascribing to them the hidden causes of divine judgments.[273]

While the beautiful translation of the Scriptures by King James is gradually being forgotten, we have also neglected his edict against witchcraft, done in 1604. It decrees that anyone who is involved in witchcraft or in taking

---

[269] Desiderius Erasmus, A Terrible Case of Sorcery in Orleans, in Alan Charles Kors and Edward Peters, *Witchcraft in Europe*, part 6, p. 235
[270] Caesarius of Arles, An Admonition to those who not only pay attention to omens, but, what is worse, consult seers, soothsayers, and fortune tellers in the manner of pagans, in Alan Charles Kors and Edward Peters, *Witchcraft in Europe*, part 1, p. 52
[271] In Alan Charles Kors and Edward Peters, *Witchcraft in Europe*, part 1, p. 54
[272] Sentence of Catalina Munoz for False Sanctity, 1588, in Homza, *The Spanish Inquisition*, document 25, p. 255
[273] Gregory VII, book 7, 21, p. 497

any dead man woman or child out of his [or] her or their grave or any other place where the dead body resteth, or the skin, bone or any other part of any dead person, to be employed or used in any manner of witchcraft, sorcery, charm or enchantment; or shall use practice or exercise any witchcraft sorcery, charm or enchantment whereby any person shall be killed[,] destroyed[,] wasted[,] consumed[,] pined[,] or lamed in his or her body, or any part thereof; then that every such offender or offenders[,] their aiders[,] abettors and counsellors, being of the said offenses duly and lawfully convicted and attainted, shall suffer pains of death as a felon or felons, and shall loose the privilege and benefit of clergy and sanctuary.[274]

This decree shows that even in those days they had deviant people. The only difference between then and now is that in those days such reprobates were put to death and not tolerated as "insane" and needing of "treatment." St. Thomas Aquinas, the Doctor of the Church, affirmed Exodus 22:13 when he wrote in support of witch burning, writing: "It is said at Exodus 22:18, 'Thou shalt not suffer a witch to live,' and at Psalm 101:8: 'I will early destroy all the wicked of the land.'"[275]

In 1523, Gianfrancesco Pico della Mirandola based his affirming of capital punishment for witchcraft on Mosaic Law:

> In Deuteronomy [18:10–12] we read that sorcerers and enchanters are to be killed, in Leviticus [20:6] diviners and soothsayers; and the law commands that those who use the prophetic spirit are to be stoned.[276]

This "prophetic spirit" is quite frequently seen today, with so many people claiming to be "prophets" and "prophetesses." Such persons are committing witchcraft when they, on a whim, all of a sudden claim to be seers. Under the Law of God such insidious people are to be stoned to death, but this terrifies the moderns and the trendy Christians of our superficial society, but what they do not know is that when Christ Himself returns, all those who claim to be "prophets" will be obligated to be killed by their own parents, as we read in Zechariah:

> It shall come to pass that if anyone still prophesies, then his father and mother who begot him will say to him, 'You shall not live, because you have spoken lies in the name of the Lord.' And his father and mother who begot him shall thrust him through when he prophesies. (Zechariah 13:3)

The New Testament never made null and void the Law, but He will return to restore the Law that we have so rejected.

---

[274] *Witchcraft Act of 1604* - 1 Jas. I, c. 12, brackets mine. I also edited the English for the sake of convenience
[275] Aquinas, *Summa Theologiae*, IIa IIae 64, article 2
[276] Gianfrancesco Pico della Mirandola, Strix, in Alan Charles Kors and Edward Peters, *Witchcraft in Europe*, part 5, p. 244

In a panel meeting conducted in 1526, the Spanish inquisitor Valdes affirmed that crosses should be posted on any areas where witches previously observed their dark rituals to consort with the Devil.[277]

The modern laughs at all of these laws. His mind is so limited to today's prejudices that he, with his open mind, never takes the chance to find that witchcraft is real, and is dangerous. This is where the crooks of the matter comes into realization. The reason why the Bible deems witchery as worthy of capital punishment is not because it wants its followers to have some sort of power, but because it desires so much to prevent the tyranny which comes as a result of witchcraft. When Israel was under the despotism of the Phoenician queen Jezebel, Joram asked Israel's future liberator, Jehu, "Is it peace, Jehu?" to which the warrior responded, "What peace, so long as the whoredoms of thy mother Jezebel and her witchcrafts are so many?" (II Kings 9:22) Tyranny, then, will reign over a nation if its leaders practice sorcery, since it is of the Devil, and anything which exalts that murderer will only bring death and cruelty. This same spirit of violence possessed the man who confronted Paul in Ephesus, as Luke describes:

> And the man in whom the evil spirit was leaped on them, and overcame them, and prevailed against them, so that they fled out of that house naked and wounded. (Acts 19:16)

The ancient Christians understood that violence springs from occultism, and thus it was amongst the reasons why they attacked it so much. The medieval theologian Hugh of St. Victor confirmed this when he wrote that witchcraft and demonism "fosters corruption of morals, and impels the minds of its devotees to every wicked and criminal indulgence."[278]

Thomas Aquinas concurred to this when he affirmed that occultism is "often employed in order to further adultery, theft, murder, and like malefices, wherefore those who practice these arts are called malefics. Now those who practice these arts are often men of evil life. [W]e read of innocent children being slain by those who practice them [dark arts]."[279]

Isidore of Seville wrote of men who threw blood on dead bodies, "for," he says, "they say demons love blood, and therefore as often as necromancy is practiced blood is mixed with water, that they may be more easily attracted owing to the color of blood."[280]

In the year 1233 Pope Gregory IX wrote in a letter that within the occult world "men engage in depravity with men." That is, the devil worshippers were homosexuals, as is the case today. He further described that these same occultist took the Eucharist and threw "it

---

[277] Deliberations on the Reality and Heresy on Witchcraft, 1526, in Homza, *The Spanish Inquisition*, document 13, p. 163
[278] Hugh of St. Victor, The Didascalicon, 6.15, in Alan Charles Kors and Edward Peters, *Witchcraft in Europe*, part 2, p. 69
[279] Thomas Aquinas, Summa contra gentiles, part 2, ch. 104–6, in Alan Charles Kors and Edward Peters, *Witchcraft in Europe*, part 3, p. 91. Ellipses and brackets mine
[280] Isidore of Seville, Etymologies, 8.9, in Alan Charles Kors and Edward Peters, *Witchcraft in Europe*, part 1, p. 52

into the latrine in contempt of the savior. These wretches also believe in him [Lucifer] and affirm that he is the creator of heaven, and will return there in his glory when the Lord has fallen."[281]

Hugh of St. Victor also wrote that divination "is achieved through the sacrifice of human blood, for which the demons thirst in which they delight when it is spilled."[282] And what we find, when analyzing the actions of occultist, is that this is most accurate.

When the Spanish inquisitor, Luis Coronel, in a panel meeting, was asked on what should be done to witches who committed ritual murders, he declared most sternly: "They must be completely destroyed. And for the killings of infants, etc. [sic], with damages, a secular judge may punish them with a suitable penalty."

Gerbald, the bishop of Liege, wrote a law at the urging of Charlemagne in which there is the mention of witches committing abortions in occult rituals:

> Women should be inquired about who give out potions to other women in order to kill a fetus and who perform divinations so that their husbands may have more love for them. [283]

The law of the emperor Charlemagne made mention of how witches cannibalized people, and declared such evil worthy of death:

> If any one deceived by the devil shall have believed, after the manner of the pagans, that any man or woman is a witch and eats men, and on this account shall have burned the person, or shall have given the person's flesh to others to eat, or shall have eaten it himself, let him be punished by a capital sentence. [284]

John of Salisbury made the observation that infants "appear to be cut up into pieces, eaten, and gluttonously stuffed into the witches' stomachs."[285]

In those days, you had the same sort of evil and depraved people as you do now, committing the same sort of grotesque and sadistic crimes. The only difference between now and then is that they killed them, while we tolerate them. You may argue that in our days we still execute individuals for killing and cannibalizing people. However, in our modern world, people who just cannibalize human beings, without killing them (for example, people who eat other humans who are already dead), are not necessarily executed, but given a lighter punishment. This is because the cannibal, in this case, did not commit murder, and the modern perspective teaches that as long as the person did not hurt or murder a human being, he is not to be given a harsh punishment. In our own times, the person is punished only after the damage is already done, whereas in Christendom, they prevented the evil from

---

281 Pope Gregory IX, Vox in Rama, in Alan Charles Kors and Edward Peters, *Witchcraft in Europe*, part 3, p. 116, brackets mine
282 Hugh of St. Victor, The Didascalicon, 6.15, in Alan Charles Kors and Edward Peters, *Witchcraft in Europe*, part 2, p. 69
283 In Alan Charles Kors and Edward Peters, *Witchcraft in Europe*, part 1, p. 54
284 In Boretius, n. 26, p. 68, in D.C. Munro, Selections from the *Laws of Charles the Great*, p. 2
285 John of Salisbury, *Policraticus*, In Alan Charles Kors and Edward Peters, *Witchcraft in Europe*, part 2, p. 78

happening by punishing the cause of the evil: devil worship. This is called preventative societal maintenance.

The Franciscan preacher, Bernardino of Siena, spoke in 1427 of a women who confessed, without any torture, "that she had killed thirty children by sucking their blood; she also said that she had let sixty go free. She said that every time she let one of them go free, she had to sacrifice a limb to the devil, and she used to offer the limb of an animal. Yet she confessed more, saying that she had killed her own little son, and had made a powder of him, which she gave people to eat in these practices of hers."[286]

What is a society to do in order to maintain civil peace, if such wretches are out and about? Of course the Christian lands had the prudence to outlaw occultism, and punish those who practiced it in order to prevent violence. The woman who Bernardino spoke of was burnt at the stake, and this punishment—rightfully so—was esteemed as an act of love, because it protected children and other potential victims of these devilish reprobates. "Whether within the city or outside its walls," continues Bernardino, "accuse her—every witch, every wizard, every sorcerer or sorceress, or worker of charms and spells. Do what I tell you in order that you not be called upon to answer for it on the Day of Judgment, having been able to prevent so great an evil which might have been prevented if you had accused her. If it had happened that she killed one of your little children, what would you think about the matter then? From your own feeling take thought for another."[287]

A certain judge of the fifteenth century, named Peter, reported on how in a very short time thirteen infants were cannibalized by witches. In an interrogation, a witch explained to Peter a ritual which her and her sect would conduct, in which cannibalism and witchcraft go hand in hand:

> We then remove them [the infants] secretly from their graves and cook them in a cauldron until the flesh, cooked and separated from the bones, is made into a powerful liquid. From the solids of this material we make a certain unguent that is useful for our desires, arts, and transfigurations. From the liquids we fill a container, and from this, with a few additional ceremonies, anyone who drinks immediately becomes a member of our sect.

An inquisitor of the same period recounted on how witches in Lausanne would devour children, and then they would see demonic visitations after which they would deny Christianity, vow that they would never adore the Eucharist, and trample under their feet a crucifix.[288]

---

[286] Bernardino de Siena Preaches Against Women Sorcerers, in In Alan Charles Kors and Edward Peters, *Witchcraft in Europe*, part 4, p. 136
[287] Bernardino de Siena Preaches Against Women Sorcerers, in Alan Charles Kors and Edward Peters, *Witchcraft in Europe*, part 4, pp. 136–7
[288] Johannes Nider, The Formicarius, in Alan Charles Kors and Edward Peters, *Witchcraft in Europe*, part 5, p. 157

A witch named Johanna Vacanda confessed that she had eaten the son of her daughter alongside another witch; she was burnt at the stake.[289]

A young girl in fifteenth century Germany informed an inquisitor that her aunt was a part of a witch cult, and that one day her aunt beat her after she opened a pot "and found the heads of a great many children."[290]

Wizardry leads people into all kinds of violent and bizarre rituals. Nicolau Eymeric, who believed in legislation against witchcraft, wrote in 1376 of how wizards "observe chastity out of reverence for the demon or abstain upon his instructions or they lacerate their own flesh."[291] Burchard of Worms, writing in the eleventh century, described an occult ritual in which people would dance around the corpses of Christians and sing songs in praise of Satan. He also wrote of another dark rite in which the occultist would take a dead infant, place its body in a secret place, and transfix it with a stake; and they believed that if they didn't do this the deceased baby would arise and assault others.[292]

Pope Eugenius IV, in 1437, made an informing letter on how occultists sacrificed to devils, hung crosses upside down, made written pacts with the devil, in which they would give their souls to him.[293] People today do these same sort of demonic rituals, and they learn it from the sorceries of the Middle Ages. And as they were burned at the stake in the old days, so should they be executed in our own times in order to prevent them from murdering and sacrificing children, and other evil practices.

Claude Tholosan, a senior judge of the area of Brianconnais, wrote in 1436 of a cult who, in a ritual, "turn their naked asses to heaven, in order to show their scorn for God, drawing a cross on the ground, spitting on it and treading it underfoot, as it is said, in contempt of God, whom they call the Prophet. They kiss him [the devil] on the mouth, giving him their bodies and souls and one of their children, usually the firstborn, whom they immolate and sacrifice."[294]

In Gianfrancesco Pico della Mirandola's sixteenth century dialogue on witchcraft, a witch gives the terrifying illustration as to how they would slaughter children for the sake of the devil:

> We entered the houses of our enemies by night, and when the parents were sleeping we stole the infants, carrying them to the fire where we pierced them with a needle, and putting our

---

289 The Errores Gazariorum, in Alan Charles Kors and Edward Peters, *Witchcraft in Europe*, part 5, p. 162
290 Kramer and Sprenger, Malleus Maleficarum, in Alan Charles Kors and Edward Peters, *Witchcraft in Europe*, part 5, p. 162
291 Eymeric, The Directorium inquisitorum, in Alan Charles Kors and Edward Peters, *Witchcraft in Europe*, part 4, p. 123
292 Burchard of Worms, The Corrector, sive Medicus, 91, 180, in Alan Charles Kors and Edward Peters, *Witchcraft in Europe*, part 5, p. 191
293 Pope Eugenius IV, A Letter to All Inquisitors of Heretical Depravity, in Alan Charles Kors and Edward Peters, *Witchcraft in Europe*, part 4, p. 154
294 Claude Tholosan, Ut magnum et maleficiorum errores, in Alan Charles Kors and Edward Peters, *Witchcraft in Europe*, part 5, p. 164

lips to the wounds, filled our mouths with their blood, and we put the bodies into a container so that we could make an ointment with which to anoint ourselves. [295]

It is no wonder as to why the occult was once outlawed. It was not just for the sake of punishing the crime, but abolishing that which leads to the crime, and that is human sacrifice, cannibalism and other demonic rites. Jean Bodin, in 1580, wrote concerning the punishment for witchcraft that "those people greatly delude themselves who think that the penalties are only established to punish the crime." He gives a myriad of benefits from punishing witchcraft, some of which are "to reduce the number of the wicked so that the good can live in security to punish the wicked." He then describes the bloody rituals of human sacrifice which the witches were involved in.[296]

In St. Matthew's Gospel, there is the possessed man who, before being exorcised by Christ, throws himself into the fire, and tries to drown himself in water:

> And when they were come to the multitude, there came to him a certain man, kneeling down to him, and saying, Lord, have mercy on my son: for he is a lunatic, and sore vexed: for oft times he falleth into the fire, and oft into the water. (Matthew 17:15)

How did this person get possessed but by interacting with the diabolical? If witchcraft was prevented, all of the suicides that we hear of being done for some demonic idea, would be prevented.

Wizards and occultists will only be tyrants to the Church. For example, the Jewish wizard Elymas tried to prevent St. Paul from preaching to the deputy of Paphos, Sergius Paulus:

> But Elymas the sorcerer (for so is his name by interpretation) withstood them, seeking to turn away the deputy from the faith. (Acts 13:8)

This is the destructive behavior of wizards, yet with the modern mentality we continue to call them "mentally insane," or mentally deranged, when in reality they are plunged into evil. The psychologists wish to attribute this violence to some particular lunacy, but all they do is distract us from the wiles of the devil, and enable the violence of the possessed.

And for those who may question, or even mock the realities of possession, are the words of Professor Emilio Servadio, an internationally renowned psychiatrist:

> I believe that every scientist who is aware of his responsibilities knows that his tools go so far and no farther. When it comes to demonic possession I can speak only for myself and not on behalf of science. I have seen some instances where the evil and the destruction caused by certain phenomena present characteristics that truly cannot be mistaken for those encouraged by a scientist such as a parapsychologist or a psychiatrist—for instance, when we deal with poltergeists or similar activities. It would be like trying to compare a

---

[295] Gianfrancesco Pico della Mirandola, Strix, in Alan Charles Kors and Edward Peters, *Witchcraft in Europe*, part 5, p. 243

[296] Jean Bodin, On the punishment That Witches Merit, in Alan Charles Kors and Edward Peters, *Witchcraft in Europe*, part 5, pp. 291, 293

mischievous boy with a sadistic criminal. There is a difference that cannot be measured with tools but that can be felt. In these situations I believe that a man of science must admit the presence of powers that cannot be ruled by science and that science cannot be called to define.[297]

Moses said to execute those who have a "familiar spirit," but at the same time there was exorcism conducted in Israel, since Christ tells a certain group of Jews, "by whom do your sons cast them [the demons] out?"[298] meaning, that there were exorcists, and that the concept of exorcism was there. But, this does not mean that we should tolerate witchcraft. Those who are demon possessed should be exorcised and brought to Christianity. But those who are wicked and evil, filled with maliciousness against God and partaking in witchcraft, if they cannot be reformed, must be punished with death.

---

[297] Servadio in Gabriele Amorth, *An Exorcist Tells His Story*, Targets of the Evil One, pp. 62–63, trans. Nicoletta V. MacKenzie.
[298] Luke 10:19, brackets mine

PART 10 – THE CHRISTIAN SPIRIT AND WAR

"This world is an army, an eternal battle."—Joseph de Maistre

THE WARRIOR NATURE OF GOD

All of Christian militancy can be summarized into one commandment of our Lord: "seek first the kingdom of God and His righteousness" (Matthew 6:33). It places the flesh into the servitude of the Spirit, and instills into our hearts that the Kingdom of God and His Law are the priority and purpose of our lives. As the wise Solomon beautifully tells us: "Fear God, and keep his commandments: for this is the whole duty of man." (Ecclesiastes 12:13) Because God is our sole duty, we deny ourselves for the divine purpose, and take upon ourselves the Cross; because the Kingdom of Heaven takes precedence over our own lives, then we are obligated to fight for the holy cause of the Lord, even at the expense of our own lives. When the devils tried to take Heaven and overthrow God, the angels fought for it, because they sought first the Kingdom of God. God made man "a little lower than the angels," (Psalm 8:5) on account of his flesh, and so what keeps us from the obligation of the angels, to combat for the Kingdom of God as they did? Angels are the messengers of God who fought and defeated the devil and his demons, emulating the warring nature of God—Who was the ultimate victor. And so we mortals, who are "ambassadors for Christ" (2 Corinthians 5:20), and being a little less than angels, imitate God, and in so doing, emulate His justice and wrath. The first step to Christian militancy is to comprehend that God is the God of war, and that we, His children, emulate this very militant nature and war against the emulators of Satan. St. James said,

> Show me your faith without your works, and I will show you my faith by my works. You believe that there is one God. You do well. Even the demons believe and tremble! (James 2:18–19)

You may say that you believe in God, in the Crucifixion, in the Trinity, but the devils themselves know that these things are real and true. So what separates us from the demons? Our actions. The angels know that God is real, that He is the Holy Trinity, they believe in the Crucifixion, in the Resurrection, and so what separates the angels from the devils, since they both have the same knowledge? What separates the angels from the demons, is that angels obey, and moreover, the angels were loyal to God and fought for Him and His Kingdom in the war over Heaven. That the angels fought against evil, against the devils and Satan, showed that they had love for God and His laws. Human beings, then, have two choices: they can either emulate the angels, and fight for God, or emulate the devils, and rebel against God and end up in the everlasting abyss. To emulate the angels makes one a son of God, and to emulate the demons makes one a son of Belial.

The warrior nature of God against tyrants, and His stance in support of the oppressed, is found in the Song of Mary, when she proclaims: "He hath shewed strength with his arm; he hath scattered the proud in the imagination of their hearts. He hath put down the mighty from their seats, and exalted them of low degree." (Luke 1:51–52)

In accordance to Mary's Canticle, the Song of Moses declares God as a warrior who defeats with His mighty arm the heathens of Canaan, Moab and Edom:

> The Lord is a man of war: the Lord is his name. ...Then the dukes of Edom shall be amazed; the mighty men of Moab, trembling shall take hold upon them; all the inhabitants of Canaan shall melt away. Fear and dread shall fall upon them; by the greatness of thine arm they shall be as still as a stone; till thy people pass over, O Lord, till the people pass over, which thou hast purchased. (Exodus 15:3, 15–16, ellipses mine)

In the Song of Judith it says that "The Lord is a warrior who ends war." (Judith 16:3) Because God is our Eternal Warrior, and we are to be His emulators, then we are to be warriors, not ones who war for the sake of war, but to end war and establish peace over the evildoers.

Even in the Temple of God, there were "spears and shields" (2 Kings 11:10), illustrating the warrior nature of God. God is a warrior who fights with a strong arm, for David says to the Lord, "You have broken Rahab in pieces, as one who is slain; You have scattered Your enemies with Your mighty arm." (Psalm 89:10)And in the same verse he says, "You have a mighty arm; Strong is Your hand, and high is Your right hand." (Psalm 89:13) And in another passage King David declares,

> Oh, sing to the Lord a new song! For He has done marvelous things; His right hand and His holy arm have gained Him the victory. (Psalm 98:1)

The Spirit of God is a warrior, for as David tells God

> Arise, O Lord; Save me, O my God! For You have struck all my enemies on the cheekbone; You have broken the teeth of the ungodly. (Psalm 3:6)

CHRISTIANITY IS AT WAR: THE MANIFESTO FOR CHRISTIAN MILITANCY

The warring Spirit of God came upon David when he fought his enemies, and the same Holy Spirit was with Samson when he "found a fresh jawbone of a donkey, reached out his hand and took it, and killed a thousand men with it." (Judges 15:15)

St. Paul said: "be imitators of God as dear children." (Ephesians 5:1) When the Christians truly imitate God, they emulate not only His mercy, but His justice and His wrath against evil, for as St. John says: "as He is, so are we in this world." (1 John 4:17) When Moses slaughtered the pagans, he emulated God; when Josiah demolished the houses of the sodomites, he emulated God; when Elijah butchered the prophets of Baal, he emulated God; when Ehud thrusted his sword into the corpulent belly of Eglon, he emulated God; when Jael hammered the nail into the head of Sisera, she emulated God; when Joshua slew the Canaanites, even women and children, he emulated God; when Jehu slaughtered the house of Ahab, and the priests of Baal, he emulated God. To slay the wicked, is to emulate God. When you look at a man, what you are seeing is Heaven and earth intertwined. "And the Lord God formed man of the dust of the ground, and breathed into his nostrils the breath of life; and man became a living being." (Genesis 2:7) In man there is heaven and there is earth, and so within him lies a divine nature that enables him to be like the Holy Trinity. The Son, the second person of the Blessed Trinity, battled alongside Joshua in the conquest of Jericho, and He destroyed Sodom and Gomorrah; and so we, emulating Christ, fight and war against the forces of darkness. St. Paul said: "in Him we live and move and have our being" (Acts 17:28), and so when the Christian soldier wars with the forces of darkness, he lives and acts in the Crucified Master. Christ surpassed all human will to sacrifice Himself for the eternal life of humanity; and so we, being His warriors, emulate Christ by charging into the battlefield of sacred combat and laying down our lives for the glory of His Church. As St. Bernard wrote:

> We are said to love, so is God: we are said to know, so is God: and much to the same purpose. But God loves like Charity, knows like Truth, sits in Judgment like Equity, rules like Majesty, governs like Authority, guards like Safety, works like Virtue, reveals like Light, stands by us like Affection. All these things the Angels also do, and so do we, but in a far inferior way, not, of course, by our native goodness, but by the goodness whereof we partake.[1]

TRUE LOVE IS WARFARE

No one is a slave to God. All of the false religions say that we must rigidly follow their gods out of cold obedience. But in the True Faith, all actions emanate from love. A husband is not a slave to his wife, and when he defends her, he does not do so out of a rigid obedience, but out of love. Such love demands a husband to commit violence and even die for his wife by laying his life to repel an intruder. Therefore, true love is warfare. It is the same in the relationship between the Church and God, with Christian fighting for God out of pure love. Even when the knight of Christ fights for the Holy Path, he does so because he burns with love. He follows with all ardency the first commandment of the Divine Law, "Thou shalt love the Lord

---

1 Bernard, *On Consideration*, 5.5

thy God with all thy heart, and with all thy soul, and with all thy mind." (Matthew 22:37) The Christian knight fights for the purpose of love, in emulation of his Father in Heaven, Who is only angry out of the zeal of love. St. Paulinus wrote: "So great is the love of our highest Father that even His anger springs from mercy, and He punishes to spare."[2]

It is the divine wrath that the Christian warrior imitates, for he has God within Him, and God works through His soldier, stirring in his spirit the desire to bring righteous judgement. When one imitates God in His justice and mercy, he becomes closer to the divine union, of which Christ said:

> If a man love me, he will keep my words: and my Father will love him, and we will come unto him, and make our abode with him. (John 14:23)

This was affirmed by St. Maximus of Turin in a sermon he preached, declaring: "whoever wants to be very near to God must imitate what God is."[3] When the knights of Christ war against evil people, they fight for justice and defend those inflicted by injustice, and they imitate the justice and mercy of God. Ramon Llull wrote: "O what great strength of courage resides in the knight who vanquishes and overcomes many malfeasant knights!"[4] This courage and strength are the hot flames that arise from the spark of zeal which emanates from a love of God and a thirst to be like Him, punishing the wicked and helping the oppressed.

St. Gerald of Aurillac, one of the greatest of the warrior saints in Christianity, decided to use his knightly strength and authority, not to tyrannize, but to help those who were without defense, the fatherless and the prey of the wicked. St. Odo, his biographer, described this passion as such:

> Committing himself entirely to the will of God and the divine mercy, he sought only how he might visit the fatherless and widows and hold himself unspotted from this world, according to the precept of the Apostle. [James 1:27] He therefore exerted himself to repress the insolence of the violent, taking care in the first place to promise peace and most easy reconciliation to his enemies. And he did this by taking care, that either he should overcome evil by good, of his enemies would not come to terms, he should have in God's eyes the greater right on his side. And sometimes indeed he soothed them and reduced them to peace. When insatiable malice poured scorn on peaceful men, showing severity of heart, he broke the teeth of the wicked, that, according to the saying of Job, he might snatch the prey from their jaws.[5]

Notice that there was a balance in St. Gerald's desire to commit to chivalry, between justice and mercy. He always gave his enemies a chance to come to peace, just as Moses gave the worshippers of the golden calf a chance to come back to God. But, when these very enemies became malicious, he imposed upon them needful retribution, just as when the apostates refused to return to the Law and Moses had them killed. Christ said "Love your enemies,"

---

2 Paulinus, letter 29, 8
3 Maximus of Turin, sermon 81.3
4 Ramon Llull, Chivalry, 2.15
5 Odo of Cluny, *The Life of St. Gerald of Aurillac*, 1.7–8

(Matthew 5:44) but so many take this without any balance. At times to love your enemy is to show mercy unto him; but in loving ones enemy we cannot deprive his victims of love. We so many times want to focus on loving the enemy, while we ignore the torment of those he abuses and tyrannizes. So, then, to punish the wicked is to fulfill the Law of Love, because it shows love to the innocent who are assaulted by the enemy.

Knightly action is so absorbed in love that even the strike of the Crusader's sword is done through love. The flame of this love is ignited by the love of God. The Apostle said, "the purpose of the commandment is love" (1 Timothy 1:5), and thus the law of God directs all men to acts of love, and this consists of slaying evildoers, Christ declares, "because lawlessness will abound, the love of many will grow cold." (Matthew 24:12) It is because of the Divine Law that there is love, but because so many today have cast away the Law, hearts have become cold, and evil assails the multitude. This is why the Law is necessary, for it guides people to love, and directs them away from callousness; it prevents violence, by uprooting the wicked theologies of heretics and the religions of pagans that cause violence and indifference to human suffering. All of the Law, be it in the execution of sodomites, murderers, heathens and heretics, and the haters of God, is imposed through the Law of Love.

The Law is noble and righteous, and is done well only through the lawful, and not the abusive. What causes the Law to be imposed with justice, and not abuse and tyranny? The answer is love, and only love, "for God is love" (1 John 4:8), and because man is made in God's image, and those who live in a state of grace are "partakers of the divine nature" (2 Peter 1:4), righteous men, then, can become partakers in God's justice, administering His wrath against evil. It is love that stirs the knight to pity, compelling him to sacrifice himself for the defense of his brethren. When a knight named Payns heard of how Christians were constantly being killed by Muslims in Jerusalem, he "took pity on them," and, "Moved by a strong feeling of justice, he defended them to the best of his ability, often lying in ambush himself and then coming to their aid, killing several of the enemy."[6]

The will to fight for God is sparked by one thing, and one thing alone: love. It is the love of the angels, and it is the love that stirs us to fight against evil and the forces of darkness. This love brings about our zeal for God, in our coming to realization of Him and His glory. When one becomes unified with God (to use the words of St. Gregory Palamas)

> He knows this from the impassible joy akin to the vision which he experiences, from the peace which fills his mind, and the fire of love for God which burns in him.

In this state of love for God, the body becomes a tool by which this love illustrates zeal for the divine laws of Heaven, and for the victory over evil. For, in the words of St. Gregory Palamas,

> Our soul is a unique reality, yet possessing multiple powers. It uses as an instrument the body, which by nature co-exists with it.

---

6 Walter Map, De nugis curialium, in Barber and Bate, The Templars, ch. 1, 3

The body becomes a weapon to combat the wiles of the devil. Our whole beings become a weapon to prove our love for God, by fighting against the devil, and all of the darkness that he has inundated the earth with.

This is why Christ said,

> You shall love the Lord your God with all your heart, with all your soul, with all your mind, and with all your strength. This is the first commandment. (Mark 12:30)

It is the first commandment, because it is the Law of Love. It is with love that we sacrifice our entire beings for the cause of God; it is with love that we war against the darkness that brings men to maliciousness, to heresies, to callousness, to violence and to the love of oppression.

And it is with love, that the warriors of the Church strike the enemies of God as Joshua struck the heathens of Jericho, as Gideon vanquished the Midianites, as Samson crushed the Philistines, as Jehu slew the priests of Baal, and Judas Maccabeus killed the Jews who plunged themselves into the abysmal depths of pagans and sodomites. It was with love that the holy king, Hezekiah, amongst the greatest warriors for the path of Light and for the peace of humanity, shattered the idols and slew the wizards, took the lives of the pagan priests and destroyed the houses of the sodomites who "are deserving of death" (Romans 1:32).

With his zeal and his piety, his gallantry and with the fiery love that burned within his bosom, the glorious Josiah "turned to the Lord with all his heart, with all his soul, and with all his might, according to all the Law of Moses; nor after him did any arise like him." (2 Kings 23:25)

When he slew the wicked, he followed the First Commandment that Christ exhorted us to follow, as well as the Second Commandment, loving his neighbor by destroying the evildoers who oppressed the helpless, "that no man might make his son or his daughter to pass through the fire to Moloch" (2 Kings 23:10). He followed the path of faith in all perfection, observing the First and Second Commandments, for "On these two commandments hang all the Law and the Prophets." (Matthew 22:39)

When justice is decreed, and righteousness established, and the king says with David, "in the name of the Lord I will destroy them" (Psalm 118:10), and "Early I will destroy all the wicked of the land" (101:8), the righteous ruler who unsheathes the sword of the law, does so under the Law of Love. There are many theologians and pastors today that complicate the Gospel, saying that Christ got rid of all the laws and replaced them with two laws: love God and love your neighbor. But what they will never bring in is Romans 13:9, where Paul says that all of the laws are not replaced but summarized by one law: love your neighbor as yourself:

> For Thou shalt not commit adultery: Thou shalt not kill: Thou shalt not steal, Thou shalt not bear false witness: Thou shalt not covet: and if there be any other commandment, it is comprised in this word, Thou shalt love thy neighbour as thyself. (Romans 13:9)

All of the Law, be it in uprooting the sodomites, Islam, feminism and atheism, or in punishing any sort of wickedness, is done so for love of one's neighbor. To give license to the homosexual agenda, or to jihadism, or to abortion, or the destruction of Christian institutions (such as marriage and the honor given to human life), or to mockery of Christianity, or to deviancy, is anarchy, and shows an utter callousness to one's neighbor.

When the valorous Hezekiah destroyed the idols and extirpated the pagan priesthood from the Holy Land, he did so "that no man might make his son or his daughter to pass through the fire to Moloch" (2 Kings 23:10); but today, we allow the pagan priesthood to reign, murdering babies before they get to even see the beauties of God's creation, or breath the air outside the wombs of their mothers. Today, people are more comfortable with blasphemy than they are with holiness; piety is mocked; blasphemy is seen as courage; to boastfully say that you are homosexual is esteemed as heroic and it is no wonder that St. Paul calls the homosexuals, "proud, boasters," (Romans 1:30); Hindus and Buddhists are revered as exemplars of peace; and Muslims who slaughter Christians receive funding from the most powerful of nations.

Truly what the world needs now is not superficial love, but true love. The world needs the love that strikes the wicked and the cruel; we need the love that instills fear into the evildoers "that we may lead a quiet and peaceable life in all godliness and reverence." (1 Timothy 2:2–4)

We need the love that infuses the zeal within the pious warrior that "shall wash his feet in the blood of the wicked" (Psalm 58:10); we need the love that declares: "So strike, that you heal; slay, that you may give life, by the example of him who said, I will kill and I will give life; I will strike and I will heal." We need love that has such strong affections for humanity, that it will slay all the cruel and demon possessed people who wish harm to precious human kind; we need love that does not compromise with superficial hypocrisy, but that enters into battle to fulfill its righteous aspirations; we need love that sacrifices itself for the victory over the sinister; we need that love in which one gives his life in defense for his neighbor; we need love that burns with the jealously of God; we need love that is as Christ, fighting against the devil to obliterate his works, so that the light of truth may dispel the ocean of darkness that the spirits of the inferno have clouded mankind with.

TO FIGHT EVIL IS TO PARTICIPATE IN GOD

When the king destroys evil, he is being like God, and participates in God Who alone can be called good. St. Gregory of Nyssa wrote: "Certainly whoever pursues true virtue participates in nothing other than God, because he is himself absolute virtue."[7] The Scripture says, "Be imitators of God as dear children." (Ephesians 5:1) Through the holy Solomon did God declare, "By me kings reign, and princes decree justice." (Proverbs 8:15) And so when a righteous king decrees that homosexuals, the killers of Christians and the promoters of death, be punished and executed, he is both being used by God as a means toward His justice, and is participating in God, in Christ, for "in Him we live and move and have our being" (Acts

---

7   Gregory of Nyssa, *Life of Moses*, 1.6

17:28). St. Gregory of Nazianzus declared that it is Christ Who gives the sword to the state, and Christ Who rules with the ruler, as he said in one homily, addressing temporal rulers,

> You rule with Christ and you govern with Christ; it is from him that you receive your sword, not to use, but to brandish. [8]

When the righteous ruler slays homosexuals, it is Christ Who commands him; when he extirpates heretical and evil cults, it is Christ Who commands him; when he wars against an aggressive and pagan nation, it is Christ Who commands him. Why then is it so wrong to have a Christian state? For truly it was by God that Christendom reined, and all of its just edicts came from the Almighty. There is no evil in forming Christendom again, and when it does revive, it will be by the will of Heaven.

How then does a ruler imitate God except by punishing the wicked and rewarding the just? For as St. Thomas tells us, "the magnitude of the king's virtue appears from the great likeness which it bears to that of God, since he does in his kingdom what God does in the world."[9] The holy David tells princes: "Deliver the poor and needy; free them from the hand of the wicked." (Psalm 82:4) How then does the king fulfill this except by punishing the tyrants and freeing his victims? And who would not argue that to do such a noble deed would be to love one's neighbor and imitate God, "a warrior who ends war" (Judith 16:3)? St. Odo of Cluny, one of the great monastic fathers of the Western Church, wrote of the knight of Christ as such:

> It would be more holy and honest that he should recognize the right of armed force, that he should unsheathe the sword against enemies, that he should restrain the boldness of the violent; it would be better that the bold should be suppressed by force of arms than that the undefended districts should be unjustly oppressed by them. [10]

To strike and slay the wicked for the defense of the helpless, is love. St. John said, "God is love, and he who abides in love abides in God, and God in him." (1 John 4:16) God destroyed Sodom, He ordered the massacre of pagans and heathens, the killing of sodomites, and all such actions were the highest expressions of love. And those who fulfilled such commands of holy war and just punishment, had God abiding in them. When Phinehas slew those who worshipped Midianite gods, the Lord said that "he was zealous with My zeal among them," and that "he was zealous for his God" (Numbers 25:11–13). Phinehas was with God, and unified with Him, for God worked through him to strike down the wicked. For this reason, Phinehas abided in God Who is love, and when he struck, he illustrated love. How then do we obtain this unity and divine union with God? By keeping His commandments. For the glorious Son of God said:

> If a man love me, he will keep my words: and my Father will love him, and we will come unto him, and make our abode with him. (John 14:23)

---

8   St. Gregory of Nazianzus, Oration 17, 9
9   Aquinas, *De regimine principum*, 1.8
10 St. Odo, Life of St. Gerald od Aurillac, 1.7, trans. Dom Gerard Sitwell

CHRISTIANITY IS AT WAR: THE MANIFESTO FOR CHRISTIAN MILITANCY

This is theosis, this is the truest enlightenment, where man is unified by God and is used by Him as a means to a glorious end. The highest state of love is indicated by obedience to Gods commandments, His Law. And so when a nation dedicates itself to Christ, they will unite themselves with God, and in their obedience, and their zealous exertion and effort and holiness, they will fight and combat the evils amongst them.

To uproot Islam, the sodomites, and every group and organization that wars against Christianity and the Divine Law, is to follow the Law of Love, and is ultimately the most beautiful expression of love for God and for neighbor, on which "hang all the law and the prophets. (Luke 16;14)

It is love for neighbor because it protects him from harm, both spiritually and physically; it is love for God, for there is only one God and there is no other, and to say that all religions and ideas must be given equal opportunity, is to ask God to step down and to no longer be supreme.

To slay the wicked and insidious foes of Heaven is to say with holy Solomon, "A wise king scattereth the wicked." (Proverbs 20:26)[11] To do so, is love, for it advances peace over bloody chaos. Augustine says, "the soldiers owe it to peace and common safety to execute military orders."[12] St. Augustine also affirms that war must always be done to conform people into peace, declaring,

> For peace is not sought in order that war might be undertaken, but a war is undertaken so that peace might be acquired. Therefore you should be peaceful even when fighting, so that by winning the war you may bring those whom you conquer into the unity of peace. [13]

It is for peace—not false superficial peace, but true peace—that Christian armies fight, and at times the obtaining of peace is only done through bloodshed. St. Paul himself tells us that the punishment of sodomites, murderers, kidnappers, and other evil people through the law, is done for the purpose of love:

> Now the purpose of the commandment is love from a pure heart, from a good conscience, and from sincere faith, from which some, having strayed, have turned aside to idle talk, desiring to be teachers of the law, understanding neither what they say nor the things which they affirm. But we know that the law is good if one uses it lawfully, knowing this: that the law is not made for a righteous person, but for the lawless and insubordinate, for the ungodly and for sinners, for the unholy and profane, for murderers of fathers and murderers of mothers, for manslayers, for fornicators, for sodomites, for kidnappers, for liars, for perjurers, and if there is any other thing that is contrary to sound doctrine, according to the glorious gospel of the blessed God which was committed to my trust. (1 Timothy 1:5–11)

---

11 See Aquinas, *De regimine principum*, 1.7
12 Augustine, Against Faustus, 22.75, quoted by Bellarmine, *On Laymen or Secular People*, ch. 15, ed. Tutino, p. 68
13 Augustine, Against Faustus, 22.74, quoted in St. Robert Bellarmine, *On Laymen or Secular People*, ch. 15, ed. Tutino, p. 70

These words are prophetic for the conditions of today, where so many self-appointed teachers want to make themselves an authority on Christian law, casting aside justice, and abusing the mercy of God to transform it into anarchy. It is far more loving to fight for the cause of the Church, then to allow it to be under the tyranny of the raging heathen, and do nothing to bring the heathen into the Light of God. As St. Gregory VII wrote:

> But still we hold it to be far nobler to fight on for a long time for the freedom of Holy Church than to sink into a miserable and devilish servitude. For the wretched fight as the limbs of the Devil, and are crushed down into miserable slavery to him. The members of Christ, on the other hand, fight to bring back those same wretches into Christian freedom. [14]

St. Robert even said that to desire the death of the enemy must be done out of love for justice and humanity:

> But wishing death on one's enemy and even accomplishing it is not evil according to the order of justice, if it is done not because of hatred toward men, but because of love of justice and the common good. [15]

The Law is for the lawless, for those who are slaves of the devil, and not servants of God. St. Chrysostom says that the Law is not for the one who "has the grace of the Spirit within to direct him."[16] Moreover he says that "the Law is still necessary for the confirmation of the Gospel, yet to those who obey it is unnecessary."[17] In one sermon this same father said,

> The laws, in fact, are rulers for rulers, but the person living a simple life has no need even of laws; hear what Paul says on this, 'a law is not there for the righteous.' [18]

Sodomites and murderers, and other evildoers, do not obey God's Law, and thus neither do they have the Holy Spirit, so do such need the Law to curb their wickedness. Christ did not abolish the Law, but fulfilled it; nor did He deprive kings of their power to impose the righteous and moral laws, but instead, as we learn from St. Robert, he regulated their power, so that it is always executed for the cause of love.[19]

CHRIST'S DEATH WAS A WAR DONE FOR LOVE

Christ said, "For God so loved the world that He gave His only begotten Son, that whoever believes in Him should not perish but have everlasting life." (John 3:16) But how is this love shown except through violence? Through war with the devil? The Divine Love was illustrated by the horrific bloodshed witnessed on the Holy Cross. It was done, not by words, but by warfare, warfare against the diabolical. The Divine Love was witnessed when Christ told the devil, "Away with you, Satan!" in the wilderness (Matthew 4:10) and He compelled the devil

---

14 Gregory VII, book 9, 3, p. 573
15 St. Robert Bellarmine, *On Laymen or Secular People*, ch. 14, ed. Tutino, p. 66
16 St. Chrysostom, Homily 2 on Timothy, on 1 Timothy 1:8–9
17 St. Chrysostom, Homily 2 on Timothy, on 1 Timothy 1:11
18 Chrysostom, *Eight Sermons on the Book of Genesis*, sermon 4, pp. 71–72
19 See Bellarmine, On the Temporal Authority of the Pope, ch. 3, ed. Tutino, p. 164

to flee; it was seen when Christ came to humanity "that He might destroy the works of the devil." (1 John 3:8) The Divine Love was beheld when Christ "had made a whip of cords," and drove them all out of the temple, with the sheep and the oxen, and poured out the changers money and overturned the tables." (John 2:15) Christ so loved humanity that He expressed this love through ferocious violence. Love is not toleration, nor superficial agreement; love is an unsheathed sword, it is war—love is violence. In the words of Chesterton, "sham love ends in compromise and common philosophy; but real love has always ended in bloodshed."[20]

The righteous, through the Law, slay those who live by the sword and who love cruelty; the destruction of the lawless, and the protection of the lawful, which is really the love for neighbor, is the reason for the law, and evinces why the law is love. A king loves his neighbor when he abides by the words of David, "Deliver the poor and needy: rid them out of the hand of the wicked." (Psalm 82:4) As St. Augustine said, "the wars of Moses will not excite surprise or abhorrence, for in wars carried on by divine command, he showed not ferocity but obedience; and God, in giving the command, acted not in cruelty, but in righteous retribution, giving to all what they deserved, and warning those who needed warning. What is the evil in war? Is it the death of some who will soon die in any case, that others may live in peaceful subjection? This is mere cowardly dislike, not any religious feeling. The real evils in war are love of violence, revengeful cruelty, fierce and implacable enmity, wild resistance, and the lust of power, and such like; and it is generally to punish these things, when force is required to inflict the punishment, that, in obedience to God or some lawful authority, good men undertake wars, when they find themselves in such a position as regards the conduct of human affairs, that right conduct requires them to act, or to make others act in this way."[21]

The holy warriors who bring upon the wicked just retribution, object to no other peace than that false peach which Christ "came not to send" upon the earth (Matthew 10:34).

They will establish His holy commandments, and fight against the forces of evil for the glory of God and His Kingdom. They will eschew the world and cling onto God, for "No one engaged in warfare entangles himself with the affairs of this life" (2 Timothy 2:4). This is the wonderful and sublime outcome of the divine union with the Holy Trinity; this is the aspiration of the warrior monk and the faithful knight; this is the goal of the Christian. As St. Gregory Palamas said on the Christian who reaches this divine union with God:

> Thanks to this remembrance, he will come to possess a divine disposition, and cause the soul to progress towards the highest state of all, the love of God. Through this love, he will accomplish the commandments of Him whom he loves, in accord with Scriptures, and will put into practice and acquire a pure and perfect love for his neighbour, something that cannot exist without impassibility. [22]

---

20 Chesterton, Orthodoxy, ch. viii, p. 139
21 Augustine, Against Faustus, 22.74
22 Gregory Palamas, The Triads, 1. ii, 19, trans. Nicholas Gendle

So then, Christians, do not unite with politicians, but unite with God, unite with your Lord and Master, unite with the Warrior Who won victory for you on the Holy Cross! Unite with the Holy One, obey His commandments, and fight the evildoers so that no longer they will be able to corrupt and attack the Christian foundation of your society.

Will there be suffering? Yes. God Himself suffered for our sakes, and so what makes us so special that we cannot say with St. Paul, "I bear in my body the marks of the Lord Jesus" (Galatians 6:17)? There will be suffering, but this will only be obedience to the Apostle said when he said, "You therefore must endure hardship as a good soldier of Jesus Christ." (1 Timothy 2:3)

Let us remember the words of Pope Pius II when he, in 1463, cried out against the Christians who were so careless before the face of the Islamic horde:

> O stony-hearted and thankless Christians, who can hear of all these things, and yet not wish to die for Him Who died for you!

Will there be martyrs? Yes, there will be many martyrs. But let us remember that when the saints are struck, zeal increases. Keep into your hearts what David said:

> It is good for me that I have been afflicted; that I might learn thy statutes. (Psalm 119:21)

Through suffering, we become closer to God, and through martyrdom we obtain divine union with God. When the Jews wanted to kill St. Stephen, he being full of the Holy Spirit, gazed into heaven and saw the glory of God, and Jesus standing at the right hand of God, and said, "Look! I see the heavens opened and the Son of Man standing at the right hand of God!" (Acts 7:55–56)

He saw God, and was united with Him, crying out before his blessed death was completed, "Lord Jesus, receive my spirit." (Acts 7:59) The divine union for those Who suffer and die was promised by our Master when He said, "Blessed are they which are persecuted for righteousness' sake: for theirs is the kingdom of heaven." (Matthew 5:10)

Those who suffer in the spiritual battlefield will see the Kingdom of Heaven, for they abide by what Christ said, "Seek ye first the kingdom of God, and his righteousness" (Matthew 6:33). This commandment is the solution to all the travesties that our civilization is now enduring. If we pursued the Kingdom of Heaven and not callous politicians, tell me, would we have Islamic terrorism? Would we have the murder of unborn infants and the onslaught of the sodomites?

No, for these evildoers would receive the sword before they could even inflict their bloodshed. Because in a society where the Kingdom of Heaven is sought out for first and foremost, any idea that is not of God, but of the Antichrist, would be extirpated before their fanatic followers could gain any sort of license for their wickedness and violence.

So I tell you now, Christians, forsake your tolerance and your indifferentism, and pursue the Light, that you may "shine before men, that they may see your good works and glorify your Father in heaven" (Matthew 5:16), and with its holy illumination, dissipate the darkness so that no more may it try to eclipse the bastions of the Holy Faith.

Let error be destroyed, and let Christian supremacy be established. Let us carry with us the goal of the monastic military Order of Santiago, "to fight under the banner of St. James for the honor of the Church and the propagation of the faith."23

TO KNOW THAT CHRIST LIVES IS WHAT STRENGTHENS THE WARRIORS

We ask ourselves: What is it that fortifies the soul of the holy warrior that allows his eyes to look upon death without trembling; his soul to come to the end of its stay in its mortal home, without being moved to desperation in desire to repose without being ripped away and pulled back to its eternal originator? Is there some way to gain this indomitable spirit? Perhaps a certain rite that brings this undying strength to the pious man? There is indeed a way for the soul to ready itself for its return back to the timeless realms. We find it in the Apostles, but more specifically, we find it in the Apostle Peter. This holy saint saw with fleshy eyes the Christ, and with earthly ears he heard the teachings of the Christ, but even then his soul was not conditioned for death, for he denied Christ three times. Once he saw the Resurrected Christ, it was then that his spirt was emboldened, and his soul invigorated. Here it was in this state that he declared before those who wanted him dead, "We ought to obey God, rather than men" (Acts 5:29); that he proclaimed the words of death upon Saphira, "Behold the feet of them who have buried thy husband are at the door, and they shall carry thee out" (Acts 5:9), and brought "fear upon the whole church, and upon all that heard these things." (Acts 5:11) It was in this state of both spiritual fortitude and physical endurance, where the saint upon whom the Church was built, emulated the Savior and underwent the beatings of tyranny along the ranks of his soldiers when "they had scourged them" (Acts 5:40), and in such moments of the most harrowing tests, did he exemplify the dauntless spirit.

And even though Peter wavered, when he fled upon seeing the Judaizers, his soul was prepared for its everlasting departure, finally leaving the temporal universe for the heavenly cosmos when he suffered crucifixion, ordering his executioners to place the cross upside down since he, with a long-suffering soul that always walked endurably on the path of piety and discipline, saw himself unworthy to die like the man he once denied. As the waters of the roaring rapids at times go through falls, and yet still reaches the strongest and highest mountain, the soul of the saint comes upon moments of weakness, but triumphs and ascends the loftiest and never-ending heavens. And so it was with Peter, who, after denying his Savior, and at one time fleeing the heretics, rejected the entreaties of the heathen, and was martyred on a cross upside down when his soul returned home to reunite with the Holy One, the Greatest of all warriors and the King of kings. Such strength is only obtained through the realization of a certain truth: Christ lives.

---

23   See Michael Walsh, *Warriors of the Lord*

ZEAL IS THE SOURCE OF ALL CHRISTIAN FEROCITY

Zeal is what feeds the fires of the militant spirit, and it is this tenacious spirit that God gives His warriors. "My zeal has consumed me, because my enemies have forgotten Your words." (Psalm 119:139) With the indefatigability of zeal's glimmering light within the hearts of Christendom's combatants "The wicked flee when no one pursues, but the righteous are bold as a lion." (Proverbs 28:1) Zeal is the flame by which the tares and thickets of fear are burned; it is zeal that frees us from the chains of human concern, and brings us into the abode of love, where the concerns of God are endless like the fields of Heaven. Gideon overthrew the altar of Baal, even though there was fear within him. How did he do this? Through zeal. Moses confronted the Pharaoh, although he had trepidation, and how did he do this? The flames of zeal burned whatever pieces of ice lied within his soul. "For our God is a consuming fire." (Hebrews 12:28) We see the invigorating spirit of zeal in the warriors of Israel, especially in Shammah, who defeated a whole hoard of Philistines by himself while he was protecting a lentil field. As the Scripture says:

> The Philistines gathered together at Lehi, where there was a plot of ground full of lentils, and the men fled from the Philistines. But he took his stand in the midst of the plot and defended it and struck down the Philistines, and the Lord worked a great victory. (2 Samuel 23:11–13)

St. Gregory the Great prayed for the Byzantine general Gennadius, that the Lord strengthen his arm to war and fill his soul with zeal to fight the enemies of the Faith:

> Furthermore, bestowing on you, as is due, the affection of our paternal charity, we beseech the Lord to make your arm strong for subduing your enemies and to sharpen your soul with zeal for the faith like the edge of a quivering sword. [24]

In the same letter St. Gregory prayed that God fortify the soul of Gennadius in the Christian empire's holy war to Christianize pagan nations:

> Now, addressing to you the greeting of our paternal charity, we beseech our God and Savior mercifully to protect your Eminence for the consolation of the holy republic, and to fortify you with the strength of His arm for spreading His name more and more through the neighboring nations. [25]

After Jehu annihilated the prophets of Baal, and the whole house of Ahab, he called such swift and brutal action, "my zeal for the Lord," (2 Kings 10:16) and with such a successful extirpation of the pagans, and with such words, one can see how deep the truth of God was harbored in His soul. David wrote, "Because zeal for Your house has consumed me, and the reproaches of those who reproach You have fallen on me." (Psalm 69:9) And this verse was fulfilled by Christ, when he "had made a whip of cords," and "drove them all out of the temple, with the sheep and the oxen, and poured out the changers' money and overturned the tables. And He said to those who sold doves, 'Take these things away! Do not make My

---

[24] St. Gregory the Great, epistle 74
[25] St. Gregory the Great, epistle 74

Father's house a house of merchandise!' Then His disciples remembered that it was written, 'Zeal for Your house has eaten Me up.'" (John 2:15–18) Because the Church is "in Christ Jesus, who became for us wisdom from God" (1 Corinthians 1:30), and "we have the mind of Christ" (1 Corinthians 2:16), and "His divine power has given to us all things that pertain to life and godliness" (2 Peter 1:3) "that through these you may be partakers of the divine nature" (2 Peter 1:4), this same zeal that Christ had, is with His warriors when they, as their Master was armed with a whip when He drove the thieves out, arm themselves with weapons to drive off the thieves of men's lives, and the persecutors of Christian peoples. In the words of St. Bernard, when he passionately wrote of the crusader knights who fought for the Temple of Jerusalem:

> By all these signs the knights clearly show that they, animated by the same zeal for the house of God which of old vehemently inflamed the Leader of knighthood himself, who, having his most sacred hands armed, not with a weapon, but with a whip which he had fashioned from lengths of cord, entered the temple, ousted the merchants, scattered the coins of the money changers, and overturned the chairs of the pigeon vendors, considering it totally unfitting to defile this house of prayer by such traffic. [26]

Pope Innocent III, in a profound discourse, explained the application of Christ driving out the merchants to Holy War by interconnecting it with what Phineas did to the pagans:

> Let negligence sleep, therefore, and let anger be aroused, as in 'Be angry and sin not.' [Ephesians 4:26] That is, be angry at vices lest you sin. This is the zeal which Christ was inflamed when he drove the sellers and buyers from the temple as, 'The zeal of your house has eaten me up.' [John 2:17] [This was the zeal] in which Phineas, enraged, transfixed the Israelite with a lance when he had gone in to the Midianite. In this way the discerning priest exercises severity against rebels and the obstinate, while showing compassion towards the humble and the penitent. [27]

When holy Phineas slaughtered those evildoers and fornicators, God worked through Him as an instrument to execute sacred wrath, stirring within his spirit the zeal of divine love; when he struck, he spilt blood to appease the anger of the Holy One upon Whom he clanged; when he thrusted his spear through the enemy, it was the act of the most fiery love, and the fulfillment of the highest contemplation. It was divine retribution, and in the words of St. Gregory of Nyssa:

> The zealous Phineas, however, did not wait to have sin purged by heavenly decision; he himself became at once judge and jury. Having been moved to wrath against the men who were filled with lust, he did the work of a priest by purging the sin with blood, not the blood of some guiltless animal which had no part in the stain of licentiousness, but the blood of those

---

26 St. Bernard, *In Praise of the New Knighthood*, ch. 5, 9
27 Pope Innocent III, sermon 7: In Synod

who were joined with one another in evil. The spear, by piercing the two bodies conjointly, stayed divine justice, mixing pleasure with the death of those who sinned. 28

And where does this zeal come from but the light of God? Through "thy light shall we see light." (Psalm 36:9) With the eyes of the spirit shall we see the light that scatters away the darkness, or the devils, their false doctrines, and their sinister ideas, and their followers. Through this enlightenment do we receive the will to fight the ranks of the sinister, burn down their banners shaded with the darkness of antichrist, and wipe them off from the memory of mankind. In this verse of the Psalm, David, fully enlightened by the light of God, says, "let not the hand of the wicked remove me." (Psalm 36:9) These are the words of struggle with evil-doers, the same struggle of the Church with her enemies, and the foreseeing of victory through the spiritual fire of God. Thus, through the light of God, the warriors receive truth, and for that truth, do they struggle with the advancers of the devil's lies.

TO FIGHT FOR GOD IS A SACRIFICE TO GOD

The virtue done by the Christian soldiers are sacrifices to God, inspired by the light of righteousness embedded onto our hearts. David said, "Offer the sacrifices of righteousness," (Psalm 4:5) and it is then asked, "Who will show us any good?" as if to question from where does the will to do go good come. David then says, "Lord, lift up the light of Your countenance upon us." (Psalm 4:6) It is the light of the holy precepts within us, "the law written in their hearts," (Romans 2:15) or "the light of natural reason," as St. Thomas interprets it.[29] And it is this internal and natural law, that helps stir the spirit of the warrior to defend the Divine Law of God.

Some people compare Hindu sages with Christian monks. There is no comparison. What is the difference between the two? If a Hindu sage is on a beach meditating, and he sees someone drowning, he will say, "That is his karma," and continue meditating. If a Christian monk is on a beach praying and contemplating, and he sees someone drowning, he will stop what he is doing and go into the water to rescue that person. In Christianity, it is the silence of the mind and the heart—a silence that brings him away from the world and into the voice of God—that stirs him to action. This love is sparked by the eternal light of Love Himself, "of whom are all things, and we in him" (1 Corinthians 8:6) and this love is manifested through action. This action is worship unto itself, and the greatest of all meditations.

The Emperor Constantine wrote of the participating in the Light of God, when intimidating the pagan Persian tyrant Shapur to prevent him from killing Christians. He wrote:

> By keeping the Divine faith, I am made a partaker of the light of truth—guided by the light of truth, I advance in the knowledge of the Divine faith.

The monastic knight, St. Gerald of Aurillac, sought after Heaven when he defended the poor and brought low the wicked with his strength and zeal. Because of this righteousness, as

---

28 Gregory of Nyssa, *Life of Moses*, 2.299–300
29 Aquinas, *Summa Theologiae*, Ia Iae, 91, article 2

we are told by St. Odo, "an inward light illumined him,"[30] that is, the light of God glimmered in his soul as he pursued a life of piety and justice. The noble actions of the Christian soldier in the battlefield, is a sacrifice to God. St. Gregory VII wrote that the gift of soldiery for the protection of the Church may be offered as "a voluntary gift to God."[31] To fight for God is to be a doer of the Word, not just a hearer, who "is like a man observing his natural face in a mirror; for he observes himself, goes away, and immediately forgets what kind of man he was." (James 1:23–24) To do this great action, is to worship God. Action is the highest form of worship. It illustrates the Faith that lies within the heart, and is the purest manifestation of internal convictions; action is without guile; action confronts to us the highest state of belief. Action emanates from every spiritual realization that we have within our very beings, and is the result of contemplation on God and His divine laws. Action is worship in its purest fashion. As St. Thomas Aquinas once wrote, "the highest form of contemplation is that which superabounds in Action." Worship has been so diluted; it has been reduced to mere singing, chaotic dancing and nonsensical and selfish prayers. Truly the greatest form of worship is to live life as a sacrifice before God. As St. Theophan the Recluse wrote in regards to prayer: "The principal thing is to stand before God with the mind in the heart and to go on standing before him unceasingly day and night until the end of life." There is no love without sacrifice. All love is sacrifice. To sing and to dance is not sacrifice, but to give your entire self to God, is love, and thus it is sacrifice. It is then quite true to say, that the greatest way to worship is to sacrifice yourself, for "to live is Christ, and to die is gain." (Philippians 1:21)

SAINTS AND WAR

The one whose allegiance belongs to God, walks not through the meadows of ease and comfort; nor under the pleasant sky of sapphire hue, and the shade of clouds as white as milk to provide him shelter from the cruel heat of the sun's flames; nor does his feet touch the soft soils that are as richly dark as the tresses of longed for maidens, or sense the caresses of grass which emanate like the enchanting glow of emerald; nor do his ears pleasure in the words of flattery or sycophants, for he is hated by the world, or he puts no trust in it; nor is his eye given the liberty to be tranced by the lofty towers of Babylon, which bring one's being to that same state when the mind is lost in dreams, to be captivated by her entrancing gardens, or gripped by the gratifying delight of being lost in the fields of idle wanderings and endless vagrancies.

The saint treads upon the parched earth, not of rest in the midst of a fluid and cool breeze, or in the repose of the day's end when sins are covered by the shade of the night, but of despair, forever plunged in the one thing for which existence came forth from destined creation: war between good and evil. Never does the saint recede or start again, he walks the bitter path of the moribund life, empty of all comprehension as to how long he will remain within the bounds of time—neither thinking nor contemplating on the concern—or as to when it shall soon soar into timelessness through a martyr's death under the blades of devil

---

30 Odo of Cluny, *Life of St. Gerald of Aurillac*, 2.2
31 Gregory VII, book 9, 4, p. 577

ridden heathens. The saint is surrounded by a wilderness that to the eye seems to never end, under a scorched and hazy sky, and as far as wounded ambition can gaze, the vacuity of hope abounds in everlasting fields of lifeless trees, under a blinding sun that semblances the dismal sands of abandoned shores, and seas whose waves of waters have been pillaged by the waves of the merciless sun. He is forever encompassed by beasts whose growls and harrowing roars resound through the dismal land that he must cross, and he is forever armed with the sword, ready to slay them to save even a single sheep of the hunted flock. As he stands guard, ceaselessly watching, and incessantly waiting, the snarls of the enemy strikes a fear that seeps into the beating heart of the one who strives forward, in whose being the battle between flesh and spirit continues on, never letting it end with lethargic defeat, but always endeavoring to finish victoriously, after so many labors. Despite so much toil, his soul ascends above the heights of his own sorrows, he walks on the bitter path of sainthood, physically far away from Heaven and so close to the rapacious eyes of insatiable devils, he looks up to the aurora above, and not yet obtaining fully the Beatific Vision, his soul is content with hope.[32]

The saint indulges not in the modish passions of the mob, but endures the Passion of the Holy One, Whose life we suffer to emulate as we walk in this valley of anguish.

The saint suffers as Christ suffered, and he fights as Christ fought; he walks the path of heavenly strife, always vigilant, and always bearing the cross that vanquishes the spite of mortal nature, and cuts asunder, as a shining blade, the malicious spirits that lure man away from the Ark that saves us from the floods of perdition. The saint advances across the rugged wilderness of holy struggle, not to see the lax meadows of Babylon, but to be under the meridian of Jerusalem, to grasp the sublime Law of Eternal Justice, to arm his soul with it, and to dissipate the forces of darkness with its ineffable effulgence. By this, does he bond himself with Heavenly Mount Zion, to be a citizen of Eternal Jerusalem, the city of the Holy Trinity, the city where sits the Son, to Whom the Father proclaims:

> I shall give thee the heathen for thine inheritance, and the uttermost parts of the earth for thy possession. Thou shalt break them with a rod of iron; thou shalt dash them in pieces like a potter's vessel. (Psalm 2:8–9)

It is here, on holy Mount Zion, where stands the armies of Christ, triumphant and victorious, crowned and worthy to be called saints. They are the warriors who fought in sacred war against the enemies of God, alongside those who refused to reject Christ for heathen idols, reside as precious martyrs on the eternal mountain. When we come to Heavenly Mount Zion, we come to the Holy Trinity, to a prodigious army of angels, and to the souls of those valiant warriors who fought and died for Christ. For as St. Paul tells us:

> But ye are come unto mount Sion, and unto the city of the living God, the heavenly Jerusalem, and to an innumerable company of angels, To the general assembly and church of the firstborn, which are written in heaven, and to God the Judge of all, and to the spirits of

---

[32] "he is contained with hope," was inspired by Dante's *Paradiso*, canto xxiii, 15–16

just men made perfect, And to Jesus the mediator of the new covenant, and to the blood of sprinkling, that speaketh better things than that of Abel. (Hebrews 12:22–24)

It is not just the saints in Heaven who watch over us, but the angels of whom St. Paul wrote: "Are they not all ministering spirits sent forth to minister for those who will inherit salvation?" (Hebrews 1:14)

The warriors on earth look up to the warriors in Heaven, who have already been rewarded the crown that those who still live mortally labor and travail, fight and struggle, to win. The armies of God do not just consist of men, but angels, as David wrote:

> The chariots of God are twenty thousand, even thousands of angels. the Lord is among them, as in Sinai, in the holy place. (Psalm 68:17)

Before Christ entered the battlefield of the Holy Cross, He was already experiencing the agony of spiritual combat, and then "an angel appeared to Him from heaven, strengthening Him." (Luke 22:43) And so, the angels and saints of mighty Heaven watch after the warriors of God, strengthening their spirits prior to their righteous engagement. When Elisha was surrounded by the pagan Syrians, his servant was sorely afraid, and Elisha, in strengthening him, asked God to reveal the army of Heaven that surrounded him, and when he saw what was unseen, he witnessed the true protection of the saints. As the Scripture says,

> Therefore he sent horses and chariots and a great army there, and they came by night and surrounded the city. And when the servant of the man of God arose early and went out, there was an army, surrounding the city with horses and chariots. And his servant said to him, "Alas, my master! What shall we do?"

> So he answered, "Do not fear, for those who are with us are more than those who are with them. And Elisha prayed, and said, "Lord, I pray, open his eyes that he may see." Then the Lord opened the eyes of the young man, and he saw. And behold, the mountain was full of horses and chariots of fire all around Elisha. So when the Syrians came down to him, Elisha prayed to the Lord, and said, "Strike this people, I pray, with blindness." And He struck them with blindness according to the word of Elisha. (2 Kings 6:14–18)

The fighters of God's army desire to emulate the saints in Heaven, "the spirits of just men made perfect," follow their actions and aspire to be instilled by the same zeal they bore when they "through faith subdued kingdoms, wrought righteousness, obtained promises, stopped the mouths of lions. Quenched the violence of fire, escaped the edge of the sword, out of weakness were made strong, waxed valiant in fight, turned to flight the armies of the aliens." (Hebrews 11:33–34)

The "the spirits of just men made perfect," are the souls of the confessors and the warriors, who fought against idolatry, defended true religion from the advances of pagans, "who willingly offered themselves for the Law," "and smote sinners in their anger, and lawless men in their wrath" (1 Maccabees 2:42–44), whose tongues forever praise the Lord, and whose hands grip a two edged sword.

PART 10

The souls of the martyrs compel the demons to flee, and this is what St. Paulinus said when he wrote at around the year 400:

> What power constrains evil spirits, seizes them against their will, forces them vainly protesting with rebellious cries to the tomb of the martyr, and plants them on this holy threshold, where they are almost immovable? [33]

Since the souls of the martyrs force the demons to retreat, then they most definitely can force the followers of demons to flee from the soldiers of God.

When the Hebrews under Judas Maccabees were in the middle of a battle with the pagans, they saw angels defending them, and two angels went in between Judas and protected him from the enemy:

> But when they were in the heat of the engagement there appeared to the enemies from heaven five men upon horses, comely with golden bridles, conducting the Jews: But as soon as the sun was risen both sides joined battle: the one part having with their valour the Lord for a surety of victory and success: but the other side making their rage their leader in battle. But when they were in the heat of the engagement there appeared to the enemies from heaven five men upon horses, comely with golden bridles, conducting the Jews: Two of whom took Maccabeus between them, and covered him on every side with their arms, and kept him safe: but cast darts and fireballs against the enemy, so that they fell down, being both confounded with blindness, and filled with trouble. And there were slain twenty thousand five hundred, and six hundred horsemen. (2 Maccabees 10:28–31)

This belief in the protection of the saints continued from Israel into Christendom. To ask the saints in Heaven for their protection and their intercession is something that is not new to the Church, but very ancient. The fourth century Doctor of the Church, St. Ambrose of Milan, saw the martyrs in Heaven as the warriors of Christ who defend Christ's Church. St. Ambrose declared:

> Such defenders do I desire, such are the soldiers I have, that is, not soldiers of this world, but soldiers of Christ. I fear no ill-will on account of them, the more powerful their patronage is the greater safety is there in it. And I wish for their protection for those very persons who grudge them to me. [34]

In the battle against the tyrant Eugenius, who was fighting to reestablish paganism in the Christian Roman empire, the emperor Theodosius and his men were few in number, and worn down by exhaustion. In such a difficult situation, the pious emperor took the monastic way, and he ascended a high mountain where he spent the whole night praying to God for intervention. He fell asleep, and awakened only to see two men clothed in white and mounted on white horses. They exhorted the emperor to "be of good courage, to renounce all fear," and when the dawn came, to lead his men into battle. One of them told him that he was St. John

---

33 Paulinus of Nola, poem 18
34 Ambrose, Letter 22.10, trans. Romestin

the Evangelist, and the other said that he was St. Philip the Apostle. There was another soldier who had the same vision, and he immediately rushed to a centurion and reported it to him. The centurion then took the soldier and brought him to the tribune; the tribune heard the story and recounted it to a general, and the general told of the vision to the emperor. "It is not for my sake," said the emperor, "that these things were shown to him, for I fully believed those who promised me the victory. But that no one might suspect that from the desire of engaging in battle I feigned to have seen such things, the Protector of my empire revealed the same to him also, that he might bear witness to the truth of my assertion; for it was to that the Lord of all first gave the vision. Let us then throw off all fear, and follow our military leaders, and let us not estimate the chances of victory by the number of combatants, but let us take into account the power of our leaders." The battle was soon commenced, and as the enemy shot forth their arrows, all of a sudden a strong wind came and shifted their direction away from the Christian warriors, and the armies of Theodosius took the victory against the pagan revivalists.[35]

After the Byzantine emperor, John I, defeated the pagan Russians, he offered his thanks to St. George, "the gloriously triumphant martyr" for the victory.[36] When the same emperor was fighting against the pagan Scythians, it was said that a man riding on a white horse was seen, terrifying the enemy and utterly confounding them. In the words of John Skylitzes, an ancient Christian historian,

> And a man appeared to the entire Roman army mounted on a white horse, thrusting foreword, routing the enemy ranks and throwing them into confusion, a man previously and subsequently unknown to anyone; they say he was one of the [two] gloriously victorious martyrs named Theodore, for the emperor always used [the icons of] these martyrs as allies and protectors against the foe. ...To honour the martyr and repay him for his timely aid, the emperor tore down to the ground the church in which his sacred body lies and built a large and most beautiful new one which he endowed with splendid estates.[37]

In the reign of Michael IV, when the empire was warring with the pagan Bulgarians, it was said that the Christians asked the warrior saint, Demetrios, to pray to God for victory against the heathens. While the battle was happening, it was said that the morale of the enemy was diminished, and that the Bulgarians themselves said that they saw a horseman leading the Christians and shot forth a fire which burned the pagans to death. As John Skylitzes describes the event:

> Now one day the people of the region went to the tomb of the great martyr Demetrios and held an all-night intercession, anointing themselves with the myrrh which flows from the sacred tomb. Then with one accord they flung open the gates and out against the Bulgars. [The Bulgars] were not in the least willing to offer a sustained or courageous resistance for the martyr was leading the Roman army and smoothing a path for it [cf. Isaiah 40:3]. This

---

35 Theodoretus, Eccles. Hist. 5.24
36 John Skylitzes, *Byzantine History*, 15.12
37 John Skylitzes, *Byzantine History*, 15.17, ellipses mine

was attested to with oaths by some Bulgars who were taken prisoner. They said they had seen a young horseman leading the Roman ranks, exuding a fire which burnt up the enemy. [38]

In the Middle Ages when Christians would go off to fight in Holy War, the popes would give them "the golden standard of St. Peter," and they would carry it up as they went off to war against the infidels.[39]

In the Battle of Cintla, between the Spanish Conquistadors and the pagan Indians of Tabasco, it was said that an unknown horseman appeared in the middle of the fight and chased the enemy away, giving the Christians the victory.

After making his attack, and forcing the pagans to flee, the horseman disappeared. It was believed by the Conquistadors that this mysterious horseman was the patron saint of Spain, St. James the Apostle, or as the Spaniards called him, St. Jaime Matamoros, or "James the Muslim killer," since it was said that St. James would appear in the battles against the Moorish Muslims and slay them. Gomara, the Spanish historian, writes on the mysterious horseman as such:

> Our men told him [Cortes] what that single horseman had done and asked him whether it was one of his company. Cortes answered that it was not, and they believed, since no other horseman had appeared, that it was the Apostle St. James, patron saint of Spain. [40]

THE ARK OF THE COVENANT WAS BROUGHT TO ISRAEL'S WARS, AND STATUES OF MARY WERE BROUGHT TO CHRISTENDOM'S WARS

As the warrior David danced before the Ark, so did the warriors of God carry up the holy image of the Ark of the Covenant, in the Battle of Jericho.

Glorifying God in both spirit and body, the warriors of the thundering Creator lifted up the Ark, in whose image God resided, and they stood before their pagan enemies with the King of Heaven as their Captain, with each warrior strengthened in the Holy One, their eyes looking forward to the holy test of arms, and their soul giving no thought to their own lives. There walked the sacred priesthood, marching before the Ark for seven days around Jericho, preparing for the slaughter that was to be done by the men of war upon the heathen horde, and through sacred battle and holy combat, was the way being made for that coming Priest, Whose Church would carry on the blessed task of the saints, to exert their minds, their souls, their spirits, and their bodies, to subdue the wicked, and glorify the Eternal General Whose Kingdom will come to earth, as it is in Heaven.

The men of war raised high the Ark, in which God resided, and the roaring sound of sacerdotal trumpets stirred the souls of the valorous troops, shook the earth, thundered throughout the air, echoed in the ears, resounded in the heavens, compelled the devils to flee, and struck with terror the hearts of those who were about to receive the sword of justice.

---

38 John Skylitzes, *Byzantine History*, 19.27
39 See Anna Komnenus, *Alexiad*, 10.7, see also f.31 of Sewter's translation
40 (Gomara, Life of Cortes, 20, trans. Simpson, brackets mine)

The walls crumbled, and the mighty arms of God's valiant men "utterly destroyed all that was in the city, both man and woman, young and old, ox and sheep and donkey, with the edge of the sword." (Joshua 6:21) And in the great victory, there stood the Holy Ark.

Christendom continued the reverence of the Ark in war, but this time they raised up the fulfillment of the Ark in holy war: the Virgin Mary. The medieval theologian, Adam of St. Victor, saw the Virgin Mary as the one who prays for warriors who combat the evil of Satan, as he wrote in one of his hymns:

> O Mary, star of the ocean, you are one unique in merit; your position is exalted over all ranks in heaven above, Stationed in the peak of heaven, to your offspring recommend us, lest our enemies' fright or cunning make us stumble in our course. As we gird ourselves for battle be we safe in your defenses; may the obstinate and crafty Satan's force yield to your power, his guile to your providence. [41]

During the great battles between Christians and Muslims, the Christians would call upon the Virgin Mary for her intercession during the fray, while the Muslims absolutely hated the Christians' reverence and exhortations toward her.

In the ninth century, a Muslim military leader who was the emir of Tarsus, sent a letter to the Byzantine general Andrew, mocking the Virgin Mary and proclaiming that she nor her Son Christ, would not help them in the impending battle:

> I will see whether the son of Mary or she who bore him will help you in any way when I march out against you with forces.

When Andrew read the letter, he hung it on an Icon of the Virgin Mary and declared:

> Behold, mother of the Word and of God; and do you, her son and God, behold; behold how this insulting barbarian disparages and abuses both you and the people who are special to you.

After he made his cries to Heaven, he readied his army and went forth into the battle against the emir of Tarsus. The two armies gathered together in a placed called Podandos, and there the holy fray commenced with the clashing of swords and the raising of war cries. The Christian sword slaughtered an innumerable amount of Muslims. As infidel blood puddled the earth, the emir managed to escape with only a few Muslims,[42] putting to shame the crescent of Allah, and bringing to naught his scoffing against the Virgin Mary.

The emperor, Basil II, after conquering the pagan Serbs and destroying their fortress in Belgrade, gave his thanks to the intercession of the Virgin Mary, the Theotokos (the Mother of God). The historian John Skylitzes recounts:

> When he came to Athens, he offered up thanks for his victory to the Mother of God and adorned her church with magnificent and splendid offerings, then returned to Constantinople. [43]

---

41 Adam of St. Victory, *Hail O Mother of Our Savior*, 11–12
42 Skylitzes, *Byzantine History*, 6.24
43 John Skylitzes, *Byzantine History*, 16.43

When Basil II was about to go to war against Phocas, a rebel and usurper, he clenched on one hand an icon of the Virgin Mary. As the Byzantine historian Psellus wrote:

> He took his stand there, sword in hand. In his left hand he clasped the image of the Saviour's Mother; thinking this ikon the surest protection against his opponent's terrific onslaught. [44]

After Basil II took the victory, the historian Psellus attributed the triumph to no other than the Virgin Mary. "For my own part," he wrote, "I prefer to express no opinion on the subject and ascribe all the glory to the Mother of God."[45] When the emperor Romanus III fought against the Muslims in Syria, in the 11th century, there was present within the army the "Theometor, the image which Roman emperors habitually carry with them on campaign as a guide and guardian of all the army."[46]

When the emperor Nikephoros Phokas was about to drive the Muslim invaders in Crete, he declared to his army, in the words of the ancient historian Michael Attaleiates, "that their first line of defense, their invincible courage, and most secure anchor was to seek refuge with the Mother of God, the All-Pure Lady, and plead with her. Immediately, without any delay, he ordered that a church be built there in honor of the all-immaculate Lady and Mother of God. … [A] beautiful and holy church was erected in three days."[47] The temple was erected, and the warriors beheld its beauties as the trumpets played with inspiring sound when the sublime liturgy was being conducted, and as they witnessed with awe the splendid Mass, they declared that the land of Crete would be brought back to Christian Roman power. The heroic sovereign unleashed the temporal sword on the Muslim heathens, slaughtered many of them with his army, and took Crete back into the fold of Christendom, and it was all done after seeking the prayers of the Virgin Mary. The entire island became subject to the glorious Byzantine Empire, and Phokas made it a home, not for Muslim heretics, but for Orthodox Christians.[48] This pious emperor was so filled with zeal and love for God, and devotion to the empire He placed under his authority, that he destroyed about twenty-thousand Muslims in numerous of his battles against the Islamic invaders.[49]

When the emperor Alexius Komnenus was doing battle with the Scythians, he is said to have "stood with sword in hand beyond his own front line. In the other hand he grasped like a standard the Cape of the Mother of the Word."[50]

The emperor Botanaeiates, after defeating the rebel general Bryennios, "gave fitting thanks to the all-pure Lady, the Mother of God."[51]

---

44 Psellus, *Fourteen Byzantine Rulers*, 1.17, trans. Sewter
45 Psellus, *Fourteen Byzantine Rulers*, 1.17
46 Psellus, *Fourteen Byzantine Emperors*, 3.10
47 Attaleiates, *History*, 28.4, trans. Krallis & Kaldellis, ellipses and brackets mine
48 See Attaleiates, *History*, 28.5–6
49 See Attaleiates, *History*, 28.8
50 Anna Comnena, 7.3, trans. Sewter
51 Attaleiates, *History*, 34.7

PART 11 – THE WAR BETWEEN CHRISTENDOM AND BABEL

To understand Christian militancy is to understand who we are at war with. The war is with Satan, and against all of the forms he has masqueraded himself with. Amongst his forms is Allah, the god of the religion of the Antichrist—Islam

To understand Christian militancy is to understand who we are at war with. The war is with Satan, and against all of the forms he has masqueraded himself with. Amongst his forms is Allah, the god of the religion of the Antichrist—Islam.

Riccoldo di Monte Croce, an obscure thirteenth century Italian monk, once wrote that "all the dirt of times gone by which the devil has scattered in other places here and there, he also spewed out in its entirety onto Mohammed."[1] It is no wonder that John called Mecca—"the desert" and "a woman sitting upon a scarlet coloured beast, full of names of blasphemy" (Revelation 17:3)—the "Mother of Harlots." All of the wiles of the devil are found within Islam, and all of these evils at one point found their home in Babel, where Nimrod ruled and wherein the Tower of Babel was erected.

This Babel was no different than the Islamic Mecca—the holiest city of the Islamic heresy. In Mecca, Muslims from all nations and different tongues, come together to worship one idol—the Blackstone in the lofty Kaaba—in one single language, Arabic. In Babel, contrary to what most theologians think, people from throughout the known world, and of different languages, came to worship their idols in one single language. Babel, then, was really a pilgrimage for all of the pagan world at its time, and not merely a place where all peoples lived.

Mecca is simply a continuation of Babel, and Babel was simply the first Mecca. So what are we at war against? The religion of Babel that seeks to destroy Christendom. But such a seeking will not prevail, for the Cross shall assail the Crescent, in that final destruction of the new Babel—Mecca.

---

1 De Croce, *Refutation of the Koran*, ch. i, trans. Londini Ensis

Islam is a religion completely bent on establishing a universal utopia in which all peoples will be, just as it was in Babel, united under a single language and ideology,[2] centering around the single pilgrimage site of Mecca to where they will all bow in unison. The Muslim claims that Muhammad purged Arabia from idolatry, but all that he really did was call for the worship of one idol, the Blackstone in the Kaaba, and for the destruction of the rest. By this, he united the docile whole of Arabia under this single image.[3] Under Muhammad, no man could go to the Kaaba unless he worshipped Allah and followed the teachings of his prophet. "There remained but one religion for Arabia," writes Muir, "and that was Islam."[4]

All Muslims, in the teachings of Muhammad, are to be a part of a collective body in which all are completely equal. They are to be, in the words of Muhammad, "on the same equality… ye are one Brotherhood."[5] Those who are not members of this collective group, specifically Christians and Jews, are not seen as equals, but as enemies to the body politic who deserve enslavement and death. It was for this idea that Muslims overran entire nations, subdued the powers of kings, deceived men who thought themselves pious but had ears itching for the gravest delusions, vanquished armies of the greatest empire, and reduced people from the unlearned to the most enlightened to levels lower than slaves.[6] This is Babel and its continuation is being done through Islam.

BABEL -- THE FIRST MECCA

"This one is Nimrod, by whose evil thought One language in the world is not still used."— *Dante's Inferno*.[7]

Babel was a pagan pilgrimage site to where all pagans of different tongues and nations would gather to worship in one single universal language. This goes contrary to the common belief that all the world once resided in Shinar.[8] When one reads Genesis 10, the chapter prior to the account on Babel and the dispersion of languages, one can easily identify that this was not what occurred.

For it is found in Genesis 10:25, that "unto Eber were born two sons: the name of one was Peleg; for in his day was the earth divided;" it is an indication that mankind was already residing in different geographic locations.[9] The world was of one speech, but this does not

---

2 See De Croce, *Refutation of the Koran*, ch. vi, p. 34
3 Muir, *Life of Muhammad*, introd. ch. ii, p. xcviii
4 Muir, *Life of Muhammad*, ch. xxvii, p. 432
5 Muir, *Life of Muhammad*, ch. xxxi, p. 473
6 The state of the dhimmi is explained by Moczar, *Islam at the Gates*, prologue, p. 16
7 Canto xxxi, 77–78, trans. H.W. Longfellow
8 It was stated by Lenorment *A Manuel of the Ancient History of the East to the Commencement of the Median Wars*, vol. i, b. i, sect. iii, p. 8), that nothing in Scripture "forbids us to suppose that some families had already separated themselves from the mass of the descendants of Noah, and had gone to a distance and formed colonies apart from the common center, while the greater number of the families destined to repopulate the Earth still remained united."
9 See Haley, *Bible Handbook, The Old Testament*, p. 100, on Gen. x.

imply that it was in one land. They were of one ideology, that of Nimrod and his envisioning of a glorified shrine and city, but this does not mean that they all resided in Babel.

Also, as one cannot be emphatic that all peoples resided in Shinar prior to the dispersion, one as well cannot conclude that the single tongue referred to in Genesis 11 was the sole language spoken by man as evidenced by Scripture, which, after describing the migrating and settling of each of the sons of Ham, Shem, and Japheth, recounts that such was done "after their families, and their tongues, in their countries, and in their nations" (Genesis 10:20); and at the end of Genesis 10, it declares thus:—"These are the families of the sons of Noah, after their generations, in their nations; and by these were the nations divided in the earth after the flood." (Genesis 10:32) These two verses are an indication that before the dispersion in Babel the world was already divided geographically, with each people having "their tongues, in their countries."

Observe also, that the Scripture describes these nations, composed of their own tongues (multiple languages) and lands, as being established "after the flood," not after the great dispersion in Shinar. Genesis 9 contains a summary of the Table of Nations:[10] "And the sons of Noah that went forth of the ark were Shem, and Ham, and Japheth: and Ham is the father of Canaan. These are the three sons of Noah: and of them was the whole earth overspread." (Gen. 9:18–19)

What is also quite revealing is how Nimrod is addressed before the Tower of Babel story is mentioned. In Genesis it says:

> Cush begot Nimrod; he began to be a mighty one on the earth. He was a mighty hunter before the Lord; therefore it is said, "Like Nimrod the mighty hunter before the Lord." And the beginning of his kingdom was Babel, Erech, Accad, and Calneh, in the land of Shinar. From that land he went to Assyria and built Nineveh, Rehoboth Ir, Calah, and Resen between Nineveh and Calah (that is the principal city). (Genesis 10:9–12)

It already speaks of Nimrod as building his cities, including Babel, while at the same time describing numerous lands, to where the other peoples settled, that are different from Shinar. If the whole of humanity was living in Shinar, then who was living in Nineveh, Rehoboth Ir, Calah and Resen? Obviously people inhabited these cities, and they did not live in Shinar. It is obvious that Shinar was a type of pilgrimage site, to where people would gather and be united by a single language.

Both the descendants of Shem and Japheth, according to Genesis, settled in lands different from Shinar. Elishah, Kittim, Tarshish, and Dodanim, who all are sons of Javan, and grandsons of Japheth, "were the isles of the Gentiles," according to Genesis.[11] Josephus identifies Kittim with Cyprus; Tarshish with Tarsus, Elishah with the father of the Aeolians (a

---

10 See Matthew Henry's introduction to his commentary of Gen. X.
11 Gen. 10:4–5.

tribe of Greece).[12] And Gesenius suggests that the descendants of Dodanim are the Rhodians[13] of Rhodes, a Greek island. Genesis also locates where some of the grandchildren of Shem migrated to: the sons of Joktan, an issue of Shem, are named Almodad, Sheleph, Hazarmaveth, Jerah, Hadoram, Uzal, Diklah, Obal, Abimael, Sheba, Ophir, Havilah, and Jobab. We are told that these persons found their dwelling "from Mesha, as thou goest unto Sephar, a mount of the east." (Genesis 10: 26–30) Mesha is a region of Arabia according to Gesenius.[14] Thus, from inquiring this subject by reading Genesis, we know that not all of the descendants of Shem and Japheth, dwelt in Shinar; furthermore, the Book of Genesis does not say that all people lived in this land, but that "the whole earth was of one language, and of one speech. And it came to pass, as they journeyed from the east, that they found a plain in the land of Shinar; and they dwelt there." (Gen. 11: 1–2.) "They" does not mean the entire globe, but some of humanity.

With all such evidence adduced, Genesis 9 and 10 show that Noah's posterity had expanded themselves as different nations,[15] before the forced dispersion that God had enacted upon the heretics of Shinar, who had attempted to establish a collectivist and universal mecca in Mesopotamia.

One can only conclude, based on the evidence presented, that as all the peoples spoke their own individual language, and resided on their own lands, there was at the same time a universal tongue spoken in order to unify all the earth under the religious sway of the cult of Babel, just as Arabic is the universal language for all Muslims. As the attempted tower in Babel was to be a unifier of the masses, regardless of their diversity of nations, so too was their universal language a unifier, regardless of their own individual languages.

The universalist cult of the Tower of Babel is a foreshadower of the greatest of all cults: that of Muhammad and his doctrine Islam, which affirms that all people, while they speak their own languages, must at the same time proclaim their praises to Allah and his prophet in Arabic. Under a universal Islamic empire, or Ummah, all peoples must collectively pray in Arabic for the same reason why those of Babel had one language: to easily subjugate the masses under a pure despotism, in which all those who spurn this tyrannical utopia of Muhammad, will be subject to the most severe of cruelties.

---

12 Joseph. Antiq. of the Jews, 1.6.2, trans. by William Whiston. "Of the three sons of Javan also," writes Josephus, "the son of Japheth, Elisa gave name to the Eliseans, who were his subjects; they are now the Aeolians. Tharsus to the Tharsians; for so was Cilicia of old called; the sign of which is this, that the noblest city they have, and a metropolis also, is Tarsus, the tau being by change put for the theta. Cethimus possessed the island Cethima; it is now called Cyprus: and from that it is that all islands, and the greatest part of the seacoast, are named Cethim by the Hebrews; and one city there is in Cyprus that has been able to preserve its denomination; it is called Citius by those who use the language of the Greeks, and has not, by the use of that dialect, escaped the name of Cethim"
13 Gesenius, *A Hebrew and English lexicon of the Old Testament*, 1882, p. 215. Also see G. Rawlinson, *Origin.*, part ii, ch. iii, pp. 187–188.
14 See Gesenius, *A Hebrew and English lexicon of the Old Testament*, 1882, p. 622: "Mesha, pr. n. of a place mentioned in describing that part of Arabia inhabited by the descendants of Joktan."
15 See R. Jamieson, Commentary, vol. i, pr. i, p. 107, on Gen. ix. 19; Rev. Thomas Whitelaw, The Pulpit Commentary, on Gen. ix. 19.

Mankind in Babel, therefore, was under a universal sway, and as long as they were of one language and culture, they were, thus, ones easily controlled by the tyrant, Nimrod.

Shinar, with its Tower of Babel, was the mecca of its time, and the truth behind this assertion is clarified by several lines from Genesis. Firstly, that there was a dispersion of languages, thus indicating that there was a mixed multitude of races[16] who, by the altering of the universal language, separated from the once universal order of Nimrod. Secondly, the words of Babel's builders: "Go to, let us build us a city and a tower, whose top may reach unto heaven; and let us make a name, lest we be scattered abroad upon the face of the whole earth." (Genesis 11:4) The ambition to make a name for oneself is a vital statement, and it poses the question: 'to make a name for whom? Subjects of Nimrod's kingdom?' It is illogical to believe that Nimrod would build a lofty building constructed for the sake of impressing his own people; a monument is usually made to attract those of the exterior of a nation, not the interior.

This is evidenced, furthermore, by a statement from the ancient historian Hestiaeus, which is preserved for us, thankfully, by the two Roman historians, the Jewish Josephus and the Christian Eusebius. It speaks of an incident in which pagan priests who escaped Shinar, took with them idols of "Jupiter Enyalius,"[17] and for some reason wanted to return to Babel. But because of the scattering of the people which precluded the completion of Nimrod's tower, "they were again driven from thence by the introduction of a diversity of tongues, upon which they founded colonies in various parts, each settling in such situations as chance, or the direction of God, led them to occupy."[18] This compels one to wonder why these priests of Jupiter were returning to Shinar, after they made their escape, for reasons unknown. We also notice that these priests, on their return, were taking with them idols of Jupiter, indicating a religious devotion to Nimrod's cult. To desire to come back to Shinar after the fact that they escaped, makes one realize the religious fervor of these priests. It also shows that there were inhabitants who lived outside of Shinar. Thus, Hestiaeus' recounting of the diversity of tongues, evidences that Shinar was a place for the journeying believer, a site of pilgrimage, to observe the rituals of his faith.

---

16 See Jastrow, *Religion in Babylonia and Assyria*, lecture i.i, p. 4. "The germ of truth in the time-honoured Biblical tradition," writes Jastrow, "that makes the plain of Shinar the home of the human race and the seat of the confusion of languages, is the reconciliation of the fact that various races had settled there, and that various languages were there spoken"
17 See Joseph. Antiq. of the Jews, 1.4.3, trans. by William Whiston.
18 Cory's *Ancient Fragments*, ed. by Hodges, p. 74, found in Josephus, Antiq. of the Jews, and Eusebius' Preartio Evangelica, 9.

Thus, a verse from a sibyl,[19] preserved by Josephus, which recounts that "When all men were of one language, some of them built a high tower, as if they would thereby ascend up to heaven."[20] Observe that it details that not all of the men aspired to build, but that a number of them did, while at the same time, the language of humanity was the same.

The pagan Greek scholar Alexander Polyhistor (1 BC) as well made use of a sibyl's verse, and it too agrees that it was various, but not all men who took upon the construction of the Tower of Babel, while all peoples spoke the same tongue. "The Sibyl says," writes Polyhistor, "that when all men formerly spoke the same language, some among them undertook to erect a large and lofty tower, in order to climb into heaven."[21] There is no indicatives in Genesis that tell us all the world's people were in Shinar, building mankind's first step-tower.[22] A certain pagan Sibyl, which Sir Walter Raleigh quotes, affirms this as well, for it reads that "certain of them built a most high tower, as if they meant thereby to have scaled the heavens."[23]

SUMERIAN HISTORY BELIEVED THAT NOT ALL PEOPLE LIVED IN SHINAR

If all people, at that time, inhabited Shinar, then why would the author of Genesis describe the migrations of certain grandsons of Noah, before his elaboration on the Tower of Babel and the dispersion of tongues? Our answer may be acquired from the ancient Sumerians themselves. While the preserved texts of ancient Greek historians can be, in the eyes of a modern, easily put off as works later manipulated by Christian and Jewish historians, such

---

19 It is requisite to expatiate the history of the sibylline books. Numerous of the sibylline writings, which were prophetic books written by pagan prophetesses and read throughout antiquity, had their origins in the near east, and new copies soon enough produced in Europe and other lands in Asia. The first sibyl, which was the name used to refer to these witches, was born from the Persians; the second of Libya; the third of Delphi; the fourth of the Cimerians in Italy; the fifth of Erythrae, which was said to have foretold the destruction of Troy; the sixth of Samos; the seventh of Cumae, who was said to have brought nine books to Rome before the emperor Tarquinius Priscus, to whom she had charged for the oracular readings three-hundred Philippines, which was to the refusal of Tarquinius. In turn the prophetess had burnt three of the books, and demanded still the same price; the king of Rome again rejected the offer, and the mad witch again scorched another three, an action which had gained the respect of Tarquinius, who had thus bought the remaining books. The eighth sibyl was from Hellespont, "born in the Trojan territory," who was said to have lived in the time of Solon and Cyrus; the ninth was of Phrygia; the tenth, and last, was of Tibur in Italy, she was eventually deified, a statue of her was said to be found within the banks of the river Anio. Each of the sibylline books were done by different authors, all of whose names were unknown except for the one of Erythrae, who was Babylonian by birth. This work of the Babylonian prophetess was, among the other sibylline works, the more celebrated and praised; so renown was it that after the Romans had finished constructing their capital, Caius Curio, a consul, told the senate that representatives should be sent to Erythrae to acquire the oracular writings, and bring back to Rome (See Lact. Div. Inst., 1.6, trans. William Fletcher). It is said that representatives Publius Gabinius, Marcus Otacilius, Lucius Valerius, were able to bring together a thousand verses of this pagan writing. (See Lact. Div. Inst. 1.6, trans. William Fletcher).
20 Sibyl in Joseph., Antiq., 1.4.3, trans. William Whiston.
21 Polyhistor in Cory's *Ancient Fragments*, Hodges ed., p. 75.
22 See Raleigh, Hist. World., b. i, ch. vii, sect. x: 9, p. 235.
23 Sibylla in Raleigh, Hist. World., b. i, ch. vii, sect. x: 9, p. 235.

as Eusebius and Josephus, there lies one Sumerian text, which confirms not only the account of Genesis' author,[24] But also those fragments of the obscure Greek historians and scholars.

It is entitled "Enmerkar and the Lord of Aratta," a story of how Enmerkar, a king of Erech, wishes to subdue, by the persuasion of his tongue, the Iranian land of Aratta. He dispatches a messenger to the unnamed king of Aratta, having him declare to the ruler not only threats, but also an incantation entitled the "spell of Enki," which speaks of a past golden age when the world, under complete unison, worshiped Enlil,[25] The Sumerian god of the winds, in one tongue. It is but a corruption of the authentic story of Genesis,[26] which reads thus:—

> Once upon a time, there was no snake, there was no scorpion, there was no hyena, there was no lion, there was no wild dog, no wolf, there was no fear, no terror, and man had no rival. In those days, the land Shubur-Hamazi, harmony tongued Sumer, the great land of the me of prince-ship, Uri, the land having all that is appropriate, the land Martu, resting in security, the whole universe, and the people well cared for, to Enlil in one tongue gave speech. (But) then, the lord defiant, the prince defiant, the king defiant, Enki, the lord defiant, the prince defiant, the king defiant, the lord defiant, the prince defiant, the king defiant, Enki, lord of abundance, whose commands are trust worthy, the lord of wisdom, who scans the land, the leader of the gods, the lord of Eridu, endowed with wisdom, changed the speech in their mouths, put contention into it, into the speech of man that (until then) had been one. [27]

Because the spell of Enki parallels so greatly with Genesis' account of the Tower of Babel, it has been believed by some that king Enmerkar is in reality Nimrod. But this is incorrect. Enmerkar is speaking of a time before his own—hence, they were already speaking different languages during his reign over Erech. Another point made for the identification of

---

24 See Lenormant, *A Manual of the Ancient History of the East to the commencement of the Median Wars*, vol. i, b. i, ch. ii, sect. i, pp. 8–9. "The Bible narrative," writes Lenorment, "which we now resume, is not one isolated tale unconnected with the traditions of other nations, and proceeding only from the pen of Moses. It is on the contrary, as we have already said, the most complete and authentic form of a grand primitive tradition, which can be traced back to the earliest ages of humanity, and has originally been common to all races and all people, and been carried all over the world, by the dispersion of these races on the surface of the earth."
25 Kramer, *The Sumerians*, ch. viii, p. 270: "Enmerkar instructs his herald to repeat to him the 'spell of Enki,' which relates how the god Enki had put an end to man's 'golden age' under Enlil's universal sway over the earth and its inhabitants."
26 See F. Lenorment, *A Manuel of the Ancient History of the East*, vol. i, b. i, ch. i, sect. 1, p. 12. Lenorment affirms that the myths which parallel the stories found in the Bible, were merely "perverted to another meaning to symbolize the introduction of material progress, instead of applying to a fundamental principle of moral government, and further disfigured by that monstrous conception, too common in Paganism, which represents the Deity as a formidable power, and a jealous enemy of human happiness and progress,"
27 See Kramer, *Sumerian Mythology*, revised ed., preface, p. xiv.

Enmerkar with Nimrod is the fact that Enmerkar was considered to be the builder of Erech,[28] Nimrod's Erech, therefore, must not have been that of king Enmerkar, but the more ancient version of that city.

The spell of Enki included the city of Sumer, which has been identified with Shinar;[29] Uri, which is identified with Akkad,[30] it also encompassed Assyria,[31] which, as we are told by certain translations of Genesis, was first built by Nimrod.[32] But, it is as well recounted that the founder of that renown Assyrian city was built by Asshur, a son of Shem. It was he who came out of Nimrod's land "and builded Nineveh, and the city Rehoboth, and Calah, and Resen between Nineveh and Calah: the same is a great city." (Genesis 11:11–12) This is as well affirmed by Josephus.[33]

Shubur-Hamazi, a city mentioned in the spell, was east of Sumer and Uri,[34] and consisted of northern,[35] and much of western Iran,[36] which in no way, was under Nimrod's kingdom.

Enki's incantation also mentions Martu, which was to the west and southwest of Sumer.[37] This land belonged to the Amorites, a posterity of Ham,[38] who ruled over an immensely significant part of the Near East. We learn from Barton that Martu is generally regarded as

---

28 See Kramer, The Sumerians, ch. ii, pp. 44–45: "According to the King List, he [Enmerkar] built the city of Erech; and according to the epic tales, he led a campaign ageist Aratta, somewhere in the neighborhood of the Caspian Sea, and subjugated it to Erech." Brackets mine. A city whose founding is attributed to Nimrod in the Book of Genesis. But it must be remembered that Enmerkar was a succeeding king, his father being king Meskiaggasher, called "the son of Utu (the Sumerian sun-god)," who determinedly built a powerful and aspiring dynasty in Erech, which in his day was still known by its older name Eanna ("House of An," the heaven-god). When one inquires the details of Nimrod in both the author of Genesis, and Josephus, one finds that "the beginning of his kingdom was Babel, and Erech, and Accad, and Calneh, in the land of Shinar." (Gen. 10:10.) Nowhere does Nimrod's father Cush, rule anywhere in Mesopotamia; for he reigned over the Ethiopians, according to according to Josephus. (Joseph. Antiq., 1.6.2.)
29 See Jastrow, *Religious Belief in Babylonia and Assyria*, lecture i, p. 3.
30 See Thorkild Jacobsen, *The Harps that Once*, p. 289, footnote 28; Kramer, *The Sumerians*, ch. viii, p. 285.
31 See Kramer, History Begins at Sumer, ch. 27, p. 225. "Directly north of Sumer was Uri," writes Kramer, "which probably consisted of the territory between the Tigris and Euphrates north of the thirty-third parallel, and included the later Akkad and Assyria"
32 See Keil and Delitzsch, *Biblical Commentary on the Old Testament*, vol. i, ch. iv, p. 167, on Gen. 8–12; Poole, *A Commentary on the Holy Bible*, p. 27, on Gen. x: 11; H.C. Leupold, *Exposition of Genesis*, vol. i, ch. x, p. 368, on Gen. x: 10–12.
33 Joseph., Antiq., 1.6.3, trans. William Whiston.
34 Kramer, History begins at Sumer, ch. 27, p. 225: "East of Sumer and Uri was Shubur-Hamazi."
35 Martin Sicker, *The pre-Islamic Middle East*, p. 16: "At about the same time that Ebla reached the peak of its power, a powerful ruler named Mesilim arose in Kish and appears to have dominated most if not all of southern Mesopotamia, including Adab, and may have extended his conquests as far as Hamazi in northern Iran"
36 Kramer, History begins at Sumer, ch. 27, p. 225: "Shubur-Hamazi, which no doubt included much of Western Iran"
37 Kramer, History begins at Sumer, ch. 27, p. 225: "To the west and southwest of Sumer was Martu"; see also Thorkild Jaconsen, *The Harps that Once*, p. 289, in which Martu or Mardu is identified with the "region east of Mesopotamia."
38 See Joseph., Antiq., 1.6.2, 5.1.23, trans. William Whiston.

being located on the north of Canaan; and so great was the prominence of their kingdom that they received the envy of the far-off Babylonian.[39]

The Book of Joshua speaks of "all the kings of the Amorites, which [were] on the side of Jordan westward," (Joshua 5:1) and the same source describes how Jordan, which is a part of Arabia, was under the control of Sihon, an Amorite king.[40] Josephus makes mention that the Amorites also had control of lands outside of Jordan.[41] The sublime book of Genesis speaks of "the Amorites, that dwelt in Hazezontamar," (Genesis 14:7) which is located in the desert of Judah.[42] The land of the Amorites also consisted of the land between the Euphrates and Mediterranean sea, as well as the Arabian and Syrian desert.[43] Thus why the Dead Sea is said to be between the lands of Moab and those of the Amorites.[44] The Amorite city of Marathus in Syria, and Phoenicia, too, were bestowed with this title of Martu.[45] Numerous of these lands mentioned, were not part of Shinar, as is recalled to us in Genesis, and, thus, undisturbed by Nimrod's despotism. In other words, they were outside of Babel and thus not in Shinar when the Tower was being built. Overall, when the spell of Enki, which was emphatically a verse remembered by the Sumerian poets, speaks of the whole universe, it signifies a territory whose farthest part included the Armenian highlands on the north, to the Persian Gulf, and from the Iranian highlands, on the east to the Mediterranean sea.[46] This compels one to conclude, that when Genesis speaks of the whole earth being of one tongue, it is not meant to be interpreted that all peoples inhabited Nimrod's kingdom in Shinar, but that all persons were followers of his cult.

The Sumerians and Akkadians were not ignorant of the world around them; their knowledge of the outside nations went as far as India.[47] This means that people in India

---

39 Barton, *A Sketch of Semitic Origins*, ch. iv, p. 146. "Sargon of Agade, about 3800 B.C.," writes Barton, "conquered the Westland, or, as scholars generally regard it, the land of the Amurru or Amorites on the north of Canaan."
40 Joshua, xiii: 27. See also J.A. Kring, *The Conquest of Canaan*, p. i, ch. v, p. 39
41 Joseph., Antiq., 5.1.25, trans. William Whiston.
42 See Gesenius's Hebrew and Chaldean lexicon to the Old Testament scriptures, p. ccxcix: "[Hazazon-tamar, Hazezon-tamar], Gen. 14:7; 2 Ch. 20:2, pr. n. of a town situated in the desert of the tribe of Judah, celebrated for its palms."
43 Kramer, History begins at Sumer, ch. 27, p. 225; also see, by the same author, *The Sumerians*, ch. ii, p. 69. "Shulgi was followed by his son Amar-Sin," writes Kramer, "who ruled only nine years, but succeeded in retaining control over Sumer and its provinces, including far-off Ashur to the north. His brother Shu-Sin, who succeeded him, also ruled nine years. It is in the course of his reign that we hear for the first time of a serious incursion of Sumer by a Semitic people known as the Amorites from the Syrian and Arabian Deserts." Also see Jastrow, *Religion in Babylonia and Assyria*, lecture i.iii, pp. 29–39; Ian Barnes, The Historical Atlas of the Bible, Patriarchs and Their World, p. 46; G. Rawlinson, *Monarchies*, vol. i: Chaldea, ch. viii, p. 163, n. 5.
44 See Joseph., Antiq., 4.5.1, trans. William Whiston. Eusebius identifies Asphaltitis with the Dead Sea (Euseb. Eccles. Hist. 1.8, trans. C.F. Cruse).
45 See Tomkins, *Studies on the Times of Abraham*, ch. 5, p. 93. "The name Martu (and its Semitic equivalent Akharrie) was given to Phoenicia," writes Tomkins, "and in an especial locality to the city Marathus."
46 Kramer, History begins at Sumer, ch. 27, p. 225: "In short, the universe as conceived by the Sumerian poets, extended at least from the Armenian highlands on the north to the Persian Gulf, and from the Iranian highlands, on the east to the Mediterranean sea."
47 Kramer, *The Sumerians*, ch. 8, p. 284.

were revering the religion of Babel. This reminds us of the Paschal Chronicle, which mentions that "About the time of the construction of the Tower (i.e., of Babel), a certain Indian, of the race of Arphaxad, made his appearance; a wise man, and an astronomer, whose name was Andubarius. It was he who first instructed the Indians in the science of Astronomy."[48] This statement, written in seventh century Byzantium, shows us that there was intermingling between diverse peoples during the construction of the Tower of Babel; for Arphaxad, the race whom this Andubarius is said to have descended from, was a son of Shem, who was born before the great commencing of the great construction at Shinar.[49]

The Sumerians also knew of the lands of Anatolia, the Caucasus region, the farther west parts of central Asia, Egypt, and Ethiopia. These lands must have also been revering the religion of Babel, and they were no near Babel, but unified by the city and its language.

IDOLATRY ORIGINATED IN ARABIA, AND NOT BABYLON

It is a common belief that Babylon is the home of all idolatries, since the Tower of Babel is the earliest pagan temple recorded. But by reading Scripture carefully, and seeing the evidence found from history, we will find that this is not correct. Arabia was idolatry's birth place, Babylon was its result.

It was from the Cushite south Arabians, and not the Babylonians, that the sinister idea of paganism commenced after the flood. It was they who first devised that system which is so besotted by the modern philosopher; it is prettified by the wicked idealist who obsequiously praises it as the most laudable of religious thought. Yet, for the human soul it is most rapacious; and to God does it express the highest form of impudence and defiance. From such wizards does influence arise, to only infect the souls of other deviants. So it was with the Cushites; for they began a rebellion which, like an infectious disease, expanded to the minds of the later peoples of Mesopotamia.

Nimrod was a Cushite, but not in the sense that we may think. He was not directly from the land of modern Ethiopia, but from South Arabia, which was anciently a part of Ethiopia. This makes Nimrod not an Ethiopian in the modern sense, but a South Arab. Thus, the religion of the Tower of Babel was Arabian.

The gap between Ethiopia and south Arabia is not of far expanse, the lands being separated only by the Straits of Bab-el-Mandeb.[50] The whole territory of the Ethiopians, according to Pliny,[51] also included that of the Red Sea, hence why he made mention of "the Arabian side of the Nile,"[52] which would indicate that Arabia was, in that age, part of Africa since the Nile lies only in that continent. Herodotus makes mention of a city called Nysa "above Egypt in

---

48 See Cory's *Ancient Fragments*, ed. by Hodges, p. 167.
49 See Gen. 10:21 to 11:8.
50 See Philip Smith, *The Ancient History of the East*, intro.10, p. 6.
51 Pliny, *Natural History*, vi.xxxv, trans. H. Rackham.
52 Pliny, *Natural History*, vi.xxxv, trans. H. Rackham.

the land of Ethiopia;"[53] the same historian as well wrote of the "Long-lived Ethiopians, those who dwell about Nysa,"[54] while Diodorus locates the same metropolis in "Arabia Felix near Egypt."[55] This places ancient Ethiopia as part of south Arabia.

St. Egeria, writing in the fourth century, wrote of the land of Gessen or Goshen, which is in modern day Egypt, as "the city which is called Arabia." She also wrote that "the 'land of Arabi' is the 'land of Gessen.'" There was a city in Ghoshen called Arabia, and when one reads Egeria rendition of Genesis 47:5 it reads: "In the best land of Egypt, gather your father and brothers, in the land of Gessen, in the land of Arabia."[56] From the time of Nimrod, Cushite inhabitation occurred in Arabia, and though they were gradually displaced by Semitic tribes,[57] Tomkins quotes Rawlinson, Her., vol. i, p. 365: "This age seems to have been in a peculiar sense the active period of Semitic colonization. The Phoenicians removing from the Persian gulf to the shores of the Mediterranean, and the Hebrew patriarch [Abraham] marching with his household from Chaldea to Palestine, merely followed the direction of the great tide of emigration which was at this time setting in from the east westward. Semitic tribes were, during the period in question, gradually displacing the old Cushite inhabitants of the Arabian Peninsula. Assyria was being occupied by colonists of the same Semitic race from Babylonia, while the Arameans were ascending the course of the Euphrates and forming settlements on the eastern frontier of Syria." Brackets mine.[58] their presence there in antiquity, remained great."[59] And the sons of Cush; Seba, and Havilah and Sabtah, and Raamah, and Sabtechah"; (Genesis 10:7) the posterity of these patriarchs made their abode in the Near East, which is an evidence unto itself of the Ethiopic presence in that region. While northern and central Arabia was the abode of mainly Semites, the southern area most certainly was inhabited by Cushites.[60]

The descendants of Havilah, who have been identified with the Macrobians of Ethiopia,[61] made their way into Arabia,[62] specifically, as one commentator[63] says, in the Arabian tract of Khawlan in the north-western part of Yemen. The children of Sabtah would also settle in Arabia Felix, or southern Arabia,[64] and it may be stated that they resided in Hadramaut.[65]

---

53 Herod., ii.146, trans. G.C. Macaulay.
54 Herod., iii.97, trans. G.C. Macaulay.
55 Diod. Sic. i.15, trans. C.H. Oldfather.
56 Genesis 47:5, in Egeria, *Diary*, ch. 7
57 See H.G. Tomkins, *Studies on the Times of Abraham*, ch. ii, p. 51.
58 See also Philip Smith, *The Ancient History of the East*, intro.18, p. 10.
59 See Diod. Sic., 3.8, trans. Oldfather.
60 See G. Rawlinson, *The Origen of Nations*, part ii, ch. iv, p. 209.
61 See Keil and Delitzsche, *Biblical Commentary on the Old Testament*, vol. i, ch. x, p. 165, on Gen. x:7.
62 This is agreed by Poole, *A Commentary on the Holy Bible*, p. 27, on Gen. x:7; H.C. Leupold, *Exposition of Genesis*, vol. i, p. 364, on Gen. x:7; G. Rawlinson, *Origin.*, part ii, ch. iv, p. 206.
63 See G. Rawlinson, *Origin.*, part ii, ch. iv, p. 206.
64 See Poole, *A Commentary on the Holy Bible*, p. 27, on Gen. x:7; H.C. Leupold, *Exposition of Genesis*, vol. i, ch. x, p. 364, on Gen. x:7.; Keil and Delitzsche, *Biblical Commentary on the Old Testament*, vol. i, ch. x, p. 165, on Gen. x:7; G. Rawlinson, *Origen.*, part ii, ch. iv, p. 206.
65 See G. Rawlinson, *The Origen of Nations*, part ii, ch. iv, p. 206.

Raamah's descendants also made a dwelling in Arabia Felix,[66] or as some authorities[67] declare, modern-day Oman. The people of Raamah were eventually intermixed, or overlaid, by their brothers, the Sabaeans and the Dedanites.[68] The Sabaeans and Dedanites would intermix with the descendants of Joktan,[69] a son of Shem, who inhabited the innermost parts of Arabia, where they had built the city of Jectan, near Mecca.[70]

Though Nimrod is called a son of Cush, he is truly a south Arabian Ethiopian, who espoused Sabaeanism, a religion founded by the first of sons of Cush mentioned in the Table of Nations, Seba or Saba.[71] The Sabaeans built and dwelt in Saba, the capital city of ancient Ethiopia,[72] which was renamed by Cambyses into Meroe.[73] The people of Saba or Meroe declared this city as having been the original home of all Ethiopians.[74]

The Sabaeans resided not just in Africa but south Arabia as well.[75] The Sabaeans, according to Diodorus, "are the most numerous of the tribes of the Arabians."[76] The ancient scholar Juba wrote that the people who lived on the banks of the Nile from the Egyptian city of Aswan to the Cushite city of Meroe, were not Ethiopians, but Arabians.[77]

The Ishmaelites to whom Joseph was sold were Sabaeans, since they came bearing "spicery and balm and myrrh," (Genesis 37:25) products which, in the Near East, came from Saba in south Arabia.[78] St. Clement wrote of a bird in Arabia which made its nest out of "Frankincense and myrrh."[79] When Judah was ruled under Jehoram, it was attacked by the Philistines and the Arabians "that were near the Ethiopians" (2 Chronicles 21:16), who could

---

66 Poole, Commentary on the Holy Bible, p. 27, on Gen. x:7; G. Rawlinson, *The Origen of Nations*, part ii, ch. iv, pp. 206–207;
67 Keil and Delitzsch, *Biblical Commentary on the Old Testament*, vol. i, ch. x, p. 165, on Gen. X:7.
68 G. Rawlinson (*The Origen of Nations*, part ii, ch. iv, pp. 207–208) tells us that the people of Raamah "was overlaid and eclipsed" by "the most celebrated of the South Arabian tribes, Sherba and Dedan." While H.C. Leupold (*Exposition of Genesis*, vol. i, ch. x, p. 364, on Gen. x:7) describes Raamah as one which "seems to be a tribe of Sabaeans in southwest Arabia."
69 See Keil and Delitzsch, *Biblical Commentary on the Old Testament*, vol. i, on Gen. x: 6–20.
70 See Poole, *A Commentary on the Holy Bible*, p. 29, on Gen. x: 26.
71 Joseph., Antiq., 1.6.2; see Poole, *A Commentary on the Holy Bible*, p. 27, on Gen. x:7; G. Rawlinson, *The Origen of Nations*, part ii, ch. iv, p. 205; Adam Clarke, Commentary, vol. i, p. 85, on Gen. x.7; James Strong, Main Concordance, p. 111, no. 7614.
72 See G. Rawlinson, *The Origen of Nations*, part ii, ch. iv, p. 205.
73 See Joseph., Antiq., 2.10.2; G. Rawlinson, *The Origen of Nations*, part ii, ch. iv, p. 205.
74 See Herod. Hist. 2.29, trans. G.C. Macaulay.
75 Diod. Sic., 3.46, trans. C.H. Oldfather.
76 See Poole, *A Commentary on the Holy Bible*, p. 27, on Gen. x:7. "Seba; or, Saba, or Sheba," writes Poole, "whose seed were the Sabeans in Arabia the Desert."
77 Pliny, Nat. Hist. 6.35
78 Sir Walter Raleigh, Hist. World., book i, ch. iii, sect. xiv; Diod. Sic. 3.46; Tert. Apol. ch. 42, trans. T.R. Glover & G.H. Rendall.
79 Epistle to the Corinthians, xxv, trans. Archbishop Wake

have been no other than the peoples of south Arabia.[80] The commentator Steuchius affirms that the "Ethiopia in the scriptures is taken for that country which joineth to Arabia."[81]

The Sabaeans, like the Chaldeans, devised an astral cult whose superior presence was founded in Arabia's religious circles.[82] The religion of the Sabaeans was the worship of the sun, the moon, the stars and the planets.[83]

Their religion, commonly termed Sabaeanism, is the oldest of idolatries,[84] and such an observation is not adventuresome, since it was indeed the Cushite Nimrod who originated the ziggurat, a temple-tower dedicated to the host of heaven. The ancient Roman scholar Lucian, in writing on the origins of astrology, does not attribute it, as is commonly done, to the Chaldeans, but to the Ethiopians or Cushites:

> It was the Aethiopians that first delivered this doctrine [of astrology] unto men. The ground thereof was in part the wisdom of their nation, the Aethiopians being in all else wiser than all men.[85]

By Ethiopians, Lucian is speaking of the Sabaeans who lived in south Arabia.[86] This is further strengthened by the fact that ancient Ethiopia encompassed south Arabia,[87] specifically Yemen,[88] and that the Sabaeans were a part of the Cushite migration from East Africa, to South Arabia,[89] and ultimately to Chaldea, where Nimrod's astrological temple tower was built.

From inscriptions found on pavements of the temple at Timna from the third century B.C., it is known that the South Arabian alphabet closely resembled that of the Ethiopic or Abyssinian.[90]

In fact, the language of the Akkadians, who made their presence from South Arabia to Mesopotamia,[91] is closely connected with the Sabaean tongue.[92] The Sabaeans of South

---

80 Josephus, in regards to this verse, speaks of the "Arabians that lived near to Ethiopia" (Joseph. Antiq. 9.5.3). That these Ethiopians were from south Arabia, see Lang, Commentary on the Scriptures, vol. ii, on II Chronicles 21:16.
81 Steuch. Eugub. in Gen. ii, in Raleigh, Hist. World., book i, ch. iii, sect. xiv. See also Gill, Commentary, on Acts 8:27
82 G. Rawlinson, *Origin.*, part ii, ch. iii, pp. 206–207. The presence of the Sabaeans, according to Rawlinson, was, "as early as Solomon," "the chief in Arabia."
83 See Gibbon, *Decline and Fall*, vol. v, ch. l, p. 896
84 See Adam Clarke, Commentary, vol. iii, p. 139, on Job xxxi.26.
85 Lucian, *Astrology*, trans. A.M. Harmon, ed. Loeb, p. 351, brackets mine.
86 See Andrew Crichton, *History of Arabia*, ch. v, p. 201
87 G. Rawlinson, *Origin.*, part ii, ch. iii, p. 193.
88 See Raleigh, Hist. World., b. i, ch. iii, sect. xiv, p. 125.
89 See Poole, *A Commentary on the Holy Bible*, p. 27, on Gen. x:7. "Seba; or, Seba," writes Poole, "whose seed were the Sabeans in Arabia the Desert; see Psal. lxxii. 10; Isa. xlii. 3; and as some think, the Abyssines in Africa"
90 Wendell Philips, *Qataban and Sheba*, ch. v, p. 42. See also Diane Moczar, *Islam at the Gates*, prologue, p. 5, where she writes that the southern tip of the Arabian Peninsula "had been influenced, and perhaps controlled, by the ancient African civilization centered in Ethiopia."
91 See Langdon, *The Mythology of All Races*, vol. v: Semitic, ch. i, pp. 1–4.
92 See Langdon, *The Mythology of All Races*, vol. v: Semitic, ch. i, p. 2.

Arabia, and the Chaldeans both worshipped the same seven planets, and even addressed them with the same titles.[93] Therefore, a connection is found between the religion of Mesopotamia, and that of the Cushite Sabaeans of Arabia. Cushite influence in Arabia is furthermore found in the language of a certain Southern Arabian people, the Mahras, whose dialect, once compared to those of the Abyssinian tribes of the Galla, Agau, and their congeners, has such a considerable affinity with the Ethiopic tongue, that it compelled George Rawlinson to describe it as deserving "to be called Ethiopian or Cushite."[94] The South Arabian dialects called Himyaric, Sabaean, and Qatabanian, which are of great antiquity, resemble the languages of both Ethiopian aboriginals, and that of the Akkadian language, which stems from Arabia, but was brought to Mesopotamia.[95]

After inquiring the primitive language of Chaldea, the great pioneer of deciphering cuneiform, Henry Rawlinson,[96] came to a conclusion in 1858 that the primitive vocabulary which he evaluated on the Babylonian monuments was Cushite or Ethiopian. He was enabled to translate the inscriptions on these monuments, which stemmed back to Babylon's earliest times, by the assistance of published works on the dialects of the Abyssinian Galla, and the South Arabian Mahra, languages of which are both Cushite.[97] The fact that the decipherer of Babylonian cuneiform was assisted by writings on south Arabian Ethiopic languages, just shows how connected South Arabia is to Mesopotamia.

The South Arabian religion of Sabaeanism, while giving birth to Babel, also gave birth to the Islamic Mecca, the holiest site to the Muslim. The builders of Mecca came from Yemen, bringing alongside with them their Sabaeanism, by which they erected the Kaaba and placed it within it the Blackstone, the meteoric idol which Muhammad chose to revere over all other idols.[98]

---

93 See Langdon, *The Mythology of All Races*, vol. v, ch. ii, p. 154; G. Rawlinson, *Ancient Monarchies*, vol. i: Chaldea, ch. vii, p. 138.
94 G. Rawlinson, *Origin.*, part ii, ch. iii, p. 209.
95 G. Rawlinson (*The Origin of the Nations*, part ii, ch. iii, p. 209) affirms the Cushite connection with the Himyaric tongue. Langdon (Semitic Mythology, ch. i, pp. 2–4) affirms that the Akkadian language is "closely allied to Himyaritic, Sabaeans, and Minaean or the South branch of the Semitic people." Wendell Philips (*Qataban and Sheba*, ch. v, pp. 41–42) presents a chart of South Arabian letters by Dr. Albert Jamme, W.F., and states its close resemblance with the Ethiopic, or Abyssinian alphabet. According to Albright (*Archeology and the Religion of Israel*, ch. ii, p. 56) the language of the South Arabian inscriptions discovered are related both to Arabic and Ethiopic, but at the same time is much more ancient than either.
96 See Philip Smith, Anc. Hist. b. ii, ch. xvii, p. 353, sect. 5.
97 See G. Rawlinson, *Origin.*, part ii, ch. iii, pp. 212–213. "Sir Henry Rawlinson," writes G. Rawlinson of his brother, "the earliest decipherer of the ancient Babylonian monuments, came to a completely different conclusion [than Bunsen] in 1858. A laborious study of the primitive language of Chaldea led him to the conviction that the dominant race in Babylonia at the earliest time to which the monuments reached back was Cushite. He found the vocabulary of the primitive race to be decidedly Cushite or Ethiopian, and he was able to interpret the inscriptions chiefly by the aid which was furnished to him from published works on the Galla (Abyssinian) and the Mahra (South Arabian) dialect." So A.R. Fausset affirms: "G. Rawlinson shows from the Babylonian language and inscription that Babylon was originally of Hamitic, not (as was opposed by Bunsen and others, in opposition to Scripture) Semitic, origin." (A.R. Fausset, A Commentary, vol. ii, p. 18, on Jeremiah v: 15) See also Fausset's commentary on Amon ix. 7.
98 Muir, *Life of Muhammad*, introd. ch. iii, p. civ

The Arabian connection with Mesopotamian religion is further supported by the fact that the Mesopotamians beheld the island of Dilmun, or the modern day Arab island of Bahrein,[99] as a holy place, greatly esteemed by the gods,[100] or in the words of one scholar, "as the Terrestrial Paradise."[101] It was the archetypical holy land for both the people and the gods of Mesopotamia.[102] There is a Sumerian tradition which states that in the earth's beginnings the land of Dilmun was an abode for the god Enki and his spouse Ninsikila, or "pure virgin lady," a native goddess of Bahrain.[103] It can be said that the "mecca" for the Mesopotamians, was an Arabian island. Dilmun is in fact referred to as Enki's home:[104]

"Pure was Dilmun land! Virginal was Dilmun Land!... When all alone he had lain down in Dilmun, the spot where Enki had lain down with his spouse [Ninsikila,] that spot was virginal, that spot was pristine!"[105]

Ninsikila was believed to have given birth, through the "sides" of Enki, to the chief deity of Bahrain, Ensak, or Inzak, who became "lord of Dilmun [Bahrain]."[106] Ensak was a native god of Bahrein, and worshipped by the people there as Inzag, as we find from two letters sent from Dilmun to Babylon.[107] An inscription upon a stone found in Bahrain speaks of an Arab pagan named Rimun, and refers to him as "the Servant of Inzak," his native goddess.[108]

When the Sumerian king Gudea was acquiring the materials needed to construct his temple-tower, Ninsus, he is said to have commissioned the Arabian god Ensak, who is also called Ninzaga, to provide the necessary copper from Bahrain:

> Ninzaga was given commission, and his copper, as were it huge grain transports, to Gudea, the man in charge of building the house, he had conveyed.[109]

Gudea as well summons the goddess of Bahrain, Ninsikila, to provide various types of wood for the building.[110]

When Enki, as it was believed, established the organization of societies, amongst the first lands he had blessed was Magan, or Egypt, and Dilmun, or Bahrain: "The lands of Magan and Dilmun looked up to me, Enki, moved the Dilmun-boat to the ground[,] loaded the Magan-boat sky-high. ...He cleansed, purified the land Dilmun, and placed Ninsikil in charge of

---

99 Thorkild Jacobsen, *The Harps that Once*, part iv, Enki and Ninsikila/Ninhursaga, p. 181; Emil G. Kraeling, Rand McNally Bible Atlas, Map iii, pp. 228–229.
100 Rice, *In Search for the Paradise Island*, ch. v, p. 103.
101 Rice, *In Search for the Paradise Island*, ch. v, p. 105.
102 Rice, *In Search for the Paradise Island*, ch. vi, p. 154.
103 Thorkild Jacobsen, *The Harps that Once*, part iv, Enki and Ninsikila/Ninhursaga, intro, p. 183, see also n. 7.
104 Rice, *In Search for the Paradise Island*, ch. v, p. 107.
105 Enki and Ninsikila/Ninhursaga, in Thorkild Jacobsen, *The Harps that Once*, part iv, p. 185, ellipses and brackets mine.
106 Enki and Ninsikila/Ninhursaga, in Thorkild Jacobsen, *The Harps that Once*, part iv, p. 204, brackets mine, see also n. 67.
107 Rice, *In Search for the Paradise Island*, ch. iv, pp. 87–88.
108 Rice, *In Search for the Paradise Island*, ch. vi, p. 119.
109 The Cylinders of Gudea, Cylinder A, in Thorkild Jacobsen, *The Harps that Once*, part vii, p. 406.
110 The Cylinders of Gudea, Cylinder A, in Thorkild Jacobsen, *The Harps that Once*, part vii, p. 406.

it."[111] The latter goddess mentioned, Ninsikil, was a patron and native deity of Bahrain.[112] So holy was Bahrain to the Sumerians that they saw it as being the place from where the sun-god Utu would arise; they saw this Arabian island as being fathered by the sun. An ancient text refers to Utu as "The father of the great city [Dilmun], the place where the sun rises."[113]

Inanna, who was originally an Arabian goddess worshipped by the Babylonians as Ishtar (Athtar), was declared by the Sumerians to have her origins in Dilmun, as we find in one text in which the deity states: "I am Inanna of the place where the sun rises,"[114] a term referring to Dilmun. In another verse the goddess is said to have "washed her head in the fountain of Dilmun."[115] A further link is made between Inanna and Bahrain by the fact that there lied a temple in Ur dedicated to the goddess named E-Dilmun-na. It was restored by the Mesopotamian king Warad-Sin, who said in an inscription: "Unto days to come for my life I built it: its head I raised and made like a mountain. Over my works may Inanna my lady rejoice."[116]

Dilmun was no mere land, but a literal heaven on earth, the place where the sun resided and the gods made their abode. Dilmun is called "The mountain,"[117] which signifies that it touched the heavens, and was the home of the gods. In the flood myth of the Mesopotamians, the hero of the tale, and his wife, are made into gods, and the celestial home given to them is none other than Dilum, or Bahrain. In the ancient text Ziusudra, the survivor of the flood, is given the "breath eternal like that of a god," and for his home "the land of Dilmun, the place where the sun rises."[118] After Ziusudra exits his ark, he makes sacrifices to the gods who at once, like flies, swarm around Dilmun to indulge in the offerings.[119] It is to Dilmun where Gilgamesh travels to attain the knowledge of eternal life from the flood hero, whom he calls Uta-napishti. "[I am seeking] the [road] of my forefather, Uta-napishti," says Gilgamesh, "who attended the gods' assembly, and [found life eternal:] of death and life [he shall tell me the secret.]"[120]

Furthermore, the god Nebo, believed by the Sumerians to have been a divine scribe from the beginning of their religion, was connected with Dilmun.[121]

All of this information proves that Arabia was the holy land of the ancient Mesopotamians, and its significance in Babylonian religion shows how interconnected it was with the religion of the Arabs, adding to the fact that the builder of the Tower of Babel himself was a Cushite south Arab.

111 In Rice, Search for the Paradise Land, ch. v, pp. 106–107, brackets mine. The last ellipses used is mine.
112 Rice, Search for the Paradise Land, ch. v, p. 108.
113 Rice, Search for the Paradise Land, ch. v, p. 107.
114 In Rice, Search for the Paradise Land, ch. v, p. 103.
115 In Rice, Search for the Paradise Land, ch. v, p. 103.
116 Rice, Search for the Paradise Land, ch. vi, p. 152.
117 See George A. Barton, *Archeology and the Bible*, ch. viii, p. 337.
118 In Rice, Search for the Paradise Land, ch. ix, p. 261.
119 Rice, Search for the Paradise Land, ch. ix, p. 270.
120 *The Epic of Gilgamesh*, tablet ix, 75–77, trans. Andrew George. See also Rice, Search for the Paradise Land, ch. ix, pp. 264–265.
121 Langdon, *The Mythology of All Races*, vol. v: Semitic, ch. ii, p. 158.

Moreover, the connection between Arabian religion and Mesopotamian or Chaldean religion can be found in the Book of Job. A perusal from the Book of Job, which is said to be the most ancient book of the Bible,[122] affirms that the Chaldeans and the Sabaeans of South Arabia, at one point in antiquity, resided in Arabia,[123] and as we find from the text, in the land of Uz, which, as we are told by one authority,[124] was located in central Arabia. Scripture specifically locates it in Edom, which was a part of ancient Arabia. As Lamentations states: "Rejoice and be glad, O daughter of Edom, that dwellest in the land of Uz." (Lamentations 4:21)

It was therefore in Edom, and thus Arabia, where Job's servants and property were attacked by Sabaeans. "And the Sabeans fell upon them," recounts a messenger of Job on the rapacious and savage nature of such people, "and took them away; yea, they have slain the servants with the edge of the sword; and I only am escaped alive to tell thee." (Job 1:15)

A further verse gives an account on how Chaldeans committed the same acts of blood lust and plunder: "The Chaldeans made out three bands, and fell upon the camels, and have carried them away, yea, and slain the servants with the edge of the sword; and I only am escaped alone to tell thee." (Job i: 17)

Such verses compel one to confirm that Arabia, in far antiquity, was a home to both the Semitic Chaldean and the Cushite Sabaeans,[125] or south Arabians.

MESOPOTAMIA, TO THE ANCIENTS, WAS A PART OF ARABIA

Arabians dominated much of ancient Mesopotamia, and to ancient geographers, Mesopotamia was a part of Arabia itself. Most interestingly is the fact that Strabo writes that "as far as Babylonia and the river-country of the Euphrates towards the south, lies the whole of Arabia."

The same ancient scholar says that "Arabia commences on the side of Babylonia with Maecene."[126] Maecene lied in Mesopotamia, and had Arabians occupying it on one side and Chaldeans on another.[127] We learn from the Roman scholar Pliny that Arabia consisted of Harran, the land where Abraham stayed and a place in Mesopotamia, and Antioch, a city in Syria. This would make Babel not separate from Arabia, but rather a part of ancient Arabia

---

122 Young, *Historical Dissertation on Idolatrous Corruptions*, vol. i, ch. i, p. 28.
123 See Poole, *A Commentary on the Holy Bible*, p. 921, on Job i:1. Uz, according to Poole, "was either in Edom, or in some part of Arabia, not far from the Chaldeans and Sabeans, as this chapter witnesseth;" while Matthew Henry locates Uz in "the eastern part of Arabia." John Gill tells us that the Sabaeans lived in Arabia Felix, and that Uz "was near to the Sabeans and Chaldeans" (Gill, Exposition of the Entire Bible, on Job i:1).
124 See G. Rawlinson, *The Origen of Nations*, part ii, ch. vii, pp. 241–242. Rawlinson tells us that Uz, where Job resided, was "probably also of a people, in the neighborhood of the Sabaeans and the Chaldeans. (See Job i. 1, 15, 17.)." He as well informs us that "there were in Central Arabia, beyond the Jebel Shomer, about the modern countries of Upper and Lower Kaseem, two regions called respectfully Bazu and Khazu, which, considering the very close connection of Huz and Buz in Scripture (see Gen. xii. 21), it is only reasonable to regard as the countries those two names indicate."
125 See Adam Clarke, Commentary, vol. iii, p. 27, on Job i.17. "The Chaldeans inhabited each side of the Euphrates near to Babylon," writes Clarke, "which was their capitol. They were also mixed with the wandering Arabs, and lived like them on rapine"
126 Strabo, 16.4.1
127 Pliny, Nat. Hist. 16.4.1

itself. So, when God told Abraham to "Get out of your country," (Genesis 12:1), He was essentially ordering him to flee Arabia.

The Arab tribe called the Praetavi had the capital of their nation, Singara, in Mesopotamia.[128] Strabo tells us that Mesopotamia, on the far side of the Euphrates, was "occupied by Arabians."[129] He also writes of how parts of Mesopotamia were occupied by the Arabian Scenitae. The road for people who were traveling from Syria to Babylon ran through the country of the Scenitae Arabs.[130] According to Zachariah of Mitylene, there was a part of Mesopotamia called 'Arab.'[131] Strabo also spoke of Arabian chieftains who held parts of the Euphrates Valley "as far as Babylonia," and how in Arabia there was "a tribe of the Chaldeans, and a territory inhabited by them, in the neighborhood of the Arabians of the Persian Sea."[132] These statements indicate that Chaldeans lived in Arabia and Arabians lived in Mesopotamia. This adds further light to the Book of Job where it speaks of Chaldeans and Arabians living in the land of Uz in Edom, which lied in ancient Arabia. The religious ideas of these two people must have been tantamount.

In the Book of Job we find the name of Bildad the Shuhite, who lived in Arabia, which means "Bel has loved,"[133] and thus it contains the name of a Babylonian deity whose planet was Jupiter. And since the period in which Job had lived has been dated as before the time of Moses, and the Book of Job is the oldest of the Scriptural Canon, Bildad's name as well indicates that deities worshipped by Babylonians had been known in Arabia in a far point of antiquity.

ALLAH WAS WORSHIPPED IN SHINAR AT THE TIME OF THE BUILDING

Imagine yourself being transported back to man's most ancient times, and viewing with your own eyes people in Mesopotamia declaring the name "Alla," and worshipping him. Mankind today is enduring the evils of Islam, with its Jihad, its persecution toward Christians and all other non-Muslims, and its most violent struggle to attain a world empire. Yet, we find that this same deity was worshipped in the very place where man, after the flood, had first tried to establish a tyranny: Babel.

Since Nimrod is recounted as a son of Cush, Genesis is showing the Cushite migration from the shores of Southern Arabia, specifically Yemen, and the west coast of the Persian Gulf, to the land of Chaldea where Nimrod began to reign.[134] The beginning of Nimrod's kingdom consisted of Akkad,[135] and therefore this Cushite establishment must have been

---

128 Pliny, Nat. Hist. 5.21
129 Strabo, *Geography*, 16.1; 16.3.1 trans. Horace Leonard Jones.
130 Strabo, 16.1.26–27
131 Zach. Mityl. Syri. Chron. 7.2
132 Strabo *Geography*, 16.1.6.
133 Francis Brown, S.R. Driver, C.A. Briggs, Hebrew and English Lexicon of the Old Testament, p. 115.
134 See G. Rawlinson, *Ancient Monarchies*, vol. i, Chaldea, ch. iii, pp. 51, 54–55; *The Origin of Nations*, part ii, ch. iii, p. 208.
135 Gen. 10:10.

accompanied with Akkadians, whose migration was quite similar to that of the sons of Cush. The Akkadians too had journeyed from south Arabia, specifically Yemen, into Mesopotamia, where south Arabian inscriptions have been discovered, as in Kuwait on the Arab shores of the Persian Gulf close to the borders of Iraq.[136]

This is linked with the fact that the south Arabians are descendants of both Cushites and Semites,[137] which would explain why the Akkadian language is related to both the South Arabian Sabaean and Minaean—both Cushite—languages.

Al Ubaid, which lies about four miles from Ur, is said to have been once the home of the earliest inhabitants of Mesopotamia; and though there has been found no physical evidence for who they were racially, Sir Leonard Woolley affirmed that "it is natural to connect them with Semitic-speaking Akkadians."[138] The pottery of al-Ubaid has been found not only in Mesopotamia, the Levant, and Iran, but most significantly for the subject at hand, in Arabian sites, specifically in al-Da'asa, Ras Abaruk, Dukhan, the region of Bir Zikrit in the south Arabian land of Qatar, and Diraz East.[139]

The founding of Akkad by the Cushite Nimrod, the analogous migration of both Akkadians and Cushites into Mesopotamia, and the connection made between the Akkadians and those of al-Ubaid, where the oldest inhabitants of the land once resided, makes it conclusive that when the Cushites had journeyed from south Arabia into the valley of the Tigris and Euphrates, that they were the original Akkadians. Therefore, the religion upon which the Tower of Babel was based had to be Arabian.

The deities Shamash, the sun-god, and Ashdar or Athtar, Venus, were brought by the Akkadians from South Arabia, where they were native deities, into Mesopotamia.[140] South Arabian inscriptions mentioning Athtar have been found in Qataban, and the largest temple in Timna in Yemen was built for this goddess of Venus.[141] And the fact that the city of Akkad was founded by Nimrod, shows definitively that these gods were those worshipped in Shinar, in the time of Nimrod, when the infamous tower was being built. Some may think that these gods came from Ethiopia in East Africa into Arabia. But this is impossible, since Athtar had originated in South Arabia and came from there into Abyssinia (today's Ethiopia).[142] With that said, it is affirmed that the idolatry of Babel originated in Arabia, and was brought by the Cushites into Mesopotamia.

That the idolatry of the Arabians was the religion in Babel, is assuredly shown by Maimonides, who attributed heathenism to a people called the Zabii, or the Sabaeans of South

---

136 See Langdon, *The Mythology of All Races*, vol. v: Semitic, ch. i, pp. 3–4. Further evidence used by Langdon is that fact that South Arabian deities were worshipped in Mesopotamia.
137 See Albright, *Archeology and the Religion of Israel*, ch. v, p. 134.
138 Sir Leonard Woolley, Ur of the Chaldees, ch. i, p. 16.
139 Michael Rice, Search for the Paradise Land, ch. iii, p. 45; ch. vi, pp. 156–157.
140 See Langdon, *The Mythology of All Races*, vol. v: Semitic, ch. i, pp. 2–4.
141 Wendell Philips, *Qataban and Sheba*, ch, ix, p. 101; ch. xx, p. 186. Farnell writes of an ancient pre-Islamic inscription in south Arabia describing the marriage ceremony of Athtar (Greece and Babylon, ch. xiii, p. 263)
142 See Barton, *Semitic Origins*, ch. iv, pp. 135–136.

Arabia. Interestingly, the name Saba, from which their name comes from, means host or army, because they had worshipped all of the host of heaven.[143] Maimonides affirmed that "these were the wise men of Babel," whose doctrines "were universally propagated, and their baneful influence diffused on every side."[144] To those who may object, that the Zabii referred to are Arabians, it is shown that every ancient book of the Zabii which Maimonides references to was written by the Nabateans, a people of Arabia Petra whose religion originated from South Arabia,[145] the birth place of idolatry. The titles of the books were Of the Worship of the Nabateans, and Of the Agriculture of the Nabateans.[146] These books were produced before Islam, and were originally written in the Nabatean language, which was hieroglyphic,[147] and the copies which Maimonides had were translated into Arabic.[148] They believed that there were no gods but the stars, moon, and the planets, with the sun being their chief deity.[149] Because their books were written in Nabatean, it is only logical for us to inquire on the Nabatean religion to further show that it was the gods of the Arabs, and ultimately Allah, who were worshipped in Shinar. The Nabateans worshipped primarily Dhu-shara, the sun, and Venus, or Allat, who they called "Mother of the gods." They worshipped both Dhu-shara and Allat as a cube shaped idol which they praised with the word "ka'bu," or "square stone."[150] This is undoubtedly another version of the Kaaba of the Muslims in Mecca, the name of which also signifies a cube or square structure. It is the holiest image for the Muslims, and was the most popular temple in pre-Islamic Arabia. And as we learn from St. John of Damascus, the Kaaba of Mecca represented Aphrodite, or Allat, the goddess of Venus.

Another evidence for Allah's existence in Shinar at the time of Nimrod is found in the Epic of Atrahasis. Our oldest copy of this story has been dated to around 1700 B.C., was written in Akkadian, and contains the oldest reference we have to Allah, calling the deity in the same name, 'Alla.'[151] The beginning of the Epic of Atrahasis describes how all of the gods labored endlessly in grueling work, under the rule of the patron deity Enlil or Elil. But soon a revolt had begun, started by Allah or Alla:

> Then Alla made his voice heard and spoke to the gods his brothers, Come! Let us carry Elil, the counselor of gods, the warrior, from his dwelling. Now, cry battle! Let us mix fight with battle! The gods listened to his speech, set fire to their tools, put aside their spades for fire, their loads for the fire-god, they flared up. [152]

---

143 Young, *Historical Dissertation on Idolatrous Corruptions*, vol. i, ch. i, p. 32.
144 James Townley's *Maimonides, Reasons of the Laws of Moses*, ch. iv, pp. 159, 164.
145 See Muir, *Life of Muhammad*, introd. ch. iii, pp. civ–cv
146 James Townley's *Maimonides, Reasons of the Laws of Moses*, ch. iv, p. 162.
147 James Townley's *Maimonides, Reasons of the Laws of Moses*, note vii.
148 James Townley's *Maimonides, Reasons of the Laws of Moses*, ch. iv, pp. 155, 162.
149 James Townley's *Maimonides, Reasons of the Laws of Moses*, ch. iv, p. 155.
150 See Langdon, Mythology of All Races, vol. v: Semitic, ch. i, p. 16; Barton, *Semitic Origins*, ch. iv, p. 133.
151 See Theodore Shoebat, *The Oldest Reference to Allah*.
152 Atrahasis, tablet i, OBV i, i–ii, trans. Stephanie Dalley, in her *Myths from Mesopotamia*, p. 10.

We should note two things here. Firstly, the spelling of Allah without the "h" in the end is simply an English rendering of the same Semitic name. Secondly, the story resembles the rebellion in Heaven led by Lucifer, and looks to be a corruption of the original story found in Scripture, with Alla being Satan leading the revolt. Since this copy of the epic was written in Akkadian, then we know that there existed within the language and religion of Akkad, a deity named Alla. Allah/Alla, then, was in existence at the time of Akkad's founding by Nimrod, and was known and worshipped in Shinar when the Tower of Babel was being built. Because the Akkadians introduced Allat into Shinar, Alla must be the requisite male counterpart which always accompanies a female deity.

The worship of Allah is in fact the worship of an ancient Mesopotamian king. As has been stated before, the oldest reference to Allah is found in the Babylonian epic of Atrahasis, in which the deity is referred to as 'Alla.' We have a Sumerian verse which directly identifies Alla with the bridegroom of Inanna, Dumuzi or Tammuz who was an ancient deified king who once ruled the city-state of Erech, or Uruk, as the fourth king of its First Dynasty,[153] at around—according to Kramer—the third millennium B.C.,[154] and whose death was ritually lamented by the Sumerians.[155]

This Alla, or Allah, has also connections in Egyptian religion, since his equivalent Tammuz was identified by Plato as the god Ammon.[156] This would link Allah with the pharaohs of Egypt, since they had been equated with the deity Ammon.

It must be emphasized that this identification of Dumuzi with Alla is not made by university scholars, but by the ancient Sumerians themselves. In the following text which gives Alla as another Tammuz, amongst others, it reads:

> Alas the lad, the warrior Ninazu! Alas the lad, my lad, my Damu! Alas the lad, the child Ningishzida! Alas the lad, Alla, owner of the net! ...The shepherd, lord Dumuzi, bridegroom of Inanna. [157]

Alla's identification with Dumuzi is made specifically in a lament for the king, who is called "the lad," after his death, in which it refers to him as Alla, amongst other names:

> [The bitter cry for him! The bitter] cry [for him!] [The bitter] cry for the captive D[umuzi!] The bitter cry [for] the captive Ama-ushumgal-anna! Woe the lad, the child Ningishzida! Woe the lad, Ishtaran of shining visage! Woe the lad, Alla, owner of the net! [158]

The more one peruses this ancient text, the more one realizes that this "Alla" is, in fact an ancestral deity who was worshipped in Mesopotamia. Within the same text we find mention

---

153 Langdon, *The Mythology of all Races*, vol. v: Semitic, ch. xi, p. 341; Gadd, Ideas of Divine Rule in the Ancient East, lect. i, p. 17, n. 2; Kramer, *The Sumerians*, ch. ii, p. 45; ch. iv, p. 140.
154 Kramer, *The Sumerians*, ch. iv, p. 140.
155 See Kramer, *The Sumerians*, ch. iv, p. 156.
156 See Young, *Historical Dissertation on Idolatrous Corruptions*, vol. i, ch. ii, p. 86.
157 In the Desert by the Early Grass, in Thorkild Jacobsen, *The Harps that Once*, part i, p. 61, Ellipses mine.
158 Vain Appeal, in Thorkild Jacobsen, *The Harps that Once*, part i, p. 53.

of the deity's grave, in which Dumuzi, or Alla, in the mythic narrative, tells his sister Geshtinanna that his mother "will make you search for my corpse."[159]

The tomb of Alla is mentioned specifically in another text, in which it states:

> …in the cupbearers house, among the little bronze cups, Alla, lord of the net, is laid to rest.[160]

By the testimony of the Sumerians, it is clear that this Alla, or Tammuz, was once an infamous king, to only be deified by the superstitious masses of Mesopotamia. By reading the Kings' List of both the city-states of Ur and Isin, we find that later rulers were in fact equated with this Tammuz after their deaths. Kings of Isin and Ur, such as Ishbi-Girra, Gimil-ili-shu, Idin-Dagan, Ishme-Dagan, Bur-Sin, Ur-Nammu, and Idin-Ishtar, were all deified after their deaths, as Tammuz.[161] And because the Sumerians identified Tammuz with Alla, it becomes logical to affirm that these kings were indeed deified as Alla as well. But besides being identified with later kings of Sumer, Tammuz is also recorded by an Arab writer named Ibn Washiyya to have been an ancient and idolatrous prophet, a cult of whom was observed by an Arabian people called the Nabateans.

The same Arab writer recounts how Tammuz had told a king to worship the seven planets and the twelve signs of the zodiac, which was to the fury of the king who had the wizard killed. To commemorate his death, the Nabatean Arabs, just as the Sumerians and Assyrians did for Tammuz, ritually wailed for him, and also lamented the death of another prophet called Yanbushad, whose name is prefixed with that of the god Nabu.[162] As the worshippers of Tammuz cut themselves in remembrance of him, Shiite Muslims today endure self-mutilation in reverence of the dead Ali, the founder of their sect and the nephew of Muhammad. It is a most diabolical act, completely contrary to what Moses stated, that we are not to cut ourselves "for the dead." (Deuteronomy 14:1) The renowned Jewish writer Maimonides, wrote on the origins of the ritual of mourning for the deceased Tammuz:

> When the false prophet named Thammuz preached to a certain king that he should worship seven stars and the twelve signs of the zodiac, that king ordered him to be put to a terrible death. On the night of his death all the images assembled from the end of the earth unto the temple of Babylon, to the great golden image of the sun, which was suspended between heaven and earth. That image pretreated itself in the midst of the temple, and so did all the images around it, while it related to them all what had happened to Thammuz. The images wept and lamented all night long, and then in the morning they flew away, each to his own

---

159 Vain Appeal, in Thorkild Jacobsen, *The Harps that Once*, part i, p. 55.
160 In the Desert by the Early Grass, in Thorkild Jacobsen, *The Harps that Once*, part i, p. 77; see also the same historians intro to this text, p. 59.
161 See Langdon, *The Mythology of all Races*, vol. v: Semitic, ch. xi, pp. 345–346.
162 See Langdon, *The Mythology of all Races*, vol. v: Semitic, ch. xi, pp. 337, 339; James Townley, Reasons of the Laws of Moses, ch. iv, pp. 164–165; Arthur Young, *Historical Dissertation on Idolatrous Corruptions*, vol. i, ch. v, pp. 249–250.

temple again to the ends of the earth. And hence arose the custom every year, on the first day of the month Thammuz, to mourn and weep for Thammuz. [163]

Because Tammuz was identified by the Sumerians with Alla, we must conclude that the false prophet described by Maimonides and Ibn Washiyya, was also this same Alla. It was, then, Allah whom the idolatrous Hebrews worshipped when they had venerated Tammuz, bowing toward east—as Muslims do when they prostrate toward Mecca—as Ezekiel witnesses:

> Then he [the Lord] brought me to the door of the gate of the Lord's house which was toward the north; and, behold, there sat women weeping for Tammuz. Then said he unto me, 'Hast thou seen this, O son of man? Turn thee yet again, and thou shalt see greater abominations than these.' And he brought me into the inner court of the Lord's house, and behold, at the door of the temple of the Lord, between the porch and the altar, were about five and twenty men, with their backs toward the temple of the Lord, and their faces toward the east; and they worshipped the sun toward the east. (Ezekiel 8:14–16)

The account of Ezekiel is reminiscent to what one witnesses in Islamic prayers: Muslims bow toward east to worship Allah—another name of Tammuz—with their backs mockingly toward Jerusalem. The event, therefore, is prophetic to the rise of Islam as the antichrist religion.

THE IDEA OF UNIFYING SOCIETIES UNDER A TEMPLE TOWER WAS ALREADY IN ANCIENT ARABIA

Since the Tower of Babel was based on Arabian religion, it should be expected to find temple towers in southern Arabia that would be used, as it was in Babel, to unify entire societies. South Arabian archeology shows this observation to be true.

It was by the goddess 'Athtar, who is the same as Allah, that major South Arabian kingdoms formed universal societies in which the people were made to be united under this deity.

In the inscriptions of the Minaeans, a South Arabian people whose language is related to the Sabaeans and Akkadians,[164] we find an occurrence in which a priest dedicates a temple-tower to the god Waddum, a moon-god, and also to the South Arabian Attar or 'Athtar (Allah), which is reminiscent to what took place in Babel under Nimrod.[165] "He of [the temple of] Qabdum, and to Waddum and Nakrahum," reads one Minaean fragment, "all the building of the tower Yahir and of its passage Rata', in wood and in hewn stones, from the foundation to the top, from the jamb of the door to the tower [which] he dedicated [in]

---

[163] Maimonides, More Nevochim, in J. Garnier, *The Worship of the Dead*, part i, ch. iv, pp. 70–71.
[164] See Langdon, *The Mythology of All Races*, vol. v: Semitic, ch. i. pp. 2, 6–7. See also Wendell Philips, *Qataban and Sheba*, ch. v, p. 41.
[165] That the Cushite founded the art of building in Mesopotamia, see Philip Smith, Anc. Hist. b. ii, p. 358, sect. 11.

Du-Hadr; when he sacrificed to 'Attar, He of Qabd."[166] These temple towers were used as unifiers to collectivize the community, as was done in Babel.

Sabaean inscriptions tell us of how Yada'il Darih, a "mukarrib" or priest-king,[167] who ruled over Saba within the eighth century B.C., united his people into one community by erecting a temple to the moon-god Ilumquh, and also by observing a sacrifice to the Arabian goddess of Venus, Attar or 'Athtar.

"Yada'il Darih, son of Sumhu'alay, mukarrib of Saba," says the inscription, "walled 'Awwam, the temple of Ilumquh, when he sacrificed to 'Attar and [when] he established the whole community [united] by a god and a patron and by a pact and a [secret] treaty. By 'Attar and by Hawbas and by] 'Ilumquh."[168] Because Yada'il Darih was a priestly ruler, his unifying of the people by a temple and its astral deities was an enactment of a state ruled under idolatry. What was done by these two South Arabian governments must have been done by Nimrod in his kingdom: he was a priestly ruler who ordered a tower dedicated to astral deities in order to unite his people as one. The same is happening now in Arabia today in Mecca: one idol of Allat or Athtar—the Blackstone—unites the entire Muslim world.

Numerous rituals of Erech, Nimrod's city, are found to be very similar to those of Islam. In the yearly sacrifices, priests would ascend to the rooftop of the topmost stage of the ziggurat and declare "O star of Anu, prince of the heavens."[169] The rooftop would also be attended by priestly singers who would chant hymns to their gods.[170] Similarly, in Islam there is the muezzin, or the one who goes to the top of a temple tower or minaret, and chants the Islamic Call to Prayer. The connection between the Islamic and Mesopotamian religions is made stronger by the fact that the Islamic minaret is a survival of the Babylonian ziggurat.

Also upon the rooftop the Mesopotamian priests would observe the rite of "Washing of the Mouth," and then recite a praise to Anu; he then would wash his hands.[171] According to the Mesopotamians, these washing rituals were done before the flood, but were later forgotten and then revived by the king of Erech, Gilgamesh:

> The rites of Sumer, forgotten there since distant days of old, the rituals and customs—it was you [Gilgamesh] brought them down to the land. The rites of hand-washing and mouth-washing you put in good order, [after the] Deluge it was you made known all the tasks of the land [172]

The rituals parallel the Islamic ritual of Wudu, or the washing of the body, in which the Muslim washes his mouth, nostrils, face, hands and feet, while at the same time reciting

---

166 Minaean Inscriptions, trans. A. Jamme, in James B. Pritchard, *The Ancient Near East*, ch. xi, p. 317.
167 Wendell Philips, *Qataban and Sheba*, ch. x, p. 105. See also Unger, Bible Dictionary, on Sabe'ans.
168 Sabaean Inscriptions, trans. A. Jamme, in James B. Pritchard, *The Ancient Near East*, ch. xi, p. 313.
169 Langdon, *The Mythology of all Races*, vol. v: Semitic, ch ii, p. 94.
170 Temple Ritual for the Sixteenth and Seventeenth Days of an Unknown Month at Uruk, trans. A. Sachs, in Isaac Mendelsohn, *Religions of the Ancient Near East*, part iii, p. 141.
171 Temple Ritual for the Sixteenth and Seventeenth Days of an Unknown Month at Uruk, trans. A. Sachs, in Isaac Mendelsohn, *Religions of the Ancient Near East*, part iii, p. 141.
172 The Death of Bilgames, lines 57–61, trans. Andrew George, in his Epic of Gilgamesh, p. 199.

prayers to Allah. In the ritual observed in Erech, certain priests would circulate around the ziggurat,[173] paralleling with Islam's Hajj ritual of circumambulating around the Kaaba seven times. It is no wonder that all of the rituals done in Mecca were invented, not by Abraham as the Muslim would tell us, but by the superstition of Arabia's oldest idolaters.[174]

THAT ALLAH WAS ONE OF THE GODS DEDICATED TO THE TOWER OF BABEL

Allah was worshipped in Nimrod's kingdom, and was one of the gods dedicated to the Tower of Babel. This is proven by a certain ziggurat which held the epithet of the "House of the Seven Lights of the Earth."[175] It was an edifice found unfinished and abandoned by its builders.

The infamous Chaldean king Nebuchadnezzar called it "the House of the Seven Lights of the Earth," which he founded in a detached suburb of Babylon called Borsippa,[176] where, according to the Talmud, the Tower of Babel was built.[177] Borsippa should grasp ones attention in our inquiry; for its name, according to M. Oppert, translates to "Tower of Tongues,"[178] or as another translation has it, "the town of the dispersion of tribes."[179]

Nebuchadnezzar confirms this; for his description of this tower as well includes the mention of the confusion of tongues, and an affirmation that this tower was the oldest in Borsippa. "The Tower," proclaims the Babylonian tyrant, "the eternal house, which I founded and built, I have completed its magnificence with silver, gold, other metals, stone, enameled bricks, fir, and pine. …[T]his edifice, the House of the Seven Lights of the Earth, the most ancient monument of Borsippa:—a former king built it (they reckon 42 ages), but he did not complete its head. Since a remote time people had abandoned it without order expressing their words. Since that time the earthquake and the thunder had dispersed its sun-dried clay; the bricks of the casing had been split; and the earth of the interior had been scattered in heaps. Merodach, the great Lord, excited my mind to repair this building. I did not change the site, nor did I take away the foundation-stone. In a fortunate month, an auspicious day, I undertook to build porticos around the crude brick masses and the casing of burnt bricks. I put the inscription of my name in the Kitir of the porticoes. I set my hand to finish it, and to

---

173 Temple Ritual for the Sixteenth and Seventeenth Days of an Unknown Month at Uruk, trans. A. Sachs, in Isaac Mendelsohn, *Religions of the Ancient Near East*, part iii, p. 141.
174 See Gibbon, *Decline and Fall*, vol. v, ch. l, p. 897
175 Philip Smith, Anc. Hist., ch. x, pp. 200–201.
176 Philip Smith, Ancie. Hist., ch. x, pp. 201–202, also see footnote 30 which reads that "Layard has observed that the name of Borshippa occurs in every mention of Babylon on the inscriptions, from the earliest time to the latest ('Asiatic Journal,' vol. xiii. part ii. pp. 436, 437.)."
177 Philip Smith, Ancie. Hist., b. ii, ch. x, p. 200, sect. 6.
178 Philip Smith, Ancie. Hist., b. ii, ch. x, p. 200, note 20; also F. Lenormant and E. Chevallier, Manuel of Ancient History, vol. i, b. i, ch. ii, p. 24.
179 See F. Lenormant And E. Chevallier, Manuel of Ancient History, vol. i, b. i, ch. ii, p. 24. Fox Talbot renders it "the land of tongues" (see R. Jamieson, Commentary, vol. i, pr. i, p. 125, on Gen. xi.9.

exalt its head. As it had been in former times, so I founded, I made it; as it had been in ancient days, so I exalted its summit."[180]

This tower that Nebuchadnezzar discovered and repaired was most definitely the Tower of Babel. The tyrant of Babylon, Nebuchadnezzar, made clear his belief in keeping preserved the tower as it was initially supposed to be built before its builders and followers were dispersed, which leads one to affirm that when Nimrod devised his building, he was formulating a tradition that would be perpetuated and followed in later eras.

By the observation of this tower, done by Rawlinson,[181] we can know the deities that were worshiped at the time of its construction, and the gods for which it was built.[182] Any connection with Islam that these gods may have will be shown.

The planet or star which each stage represented can be found out by the color which they were individually coated with.[183] The present author will accompany the name of the star or planet with its color and Babylonian term; for although the names for these astral-gods may have changed, from the time of Nimrod to the later civilizations of Babylon and Sumer, it nevertheless does not nullify the fact that the Tower of Babel was being built based on the same astrological system, as would be used by later generations in Mesopotamia. The base or the first stage of the tower was black and belonged to Saturn or Ninurta.[184] The Kaaba, was originally dedicated to Saturn.[185]

The second stage was orange and was dedicated to Jupiter or Marduk;[186] the third red and to Mars or Nergal,[187] a god of Cuth or Cush, which is an indication of the Cushite connection with this tower. The fourth stage was colored golden and was consecrated to the sun, which belonged to the gods Shamash, Tammuz, and Bel.[188] Tammuz, as we have shown, was one and the same with the Arabian Allah. Shams, the south Arabian sun-god, was equalled with Athtar,[189] Allat's archetype and the original form of Allah. The fifth stage was painted

---

180 Quoted in Philip Smith, Ancie. Hist., ch. x, pp. 200–201. Brackets and ellipses mine.
181 See Budge, *Babylonian Life and History*, ch. iii, pp. 57–58.
182 That the seven stages of the House of the Seven Lights of the Earth represented seven planets, see Philip Smith, Anc. Hist. b. ii, ch. xvi, pp. 332–333, sect. 5; ch. xvii, p. 362, sect. 14. See also Diod. Sic., 2.29; Henry George Tomkins, *Studies on the Times of Abraham*; Philip Smith, Anc. Hist. b. ii, ch. xvii, p. 358, sect. 11.
183 The colors of the stages are from Budge, *Babylonian Life and History*, ch. iii, p. 58; Philip Smith, Anc. Hist. b. iii, ch. xvi, p. 333, sect. 5; Langdon, *The Mythology of All Races*, vol. v: Semitic, ch. ii, p. 159.
184 See G. Rawlinson, *The Religions of the Ancient World*, ch. ii, p. 66; Frankfurt, *Kingship and the gods*, book ii, part vii, ch. xxii, p. 319.
185 See George Sale, *Preliminary Discourse*, sect. 1, p. 22
186 See G. Rawlinson, *The Religions of the Ancient World*, ch. ii, p. 69.
187 See G. Rawlinson, *The Religions of the Ancient World*, ch. ii, p. 69; Langdon, Semitic Mythology, ch. ii, p. 147.
188 See Ezekiel 8:16; Langdon, Semitic Mythology, ch. xi, p. 351; Henry and Scott, *Logos Commentary on the Whole Bible*, p. 294, on Ezekiel viii:13–18; Jastrow, *Religious Belief in Babylonia and Assyria*, lecture ii, pp. 128, 371; Henry George Tomkins, *Studies on the Times of Abraham*, ch. i, p. 14; Adam Clarke, Commentary, vol. i, p. 89, on Gen. xi.4; John Landseer, *Sabaean Researches*, Essay ii, p. 34; Arthur Young, *Historical Dissertation on Idolatrous Corruptions*, ch. iii, p. 110
189 See Barton, *Semitic Origins*, ch. iv, p. 129.

yellow and dedicated to Venus or Ishtar, or Allat or 'Athtar.[190] According to Strabo Borsippa was dedicated to Artemis,[191] which would have been this very goddess, who was worshipped as Allat since a Greek engraving from 6 B.C. reads "Allat who is Artemis."[192] This has a direct connection with Allah since he was the same as Allat.

The sixth stage was blue and dedicated to Mercury or Nebo or Gud;[193] and the seventh, or the topmost stage, was likely silver and dedicated to the moon, which was worshipped as Nanna or Sin,[194] who was, in actuality, depicted as the crescent moon: "the Divine Crescent, Sin," as he is called in several inscriptions.[195] This parallels with a temple tower in Ur, in which the topmost stage was a temple dedicated to Nanna, a moon-god of the Sumerians, as one ancient inscription says: "from Nanna's radiant temple on high."[196] This may have a connection with what is written of the Tower of Babel by the Targum of Pseudo-Jonathan, which describes how the builders in Shinar, in their war against Heaven declared:—"Let us make ourselves an idol at its top, and let us put a sword in its hand, and let it draw up battle formations against (him) [the Lord] before we are scattered from upon the face of the earth."[197]

The sword used in the ancient Near East was the scimitar, and the images of the god Ashur armed with this same weapon have been found in strata from the twenty-fourth century B.C. in Nineveh, the ancient capital of Assyria.[198] The idea of a deity being on top of a temple tower, while holding a crescent shaped scimitar, was not uncommon in Mesopotamia, as one finds in an Akkadian seal in which a divine being stands on top of a ziggurat with his right hand clutching a scimitar, and his left a scepter.[199] This correlates with the minaret, or Islamic ziggurat, on the top of which is placed the lunar crescent idol of Allah.

Like the muezzins of Islam, who chant to Allah from the top of the minaret, the Mesopotamian priests would ascend to the rooftop of the ziggurat, singing hymns and declaring praises to their gods. In fact, Arabic writers trace the minaret to the Mesopotamian step-towers. The term minaret literally means "light-house" or "light-tower,"[200] reminding us of how the Babylonians referred to their ziggurats as towers of light, and to how the Tower of Babel was called "the House of the Seven Lights of the Earth." Today, the minaret of Samarra

---

190 See G. Rawlinson, *The Religions of the Ancient World*, ch. ii, p. 71.
191 Strabo, *Geography*, 16.1.7
192 See Javier Teixidor, *The Pantheon of Palmyra*, ch. iii, pp. 61–63.
193 See G. Rawlinson, *The Religions of the Ancient World*, ch. ii, p. 72; Langdon, Semitic Mythology, ch. i, p. 58. That Mercury was Gud see Frankfurt, *Kingship and the gods*, book ii, part ii, ch. xxii, p. 319.
194 See G. Rawlinson, *The Religions of the Ancient World*, ch. ii, p. 61; Langdon, Semitic Mythology, ch. i, p. 5; Henry George Tomkins, *Studies on the Times of Abraham*, ch. i, pp. 8–10; Thorkild Jacobsen, *The Harps that Once*, part iv, Enki and Ninsikila/Ninhursaga, p. 187, n. 14. Sin was the head of the host of heaven (Jastrow, *Religious Belief in Babylonia and Assyria*, lect. ii, sect. x, p. 130).
195 Nabonidus and His God, i, trans. A. Leo Oppenheim, found in James B. Pritchard, *The Ancient Near East*, ch. viii, p. 279.
196 Enki and Ninsikila/Ninhursaga, in Thorkild Jacobsen, *The Harps that Once*, part iv, p. 187, see also n. 14.
197 Targum Ps.-J, to Gen. x: 4. trans. Michael Maher.
198 See Langdon, *The Mythology of All Races*, vol. i: Semitic, ch. i, pp. 70–71.
199 See Alberto R.W. Green, *The Role of Human Sacrifice in the Ancient Near East*, ch. iii, p. 36.
200 Jastrow, *Religious Belief in Babylonia and Assyria*, lect. v, sect. iv, p. 291; n. 2

in Iraq reveals this structure's origin from Babel, since it is almost perfectly identical to a ziggurat.[201]

The Tower of Babel consisted of seven stages, each one representing a heaven or planet. The people of Babel, then, wished to ascend seven heavens, just as Muhammad had his ascension to the seven heavens in which he ultimately made it to the topmost one.[202] The Sabaeans, who in truth invented all of the rites still practiced in Mecca today, worshipped these same seven planets mentioned.[203]

In Saudi Arabia today, the Arab Muslim government has built seven towers for the observing of the planets. Al-Sharq Al-Awasat, the prominent Middle East Newspaper, even names it as "Mount Babel," and has this to say about the massive project that was completed in Mecca:

> The Project Towers Of The House is the first project in Mecca…which carry seven towers… Towers Of The House is on the area of Mount Babel in Ajyad. The site overlooks directly on the Haram al-Sharif (Holy House [Kaba]).

Just as the topmost stage of the Tower of Babel was dedicated to the crescent moon, the highest tower of the seven towers just built in Arabia has a crescent moon on its head. Arabia has already rebuilt the Tower of Babel, with its seven towers and all; the land from where the religion of Babel originated, is continuing from where the builders of Babel left off.

Now that we have confirmed that Allah (Athtar) was one of the gods that the Tower of Babel was consecrated to, we must now show how this same deity distributed itself throughout the world.

JESUS CHRIST—TRIUMPHANT KING OVER BABEL

Those builders of Shinar, brick upon brick did they place upon one after the other, and how convinced they were, that surely they had a firm foundation in their building. But indeed there lied a void in their plan: that of an absolute moral. For surely they were erecting a tower of ideas, and such was absent of a trusting foundation.[204] And it is Christ who is this foundation; for He is the Word of His Father, and the incarnation of Virtue.[205] "For other foundation can no man lay than that is laid," writes St. Paul, "which is Jesus Christ." (1 Corinthians 3:11) The builders of Shinar upheld no fixed principle;[206] and therefore did their envisioning have no hope for being attained; their ideals were not founded upon that Rock of Truth, but on the folly of their chaotic waves of unsettled persons, lost in their own demise; confounded by a doctrine which seeks to accomplish things not whole, and things not real. Confusion arises in those who believe in things uncertain; they make themselves lost when they search for a

---

201 Jastrow, *Religious Belief in Babylonia and Assyria*, lect. v, sect. iv, p. 291
202 See De Croce, *Refutation of the Koran*, ch. vi, p. 31
203 See Gibbon, *Decline and Fall*, vol. v, ch. l, p. 898
204 See Jonathan Edwards, *The History of Redemption*, period i, part ii, v, p. 51.
205 See Cyprian, treat. ii:vi, trans. and ed. John Henry Parker, J.G.F., and J. Rivington.
206 See M. Henry and T. Scott, Logos Commentary, pp. 278–279, on Luke xiv: 28–29.

destination not there; they wander with minds and souls dumbfounded, their nature frenzied, when embarking to configure a utopia, and upon the sand do they build their houses. "Therefore whosoever heareth these sayings of mine, and doeth them," proclaims the Christ, "I will liken him unto a wise man, which built his house upon a rock; and the rain descended, and the floods came, and the winds blew, and beat upon that house; and it fell not: for it was founded upon a rock. And every one that heareth these sayings of mine, and doeth them not, shall be likened unto a foolish man, which built his house upon the sand: and the rain descended, and the floods came, and the winds blew, and beat upon that house; and it fell: and great was the fall of it." (Matthew 7:24–27)

And as such fools build, brick upon brick, do they rejoice how they have teared down and deconstructed the monuments of truth which were there before them. To the righteous they scorn with contempt, as though they are an obstacle before the arising of their utopia; and for such an evil they persecute those builders and admirers of those old monuments of truth. But such is the hour for those who trod upon that path of Belial, and even Christ acquiesced when placed under the mercies of the masses who declared their wishes for His death, rather than the punishment of Barabbas, a murderer. "Away with this man," did those seas of despots cry out, their tyranny being equal to that of one tyrant, "and release unto us Barabbas!" (Luke 23:18) Their bloodlust was to the disagreement of Pontius Pilate who chastised the crowed. "Crucify him," did they in turn command, "crucify him." The protest of Pilate was vanquished by the wants of the crowd, the sentence was made, for tyranny is founded not in the government, but in the masses.

The tyrant's actions are those demanded by the masses, the enemies of whom are usually the wisest of mankind. But the murder of the Nazarene was done in the hour of the sinister, and it was proudly declared by the Jews, after the Crucifixion, that an evidence to Christ not being the Son of God, was that betrayal by Judas which occurred in the Garden of Gethsemane. How could the Savior be betrayed by His own disciple?[207] The execution of Christ was done not because Judas' conspiring was unknown to the Nazarene, but because the Light of the Heavens was too bright for the darkness to withstand. It's not as though Christ committed suicide, but that He was so righteous, so noble, so immaculate, that the world, being so fettered by evil, had to kill Him. So pure was that man that He swept the minds of those wicked ones amongst him. It was not the Father killing his Son, as the moderns have so said, but the perfect man following that foundation which is of the heaven; so perfectly, so pristinely, did he follow that fixed principle of his Father, that he met the gaze of the callous masses as one who threatens their confusion. Because of His perfection was He slain. He was not a hypocrite, and therefore was he hated.

Lie did he not, and within his heart lied not an appeasement for the heretic. "He had done no violence," proclaims Isaiah, "neither was any deceit in his mouth." (Isaiah 53:9) To lower His teachings to the level of the world, He would have indeed saved himself; but

---

207 See Celsus, *On the True Doctrine*, ch. iii, pp. 61–62, trans. Hoffmann.

because He wished to bring man to the standards of his Father, was He, in haste, conspired against. The followers of darkness were allowed to advance, and the Savior to acquiesce. "When I was daily with you in the temple," declared the Christ to the chief priests and armed guards,[208] "ye stretched forth no hands against me: but this is your hour, and the power of darkness." (Luke 22:52–53)

The hour of power was but a time for the indulgences of the sinister; He who had done no wrong was mocked, and no proclamation was made for those who knew the innocence of the accused to come forth, as was according to custom.[209] "But he was wounded for our transgressions," prophesied the inspired Isaiah, "he was bruised for our iniquities: the chastisement of our peace was upon Him; and with his stripes we are healed." (Isaiah 53:5) The infliction which Christ had endured—how they had "scourged him" (John 19:1) with whips;[210] how they had mocked him;[211] how they had placed upon His head a crown of thorns;[212] how they had crucified Him—was all inflicted by those possessed by "the power of the lord of darkness;"[213] It was allowed, but only for a moment.

Christ was the most renowned victim of tyranny, for He is the greatest enemy to tyranny. How then was His coming foreshadowed? It was through a star shining in the heavens, with brilliance greater than all of the other stars, even the sun and the moon, all of which gave their praise to that one single luminary that foretold to the wise men of the East, that the Seed of the woman proclaimed in the garden, was about to be born to crush the head of the serpent. Men were troubled by this one star in the midst of the dark sky, how it was brighter than all the rest, and hence were all the deceitful and feigned impressions of paganism exposed under the light of that shining sign of mankind's Redeemer.[214] Did Christ not prevail against that first tyranny in Shinar?[215] "And the Lord came down to see the city and the tower," recounts Moses, "which the children of men built." (Gen. 11:5) The tower was the symbol of tyranny. It was not built for the glory of sublime Heaven; the builders of Shinar did not meditate upon the things of that glorious Kingdom above, but their minds were possessed by things below, by entities of the darkness and the lord thereof.[216]

It indeed was a tyranny, and certainly did they vanquish humanity with their confusion, and in such turbulence of souls, and madness, was their reign of hopelessness remedied by the Lord of truth; and in their scattering was it made known that never again shall universal utopia rule. The Rock of Truth had crushed those sinister persons and their monument built

---

208 The group consisted of both armed Roman guards and temple officers (see John Gill, Commentary, vol. v, p. 572, on Luke xxii: 47).
209 See Lowth in M. Henry and T. Scott, Logos Commentary, p. 119, on Isaiah liii: 4–9.
210 See John Gill, Commentary, vol. v, p. 290, on St. Matthew xxvii: 26.
211 Luke xxiii: 11; Matthew xxvii: 28–29.
212 Matthew xxvii: 29.
213 From the Ethiopic version of Luke xxii: 53, found in John Gill, Commentary, vol. v, p. 573, on Luke xii: 53.
214 See St. Ignatius, Epistle to the Ephesians, 19
215 See Euseb. Eccles. Hist. 1.2, trans. C.F. Cruse.
216 See John Gill, Commentary vol. v, p. 509, on Luke xiv: 28.

on the sand. That tower did crumble, and indeed did those enemies of Heaven flee. Their city was built to be perpetuating and magnificent; it was supposed to be a mecca, constructed for the purpose of being a fortress against the godly, and from a metropolis of tyrants and slaves, did it become a habitation for demons.

But soon shall exalting bliss arise, and those dry lands be flooded with the cultivating waters of the Savior. Green fields of joy shall occupy our time; fruits, emanating from trees of virtue, shall quench that thirsty soul of the saint who lives in this maddened world, with an eternal satisfaction, and from such a quenching shall his mouth for evermore proclaim truth.

Our souls shall not be like the mad followers of confusion, but like unto those trees which are given waters of pristine rivers. A tyrant shall no more receive the docile trust of dry souls under the reign of the Savior; for no more shall the confidence in man be suffered, for such is the spark that commences those fires of despotism which set ablaze all beautiful civilizations.

"Cursed be the man that trusteth in man," declares the Almighty, "and maketh flesh his arm, and whose heart departeth from the Lord. For he shall be like the heath in the desert, and shall not see good cometh; in a salt land and not inhabited. Blessed is the man that trusteth in the Lord, and whose hope the Lord is. For he shall be as a tree planted by the waters, and that spreadeth out her roots by the river, and shall not see when heat cometh, but her leaf shall be green; and shall not be careful in the year of drought, neither shall cease from yielding fruit." (Jeremiah 17:5–11)

Nimrod in the desert of Shinar, Muhammad in the wilderness of Arabia, all such men had souls vanquished by thirst as the deserts in which they were conquered by the Lord of Darkness. But, no more shall these be permitted to inflict their tyranny; no more shall they make paradises into heaps of sand. For when that Prince returns as a conquering savior; once that Chief Cornerstone, who was rejected in the days of old, and laughed at by the wise, and marked as a fool by the elite, comes again, shall every tyrant bow at the feet of the greatest liberator of mankind. "Look unto me," declares the Savior, "and be ye saved, all the ends of the earth: for I am God, and there is none else. I have sworn by myself, the knee shall bow, every tongue shall swear. Surely, shall one say, in the Lord have I righteousness and strength: even to him shall men come; and all that are incensed against him shall be ashamed. In the Lord shall all the seed of Israel be justified, and shall glory." (Isaiah 45:22–25)

And also St. Paul writes:

> Then cometh the end, when he shall have delivered up the kingdom of God, even the Father; when he shall have put down all rule and authority and power. (I Corinthians 15:24)

The yoke of the subject, the cutting whip upon the slave, all shall be obliterated. And all those idols of tyrants, no more shall they inspire the sinister to cause bloodshed and slavery.

The Kaaba of the Muslim, the Gaia of the pagan, shall all these be ceased from making drunk the despot with sanguinary frenzy. "Bel boweth down," declares the Almighty, "Nebo stoopeth, their idols were upon the beasts, and upon the cattle: your carriages were heavy loaden; they are a burden to the weary beast." (Isaiah 46:1) And with the sway of such diabolical images gone, shall peace and bliss arise in their fullest form, never again to be warred against by those confused and confounded; never again shall the monuments of truth be conspired to be torn down by the modern savage. "And through the mercy of God, his house," writes Lactantius, "that was laid in ruins by his enemies, is now rebuilt with a new magnificence."[217] The servants of Allah shall rise and attempt with hysteria to force mankind in chains, but they shall be struck by the eternal Judge, only for themselves to be trapped. Their minds shall forever be confounded, and as they attempt to flee from their misery, they will only be bound by their confusion, as those of Babel, only on that day shall they babel no more.

> In Gabriel's hand, a mighty stone
> Lies—a fair type of Babylon:
> Prophets rejoice, and all ye saints;
> God shall avenge your long complaints.
> He said,—and dreadful as he stood,
> He sunk the mill-stone in the flood:
> Thus terribly shall Babel fall,
> Thus—and no more be found at all. —L.M. Blendon's Babylon Fallen[218]

ARABIAN PAGANISM IS INHERENTLY HATEFUL OF CHRISTIANITY

Arabians who were of false beliefs harbored a violent disdain for the true Faith, even before Islam. In the early sixth century there was a festival held in Jerusalem in honor of Christ. As it was taking place some Egyptians and Arabians arrived, and when they saw a cross, placed in remembrance of Christ, it is said that they were possessed by a demonic power, and they began to bark like dogs toward it.[219] The early sixth century Byzantine historian, Procopius, described how a church had to be fortified with walls to prevent attacks done by Arabian pagans:

> There is a certain church in Euphratesia, dedicated to Sergius, a famous saint, whom men of former times used to worship and revere, so that they named the place Sergiopolis, and they had surrounded it with a very humble wall, just sufficient to prevent the Saracens of the region from capturing it by storm. ...And there is a city in Phoenicia by Lebanon, Palmyra by name, built in a neighbourless region by men of former times, but well situated across the track of the hostile Saracens. Indeed it was for this very reason that they had originally built this city, in order, namely, that these barbarians might not unobserved make sudden inroads into the Roman territory.[220]

The pagan Arabs, before Islam, endeavored to destroy Christianity. Mundhir, a Lakhmid king, executed numerous raids upon Roman Christian lands. When the Roman emperor

---

217 Lact. *A Relation of the Death of the Primitive Persecutors*, ch. i, trans. Gilburt Burnet.
218 From Samuel Worcester, *The Psalms, Hymns, and Spiritual Songs, of the Rev. Isaac Watts*, b. i, Hymn 59, p. 319.
219 Zach. Mityl. Syri. Chron. 7.15
220 Procopius, *On Buildings*, 2.9.3–2.11.10, trans. Loeb

Justin sent a messenger to Arabia to make peace, one of the pagans said to him: "What can you do? Behold! Your Christ has been expelled by the Romans and the Persians and the Homerites." Mundhir, in his pillaging and conquests, made an alliance with a heretic Jewish warlord who, sharing the same tyrannical sentiments, massacred the believers of the Himyaric kingdom of South Arabia, killing two hundred and eighty men, alongside the priests and church guards who were with them; he then converted the church into a synagogue. He took Nagrin, seized its gold and silver, and unburied their former bishop, Paul, burning his bones. Before butchering the inhabitants, this warlord asked them to deny Christ, with all of them refusing. He killed 340 of the city's magnates, the king, his wife, all of their daughters, and countless others by having them tossed into trenches filled with fire. In the end, the death count was added up to about twenty thousand.[221] When Mundhir was informed about this, it emboldened his zeal against the saints, and he told the Christian members of his army: "Behold! You have heard what has happened. Deny Christ; for I am no better than the other kings who have persecuted the Christians." The evil disposition of Mundhir was fully exemplified in the onslaught which he made in Roman Syria, in which he, after attacking and taking many captives from the Church of Thomas the Apostle, ritually sacrificed four hundred nuns to the goddess Uzza[222] who was a female version of Allah, whose image, the Blackstone, is still revered by Muslims today in Mecca.

Theophilus of Edessa, one of the oldest Christian chroniclers we know of, wrote of how "A band of Arabs came out of Arabia into the [Christian] regions of Syria. They pillaged and laid waste many lands, committed many massacres of men and burned without compassion or pity."[223]

At around 570 A.D., there was an attempt made by an Arab Christian named Abraha to destroy the Kaaba. He sent a messenger to the Meccans who told them he "had no desire to do them injury. His only object was to demolish the Ka'ba; that preformed, he would retire without shedding the blood of any man." The Meccans saw the peacefulness of Abraha, but were still willing to defend their idolatrous temple. Abd al-Muttalib, the grandfather of Muhammad, the founder of Islam, was so fearful that Abraha would destroy the Kaaba that he proclaimed to Allah: "Defend, O Lord, thine House, and suffer not the Cross to triumph over the Ka'ba!" According to legend, Allah struck Abraha with smallpox and killed him.[224] Many may condemn the desire of Abraha, but imagine if he succeeded; there would be no Kaaba, and thus Islam would have never been founded, we would never be dealing with its violence today, and the site of Mecca would have been

---

221 Zach. Mityl. Syri. Chron. 8.5; Muir, *Life of Muhammad*, introd. ch. ii, p. xciii
222 Zach. Mityl. Syri. Chron. 8.5
223 Theophilus of Edessa's *Chronicle*, section 1, from MSyr, p. 63, trans. Robert G. Hoyland, Liverpool University Press, brackets mine
224 Muir, *Life of Muhammad*, introd. ch. iv, pp. cxvi–cxvii

conquered by the genius of Christianity.²²⁵ And just think, that only fifty-five days after the attack of Abraha, Muhammad was born.²²⁶

He was the forerunner of the Antichrist; he arrived as a false Christ, as the promised Messiah who the prophets foretold. He desired the destruction of Christianity just as much as the pagans before him. The birth of Islam by Muhammad was simply a continuation of the persecution of Christians that was being done by the same pagan Arabs. The conquests of Christian Byzantine territory by the Muslims, was already being done by the pagan Arabs, and the mission to destroy the Cross, was merely continued by Muhammad.

---

225 See Gibbon, *Decline and Fall*, vol. v, ch. l, p. 900
226 Muir, *Life of Muhammad*, ch. i, p. 5

PART 12 – ISLAM: THE GREATEST OF ALL HERESIES

"Millions of modern people of the white civilization, the civilization of Europe and America have forgotten all about Islam. They have never come in contact with it. They take for granted that it is decaying, and that, anyway, it is just a foreign religion which will not concern them. It is, as a fact, the most formidable and persistent enemy which our civilization has had, and may at any moment become as large a menace in the future as it has been in the past."—Hilaire Belloc, 1938[1]

Islam is a heresy, and not only that, it is an apostate church. In its founding it prostituted itself with the most major heretical beliefs the Church has ever faced. It is Arianism, for it denies the divinity of Christ; it is Nestorianism, for it denies the Incarnation and rejects that the Word became flesh; it is Pelagianism, for it rejects original sin; and it has a trace of Gnosticism, in that it affirms that there was no Crucifixion of Jesus, but that people only imagined or thought they saw Him crucified; in other words, it is the ultimate whore of a religion.

Islam has been commonly accepted to be a religion completely separate from Christianity, or a purely pagan religion though it was founded outside of Christendom, Islam is a Christian heresy no more than Mormonism or the Watchtower Movement. That Islam is a heresy was known by the Church from its very beginning all the way to the modern era. St. John of Damascus put Islam in his list of heresies. In 1376 the inquisitor Niocalu Eymeric, legislated that anyone who believed in Muhammad was a heretic and was deemed as dangerous:

---

[1] *The Great Heresies*, The Great and Enduring Heresy of Muhammad, p. 46

Whoever invokes the aid of Mohammed, even if he does nothing else, falls into manifest heresy. So does anyone who in his honor constructs an altar to him. In similar cases the same thing may be said of invoking any demon, building him an altar, sacrificing to him, etc. [2]

Muhammad lived before the East-West Schism of the eleventh century, and before the Reformation, and so the only Christianity he knew was Catholicism. The religion of Muhammad was really a mere simplification, and degradation of what the Catholic Church taught, thus it is a heresy.[3] Islam was founded as a protest against the Catholic Church's teachings.

Islam was founded to be a direct attack against the Catholic Church and its doctrine. Muhammad denied the Trinity, rejected the Incarnation, and wanted nothing to do with the Eucharist. He hated the Mass, attacked the Priesthood, and despised any reverence to the Virgin Mary. He went against the Church's teachings on marriage and made divorce as easy as possible, and like Calvin, placed great emphasis on predestination. He despised the image of the Holy Cross and sought to destroy all church icons. According to the Arab historian al-Waqidi, the prophet Muhammad had such "a repugnance to the form of the cross that he broke everything brought into his house with that figure upon it." He saw the Catholic Church as a corrupt institution of Satan that needed to be destroyed.[4]

The rejection of the Trinity is the acceptance of anarchy. Many may say that the Trinity is a non-issue or irrelevant—this belief unto itself will lead to our very demise. The Trinity is what gives Christianity its uniqueness and order. Take away the Son and the Holy Spirit, and God can be equated with Allah or any other deity, or even the Devil himself. Take away the Father, and the Holy Spirit can be defined as a mere spiritual entity by itself, and the Son can be deemed as just a man. Keep the Son, the Holy Spirit, and the Father and the Godhead is pure, distinguished from false and satanic creeds, and is the solid gate that can never be penetrated by heretics.

The Trinity is what separates the Church from the rest, and if we do away with it we will become a part of the collectivist and universal system of paganism, engulfed by the builders of Babel, and no different than the slaves who revolve around the Kaaba and are lost in utter confusion. Mutilate the Holy Trinity, and civilization will return to the hellish days of false gods, human sacrifice, and cannibalism.

The Trinity, then, is not just some mere belief that one can keep or throw away and still be "a believer," it is what prevents us from accepting tyranny and treading upon the path to the ultimate tyrant: the Antichrist. "Who is a liar but he that denieth that Jesus is the Christ?" asks St. John, "He is antichrist, that denieth the Father and the Son." (1 John 2:22)

Just to give an example of how heretical cults eventually execute violence against the saints, there is the story of the anti-Trinitarian Eutychian heretics. These were founded by

---

2   Nicolau Eymeric, The Directorium inquisitorum, in Alan Charles Kors and Edward Peters, *Witchcraft in Europe*, part 4, p. 126
3   See Belloc, *How the Reformation Happened*, intro, p. 25
4   See Belloc, *The Great Heresies*, Scheme of this Book, p. 13; the Great and Enduring Heresy of Muhammad, p. 40

one Eutyches, and he believed that Christ did not receive His flesh from the Blessed Virgin Mary, he rejected that God could have a human body from the womb of a woman, but that His flesh was purely of a divine substance and not like our own.[5] Eutyches stated:

> I allow that our Lord was produced from two natures [human and divine] before their union, but I confess only one nature [divine] after their union."[6]

The belief was a false doctrine, for it is against what our Lord told the Serpent:

> And I will put enmity between thee and the woman, and between thy seed and her seed; it shall bruise thy head, and thou shalt bruise his heel. (Genesis 3:15)

Christ is the seed of Mary, so to say that His flesh was not received from her is contrary to Holy Writ. The devil hates Mary because it was in her womb where God became flesh, and the divine and corporal united, in order to bring forth the Messiah. To reject the Incarnation, is to then take part in the hatred which the serpent possesses for Mary and the Fruit of her womb, Jesus Christ. Moreover, if Christ did not have a human nature, then He did not suffer as a man, and if there is no suffering, then there is no sacrifice, and thus no salvation. A heresy like that of Eutyches, was condemned by St. Ignatius in his epistle to the Smyrnaeans, as heretics who deny Christ Himself:

> For what does a man profit me, if he shall praise me, and blaspheme my Lord; not confessing that he was truly made man? Now he that doth not say this, does in effect deny him, and is in death.[7]

Now, most people today would perceive the Eutychians as a harmless group; their doctrines would be seen as a personal preference, and their teachings would be welcomed with the usual cliché of, "They believe in Jesus, and that's all that matters." The modern perspective would hold this view, because modern people no longer hold Christianity as the system that dominates their lives, but a mere individual opinion amongst the others.

'You have your belief, and I have mine,' says today's conservative, and if anyone questioned the Eutychians, they would be berated with the common saying, 'theology is irrelevant, what matters is good morals.' The root problem with the modern conservative, is that he severs theology from morality, and we can see why this is dangerous in the eventual result of the Eutychian heresy. A Eutychian named Timotheus, who had been a presbyter of the church of Alexandria, in his hatred of the orthodox Christians, attacked the bishop Proterius, a major opponent of their heresy, with a mob. The bishop fled to the holy baptistery, and when the violent multitude found him, Timotheus thrusted his sword into Proterius' bowels. They then hung his body on a chord, and like Muslims, cheered and wildly cried in pride of their murder of Proterius. After they had dragged the perished bishop through the whole

---

5 See St. John of Damascus, *On Heresies*, 82
6 Quoted in Evagrius, 1.9, trans. Edward Walford
7 St. Ignatius, Epistle to the Smyrnaeans, 5

city, they burnt it and then, being most definitely under the control of demonic power, ate his intestines.[8]

So then, let this story be one lesson, that we should never, as Christians, adopt the modern mindset which tells us to treat theology as a minor or even insignificant issue, for from theology comes the sanity and civility of a nation.

Islam, to an extent, parallels the Eutychian heresy in that it utterly rejects the belief that God can take on a purely corporal body.

Muhammad and his cult have nothing but enmity for that sublime moment, in which Christ told the disciples, "If ye had known me, ye should have known my Father also: and from henceforth ye know him, and have seen him"; when Philip urged our Lord, "shew us the Father, and it sufficeth us," and Christ said, "Have I been so long time with you, and yet hast thou not known me, Philip? He that hath seen me hath seen the Father; and how sayest thou then, Shew us the Father." (John 14:7–9)

To become a Unitarian is to become Muslim and accept Islam—the religion of the coming tyrant, the Antichrist. "But how do you know that the rejection of the Trinity leads to tyranny?" one may ask. The annals of history show us how when Unitarianism, or any anti-Trinitarian doctrine arises, despotism arises with it. Let us see what heresies Muhammad adopted, and how those same heresies escalated to tyranny and the persecution of the saints.

ISLAM AND NESTORIANISM

While Islam consists significantly of Sabaean idolatry, it also has its roots in Christian heresy. Islam, in truth, is the belief that all the world should become Unitarian,[9] while observing some of the native pagan rituals of Arabia, specifically praying toward and revolving around the Kaaba. Arabia was the center for ancient Christendom to where heretics would run away, creating the perfect environment to shape the founder of Islam.[10]

Muhammad, like all other past heretics, merely built his religion upon the works of former apostates. As Gratian once said: "Every heretic either follows a heresy already damned or frames a new one."[11] He accepted the apostasy of Eunomius, which believed that since Christ is begotten of God, He cannot be one with the Father, a heretical doctrine justifiably condemned in 381 by the First Council of Constantinople.[12]

The heretic Nestorius, rejected utterly that the baby Jesus in the womb of Mary was God. In the Synod at Ephesus, when all of the fathers of the Church declared Christ to be God, Nestorius raged and said:

---

8   Evagrius, Eccles. Hist. 2.8
9   Gibbon calls the Muslims Unitarian, *Decline and Fall*, vol. v, p. 904
10 See Gibbon, *Decline and Fall*, vol. v, ch. l, p. 899
11 In John of Brevicoxa: On the Church and Heresy, in Edward Peters, *Heresy and Authority in Medieval Europe*, ch. x, p. 300
12 De Croce, *Refutation of the Koran*, ch. i, p. 9; see also n. 14 by the translator Londini Ensis.

CHRISTIANITY IS AT WAR: THE MANIFESTO FOR CHRISTIAN MILITANCY

I cannot term him God who was two and three months old. I am therefore clear of your blood, and shall in future come no more among you. [13]

Nestorius' most fanatic follower, Anastasius, viciously said that Mary cannot be called Theotokos, or the Mother of God, because there was no way God could be born of a woman:

> Let no one call Mary Theotokos: for Mary was but a woman; and it is impossible that God should be born of a woman. [14]

He once said:

> What is Mary? Why should she indeed be called the Theotokos [Mother of God]? [15]

The Nestorians attributed Christ's miraculous actions solely to His divine nature, and His more humble accomplishments to His humanity alone, splitting the two natures into separate Christs.

The Nestorians, too, had a history of forcing Christians through violence to accept their doctrine. The Christian Theodosius was arrested in Sidon for his preaching against Nestorianism. While he was in prison, where he would be confined until death, the Nestorians disputed with him for the purpose of convincing him to reject the truth, but he, with beautiful prose, rebuked them thus:

> Even though I am imprisoned and thereby prevented from going about in the different places, according to my former custom; yet as long as the breath is in my nostrils, the word of God shall not be imprisoned in me; but it shall preach that which is true and right in the ears of the hearers. [16]

Intolerance toward Nestorianism had to be utilized by the Church if orthodoxy, and the peace of the saints, were to be preserved and protected from the bloodthirsty heretics. The emperor Theodosius wrote this edict and put it into law:

> Further, we ordain, that those who favor the impious creed of Nestorius, or follow his unlawful doctrine, be ejected from the holy churches, if they be bishops or clerks; and if laics, be anathematized. [17]

It was this same Theodosius who decreed for Nestorius himself to be "banished to the place called Osasis."

Many of these Nestorians would flee to Arabia,[18] and their doctrine influenced Muhammad whose many followers actually consisted of Nestorians. Because of Muhammad's contempt for the Trinity and his overall agreement with them, some Nestorians

---

13 In Socrates, 7.33
14 In Socrates, 7.32
15 Syriac Chronicle, 3.1
16 Zach. Mityl. Syr. Chron. 3.9
17 In Evagrius, Eccles. Hist. 1.12
18 Gibbon, *Decline and Fall*, vol. v, ch. l, 899

became his followers, since they believed, like the Muslims, that Mary never gave birth to God in the flesh, but that Christ was just a man.[19]

ISLAM, A JUDAIZING HERESY

While Islam is usually criticized for being pagan, what is never addressed is the fact that Islam is a Judaizing heresy. Islam, in an attempt to follow the Jews, forbids the consumption of pork, and it makes circumcision obligatory, just as the Judaizers of the Apostles' time. When the Apostles, in the Council of Jerusalem, condemned and anathematized the people who wanted circumcision obligatory, their declaration was not only a warning against the Judaizers of their times, but the Judaizers of all time, including Islam.

Although the Muslims may be circumcised in the flesh, they are not so in the spirit. The Byzantine scholar, Anna Komnenus, made this same observation when she spoke of how the Muslims, without restraint, gratify every form of sexual lust:

> The Ishmaelites are indeed dominated by Dionysus and Eros; they indulge readily in every kind of sexual license, and if they are circumcised in the flesh they are certainly not so in their passions. [20]

All Judaizing, no matter how seemingly pious it make be solicited, leads to tyranny and despotism.

In the 9th Century there was a group of Judaizing heretics called the Athinganoi. Though they did not require obligatory circumcision, they stressed that the Saturday Sabbath should be observed rather than the Sunday rest day, that Easter was a pagan holiday, and that the icons of the Catholic Church were idols.

There was in fact an emperor of the Byzantine Empire, named Michael II the Stammerer, who was a member of the Athinangoi. Judaziers are wont to ceaselessly talk of their fabricated histories, how the Catholic Church murdered "millions of their people." If they are correct (and they are not), then we would certainly find the utmost of peace and civility under the reign of Judaizing emperor Michael II. Whoever thinks such a thought, should only look into the historical record of this man's rule, within the work of the primary source, *A Synopsis of Byzantine History*, by the ancient historian John Skylitzes. We learn from Skylitzes that when Michael took power, he promised that he would leave the traditions of the Church, and that he had no intention of changing them. Michael made this statement to the head patriarch, Nikephoros,

> Let each one do what seems right and desirable to him, free of punishment and knowing no affliction.

But like Antiochus Epiphanies, Michael gave a false sign of peace, and in short time he executed a reign of terror over the Orthodox, killing and imprisoning those who affronted him, and even forbidding children from learning Catholic teachings in order to prevent

---

19 De Croce, *Refutation of the Koran*, ch. xiii, p. 74
20 Ann Komnenus, 10.5

future generations from condemning his heresies. Skylitzes writes of this despotism of the Judaizers thus:

> Now he [Michael II] would assault the monks, afflicting them with a variety of terrors and devising one punishment after another; he would throw others of the faithful into gaol or send them into exile. Methodius, who a little later was thought worthy of the patriarchal throne, and Euthymios, then bishop of Sardis, withstood him, refusing to renounce the practice of revering the sacred icons; these he expelled from the capital city for their pains. He imprisoned the sacred Methodios on the island of Akritas and put the blessed Euthymios to death by a merciless flogging with bull's sinews at the hand of Theophilos, his [Michael's] son. ... Thus he [Michael] attained the very acme and meridian of godlessness, now ordering fasting on Saturdays, now sharpening his tongue against the sacred prophets; now denying the resurrection to come and decrying the good things promised in the next world. He would affirm that there was no such thing as the devil because there was no mention of him in the Mosaic [law]. He embraced porneia, stipulated that swearing should always be by God, with his unbridled tongue, located Judas among the saved. He ridiculed the feast of salvation-bringing Easter for being celebrated badly and out of season, portraying it as a pagan tradition. He was so alienated from our own sacred teaching that he would not even allow the young to be educated, this so that nobody would be able to withstand and condemn his mindlessness; nor any man whose eye had been sharpened and his speech quickened by education get the better of him. [21]

This entire text is significant, in that it shows what tyrannies and despotisms the Apostles prevented when they condemned the Circumcision Party, for if the Judaizers of Peter's day were allowed to overrun the Church, they too would have been a terror to the Orthodox. Let us not forget that the Judaizers struck terror into the heart of St. Peter, for St. Paul recounts:

> For before that certain came from James, he [Peter] did eat with the Gentiles: but when they were come, he withdrew and separated himself, fearing them which were of the circumcision. (Galatians 2:12)

Moreover, we find that Michael II enforced the Saturday Sabbath on Orthodox Christians, and punished monks and other Church leaders with death and tyranny for doing what he deemed as paganism—that is, having icons and observing Easter. That a Judaizer would implement such despotism on Orthodox Christians is inherent an quality of their sect once it takes a position of power. St. Paul warned the Church on the tyrannical goals of the Judaizers, when he wrote:

> And that because of false brethren unawares brought in, who came in secretly to spy out our liberty which we have in Christ Jesus, that they might bring us into bondage (Galatians 2:4)

Such heresy brings one to bondage, because it brings the Church into tyranny.

---

21 Skylitzes, *A Synopsis of Byzantine History*, ch. 3.4, [28], trans. Wortley, first and third brackets, and ellipses, mine. See also ch. 3.2, [25]

A REFLECTION ON ICONS

When I see the portraits of passed martyrs, and see them enduring with all zeal through the most excruciating of tortures, I do not see a reason for sadness, but instead I see an image of Christ, a window into Heaven, an icon of God. When we think of icons, we automatically think of paintings or statues, and while these are certainly icons, let us never forget that the greatest icon is the one who shines with the unseen light of God, so bright that it brings people to the One by Whom man knows the Father in Heaven.

The human icon is not only a hero for the Faith, but a preserver of Christian civilization. By him does man see the glory of God, by him does man thirst and seek for the eternal love of Paradise, by him does man look to the world, not with earthly eyes, but with the eyes of the soul. "You are the light of the world." And so "Let your light so shine before men, that they may see your good works and glorify your Father in heaven." (Matthew 5:14, 16) Christ tells this to His Church, to human beings who are made in the image and likeness of God. He said this to icons, icons that bring man to a contemplation on the heavenly, and constantly remind him of who he is in Christ. We have so many statues erected of men made famous for secular accomplishments, and many times of plainly evil men. But where are the statues of the martyrs, where are the paintings of their contests, over which they conquered and for which they received their crowns of glory? Why do we have statues of presidents, politicians, feminists and explorers, yet we do not dare inundate the society with the images that would remind us of the most important thing? that is, the realization that we are not here for ourselves, that our "bodies are members of Christ" (1 Corinthians 6:15), that "you are not your own" (1 Corinthians 6:19), that we are given a destiny that breaks through the physical, the beautiful purpose to stand in the midst of this capricious world, as a beacon of order, as an exemplifier of harmony, as a living candle that shines with the unseen light that repulses the infernal spirits naked to the eye, and pulls in those whose souls are parched by the waves of the watery abyss, into the bright rays of the Holy Cross, so that we can say with the Gospel, "people who sat in darkness have seen a great light, And upon those who sat in the region and shadow of death Light has dawned." (Matthew 4:16) It is that sublime purpose, to be an icon.

Christianity is the originator of civilization; the holy Faith calms the spirit, brings men away from what is disorderly and depraved, it cuts off the dried tree of apathy, it goes into the desert, and transforms it into a luscious field, so fecund and fertile, that when the seeds of the soul fall upon it, they yield "a crop: some a hundredfold, some sixty, some thirty." (Matthew 13:8) Christianity drives savages away from their savagery; it has brought pagans away from cannibalism, it has compelled their spirits to no longer have the lust for human blood, it brings them away from the mindset of a creature lower than an animal, to the eternal love only unseen to the eyes, but desperately being sought out for by the thirsty mouth of the soul, and sung of by the choirs of angels in the boundless Heavens. For "He who follows Me shall not walk in darkness, but have the light of life." (John 8:12) Christianity brings man back to that light that was placed in humanity that lied in the mind of the Triune God when He said:

✝ CHRISTIANITY IS AT WAR: THE MANIFESTO FOR CHRISTIAN MILITANCY

> Let Us make man in Our image, according to Our likeness (Genesis 1:26)

The Faith destroys savagery, for it brings man to his beginning, a beginning that has no end, but that leads one into eternity. This beginning is the likeness and image of God, it is what makes man an icon of his Creator. And it is the icon that men see on account of his brightness, for his good works, that make him a light to the world. The Christian is an icon that has men turn away from what is evil, and walk upon the path of life. When the Conquistadors destroyed the idols of the Indians and brought them to the Faith, they were icons of God, bringing those who were lost in darkness to the light that reinvigorated the eternal flame within them, so that they could throw away the likeness of demons and be in the likeness and image of God. To be an icon is to be as Christ, "To give light to those who sit in darkness and the shadow of death, to guide our feet into the way of peace." (Luke 1:79)

This is the truest form of worship, to be an icon, standing before God until we reach our eternal homes. For to be an icon is to emulate God, to "be imitators of God as dear children" (Ephesians 5:1), to be His likeness and His image. This is what is meant when St. Paul wrote: "Rejoice always, pray without ceasing" (1 Thessalonians 5:16–17). People read this and think that this means that we must be constantly mumbling requests to God. But what this means is that our entire lives must be an act of worship, in both faith and action.

We love to make a separation between regular life and worship, but what most never realize is that life is worship. The entirety of our lives should be to continuously strive to be like God, to the point that being unto itself is a rite of worship. As St. Theophan the Recluse wrote in regards to prayer: "The principal thing is to stand before God with the mind in the heart and to go on standing before him unceasingly day and night until the end of life." Being made in God's image and likeness means that we have within ourselves the creative nature of God. God creates, so we create. The creation is a living symphony, it is a harmonious melody that sings with silence, only to be heard in the Heavenly Mount Zion. But God wants us in the symphony, not being separate from His plan, but a part of it, to be the conductors and the musicians, to sing with the angels, to partake in the chorus of martyrs, to not only behold the beauty of creation's harmony, but to be the harmony itself, so that when the world hears the unsurpassable sound, they will flock to hear the music of Heaven, emanating from God—the Eternal Composer—through you, as a ray of the sun beams so sharply through a piece of transparent glass. To be like God is to be creative as God is creative, doing everything for His glory. As the Apostle says, "whatever you do, do all to the glory of God." (1 Corinthians 10:31) God's creation is beautiful, and let everything we do be beautiful, and let this beauty be a light to the world, as the stars guide the ships in the gloomy darkness.

God created us in His image, and thus do we, bearing His image, emulate God when we create things with beauty, harmony and order. Because God is the Creator, we, being made in His image, create.

And so, the greatest form of worship is to emulate God, doing everything that we do to partake in the creative nature of God, forming everything with beauty. "Therefore be imitators of God, as beloved children" (Ephesians 5:1) Even when we cook, we can worship God by forming the dish with all our effort to make it beautiful and delicious, in order to imitate the beautiful creativity of God. The Scripture says, "Rejoice always, pray without ceasing" (1 Thessalonians 5:16–17) How does one worship God always? By exerting all our energy to make everything we do beautiful. As I write these words, I worship God, as I write these words I am praying. The greatest worship is to imitate God in action. Worship God, create beauty. This is what we learn from the readings of the holy Fathers, a teaching lost and forgotten to the mumblers of today.

This is why in Christendom, art was at its peak in beauty, be it music, paintings and architecture; the standard of art was to be God's standard, it was to have order as God has order, it was to be harmonious and awe inspiring. Why was this? Because the men of Christendom wanted to emulate God, they wanted to be sacred icons. The greatest form of worship is to be a holy icon, putting all vigor and tenacity into all that we do. To be an icon of God is to say with St. Paul, "it is no longer I who live, but Christ lives in me" (Galatians 2:20). As an icon of God, your body is not your own, the self has been denied and the Cross is being carried; all the good that you do is done for God's glory, you are a ship and your sail is being guided by the hands of God, carried up over the waves to be above the oceans of the world, to cross the vicious floods and reach the top of the Ararat of theosis. And even if the ship crashes, it is done for Providence, for you will swim across the violent waters, and like St. Paul, reach Malta to seize the serpent and throw him into the flames.

The Italian mystic, Lorenzo Scupoli, once said: "I will tell you plainly: the greatest and most perfect thing a man may desire to attain is to come near to God and dwell in union with Him."[22] This is what it means to be an icon, for "he who is joined to the Lord is one spirit with Him." (1 Corinthians 6:17) To be an icon of God is to be a part of the Lord's army. God loved the icon of humanity so much, that He became an icon, "the image of the invisible God" (1 Colossians 1:15), to show us what it means to be an icon, that is, to "destroy the works of the devil." (1 John 3:8) For this reason does Satan hate the icons of God, he wishes to destroy them through persecutions and oppressions; he influences his slaves to kill them and make them miserable. The slaves of the devil are not icons of God, but they are the idols of the abyss, who failed to listen to the command of Christ, "take heed that the light which is in you is not darkness." (Luke 11:35) Thus, the wicked—while they were created in the image of God—lose their image of God, and become idols. The war between good and evil, is therefore a war between the icons and the idols.

The icon of God leads the society to be reminded of Christian identity, and the idol of Satan brings a society to forgetfulness of this identity. As icons we constantly remind people of who they are to emulate—God—and who they are not to emulate—Satan. The idols do the exact opposite of this. The icons of Christ carry their cross, and so when men see them, they think of Christ, they think of His Cross and His zeal, His tenaciousness and valor, and

---

[22] *The Unseen Warfare*, ch. 1

learning from this, they deny the self. When people see somebody who is vile, who emulates the devil, and are influenced by this, they worship the self. This is why I do not like this idea that is constantly being touted today, the idea of "finding yourself." Why should we find ourselves, when Christ commanded us to deny the self? In Christ we forget the self, saying with St. Paul, "it is no longer I who live, but Christ lives in me" (Galatians 2:20), becoming an icon, conveying to the world that their identity is not to be in themselves, but in Christ, that this life is a constant war, and for victory we are to cleanse the earth of idols. As the Apostle says, "your body is the temple of the Holy Spirit who is in you" (1 Corinthians 6:19), to have the Holy Spirit is to be an icon of God. Humanity unto itself is an icon, and it is to be a temple of God, made in God's image, but now it is filled with idols, and what are we to do—as emulators of Christ—but to take a whip and drive the idols out of God's Temple? The men who make themselves into idols, are sellers of the human soul, giving them away to the devil, and it is the icon of God who purges the world of them.

As icons, we fight the idols by creating beautiful art, art that teaches the Faith through wonder and majesty. Look to the Church, and you will see beautiful paintings and images of Crosses. Oh, how the devils hate such art, because they—with their immaculate imagery—instill in us a sense of Christian identity, and constantly remind us that we are in Christ, and are not to be dictated by the trends of this world. This is why the wicked and evil atheists and Muslims are always pushing for governments to censor any sort of Christian imagery and expression. They want us to be devoid of icons, to forget our hope, and to place our faith in the idolatry of the self. I have heard people say that crosses, church bells, Christian paintings and statues, are idols. But the hatred against the icons is the real idolatry. For to make a society devoid of Christian imagery, is to enable the enemy to replace the icons with true idols, with the worship of celebrities, of buildings, of politicians, of false prophets. Man, by his very nature, venerates. Take away the icons and he will venerate himself, he will venerate other men, he will venerate Mammon, he will venerate the devil. But restore the holy icons and you will see Christendom revive. The icons will be everywhere, and even the least religious person will see it and feel within himself a small measure of awe, enough to compel him to express his gratitude to the One Who died for Him. Embellish the earth with holy icons, and man will be reminded of what is sacred, man will come to contemplation, and with contemplation comes wonder and inspiration, and from this does the person know that he is but an icon himself, a window into Heaven, who is to shine so brightly that men will worship their Father in Heaven. Anyone who hates Christian icons, hates humanity, for humanity itself is an icon. This is the heresy of iconoclasm.

ISLAM IS ICONOCLASM

Islam is most frequently berated as a false religion by Christians, because it denies the divinity of Christ, the Crucifixion, and other Orthodox doctrines of the Faith. But, what most, if not all, Christian critics of Islam fail to point out, is that Islam is an iconoclast heresy, meaning it seeks to destroy all Christian icons, from crosses and crucifixes, to statues of Christ, saints and angels. Islam deems Christian icons as "idols," that need to be destroyed, and teaches that Christian iconography must be replaced by a puritan Unitarianism, in which only the one god, Allah, is worshipped. This way of thinking is akin to the theology of the Puritans. This parallel becomes clearer with the fact that both the Muslims and the Puritans believed in a fanatical form of predestination. This is why Islam can be called Unitarian Calvinism.

When Muslims today attack Christian villages and churches, they always desecrate and shatter the Christian icons, believing them to be idolatry and worthy of destruction. This is nothing new, though. Islam is simply a continuation of iconoclast groups that were active in Christendom during the Middle Ages, and like Islam, these iconoclasts believed in absolute tyranny, terror, and persecution against Orthodox Christians.

THE POWER AND TYRANNY OF ICONOCLASM IN THE BYZANTINE EMPIRE

Iconoclasm was greatly propagated by the 9th century monk, Sabbatios. He maliciously hated the emperor, Leo V (who was surnamed "the Armenian") for his reverence to Christian icons. Sabbatios, with vitriol, said that the emperor was "addicted to idols," and expressed his spite at how Leo V piously obeyed the patriarch of Constantinople, Tarasios, and viciously called him "taraxios" or "trouble maker." After Tarasios passed away, he was replaced by Nikephoros who began to warn that soon Leo V would begin to enforce iconoclasm and persecute the Church. The quarrelsome monk also had nothing but hatred for the emperor's wife, Eirene, and scoffingly named her, "panther" and "folly." He even threatened that the emperor would lose his life if he did not abide by his heresy and throw away all of the Christian icons. Sabbatios soon had a meeting with one Theodotus Melissenos, a fanatic proponent of iconoclasm, who for a long time kept his heretical sentiments to himself, and was always waiting for the opportunity to vomit them out in public. He told the monk to affirm to the emperor that he must adopt the iconoclasm of the past emperor, Leo the Isaurian—who enforced iconoclasm and persecuted the Orthodox—and destroy all of the icons of the Church:

> Tomorrow night the emperor will come to you in ordinary clothing, to ask about the faith and other pressing matters. For your part, you are to remember to threaten him with the imminent loss of his life and his fall from the throne, unless he choose of his own free will to embrace the dogma of the emperor Leo the Isaurian and to cast out the idols… from the churches of God. Nor must you forget to promise him that, if he adopts the way of life you suggest, he will enjoy a long life and a fortunate reign for many years. [23]

When Sabbatios, the iconoclast monk, approached the emperor (who was wearing civilian clothing) he told him, as though it was revealed to him by divine inspiration,

> What you are doing is not sensible, O emperor, deceiving us with private citizens' clothes and concealing the emperor hidden within them. Do what you will, the grace of the divine Spirit has not allowed us to be outsmarted by you any longer. [24]

---

23 Skylitzes, *Byzantine History*, 2.2, trans. Wortley
24 Skylitzes, *Byzantine History*, 2.2

CHRISTIANITY IS AT WAR: THE MANIFESTO FOR CHRISTIAN MILITANCY

When the emperor heard this he was baffled at how the monk could easily identify him regardless of his humble clothing, and thought that he was some sort of holy man, and at that point, the iconoclast obtained their influence, and thus gained the power they were seeking. Leo V made himself ready to obey whatever the monk commanded of him, and so decreed that the sacred icons would be taken down. The emperor then presented a document that explained the doctrine of iconoclasm, to the leading citizens of Constantinople, and urged them to sign it. Many signed it willingly, while those who refused were forced to write their names on it. The patriarch Nikephoros, who forewarned of this tyranny beforehand, was now presented with the document, and he, like a good soldier, refused to sign it and utterly rejected its teachings. He was seized and exiled to Prokonnesos. A monastic named Theophanes the Confessor, of the monastery of Agros, accompanied Nikephoros with incense and candlelights, alongside many others who did not bow the knee before the idol of iconoclasm, and in his banishment he died as a martyr. While the patriarch Nikephoros was in exile, he was replaced by Theodotus Melissenos, who took the seat illegitimately and proclaimed the heresy of iconoclasm out in the open. Not only this, but he used his position to execute harsh violence on those who opposed iconoclasm, having people's feet and hands amputated, and even their private parts cut off, and then the severed parts were to be hung along the main thoroughfare for all to see.[25] Islam, which is a continuation of iconoclasm, demands for the amputation of Christian—who they deem as idolaters—in the following verse:

> The recompense of those who fight Allah and His messenger, and seek to make corruption in the land, is that they be killed or crucified or that their hands and feet be cut off from alternate sides or that they be banished from the land; that is their disgrace in this world and in the Hereafter they will have a great torment. (Qur'an 5:33)

A man was then chosen to be the iconoclast agent, who would further influence the emperor to further advance iconoclasm. In one particular Mass there was a reading from the Book of Isaiah when the prophet said:

> To whom will ye liken the Lord? Or with what will ye compass him? Was it not the carpenter who made the image, the goldsmith who melted gold and gilded it, and made a likeness of himself

The iconoclast agent then used this verse to justify iconoclasm, and whispered into the ear of the emperor these words:

> Give understanding to what is said [here], oh emperor, and do not let the truth elude you. Embrace the pattern of devotion which the prophet proposes to you. [26]

With this pernicious influence, which flowed like a sweet potion tainted with venom, the emperor intensified the persecution over those who revered the icons. The people who accepted iconoclasm, lived quiet and peaceful lives and were not bothered, but those who

---

25 Skylitzes, *Byzantine History*, 2.2–3
26 Skylitzes, *Byzantine History*, 2.4

combated the doctrine, and struggled with Satan and his doctrine, were received with threats and afflictions.[27]

THE TYRANNY OF THE ICONOCLAST EMPEROR, THEOPHILOS

What is interesting is that the emperor Michael II was both an iconoclast and a Judaizer, and his son, Theophilos, following his father, fanatically subscribed to iconoclasm. Throughout his reign, Theophilos would afflict and persecute Orthodox Christians who revered the icons, never permitting them a moment of peace, or in the words of Skylitzes,

> He relentlessly afflicted the pious and all holy people, allowing them not a moment of calm throughout his reign. [28]

Continuing the persecution of his Judaizing father, Theophilos decreed that no paintings of saints could be allowed to have the words "saint" or "holy" on them, since to the tyrant, only God deserved such titles. With such a measure it was evident that Theophilus did not follow Orthodox theology, for if a Christian who was used by God for many noble and meritorious works could not be called holy, then he should have been angry at God for calling His priests "gods" in the Old Testament:

> Ye are gods; and all of you are children of the most High (Psalm 82:6)

If calling Mary or one of the prophets or apostles "holy" is blasphemy because the title only belongs to God and hence it is idolatry, then by this logic God Himself is an idolater because He called human beings "gods,"[29] not in the sense that they were actually divine, but that they were God's representatives on earth. Concordantly, saints who are given the title of "holy," are done so in accordance with the definition of holy, in that they are used by God for a specific purpose.

Theophilos would soon utterly abolish icons and the painting of saints, and all of the Christian images were subsequently, and forcefully, removed, and disturbingly replaced with depictions of animals, wild beasts and birds. This only was a reflection of the beastly and, really, pagan mindset of the tyrant. Where did the icons go? They were thrown into the local market places where they were defaced and scoffingly and abominably desecrated and abused by the godless mobs. After the forceful removal of the icons, came the forceful removal of the Orthodox. The prisons, instead of being filled with just criminals, were now being flooded with monks, bishops, and laymen who resisted the heretical devils and chose not to reject the holy icons. The Orthodox were violently seized and banished to the desolate wilderness, left to the cruel dictates of nature, where hunger and thirst reigned. Full of the bodies of martyrs were the mountains and caves, of those holy Christians who chose death rather than compliance with the tyrant. The emperor Theophilos decreed that the cities block any monks from entering into their premises, and ordered that they be kept a distance by any

---

27 Skylitzes, *Byzantine History*, 2.4
28 Skylitzes, *Byzantine History*, 4.3
29 Skylitzes, *Byzantine History*, 4.10

means. But these holy men, living the arduous lives of monastics, following their predecessor Elijah, who was driven into the desert by Jezebel, preferred death than apostasy.[30]

A group of very zealous monks, some of whom were a part of a monastic order called the Abramites, came before the emperor and, with zeal and blazing strength and dedication, exclaimed that monasticism was no recent invention, but was supported by the sayings of the holy fathers, Irenaeus, Dionysus the Great, and Hierotheos, and that their spiritual lives were there from the time of the ancient days of the Church. The pious monks declared that Luke, the apostle, carved out an image of the Virgin Mary, and that Christ Himself left us an image of His face imprinted on a piece of linen "without the intervention of hands."[31] After hearing such a speech, the emperor Theophilos had all of the monks tortured and beaten, and so severe were the blows that they teared extremely deep wounds into their flesh, and their bodies became as the Body of Christ when He was scourged. The monks were then sent off into the wilderness, bearing their inflections with all endurance, and exemplifying the greatest form of long-suffering. They kept on walking through the grueling land, until they reached the Church of the Forerunner (John the Baptist). They entered the sacred edifice, and from the suffering of their wounds, they died.[32]

Another monk, whose heart was fortified by tenacious conviction, went right to the emperor's face and withstood him with chastisement, and quoted to the tyrant the words of St. Paul: "If any man preach unto you any other gospel than that which you received, let him be anathema." (Galatians 1:9) Theophilos was ignited by rage at this man's holy recitation, and so he had the monk brutally flogged. But he noticed that this monk's zeal only increased when he was persecuted, and so he decided that he would beat his intellect. The emperor chose one of his best theologians, Jannes, to debate the monk. This Jannes, while hating the sacred icons, was addicted to witchcraft, in particular a fashion of sorcery called lecanomancy in which the sorcerer throws precious stones or pieces of gold and silver into a basin filled with water, and then observes the patterns formed once the objects reach the bottom. The monk broke through the bastion of Jannes' sophisms and subtle arguments, not only with his own words, but with those of Scripture, and revealed how empty the cunning deceptions of the iconoclasts were. After the debate, the steadfast monk was given another beating, banished into exile. He would later take refuge with Iganatios the Great, and after giving several prophecies of future emperors, for it was said that he was blessed with the gift of prophecy, he died.[33]

The emperor Theophilos ordered that all of those who made paintings of Christ, under pain of death, were to spit on the very holy icons they painted. Amongst the many painters who were arrested was a monk named Lazaros, and he was not planning on acquiescing to the demands of a heretic, and nor was it in his mind to spit upon an image of the One Who died for him. At first the tyrant tried to convince him to obey the order through flattery, but

---

30 Skylitzes, *Byzantine History*, 4.10
31 Skylitzes, *Byzantine History*, 4.10
32 John Skylitzes, *Byzantine History*, 4.10
33 Skylitzes, *Byzantine History*, 4.10; 5.3, see footnote 19 by Jean-Claude Chaynet on Lecanomancy

when that did not impact the mind of this monastic warrior, Theophilos, like a Muslim and a true heretic, resorted to violence. So brutal and severe was the torture afflicted on this man's body, that it was thought that he was not going to survive. They sent him out, thinking that with such a broken body he would never try to paint an icon of Christ. But soon his health recovered, and immediately he began to make a holy icon. The emperor had him arrested, and the torturer placed burning hot coals on his hands, and so excruciating was the pain, that this poor saint of God lost consciousness and dropped to the floor half-dead. He was near his last breath, but the wife of the emperor took pity on him, and demanded her husband to have the holy monk spared. He was released from prison and placed in the Church of the Forerunner (John the Baptist).[34] The endurable athlete Lazaros painted an immaculate image of St. John the Baptist in the Church of the Forerunner, and it remained there for a long time, and those who were stricken with infirmities came to touch it and were healed.

The monk Lazaros was a likeness to John the Baptist: he confronted the tyrant, as the pious warrior confronted Herod; he lived in the state of hermitage, and John cried out from the wilderness, attired himself with the humblest clothing of goatskin; he suffered persecution and endured until the end, as the Baptist was thrown into prison for exposing the wickedness of the despot.

We must ask ourselves the question: how different were the iconoclasts from the Muslims who have been destroying Christian icons, and still continue to desecrate the icons till this day? There is no difference: the antichrist spirit is the same, and the vehement malice against the icons is identical to the jihadis of today.

THEOPHANES AND THEODORE—MARTYRS AGAINST ICONOCLASM

There were brothers very learned in the Scriptures, their names were Theophanes and Theodore, and their eruditeness in Holy Scriptures and the Faith manifested itself as light to the darkness of iconoclasm. The emperor was stricken by this light, and he, uttering the vitriol of darkness, said to the two brothers,

> Come on then, you accursed ones, by what sayings of scripture are you persuaded to worship the idols, and to persuade the innocent common people to do likewise?[35]

But the two brothers did not fall in fear, or quiver in terror—no—instead they turned to the tyrant, and proclaimed,

> Let the mouth be dumb which speaks iniquity against God.

After much struggle and debate, the emperor's wrath could no longer be concealed, but compelled to be revealed by the light of truth that shined forth from the two saints. In his anger, the tyrant said:

> An emperor ought not to be subject to the insults of men like you.

---

34 John Skylitzes, *Byzantine History*, 4.10
35 Skylitzes, *Byzantine History*, 4.10

He had the two brothers arrested and brought to the inner garden of the Lausiakos where they were heavily beaten with two hundred blows with the heftiest of rods. And then, to further the humiliation of the punishment, he had their foreheads tattooed with these mocking and scolding words:

> When all the world went running to that town where the all-holy feet of God the Word once stood to ensure the safety of the world, in that most pious place these did appear who are an evil vessel of superstitious error. Which superstitious men, achieving there with impious mind the deeds of unbelief most horrid, were expelled as apostates and exiles. Thence they fled, sad refugees, unto the capital and seat of government—but did not leave aside their foolishness hence, indicted and condemned, an evil perpetrator of the image, they are banished once again.[36]

Does this not remind us of the mocking which Christ endured? What scoffing, what deriding, and yet, it is the suffering of Christ, seen before our eyes in the person of His children who, being as innocent as doves, piously declare the words of truth without guile, and being as wise as serpents, strike, in the zeal of the Spirit, with the words of Orthodoxy at the vipers.

And after the holy brothers were marked with the lines of the scoffers, they were both executed, and crowned with a martyr's embellishment. Not so long after, the emperor Theophilos arrested one Michael, a synkellos or episcopal vicar of the Church of the Holy City, and many other hermits and ascetics, and shut them up in prison, with the pernicious hope that by depriving them of their freedoms they would eventually acquiesce to the tyrant's wicked demands. And for the rest of his life did this despotic sovereign ceaselessly subject them to irremediable afflictions.[37]

When the tyrant Theophilos died, his son, Michael III, and his wife, Theodora, reigned. By the suggestion of some Orthodox holy men, she began to closely examine the heresy of iconoclasm that her husband so fanatically subscribed to. So many people within the government followed it, and even most of the senate, and the Church synod (including the patriarch) were iconoclasts. Soon a terrible illness struck the empress' scholastic, Manuel, and as he lay bed-ridden, surrounded by monks, he said,

> And how can this be for me, godly fathers? My mental forces are all gone, my body is wasted away and emaciated. Here I lie, devoid of flesh, a mere skeleton; there is no difference between me and a corpse, except that I am breathing. What hope is there, what reason to believe in my recovery and return to my former health?

The monks took up his argument and responded:

> With God, all things are possible and there is nothing that is impossible. We proclaim the good news that you will live, provided that you endeavor to extinguish the conflagration the

---

36 John Skylitzes, *Byzantine History*, 4.10
37 John Skylitzes, *Byzantine History*, 4.10

PART 12

enemies of the icons have ignited when you recover your strength, and that you restore the sacred icons to the status they enjoyed in the time of our forefathers. [38]

Manuel told the empress Theodora that she must overthrow iconoclasm and restore Orthodoxy, but she resisted, for she feared the multitude of iconoclasts and their reign of terror. But when Manuel insisted with ardency, she exclaimed:

> O magister, my late husband, the emperor, a stickler for precision, never did a thing in all his life without careful examination of the matter. If this practice [of revering icons] were not forbidden in sacred laws, and the Holy Scriptures, he would not have expelled it from the church. [39]

Manuel wasted no time, he had to restore Orthodoxy and would not allow the fears of a woman to prevent that. He declared to her that if she did not drive out iconoclasm, that both her and her son would die. The threat enabled the empress to commit to her own desires, and that was that the blade of Orthodoxy be unleashed and vanquish the wiles and bastions of heresy that so plagued the empire. She provided her full support in the ousting of iconoclasm, and summoned a meeting with the fathers of the synod and members of the senate, so that the iconoclasts and those who revered the icons could debate. After much fierce and zealous arguing, it was obvious as to who took the victory: the Orthodox. After the debate, many of the monks, bishops, and senators who subscribed to iconoclasm threw away their heresy and adopted Orthodoxy, while those who remained within the heretical movement, were exiled. The wicked patriarch, who was responsible for the persecutions against the Orthodox, was ousted out of his seat and banished. Once he was gone, he was replaced by the godly Methodios, on whose body one could still see the marks from the beatings he received from the iconoclasts. As for Jannes, the theologian chosen by Theophilos to debate with sophisms against the Orthodox, he was shut up in a monastery, and in the monastery were icons of Jesus Christ, Mary His mother, and Michael the Archangel. Jannes said that such icons are devoid of sight, and so he ordered his personal deacon to tear out the eyes of the sacred images. The empress Theodora heard of this, she was ignited by godly zeal, and ordered that his eyes be removed. But a number of Orthodox holy men interceded for him, and begged the empress to show mercy, and so instead he was punished with 200 lashes.[40]

Orthodoxy was restored, Lazaros painted a beautiful image of Christ. He was invited by the very empress, Theodora, who rescued him, and she asked him to pardon her husband, and to intercede for him. To this Lazaros replied:

> O empress, God is not so unjust as to forget our love and our labour on his behalf, while holding in higher honour the hatred and the presumptuous folly of that man.[41]

---

38 Skylitzes, *Byzantine History*, 5.2
39 Skylitzes, *Byzantine History*, 5.2
40 Skylitzes, *Byzantine History*, 5.2–3
41 John Skylitzes, *Byzantine History*, 4.10

But the iconoclast, led by their leader Jannes, never ceased in their onslaught against the Orthodox. They still raged against the icons, and devised all sorts of slanders and false accusations to frame the Orthodox patriarch Methodios with the attempt to reestablish iconoclasm.

THE SLANDERED VERSUS THE HARLOT

The emperor hated with great intensity the noble life of monasticism, and did not allow the monks to conduct their assemblies where men gathered together to conquer the passionate flames of violent desires. They took a woman and payed her with much gold to denounce Methodios before the empress, and say that he had licentious relations with her. This accusation brought much fear to the Orthodox, seeing that they could become but a laughing stock before the heretical mobs. Methodios was brought before a tribunal, amidst a crowd of iconoclasts who laughed and mocked him with scathing insults. Methodios ignored the mob, and in the presence of everyone, took off his garments and exposed his private parts to all, and he revealed that his genitals were atrophied by some infirmity that made him utterly incapable of copulating. The mob of heretics shut their mouths, and the Orthodox rejoiced.[42] The false accusers were about to be arrested and punished for false testimony, but Methodios, emulating Christ, expressed mercy for his enemies, and affirmed that their only punishment should be that every year they should come to the Church of the All-pure Mother of God at Blachernae, and hear the anathemas against iconoclasm. This was done by the slanderers for the rest of their lives.[43]

CONSTANTINE V AND HIS ISLAMIC PARALLELS

While many go against Constantine the Great, nobody reveals the evils of Constantine V. He shared beliefs akin to Nestorianism, an influence to Muhammad. He also was an iconoclast, or somebody who disdained the monastic life and despised any icons or paintings of Christ or Mary—they saw this as idolatry. Islam embraces this doctrine whole heartedly. Like Muhammad, Constantine V "was deceived by wizardry, licentiousness," and "summoning demons." He would also be involved in making sacrifices of urine and dung,[44] a form of divination which Muhammad partook in, as we read in one Hadith. One woman consumed some of Muhammad's urine and he told her, "You will never complain of a stomach ache. He did not order any of them to wash their mouths out nor did he forbid them to do it again."[45]

Like Muslims, Constantine V would kill those who went against his heretical doctrine.[46] Those who criticized the emperor's apostasy would suffer the same fate as those who question Muhammad's creed in Sharia code: death. The monk Andrew was whipped to death in the arena for accusing Constantine V of impiety.[47] There was also the situation with the monk

---

42 Skylitzes, *Byzantine History*, 5.4
43 Skylitzes, *Byzantine History*, 5.4
44 Chron. Theophan. Annus Mundi 6232
45 See Walid and Theodore Shoebat, *For God or For Tyranny*
46 See Chron. Theophan. Annus Mundi 6256
47 Chron. Theophan. Annus Mundi 6253

Stephen who, for praising the monastic life over the evils of politics, bounded at his feet with a cord, and dragged him to death on the street; his body was then torn to pieces and thrown into a pit.[48] Such a method of killing for the sake of heresy closely resembles what is done in the Muslim world today.

Constantine V ordered that one patriarch, also named Constantine, be beaten until he could no longer walk. He was made to sit down within a church—now a heretical sanctuary—where he was told all of his "crimes," he was then condemned and called "Skotipsis," which means "Of darkened vision." On the following day there was a horse race, and the persecuted patriarch was to be a part of the savage spectacle. He was spat on, his beard, head, and eyebrows were shaven, and he was made to put on silk and a sleeveless garment. He was forced to mount on a donkey backwards and ride to the arena where he was beheaded.[49] The impious emperor savagely and sadistically killed many others. He had one Peter seized, dragged through the streets and then buried alive. He bound others in bags from which they could not escape, and thrown into the sea to drown. Anyone who was found to be living as a monk or with zealous orthodoxy was killed in such ways.[50]

THE DESPOTISM OF LEO III AND THE ICONOCLASM OF ISLAM

Another iconoclast king, Leo III, ordered for all the statues of martyrs to be effaced, and when the Pope of Rome heard of this, he ordered the Christians to refuse to pay taxes to the empire.[51]

Iconoclasm was, and still is, exemplified by Muslims. The Muslims under the Ottoman Empire, were famous for stabbing church icons. One Italian poet wrote with sadness on "the outrage done to God... the crucifixes and the images of the saints, of God, of the Madonna and the Holy Sacrament," by the Muslims, who took joy in stabbing, burning, and firing arrows upon Christian icons.[52]

Both Muhammad and Constantine V affirmed with fervent conviction that Mary was not the mother of God, and Protestants today would agree with them, saying that we should simply call her the mother of Christ. Now, while there is nothing wrong with calling her the mother of Christ, there is a danger in affirming that we must never address her as the mother of God. To affirm this implies that Christ is somehow different, or even less significant, than the Father. I do not agree that the source of God was Mary, but I do certainly believe that she brought forth Christ, God in the flesh, and that in this regard she indeed is the mother of God. Christ said "I and my Father are one."[53] This means that Jesus is God, and as He was on the cross, He saw his mother and declared, "Woman, behold thy son!"[54] By these two verses, Mary was the mother of God. Protestants have no problem in calling God the

---

48 Theophan. Chron. Annus Mundi 6257
49 Chron. Theophan. Annus Mundi 6259
50 Chron. Theophan. Annus Mundi 6259
51 Theophilus of Edessa's *Chronicle*, section 2, p.225
52 See Moczar, *Islam at the Gates*, ch. vii, p. 147
53 John 10:30
54 John 19:26

CHRISTIANITY IS AT WAR: THE MANIFESTO FOR CHRISTIAN MILITANCY

Father of Christ, and we know that they are not referring to Christ as not eternal or as being created. So then where is the issue if we call Mary the mother of God? It was not adopted from paganism, as the subscribers to Hislop say, but to combat Arianism and Nestorianism. Anatasius, a follower of Nestorianism, defiantly declared:

> Let no one style Mary the Mother of God; for Mary was human, and it is impossible for God to be born of a human being. [55]

There is a story which reveals the reason why the ancient church addressed Mary as so. One day the emperor Constantine V asked the patriarch of Rome, "But why would it harm us if we were to call the Mother of God 'the mother of Christ'?" The patriarch embraced his question and replied, "Have mercy, lord, that title should not have crossed your mind. Do you not see that Nestorius was declared infamous and was anathematized by the entire church?"[56] To call Mary the mother of God, thus, is to prevent the sheep from going astray to the wolf of Unitarianism. Not only was it a response against Nestorius, but the heretic Arias as well.

But not only this. The term "Mother of God" directly spearheads the heresy of Islam, because it is the doctrine of Muhammad that hates calling Mary the Mother of God, for like its predecessors, it seeks to destroy the doctrine of the Incarnation that God was born from the womb of Mary.

ISLAM AND MANICHAEANISM

Islam teaches that Christ was never killed nor crucified, but that He only appeared to be crucified, and that He ascended to heaven and never died, as the Koran writes:

> Because they rejected Faith; that they uttered against Mary a grievous false charge; That they said (in boast), 'We killed Christ Jesus the son of Mary, the Messenger of Allah', but they killed him not, nor crucified him, but so it was made to appear to them and those who differ therein are full of doubts, with no (certain) knowledge, but only conjecture to follow, certainly they killed him not. No, Allah raised him up unto Himself; and Allah is Exalted in Power, the Wise. [57]

This verse is indicative that the Muslims are of the same spirit as those whom St. Paul referred to as the haters of the Holy Cross in his epistle to the Philippians:

> Brethren, be followers together of me, and mark them which walk so as ye have us for an ensample. (For many walk, of whom I have told you often, and now tell you even weeping, that they are the enemies of the cross of Christ: Whose end is destruction, whose God is their belly, and whose glory is in their shame, who mind earthly things. (Philippians 3:17–19)

Moreover, when the Koran states that Christ only appeared to be crucified, it was upholding a heresy which existed long before Muhammad, and can be traced explicitly to

---

55 Quoted in Evagrius, Eccles. Hist. 1.2
56 Chron. Theophan. Annus Mundi 6255
57 Surah 4

the apostolic age. St. Ignatius (a student of St. John, St. Peter and St. Paul, who was commissioned by the Apostles to be bishop of Antioch) warned against them as evil and dangerous deceivers in his epistle to the Trallians:

> But if as some who are atheists—that is to say, infidels—pretend that he [Christ] only seemed to suffer, (they themselves only seeming to exist,) why then am I bound? Why do I deserve to fight with beasts? Therefore do I die in vain: therefore I will not speak falsely against the Lord. Flee, therefore, these evil sprouts which bring forth deadly fruit, of which if any one taste, he shall presently die. [58]

In his letter to the church in Smyrna, St. Ignatius again warned against such heretics who believed, as the Muslims do, that the Crucifixion only appeared to be seen and did not take place, and that Christ did not suffer death:

> And he [Christ] suffered truly, as he also truly raised up himself; and now, as some unbelievers say, that he only seemed to suffer, they themselves only seeming to be [Christians]. [59]

This impious denial of Christ's Crucifixion, this slandering utterance that the Holy One only seemed or appeared to be crucified, was adopted by that heresiarch Muhammad. No heretic is original, he only plagiarizes lies from an older heretic, and if one was to trace the first from whom this succession of lies comes, we would find that it was that old serpent in the garden. This gnostic heresy would be adopted by numerous sects who were called Manichaeans, Cathars, Paulicians, Bogomils, and other names.

Let us see the history of this heresy, in order to see how the results of the Gnostic false religion, are the same as those of Islam: violence and tyranny against Christians. For, it is of that same spirit which took Cain, and which possessed Judas, before they conspired to kill the Father's chosen ones, the former slaying Abel and the latter Christ. By showing such a history, it will also be revealed why Christendom had no tolerance for false religions, in this case the evil doctrine of Mani, and how from error of the heretic, comes terror to the Christian.

So then let us see what violence this heresy caused, and why the Church did not tolerate it.

ARABIA: THE ORIGINATOR OF THE MANICHAEAN HERESY

The Cathars' doctrine did not originate with Mani in Persia, but like Islam, with an Arabian from Arabia. It began with a man of the same race as Muhammad, named Scythianus, an Arabian who was educated in Arabia, and traveled to India and Egypt where he would learn their false philosophies. Scythianus founded the gnostic cult which believed that God and the devil were both deities and were both co-eternal, and amongst other blasphemies, that Christ did not come in the flesh. As Archelaus, a man who debated Mani personally, said:

> This man [Mani] is neither the first nor the only originator of this type of doctrine. But a certain belonging to Scythia, bearing the name Scythianus, and living in the time of the apostles, was the founder and leader of this sect. For he introduced the notion of a feud

---

58 Epistle to the Tallians, 10–11, trans. Archbishop Wake
59 St. Ignatius, Epistle to the Smyrnaeans, 2, brackets mine, see n. 1 in Archbishop Wake's translation

between the two unbegottens… This Scythianus himself belonged to the stock of the Saracens [Arabs], and took as his wife a certain captive from the Upper Thebaid, who persuaded him to dwell in Egypt rather than in the deserts. [60]

Scythianus' Arabian origin was also attested by Epiphanius of Salamis, who explained his origins as such:

…Scythianus, who was a Saracen but had been brought up on the borders of Palestine, that is, in Arabia. [61]

The ancient Church historian Socrates describes the founder of the gnostic heresy as an Arab or Saracen named Scythian (same person as Scythianus), who settled in Egypt and intermixed some Christian teachings with Egyptian philosophy, as it was presented by Pythagoras and Empedocles:

A Saracen named Scythian married a captive from the Upper Thebes. On her account he dwelt in Egypt, and having versed himself in the learning of the Egyptians, he subtly introduced the theory of Empedocles and Pythagoras among the doctrines of the Christian faith. [62]

Drunk off the wanton nature of luxury, and rebelling against the Orthodox Faith, Scythianus taught that there were two principles, or gods, one evil and one good, and such an idea was sparked by a question he asked himself, to which he himself also answered, not with orthodoxy but heresy:

What is the reason for the inequalities throughout the visible vault of creation—black and white, flushed and pale, wet and dry, heaven and earth, night and day, soul and body, good and evil, righteous and unrighteous—unless, surely these things originate from two roots, or two principles? [63]

This Arabian heretic would end up writing four books: the first was called "Book of the Mysteries," the second, "Book of the Summaries," the third, "Gospel," and the fourth was called, "Treasury."[64]

Scythianus the Arab read through the Old Testament, and in his pompous and arrogant mind, he laughed and mocked the holy prophets, boasting that he was greater than they. In his haughty spirit he went to Jerusalem when the Apostles themselves were still alive and teaching, with the plan to dispute with the Apostles themselves. As Epiphanius says:

[H]e chose to travel to Jerusalem, about the apostle's time, and dispute there, if you please, with the preachers of God's sovereignty and the [creation of] God's creatures. On his arrival the unfortunate man began to challenge the elders there—who were living by the legislation

---

60 The Disputation with Manes, 54, ellipses and brackets mine
61 *The Panarion* of Epiphanius of Salamis, Against Manichaeans, 46, but 66 of the series, 1,6, trans. Frank Williams
62 Socrates, 1.22
63 Quoted By Epiphanius, *The Panarion*, Against Manichaeans, 46, but 66 of the series, 2,3, trans. Frank Williams
64 Epiphanius, *The Panarion*, Against Manichaeans, 46, but 66 of the series, 2,9; *The Disputation of Manes*, 52

which God had given to Moses and confirmed by the inspired prophet—with, How can you say that God is one, if he made night and day, flesh and soul, dry and wet, heaven and earth, darkness and light?' They gave him an explanation—the truth is no secret—but he was not ashamed to contradict them. And though he could not achieve his aim, he still behaved with stubborn shamelessness. [65]

Scythianus was enraged at the Apostles, and at the Christians who rejected his teachings, and he, holding to the suspicions of wizards, went up to the top of a roof and began to conjure curses against them. It is said that as he was doing this, he suddenly fell off the roof and died.[66]

This pernicious Arabian only had one disciple, a man named Terebinthus who, being influenced by the Indian teachings of his former master, changed his name to Buddha. Terebinthus took the books of his Arabian teacher, and began to form his own cult, teaching his followers that he was born of a virgin and was brought up by a certain angel in the mountains. Terebinthus would later marry a certain elderly woman, and when he died, she took the four books of Scythianus the Arab, and adopted a young boy named Corbicus. Soon she perished, and Corbicus, at that time twelve years old, took the books of Scythianus, learned them, became a teacher of his heresy, and changed his name to Mani. And thus was the origin of the Manichaean heresy.[67]

The Gnostic heresy was founded by an Arabian, and therefore when John wrote that "every spirit that confesseth not that Jesus Christ is come in the flesh is not of God: and this is that spirit of antichrist,"[68] and that "many deceivers are entered into the world, who confess not that Jesus Christ is come in the flesh. This is a deceiver and an antichrist,"[69] he was speaking against an Arabian heresy, since Scythianus was living in his time. Thus, the Apostle was forewarning on an Arabian sect, and at the same time, his words are prophetical, for the religion of the coming Antichrist, Islam, being also founded by an Arabian, Muhammad, teaches that the Crucifixion was an illusion. The account of the Crucifixion in the Gospels was denied by Mani, for to him (and to Muhammad) people saw Christ crucified only as an illusion.[70]

Islam rejects the Crucifixion, believing, as the Gnostics, that it was an illusion, and it also disbelieves in the words of St. John, that God came in the flesh, and therefore Muslims reject that Christ—God the Son—came in the flesh.

THE HERETICAL TEACHINGS OF MANI

Mani was brought up in the religion of the Mandaeans, which intermixed Christianity with Zoroastrianism,[71] visited India and felt compelled to add to this heretical concoction traits

---

65 Epiphanius, *The Panarion*, Against Manichaeans, 46, but 66 of the series, 3,4
66 Epiphanius, *The Panarion*, Against Manichaeans, 46, but 66 of the series, 3,7
67 *The Disputation of Manes*, 53, 55
68 I John 4:3
69 2 John 1:7
70 Augustine, Concerning Heresies, ch. 46, in Edward Peters, *Heresy and Authority in Medieval Europe*, ch. i, p. 37
71 Archelaus tells us that Mani and his followers worshipped Mithra, a Zoroastrian angel (Disputation with Manes, 36)

of Buddhism and the Hindu belief of reincarnation. He beheld himself as "the apostle of Jesus Christ," because, as he falsely claimed, Christ promised to send, and did send, the Holy Spirit to him; to mimic Christ, Mani even had twelve disciples, did the unforgivable sin and declared that he was the Holy Spirit, or the Paraclete.[72]

Muhammad, just like his predecessor Mani, declared himself to be the Paraclete. Many Muslim writers have interpreted the statement of Jesus, of "another Paraclete" (John 14:16) as a reference to Muhammad. The earliest of Islamic scholars to have done this is probably Ibn Ishaq. More scholars who have taught this heretical interpretation include Ibn Taymiyyah, Ibn Kathir, Al-Qurtubi, Rahmatullah Kairanawi, and contemporary Muslim scholars such as Martin Lings. A few Muslim commentators, such as David Benjamin Keldani (1928), believe that the original Greek word used was *periklytos*, meaning famed, illustrious, or praiseworthy, was actually called in Arabic "Ahmad," and that this was substituted by Christians with parakletos.

Mani, just like Muhammad, blasphemously said:

> If vain presumption is rejected by every one of you, and those things is rejected by every one of you, and if those things which are to be declared by me be heard with a real love for the truth, ye will receive the inheritance of the age to come, and the kingdom of heaven. I, in sooth, am the Paraclete, whose mission was announced of old time by Jesus, and who to come to 'convince the world of sin and unrighteousness.'[73]

As Joseph Smith and Muhammad both saw themselves bringing into the world a new revelation or divine testimony, Mani boasted that he was ushering into the world a "third testimony," the rejection of which would be punished by hellfire, as he announced:

> Therefore receive ye this third testimony, that I am an elect of Christ; and if ye choose to accept my words, ye will find salvation; but if ye refuse them, eternal fire will have you to consume you.[74]

If we are to inquire deeper into Mani's theology, then we must read the horrid heresies he composed in his antichrist Gospel of Mani. In this false gospel, Mani puts blasphemous words in the mouth Christ Himself, making it as though Jesus declared that He was not crucified:

> Amen, I was seized; amen again I was not seized!
> Amen, I was judged; amen again I was not judged!
> Amen, I was crucified; amen again, I was not crucified![75]

The rejection of the Crucifixion sprung from Mani's belief that all of the material world was created by the devil, and by extension, his affirmation that the human body was not holy, but a prison for the soul. As his damnable book says:

---

72 Euseb. Eccles. Hist. 7.31
73 Mani in Archelaus, The Acts of the Disputation, 13
74 Mani in Archelaus, The Acts of the Disputation, 13
75 Mani, 34.5

Ever since they bound me in the flesh I forgot my divinity; like a bird in a snare, so too am I while in the body of death, the dwelling of the robbers, over which everyone has wept. The mind itself is great and exalted, but it becomes crooked and petty because of this small contemptible body, causing me to be dull and drugged and to lose all my senses. I am not sick at heart over the bodies, but over the treasure of the Living Ones that is lodged in them, (for) they are called the slaves of the flesh of death. The body prevents the Soul from rising; it is a prison and a heavy penalty for the Soul; it is the gateway of all the hells and the road to all rebirths. While we are in the body we are far from God, rest has not overtaken us because we are lodged in it. There is none who can glory while he has still an hour in this prison.[76]

How different is this wicked talk, from the Holy Scriptures, which declare that man must glorify God not only in spirit, but in body as well:

Or do you not know that your body is the temple of the Holy Spirit who is in you, whom you have from God, and you are not your own? For you were bought at a price; therefore glorify God in your body and in your spirit, which are God's. (1 Corinthians 6:19–20)

In this same feigned gospel Mani is literally deified as the tree of life, perfect and sinless, the first and the last, "glorious Father," and other titles that did not belong to him:

Our Lord Mani, the Messenger of Light, the Tongue that speaks no lie, our glorious Father, the Gentle One who loves (his) children, the Tree of Life full of gay fruit—he gives life to the dead and illumines those in darkness. Mani (is) the Sovereign Light, the Spirit of the Light, Father of the blessing, …compassionate and incorruptible place of Repose, (also) the Mind and the Wisdom that dwell in his Scriptures, his five holy Books![77]

By five books, it is not speaking of the Pentateuch, but five books of the Manichaeans that have been listed as, "the Living Gospel, the Treasury of Life, the Mysteries, the Pragmateia, and either the Shahpuraqan or the Book of Letters."[78]

Mani, just as Muhammad affirmed, believed that the Scriptures were corrupted, and could not be fully trusted, as the prominent Manichaean Faustus said:

For myself I am rescued from the necessity of this alternative by the Manichaean belief, which from the first taught me not to believe all those things which are read in Jesus' name as having been spoken by Him; for that there be many tares which to corrupt the good seed some nightly sower has scattered up and down through nearly the whole of Scripture.[79]

He taught, adopting this belief from the Persians, that there were two gods, one good and the other evil,[80] that all the physical world was of the devil who, as he believed, was equal to God, in that he was co-eternal with Him. He, in fact, worshipped both God and the devil,

---

76 Mani, 49:1–2
77 Mani, 37:1
78 See footnote 1 by Duncan Greenlees, for the Gospel of Mani, 37:1
79 Aug. Cont. Faust., 19, 7
80 Augustine writes that in the ancient Persian books there is the belief in two gods, "the one good and the other evil" (*City of God*, 5.21)

and even so far as to call Satan a god.⁸¹ According to Mani, all flesh and physical matter was evil and of the Devil, spirit was of God, and because of this Christ could have never come in the flesh, but was a phantom.

He did not see Adam's and Eve's eating of the forbidden fruit as the fall of man, but as man getting closer to redemption, for to Mani, the God of the Old Testament was the devil from whose tyranny mankind needed to be rescued, and that the Law of Moses came through the inspiration of a demon. His doctrine was so satanic that to him the serpent was literally Christ, who was showing Adam and Eve the way to enlightenment and divine wisdom, that they could become gods.⁸² Surely was this utterly blasphemous—a heresy of all heresies! St. Augustine was a Manichaean before being baptized in the Catholic Church, and he confessed to God his past hatred for the Old Testament:

> I knew nothing of all this, and so I derided your holy servants and prophets. ⁸³

To this troublesome character, Mani, and to Muhammad, the Incarnation never occurred, and nor was Christ—God in the flesh—even the son of Mary. Mani said:

> God forbid that I should admit that our Lord Jesus Christ came down to us through the natural womb of a woman! …If you, however, mean to say that Mary was actually His mother, you place yourself in a position of considerable peril. ⁸⁴

Like Muhammad, Mani taught against free-will, and promulgated the false belief of fatalism.⁸⁵

As Muhammad did, Mani rejected the belief that Christ has a Father, and in regards to this belief, he proclaimed with wicked tongue:

> For to me it seems pious to say that the son of God stood in need of nothing whatsoever in the way of making good His advent upon earth; and the He in no sense required ether the dove, or baptism, or mother, or brethren, or even may have a father. ⁸⁶

Mani believed that the Eucharist was an illusion, and in so doing he replaced the Eucharist with his own, and so reprobate was he that his followers were forced to eat a communion bread with semen on top of it, with the belief that parts of their god were locked inside of male seed. His followers were made to suffer other sexual deviances. One Margaret, under the age of twelve, was violated by Manichaeans in a strange ritual for their god. Manichaean books spoke of men becoming women and women becoming men, in order to free through sexual intercourse "the princes of darkness of both sexes so that the divine substance which

---

81 See Archelaus, in The Acts of the Disputation with the Heresiarch Manes, 6, 13, ANF, vol. vi
82 Carroll, *A History of Christendom*, vol. iii, ch. v, pp. 164–165; Augustine, Concerning Heresies, ch. 46, in Edward Peters, Heresy and Authority, ch. i, pp. 37, 39; see Prudentius, *The Divinity of Christ*, 956–958, trans. H.J. Thomson, ed. Loeb, vol. i; Euseb. Eccles. Hist. 7.31
83 St. Aug. Confessions, 3.18, trans. Maria Boulding
84 Disputation with Manes, 47, ellipses mine
85 Socrates, 1.22
86 The Disputation with Mani, 50

is imprisoned in them may be set free and escape." Luckily there was foresight amongst the Church, and their vile religion was outlawed, and their members arrested by an inquisition,[87] since no toleration was to be given to error and blasphemy. What sane society could allow for such a gang of reprobates to grow and to thrive? In our society today, cursed by the conniving, imprudent, and sophistical ideas of the Enlightenment, we pompously show off our religious tolerance, thus permitting the growth and multiplying of dangerous cults.

In the year 438, a law was written that prohibited the Manichaeans, declaring that they "shall not assemble in any groups, shall not collect any multitude, shall not attract any people to themselves, shall not show any walls of private houses after the likeness of churches, and shall practice nothing publicly or privately which may be detrimental to Catholic sanctity."[88]

The Manichaeans were vegans who madly believed that even a fig contained the divine, that it wept when it was plucked, and that after it was eaten one would belch out "particles of God." They were not allowed to eat eggs, to drink milk, to clear a field of thorns, nor did they eat any animal meat because they believed, like the Hindus, that other souls passed into cattle. They also did not kill animals to avoid offending "the princes of darkness who are bound in the celestials."[89] They partook in openly pagan activity, worshipped the moon, the sun, and the stars, and even went so far as to pray to demons.[90]

Life itself was considered by Mani to be an abomination from which all of humanity should seek to be free. Couples within the cult were told never to conceive offspring, and forbade the propagation of children, since this would bring more life into the world. So immense was their hatred for life, that they said that to bring food to a starving human being who was not a Manichaean was to murder the food itself.[91] They were a cruel bunch, and saw themselves as superior, paralleling the self-exalting spirit of Islam. Like Muhammad, Mani intermixed his heresy with pagan traits; his followers prayed toward the sun in the daytime and toward the moon in the evening.[92]

THE MASSALIAN GNOSTICS
The cult came to Syria, where they called themselves Massalians. These demonically believed that Satan dwelt personally with man, and dominated all things; that the devil lived and binded together with the Holy Spirit, and that even the Apostles were not liberated from the power of Lucifer. They rejected baptism and Holy Communion, and held that the soul could only be purified through prayer, which they did to an excessive and dangerously charismatic degree. They were convinced that it was obligatory for the soul to have communion with "the

---

87 St. Aug., Concerning Heresies, ch. 46, in Edward Peters, *Heresy and Authority in Medieval Europe*, ch. i, pp. 35–6, 39
88 *Theodosian Code*, 16.5, in Edward Peters, *Heresy and Authority in Medieval Europe*, ch. i, p. 45
89 St. Aug. Confessions, 3.18; Concerning Heresies; The sermon of Cosmas the Priest against Bogomilism, in Edward Peters, Heresy and Authority, ch. i, pp. 36–7, ch. iii, p. 114
90 St. John of Damascus, *On Heresies*, 66
91 St. Aug. Confessions, 3.18; Concerning Heresies, ch. 46, in Edward Peters, Heresy and Authority, ch. i, p. 37
92 Augustine, Concerning Heresies, ch. 46, in Edward Peters, Heresy and Authority, ch. i, p. 38

heavenly bridegroom," with sexual sensations. Perpetuating the Zoroastrian beliefs of Mani, they affirmed that fire is a creator, and they also believed in the most wicked idea of evil being natural. Like the Mormons, the Messalians held that Mary had received physical seed into her womb, alongside the Word, when she conceived Christ. They were bereft of all affection, and deemed it improper to give assistance to abandoned widows, to help beggars, the mutilated or the diseased, or those who had suffered under thieves or barbarians. They were so sinister, that they would persuade fathers and mothers to neglect the caring of their children,[93] which is reminiscent to how the Jehovah's Witnesses would rather have their infirm children, in need of blood, die than have a doctor give them blood transfusion. They were given the title of "possessed ones," because they would go into wild frenzies in their states of demonic possession. They hated the Eucharist of the Catholic Church, and withdrew from it, and so great was their madness, that some of them would chop off their own testicles. There were a number of congregations of these Messalians in Melitene, in Asia Minor. Once the bishop of this city, named Litoius, discovered them, he burnt down their churches and drove them out as king Asa drove out the sodomites. The Bishop of Antioch, Flavian, sent a group of monks to conduct an investigation to see if they were any of these heretics in Syria, and once they found them, they drove the Messalians out of Syria,[94] as Christ cast out the thieves from His temple.

THE PAULICIAN GNOSTICS

The antihuman doctrine of Mani spread to Armenia where its subscribers called themselves Paulicians.[95] They were founded by two Manichaeans, named Paul and John, and they were unusually cruel and savagely violent.[96]

The empress Theodora, the great defender of Orthodoxy and a zealous protector of Christendom, resolved that if these Paulicians did not throw away their heresy that she would have them obliterated. The Paulicians were malicious followers of the gnostic heresy, and they refused to bring themselves back to the path of Orthodoxy. Thus, the extirpation of these evil-doers commenced. Theodora commissioned three men—Leo, Adronikos, and Soudales—to execute the sword on the heretics, and it was carried out, as Skylitzes describes:

> Some [of the Manichees] they hung on gallows, some they put to the sword, while others were dispatched with various kinds of afflictions and by diverse and multiform methods of torture, until ten times ten thousand men had been destroyed, their possessions appropriated by the state. [97]

Amongst the surviving Palicians was a man named Karbeas, and when he heard how his father was impaled, he was enraged beyond any hope of calm, and went to the side of the Muslims. He joined the ranks of the jihadist leader Amr, the emir of Melitene, together with

---

93 See St. John of Damascus, *On Heresies*, 80
94 See St. John of Damascus, *On Heresies*, 80
95 That Paulicians were Manichaeans, see Skylitzes, *Byzantine History*, 5.8
96 Anna Komnenus, *Alexiad*, 14.8
97 Skylitzes, *Byzantine History*, 5.8, trans. John Wortley

five thousand fellow Paulicians. They declared loyalty to the Muslims, and the two heretical armies charged against the Christians. They overtook the towns of Aeagoun and Amara, and from there they rendezvoused with Amr and Aleim, the emir of Tarsus. Together, they ruthlessly expanded into Christian Roman territory. Aleim, however, was soon killed in his attempt to invade Armenia.[98]

A fierce crusade by the Greek Christians took place against the Muslims and their Manichaean allies. The Byzantine general Bardas, and the emperor Michael III, fought against Amr the Muslim and Karbeas the Paulician, in the city of Samosata which lied on the banks of the Euphrates River. The Muslims feigned cowardice and kept themselves inside the city, and the Christians ferociously besieged it. On the third day, Sunday (the Lord's Day), as the Christians were observing mass, and as they were about to partake in the Eucharist, the Muslims opened the gates and charged out, and fell upon the Christian warriors. The Paulicians, exhibiting the most horrendous portrayal of viciousness, slaughtered many of the Christians with ruthless blows and attacks. The Christians were confounded, and in their deep hysteria and confusion, they desperately ran about trying to flee. The emperor Michael mounted his horse, and with much difficultly, fled.

Two years passed since that terrible day, when the Muslim leader Amr raised thirty thousand Muslim soldiers thirsty for Christian blood, and led them into another attack against Christendom. The emperor Michael was determined to be superior to the Islamic army, and so raised a force of forty thousand warriors from Thrace and Macedonia. As the Christian troops were headed to battle, Amr took on a different route through rigorous terrain and executed an unexpected attack upon the Romans. So shocking was the ambush that the emperor himself would have been taken prisoner if it wasn't for the tenacious Manuel, a combatant of the elite warrior division called scholai, who cut through the enemy and took ahold of Michael and rescued him.[99]

After Karbeas died, his nephew, Chrysocheir, succeeded him, and continued the Manichaean war against Christendom. The Byzantine emperor Basil I, attacked the towns that surrounded Tephrike, the Paulician center over which Chrysocheir ruled. The holy emperor then smashed against the land of the Paulicians, attacking the areas of Aragouth, Koutakios, Stephanos, and Arachach, and reduced the entire area to ashes. After such a great victory, in such a sacred war for the defense of the Divine Law of God and the true Faith, Basil I proceeded to the Church of the Personified Wisdom of God, and like King David, offered hymns of thanksgiving to God, and was adorned with crowns of triumph by the patriarch Ignatios.[100]

Chrysocheir deployed a very powerful army and expanded further into Roman territory. But the emperor hindered his expansion and commissioned the head of the scholai who efficiently stopped him before he could rampage through the countryside.[101]

---

98 Skylitzes, *Byzantine History*, 5.8
99 Skylitzes, *Byzantine History*, 5.12
100 Skylitzes, *Byzantine History*, 6.18
101 Skylitzes, *Byzantine History*, 6.19

✟ CHRISTIANITY IS AT WAR: THE MANIFESTO FOR CHRISTIAN MILITANCY

The sun deprived her illuminating hands from the sky, and no longer did the harsh earth feel the warmth of her embraces, when evening came about, and the advancers of heresy—those followers of Mani and agents of Antichrist!—stood on the foot of the mountain, in a land called Bathyrryax, ravenously scheming their next pounce upon another victim of their demonic terror. While the soldiers of the devil stood at the bottom of the mountain, the gallant soldiers of Christendom stood on the top of the arid pinnacle, while a smaller body of six hundred elite fighters anticipated for the diabolical enemy on a lower point, awaiting for the order to charge upon the haters of God. The smaller garrison concealed themselves behind the blackness of the night, when they, like the warriors of Gideon, approached the camp of the Paulicians, and before the rays of the dawn could even graze the rugged peaks of this wilderness, the charge of the Christians from the top of the mountain met the gazes of the heretics. There went forth the Christian army, the ones who glorified the Holy Cross of Christ—the most elite of warriors—"who for the joy that was set before him endured the cross" (Hebrews 12:2), and now these soldiers, who were "one body by the cross" (Ephesians 2:16), emulating the forbearance of Christ, denied themselves and carried up their own cross, in the battle against the devil. Their troops charged foreword, and like the Israelites before them, they shook the ears of the heretics with a loud shout from their thundering voices, and with the braying of their trumpets the air echoed with their resounding noise throughout the peaks of the wilderness, and it seemed as though the very earth shook. And there stood the enemy, baffled and fear-stricken, who were only fighting for the cause of Antichrist, for they were the ones of whom St. John warned when he wrote of those who "do not confess Jesus Christ as coming in the flesh. This is a deceiver and an antichrist." (2 John 1:7) They were of the armies of the diabolical, "the enemies of the cross of Christ" (Philippians 3:18), who like the Muslims had nothing but indignation for that majestic moment when God Himself crushed the devil on the Cross, by saying that it was only an illusion. And now, as Christ defeated the devil through sacred combat on the Cross, these holy and gallant warriors were to defeat the advancers of Satan with the Cross. For under the gleam of the moonlight, as the roaring of the trumpets filled the air and pierced the ears, and the ascending hollers of Christendom's defenders terrified the Paulicians, the Christian warriors, with all the might of their voices, sung with reverent harmony, "The Cross has conquered!" They charged and smashed into the enemy ranks, and as they fought and slew the blood of infidels, the warriors who stood upon the mountain joined in the warlike and sacred hymn, and the words of the song permeated the battle. There a heretic was struck, and one would hear the words of the song, and be reminded that truly the Cross has conquered over those who denied the Cross. The Paulcians did not even take the time to organize themselves, or to gain strength, and they began to retreat. The Christians called upon the warriors who stood upon the mountain, and these descended from the top, and now joined the pursuit, adding even more fear and terror to the hearts of the Paulicians. For thirty miles they chased after the enemy, and made an entire trail of corpses. Chrysocheir rode on a galloping horse with a few of his followers, and then, turning around, he recognized one of the Roman soldiers. His name was Poulades, he was once a prisoner of Chrysocheir, and because of his culture and charm, the two developed something of an acquaintance. Chrysocheir looked to this soldier and said,

> What harm have I done to you, wretched Poulades, that you pursue me insanely like this, anxious to do away with me?

Pouledes zealously snapped back and said,

> I have full confidence in God, sir, that this very day I am to deliver you the reward of your good deeds.

The countenance of Chrysocheir, at that moment, looked as though he was struck by lightning as he rode away with desperation. He soon came upon a ditch that his horse could not leap over, and Pouledes swiftly struck him in the side with a lance. He fell into the ditch, and one of the Paulicians, Diakonitzes, immediately jumped off his horse and embraced his dead leader with cries and wails. Pouledes came down from his horse and struck Chrysocheir's head off. With the death of this tyrant, came the death of the Manichaean kingdom of Tephrike, and their empty glory dissipated like hollow smoke.[102]

When the Byzantine empire was under the rule of John I, a monk named Thomas, the archbishop of Antioch, exhorted the emperor to take all of the Paulicians, who were ravishing the eastern provinces and teaching their heresy, and move them to a remote wilderness. Here the archbishop used the spiritual sword of St. Peter, to have the state unsheathe the temporal sword against a threat to the spiritual state of Christendom and its liberty. John I complied and moved the Paulicians to Philippoupolis.[103]

THE BOGOMILS

The Paulician sect made its way to the Balkans where it influenced a man in Bulgaria named Bogomil, who would start his own cult in his country. The doctrine of the Bogomils was really an amalgamation between Manichaeanism and the Massalian heresy.[104] The Bogomils fabricated their own gospel called "The Bogomile Book of John," in which Jesus tells John that God the Father, pitying the devil, gave power to Satan to create the world, and even to create human beings. It goes on to say that the devil was the one who created the Garden of Eden and commanded the people not to eat of the Tree of the Knowledge of Good and Evil:

> 'Then I [John] asked of the Lord [Jesus]: "When Satan fell, what place did he dwell?" And he answered me: "My Father changed his appearance because of his pride, and the light was taken from him, so his face became like heated iron and his face became altogether like a man's. And with his tail he drew the third part of God's Angels, and he was thrown out from God's seat and from the stewardship of the heavens. So Satan came down into this firmament, and he could find no rest for himself, nor for those who were with him. Then he

---

102 This whole battle is recounted by Skylitzes, *Byzantine History*, 6.19. For more on the battles against the Paulicians, see Anna Comnena, 6.1–2, 4
103 John Sklitzes, *Byzantine History*, 15.3
104 Anna Komnenus, *Alexiad*, 15.8

implored the Father: 'Have patience with me, and I will pay Thee all!' So the Father had pity on him and gave him rest and those who were with him, as much as they wanted, even to seven days. And so as he sat in the firmament and commanded the Angel who was over the Air and him who was over the Waters, and of the half of it he made the moonlight and of the (other) half of the starlight; and of the gems he made all of the hosts of the stars. And after that he made the Angels his servants according to the form of the order of the Most High, and by the command of the invisible Father (he made) thunder, rain, hail and snow; he sent forth Angels to be servants over them. And he commanded the Earth to bring forth every beast for food, and ever creeping thing, and trees and plants; and he bade the seas bring forth fishes and the birds of the skies. And furthermore he planned and made man in his (own) likeness, and commanded an Angel of the third heaven to enter into the body of clay. And he took of it and made another body in a woman's shape, and commanded an Angel of the second heaven to enter the body of the woman. But the Angels lamented when they saw a mortal form upon them and that they were unlike in shape. So he commanded them to do the deed of the flesh in the bodies of clay but they knew not how to commit sin. Then did the contriver of evil plan in his mind to make a Garden, and into it he brought the Man and the Woman. He commanded a reed to be brought, and this the devil planted in the center of the Garden, and the devil so hid his plan that they did not know his deceit. Then he came in and spoke to them, saying: 'Eat of every fruit that is in the Garden, but do not eat of the fruit of the Knowledge of Good and Evil.' Again the devil entered into a wicked serpent and seduced the Angel who was in the woman's form, and (persuaded her) and worked his desire with her even in the form of the serpent's sons even to the end of this world who work the lust of the devil their father. [105]

In this antichrist book, Jesus even says that those who say that His Father created human bodies are fools:

Listen, John, my Father's beloved; foolish men speak thus in their deceitfulness that my Father made bodies of clay: but by the Holy Spirit He made all the Powers of the heavens, and holy ones were found with bodies of clay because of their transgressions, and therefore were they surrendered to Death. [106]

Though Bogomilism went underground, it continued to grow like bacteria multiplying in static murky water under the summer heat. Like the Mormons and the Jehovah's Witnesses, whenever the Bogomils met someone who they desired to deceive, they flooded the man with all sorts of politeness to undermine his vigilance. As the heretics of America do today, the Bogomils also did not hesitate to call themselves Christian. A certain priest named Cosmas preached a warning on this deceptive polite fiction:

The heretics in appearance are lamb-like, gentle, modest and quiet, and their pallor is to show their hypocritical fastings. ...The people, on seeing their great humility think that they are orthodox, and able to show them the path of salvation; they approach and ask them how

---

105 The Bogomile Book of John, 7–11
106 The Bogomile Book of John, 12

to save their souls. Like a wolf that wants to seize a lamb, they pretend at first to sigh; they speak with humility, preach, and act as if they were themselves in heaven. Whenever they meet any ignorant and uneducated man, they preach to him the tares of their teachings, blaspheming the traditions and orders of the Holy Church. [107]

But under all of that feigned kindness, was a roaring devil filled with foaming hatred against Christ. They denied the Trinity, called John the Baptist "the forerunner of Antichrist," and harassed Christians with words such as these: "How can we bow to the cross? Is it not the tree on which the Jews crucified the Son of God? The cross is detestable to God. … Christ neither gave sight to the blind, nor healed the lame, nor raised the dead, but these are only legends and delusions which the uneducated evangelists understood wrongly." They rejected any honoring of Mary, hated all church icons, and declared with the utmost sacrilege: "We reject David and the prophets. We admit only the gospel; we do not carry out our lives according to the law of Moses, but according to the law given through the apostles."[108]

In accordance to the teachings of Mani, whenever a Bogomil would see an infant they would turn away, spit, and cover their faces, since they believed that babies were "little devils."[109]

They hated the rich and the tsar of Bulgaria, yet they did not hesitate to take the property of their followers; for that is what heresy desires: power and to replace the Church.

Cosmas' ultimate solution for the Bogomil heresy was to purge Bulgaria of their presence: "Since we know the heretics well, let us drive them away, because they are the enemies of the holy cross."[110]

The Bogomil heresy reached its apex in popularity through the charisma of a certain corrupt monk named Basil. He, like Mani, had twelve elite followers who he called "apostles," and he also had with him numerous female believers who were known for their depravity. They went about inculcating their heresy, and many people embraced this rotting doctrine into their souls. Soon the emperor, Alexius Komnenus, had enough of the heresy spreading, and had some of the Bogomils arrested. All of those apprehended, except one named Diblatius, denounced the heresy and were released. Diblatius, on the other hand, was thrown into prison, and rightfully so. The emperor eventually brought in Basil himself and had him sit down next to him, as to inquire more on what wicked beliefs he promulgated. The emperor's brother, Isaac, acted as though he was enthusiastically interested in the Bogomil doctrine, and such a trick worked. For Basil happily told him what evil doctrines he subscribed to, and not a single blasphemy was left covered by this heretic. He went so far as to call the churches

---

107 The sermon of Cosmas the Priest against Bogomilism, in Edward Peters, Heresy and Authority, ch. iii, pp. 109, 114, ellipses
108 The sermon of Cosmas the Priest against Bogomilism, in Edward Peters, Heresy and Authority, ch. iii, pp. 110, 112, 115, 116, ellipses mine
109 The sermon of Cosmas the Priest against Bogomilism, in Edward Peters, Heresy and Authority, ch. iii, p. 114
110 The sermon of Cosmas the Priest against Bogomilism, in Edward Peters, Heresy and Authority, ch. iii, pp. 112

of the Orthodox "temples of demons," and declared that the Eucharist was not the body and blood of Jesus Christ.

The emperor ordered that the senate, all of the chief commanders of the army, and all of the elders of the Church, be summoned together for a council. Look at how matters such as this were treated! In the greatest empire of that time, the emperor himself did not say, "let them believe what they want," or "let us not waste time on such personal matters," but took the time to convey an entire council to determine what to do with corrupt beliefs. In the council the teachings of the Bogomils were read aloud, with Basil present, but the disgusting heretic still refused to denounce what was declared. He was sent to prison, and there were many times in which Alexius called for him and tried to convince him to leave the heresy, and all such attempts did not work. The emperor ordered that all the Bogomils, including the twelve 'apostles' be brought over and burned to death. When all of them were assembled, there were many who refused to reject their heresy, and others who said that they were not Bogomils, but wrongfully accused of being such. How was Alexius to deal with this? Was he to burn people who could have been innocent?

Like King Solomon, he thought of a way to separate the wheat from the tares: he made two pyres, one with a cross before it, and the other without one. He then ordered that the Christians go to the pyre with the cross, since it would be better for them to die for their Faith than for a false accusation, while the Bogomils were told to go to the other pyre. The Christians, without any fear of death, went to the pyre with the cross, and before they were all thrown into the flames, those who were watching wailed and cried for the Christians. Alexius then knew who were the true Christians, and let them go free. The others he did not burn, but instead threw them into prison where they were treated very well, with much food and clothing. The imprisoned Bogomils who turned to Christianity were released, while the others were kept in their cells until death. Basil, their leader, was brought to the Hippodrome where he was burnt to death.[111]

Again, some may object to this as bigotry and Christian exclusivism, but we will see what results came about from allowing such a sect to grow.

They began in the East and slowly moved toward the West, beginning as small, seemingly harmless communities with a new and, as they called it, purified religion. With such minuscule groups, today's people would see them as not a threat.

The acetic Priscillian, at around 380, taught a doctrine in Spain which was a combination of Manichaeism and Gnosticism, and in 383 he was executed, the first to be killed for heresy by a Christian government.[112]

Why such intolerance and fear for doctrines contrary to orthodoxy? Was this all a power grab by Christian governments and the Catholic Church? What will be soon known is that

---

111 See Anna Komnenus, 15
112 Edward Peters, Heresy and Authority, ch. i, p. 42; St. Isidore of Seville, On the heresies of the Christians, in the same work of Peters, p. 49

the anti-heresy laws were absolutely justifiable, because Manichaeism would in time begin a tyranny within Europe.

THE CATHARS

The heresy spread to Italy, where its subscribers would become better known as Patarenes. These became violent and began to physically attack wealthy clergy who, in their eyes, should have been living in poverty. When clergymen did not heed to their demands, the Patarenes looted their homes.[113] They took over Ferrara, Verona, Rimini, and Treviso. At Piacenza they drove out all of the clergy and kept them from returning for three years. Even the city of Assisi had a Cathar for its high official. Eventually their violence and false doctrine compelled Pope Innocent III to tear down their homes in Viterbo,[114] and the government to decree in 1231 that "these Patarines should be condemned to suffer the death for which they strive."[115]

By the twelfth century the cult made its way to the richest and most central part of Catholic Europe: Central France, where its followers would adopt the Manichaean title of Cathar, from the Greek word for "pure."[116] It entered southern France when two heretics named Peter of Bruys and Henry came into the land and began to preach Catharism. The natives were so angered by their errors that they seized Peter and burnt him alive. But still the preaching of this heresy continued, and the community was allowed to grow in numbers without any significant intervention on the part of the Church to stop its growth.

Like Mani and the Bogomils, the Cathars forged their own bible called "The Catharist Bible." In this damned book, it says that Jesus was not the eternal Son of God, but only one spirit out of innumerable other spirits in Heaven, Who chose to become the Father's son after deciding to endure suffering. It also says that John the Baptist was a devil who baptized Jesus:

> Then, seeing this, the Holy Father said: "So then there is not one of you who desires to be My Son?" Then one of the spirits standing by, who was called Jesus, rose up and said: "I myself am willing to be the Son of the Father and to complete all things which are written in that book." ...After baptism by the great demon John, the devil carried Jesus hanging on his neck."[117]

It then goes on to say, like the Quran, that Christ never died, but that only His death was an illusion to the Jews. It reads that "it seemed to the Jews that the Son of God was dead and that after death they had placed him in a sepulcher, nevertheless he was not truly dead, nor was he buried, though he seemed to be so."[118]

---

113 Moczar, *Seven Lies about Catholic History*, ch. iv, p. 85
114 Englebert, *St. Francis of Assisi*, ch. v, p. 62
115 The Liber Augustalis of Frederick II, 1231, in Edward Peters, Heresy and Authority in Medieval Rome, ch. v, p. 208
116 Augustine makes mention of a sect within the Manichaeans called "Catharists" (Concerning Heresies, ch. 46, in Edward Peters, *Heresy and Authority in Medieval Europe*, in p. 35)
117 Catharist Bible, 4–6, ellipses mine
118 Catharist Bible, 18

CHRISTIANITY IS AT WAR: THE MANIFESTO FOR CHRISTIAN MILITANCY

In a council conducted in Toulouse in 1119, presided by Pope Calixtus II, the Cathars were anathematized as heretics. By 1165 the Cathars had become so numerous that they began to preach in the open, with the Catholic bishops too fearful to protest. They soon commenced to form their own church separate from Roman Catholicism, establishing as their own bishop one Barthelemy in their city of Albi, where they built the Cathar community—the strongest in southern France. It was because of this community in Albi that these heretics were called Albigensians.[119] As the Manichaeans before them, they believed in the existence of two creators, one good and the other evil. The God of the Old Testament, they believed, was the devil and a "liar," they also called him a "murderer" because of the destruction of Sodom and Gomorrah, the flood, and the slaughter of the Egyptians through the Red Sea. They called the Law of Moses "evil" because of its intolerance toward depravities and heresies, and they considered Joshua, David, and Moses, as advancers of the evil god, or the devil. Cathars held the deity of the New Testament as the good God, and for this reason they rejected the Old Testament, and their bible would only be a copy of the New Testament.[120] And for those who may say that these accusations have no merit because they are from Catholic documents, here are the words from an actual Cathar book:

> Our opponents [i.e., the Catholics] say that according to Genesis the Lord is the creator of the visible things of this world ... But I say that the creator of the visible things of this world is not the true God. And I prove this from the evil of his words and deeds, and the changeableness of his words and deeds as described in the Old Testament. [121]

These blasphemous haters of truth deemed John the Baptist as one of the chief devils; they hated Christ and called Him "evil," and libelously said that Mary Magdalene was His concubine (with this they agree with Mormonism), and that the true Christ was the one who appeared to St. Paul, since He came in the spirit and not the flesh in His visitation. Marriage was evil, and like the Muslims and Mormons, wine was forbidden. Like the Mormons, they most sacrilegiously said that God had two wives and even begat children with them. And also like the Mormons, they believed that Jesus was the brother of Lucifer. Similar to the teachings of Muhammad, they also denied the Incarnation. All of these beliefs led the Cathars into some very dangerous activities, such as magic and even open devil worship.[122]

---

119 Carroll, *A History of Christendom*, vol. iii, ch. v, pp. 164–165; Moczar, *Seven Lies about Catholic History*, ch. iv, p. 89–91; see the notes in The Principle Works of St. Ambrose, *On the Christian Faith*, 1.8, Nicene and Post-Nicene Fathers, vol. x; Belloc, *How the Reformation Happened*, intro, p. 27; *The Great Heresies*, The Scheme of this Book, p. 13, The Albigensian, pp. 72–76; J. Balmes, *Protestantism Compared With Catholicity*, ch. xxxvi, p. 206; Edward Peter's intro to Augustine: On Manichaeism, in *Heresy and Authority in Medieval Europe*, ch. i, p. 32; St. Aug. Concerning Heresies, ch. 46, in Ibid, p. 33; Maistre, *Letters on the Spanish Inquisition*, letter i
120 Peter of les Vaux-de-Cernay, 1.10–12; 2.28, 52, brackets mine; Belloc, *The Great Heresies*, The Albigensian, pp. 72, 76–7; The sermon of Cosmas the Priest against Bogomilism
121 In Edward Peters, *Heresy and Authority in Medieval Europe*, ch. iii, document 22, B, p. 135
122 Peter of les Vaux-de-Cernay, 1.10–12; 2.28, 52, brackets mine; Belloc, *The Great Heresies*, The Albigensian, pp. 72, 76–7; The sermon of Cosmas the Priest against Bogomilism; A Standoff at Lombers, 1165; Ranier Sacconi: A Thirteenth-Century Inquisitor on Catharism, these last three references are in Edward Peters, Heresy and Authority, ch. iii, pp. 109, 111, 112, 114, 117, 132

A sect of the Cathars, called Publicans, were said to worship a demon named Luzabel who they believed "presides over all the material creation, and all things on earth are done by his will." They also made "execrable sacrifices" to this devil.[123] It is no wonder, then, that Cosmas, when preaching on the Bogomil Cathars, says: "And they worship the devil to such an extent that they call him the creator of the divine words and ascribe the divine glory to him." They also believed that "everything exists by the will of the devil."[124] One Cathar named Guillelme Carreria was plowing his fields and the plower's yoke was displaced, and upon this he said: "Devil, put back that yoke in its proper place!"[125]

Concurring with many of today's Evangelical Christians, and with the Latter Day Saints, they also believed that the Roman Catholic Church was the Harlot of Babylon of the Book of Revelation. They were so entrenched in this belief, that they affirmed that Christ assumed a bodily presence merely to incite us to fight against the Church of Rome, and to ask us to join the Cathar church. In a debate between the Catholic Abbot of les Vaux-de-Cernay and a certain Cathar named Theodoric, the heretic was so trumped and unable to answer his opponent's arguments, that he said: "The harlot [of Babylon] has kept me long enough, she shall keep me no longer."[126]

Though they rejected the Catholic Church, they modeled their church government very much after the institution they had left; they had their own deacons, bishops, and even made their own pope.[127] In 1167, the Cathar church had its own council, with one pope Niquinta guiding it.[128] Again, the heretics wanted to subvert and replace the established authority, of both Church and state, with their own institution triumphing and dominating.

In contrary to Church teaching, they rejected holy water, the sacraments, the Eucharist, confirmation and confession of sins. They looked with contempt on holy matrimony, and called it "mere harlotry," and with great demonic fervency, held that souls were nothing but the demons who were driven out of Heaven.[129] They, in a way, agreed with Muhammad who said that every Muslim is possessed by a legion of demons. They considered church icons as idols and maintained that church bells were the trumpets of devils. Like many modern pastors today, they considered all sin to be equal, and went so far as to say that a man fornicating

---

[123] Ralph of Coggeshall, The Heretics of Rheims, in Alan Charles Kors and Edward Peters, *Witchcraft in Europe*, part 2, p. 81. That the Publicans were Cathars, see Edward Peters, *Heresy and Authority in Medieval Europe*, ch. iii, p. 104
[124] The sermon of Cosmas the Priest against Bogomilism, in Edward Peters, Heresy and Authority, ch. iii, p. 113
[125] The Inquisitorial Register of Jacques Fournier, Invocation of the devil: testimony of Arnaud Laufre, in Edward Peters, *Heresy and Authority in Medieval Europe*, ch. ix, p. 264
[126] Peter of les Vaux-de-Cernay, 1.10–12; 2.28, 52, brackets mine; Belloc, *The Great Heresies*, The Albigensian, pp. 72, 76–7; Englebert, *St. Francis of Assisi*, ch. v, p. 61
[127] Peter of les Vaux-de-Cernay, Hist. Albi. Crus. 1.14
[128] The Cathar Council at Saint-Felix-de-Caraman, 1167, in Edward Peters, *Heresy and Authority in Medieval Europe*, ch. iii, p. 121
[129] Peter of Vaux-de-Cernay, Hist. Albi. Crus. 1.10–12; Edward Peters, *Heresy and Authority in Medieval Europe*, ch. iii, document 22, Chroniclers and Cathars on Catharism: The Heretics of Lombardy, pp. 133–4

with his sister or mother was the same sin as copulating with any other woman.[130] Surely these were great reprobates, and a danger to all civilization.

Like Muslims, Mormons, Jehovah's Witnesses, and all other heretics, they despised with mad hatred the icon and the sign of the Cross. When a certain Abbot made the sign of the Cross, a Cathar knight saw him and said to him, "may the sign of the cross never come to my aid."[131] They rejected prayers to Mary, being in line with their false prophet Mani who once said with blasphemous false piety:

> God forbid that I should admit that our Lord Jesus Christ came down to us through the natural womb of a woman![132]

When one wanted to convert to the Cathar church, an official of the heresy went before the initiate and said: "Friend, if you wish to join us you must renounce all beliefs of the Roman Church." The initiate replied: "I so renounce." "Therefore receive the Holy Spirit from the good men," and the official then breathed seven times into the initiate's mouth. The official then said: "Do you renounce the sign of the cross which the priest who baptized you [in the Catholic Church] made with oil and unguent on your chest, shoulders and head?" "I renounce." "Do you believe that the water of baptism helps to gain salvation for you?" "I do not believe." "Do you renounce the veil which the priest placed on your head after baptism?" "I so renounce." He was then baptized into the Cathar church, and all those around him placed their hands on him, kissed him, and put a black robe on him.[133]

They preserved the doctrine as it was founded by Mani[134] in the Near East, hating the humanity of Christ, and because they saw all life as evil, they prohibited procreation. To satisfy their sexual passions and observe their perverse creed, many of the Albigensians resolved to the sins of the Canaanites: homosexuality and bestiality, in order to prevent life from ever being born. So true are the words of God: "all they that hate me love death." (Proverbs 8:36) They were the elite members within the cult called "the Perfect," who stayed away from meats or any other animal food, and refrained from marriage and falsely practiced chastity.[135] Such a deplorable group is a fulfillment of what Paul foretold by Providence:

> Now the Spirit speaketh expressly, that in the latter times some shall depart from the faith, giving heed to seducing spirits, and doctrines of devils; Speaking lies in hypocrisy; having their conscience seared with a hot iron; Forbidding to marry, [and commanding] to abstain from meats, which God hath created to be received with thanksgiving of them which believe

---

130 Peter of les Vaux-de-Cernay, Hist. Albi. Crus. 1.10–12, 17; Ranier Sacconi: A Thirteenth-Century Inquisitor on Catharism, in Edward Peters, Heresy and Authority in Medieval Spain, ch. iii, p. 125
131 Peter of les Vaux-de-Cernay, 2.53
132 Mani in The Disputation With Manes, 47
133 Peter of les Vaux-de-Cernay, 1.19
134 See Belloc, How the Reformation Happened, intro, p. 27
135 See Peter of les Vaux-de-Cernay, Hist. Albi. Crus. 1.13

and know the truth. For every creature of God [is] good, and nothing to be refused, if it be received with thanksgiving: For it is sanctified by the word of God and prayer. [136]

The Albigensians subscribed to a form of universalism tantamount to that of today and contradictory to Christian doctrine. One belief amongst them was that "Christ will have mercy on the souls of all heretics, Jews, and pagans; therefore none of them will be damned." The Catholics, in response to this very error, affirmed that "All heretics, pagans, and Jews, who did not want to believe in Christ, will be damned. They will be punished eternally in hell."[137]

There were cases where Muslims and Cathars would work together against Christians. The Manichaeans, their founders, were favored by the Caliph Walid II. This pact was so strong that Walid had St. Peter of Damascus' tongue cut off because he publicly denounced the heresy of Manichaeism.[138]

Catholic legates would threaten Cathars with the loss of their possessions and with the "wrath of kings and princes," because of their unorthodox beliefs.[139] To us, the very thought of people being threatened simply for what they privately believe in, deserves protest and condemnation no matter how demonic or dark they be. But, those who privately believe in diabolical religions, if allowed to grow and dominate as a group, will soon coerce the rest, through tyranny and violence, to publicly accept their poisons. In fact, this is what happened in France: powerful consuls of southern France tolerated them, and even protected them from the authorities,[140] thus enabling them to grow numerous and to thrive.

The most prominent of these was the very powerful Count of Toulouse, Raymond VI. Not only did he protect these heretics, but he also fully accepted their error. Everywhere he went, he held a New Testament, since he detested the Old Testament, and he was accompanied with Cathar priests so that if he was ever about to die they would pray over him and ensure his salvation. He wished his son to be under their spiritual guidance, to make sure that he would become a Cathar. He shared the belief that Satan created the world, saying: "It is clear that the Devil made the world, since nothing I wish comes about." One day he was playing a game of chess with one of these Cathar priests, and when the latter told him, "The God of Moses, in whom you believe, will not be able to help you to prevent me winning this game," Raymond replied, "Never let that God come to my aid." When he was in Mass one day, and watched the Catholic priest lead a congregation in reciting the "Lord be with you," Raymond ordered a clown to mimic the priest to mock him.[141]

---

136 I Timothy 4:1–5
137 The Inquisitorial Register of Jacques Fournier, Testimony of Arnaud Gelis, of Pamiers, in Edward Peters, *Heresy and Authority in Medieval Europe*, ch. ix, p. 258
138 Theophilus of Edessa's *Chronicle*, section 2, p. 242
139 Peter of les Vaux-de-Cernay, Hist. Albi. Crus. 1.7, trans. W.A. Sibly and M.D. Sibly
140 Peter of les Vaux-de-Cernay, Hist. Albi. Crus. 1.7, 9
141 Peter de les Vaux-de-Cernay, 2.28–20, 32, 35, 43

According to Bishop Diego, amongst the reasons why Albigensianism spread so vastly was because of its appearance of holiness which the Perfect projected,[142] which was merely a shell covering their truly reprobate desires. This same facade of holiness can be found in both Muslims and Mormons today, and many fall for this type of masquerading. I myself have seen Americans become so beguiled by Mormonism and Islam because of the politeness of the two cults' followers, that they foolishly accept them as sects of Christianity or as inspired or harmless religions, while ignoring their sinister and terroristic history and ideology. The heretics present a face of righteousness to trick many with good works, and flaunt on how they left a life of sin thanks to a particular heresy they joined, when St. Peter already warned on this seeming nobleness of the heretic:

> For if after they have escaped the pollutions of the world through the knowledge of the Lord and Saviour Jesus Christ, they are again entangled therein, and overcome, the latter end is worse with them than the beginning. For it had been better for them not to have known the way of righteousness, than, after they have known it, to turn from the holy commandment delivered unto them. [143]

If a lay Albigensian was seriously ill, the Perfect saw to it that they should never heal; for suicide was esteemed as the highest form of death to these malevolent sadists, and was carried out in a ritual called endura.[144]

The Albigensian priests were adamant about preventing life, that they seized a baby and began to starve him, and as he was on the verge of death, the mother swiftly took her child and fed him. When priests began the process of starvation, some of them would change their mind and attempt to eat, but these were forced by the other priests to continue the ritual.[145] Rainier Sacconi, a former Cathar who turned Catholic, wrote concerning this ritual:

> Many of them, on this account, have directed those waited upon them in sickness not to put any food or drink into their mouths if they (the sick person) could not at least say a Pater Noster [Our Father]; whence it is very probably that many of them kill themselves by this means, or are killed by their heretical brethren. [146]

THE CATHARS STRIKE

The Albigensians were condemned again in the Third Lateran Council by Pope Alexander III in 1179,[147] and it was not just a condemnation, but a call to arms against the destructive Cathars and all of the foreign mercenaries who assisted them in their persecution of Christians:

---

142 Carroll, *A History of Christendom*, vol. iii, ch. v, pp. 165–166
143 II Peter 2:20–21
144 Carroll, *A History of Christendom*, vol. iii, ch. v, pp. 165–166
145 See Moczar, *Seven Lies about Catholic History*, ch. iv, p. 90
146 Rainier Sacconi: A Thirteenth-Century Inquisitor on Catharism, in Edward Peters, *Heresy and Authority in Medieval Europe*, ch. iii, p. 129, brackets mine
147 Carroll, *A History of Christendom*, vol. iii, ch. iii, p. 115

Wherefore, since in Gascogne, in the territory of Albi, in Toulouse and its neighborhood, and in other places, the perversity of the heretics, whom some call Cathari, others Patarini, and others again Publicani, has assumed such proportions that they practice their wickedness no longer in secret as some do, but preach their error publicly and thus mislead the simple and the weak, we decree that they and all who defend and receive them are anathematized, and under penalty of anathema we forbid everyone to give them shelter, to admit them to his land, or to transact business with them. …With regard to the [mercenary] Brabantians, Aragonians, Basques, Navarese, and others who practice such cruelty toward the Christians that they respect neither churches nor monasteries, spare neither widows nor orphans, age nor sex, but after the manner of pagans destroy and lay waste everything, we decree likewise that those who hire or patronize them throughout the regions in which they rave so madly, shall be publicly denounced in the churches on Sundays … These and all the faithful we command in remission of their sins that they vigorously oppose such pests and defend with arms the Christian people.[148]

Alexander sent two Cistercian bishops, Peter of Castelnau and one Henry, to minister unto the heretics,[149] but they obstinately resisted with scoffing. Evangelism, commissioned by the Catholic Church, was done most frequently, but with very little success. However, there was an eight day debate which took place in Servian between the Catholic Bishop of Osma and some monks, and the Cathars Baldwin and Theodoric. By the end of the debate, Theodoric told the Bishop: "I know of whose spirit you are; you have come in the spirit of Elias [Elijah]." The Bishop responded with: "If I have come in the spirit of Elias, you have come in the spirit of the Antichrist." After the debate, the whole of Servian hated the Cathars, and would have driven them out if it wasn't for the powerful Stephen of Servian who protected them.[150]

The Cathars became very powerful throughout southern France, and soon wanted to establish their own state and implement their own laws against Catholics. Those who were laymen and not of the Cathar priesthood were called "believers" and these rejected faith in Christ and good works as necessary for salvation, and because of this lenient belief system, they indulged freely in murder, robbery, perjury, and adultery.[151]

Rainier Sacconi, a former Cathar turner inquisitor, recounted how they had no concept of confession:

> I never saw any one of them engaged in private prayer apart from others, or manifest sorrow for his sins, or weep, or smite upon the breast, and say, 'God be merciful to me a sinner'; or anything of the kind which could denote contrition.[152]

---

148 The Third Lateran Council, 1179: Heretics are Anathema, canon 27, in Edward Peters, *Heresy and Authority in Medieval Europe*, ch. v, p. 169, ellipses mine
149 Peter of les Vaux-de-Cernay, *History of the Albigensian Crusade*, 5, trans. W.A. Sibly & M.D. Sibly
150 Peter of les Vaux-de-Cernay, 2.20, 22–23
151 Peter of les Vaux-de-Cernay, 1.13–14
152 Rainier Saccone: A Thirteenth-Century Inquisitor on Catharism, in Edward Peters, *Heresy and Authority in Medieval Europe*, ch. iii, p. 125

As one priest of that era wrote of southern France:

> Its citizens were not only heretics, they were robbers, lawbreakers, adulterers and thieves of the worst sort, brimful of every kind of sin.[153]

Southern France, in other words, was a violent, dangerous, and wild place. Catholics in southern France were under threat being surrounded by so great a wave of heretics very hostile to the Church. One day a certain Cathar named Hugo went into such demoniacal frenzy that he entered a church and defecated beside the altar, and to show his mad enmity toward God, wiped himself with the altar cloth. The Abbot of Citeaux reported this crime to the Cathar Count of Toulouse, Raymond, and he told the clergyman that in no way would he punish him for such a matter.[154] This toleration for the Cathars and their heretical deviancy, of course enabled them to become superior in power. In such a position, the heterodox will kill and persecute the orthodox. From toleration comes desecration of everything holy and sacred. Raymond began to command his private mercenaries to loot and destroy churches and monasteries.[155] It was for his persecutions and acceptance of heresy that Pope Innocent III called him "an unbeliever, a persecutor of the cross, an enemy of the faith,"[156] and with that we can shed light as to what would happen if power was given to those who St. Paul described as "the enemies of the cross of Christ."[157]

It was once discussed between one Thedisius and an Abbot on whether or not Raymond should be allowed to go back into the Catholic Church. The Abbot, with all prudence and concern for the preservation of the Faith, concluded that if the Count were allowed to reenter, and he was lying, the Church in southern France "would be destroyed and the faith and Christian worship would perish."[158] If only we had men of this caliber dealing with the heresy that is currently in our midst.

In a later time, he angrily ordered an Abbot to hand over to him the keys of his monastery. The Abbot refused, entered his monastery and placed the keys over the body of St. Anthony, in honor of whom it was built. Raymond followed him, took the keys, locked him and the rest of the clergy inside and barred the doors of the church. As they lied imprisoned, Raymond looted the money of the sanctuary, and to show his contempt for the Faith, had an orgy with some prostitutes. He then drove the clergymen out and forbade any one to provide them with shelter "on pain of a most severe penalty." On another occasion Raymond came with a number of his mercenaries to attack the Monastery of Saint-Marie. The clergymen fled inside the sanctuary, the Cathars besieged them, and for so long were those poor legates trapped that they began to drink their own urine out of thirst. When they eventually gave up, the Cathars entered the church, looted the furniture, took out the crosses and sacred vessels,

---

153 Peter of les Vaux-de-Cernay, 3.84
154 Peter of les Vaux-de-Cernay, 2.40
155 Peter of les Vaux-de-Cernay, 2.42
156 Peter of les Vaux-de-Cernay, 137
157 Philippians 3:18
158 Peter of les Vaux-de-Cernay, 163

destroyed the bells, and left nothing but the walls. They took the statue of Christ crucified and hacked off the arms and legs and used them to grind pepper and herbs. They led their horses inside the church and fed them by the altars. They ransomed the church for fifty thousand sous, and when the violence was done, a Cathar knight said: "We have destroyed St. Anthony and St. Mary; it only remains for us to destroy God." In another church, a Cathar knight placed on the head of a crucifix his helmet, placed on the body his shield and spurs, and then struck the image with his lance and said: "Redeem thyself!" In one instance, Raymond requested the Bishops of Toulouse and Couserans to come for a meeting. When they arrived, Raymond spent the whole day attacking a Catholic commune.[159] Their violent hatred toward Christianity was no greater than the heretics of the East—the Muslims.

Raymond sent a knight to the Bishop of Toulouse, to tell him, on pain of death, to leave his city. "The Count of Toulouse did not make me Bishop," he said, "nor was I ordained by his hands or by his behalf. It was the humility of the Church that brought about my election, not the power of princes. I will not go on his account. Let him come if he dares. I am ready to embrace the sword if I can attain glory by drinking the cup of suffering. Let the tyrant come, surrounded by knights and armed; he will find me alone and unarmed. I await my reward. I have no fear of what man may do unto me." Raymond did not dare touch him.[160]

In the southern French city of Breziers, a priest one evening was walking to his parish when a number of Cathars violently upheld him, beat and wounded him, broke his arm, took his chalice, scoffingly disrobed him, and to express their hatred for the body and blood of Christ, urinated on him. In the church of St. Mary Magdalene, the Cathars ambushed and murdered the Viscount of Breziers, Raymond Trencavel. When the Bishop tried to fight the heretics, they broke his teeth.

In another instance, a convert to Catharism and a knight named Giraud de Pepieux, took two Catholic knights, put out their eyes, cut off their ears, sliced off their noses and upper lips, stripped them completely naked and sent them off into the freezing cold to die. They were blind and could not find their way through the cruel wilderness; one of them perished and the other was found and rescued by a poor local. One Abbot named Stephen of Eanes, alongside two monks and a layman, were ambushed by the Cathar William of Roquefort. By the time he was done, the Abbot was inflicted with thirty-six wounds and the layman twenty-four, and both were dead. One of the monks was left half-dead, and the other was spared. A woman—or more accurately, a Jezebel—who was an influencer for the Cather heresy, had a son who was a knight and a fanatic for her corrupt cause. He one day attacked a priest as he was observing mass, and hacked him to pieces. In another occasion, he took a Catholic from a monastery and tore out his eyes. The Cathar Count of Foix once ordered the inhabitants of Pamiers to exit the house with the promise that they would be left unharmed. As soon as the townsmen came out, they were ambushed and many were made captives. This same Count

---

159 Peter of les Vaux-de-Cernay, 199–205
160 Peter of les Voix-de-Cernay, 221

once said that if he could kill, with his own hands, all the Christian crusaders who opposed the Cathars, he would esteem himself as "having rendered service to God."[161]

From such a statement we are reminded of the words of Christ when He said that "the time cometh, that whosoever killeth you will think that he doeth God service."[162]

So filled with hatred for the Faith was this man, that it is said that he "panted after the death of Christians and never lost his thirst for blood."[163] His son, Roger-Bernard, followed his father in cruelty and heresy. In an attack on the Catholic commune of Montgey, he approached a priest who was taking refuge in a church and asked him who he was. "I am a crusader and a priest," he said. "Prove to me that you are a priest." He removed his clerical hood from his head and showed his tonsure. Roger-Bernard, like a devil before a cross, plunged his knife into the priest's head and killed him. In one Catholic monastery there was found a hundred and fifty people mutilated by the Cathars. Their hands and feet were cut off, their eyes torn out; women were found with their nipples lacerated and their thumbs amputated. After they seized one knight, they hung him and then cut off his hands and feet.[164]

So violent was anti-Catholic fervor, that the Bishop of Osma and his colleague Ralph, warned their clergyman Peter to leave the Cathar city of Brezier, because the hatred of the Cathars towards him was so intense that they feared he might be murdered by them.[165]

THE CATHARS ARE DESTROYED

A great example of Christian militancy is found in Christendom's war against the Cathars. When people speak of this event they almost always describe it as though the Catholic Church hunted down poor and innocent Cathars who just wanted to be left alone and attend their small group of underground Bible studies.[166] This is far from the truth.

Pope Innocent III, in the first full year of his pontificate in 1199, sent legate Pietro Parenzi to Orvieto in Italy where Cathars thrived, and to install peace in the city. While there, the Cathars murdered and mutilated Parenzi,[167] revealing the true violent nature of their religion, and of ultimately all heresy. A justly given reaction was made by the Pope who demanded that Hungary and Bosnia suppress the heresy in their own countries, where it was still called Bogomilism. A missionary to southern France, Peter of Castelnau, was advised to leave Albigensian territory on account of "fear of assassination" because "the heretics hated him above all others." Despite this intolerance, the Catholic Church was still willing to dialogue with the Albigensians. In 1207 St. Dominic and a number of legates partook in an official theological debate in Montreal with a Cathar bishop named Guilabert de Castries. The four judges of the debate, all Cathars, refused to give a verdict, although one hundred and fifty Cathars converted

---

161 Peter of les Vaux-de-Cernay, 3.85–86, 127, 130, 200, 207
162 John 16:2
163 Peter of les Vaux-de-Cernay, 209
164 Peter of les Vaux-de-Cernay, 219, 530, 582w
165 Peter of les Vaux-de-Cernay, 2.24
166 See Moczar, *Seven Lies about Catholic History*, ch. iv, p. 76
167 Carroll, *A History of Christendom*, vol. iii, ch. v, pp. 165–166

to Christianity. When St. Dominic was in southern France he reproached a man for working on a Catholic feast day, to which the Cathar populace responded by trying to murder him. A Catholic legate named Peter of Catelnau was ordered to go to southern France to preach peace and maintain order. While in Toulouse, the Count Raymond VI threatened him with death, and in the legate's departure, the threat was matched with action. In one early morning, after Mass, a Cathar knight rode to Peter and plunged his lance into his ribcage. Before he gave his last breath, he looked at the assassin and said: "May God forgive you, even as I forgive you." When this murder was reported to Rome, Pope Innocent III buried his head into his hands in grief.[168] On March 10 of 1208 the Pope made this proclamation to commence a crusade:

> Let us turn now to those who, fired with zeal for the true faith, are ready to gird themselves to avenge this righteous blood (which will not cease to cry from earth to heaven until the Lord of Vengeance descends from heaven to earth to cofound the corrupt and their corrupters); and to resist those villains who are attacking peace and truth…Let us emphasize that those villains are striving not merely to snatch our possessions but to take our lives; they are not merely sharpening their tongues to attack our souls, they are raising their hands to attack our bodies; they have become corrupters of souls and despoilers of lives. If we follow true belief, we should fear not them which kill the body, but him which is able to send both body and soul to Hell. Let us therefore trust in Him who, in order to free His believers from the fear of death, Himself died and rose again on the third day; and hope that our venerable brother the Bishop of Couserans and our beloved son the Abbot of Citaeux, legates of the Apostolic See, and the other followers of the true faith, will find no cause for fear in the death of Peter, man of God, but that on the contrary it will set fire to their ardour, so they will be ready to follow the example of one who gladly exchanged a temporal death for eternal life, and will not shrink from laying down their lives for Christ in so glorious a struggle, if needs must…Forward then soldiers of Christ! Forward, brave recruits to the Christian army! Let the universal cry of grief of the Holy Church arouse you, let pious zeal inspire you to avenge this monstrous crime against your God! In the name of the God of peace and love, apply yourself vigorously to pacifying those nations. Work to root out perfidious heresy in whatever way God reveals to you. Attack the followers of heresy more fearlessly even than the Saracens—since they are more evil—with a strong hand and a stretched out arm. [169]

Notice from this zealous speech and battle-cry, how the Pope associates the God of peace and love with driving out heresy. When heresy is strong and dominant, peace lies dead, and love is as unknown as the God Who is love. His words are in accordance with Christ's warning on heretics that they come to kill, steal, and destroy.

Pope Innocent III was more forceful against Cathars than he was against Muslims, and this is adequate for several reasons: the Muslims were outside of Europe, while the Cathars were within Christendom. How would have the Church, if the Cathars greatly flooded Europe,

---

168 Carroll, *A History of Christendom*, vol. iii, ch. v, p. 167, 169–170; Moczar, *Seven Lies about Catholic History*, ch. iv, p. 91; Peter of les Vaux-de-Cernay, 2.26; 3.57, 59
169 Quoted by Peter of les Vaux-de-Cernay, 3.63–64

CHRISTIANITY IS AT WAR: THE MANIFESTO FOR CHRISTIAN MILITANCY

been able to fight against one heresy in the East if it had been so infiltrated by another heresy within its own ranks? If the Cathars ever managed to take a significant part of Europe, and deeply wound the Christian Faith, then warring with the Muslims would have been hindered, because it would not have been agreeable to the heretics, for devil cannot fight devil.

This claim is not an educated guest, but an affirmation based on the actual history of the Cathars, in which we find them forming alliances with Muslims for the destruction of Christianity.

We even find a case in which the Muslim ruler Walid ordered that the holy metropolitan of Damascus, Peter, have his tongue cut off because he condemned, not only the impiety of the Muslims, but also that of the Manichaeans, or Cathars, who were quite numerous in Arabia.[170] During the First Crusade, the Cathars of the Middle East, called Paulicians, allied with the Muslims to fight and crush Christendom. Raymond, the leader of the Cathars in the thirteenth century, went so far in his vehemence for the Church that he sent his emissaries to the king of Morocco, to beg not only for his help to fight against the Christians, but to obliterate all of Christianity.[171]

In 1215 the Fourth Lateran Council took place, and what occurred here illustrates how militant Christianity once was. Pope Innocent III opened the Council with the words of Christ from the Last Supper: "I have desired to eat this pasch with you before I suffer," and then the Pope added, "before I die." He began his proclamation for a new crusade against the Cathars with the Book of Ezekiel, reading the verses in which God ordered a pious man clothed with linen to place the mark of God—the TAU, a Hebrew letter shaped as a T, and also a T in Latin—upon those who lamented for the wickedness of Israel, and commanded six saintly warriors to destroy the heretics in Israel:

> And, behold, six men came from the way of the higher gate, which lieth toward the north, and every man a slaughter weapon in his hand; and one man among them was clothed with linen, with a writer's inkhorn by his side: and they went in, and stood beside the brazen altar. And the glory of the God of Israel was gone up from the cherub, whereupon he was, to the threshold of the house. And he called the man clothed with linen, which had the writer's inkhorn by his side; and the Lord said unto him, through the midst of Jerusalem, and set a mark upon the foreheads of the men that sigh and that cry for all the abominations that be done in the midst thereof. And to the others he said mine hearing, Go ye after him through the city, and smite: let not your eye spare, neither have ye pity: slay utterly old and young, both maids, and little children, and women: but come not near any man upon whom is the mark; and begin at my sanctuary.[172]

---

170 Chron. Theophan. Annus Mundi 6234, see also n. 213 of the editor Harry Turtledove; Gibbon, *Decline and Fall*, vol. v, ch. l, p. 899
171 See Peter of les Vaux-de-Cernay, 395
172 Ezekiel 9:2–6

After the reading of this great biblical event, the Pope then began to speak his own words against the heretics of his day—the Cathars:

> And who are the six men charged with the divine vengeance? They are you, fathers of the Council, who with all the arms at your disposal—excommunication, depositions, suspension and interdict—shall smite without pity those unmarked with the atoning cross who persist in dishonoring the city of Christendom.

St. Francis of Assisi was present to hear this call to war, and was so moved to zealotry that he made the Latin cross shaped TAU the symbol of his order.[173] "The TAU," said the Pope, "has exactly the same form as the Cross on which our Lord was crucified on Calvary. And only those," he continued, "will be marked with this sign and will obtain mercy, who have mortified their flesh and conformed their life to that of the Crucified Savior."[174]

Many a man took up his cross—warriors of France, Brittany, and Germany—and like the prophets clothed with linen, placed the holy sign of God upon their breasts under which lied throbbing hearts hotly pulsing for the crushing of the wicked and the purging of demons. Each man cried battle, took his weapon, and peered down with pious eyes toward the land where error abounded and was embraced with deceptive hands, to drive out the heretics as Jehu crushed the prophets of Baal.[175] Such a rising was not done for the sake of bloodshed, but for the upholding of peace; not for murder, but for justice over murderers and those haters of God who sought out the destruction of His Church. As one monk, who lived in these zealous times, wrote:

> With so many thousands of the faithful in France already taking up the cross to avenge the wrong done to our God, and others yet to join the Crusade, nothing remained but for the Lord God of Hosts to dispatch his armies to destroy the cruel murderers—God who with His customary goodness and inborn love had shown compassion to his enemies, the heretics and their supporters, and sent his preachers to them—not one, but many, not once, but often; but they persisted in their perversity and were obstinate in their wickedness; some of the preachers they heaped with abuse, others they even killed.[176]

It was "on account of the wickedness"[177] of the Canaanites that God permitted the Hebrews to take Canaan, and thus the Church was now warring upon southern France for its sinister actions and beliefs, and for its tyranny over the Christian inhabitants who resided there. Forty years before this crusade took place, the Christians were always striving to bring the Cathars back to the truth, but this was to no avail.[178]

---

[173] See Carroll, *A History of Christendom*, vol. iii, ch. v, pp. 188–189
[174] In Englebert, *St. Francis of Assisi*, ch. ix, p. 141
[175] See Peter of les Vaux-de-Cernay, 3.73, 80, 168
[176] Peter of les Vaux-de-Cernay, 3.81
[177] Deuteronomy 9:5
[178] See Fletcher's notes on Maistre first letter on the Spanish Inquisition, B

CHRISTIANITY IS AT WAR: THE MANIFESTO FOR CHRISTIAN MILITANCY

We can already hear the cries of the objectors, the moderns and the indifferent Christians, asking their empty questions: how can such a war be justified just because of the murder of one man (Peter Castelnau), committed by only a few people and not the whole of the Cathar population? One could have made the same plaintiff cry before the honorable Battle of Gibeah. Did not the Israelites make war against the entire tribe of Benjamin for the rape and murder of one woman that was done by a few men and not the whole tribe? A number of savage men, sons of Belial, attempted to rape a man, but instead raped a woman, and murdered her. What did Israel do? At first they requested from the leaders of Benjamin the wicked men who did this, but they refused, just as Raymond VI and other leaders of Southern France refused to bring the Cathar criminals who persecuted Christians to justice. What did Israel do? They went to war. What did the Pope do? As Israel did before him, he launched a crusade against the heretics.

Before the battle commenced, an old man in the presence of the Cathars in the city of Breziers, said: "You are defending the city against the crusaders, but who will be able to defend you from above?"[179]

What was the result of allowing heresy to become dominant? War; war between the predecessors of Cain and the predecessors of Abel. A certain bishop was preaching to the heretics at the Cathar city of Carcassonne, and when they scolded him he, like the prophets of old, declared:

> You will not hear me? Believe me, I will utter against you such a mighty roar that men shall come from the ends of the earth to destroy this city. Know you for sure that even if the walls of the city were built of iron and very high, yet you would not be able to avoid receiving from the most Just Judge a worthy punishment for your unbelief and wickedness.

And so did it happen. Many a battle was fought most bloody and violently, led by the valiant Simon de Montfort who, with arms and piety, fought against the heretics. Swords were struck; arrows were fired; stones flew and pierced men as bullets do today; boulders descending from terrifying catapults smashed through walls. As man quarreled with man for the sake of the Truth triumphing, priests chanted their ancient hymns with reverent and rustic voices. The warriors of the Cross were not only laymen, but archbishops, bishops, deacons and archdeacons, who like Samuel the prophet, took up the sword to put down those who corrupted the truth for a lie and were worthy of death. The militancy was great amongst these ancient clerics; and just to show an example, here are the words of a French monk named Peter of les Vaux-de-Cernay, on his experience with certain Cathar mercenaries:

> On another day I myself, a mere monk of the Cistercian order, went quite close to the castrum to encourage the crusaders who were supplying the petraries; one of the mercenaries in Moissac, showing no respect for my calling, fired an extremely sharp bolt from his crossbow at maximum power and tried to hit me; I was on my horse at the time—the bolt pierced my robe, missed my flesh by a finger's width or less, and fixed itself in my saddle. Through God's

---

[179] Peter of les Vaux-de-Cernay, 3.87

PART 12

grace neither I nor my horse was harmed; this I do not attribute to my own merit—rather it seems that Divine clemency ensured that the enemies of religion would not be able to rejoice in striking a monk as if this were a significant victory, and thus justify continuing their attacks on our men.

From sunup to sundown the Cathars roamed the land, seeking out the Catholic troops to murder them and mutilate their bodies. But still Montfort and his men carried on the cause of the Cross, and when a certain monk came to pray for him, he said:

> Do you think I am afraid? We are about Christ's business. The whole Church is praying for me. I know that we cannot be overcome.

The local Cathars were possessed by the spirit of treachery, as the Mohammedans are today. In the area of Lagrave, a French Catholic knight, being more trusting of the heretical locals, hired a Cathar to repair his wine casks. When the carpenter was done, he asked the knight to see if he found the repairs sufficient. The knight bent down and placed his head inside the cask, and the carpenter raised his axe and decapitated him. The other locals at once rose up and began murdering the few French soldiers present in the area. As soon as the news of these killings spread, the Crusader Godfrey rushed to the sight with armed men. When the locals saw them arrive, they embraced them, perceiving that they were one of them. The crusaders raised their arms and slew them all, both young and old, as the Israelites did unto the Benjamites in the Battle of Gibeah. Godfrey was later ambushed by a great force of heretics. They fought like saintly knights, and when all were dead but Godfrey, he was asked to surrender to which he replied: "I have given myself to Christ; far be it from me to give myself to His enemies." They slaughtered him, and he gave up his spirit in glory. Knights who were captured in this war were dragged in the streets by heretic mobs and then hung. The Count Godfrey was captured, and when he requested to observe Holy Communion he was refused. "If I am not to be permitted communion and the holy sacraments, at least let the Eucharist, my salvation, be shown to me, so that in the life to come I may look upon my Saviour." The chaplain present raised the Eucharist, and the Christian warrior beheld it with sublime reverence. On the orders of the tyrant Raymond, Godfrey was to be hung. Before being executed, he asked to see a priest, this too was denied him. "Since I am not allowed to see a priest, God will be my witness that I have always served Christianity and my lord the Count of Montfort with a ready will and an eager heart, and that I am willing to die for this and for the defense of the faith." They raised him up forcefully and hung him from a walnut tree.

The Christian soldiers celebrated the feast of St. John the Baptist, to honor that holy man who rose up against the tyrant and cried out faithful chastisement toward his iniquities, and died for it. And on the next day, after the glimmering light arose over both the wicked and the righteous, armies of men whose hearts were as black as the birds of the air which consume the flesh of dead men, prepared their attack upon the warriors who took up the Cross and bore the sign of God. Montfort ordered for his armour to be brought; the others made ready. Though they were covered with such thick metal, Montfort did not forget the armour of light which he had put on, to combat the darkness that overran the earth and brought men to madness so great that they would war with the very One who created them. There they were before the trenches, their standard with heads up to Heaven, their hands gripping ever so tightly the tilts of their swords. Montfort arose and hurried to a church, sat inside the sanctuary and heard voices of pious men singing unto that God who the enemy sought to make unknown. But no longer was this earth to be a place where God is but darkly acknowledge, for the men of the Cross were lights to the world over which the gates of hell could not prevail.

As the warrior stood and heard the liturgy so serene to the soul, the men outside saw before them a charging horde of the heretics with cries of violence and clamor. They came upon them with much ferociousness and all that is expected in such melees were committed. A messenger ran to Montfort and begged him to join the battle. "First let me hear the divine mysteries and see the holy images of my Saviour." Another man speedily arrived and said: "Make haste! The battle grows more intense, and our men can hold out no longer." "I will not go until I have seen my Redeemer." Upon that moment the priest raised the Eucharist, and to such a sight Montfort was so pressed, he raised his arms to Heaven and said: "Lord now lettest thou thy servant depart in peace, according to thy word, for mine eyes have seen thy salvation. Let us go and if needs must die for Him who deigned to die for us." He came to the battlefield and saw before his eyes a myriad of dead and wounded, and two waves of men struggling with the greatest forcefulness. Not just man against man, but minds focused on Heaven against minds rooted in hell; ideas loving life against ideas revering death; a Faith that brings salvation versus a faith that brings damnation. The warriors saw their leader, and hope did arise within them. They raised their swords and shields, and with faith upon that armour of light, struck against the advancers of darkness and drove them back into their trenches. Arrows and stones hailed on the Christians, and as they stood their ground a stone pierced right through the head of Montfort, and he died. He perished as all righteous men do when they stand before the violent slaves of error, just as that prophet of old lost his head under the orders of Herod; that prophet to whom they celebrated the day before this event, prior to that moment when the dawning light illuminated upon the church where Montfort heard the hymns of holiness as the battle commenced. The very presence of that sanctuary in the midst of heretics, is but one example out of many of that light of the world that is seen even in the thickest oceans of darkness; that light which forever glimmers; that light which we are all to be in and for which we are to fight.

In 1218, prince Louis of France took up the Cross and finished the behooved war, and where cities were captured falsehood was purged away and the most Holy Cross put in its place.[180]

---

[180] See Peter of les Vaux-de-Cernay, 3.89–93, 95–96, 99, 103, 105, 116, 123, 126, 134, 136, 142, 144, 145, 148, 153, 154–55, 173, 176–179, 188–189, 216, 218, 224, 226, 227, 235, 238, 240–245, 250, 253, 256–258, 261–263, 270–277, 280, 282–283, 284, 288, 291, 292, 310, 313–315, 322–327, 333, 336–339, 347–348, 351, 353, 427, 448, 501, 513, 608–612, 619

Were Cathar priests burnt at the stake for refusing to reject their heresy? Absolutely, and rightfully so, for to prevent Cathar violence, the holders and teachers of the poison had to be extinguished before their fangs full sunk themselves into the flesh of the naive. In one setting, at least one hundred and forty-four Cathar priests were burnt in a pyre by Simon de Montfort.[181] In 1244 the Catholics took the last Cathar stronghold in Montsegur; all of its residents were allowed to leave in peace except for about two hundred Cathars who refused to recant their heresy. These were burned at the stake, leaving the sect with a fragmented following here and there.[182]

In 1229 a council in Toulouse made obligatory that every person in Languedoc, the largest province in southern France where most Cathars lived, to vow that they would remain Catholic and to condemn heresy. The council also demanded that teams consisting of two laymen and one priest search out homes and buildings for Cathars. A former Cathar named William of Solier warned the Papal legate, Cardinal Romano Frangipani that revealing the names of witnesses against the heretics would put their lives in danger, since the Cathars were a violent bunch. Because of this, an inquisition was established to investigate the Cathars, conducted by Dominican monks, whose order St. Dominic founded initially to combat Catharism. This all may sound intolerant or tyrannical by modern perspectives, since today's thinking sees one's religion as insignificant to civilization's preservation. The Cathars were no harmless or gentle people. According to historian A.L. Maycock, the Cathars assumed "the form of a definitely anti-social philosophy, aiming at the literal destruction of society."[183] To outlaw their beliefs, and arrest those preaching the heresy, the Catholics were in reality preventing Cathar heresy from arising. In the general council held at Pamiers in the year 1212, the very connection between driving out heresy and keeping civil peace in society was made, as one medieval historian explained:

> The purpose of the council was this: our Count [Montfort] wished to develop good customs in the territories he had won and brought under the Holy Roman Church; and, now that the heretical filth which had corrupted all those territories had been driven out, to ensure the establishment of a sound set of customs to promote order in civil life. The area had indeed long been exposed to plunder and rapine; the powerful oppressed the powerless, the strong the weak. [184]

Twelve men were appointed to "establish customs that would allow the Church to enjoy its proper freedom and would improve and strengthen the condition of the whole area."[185] This inquisition against Catharism, therefore, precluded the heretics from doing what Cain did to Abel.

---

181 Peter of les-Vaux-de-Cernay, 156
182 Carroll, *A History of Christendom*, vol. iii, ch. vi, pp. 217–219
183 Quoted by Moczar, *Seven Lies about Catholic History*, ch. iv, p. 91
184 Peter of les Vaux-de-Cernay, 362
185 Peter of les Vaux-de-Cernay, 363

After reading of all the evils brought by the Cathars, we could at least understand as to why the Church, after its victory over the heretics, made laws against them, reminiscent to the laws of Moses:

> And the house, in which a male or female heretic shall be discovered, shall be leveled with the ground, never to be rebuilt; unless it is the master of the house who shall have arranged the discovery of the heretics. [186] Whoever shall be caught giving any male or female heretic counsel, help, or favor, besides the other punishments mentioned duly in their logical places in other passages of this decree, shall become infamous by that same law, and shall be admitted neither to public office, nor public affairs, nor the election of persons to these, nor may he testify in a legal process; to that extent shall his incapacity to testify go, that he shall neither bequeath legacies to heirs nor inherit them himself. [187]

Their religion was not about a personal relationship between a man and his god, but about revolution and the replacement of Christianity with their dualistic and oriental pagan heresy. Like the Mormons in the nineteenth century, the Cathars wanted to separate themselves from the State and form a new government.[188] They hated life and the continuance thereof; imagine if everyone had converted to the religion of the Cathar, births would decline to a dangerous level, suicide would abound, and the world would be ruled under the rulership of multiple tyrants who call themselves the Perfect. Catharism would have quickly spread like wild fire if it wasn't for the Church's response to fight against it. And if it never warred with the vile error, then Catholicism and European civilization would might have well today be seen only in isolated corners of Europe. With this in perspective, it makes all the sense as to why a crusade and inquisition was launched against the Cathars. Even Henry Charles Lea, one of the most fervent critiques of the Inquisition, admitted that the Church was on the right in this regard.[189]

The inquisition, contrary to the exaggerations of professors and anti-Catholic ministers, was actually quite equitable and orderly. All those accused were given the liberty to list all of his enemies, and all those named were not allowed to serve as witnesses. Torture was not used frequently and never had any lasting effects on the person. One of the inquisitors, Jacques Fournier, interrogated some nine hundred and thirty suspected Cathars, and none of them were executed, and in the fifty years which this inquisition lasted (from 1227 to 1277), five thousand Cathars were executed. This is not a huge number. There are more murders that are done in America every year then the number of Cathars killed by the Inquisition. There are millions of more infants murdered throughout the world (in the name of "women's rights") through abortion every year, than all of the heretics executed by the Inquisition combined. We may scoff the Middle Ages as "the dark ages," but truly it is the modern era—dominated by secularism—that is the real dark ages.

---

186 1243–1254, SS Innocentius IV, Bulla, Ad Extirpanda [AD 1252–05–15], Law 26
187 1243–1254 SS Innocentius IV Bulla Ad Extirpanda [AD 1252–05–15], Law 27
188 See Moczar, Seven Lives about Catholic History, ch. iv, p. 91
189 Moczar, *Seven Lies about Catholic History*, ch. iv, p. 102; Belloc, *How the Reformation Happened*, intro, p. 28

The Cathar heresy was finally crushed, all of France was under the Crown and was now a truly united country. Remnants of Catharism still survived—though it was very fragmented—and it was not until the fourteenth century that it was eliminated, thanks mainly to the efforts of the inquisitor Bernard Gui. Out of the many he interrogated, six hundred and thirty six were punished: forty by death, three hundred by imprisonment, and the rest with lighter sentences.[190]

Despite all of these facts on the Cathar Crusade, we still have Christians today who will go so far as to even identify themselves as Cathars.[191] By their own behavior and madness, we can say that such a title fits them.

ISLAM WAS NOT FOUNDED BY MUHAMMAD, BUT BY A FOURTH CENTURY HERETIC NAMED ARIUS

One of the biggest myths about Islam is that it was founded by Muhammad. When studying about Islam's history, every historian begins with Muhammad having a vision of the angel Gabriel in the cave. But, when studying Islam's origins, one needs not to begin with Muhammad's vision in the cave of Hira, but in the fourth century with the heretic, Arius, the heretic who denied the Trinity and believed that Jesus was a creature. The true founder of Islam was not Muhammad, but Arius. His heresy would become the foundation of Islam. Islam is really an Arabian extension, or continuation, of the Arian heresy. Islam's link with Arianism, which is the denial of Christ's divinity, was affirmed by one of the oldest non-Muslim writers on Islam, St. John of Damascus, when he, in the 8th century, wrote:

> This man [Muhammad], after having chanced upon the Old and New Testaments and likewise, it seems, having conversed with an Arian monk, devised his own heresy.[192]

John the Deacon also recounts an Arian origin to Islam:

> The Saracens [Muslims] are intent and zealous to deny the divinity of the Word of God. On all sides, they array themselves against him, eager to show that he is neither God nor the Son of God. Indeed, it was only because their false prophet [Muhammad] was the disciple of an Arian that he gave them this godless and impious teaching.[193]

Constantine Porphyrogentinitus, the fourth emperor of the Byzantine Empire, wrote in the 10th century, in his *Administrando Imperio*, that "he [Muhammad] was believed because a certain Arain, who pretended to be a monk, testified falsely in his support for love of gain."[194]

---

190 Carroll, *A History of Christendom*, vol. iii, ch. vi, pp. 217–219; See Moczar, *Seven Lies about Catholic History*, ch. iv, p. 92–3
191 See Moczar, *Seven Lies about Catholic History*, ch. iv, p. 77
192 St. John of Damascus, *On Heresies*, 101, trans. Frederic H. Chase, Jr., brackets mine
193 *Refutations of the Saracens* by Theodore Abu Qurrah, the Bishop of Haran, as Reported by John the Deacon, GK86–88, trans. John C. Lamoreaux
194 Constantine Porphyrogentinitus, *De Administrando Imperio*, 14, trans. R.J.H. Jenkins, brackets mine

CHRISTIANITY IS AT WAR: THE MANIFESTO FOR CHRISTIAN MILITANCY

It was this same Arius who would forge the heresy that would give birth to Muhammad's cult.[195] The Medieval scholar, Peter of Cluny, affirmed that Muhammad consumed the deceptions of Arius and gagged them out from his conniving tongue:

> Indeed [this heresy], long ago conceived by the plotting of the devil, first spread by Arius, then promoted by this Satan, namely Muhammad, will be completed by Antichrist, in complete accordance with the intentions of the devil. [196]

Arianism, just like Islam, overran the Roman Empire and almost destroyed it from within. It was so dangerous and destructive, that it compelled the Emperor Theodosius to establish this law:

> It is Our will that all the peoples who are ruled by the administration of Our Clemency shall practice that religion which the divine Peter the Apostle transmitted to the Romans as the religion which he introduced makes clear even unto this day. ...[A]ccording to the apostolic discipline and the evangelical doctrine, we shall believe in the single Deity of the Father, the Son, and the Holy Spirit, under the concept of equal majesty and of the Holy Trinity. [197]

The modern man, upon reading such a law, falls into shame, or confusion, as to why the Church upheld such edicts against people for not accepting the Trinity. To him, to accept the Trinity is merely a religious preference, and to not accept the Trinity is seen with the same nominal view. Indifferentism seizes his mind, and when he is confronted by a progressive or liberal thinker about this early intolerance of the Church, he does not hesitate to blabber out apologies.

But the fact is, that the Church had every reason, and every right, to see to it that the doctrine of the Trinity be upheld to maintain orthodoxy and repulse heresy. St. Paul, when confronted by the Judaizing heretics, "did not yield submission even for an hour, that the truth of the gospel might continue with you." (Galatians 2:5) And so, Christians are not to give ground to heretics, but completely stop them from inundating into society their insidious beliefs. Heretics, if not prevented from spreading their beliefs, will cause tyranny.

The law quoted from the Theodosian Code was established to combat the heresy of Arianism.[198] It was this heresy that caused St. Jerome, when commenting on the verse from Galatians, "A little leaven," to write:

> Cut off the decayed flesh, expel the mangy sheep from the fold, lest the whole house, the whole paste, the whole body, the whole flock, burn, perish, rot, die. Arius was but one spark in Alexandria, but as that spark was not at once put out, the whole earth was laid waste by its flame. [199]

---

195 See De Croce, *Refutation of the Koran*, ch. i, p. 9
196 Quoted John Victor Tolan, Saracens: Islam in the Medieval European Imagination
197 *Theodosian Code*, 16.1, in Edward Peters, *Heresy and Authority in Medieval Europe*, ch. i, p. 44
198 Moczar, *Seven Lies about Catholic History*, ch. iv, p. 81
199 Quoted by Aquinas, *Whether Heretics Should Be Tolerated*, in Edward Peters, *Heresy and Authority in Medieval Europe*, ch. v, p. 183

Alexander, the bishop of Alexandria who fought Arianism, described the promoters of this heresy as "teaching apostasy such as one may justly consider and denominate the forerunner of Antichrist."[200]

Arianism is the religion of the Antichrist, and since Muhammad continued Arianism, Islam, thus, is the religion of the Antichrist.

In order for us to fully comprehend the tyranny of Islam, and thus the Antichrist, we must first expound on the history of Arianism, and how, like Muhammad's cult, it implemented violence on Christians in trying to force them to renounce the Trinity when it eventually took substantial control over the government.[201]

ARIANISM'S FOUNDING

Arius coveted the priestly position of the bishop Alexander, his jealousy taking such a hold on him that he sought to destroy the Church by contriving his own heresy. Since Alexander had strictly upheld and preached the Holy Trinity, Arius attempted to refute this eternal truth by teaching that Christ was created and thus at one point did not exist, and therefore could not have been equal with the Father or God. "If," he said, "the Father begat the Son, he that was begotten had a beginning of existence: and from this it is evident, that there was a time when the Son was not. It therefore necessarily follows, that he his substance from nothing."[202] The bishop Alexander went on to define the heresy as such:

> That God was not always the Father, but that there was a time when he was not the Father; that the Word of God was not from eternity, but was made out of nothing; for that the ever-existing God (the 'I AM'—the eternal One) made him who did not previously exist, out of nothing; wherefore there was a time when he did not exist, inasmuch as the Son is a creature and a work. [203]

Like Muhammad, Arius reduced Christ to only the status of a prophet. This belief, because of its confusing of the person of Christ, appealed even to pagans. He began to teach this to as many people as he could reach, making public declarations of his blasphemy. After many disputes and attempts at reasoning with him, Alexander had no choice but to oust out Arius from the Church.[204] Other very learned men contended strongly with Arius and his followers, such as St. Augustine, St. Jerome, St. Hillary of Poitiers, and St. Gregory of Nazianzus.[205]

The Satanic nature of Arias and his ilk was exposed by Alexander in his letter to another Alexander, the bishop of Constantinople, describing how the Arians "trampled upon the

---

200 The Epistle of Alexander, in Socrates, Eccles. Hist. 1.6
201 See Moczar, *Seven Lies about Catholic History*, ch. iv, p. 81
202 Quoted by Socrates, Eccles. Hist. 1.5
203 Quoted by Socrates, Eccles. Hist. 1.6
204 Theodoret. Eccles. Hist. 1.2; Moczar, *Seven Lies about Catholic History*, ch. iv, p. 81; Belloc, *The Great Heresies*, The Arian Heresy, p. 18
205 De Croce, *Refutation of the Koran*, preface, p. 5

religion of the church," being "instigated by satanic agency" and "skillful in deception," circulating "specious letters, calculated to delude the simple and unwary." They lied to bishops about their hatred for the Trinity, convincing them to accept their sect so that they could simply say that high members of the Church agreed with them. Not only were they of a demonic and deceptive nature, but a violent one as well. Like Islam, and his patriarch Cain, they would come in the name of peace to deceive with the intent of bloodshed, daily rallying for persecutions against Christians, and making false accusations toward them before judges so as to get them punished.[206] Such is no different than what the Muslims have been doing against Christians. Islamic Sheiks today have, with their savage speeches, provoked mobs to execute crimes against churches and the saints. Islam is nothing new, Arianism influenced many, as is often the case, to slaughter and persecute Christians.

ARIANISM SPREADS LIKE WILDFIRE

Arianism—like Islam, except without the physical sword, but rather with the tongue—soon overran the whole of Egypt, Libya, and the further Thebaid, eventually extending to the other cities and provinces of the empire, and completely dividing Christendom.[207] The reason for this swift expansion was the decay of the populace and the decay of Christian supremacy and identity in the society. Where Arianism spread, there were mockeries made of Christianity done in the form of comedic plays, as is always the case where the Faith declines in influence and power. As the Church historian Socrates recounts:

> Christianity became a subject of popular ridicule, even in the very theaters. [208]

In our own times, it is a trend to mock Christ in the theaters and the films, in the universities and the media, and just as it was then, Orthodoxy has declined in the midst of this sacrilege. It was a time when the people took the supernatural for granted, and declined theologically to the point that it esteemed Christ as not one of the three persons of the Godhead, but as a mere creature. It appealed to the elites and the intelligentsia of the empire—just as it is today with the atheists and Darwinists—since the denial of the Trinity distinguished them from common society, and thus gave them an imagined luster of social and intellectual superiority. Soon, even the army of the empire became solidly Arian because, like the Muslims, Arianism provided them with a sense of superiority over the civilians. This is because the Trinity appears as unscientific, while Deism (which is what Arianism and Islam are) always appeals to the pompous elites who erect their idol of vanity on the altar of intellectualism. When the emperor Constantine had heard of this grave predicament, he sent a letter to Arius and Alexander calling for mutual respect between the two divisions; but this was done to no avail, and Arianism extended to all of the eastern provinces of the empire. From Egypt, to Syria, to Palestine, both laypeople and priests went to the side of Arius and denied Christ's divinity. The heresy's growth in the Middle East was assisted by Constantin's co-emperor

---

206 Theodoret. Eccles. Hist. 1.4
207 Eusebius, *Life of Constantine*, 2.31; Socrates, Eccles. Hist. 1.6
208 Socrates, Eccles. Hist. 1.6

Licinius, a secret pagan who professed Christianity and who governed the eastern part of the Roman Empire only to later be crushed by Constantine.[209]

Alexander, the bishop of Alexandria, was stirred to action, and composed an epistle warning his fellow bishops that Arianism was the religion of Antichrist; that it needed to be cut off before it could further taint the laity, and that it was being enabled by heretical bishops from within the Church, namely one Eusebius, the bishop of Nicomedia:

> Inasmuch as the Catholic Church is one body, and we are commanded in the holy Scriptures to maintain 'the bond of unity and peace,' it becomes us to write, and mutually acquaint one another with the condition of things among each other, in order that 'if one member suffers or rejoices, we may either sympathize with each other, or rejoice together.' Know therefore that there have recently arisen in our diocese lawless and anti-Christian men, teaching apostasy such as one may justly consider and denominate the forerunner of Antichrist. I wished indeed to consign this disorder to silence, that if possible the evil might be confined to the apostates alone, and not go forth into other districts and contaminate the ears of some of the simple. But since Eusebius, now in Nicomedia, thinks that the affairs of the Church are under his control because, forsooth, he deserted his charge at Berytus and assumed authority over the Church at Nicomedia with impunity, and has put himself at the head of these apostates, daring even to send commendatory letters in all directions concerning them, if by any means he might inveigle some of the ignorant into his most impious and anti-Christian heresy, I felt imperatively called on to be silent no longer [210]

Every heresy has its enablers, the ones who support and promulgate it. Those who were inculcating Arianism worked, in the words of Alexander's epistle, "to blend falsehood with truth, and that which is impious with what is sacred."[211]

After Alexander's epistle was read by all the bishops in every city, his words of contention against the heresy only enraged the demons that possessed the Arians. The Sword of Christ, which brings division between light and darkness, struck their heretical hearts, and they became even more fanatical. Those who read the letter either went deeper into Orthodoxy, or rebelled against the Church and plunged themselves into the religion of Antichrist. Eusebius the Arian wrote letters to Alexander, that he might receive Arius and his followers into communion with the Church, and he also wrote to the other bishops that they might reject the epistle of Alexander. The theological struggle was a spiritual war, that split not only the clerics but the laity, with many vacillating, moving to and fro, not remaining sturdy in the truth, like the man whose house is on the sand, and actually converting to Arianism,[212] being as "clouds without water, carried about by the winds" (Jude 1:2).

---

209 Eusebius, *Life of Constantine*, 2.34–35; Belloc, *The Great Heresies*, The Arian Heresy, pp. 18, 21, 24–26
210 Quoted by Socrates, Eccles. Hist. 1.6
211 Alexander, in Socrates, Eccles. Hist. 1.7
212 Socrates, Eccles. Hist. 1.6

THE COUNCIL OF NICEA

Theological disunity—in which people break away from the Orthodox Faith and the society is fragmented by various cults—is the cause of civil and political decay. If the people are so willing to rebel against Divine Law, fracture from His Church and create and partake in cults and promulgate heresies, then they will just as easily rebel against civil law. The spread of heresy would worry any Orthodox Christian government. The colossal theological division caused by Arianism was to the consternation of Constantine, and with the attempt of fixing the matter between Arius and Alexander, he wrote an epistle to the two in which he said:

> I am informed that your present controversy originated thus: When you, Alexander, inquired of your presbyters what each thought on a certain inexplicable passage of the written Word, rather on a subject improper for discussion; and you, Arius, rashly gave expression to a view of the matter such as ought either never to have been conceived, or when suggested to your mind, it became you to bury it in silence. This dispute having thus been excited among you, communion has been denied; and the most holy people being into two factions, have departed from the harmony of the holy body. The great God and Savior of us all has extended to all the common light. Under his providence allow me, his servant, to bring this effort of mine to a successful issue; that by exhortation, ministry, and earnest admonition, I may lead you, his people, back to unity of communion. For since, as I have said, there is but one faith among you, and one sentiment respecting religion, and since the precept of the law, in all its parts, combines all in one purpose of soul, let not this diversity of opinion, which has excited dissension among you, by any means cause discord and schism, inasmuch as it does not affect the force of the law as a whole. [213]

Constantine efficiently responded to Arianism by conveying more than three hundred bishops from all parts of the empire into an assembly: thus was the Council of Nicaea in 325.[214]

During the assembly, a group of Arian bishops wrote up their statement of faith and presented it to the rest of the attendants. Instead of giving it recognition, or respect, the other bishops honorably teared it to pieces, and all but two of them stood up and declared that Arius must be excommunicated. So imposing was their zeal and protest, that Arius himself was overwhelmed and unsettled before the presence of this fervency.[215]

Many in the modern era have been inclined to mock and laugh at the controversy between Orthodoxy and Arianism, that it was all hairsplitting arguments and bigots controlling doctrine for the purpose of preserving power. But as we move forward in this history, what we will find is that Arianism was a rebellion, against all Orthodoxy and therefore

---

[213] Victor Constantine Maximum Augustus to Alexander and Arius, in Socrates, Eccles. Hist. 1.7
[214] Eusebius, *Life of Constantine*, 2.8; Theodoret. Eccles. Hist. 1.8. Eusebius says the number was 250 bishops, while Theodoretus suggests that it was 270, Socrates 318, the latter of these, I believe, is accurate, since the emperor Constantine, in a letter of his which was registered by Socrates, recounts that "more than three hundred bishops" were present (Socrates, 1.9)
[215] Belloc, *The Great Heresies*, The Arian Heresy, p. 26

against all order,[216] and ended with bloodshed and tyranny. The Council concluded their statement of faith, or the Nicene Creed, in which it was stated:

> I Believe in one God, the Father Almighty, the Maker of all things, whether visible or invisible; and in one Lord Jesus Christ, the word of God, God of God, Light of light, Life of life, the only begotten Son, the First-born of all creatures, begotten of the Father before all ages; by whom all things were made: who for our salvation took upon him our nature, and dwelt with men. He suffered and rose again the third day, and ascended to the Father; and he will come again in glory to judge the living and the dead.[217]

This beautiful Nicene Creed was what Arianism would want to destroy, and eventually it would be the reason why Muhammad founded Islam, since he was viciously bent on destroying the doctrine of the Holy Trinity. All of the crusades that were fought between Christian and Muslim, all of the holy wars that were waged between the slaves of Allah and the sons of God, were done over the Nicene Creed. The knights of Christ who unsheathed the sword, did so to defend the Creed, and the ghazis—or the Muslim warriors—wielded the scimitar to destroy it.

Constantine accepted the Creed, and was the first to testify that it was most Orthodox, imploring others to sign it in agreement with the addition that the term "consubstantial"—which meant that the Father, Son, and Holy Spirit are of the same substance—be used when describing the Holy Trinity.[218] The Council also affirmed that the "holy catholic and apostolic church condemns all those who say that there was a period in which the Son of God did not exist; that before he was begotten he had no existence; that he was called out of nothing into being; that he is of a different nature and of a different substance from the father; and that he is susceptible of variation or change."[219] This went against all that Arius stood for, and in the future, the Creed would also spearhead the doctrine of Muhammad. Arius was anathematized, and he, together with Eusebius the Arian, another Arian leader named Theognis, and all of their followers were prohibited from entering the city of Alexandria.[220]

Constantine exalted the holy Creed, and in celebration, wrote a letter to the Catholic Church in Alexandria, writing:

> We have received from Divine Providence the inestimable blessing of being relieved from all error, and united acknowledgement of one and the same faith. The devil will no longer have any power against us, since all that which he had malignantly devised for our destruction has been entirely overthrown from the foundations. The splendor of truth has dissipated at the command of God those dissensions, schisms, tumults and so to speak, deadly poisons of discord. Wherefore we all worship one true God, and believe that he is. But in order that this

---

216 See Belloc, *How the Reformation Happened*, intro, p. 24
217 In Theodoret. Eccles. Hist. 1.12
218 Theodoret. Eccles. Hist. 1.12; Socrates, Eccles. Hist. 1.8; see also Moczar, *Seven Lies about Catholic History*, ch. iv, p. 82
219 In Theodoret. Eccles. Hist. 1.12
220 Socrates, 1.8

might be done, by divine admonition I myself also, who am but one of you, and who rejoice exceedingly in being your fellow-servant, undertook the investigation of the truth. And may the Divine Majesty pardon the fearful enormity of the blasphemies which some were shamelessly uttering concerning the mighty Savior, our life and hope; declaring and confessing that they believe things contrary to the divinely inspired Scriptures. Arius alone beguiled by the subtlety of the devil was discovered to be the sole disseminator of the mischief, first among you, and afterwards with unhallowed purposes among others also. Let us therefore embrace that doctrine which the Almighty has presented to us: let us return to our beloved brethren from whom an irreverent servant of the devil has separated us: let us go with all speed to the common body and our natural members. [221]

THE ARIANS STRIKE BACK

After Arius was defeated at the Council of Nicaea, he began to learn the weaknesses of the Orthodox, like the clever serpent before the credulous woman. He slyly began to change his angle, and through sophism altered the wording of his doctrine so that its heresy may not appear conspicuous, but like tasteless poison in the sweetest of wine, be hidden in false orthodoxy. It was a verbal compromise, a mere play on words,[222] the conniving wiles of the devil. In the words of Socrates:

> For Arius, as I have before related, entertaining one opinion in his heart, professed another with his lips; having hypo-critically assented to and subscribed the form of faith set forth at the council of Nicaea, in order to deceive the reigning emperor. [223]

He would write a letter to the emperor Constantine, conveying to him his statement of faith, the wording of which sounded very Orthodox. He connivingly put it together to deceive, which is what heretics do, presenting themselves as Orthodox to infiltrate the Church. The letter read:

> We believe in one God the Father Almighty: and in the Lord Jesus Christ his Son, who was begotten of him before all ages, God the Word through whom all things were made, both those which are in the heavens and those upon the earth; who descended, and became incarnate, and suffered, and rose again, ascended into the heavens, and will again come to judge the living and the dead. [We believe] also in the Holy Spirit, and in the resurrection of the flesh, and in the life of the coming age, and in the kingdom of the heavens, and in one Catholic Church of God, extending from one end of the earth to the other. [224]

In 335, Arius traveled to Constantinople where he would meet Constantine who, upon his arrival, asked the heretic if he believed in the true doctrine of the Church. Arius responded that he upheld orthodoxy, presenting to the emperor his statement of faith, which omitted his belief against the Trinity. After declaring upon oath that he did not subscribe to the heretical

221 The Emperor's Letter, in Socrates, 1.9
222 Belloc, *The Great Heresies*, The Arian Heresy, p. 27
223 Socrates, 2.35
224 Quoted in Socrates, 1.26

views which he in fact taught, Constantine gave him leave with these words: "If your faith be orthodox, your oaths are honourable; but if you do not really hold that belief which you have professed upon oath, God will judge you from heaven."

The emperor, docile and credulous for the sophistry and deception of this heretic, allowed Arius reentry into Alexandria, and when he arrived he did not hesitate to spark a commotion by rapidly preaching his heretical doctrine.

The deceived Constantine ordered Athanasius to readmit Arius to communion with the Church. But he, honoring "God rather than men" (Acts 5:29), and being unsubmissive to the corruptions of government, refused. The emperor, believing the heretic to be Orthodox, became very angry with Athanasius' resilience and declared to him:

> Since you have been apprised of my will, afford unhindered access into the church to those who are desirous of entering it. For if it shall be intimated to me that you have prohibited any of those claiming to be reunited to the church, or have hindered their admission, I will forthwith send some one who at my command shall depose you, and drive you into exile. [225]

Constantine is always falsely condemned as the one who "invented the Catholic Church," or the one who mixed paganism with Christianity. But rarely is he ever criticized for attacking Athanasius and for believing the deceptions of Arius. Arius' major followers, especially Eusebius the Arian, even tried to have Athanasius removed from his bishopric. The Arians incessantly tried to frame Athanasius of crimes that he did not commit. There is one story that had quite a comedic ending.

The Arians accused Athanasius of murdering a man named Arsenius who was staying in Tyre. While there, some servants of the local governor heard some people at an inn say that Arsenius was actually hiding in someone's home, and Arsenius was then arrested by the authorities. In the trial, Athanasius stood ready to make his defense. The Arians came and presented a severed hand, crying out that it was the hand of Arsenius, and that it was Athanasius who killed him. Athanasius then asked who in the room actually knew Arsenius, and a number of the heretics did not hesitate to present themselves. Athanasius then summoned for Arsenius to be presented, and there he stood, still alive and with hands intact. Anthansius, with all of his wit, said: "Arsenius, as you see, is found to have two hands: let my accusers show the place whence the third was cut off."

The Arians would soon raise more slander against Athanasius so as to frame him. They ran to the emperor and raised an uproar, saying that Athanasius was stopping corn from being shipped from Alexandria to Constantinople. This time there calumny penetrated the mind of Constantine. Athanasius was then exiled into Gaul where he was a light to the world and helped the western church see the evils of Arianism.[226]

Arius' supporters desired to restore the heretic to the Church, an idea unthinkable to Alexander, the bishop of Constantinople. Eusebius the Arian threatened Alexander that if

---

225 Quoted in Socrates, 1.27
226 Theodoret. Eccles. Hist. 1.14; Socrates, 1.35

CHRISTIANITY IS AT WAR: THE MANIFESTO FOR CHRISTIAN MILITANCY

he did not allow Arius back into communion with the Church, that he would have him disposed. But Alexander did not let positions of power and influence hinder him from the true mission of his office: the perpetuation of Orthodoxy and the prevention of heresy.

He mortified his body, fasting and praying, and offering to God not just his exhortations, but his tears. He committed himself to this penance for many days. Mournful, Alexander retired into his church, and in lamentations beseeched God to prevent Arius' restoration. "If Arius," he said, "is to be joined to the Church tomorrow, dismiss me thy servant, and do not destroy the pious with the impious. Cut off Arius, lest if he enter into communion with the Church, heresy enter also, and impiety be found conjoined with piety."

Constantine, observing his duty as a Christian king, summoned Arius to his palace and asked him whether he believed in the Council of Nicaea, and without any hesitation, Arius affirmed that he did. Arius said this with immense duplicity, and with the cunning of the heretic. It is not hard for heretics to proclaim Orthodox doctrine in order to gain the trust of the people so that they can later on seep their poison into docile ears.

Foolishly convinced, Constantine demanded that Alexander bring Arius back into communion. The day had come, and Arius triumphantly and boldly paraded himself throughout the city. He began to give a series of speeches; but as he spoke he was abruptly distracted by something. He suddenly fell down, and in his faintness, his insides bursted out of his belly.[227] The Arians mourned his death, but even Constantine, as time went on and his zeal for Christianity grew, would eventually praise the death of Arius.[228]

CONSTANTINE ATTACKS ARIANISM

Although Arius had died, his seeds of evil continued to grow. Eusebius, the bishop of Nicomedia, being a fervent supporter of the Arians and their doctrine, gained the concern and weary of the emperor. Constantine took measures against the spread of Arianism, this being attested by these concluding words of his letter to the Nicomedians: "If any one should make mention of those destroyers [the Arians], or presume to speak in their praise, let him know that his audacity will be repressed by the authority which has been committed to me as the servant of God. May God preserve you, beloved brethren!"[229]

Eusebius was then deposed and banished, being replaced by one Amphio.[230] Constantine also nobly utilized the burning of Arian books,[231] and most righteously decreed that if anyone possessed a writing by Arius, and did not bring it to the flames, that person was to be put to death. The decree said:

> And in addition to this, if any treatise composed by Arius should be discovered, let it be consigned to the flames, in order that not only his depraved doctrine may be suppressed, but

---

227 Theodoret. Eccles. Hist. 1.14, ellipses mine; Socrates, 1.27–38; Belloc, *The Great Heresies*, The Arian Heresy, p. 28
228 Socrates, 1.38
229 In Theodoret. Eccles. Hist. 1.20, brackets mine.
230 Theodoret. Eccles. Hist. 1.20, brackets mine.
231 See Kamen, *The Spanish Inquisition*, ch. vi, p. 112

also that no memorial of him may be by any means left. This therefore I decree, that if any one shall be detected in concealing a book compiled by Arius, and shall not instantly bring it foreword and burn it, the penalty for this offense shall be death; for immediately after the conviction the criminal shall suffer capital punishment.[232]

This decree has been used to try to label Constantine as an evil tyrant. But such was the action of a prudent Christian emperor, one who fought for Christendom and for the Orthodox Faith, and who did not stand lax when serpents were slithering about trying to inject their poison into the Body of Christ. He did not stand idle, but stood strong, proud of the Faith, and not careless toward a conspiracy to destroy the Church. He combated the heretics, and was in fact fighting the tyranny of heresy. The despotic and totalitarian nature of the Arian cult was always desperately trying to manifest itself, and it would have opened itself up in its entirety, if it were not for the Orthodox men who combated it. Arianism, after being uprooted in the Roman Empire, would eventually find itself in Arabia, and who did it influence? Muhammad. And till this day are we dealing with Islam, the continuation of Arianism. Islam would have never spread as much as it did, if Christendom was extremely severe against Arianism. If Arius was put to death and all of his followers destroyed or coerced back to the Faith, Islam would have never come into existence.

The treachery of the Arians was later exemplified by their conspiring against Athanasius, bishop of Alexandria, in that they had accused him before Constantine of trying to usurp the royal throne. Constantine, after hearing the bishop's defense, acquitted Athanasius of the charge, and then sent a letter to Alexandria in which he announced: "Believe me, my brethren, the wicked were unable to effect any thing against your bishop."[233]

ARIANISM INFILTRATES THE ROMAN GOVERNMENT

But the justice of Constantine, as well as his defense of the Faith against the deceit of Arianism, would come to an end after his death. For, Constantius II, his son, was soon beguiled, and accepted the Arian heresy.[234] How this happened, can be briefly explained.

The Arians, in order to take power, did what any heretics would do: infiltrate the government. Constantine's sister, Constantia, had a deep friendship with a certain Arian monk, though this fact was concealed from the emperor. This false monk was actually the one who helped get Arius out of exile, and now he was in the government, and was being used by the other Arians to inundate their heresy into the state, and in turn use the state to advance Arianism. The monk then convinced a certain eunuch of the royal bed-chamber to convert to Arianism. Soon the other eunuchs followed, adopting the religion of the Antichrist, and they did not wait long to introduce this heresy to Constantius's wife, and she too became Arian.

As the serpent went to Eve in order to get to Adam, the Arians used the sister of Constantine to influence the entire empire. Because of her liking of this heretic, she bade her brother

---

232 The Emperor's Letter, in Socrates, 1.9
233 Theodoret. Eccles. Hist. 1.27
234 Belloc, *The Great Heresies*, The Arian Heresy, pp. 28–29

to bring him under his protection, a request which he fulfilled. When Constantine was on his death bed, he was unable to show his will to his sons on account of their absence, leaving him no choice but to request the Arian monk, who was present, to give it to them.

After the Arian monk gave the will to Constantius, a bond grew between the two, and the monk would have an immense influence on the new emperor, instructing him in the apostasy of Arius. Constantius' wife soon also began to influence her husband, for the serpent, continuing what he did in the garden, went first for the wife to get to the husband. His wife and the Arian monk guided him into Arianism.

Having now the zeal of a heretic, Constantius II went against everything his father stood for, taking in a group of Arian bishops as his advisors, and afflicting all kinds of cruelty on the saints.[235] In little time, Arianism began to spread throughout the royal court; the imperial guards and the officers of the royal household embraced the heresy, and from there it flooded like a torrent into the population of the city. Everywhere now, there were people jumping off the Ark of the Church and falling into the deathly waves of the flood, their souls being taken by the volatile torrents of the devil's ocean.

Everywhere one turned, there were the traitors turning away from Christ, there was dissension, there was contention, malicious debate and sophistical questions.[236] The spirit of debate seized the souls of the masses, and from theological objections came anarchy, and from such there sprung violence. Christians who had immense influence, freedom, and state support under Constantine, in a breath, lost it all under his son.[237] The despotism of heresy revealed itself, now that it had the backing of the powerful emperor.

THE NOW ARIAN GOVERNMENT COMMENCES TYRANNY OVER THE CHRISTIANS

Every heresy strives for power; for this is the entire goal of heresy. The reason why Islam is so bent on tyranny is because it is a heresy, with its entire creation being done to destroy Christianity and Christ's Church. We see this truth in history, in the rise of Arianism. Once it took over the government by converting the Emperor Constantius II, the reign of Arian terror began.

The emperor banished Paul, the bishop of Constantinople, to Cappadocia where he would shortly be murdered by Arians. In the words of Athanasius, "they had him [Paul] strangled, by order of Philip the pro-consul, who was the protector of their heresy, and the active agent of their most atrocious projects."[238]

A Christian council was held in Sardica to dispute for the cause of Athanasius, a bishop who was banished by the Arians. The assembly was attended by not only bishops, but victims, alongside their families, of Arian tyranny. Arian bishops had attended the meeting, but

---

235 Theodoret. Eccles. Hist. 2.3
236 See Socrates, 2.2
237 See Moczar, *Seven Lies about Catholic History*, ch. iv, p. 82
238 Theodoret. Eccles. 2.5

once they realized that the members of the synod upheld the Trinity, and that they were with those who they had persecuted, they left in rage.[239] In the synodical letter from the bishops assembled in Sardica, it was written that the Arians:

> used chains, and the sword, as the engines of their cruelty. Several individuals were present whom they [the Arians] had exiled: others came forward as deputies from those still kept in exile. The relations and friends of those whom they had put to death also attended: and what was of most importance, bishops also appeared against them; one of whom exhibited the irons and the chains with which they had bound him. There were also witnesses to testify that the death of many others had been occasioned by their calumnies. Their infatuation led them to such excess that they even attempted the life of a bishop; and he would have fallen a sacrifice to their fury, had he not escaped from their hands. Theodulos, our fellow-minister, of blessed memory, died while striving to make his escape from them; for, on account of their calumnies, he had been condemned to death. Some showed the wounds which with the swords of these persecutors had inflicted on them; others deposed that they had been exposed to the torments of famine. [240]

All of these atrocities and oppressions were not done by mere individuals, but entire Arian churches, the ministers of which used the Roman military to kill and persecute Christians. The Arians would denude virgins, set churches on fire, and have Christians imprisoned, all for the purpose of exalting Arianism, and punishing those who refused to accept their heresy. In the synod, two men who had left Arianism for the true faith, Macarius, bishop of Palestine, and Asterius, bishop of Arabia, spoke of the violence they received by the heretics for their reconversion. They informed the synod that they were many within the Arian movement who still held orthodox beliefs, but were kept from joining the council by both threats and empty promises, being even forced to remain in a single house, never being allowed, even for the briefest moment, to be alone.[241]

The bishop Athanasius was justly permitted to return back to his church in Alexandria by the emperor, who wrote a letter to the Church of Alexandria:

> It cannot, I conceive, have escaped the knowledge of your devout minds, that Athanasius, the expositor of the venerated law, was sent for a while unto the Gauls, lest he should sustain some irreparable injury from the perverseness of his blood-thirsty adversaries, whose ferocity continually endangered his sacred life. To evade this [perverseness], therefore, he was taken from the jaws of the men who threatened him into a city under my jurisdiction, where, as long as it was his appointed residence, he has been abundantly supplied with every necessity: although his distinguished virtue trusting in divine aid would have made the pressure of a more rigorous fortune. And since our sovereign, my father, Constantine Augustus of blessed memory, was prevented by death from accomplishing his purpose of

---

239 Theodoret. Eccles. Hist. 2.7–8
240 In Theodoret. Eccles. Hist. 2.8, brackets mine.
241 Theodoret. Eccles. Hist. 2.8

restoring this bishop to his see and to your most sanctified piety, I have deemed it proper to carry his wishes into effect, having inherited the task from him. [242]

Athanasius received the letter and used it to gain reentry into Alexandria, and he was most joyfully received by the faithful Christians. But the heretics, who were many in that infamous city, made an outcry of feigned piety, blaming Athanasius of taking the Alexandrian church. The Arians vomited up their slander, and the emperor, even after writing his gracious letter, sucked it up as though it was honey, and banished Athanasius from Alexandria.[243] Why such a shifting of the mind? Because he was a heretic, and a heretic "is a double-minded man, unstable in all his ways." (James 1:8)

THE ARIANS CREATE THEIR OWN COUNCIL TO DESTROY THE NICENE CREED

Eusebius the Arian conveyed his own council in Antioch as a means to declare that the Arian cult was indeed Orthodox. Such is the nature of heretics: they will incessantly go out of their way to convince the world that they are Orthodox to hide their pernicious intentions. As drops of water continuously land on the surface of a rock, to only crack the rock, so do heretics receptively say that they are Orthodox, to only penetrate the guards of the Church, and shatter it from within with their maddening altercations. Maximus, the bishop of Jerusalem, spurned such a false council, and affirmed that the Arians were deceivers because they had connivingly convinced the emperor to depose Athanasius. Julian, the Pope of Rome, refused to attend the council, and did not even send a substitute to take his place. Regardless of the Pope's serious affirmations against the council, ninety bishops, filled with corruption, attended the council, and surely they were breaching ecclesiastical law, for in the words of the Church historian Socrates,

> Neither was Julius, the bishop of the great Rome, there, nor had he sent a substitute, although an ecclesiastical canon commands that the churches shall not make any ordinances against the opinion of the bishop of Rome. [244]

So deceptive were the Arians that the declaration that was made in this nefarious council went so far as to even disassociate itself, though subtly, from Arius:

> We have neither become followers of Arius,—for how should we who are bishops be guided by a presbyter?—nor have we embraced any other faith than that which was set forth from the beginning. [245]

Notice how elusive they were. They never outright rejected Arius or his teachings, but simply used the excuse that because he was a mere presbyter, they were not going to follow him simply for the reason of his inferior position. The rest of the declaration sounded Orthodox, and it was done in such a way to have people think that they were on the side of

---

242 Socrates 2.3
243 Socrates 2.3
244 Socrates, 2.8
245 Socrates, 2.10

the Church. What these wicked bishops did not reveal was that it was part of a long-term sinister plan. They would do one council and sound Orthodox, with the intent of doing future councils, with each one slowly and elusively chipping away the Nicene Creed, in order to gradually destroy what the Fathers declared against Arianism. This is the nature of heretics: they will sound extremely right for the sake of your acceptance, and then once they obtain the power they desire, they bring destruction. The statement of the false synod continued on to evasively say that while they would not adopt Arian teachings directly from Arius, that they recognized the "soundness" of them:

> But being constituted examiners and judges of his [Arius'] sentiments, we admit their soundess, rather than adopt them from him: and you will recognize this from what we are about to state. We have learned from the beginning to believe in one God of the Universe, the Creator and Preserver of all things both those thought of and those perceived by the senses: and in one only-begotten Son of God, subsisting before all ages, and co-existing with the Father who begot him, through whom also all things visible and invisible were made; who in the last days according to the Father's good pleasure, descended, and assumed the flesh from the holy virgin, and having fully accomplished his Father's will, that he should suffer, and rise again, and ascend into the heavens, and sit at the right hand of the Father; and is coming to judge the living and the dead, continuing King and God for ever. We believe in the resurrection of the flesh, and the life everlasting. [246]

Most of the statement sounds orthodox, except for the one single line stating that Arius' teaches are "sound," a line that contradicts everything that is written afterwards. This statement was written as an epistle and sent to all the bishops with the intention to deceive, and as they were trying to give an appearance of Orthodoxy, they were already conspiring against the truly Orthodox Christian, Athanasius. Heretics, for the public view, will always try their best to appear as true Christians, as they conspire amongst themselves how to destroy the true Christians. The Arians commissioned one of their own ilk, a man named George, to be the replacement of Athanasius, who was still in Alexandria at this time.[247]

THE ARIANS CONSPIRE TO MURDER ST. ATHANASIUS, BUT THE CHRISTIANS PICK UP THEIR SWORDS AND FIGHT THE HERETICS IN COMBAT

The Emperor Constantius' Arian advisors, violently wanting to end their great opponent, convinced him to put the saint to death. The plan was to bring George into Alexandria with an escort of armed guards; the soldiers would then bombard the church, seize Athanasius, and eventually have him killed.

On one evening, as Athanasius was with his congregation directing mass, an army of soldiers surrounded the church demanding for his life. The commander set his soldiers in battle formation on all sides of the church. Athanasius, with much wit and prudence, thought on what he was suppose to do. He ordered a psalm to be chanted, and as the melodious voice

---
[246] In Socrates, 2.10
[247] Socrates, 2.10–11

was being enjoyed by the soldiers, Athanasius, though he had the chance to escape immediately, waited for the congregants to exit the church for safety. "It is better," he said, "for me to meet the danger alone, than that any of our people should experience the least injury." Athanasius was no hireling, who flees at the coming of the wolf, but a true shepherd who sacrifices himself for his flock.

When the greater number of the people left, and with the rest following after them, Athanasius was led by monks and some of the clergy out of the church, and under the cover of darkness, he made his way to a life of exile. The Arian people, who were but laity and not soldiers, were wroth once they discovered that Athanasius was not in the church, and they set the sacred edifice on fire.[248]

Shortly after, Eusebius the Arian, who was at that time bishop of Constantinople, died. The people there chose one Paul to be their new bishop. But the Arians would have nothing of it, and nominated an Arian named Macedonius. The people, fired up by the zeal of Orthodoxy, revolted and executed the spirit of Christian militancy. The heretic Emperor Constantius sent an army under the general Hermogenes, to arrest Paul and expel him from the church. When the army arrived, the general had the intention to expel all of the bishops and end the sedition, but he was met with fierce opposition from the Orthodox, who fought with much ardency for the defense of their bishop. The people went to the house of the general and set it on fire, they then dragged the general out and put him to death.[249]

The emperor, adamant about replacing Paul with the Arian Macedonius, ordered Philip, the Praetorian Prefect who was known as second to the emperor in power, to arrest Paul. Knowing the ferocity of the multitude, Philip had to tactfully plan out the arrest. He went to a local bathhouse and from there sent for Paul with much respect for his office, adding that his presence was greatly needed. Once Paul arrived, Philip presented him with the edict of the emperor demanding for his arrest. Paul accepted his fate with humility, but the people no doubt were not willing to exhibit the same toleration. Just as the Pharisees hesitated to seize Jesus because they "feared the people" (Mark 12:12), Philip also feared the fierce spirit of the Christian multitude, who by then had gathered around the building awaiting for what was about to transpire.

The doors bursted open and Paul was rushed out, placed on a vessel, and sailed off into exile to Thessalonica. Macedonius was taken by buggy to the church, and the people, consisting of both Arian and Orthodox, rushed to the sanctuary. As soon as the multitude entered, there was a rush of ecstatic confusion and enthusiasm that struck them, and the soldiers, fearing a riot, unsheathed their swords and attacked them without discrimination, making a great slaughter of 3,150 people.[250]

---

248 Theodoret. Eccles. Hist. 2.14; Socrates, 2.11
249 Socrates, 2.13
250 Socrates 2.16

THE POPE DEFENDS ORTHODOXY AND COMBATS THE ARIANS

Athanasius, living under the oppressions of the heretics, constantly looking out for his own life, went to the last place he could go, and turned to the only person who would truly help him and who was above the rest of the bishops, the Pope of Rome. Athanasius, alongside numerous other bishops who were exiled by the Arians, turned to Pope Julius who issued to each of them letters that allowed them to return to their respective churches with their authority as bishops intact. They left Rome and returned to their lands with the papal epistle, and validly took possession of their churches. The Pope's authority expediently obtained for Athanasius his position as bishop by, in the words of Socrates, "the Church of Rome's peculiar privilege."[251]

Athanasius returned to Egypt, but while he was there, the Arians again began to concoct all sorts of calumnious accusations to frame him. They accused him of taking the church's supply of corn, which was there to be freely given to the poor, and selling it for his own gain. The emperor Constantius gave credence to such slanders, and threatened Athanasius with death. And who was willing to take Athanasius in, to protect him? Pope Julian who, seeing the wicked machinations of the Arians, found out where Athanasius was hiding, and opened the doors of Rome for him.

He fled to Rome and kept himself under the refuge of Pope Julian, who took him under his care and protection. Pope Julian wrote a stern letter against the Arian bishops for their illegitimate council in Antioch, which they had conveyed without his approval, for, in the words of Socrates, "they had not requested his attendance at the council, seeing that the ecclesiastical law required that the churches should pass no decision contrary to the views of the bishop of Rome."[252]

Pope Julian then berated them with severe condemnation for their perverting of the Faith.[253] As Athanasius remained under the protection of the Pope, the emperor of the Western parts of the Empire, Constans, sent a letter to his brother Constantius, that if he did not end the persecution against Athanasius and Paul, the bishop of Constantinople, and reinstate them back to their bishoprics, he would declare war on him, or really, a holy crusade against the Arians. The letter read:

> Athanasius and Paul are here with me; and I am quite satisfied after the investigation, that they are persecuted for the sake of piety. If, therefore, you will pledge yourself to reinstate them in their sees, and to punish those who have so unjustly injured them, I will send them to you; but should you refuse to do this, be assured, that I will myself come thither, and restore them to their own sees, in spite of your opposition.[254]

---

251 Socrates 2.15
252 Socrates, 2.17
253 Socrates, 2.17
254 Quoted in Socrates, 2.22

CHRISTIANITY IS AT WAR: THE MANIFESTO FOR CHRISTIAN MILITANCY

Surely was this an illustration of a king using the temporal sword to defend the Church, or really, the unsheathing of the political sword of St. Peter to end an unjust persecution. Such a forceful command had to have come from the influence of the Pope, who initiated the protection of Athanasius. The use of political power against persecution was effective, for Constantius, being perplexed by the threat, decided that Athanasius and Paul be allowed to return to their homes and observe their office as bishops, and wrote a letter to Athanasius:

> Our compassionate clemency cannot permit you to be any longer and disquieted as it were by the boisterous waves of the sea. Our unwearied piety has not been unmindful of you driven from your native home, despoiled of your property, and wandering in pathless solitudes. And although I have too long deferred acquainting you by letter with the purpose of my mind, expecting your coming to us of your own accord to seek a remedy for your troubles; yet since fear perhaps has hindered the execution of your wishes, we therefore have sent to your reverence letters full of indulgence, in order that you may fearlessly hasten to appear in our presence, whereby after experiencing our benevolence, you may attain your desire, and be re-established in your proper position. For this reason I have requested my Lord and brother Constans Victor Augustus to grant you permission to come, to the end that by the consent of us both you may be restored to your country, having this assurance of your favor. [255]

The swift reaction of Constantius to safely return Athanasius, is a lesson that teaches the importance of the State protecting the Church from persecution. For if it were not for Constans and his willingness to commence a crusade against his brother, Constantius would have never allowed to Athanasius to repossess his ecclesiastical office.

Upon hearing the news of Athanaius being allowed to return, Pope Julius rejoiced, declaring to the Christians of Alexandria:

> I also rejoice with you, beloved brethren, because you at length see before your eyes the fruit of your faith. For this is really so, any one may perceive in reference to my brother and fellow-prelate Athanasius, whom God has restored to you, both on account of his purity of life, and in answer to your prayers. ...For having suffered so many and diversified trials both by land and by sea, he has trampled on every machination of the Arian heresy; and though often exposed to danger in consequence of envy, he despised death, being protected by Almighty God, and our Lord Jesus Christ, ever trusting that he should not only escape the lots [of his adversaries], but also be restored for your consolation, and bring back to you at the same time greater trophies from your own conscience. [256]

---

[255] Constantius Victor Augustus to Athanasius the bishop, in Socrates, 2.23
[256] Epistle of Julius, Bishop of Rome, to those of Alexandria, in Socrates, 2.23, ellipses mine

THE ARIAN TYRANT CONSTANTIUS TAKES OVER THE WHOLE ROMAN EMPIRE AND UNLEASHES AN UNRESTRAINED PERSECUTION ON THE CHRISTIANS

But the amity and seeming fairness of Constantius was only a shield against the ferocity of his brother. A commander of the imperial guards unit, Magnentius, conducted a sedition against Constans, and through treachery killed him. After a bloody civil war, Magnentius made himself master of all Italy. Constantius would eventually defeat Magnentius, and with his brother now dead, the entire empire was now in his hands. The measures he took under the threat of Constans were soon reversed, and the tyranny of the Arian was given full license.

It was at this time that Constantius, being imbued with Arian doctrine, forced Paul out of Constantinople and exiled him to Cappadocia, and had him strangled to death. Lucius of Adrianople, another Orthodox prelate, was chained up and thrown into prison where he perished. Athanasius was not naive to the conspiring of the heretical state against his life, and so he fled.[257]

The tyrannical state at first began driving the Orthodox not only from the churches, but even from their cities. But expulsion did not gratify their evil lusts, and it did not take long for them to resort to more violence. They began to force the Christians to be in communion with the Arian heretics, a horrible sin, and then it intensified. Christians were tortured to death, others were executed, and such inhumanities were done throughout the eastern parts of the Empire, especially in Constantinople.[258]

With Athanasius gone, the Arians replaced him with George. He was a ministerial tyrant for his cult who hated Christians with such demoniacal frenzy that he executed various sadistic cruelties on the congregation.

To do this, George hired a military chief by the name of Sebastian, a Manichaean heretic, to see to it that the doctrine of Arius was enforced. Women who took an oath of chastity were thrown into prison, bishops bound and dragged, the homes of widows and orphans were pillaged and attacked, and Christians were, under the den of night, arrested and taken away from their houses. A week after Pentecost, the congregants gathered together to pray that God deliver them from the despotic hand of George.

The sinister bishop ordered that these poor saints be punished for going against him and his heresy. Sebastian charged them with his soldiers, and though by the time they arrived most of them had left on account of the late hour, his sadistic desires remained to be quenched. He ordered a huge fire to be made, brought next to it two virgins, and as Muslims do to their victims, ordered them to denounce their faith and accept Arianism. Their obstinate refusal was to his wrath, and Sebastian had his men beat the virgins until "they became scarcely recognizable." Forty men were then seized, and ordered to be flogged with palm tree branches covered in thorns. They were beaten so horrendously that some even died, while others had thorns driven so deeply into their bodies that they could not remove them without

---

257 Socrates, 2.26
258 Socrates, 2.27

surgical operation. The survivors were banished to the Greater Oasis, while the dead were refused burial. Thirty Orthodox bishops were seized and exiled, for the Arians, like Ahab, persecuted the Church to see the truth obliterated.[259] In the words of Athanasius:

> When Easter-week was passed, the virgins were cast into prison, the bishops were led in chains by the military, the dwellings even of orphans and widows were forcibly entered and their provisions pillaged. Christians were assassinated by night; houses were sealed; and the relatives of clergy were endangered on their account. [260]

How could one read such a story, and not recognize the immense strength of spirit which these saints of old harbored within their souls? The eyes of the wicked noticed the saints for the pureness of their works, and as they bore their cross, they suffered under cruel men whose minds were rooted in the earth, only to die the death of the flesh and have their souls ascend to the eternal realm of Heaven. To those who endured this persecution and were not allowed to bury their dead, Athanasius wrote:

> Let none of you be grieved on account of these impious heretics having prohibited the honours of sepulture from being rendered to you. The impiety of the Arians has reached such a height, that they block up the entrances, and sit like so many demons around the places of sepulcher in order to prevent the dead from being interred. [261]

The Arians would eventually throw George out because he became quite unpopular, and also because he burned a church down.[262] Athanasius would remain in exile until being allowed to return to his church in Alexandria by the emperor Julian in 361.[263]

Hosius was another prelate that the Arians exiled. He was the bishop of Cordoba, in Spain, before the Arians drove him out. But at the request of the Arians gathered in a heretical council in Sirmium, the emperor called for Hosius to come to them so that he could give his acceptance of their heresy, thinking that if they could gain his credence, it would give strength to their blasphemies. But he refused to be present at their fake council, and for this he was punished, being deeply whipped with stripes, suffering as Christ did. So horrendous were the beatings that he could no longer forbear. The saint was worn out, and acquiesced to the demands of the heretics.[264]

As time went on the Arian cult would have various changes, with schisms beginning to form. Such is the nature of all cults and heresies. Aetius the Syrian was a follower of Arius' teachings, but he disassociated himself from the cult because Arius went into full communion with the Catholic Church. Like a Muslim Aetius began to question the very Orthodox concept of how Christ could live eternally with His Father, asking "how that which was begetton can

---

259 Theodoret. Eccles. Hist. 2.14; Socrates, 2.28
260 Athanasius, *Apology for His Flight*, in Socrates, 2.28
261 Theodoret. Eccles. Hist. 2.14
262 Socrates, 2.14
263 Theodoret. Eccles. Hist. 3.4
264 Socrates, 2.31

be co-eternal with him who begat."[265] The heretical objections to the doctrine that Christ was both the Son of God and God, was the same objection adopted by Muhammad when he wrote that God "begets not, nor is He begotten."[266] Like Islam's predecessor, Arianism was really a simplification of Christianity, an entertaining of sophistical sentiments in which it boasted, much like the pompousness of deism.

As all heresies aspire to obtain the power of the state to further advance their beliefs, he composed a letter to the emperor Constantinius, using sophisms interwoven with tedious disputes over Orthodox doctrine that was already declared. Aetius began to teach and influence one Eunomius, who would become the leader of the entire Arian cult, who would go so far as to blasphemously say that whatever God knows about His own substance, we know about our own no differently,

> God knows no more about his own substance than we do; nor is this more known to him, and less to us; but whatever we know about the Divine substance, that precisely is known to God; and on the other hand, whatever he knows, the same also you will find without any difference in us. [267]

THE ARIANS MAKE HERETICAL COUNCILS TO DESTROY THE NICENE CREED

Life is but a perpetual spiritual war. It continues on, with battles, retreats, surrenders, false treaties, the breaking of truces, fierce struggles and quarrelsome engagements. But one thing that it never does, it never rests.

The Arians, by the order of the emperor Constantius himself, conveyed a synod in Milan, Italy. Once the meeting commenced, the Eastern bishops immediately called upon everyone to condemn Athanasius, that he might be completely cut off from entering Alexandria. But the western bishops—such as a bishop in Gaul (or France), and a number of Italian bishops—objected to such theological tyranny, and called for a reversal of the sentence against Athanasius, exclaiming that "this proposition indicated a covert plot against the principles of Christian truth. For they insisted that the charges against Athanasius were unfounded, and merely invented by his accusers as a means of corrupting the faith."

They made their righteous protest against heresy, and the evil council was dissolved.[268] The heretics pulled the bow to fire their poisonous darts, but the righteous unsheathed the Sword of the Spirit, and the devils fled.

But the Arians would not give up. Another synod was conveyed in Arminum and in this one the Arians went so far as to make another creed. They did it quite elusively, with the idea of deceiving the Orthodox bishops. In the beginning of their creed they said: "We believe in one God, the Father Almighty, the Creator and Framer of all things: and in one only-begotten Son of God, before all ages, before all beginning, before all conceivable time, and before all

---

265 Socrates 2.355
266 Koran 112.3
267 In Socrates, 4.7
268 Socrates, 2.36

comprehensible thought, begotten without passion: by whom the ages were framed, and all things made: who was begotten as the only-begotten of the Father, only of only God, God of God, like to the Father who begat him"; and then in the end they rejected that the Son is consubstantial with the Father, saying, "As for the term 'substance,' which was used by our fathers for the sake of greater simplicity, but not being understood by the people has caused offense on account of the fact that the Scriptures do not contain it, it seemed desirable that it should be wholly abolished, and that in future no mention should be made of substance in reference to God, since the divine Scriptures have nowhere spoken concerning the substance of the Father, and the Son."[269]

Notice the sophisms used in their malicious creed: they say they believe in one God, and even speak of how Christ is the Son of God, but they reject that the Son is of the of same substance as the Father. The Arians transformed the statement within the Creed, that the Son is "of the same substance" as the Father, to "of different substance."[270] The modern Christian would see this and think nothing of it. He would say, "they believe in one God, and that Christ is the Son of God, so why bother attacking them? Where is the love?"

It is no wonder why the Apostle James wrote, "You believe that there is one God. You do well. Even the demons believe and tremble!" (James 2:19) These words were not written only for the times in which he lived, but for all time. Thus the verse of St. James is a warning against the heresies, such as Arianism and Islam, that proclaim one God, but corrupt the image therefore into their own wicked devices.

The Arian change of the Creed may seem like a small alteration, but the heretic just takes, and keeps taking, until he has everything. This may not be understood by many today, but it was understood fully by the righteous prelates of Christendom. The Orthodox bishops who were present in the mock council, rose up and got right into the heart of the matter, demanding that if those who constructed the distorted creed be willing to condemn Arius:

> We came not hither because we were in want of a creed; for we preserve inviolate that which we received from the beginning; but we are here met to repress any innovation upon it which may have been made. If therefore what has been recited introduces no novelties, now openly anathematize the Arian heresy, in the same manner as the ancient canon of the church has rejected all heresies as blasphemous: for it is evident to the whole world that the impious dogma of Arius has excited the disturbances of the church, and the troubles which exist until now. [271]

But the Arians refused to comply, and instead they affirmed with pompous piety, "The faith has now been published," as though (and this is how all heretics think) they were declaring the faith of the first Christians. The Orthodox synod deposed from their office the bishops who would refused to anathematize the Arian heresy, such as Valens Ursacius,

---

269 In Socrates, 2.37
270 See Bellarmine, *On Laymen or Secular People*, ch. 19, ed. Tutino, p. 89
271 Socrates, 2.37

Auxentius, Germanius, Gaius, and Demophilus.²⁷² The Orthodox Synod of Ariminum sent a letter to the emperor Constantius, demanding that the Nicene Creed remain intact without any Arian changes being made. In the same letter they also deemed the Arians as enemies of peace, and that their doctrines fill people with cruelty:

> For how can those be at peace who destroy peace? Rather will strife and tumult be occasioned by these things in the church of Rome also, as in the other cities. For the innovations they introduce at present fill the believing with distrust and the unbelieving with cruelty. ²⁷³

The objective of the Church was to obliterate the Arian heresy, and depose those bishops who believed in Arianism from their offices. The Arians used false peace, but the Christian bishops wanted to bring true peace by destroying false peace. "I did not come to bring peace but a sword." (Matthew 10:34) And so did those fathers of the Church strike falsehood with the Sword of the Spirit.

THE ARIANS USE THE STATE TO OPPRESS THE CHURCH, BUT THE CHRISTIANS DO NOT TOLERATE IT, AND PICK UP THEIR WEAPONS AND FIGHT BACK

Though the Arians had lost the battle over the power of the council, they still had the advantage: they possessed the temporal arm, since the emperor Constantius agreed with their heresy. The tyrant intended to disseminate the Arian doctrine throughout all of the churches, and enthusiastically desired to make it the supreme religion.

He upheld the exiling of orthodox bishops under the pretext that they disrespected him when they dissolved the council in Milan, the one that he ordered. Constantius decreed that the Arian creed be read in all the churches in Italy, and that those bishops who "would not subscribe to it should be ejected from their sees, and that others should be substituted in their place." The first one they attacked was non other than the Pope himself. Pope Liberius refused to accept Arianism, and as punishment he was seized and forced into exile.²⁷⁴

One of the greatest examples of Christian fortitude is found in the actions of Pope Felix II; for he had fearlessly declared that Constantius II was a heretic. Enraged, the emperor ordered him to be arrested and beheaded, alongside other saints, beside the adequate of Trajan. His body was soon recovered by Christians who came to his place of execution at night, and he was buried on the Via Aurelia.²⁷⁵

Maximus, the bishop of Jerusalem, was a zealot of the Faith and an enemy of the Arian cause. He persevered in his fight against the evil doctrine, and continued even after the Arians cut off his eye and severed his right arm.²⁷⁶ All of the cities near Constantinople were bom-

---

272 Socrates 2.37
273 In Socrates, 2.37
274 Socrates, 2.37
275 *The Book of the Popes*, 38: Felix, trans. Louise Ropes Loomis
276 Theodoret. Eccles. Hist. 2.26; see Socrates, 2.38

barded with the despotism of the Arians, by the hands of one Macedonius. He organized a persecution upon not just Catholics, but also Novatians, since they too believed in the Trinity.

The Novatians were schismatics that broke off from the Catholic Church, but subscribed to many of the teachings of the Church. Many pious people were seized by the Arians, who would force open their mouths and shove into them the Arian communion bread and wine. They took Christian women, and forcefully baptized them under the anti-trinitarian Arian baptism.

The women who resisted, the Arians would saw off their breasts, and those who spoke against it would get beaten with whips. They would also take Christian women and sear their breasts with hot iron. They took a Novatian presbyter, an aged man named Auxanon, and threw him into prison alongside his companion in monasticism, named Alexander, and beat them so severely with stripes that Alexander perished. The Arians attacked churches and demolished them, and doomed to destruction any church that proclaimed the Holy Trinity.[277] Surely was this violent hoard of the Antichrist spirit.

The Arians were headed toward a certain Novatian church, and the Novatians, with immense zeal for the Holy Trinity, deconstructed the entire edifice and reassembled it in another place. The persecution was intensifying so much, that the Catholics and the Novatians united together, readied themselves for holy combat, and became willing to die for one another.

The Catholics and the Novatians in the province of Paphlagonia and Mantinium heard of how the Arians had just destroyed a church in Cyzicus, and so realizing that their churches were the next targets, they gathered together, armed themselves with hatchets, sharp hooks and whatever weapon they could get their hands on, and prepared for battle. Surely was this Christian militancy, with Christians fighting for the Faith and for the love of their neighbors. Macedonius and the other Arians realized that it would be difficult to drive the Christians from their homes, and so with the permission of the emperor, he took an entire company of soldiers into Paphlagonia, that through the sword the people there might accept Arianism. The two forces clashed, with the swords of Christians and Arians colliding against each other. Much blood was spilt, and many agonies were inflicted. Many of the Christians lost their lives, but almost every soldier on the Arian side, was slaughtered.[278]

After this victory, Macedonius, in utter disrespect, removed the remains of Constantine the Great from his coffin, and transported them into a certain church. The Christians, in their love for Constantine, and in their zeal for Christendom, rose up and charged to the site of the church, and a bloody battle ensued with the Arians. They attacked one another and the entire churchyard was covered with human gore, and even the well overflowed with blood, so much that it ran into the adjacent portico, and from there into the street itself.[279]

---

277 Socrates, 2.38
278 Socrates, 2.28
279 Socrates 2.38

Thus was the spirit of the ancient Christians; they were not what some today portray them as (people of pacifism and superficial peace), but combat—combat against the devil and his followers. And so much did they love Christianity that they fought and killed just to protect the remains of Constantine, the great defender, and the commencer, of Christendom.

Hearing about the bloodshed, Constantius was greatly upset with Macedonius, on account of the violence he provoked, and for his disrespect of his father's remains. Macedonius would eventually be ejected, and he plunged himself deeper into the abyss of heresy. For soon he devised a new heresy, not just rejecting the divinity of Christ, but the divinity of the Holy Spirit,[280] paralleling himself with Islam even further, since Muhammad, too, denied that the Holy Spirit was God. Macedonius attracted a substantial following called the Macedonians.

This was not the only battle that would be fought between Christian and Arian. In the time of the emperor Arcadius, it was common for the Arians to make a procession throughout the city of Constantinople every Saturday and Sunday, and sing Arian hymns to attack people to join their heretical movement. The hymn they would sing deliberately attacked the Holy Trinity, the lyrics being:

Where are they that say three things are but one power?

St. John Chrysostom, fearful of simple people falling for such deceptions, organized his own parade to combat the Arian attractions. He gathered together a large number of the faithful and sung hymns right in the same where the Arians sung their antichrist music. The Arians were greatly upset at this and violently attacked the Christians, and a small battle ensued. Christians killed Arians, and Arians killed Christians; death came on both sides. The emperor was furious at the Arians for provoking such a quarrel, and making the first attack, and banned the Arians from ever conducting such heretical processions.[281]

UNITARIANISM LEADS TO CRUELTY

The cruelty of the Arians was a result of their theology; their violence towards men flowed from their belief that the God of love was far from that humanity of which Christ came, being both Very God and Very Man. The sacredness of man was degraded in their doctrine that diminished the authority of Christ, and reduced our Savior almost to the status of myth rather than divinity. In the words of Belloc, "What began as Unitarianism ends as Paganism."[282] The cruelest religions are those that sever God from humanity. Islam has this same callous theology, in which God is said to be entirely separate from His creation, having absolutely no participation with humanity. Man, and not God is now the one who determines how the world should be governed. Thus, tyranny reigns.

Christ tells us: "seek ye first the kingdom of God" (Matthew 6:33). But, under this theology, how is the ruler to seek God first when God is so far away? He then only seeks himself;

---

280 Socrates, 2.45
281 Socrates, 6.8
282 Belloc, *The Great Heresies*, The Arian Heresy, p. 26

Christ is no longer divine, rather, man is now divine. His passions and his evil desires become the priority, and so despotism is established. This is what happened in the eighteenth century with the rise of Deism, the heresy that teaches that God is completely apart from his creation. With God so distant from human beings, it is now man's duty to rule the earth, with his own morality. The result of this thinking led to hundreds of thousands of people begin decapitated under the guillotine in the French Revolution. The same is with Islamic history, with millions being slaughtered by the scimitar.

THE HERETICAL EMPEROR CONSTANTIUS DIES, BUT THE REIGN OF TERROR CONTINUES ON

The Arian tyrant Constantius eventually died of apoplexy,[283] but the Arian reign of terror did not end, but only grew more and more violent.

There were two brothers who ruled the empire, Valens and Valentinian, and their story was like Cain and Abel. Valentinian was Orthodox, and held firm to the Nicene Creed; while his brother Valens held strongly to the Arian heresy. Valentinian believed in protecting the freedoms for not just Christians, but Arians as well, while Valens believed ardently that those who did not reject the Holy Trinity were to be punished.[284]

Liberty may be given to the heretic, but this does not necessarily mean that the heretic will favorably give peace to the Orthodox. Cain will always try to steal the life from the Abel, regardless if the righteous brother showed fairness to the wicked one. In a certain time of Valen's reign, there were no wars, but all was a time of peace, and he used this peace to "prosecute a war of extermination against all" who believed that the Son was of the same essence as the Father.

He had one Melitius punished with exile, and all those in Antioch who refused to be associated with the Arian leader Euzoius, he drove out of their city. The bishop Eustathius was banished to Bizya, a city in Thrace, and another man named Evagrius was also driven into exile. Five thousand monks went into hiding, for the persecution was so harsh. One Melania fed them for three days with bread, as Christ fed the five thousand.[285]

Numerous other Christians were exiled into the wilderness where they would be attacked and eaten by wild beasts. Valens took many Christians and had them drowned in the river Orontes.[286] The Arians were emboldened by this, and felt empowered as they saw their utopia of Arianism being carried out right before their eyes. The Arians, with this sensation of empowerment, would frequently attack Christians in mobs, beating them, scoffing at them with revilement, and having them imprisoned and fined.[287]

The Christians became so worn out and tormented by these incessant attacks, that they determined that a protest be made to the emperor Valens. Eighty Christian clerics gathered

---

283 Socrates, 2.47
284 Socrates, 4.1
285 Paulinus, letter 29, 11
286 Socrates, 4.2; 4.15; 4.36
287 Socrates, 4.15

themselves before the emperor in Nicomedia, and presented to him an imploring petition that protested the suppressions they suffered. The emperor did not respect their liberty or vow that he would take measures to protect their freedoms, but expressed a harrowing rage. He ordered that the eighty clerics be put to death in a secret order to the governor Modestus.

The governor, fearing the Christian multitude who revered these clerics as holy men, made it seem as though the clerics were just going to be exiled, and not killed. He commanded that they be put on a ship and sailed away so as to make it appear that they were simply being banished. But in secret, he gave an order to the sailors of the ships that they set the entire vessel on fire. When the clerics were in the ship and it was sailing in the midst of the Atacian Gulf, the sailors shut them in, set the vessel ablaze, and took refuge in a small boat that followed them. The direction of the burning ship was now dictated solely by the winds, and sailed away into the port named Dacidizus, where it was found to be completely consumed by the flames, the clerics within dead and charred.[288]

Immediately after these men died in the flames, and escaped the fires of hell through their martyrdom, a great famine plagued the entire land of Phrygia, where the emperor was staying. Valens moved from there and journeyed to Antioch where he resumed the persecution, having numerous Christians executed by drowning.[289]

In one event Valens visited a beautiful church at Edessa, in Mesopotamia, knowing that the people who attended it rejected Arianism and triumphed in Orthodoxy. When he arrived he struck the prefect with his own hand for allowing the Christians to enter the church. The prefect ordered the people to enter the church, and the next day, obeying "God rather than men" (Acts 5:29), the Christians flocked to the church. The governor, in order to satisfy the emperor's wrath, went with a large company of soldiers to slaughter the people. What they did not realize was that the entire community of Christians in Edessa were willing to die for their Faith.

One woman holding a baby rushed passed the ranks of the soldiers, and the prefect, seeing her putting herself and her child in such peril, was upset at her, saying,

Wretched woman! whither are you running in so disorderly a manner?

She said, "To the same place that others are hastening." "Have you not heard, that the prefect is about to put to death all who shall be found there?" "Yes," said the woman, "and therefore I hasten that I may be found there." "And whither are you dragging that little child?" asked the prefect. "That he may also be worthy of martyrdom."

The prefect, shocked at their fortitude, rushed to the emperor and told him that "all were ready to die in behalf of their own faith." He added that it would be "preposterous to destroy so many persons in one time," and convinced the emperor to prevent his wrath from being unleashed on so great a multitude.[290]

---

288 Socrates, 4.16
289 Socrates, 4.17
290 Socrates, 4.18

Valens had Peter, bishop of Alexandria and the successor to Athanasius, thrown into prison, and replaced with one Lucius.[291] The Arians in Alexandria received from Valens an edict, that was to be given to the governor, and it commanded that those who believed that the Son was of the same essence as the Father, be driven out not from Alexandria but from all of Egypt.

Soldiers rushed the land and violently seized Christians who would not lift a finger to fight back, and because of this numerous people were slaughtered. Poor monks who exerted their energy in pious labors, praying, healing diseases and casting out devils, were prohibited from doing these rites, and banished.[292]

BASIL AND GREGORY COMBAT THE HERETICS AND LAY DOWN THEIR LIVES FOR GOD

There were two holy men, Basil of Caesarea and Gregory of Nazianzus, who combated the Arian heresy. Basil founded monasteries where people were instructed on the Holy Trinity, and learned refutations of Arianism, while Basil went through various cities instructing the faithful on the true Faith, and strengthened his brethren to endure the persecutions and stand strong for Orthodoxy.

The emperor Valens, who was an Arian, asked Basil to not bring the Arian churches to anger over small differences of doctrine. But to this Basil replied: "Those who are nourished by divine words do not allow the corruption of even a syllable regarding divine doctrines, for if this should happen, they would rather suffer any kind of death for these doctrines."[293]

When Valens heard of these men of zeal, and their most zealous actions, he had Basil arrested and summoned before the governor of Antioch. In the face of the tribunal Basil was asked why he refused to subscribe to the religion of the emperor. Basil did not hesitate, but expressed his utter contempt for Arianism, anathematized the antichrist doctrine, and condemned the heretical creed it professed. The prefect snapped at him, and told him that he would put him to death. "Would," said Basil, "that I might be released from the bonds of the body for the truth's sake." The prefect begged him to change his mind and shift his opinion, but Basil responded, "I am the same today that I shall be tomorrow: but I wish that you had not changed yourself."

Basil was kept as a captive, when suddenly news came that Valens' infant son was struck by some dangerous illness. His wife, Dominica, fearfully cried to him that she had been receiving disturbing dreams that convinced her that their child was inflicted by God as punishment for the persecution done to Basil. Valens came to Basil and said, "If the doctrine you maintain is true, pray that my son may not die." "If your majesty should believe as I do," replied Basil, "and the church should be unified, the child shall live." The emperor spurned

---

291 Socrates, 4.22
292 Socrates, 4.23–24
293 Theodoretus, book 4, ch. 17, in Bellarmine, *On Laymen or Secular People*, ch. 19, ed. Tutino, p. 90

such an idea. "God's will concerning the child will be be done then," responded Basil. The child, like the infant of Pharaoh, was struck with death.[294]

POPE GELASIUS I DEFIES THE TYRANNY OF THE ARIANS
Another example of fortitude was from Pope Gelasius I who, when the Arian Euphemianus asked him to submit to certain Arian beliefs, wrote to the heretic the following chastisement:

> While you say that we should bend down to you, you reveal that you meanwhile are lowering yourself further down, or that you have already done so. So I ask, what is this slippery slope? Surely you see, you understand, you do not deny that you have been lowered from a superior place to an inferior one, that you have fallen from the Catholic and Apostolic communion to the heretical and condemned one, and you wish us, who remain in the superior place, to be persuaded to descend with you; you invite us from the highest to the lowest, but we ask you to ascend with us from the lowest to the highest. [295]

ST. AMBROSE DEFIES THE TYRANNY OF THE ARIANS
The archbishop of Milan, St. Ambrose, proved to be one of the most formidable enemies to Arianism. The Arian emperor Valentinian II, alongside his Jezebel of a wife, demanded for an Arian church in Milan, to which Ambrose expressed a most obstinate rejection. Counts and Tribunes approached Ambrose and urged him to surrender his basilica to the emperor under the pretense that "everything was under his power." Ambrose declared, "Those things which are God's are not subject to the imperial power. If my patrimony is required, enter upon it, if my body, I will go out at once. Do you wish to cast me into chains, or to give me to death? It will be a pleasure to me. I will not defend myself with throngs of people, nor will I cling to the altars and entreat for my life, but will more gladly be slain myself for the altars."

Armed Arians, many of them Goths, surrounded the Basilica and made threats of violence. Calligonus, the chief chamberlain, approached Ambrose and like a Muslim viciously said that he would decapitate the archbishop himself. "Do you," he told Ambrose, "whilst I am alive treat Valentinian with contempt? I will take your head from you." The saint's response was simple yet direct: "God grant you to fulfil your threat; for then I shall suffer as bishops do, you will act as do eunuchs."[296]

THE ARIANS UNITE WITH THE PAGANS TO SLAUGHTER AND OPRESS THE CHRISTIANS
Christ said that "if Satan cast out Satan, he is divided against himself," (Matthew 12:25) the Arians united with other followers of demons, the pagans, as allies against their common enemy: the Church. Lucian, the Arian bishop of Alexandria who replaced the exiled Athanasius, used a heathen mob to decimate the saints.

---

294 Socrates, 4.26
295 In Bellarmine, *On Laymen or Secular People*, ch. 19, p. 90
296 Ambrose, epistle 20, 7–8, 20, 28; see also Socrates, 5.11

CHRISTIANITY IS AT WAR: THE MANIFESTO FOR CHRISTIAN MILITANCY

He accompanied himself with one Magnus, a pagan who was known as a hater of liberty and piety: when the idolater Julian was emperor, he burned a church down in Phoenicia; and in the reign of the Christian Jovian he was forced to rebuild it at his own expense.

But under the succeeding Arian emperor Valens, the pagans were again empowered and encouraged. Idolatrous rituals which were done in secret under Constantine, were now done out in the open under the Arian power, and Valens, in his hatred for the Cross, called the pagans to revive their reign of terror against the Church.[297]

The heathens in Alexandria, by the demand of Lucian, seized Christian virgins, stripped them completely naked and clubbed them to death; and anyone who protested was automatically assaulted by the savage crowd. In their ambush of the city's church, one pagan sodomite, who renounced his male identity and dressed himself as a woman, danced upon the altar mockingly calling for the Holy Ghost. Another made himself entirely nude and seated himself on the episcopal chair.

All of the other scoundrels saluted him, and he then gave a speech declaring homosexuality, licentiousness, theft and gluttony as superior to chastity. When Lucian entered the church, the vandals all saluted him, praised his Arianism and proclaimed that he was under the favor of the Egyptian god Serapis. "Welcome, O bishop," they said, "welcome to you, who deny the Son [Jesus Christ]! Serapis, who loves you, has brought you here!" His accomplice Magnus seized nineteen presbyters and deacons and compelled them to renounce the Trinity, his words being:

> Assent, O wretched men, assent to the Arian doctrines. Even if your religion be true, God will forgive you for having renounced it, for you are not now acting voluntarily, but by compulsion. What is done from constraint is excusable; voluntary actions alone carry with them their own condemnation. Therefore, reflect upon the reasons which I have brought before you, and sign, without delay, the doctrine of Arius, which is now preached by Lucius. You may be certain that, if you accede to this injunction, you will receive riches, gifts, and honours, from the emperors. But if you will refuse obedience, you will be imprisoned, tortured, and scourged; you will be deprived of all your wealth and possession, driven from your country, and banished to a sterile and inhospitable region.[298]

They refused, and were eventually sentenced to be put in a ship and banished to Phoenicia. As they were being conveyed into the ship, their fellow Christians wept for them. Their tears and lamentations were to the cruelty of the pagan, for Palladius, prefect of Alexandria, prohibited at that moment any citizen from expressing grief for their ministers. Those who refused to take heed to this tyrannical restraint endured the end of whips and blades and were then sent to the mines as slaves. A deacon was then arrested for carrying a letter from

---

297 Theodoret. Eccles. Hist. 4.22, 27
298 Theodoret. Eccles. Hist. 4.22

Damasus, bishop of Rome; his hands were bound behind his back, his head was beaten with stones and masses of led, and he was then thrown into the ship with his other brethren.[299]

Later, this same Lucian was commissioned by the emperor to ordain a man named Moses to be a bishop. But when Moses came to the church in Alexandria and saw that it was Lucian, he confronted him with these words: "God forbid that I should receive ordination at your hands; for the grace of the Spirit is not given in answer to your prayers." When Lucian asked why he had such sentiments, Moses declared, with righteous indignation:

> I say what I positively know, not what I conjecture. You oppose the apostolical doctrines, and you speak against them; and the iniquity of your actions coincides with the blasphemy of your words. Whom have you not employed to disturb the assemblies of the church? Which of the eminent men have you not exiled? What inhumanity can be compared, in point of cruelty, to that exhibited in your daily actions? [300]

In Antioch, a number of clergymen and monks were banished to Asia Minor for protesting against Arianism, where they all perished upon arrival.[301] The Arians in Constantinople forced numerous presbyters to get on a ship and sail to sea as exiles. Subsequently, another ship manned by Arians followed them, and when they got close enough, they set the Christians' ship to flames. The Christians, unable to escape the burning ship, made their grave in the sea, and their home in Heaven.[302]

All of this violence commenced on the permission of the emperor Valens, who was so evil that many of the saints came before him with fearless zealotry, chastising his wickedness. When Vetranion, the bishop of Scythia, saw Valens he was moved by that sublime zeal against tyranny which God gives us, and repeated with a loud voice a Psalm of David: "I shall speak of thy testimonies before kings, and shall not be ashamed."[303]

ARIANISM SPREADS TO GERMANY, AND THE GERMAN ARIANS ARE FAR WORSE IN CRUELTY AND BARBARISM

A civil war commenced amongst the Goths, between two leaders, Fritigernes and Athanaric. When the latter was being overpowered by the former, he pleaded to Valens for help, and he complied. The emperor ordered that troops stationed in Thrace march to assist the weaker German army. They utterly routed the armies of Fritigernes, and brought victory. Athanaric desired to express his gratitude toward Valens, and so left paganism and converted to Arianism. At this time there was a Goth named Wulfia, whose name literally means, "little wolf," and surely this is what he was. For this little wolf was the one who preached Arianism to the

---

299 Theodoret. Eccles. Hist. 4.22
300 Theodoret. Hist. Eccles. 4.23
301 Theodoret. Hist. Eccles. 4.23
302 Theodoret. Hist. Eccles. 4.24
303 In Theodoret. Eccles. Hist. 4.35

Goths. He translated the Bible from Greek to Goth to misconstrue its passages in order to teach Arianism, and the Goths embraced the heresy whole heartedly.[304]

Now, instead of easterners enforcing Arianism with exile and sometimes executions, the Christian world was faced with hearty barbarians, strong in body and violently fueled by the wiles of heresy, and who were much crueler then the Arians of the East. St. Ambrose would later write of their barbarisms and how much it spread throughout the empire:

> No desire have I to recount the deaths, tortures, and banishments of confessors, the offices of the faithful made into presents for traitors. Have we not heard, from all along the border,—from Thrace, and through Dacia by the river, Moesia, and all Valeria of the Pannonians,—a mingled tumult of blasphemers preaching and barbarians invading? What profit could neighbors so bloodthirsty bring us, or how could the Roman State be safe with such defenders.[305]

Some time after this, the Huns charged into the territory of the Goths, and drove them from their rugged abode. The current emperor at the time, Valens, having compassion for his fellow Arians, took the Goths and placed them in parts of Thrace. The emperor believed that these heretical Germanians would make great guards to protect the empire, and he showed much more favor for them than the veteran soldiers who struggled so long to defend the empire. He despised the veterans, and put his reliance on his fellow heretics.[306]

THE GERMAN GOTHS TRY TO CONQUER CONSTANTINOPLE

And what was the result of allowing Arianism to take such a hold of the empire? The result was war. Arian Goths turned against the empire that helped them, and devastated all of Thrace with pillage and slaughter.[307] They sacked the region, and now headed toward that most holy city of Christendom, Constantinople. What is quite profound in all this is that the city of Constantinople was always the target of Christendom's enemies. The Persian Zoroastrians tried to conquer it; the German Arians wanted to take it, and eventually the Muslims, under the command of Muhammad, conquered it. Constantinople was one of the holiest cities in Christianity, and thus it is of no surprise as to why Satan would want to take such a metropolis for his diabolical influence.

The people of the city expressed their rage at the emperor, for it was he who brought the heretical Germans into the empire. And so great was this frustration that one could hear in the colosseum the people cry out, "Give us arms, and we ourselves will fight."

Valens had no choice but to attack his fellow Arians. He marched against them with an army, vanquished them, and drove them out as far as Adrianople in Thrace.[308] But this did not discourage the heretics, for they gathered another army and returned to the very walls of

---

304 See Procopius, 3.2; Socrates, 2.41; 4.32
305 St. Ambrose, *On The Christian Faith*, 2.16
306 Socrates, 4.34
307 Socrates, 4.35
308 Socrates, 4.38

Constantinople, ready for another fight. This invasion was not responded to by the government military, but by the people, who armed themselves with whatever weapons they could possess, formed an efficient militia, and prepared for a defensive crusade against the heretics.

There was even an army of Arabs who joined their ranks. The Arian Goths attacked, but the people defended Christendom with all their exertion, fighting and striking with as much force as they could gather. Their defense was effective, and the Goths retreated a great distance away from the glorious city.[309]

AN ORTHODOX CHRISTIAN TAKES THE THRONE AND LAUNCHES A CRUSADE AGAINST THE HERETICS

Before Valens helped the Goths enter the empire, he, filled with paranoia as to who would take his place in the throne, consulted with a demon through necromancy, or communicating with the dead. He asked the demon who would take the throne from him, and it presented him with four letters—Q, E, O, D,—and said that the name of his successor would have these letters, and that it was a compound name.

The answer was ambiguous and left Valens no actual conclusion, and so it drove him to madness, not knowing who exactly was to take his place. With the devils now influencing him, he concluded that the omen was speaking of someone named Theodore, or a name like it. With this, he massacred anyone with the names Theodore, Theodotus, Theodosius, Theodolus, and the like, and so much was the bloodshed that people began to change their names.[310]

But there was one man, who did not change his name, and that was Theodosius, and it was this man who took the throne after Valens died. Theodore means "Gift of God," and surely did this man fit this title. Theodosius was a defender of Orthodoxy, protector of Christendom, and guard against the heretics. He, alongside Gratian, took up sword, and his cross, and led an army into battle against the Arians, and made victory over them.[311]

Theodosius exemplified a true Christian leader. For he not only defeated the physical threat of the Arian Goths, but the spiritual threat from within the empire that brought about the actual invasion to begin with. He attacked the problem—heresy—as opposed to just dealing with the symptom to the problem—physical violence against the Church.

Theodosius told the leader of the Arians at that time, named Demophilus, that he had to accept Orthodoxy and reject Arianism. Demophilus refused, and what did Theodosius tell him? He did not respect his religious liberty, but instead told him: "Since you reject peace and harmony, I order you to quit the churches."[312]

This goes contrary to the modern mind, which sees peace as requiring freedom of religion. But this is not so. The reality is that true peace comes from true religion. For all of order

---

309 Socrates, 5.1
310 Socrates, 4.19
311 Socrates, 5.6
312 Socrates, 5.7

and harmony comes from God, and the refusal to worship this God, leads to disharmony and chaos. To maintain peace and harmony, the true religion must be maintained, and the promoters of destructive religions cast out or killed.

Demophilus saw himself as a persecuted victim, and he told his followers, "Brethren, it is written in the Gospel, 'If they persecute you in one city, flee ye into another.' Since therefore the emperor needs the churches, take notice that we will henceforth hold our assemblies without the city." After he said this, he fled. The rule that the Arians had over the empire, lasted forty years, but now it was ceased by the gallant Theodosius, and the soldiers of Orthodoxy took possession of the churches.[313]

THEODOSIUS STRENGTHENS THE CHURCH

Theodosius saw what disunity the schismatics had brought to the empire and aspired to unite the flock, and help guide the wandering sheep who swayed to the sects of the wolves. He conveyed a meeting with the leaders of the Arians, Eunomians, and the Macedonians, and asked them whether they held any respect toward the Fathers of the Church who expounded on the Christian Faith before their schisms came about.

They responded, with the skill of subtlety and sophism, that they revered the Fathers and esteemed them as their masters. The emperor, not satisfied with their answer, asked them whether they would consider the Fathers as legitimate witnesses of Christian doctrine. The leaders of the heresies were frustrated by such a question, since the Church Fathers always repulses the deceptions of heretics.

They argued amongst themselves, agreeing on one thing but disagreeing over another, finding it impossible to collectively come to a consensus. The emperor saw how the strength of the heretics was solely based on sophisms and subtle arguments, and not on any sound teachings of the ancient Fathers of the Church. Theodosius then requested that they each write a statement describing what they believed. They each composed an account of their doctrines and presented them to the emperor. He read the writings of all the heretical parties—the Arians, Eunomians, and the Macedonians—and proclaimed his condemnation of them all, seeing how they rejected the Holy Trinity, and departed from Orthodoxy.

Theodosius, that great defender of the Path of Truth, did not permit the heretical sects to use the churches, while allowing freedom to only the Catholics and the Novatians.[314] The Arians in Constantinople burned with rage as they saw the Christians taking the churches and conducting their masses. They revolted with violence and, committing all sorts of outrages and assaults, set the home of the bishop Nectarius on fire.[315]

While it was noble and just for Theodosius to give the possession of the churches to the Christians, he made a detrimental decision that would have ramifications lasting centuries

---

313 Socrates, 5.7
314 Socrates, 5.10
315 Socrates, 5.13

later: he allowed the Arians to organize their own gatherings and services.[316] Because he did not obliterate and uproot the Arian heresy entirely, Arianism would, hundreds of years later, expand into Arabia, influence Muhammad, and spawn Islam.

Another disastrous consequence of Theodosius' leniency on the Arians was the Germanic Arians who lived within the empire were left untouched, and allowed to observe the pernicious and violent heresy.

THE ARIAN GERMANS RISE AGAIN AND TRY TO CONQUER CONSTANTINOPLE

There was a Goth within the Roman military named Gainas; he was a master warrior, and rose above the ranks, eventually becoming a general-in-chief of the Roman cavalry and infantry.[317] While he was allowed and enabled, with Roman freedom, to obtain such a prestigious position, there was one thing about Gainas that was very dangerous: he was an Arian.

The modern mind would ignore his religion, as though it was not relevant to his military accomplishments. It would be said, "He has risked his life to defend his country, keep his religion out of it!" But let us see the consequences of tolerating the Arian heresy, and we shall witness just how detrimental religious freedom was.

Gainas was not just a good soldier, but a very religious man, a fanatic for the Arian heresy. He sympathized with his fellow Arians, since they did not have an Arian church in Constantinople, and was determined to use his military position to obtain for them an edifice for their heretical worship. He requested from the emperor, Arcadius, that one of the churches in Constantinople be given to the Arians, but this was opposed by St. John Chrysostom, and thus it was denied.[318] The request to build an Arian church is the equivalent of Muslims today requesting a mosque. Why would any Christian allow such an advancement of heresy? But, people today would argue that the denial of such a request is unfair. "How could a country deny a people such a simple request as a house of worship?" says the modern. "This man has fought and risked his life for his country, the least you can do is give him a place of worship!" says another superficial modern.

But again, the modern mind will never be willing to comprehend the dangers of religious freedom, and what evils it brings forth. Gainas called for the Arian Goths of his own country, brought them into the empire, and gave his relatives high positions in the military. One of these relatives was Tribigildus, and he was given the command over the forces of Phrygia, and Gainas secretly ordered him to spark a violent revolt in this land.

When the emperor, Arcadius, heard of the revolt, he sent Gainus and the whole army of heretic Goths to stop the riots. This was all in accordance to the plan: create a disaster in the region, and then use the disaster as an opportunity to invade the region under the guise of bringing stability. It was a classic strategy.

---

316 Socrates, 5.20
317 Socrates, 6.6
318 Socrates, 6.5–6

Gainas charged into Phrygia, and instead of stopping the revolt, he joined it, intensifying the violence, and escalating the chaos and confusion that inflicted the Christian Greeks.[319] Now the heretics ruled Phrygia, and such was a result of religious toleration toward Arianism. The emperor Arcadius, desiring to appease the heretics, sent an embassy to Gainus and asked of him as to what he demanded. Gainus commanded that the two senators, Saturninus and Aurelian, men who never saw him with favor, be given to him.

The emperor reluctantly fulfilled this stipulation; the two senators submitted to the command, and were sent to the barbarian heretic. But Gainas did not harm nor kill them, instead he expressed that he was not content with the hostages, and desired a meeting with the emperor. The two men—the emperor of Christendom and the usurping tyrant of Antichrist—met at a certain church in Chalcedon, and made an oath that they would never harm each other.

But such was the peace of Cain, the false peace that Christ came to destroy, reminiscent to the Hudna in Islam that feigned peace made by Muslim heretics, the successors of Arianism. For Gainas gathered his men and set his thirsty eyes on the holy city of Constantinople. When the evening came, he sent an immense body of Arian Goths to the palace within the city to set it to flames.

When the heretics arrived to wreak their havoc, they saw something that surpassed their carnal minds, and transcended all temporal existence: they saw men of a colossal stature, and of incredible height, taller than any men they had ever seen. These gigantic men pierced the hearts of the savage heretics with such fear, that they could no longer gaze upon their magnificent bodies, but fled. They returned to Gainas and told him everything their weary eyes had seen, and such news could not penetrate the mind of the barbarian.

He refused to believe it, knowing that the Roman army did not have such unimaginable warriors. Gainas sent another army, and when they arrived their minds were immediately staggered by the site of them, and it was obvious that these surely were not men, but angels, sent by God to protect His glorious city. They were soldiers of Heaven's army, of whom David spoke when he wrote, "The chariots of God are twenty thousand, even thousands of angels" (Psalm 68:17) Their souls were struck by the blade of such a heavenly sight, and they retreated in utter freight. Gainas was most exasperated by this, and decided that he now would lead his troops himself into Constantinople, and take the sacred metropolis.

When he arrived and saw the lofty men that his warriors were trepidatious over, he deemed them only as mere men. But he was baffled by them, and desisted from his first attempt and decided that another strategy would have to be utilized. Gainas pretended to be possessed by demonic spirits, and rushed into the Church of St. John the Apostle, where he acted as though he was praying.

This was done as a distraction from what his soldiers were doing. Several Goths went to the front of the city gates, pulled out some concealed swords and slew the guards. The

---

319 Socrates, 6.6

Christians within the city were terrified at the news of this bloodshed, sudden doom seemed so near, and a tumult of horror spread across the populace. The emperor Arcadius had to make a decision in order to preserve the empire and save the city from the coming horde of heretics.

He declared Gainas an enemy of the state, and ordered that all of the Arian Goths in the city be exterminated. The next day, not soldiers, but regular Christian folk, took up their weapons and attacked the Goths, unleashing a proficient tempest of onslaughts, and slaughtering many of them. The Goths tried to hide in their church, but the people killed a numerous amount of them, and set their entire church on fire. Gainas, hearing what had happened, fled to Thrace where he was stopped by a body of Roman soldiers, and put to death.[320]

THE ARIANS INVADE ROME

Out of all the cities in the world, the Muslims target the holiest: Jerusalem, Constantinople, and Rome. In the mind of every Muslim, Rome must be conquered and made into an Islamic city. This is because it is the center for Christianity in the West. Arianism, Islam's parent, also wanted to conquer and destroy Rome.

Like the Muslims today and of antiquity, the Arians treated all of Christendom as enemy land, and in particular, wanted to destroy Rome, one of the holy cities of God. A black haze of sinister spirits permeated throughout the sacred land of the true Faith, and the eternal path of the Spirit, was sought out for destruction by the advancers of Antichrist. The German Arian named Alaric, pointed his sword upward as to defy Heaven, and aspired to shatter Orthodoxy for his love of heresy.

He marched with an army towards Rome, center of the Church Militant for the western saints. As he treaded upon the earth and came closer to the eternal city, a pious monk approached him, and encouraged him to throw away his fleshy ambition for bloodshed and dominance. Alaric's response only evinced what demonic forces were involved in his envisage to destroy Rome:

> I am not going in this course of my own will; but there is something that irresistibly impels me daily, saying, 'Proceed to Rome, and desolate that city.' [321]

His words reflected the diabolical influence that was in his mind. The devil wanted Rome, and still does, and he was using the Arians as a means to this end. As he marched he was ambushed by a mighty army of Thessalians, filled with apostolic fury and Christian zeal. They overtook the Arians, and slaughtered three thousand of Alaric's men. But the Arian Goths continued on, and struck Rome.

They pillaged without stopping; they saw some of the most magnificent Christian structures, and set them on fire, burning them to the ground; they seized many of the prestigious

---

320 Socrates, 6.6
321 Socrates, 7.10

senators, accused them with all sorts of calumny, and put them to death. After much Christian blood was shed, there came the Christian army, headed toward the spiritual head of Christendom. Alaric heard of the approaching forces, and being filled with terror, retreated out of the city alongside his men.[322]

They destroyed the cities which they captured, and so much destruction did they cause south of the Ionian Gulf, that it was hard to believe that one could find a tower or gate remaining amidst the chaos.[323]

THE ARIANS INVADE SPAIN, ITALY AND SICILY

From the earliest history of Islam the Muslims invaded Christian lands, conquering Spain, North Africa, all of the Middle East and much of Eastern Europe, forging a major empire. The Arians were no different. They overran Spain and wrested Libya from the Roman Empire.[324]

After making alliances with the Moors, the leader of the Vandalic Arians, Gizeric, made several invasions over Sicily and Italy, enslaving entire cities and razing others to the ground. He plundered Illyricum and most of the Peloponnesus. His motivation had a religious basis, and as the Muslims believe that the countries they fight with are Allah's enemies, Gizeric said that he wished to war "Plainly against those with whom God is angry."[325]

Gizeric overtook the Greek island of Zacynthus, took five hundred people, and when he reached the Adriatic Sea, he cut them all into small pieces and dumped them into the sea.[326]

Gizeric's successor, Honoric, was most cruel to the Christians of Libya. Like the Muslims, he ordered them to deny the Trinity and accept the heresy of Arius. Those who refused he burnt alive, and upon others he cut their tongues from the very roots. They marched into Tunisia, seized the priests and beat them ruthlessly with many blows. The king of the Moors, Cabaon, was not a Christian, but he respected the Faith, and wished for God to help drive out the Arians. A clash eventually took place with the heretics fleeing for their lives and many of them being killed by the Moors.[327]

In later time, in Libya, the emperor Justinian prohibited any Arians from receiving baptism or any other sacrament. They became vexed and enraged like Cain, and murdered Theodorus—commander of the guards—and once they had tasted blood they did not stop, and murdered numerous others after that.[328]

---

322 Socrates, 7.10
323 Procopius, 3.2
324 Procopius, 3.2; 3.4
325 Procopius, *Wars*, 3.5
326 Procopius, *Wars*, 3.22
327 Procopius, *Wars*, 3.8
328 Procopius, *Wars*, 4.14

PART 12

THE GOTHIC EMPEROR THEODORIC UNLEASHES A REIGN OF TERROR ON THE CHRISTIANS

Pope John I, an indefatigable opponent to the Arian cause in the sixth century, showed no fear when he reconverted Arian churches. These actions were noticed by the Gothic emperor Theodoric, an ardent follower of Arianism, and he threatened to destroy all of Italy if the pope did not cease. He killed many Christians and priests by the sword, and had executed the two senators Boethius and Symachus. John was soon thrown into prison, with other devout senators, and was forced into confinement until death.[329]

A MAJOR HOLY WAR COMMENCES AND THE CHRISTIANS UPROOT ARIANISM COMPLETELY FROM CHRISTENDOM

All of the tyrannies that Arianism caused eventually provoked a major holy war between Christians and Arians that led to the ultimate extirpation of the Arian heresy from Christendom. It began with France, where Arianism was very powerful.

A Frankish general in France by the name of Clovis left his native pagan religion and became Arian. Soon with an army he invaded the mass of northern France. Because he was never a part of the Christian religion, but originally a heathen, he never had that great knowledge of, and immense viciousness against the Church, and so it was expedient for the Christians to convince him of his falsehoods, and to convert him to Catholicism. As soon as this happened he swayed his subjects to reject the heresy, and with his troops defeated the Arian generals of southern Europe. Though he was not strong enough to conquer Arian Italy and Spain, he nonetheless greatly weakened Arianism's power in the continent.

By 630 AD all of France became Catholic; the last remnant of the Arian generals in Italy and Spain turned to Orthodoxy. The Visigothic king, Reccared I, expelled all of the Arians from his realm in Spain, and the Arian generals of North Africa were defeated by the Christian armies of the Roman Empire.[330]

Take notice what the eventual cause of heresy's thriving and growing powerful: it was war, war between the saints and the heretics. The Church was better off following the Law of Moses and executing the heretic Arius at the moment he began to spread his poison. For, because they did not, look at all of the bloodshed and the violent struggles the Church had to endure, simply because it did not extinguish the leaven before it corrupted the whole batch.

ARIANISM CONTINUES THROUGH ISLAM

The eventual death of Arianism was not exactly a victory over it, for it would extend and revive itself in a new life: Islam.

---

[329] Book of the Popes, 55: John I, trans. Louise Ropes Loomis.
[330] Belloc, *The Great Heresies*, The Arian Heresy, p. 35; *The Great and Enduring Heresy of Muhammad*, p. 37; *The Chronicle of San Juan de la Pena*, ch. 2

CHRISTIANITY IS AT WAR: THE MANIFESTO FOR CHRISTIAN MILITANCY

Islam is merely an extension of Arianism, and it was this same Arian heresy which St. Ambrose thought was the religion of the Antichrist in Revelation:

> John, likewise, saith that heretics are Antichrists, plainly marking out the Arians. For this [Arian] heresy began to be after all other heresies, and hath gathered the poisons of all. As it is written of the Antichrist, that 'he opened his mouth to blasphemy against God, to blaspheme His Name, and to make war with His saints,' [Revelation 13:6] so do they also dishonour the Son of God, and His martyrs have they not spared. Moreover, that which perchance Antichrist will not do, they have falsified the Holy Scriptures. And thus he who saith that Jesus is not the Christ, the same is Antichrist; he who denies the Saviour of the world, denies Jesus; he who denies the Son, denies the Father also, for it is written; 'Every one which denieth the Father likewise.' [I John 2:23][331]

In this regard, Ambrose is correct, Arianism is the religion of Antichrist, for Islam is simply an Arabian form of the heresy.

Unlike the other heresies, Islam was not extinguished by the Church. The reason for this is that Islam never arose from Christendom, as Arianism or Catharism did. Muhammad, unlike Arius, was never a part of the Catholic Church, he was a pagan and so he was never a schismatic. Therefore the system of the Church was not able to reprimand or punish Muhammad for heresy, since it had no jurisdiction over pagan Arabia. Furthermore, the heretics who broke from the Church, as we have seen in history, have a higher chance of going back into Orthodoxy, because of their history in the Faith. Muhammad, and most of his earliest followers, on the other hand, had no recourse back to Christianity. They were born into error and simply transferred into a more deceptive error. They were not inclined to return to the truth because they never had any complete familiarity with the truth to begin with, and so the chances of them joining the Church was almost nil.[332]

Islam is really the Arabian continuation of Arius' false doctrine, and concordantly, the historian John Whitaker had this to say on the Arian origins of Muhammad's doctrine in his book, *The Origin of Arianism*:

> Among these Saracens of Arabia, under this general darkness of ignorance, and amidst this national night of polytheism, did that grand impostor arise, who has made the name of Mahomet to be nearly consonant to that of Antichrist, in the ears of every true Christian; and who has become the father of a new and numerous race of Arians, in the earth. His scripture is one grand system of Arianism.[333]

Muhammad intermixed this heresy with his native paganism, making a religion which did away with some of the most complex concepts in Christianity: the Trinity and the Incarnation.[334] Therefore, Satan used Islam not just to spread paganism, but unitarianism

---

[331] Ambrose, *On the Christian Faith*, 2.15, trans. Rev. H. De Romestin, brackets mine
[332] See Belloc, *The Great Heresies*, The Great and Enduring Heresy of Muhammad, p. 49
[333] Whitaker, *The Origin of Arianism Disclosed*, ch. iii, p. 335
[334] Hilaire Belloc, *The Crusades*, ch. ii, p. 8

all throughout the world by the sword, just as the Arians enforced their heretical doctrine through violence. The great Muslim leader Akbah expressed this militant unitarianism when he spoke of his desire to go "to the unknown kingdoms of the West, preaching the unity of thy [Allah's] holy name, and putting to the sword the rebellious nations who worship any other gods than thee."[335]

The "unity" here mentioned refers to the anti-Trinitarian nature of Allah, while the "rebellious nations" and "gods" allude to the countries of Christendom and the Godhead—that is, Father, Son, Holy Spirit.

All of the atrocities committed by the Arians can be found being done in a similar fashion in the earliest history of the Muslims. There lies a story which sums up the war between Orthodoxy and heresy. It begins in 743 AD with a tax official named Peter of Maiouma, who being ill one day, was visited by some friendly Arabs.

Peter did not angle his position when speaking with them, nor did he hide his true convictions in the fear of offending them or making these Muslims feel isolated. "You should gain a reward from God for visiting me," he said to the Arabs, "even if you friends are outside the faith. I want you to be my eyewitnesses that this is the situation: everyone who does not believe in the Father, the Son, and the Holy Spirit, in consubstantiality, and in the Trinity in Unity which rules life, has maimed his soul and deserves eternal punishment. Even your false prophet Muhammad is such a person, and a forerunner of the Antichrist. If you are convinced by my testimony about the heaven and earth, abandon his mythology today, lest you be punished with him: for I feel goodwill toward you."[336]

This saint did not proclaim such words to receive their favor or their acceptance, he did it in the truest sense of Christian love. Modern Christians today repeatedly say that "God is love," and therefore we should never expose or chide evil when we see it. This is not love, but evil in its purest form; for who does not want us to fight against the forces of darkness but the Devil himself?

To love is to combat and contend, to strive and to struggle, without remorse, the entities in this world that want us to come not to God, but to sinister creeds that leave man to nothing but misery. What happened to our saint Peter of Maiouma? The Muslims left him alone, and thought that his illness may have caused his bout of zeal. They returned the next morning expecting a nicer, more tolerant and diplomatic Peter. "Anathema to Muhammad," he cried, "to his false writings, and to everyone who believes in him." His zealotry stirred the demoniacal spirits within the friendly Arabs, and they, following the oppressive ways of the Arians before him, took their swords and killed him.[337]

Such a story captures the reality of this war between good and evil, and in many battles for man's soul, the wicked usually prevail over the saints. To many this may seem as a proof that saints are the losers, and their doctrine is false; but as a few jewels in a desert of dust

---

335 In Gibbon, *Decline and Fall*, vol. v, ch. l, p. 953, brackets mine
336 Chron. Theophan. Annus Mundi 6234
337 Chron. Theophan. Annus Mundi 6234

bring out their beauty more pristinely, so does the truth show itself more unique and beautiful when its followers are few.

The fight between Islam and Christianity is a major part of this war, but it will be determined by the zeal of the Church. Islam is just as vigorous now as it was when it began, and it is more so active over the lands where Christianity once reigned, than the Western Church is over the countries which it so fragilely influences. The force of Islam only grows stronger as the Church grows weaker.[338] So let us see the true history of the war between the Christians and the Muslims, and honor the martyrs of old who, though forgotten, fought for the glory of the Cross, and the downfall of that Antichrist religion of Muhammad. Let us do this to prepare our minds and souls for the coming Final Crusade that will take place between a restored Christendom led by Christ and a revived Ottoman Empire under the Antichrist.

---

338 Belloc, *The Great Heresies*, The Arian Heresy, p. 29

PART 13 – ISLAM VERSUS CHRISTENDOM

ISLAM'S EXPANSION

So swift would be Islam's expansion, that within only a hundred years half of the Roman Empire would fall to the heresy of Muhammad.[1]

In 633, the caliph Abu Bakr sent out four despots to commit jihad; they took over the whole of Gaza and Hira. The Romans tried to stop them in Caesarea but were defeated, suffering three hundred and one casualties.[2]

The next year the Muslims, under Umar, marched into Christian Byzantine Arabia (which encompassed modern day Jordan), and invaded numerous cities. The Romans again attempted to counterattack them, but endured another loss.[3] A countless host of Muslims campaigned in Damascus. Once the Romans were informed of this they hastily met them, but were hindered from fighting on account of a troublesome wind storm that prevented them from looking their enemies in the eye. The Arabs, conditioned to the dry and turbulent desert, easily prevailed over the Romans, adding Damascus to their list of victories over Christian lands.[4]

There was then the great Battle of Yarmuk in 636, in which the Arabs killed so many Romans that their bodies formed a bridge upon which one could walk across.[5]

Upon that land to where pilgrims sojourned to touch the earth upon which prophets of old walked and saw with inspired eyes visions of angels; where pious warriors overturned

---

1 Belloc, *The Great Heresies*, p. 38
2 Chron. Theophan. Annus Mundi 6125
3 Chron. Theophan. Annus Mundi 6125, see also n. 94 of the editor Harry Turtledove
4 Chron. Theophan. Annus Mundi 6126
5 Theophilus of Edessa's *Chronicle*, section 1, Agapius, p. 101, trans. Robert G. Hoyland, Liverpool University Press

kingdoms and brought low the tyrants; where with elated ears holy men heard the voice of God; where prophets with minds transcendent by divine revelation dreamt dreams for which one amongst them was seized by his brothers, thrown into a pit and then sold to Arabs, there stood the holiest sight of them all to the saints, and that was Jerusalem, and soon was this sublime city taken, like Joseph, by the same men who journeyed from the scorched sands of Arabia.[6]

In 635, the caliph Umar Bin al-Khattab captured Jerusalem, and when Saint Sophronius looked upon this Arab conqueror dressed in filthy camel hair and defiling the city of God with his idolatry and heresy, he proclaimed: "In truth, this is the abomination of the desolation established in the holy place, which Daniel the prophet spoke of." Umar built a mosque in Jerusalem, just as Antiochus erected temples of Jupiter in the same city.

The mosque crumbled down, and when he asked as to why this took place, a number of Jews approached him and said, "If you do not tear down the cross on top of the Mount of Olives, your building will not stay up."

He removed the cross, and thus did great defilement taint the Holy Land. It is of no wonder that with bitter tears saint Sophronius wept for the loss of the Holy City, and over the Christian people who would suffer greatly.[7] Indeed, he was correct, Islam is the Antichrist system as prophesied by the Scriptures—and the evils which the Muslims committed in Jerusalem further attests to this. When a Christian in Jerusalem was not killed, he lived his life yoked by the heavy brick of taxation, called the Jizya tax.[8]

The Muslims would steal the city of Antioch in Syria in 638; in the next year they took possession of both Edessa and Constantia. Within a score of years they took all of Syria, the Cradle of the Faith, and in 641 they wrested the city of Caesarea in Israel, massacring seven thousand Romans.[9] In 648 the Muslims under Muawiyah Ibn Abi Sufyan, attacked Cyprus with one thousand seven hundred war ships, taking and devastating the entire island.[10]

When Arab ships first approached Cyprus, the poor people thought they were Romans, and so when the Muslims came ashore they overran the entire island without resistance, spoiling, killing, and enslaving everywhere they went. Another Muslim force came to Cyprus where they would defeat another Roman army and slay with the sword their general Theophilos.[11]

Abu 'l-Awar charged right into Lykia, in Asia Minor, where he fought a naval battle with the Roman emperor Constans. The Romans were vanquished, and the emperor almost killed,

---

6   For a description of Jerusalem, see Alfred J. Andrea, Christendom and the Umma, in Thomas F. Madden's *The Crusades*, part 1, p. 22
7   Chron. Theophan. Annus Mundi 6127, 6135
8   Moczar, *Seven Lies about Catholic History*, ch. iii, p. 57
9   Chron. Theophan. Annus Mundi 6129, 6131, 6133; Belloc, *The Great Heresies*, The Great and Enduring Heresy of Muhammad, p. 38
10 Chron. Theophan. Annus Mundi 6140
11 Chron. Theophan. Annus Mundi 6282; Theophilus of Edessa's *Chronicle*, section 1, Chron. 1234, p. 132, trans. Robert G. Hoyland, Liverpool University Press

if it was not for the audacity of a zealous soldier who physically picked him up and carried him away to a safer ship.[12] They took over the Phrygian city of Amorion in Asia Minor, only to lose it when the Romans entered the metropolis and slaughtered five thousand Muslims.

Seditious and treasonous behavior plagued the Christians. Sergios, who was under the empire, worked with the Muslim conqueror Muawiyah, and when Andrew the chamberlain of the emperor Constans arrived to try to convince the Islamist not to work with this traitor, Sergios mocked him and called him a woman. Muawiyah and Sergios worked a deal against Byzantium, but when he was confronted by Andrew again, this time accompanied by an army, he begged for his life. "You are Sergios," said Andrew, "who was so proud of your genitals in front of Muawiyah, and you called me effeminate. Well! Now your genitals are no good to you at all, and will even be your death." Andrew had the traitor castrated and hung on a stake.[13]

By 672 the Arabs were making expeditions in Kilikia and Smyrna,[14] a city which the Turks would burn down in 1922. They captured Kyzikos but were ousted by the Romans in 678.[15] Around this time a peace treaty was made between the Roman Empire and the Muslim empire;[16] this was nothing but a Hudna—or false peace—which gave the enemy time to restore himself back to his former strength.

In 707, the Muslims had awaken from their feigned peace. The Arab leader Walid, after venting much jealousy for a church's beauty, captured Damascus from Rome and decreed that public record books could no longer be written in Greek, but only Arabic.[17] How could Christendom trust such an enemy which is constantly devising evil and never keeping peace deals? A Crusade to cut the head off the Islamic snake had to happen.

When the Muslims were trying to take Pergamos, the inhabitants took a pregnant woman, cut her open and boiled the child. All of those who wanted to fight dipped their right sleeves in this human sacrifice, but such was the divination of their ancestors still preserved in this time, and when they came face to face with the Muslims not only did they lose the battle, but Pergamos.[18] Let this story be a lesson to the West today; if we are to fight against the Muslims who are trying to invade Christendom today, then we first must purge ourselves of all paganism, and become zealots in the Faith.

Suleiman, an enemy of Christ, came with 1800 warships to further expand Islamic dominion in Asia Minor. Because of a very strong storm, he was unable to withstand the Roman defenses, but once weather got better the Muslims pushed forward. They were surprised by a weapon they were not used to: liquid fire. It set their ships ablaze; many sank,

---

12 Chron. Theophan. Annus Mundi 6146
13 Chron. Theophan. Annus Mundi 6159
14 Chron. Theophan. Annus Mundi 6164
15 Chron. Theophan. Annus Mundi 6165, see n. 119 by the editor Harry Turtledove
16 Chron. Theophan. Annus Mundi 6169
17 Chron. Theophan. Annus Mundi 6199
18 Chron. Theophan. Annus Mundi 6208

smashed into sea walls, or continued to sail into other islands uncontrollably.[19] Around 779, fifty thousand Muslims stampeded Asia Minor under the leadership of Thumama, and raided the land.[20]

In 662 they began their campaign against Romania, taking many prisoners and plundering numerous lands.[21] A major attack was done by Abd ar-Rahman in Romania, and there was also the Islamic incursions into Romania of 666, 694, 730, 736, and 738. On the subsequent year Suleiman orchestrated a severe assault on Romania with ninety thousand men. Another strike was done against the Romanians by the warlord Salim with eighty thousand jihadists in 757. The Arabs eventually sacked Romania in 759.[22]

Probably the largest attack that the Muslims orchestrated was at around 805, in which the tyrant Harun entered the country with three hundred thousand men from Libya, Syria, Israel, and other lands.[23] Imagine to yourself such a vast force entering England or America. No doubt, if such a thing were to happen, the western allies would have no choice but to strike back with fierce military might. No nationalist, be he American or English, would disagree that war would have to be chosen to crush an Islamic power infiltrating his country.

The Christians who lived in the Muslim provinces suffered gravely. The Christians of Tyre, for four hundred years, suffered tremendously under Islamic rule. Families who refused to convert to Islam were forced to leave their homeland, and if they defied this order, their children were taken after their fathers were murdered and their mothers humiliated. Churches were made into mosques, Christian statues destroyed, and youths compelled to live lives of prostitution in brothels.[24] The caliph Umar decreed that all Christians should convert to Islam; those who refused were imposed with death, and many martyrs were made. In trials the witness of any Christian was made null, and the fanaticism of Umar was so elevated that he even sent a letter to the Roman emperor Leo inviting him to Islam.[25] How could anyone, seeing the barbarity of this heathen faith, be persuaded to convert to Islam unless he himself is a savage?

One ancient chronicle describes this tormenting state of the Christians under Umar Bin Al-Khattab:

> He [Umar] ordered oppression of the Christians in every way to make them become Muslims. He legislated that every Christian who became a Muslim would not pay poll-tax and many converted. He also decreed that Christians should not testify against Muslims, act as governors, raise their voices for prayer, strike the sounding-board (to call people to prayer),

---

19 Chron. Theophan. Annus Mundi 6209
20 Chron. Theophan. Annus Mundi
21 Chron. Theophan. Annus Mundi 6154
22 Chron. Theophan. Annus Mundi 6157, 6158, 6186, 6222, 6228, 6230, 6231, 6248, 6251
23 Chron. Theophan. Annus Mundi 6298
24 See Edward Peters, *The First Crusade*, ch. iv, pp. 195–6, The March to Jerusalem: The Version of Raymond d'Aguiliers
25 Chron. Theophan. Annus Mundi 6210

wear the overcoat or ride on a saddle and (that) if an Arab killed a Christian he could not be executed for it, but just paid compensation of 5000 silver coins. [26]

Is it not then ironic, that this Umar died in a monastery?[27]

At around 741 the ruler of the Arabs, Hisham, massacred all of the Christian prisoners in every city under his jurisdiction. Among these was the count Marianos in Harran, the city from where Abraham left for the Promised Land; he was tortured and afflicted for a prolonged time, but never gave in to renounce Christ, ending his life as a martyr.[28] At around 757 the Muslim leader Salim commanded that no new churches should be built, that the cross should never be displayed, and that Christians are prohibited from discussing religion with Arabs.[29]

The caliph Abd Allah continued with these same edicts, taking all of the crosses from churches, preventing the Christians from observing their holidays and studying their scriptures.[30]

The Christians under 'Abdallah Mansur suffered so greatly that they were forced to exhume dead bodies and eat them, consume dogs, and desperately search for specs of gold to pay their taxes. In the years 779 to 780, under the Caliph Mahdi, the Muslim commander Mouchesias horrendously persecuted the Christians of Hims and other parts. He destroyed their churches and had them endure a thousand lashes until they converted to Islam, and all of them died under such torture.[31]

Overall, within the seventh century the Arabs had established their rulership over large sections of the southern Byzantine Empire, including Syria, Israel, and Egypt.[32]

In 806 another peace treaty was made between the Roman Empire and the Islamists; but as usual, the Muslims fabricated their agreement and resumed their attack. The terrorist leader Harun sent a fleet into the island of Cyprus where these slaves to Satan tore down churches, seized many of the inhabitants and resettled them in other lands.[33] The Muslims continued their terrorism upon Christian inhabitants living under the Islamic empire, and mobs even rose up to lay waist the churches and monasteries. The monasteries of Saint Khariton and Saint Saba were made into Islamic centers, and even Golgotha, where Christ was crucified, was profaned. Many of the persecuted escaped to Byzantium, and we cannot forget the loving help these Christians received from the Emperor Michael and the patriarch Nikephoros, who provided the monks in the city with a new monastery and gave a talent of gold to the believers who fled to Cyprus as refugees.[34]

26 Theophilus of Edessa's *Chronicle*, section 2, MSyr, pp. 216–217, trans. Robert G. Hoyland, Liverpool University Press, brackets mine
27 Theophilus of Edessa's *Chronicle*, section 2, MSyr, p. 217, trans. Robert G. Hoyland, Liverpool University Press
28 Chron. Theophan. Annus Mundi 6232
29 Chron. Theophan. Annus Mundi 6248
30 Chron. Theophan. Annus Mundi 6258
31 Theophilus of Edessa's *Chronicle*, section 3, pp. 307, 314
32 Moczar, *Seven Lies about Catholic History*, ch. iii, p. 57
33 Chron. Theophan. Annus Mundi 6298
34 Chron. Theophan. Annus Mundi 6301

✝ CHRISTIANITY IS AT WAR: THE MANIFESTO FOR CHRISTIAN MILITANCY

In 823 they followed the spirit of Hannibal and invaded Sicily, taking the entire island, and if it wasn't for the sectarian divisions amongst the Muslims all of Italy would have fell to them. From that time did the Sicilian Christians groan with anguished spirit, and neither Greek nor Latin succeeded in their liberation. But in time there arose Robert Guiscard who, with the encouragement of Pope Nicholas II, vigorously attacked, with all the ferociousness and intrepidity of a Christian warrior, the Muslims in Sicily, purged the island of all its tyrants, and restored and established the Christian religion as the faith of the land, bringing a glimmering light to a place overtaken by darkness. He placed bishops, founded monasteries, and erected pristine and glorious churches.[35] The faith which seemed to have been on the verge of being completely extinguished in Sicily, now triumphed; the church was established and the gates of hell did not prevail.

ISLAM INVADES ARMENIA AND THE CHRISTIANS WAR AGAINST THE MUSLIMS

Armenia was the first to declare itself a Christian nation, and for this, it was amongst the greatest desires for the fangs of the Devil. The Persians tried to extirpate Christianity from the land, but they failed. Satan now had to use a different people and system to obliterate the saints of this nation: Islam and its followers.

At around 637 A.D., eighteen thousand Muslims lead by one Abdul Rahman invaded Armenia, committing many atrocities, taxing all of the men while seizing the women and children. The chief of Armenia, Vahan the Camsaracan, grandson of Vahan the Wolf, alongside Sahur, Tiran, and a general named Mushel, led a force of three thousand men to engage the Islamic horde. The battle commenced, and as fighting went on, Sahur betrayed his own people for the Muslim cause. Tiran confronted this traitor, and with one strike with his sword split Sahur's skull in two.

They kept on with the battle arduously, but soon, Mushel the general was slain; Tiran too fell, and the Armenians were eventually defeated. The heart of the Armenian pope, Ezr, became so heavy by this that he died of grief. The Muslims then advanced with an immense army into Duin, besieged the city and caused the most dreadful havoc, massacring twelve thousand saints. They burnt and pulled down the beautiful architecture, destroyed everything valuable, and took captive thirty five thousand people.[36]

CHRISTENDOM EXECUTES A CRUSADE TO DEFEND ARMENIA

After a little peace was enjoyed, the Muslims resumed their holocaust of the Armenians, and by 646 they had afflicted violence upon the people of Aliovit and the Buznunians, and then expanded themselves along the parts by Mount Ararat.[37] By 693, one Abdullah entered Duin

---

35 See Gibbon, *Decline and Fall*, vol. v, ch. lii, p. 973; Mosheim's *Church History*, The 11th century, part i, ch. 1.3, p. 253
36 Chamich, *History of Armenia*, part iv, ch. xvii, pp. 359–360
37 Chamich, *History of Armenia*, vol. i, part iv, ch. xviii, p. 362–363

with an army. He came with peace in order to deceive, and shortly after entering showed his his true intent.

The pope, Isaac, and the Armenian general Sumbat were both chained and sent to Damascus. Abdullah marched to the great churches of Ararat, stole all of their treasures, and then ordered that a Christian, named David Duinensis, be crucified,[38] symbolizing the suffering Christ. Sumbat somehow escaped from prison and returned to Armenia where he sent a letter to the Byzantine emperor Justinian pleading for help. Justinian, without hesitating, ordered his celebrated general Leontius to proceed to Armenia with a large army, and a new crusade was now coming to pass.

The Byzantine warriors destroyed the home of Abdullah and all of his followers. They marched to the city of Vardanakert where they rendezvoused with the Armenian Sumbat and his troop, and battled with Abdullah and his horde. The slaves of Allah never grasped victory when contending with the bearers of the Holy Cross; the Muslims were crushed, slain by the swords of the saints. The only survivors were Abdullah and ten other of his serfs.

THE MUSLIMS RESUME HORRIFIC PERSECUTION ON THE CHRISTIANS

Abdullah would later become the caliphate of Damascus, but being so sore by his former loss, he appointed Cashm to be the governor of Armenia, and directed him to do whatever it took to slaughter the chieftains and noblemen of the nation. Cashm had tricked a number of the Armenian nobility to enter the church of Nakhjuan, and then set the sanctuary ablaze burning all of them alive. The property of these martyrs were seized and their families made captives, amongst whom was a four year old boy who was soon executed, and a young girl who was taken to Iraq and tortured to death for her refusal to convert to Islam.[39]

Not surprisingly there was treachery amongst the Armenians, since the falling away has always been amongst us. In 651, the patrician of Armenia, Pasagnathes, made agreements with the Arab conquerer Muawiyah bin Abi Sufyan, giving the leeway to the Muslims to further establish themselves in the country.[40]

In the records of Armenia, which scream of its sufferings till this very day and still is ignored by comfortable Christians, we find that entire groups of Christians were herded into churches and burnt alive for refusing the heresy that denied the Cross that they so revered.[41]

THE MUSLIMS IMPOSE ICONOCLASM ON THE CHRISTIANS AND DESTROY CHRISTIAN IMAGES

When the Muslims controlled Armenia they imposed on the Christians the demonic heresy of iconoclasm, ordering the destruction of Christian images from the churches. When the caliphate Al Mansur began constructing the city of Baghdad, he imposed a heavy tax on the

---

38 Chamich, *History of Armenia*, vol. i, part iv, ch. xix, p. 374
39 Chamich, *History of Armenia*, vol. i, part iv, ch. xix, pp. 374–375, 378–379
40 Chron. Theophan. Annus Mundi 6143
41 See Moczar, *Islam at the Gates*, prologue, p. 16

clergymen, even those who were hermits, in order to pay for the building expenses. All of the crosses which were placed upon the churches were ordered to be removed.

When Arshot the Christian governor of Armenia planned on executing a revolt, he was seized by two apostate Christians named Gregory and David, and his eyes were plucked out.[42] The Armenians made an attempt at rebelling against their Islamic masters, and asked the Romans for help. When these arrived, they encountered the Muslims and had a heavy engagement with them, only to be defeated. The Armenian nobles were gathered together by the ruler of Armenia, Muhammad, and were all burned alive.[43]

THE ARMENIAN CHRISTIANS REVOLT AGAINST MUSLIM TYRANNY

In the 770s, Bekir, the governor of Armenia, sent troops to commit massacres in the provinces of Kalen and Thalen where they slaughtered seven hundred Christians and made slaves out of another 1,200. His successor Hassan exceeded all of his predecessors in tyranny. He permitted his soldiers to indulge themselves in whatever sadism they wished to commit on the Armenians. The licentious conduct of the savages provoked a Christian named Mushel to such rage that he assembled a few men and attacked them, defeating and killing two hundred of the Muslim barbarians. He acquired more like minded warriors and massacred four thousand of the Muslims.

The valiant Mushel then stormed Duin and drove out the despotic Hassan. Inspiration came upon the other Armenian chiefs, and they took up arms and revolted for their freedom. Thirty thousand Muslims engaged a small army of five thousand Christians headed by Mushel. It was a great contest, and though the Armenians lost, they exemplified how fierce the soul of the martyr truly is. The Muslims immediately after this victory began to spoil the country. As they were elated by the property they were stealing, two Christian brothers named Ashot and Shapuh gathered together an army and attacked the plunderers with such fury that it put them to flight. The warriors of the Cross then journeyed to the province of Shirak where they crushed the Muslims there, and ousted out the Islamic governor Jahap.[44]

THE MUSLIMS COMMENCE A CRUEL AND BLOODY PERSECUTION ON THE ARMENIAN CHRISTIANS

Let us be proud of our Christian heritage when we remember the Armenians who revolted in 849, after their governor converted to Islam under duress before the Caliph. They compelled the Muslims who controlled Mount Shem to flee and then executed the apostate governor. The Caliph was incensed when he was informed of this, and placed Bulah, a man bent on implementing shear despotism, to govern over Armenia ordering him to take vengeance, arrest all of the chiefs, and kill any owner of weapons.

---

42 Chamich, *History of Armenia*, vol. i, part iv, ch. xx, pp. 386
43 Chron. Theophan. Annus Mundi 6195
44 Chamich, *History of Armenia*, vol. i, part iv, ch. xx, pp. 386, 389–391

Bulah, being homosexual, spared all the handsome men who converted to Islam, while those who were ugly, even if they became Muslim, were to be slain.[45] He sent troops to the valleys around Mount Shem, where the revolt began, and massacred every soul found. The inhabitants who lived on the summit, seeing their countrymen butchered and knowing that the same was to happen to them, rushed down and fell upon the Muslim murderers, only to be killed and made captives in great numbers.

Bulah selected the best looking of the prisoners and put them in confinement, and commanded that the remainder be butchered in his presence. He did the same in Taron in 851, separating the most comely men and killing the rest. The slaughter was so great that according to Armenian records, "human blood manured the land, and the valleys were literally choked up by the corpses of their inhabitants." Those who weren't killed in this were forced to endure torture until they gave up and embraced Islam. The believers remained steadfast, and so were afflicted with torment to the death.

Bulah then penetrated through Duin in 852, taking those who aroused his sadistic lusts and titillated his sinister appetites, and slaying those who didn't. He commenced a massacre in 853 upon the captives he took from Ararat, having violent hatred for them on account of their Faith. After being tortured to the point where they could not even be recognized, Bulah had them burnt alive. Amongst these victims were seven Christians, who Bulah gently asked to convert to Islam, and when they refused, he had them tortured and then crucified.[46] Such an event reminds us of the seven martyrs who were killed by Antiochus Epiphanies, and ultimately, became witnesses for Christ.

The severity of this tyrant led those Armenians who had not fallen into his hands to spark a revolt and defy him. They took a position on a certain valley and ambushed a detachment of Muslim soldiers returning from an attack, taking a few prisoners, killing many, and then liberating a group of Christian captives. Before they could make their retreat, the brave fighters found themselves surrounded and seized, and by the orders of Bulah, they were all beheaded. And as all of this carnage and devastation was taking place, there stood Johannes, the pope of Armenia, wandering about his ravished country, where he once flourished and was a shepherd to his people, his soul bitterly pierced with sorrow, and his mind forever taken by the deepest agony. He eventually found a safe abode in the convent of Makenoses; his heart was so broken, his eyes so drowned in tears that he died, in the year 854.

A CHRISTIAN BREAKS THROUGH FEAR AND SLAUGHTERS THE MUSLIMS

Muslim troops were soon after dispatched by the governor to massacre the Armenian people of Seunies and Sisakans. Vasak, the chief of the Sisakans, was pursued by the enemy as he fled on his horse. His heart was racing, his mind taken by angst and anticipation. But then he stopped, turned back, and with determination and boldness drew out his sword and like a wild bear protecting her young rushed upon them wildly. The blade of his weapon ripped

---

45 Chamich, *History of Armenia*, vol. i, part iv, ch. xxi, pp. 403–404
46 Chamich, *History of Armenia*, vol. i, part iv, ch. xxii, pp. 405–408

right through any Muslim who tried to put him down. They were all astonished and terrified, running away before the presence of this desperate warrior. The general of the Muslims stood his ground, only to be single handidly brought to the ground by one blow from the sword, and trampled to death by the horse of Vasak.

But this loan fighter was later betrayed by Carich, one of his own countrymen, and made a prisoner of Bulah who afterwards marched with his men into the province of Cachen where he butchered thousands, filling the earth with blood and anguish. He then seized the castle of Carich, the traitor, and after besieging it fettered him with chains and massacred most of his followers. He destroyed a city named Tus, then marched into the country of the Aluans, murdered the royal family and the chiefs, and desolated it like a viscous flood destroys all things before it. From there, Bulah proceeded to Tiflis and crucified the chieftain Vanand and martyred the tribesmen Mockathel. It was an utter horror. Armenia, in that day, was said to be so filled with darkness and human cruelty, that it had the appearance of a slaughter house rather than a nation.

In 856, Sumbat, the Armenian general, was persuaded by Bulah to accompany him to the Caliph in Baghdad, promising him that he would be made governor of Armenia by the monarch. He assented, with Bulah also taking with him a Syrian deacon named Nana and a large number of captives. When all of these were brought before the Caliph, he gave them only two choices: convert to Islam or die. Many embraced the cult of Muhammad, while others remained steadfast and accepted the crown of martyrdom, amongst these was one Stephan who had an unshaken fortitude. Sumbat declared that he would remain a Christian and was thrown into prison where he bitterly wailed in regret for having trusted the conniving Bulah, and continuously cried out to God for pardon.[47]

While these saints wept for justice, more persecution continued throughout the nations.

THE ISLAMIC CONQUEST OF CHRISTIAN EGYPT AND THE EVILS OF TOLERANCE

When the Byzantine emperor Heraclius defeated the Persian king Chosroes, the head of paganism in the Near East was given a fatal blow. The Devil thus ushered in a new concoction between heresy and heathenism, Islam, to bring the region back to idolatry and to set the stage for the Antichrist religion to spring forth from the pit of Hell and flood the world.[48]

Early in the year 640, The Muslims invaded Roman Syria with an army of seventy thousand. The caliph Abu Bakr sent a letter to all of Muhammad's followers expressing his intent "to send the true believers into Syria to take it out of the hands of the infidels. And I would have you know that the fighting for religion is an act of obedience to God." At 633 the invasion began, and in 639 the Christians were subdued to the sound of these words from the mouth of Khalid bin al-Walid: "Ye Christian dogs, you know your option; the Koran, the tribute,

---

47 Chamich, *History of Armenia*, vol. i, part iv, ch. xxii pp. 408–413
48 See De Croce, *Refutation of the Koran*, ch. xiii, p. 73

or the sword."[49] For those families unable to pay, on account of their impoverishment, the rapacious Muslims were satisfied in taking their children as their slaves.[50]

After this, the Muslims set their eyes upon Egypt, then under the Roman Empire, and upon Heraclius. The Muslims were aided in their onslaught, not by another Muslim, but by a traitorous bishop named Cyril. He promised them that Egypt would pay the Muslims 120,000 denarii in gold per year.

This went on for three years, and once the emperor Heraclius was informed of this treason he replaced Cyrus with a true zealot against evil named Manuel. When the Muslims came to Egypt to receive their annually expected tribute, what they met was not the seditious and backstabbing Cyrus, but a fierce believer in Scripture, who believed in godly anger toward the wicked and tyrannical. "I am not weaponless Cyril," he said to the jihadists, "to give you taxes; rather, I am armed."

With a few warriors Manuel fought against them, but they were overpowered. Heraclius, in response, sent Cyril to try to get them to leave Egypt. When the feigned bishop attempted to reason with them, a Muslim pointed to a large pillar and asked, "Could you gulp down that huge pillar?" to which Cyrus replied, "That is impossible." The response from the Muslim was: "Nor is it still possible for us to withdraw from Egypt."[51] And so it began.

In the war between Christendom and the Muslims, the victor would be the master of Egypt. City after city was taken, and in one major battle the Muslims made a fake retreat; when the Byzantine troops felt confident they were swiftly surrounded on all sides by Arab warriors. They broke through and fled, with only three hundred surviving. Many other Christian soldiers attempted to escape the invaders, only to be cut off and massacred in cold blood. One garrison of only a few hundred chose to stand their ground, and fought for three weeks with the Islamic hordes, who were superior in numbers, and made their way back to liberty.

But in the end, in December of 641, the fighters for Allah's crescent put Egypt in chains, and the Christian See was finally taken.[52]

How did this happen? Tolerance. When the Egyptian populace heard that the Muslims were arriving, they accepted them with open arms, not seeing them as deceiving heretics, but as people who merely believed in one God.[53] It was as though the heresy of Arius still resonated in their minds. Heresies leave prints on the souls of the people, and Arianism's impact resulted in Egypt being conquered by the new Arians.

Their open mindedness would have received the applause of the moderns, but the end result was the consequence of all ultra-equality and tolerance: violence. The Muslims broke

---

49 In Gibbon, *Decline and Fall*, vol. v, ch. li, pp. 947–948, ed. Hans-Friedrich Mueller, see the editors annotations; Alfred J. Andrea, Christendom and the Umma, in Thomas F. Madden's *The Crusades*, part 1, p. 19
50 Moczar, *Islam at the Gates*, prologue, Act 2, p. 16
51 Chron. Theophan. Annus Mundi 6126
52 Butcher, *The Story of the Church of Egypt*, vol. i, part i, ch. xxxi, p. 352; ch. xxxii, p. 358, 363–365, 370; Belloc, *The Great Heresies*, The Great and Enduring Heresy of Muhammad, p. 38
53 Butcher, *The Story of the Church of Egypt*, vol. i, ch. xxxii, p. 365

right into the country, plundering, burning, and massacring wherever they went. They took the city of Nikius with much bloodshed, putting to the sword everyone they met, "in the streets and in the churches, men, women, and children alike, sparing none." It did not take long for the Egyptians to recognize that their acceptance of Muslims was a grave mistake.[54]

It was in Egypt where St. Athanasius combated the deceptions of Arianism, and now all of his labors, his holy toils, his ideas which have lived on till these dark days, were eclipsed by the adopters of the new Arianism—Islam.

Today we do not esteem nations by how intolerant they are of evil, but how permissive they are to it. We curse, revile, and admonish a country if they do not open themselves, as the Egyptians did, to sinister precepts. But this is a fallacy which only favors the side of despotism and gives it leeway to stealthily enter civilization. Proponents of 'pure equality' ultimately want only oppression, since if their ideas were to be enacted, those who would criticize Islam or any Leftist belief would face punishment, since all things, which only they approve, must be equally accepted.

Tolerance is the cracks through which tyranny gains access into any nation. Accept a violent religion and expect violence to run rampant; accept a deceptive religion, and expect deceivers to be everywhere; accept a religion which commands massacres, and do not be surprised to find individual freewill squashed, and towers of bodies being made. In order for liberty to be perpetuated, disdain toward tyrannical ideologies must be embraced, and the prevention of their infiltration into any government or academia established. If this does not happen, and Islam and Leftism and their edicts are continually entertained, and Christianity is seen as no longer worthy of our attention, then free societies will eventually be plunged into a socialistic state where only idolatry is permitted.

Tolerance and religious liberty—these two words are the cliches used by the modernists to camouflage their true intentions, and that is control over Christians; for it is only the Christian—the true zealot—who is viewed as obligated to respect every creed but his own. It is the zealot who is deemed as the one who is to stay silent on his doctrine, and to accept with open arms the same religions which call for his death. It is only the true believer in Scripture who is told to put away his zealotry, and join the herd in revering every other form of zealotry be it Islamic, Mormon, atheist, Buddhist, Hindu, or any other dark superstition.

The only people who win the war over culture are the zealous ones. Christians then must stop being compliant moderates, and start becoming fundamentalists, believing in the whole doctrine of Scripture and the Apostolic teachings, if we are to advance the Church over the dark forces which have been pervading the world.

The Christian Egyptians, in a way, believed in a form of Chrislam, viewing Islam as acceptable simply because it had one god, and this is what led to their subjugation. Right now the Western Church has accepted this same lie, and in consequence Islam is rising.

---

54 Butcher, *The Story of the Church of Egypt*, vol. i, part i, ch. xxxii, pp. 365–366

We love to mention how both Islam, Judaism, and Christianity, are all monotheistic, as if monotheism takes precedence over truth. It is a great evil to classify Christianity, which has brought much of the world from darkness to light, under a technical term such as monotheism. If this is all that mattered, then that means Islam, Zoroastrianism, Judaism and Christianity are all universally good.

This is what Dennis Prager has taught, stating that the "Jewish people has a task to bring the world to ethical monotheism, to the belief that there is one god for everyone, who demands one ethic for everybody." If Moses heard such a statement, Dennis would have been put to death. If Judaism's purpose is to spread monotheism, then would it be appropriate for all Jews to preach Islam, since it is indeed monotheistic? He also writes that if all peoples accepted monotheism "the world would experience far less evil."[55] So then, if all the world became Muslim, would there be a greater rise in peace in the world?

Tell the Armenians who were massacred since Islam's earliest days, the Egyptians who were, and still are, greatly oppressed by jihadists, the Pakistani Christians who live each day as though it were their last, the millions of Sudanese Christians who have been butchered, the Iraqi Jews who were systematically and sadistically murdered by the thousands, that Islam is a vehicle of peace because of its monotheism. Prager later writes:

> During some of the Western world's darkest periods, Islam was a religious light in the monotheistic world. The seeds of ethical monotheism are deeply rooted in Islam. For whatever reason, however, the soil for their nourishment has, over the last several hundred years, been depleted of necessary nutrients. Islam could be a world force for ethical monotheism, but in its present state, the outlook is problematic.[56]

Notice he refused to admit that Islam is inherently evil, but expresses the fact that there is surely a problem within the Muslim world. It doesn't matter whether a religion claims to believe in only one god, what matters is which god. If all of us subscribed to Prager's focus on monotheism, then we would all have no problem in getting on our knees and bowing to Mecca. If Prager hesitates to proclaim that there is no god but Allah and Muhammad is his messenger, then monotheism is not the focal point, and there is indeed a difference between the God of the Bible and the devil of Islam.

THE MUSLIMS COMMENCE HORRIFIC VIOLENCE OVER EGYPT

The Muslims marched to the library of Alexandria, the greatest library of antiquity; the librarian begged them not to harm the books, stating that they were worth more than all of the riches of Egypt. "If these books contain nothing more than that which is written in the book of God (el Koran)," said the caliph Omar, "they are useless; if they contain anything contrary to the sacred book, they are pernicious; in either case burn them."

---

55 Prager, *Ethical Monotheism*
56 Prager, *Ethical Monotheism*

CHRISTIANITY IS AT WAR: THE MANIFESTO FOR CHRISTIAN MILITANCY

All of the books, without care of the immense knowledge within them, were used for six months as fuel for the bath houses. By 647, the first mosque in Egypt was built—a monument of tyranny—by the Muslim general Amr bin Aas. Columns, ripped out of Christian churches, were later added to this building which still stands today as the "mosque of Amr."[57]

Persecution ensured upon the time of the Islamic conquest, progressively getting more and more brutal. Christians had their hands and feet severed off, their feet burned with hot coals, and, such as what happened to the Egyptian patriarch Theodore in 703, were subject to crucifixion.[58] All of this was in accordance with the inhumanity commanded by the Quran to be imposed on all those who oppose Islam:

> The punishment of anyone who fights against Allah and His apostle and do mischief in the land is to be killed or crucified or to have their hands and feet cut off from opposite ends or be banished from the land. [59]

THE MUSLIMS IMPOSE BRUTAL TAXES OVER THE CHRISTIAN CHURCH IN EGYPT

At the beginning of the eighth century Egypt became under the governorship of the Muslim Asabah, whose main liaison consisted of a deacon turned apostate named Benjamin. From this heretic, not surprisingly, Asabah learned methods on how to reduce the Christian population with the purpose of making it powerless: he taxed every monk in Egypt one piece of gold, ordered a census to document their population, decreed that no man was to become a monk unless without approval by the government, and imposed a tax of two thousand gold pieces on bishops.[60]

These tyrannical edicts should remind us of what the progressives in the West wish to do to Christianity and to society as a whole: destroy the Church and control the population through a census. One day Asabah entered a church in Helwan, and when his wicked eyes saw a magnificent painting of Mary with her Son Jesus, he asked a bishop on the significance of the portrait. After receiving the meaning, he spat upon the picture and swore that the time would come that he would "exterminate Christianity from the country."[61]

That same night he was attacked by a violent fever and died hours later.[62]

THE CHRISTIANS REVOLT AGAINST MUSLIM RULE

In 705 one sadistic Abdallah became the emir over Egypt. He was of the cruelest sort, finding it entertaining to invite a Christian for dinner and decapitate him as he sat down to eat. He ordered entire churches to be torn down; his rulership was so severe that the wealthier Egyp-

---

57 Butcher, *The Story of the Church of Egypt*, vol. i, part ii, ch. i, pp. 373–374
58 See Butcher, *The Story of the Church of Egypt*, vol. i, part ii, ch. iii, pp. 387, 392–393
59 Quran: The table spread
60 Butcher, *The Story of the Church of Egypt*, vol. i, part ii, ch. iii, pp. 398–394
61 Butcher, *The Story of the Church of Egypt*, vol. i, part ii, ch. iii, p. 394
62 Butcher, *The Story of the Church of Egypt*, vol. i, part ii, ch. iii, p. 394

tians fled the country.⁶³ It is a reminder of what has been taking place in Egypt now: Christians are being persecuted, while the believers who are wealthy enough have already left.

As the Babylonians took the resources of other nations to build their pagan temples, the Muslims stole the pillars of precious marbles and porphyry to add them to their mosques. Under Asama bin Yezid taxes imposed on Christians were increased, and every monk was forced to wear a silver ring on their hand, upon which was engraved the name of their convent and the date in which they paid; failure to wear meant beheading. In 725 the Christians tried to make a stand against their masters, but being unarmed, the revolt became a pure bloodbath. One bishop was seized and relentlessly whipped until his fellow Christians could pay the emir a thousand pieced of gold. On the verge of death the ransom was finally made (although it was three hundred pieces) and the bishop let go.⁶⁴

A temporarily successful revolt was led by the patriarchs Michael and Cosmas which led the Egyptians to obtain semi-independence for several years. The warlord Abd el Melek attempted to reconquer them only to lose, with a great amount of his army killed by the frustrated saints. Many a believer was murdered, and many a church burned down, but they still held out, until finally being defeated in 750 by Merwan, the caliph of the Islamic empire.

Crops were set ablaze, monasteries pillaged, and nuns dragged out and raped. One nun, Febronia, was so beautiful that Merwan set her aside for himself. She took some ointment and claimed that it had the power to protect a man from a sword, and promised Merwan that she would test it on herself only if she and her fellow nuns were spared. Merwan conceded to this, and when Febronia rubbed the ointment on her neck and lowered herself, the edge of a scimitar struck down and her head rolled upon the floor. The sight so shocked the Muslims that they were moved with pity and spared the remaining nuns from being ravished.⁶⁵

THE MUSLIMS DESTROY CHRISTIAN IMAGES AND IMPOSE ANTICHRIST DESPOTISM ON THE CHRISTIANS

By 750, Muslim power was over significant portions of Mesopotamia and Armenia, costal lands from Syria to Egypt, and from that point it captured North Africa,⁶⁶ which before that time was the great flower of Christendom, the home to some of the greatest minds on the Scriptures, from Tertullian, Cyprian, Lactantius, and Augustine. These conquests were only an addition to the horrific persecutions that were already happening to the Christians in Egypt.

A very significant revolt took place in 831, when the Copts (the proper name for Egyptian Christians), in defiance to tyranny, fought against the Muslims in their last attempt to regain their freedom. They were pushed back to the Egyptian city of Babylon and hid in a citadel, upon which a siege began.

---

63   Butcher, *The Story of the Church of Egypt*, vol. i, part ii, ch. iv, pp. 395–396
64   Butcher, *The Story of the Church of Egypt*, vol. i, part ii, ch. iv, p. 401
65   Butcher, *The Story of the Church of Egypt*, vol. i, part ii, ch. v, pp. 413–414
66   See Moczar, *Islam at the Gates*, prologue, p. 12

The Muslims eventually broke through and slew every male found. A slaughter took place upon the saints in which many were sold into slavery, executed, or unwillingly converted to Islam. It was at this point that the Christians became officially a minority, with Muslims taking over many villages.[67]

From being the sovereign rulers of their nation, the Egyptian Christians were now reduced to the lowest level of servitude. The Coptic Church was kept in constant poverty on account of heavy taxes; no Christian was allowed to ride on any animal save a donkey or mule, and even the saddles were to be given a distinguishable mark. Every Christian was to place on his door the wooden image of an ape, dog, or devil.

No public prayers were allowed to be given, all crosses were forbidden (the Left in the West would love such edicts), and like weeds in a luscious field, minarets sprouted and churches were burnt down. And as the Nazis forced every Jew under the Third Reich to put on a yellow patch of the Star of David, so did the Muslim make every Christian wear a patch.[68]

From this, we must not cover our ears from hearing the judgments of history; no nation is immune from her lessons. Let us not see the world through a text book and tedious statistics, but through the results and consequences of the wrong decisions made by men in the past. Let us not accept tolerance because of fear from accusations of racism and discrimination, but let us reject tolerance on account of prudence and the foresight to see its destructive results.

THE MUSLIMS DESTROY TENS OF THOUSANDS OF CHURCHES IN EGYPT
Great tyrants of the Muslim faith ruled over Egypt. Al-Hakim, who believed himself to be Allah reincarnate, and was called an antichrist by the Christians, massacred many of the faithful; he burned down the Egyptian city of Babylon for its Christianity, beheaded saints, seized the property of the followers of Christ and tore down thirty thousand churches. He forced Christians to wear a huge cross around their necks, Jews to put a round piece of wood around theirs, outlawed Christian holidays and put to the flame any cross discovered.[69]

Years later, under a different ruler, a man named Nekam denied Christ to preserve himself, but once guilt seeped into his heart, and he realized that "whosoever will save his life shall lose it," (Matthew 16:25) he confronted tyranny to its face, threw away his Muslim garbs and wore Christian dress, and openly proclaimed Christ. He was arrested and sentenced to death, and when his father came to visit and convince him to leave his zealotry, he had already professed who his Redeemer was, and was beheaded.[70]

The patriarch of Egypt in the early thirteenth century, Nicholas, had this to say on the persecution occurring in a letter to Pope Honorius in Rome:

---

67 Butcher, *The Story of the Church of Egypt*, vol. i, part ii, ch. vii, pp. 436–437; ch. viii, p. 440
68 Butcher, *The Story of the Church of Egypt*, vol. i, part ii, ch. ix, pp. 449–451
69 Butcher, *The Story of the Church of Egypt*, vol. ii, part ii, ch. xv, pp. 26–28
70 Butcher, *The Story of the Church of Egypt*, vol. ii, part ii, ch. xvi, pp. 41–42

If any Christian church from any accident happens to fall, we dare not rebuild it; and for these fourteen years past each Christian in Egypt is compelled to pay a [Jizya] tax of one bezant and fourteen karabbas; and if he be poor, he is committed to prison and not set at liberty until he has paid the whole sum. There are so many Christians in this country that the Sultan derives from them a yearly revenue of one hundred thousand golden bezants. What further shall I say when Christians are employed for every unfit and sordid work, and are even compelled to clean the streets of the city?[71]

MUSLIM MOBS RUSH THE CHRISTIANS WITH DEMONIC RAGE

"Why do the heathen rage, and the people imagine a vain thing?" (Psalm 2:1)

On one afternoon of June in 1320, mosques throughout Egypt were observing the Friday prayers, and in multiple congregations men arose and cried out "God [Allah] is great! God is great! O my brethren, let us go forth and destroy the churches!" In Cairo the same rallying cry was heard in three places at the same moment.

It was a calculated plot, the conspirators understood the easily shaken conscious of the masses, and it worked sufficiently to rouse the mob to violence. They attacked the church of Zehry, and not one stone of the sancturary was left upon another. They then raided and ruined the church of St. Mena in the Hamra quarter. The mob broke through the Church of the Maiden, took out every nun and stripped them all naked, plundered the church of its valuables and then set it on fire.

The same rabble destroyed another 56 churches and countless convents. A crowed rushed to the sultan and screamed "Let there be no faith except that of Islam! God protect the faith of Mohammad! O thou commander of the faithful, help us against the infidels. No favour to the Christians!"

The sultan unwillingly acquiesced to the wants of the masses just as Pilot had done, and the crowd was ecstatic at such freedom given to them. The details of the violence is left only to our imagination, but we know that they ferociously reduced the Christians into servility, with any Christian caught wearing a white turban or riding a horse swiftly put to death.[72]

This mob violence continued on for years. One Christian was tortured for a whole week and then beheaded for denouncing the wickedness and anarchy of the Muslims. Churches were frequently leveled to the ground and Christian tombs were torn open and the bodies burnt. One multitude of jihadists even went so far as to make a large pit to throw Christians in.[73] One Christian named Gabriel was seized, and under the order of the sultan, tortured and forced to parade naked through the streets as an official screamed, "Thus shall it be done to every Christian in the employ of the Sultan."[74] These Christians suffered as Christ suffered, for as they were paraded naked, so was our Savior crucified naked.

---

71 In Butcher, *The Story of the Church of Egypt*, vol. ii, part ii, ch. xxiv, p. 134
72 Butcher, The of the Church of Egypt, vol. ii, part ii, ch. xxix, pp. 188–199
73 Butcher, *The Story of the Church of Egypt*, vol. ii, part ii, ch. xxx, pp. 205–206, 209
74 Butcher, *The Story of the Church of Egypt*, vol. ii, part ii, ch. xxxi, pp. 226

† CHRISTIANITY IS AT WAR: THE MANIFESTO FOR CHRISTIAN MILITANCY

THE CHRISTIAN CRUSADERS TRY TO DEFEND CHRISTIANITY IN EGYPT

The Christian crusaders under Amaury invaded Muslim Egypt, took Cairo, and in 1166, invaded the city of Balbeis where they slew many Muslims. But the Muslim leader Shawer, in fear that the Copts and Crusaders would unite against all Egyptian Muslims, rallied up his men for a jihad toward the saints and burned down the entire city of Balbeis.

No number can be given on how many Christians died in the flames, but what we do know is that the city burned unceasingly for fifty four days, and to this day does its site lay desolate, with only a coin found here and there, and some ruins of old churches to spark the memory of today's zealot on how Egypt was once a Christian nation.[75] The man who sees such remnants and walks passed them coldly, and views with lifeless eyes half demolished convents and monasteries, and has not the urge to read the annals of history to comprehend what such monuments once were and what they still symbolize, has no concept truly of what Christianity is, nor does he hold connection with beauty and sublimity.[76]

The Christians of Egypt today suffer severe persecution, while most Christians look on like those who neglected the wounded man in the story of the Good Samaritan. These have not the slightest idea that Christ Himself was a victim of persecution, and they have the same mindsets as those who did not care about the suffering Messiah.

THE ISLAMIC CONQUEST OF CHRISTIAN SUDAN

Upon the desert of Gaza there was once an Ethiopian reposing on his chariot reading this verse of Isaiah: "He was led as a sheep to the slaughter; and like a lamb dumb before his shearer, so opened he not his mouth: in his humiliation his judgment was taken away: and who shall declare his generation? for his life is taken from the earth." (Acts 8:32–33)

He was then approached by a certain Philip, a follower and Apostle of Christ, who asked the Ethiopian if he understood what he was reading. "How can I," he said, "except some man should guide me?" (Acts 8:31) After perusing the same verse, the Ethiopian posed the question: "I pray thee, of whom speaketh the prophet this? of himself, or of some other man?" (Acts 8:34)

And Philip showed him, that Isaiah preached Christ. (Acts 8:35) As they went on their way, riding on the chariot, they passed by some natural pool. "See," said the Ethiopian, "here is water; what doth hinder me to be baptized?" (Acts 8:36) The Apostle replied that if he truly believed, and had absolute conviction, that Christ is Lord, then he could be baptized. The Ethiopian in turn proclaimed: "I believe that Jesus Christ is the Son of God." (Act 8:37) The chariot stopped, the man was baptized, and with such sublime satisfaction in his spirit he went on his way rejoicing. (Acts 8:38–39) It is said that he retuned to his home in Ethiopia, or

---

75 See Butcher, *The Story of the Church of Egypt*, vol. ii, part ii, ch. xx, pp. 93–98
76 See the Rev. J. Balmes, *Protestantism and Catholicity*, ch. xxxviii, p. 220

what is today called Sudan,[77] and preached to the people there that Christ is the Son of God, bringing the truth of Scripture and the Church to that land.[78]

Christianity made a profound impact on Sudan, with many of its inhabitants accepting the Son of God. But little did they know at that time, that hundreds of years after that inspiring conversation between Philip and the Ethiopian, the teachings of the Apostle would be to the anger of Muslim warlords who came to Sudan with the teaching of that impostor Muhammad, that God did not have a son.

In 653, twenty thousand cruel Muslim warriors marched into Sudan, and were given complete freedom by their leader Abdallah bin Said to indulge in whatever sadism and brutality they wished. They were confronted by one hundred thousand fierce Christian Sudanese fighters—masters in close quarter combat and archery. The Muslims were so aggressively opposed that they only obtained a pyrrhic victory, having won the battle without an efficient foothold into the country. They returned, and this time Abdallah brought with him a catapult, a weapon completely unknown to the Sudanese, and with such a machine did the Muslims come out the victors. The catapult launched boulders right into the principle church of Sudan, compelling the king Balidaroub to come to terms of peace with the Islamic invaders. The agreement was ruthless and cutthroat.

The Sudanese were to allow a mosque—the symbol of Islamic superiority and Christian servility—to be built, and were also made to see to it that the despotic building was properly cleaned and well lighted. The 'treaty' also lay the foundation for the Arab slave trade. The Christians were to provide each year three hundred and sixty of their own people to the Muslims so that they would be their slaves.[79]

There was such savagery done in Africa, yet those who scream racism in America never bring up the atrocities committed in Africa by the Muslims. In one case, in 773, the Islamist pagans beheaded two hundred and eighty Africans and sent the heads to Syria where they were paraded as trophies.[80]

THE ISLAMIC CONQUEST OF CRETE, AND HOW A HERETICAL MONK BETRAYED HIS PEOPLE

After the Islamic conquest of Spain of 711, the Muslims who lived in the western part of that country grew tired of their poor conditions, and desired to find a land more fertile. They went to their leader, Abu Hafs, and asked him to settle them in a more fecund land, a request which he granted. He led them on a fleet to Crete, and the Muslims overran the entire land, shedding much Christian blood and taking many captives. Abu Hafs set his gaze upon the land, and said, "Behold, a land flowing with milk and honey."

---

77 See the commentaries on this story of Gill, Clarke, and Fausset
78 Euseb. Eccles. Hist. 2.1
79 Butcher, *The Story of the Church of Egypt*, vol. i, part ii, ch. ii, pp. 378–380
80 Chron. Theophan. Annus Mundi 6266

CHRISTIANITY IS AT WAR: THE MANIFESTO FOR CHRISTIAN MILITANCY

The Muslims left for the winter, and when spring time arrived, Abu Hafs returned to Crete with forty ships filled with fighting men eager to partake in jihad. When they arrived they came upon a lofty hill called Charax, and since there was no resistance attempted by the local Christians, they set up a fortified encampment, and sent out men to forage for food. As they were gone to search for their bellies' satisfaction, Abu Hafs burned all of the ships, not leaving one left. When the men returned they were greatly astonished, and frightfully asked him why he did this, to which Abu Hafs said:

> You yourselves are the cause of these events, for you sought to settle elsewhere and in a good land. As I could think of no land better than this, I chose this way of granting you your heart's desire and ridding myself of your objections.

When the Muslim mentioned to him their wives and their children, and how they were to bring them into Crete, Abu Hafs callously said:

> You take these prisoners here for your wives and soon enough they will give you children.

The Muslims fell to silence, for they were deeply satisfied with his words, as they gratified the desires of their earthly minds.[81]

As some time went by, a monk journeyed from the mountains and approached the Muslims, and told them that they were making a mistake if they were going to settle on the land they were on, and said it would be more profitable for them to invade the area of Chandax, a rich land filled with fertile soil and an abundance of crops. The Muslims happily received this information from the heretical monk, and invaded Chandax and the entire nation of Crete (except for one city), enslaving the whole population. The Muslims charged the Cretan bishop of Gortyn and demanded that he convert to Islam. The bishop refused, and the Muslims executed him.[82]

CHRISTENDOM DEFENDS CRETE AND FIGHTS THE MUSLIMS

The emperor Theophilus[83] sent a warring Christian fleet against the Muslims in Crete, led by the military commander, Krateros, who sailed into the conquered land with seventy ships. When the Roman warriors arrived in Crete, they were met with resistance by a Muslim war, and not only Islamic troops, but by native Cretans who attacked them with fury. As the sun illuminated the ridges of the mountains, so did the Romans and the Muslims, and their Cretan troops, lock horns in a bloody bout of arms and melee.

When the waning of the moon appeared before the weary eyes of the warriors, the Cretans who were fighting for the jihad were drained of all their fortitude, and ran with angst and dread. With victory came negligence, for the Romans, acting as though they had already fully taken Crete from the control of the crescent, began to celebrate with the highest pas-

---

81 Skylitzes, *Byzantine History*, 3.16
82 Skylitzes, *Byzantine History*, 3.16
83 That the emperor was Theophilus, see footnote 86 by Jean-Claude Cheynet for Skylitzes' *Byzantine History*, 3.18

sions. They consumed wine to their hearts' delight, and being inebriated, they thought of nothing else except the gentle comforts of reposing. As they slept and reclined, their bodies enervated by intoxication, the Cretans crept up to their slumbering bodies and slew them all, not sparing even the messengers. The only one who managed to escape was Krateros, the commander, but the Muslims did not forget him, and the leader of the Muslim army sent out assassins to find them. They eventually discovered poor Krateros in the island of Kos, and brutally slaughtered him by crucifixion.[84]

Because of the incompetence of these troops, and the viciousness of the Cretans against the Romans, the emperor commissioned an extremely shrewd and intelligent warrior named Orryphas to attack Crete and pay the peoples there a lesson. Orryphas payed his warriors very well, giving each one of them forty pieces of gold, a generosity which earned the garrison the name, "the fortiers." When this hardy and proficient body of fighters entered Crete, they slaughtered the Muslims as they were caught foraging for food, and when the elite "fortiers" spotted the traitorous Cretans, the Cretans put up a resilient and formidable onslaught, but they were no match to the superiorly trained force, and they ran with all fear and trepidation before the swords and ferocity of the Christian combatants.[85]

HOW THE MUSLIMS INVADED SICILY BY THE HELP OF A HERETICAL CHRISTIAN

In the ninth century there was a man named Euphemios, a military commander who was in charge of a unit of soldiers in Sicily. He fell in love with a nun, and to gratify his rapacious and insatiable desires, he seized her against her will and forced her into his house where he ravished her.

Her brothers, hearing of how their sister was abused in this horrid way, made their complaint before the emperor, Michael II, and he justly ordered that Euphemios be arrested and his nose cut off. Once Euphemios heard of the order against him, he bid his soldiers fair well and fled to Tunisia, where he promised the ruling Muslim emir that he would invade and conquer all of Sicily for him, and pay him much tribute, if he would just do one thing to satisfy his thirst for power: declare him emperor of the Romans.

The emir happily agreed and furnished Euphemius a substantially large army of Muslim warriors. Euphemios then led the Muslim fighters into Sicily and successfully conquered the whole nation, and thus the emir—and the Muslims—ruled Sicily, and he in fulfilling his agreement, declared Euphemios emperor of the Romans.

Euphemios walked about Sicily dressed in the ostentatious attire of an emperor, surrounded by a company of bodyguards and a multitude of sycophantic officials. He entered the city of Syracuse as a conquering hero, who conquered nothing, but only betrayed his people to the heretics. Two brothers cried out to him with praises, and Euphemios enthusiastically embraced their adulations; and then he, with a show of friendliness, called for them

---

84 Skylitzes, *Byzantine History*, 3.18–19
85 Skylitzes, *Byzantine History*, 3.19

CHRISTIANITY IS AT WAR: THE MANIFESTO FOR CHRISTIAN MILITANCY

so that he could welcome with open arms. He greeted them with a bow, and as he brought his lips toward the face of one of the brothers (as is customary in the east), one grabbed a hold of his hair with firmness while the other one took out a blade and decapitated the traitor.[86]

Regardless of this heroic action, the Muslims ruled all of Sicily, and it was all because of a traitorous Christian.

By the later ninth century, nearly all of the southern part of Italy that was controlled by the Byzantine Empire, was being overtaken by Carthaginian Muslims, the successors of the pagan Hannibal. In the words of Skylitzes:

> Nearly the entire area of Italy which belonged to the Roman Empire and the greater part of Sicily had been overcome by the Carthaginian forces and the people there were now paying taxes to the barbarians.[87]

The Muslims invaded and conquered the Roman provinces of Pannonia, Dalmatia, and even all the way to the lands of the Scythians, the Croatians, the Serbs, and numerous others. As time went on, the Muslim leaders, the sultan of Bari, Saba of Tarento, and a Berber named Kalfun, sent out thirty-six warships to attack Dalmatia, and in their jihadist incursion they managed to seize and overtake the cities of Boutoma, Rhosa, and Kato Dekatora.

THE MUSLIMS TRY TO CONQUER ROME, THE CHRISTIANS RESPOND WITH A CRUSADE

In the ninth century, in the Sicilian city of Ragusa, the watchers of the metropolis looked out and saw before them an entire army of Muslims. They blockaded the city and executed a fierce siege, but the native Christian Sicilians, with tenaciousness and ardency, put up a formidable resistance. But as much time passed, the advancers of antichrist wore out the saints; the Ragusians began to be extremely exhausted, and in their turmoil they sent a number of delegates to the emperor to gain his assistance against the enemies of Christ.

By the time the delegates arrived, the emperor gave up the ghost, but with all fortune, the succeeding emperor, the pious Basil I, heard their pleas. He sent a fleet of a hundred warships into Ragusa, but when the Muslims heard of this, they shook in terror and fled deeper into Italian territory. They attacked the town of Bari and set up a camp there, and made vicious incursions on the surrounding areas. They continuously expanded and eventually took control of the whole of Lombardia, and almost reached Rome,[88] the center of Western Christianity, a city the Muslims, no doubt, wanted to destroy on account of its primacy and orthodoxy.

The emperor realized that the hundred ships would not be efficient enough to vanquish the Muslim problem in Italy. The heretics were now using Ragusa as a base from which to execute their attacks around Italy, and as a foothold into Christendom, and a Christian army

---

86 Skylitzes, *Byzantine History*, 3.20
87 Skylitzes, *Byzantine History*, 6.26
88 Skylitzes, *Byzantine History*, 6.26, 146–147

strong enough to accomplish this dangerous feat needed to be assembled. Basil I went to the person who would care the most about a wounded Christendom, and about the Church being conquered by the heretics: the Pope of Rome, Pope Adrian II.

With the authority of the Pope behind him, Basil I pushed the king of France, Louis II, to send reinforcements to fight alongside his Christian brethren against the haters of Christ, an exhorting request which the king piously fulfilled.[89] Surely was this a moment in which the Two Swords of St. Peter worked as one, with the Pope of the Church, weaving his spiritual sword and giving the nod to the king to unleash the temporal sword against the godless enemies of Christ. Indeed, this truly was what Christendom was about; and most definitely was this a crusade.

They are those who say that the First Crusade of 1095 was the first of its kind, with the Pope calling for soldiers to fight against the Muslims from conquering eastern Christendom. While there were aspects of the First Crusade that could be labeled distinct the battle for Ragusa and the rest of southern Italy shows that the Pope using his spiritual authority to call for armies to protect the Byzantine Empire from Islamic conquests was not exclusive to 1095. Since here we have Pope Adrian II pushing for an army to drive back Islamic expansion from flooding Byzantine territory, a moment parallel to Pope Urban II, in 1095, calling for armies to stop the Muslims from taking Constantinople and the rest of the eastern Christian lands.

The hardy warriors of France were ready for the intensity of the battle, and Basil I ordered that the native Christians of Ragusa do their part and put up a resilient fight. When all of them had gathered together, they charged into the town of Bari, which was earlier conquered by the Muslims, and drove the heretics out, taking the town for Christendom, and for Christ. The Frankish fighters attacked the sultan of Bari and his men, and drove them into France where they would make them captives.[90]

THE SULTAN FOOLS THE FRENCH

Though he was captured by the French, this sultan was no fool. There was a thing that always baffled the king of France about this sultan: he never smiled nor ever expressed himself in laughter. But one day the sultan saw the wheel of a wagon, and silently contemplating its movement, he laughed. The king was shocked upon hearing the news of his laughter, and after summoning the sultan, asked him as to what made him laugh, to which the sultan responded:

> I saw a wagon, and noticed its wheels; how the lower part is raised up while the upper part is brought low. In this I saw a metaphor of the instability and uncertainty of human happiness. Then I laughed at the thought of how we are puffed up by such uncertain things; and I also recognized that it was impossible that I who have been brought low from so great a height should not be raised up again to greatness from ground level.

---

89 Skylitzes, *Byzantine History*, 6.26, 147
90 Skylitzes, *Byzantine History*, 6.26, 147

The king was taken aback by his words, and contemplating on this nugget of oriental wisdom, came to a realization that the sultan was quite erudite and intelligent, and granted him freedom to come to him liberally for conversation, and to freely roam about the country. With this freedom, the sultan exerted all of his talents as a cunning rascal. He looked to the Italian cities that were under the power of France, Capua and Benevento, and observed how they hated the king and were always seeking independence. He then went to the king and proposed what seemed to be a prudent idea, saying,

> I notice, O king, that it is a constant source of worry and concern to you how you are to maintain a firm hold on these Italian cities. I will give you some advice: you should be aware, most noble prince, that you will never have an unshakable hold on these cities until you remove the leading inhabitants of them to the hands of the Franks. For those who are enslaved against their will naturally long for freedom and will break out in revolt to attain it if they are given the opportunity.

Louis II expressed himself favorable to this plan, and ordered a prodigious number of blacksmiths to make chains and fetters by which to bind the Italians and bring them into France. The sultan, with his double minded character, went to the leading citizens of Capua and Benevento and said,

> I wish to give you some top secret information which, if it were dissevered, would, I fear, be my destruction and put you in great danger.

They swore silence upon hearing this, and anxiously wondered what he had to say. The sultan continued:

> The king wishes to send you all in chains to his own land of Francia, fearing that there is no other way for him to maintain a firm grasp on your cities

But the leading citizens of Capua and Benevento did not fully trust the sultan, and asked that he show them some concrete evidence for his claims. The sultan took one of the leading citizens to the area where the blacksmiths were making the chains and fetters, and asked him to ask the blacksmiths why they were working with such haste. When the plan was revealed to him, he rushed back and told his people what was happening, and confirmed what the sultan said.

The people then planned how they were going to counter-attack King Louis II. When the king of France arrived to take the people, they shut the gates to his face and refused to let him in. The sultan then approached the leading citizens asking that as a reward for his information, he be allowed to leave for North Africa. They helped him escape, and he returned to his home in Carthage, resumed his authority and command, and commenced a military campaign against Capua and Benevento, the very cities that set him free. He established a military bastion and viciously besieged the two Italian metropolises. They were being grievously oppressed by the Muslim sultan, and could do nothing else but seek help from the king of France. But when the king heard their envoy, he said that he rejoiced in their destruction because they refused him earlier.

They then sent an envoy to the pious emperor Basil I, who received him well and told him to return to his people and urged them not to worry, for reinforcements would be on their way to defend them. As the envoy was returning to Italy he was captured by the men of the sultan and made a prisoner. He was brought before the sultan who told him,

> There are two paths open to you, of which you should take the one more beneficial to you. If you wish to save your own life, also to receive many gifts and favours, say—in my hearing—to those who sent you that the emperor of the Romans refuses to ally himself with you; thus, you will live. But if you insist on delivering your true message, sudden death awaits you.

The messenger agreed to comply with the sultan, and asked that the leading citizens be brought before so that he could tell them what the sultan wanted him to say. When they were summoned, he said to them:

> O fathers, even though death is obviously at hand and the sword ready to strike, I will not conceal the truth. I only ask that you show your gratitude to my wife and children. I am in the hands of the enemy, my lords; but I have completed my embassy. You may expect help from the emperor of the Romans forthwith, so be of good cheer; your deliverer is coming, but not mine.

As he was saying the final lines the Muslims slashed him with their swords, and by the time the last word was spoken from his mouth, he was cut to pieces. He sacrificed himself for his people, for when the sultan heard what he said, he was deeply afraid of the Romans, and ended the siege of Capua and Benevento.[91]

THE GREEK CHRISTIANS TAKE UP THEIR SWORDS TO DEFEND THE SICILIAN CHRISTIANS

When the crescent of Islam hovered over the island of Sicily, and blocked the effulgent rays of Christian liberty, the pious emperor Basil I looked with his sovereign eyes as to who would have the strength to drive out the darkness of Islam and allow the pleasant beams of Christendom to illuminate that beautiful land. Out of all the mighty men, he chose Nikephoros Phokas. He was strong in battle and valiant in war, and filled with piety and the utmost reverence for the Holy Trinity.

His physique was robust, and fit for combat; his mind sharpened by prudence and strategy, his spirit and heart, fortified by the grueling labor of penance and piety. Truly was this man like Josiah, fighting against the enemies of Heaven, he "turned to the Lord with all his heart, with all his soul, and with all his might" (2 Kings 23:25).

He looked to Sicily and saw what havoc and misery the Muslims were causing for the Christians: its cities were ravaged and devastated, and the only city that was spared the pil-

---

91 Skylitzes, *Byzantine History*, 6.28, 149–151

lage of the scimitar was Palermo, for from there the Muslims coordinated their attacks. And what infuriated Nikephoros was the sight of Christians paying taxes to Muslim overlords. He would have none of this. He sailed to Italy with a force of hardy fighters, and drove the Muslims completely out of Sicily.

After the victory, to glorify God with gratitude, the Sicilians built a church to forever perpetuate the memory of when the Christians defeated the haters of Christ.[92]

MUSLIMS AGAIN TRY TO CONQUER ITALY

Italy remained in peace until the reign of Constantine VII Porphyrogennetos, when the Bulgarians distracted the Byzantines with sword and violence, and forced them to turn their eyes from the Muslims behind them, who always waited for moments like this to pounce on the flock of Christendom. Because the threat of the Bulgarians was severe, the Christians could not deal with two enemies at once, so they compromised with the Muslims for peace, and agreed to pay them a tribute of twenty-two thousand pieces of gold a year.[93]

During the Byzantine Empire's war with the Bulgarians, there were people who deserted Muslim Carthage and fled to Christian lands. The Muslims did not protest this, nor did they demand for the return of the deserters, out of fear that the Christians would stop sending them their tribute, and thus starve them. But once the war with the Bulgarians was over, and the Christians broke the treaty by cutting off the Jizya (tribute) from being sent to Carthage, the Muslims demanded both the deserters and the twenty-two thousand pieces of gold.

When the Christians ignored their demands, the Muslims launched a major assault against the southern Italian land of Calabria. Constantine VII had no desire to treat the Muslims with gentleness and renew the treaty, but to finally settle the problem through a holy war.

He gathered together a well-equipped army conditioned for war and meritorious of heavy combat, and sent them off to Calabria under the nobleman Malakenos, and ordered that upon their arrival they would join forces with the local troops and their brave commander, Paschalios. When the emir of the Muslim army, Aboulchare, heard of this, he exhorted his men to not fear death when battling with the Christians, but to fight with all strength and exertion.

The Christian troops fell upon the Muslims, but the emir led his troops to overpower the armies of Christendom, and soon there was a great slaughter of the Byzantines, and only the senior officers escaped from being captured alive. A peace treaty was signed, and it was agreed that the Muslims would leave Calabria in peace. But once the treaty was expired, the Muslims manned their ships and sailed into Calabria, wreaking havoc and causing much destruction and death.

---

92 The battle is recorded by John Skylitzes, *Byzantine History*, 14.3–4
93 John Skylitzes, *Byzantine History*, 14.4

Constantine VII sent another force, this time under the command of Krambeas and Marianos Argyros. They gathered together at Hidgrous, or the coast of Otranto in southern Italy, and from there travelled to Sicily. As they were approaching, a sudden fear struck the hearts of the Muslims in the city of Reggio in Calabria, from where they commanded, and such a trepidatious sensation was unusual, since the Muslims were almost always ready to battle it out with their Christian enemies.

They fled Reggio, and got on their ships and headed for Palermo. But on the way, a storm ambushed them, and their ships were capsized, in the words of Skylitzes, "by Christ who is God, blasphemed by them," and they all perished in the fierce waters.

THE CHRISTIANS SLAUGHTER THE MUSLIMS IN CILICIA

After the battle was done, the Muslims made a treaty, the Christians agreed to pay them an annual tribute, and peace was established. But this peace did not last, and it was soon broken when Nikephoros Phokas ascended the throne and became emperor. Phokas saw it as shameful for Christendom to pay tribute to heretics, cut off the money from being sent to the Muslims, and thus broke the treaty.

He called one Manuel to lead the army into battle in Sicily. He was a vicious and daring fighter, who was said to be too reckless to be leading armies, but audacious enough to be a soldier. He was too imperious to hear the advice of any formidable strategist, and so when he commanded the troops in Sicily, the whole army was annihilated by the Muslims.[94] In that same year, the emperor appointed John Tzimiskes, a very resilient combatant who was quite adroit in things pertaining to war, to fight the Muslims in Cilicia. He brought forth his army into the town of Adana, and there he encountered a force that did not consist of regular soldiers, but handpicked warriors. This was an elite Islamic garrison.

With both avidity and skill, he charged into the attack, and overtook the Muslim warriors so effectively that his men quickly cut to pieces a good portion of them. The rest of the enemy, who were now about five thousand, fled up a very rugged and steep mountain. John and his men chased them up the peak, and slaughtered all of them, sparing none, and leaving not a single one of them alive, and so much blood was shed that day, that a river of blood flowed down the mountain.[95]

THE MUSLIMS TAKE REVENGE

The next year, the emperor Nikephoros Phokas took a massive army of Christian warriors from Armenia and Spain, alongside a prodigious amount of Greek fighters, into Cilicia to further vanquish the Muslim enemy. He commissioned his brother, Leo, to crush them in Tarsus while he combatted this hellish foe in the land of Mopsuestia. This city was divided in two by quite a long and wide river called Saros, which made it appear to be two cities. A devastating famine plagued the land and like a vicious contagion, tormented the people with hunger.

---

94 John Skylitzes, *Byzantine History*, 14.9
95 John Skylitzes, *Byzantine History*, 14.10

CHRISTIANITY IS AT WAR: THE MANIFESTO FOR CHRISTIAN MILITANCY

The emperor, not allowing this to vitiate him nor his troops, instead used the starvation to his advantage, since it would weaken his enemies. He attacked with full force, and striking the enemy with heavy blows, took half of the city without hindrance. The enemy, using all their wits, simply set the half of the city that was taken by the Christians on fire, burning everything, and then ran to the other side of the river. The sun descended, and no longer could the eyes of the Christians be guided by its light. The Christian troops in Tarsus went out looking for food, and as they were foraging they were quite spread out—too spread out that is. The Muslims snuck behind them, and commenced an ambush. Many of the Christians, and even their commander Monasteriotes, were captured. But captive Christians could not gratify the grueling hunger that the people were enduring, and they flocked to the emperor and begged him to permit them to leave, to which Phokas agreed. They left, and the city was surrendered to him. During his taking of the city, there were numerous Christian crosses, beautifully carved and wonderfully embellished, and after the victory was taken, it was these magnificent crosses that the emperor offered to God, in great thanks and gratitude for his triumph over the enemies of the Holy Trinity.[96]

THE CHRISTIANS STRIKE THE MUSLIMS IN CYPRUS

Before the year passed, and before the crescent of Allah could fully eclipse the flower of Christendom that basked under the light of the Church's rays, Phokas—God fearing king that he was—struck the enemies of God in Cyprus, leading his army into that land, and driving the followers of Muhammad out. From there, he led his troops—who truly denied themselves and placed their lives as sacrifices for God—into Syria, where he unleashed a fury of attacks and incursions all the way down to the coast toward Lebanon. But the Syrians were very bellicose, being more than willing to fight against the Christians with much enthusiasm. Facing such an avidity to fight, and with the hunger that his troops were suffering, Phokas could not force his starving men to endure such a task. He retreated from Syria, and returned to Constantinople.[97]

But the taking of Antioch was still most pertinent to this Christian king. He was not going to give up on a whim, but was sturdily determined, like a house built upon a rock, to capture the city. On a night when the moon was absent from the blanket of stars that flooded the sky, and the air and the earth was flooded by heavy rain, Phokas, alongside three hundred of his warriors, scaled the two watchtowers that guarded the city, and slew the guards.

Once the towers were secured, Phokas called for the reinforcements, led by a eunuch named Peter, to charge into the city and break open its gates. But Peter lost it, fear took him and he hesitated on whether or not he should go forth. As the three hundred soldiers and their emperor were awaiting for the auxiliaries in the watchtowers, alas a whole multitude of Muslims, many of whom were simply part of a local militia, surrounded the towers. They set fire to the edifices, and surely were the warriors in danger of being destroyed.

---

96 John Skylitzes, *Byzantine History*, 14.11–14
97 John Skylitzes, *Byzantine History*, 14.15

In such a moribund situation, and the flames of the fires below approaching closer to their fearful bodies, and the arrows of the enemy piercing through the air and striking against them, hope seemed to dissipate as water evaporates once touched by flames. The commander of the Christian camp could not bear the idea of allowing the men to be slaughtered, so he led his entire army into the fray. The Syrians, hearing of his approach, fled in fear, giving the chance to a commander named Bourtzes, to rush toward the gates and break them open. Once they were open, Peter the eunuch entered Antioch with his entire force, and the illustrious city was taken.[98] In his glorious path of holy war, the emperor took over a hundred cities and fortresses throughout Cilicia, Syria and Phoenicia, the largest of which were Anazarbos, Adana, Mopsuestia, Tarsus, Pagras, Synnephion, Laodikeia, and Aleppo.[99]

THE MUSLIMS ATTACK THE TOMB OF CHRIST, AND THE WIFE OF THE KING BETRAYS CHRISTENDOM

Though Christendom now ruled over lands that rightfully belonged to her, the Muslim thieves, like those in the Temple of God, wanted to steal what was God's to fulfill their rapacious lusts, and so the demons of the abyss seized their souls and had them cause violence against the Christians. A mob of Muslims attacked the archbishop of Antioch, and attacked both his church and his home. The Muslims in Jerusalem, being influenced by the same demonic spirit, seized the archbishop of Jerusalem, and burnt him alive, and then they assailed the beautiful and sacred Church of the Holy Sepulcher, and set it to the flames.[100] The place where Christ was buried, where God in the flesh vanquished death, where Satan was crushed, where eternal life from the sacrifice of the Savior was first evinced—this whole edifice was burnt and defaced by the devilish heretics. And now the Christian clergy was under threat of miserable violence. The two clerics, Pankratios and Gregory, were taken in under the protection and refuge of the righteous Christian emperor, Phokas.

As this Christian sovereign labored arduously to preserve Christendom from the advances of the Muslim heretics, who was behind his back conspiring against him? It was his wife, Theophano who, like Delilah, connived in secret with an enemy named Tziniskes, who hated the emperor because he relieved him of his high position in the government.

She hired him to kill her husband, having nothing but contempt and despicable ingratitude of all the things her husband had done for Christendom. She worshipped only her flesh, and fixated herself solely on the gratification of her own wants. The demon of Mammon possessed her soul, and she bowed down to the devil, who manifested himself as temporal power to which she gave worship. As the pious emperor slept, he was awakened by a kick from Tziniskes. He tried to get up, but fell off his bed; another evildoer, whose name is not worth mentioning, struck him in the head with the sword and split open his skull. They

---

98 John Skylitzes, *Byzantine History*, 14.17
99 John Skylitzes, *Byzantine History*, 14.16
100 John Skylitzes, *Byzantine History*, 14.21

picked him up, abused him and scoffed at him, as Samson was mocked and maltreated by the pagans Delilah conspired with.

All one could hear from the God-fearing emperor was "Lord have mercy" and "Mother of God, help!" The slaves of the demons then cut his head off and showed it off from the balcony, with diabolical boasting, to the palace guards.[101] There, in that room, lied the body of a martyr, and the head of one who gave himself to God, and through the hands of malicious reprobates, did he obtain martyrdom and obtain the crown of glory. Let us remember the great emperor, Phokas, and his mighty feats and deeds for the glory of Christendom, and for the vanquishment of the Islamic hoard who, for so long a time, plagued and tormented the Christians. Let us remember his actions, as ones worthy of emulation for the world today, and let us hope that a sovereign rises up, with the same passion and zeal for Orthodoxy that this man committed himself to. After his martyrdom, the bishop of Melitine inscribed these words onto his coffin:

>Who once sliced men more sharply than the sword
>Is victim of a woman and a glaive.
>Who once retained the whole world in his power
>Now small, is housed in but a yard of earth.
>Whom once it seems by wild beasts was revered
>His wife has slain as though he were a sheep.
>Who chose to sleep but little in the night
>Now sleeps the lasting slumber of the tomb.
>A bitter sight; good ruler, rouse yourself!
>Take footmen, horsemen, archers to the fight,
>The regiments and units of your host—
>For Russians, fully armed, assail our ports,
>The Scyths are anxious to be slaughtering
>While every people does your city harm
>Who once was frightened by your graven face
>Before the gates of your Byzantium.
>Do not ignore these things; cast off the stone
>Which now detains you here and stone the beasts,
>Repel the gentiles; give us, built in stone,
>A firm foundation, solid and secure.
>Or if you would not leave your tomb a while,
>At least cry out from earth against the foe—
>For that alone might scatter them in flight.
>If not, make room for us there in your tomb
>For death, as you well know, is safety and
>Salvation for th'entire Christian folk,

---

101 See John Skylitzes, *Byzantine History*, 14.22

Nikephoros, who vanquished all but Eve.[102]

THE MUSLIMS USE DECEPTION TO RECONQUER ANTIOCH FROM CHRISTENDOM

There is one story that really illustrates the deception of Muslims, and it is of how they retook Antioch from the Christians. There was a prisoner of war from Antioch named Mousaraph, a Muslim who was made a prisoner of war after the conquest of the city.

He told the leader who was made over Antioch, named Spondyles, that if he let him go from captivity, he would fight for the Byzantine Empire against the Muslims. Spondyles believed him, and freed him. Mousaraph told him that he would effectively fight against the enemy if a military fortress was built for him, and again, they listened to him, erecting the bastion in the location that he wanted it to be constructed. After this was complete, Mousaraph went behind the backs of the Christians and made a deal with the emir of Tripoli and a Turk named Duzbari, who at that time was commanding the Egyptians, that they would send him an army with which he would use to assault the Christians and hand over the fortress to them.

One thousand Christian guards protected the fortress, and they were soon attacked and ambushed by Muslim soldiers being led by the very traitor, Mousaraph, and the heretics wiped out and annihilated every guard there. After the bloodbath was created, Mousaraph handed over the fortress to the Muslim leaders, and from there the heretics ensued a warpath throughout the Christian controlled lands of Syria. Constantine Karantenos, whose job it was to protect Syria, was very lax and grew careless, and it was in his inefficiency that the Muslims struck Antioch. Spondyles, the fool who trusted the Muslims, confronted the Muslims, who were led by the Islamic prince of Aleppo, and fought them. He was quickly routed and crushed in the heat of battle.[103]

The very idea of fighting the Muslims struck terror in the heart and trepidation in the mind. Even the patrician, John Chaldos, urged the emperor Romanos III to make a treaty with the Muslims since, as he said, the heat of the desert would be unbearable to an army not conditioned to such a parched and harsh climate and to fighting a people so enduring to the ruthless sun of the Near East. But this did not stop the emperor; he was tough and robust, forbearing and determined, and never did he allow the parlous intensity of warfare inveterate his will for victory. He went off to Syria and established his camp about two days journey from Aleppo, where he sent out the commander Leo Choirosphaktes and corp of troops, to spy on the Arabs and determine whether any of them were planning on making an attack. As they were searching, and wandering about the desert, the air was silent and the whole plain seemed empty. The absence of men relaxed the soldiers, and that is when the enemy attacked; they captured Leo and scattered the troops. The Arabs grew so proud and confident that they hin-

---

102 John Skylitzes, *Byzantine History*, 14.23
103 John of Skylitzes, *Byzantine History*, 18.4

dered the Christians from even foraging for food and water. So thirsty were the men that they, in utter dread and agony, exposed openly themselves to the eyes of the enemy just to obtain a little water. These were swiftly slaughtered without mercy. The patrician Constantine Delassenos was commissioned to drive back the Muslim advancement. He fought the Muslims face to face, but was in little time compelled to flee. He ran back to the camp, breathing heavily, and because of all the terrifying descriptions he brought to the men, utter confusion now flooded the camp. A meeting was conveyed and it was agreed that they would leave back to Antioch.[104]

THE SONG OF ROME

There was a rustic room, designed in the common fashion of the Mediterranean, simple in appearance and yet profound, in that it instilled in the spirit a want for reverence. From a nearby window one could behold the sun awakening from the crevice of the evening, and how it set ablaze the countless little clouds that crowned the sky, and its short rays stirred within the soul a sense of awe, illuminated the hills of a beautiful landscape, an array of farms and majestic villas, and an ancient temple surrounded by devilish statues, with its stone columns and lofty rooftop, in which the pagans worshipped what to them were gods, but in truth, devils. Twilight's silence abounded the crisp air; suddenly the pious chant of monks could be heard. The rhythm of their hymn brought harmony to disorder, peace to chaos, and abated what storms that rage within the soul. Whatever reverence one had by seeing the pagan temple, was disrupted by the chants. It was as though a cosmic war had ensued, between the chant and the paeans of the heathen; between the Cross and the idol, between liberation and bondage. Such a simple moment captured the epitome of a war that has lasted even to this very day, and will continue on till Kingdom come.

In the room there sat a man behind an old rugged desk; his face was aged and his hair grey; his eyes seemed as everlasting as the sky above him, and one could see in them a will as determined as the monks who chanted, and a mind enlightened as the horizon. He was writing on some old parchment, and if one just peered closely at the words he was composing, one could read:

> To all who are in Rome, beloved of God, called to be saints: Grace to you and peace from God our Father and the Lord Jesus Christ. First, I thank my God through Jesus Christ for you all, that your faith is spoken of throughout the whole world. (Romans 1:7–8)

The man was St. Paul, and with his mind inspired by mighty Heaven, he planted the seeds of the Gospel into Rome, and from that infamous city those very seeds would grow into the tree of majestic Christendom. Its strong roots would burrow into the depths of the abyss, uproot the foundations of pagan temples, and cut them asunder. From Rome the light of truth inundated the nations, as the rays of the sun flooded the sky; from Rome the Sword of Christ was unsheathed, and the blade wielded in the eternal war against the armies of hell. To destroy the bastions of false religion was the aspiration of St. Paul, and it was the very

---

104 John Skylitzes, *Byzantine History*, 18.5

mission of those forgotten monks who sung as good soldiers in the battlefield of salvation: it was the chant of Christendom, it was the song of Rome.

MUHAMMAD COMMANDS HIS FOLLOWERS TO CONQUER ROME

The sky was boundless, and absent of all clouds, and the entire earth was scorched by the sun in that land called Arabia. The lusciousness of nature was purged by the ruthless heat; the night owl and the jackal made their home on this desolate land. But they were not alone; for in a certain city, there the devil made his abode. The city was Mecca—the capital of pagandom—and on its center was the last remaining idol that survived the onslaught and victory that Christianity had over the heathen religion. It lied in the Kaaba, and was called the Baitullah, or the 'house of Allah,' that is, the house of Satan. From here all the forces of darkness would wield its blood-stained blade, to take revenge against the holy victories the Sword of Christ won over the wiles of Lucifer.

In this city lived Muhammad, and one day he was asked by his followers: 'Which cities will we conquer?' To this question, Muhammad replied: "You will invade the Arabian Peninsula and Allah will grant it to you. Then you will invade Persia and Allah will grant it to you. Then, you will invade Rome and Allah will grant it to you."[105]

846 AD—THE MUSLIMS INVADE

It was August 23rd, the year 846, and on the roaring shores of Italy a multitude of ships could be seen landing. Armies of soldiers from North Africa departed their vessels, and with them a great many horses. These were the Muslims, and they were here to fulfill what Muhammad foretold to them; they were here to do the will of their father, the devil, and retake the land that St. Paul and St. Peter took, and bring it back to the fold of pagandom.

The earth upon which Rome stood was consecrated by the martyrdoms of these very Apostles; it was here that St. Paul was beheaded; here that St. Peter was crucified upside down, never feeling worthy to be executed like his Lord. Their blood sanctified the city; their blood conquered the city, and now the slaves of heathendom came to reconquer what was brought to the flock of the Mighty Shepherd. The fury of the godless cried out to the highest skies, and made war upon Heaven; the flames of insatiable violence fanned at the sight of a city blessed by crowned martyrs, touched by unconquered saints. To this do we ask with David: "Why do the heathen rage, and the people imagine a vain thing?" (Psalm 2:1) They rode on their horses, and with sacrilegious cries to Allah and Muhammad, charged toward that ancient city, and broke right into Rome. Ah, how the pagans plunged into a frenzy as soon as their eyes spotted the relics, the churches, and the tombs of holy men. The devils within them agitated their spirits, and so the Muslims, obeying their anger, foamed at the mouth in dripping rage. When they saw the tomb of St. Peter, they sacked his sepulcher and stripped away the silver altar that lied over it, desecrated every altar they could find, and overran Saint Peter's Basilica in the name of Allah and for their hatred of the Gospel.

---

[105] Quoted from a hadith narrated by Nafi, the son of Utbah

☦ CHRISTIANITY IS AT WAR: THE MANIFESTO FOR CHRISTIAN MILITANCY

Why should we be surprised at this? We should never forget what significance Rome has in the story of Christendom. It was Peter who preached to the first church in Rome, and as he quenched the souls of the earliest Christians with the watering of the Word, St. Mark stood by him, recording everything he said that pertained to the life of Christ. From his hearing of St. Peter in Rome, Mark produced his Gospel that still blesses us today with eternal truths.

It is in Mark's Gospel where we read that beautiful story in which the Jews ask Christ: "Art thou the Christ, the Son of the Blessed?" and to which Christ declares: "I am: and ye shall see the Son of man sitting on the right hand of power, and coming in the clouds of heaven." (Mark 14:61-62) And it was now, in this invasion of Rome, where the people who rejected the Christ were invading the city, to destroy the teachings of the Crucified One, and replace it with the blasphemous doctrine that states that Jesus is not the Son of God. They pillaged and plundered; and the numbers slaughtered were as great as the cries of agony that reached to the empyrean. Pope Sergius II, following the commission to be a good shepherd, called a holy war against the heathen invaders. King Lothair I, a righteous ruler of Christendom, declared war on the Muslims and aspired to defend Rome and the Church of St. Peter. In a letter he expressed his woes over the now tormented city:

> No one doubts that it is because our sins and iniquities deserve it that so great an ill has befallen Christ's church and even the very Roman church which is the head of christendom has fallen into the hands of infidels and throughout all the borders of our realm and that of our brothers the people of the pagans has prevailed. Therefore we have firmly judged it necessary that he is particularly offended by us and that by making fitting satisfaction we may endeavor to placate the divine justice, so that we can have him placated whom we realize to be angry."

THE CHRISTIANS FIGHT BACK IN A HOLY WAR TO DEFEND ROME

Lothair had an army of mighty men, conditioned for hardship and eager to fight, march against the Muslims and vanquish them. The battle was swift and deadly, and it was so fierce that the Muslims fled the great city, and stayed in the nearby land of Gaeta where they made their position on a very well-fortified mountain. A large army of Franks saw the Muslim forces and, avid and fervent for justice, commenced a sharp attack on the enemy. The Muslims were prepared; they, with great prowess, overtook the Christians, slew their standard bearer, and slaughtered the rest of them. King Louis II, Lothair's son, tried to complete the battle from where his father failed, but he too was faced with terrifying opposition.

The crescent shaped scimitars of pagandom clashed against the cross shaped swords of Christendom, and many rivers of blood flowed from the torrential nebulous of gore, severed flesh, mutilated bodies, and bone chilling screams. King Louis fled to Rome, his spirit cut in two, his will broken, his morale crushed by the despair of defeat. After they spilt the blood of so many selfless warriors, the Muslims were determined to take the entire city of Gaeta. But, right on the shores of land, they were met with numerous ships from Naples and Amalfi, headed by the dauntless Caesarius, who so efficiently defended the city that the heathens made a run for it.

THE MUSLIMS RAVAGE ITALY
Although they were now defeated, this did not stop the heretics as they treaded the land of Christian Italy, hungry for saintly blood. Like hyenas, they preyed upon the church of St. Andrew and consumed it with flames. They then set their sights on the church of St. Apollinares, seeking to burn down the sacred edifice. The monks within the church knew that the Muslims were coming for their doom. They were filled with terror and knew that by themselves they were helpless. They expected death, but still within their consternated souls there was still some hope. As the savages preyed upon them, they prayed to the Lord and sought out his mercy. The abbot of the monastery, Bassacius, suddenly had a vision: his predecessor, Apollinaris, told him to have the monks have masses and to conduct litanies. The monk obeyed; they did their masses and made their petitions before God; they, like good penitents, walked barefoot and put ashes on their heads. They cried out to the Almighty, and waited on Him, clinging onto the Lord and depending on no one else. As the Muslims were approaching, all of a sudden a raging storm came down upon them, and the land flooded with raging waters. The pagans could not get any nearer, for fear of being caught in the relentless waves. The slaves of Allah had no choice: they made a truce with Caesarius, and departed from the blessed land.

A HERO ARISES TO LEAD CHRISTENDOM INTO BATTLE
Although the savage enemy was now gone, they did not leave the land unconquered; for the armies of agony now vanquished the hearts of the people, and drops of sorrow tainted their beings, and covered the city as moist dew overspreads the green grass of a humid morning. The Church of Rome was first headed by St. Peter who exclaimed with inspired mind: "Thou art the Christ, the Son of the living God." (Matthew 16:16) This was the declaration of faith, upon which the Church still stands, and it was this declaration that the Muslims sought to destroy when they desired the city in which Peter lied buried. But let us never forget the words of our Lord after Peter declared his holy words: "That thou art Peter, and upon this rock I will build my church; and the gates of hell shall not prevail against it." (Matthew 16:18) And so, with the storm of pagan fury looming, surely this was an attack from the realm of the diabolical, a declaration of war, not just against humankind, but against Heaven itself.

As one viewed the old metropolis, one could see a little monastery. Its appearance was modest, and yet through its simplicity it did not fail to pull one into a sense of divine mystery. It lied at a close distance from the ruins of the Colosseum, as though it were making a declaration of victory: 'Here once stood the pride of pagandom, and now it lies dead and only in decayed remains for all the world to remember your defeat at the war of the Cross; and here lies the Church—simple and humble, fierce and just—enduring forever, and always withstanding the onslaught of hades.'

CHRISTIANITY IS AT WAR: THE MANIFESTO FOR CHRISTIAN MILITANCY

The monastery was called the Quattuor Coronatti, or The Four Crowned Martyrs; it was dedicated to four Christians who were executed by the emperor Diocletian for refusing to make a sacrifice to the demon, Aesculapius. The names of these four martyrs were unknown, and till this day they remain anonymous, as so many heroes of old, who fought and died for the Faith, remain without praise and with names not remembered. Inside the monastery the walls were decorated with frescos bearing the icons of saints, martyrs, and angels. An aged man sat down in a rugged room, perfect for the monastic. The room was without noise, and he took refuge in the silence; his spirit stilled through prayer, his mind contemplative, his heart heavy with sorrow, not for himself, but for others. He may have looked at the angels, and wondered to himself how many angels were now looking upon the city from above. Suddenly, the door abruptly opened, and a multitude of enraged people rushed up and eagerly seized him. They did not yell curses or insults, but instead, they sang hymns and exalted him. They brought him to the Lateran palace, let him go so that he could stand, and kissed his feet with pious reverence. The Pope, Sergius II, was now dead, and they all wanted him to take the pontificate. It did not matter if he refused, the people wanted him to be their bishop, and so he ascended the pontificate, and took the name Leo IV.

In this day, after the city had suffered such a great attack, one could see throughout the populace the hearts of the people melted in the glowing flames of contrition; the desires of the flesh no longer seized them, but their passions now shifted from sin to sainthood. The people wanted to honor God, to perpetuate Orthodoxy and preserve Christendom, and they understood that the only way to do this was not through some superficial secular war, where victory is won and vice embraced, but a religious war—a holy war. They did not ask a king, but a pope to lead them into a battle. Surely was this a nation carrying its cross, surely was this a crusade.

THE VENGEANCE OF GOD DESTROYS THE MUSLIMS

Leo prayed earnestly to God for justice, and requested from Him due punishment upon those Muslims who had just pillaged and ransacked the holy churches of Rome. The Muslims who pillaged the city were now leaving Italy. They entered their ships and sailed off with their bellies satisfied and their flesh gratified. In time, they were so close to their country in North Africa that they could see the mountains of their land ever so clearly, and they cheered with joy.

Then suddenly another boat appeared amongst theirs; it was not one of their own, and on its deck were two men. One was dressed like a priest and the other like a monk. The pirates were dumbfounded at this, not having the slightest idea of who these men were. The two mysterious men asked them: "Where have you come from and where are you going to?" The Muslims replied: "We come back from Peter in Rome, where we have laid waste his entire shrine and despoiled the people and the region. We have defeated the Franks and burnt down Benedict's cells. But tell us who you are."

"You will soon see who we are"

The rise of roaring waves struck at their ears, they looked up and saw high waves from a rushing storm. The mighty waters broke right through their ships and smashed all of them;

the ocean swallowed them up, and their bodies plunged into the boundless abyss, as the waves of the Red Sea crushed the Egyptians.

ST. PETER'S BASILICA IS RESTORED AND REPAIRED
After the savages drowned in the waves and received the deaths they justly deserved, Leo dedicated his time to the Basilica of St. Peter, to restore what the heretics had stolen. He embellished the sanctuary with the ornaments fitting for such a holy place; and he arrayed the church with ten veils, and on each was embroidered the image of a lion. The meaning of his name, Leo, is lion, and this is what Christendom needed at so forlorn a time. "The wicked flee when no man pursueth: but the righteous are bold as a lion." (Proverbs 28:1) The wicked were on their way, and the mighty lion was patiently awaiting for the hyenas to arrive.

He approached the tomb of St. Peter and encompassed its altar with golden panels on which were engraved depictions of the Holy Cross, Jesus Christ and His Resurrection. They were placed together, as if to say: From noble suffering, springs liberation. The Christians of Rome had just underwent a most harsh violence, and all hoped to resurrect from the tomb of despair.

THE POPE STRENGTHENS HIS BRETHREN
Pope Leo IV had the city's walls repaired; fifteen towers were built or renewed, and an iron chain was drawn across the Tiber River to hinder any enemy naval ships from sailing into Rome. The devil never gave up in taking the city for his rule; he inspired the minds of the Muslims, and reminded them of what great treasured lied in Rome, and how many riches they would acquire if they conquered the metropolis. They entered their ships and praised the demon they called Allah, and sailed into the nation of Italy. The savages soon arrived to the shores of a place called Totarum close to the island of Sardinia, and there they lingered about waiting, like wolves, for the right moment to make their attack. After some time they resumed their journey, and eventually arrived at the Port of Rome.

From a distance the local Christians saw the barbarians arrive, and they were so filled with fear. The news spread throughout, that the Muslims were here, but not everyone reacted with fear. Divine Providence stirred the hearts of the mighty men of Naples, of Amalfi and Gaeta, and they all offered themselves up as warriors for a holy cause: a war against the forces of evil. The armies of God gathered together, entered their ships and sailed to Rome where they informed the Pope of their arrival. Leo received the elite of their number, amongst them the valiant Caesarius, with a hospitable reception in the Lateran palace, and asked them as to what they desired. They replied that they desired for nothing else but to warn him of the invasion to come, and to assemble their fighting men and "to win a victory with the Lord's help over the pagans." The Christian fighters ascended their praises on high, thanking Almighty God for sending them such a shepherd to strengthen them. Leo simply followed the command our Lord gave to his predecessor, St. Peter: "strengthen thy brethren." (Luke 22:32) And now a successor of St. Peter, Leo, was obeying the orders of his Eternal General,

CHRISTIANITY IS AT WAR: THE MANIFESTO FOR CHRISTIAN MILITANCY

and gave strength to the warriors to protect the city in which (in the words of Tertullian) "Peter endures a passion like his Lord's!"[106]

When Christ told St. Peter, "Put your sword into the sheath" (John 18:11), he never discarded the sword, only sheathed it within the Church for a time when it must be properly used. Now was that time, and Leo was rightfully unsheathing it.

THE SUCCESSORS OF CORNELIUS PREPARE THEIR SOULS FOR COMBAT

Is it not profound that the first gentile to enter the doors of the Church was a warrior? His name was Cornelius, and he was no effeminate, but a centurion of the Italian division. Through him, the gentile world was opened to the embraces of the Church; through him, the warriors of Europe took up their crosses and became the strong arm of Christendom. A warrior named Cornelius stood before St. Peter to receive his intercession, and now a multitude of Cornelius' successors stood before the successor of St. Peter, also awaiting his intercession, to pray and ask God for the salvation of the city. They all gathered together at the church of St. Aurea, and there the priest stood before his warriors; he chanted the beautiful hymns of monks—the music that agitated the devils who so possessed the Muslims who were now on their way. He prostrated on his knees, and like the prophets of Israel declared:

> O God, whose right hand raised up St. Peter the apostle lest he sink when walking on the water, and delivered from the depths of the sea his fellow-apostle Paul when three times shipwrecked, graciously hear us and grant that, by the merits of them both, the limbs of these thy faithful contending against the enemies of the holy church, may be fortified by thy almighty right hand and gain strength; that by their gaining triumph thy holy name may be seen glorious among all races; through [our Lord Jesus Christ]."

As Melchizedek "brought out bread and wine" (Genesis 14:18) before the warrior Abraham, Leo took bread and wine and consecrated it, and gave the Lord's body to the mouths of valorous fighters, ready to give their lives after the holy supper, as Christ gave His after the Last Supper.

THE FINAL BATTLE FOR ROME

On the waves of the shore could be seen a great number of colossal ships. The sound of the clamoring waters was heard alongside the noise of people speaking Arabic. It was the next day, and the Muslim ships were on the beach of Ostia, a suburb of Rome. Though the sun had already arisen, it seemed as though dawn did not flee, and nor did it haste on that day that seemed endless, when it brought forth its hopeful light. The tremulous waves of the heathen torrent were on the horizon, wanting to clash into that rock, upon which, Christ said, "I will build My church, and the gates of Hell shall not prevail against it." (Matthew 16:18)

Here the warriors stood, to defend that city consecrated by the blood of Peter and Paul, who fought a good warfare and endured for Jesus Christ, enduring the axe and the gibbet in

---

106 Tertullian, *On the Prescription Against Heretics*, ch. 36

the battlefield of the spirit. And now these men of valor, carrying their crosses as their two Apostles had done, were prepared to receive the blows of the enemy, and to strike with all fortitude in the spirit of zeal. The Muslim armies were still in their ships and as they thought of gain and plunder, an array of other ships manned by Christian warriors from Naples suddenly appeared in their presence and launched an attack upon them.

The Italian Christians shot forth their missiles and struck the enemy; Muslims lied down wounded, but still none tasted death. The Muslims made their maddening prayer to Allah and advanced for a naval attack. The clash continued. Suddenly, out of nowhere, a gust of mighty winds stirred the air, and a ruthless tempest smashed right into their midst. So overpowering were these winds that the seas arose and waves cried as they scattered about the helpless ships. The vessels ascended up as the lofty waves carried them, and descended ever so low as the waters dropped under the force of the screaming storm. While the Christians were in disarray, the Muslim ships were devastated in the broom of destruction that tore them apart. So miraculous was this sight that the Christian onlookers could sing with Moses: "And with the blast of Your nostrils The waters were gathered together; The floods stood upright like a heap; The depths congealed in the heart of the sea." (Exodus 15:8)

The enemy was now utterly defenseless, and the time to attack was now. The Muslims who had not been consumed by the thundering seas made their way to some nearby Italian islands. On these isles the Christians met their enemy, and with their swords—shaped like crosses—they made a great slaughter of those who held swords in the shape of crescents. The survivors were seized and taken to Rome where many of them were hung. The rest were taught Christianity and made to repair what damages their people brought to the churches.

Victory had been won; the crowning city of Christendom was saved by God through the arm of zealous men. After some time, Pope Leo IV went to the gate of the city that overlooks St. Peregrinus, and with fervent heart and impenetrable spirit, he cried out:

> O God, who didst confer on thy apostle Peter the keys of the kingdom of heaven and didst grant him the pontificate of binding and loosing, grant that by the help of his intercession we may be delivered from the bonds of our sins; and cause that this city which we have newly founded with thy assistance may ever remain safe from thy wrath and have new and manifold triumphs over the enemy on whose account it has been constructed; through [our Lord Jesus Christ].

The Muslims tried to invade Rome seven times, and seven times did they fail. Never will they ever succeed in breaking the Cross of this eternal city; never will the crescent vanquish the holy emblem of our warfare. The successors of Cornelius the Italian repulsed the pagan invader, and his successors still live on today, destined to fight in the Final Crusade against the Antichrist, and fulfill the prophecy that says: "the galleys and the Romans shall come upon him" (Daniel 11:30). Soon the Muslims will try again to take Rome, but never will they conquer the Christians of this city, "beloved of God, called to be saints" (Romans 1:7).[107]

THE BATTLE OVER EURIPOS
In the late ninth century, Esman, the emir of Tarsus, exalted himself in past victories over Christian armies, and being puffed up with pride, he readied thirty ships and set out to conquer the Greek city of Euripos. The emperor at the time, Basil I, received knowledge of this planned a heavy bombardment, and so he appointed the general, Oniates, to fight and defeat the Muslim enemy.

Oniates spared no time, and did not deprive the city of any machine or weapon that would defend the city from the impending Islamic siege. He placed catapults that would launch stones that could crush the heads of the attackers, and defense machines that could fire arrows and pierce the bodies of any charging adversary. When the Muslim fleet arrived around the city's walls, and launched their bombardments against the metropolis, the Greek Christians burst with energy and exuberance, enthusiastic about the heat of the fray, and more than willing to fight and combat the enemies of God.

The Christians sailed their ships into the ranks of the Islamic fleet, and presented to them a weapon the Muslims were not prepared for: Greek fire. They fired at the Muslims with indistinguishable flames, and the enemy within a swift moment found themselves combusted and consumed in fire, their flesh burning with an insatiable blaze. They were at a loss at what to do, and so deeming the Christians as greedy, like themselves, they took up a large shield filled with gold, and said that this, alongside the finest one hundred virgins taken from their captives, would be given to the first man who would scale the walls and fight them hand to hand.

The Christian defenders who stood behind the walls of the city took up the challenge, and encouraging each other to fight with strength and might against the enemy, they opened the gates and unleashed the most ferocious attack they could muster, executing with all the fury that they could execute upon the Muslims. The emir Esman was immediately hit with a mortal wound and fell dead, and in a little time the Christians managed to make a great slaughter and massacre of the Islamic attackers. The survivors manned what few ships were left and took off in shame and humiliation.[108]

THE MUSLIMS MAKE A SURPRISE ATTACK ON THE CHRISTIANS, BUT ONE CHRISTIAN GENERAL LEADS AN ARMY AND CRUSHES THE ISLAMIC ENEMY
The king of Tunisia, Husayn bin Rabah, sent sixty ships that were exceedingly large against the Christians. They destroyed and devastated the islands of Kephalonia and Zakynthos, and seized many Christians who they made captives and prisoners. Swiftly did the emperor

---

107 This entire rendition of the Battle of Ostia is based on the *Liber Pontificalis*, 104–105, trans. Raymond Davis (see also his commentary); Gibbon, *Decline and Fall*, vol. v, ch. lii, pp. 973–75; Mosheim's *Church History*, The Ninth Century, part i, ch. ii, p. 209
108 Skylitzes, *Byzantine History*, 6.29

Basil I act when he saw this vicious enemy wreaking such havoc and death upon his empire. He sent out a whole squadron of ships headed by one Nasar, a very shrewd and brutal naval commander, who had both the fortitude and the prudence efficient enough to crush the Islamic enemy. He led his fleet into the area of Methone, but was hindered from continuing on because many of his oarsmen made a quick escape and deserted the ships.

Nasar immediately sent a letter to the emperor informing him on the desertion, and in less time than it would take to describe the entire story, he caught all of the deserters as they were trying to flee and disappear. To instill fear into the runaway oarsmen, he took thirty Muslim captives, covered their faces with soot to make it impossible to distinguish or recognize them as Muslims, and sent them off to the Peloponnese—as though they were the deserters—where they were publicly whipped and then impaled.

Terror struck the entire Roman fleet, and every thought of convenience and repose was cast aside from their minds, and the sailors begged Nasar to attack the enemy. While in the Peloponnese, Nasar was given assurance by the local Peloponnesian commander that he had his and his fighting men's full cooperation for the attack against the Muslims. The Christians were thus ready for battle.

The Muslims scolded the Roman fleet with utter contempt because of their past victories, and with pomposity, they attacked the surrounding area. As they brought much havoc and torment to the local Christians, there came, under the shield of night, the Christian fleet, and they were very close to the Muslim ships. Nasar ordered a dauntless attack on the enemy, and the Muslims, not being able to make a quick counter, were getting slaughtered. Nasar commanded that Greek fire be unleashed upon the enemy, and when the flames burst forth they wrapped themselves around the Muslim sailors, and consumed their flesh. The Muslim army was annihilated, and who did Nasar dedicate such a victory to? He dedicated it solely to God,[109] for surely was this a holy war. Nasar later guided his fleet to Sicily where he attacked and besieged all of the Christian cities under Islamic control. He continued on into southern Italy, where he executed fierce and tenacious attacks against the Muslims, destroying all of the Arab controlled fortresses in Calabria and Longobardia.[110]

THE MUSLIMS TRY TO RETAKE SICILY, BUT THE CHRISTIANS CARRY UP THEIR CROSS AND FIGHT THEM WITH ALL COURAGE

After the victory, when the winter season passed, and the spring arrived, the Muslims, not hearing of any military fleets being sent by the emperor, assumed that he must have been engaged with something else, and so executed another invasion into Sicily where they bombarded the city of Syracuse with a brutal siege. The emperor sent a fleet led by the commander Adrian, to defend the city, but it was easily hindered by the capricious weather, and in due time the Muslims managed to take all of Syracuse.

---

109 Skylitzes, *Byzantine History*, 6.33
110 Skylitzes, *Byzantine History*, 6.33

Much blood was shed, and many martyrs were made, as the Muslims slaughtered many of the stout and stubborn Sicilian Christians who refused Islam. Those who were not killed were bound by chains and fetters, and all of the holy churches, wherein the people would communicate with God, were put to the flames. When the news of the devastation was confirmed to Adrian, he turned his fleet around and fled to Constantinople, where he hid in terror in the Hagia Sophia. He was dragged out and exiled for desertion.[111] The general Nikephoros with his entire force, alongside even a body of Manichaean soldiers under the command of Diokonitzes, went into southern Italy and launched many incursions against the Muslims. Nikephoros baffled and shook the sturdy spirit of the Muslims with his effective attacks; he then seized the cities of Amantia, Tropai, and Saint-Severine, from Muslim control into the rule of Christendom.[112]

A SAVAGE HERETIC HELPS THE MUSLIMS SLAUGHTER INNOCENT CHRISTIANS

In the reign of the emperor Leo VI, the Muslims struck Sicily again, and with their blood stained hands conquered the city of Taormina, where they butchered a large number of Christians. Their eyes were not satisfied with the sight of their conquest, and so they turned to the island of Lemnos; they overran this land, and a considerable number of people were made into slaves.[113]

A dreadful hindrance distracted the empire when the Romans were occupied with fighting the Bulgarians, for while they were focused on this enemy, the Muslims took the advantage and began tearing apart the Roman shores with surprise attacks. Helping the Muslims was an apostate Christian who converted to Islam named Leo of Attaleia, who lived in Tripoli, and because of this received the nickname, Tripolites.

The emperor appointed one Eustathios to combat the Islamic horde, but he was not able to endure the attacks of Tripolites, the apostate, and instead of pursuing the enemy he ended up as the pursued, fleeing the enemy all the way to the Hellespoint and as far as Parion. The emperor sent another force, this time under the commander Himerios. He spotted Tripolites and his Muslim allies in the harbor of Thasos, but when he gazed upon their great numbers and the sheer superiority of force and strength, he refused to commence an attack, knowing within himself that victory would not be established upon so great a multitude. Because of this, Tripolites freely sailed to Thessalonike, blockaded the entire region, captured it, and then took for his prisoner the commander Leo Chatzilakios.

So much Christian blood was spilt on that day, and so many of these poor saints were forced into slavery. A poor sick businessman, named Rhodophyles, was resting in Thessa-

---

111 Skylitzes, *Byzantine History*, 6.37
112 Skylitzes, *Byzantine History*, 6.38
113 John Skylitzes, *Byzantine History*, 7.21

lonike when the invasion occurred. Tripolites entered his room and tortured him to death with his own bare hands. He then stole all of his gold and went his way.[114]

The savage heretic Tripolites would later lead three hundred Muslim ships alongside Damian, the emir of Tyre, and smash right into Christian territory. The admiral of the Roman navy, Himerios, spotted causing their trouble off the coast of Samos. The battle ensued, the Christians found themselves to be at the receiving end of the vicious assault, and the result was purely dreadful. So bad was the defeat, that by the end the Christian ships were scattered about, without order nor organization, wandering about for desperate survival, or absent of all life.[115]

THE POPE DECLARES A MAJOR CRUSADE AGAINST THE MUSLIMS

In the tenth century, Pope Sylvester II, in the first year of his pontificate, declared for a crusade to liberate the Holy Land. When we think upon that glorious history, of the Cross combating the acolytes of Satan, we so commonly mention the wars between Christian and Muslim. How little is the age known, of that war between the Catholic and the waves of Allah's slaves, between that Church which Peter and Paul founded in Rome as that great city was plunged into darkness. It was Pope Sylvester II, in the first year of his pontificate in that peak of the tenth century, who was the first to have sat on the throne of St. Peter and declare a war upon the Muslims to liberate the Holy Land,[116] where God Himself walked and instilled and advanced the most holy laws; where He defeated the devil as Samson destroyed the temple of Dagon; where He bore the Holy Cross and rose to the most serene Heaven, of which time the saints cry Hallelujah.

From the city of Rheims, in 984 A.D., he wrote with sublime words an epistle through the perspective of the anguished Jerusalem, calling for Christian warriors to rise against the heretics who wrongly ruled the Holy City:

> Behold! The world still regards me [Jerusalem] as the best part of itself, prostrate though I am. With me are the oracles of the prophets, the manifestations of the patriarchs; here the clear lights of the world, the apostles, made their appearance; here it [the world] discovered the faith of Christ; with me found its Redeemer. For, although He may be everywhere in His divine nature, yet in His human nature here was He born, did He suffer, was He buried, and from here was He raised up to heaven. But, though the prophet has said: 'His sepulcher be glorious' [Isa. 11:10], now that the infidels have overthrown the sacred places, the devil strives to render it inglorious. Shine forth, therefore, soldier of Christ, be His standard-bearer and cofighter; and because you are not powerful in arms, assist with counsel and the aid of riches. [Consider] what you are giving, and to whom you give it. Assuredly it is only a little from great wealth, even though [you give it] to that Man who notwithstanding His giving freely all that you have, nevertheless receives not ungratefully. For He multiplies, and He

---

114 John Skylitzes, *Byzantine History*, 7.23–24
115 John Skylitzes, *Byzantine History*, 7.33
116 See Mosheim's *Church History*, vol. i, 9th century, part ii, ch. 1.10, p. 238

rewards in the future. Through me He blesses you that you may grow by giving, and He forgives sins so that you may live by reigning with Him. [117]

His urging for holy war against the infidel was heard by only a few pious Italians from Pisa, but not enough to launch an efficient strike. They partook in some fighting on the Syrian coast, but nothing beyond that.[118]

THE MUSLIMS SLAUGHTER CHRISTIAN PILGRIMS TRYING TO GO TO THE HOLY LAND

In the eleventh century Muslim persecution toward Christians increased in momentum. The Church of the Holy Sepulcher, along with other sanctuaries, were destroyed, and in 1064 seven thousand Christian German pilgrims, piously visiting the Holy Land, were so viciously attacked by the Arabs that only two thousand returned alive.[119] Those poor pilgrims traveled with weary feet and pious poverty; money had they not, their souls elated with charity; their eyes were toward heaven, their faith was simple and rustic, their bodies content with the food of the Spirit, their minds meditative on those sublime words of Christ:

> If thou wilt be perfect, go and sell that thou hast and give to the poor, and thou shalt have treasure in heaven: and come and follow me. (Matthew 19:21)

They chose rather to behold the sacred land and its holy sanctuaries with their own eyes, as opposed to just reading of them in the Scriptures. Even the dust of this land was adored as deserving reverence, "For thy servants take pleasure in her stones, and favour the dust thereof." (Psalm 102:14) And the rustic pilgrims took with delight some of it back to Europe to receive adoration. They returned home with palm-branches, as the earliest reverencers of Christ held these up in His presence, and placed them above the altar of their churches. So holy was Israel to the early Christians that pilgrims from Germany, England, Spain, and even as far as Ethiopia and India would travel just to see the place where the Lord lived.[120] Such temples of God were to the enmity of that old serpent, and so did many of them become those saints in Heaven who cry to their Saviour for the peace of the eternal Church.

When Christians were afflicted by the Muslims in Jerusalem, St. John of Almoner, patriarch of Alexandria, exemplified a most admirable expression of charity, and sent much money to them. The slightest complaint from the tormented Christians resulted with the Muslims threatening to destroy the Church of the Resurrection.[121]

But, after much time and many battles and revolts, Islam began to lose its grips over the Christian provinces that it conquered. While the ideology of Islam came from the Arab, the power of Islam fully came about by the sword of the Mongol Turks.

---

117 *The Letters of Gerbert*, Letter 36, trans. Harriet Pratt Lattin, the first brackets are mine
118 Moshem's *Church History*, 9th century, part ii, ch. 1.10, pp. 238–39; Mills, Hist. Crus. ch. i, p. 20
119 Moczar, *Seven Lies about Catholic History*, ch. iii, p. 58; *Islam at the Gates*, prologue, act 3, p. 21; Mills, Hist. Crus. ch. i, p. 17
120 Mills, Hist. Crus. ch. i, p. 14, 15
121 Mills, Hist. Crus. ch. i, pp. 17, 19

THE RISE OF THE TURKS AND THE RESTORATION OF ISLAMIC POWER

When the Arabs controlled Syria, Armenia, North Africa, Iraq, Arabia, Iran, and other lands of the East, they were not capable of controlling their provinces due to their lack of unity and military strength. The Arab would conquer a land only to lose it just as fast as he captured it.

The intermixture of other peoples with the Arabs, on account of the conquests of Persia, the Berbers and other Asian tribes, diluted Arabian unity on which Islamic strength rested, and division sprung amongst the Muslims.

Hope was lost for the utopian vision of Muhammad, and it was believed that the Arab Islamic empire was finally about to crumble and allow the Christian Byzantine Empire to recover what it had lost from Muslim invasions. Until all of a sudden bands of Mongol hordes, experts in archery and cruelty, swiftly swarmed into the Middle East where they would find a religion that fit their savagery, Islam. By becoming Muslims, the Mongols, being stronger in body and more warlike than the Arab, reinvigorated the Islamic empire. By the eleventh century they would replace the Arabs in power, and with their sadism and destructive temperament, they ravaged, pillaged and massacred everywhere they went, dominating the central power of the Muslim world.

Between 1038 and 1092, all Persia, Arabia, and most of Syria, was under the Turks. They captured Jerusalem from the Arabs in 1076 and ruled it for eighteen years, only to lose it to the Egyptian Muslims, or the Shiite Fatimids.

The Sunni Power of the Abbasids was fragmenting on account of the Shiite, and it appeared that the latter was about to fully triumph, until the Turks arrived. These Turks were part of the Oghuz people, a race of the Huns who had the appearance of the Mongolians or the Japanese. Like the Mongols, they originally worshipped the Blue Sky, but many of them converted to Buddhism, the first external religion that they accepted. By the mid-eighth century a significant portion of them converted to the Manichaean and Nestorian heresies. But the religion that truly united them, and gave rise to the Turkish Empire was Islam.

The Oghuz Turks who converted to Islam were part of a branch of Turk called the Seljuk. These originated from a Turkic people called the Qarakhanids, who initially were ruled by a Manichaean elite, but they also consisted of many Buddhists. The Qarakhanids then conquered the area of Balasaghun in Kyrgyzstan, and it was after this, in the mid-tenth century, that they converted to Islam. From the Islamic Qarakhandids, came a fringe family who broke away from them, these were Seljuks, founded by Saljuk ibn Duqaq, and it was these Turks who would commence the first Turkish Islamic empire. The type of Islam that the Turks accepted, however, was not exactly the mechanical form of Sunni Islam that most Muslims follow, but the severely mystical Sufi Islam, which appealed to them more since it was quite paralleled to Buddhism. From Attila the Hun to the Muslims who massacred the

Armenians, they brought nothing constructive, only death. They slaughtered by the millions, and made the most fertile of land into a desert—these are the Turks.[122]

THE SELJUKS STRIKE

Out of all the Turkish people which penetrated into the East from Asia at this time, the ones which made the most effect on Christendom were the Seljuk Turks. Three generations before the eleventh century, a small tyrant named Seljuk, who converted from worshipping the sky to venerating Allah, became the kingpin of various Mongol bandit groups which formed a formidable army once put together. They were really Huns "living to the north of the Caucasus mountains, populous and autonomous, never enslaved by any nation."[123]

Seljuk had three sons, Musa, Mik'ail, and Arslan Isra'il. The Turks would be led by the two sons of Mik'ail, Togril Bey and Chagrhi Bey.[124] Their onslaught began when the Muslim king of Persia, Mahmud the Ghaznavid, requested from Turkmenistan (the mother land of the Turks) three thousand troops to assist him in his wars against the Indians and Babylonians. This request was granted, and three thousand Turks under Togril Bey were dispatched.

The Turks did this with the hope that if they could defeat the enemies of Persia, they could gain entry through the bridge on the river Araxes, by which the Turks could enter Persia and conquer it. In a battle done for Persia, Togril defeated the Buyid emir, al-Basasiri.[125] The Buyids were a very a powerful Shiite empire in the Muslim world, and an eternal enemy of the Sunnis. The Sunni Persians, then, were using the Turks to obliterate the Shiite power, and replace it with the Sunni Caliphate. Because the Turks were a small number in comparison to the local Muslims of the Near East, they made their base in the Steppes between the Caspian and the Aral seas, to the north of Khorasan, and from there conducted their raids.[126] They seized carriages, pillaged and executed horrific massacres.

They conquered territories by a very simple but effective strategy: thousands of them would come upon their victims on horseback quickly firing arrows from numerous directions, and then speedily retreat. Once they spotted fear, they would as one body charge directly at the people, and with a very sharp, carved, and thin sword, cut right through their bodies and make a great slaughter. Once the Muslims proclaimed him king of Persia, Togril ordered the slaughter of all the guards of the bridge on the Araxes River, thus enabling any Turk to cross into Persia without hindrance.

The Hunnic savages flocked to the bridge, flooded Persia and then began an outright massacre of the Persian and Arab populations. He ousted out all of the local governors and

---

122 See Belloc, *The Crusades*, ch. ii, pp. 9–11; *The Great Heresies*, The Great and Enduring Heresy of Muhammad, p. 50; Moczar, *Islam at the Gates*, prologue, act 3, p. 19; Mills, Hist. Crus. ch. i, p. 2; Nicolle, *Manzikert 1071*, ch. 1, pp. 8, 12
123 John Skylitzes, *Byzantine History*, 21.9. Michael Attaleiates calls the Seljuks "Nephthalite Huns" (History, 8.1; 14.1)
124 See footnote 106, by Jean Claude-Cheynet, in John Skylitzes, *Byzantine History*, 21.9
125 John Skylitzes, *Byzantine History*, 21.9, f. 107
126 John Skylitzes, *Byzantine History*, 21.9, f. 110

replaced their seats with Turks, and entirely humiliated the people of that land. Togrul Beg, Seljuk's grandson, would expand the Turkic power throughout the Middle East and forge an empire that would always remain in the memories of the ancient Christians. He drove out the Ghaznavid government from Persia, forced Iraq under Turkish jurisdiction, and would place Media under his rule.[127]

THE SELJUKS ATTACK CHRISTENDOM

It was not as though Christendom was in comfortable peace during the Islamic onslaught; for the devil's forces, just as today, abounded, and never ceased in their endeavor to destroy the Church. In the Germany the Christians were fighting the Asiatic pagans; Christianity in England was nearly wiped out by the Vikings from the north who would also attack the Faith in northern France; and from the South and the South-East sprang forth the plague of Islam.[128]

The Seljuks under Togril invaded and overtook significant regions of Georgia, they also seized Mesopotamia, Melitene, Koloneia, and all of the regions adjacent to the Euphrates River. If it was not for the brave Romans who fought and died striving to defend their lands, the Turks would have reached all the way to the Christian lands of Galatia, Honorias, and Phrygia.[129]

The weakness of the Byzantine Empire was not on account of its warriors, for these were brave and very willing to fight and take victory, but the moral decay within its own government. The soldiers were deprived of the necessary supplies with which to fight sufficiently, the best soldiers were let go from their duties, and they were horrendously deprived of adequate pay. In the words of the ancient Christian historian, Michael Attaleiates,

> When the need was pressing, an army was indeed sent out, which was not at all unreasonable, but the fact that it was lightly equipped and demoralized by the inadequacy of its supplies, and that it was, moreover, the worst part of the army, given that the best had been discharged because they were higher ranked and so cost more; well, all this had to be condemned, for it accomplished nothing of account or worthy of the former magnificence and power of the Romans. [130]

The lack of morale amongst the Roman ranks, only fueled the arrogance of the Turks under Togril, and this would empower them to attack with more confidence and haughty dispositions.[131]

The Seljuks did not cease with their conquests and pillaging, but like the wolves they so revered, they continued their hunt for domination and their establishing of an Islamic empire.[132] They continued their Mongol strategies of battle, eventually coming to the terri-

---

127 See John Skylitzes, *Byzantine History*, 21.9; Michael Attaleiates, *History*, 8.1
128 Belloc, *The Great Heresies*, The Great and Enduring Heresy of Muhammad, p. 53
129 Michael Attaleiates, *History*, 14.1
130 Attaleiates, *History*, 14.1
131 Attaleiates, *History*, 14.1
132 See Michael Attaleiates, *History*, 8.2–3

tories of Christendom. Thus a writer of old Christendom, Matthew of Edessa, wrote of this brood of vipers:

> In the beginning of the year a calamity proclaiming the fulfillment of divine portents befell the Christian adorers of the Holy Cross. The death-breathing dragon appeared, accompanied by a destroying fire, and struck the believers in the Holy Trinity. The apostolic and prophetic books trembled, for there arrived winged serpents come to vomit fire upon Christ's faithful… At this period there gathered the savage nation of infidels called Turks. Setting out, they entered [our] province and put the Christians to the sword. Facing the enemy, the Armenians saw these strange men, who were armed with bows and had a flowing hair like women. [133]

With this said, surely were these the people of Antichrist who St. John saw when he wrote:

> And they had hair as the hair of women, and their teeth were as the teeth of lions. [134]

The Romans were suddenly attacked by this unknown race of barbarian, one more sinister, fierce and savage than the regular Muslims they were used to fighting. The Turkish horsemen overran a frontier of six hundred miles from Tauris to Arzeoum. With their endurance fit for the highest peaks of Asia, and their horses conditioned for the most fatiguing sprints of war, these Mongols shed the blood of a hundred and thirty thousand Christians for the appeasement of Allah.[135]

THE CHRISTIANS FIGHT THE TURKS WITH VALOR TO DEFEND MEDIA

After Togril took over Persia, his cousin Koutloumous battled with the royal patrician Stephan of the Christian Byzantine Empire. When Koutloumous desired to pass through Media, which was being ruled by the Byzantines, he asked permission from Stephen to be allowed to pass. Stephen took this as weakness, prepared an army, and attacked the Turk.

Koutloumous was dismayed at this, and even though he did not have the amount of weapons the Christians had, for many of the Turks were unarmed, he fought regardless, and quite surprisingly, defeated Stephen, and sold him to one of the local rulers. Togril sent a much more powerful force back into Christian ruled Media, under the commander Asan, and when they arrived, a sea of innocent blood covered the earth. The Turks set everything ablaze and butchered everyone they came across, not even sparing those of tender age. In the next battle over Media, the Christian Romans, well prepared and fit for the battle against the formidable Huns, hurled themselves onto the charging Turkish horseman, in a desperate struggle for the survival of Christendom. Asan, stout hearted and tough, was in the front line, and he was amongst the first to be slain. The Christians struck and killed, slashed and terrified, and in striking horror into the hearts of the Turkish Muslims, they drove them away in their fear and disarray. The Turks could not stand before the advanced charge of the Romans.

---

133 In John France, "Impelled by the Love of God," in Thomas F. Madden's *The Crusades*, part 2, p. 35
134 Revelation 9:8
135 See Gibbon, *Decline and Fall*, vol. v, ch. lvii, pp. 1034–1036

PART 13

The remnant of the Turkish fighters retreated and hid through the mountains, eventually finding refuge in the cities of Persarmenia.

THE CHRISTIAN WARRIORS FIGHT TO DEFEND GEORGIA FROM ISLAMIC INVASION

After they invaded Persia, the Seljuks would invade the borders of Georgia, where they seized as much Christian Roman territory as they could, and captured a local Roman commander, who was the governor of Syria, named Leichoudes. Each year the Turks would return and create much havoc and unleash a torrent of destruction.

The Romans made an attempt to defend their lands, but were utterly defeated because of the Turk's formidable skill with the bow and the arrow. The Muslim Huns overran Georgia where they spilt blood, brought nothing but turmoil, invaded entire villages and towns, and overpowered the people with oriental tyranny. The defeat of the Romans in Georgia occurred not because they were terrible fighters, but because of moral decay within the government. There was actually a very powerful and proficient force of Roman troops in Georgia, but on account of corruption, the empire removed these troops out of Georgia, thus leaving the terrain exposed to the advancing Turks.[136] America and the West have and are still conducting the same sort of evil and corrupt policies as the Byzantine empire.

The Turks aspired to invade all of Georgia through the city of Ani, and for this reason, Roman warriors defended this land. But the governor of Ani deprived funds for the city's defense, and thus made it more vulnerable to the approaching Turks. But all of a sudden an obscure Armenian named Pangratios promised the governor that he would defend the city. But this he did quite poorly, and in an unworthy manner. He did not supply the city's main fortress with grain, nor did he establish a defense to protect it, leaving the citadel entirely defenseless. When the sultan, Togril, passed Ani with his entire army, Pangratios and his forces fell upon them, attacking the rear and slaying many a Turk who were straggling due to exhaustion.

Togril was not able to bear the insult, and being filled with pure rage and wrath, he commenced a full on siege against Ani. The soldiers within the city were not equipped enough to put up a formidable defense, since Pangratios stole many of the funds for himself instead of investing them into the troops. The local Christians tried to fight, but they were unfit for war and not conditioned to the arduousness of combat. There were only two commanders, Pangratios and his slave, both disloyal to their people since they were not focused on fighting the Turks as much as they were competing for full power.

The Turks pounded the city's walls, and they were about to crumble and be cut asunder, leaving the entire city open for slaughter. Pangratios and his slave, looking to each other, both declared that it was time to flee the city, but as soon as the Turks were informed on their cow-

---

136 Attaleiates, *History*, 8.1; see also Nicolle, *Manzikert 1071*, ch. 1, p. 11

ardly plan, they all, in unison, rushed the entrance and broke through the city's gates. What happened afterwards was described by the ancient historian Attaleiates:

> Aggressively destroying the gates and parts of the walls, they took the city by storm, and the slaughter of those inside was beyond telling. For no mercy was shown on account of age, sex or creed: all were killed from the young and up and a river of blood flowed through this pitiable and unhappy city. A tiny part of its ruling class saved itself, along with those unworthy commanders, by going up to the citadel. Those who fell into the hands of the enemy and who, through some most lucky chance, escaped being put to the sword, were given over to bitter slavery. But also those in the citadel, as they did not have supplies and were hard pressed by the lack of necessities, eventually made terms and surrendered their refuge, in exchange for which they were granted only their lives. And so such a city was taken by the enemy along with all its villages and their lands on account of greed and an untimely economizing. [137]

THE MUSLIMS MASSACRE CHRISTIAN SOLDIERS BECAUSE CHRISTENDOM IS FILLED WITH CORRUPTION

When Islam arises, it is only an indication that Christendom is weak in its zeal.

There was a Roman garrison in Mesopotamia that reached the rapacious eyes of the Turks. These poor soldiers, on account of the corruption within the government, were terribly lacking provisions, and for this reason were they filled with misery, boiling in rage and stirred with anger at their own government.

The reinforcements who were supposed to join them to fight the coming enemy, did not do so. Why? Simply for the reason that they were sloth and did not want to cross the Euphrates river. The Turks subtly approached them alongside the river, and from a distance fired their arrows at the forsaken troops. Many fell dead, numerous of them were taken captive, and those who remained managed to flee with desperation into the city of Melitene, utterly beaten and their spirits broken by humiliation and defeat.[138]

But it was not only the Turks who killed these men, for their murders were merely a symptom to the deeper problem, and that is political corruption and indifference. Because of this, the Turks broke the feeble Roman defense and ravished Christian territories as far as Kaisareia. They pillaged and destroyed everything that lied on their path; they set whatever they saw on fire, and because of their great hatred for Orthodox Christianity, they opened the tomb of St. Basil, tore it apart, defaced it, and looted all of its sacred furnishings.

They saw a strong structure, in which was placed the sacred relics of the saint, and they were unable to tear it open. But they did rob the paneling that covered the opening that was beautifully made of gold, pearls, and precious stones. After desecrating the tomb, defiling the ancient church, and after slaughtering an innumerable amount of people, they left. They

---

137 Attaleiates, *History*, 14.4, trans. Anthony Kaldellis and Dimitris Krallis
138 Attaleiates, *History*, 16.3

charged into Kilikia where they conducted a very systematic massacre of the Christians, and spent several days plundering and stealing, quenching their thirst for robbery and rapine.[139]

Since the Seljuks really became the backbone that strengthened the once weakening Muslim caliphate, they were invited by the Arabs of Aleppo to join them in devastating the city. The Turks answered the invitation with avidity, and with the Arabians they sacked all of Aleppo, massacring, taking captives, and utterly ravishing the land. A force was sent to defeat the Muslims, but the effects of corruption was soon manifested. The parsimonious government refused to pay the soldiers fairly, for those who had to endure battle for the safety of the empire were not esteemed worthy of a full salary. What was the consequence? They completely failed. When the Muslims charged against the troops, the poor soldiers raised a useless shout, in the attempt of trying to scare them, and then ran away and dispersed.[140]

The emperor's men, knowing that they had to do something to fix this serious problem, did not gather together a band of well cared for men, but young youths. With the fires of youth they tried to fight, but not one of them could ride a horse and none were trained for battle, and they were practically unarmed and without weapons. Many of them were killed and utterly vanquished by the hardened Turks. The youths lost their haughtiness, and realizing that they were not strong enough, the spell of adolescence left them, and they soon returned to their homes.

There was one righteous general, named Nikephoros Botaneiates, who employed local soldiers and with the virtue of being a good leader, heroism and bravery, he successfully repulsed the Turkish advancement from it fully taking control of Antioch. But, the corrupt government of the empire wrongfully discharged him from his duty as general, and as soon as this occurred, the Turks grew bolder. You know that a nation is growing in decay when it begins to fire its righteous generals. They conquered more cities, which were perniciously deprived of provisions, and reduced them to mere narrow straits.[141] But the horrid predicament became so severe that this great general, Nikephoros, was appointed emperor, and as is expected in governments plagued and riveted by ambitious corruptions, wicked men amongst the state stopped this from happening.[142]

There was one man who stood at a distance, observing what blood was spilt from the blade of corruption; and he straightaway knew that it was the fault of the avaricious politicians, that the Turks were allowed to overrun Christendom, and that it was they who were truly giving the enemy strength. His name was Diogenes Romanus, but we shall discuss him at another time.

---

139 Attaleiates, *History*, 16.3–4
140 Attaleiates, *History*, 16.5
141 Attaleiates, *History*, 16.6
142 Attaleiates, *History*, 16.6

CHRISTIANITY IS AT WAR: THE MANIFESTO FOR CHRISTIAN MILITANCY

A TURK FINDS THE LIGHT OF JESUS CHRIST AND LEAVES THE DARKNESS OF ISLAM

While reading on all of these horrific stories of Christendom's travails, there is a beautiful story worth telling, of two Turks, one who saw the light and absorbed himself into its magnificent rays, and another who lied to the very brilliance of Heaven. One was Boulosoudes, a powerful chieftain of the Turks. He travelled all the way to Constantinople—city of Constantine the Great—and declared that he casted away the deceptions of Muhammad, and embraced the Eternal Son of God.

He converted to Christianity, was baptized, and right there next to the baptismal font, was he received with open arms by the emperor himself, Constantine VII. He departed from the great capital of Christendom, and returned back to his people. But when he was amongst his fellow barbarians, he was not a "light to all who are in the house," nor did he "shine before men, that they may see your good works and glorify your Father in heaven." (Matthew 5:16) Instead, he lied before God and before the Holy Cross, and was amongst the false brethren who went "by stealth to spy out our liberty which we have in Christ Jesus, that they might bring us into bondage" (Galatians 2:4).

He dedicated himself to the cause of Allah, and led the Turks into Christian lands, pillaging and causing much bloodshed and anguish. He set his eyes for some of the toughest fighters of Christendom: the Franks, but it was to his demise. For the emperor of the Franks, Otto, had the heretic seized and impaled,[143] and rightfully so. Not long after this, Gyles, another prestigious chieftain of the Turkic race, travelled to the glorious city of Constantinople, and drew "near with a true heart in full assurance of faith" (Hebrews 10:22) and was "truly baptized with water" (Acts 1:5). Here he learned the precepts of holy Orthodoxy, here was his soul, mind and body, sanctified by "one Lord, one faith, one baptism" (Ephesians 4:5). He humbled himself before the fathers of the Church, and before departing away from the heavenly destined city of God, he took with him a monk Hierotheos, for he humbled himself in his own lack of knowledge, to teach the Muslim Turks the true path to God. When he was amongst his people, he brought many to the light of Heaven; he took Christian captives who were taken by the Muslim Turks, and purchased their ransom to set them free.[144]

Truly was this man one who "had found one pearl of great price, went and sold all that he had and bought it." (Matthew 13:45) Surely was he amongst those who "will shine forth as the sun in the kingdom of their Father." (Matthew 13:43) There were two men, and both were called to "work today in my vineyard." (Matthew 21:28) The first one, stuck in the reposing lies of heresy, and saying, "I will not," (Matthew 21:29) to God, soon realized what filth his soul was drenched in, and being filled with repentance and regret, he left the cesspool of Islam for the sacred springs of the Eternal Kingdom, and there did he drink the sacred waters, of which "whoever drinks of the water that I shall give him will never thirst." (John 4:13)

---

143 John Skylitzes, *Byzantine History*, 11.5
144 Skylitzes, *Byzantine History*, 11.5

The second Muslim went before God and said, "'I go, sir,' but he did not go." (Matthew 21:30) How greatly are our minds reminded of that most sublime and awe-inspiring event, in which Christ stood before two thieves. As these two Turks were plunged into the thieving heresy of Muhammad, so these two men stood crucified as robbers. Both of the Turkish chieftains reviled Christ as Muslims, and hated the Cross, as "the robbers who were crucified with Him reviled Him with the same thing." (Matthew 27:44)

One Muslim, although he looked to Christ, ended up reviling the Messiah, and staying on the path of Antichrist, rejecting Jesus as the Christ, as the one thief, who saw Christ with his own eyes, refused to see the suffering Savior as the Christ, when he said, "If You are the Christ, save Yourself and us." (Luke 23:39)

But the other man, although at one point being a hater of Christ as a Muslim, realized that his soul was entrapped in the darkness of Satan, and surpassing the fetters of his own pride, he got passed his own suffering and looked to the agony of the Holy One, and transcending his earthly eyes, he approached Heaven with a sublime awareness of his own need for salvation, and cried "Abba, Father!" (Galatians 4:6), as the other thief realized the taint of sin that darkened his own soul, the godlessness of the other robber, and the perfection of Christ's soul, crying out,

> Do you not even fear God, seeing you are under the same condemnation? And we indeed justly, for we receive the due reward of our deeds; but this Man has done nothing wrong.' Then he said to Jesus, 'Lord, remember me when You come into Your kingdom.' And Jesus said to him, 'Assuredly, I say to you, today you will be with Me in Paradise.' (Luke 23:40–43)

THE SONG OF ORDURU

"Come with me, and see my zeal for the Lord." (2 Kings 10:16) Such were the words of the holy Jehu, before he slew the pagans within Israel, and let us now come and see the zeal that permeated the souls of those warriors who fought for "the city of the living God, the heavenly Jerusalem" (Hebrews 12:22). The sultan of the Turks, Togril Bey, who called himself "king of kings"[145] declared his war against the true King of Kings, and in his defiance of Heaven, he committed himself to an onslaught against the sovereignty appointed by God, the Byzantine empire, and to burning the very pedals of Christendom's glowing flower. The towers of heresy approached the fortress of Orthodoxy, and the eagle of mighty Christendom flew high above the rivers that harshly flowed with tainted waters from the city of Babylon, and under the blazing rays of the sun, and in the midst of the torrid haze that ebbs from the heat, she saw how they shifted their course toward the vast plain that lied on old Armenia, Orduru.

These rivers were not of water, but consisted of entire multitudes whose hearts were rooted in the contagion of Islam, that sprung forth from the new Babylon, Mecca, and that stood proudly encompassed by the fires of the abyss. There, to the lonely plain, did they make their charge, barbarian Huns from the frigid Steppes of Central Asia, who no longer

---

[145] John Skylitzes, *Byzantine History*, 21.9

CHRISTIANITY IS AT WAR: THE MANIFESTO FOR CHRISTIAN MILITANCY

prostrated before the pagan gods of their fathers, but now bowed down toward an Arabian idol of the arid desert, denying Christ and rejecting the shining pinnacle of Orthodoxy, for the callous tomb of antichrist.

There they made their charge, to trample upon the Holy Cross, and with their vain hopes exalted, to uproot the true Faith; there they made their advancement, and with the flames of sinister ambition burning the desires of their flesh, they thought they could vanquish the God that they so hated. The eagle of Christendom hovered over this dismal hoard, only to see about one hundred thousand Turks, led by Togrul's brother, Abram Aleim.[146]

Their numbers were as high as their spirits, and loftily raised with their voracious hands was their banner of war, on which was sewed the image of the crescent, for like the pagans of old, they venerated this luminary as a representative of their god. So many of them tread the earth on foot, while a great body of them journeyed on their galloping horses.

The horsemen who were much more severe in their ferocity, and exhibited a higher spirit of prowess, pompously presented themselves in ways that seized the attention of the eyes, and exuded an air of superior swordsmanship and warlike dexterity. The saddle of their horses were embellished by the bright shade of turquoise and ornamented with the scarlet dye of a blooming rose, and their robust necks were adorned with a golden necklace.

The rider himself was attired with a long garment stained with hyacinth blue and embroidered with sulfur yellow that was terrifying to the eye and imposing to the onlooker; the scales of their armor appeared as the beautifully plumed wings of the blue peacock, the very sight of them looked as if an innumerable multitude of eyes were embedded onto their bodies; and the color of their boots were as red as the blood they so yearned to shed. Their hair was long like women, and every day did their mouths spew forth blasphemies when they declared the god of their heresy to be superior to the most Holy Trinity, as the dragon breathes out its blazing flames. One imagines these warriors, with such hue and such impactful elaborations, and cannot help but wonder, is this not what John saw when he wrote:

> And thus I saw the horses in the vision: those who sat on them had breastplates of fiery red, hyacinth blue, and sulfur yellow; and the heads of the horses were like the heads of lions; and out of their mouths came fire, smoke, and brimstone. (Revelation 9:17)

But on the plain of Orduru, there was the Christian army[147] of Constantinople, that great metropolis of eternal memory, that withstood the onslaught of the transient passing of time, and the bombardments of so many enemies who desired to see her destruction. Those noble troops, who denied themselves and took up their crosses, stood posted as loyal soldiers, to defend that very light that glimmered in a vast sea of infinite darkness, from the tenebrous advancers of the morbid night. These warriors of God exposed themselves to the highest

---

146 John Skylitzes, *Byzantine History*, 21.13
147 John Skylitzes, *Byzantine History*, 21.13

perils, to fight for the God Who "broke the arrows of the bow, the shield and sword of battle." (Psalm 76:3)

The Christians were not seen raising their heads as to rival with Heaven, nor did they show themselves off with pomposity. Instead, they were seen placing the local people, the women and the children, and anything that was of value, into the fortifications so as to hide and protect them from the impending attack that was to be unleashed by the Turkish scimitar. Their commander, Aaron, governor of Vaspurakan, had received orders from the emperor, Constantine Monomachos that they should remain inactive until Liparites, a fierce man who was a prince of Georgia, met with them with his Iberian troops. Before they arrived in Orduru, the warriors were stationed in Vaspurakan, to where the Turks were initially making their journey, but they shifted their course after Aaron determined it a wise decision to change the location of their camp.[148]

Like lions patiently crouching under the cover of lofty grass when stealthfully hunting their prey, Abram and his Turkish hoard cunningly approached Vaspurakan. But, his gaze did not meet those Christian fighters he desired to crush, and once he found out that they had shifted their course to Orduro, this Turk, like the wolves his people so emulated and revered, smelled fear.

He and his men without hesitation chased after the Christians charged into the field of Orduro. When the Christian soldiers were informed of this, they were struck with fear because Liparites had not yet arrived with his men, and to combat such a fierce and numerous band of Hunnic savages without the auxiliaries seemed to be imprudent—no—suicidal.

So they took refuge within an isolated spot surrounded by ravines that would be very difficult for the Turks to break through, and waited there. The Christians wrote a letter to Liparites, exhorting him to rush himself and his men with all haste to their aid against the band of Muslim barbarians.[149]

When Togril arrived in Orduro, and his thirsty eyes beheld not the warriors of the Byzantine Empire, he ferociously led his men to the very wealthy town of Artze, where Syrian and Armenian Christians resided, to pillage it, and slaughter all of the inhabitants. The general Kekaumenos urged the people to enclose their town by walls, but they refused to do this; and even though they could have taken refuge in the neighboring and heavily fortified city of Theodosioupolis, the local Christians refused to leave their homes, and were zealously determined to defend their land from the Muslims.

There came the Turks, under their ruthless commander Abram, and they, for six straight days, bombarded the town with their onslaughts; they fired their arrows and pummeled the courageous locals with their fierce attacks. But the native Christians, took up their crosses and with so intense a tenacious resilience they made their defense. They barricaded the entrance of the town so as to preclude the breaking in of the Turks, ascended up to the roofs

---

148 John Skylitzes, *Byzantine History*, 21.12
149 Skylitzes, *Byzantine History*, 21.13

of their homes, and with strong arms, aimed their arrows at the Muslims and fired with much force. The enemy, besieging the town with all sinister intent, were crushed by stones and pierced with arrows, but they persisted in their bombardment.

The Christians kept firing, and the Turks continued to beleaguer the firm Christians, whose faith was as sturdy and as unshakable as a house built upon a rock. The general Kekaumenos urged Aaron and his men to come swiftly to the rescue of these stubborn Christians. But Aaron refused, and firmly declared that he was to loyally follow the orders of the emperor and remain in his position until Liparites arrived with the auxiliaries.

The Christians were going to have to fend for themselves, and they had no problem doing so, and nor did they ever beg for help, but staunchly determined, with all noble pride and dignity, to fight for their land against the Hunnic Muslims. And what awaited such an adversary, but the "Sharp arrows of the warrior" (Psalm 120:4)? For the Christian men defending Artze pulled back the bows, took aim with their sharp eyes and pierced through the flesh of savage infidels; they took up heavy stones and launched them up to the air, and with their great mass crushed whatever Turk they landed on. Their fury was to the angst of the enemy.

Abram, being so exasperated by the stubbornness of the local Christian militia, cast aside all of his desire for the wealth that lay within the town, and was suddenly seized by the desire for its destruction. He had ordered that the roofs of the homes, from which the Christians made their attacks, be set on fire. They lit their torches with bright flames and threw them onto the roofs. The Christians tried to fight, tried to endure, but before their eyes lied insatiable flames, and moving beyond them were the piercing arrows of the Turks.

The roofs were set ablaze, and being unable to withstand such an imposing sight of rising flames with their piercing glow, asphyxiating smoke, the unbearable heat, and the tearing arrows, the Christian defenders fled. The Turks overtook the town, and they say that about one hundred and fifty thousand people were slaughtered, either by flame or by arrow. The Christians, so stirred by an ineffable hatred for the Muslim enemy, they perceived it as a great shame to die under them, and thus many of the men slaughtered their own wives and children, and then threw themselves into the flames. The ancient Armenian historian, Aristakes, provides us with probably the most animated and moving description as to the bloodbath that occurred in Artze:

> The flaming columns of fire vanquished the rays of the sun. One could see there a pitiful and terrifying spectacle in the extreme, for the entire city the bazars, the lanes, and the great chambers was full of the corpses of the slain. Who can count those burned to death? Those who had escaped from the glittering sword, and taken refuge in houses, were immolated, one and all. As regards the priests, those whom they caught in the churches, they burned to death; those they found outside, they killed and, to insult and disgrace us, put huge hogs in their arms. The number of priests who died by fire and sword, lords of diocese and church, we found to be more than 150. But as for those who had come from all other lands, and happened to be there, who can count them? [150]

---

[150] Aristakes Lastivertc'i's' *History of Armenia*, ch. 12, 84, trans. Robert Bedrosian

PART 13

Let us never forget the Christians who bled at Artze, all of those martyrs who were made, and the saintly blood that "cries out to Me from the ground." (Genesis 4:10) They chose the noble death of the warrior, who dies while fighting the pagan enemy, rather than the harsh yoke of the Muslim, for upon their hearts were inscribed the words of the Apostle, "to live is Christ, and to die is gain." (Philippians 1:21) They "crucified the flesh with its passions and desires" (Galatians 5:24), and disregarding earthly life for heavenly life, they defended their religion and their churches to the death. Christ says, "For whosoever will save his life shall lose it: and whosoever will lose his life for my sake shall find it." (Matthew 16:25) And surely it can be said that the Christian who died while fighting, or were killed by the persecuting sword, lost their lives only to find everlasting life.

After they took Artze, Abram and his Muslim bandits stole all of the gold they could find, and to strengthen their own army, took all of the horses and the weapons.[151] They took off and resumed their search for the Christian army, and it was around this time that Liparites finally arrived with his troops. The Romans left their hiding place, gathered with Liparites and his auxiliaries, and made their position at the foot of the mountain, right where the Kapetros fortress stands. The day was September 18th.

One would look up to the heavens only to see the bottomless and murky ocean of darkness, bedizened by the glimmering lights of luminaries, and the dazzling labyrinths of the stars, and the constellations that appeared to the lonely vision of the mortal to be as glowing spider webs. And such an image would impact the mind, to imagine oneself as but a mere prey, about to get caught on the spider's web, and consumed by some frothing monster. Foreshadowing imaginations that emanate from fear torment the mind when the path of anguish is paved under one's feet, and the torrent of destruction lies right in the horizon just before getting caught on the spider's web.

Their eyes peered out only to see the Turks slowly making their advancement toward them, not as one body, but little by little, as the raindrops descend from the sky only to hoard into a massive flood. Now the time for battle was about to commence; now the fierce clash of arms were about to be witnessed; now the screams of pain, and the cries of victory, were about to ring through the ears; and the wide and open field was soon to be a pool of blood and carnage. Kekaumenos quickly advised that the attack be made now, as the Turks were fragmented and not one collective body. Liparites objected, not for any strategic reason, but on account of his own superstition, for it was a Saturday, and to him such a day was deemed as one of bad luck. From his fear of misfortune, he refused to make the attack.

While old wives' tales struggled against prudence, what they didn't know was that as they argued, Muslim scouts were observing them from distance, hearing everything they said. Pleased with the discord that fettered them, they returned back to Abram, and he was pleased to know that the Christians lacked harmony, and that superstition prevailed over wise council amongst them.

---

151 John Skylitzes, *Byzantine History*, 21.13

CHRISTIANITY IS AT WAR: THE MANIFESTO FOR CHRISTIAN MILITANCY

The Christians were not going to fight on account of Liparites' fear of omens, and this only gave the Turks the time to gather themselves in their entirety, and become a formidable and united force, ready for the fight. The Christian camp stood without order, and nor were they ready for battle, when they turned around only to see the whole hoard of the Turkish warriors, with all of its awe and imposing colors, its ornaments and lofty banners with their crescents.

They marched with meticulous battle formations, and shook the earth with the stomps of their feet, and the galloping of their robust and colossal horses. They vanquished the eyes with the shades of their brightly adorned garments and ascending standards. Terror permeated the Christian camp, pierced inside their souls and emptied their very beings of all the hope they may have had. Now they stood, their hearts as hollow as trees conquered by parasites, gazing upon the eternal enemy of their Faith, and of Christendom. With all its embellishments and bright ornaments, and how they marched with great unison, it could be said that the Turkish ranks appeared as a giant bird, connivingly hunting for that beautiful eagle of Christendom.

The Christians wasted no time. All superstition was thrown aside, and they made their positions and gathered into battle formations. Kekaumenos took the right wing, Aaron the left, and Liparites was stationed right at the center. They were ready to fight, ready to lose their lives to save them, ready to kill and strike with the sword; their souls were prepared, for death nor life, victory nor defeat, was to take away the triumph they would receive through the martyrdom gained in holy war.

There the selfless defenders of the true Faith stood, with hearts beating like pounding drums, ready to pour out the flowing blood of valor and loyalty; there stood the majestic eagle of Christendom, soaring high above the clouds of the superficial, to tear to pieces the vicious bird who preys after her magnificent nest. The two sides gave one last still glance, looking to their enemies, and gazing up to the abyss of darkness hovering over them in that evening hour.

The charge was made; they sprinted toward each other, with fortifying howls and strengthening cries resounding through the night's mist. They collided and clashed; swords teared right through flesh, and horses smashed into enemy ranks. Liparites' nephew was hit with a strong blow, and his horse was struck with a mortal wound; both the rider and the powerful animal fell dead. Liparites lost all sense, and with the most ferocious rage he charged with horse right into enemy ranks, slashing with his sword with the fullest exertion of his might.

Wrath assailed his eyes, as to only thirst for the utter destruction of his enemies, his heart pounding with fury, his anger could only be satisfied with Turkish blood. His wit was gone, and this was to the advantage of the Muslims. As he exposed himself, the Turks struck his horse; Liparites fell down to the earth, and they took him captive. Within a little time, Kekaumenos and Aaron overpowered the left and right wings of the Turkish army, and pursued them with perseverance and tenacity. The rays of the dawn broke the chains of the night's abyss, cut asunder the webs of the stars, and with its illuminating light, all of the miseries and anguishes of battle fully manifested themselves. The Christians called off the pursuit, got off their horses, and cried out to Heaven,

What god is great like our God?

They awaited for Liparites, hoping that he too was pursuing the enemy. But as time lapsed, their fears increased, and soon a messenger arrived to inform them: Liparites has been captured, and many Iberians with him were also made into prisoners. The commanders were struck by dread and sadness, and all the night did they keep watch, with a glimmer of hope flaming in their hearts that some good news may come. The sun arose and the hammer of twilight broke down the walls of the black and dim shades of the dusk, and all of the commanders decided that it was time to return home. Liparites was taken before Togril who asked him as to how he should be treated, to which Liparites said, "Royally."

After hearing this Togril had him released. The battle was over,[152] the enemy routed, and the eagle of Christendom hovered above the land, wounded yet still flying, forever witnessing the zeal the Christian warriors exhibited for heavenly Jerusalem. What happened near Kapetros fortress, let it never escape our memories. Let our minds never be empty of that profound image, of men loving their brethren, and fighting and dying for them, for justice, for truth, for faith, for God, following the words of St. Peter: "Honor all people. Love the brotherhood. Fear God. Honor the king." (1 Peter 2:17)

MORAL AND SPIRITUAL DECAY WITHIN CHRISTENDOM WEAKENED THE CHRISTIANS AND EMPOWERED THE MUSLIMS

In the tenth century, Byzantium had no difficulty in repulsing Muslim attacks; the Turks unstoppably kept conducting raids against it, but were unable to establish a permanent foothold. Asia Minor was the bastion of the Christian world until hundreds of thousands of Seljuk Turks in the later part of the eleventh century, rammed right into the country, looting and butchering all in their path.

The strength of Byzantium would in time begin to dwindle because many of its politicians had adopted a pernicious philosophy equal to what is referred to today as "Pacifism" and "Anti-Militarism." This fomented corruption within the government, leaving Byzantium weak and open to being conquered. Around this time, a bright comet was seen blazing with all of its brilliance, flying across the sky. The soaring luminary caught the eye of the world, and an ancient chronicler, Matthew of Edessa, immediately saw it as inauspicious sign:

---

[152] This battle was recounted by John Skylitzes, *Byzantine History*, 21.12–14; Michael Attaleiates, 8.2

...many said that it was the same omen which had appeared before of the second devastation and final destruction of our country by the wicked Turkish forces, because our sins had increased and spread.[153]

The results of this decay were seen in 1071 in the Battle of Manzikert, in which the great-grandson of Seljuk, Alp Arslan, warred with the Christian emperor Romanus Diogenes who confronted the Turks to save Armenia from them. Sixty-thousand very well-trained warriors of Byzantium clashed with Asiatic nomads whose numbers were superior. This leads us to the recollection of another great battle.

THE SONG OF MANZIKERT

In a dark, small and dismal room there was seen a man, devastated and terrified, lying on the floor. All of his limbs were bound by ropes, and numerous soldiers, all dressed in Roman military attire, held his body down with shields. The man was screaming with the most chilling of cries, as a cold and callous person hovered above him with a sharp metal pin. Some other men forcefully opened his eyes, as the other slowly brought the sharp point of the pin to his pupil, giving no thought to the chilling pleas for mercy. But such a sight passes through our minds and we now enter into an occurrence before this horrid event, and in due time shall we return to see the fate of this poor and oppressed soul.

THE NOSTALGIA OF THE SHEPHERD

There once stood a city, long ago, in times now forgotten and covered by the webs of ingratitude, in the midst of fields as vast as the very sky one beholds when contemplating the cosmos. It arose on the eastern shore of a majestic lake and stood near a multitude of inaccessible mountains.[154] It was surrounded by luscious springs that lied on its plains, which made its very sight most pleasant to the weary eye, with the subtle and delicate ripples of the waters, and the fluttering of the tall grass and the pedals of the bloomed flowers, that ornamented the dark earth and colored this animate painting of divine creation, ebbing to the morning winds of the summer season.

The eyes beheld the waters of the spring as they glimmered under the twilight, in one moment shimmering to the sounds of muttering sheep grazing on the nearby pastures, and in another, darkened by the distant mountains that cover the sun's rays as they traveled in their destined journey.

What a pleasure it must have been, to sit upon a rock amidst this lovely oasis, and watch the rustic magnificence that charmed the eyes of the onlooker; to hear the heart of the shepherd as it poured out its passion through the sound of his rugged yet harmonious voice, in simple verses embellished by a kernel of beauty.

---

153 Matthew of Edessa, (tr. Dostourian, A.E), *Armenia and the Crusades*, tenth to twelve centuries: The Chronicle of Matthew of Edessa (New York, 1993) sect. 55, in Nicolle, *Manzikert 1071*, p. 32
154 See Nicolle, *Manzikert 1071*, ch. 1, p. 10

Here he sings softly; here he sings of life, of love, of death; here he sings of times once cherished, but now gone, as the gentle bird swiftly flies from the hand of its owner, or as the presence of the lover leaves the flames of affection dwindled and cold.

His voice transitions, he sings with agony, comforting the tempestial storm of his heart with the bittersweet woes of his soul, and our minds are stopped, and are struck by the sublime sound of ascendency and stirring anguish. Here he sings with cheeks tinged with tears, here he cries the song of Manzikert.

THE BATTLE OVER MANZIKERT—THE BEGINNING

With its abundance of waters, its people never were in want, and never once were their lips ever parched with thirst in that field that seemed as endless as the heavens. Within the lofty and sturdy walls of the city, a multitude of churches stood erect, and amidst its streets and inside the many holy edifices and monasteries, priests and monks flooded the metropolis, cleansing the people "with the washing of water by the word" (Ephesians 5:26).

As the people never suffered thirst on account of the city's abounding springs, they had "a fountain of water springing up into everlasting life." (John 4:14) For they had with them the well of Orthodoxy, in that once great city of Manzikert.

But as Heaven was sought out by the devils, so did the mortal emulators of the demons prey upon this city, and wish to seize it for their own despotic possession.

There came a great hoard of Muslim Turks, slanted eyed Huns of the oriental Seljuks; hardy and stalky, filled with perseverance and ever-ready to unleash their ferocity, and illustrate their cruelty.

They arrived under the leadership of their sultan Togril Bey, and one of his elite commanders, Al-Khan Osketsam.[155]

There they were seen, riding their horses with pride and pomp, with spirits high under the potion of hubris, with all of their banners and standards, with a multitude of imposingly bright colors. It appeared as an ocean of different hues and shades, marching in meticulous formation.

Amongst their ranks their peering eyes could immediately be recognized: they were tense and cold, and devoid of all compassion, like lifeless stones, or sharks solely fixated by the smell of blood.

Togril Bey was very assured that he would take the city without much challenge. He set up a palisaded camp as close to the city as possible, and commenced a ferocious onslaught against the city. From the ocean of this massive body of Turks, came a wave of arrows that covered the sun's rays and kept them from shining upon the city.

The Muslims launched devastating stones against Manzikert's walls with their colossal catapults, and never did they rest in their vicious onslaught. But the Christians behind the

---

[155] John Skylitzes, *Byzantine History*, 21.19. Jean-Claude Cheynet provides the actually name of the commander in n. 169

walls stood fast against the attacks, and repelled whatever bombardments the Muslims executed, thanks to their erudite commander, Basil Apokapes, who "strengthened his hand in God." (1 Samuel 23:16)

These were not frail and frightful men who defended Manzikert, but warriors stern and zealous, with hearts like lions, "strong in the Lord and in the power of His might." (Ephesians 6:10) For thirty days straight did they bombard the fortified city, and after so many sunrises, and so many nights illuminated by the blue light of the moon, the sultan, Togril, frustrated, and his spirit weakened by the zeal and tenacity of the Christians, and with both fury and sighs, ordered that the siege be ended.

But Al-Khan, experienced and adroit in the things of war, expressed his objection to such a decision, and requested that one more day be committed to the siege. The sultan found favor in his confidence, and called off the retreat.

THE ARROWS COVER THE SUN

The next morning, when the starry sky came to its end, the stars disappeared and the earth basked under the sun, Al-Khan assembled the entire force under his command, and placed the sultan, and all of the most prestigious of the Turks, in a camp positioned on a high hill facing the eastern gate of the city.

Upon this time he began to prepare for his plan. He broke the army into two groups: the first was to stand on a high eminence, and solely use the bow, and fire arrows upon the Christian warriors who stood defending the walls. He then ordered that strong and thick tents out of wickerwork and equipped with wheels be constructed. These were to be advanced to the walls of the city, so that the troops inside of them could dig right through the walls without having to worry about the defenders attacking since they would be too distracted by the danger posed by the waves of arrows launched by the Turkish archers.

This was the plan, but it did not escape the prudent mind of the Christian commander Basil, who having enough knowledge on strategy, understood perfectly well what the Muslims were about to do just by watching them prepare their attack. Al-Khan had all of his siege weapons moved to the eastern gate, for here the wall seemed the least high and the weakest.

It was against this wall that Al-Khan directed his attack, and commenced the siege. Out of all of the siege-tents, there was one catapult that was so massive and powerful that it could launch giant boulders strong enough to crush many men at once and shatter the walls of the beloved city.

Basil remained patient, waiting as a lion waits before pouncing upon the prey. The siege tents were close enough for the Turks to now dig out the walls, and upon this moment, when the Turks began their onslaught, a beautiful cry resounded through the winds: "Christ help us!"

It was the voice of Apokapes, and his cry was the anguish of the heart of Christendom, bleeding forth all of her sorrows. But in the bitter sound of his cry, was there a taste of sweetness; the taste of hope, and the taste of victory. To this cry did the soldiers of God take up stones that could be gripped with hand, and place them on their stone-throwers; and to this cry did the Christian archers place the arrows onto their bows.

A swift moment of silence followed the wail of the captain, and his call to attack echoed through their souls, and shook their spirits to action. The stones and the rocks were launched, and the bows released from their trembling holds. The Muslims fired their arrows, and one looked upward only to see a lightless sky, and the earth covered by the shade of arrows and stones.

Two clouds of arrows collided amidst the lofty empyrean of the sky, before the awe-inspiring presence of the scorching sun. It was as though one was lost in a shadowy dream, and witnessed angels and demons battling over Heaven. The sun was lost in the wave of projectiles, and the bravery of the enemy was taken by the rapids of Christendom's harrowing cry to holy conquest.

Time went on; the arrows zipped through the air and pierced through flesh; a storm of carnage was seen no matter where one turned his livid eyes. The earth was fattened by blood, and the whole area was permeated with the wailings of the wounded and dying.

From the walls of the city it was witnessed: the bodies of the Turks were cut asunder by the arrows, and crushed by the stones, and the Christians kept firing upon the advancing enemy. The Christians carried up long and heavy beams sharpened at one end, and dropped them upon the siege tents. They pierced right through, and tipped over the tents so that those who were within them were completely exposed.

The Turks looked up, only to see the last thing their gaze would ever capture, and were cut to pieces by arrows, and pummeled to their deaths by stones. Not one of them was left alive, except Al-Kahn who ran away. The giant catapult was nigh, and neither shield, nor battlement, nor any screen or cover, was able to withstand the boulders it was to launch against the Christian warriors.

Basil was at a loss as to what to do, and not even with his experience, could he devise a plan as to destroy this massive machine of war. All of a sudden inspiration came upon one of the soldiers, and he with quick hands and fast movement, took a jar filled with an incendiary liquid, ran with all of his might and will, passed the gates and right into the very ranks of the Turks, valiantly stood before the catapult, and with pure speed and perseverance, ignited the jar with fire, and hurled it at the machine.

The jar shattered, and the entire catapult combusted into flames; it engulfed the entire contraption, consumed it, and rendered it useless. The Turks chased after this unknown Christian warrior, but he sprinted away and returned inside and took refuge behind the walls unharmed. Suddenly two young fighters, swift of foot and skilled with prowess, leaped out from the gates and seized Al-Khan by the hair.

They brought him before Basil who, without a moment of hesitation, unsheathed his sword and beheaded the infidel. He then took his head and hurled it at the Turks, as Judith, when slaying Holofernes, "struck twice upon his neck, and cut off his head, and took off his canopy from the pillars, and rolled away his headless body." (Judith 13:10)

Togril Bey, filled with terror at the very sight of the head, called off the siege and retreated with all of his men.[156]

What an impactful example of compassion did Basil have when he beheaded Al-Khan and defeated his armies; for his actions were selfless, and completely committed to the safety and preservation of the Christian city. Such a dauntless expression of compassion, could be paralleled to how the great St. Clement, a student of the Apostles themselves, praised Judith's beheading of Holofernes as a pure action of charity and selfless love for her country:

> Many women, being strengthened by the grace of God, have done many glorious and manly things on such occasion. The blessed Judith, when her city was besieged, desired the elders that they would suffer her to go into the camp of their enemies, and she went out, exposing herself to danger, for the love she bare to her country and her people that were besieged; and the Lord delivered Holofernes into the hands of a woman.[157]

The silence of peace instilled the air that permeated Christendom, and abated the ferocity of the warrior's heart. But it was only for but a swift moment, a small measure of tranquility, departing from the banks of the beholder, as an old friend sails away, without ever knowing when he will return.

A NOBLE KING TAKES THE THRONE

Years had passed since that battle at Manzikert; many a Christian was slaughtered, many a sword unsheathed, and many noble battles ended with the pious on their knees, beneath the heartless eyes of the Altaic wolf.

The land was filled with heretics, false brethren who followed Nestorianism and who tended to support their Muslim overlords. Blood stained the swords of the Muslim, but it was found overfilling the treasure chests of politicians, who cared more for gratifying their own burning lusts for gain than the care of these precious warriors, and the glory of Christendom.

The Turks' expansion into Roman territory now placed the empire into a very dangerous predicament, and a new leader—one free from the fetters of greed and temporal benefits—needed to ascend the throne, not for secular gain, but for religion, for the path of Orthodoxy, for the brotherhood, for Christendom, for God. In the words of Attaleiates, "the man's goal was not love of self but solely love of his brothers and love of true religion, as we have said, distressed as he was on behalf of the Orthodox who were suffering terribly, the prayers of the people who wished this were answered."[158] This was Romanus Diogenes.

Heretics, heresies, the "equal rights" of all religions—this was not found amongst the cares of this zealous ruler, but the perpetuation of the illuminating blade of Orthodoxy, cut-

---

156 This entire battle can be read in John Skylitzes, *Byzantine History*, 21.19; Michael Attaleiates, *History*, 8.3
157 Clement, Epistle to the Corinthians, 45
158 Attaleiates, *History*, 16.10; Nicolle, *Manzikert 1071*, ch. 1, p. 8

ting asunder the advancing armies of devils and reprobates, the advancement that was so enabled by gluttonous politicians who cared not of the beauties of piety and true religion. There stood the new emperor, standing before the throne, tall and broad-chested, looking to the widowed empress Eudokia, who was to be his wife, and with unrestrained affection he embraced her whose cheeks now washed themselves with flowing tears.[159]

The scepter was now in his hands, Christendom in his grasp, his gaze was held captive by the sight of the enemy, and the holy war was now his. Eudokia's sons could not find out that Romanus was to be emperor, so under the secrecy of the night, he entered the capital bearing arms, and was proclaimed emperor. As the people marveled at their new emperor, the sultan peered through his oriental eyes at the flower of Christendom, only desiring to see her pedals burn, to watch with a cruel smile her fortresses torn down and her people wailing within the blazing ship of anguish and servitude.[160]

THE SULTAN RISES UP AND UNSHEATHES THE SCIMITAR AGAINST CHRISTENDOM

The sultan could be seen sitting with his legs squared on the floor, attired in a long and dark grey garment that reached his ankles, and was wrapped around his body with the left side covering the right, appearing almost like a Japanese shitagi.

His head was adorned with a conical helmet, and the features of his countenance were Oriental, almost Mongolian, and if one today were to see him, his appearance would be reminiscent to that of a Samurai. He stood firm, though not without an elegant composure; his eyes, slanted like those of his race, were callous but projected a cunning and very assiduous spirit.

There he sat within a room decorated by the oriental art of the Seljuk. Here paintings of graceful gardens embellished the walls and softened the eyes. In another part gazelles galloping through the wonderful groves captivated the sight, and the aesthetic depictions of beautiful peacocks with plumes and feathers beautified by the colors of the citrus tree, took prisoner the mortal gazes.

This sultan was Alp Arslan. The sharif, or the chief of Mecca, the holiest site of Islamic pagandom, had informed him that so great was his prestige that the sermon done in the site of the Kaaba was proclaimed in his name and that of the Abbasid Caliph. The entire Sunni Muslim world made their allegiance to him,[161] and so shall it be in our own times, after the great vicissitudes of the world transpire, and the power of the Turk shall rise again with all the Muslim world pledging allegiance to the Ottoman Empire.

But Alp Arslan did not want this to be a war of race, but a struggle of religion. For he declared himself a mujahid, a ghazi or warrior for Islam, and sternly affirmed that this war would be done for the advancement of Islam, and not the Seljuk Turk.[162]

---

159 Attaleitas, *History*, 16.10
160 See Attaleiates, *History*, 16.12
161 See Nicolle, *Manzikert 1071*, p. 32
162 See Nicolle, *Manzikert 1071*, p. 48

But from this room our imaginations are taken, and brought now to a wilderness of the Near East, where we see Alp Arslan upon his horse with an air of unrestrained pride. He looked back to see a prodigious multitude of his men, and then turned the other way and faced an endless plain of untouched earth that flowed right into the gleaming horizon.

THE SULTAN FORMS HIS MILITARY WHILE CHRISTENDOM'S SOLDIERS ARE ABUSED BY CORRUPT POLITICIANS

The emperor Romanus was marching with his men through Phrygia, and what a tormenting sight it was, to see warriors—members of the most elite divisions—sunk into the absolute depths of misery. For they were deprived of food, impoverished in their state of dereliction, and forsaken by leaders unworthy of their titles and diseased by want.

Forsaken, they were enervated and made almost entirely useless. Weakened and neglected, they were sapped of all morale by the bats of the empire for which they gave everything, even their very lives. Their very banners reflected their feeble state, for they were filthy, as though they had been exposed to smoke.

Their numbers were but a few, and they were like those forces that were small yet efficient enough to take out armies more massive than them. The young men amongst the ranks had no experience in battle, unlike their Hunnic enemies. From an innumerable distance, there stood Alp Arslan, with armies more skilled and experienced, with hands tougher and bodies more hardy, with eyes cold as stones and souls possessed by callous devils.

This sultan did not deem the Christian army as something to be taken lightly, but knew that even with their weakened army, they executed an effective fashion of attack: they would rush the Muslims with explosive and vicious ambushes that confounded and disconcerted them.

With all of his prudence, Alp Arslan sent out a very large army of Muslims into Upper Asia Minor, one part being in the upper regions and the other in the lower. He as well hired Muslim fighters from Baghdad, and during this session, there was a recruit who was small and appeared incapable for war.

The recruiter, Nizam al-Milk, mocked this man, and said: "What can be expected of him? Will he then bring captive to us the Roman Emperor?" This unknown soldier was accepted and added into the fold of the army. In all, the Seljuk army numbered up to about thirty thousand men, including fifteen thousand elite warriors.[163]

In every mosque throughout the Sunni world, there the imams went before crowds of Muslims fanatically raged about the coming battle, and declared with unified voices to their pagan god:

---

[163] See Attaleiates, *History*, 17.2–3; for the story of the anonymous recruit and the Turkish numbers, see Nicolle, *Manzikert 1071*, pp. 48–49

Grant the sultan Alp Arslan, the Proof of the Commander of the Faithful, the help by which his banners are illuminated. Cause his troops to be helped by Your angels and his decisions to be crowned with good fortune and a happy outcome. [164]

THE EMPEROR FORTIFIES HIS ARMY

Romanus, on the other side, aspired to restore the strength of his men, and bring the armies of the empire back to their former robustness. From every city and from every region, young men were recruited, and the most formidable commanders were brought out from the shadows of neglect, and placed in positions worthy of their authority.

In short time, no longer was Christendom's armies weak and feeble,[165] but vigorous and sturdy; like starving lions brawny and burly, they were filled with the highest enthusiasm to partake in the holy war.

Their hands were not trembling, but tightly gripped around the tilt of the sword; their form was no longer sloppy and sluggish, but structured and organized, with men wonderfully attired in splendid and thick armour, imposing the eye with prestige, and glimmering with the sun's magnificent rays that flowed above the high mountains that could be seen from a distance, as they marched with impeccable form.

It was awe-inspiring to the citizen of Christendom and terrifying to the slave of the devil. Their bodies were not weak and slouchy, but conditioned and fit for the fray. With minds no longer filled with wails and pitiable cries, with bodies no longer suffering from hunger, and with souls no longer inflicted by abandonment, they grumbled no more, but with internal fortitude, and with an unyielding heart, cried out with fury the cry of their spirits' will to war.

The long and arduous fight was about to begin. It was not to be just battles, but a single and continuous struggle made up of many combats; a struggle between truth and falsehood; a struggle between light and darkness; a struggle between cosmos, between Christendom and the empire of Antichrist.

THE EAGLES OF CHRISTENDOM SOAR THROUGH CANYONS

The lands of Koile Syria, Kilikia, and Antioch were being struck by the scimitar of the Turk and their Persian troops, and because of this Romanus decided to march into Lykandos with the intentions of remaining there for the summer, and then attacking the enemy in the autumn season, so as to not allow his troops to suffer under the scorching heat.

While the emperor and his men spent their days in Lykandos, the Muslims, seizing the moment when their enemies reposed, attacked and destroyed Neo-kaisareia. When this reached the ears of the Christian army, they did not wait nor did they remain, but with horses and men, with strength in heart and knightly zeal, they committed themselves to the charge.

---

164 Sited by Hillenbrand, op. cit., 53, in Nicolle, *Manzikert 1071*, p. 49
165 See Attaleiates, *History*, 17.2–3

CHRISTIANITY IS AT WAR: THE MANIFESTO FOR CHRISTIAN MILITANCY

They rushed through the air, as lone birds soar the boundless sky passed the blush red hue of the glowing sunset. The hands of the knights' thralled over the straps of their horses, as they rushed through the land of Tephrike, galloping with majestic movement through the rugged earth, and they traversed mountains with peaks encompassed by the clouds, and absorbed by the rays and the perfusing light of the eastern sky.

Much toil did the horses endure, being pushed with all exertion by their gallant riders; their muscles became weary, and their bodies worn down and exhausted. With such fatigue did the riders reduce their pace, but as they slowly galloped through the beautiful wilderness, they saw the enemy, and the Muslim Huns, with slanted eyes peering across what vast mountainous distance stood in between them, spotted his Christian adversaries.

A small glimmer of the day's remaining light sparkled on the farthest corner of their eyes, and the very sight of Romanus and his warriors mirrored on their squinting pupils. One still moment transpired, and the brazing flame of fear took ahold of the Muslims as the Christians charged with all fury toward them.

They were not expecting the Christians to reach them so quickly, but as this occurred they were truly ambushed by the weapon of surprise. The Muslims were surrounded, and although they could have put up an efficient fight, they were already conquered by the blade of shock. The Christians slaughtered them outright, and all of the remaining Muslims were seized; the Christians cast away any idea of quarter, and executed all of them.

The noble Romanus, after making such a great bloodbath of the enemy, looked upon all of the prisoners that the Muslims had in captivity, and with pure justice and mercy, ordered that they all be set free.[166] Does this not remind us of the righteous Abraham? For he, after gallantly defeating pagan tyrants, "brought back all the goods, and also brought again his brother Lot, and his goods, and the women also, and the people." (Genesis 14:16)

THE CHRISTIANS CHARGE THROUGH MUSLIM TERRITORY

In the following month of October, Romanus and his army made their repose in the city of Sebasteia. He allowed his men to rest for only three days, and from there they resumed their holy warpath, and headed for Syria.[167] He and his band of heroic fighters reached Aleppo, the city where the Arabs and Turks esteemed themselves brave and courageous when they tormented and made a great slaughter of the defenseless local Christians.

When the emperor and the holy knights marched through enemy territory, and were approaching the city of Hierapolis, they looked from far away at a force of Arab horseman, circling about like hawks before striking down upon their helpless prey, exuding a willingness to fight the Christians and take part in a fierce battle.

The Arabs spotted the Christian forces, with their majestic standards on which Christ and the Holy Cross were embroidered, and the banner of the soaring eagle of Christendom

---

166 Attaleiates, *History*, 17.4–5
167 Attaleiates, *History*, 17.6

was seen raised up. The Christians gathered together in the formation of the phalanx, with shield touching shield, and spears paralleled together and pointing toward the enemy, they marched with sharp movement.

The Arabs already knew that these were not the harmless Christians they were used to, who would tremble in terror as they cruelly slaughtered them, but fierce fighters of elite training, and the guards of glorious Christendom.

The Arabs and Turks united together, and they did not dare collide with the Christian forces, but instead rode around in their horses from a far distance, acting as though they were fighting. When the last remnant of the sun's rays beamed through the scorching autumn sky, and the men stood before Hierapolis, Romanus had a deep trench dug up and a well-fortified palisade erected; the imperial guard and the Armenian troops did not linger about, nor did they repose in their tents, but they, with all unified force, assailed the city.

The Arabs and Turks within the metropolis turned their heads only to see the rageful soldiers of Christ; they widened their eyes in trepidation, and one can only ask the question: did they remember all of those Christians they slaughtered, when they looked upon the fierce countenances of the holy warriors? Did they remember all of the sacred places, the tombs of the saints, the precious churches that they defaced and desecrated?

Right before their eyes were the faces of Christians, tired of being forsaken, over filled with the wine of their suffering from their beating hearts and spilling over the wrath of the winepress upon the rotten grapes. These were the successors of the "two hundred soldiers, seventy horsemen, and two hundred spearmen" who protected Paul (Acts 23:23), and now they were here, protecting the Church from the bandits, and unlike their pagan ancestors, they fought for Christ, Who "did not come to bring peace but a sword." (Matthew 10:34) And looking upon the Cross they said with the centurion, "Truly this was the Son of God! (Matthew 27:54)

The Muslims, seeing this torrent of holy rage scouring to their side, could not bear the very thought of fighting Christians who abided by the words of Christ when He said, "he who has no sword, let him sell his garment and buy one." (Luke 22:36) The enemy fled and took refuge in several very high and well-fortified towers, and a battle ensued.

The Muslims fought for their god, and the Christians combatted for the true God, with arrows flying from both sides. The Christians surrounded the towers and overwhelmed the enemy with fierce and proficient attacks, and soon they surrendered. But there was one tower more powerful than the others, and it proved to be more challenging. But still, after many bombardments, the Christians bound them tight with their siege weapons, hurling countless arrows from their bows and launching boulders with catapults into the confined enemy.

An entire storm of arrows and massive stones struck and shattered the tower, and the Muslims did not hesitate to surrender. They asked for pardon and begged to be able to pay a ransom for themselves, their wives, and their children, and Romanus, being so stirred by Christian pity, let them go in peace and granted their request for mercy.[168]

THE FINAL TOWER

One last and final tower put up a fight against the Christian army. They shot forth arrows and the valiant knights swiftly countered with their sharp and bludgeoning projectiles. Romanus had his men in battle formation, and stood them in between the towers and an army of Arab horsemen who tried to take out the Christians with arrows from a far distance, as they rode about the outskirts of the city.

As all of this was happening, the emir of Aleppo had already gathered together a large body of Arabs and Muslim Huns, and was beginning to march toward the very heart of the fray. As the battle occurred, one could look out as he stood in the midst of light that rained down from heaven's summit, and see with both awe and fear, hope and despair, a vast and flat plain with a line of small hills that aligned itself with the edge of the horizon, under the blazing heat of the eastern sky, and on this flatland that stretched for great distances, the whole force of Muslim Huns and the Arabs, riding on their horses and heading toward the city.

THE SCREAMS OF WARRIORS ARE IGNORED BY COWARDLY SOLDIERS

The two Christian battle lines assembled themselves in the phalanx formation, and were ready to fight. The Muslims fired their arrows, and this provoked some of the Christians to charge after them; again, the enemy unleashed another wave of arrows two or three times, and the horsemen of Christendom came out against them.

Following their common strategy, the Turks wheeled around the Christians, and fired another flood of arrows. This further provoked the Christians to come to the attack again, but this time the Turks did not circle around them, but charged directly into the phalanx, and a head on melee of swords and spears commenced. They overwhelmed the tagma—the elite division of the battalion—and slaughtered many of them, and forced the rest into an ignominious retreat.

As these warriors were being hewn down and butchered by the ferocious Huns, the other division of the Christians watched and did nothing; they stood calmly at ease as they witnessed the savage massacre of their men. They thought within themselves that if they remained quiet and still they would not be noticed by the enemy. As they heard the anguish and miserable cries of their men, they remained inactive; but when the Turks returned from their slaughter, they did not stand afraid of them, but charged into their indifferent ranks and hacked them to pieces, and struck them dead no matter how hard they tried to resist.

The Arabs then dismounted their horses, took a large number of the Roman soldiers and decapitated them, sending their heads back to Aleppo as a sign of their victory.

As these men were being butchered and cut to pieces, there was another camp—the remaining camp—that watched from a safe distance, and these did not solely just stare, but

---
168 See Attaleiates, *History*, 17.7–8

wandered about in their base, as though they were camping in a friendly country, and as though nothing was happening. The screams of sorrow and the wailings of the oppressed was not allowed to flow into their impervious ears. Romanus and his troops still remained within the city when all of this violent chaos and carnage occurred; he received the news, and instead of being overjoyed with triumph, he was soon struck by the arrows of despair. It was also informed to him that the entire Armenian division was already planning on leaving.

A TERRIFYING NIGHT

The last beams of the sun abandoned them, and deprived their warmth from their agonized spirits; the stars invaded the pitch black blanket of the empyrean's peak, and the comets soared across the sky, and the eve descended on that vast meadow of Syria, and fell upon their disdain.

Silence filled the dim air and all that could be heard was the pounding of their hearts, and the weeping of their souls. The internal wailing of the soul was a dissonance to the disharmony of misery's song, and who was to care for them in their state of dereliction, as the cruel sword of anguish wounded their abandoned hearts, and the capricious arrows of not knowing what lies ahead inflicted them with bitterness?

The sound of galloping horses ambushed their ears, getting louder and louder, and increasing in intensity. The horses were unseen to the naked eye, but their approach was getting closer. The moment of silence, in a sudden rush, dissipated as the autumn leaf breaks away from the tree and shatters into pieces to the looming winds.

The galloping of the horses was nigh, and all of a sudden the howling of wolves was heard. This noise did not come from wolves, but from the Hunnic Turks, whose custom it was to howl like this animal which they had held in high esteem. Unceasing was this howl, and it dominated the silence of the night.

It was now time to fight the enemy head on, through the darkness, and confront what was unseen. No trumpets were played, Romanus and his men simply mounted their horses, raised their standards and rode out to battle. Within the soul of each warrior was a piercing hope for victory. The Muslims gathered about in one spot heading against the Roman phalanx.

The Muslim enemy charged and clashed right into Christian ranks; the fighting was brutal, and the sounds of swords, spears, shields and death assailed the silence that once pervaded the evening. The men who stood at the frontline shouted a mighty battle cry, and as soon as it brazed their eyes and stirred their souls, the Romans burst with a rush of ferocity, and struck the enemy with devastating blows.

The Muslims mounted their tall and robust Arabian horses and fled, but the Christians pursued, and not for a very long time either. The Arabian horse is broad and lofty, strong and majestic, but with all of its weight it was unable to run for a long distance. It soon grew weary and slouchy, its energy diminished by the prolonged sprint.

The Christians fell upon them with arms and raging horses. Here a man is struck with a sword, and the blade rips right through flesh, muscle and sinews; there a man is pierced to his death with a lance by a horseman; here a man's head is cut in two; and there a fleeing soldier is trampled by a galloping horse, and perishes. Many a Muslim was taken prisoner, and many a Christian was satisfied with the triumph. Romanus ordered that the chase cease, and so the Christians pulled the reins of their horses, and left quite content with the bliss of victory.[169]

SURROUNDED BY WOLVES

After some time in their encampment, Romanus and his men resumed their journey and headed for the fortress of Azas. As soon as the Christians commenced their journey, and began turning away from Allepo, the Muslims began to gradually approach them from behind, little by little, getting closer and closer.

They then began some ambushes on the rearguard of the army, but it wasn't too difficult for Romanus and his troops to repulse them. The Muslims advanced, but the Christians repelled them with arrows and light infantry, and compelled them to flee once more.

They reached the foot of a lofty hill, and looking upwards one could see on its ridge the fortress of Azas. The entire edifice was thick and well-fortified, and surrounding it were walls made of stones that looked as though they had been joined together by hand. A small river flowed through that area, but it contained not even enough to sustain the army. The night was advancing into its earthly dominion, and the sun's beams were on the verge of withdrawing and hiding behind the cover of the moon.

The day was about to end, and the men needed to return to their camp before the enemy would attack and burn them alive. The summer's warm embraces were retreating, and the armies of the cold winter frosts were invading the air, and one could foresee the chill of the approaching breezes subverting the scorching winds, transforming the desert into a snowy blizzard, stinging the flesh and freezing the men into an ice-cold death.

As this image played itself in the mind of Romanus, he looked about and saw the depths of the enemy who, like foraging wolves, were encircling them, following them, and patiently awaiting for the right moment to make their attack. They had no choice but to not remain on the fortress of Azas, and made their leave.

TWO SPIES IN THE WILDERNESS

They marched out, and peregrinated across the land, and multitudes of Muslim horsemen rode amidst their presence; everywhere the Christian turned, there were eyes of sinister men scouting about, watching with eyes unseen, and thirsting for blood with darkened souls never satiated, but always hunting to gratify their sanguine lusts. As they continued to march, they stopped before a town called Katma; it was controlled by the emir of Aleppo, and for this it needed to be consumed by the wrath of the emperor, who did "not bear the sword in vain" (Romans 13:4).

---

169 See Attaleiates, *History*, 17.9–13

They made fires and set the entire village to the flames. They marched foreword and made their stop at a village called Terchala, and began digging a trench on which to establish their camp. They stood on a plain where the earth was raised one part and was flat on another, and looking up to the skies one could behold the high mountain peaks that surrounded them, and touched the last remaining glares of the sun before they journeyed off to the other side of the globe.

A river flowed through the land, and on the right side of it there was a raised bank on which the emperor made his post. A herd of cattle was with the troops, to be cooked and satisfy their grumbling bellies. Here the soldiers tended to their flocks, and there the emperor remained in his post, contemplating on the next quarrel, and being ever watchful for his own flock, that is, his men.

In the farthest rear end of the army's ranks, the soldiers spotted a number of Arab horsemen galloping about. The men sprung into attack and rushed the men with vicious onslaughts. The Christians held the line and fought them off, and as this small skirmish went on, two Arabs who were hiding behind a ridge of a mountain charged with their horses right into the edge of the camp. With swift movement they pierced two Christian infantrymen with their lances, and the poor warriors fell dead. The emperor witnessed this, and made the cry for battle, ordering his men to pursue the two Arab ambushers, but with their quick steeds they took off into the refuge of their own army.

ENDLESS FIELDS OF DESERTED MISERY

The final flame of the sun's gleam was put out, and in the dreary darkness of the night, cries and howls filled the air and only brought the warrior's mind to wonder, how close was the enemy? It was the howling of the Arabs, who made such noise only to bring their foes to fear, but the armies they were dealing with were no tremblers.

They remained within on their campground and awaited for the day to finally awaken from its rest. They resumed their journey and noticed a range of boundary markers, which meant that they had finally reached Roman territory.

But this land, after all of the carnage and gore they witnessed, the cruelty they saw and the miserable state they were just in, did not appear to their exhausted eyes as a paradise. As they passed by, all they could see was a land laid waste: homes were destroyed, the entire premise was absent of all vigor, vibrancy and animation.

Hardly was a place found to be livable, except for a few abodes here and there in which the remaining inhabitants lived their anguishing lives, always surviving and never living, always looking about to see whether or not their capricious end had finally come.

The men walked through such lands not for a short distance, but for miles and through endless regions that once stood as vivid and pleasant towns but now were but pains for the eyes to see, struck and scorched into wastelands by the vicious hands of Allah's slaves.

They passed by a well-built fortress in Artach; it was erected by the Roman military, and was guarded by Roman soldiers. But when Romanus and his warriors arrived, Arab fighters resided within it, as black birds scavenge through a dead crop field, and linger upon a parched scarecrow.

As soon as the eyes of these Arabs locked their sights on the approaching Christian army, they fled with their souls wounded by fear.[170] Through deserted lands and empty wilderness Romanus and his men marched; they traversed across a wasteland that stood between Koile Syria and Kilikia.

They were on top of a very high terrain, and with souls taken by great distress, they travelled through many narrow roads, dangerously steep rocks, and near the edge of cliffs that seemed never-ending. They reached Kilikia, and the next day continued their journey through the Tauros Mountains. The emperor and his band of warriors marched through these rugged eminences, carved out from the earth and divinely embellished by beautiful green meadows.

A RUTHLESS WINTER

They continued on and entered Roman territory, and suddenly the warm air no longer comforted them, but the entire ether was conquered by the icy cold breezes of the winter season.

It was near the end of December, and surely did they feel the bitter fangs of the freezing winds sinking their sharp blades into their delicate flesh. The roaring sound of the iced torrent rumbled throughout the land; the ether was invaded by the ice cold gale, and the frost of the frozen tempest latched onto their beards and their faces.

Within the ranks of the army a whole multitude of the helpless cattle animals lied dead, their lives sapped out of them by a ruthless storm of sharp and stabbing, yet soft and brittle snowflakes. They proceeded to march, fighting with all their might to endure the resilient winds, and striving with all their souls and minds to conquer their pains, and triumph over their discomforts.

Horses trembled to the frost-bound floor, their hooves and robust bodies unable to withstand the arrows of the winter that pierced their thick hides. They neighed for the last time, and soon could be found dead and alone amidst the wilderness.

Those who were too thin and not robust enough, or were not wearing sufficient clothing, did not escape the thrall of winter's deathly hands; forsaken by the blanket of the sun's rays, and deprived of all hope, they lied down on the cold and lifeless earth, breathed whatever life glimmered within them, with their chests going up and down as the final breaths were made, and in between each heartbeat a moment of silence pervaded, a rush of air flowed from the mouth, and they perished, "the dust returns to the earth as it was, and the spirit returns to God who gave it." (Ecclesiastes 12:7)

---

170 See Attaleiates, *History*, 17.14–18

PART 13

THE TURKS CONTINUE THE SLAUGHTER

As their agonizing journey went forward, a pack of Turks creeped into the Christian city of Amorion, and like the storm the men were suffering, overtook it. The Muslims conducted a horrific massacre in this metropolis, massacring, in the words of Attaleiates, "an incredible number of men, and led all the others away as captives."[171]

The pagan Muslims later came close to the city of Tzamantos, and upon their arrival an army of Christian soldiers came to fight against it. A show of arms ensued, and after some time, the Turks routed the Christians and slaughtered many of them with the sword. After Romanus and his men finally escaped the freezing cold storm, they received the news of how so many warriors were slaughtered, and though distressed pressed upon his soul, he still never let go of what he envisioned: victory over the enemies of God and His Church.

The harshest depths of the winter season made its presence everywhere, and so the only prudent decision was to keep warm. Romanus ordered that the soldiers reside within their winter quarters, while he, his bodyguards, and his family, made their abode in the holy city, Constantinople.[172]

Soon the howling wolf arose from his dreadful slumber, soon he walked about awaiting for the feeble to linger in his midst, so that he may devour them. After so many moments, the wolf pack arrived, that is, the Turks, and they howled and screeched as the animals they imitated, charging on horseback through a plain overspread with dark green meadows, near the city of Larissa, surrounded by mountainous lands so high and splendid, yet lofty as the pride of those who now pounced for their mortal prey. They went about the terrain, rampaging and devastating whatever random village they could spot,[173] being ever ready to destroy whoever they could find. They ravished and pillaged, slaughtered and enslaved, and howled with chilling spirit to the night that they so loved, freezing with fear the souls of those whom they desired to conquer: defenseless Christians who knew not war nor guile, harmless like doves but devoid of the wisdom of the serpent.

THE WARRIORS CARRY THEIR CROSS

After much time passed on, and the appointed day to resume the battle came to be, the tenacious emperor gathered together his great army, and as a shepherd guides his flock, marched out with them to Larissa, from where the news arrived that the Turks were tearing apart the adjacent lands.[174]

From the farthest distance the eye could see the majestic ranks of the troops, hands clutched to shields, gripped to a spear, waists equipped with sheaths in which lied every man his sword, and within every soul a flickering flame of eternal hope, for either triumph over the enemies of the Cross and the servants of the devil, or to ascend to thundering Heaven,

---

171 See Attaleiates, *History*, 17.20–22
172 Attaleiates, *History*, 17.22
173 See Attaleiates, *History*, 18.6
174 See Attaleiates, *History*, 18.6

and obtain union with the Almighty. They did "not fear those who kill the body but cannot kill the soul."

Rather, they feared "Him who is able to destroy both soul and body in hell." (Matthew 10:28) The Apostle tells us, "Eye has not seen, nor ear heard, nor have entered into the heart of man the things which God has prepared for those who love Him." (1 Corinthians 2:9) And what greater love for God could these men of valor exhibit, each one laying "down ones life for his friends" (John 15:13)?

They placed their lives near the gates of death, not only for Christendom, but for God, and "Greater love has no one than this" (John 15:13). "Honor all people. Love the brotherhood. Fear God. Honor the king." (1 Peter 2:17) Surely did these warriors abide by these very words, when they went out to fight and die for the defense of their brethren from the raging Turks, to fight for God, and to honor the emperor with their heroic spirits.

THE SWORD CLASHES WITH THE SCIMITAR

The brave soldiers and knights went forth towards the place where the presence of the enemy was thick, and when they reached the plain where they could set up camp, the emperor entered his imperial tent.

From a distance the Christians peered with observant eyes, they passed the brilliant rays of the noon day, and saw that in the very heights of the high hills that surrounded the jade colored fields, there were the Turks. Like savage dogs they were spread across the mountainous terrain, hiding behind the cover of nature. The Christians "arose and shouted," (1 Samuel 17:25); the emperor ordered the trumpeter to bray, "then he blew the trumpet," (Judges 6:34) the soldiers advanced in their formations, the Christian standards of the flying eagle and the assailing Cross were raised high, and the army was arrayed in the imposing order of the phalanx, and before them stood the shepherd of the flock, the emperor, leading his men to fight off the wolves.[175]

The Turks descended from the mountain, and like charging beasts sprinted toward the Christian troops; with speed and swiftness they came toward the Roman warriors. An entire unit, called the Lykaonai, and another that was named Arithmoi, headed for their faces; the Turks made a run for it and the Christians charged after them with more boldness than usual.

They forced them to turn and flee, but there was still a whole multitude of Turks forging an attack. To such as these there was the emperor Romanus, leading his men with sword in hand and majestically riding on his horse into the midst of enemy ranks, into the very thick clouds of the roaring fray. Blades held by Christian hands struck and hammered the enemy, and within a short duration, the Turks were put to flight.

Romanus gave no quarter, but took the lead with his men and pursued after them. They passed through the vast valleys and meadows of the luscious land, and charged passed plains

---

175 See Attaleiates, *History*, 18.6–7

that appeared to the eye as shaped like crescents,[176] the image embroidered onto the very banners of the Turks who now fled from those who upheld the standard of the Cross, and the soaring eagle of Christendom.

As the intense chase was happening, a unit of the Seljuk, made up of a noticeable multitude, stayed hidden, and knowing that the Christian army was away from their camp, rode up with their horses to the encampment, guarded by Frankish warriors and other Greek fighters. The Turks smashed right into the camp only to be met by the firm hand of the Frank, and his sword. The Franks put up a great resistance, blood and carnage, tenacity and ferocity, was all that could be seen; and it was only the Franks who fought while the others stood and watched, not lifting a finger to come to their aid. But the Franks were in no need to reinforcements, for they held the line with fierce fighting, repulsing the Turks and driving them out.

The emperor was chasing after the enemy through the rugged meadows, and by then the green grass disappeared as the last beams of the blazing sky dimmed and withdrew its exposure, and the cover of night flooded their blades, and looking up to the heavens one could see the glowing lunar raining down its blue florescent light upon the victory.

They ceased their pursuit, and marched back to the camp. The howling of barbarians was not heard, and the only horses' gallop that the ears met was that of the victors, and the only prisoners seen were Turks.

The next day the emperor Romanus ordered that all of the Muslim captives be executed; the sword was unsheathed and unleashed upon these evil-doers, and not a single one was spared.[177]

THE CHRISTIANS PUSH FORWARD TO DESTROY THE ENEMY

But the wrath of the emperor was not curbed nor abated; he was not done with the Turk, and wished to obliterate them all. With his whole army he marched toward the enemy; but the Muslims, being swift of foot and only retreating to regain strength to reenter the fight, crossed the Euphrates River, and were quite far away from the Christians.

The emperor contemplated within his mind as to what he should do, and explained his plan to his men: the enemy was beyond reach, too far for them to pursue, and to chase after them would only be vain. It was thus best to have the soldiers return to their homes and for him to reside in Constantinople until the army retrieved their strength for the next battle.

Everyone agreed to this plan, except for one soul named Michael Attaleiates, who expressed his disagreement through silence. The emperor noticed this and asked why he remained quiet. Attaleiates called on God as his witness, and declared that the plan was not satisfactory to his prudence.

The enemy had not been utterly defeated and destroyed, he said, and since the advent of evening had saved them, the Turks were already given a chance to regain their courage, and

---

176 See Attaleiates, *History*, 18.7
177 See Attaleiates, *History*, 18.7–8

this was made clear by the fact that they had left their plunder behind. This only meant that the Turks already had plans to fight the Christians continuously, without ceasing. He went on to say that the small victory over the enemy did not truly affect them, since the Seljuk Muslims were not fazed by fighting and had the endurance to get passed their defeat and strive against them.[178] Attaleiates also concluded that for the Christians to rest would only be perceived as cowardice by the Turks, and thus swell their boldness. He finished with these words:

> Why is it necessary, O emperor, to leave the enemy in Roman territory awhile the year is still in the middle of summer, and take it easy and enjoy ourselves and not go to some trouble now so that we may prosper in the future? For what reason should we not take by siege the city of Chilat and the towns subject to it, which also enable our soldiers to get their full share of the plunder, become more eager, and inspire fear into the enemy? Instead of being under enemy control, those cities still enrich the Roman Empire. Forces stationed there will vigorously repel the hostile forces, and the invasions of the Turks, which take place at intervals and in small bands, would be blocked; they would no longer find there a rallying point and supply base but simply military opposition, and the road through Mesopotamia will be closed by them. [179]

As a seed quickly sprouts in darkly rich fertile soil, so did this seed of wisdom geminate well in the mind of the emperor.

A BATTLE ON THE PLAIN OF BABEL

The Turks were encamped on the edge of the River Euphrates, the plain of Babel. They looked up and their eyes widened as though lightening had struck them. But this was not lightening, it was Romanus and his army of brave warriors, refusing to repose and determined to vanquish the Muslim horde.

Look up to Christendom, review her walls, observe her pillars, behold her churches, revere her eternal laws, and never forget what mighty warriors defended her. Envision to yourselves the armies and their leader Romanus, how they attacked the startled enemy, and how the Turks, unable to withstand the onslaught, fled back to their own country.

One can only imagine the soldiers, with their necks bent and pointed downwards, their bodies exhausted and drained, exerted of all energy, but still within themselves the blazing fire of zeal lit up like a torch in the darkest night, as they gazed before the great and vast wilderness that they would have to traverse. They carried on, descending through precipitous and steep roads and making their way past deep valleys that lied amidst marvelously green fields that glowed with a pleasant and soft shade when touched by the arms of the sun, and lied in between tall, jagged and rugged hills.

---

178 Attaleiates, *History*, 18.9–10
179 Attaleiates, History, 18.11

A PARADISE IN THE MIDST OF HELL

The dread of a dry tongue and the unbearable sensation of thirst wrapped themselves around the strength of the emperor, and so he went out to search for water and snow to quench this burning desire, and cool down his weary body. He left behind a garrison under the command of one Philaretos to act as a defense against any Turks that could come about for a surprise attack, and went off with his soldiers to forage for water.

As the other men suffered the suspenseful feeling of knowing that the Turks could strike at any moment unknown to them, Romanus and his troops endured an arduous struggle against nature itself.

They passed through harsh and rigorous terrain, and treaded over rugged hills absent of any tracks with which the frightful traveler could guide himself. This wilderness was not for such people, but for the warrior, who with his endurance journeyed across this desolate place. By their perseverance they arrived in a beautiful oasis called Anthiai, through which pleasant rivers flowed to satisfy the thirst of the resilient soldier, which lied right within the ranks of mountains desolate and severe.

It stood in the midst of a merciless wilderness, but was itself a field of luxury for those strong enough to reach it. He remained in this hidden paradise for three days, and after the sun arose and descended thrice, they left it and traversed to the foot of Mount Tauros.

They ascended up this eminence and suffered the laborious journey across the cruel and rugged terrain, and then descended down into the region of Kelesine. They approached the foothills of the Tauros, and from there they crossed the River Euphrates.

THIRST BRINGS NEGLIGENCE

As the weary warriors rested in their encampment, trying to nourish their exhausted bodies with sustenance and slumber, and sooth their combative souls with glints of hope, Philaretos and his army remained in their post, yet they did not rest on the skill of their arms, but were tormented by the Turks who were now on the hunt for unwatchful prey.

There a Turk swiftly rode through the grassy plains, there another, and soon like a wave of smoke grows in thickness as it hazes above its flames, they overtook the field, and the Christians found themselves assailed on all sides. The Christians with all trembling and fright tried to put up a defense, but the Turks overwhelmed them with an overbearing assault, and the light of the sun was covered with their soaring arrows, and their fearful hands could not counter against the blows from their crescent shaped swords.

The whole camp, from a blockade, became a field of agony covered with the dead and those about to be absorbed into death, coughing and gurgling blood in the presence of the oriental horsemen who stood with their heads arched up and their deranged spirits towering above the stars.

† CHRISTIANITY IS AT WAR: THE MANIFESTO FOR CHRISTIAN MILITANCY

THE WOLVES GO ON THE HUNT FOR CHRISTIAN PREY
The surviving Christians foresaw the end of mortality's path, and refusing to walk across the line of this end, they ran away to wherever they could. They scattered about the wilderness with all sorrowful desperation, and within their minds all they could picture were the Asian nomads riding up to finish their destruction. So great was the terror that seized their minds that they acted as though they could hear from a very close distance the galloping of the Turkish sword and the howling they would make before they struck.

They kept sprinting with all angst, scouring through the wilderness and running all the way to the hidden paradise of Anthiai. The hope to be safe in this hard to reach oasis balanced on a hair of hope. They turned around, their eyes widened eyes as though they spotted a wolf, and they saw before them horrifying horsemen riding right towards them.

They took off and spread out with all fearful confusion; there a man went one direction and there one went down another path; they kept bolting through the rugged terrain until they reached Kelesine. And it was at this time that some of them reached the emperor, and with confounded breath and trembling voice told Romanus the dreadful news.

SAVED BY ROYALTY
The men immediately made themselves ready for an ambush, for the Turks would have struck with swelled up boldness after such a victory. The Muslims hurried to find the rest of the Christians, and with great persistence and hunger for blood, they strived through the wilderness; but the land was without tracks, it was rugged and was overspread with high, steep and sharp terrain too harsh for them and too painful for the hooves of their horses, and their courage was assaulted by the prestige of the emperor, and so their attack was hindered by divinely designed creation, and by the might of Romanus.[180]

The Seljuk warriors scorched the earth with their burning lust for destruction, and to further fan the flames of their insatiable desires, they marched into Kappadokia, and with full exertion and strength, and blood rage taking all control of their limbs, they slaughtered many Christians and took much plunder in the city of Ikonion.

THE ARMENIANS TAKE REVENGE
Onward did the emperor and his men move against the wretched and adverse enemy, and passing through Koloneia they reached as far as Sebasteia, where they were informed that the Turks had ridden on ahead all the way to Pisidia and Lykaonio. The Sejuks were deeply fearful of the emperor and his effective attacks and battle formations, and with this dread they journeyed to the mountains of Seleukeia, but here they were greatly surprised by a sharp and calculated ambush. Spears plunged down through the air and pierced right through their bodies.

Filled with bewilderment, they did not know what to do, being trapped within the mountainous countryside and assailed by those who knew of the terrain more than them.

---
[180] See Attaleiates, *History*, 18.12–16

Here a lance penetrated a chest, and in the next instance a spear impaled a Turk from his chest and pushed through bone, muscle, and insides with an upsetting noise of flesh being cut asunder.

Who were these warriors that lingered about in the cover of nature, and through cunning overwhelmed the wretched Turks? These were the Armenian Christians, who took pleasure in slaughtering all of them, picking them out one by one, and thrusting them through with their tall lances. Now that this army of Turks was finally obliterated, the emperor was comfortable enough to allow his men to repose in their homes, and was at peace to enter Constantinople and rest.[181]

THE SEASON FOR BATTLE AWAKENS

Layers of frost suppressed the fertile soils that, when the weather is warm and the sun's rays are free from the fetters of the clouds, lied soft and smooth, brittle like sand for the farmer to easily cultivate, and enriched for the union between seed and earth.

The arrows of the solar star now broke forth from the oppressive fogs that sprang from the cold breeze. Gone were those still nights in which the callous winds were at liberty to torment poor mortals, to pain their very bones and keep them imprisoned within their homes, to hinder their eyes from beholding what glowing beauties the sky holds, and cut off from all life what crops they grow by the sweat of their brow; no more were those lonely evenings, in which the frozen chains of the icy clime held back the generous streams of the sun's beams that poured forth into the groves and the glades, the villages and the cities, the meadows and the fields, the forests and the desolate wilderness, and allowed man, wherever he was, to see nature awaken from its dismal slumber.

All that was seen was now attired by the robes of the daylight, with a magnificent garment of rose colored brilliance that clothed the earth with warmth, and overcame the darkness that so robbed man of his sight of what was truly worthy of his admiration. The air was caressed by the mists of life that intimately intermingled with the white and clear light that emanated from the sun, and all that one could see before his eyes was the hand of God at work.

Here the roses bloom and move to the gentle and warm winds; here the flowers blossom covered in the morning dew; here the blades of grass burst forth from the loose dirt, waving back and forth with a verdant radiance to the mellow breeze; here man witnesses the glow of the horizon of the setting sun, its light flooding sky with a hue bright fire overlapping a more dimmer shade that is easy for the eye, like a small flame of the candlestick in the midst of a dark room. Now was the time of the spring season, now was the time to pursue the enemy, and finally destroy him.

---

[181] See Attaleiates, *History*, 18.16, 19, 20, 21

✝ CHRISTIANITY IS AT WAR: THE MANIFESTO FOR CHRISTIAN MILITANCY

IT WAS A WAR AGAINST HERESY
Here, in the era in which the Church battled the Muslims—the acolytes of Antichrist—was the authority of the Church to use the sword seen in a shining manifestation.

The State, under the spiritual authority of the Church, fought for the Church, for God, for the Blessed Trinity, for the defense of the Holy Faith. In this time one could see that as the emperor Romanus resumed the battle and led his armies to confront the pagan enemy, the Church in sacred Constantinople began the first Sunday of Lent, a most ancient rite of the Holy Faith, in which Christians remember Christ, Elijah and Moses, in their fasting in the desert for forty days and forty nights, and their battle against the spirits of the abyss, and emulate them, depriving themselves from meats and comforting foods for forty days and forty nights, being as Daniel when he "ate no pleasant food, no meat or wine" (Daniel 10:3), casting aside their temptations and their fleshy ambitions, as Christ refused the kingdoms of this world and defied the devil, and turning "toward the Lord God to make request by prayer and supplications, with fasting, sackcloth, and ashes." (Daniel 9:3)

As the holy men of Israel "put a mark on the foreheads of the men who sigh and cry over all the abominations that are done within it" (Ezekiel 9:4), before they went to slaughter those who were found "with their backs toward the temple of the Lord and their faces toward the east," (Ezekiel 9:16) so did the priests of Christendom place on the foreheads of the faithful, the mark of God—called the TAU—the Holy Cross, made of ash, just four days before Romanus and his warriors marched out on that Sunday, March 13, 1071, to fight the Muslims who wished to defy God's holy city, Jerusalem, and destroy the holy churches within her, and bowed toward the east to worship their pagan god.

Before he left the city, the emperor's wife, Eudokia, expressed to her husband her love for him, and gave him a farewell address,[182] but whether this was the affections of a Deborah or the deceptive embraces of a Bathsheba, only time would tell.

There went the strong soldiers of glorious Christendom, there the loud noise of galloping horses rumbled the ears, there the eyes widened at the sight of their elevated banners, there the warriors marched and the earth shook. As they journeyed foreword to fight with temporal sword the mortal advancers of the devil, the priests of the Church gathered together in a council, to fight with spiritual sword the demons and their deceptions, and anathematized all heretics,[183] and in that very moment, were their soldiers marching out to combat an entire army of heretics.

A MEADOW OF MARTYRS
They journeyed all the way to the land of Sebasteia, which lied on the northern part of Cappodocia, a region covered with mountains and high hills, lofty rocks and sharp cliffs, and as they traversed through this vast terrain, they reached a fork on the road, with one path going

---

182 Attaleiates, *History*, 20.2
183 See Attaleites, *History*, 20.1, see also footnote 202 of Kaldellis' and Krallis' translation

to the left and the other going to the right. They all stopped before the two egresses, waiting for the emperor to make the decision on which one to choose.

He chose the left path, and as they treaded it, they beheld a most dreaded sight: countless human corpses covered the field; these were the bodies of those warriors who fought the Turks in an earlier battle, just a year before their eyes beheld such carnage. The emperor did not turn away in fright, but wanted to see this field of dead bodies,[184] as though to instill a lesson into his men, on the mistakes the Christians made in this previous battle. Memories enflamed the mind at this moment, and the winds of the past brought one's mind to what happened to these poor souls.

A HORRIBLE MEMORY

It was the spring of 1070. The Turks surrounded the Christian city of Hierapolis in Syria, and to relieve the people trapped within its walls, who were already suffering from starvation, the general Manuel Komnenos split his army into two and with selfless love went one half for the defense and liberation of the city.

They headed for Hierapolis and encamped in Sebasteia nearby the city, when suddenly a whole multitude of Muslim Huns ambushed them. Manuel did not run, instead he and his entire force unsheathed their swords and confronted the enemy, and after some bloodshed was done, the Turks fled. Manuel was not satisfied with a mere retreat, but wanted to finish the enemy off.

He and his men pursued them with their horses; the Turks continued to hurry away, and just when the confidence of the Christians reached its peak, the Muslims turned around and circled them, as was their typical strategy, and the tide of the battle was reversed.

Some of the Christian soldiers were captured, including Manuel himself, but most were slaughtered under the sharp crescent swords and agile arrows of the Turk.[185]

This is what had happened on this field in Sebasteia, and Romanus and his men were determined to not let this happen to them.

THE MUSLIMS RETURN TO MANZIKERT

Day after day they traversed through various lands and passed by numerous cities. It was at this moment that one could see Alp Arslan, riding his horse with head high above the cloud-born storms[186] of uncontrollable desire to rage against and to shatter the abodes of Christendom, "to steal, and to kill, and to destroy" all the Christians and their holy churches. The Turks gathered themselves together, and with their minds and their hearts burning with wrath, they said with Zebah and Zalmunna, "Let us take to ourselves the houses of God in possession." (Psalm 83:12)

---

184 See Attaleiates, *History*, 20.8
185 Attaleiates, *History*, 19.2
186 "cloud-born storms" was taken from a line from Prudentius, *The Origin of Sin*, 485–490, trans. H.J. Thomson

Alp Arslan and marched with an array of men and innumerable horsemen, and finally stood before that city, that lied on a plain as vast as the sky that captures our imaginations; that was sustained by overflowing and abundant spring water, where the people were never heated by thirst and where their souls were never pained by spiritual thirst, being washed with the water of the word through the teachings of the priests, and where the rustic shepherds now watch their flocks graze upon the fields, and sing of times now gone: this was Manzikert.[187]

Alp Arslan and his Turkish hoard rushed into the city and took it over as a storm tears apart a helpless ship in the midst of the seas.

THE CHRISTIAN ARMIES APPROACH MANZIKERT

Romanus approached the city's walls with only a select group of his men, and they rode about them, observing the structure and with keen eyes sought out the best place to commence the siege of the city, and retake it from the Muslim savages.

As they went about the walls, suddenly they heard the howling of wolves and screeching cries: these were the Turks, and with their Hunnic faces one could see them within the walls of the city, crying and mimicking the animals they so loved, and brandishing their knives.

A great number of them pulled back their bows, and with one unified movement released the arrows, and the sound of snapping strings all erupted at once. The arrows soared high, and rained down upon the Christians; a shield protecting the emperor blocked whatever projectiles would have ended his life in one swift moment.

Romanus and his men of valor had seen enough, and they rode away from the city and returned back to their camp.

THE CHRISTIANS ASSAIL THE WALLS

After dawn had awakened, the shades of the dreary darkness pulled back their murky tentacles from the sky, and the stars had fled from the clear light of the sunrise, a great many Christian warriors, all of the Armenian division of the army, came upon the walls of Manzikert with thousands of siege ladders transported by thousands of wagons. They attempted to assail the walls, but the Turks, "who handle and bend the bow" (Jeremiah 46:9), shot forth their arrows and repulsed the Armenians from fulfilling their aim, to overtake the city.

The waves of the roaring seas collide into the rocks of the shoreline, they are pulled back by the force of the full moon, only to return with the might of a storm; so it was with these Christian warriors of old, driven away by the strength of the enemy, they came back as a raging torrent.

THE SHEEP OVERPOWER THE WOLVES

The sun had set, the stars were ready to reside in their shadowy abodes, and the moon was about to take the seat of its bright rival. The worshippers of the moon could no longer pull

---

187 On Alp Arslan's arrival to Manzikert, see Attaleiates, *History*, 20.9

PART 13

back the waves of the Christian forces; the carriers of the Cross collided into the walls and flooded their tops. They overtook the city, and brought it back into the fold of Christendom.

THE MUSLIMS URGE FOR A PEACE TREATY
The emperor was in the camp when an envoy of Turks hurried to his presence, and begged him to spare their property and to show mercy, and that if he would do this, they would relinquish the city to his hands. The emperor honored the messengers with gifts, and assured them that their requests were granted.

When the emperor was about to make a triumphant entry into the city with his army, the inhabitants refused to let him in because, as they said, it was late at night and they were afraid that the Christians could attack them while it was so dark. It seemed that the Muslims were disregarding the treaty, and Romanus immediately ordered that the trumpets of battle be brayed, and the men of war resume the siege of the city.

The Muslims were surely shocked at his tenacity, and he communicated a conspicuous message that he was not going to tolerate any deception. They started to make excuses, and demanded more assurances for their own safety. Romanus assured them, and they departed from the city. Manzikert was now within the Christian thrall.[188]

THE MERCILESS KING
But the Turks did not leave empty-handed; for in their grips were their scimitars, weapons they would never give up. The emperor stood before them, watching the Turks as they left in one very large procession of sorrowful countenances, and many of them still holding their swords. Some of the Seljuks even walked very closely to the emperor, who was not even wearing armor. Michael Attaleiates was standing quite near Romanus, and he, with all of his prudence, did not approve of him being so absent of armor in the presence of, in the words of Michael himself, "those reckless, ruthless, murdering men."[189]

As some time went by, something happened in the camp: one of the soldiers was accused to stealing a Turkish donkey. The emperor had this man arrested, and ordered that his nose be cut off. The man begged for mercy, and ceaselessly cried, and as his wails struck those around him with sympathy and pity, the soils of Romanus' heart was vacuous of all compassion; the man's tears could not wet the parched earth of callousness. He cried out for clemency, and called out for the intercessions of the holy Virgin Mary, but no leniency was given. Before the cold and hard eyes of Romanus, and all of the army, and even in the presence of the icon of Mary, which stood high and usually accompanied the emperor, the poor soldier could be witnessed having his nose cut off, as he groaned and screamed, with cries that chilled the very bones and compelled the heart to weep.

---

188 See Attaleiates, *History*, 20.13–14
189 Attaleiates, *History*, 20.14

There stood Michael Attaleiates, and after the cruel punishment was done, he whispered within himself that surely the anger of God would come upon them.[190]

THE PEACE OF CAIN

Romanus had the garrison in the city removed and replaced by a purely Roman force, and when he returned to the camp from the now conquered Manzikert, he arrived to the roaring sound of praise, hymns of adoration and the cries of triumph. But the celebration was abruptly halted by dreaded news, that Alp Arslan's officers were attacking the soldiers' servants who were walking about.

A HOPELESS BATTLE

Romanus ordered his general, Nikephoros Bryennios, to lead a sufficient force against the Turks and confront them with all their might. Both the Christians and the Muslims broke off into small garrisons, and the battle commenced with each body of warriors warring against each other, in various areas. They were all on the front line, with arrows being shot from all sides in a wild tempest of confusion, with rage as red as blood, with men falling down in utter agony, and death latching itself onto great numbers.

The Romans had expected the Turks to be, as usual, quite reliant on their arrows, but these Huns were different from the others; these were more courageous, sterner and stronger. They did not rest on the comfort of firing arrows from far distance, but fought the Christians head on, with sword and hand to hand combat.

The general Bryennios was so terrified that he urged the emperor to send in reinforcements. Romanus bitterly, and maliciously, frothed out insults against the general, calling him a coward and, almost maniacally, declared that he would not send any troops to his aid. He assembled an army, and frantically described to them in harsh words the severity of the battle.

THE LAST SUPPER

As the hands of chaos confounded the minds of many a soldier, and the tempest of confusion raged in all places, as arrows ripped through men and the blades of swords cut right through flesh, as the wounded and the injured lied down, and all those nearby were not spared from the horrors of their cry, as the battle went on and escalated in intensity, and the melees only fanned the flames of wrath and swelled the flesh's desire to be satisfied through bloodshed, there stood the light of the world, the glowing lamp that made Christendom what it is, who watered it so that it could bloom and flourish—there stood the priest.[191]

He is the giver of the sacraments, the one who discharges, in the words of Ambrose, "the function of the priestly oblation."[192] To him is it given, in the words of Justin Martyr, "bread and a cup of water and [a cup] of wine mixed with water, and he taking them sends

---

190 Attaleiates, *History*, 20.14
191 See Attaleiates, *History*, 20.15; see also Nicolle, *Manzikert 1071*, p. 62
192 Ambrose, Letter 41.5, trans. Romestin

up praise and glory to the Father of the Universe through the name of the Son and of the Holy Spirit, and offers thanksgiving at some length for our being accounted worthy to receive these things from Him."[193]

The food, "eucharistized through the word of prayer that is from Him, from which our blood and flesh are nourished by transformation, is the flesh and blood of that Jesus who became incarnate."[194] There the priest, before the assembly of valorous men, conferred to each the Holy Sacrament, "the true Flesh of Christ,"[195] to prepare their souls to fight against the Muslims, those heretics who rejected the very sacraments of the Church, and like the heretics before them, to use the words of St. Ignatius, "confess not the Eucharist to be the flesh of our Savior Jesus Christ."[196]

The priest consecrated the bread and the wine, and "by blessing nature itself is changed."[197] Such a sublime and eternal event was happening at that very moment, in which the men of valor were in the Sacred Presence, and the holy and bloodless sacrifice was offered to God by men who drunk "the cup of the Lord" and partook "of the Lord's table" (1 Corinthians 10:21), preparing their souls for the battle against those who "sacrifice to demons and not to God" (1 Corinthians 10:20).

The priest gave them the Eucharist, and they took of the Body and Blood of Christ, before they carried their cross into the line of battle to combat the devil by slaying his advancers, as Christ gave His Body and Blood to the Disciples for them to eat, before He carried His Cross into battle to fight all of the powers of darkness on the Holy Wood, to "destroy the works of the devil." (1 John 3:8) The Disciples drunk the Savior's blood, before He gave His own "blood of the new covenant, which is shed for many." (Mark 14:24)

So the warriors, as the mighty fighters of Israel, "offered themselves willingly with the people" (Judges 5:9); for they emulated Christ, sacrificing themselves in holy war as He sacrificed Himself in the sacred fray against Lucifer, passing "from death to life, because we love the brethren" (1 John 3:14) manifesting the purest love, observing what St. John wrote,

> By this we know love, because He laid down His life for us. And we also ought to lay down our lives for the brethren. (1 John 3:16)

CHRIST'S WORDS ARE FULFILLED

Look up to wonderful Christendom! Look to its priests, see how they confer the sacraments! See how through them blessings are manifested, and the souls of warriors unified with the peace of Heaven before entering the field of battle! And look to the holy flower's armies, how they obey their officers, respect all men, honor the emperor and fear God! Watch how they

---

[193] Justin, *Apology*, 1.66, trans. Barnard
[194] Justin Martyr, *Apology*, 1.66
[195] Ambrose, *On the Mysteries*, 9.53
[196] Ignatius, Epistle to the Smyrnaeans, 7
[197] Ambrose, *On the Mysteries*, 9.50

"Render to Caesar the things that are Caesar's, and to God the things that are God's." (Mark 12:17)

In fighting for Christianity, did these soldiers obey this command all at once, for they gave to God all of their being, glorifying the Lord with their bodies and their spirits, fighting for Him and His Holy Faith, and striving to protect the empire of Christendom and the Caesar "sent by him for the punishment of evildoers and for the praise of those who do good." (1 Peter 2:14) The priest, in the presence of the soldiers, opened the Sacred Scriptures and turned to the Gospel of John, and from this eternal book he read the holy words of the reverent Apostle:

> If they persecuted me, they will persecute you; if they kept my word, they will keep yours also. But all this they will do to you because they do not know him who sent me. Indeed, the hour is coming when whoever kills you will think he is offering service to God. (John 16:2–3)[198]

Not everyone who heard the words of the reading thought that they were in any way connected with their present predicament. But there were those who, after hearing the holy Gospel read, immediately understood that it was not just a mere reading, but a sign of destiny, and truly providential: many martyrs were about to be made, Heaven was to be filled with a multitude of icons, and the angels of Heaven would soon be busy carrying up the souls of the slain. The field was soon to be a plain of saintly blood, and till this day the crimson river "cries out to Me from the ground." (Genesis 4:10)

THE BLOODBATH CONTINUES

Alp Arslan ascended a high place, and looking upon the Christian camp, it is said that he exclaimed:

> By Allah, they are as good as defeated, for digging a trench around themselves, in spite of their great numbers, is a sign of their cowardice and weakness. [199]

Curved swords and long lances were seen bespattered with human blood; the heads of arrows burst right into chests and torsos, faces and limbs; the heads of men could be seen on the fertile earth. There stands a man without an arm, over there one lies without a leg, and the flowing blood of pagans and martyrs reddened the earth.

The sounds of chiming resounded throughout, but it was not wedding bells that one was hearing, but swords clanging and colliding together, all in the midst of screams and wails, bellowing and howling, and the martyrs of Christ, that is, the Bride of Christ, ascended up to Heaven to join their Bridegroom, to the words of "Behold, you are fair, my love! Behold, you are fair!" (Songs of Solomon 4:1)

The cries of victory and the cries of agony merged together as one wave of clamor that shattered the soul and brought awe to the heart and to the spirit, and terror to the mind. In

---

198 This is actually quoted from Michael Attaleiates, *History*, 20.15, trans. Kaldellis and Krallis
199 Quoted by Sadr al-Din al-Husayni, in Nicolle, *Manzikert 1071*, p. 63

such battles of holy war, it is heart and spirit that brings one to victory, and not just the reliance on the mind. Romanus sent out his general, Basilakes, into the field of battle with his local forces, and he then joined with Brennios, and with the bulk of the army, they pursued the enemy.

The Turks saw this great body of gallant men and perceived no other choice but to flee; the Christians chased after them, but understanding the deception of the Seljuk, Byrennios gave the order to turn back.

But this command did not reach the ears of Basilakes. He kept on going with his own men, they approached the enemy camp, and within a swift moment the Turks wounded his horse and took him alive.[200]

THE CRIES OF ABEL WERE AMONGST THE CAMP

Those who were in the camp could see what carnage came upon the Christians: here the eyes could witness the many wounded men who were brought in, carried on stretchers; the ears could see what the eyes could not fully comprehend, for the groaning of the men,[201] with blood dripping wounds on their wearied bodies, told of stories of horror, and their agonies recounted what miseries lied on the field of carnage. The calls for mercy that the Turks exhorted from the just emperor, was nothing but the peace of Cain, for "Cain rose up against Abel his brother and killed him" as "they were in the field" (Genesis 4:8), acting as though he was not about to slaughter him.

And now in that field of Manzikert, there flowed the blood of those who believed in Christ, that Savior of humanity "prefigured by Abel the shepherd of sheep;"[202] there their bodies lied, slain by the successors of Cain after they came to them with cries of peace. If Romanus had done unto the Muslims of the city what Joshua did to the pagans of Jericho, slaughtering "all that was in the city, both man and woman, young and old, ox and sheep and donkey, with the edge of the sword" (Joshua 6:21), then they would not have been in such a difficult plight.

THE GRIM NOISE OF SILENCE UNDER THE MOONLESS LIGHT

The emperor took the rest of the entire army, and they journeyed outside of the camp, riding through some wilderness, and they ascended a number of high hills, and there was nothing—nothing but the grim noise of silence that whispers fear into the hearts of men, and brings them into the realm of heightened suspense.

There was a sense that someone was there, watching them, and remaining hidden behind the cover of silence. A vast plain of wilderness lied before their very eyes, and no one could be seen. They stood on the top of the hills, and then the sun was beheld departing from the celestial sphere, and the night covering all that was in their presence. They headed

---

200 Attaleiates, History, 20.16
201 See Attaleiates, History, 20.15–17
202 Augustine, *City of God*, 15.8

for the camp as the remnant of the effulgent beams were quickly dissipating to the light's department.

They arrived to their encampment, a silent moment lapsed; one could look up to the dark sky only to behold that this night was a moonless night. It was naked to the eye, absent from the firmament, absorbed into the darkness, as though the lamp of hope seemed plunged into the darkest abyss.

Then, out of nowhere, the wolves, who waited so long crouched in their concealment, crept near to the borders of the premise, and leapt onto the Scythian mercenaries posted outside of the camp. Within the camp, the still air of night no longer remained, it was disrupted by the sudden howl of a wolf.

Swiftly did the Christians know that this was the cry of no real wolf, but of the Turks. In a short time the inarticulate sounds of confusion assailed the ears; the Christians within the camp were confounded when they saw the mercenaries cornered to the entrance of the palisade, all in utter terror of the attacking Turks.

An array of unforeseen arrows zipped through them, and as they ripped through the air and cornered the Christians, the noise of galloping horses encompassed the camp, and their presence only fanned the flames of terror. The absence of the moon blinded their discernment, and no one could tell who was pursuing and who was fleeing, as the guidance of the lunar's shades of blue light, were gone.

A contagion of fear rushed through the entire army, talk of disasters and defeats were in the mouths of many, and the rambling cries of men seeing the blade of the scimitar about to strike their bodies and break the thread that connects all mortals to life, brought such a harrowing sound that all of the Christians felt that death would be better than witnessing the slaughter that was occurring right in their midst. "Not seeing such a thing was regarded as a stroke of luck," later wrote Michael Attaleiates, who was present in the camp, "and those who did not have to behold such a sight were deemed fortunate."

THE LINGERING WOLVES

Though the Turks could have broken through the entrance of the camp, and commenced an entire pool of blood and human gore, they restrained themselves, knowing that then was not the most opportune time. The sun's light stood apart from that rugged wilderness of the earth, depriving the guidance of its shining arms, as the daunting presence of the Turks never departed from them on that moonless night. There the Christians stood, frozen in their place with eyes wide opened like owls, only now the nocturnal bird of prey was being hunted by the wolves.

There rode the Turks, galloping on their horses throughout the surroundings of the camp; they cried with hysterical noise the eerie howl of the wolf, screaming and yelling like savage beasts. The release of arrows from tight bows was heard, and a rush of the projectiles landed into the camp. Hour after hour went by, and without ceasing did the arrows continue

PART 13

to be fired right into the Christian palisade. The Christians could not allow their eyes rest nor suffer their bodies the comforts of repose; they did not slumber and nor did their minds close in the warm embraces of dreams, in the midst of such a nightmare.

THE FRUITS OF THE SPIRIT DEFEAT THE SLAVES OF THE FLESH

When the sun finally arose from the long and frightening night, still their ears were oppressed by the howls and shrieks of the pagan Turks, and not only this, but now the river by which their thirsts were quenched, that flowed nearby the camp, was under the control of these Asian Muslims, who now used it to wet their screeching tongues. Although their mouths were deprived of the river's flowing waters, their hearts still overflowed with long suffering, that "fruit of the Spirit," "Against such there is no law." (Galatians 5:22–23) They harnessed all the courage within their spirits, their hearts and their minds, and using the body, "the temple of the Holy Spirit" (1 Corinthians 6:19), to unleash all the fury that pulsed and throbbed throughout their limbs, they executed a most coordinated assault on the Turks who still remained outside the camp.

The Scythian fighters charged against them, and their unsheathed swords tightly gripped in fighters' hands struck the Seljuks with swift, agile and devastating strikes. Christian archers approached the Turks' position, and from a safe distance, took aim and fired their arrows, and as lightening cuts asunder massive trees, they pierced through the Turks, cutting through torsos and heads, dividing flesh and penetrating the deepest organs.

THE WARRIORS THAT NEVER CAME

Many a Turk got struck by the Christian arrow, and so many of their corpses were seen scattered about the land. Romanus wanted to lead his army right into the Islamic ranks, and confront the enemy with sword and shield in hand to hand combat. But he knew that there was another body of elite warriors who were sent off to Chilat, well trained, quite conditioned for fighting in the front lines, and well instilled with prowess in the dance of war.

Romanus was hoping that this selected force would meet him and join forces to fight the Turks. But what he did not know was that the general of this elite force, as soon as he was informed that the Turks were audacious enough to attack the emperor, took all of his men and shamelessly retreated back into Roman territory. Romanus, hoping that these men would show up, refrained from commencing a battle, but as time went on, and no one came to their aid, the emperor suspected that some difficult impediment was hindering them from arriving, and was now determined to commence the bloody fray.[203]

AN UNWANTED PEACE

The next morning, the emperor sat within his imperial tent, as battle preparations were being vigorously conducted, and suddenly a number of envoys from the Turkish camp approached him, stating that the sultan Alp Arslan desired peace, not just for himself, but for the Chris-

---

203 See Attaleiates, History, 20.17–20

tians as well. The emperor dialogued with these messengers, although he was quite rough with them, and in the end agreed to have a peace settled.

He gave the sign of peace, that is an image of the Cross, to the envoy, and declared to them that the sultan should leave his position and move back farther away, to allow the emperor to move his own camp where the Turks were settled, and from there conduct a negotiation for a peace treaty. But such an agreement was not accepted by Michael Attaleiates, who was adverse to the emperor for so easily giving the sign of the Cross to the enemy.

While the envoys were still in the camp, Romanus's closest associates tried to convince him not to agree with any treaty with the Turks, for Alp Arslan, as they said, "was afraid, since his army was not strong enough, and he was waiting for his other forces to join up with him."[204]

The treaty was simply a hudna, or a false peace the Muslims use to deceive their enemies, and allow them enough time to regather sufficient strength to make a surprise assault. Cain was trying to beguile Abel, to distract him with friendliness from seeing the hidden blade he would use to slay him. But Romanus, this successor of the martyred righteous brother, quickly realized that he was not amidst people seeking true peace, but surrounded by the sons of Cain.

The Turks said they were seeking peace, but Romanus told them, "I will agree to that opinion [only when I am] in [the Iranian city of] al-Rayy." The Turks were based in Persia, and the emperor affirmed that there would be no peace until the Christians took over that land. He condescendingly asked the negotiator, Ibn al-Muhallaban, which city in Iran would be best to winter, Isfahan or Hamadan. Al-Muhallaban said that Isfahan would be the best place to stay during the winter. "As for us," said the emperor, "we will winter in Isfahan and the riding animals will be in Hamadan." "As for the riding animals," responded al-Muhallaban, "it is true that they will winter in Hamadan. As for you, I do not know."[205]

THE CHRISTIANS SEND A DARING MESSAGE
In the Muslim camp, it is said that a messenger arrived to Alp Arslan, and declared to the sultan the words of the emperor:

> I have come to you accompanied by troops that you cannot resist. If you become subservient to me, I will give you from the lands that which will be sufficient for you… If you do not do that, I have with me in the way of troops three hundred thousand cavalry and infantry. I have fourteen thousand carts on which are coffers of money and weapons. Not a single one of the Muslim troops can resist me and none of their cities and citadels will remain shut in my face.

Alp Arslan looked with deepened eyes to the envoy, and declared:

---
204 Attaleiates, History, 20.21
205 This conversation was recounted by Ibn al-Azraq, quoted by Nicolle, *Manzikert 1071*, p. 69

Tell your master: It is not you who have sought me out, but it is Allah... Some of your troops will be killed by me; others will be my captives. All your treasures will be in my possession and [become] my property. [206]

Alp Arslan's personal imam, Abu Nasr Muhammad Ibn 'Abd al-Malik al-Bukhari al-Hanafi, comforted the sultan with elating words, declaring to him with much zeal:

> You are fighting for Allah's religion. I hope that Almighty Allah will have written this victory in your name. Meet them [the Byzantines] on Friday at the hour when the preachers will be on the pulpits [during the main congregational service] praying for victory for the warriors of the faith against the infidels and the prayer will be answered. [207]

THE CHRISTIANS PRAY TO GOD WHILE THE MUSLIMS PRAY TO THE DEVIL

As the night hours passed, both Muslim and Christian raised up their heads to only see the moonless sky. They did not know to where the lunar star was hidden, but they did know that soon, all of the moon, the sun, the sky, and the earth, was to be covered in blood, and the air was to be seized by the odor of carnage.

Each side stood by, waiting, and hoping that the next morning the smell of their enemy's blood would touch their nostrils. The next morning had finally come. It was Friday, and the Muslim camp was arrayed by an entire multitude of warriors, their foreheads pressed upon the ground as their imam chanted the paean of the Sufi.

The ghazis stood up, they swore oaths and expressed their love for one another, and then with one voice cried out to Alp Arslan, "We will invoke the name of Allah Most High and we will attack the people [the enemy]."

On the other side, in the Christian camp, the warriors took of the Lord's Body and Blood, and for many of them it would be their last supper. There the saintly fighters prostrated and prayed to the God of Heaven; and there it could be seen the majestic banners of Christianity, raised up high for all to behold. Crosses and holy icons bearing the images of patron saints were held aloft; the soldiers made their prayers to God and to His saints, and by the very site of the icons, did they receive their strength.[208]

AN UNEXPECTED ATTACK

The Turks, who were still in their camp, looked up and saw the soaring force of Christians, all in battle array and aligned in the formation of the phalanx, walking with organized step, and approaching ever so closely with imposing appearance.

The Muslims fled, and the Christians pursued after them; the Turks hurried away and kept sprinting, without even firing a single arrow, as the raging emperor chased them as a multitude of lions go after a herd of frightened hyenas.

---

206 This correspondence comes from al-Husayni, who heard it from Khwaja Musharraf al-Shirazi, quoted by Nicolle, *Manzikert 1071*, p. 69
207 Quoted in Nicolle, *Manzikert 1071*, p. 70
208 See Nicolle, *Manzikert 1071*, pp. 70, 72

✝ CHRISTIANITY IS AT WAR: THE MANIFESTO FOR CHRISTIAN MILITANCY

THE CHASE IS CALLED OFF, CONFUSION AND CHAOS STRIKE

The sun began to descend upon their ambitious hunt, and the emperor, noticing that the Turks were not resisting at all, and knowing that there were no guards in his camp, realized that the enemy was only luring him away to make the Christian encampment vulnerable to being invaded, and if he were to prolong his pursuit the night would only overtake them, hide the Muslims from their site, and leave themselves open to the arrows of scouting Turks as they tried to walk a long journey back to base.

He ordered that the chase be called off, the imperial banner was turned around to signal to the men to return back to the camp. But the soldiers who were too far a distance from the main body of warriors, when they saw the banner reversed, thought that the emperor was slain, disarray and confusion conquered them.

Hysteria, frenzy and terror spread around like a disease, and so many men were running away to and fro without order. It is said that a cousin of the emperor's stepson, Michael, who hated Romanus and always wanted to get back at him, was the one who spread the report of his death to cause disorder amongst the army.

This traitor took his men and fled back to the camp, and many of the soldiers began to follow his example. The emperor saw this confounded avidity to flee, and how it was truly weakening and fragmenting the numbers and the strength of the military body. He remained with his own amongst this uncontrollable desertion and flight, and tried to take a stand to encourage the others to carry on and endure. But his cries fell on deaf ears, and no one had listened to him.[209]

ALP ARSLAN MAKES HIS FINAL SPEECH

As the chaos of the masses abounded, throughout the meadow and on the mountainous plain, a station of Turks posted upon numerous lofty hills could see what shambles the Christians had become, and so being quite elated about all of this, they quickly informed Alp Arslan, who was leading the fleeing ranks, to order his men to stop their flight, turn around and strike Christendom's disarrayed troops. Alp Arslan, dressed in the pure white garments of the Muslim, stood before his army and declared:

> We are with a depleted number of men. I want to throw myself on them [the Byzantines] at this hour when prayers are being said for us and the Muslims on the pulpits. Either I will achieve that goal or I will go as a martyr to Paradise. He amongst you who wants to follow me, let him follow me, and he who wants to leave, let him leave my company. Here is not a sultan commanding, nor an army being commanded, for today I am only one of you and a ghazi with you. He who follows me and gives himself to Allah Most High, he will gain Paradise and booty. He who goes away, the Fire [of Hell] and ignominy are obligator for him.[210]

---

209 Attaleiates, *History*, 20.23
210 Quoted by Nicolle, *Manzikert 1071*, p. 77

The Muslims looked to the Christians fleeing and chaotically dispersing, and being filled with such moral and enthusiasm, cried out, "Takbir! Allahu Akbar!"[211]

A SMALL GROUP OF CHRISTIANS HOLD THE LINE

With the purest determination did the sultan turn his men around and charge right into the dissipated army of his Trinitarian enemy. In the midst of fleeing soldiers, like countless rain drops showering around a labyrinth of lightning bolts, as the thunders roar and their ferocity heightens as the torrent grows in strength, so did Romanus and his small band of men hold the line as the rest subsumed themselves in flight. Here one could see Alp Arslan, riding ever so vigorously, with utter verve and flaming zeal, leading his men right into the remnant of the Christian ranks. One could see the Christians: small in number, weakened through exhaustion, their bodies fatigued from the endless miles of marching, and from the battles that seemed to have no end in this sublime struggle between good and evil, heresy and Orthodoxy, Christendom and pagandom.

Think to yourself what pains these men must have suffered; what travails they had to go through! What endurance they had to display! Thousands upon thousands of times did they strike with the fullest of exertion; every tendon, every sinew, every fiber of every muscle, worked together as one, in unison with the spirit, to strike with the sword the pagan foe, to advance the Sword of the Spirit over the scimitar of the abysmal demons.

There on the field of Manzikert, could one see the Christians broken and hurt, yet strong enough to hold their formation with swords, spears and shields drawn, right before a hoard of Orientals riding upon their galloping horses, holding up curved blades; the hooves of their beasts raised themselves and hit hard against the earth, and in one short moment, the forces collided.

It was as if two hurricanes crossed paths; lightning bolt struck lightning bolt, winds assailed over winds, thick and pitch black clouds intertwined into the folds of the blackened fog, covering the sun and bringing to the eye a most majestic site, with darkness complimenting the soft glowing hue.

A warrior struck at a sharp angle with his sword and slashed through a torso; a blade sunk deep into one's brains; here an arm was severed away from the body; in another place a leg was snapped right off; a soldier trained and tough, eyes crazed and face splattered with blood, with hands tightly gripped on the tilt of his sword, he raised his weapon and in one swift movement decapitated an enemy.

THE EMPEROR SHOWS HIS STRENGTH

There the emperor stood amongst his dauntless men, valiantly defending himself upon his horse with sword in hand, slaughtering the enemy by his own prowess and vigor. Wet and warm was the ground upon which they fought and used the sword, soaked was the soil and

---

211 See Nicolle, *Manzikert 1071*, p. 77

muggy was the air of that eastern land, with the fresh blood of the slain overflowing above the terrain, and its vaporous haze rising up like steam.

On that day did the eagle of mighty Christendom weep. Most of the Christians were still running, and soon they found themselves jammed together outside the camp, all running about in a delirium, not knowing how to settle the conundrum that posed so great a danger to their frantic lives. There they went with their confounded state, their hearts fragmented and their souls sinking like a house upon the flooded sands.

From a distance in the harrowing wilderness, one could see the emperor, riding on his horse with valor and majesty, attacking the enemy with sharp form and swift strikes with the edge of his sword. He lacerated flesh and gashed men right through their bodies. One could envision what appearance the emperor had in his arduous state: in the midst of such a small number of men, his hair uncouth, his eyes wild yet stern, his body wearied, his heart strong, his spirit fortified, his mind upright and determined till the end, his self-denied and absent.

Surely it can be said, that he loved God with all body, mind, soul, heart, spirit and strength.

THE SHEEP FLEE

The earth was strangled by the ever flowing river of blood that poured out from the mounds of carnage and gore on the hard ground. One could have fell, and his hands would have been stained by the blood of his brother or his enemy. The Cappadocians soldiers that were at the king's side were not struck by the arrows that kills life, but that suffocates the heart and drains the soul of what courage it has left.

No longer could they withstand the onslaught of the Turk, who relentlessly charged against them with horse and scimitar, wild cries and howls, vicious blows and heavy bombardments. The earthquake of terror shook their very beings, the shrieking of grief struck them with travails.

Death seemed so sudden and so near, and all that could be witnessed were clouds of dust, vast trails of corpses, and hordes of Turks overrunning the plain. The Cappadocians chose the road of retreat, as all the soldiers had done, and as they desperately sprinted to save their lives, they looked back only to see the Turks riding on their horses so closely that the whites of their curved eyes beamed right into their spirits. The scimitars of the galloping Seljuks cut them down to their mortal ends, and others, as they ran for dear life, were pummeled by the horses and trampled under the hooves, and to their deaths.

A GENERAL WITHOUT SOLDIERS

The mighty eagle of Christendom soared above the plain, and all she could see was entire valley of Christian corpses. They left the fate of the entire battle to the hands of only one man: Romanus Diogenes. Turkish archers from some distance took aim and fired upon his horse; the poor beast was pierced with many arrows, and it fell to the ground with the emperor tumbling to the earth, and after releasing a painful neigh, the loyal stallion died.

PART 13

He got up, with his impenetrable will still intact. Here he stood, a general without soldiers; here he lied, an emperor without an empire; here he remained, a king without a throne, a sovereign without authority; here he endured, a warrior, sacred and pure of heart, armed with his sword and his spirit. He labored no longer with the worries of a king, but now found himself burdened by the just cause of a martyr.

One could see the travailing occurrences that surrounded him: most of all his men were either slaughtered or taken captive, and his entire camp was now under barbarian hands. He was alone, like a sheep "in the midst of wolves." (Matthew 10:16) He was forsaken, yet not lost in despair; abandoned, yet not without hope. He was a saint.

He peered out to his enemy, eyes gleaming and sturdy; the hilt of his sword was tightly held in the thrall of his resilient hands, with its blade honorably splattered with the blood of pagans.

THE SHEPHERD FIGHTS THE WOLVES

As wolves encompass a single sheep lying within the safety of a fence, and growl as their hunger yearns for what they cannot easily capture, the Turks surrounded Romanus with their devilish faces, as he firmly stood on guard with sword in hand. They charged after him; he immediately defended himself as the efficient warrior he was. With the strength of his arm he slaughtered many Turks single-handedly, gloriously killing one by one with inimitable technique. He killed one, then another; here one lied dead, here another perished at a blow of the Christian sword, and there a Turk stood hesitating to attack.

He wielded the sword concisely against his enemy; he was like a tornado that cuts asunder whatever stands in its way. Many Turks were right near his body, trying to slash him with their scimitars from any direction they could, but they were so overpowered by such an indomitable spirit. Soon one Turk struck his hand, but he kept going with valorous exertion and heroic perseverance.

He gave one last burst of rage, but tired and fatigued, and no longer able to continue, he surrendered himself.

A PRISONER AMONGST PRISONERS

His eyes gazed upon the serene heavens, and beheld an empty horizon beautifully embellished by the rosy shade of the twilight, and the fiery red color of the approaching dusk. Now the end was here, and the battle was over, but maybe a measure of peace could be briefly seen in that pristine sky. The Muslim who snatched him, was that same recruit from Bagdad who was mocked as puny and feeble, and of whom the recruiter mockingly said, "Will he then bring captive to us the Roman Emperor?"

They apprehended the emperor, and in a short time he found himself with his captured men. From an emperor amongst warriors, he was now a prisoner amongst prisoners, awaiting his fate as all men do. When the Turks saw they had not only defeated the Roman army, but captured the emperor himself, they attributed their victory solely to Allah.[212]

IN THE PRESENCE OF THE SULTAN

Romanus was taken up, and while still attired with the same clothing he wore in the battlefield, weary and fatigued from combat, they placed a rope around his neck and brought him before the sultan, Alp Arslan, who was dressed in his silk white garments.

One of the Turks grabbed the emperor by the hair and the chest and threw him to the floor, and ordered that he kiss the ground. The sultan ordered that he be left alone and at peace. He then approached the emperor, and gracefully embraced him. "Do not fear, O emperor" said the sultan, "and above all be of good hope that you will suffer no bodily punishment and will, instead, be honored in a manner worthy of your high station. For a man would be foolish if he did not fear that sudden change of fortune might reverse the situation."

He ordered that he be given a comfortable tent, and attended to hospitably, as is the Oriental custom. After some rest and washing up, Alp Arslan invited him to a dinner. Romanus arrived dressed in Turkish garments, and ate with the sultan, who placed him on a seat of prestige, and not at the table of commoners. In one moment he suddenly and violently struck the emperor, and then viciously kicked him, telling him that he was a fool for not accepting the peace treaty when he had offered it to him before his defeat.

Romanus then responded: "but the victory was yours. So do what you want and stop rebuking me." Twice a day did the sultan visit the emperor, to conduct pleasant conversations with him, to raise his spirits with words of encouragement, and to even share with him proverbs and maxims on the vicissitudes of life. One day he asked Romanus, "What would you have done if you yourself held me in your power like this?" To this the emperor said, "Know that I would have inflicted much torture on your body."

The sultan replied, "But I will not imitate your severity and harshness." Such is the way of the Orient, in which there are two contradictory natures: elegance and brutality, and coming together as two snakes embracingly twirl, cruelty becomes an art. A few days had passed, a treaty was signed between the two, and after a firm handshake, Alp Arslan released him along with his soldiers.[213]

A messenger arrived to Alp Arslan with a message from the Caliph of the Abbasids:

> The son, the most lofty, supported, assisted, vicarious lord, the most mighty Sultan, the possessor of the Arabs and the non-Arabs, the lord of the kings of nations, the light of religion, the support of the Muslims, the helper of the imam, the refuge of mankind, the support of the victorious state, the crown of the resplendent community, the sultan of the lands of the Muslims, the proof of the Commander of the Faithful.[214]

With this, the Turks became, from bandits to an empire.

---

212 See Attaleiates, History, 20.24–25; Nicolle, *Manzikert 1071*, pp. 48, 83
213 See Attaleiates, History, 20.26–27
214 Quoted by Nicolle, *Manzikert 1071*, p. 89

A LONG JOURNEY BACK HOME

The emperor, still wearing his Turkish clothing, and his men, reached the town of Theodosioupolis where he was received most honorably, and there he rested for a number of days to allow his hand to heal. He redressed himself in some Roman attire, and continued his journey, passing the towns of ancient Georgia. During his travel he would come across some Roman soldier here and there, survivors from the battle, and always kept them by his side along with the other warriors,[215] as a father takes in his children after they have gone missing.

A HERO IS NEVER ACCEPTED, NOT EVEN BY THE PEOPLE HE FIGHTS FOR

He strived to arrive to his empire, after fighting so pernicious an enemy, only to find out that his greatest adversaries were right in his own home. During his journey he was informed that he was no longer emperor, and that his throne now belonged to Michael VII Doukas, his stepson. He was the son of Eudokia, Romanus' wife, and her former husband who was now dead.

After the emperor was released by the sultan, Eudokia was enraged at her husband's liberty, and so sent an order throughout all the provinces of the empire not to recognize Romanus as their sovereign. Her embraces turned out to be but a cold and callous touch—the kisses of Delilah, and the love Bathsheba would have shown Urijah after his return from the battle.

Here he was, fighting with all of his will and his strength, to defend Christendom and protect the empire, to drive out the Muslim hoard who wanted to slaughter and enslave every citizen of New Rome, only to be betrayed by his wife. But her plan to persecute her husband ended up turning against her, for those who worked with her to dispose Romanus drove her out as well, forcing her to be exiled in the city of Stenon, where she was forced to live as a nun.

ANOTHER WAR COMMENCES, NOT BETWEEN CHRISTIANS AND HERETICS, BUT BETWEEN CHRISTIANS

The greatest enemy to Christendom, is not Muslims, but traitorous Christians. A civil war commenced, between Romanus and those loyal to him, and his usurping stepson. In the end, the noble emperor, who did everything he could for his people, was defeated. He was mocked and scoffed; his enemies dressed him up like a monk and rode him around on a pack-animal. What sinister ingratitude!

THE FORSAKEN HERO

The man who risked everything, who gave his life for his brethren, to defend the people from the most warlike nation, was now being mocked. The emperor was treated with the greatest humiliation, being as Christ, the King of Heaven, Who suffered so much under the hands of those He came to redeem.

---

215 See Attaleiates, History, 20.28

Romanus was sentenced to have his eyes brutally carved out with an iron pin. The emperor crumbled to the ground upon hearing this, and at the feet of a certain archpriest who was there, he begged him to defend his life.

The priest was so willing to help his emperor, but so absent of any power. Here lied the emperor, weeping and begging, sobbing and wailing. His tears ran down his cheeks, but not his cries nor his entreaties could reveal his nobleness to the persecutors.

They dragged him to a small room and tied down his four limbs, and numerous men held him down with shields on his chest and belly. A man hovered over him, and with his iron pin he stabbed Romanus' eyes. Blood gushed out as he struggled and shook, screamed and bellowed as loud as he could. He rose up, blood streaming out from what was once his eyes, and everyone present in the room wept with uncontrollable tears. He lied down half-dead, unconscious from the excruciating pain he had to suffer.

They placed him on some beast of burden and rode him out. One could see him, almost lifeless and his eyes completely missing; his face was swollen and on his cheeks maggots crawled chewing on the rotting flesh that hung from the sockets.

A few days had passed, and as each moment dissipated into the next transient lapse of time, the most painful agony rushed through his body; his passion was made known from his incessant cries, and the anguish of both his soul and his flesh was made manifest by his travails, and through the bitter betrayal he had to endure. In his suffering, did he emulate Christ, and in being betrayed by his wife, did he experience what Christ endured when He was kissed by Judas. He soon died in his anguish,[216] bitter and abandoned, knowing what Christ had undergone when He was forsaken.

Now the shepherd weeps, as this passing moment is retold through the torment of his voice, in the song he sings upon that pleasant meadow, where the abundant springs are always replenished by his tears, always remembering, and never ceasing to speak of what happened in that city of Manzikert. About a year after his death, Alp Arslan declared to the Muslim warriors:

> Henceforth all of you be like lion cubs and eagle young, racing through the countryside day and night, slaying the Christians and not sparing any mercy on the Roman nation.[217]

As they were fighting, so too was Christian civilization fighting for its very existence. The Christian was armed with extensive knowledge in tactical warfare, while his enemy was skillful in the riding of the horse and the bow. The Turks proceeded with their common tactic of attacking and running, which exhausted their Christian enemies. Overpressed by continuous movement and heat, Romanus had no other choice but to retire to his camp. As they were marching back, his force became confused and soon fragmented. Many of his reserve soldiers broke away, and were now cut off from the center of the army, leaving the whole force completely vulnerable to the elusive Turk. The commander of this reserve ran off from the field of battle solely to destroy the reputation of Romanus by saying he

---

216 To learn about the betrayal and death of Romanus, see Attaleiates, *History*, 21
217 Nicolle, *Manzikert 1071*, p. 92

had lost the battle. When sundown came, and during the night, the Seljuks took advantage of the opportunity: the Christian soldiers were massacred. The barbarians surrounded the emperor, killed his horse and then wounded him. He was taken prisoner, his jewels were stolen, his purple taken, and all of Asia Minor lay open to the Turk. Romanus was led to the Turkish divan where he was presented before that most sinister appearing figure, Alp Arslan. He was commanded to bow down to the Mongol savage and kiss the ground before him. He reluctantly obeyed, and as his lips touched the floor the foot of the tyrant was planted on his neck. The Turks overran Asia Minor, the nursery of Christianity, and in less than a lifetime the whole vast district of its interior was ruined.[218]

THE TURKS UNLEASH A TORRENT OF CHAOS ON CHRISTENDOM

After Manzikert, utter chaos flooded the land and massive massacres of Christians were done almost without end. The Byzantine historian Anna Komnenus described this time as such:

> Cities were wiped out, lands ravaged, all the territories of Rome stained with Christian blood. Some died miserably, pierced by arrows or lance; others were driven from their homes and carried off as prisoners-of-war to Persian cities. Dread seized on all as they hurried to seek refuge from impending disaster in caves, forests, mountains and hills. There they loudly bewailed the fate of their friends in Persia; the few others who survived in Roman lands mourned the loss of sons or grieved for their daughters; one wept for a brother, another for a nephew killed before his time and like women they shed bitter tears. In those days no walk of life was spared its tears and lamentations.[219]

THE IGNORED POPE

Three years after this great travesty of Manzikert—sadly forgotten by modern Christians—Pope Gregory VII, ignited by his mourning for the persecuted Christians of the Eastern Church, felt himself behooved to begin a crusade against the Muslim powers and to finally extinguish this principality of Satan which had so tormented the saints. In 1074, he wrote:

> We hereby inform you that the bearer of this letter, on his recent return from across the sea [from Palestine], came to Rome to visit us. He repeated what we had heard from many others, that a pagan race had overcome the Christians and with horrible cruelty had devastated everything almost to the walls of Constantinople, and were now governing the conquered lands with tyrannical violence, and that they had slain many thousands of Christians as if they were but sheep. If we love God and wish to be recognized as Christians, we should be filled with grief at the misfortune of this great empire [the Greek] and the murder of so many Christians. But simply to grieve is not our whole duty. The example of our Redeemer and the bond of fraternal love demand that we should lay down our lives to liberate them. "Because he has laid down his life for us: and we ought to lay down our lives for the brethren,"

---

218 (Belloc, *The Crusades*, ch. ii, pp. 11–16; Gibbon, *Decline and Fall*, vol. v, ch. lvii, p. 1037; Moczar, *Seven Lies about Catholic History*, ch. iii, p. 63; John France, "Impelled by the Love of God," in Thomas F. Madden's *The Crusades*, pp. 34–35)

219 Ann Komnena, *Alexiad*, 15.11

[1 John 3:16]. Know, therefore, that we are trusting in the mercy of God and in the power of his might and that we are striving in all possible ways and making preparations to render aid to the Christian empire [the Greek] as quickly as possible. Therefore we beseech you by the faith in which you are united through Christ in the adoption of the sons of God, and by the authority of St. Peter, prince of apostles, we admonish you that you be moved to proper compassion by the wounds and blood of your brethren and the danger of the aforesaid empire and that, for the sake of Christ, you undertake the difficult task of bearing aid to your brethren [the Greeks]. Send messengers to us at once inform us of what God may inspire you to do in this matter. [220]

His words, inflamed with zeal and righteous indignation, gathered together over fifty thousand warriors of the Cross, ready to stop the cruelty of the Muslims. On December 7th, of the year 1074, St. Pope Gregory VII sent a letter to King Henry IV, exhorting him to observe his God-given obligation to protect Christendom, bear the cross of Christ, unsheathe the sword of St. Peter, strike down the Muslims and preserve the lives of the Christians from the Islamic scimitar. Gregory emphasized that even though the Eastern Orthodox Christians differed on some theological details, that they were still fellow brethren, and needed to be defended from the worshippers of Satan. This fact aggressively confronts those who today want to promote division between the Roman Catholic Church and the Eastern Orthodox Church; for when the Eastern Christians were being slaughtered, it was the Roman Catholic Church who came to their defense. If King Henry refused, then Gregory, as he himself said, was willing to take up the cross himself, and with an army of fifty thousand loyal Christians willing to bear their own cross, lead a holy war against the heathens:

Further, I call to your attention that the Christians beyond the sea, a great part of whom are being destroyed by the heathen with unheard-of slaughter and are daily being slain like so many sheep, have humbly sent to beg me to succor these our brethren in whatever ways I can, that the religion of Christ may not utterly perish in our time—which God forbid! I, therefore, smitten with exceeding grief and led even to long for death—for I would rather stake my life for these than reign over the whole earth and neglect them—have succeeded in arousing certain Christian men so that they are eager to risk their lives for their brethren in defense of the law of Christ and to show forth more clearly than the day the nobility of the sons of God. This summons has been readily accepted by Italians and northerners, by divine inspiration as I believe—nay, as I can absolutely assure you—and already fifty thousand men are preparing, if they can have me for their leader and prelate, to take up arms against the enemies of God and push forward even to the sepulcher of the Lord under his supreme leadership. I am especially moved towards this undertaking because the Church of Constantinople, differing from us on the doctrine of the Holy Spirit, is seeking the fellowship of the Apostolic See, the Armenians are almost entirely estranged from the Catholic faith and almost all of the Easterners are waiting to see how the faith of the Apostle Peter will decide

---

220 Gregory VII: Call for a "Crusade," This text is part of the Internet Medieval Source Book, found in the Fordham University website

among their divergent views. For it is the call of our time that the word of command shall be fulfilled which our blessed Savior deigned to speak to the prince of the Apostles: 'I have prayed for thee that thy faith fail not: and when thou art converted, strengthen thy brethren.' And because our fathers, in whose footsteps we, though unworthy, desire to walk, often went to those regions for the strengthening of the Catholic faith, we also, aided by the prayers of all Christian men, are under compulsion to go over there for the same faith and for the defense of Christians—provided that the way shall be opened with Christ as our guide—for the way of man is not in his own hand, and the steps of a man are ordered by the Lord. But, since a great undertaking calls for the aid and counsel of the great, if God shall grant me to begin this, I beg you for your advice and for your help according to your good pleasure. For if it shall please God that I go, I shall leave the Roman Church, under God, in your hands to guard her as a holy mother and to defend her honor. [221]

On December 16th, 1074, St. Gregory sent another letter, this time to the Countess Matilda. He spoke of his fiery zeal to lead the Christian army himself against the heathens, and urged her that she too had a moral obligation to God to participate in the holy war against the Muslim Turks by providing whatever aid she could provide for the soldiers:

> How serious my intention and how great my desire to go overseas and with Christ's help carry succor to the Christians who being slaughtered like sheep by pagans, I hesitate to say to some persons lest I seem to be moved by too great fickleness of purpose. But to you, my most dearly beloved daughter, I have no hesitation in declaring any of these matters; for I have more confidence in your good judgment than you yourself could possibly express. Therefore, when you have read the letter which I have written to the faithful beyond the Alps, pray use your utmost efforts to furnish whatever aid and counsel you can in the service of your Creator. …If the empress will come, her prayers joined with yours may rouse many to this work. And I, provided with such sisters, would most gladly cross the sea and place my life, if need be, at the service of Christ with you whom I hope to have forever at my side in our eternal home. [222]

But politics intervened, and as usually happens when zeal is about to combat evil, the politician and the apathy of many of Europe's knights prevented the saint from his divine mission. A quarrel with Henry IV obliged Gregory to relinquish his attack.[223]

The Seljuks arrived at the gates of Constantinople, and they would have taken it if it wasn't for a group of zealots from Western Europe: these were the Crusaders, this is how their story begins, and this is how they began where Pope Gregory was forced to leave off.[224]

---

221 Gregory VII, b. 2, 31, p. 165
222 Gregory VII, Epistolae collectae, 11, p. 532
223 Mosheim's *Church History*, 11th century, part i, ch. 1.4, p. 253; Moczar, *Islam at the Gates*, prologue, act 3, p. 20; Mills, Hist. Crus. ch. i, p. 20
224 Belloc, *The Crusades*, ch. ii, pp. 11–16; Gibbon, *Decline and Fall*, vol. v, ch. lvii, p. 1037; Moczar, *Seven Lies about Catholic History*, ch. iii, p. 63; Mosheim's *Church History*, 11th century, part i, ch. 1.4, p. 253

PART 14 – THE WARRIORS OF CHRISTENDOM TAKE UP THE CROSS

THE BLOOD OF THE SAINTS CRY OUT FOR JUSTICE
A horde of bandits trampled through the doors of an ancient church. The congregation is immediately struck with terror as the criminals run about, clutching with their hands on anybody they can latch onto. Women are viscously seized, stripped into the nude and raped. A large body of congregants are violently forced to get on their knees and bend low their necks. A few smiling men thrust down their blades and decapitate the victims. Meanwhile, the rape of the women continues on as the blood of their butchered men puddles next to them. The bandits take a defenseless monk and laugh sadistically as they hold him, and as one of them plunges a sword into his belly. They watch as he bleeds and chuckle as though it was nothing.

Screams are heard that are so filled with horror, suffering, agony, and helplessness that they pierce through our very bones, stab our souls and overrun our minds. The murderers grapple another group of men, tear open their garments and cut off their private parts. Some take in a portion of the spraying blood into containers and mockingly sprinkle it onto the church altar, while others pour it into the holy water vases. The bleeding monk is still alive, his heart beating ever so intensely. A bandit shoves his hand into his deep wound and pulls out his intestines. The others help, and when they pull out enough guts, they wrap them around a stake. One holds the stake, another whips the monk to make him walk, while the rest enjoy the sight as a comedic spectacle. They walk out of the church; a trail of blood follows. The monk murmurs some prayers, preparing his soul for the everlasting glory that is to come. His body, forced into its weakest state, is about to perish, while his soul and his faith are as strong as they were before the attack. They continue to pull him, and though we are now outside, the shrill cries from inside the church can still be clearly heard. They keep going, and as a few moments go by, the monk's body can no longer withstand the pulling, his body splits right open and all of his entrails come out. He gives out his last breath and collapses as his persecutors explode into the laughter of madmen possessed by devils.[1]

This is not some sick man's fantasy, but a reality which frequently took place in the Eastern Christian lands such as Syria, North Africa, Mesopotamia, and Armenia, which, before being under Islam, were half of Christendom.[2]

THE MONK WHO DID AND DID NOT JUST TALK

Now, after imagining this horror we find a priest short in stature, but a zealot nonetheless, this is Peter the Hermit. He travelled from France to Jerusalem as a pilgrim where he met with the Christians who revealed to the hermit all of the tremendous persecutions which the Christians were enduring. What he wasn't told of he saw with his own eyes, witnessing the turmoil of his brethren before him. He also met Simeon, the patriarch of the city, who provided him with further details on the inhumanities of the Muslims. His spirit was stirred to zeal and compassion for these saints. Their voices needed to be heard, and he was going to make sure that they were. He did not turn his eyes from the evils which took place in Jerusalem, go back home and live a merry life, nor did he tell Simeon, "I'll pray for you" and walk away. He was moved to action, and not just talk, and told Simeon:

> You may be assured, Holy Father, that if the Roman church and the princes of the West should learn from a zealous and reliable witness the calamities which you suffer, there is not the slightest doubt that they would hasten to remedy the evil, both by words and deeds. Write them zealously both to the lord Pope and the Roman church and to the kings and princes of the West, and confirm your letter by the authority of your seal. I, truly, for the sake of salvation of my soul, do not hesitate to undertake this task. And I am prepared under God's guidance to visit them all, to exhort them all, zealously to inform them of the greatest of your sufferings and to urge to hasten to your relief.[3]

The patriarch followed through, wrote of the calamities which were occurring, and gave it to Peter who proceeded to Rome and delivered the urgent message to Pope Urban II.[4]

This poor pilgrim did what our Faith demands, and that is to bring aid to the persecuted. So many famous pastors receive great revenues and do not give a cent to those Christians who live their lives every day not knowing if they are to be butchered, raped, kidnapped, and a whole litany of other cruelties. A professing Christian who does nothing for our suffering brethren is not a true believer in the Faith. When Christ returns in the Day of Judgement He will tell those who took no action to help His oppressed people:

---

[1] This description was inspired by the speech of Pope Urban II, documented by Robert the Monk, in Edward Peters, *The First Crusade*, p. 2
[2] See Hilaire Belloc, *The Crusades*, ch. i, p. 1; ch. ii, p. 9
[3] See Edward Peters, *The First Crusade*, ch. iv, p. 93, Peter the Hermit, The Version of William of Tyre
[4] See Edward Peters, *The First Crusade*, ch. iv, p. 94, Peter the Hermit, The Version of William of Tyre; Mills, Hist. Crus. ch. ii, pp. 23–24

CHRISTIANITY IS AT WAR: THE MANIFESTO FOR CHRISTIAN MILITANCY

Verily I say unto you, Inasmuch as ye did [it] not to one of the least of these, ye did [it] not to me. And these shall go away into everlasting punishment: but the righteous into life eternal. (Matthew 25:45-46)

The evils that Peter the Hermit would record, would eventually reach the ears of the Pope, Urban II, and we shall see how much of a doer he was.

THE POPE WHO WATCHED FOR THE FLOCK AND DID NOT FLEE FROM THE WOLVES

As Pope Urban II was sojourning in Piacenza on a journey to France, he was encountered by an embassy coming from the Emperor Alexius I Commenus, bringing news of these very atrocities, imploring him to come to the aid of the Eastern Church.[5] What did the Pope do? He did not call for an interfaith dialogue, as we see so much today, nor did he preach to "build bridges" with Muslims, and try to find commonality with Islam. On November 27, 1095, Urban made a profound declaration in France—the most military country of the West in that time—before a congregation of three hundred and ten Frankish bishops and abbots, as well as legates from Tuscan, Lombard, and Constantinople,[6] in the attempt to arouse their spirits to sojourn to the Holy Land and fight the Muslim horde in a grand crusade.

"Hastening to the way," he said, "you must help your brothers living in the Orient, who need your aid for which they have already cried out many times." He spoke of how Muslims invaded the lands of the Christians and "depopulated them by the sword, pillage and fire;" how they "destroy the altars, after having defiled them with their uncleanness. They circumcise the Christians, and the blood of the circumcision they either spread upon the altars or pour into the vases of the baptismal font. When they wish to torture people by a base death, they perforate their navels, and dragging forth the extremity of the intestines, bind it to a stake; then with flogging they lead the victim around until the viscera having gushed forth the victim falls prostrate upon the ground. Others they compel to extend their necks and then, attacking them with naked swords, attempting to cut through the neck with a single blow. What shall I say of the abominable rape of the women? To speak of it is worse than to be silent."[7]

In Jerusalem, which was conquered by the Seljuks in 1076,[8] Christian pilgrims coming into the Holy City were subject to the Jizya tax, or the tribute that those who reject Islam are to pay Muslims. Every time a Christian wished to enter a church, or even at the moment of his journey, he was met by a Muslim who compelled him with violence to pay. Many of these saints came with nothing but their very lives, and so when they had no money to give, the Muslim would cut open the heel of the pilgrim to see if he had any hidden inside. The Muslim would rip

---

5 See footnote 1 of Edward Peter in his First Crusade, ch. iii, p. 30, to Fulcher of Chartres' chronicle, 1.3.2; John France, "Impelled by the Love of God," in Thomas F. Madden's *The Crusades*, part 2, p. 36

6 This number comes from Fulcher of Chartres, chron. 1.1.1, in Edward Peters, Fulcher of Chartres, *The First Crusade*, ch. iii, p. 26; Mills, Hist. Crus. ch. ii, p. 25

7 Pope Urban II at the Council of Clermont, the version of Robert the Monk, in Edward Peters, *The First Crusade*, p. 2

8 See Gibbon, *Decline and Fall*, vol. v, ch. lvii, p. 1042, ed. Hans-Friedrich Mueller, see his annotation for the date

open his stomach and inspect the Christian's intestines, or force him to drink scammony until he vomited, hoping that he would spew out any money. The Turks esteemed it an entertaining spectacle to tie Christians onto posts and use them for target practice with arrows.[9] Such evils and brutalities justify a crusade without apology. After reading this, it is ironic to hear those who condemn the Crusaders while praising the American Revolution for fighting taxation without representation. The Crusaders were a response to the massacring and enslavement of Christians.[10] Urban then sent a letter of instruction to the warriors which expresses truly the purpose of the crusade: to save the Eastern Church from annihilation by the Muslims:

> Your brotherhood, we believe, has long since learned from many accounts that a barbaric fury has deplorably afflicted and laid waste the churches of God in the regions of the Orient. More than this, blasphemous to say, it has even grasped in intolerable servitude its churches and the Holy City of Christ, glorified by His passion and resurrection. Grieving with pious concern at this calamity, we visited the regions of Gaul [France] and devoted ourselves largely to urging the princes of the land and their subjects to free the churches of the East.[11]

And where are those bickerers of our time who howl about slavery in old America? Why are they not showing their gratitude to the Crusades for liberating slaves who were under the Turks?

Before the First Crusade was even commenced, seven thousand European Christians travelled to the Holy Land; they too were massacred with only two thousand returning home, thus burning the souls of the Westerners with indignation.[12] Such evils gave good reason for a crusade into the Holy Land: the wickedness of the Muslims had to be visited by the knightly saints, just as the injustices of the Canaanites were to be visited by the Hebrews, or the violence of the Aztecs by the Spaniards. It's so ironic that many today still condemn the Crusades while at the same time praising the American Revolution for Britain's taxation without representation. If the Crusades did nothing, then half of the Christian world would have ended up under the darkness of Islam. Today much of the western church isn't doing much of anything against the rise of jihadism, and thus Islam is growing more powerful in influence, while Christianity has remained static. Society is dictated by ideas; but whether or not a belief or creed prevails depends on the fervency of its followers. If Christians do not advance the Kingdom, then Muslims will advance Sharia. To use the words of Hilaire Belloc: "Human affairs are decided through conflict of ideas, which often resolve themselves by conflict under arms."[13]

---

9 Pope Urban II at the Council of Clermont, the version of Guibert of Nogent, in Edward Peters, *The First Crusade*, pp. 14–15; Robert the Monk, *History of the First Crusade*, 1.10
10 See Moczar, Seven Lies about Catholic Church, ch. iii, 73
11 Pope Urban II at the Council of Clermont, the version of Guibert of Nogent, in Edward Peters, *The First Crusade*, ch. i, pp. 15–16
12 Butcher, *The Story of the Church of Egypt*, vol. ii, part ii, ch. xviii, p. 70
13 Hilaire Belloc, *The Crusades*, ch. i, p. 1

⚔ CHRISTIANITY IS AT WAR: THE MANIFESTO FOR CHRISTIAN MILITANCY

JERUSALEM, THE HEAVENLY CITY WORTH FIGHTING FOR

Pope Urban II declared Jerusalem the center of the world where Christ redeemed mankind, and that this city of God was now taken by the haters of God.[14] Churches of olden times, he said, were now taken by "base and bastard Turks"; the saints were tormented and made subject to "pagan tyranny."[15] Urban understood that despotism comes from paganism, and is implemented by idolaters; that the Muslim heathen, being taken by devils, would naturally desire to war with Jerusalem, an image of the Kingdom of Heaven.

The Muslims had taken the Holy Land, the sanctified place where Christ was born, where He died, where He resurrected, and where He will return to purge the earth from all wickedness and drive out the crescent idols of the Muslim with His divine light and mighty hand. The land of Israel holds the blood of the first martyr Stephen, the waters of the Jordan which served John the Baptist when he baptized the Savior; it was to this holy place where the Israelites came to stamp out the barbarous heathen, and ultimately it is where the blood of Christ was spilt for our salvation. The Church loved Jerusalem so much, for they truly revered and upheld the description of Jerusalem by Christ as "the city of the great King." (Matthew 5:35) A place so used by God to defeat the forces of darkness would of course be to the eternal hatred of Satan and his servants, who would slaughter countless lives to rule over it.

Our entire faith sprung from Israel, and indeed, a land so holy must not be neglected, but protected and defended by the citizens of Heaven. The Maccabees fought so that Antiochus would no longer corrupt the land of Israel and tyrannize the believers, and now the crusaders were to push out the Muslims from despotically ruling the Holy Land, and in the words of Urban, "to defend the liberty of your country."[16]

"If all that there is of Christianity has flowed from the fountain of Jerusalem," said Urban, "its streams, whithersoever spread out over the whole world, encircle the hearts of the Catholic multitude, that they may consider wisely what they owe such a well-watered fountain."[17] Now a new enemy, the Muslims, marched forth into Israel, with a religion no less savage than that of the Canaanite. And as Joshua came to Canaan to vanquish the pagans, so would the Christians of Europe march into the Holy Land to expunge the cruel followers of Islam, and end the misery which they so caused upon the saints. "With Moses," beautifully proclaimed Urban, "we shall extend unwearied hands in prayer to Heaven, with you go forth and brandish the sword, like dauntless warriors, against Amalek."[18] Such a line shows just how much the warriors of Christendom looked up to Old Testament saints as models in the war against

---

14 Pope Urban II at the Council of Clermont, the version of Robert the Monk, in Edward Peters, *The First Crusade*, p. 2
15 Pope Urban II at the Council of Clermont, the version of Baldric of Dol, in Edward Peters, *The First Crusade*, p. 2
16 Pope Urban II at the Council of Clermont, the version of Guibert of Nogent, in Edward Peters, *The First Crusade*, p. 12
17 Pope Urban II at the Council of Clermont, the version of Guibert of Nogent, in Edward Peters, *The First Crusade*, p. 12
18 Pope Urban II at the Council of Clermont, the version of Baldric of Dol, in Edward Peters, *The First Crusade*, pp. 7–10

the devil. Unlike today, where the Old Testament is rendered useless, the Christian warriors made the writings of the prophets come alive.

THE CHRISTIANS CARRY THE CROSS AND DENY THEMSELVES

The congregation in the council expressed their agreement for the profound speech of Pope Urban II, and the First Crusade began. Urban ordered that the crusaders were to bear the Holy Cross as their image, and to sew it upon their shirts and cloaks,[19] which reminds us of how Constantine, who was the first to do this, decreed that the sign of the Cross be engraved on the shields of his soldiers,[20] and how the Israelites of Ezekiel's day put the cross-shaped Tau on their foreheads.

So militant was Christianity in those days, that the first to take up the cross for this battle with evil was not a layman or a mere warrior, but a papal legate, Adhemar the Bishop of Le Puy. A huge multitude of men joined this noble and great cause, just twenty five years after the Seljuk Turks overran Asia Minor.[21] They had left all of the beauties and pleasures of this world; they left their parents, wives and possession for an idea greater than themselves.[22] When John of Joinville was leaving to join the Crusade, he did not want to turn his eyes back to his family, "fearful that my heart would melt for the fine castle and two children I was leaving behind."[23] Fathers departed from their sons, and husbands from their wives; and if the spouses wept, it was only because they could not share the honors of their men.[24] The warrior Archard of Montmerle sold his land to a monastery, for, in his words, "I wish, fully armed, to join in the magnificent expedition of the Christian people seeking for God to fight their way to Jerusalem against the pagans and Saracens."[25]

Raymond IV of St. Gilles, though rich and very wealthy, sold all that he possessed to leave for the Crusade and liberate God's land from the heretic.[26] Truly did they deny themselves and follow Christ. You may say that all these actions of severe detachment from family, land, and self, is extreme, but Christ was extreme when He said:

> If anyone comes to Me and does not hate his father and mother, wife and children, brothers and sisters, yes, and his own life also, he cannot be My disciple. (Luke 4:26)

With all of this sacrifice, we are very much reminded of the words of St. Paulinus of Nola, a fourth century monk from Italy, when he said:

---

19 Pope Urban II at the Council of Clermont, the version of Guibert of Nogent, in Edward Peters, *The First Crusade*, ch. i, pp. 14–15
20 Eusebius, *Life of Constantine*, 4.17
21 Hilaire Belloc, *The Crusades*, ch. i, p. 1; ch. iv, p. 50; John France, "Impelled by the Love of God, in Thomas F. Madden's *The Crusades*, part 2, p. 36
22 The Chronicle of Fulcher of Chartres, b. i, prelude, 1, in Edward Peters, *The First Crusade*, ch. iii, p. 24
23 John of Joinville, *Life of Saint Louis*, 122, trans. Caroline Smith
24 Mills, Hist. Crus. ch. ii, p. 31
25 In John France, "Impelled by the Love God," in Thomas F. Madden's *The Crusades*, part 2, pp. 38–9
26 Robert the Monk, *History of the First Crusade*, 3.2

CHRISTIANITY IS AT WAR: THE MANIFESTO FOR CHRISTIAN MILITANCY

> Through the sale of all my goods I purchased the carrying of the cross. Hence earthly possessions purchased the hope of the kingdom of heaven, for the hope extended by faith is stronger than the possessions of the flesh. [27]

The Crusaders fought without care of numbers, placed their confidence on their Redeemer, and with so few men gained exceptional victories over armies larger than theirs. The patriarch of Jerusalem, during the First Crusade, expressed this sentiment and illustrated this reality in a letter written to the western church:

> Where we have a count, the enemy have forty kings; where we have a company, the enemy have a legion; where we have a knight, they have a duke, where we have a foot-soldier, they have a count; where we have a camp, they have a kingdom. However, confiding not in numbers, nor in bravery, nor in any presumption, but protected by justice and the shield of Christ, and with St. George, Theodore, Demetrius, and Basil, soldiers of Christ, truly supporting us, we have pierced, and in security are piercing, the ranks of the enemy... our spiritual Mother Church calls out: 'Come, my most beloved sons, come to me, retake the crown from the hands of the sons of idolatry, who rise against me—the crown from the beginning of the world predestined you.' [28]

They marched out to partake in the heaviest of combat with one mind—not to flee, but to die or stand victorious. They looked upon death without the slightest gesture of fear; to die was not defeat, but birth.[29] "For to me, to live is Christ, and to die is gain." (Philippians 1:21) To the Christian warrior, Christ was exposed to the world for the sake of the world; He perished for our sins, not as water which is polluted as it cleanses, but as a sunbeam which casts out the darkness and yet remains pure.[30] The life of Christ taught them how to live, His death, how to die.[31] They lived to fight evil, and they esteemed death highly as that moment when they will eternally live with the One Who crushed evil. As St. Bernard wrote of the knights who went to Jerusalem to protect Solomon's Temple:

> The knight of Christ, I say, may strike with confidence and succumb more confidently. When he strikes, he does service to Christ, and to himself when he succumbs. Nor does he bear the sword in vain. He is God's minister in the punishment of evil doers and the praise of well doers. Surely, if he kills an evil doer, he is not a man-killer, but, if I may put it, an evil-killer. Clearly he is reckoned the avenger of Christ against evildoers, and the defender of Christians. Should he be killed himself, we know he has not perished, but has come safely home. The death which he inflicts is Christ's gain, and that which he suffers, his own. At the death of the pagan, the Christian exults because Christ is exulted; in the death of the Christian the King's liberality is conspicuous when the knight is ushered him to be rewarded. [32]

---

27 Paulinus, poem 21
28 The Patriarch of Jerusalem to the Church in the West, in Edward Peters, ch. v, p. 228
29 Robert the Monk, *History of the First Crusade*, 3.2
30 See St. Bernard, *In Praise of a New Knighthood*, ch. 10, 18
31 St. Bernard, *In Praise of the New Knighthood*, ch. 11, 18
32 St. Bernard, *In Praise of the New Knighthood*, ch. 3, 4

THE CRUSADES—AN IMAGE OF TRUE CHRISTIAN FAITH

The Crusades were an image of true Christian Faith. They were the result of Christians who had so much faith that they were willing to fight, kill, and die, for God, throwing away all fear of loss. The love of the crusaders was overflowing, it was of the highest perfection, because they did not fear the enemies of God. Such is faith. "There is no fear in love; but perfect love casts out fear, because fear involves torment. But he who fears has not been made perfect in love." (1 John 4:18) If the Faith is true, and we are not to "fear those who kill the body but cannot kill the soul" (Matthew 10:28), then there is no point in fearing the enemy. This was the spirit of the crusaders, and this spirit was glimmering because they had faith. This faith was there because Christianity was there, in all of its strength and might. But today, this zeal has been almost lost, and Islam is stronger now than it ever has been in centuries. Islam rises when Christian zeal declines. As Hilaire Belloc said:

> Islam survives. Its religion is intact; therefore its material strength may return. Our religion is in peril, and who can be confident in the continued skill, let alone the continued obedience, of those who make and work our machines? [33]

So great were the Crusades that Edward Gibbon referred to it as "The World's Debate."[34] So long was this event, that it would last for five hundred years.[35]

It may seem odd to the modern Christian to find believers arising to fight, and monks and popes calling for battle against the Muslims. Christianity, as we have already discussed, was a militant movement, and many a saint would agree. St. Bernard of Clairvaux preached in support of the Second Crusade and composed precepts for the Knights Templar; St. Louis IX fought and died in a crusade; and both St. Gregory VII and the later Pope Pius V, called for Christendom to conduct a crusade against Islamic power.[36]

Islam is a movement, and so it moves, and does not stop moving.[37] Christianity is too a movement—a very radical one—but we have forgotten this, and instead have tried to make it into a new movement which restlessly preaches against Christian movement and exalts tolerance in the face of evil. Because of this the church in America has become like a static tide pool about to be swallowed by a towering tsunami. The Bedouins of the desert never stop traveling, and so the Muslims never stop moving. It is only the modern Christian who has halted, while he tries to force the rest of the church to stop with him. The modern Christian, as much as he may hate to hear this, can learn something from the zeal of the Crusaders.

The Crusaders were fundamentalists who accepted Scripture puritanically and believed that the decay of a society flows from the moral chaos of its people. To them, error had no right, and thus the upholders of error—for this case the Muslims—could not be allowed to

---

33   Hilaire Belloc, *The Crusades*, ch. i, p. 5
34   Hilaire Belloc, *The Crusades*, ch. i, p. 1
35   See Mozar, *Seven Lies about Catholic History*, ch. iii, p. 73
36   See Moczar, *Seven Lies about Catholic History*, ch. iii, p. 74
37   See Chesterton, *The New Jerusalem*, ch. ii, in James V. Schall, The Collected Works of G.K. Chesterton, pp. 217, 219

CHRISTIANITY IS AT WAR: THE MANIFESTO FOR CHRISTIAN MILITANCY

rule over God's land. To show an example of this fervency, here are the words of Pope Innocent III concerning the Islamic tainting of the Holy Land, and in which he declares Islam to be the Beast of Revelation:

> The Muhammedan heresy, the beast foretold by the spirit, will not live forever; 'its age is 666.' On the very spot on Mount Thabor itself, where the Redeemer showed his future glory to his disciples, the Saracens have raised a fortress for the confusions of the Christians name. They hope, by means of this fortress, to possess themselves of Acre, and then to subjugate all the Holy Land, at present almost destitute of sacred soldiers. 38

If Moses commanded that the Holy Land must be purged from idolatry, so did they believe that the same sacred land, and Christendom, must not be tainted by the perfidious teachings of Muhammad. Sadly, in our own day only a small body of people zealously uphold the Faith, while the rest accept only fragments of it, vaguely seeing them as mere opinions.[39] The masses of America and the rest of the West no longer see Christianity as the Light of the world which is to expunge the darkness, but only as an individual preference. Because of this, the modern church has mainly become a compliant and fruitless entity, taking absolutely no action to counter the rise of Islam and its leftist supporters, and allowing the progressive movement to continuously dechristianize our entire civilization. While the Crusades would have swiftly struck the plague of jihad and leftism, many of today's pastors, with the support of their congregations, now refuse to expose Islam in the attempt to have the church join with mosques, producing an anomaly we call "Chrislam." These same heretics deceitfully condemn the Crusades and chastise those who support them, while Christians in the Middle East and Africa are being slaughtered by Muslims who the Crusaders would not have hesitated to obliterate.

CHRISTIANITY—WORTHY OF FIGHTING, KILLING, AND DYING FOR

When people talk about the Crusades as if they were some random attack on innocent people, they strangely forget, or purposely neglect the fact, that Islam was nothing more than an aggressive raid against the beautiful and innovative civilization which Christianity itself brought. The precepts and beauties of Christianity are worth fighting for, they are worth dying for, they are worth killing for. It is hypocritical for people, especially Christians, to mock and sneer at those knights who fought, killed, and died, for Christianity, when these same people would not hesitate to praise soldiers who do the same thing for American ideals. It is hypocrisy for people today to condemn the Crusades for going to war with Muslims for controlling the Holy Land, when America righteously massacred hundreds of thousands of Japanese for crossing passed its frontiers and butchering its soldiers in Pearl Harbor.

Those who laugh at the Crusaders and slander them as 'crazy' aren't doing anything against the Islamic religion rising today. It is equal hypocrisy to smirk at the Crusades for fighting for the Cross, when we have shed rivers of blood for the glory of a flag. Once we stop

---

38 Quoted by Mills, Hist. Crus. ch. 14, p. 192
39 See Hilaire Belloc, *The Crusades*, ch. iii, p. 23; Mills, Hist. Crus. ch. i, p. 20

applying our modern day ineptitude on medieval zealotry, is when we realize how dishonest we are when condemning the Crusades. The moderns love to label the old knights of the Cross as 'Christian supremacists', since they rallied into the Holy Land because it was under the control of a non-Christian power. The crusader Fulcher of Chartres gives his praise and lamentation for the glorious sacrifices of the Crusades, words that would most definitely be mocked by modernly minded people:

> Oh, how many thousands met a martyr's blessed death on this expedition! Is there anyone with heart so stony who hears these acts of God and is not moved by bowls of compassion to burst forth in praises to Him? Can there be anyone who does not marvel how we, a few people in the realms of so many of our enemies, could not remain but could even thrive? [40]

But yet our society, and even our churches, are filled with those who look upon the crusaders with contempt, taking no appreciation for the actions they took to preserve Christendom, perpetuate the Gospel, crush tyranny, and protect the saints who suffered greatly under the Muslims. They accomplished feats which most today would never attempt, and fought with sword an enemy who most of the church is too afraid to even expose.

But many of us, though unknowingly, would be worried if a good amount of the world was ruled by something not Christian, such as Communism, the pagan religions of the Romans and the Aztecs, or Islam. Medieval Christendom was deeply trepidatious over the Islamic capturing of the Middle East, as anyone today would be if Communism invaded all of Canada, or if Islam invaded all of Israel. America entered the Middle East and destroyed numerous governments, and enabled the slaughter of Christians that we see today, and the US government doesn't care a bit. How inferior we are as a civilization to Christendom, who did not hesitate to fight for people not even in its own lands.

Critics talk of the Crusades as though they were some violently vehement attack upon poor defenseless mosques and their timidly pious followers. They refuse to mention the fact that long before the Crusades the Muslims almost invaded Paris, and were already masters over much of Spain. If the Crusades conquered the Middle East and kept it conquered, it would have been a mere response to the Muslims who had nearly captured Europe. The Crusades were the counterattack that, instead of fighting the war in its own territory, decided to bring the fight to the enemy's base.[41] The incursion of the slaves of Muhammad upon the servants of Christ was as black clouds coming against the rays of dawn. And as the thundering clouds are plunged into the beams of the rising sun, so will the saints and the Christ prevail above the ruthless armies of Satan.

THE BATTLE FOR NICAEA—HOLY CITY OF CHRISTENDOM

The Muslim Turks took the city of Nicaea to force it into the empire of Islam. It was in Nicaea where the Church held the Council to repulse the wiles of Arianism and to affirm the Holy

---

40 Fulcher of Chartres, chron. b. i, prologue, ch. 4, in Edward Peters, *The First Crusade*, ch. iii, p. 25
41 See G.K. Chesterton, *The New Jerusalem*, ch. ii, xi, in James V. Schall, The Collected Works of G.K. Chesterton, vol. xx, p. 209, pp. 360–363

CHRISTIANITY IS AT WAR: THE MANIFESTO FOR CHRISTIAN MILITANCY

Trinity; it was this city which the Muslims invaded to crush God's Word, and it was now here where the crusaders came to proclaim Christ and repulse the enemies of God. The Christians of the East defeated Arianism with the pen, but now the Christians of the West—the successors of Cornelius the Centurion—had to crush this very heresy with the sword. On July 1st, 1097, the Crusades advanced to Nicaea with their banners bearing the Cross and blowing their disquieting horns. Fulcher of Chartres, a crusader who fought to take back Nicaea into Christian hands, wrote of the devastation caused by the Muslims which he saw:

> Oh, how many severed heads and bones of the dead lying on the plains did we then find beyond Nicomedia near that sea! In the preceding year, the Turks destroyed those who were ignorant of and new to the use of the arrow. Moved to compassion by this, we shed many tears there. [42]

The Crusaders saw this type of destruction made by the Turks throughout their travels in the East. They saw heaps of rubble of what was once villages, and orchids and crops scorched and completely destroyed. They saw the city of Iconium utterly ruined and all of its provisionment gutted and seized.[43]

Before they entered Nicaea, Bohemond cried out to the men, with such fervency and emotion that his voice choked up as the tears ran down his Frankish cheeks. His words contain that spirit of Christian militancy, seeing the Faith in light of the Old Testament, with the labors and combats of the prophets of Israel, never ignoring them, neither separating their valiancy with the obligations of the Christian to partake in combat against the wicked, without ceasing nor slumbering:

> O soldiers of the Lord and tireless pilgrims to the Holy Sepulcher, who was it that led you to these foreign lands if not He who led the sons of Israel from Egypt dry-shod across the Red Sea? Who else influenced you to leave behind your possessions and the home where you were born? You have given up your relatives and neighbors, your wives and your children—more than that, you have renounced all fleshly pleasures. Now you are born again through confession and penitence, and you show daily through your hard labours. Happy are you who weary yourselves with such work, who will see Paradise before you see your homes again! What an order of soldiers, three and four times blessed! Until now you have stood out as an incitement of God's anger; but now you are the reconciliation of his grace and the rampart of his faith. So with all this in mind, undefeated soldiers as you are, now that we start for the first time to fight for God, let us not glory in our arms or our strength but in God who is more powerful than all, because the battle is the Lord's and he is the governor among the nations. [44]

They positioned their massive catapults and siege machines, and shooting through the air were the arrows of the Turks, dipped in poison. Charging toward the walls, staring death

---

42 Fulcher of Chartres, chron. 1.9.5, in Edward Peters, *The First Crusade*, ch. iii, p. 42
43 Belloc, *The Crusades*, ch. iv, p. 64–65
44 Quoted by Robert the Monk, *History of the First Crusade*, 2.16

into her cold eyes, the Latin Christians, alongside two thousand Greek warriors led by general Tatikios, brought up their siege towers, and hailing down upon the city were boulders and stones, stakes and torches. Terror gripped the souls of the inhabitants as the cries of war rang through every ear in the midst of that horrifying moment.

The Turks, under Sulaiman, gathered together in readiness for battle and numbered three hundred and sixty thousand warriors, greatly outnumbering the crusaders. In one moment, the saints clashed with the servants of Satan; swords and spears were thrusted and countless arrows covered the sky. The Turks gained ground with their exceptional skill in archery, while many crusaders found death, having never been tried by such strategy, forcing the Christians to flee in angst and leave their campsite to be plundered by the enemy.

Suddenly, the knights Hugh the Great and Duke Godfrey smashed into the Turkish ranks from behind. Despite this, the crusaders still found themselves surrounded, huddled together like terrified sheep encompassed by wolves.

Many a Christian soldier was cut down on that day, yet they still continued to fight, their hearts ever strengthened and fortified by their union. They kept striving relentlessly, and they saw to their surprise the Turks turn their backs and flee. The knights shouted their war cries and pursued them, many of them not stopping their chase until nightfall. They praised God for their victory, attributing the retreat of the Turks solely to Him.[45]

THE BISHOP ATTACKS

Notwithstanding this victory, the battle over Nicaea continued. In one fight, the Count of St. Gilles and the Bishop of Puy, with mighty armies and the sign of the Cross, executed a fierce incursion on the Turks, forcing many of them to retreat.[46] As time went on, and fighting proceeded, Sulaiman made a promise that he would surrender the city. But as the crusaders were believing this, Sulaiman was regaining strength and collecting more troops. It was a hudna (false peace). The Muslims sent messengers out of the city to call forward reinforcements, and so did they come, with sixty thousand Turks fresh for the intensity of the fray.

Down came the Turks from the mountains, but as they charged forward their courage sharply turned into sorrow, as they saw how organized the columns of the Christians were. The rays of the sun made a cutting reflection upon the sore eyes of the Turks as they went against the armor of the saints.

The Count of Gilles counterattacked and took many lives of an innumerable multitude of the enemy. Spears flew, and neither was it possible for one to turn without seeing a lance cut through the desert heat. They turned back to the mountain, and as they sprinted from the columns of the rustic crusaders, they turned only to see the presence of their Christian

---

[45] Fulcher of Chartres, chron. 1.11.2–8; 1.12.2–5, in Edward Peters, *The First Crusade*, ch. iii, pp. 45–48; John France, "Impelled by the Love of God," in Thomas F. Madden's *The Crusades*, part 2, p. 41

[46] See Edward Peters, *The First Crusade*, ch. iv, p. 147, The Siege of Nicaea, *The Gesta* Version

enemies raising their slaughter weapons and taking many of their lives. The Muslims within Nicaea looked up only to see the raining heads of their Muslim warriors shot by the catapults.[47]

THE GREEKS ARRIVE

Swords clashed and many martyrs were made, and as the siege went on a body of ships were seen sailing toward the coast. They belonged to the Byzantine emperor Alexius and were arriving for the aid of the crusaders and for a victory over the Muslims. The Turks, upon seeing these ships, were frightened to tears and lamentations, while the Christian knights gave glory to God for such assistance.

After such gruesome and ruthless fighting, the Cross ended as the victor over the crescent. The followers of Allah requested a surrender, Alexius without hesitation gave them leave, and Nicaea was now in Christian hands after seven weeks and three days of grueling warfare. Much of the poor who accompanied the knights perished on account of hunger, declaring before their deaths: "Avenge, Lord, our blood which has been shed for Thee, who are blessed and praiseworthy forever and ever. Amen."[48]

Christians entered the city holding up crosses and crying out in Greek and Latin: "Glory to Thee, O God."[49]

So pertinent is Orthodoxy to the Christian faith, that at times blood must be spilt for its preservation from the tyrannical hands of heretics. The order of Church, the peace of Christian society, the preservation of civilization, and the souls of mankind—all of these things are threatened by heresy, and yet all of them are seen for cheap today. The modern Christian sees men falling into error, and it simply sees this travesty as merely a choice deserving our respect in the name of "religious liberty."

Christians complain of all of the heresy and apostasy today, without recognizing or admitting that it is their very tolerance of falsehood that is the root of these problems. It was in this city of Nicaea where hundreds of bishops gathered together just to wrest the Church away from the hands of the heterodox—the Arians—who wished not only to deceive but to kill the believers; for it is the goal of the heretic to rob, to murder, to destroy. It is the predecessors of Abel versus the predecessors of Cain, and still today does this war continue, and if error is not crushed, then surely will the blood of the saints spilt on the wailing earth under the feet of the heretic with sword in hand, be the only result of our carelessness toward this great and eternal struggle.

---

47 Anselme of Ribemont to Manasses II, in Edward Peters, *The First Crusade*, ch. v, p. 223; Robert the Monk, *History of the First Crusade*, 3.3–4
48 See Edward Peters, *The First Crusade*, ch. iv, p. 147, The Siege of Nicaea, *The Gesta* Version
49 Anselme of Ribemont to Manasses II, in Edward Peters, *The First Crusade*, ch. v, p. 223; Robert the Monk, *History of the First Crusade*, 3.5–6

THE EASTERN CHRISTIANS THANK THEIR LATIN BROTHERS

Days later, as they continued to journey through the East, the crusaders were met by a multitude of Armenians who, having gone through so much persecution as we have already seen, came with crosses in their hands, kissing their feet and their garments because they had heard that the knights would defend them from the Turks and bring them to liberation.[50] Similar situations also occurred in other times. The crusaders once had taken the city of Roussa, which was ruled by Muslims and inhabited by Paulician heretics. Once the Muslims and heretics were subdued, the local Christian Armenians praised the accomplishments and happily accepted the crusaders as their new rulers.

This same praise for the crusaders was expressed by the Armenians in the Fourth Crusade, in which they met with the French king Louis IX and commended him to God, and he in response did the same for them.[51] It was, after all, for these persecuted Christians that the Crusades began, and yet today many do not acknowledge the help which the crusaders gave to their suffering brethren. Many talk about the Armenian genocide, while at the same time they criticize the Crusades, without taking for the slightest moment the grueling fighting which these warriors undertook to preserve these Eastern Christians. If the Armenians gave thanks to the crusaders for their assistance, then who are we, who live in modern comfort, to chastise these knights? These Christians saw with their own eyes the bloodshed, the slaughtering and kidnapping of their own brethren; they saw things that we can only imagine through the descriptions of books. Surely we cannot correct these persecuted saints on something they themselves lived through, as we live in an era so far from theirs, and so corrupted by the pleasures of luxury.

THE CHRISTIANS FIGHT WITH ALL THEIR HEART

The Christian fighters rode on swift horses toward Anatolia; the silence of the day brought comfort to the minds of the meditative warriors. Those who accompanied Bohemond turned and saw with startled eyes an army of three hundred thousand warriors, bearing the crescent as their banner, crying forth to the skies a savage shriek in a language unknown to the Christians of France, bringing forth to the eye an awe-inspiring sight. Not only were these Muslims, but Publicani or Cathar heretics who, because of their equal hatred for the Cross, joined the Muslims in their aspiration to uproot the Holy Faith.

The men looked upon a force and the thoughts of an unsettled soul rushed throughout their minds, and a number of them were not sure on whether to fight or to fly before the Asiatic horde. Bohemond commanded the mounted troops to pitch camp alongside a certain river. Before their tents were erected, one hundred and fifty Turkic warriors treading the earth upon swiftly rode to the men, bent their bows and shot poisoned arrows.

The Christians rushed to these barbarians without trembling, and with arms faster than the hooves of the enemy's horses slew every one of them. They continued on and met the

---

50   Fulcher of Chartres, chron. 1.15.11
51   John of Joinville, 565–567; Robert the Monk, 3.27

CHRISTIANITY IS AT WAR: THE MANIFESTO FOR CHRISTIAN MILITANCY

Turkish army, eye faced eye, and spirit faced spirit. So great were the numbers of the Turks that they could not flee from the fierce army of God. One moved his massive sword in one direction, and cut a Turk asunder, another did the same and his blade ripped through the human wall of Muslims. They tried to use their arrows, but the distance was so close to the Christians that the very thought remained useless. The men struck hard their lances upon the Turks, and so numerous were there blows that these lofty weapons broke upon the bodies of their enemies.

And how many was the sight of men without limbs, and bodies lying on the floor without heads, the beholders of such carnage looked at this dreadful scene, neither knowing if the dead man in their presence had family, or who his parents were, or for how much time their mother and father spent to raise them up.

THE TURKS ATTACK THE CHRISTIAN CAMP

Another army of Turks saw from across the river the bloodshed taking place, and they rode with their horses across the river, not to partake in the intense display of valor and arms, but to rush inside the Christian camp. A mother cleaved her infant, and she saw with sheer terror the Turks ride on their robust horses.

Her grip grew tighter as maternal love heightened and the presence of pure evil lingered about. They wrested ahold of the little one, hacked his infant body to pieces, took the mother and spilt her blood. They went about the village like the ancient pagans of antiquity, esteeming themselves as holy but exemplifying nothing but the actions of a heathen. They took each of the mothers, slew them; upon their infants they indulged in their cruelty, and neither were the others of the camp exempted from this violence. The cries of the slaughtered arose to heaven; they pierced the sharpest winds, the highest shrieks of the Turks, the manliest war cries of the Christians. They pulled Bohemond's ears and went through his soul like daggers stabbing the bark of the hoariest redwood tree. He turned as the swords of heretics and saints clashed, gave orders to the Count of Normandy to lead the fray, and sprinted with all his might toward the camp.

The Turks, still engaging in their wanton madness and drunk off the blood of the saints, turned a quick eye, saw this lion of Christendom with numerous of his men, and fled. The Christians ceased to run, stopped and beheld the gore, the wailings of the wounded, the mournings of the living for the dead, before their sights. Tears rushed down the widened eyes of Bohemond, and he lamented to God, and implored Him to be a refuge for those alive and those deceased.

THE BISHOP STRIKES AND THE SONG OF MOSES IS SUNG BY THE CHRISTIANS

Bohemond returned and the battle still raged on. The tendons of the Christians burned with unendurable exertion, as the Turks unceasingly rushed on with energy and fresh spirits. Under that cruel summer heat, they fought; though fatigued they hammered their swords

PART 14

upon the breastplates of the enemy, and with each blow did their minds wonder as to whether or not they should fight and die, or flee and live.

Christian women, who came to accompany their husbands in the crusade, and fill that dismal void of loneliness, brought water from the nearby river to refresh their bodies and cool their ligaments. But not even this could settle their spirits, and some of them began to retreat. But lo, the Count of Normandy, with awe-inspiring valor, turned his horse around, lifted heavenward his standard, and cried out with inspiring fury, "God wills it! God wills it!" The fleeing men turned around and beheld their commander with Bohemond.

The cry of Christian war restored their spirits, brought high their hopes and brought low their worries of death, and with regained courage they made their decision to fight and die rather than flee. The Turks attacked with such great fury, with one pushing the other in front of him. No empty space was there, just men, one with crescent scimitar, the other with cross-shaped sword. As the intense slaughter went on, arrows descended and ripped through torsos and heads. No one stood idle, not one was free from action.

The men collided, bodies were ripped open, limbs were severed, cries to Allah rang the ears, cries to God emanated throughout the air and ignited their hopes; the priests and the clergy with hands raise to heaven intently prayed for victory; women wailed for the fallen and dragged the dead to the camps.

Above their heads was a dark cloud of merciless arrows, and as these descended and cut life from the earth, there was seen from a distance two knights, Duke Godfrey and Hugh, and with them was forty thousand troops. When death was the plan of many a knight, and eternity the hope of them all, there came this force to the rescue; for many were they in that battle, whose times for perishing did not yet come.

Like descending eagles they rushed down upon the Turks to cries and wild shrills of the womenfolk who watched nearby. They drove into the thick of opposition burning with rage and anger.

No man there could fully describe the sounds of clashing arms, of splintering lances; the dying gave a great cry, but the victorious—how joyful was their rejoicing, how exhilarating their praises which reached the topmost summits.

The living pounded the earth as the dead watered the grass with blood and tears. The enemy looked upwards, their chests heavy with the pains of the defeated, and saw to their despair more Christians rushing forth from a distant mountain. The crusaders looked up, their hearts relieved by the hope of victory, and cried the sounds of bliss as they saw the newly arrived force of Christians led by the Bishop of Le Puy and Count Raymond. So terrified were the Turks that they thought their enemies were coming down from heaven. The earth was crimson with blood, and a river of this thick red substance of life flowed down the terrain by the swords of this military might of Christ.

The sun descended, and in the cool silence of a young evening, this militant hymn, with lyrics from the Song of Moses, was heard from the elated but sore knights,

Thou art glorious in Thy saints, O Lord, and wonderful in majesty; fearful in praises, doing wonders. Thy right hand, O Lord, hath dashed in pieces the enemy, and in the greatness of thine Excellency thou hast overthrown them that rose up against thee. The enemy said, I will pursue, I will overtake, I will divide the spoil; my lust shall be satisfied upon them; I will draw my sword, my hand shall destroy them. But Thou, Lord, wast with us as a strong warrior, and Thou in thy mercy hast led forth the people which thou hast redeemed. Now we realise, God, that Thou art guiding us in Thy strength unto Thy holy habitation, Thy Holy Sepulcher. [52]

Several lines of this hymn are directly from the Song of Moses, sung by the same prophet after the Egyptians were crushed underneath the waves of the Red sea. For these men never looked with contempt upon the Pentateuch, nor did they ever reject or ignore its militant lessons, but embraced them. Nor did the clergy undermine them, as they do today, with empty words and say "we are now in the age of grace, these martial lessons do not apply to us," but they instilled them into the hearts and the minds of their congregations in every parish in Europe. This is that militant Christian spirit which we have long forgotten, and it is the hope of this book to restore it.

THE BATTLE FOR ANTIOCH

In order to end the Islamic persecution over Christian lands in the East, it was necessary for the crusaders to take the city of Antioch in Syria which had fallen to the Turks only ten years before Pope Urban II commenced the First Crusade. Syria acted as a bridge by which the western and eastern legs of the Islamic empire would communicate and bring armies behind the Crusaders' radar. It provided a free passage for Muslim armies going north from south and vice versa, and it connected Mesopotamia, Persia and all Muslim lands even unto the Indus, with the religious center of Mecca. Should this link be broken, the Muslim power would have bled to death by such a wound.[53]

So crucial was Syria in this war that Hilaire Belloc wrote that "Islam would not have survived had the Crusade made good its hold upon the essential point of Damascus."[54] To control Syria is to control the Muslim world, and the same applies to today despite of technology; our airplanes and petrol.[55] Such is the reason why that Turkey even till this day, in reviving its wounded Islamic empire, wants to take Syria. The Syrian revolution was praised at its beginnings, but the end result will only be a revival of the Ottoman Empire, and a pool filled with the blood of the saints.

---

52 Robert the Monk, *History of the First Crusade*, 3.8–14
53 Belloc, *The Crusades*, ch. i, p. 2; ch. iv, p. 51; ch. v, p. 77; ch. ix, p. 173
54 Belloc, *The Crusades*, ch. i, p. 5
55 Belloc, *The Crusades*, ch. viii, p. 163

THE MUSLIMS KILL A CHRISTIAN WOMAN AND THE
CHRISTIANS RESPOND WITH THE SWORD OF JUSTICE

So infamous was Antioch for its great fortifications and immensely thick walls, and so great was this siege that it provoked a medieval monk, Robert, to write a poem so vivid and evocative that it would be an injustice to try to emulate it:

> The rising star of morning had preceded the beams of dawn
> So that dawn itself might shake out its shining dew
> And the sun make the world gorgeous with its flaming light.
> The lords rise hastily, their troops with them,
> And seize their arms and run to the walls.
> Right arms fought a hard battle inside and out:
> Those inside defend, whilst our men throw darts
> And weapons, sticks, and indeed stones and stakes.
> The effort was immense, but in vain.
> So they retreated, unable to overthrow
> The towers and walls, susceptible to no force.
> Seeing that their efforts were in vain, our men
> Stop fighting, but carry on the siege. [56]

The Turks were so confident in the strength of Antioch, that in the evening darkness they opened their gates and let loose archers who came under the shadow of night and fired their arrows toward the Christians. A woman was walking before the tent of Bohemond, and in one moment an arrow pierced her gentle body and her life was gone. The Franks responded by quickly posting watchers throughout the camp to eye the lurking enemies, and by building a castle to safeguard them from the stealth killers.

A large body of Turks rushed from the castle of Harim from a close distance and ambushed the men. The Christians sent a thousand of their men into a valley, and when they were met by the Turks they fled and so the chase began. The Turks, like good Asiatics, spurned their horses on, and the Christians took refuge with their army. Now the two forces were nigh between each other; the Turks trusted in their numbers, the Christians their God. Swords were unsheathed; cries to bloodshed were unleashed from the viscous mouths of men, while the shouts of war for God was heard on that side of the army whose standard was the Cross.

Two Christians were slain in the battle, and countless Turks were taken prisoner, and their heads were cut before the Muslim warriors who stood watching from the walls of the famous city. After this victory, the Armenians were free to approach the crusaders without fear and sell food to them.[57]

---

56 Robert the Monk, 4.1
57 Robert the Monk, 4.1–2

CHRISTIANITY IS AT WAR: THE MANIFESTO FOR CHRISTIAN MILITANCY

THE CITY OF GOD VERSUS THE CITY OF SATAN

A greater battle was forged in due time. One can only imagine the site of this battle: tens of thousands of Muslims, efficiently ranked, all from the lands ruled under the crescent—Persians, Arabs, and Medes, men from Damascus and Aleppo. And before their deceived eyes stood a force of thirty-thousand knights and soldiers, all hand-picked for this fight. The Muslims were overjoyed, thinking their enemy ready to be taken by Turkish hands and taken in chains. As their hands were shaking with the desire to kill, the hopes of the two armies were unto themselves engaged in a war: one was that of the City of Satan, striving for the obliteration of the Faith, the massacre of the faithful, and the complete triumph of falsehood; the other was that of the City of God, aspiring for the Truth to conquer all error.

The two armies rushed with the greatest intensity, with the knights cutting down the Turks as the scythe rips through the harvest. Turkish horsemen fell into the presence of foot soldiers who cut them down and made a great slaughter. The second column of Muslims came, and immediately were their ears taken by the sounds of battle and cries, the clash of armour against armour, the hooves of horses beating desperately on the cold earth. The newcomers saw, and sheer terror grabbed hold of all of them. The Muslims ran, and the Christians pursued after them, only to take the victory.

Bohemond later went before his armies and declared to his weary and starving troops:

> You men have been distinguished up to now as outstanding soldiers. God has upheld you through the many dangers of various battles and given you victory. You have an impressive track record. So why are you muttering against God simply because you are suffering from pangs and famine? When he stretches out his hand to you, you exult; now he withdraws it, you despair. It seems as if you love not the giver but the gifts; not the one who is generous but the results of their generosity. When he is generous God is treated as your friend; when he ceases to give, you seem to consider him unworthy and irrelevant. Right now he is testing you through the deprivations of famine and the incessant attacks of your enemies. If they had inflicted as many injuries on us as we have on them, if they had killed as many of us as we have on them, if they had killed as many of us as we had slaughtered of them, any of us who remained alive would have every right to complain—but not one would be able to complain because not one would remain alive. So do not lose confidence, but keep your courage up. Whether you live in him or die for him you will be blessed.

With such great words came great elation of the spirits and aspirations of the soldiers. But yet hunger did not leave, nor did it refrain from its cruel travails. And to their help came a number of Armenian and Syrian Christians, with that hospitality common to the East, they found whatever food they could find and gave to the crusaders.[58]

---

58 Robert the Monk, 4.9–11

THE CHRISTIANS OVERRIDE HUNGER FOR VALIANCY
BEFORE AN ARMY OF THOUSANDS OF MUSLIMS

But soon, from famine, desperation, anguish and hopelessness, came valor, valiancy, and the urge to war against the enemy of the Cross. A messenger arrived and reported that innumerable thousands of Turks were on their way, marching with the confidence that the Christians were now to be vanquished. Men who were unable to walk now stood upright and ready to quarrel; they raised their hands to heaven and praised God as though victory was already theirs.

To them death under the scimitar was superior to perishing under the torments of hunger. To such men, with mouths dry as deserts, stomachs as empty as the pockets of pilgrims, and hearts as swelled with the spirit of hope as the wandering preachers of ancient Europe, to die for something was greater than dying of something. The battle was between those who say with Paul, "I discipline my body and keep it under control" (1 Corinthians 9:27) and those "Whose end is destruction, whose God is their belly, and whose glory is in their shame, who mind earthly things." (Philippians 3:19)

THE CHRISTIANS MAKE THE SIGN OF THE CROSS
BEFORE THE SLAVES OF THE CRESCENT

The sun went low and darkness overran the land, and the Christians made ready their ambushes. The sun had arisen, and just as dawn brought the first light to the world, they set their sights upon the enemy, and never before had they seen such numbers of enemy troops, riding upon their horses, swift like lightning, and arms strong but light like feathers to shoot off arrows into the cruel air that hovers in the midst of brutish battles. The knights made the sign of the Cross, outstretched their hands toward heaven and gave themselves up to God—all with might, mind, strength and heart—to the God who crushed the devil upon Calvary.

In moments all that could be seen were men clashing like waves smashing into imposing summits in the midst of a mighty tempest. Turks rode on their horse; they were struck by lances and violently fell off to the ground. Other Muslims rode around the fray and with speed and agility fired arrows into the knights. The men fought, with the Christians crying out to God and the Turks barking like dogs to bring fear into their enemies. The saints heard such growls, and they were not afraid; they laughed in scorn and in mockery.

Bohemond leaped into the ranks of Muslims, and with his men fortified the courage of the others. When the Muslims looked up and saw so close to them the banners of the Christians hovering above their heads, and the swords of the saints slashing all around them, all their fortitude dissipated like the fragile foundations of their heresy. The victory was to the horror of the Muslims, and to the joy of the native Christians who brought their congratulations to the crusaders.[59] Many of the Eastern Christians loved the crusaders, dissipating the myth that has been taught of so long, that the Eastern Christians hated the Western knights.

---

59 Robert the Monk, 4.14–16

✝ CHRISTIANITY IS AT WAR: THE MANIFESTO FOR CHRISTIAN MILITANCY

THE HEADS OF MARTYRS INFLAMES THE ZEAL OF THE WARRIORS

When the crusaders were besieging Antioch, the Turks, in hatred of the Gospel, began to throw at them the heads of Greek, Syrian, and Armenian Christians. The crusaders, upon seeing this, went into great grief and trepidation,[60] but they still continued on. At a place called the "Iron Bridge," the crusaders stopped an army of Turks from oppressing Christians living in the lands surrounding Antioch.[61]

Before the city the men began to construct a castle, and as they toiled and built they were ambushed, and a thousand were slain. The news was brought to the attention of the crusaders, and so filled with rage were they, that they rushed toward the enemy with great speed.

The numbers of the Christians were seen, but quickly they increased, and so numerous did they become that the Turks fled toward the bridge. So narrow was their path that they could not escape from the ferocity of the knights. Poisoned arrows did not work, and nor could their arms outmatch the skill of a Frankish fighter.

Fight nor flight was possible, only death. Countless Muslim heads were struck off, vengeance was made for all of the Christians they beheaded, and no matter how tired the Christians grew, they did not cease in cutting down the enemy.

Godfrey, set ablaze with tremendous fury, struck an enemy with one blow, and the body of the slain was found cut in two. One Turk, riding upon his horse with a body lofty and robust, charged at Godfrey and hammered down his sword toward his neck. Godfrey blocked the strike with his shield, and in one move of agility plunged his sword into the left side of his shoulder-blade with such ferociousness that his chest split down the middle, his spine was severed by the blade, and his head slipped right down. The horse of this giant rode away with the remains of the body into Antioch, and upon its arrival all that was heard were the screams of the people, for he was their emir.

The ruler of Antioch, as he fought with valor, was struck down, and twelve other emirs never saw life again in that day. The Turks flung themselves into a river only to be struck by lances and slain. Five thousand were killed upon that bridge; blood tainted the water like black ink shooting forth the fleeing octopus, and in moments the water turned red like when the Nile turned crimson. No longer did the crusader hear the insults of the Muslims coming from behind the walls of the city, all that he heard was the silence of fear.[62]

THE CRUSADERS FOUGHT NOT A CARNAL, BUT A SPIRITUAL BATTLE

During the siege, the Count of Flanders rushed impetuously into the phalanxes of some of the enemy which was so shocking and unexpected that these Turks ran away in search of refuge. The Count did not sheath his sword until he removed a hundred jihadists from life. In returning to his companion Bohemund, the Count saw twelve thousand Turks coming from his rear, and rising up on the nearest hill was a countless multitude of enemy foot-soldiers. He quickly informed

---

60 Fulcher of Chartres, chron. 1.15.9–12
61 Anselme of Ribemont to Manasses II, in Edward Peters, *The First Crusade*, ch. v, p. 224
62 Robert the Monk, 4.17–21

the army and with a small number of men fiercely attacked the immense wave of Turks who then attempted to encircle the whole of the crusaders. The saintly fighters, thanks to their foresight, prevented this strategy from succeeding. Turks, accompanied by Arabs, attempted to use arrows, and in response the knights utilized their swords in close quarter combat, which made the archers useless. In the midst of the siege of Antioch, as arrows darkened the air, the tall and brawny[63] Bohemund made this profound command to his constable Robert:

> Go as quickly as you can, like a brave man, and remember our illustrious and courageous forefathers of old. Be keen in the service of God and the Holy Sepulcher, and bear in mind that this battle is not carnal, but spiritual. Be, therefore, the bravest athlete of Christ. Go in peace. The Lord be with you everywhere. [64]

These words beautifully illustrate how the crusaders did "not wrestle against flesh and blood, but against principalities, against powers, against the rulers of the darkness of this age, against spiritual hosts of wickedness in the heavenly places." (Ephesians 6:12) The war was spiritual because it did not war against humanity itself, but against Satan, and in so doing did they have no choice but to fight against the servants of the devil, for the aid of humanity.

FORTY KNIGHTS VERSUS SIXTY THOUSAND MUSLIMS

At this command, Robert, like a raging lion, charged and leaped over the Turkish ranks. Upon seeing this, his companions followed and in one accord attacked the enemy.[65]

This battle becomes all the more exceptional, most miraculous, by the fact that during the siege sixty thousand Muslim soldiers could not withstand the ferociousness of only forty knights, who with their arduous belief in God, compelled all of these to retreat. The Crusaders took the towers of city, and the key tower they had taken with the help of the local Christian population who opened its gates.[66]

THE CHRISTIANS BERATE THE MUSLIMS IN A MEETING

A meeting was conveyed between the leaders of the Crusade and the Muslim ambassadors. The Muslims expressed their unbelief that the Christians came as pilgrims, since they arrived holding weapons for the purpose of warfare. The Crusaders replied with this zealously direct declaration, remembering all of the defenseless pilgrims slain and abused before the war:

> Nobody with any sense should be surprised at us coming to the Sepulcher of Our Lord as armed men and removing your people from these territories. Any of our people who came here with staff and scrip were insulted with abominable behaviour, suffered the ignominy of poor treatment and in extreme cases were killed. The land may have belonged to those people for a long time but it is not theirs; it belonged to our people originally and your people attacked and maliciously took it away from them, which means that it cannot be yours no

---

63 See Belloc, *The Crusades*, ch. iv, p. 48
64 See Edward Peters, *The First Crusade*, ch. iv, p. 158, The Sufferings of the Crusaders: *The Gesta* Version
65 See Edward Peters, *The First Crusade*, ch. iv, p. 159, The Sufferings of the Crusaders: *The Gesta* Version
66 See Belloc, *The Crusades*, ch. v, p. 89

matter how long you have had it: for it is set out by divine decree that what was unjustly removed from the fathers shall be restored by divine mercy to the sons. Neither should your people take any pride in having overcome the effeminate Greek race because, by order of divine power, the payback will be exercised by Frankish swords on your necks. And let those who do not already know be aware that it is not down to me to overturn kingdoms but to Him through Whom kings reign. These people say they want to tolerate us with good humour if we are willing to cross their lands with scrip and staff. Let their concessions be flung back in their faces because, whether they want it or not, our shortages will be met and dispelled by their treasures. Since God has granted us Jerusalem, who can resist? No human strength can inspire us with terror because when we die we are born; when we gain eternal life. So go and tell those who sent you that we will not lay down the arms we took up at home until we have captured Jerusalem. We place our trust in Him who teachest my to hands war, so that a bow of steel is broken by mine arms; the road will be opened by our swords, all wrongdoing will be eradicated and Jerusalem captured. It will be ours not by virtue of human toleration but through the justice of divine decrees. It is by God's countenance that Jerusalem will be judged ours. [67]

Take notice of their words: death is seen as gain, and the very thought of toleration is given no leeway, only the will of God and the chivalric swords of justice. How many times have we heard today that Jerusalem can be a home to all religions, or to Islam, Judaism, and Christianity? This is the creed of the moderns, but it is blasphemy to the saint, and absolute sacrilege to those men of old who subdued kingdoms and valiantly drove out the heretics from the land upon which God walked.

A truce was negotiated, terms were agreed upon, and the gates of Antioch were open. Franks walked freely amongst the citizens, and the common man of Antioch visited without hindrance the camps of the knights with the utmost delight.

THE PEACE IS BROKEN AND CAIN KILLS HIS BROTHER
But this treaty proved to be but the peace of Cain, and the blood of a precious Abel was about to be spilt. Time passed, and a certain Frankish knight named Walo strolled amongst a certain valley beholding the pristine sight of nature, and looking, with a pleasant delight, at the serene field before him. In a sudden movement a band of Muslims ambushed him, spilt his blood and hacked his body into pieces.

The knowledge of his death spread like rapid winds through an eastern wilderness, and the cries of the Christians were heard throughout the city. The bitterest screams and the most wrenching lamentations ripped through the hearts of the men, who now were inflamed to arms. The wife of Walo was stricken with the deepest sadness; her throat was choked by sobs, her tongue hindered from speaking the simplest expressions of grief. The heat of life still throbbed in her breasts, and her veins pulsed to the highest intensity. No longer could

---

67 Quoted by Robert the Monk, 5.2

the comfort of silence contain her suffering; she plunged her nails into her soft cheeks, tore the golden locks of her head, and said:

> King of Heaven, three in one, have compassion on Walo
> Give him eternal life, you who are the One God.
> Did Walo deserve to die without striking a blow?
> You, sprung from a Virgin mother, cleanse Walo of his sins,
> Whom you lifted out of the changing fortunes of war
> And now have allowed to be martyred.

THE SAINTS HELP A MUSLIM CONVERT TO CHRISTIANITY AND HE ASSISTS THE CRUSADERS

During this truce, Bohemond formed a friendship with a Turkish emir named Firruz, and in one of their discussions a most profound event was brought to the attention of the French knight. The emir asked him as to why, when the Christians and Muslims fought, there was an innumerable army of soldiers who emanated bright light, shining as though they were stars in the night sky. The Turks could not withstand them, nor drive them out; as soon as they saw them fear would grab ahold of their hearts, and like an uncontrollable tempest rushed on them as the Christian knights slaughtered them.

Bohemond, upon hearing such an account, asked: "Do you think that to be a different army from our army which you see here?" "By Mohammad my teacher," said Firruz sharply, "I swear that if they were here this whole plain would not be large enough to hold them. They all have white horses of astonishing speed, and clothes, shields and banners of the same colour. Perhaps they are hiding so that we do not realise your full strength. But by your faith in Jesus, where on earth are their camps?"

"Although you do not follow our law," said Bohemond, "I can see that you are well disposed towards us and approaching things in a good spirit. So I shall explain to you some of the mystery of our faith. If you had any understanding of what lies beneath the surface you should thank the Creator of all for showing you the army of shining white soldiers; and be aware that they live not on earth but in the heavenly mansions of the King of Heaven. These are the ones who suffered martyrdom for the faith of Christ and fought against unbelievers across the earth. Their particular standard bearers are St. George, St. Demetrius and St. Maurice, who whilst they were on earth bore arms and died in the faith of Christ. Every time we need it they come to help us by order of Lord Jesus Christ, and defeat our enemies. To show you that I am telling the truth, make enquiries today, tomorrow and the next day to whether their camps can be found anywhere in this whole region. If they can, we will blush under your gaze, shown up as liars. And even though you will have been unable to find them anywhere in the region, you will see them here tomorrow if we find it necessary. How could they get here so quickly if not from the heavenly regions in which they dwell?"

CHRISTIANITY IS AT WAR: THE MANIFESTO FOR CHRISTIAN MILITANCY

To this Firruz replied: "So if they do come from the sky, where do they find all those white horses, shields and standards?"

Bohemond answered: "You are asking me about weighty issues beyond my understanding. If you do want to know the answer I shall send for my chaplain, who can reply of your questions on these matters."

After some discussion with the chaplain, and with Bohemond, Firruz realized that he lived in error and turned himself and all of his household to the faith of the Teacher from Nazareth. "I have realized," he said, "that you are a noble man and a faithful Christian. I commend myself and my household to your faith. I shall do what you encouraged me to do for you. I shall hand over to you the three towers I guard in Antioch, and open one of the gates."[68]

And so it was. The Muslim saw the light, and now he comprehended the darkness that needed to be subdued. People may think that these men of the Middle Ages were primitive or superstitious, but they lived purely in the mystical realm, making no differentiating between the natural and the supernatural. For the supernatural was natural, and to them a most excepted truth, unlike today, conquered by the Enlightenment, which is filled with materialism and modernism.

FIRRUZ HELPS THE CHRISTIANS INVADE ANTIOCH

Under the darkness of night twenty men climbed over Antioch's walls, and the gates were opened thanks to Firruz. They charged into the city shouting "God wills it! God wills it!" The cry brought a chill down the spines of the Muslims. The Eastern Christians sang with unsettled lips the ancient "Kyrie Eleison," as the knights slew their enemies. Arrows stormed upon the saintly knights; they raised their shields and the viscous sounds of the sharp projectiles ripping through the air and clashing upon metal was all that could be heard by the ears of God's warriors.

And so were they hindered greatly from using their arms as they were caught within a narrow place and the enemy above shot down their primitive missiles. The Turks rushed them, and there lied no distance between the Muslim fighters for so many were their numbers. As they sprinted they saw before them flying lances and sharp darts which pierced their exerting bodies. Bohemond, inflicted by a wound, was found limping and running into a tower for refuge. The men saw this and their fears were suddenly heightened; to and fro did their worries travel one to another.

One Christian stood on the top of a tower and unleashed upon the Turks below rocks, mortars, and whatever objects his strong hands could find. Arrows from all sides fly toward him. His breath is short and gasping, his faith in eternity fortified, his soul prepared for what comes once the heart ceases to throb. He looked below, and with one sudden movement, he leapt down, hands gripped on sword and shield, into the thickest press of the enemy, and like a violent torrent made the ground beneath his feet as red as crimson, and the air filled

---

68 Robert the Monk, 5.8–10

with the cries of the infidel. The blades of massive swords, forged in the most rugged parts of France, cut through the enemy, and no earthly tongue could recount how many lives were taken on that day.

THE CROSS INVADES THE CITY

When the Muslims saw the waving crusader banner on high, the giant crosses, the knights making slaughter on their people, and heard the blowing horns, they fled the citadel, surrendering Antioch on June 3rd, 1098.[69]

The emir of Antioch was actually beheaded by an Armenian in righteous vengeance for all of the Christians he decapitated.[70] Before this the Turks had stolen a Christian war banner which was dedicated to the Virgin Mary, and in hatred stuck it downward into the ground.[71] But now the tables were turned. When victory was won the crusaders magnified God with these words: "Three in One, who liveth and reigneth now and forever, Amen."[72] This praise was a direct attack on Islam's hatred of the Trinity, and its hellish god.

In fact, after the Turks surrendered Antioch they sent to the crusaders a number of envoys who, when seeing the extraordinary feats they had accomplished, accepted Christ.[73]

THE MUSLIMS RETURN

As the watchmen stood upon Antioch's great towers, they looked with vigilant eyes for the hordes of Muslims returning to take what they had once stole. From a distance there was seen a strange sight: a whirling wind of sand arose and ascended to the air, and twirled like some great tornado.

As this perplexed the mind, there loomed before the men a host of Persians, Arabs, Turks, Kurds, and gnostic Cathar heretics, riding upon swift horses the hooves which pounded the earth, and so great were there numbers that they ruptured the sand to rise up and form a great wave. At their head was the general of the whole Persian army, Kerbogha. The Christians, worn out by grueling fighting, decided that it was safer for them to stay within the city's walls than combat this great horde outside.[74]

---

69 Fulcher of Chartres, chron. 1.16.7; 1.17.4–6; see n. 3 on the chronicle in Edward Peter's *The First Crusade*, ch. iii, p. 56; Robert the Monk, 6.2
70 See Edward Peters, *The First Crusade*, ch. iv, p. 168, The Fall of Antioch: The Version of Raymond d'Aguiliers; Robert the Monk, 6.3
71 See Edward Peters, *The First Crusade*, ch. iv, p. 159, The Sufferings of the Crusades: The Version of Raymond d'Aguiliers
72 See Edward Peters, *The First Crusade*, ch. iv, p. 152, The Siege and Capture of Antioch, Kerbogha's Attack, and the Discovery of the Holy Lance, *The Gesta* Version; p. 155, The Version of Raymond d'Aguiliers
73 See Edward Peters, *The First Crusade*, ch. iv, p. 163, The Sufferings of the Crusaders: The Version of Raymond d'Aguiliers
74 Robert the Monk, 6.7

CHRISTIANITY IS AT WAR: THE MANIFESTO FOR CHRISTIAN MILITANCY

THE MONK FACES THE GENERAL
Peter the Hermit, the short monk who helped commence the First Crusade, came before the tyrant Kerbogha with this message:

> Our leaders and nobles wonder wherefore you have rashly and most haughtily entered their land, the land of the Christians? We think, forsooth, and believe that you have thus come hither because you wish to become Christians fully; or have you come hither for the purpose of harassing the Christians in every way? All our leaders together ask you, therefore, quickly to leave the land of God and the Christians, which the blessed apostle, Peter, by preaching converted long ago to the worship of Christ. [75]

What was the response of Kerbogha? An invitation to Islam:

> Your God and your Christianity we neither seek nor desire, and we spurn you and them absolutely. We have now come even hither because we marveled greatly why the princes and nobles whom you mention call this land theirs, the land we took from the effeminate people. Now, do you want to know what we are saying to you? Go back quickly, therefore, and tell your seignors that if they desire to become Turks in everything, and wish to deny the God whom you worship with bowed heads, and to spurn your laws, we will give them this and enough more of lands, castles, and cities. [76]

The words of Kerbogha was the temptation that Satan gave to Christ. The devil showed the Crucified Warrior "all the kingdoms of the world, and the glory of them; And saith unto him, All these things will I give thee, if thou wilt fall down and worship me." (Matthew 4:8–9) The Christian soldiers told the Muslims, "Get thee hence" (Matthew 4:10), and like Christ, responded with warfare against the works of Satan.

THE CRUSADERS SPIRITUALLY PREPARE FOR BATTLE
When the message was reported by Peter, the crusades prepared their minds for battle. The Bishop of Le Puy ordered a three day fast for everyone to observe. All committed to penitence and confessed with pure hearts, and those who had food happily shared it with others around them. They spent those three days purifying themselves, walking in processions around the churches and imploring God for this mercies.

When dawn arose on the third day and the beams of the solar star illuminated the land, the men celebrated, as one body, the Mass and took of the Body of the Lord, and drunk of the Cup of the Lord, ready to subdue those who sat on the table of devils and drunk of the cup of devils. As they came marching toward the Turks, their bishops, priests, clerics, and monks, were amongst them dressed in their sacred vestments, carrying crosses, singing hymns with hands heavenward and with the fifty-first Psalm on their lips: "Save Thy people, and bless Thine inheritance: govern them also, and lift them up now and forever; be to them a strong

---
75 See Edward Peters, *The First Crusade*, ch. iv, pp. 185–186, The Defeat of Kerbogha: *The Gesta* Version
76 See Edward Peters, *The First Crusade*, ch. iv, p. 186, The Defeat of Kerbogha: *The Gesta* Version

tower from the enemy." They chanted holy songs, as did those on the ground and those on the city's walls, ready to combat as soldiers of Christ against acolytes of the Antichrist.

When the ranks of the crusaders met the eyes of Kerbogha, he said: "Let them come out, that we may the better have them in our power!"

THE BISHOP PREACHES A SERMON

The men marched to a flat land and halted. The Bishop of Le Puy stood before them, and in complete and pious silence they listened to his sermon:

> All of us who were baptized into Jesus Christ [Romans 6:3] are both sons of God and brothers together: we are bound by one and the same spiritual link and by the same love. So let us fight together in common purpose, like brothers, to protect our souls and bodies in such desperate straits. Remember how many tribulations you have suffered for your sins, as Our Lord God has seen fit to make plain to you in the visions he has sent. But now you are cleansed, and reconciled in full to God. So what should you fear? No misfortune can touch you. The man who dies here will be happier than he who lives because he will receive eternal joy in place of his mortal life. Conversely the man who survives will triumph over his enemies in victory; he will gain their riches and not suffer any need. You know what you have suffered, and the situation you now face. The Lord has brought the riches of the Orient right up to you—in fact, put them in your hands. So fear not, nor be dismayed, be strong [Joshua 10:25], because our God is sending the legions of his saints to avenge you on your enemies. You will see them today with your own eyes: when you do, do not be afraid of the terrifying noise they make. Indeed you should be used to the sight of them, since they have already come to your aid once; but human eyes do quail at the sight of citizens of heaven. See how your enemies are watching you march forward, necks straining forward like terrified stags or does, more inclined to flight to fight. You know their tactics well, and how once they have shot their arrows they place their trust in fleeing rather than fighting. So match out against them in the Name of Our Lord Jesus Christ, and may our all-powerful Lord God be with you. [77]

Notice how these ancient Christians saw the Scriptures with such beautiful simplicity, and rustic zealotry. He quotes St. Paul's letter to the Romans at the beginning, and later references the militant Book of Joshua in which the conquest of Canaan and the obliteration of the Canaanite idols is recounted. These Christians did not disconnect the Old Testament's calling for the destruction of paganism and heresy from what is taught in the New Testament. To them, to love was to purge the world of wickedness. Christ was the ultimate sacrifice, and no heretic was to pervert this truth; Christ was the Holy Temple, and no heretic was to misconstrue Him; Israel was the Holy Land, and no heretic was to make it unclean. The mindset of Moses—who massacred the calf worshippers—was continued and kept by these Christian knights, and unlike the modern heretical pastors of today, they did not adapt and mutilate doctrine to make it relevant to present insanities and perversities.

---

[77] Robert the Monk, 7.10

CHRISTIANITY IS AT WAR: THE MANIFESTO FOR CHRISTIAN MILITANCY

THE SONS OF THE CROSS COLLIDE WITH THE SLAVES OF MUHAMMAD

The Bishop of Le Puy's sermon was received with an "Amen!" coming from all the men at once. They gathered together and advanced toward the enemy. Kerbogha and his men fell back and went toward the mountains; the Christians continued after them. The Muslims split into two columns, with one remaining on the battlefield and the other moving toward the coast, with the hopes that the Crusaders would end up between and become easy targets for their arrows. The sons of the Cross collided with the slaves of Muhammad; Turkish archers pulled back their bows and unleashed an onslaught of arrows. But a phenomena occurred which surely was a sight to behold: a sudden wind came about and blew the arrows off their target. When the archers saw this they were mesmerized, and fled.

The knight Hugh the Great galloped on his horse toward the melee, locked his eyes on one of the boldest of the Muslims and plunged his lance into his throat.

In one medieval account we find that in this same battle over Antioch sixty thousand Muslims broke right into the city, and when they flooded it, they numbered over one hundred thousand.[78] This left the crusaders in the deepest anxiety. They sent a message to the Turks, giving them the options to leave the city or be attacked the next day, or choose a small body of their finest fighters to fight an equally small group of elite knights.

The Turks rejected their offer, being confident with their number of three hundred thousand soldiers, leaving the Christians no other choice but to prepare for war. The next morning came the crusaders in their most glorious presentation: their banners were held up, bearing the ensigns of Christendom, and their ranks were superbly organized. Truly it must have been a beautiful site for the saint, and a terror to the Muslim. At the front line stood the phalanges with their shields and long spears, and the priests clothed in white vestments, their eyes weeping and their voices singing exalting hymns to God.[79] When Amirdal, the military leader for the Turks, saw the banners of his enemy, he told the top lieutenant Kerbogha:

> Behold, the Franks are coming; either flee now, or fight well; for I see the standard of the great Pope advancing. Today you may fear to be overcome by those whom you thought could be entirely annihilated. [80]

THE ARMIES OF HEAVEN JOIN THE MILITANTS

When these saints fully showed the heat of their zeal and ferociousness before the Muslims, the sight was unbearable to this despot of Islam who now lay in fear. Entire waves of arrows from Turkish archers flew and towered them, killing and wounding many. From all sides these missiles brought much trepidation, taking many lives and neutralizing the crusaders' skill in the sword. A poisoned arrow struck Odo of Beaugency, the standard bearer of the army; he fell to the ground and gave up the ghost. Another knight, William of Belesme, saw his fellow

---

78 See The Letter of the Princes Addressed to the Roman Pontiff; Fulcher of Chartres, 1.24.5; 1.19.4
79 Fulcher of Chartres, chron. 1.19.4; 1.21.1–4; 1.22.3
80 Fulcher of Chartres, chron. 1.22.7

knight lying dead, the standard next to him, and charged toward it. He charged through the thick of the enemy, hacking to death the Muslims who stood before him, picked up the standard and raised it high. No Muslim played the coward, each and every one of them exerted all his energy, and with the utmost of vigor pressed upon the Crusaders with the fiercest of strikes.

But then from out of nowhere an army of knights came from the mountains. Their horses and banners were completely white, their luster bright, their numbers seemed countless, and their identity was entirely unknown to the crusaders until, from their own eyewitness accounts, they were recognized that they were led by "St. George, Mercurius, and Demetrius."

The Bishop of Le Puy beheld these soldiers of Heaven and proclaimed with profound dispossession: "Soldiers, here comes the help of God promised you!" One crusader who fought in this battle wrote: "This is to be believed, for many of our men saw it. However, when the Turks who were stationed on the side toward the sea saw that they could hold out no longer, they set fire to the grass, so that, upon seeing it, those who were in the tents might flee. The latter, recognizing that signal, seized all the precious spoils and fled. ...The Turks and the Persians in their turn cried out. Thereupon, we invoked the Living and True God and charged against them, and in the name of Jesus Christ and of the Holy Sepulcher we began the battle, and, God helping, we overcame them."[81]

The Turks and Persians retreated from the crusaders, and so shall it be in the end, when the Persians and the Turks—Elam, Lydia, Meshech and Tubal—will be crushed by the Christian armies, and "all the saints with You" (Zechariah 14:5), and their Lord Jesus Christ in the final battle over Jerusalem.

The enemy fled in pure terror from the armies of Heaven, and the Christian warriors went after them. When the Syrian and Armenians saw the Muslims fleeing, they rose up and joined in on the slaughter of their enemies, and all those martyrs who were killed amongst them were avenged. So hard were the Muslims pressed that they could not even find refuge in their own tents. A quarrel ensued.

One knight was pierced by arrows and many others were swiftly decapitated. In the end, the Muslims retreated and upheld the victory.[82] The crusaders brought such a fierce attack upon the Turks that it pierced the courage of their enemies, regardless of their superior numbers, and killed thousands of them. The Turks darted away in a chaotic fashion, with the Franks chasing after them with all of their might and endurance. Those with swift horses escaped the fierce hands of the Christians, while those who straggled were swiftly dispatched. But the loss of the Christians was no small few: one hundred thousand knights were slain in this battle.

"Corbagath," writes Fulcher of Chartres, "who had slain the Franks many times with such cruel words and threats, fled more swiftly than a deer. But why did he, who had a people

---

81 See Edward Peters, *The First Crusade*, ch. iv, pp. 186–188, The Defeat of Kerbogha: *The Gesta* Version; p. 192, The Version of Raymond d'Aguiliers; Robert the Monk, 7.8–13
82 Robert the Monk, 7.14

so great and so well equipped with horses, flee? Because he strove to fight against God, and the Lord seeing him afar, entirely broke his pomp and strength."[83]

The Muslims who lay wounded on the field of battle were finished off by the Armenian and Syrian Christians.[84]

There, in the midst of this bloodied place, was seen the Bishop of Le Puy arrayed in the purest attire of a warrior: his chest bore a breastplate, a lance was in his hand and his face was covered with tears through sheer joy as he looked to the men and proclaimed:

> From the day you became soldiers, nobody has stood in comparison with you. Nobody has ever fought so many great battles in such a short time as you since you crossed the sea of Constantinople. Anyone who sees what you have seen today and is not affirmed in his love of God is a true stranger to the Christian faith. [85]

When the emir of Antioch, Ahmed bin Meruan, witnessed the Muslims suffer so ignominious a defeat, and saw the thousands of heavenly knights overpower his leader and his people, he was so filled with trembling that he requested from the Crusaders one of their banners. Bohemond sent him one, and Ahmed asked for a meeting with him. The two agreed that the Muslims who refused to convert to Christianity would be led out of the city and into Muslim territory, while those who did convert would remain in the city. "My friend," said Bohemond, "we shall be delighted to grant what you grant. However please wait a moment while I go and tell our leaders, and I shall come back to you shortly."

Bohemond jovially went to the princes and informed him on what he and Ahmad discussed, and all were overjoyed. The emir and three-hundred Muslim warriors met with the Bishop of Le Puy and they all renounced Muhammad and Allah and converted to Christianity. The troops were so elated that they were filled with more joy over these men rejecting error than the actual victory itself. After a three-day fast they were baptized, and confessed that as they looked with awe at the heavenly beings subdue the Muslims into submission, they realized that they could not defeat the God of the Christians.[86]

The same thing shall happen when Christ comes wars against the Muslims after the final battle over Jerusalem. For the Scripture says, "it shall come to pass, that every one that is left of all the nations which came against Jerusalem shall even go up from year to year to worship the King, the Lord of hosts, and to keep the feast of tabernacles." (Zechariah 14:16) Many Muslims, in the end days, will leave the armies of the Antichrist and worship Christ.

---

83 Fulcher of Chartres, 1.23.4; Robert the Monk, 7.16
84 Robert the Monk, 7.19
85 Quoted by Robert the Monk, 7.16
86 See Fulcher of Chartes, 1.23.2; 1.24.11; Robert the Monk, 7.18

PART 14

THE CRUSADERS SEND A LETTER TO THE POPE TELLING HIM ABOUT THEIR VICTORY

After this victory was obtained, a letter was sent by the crusader princes to the Pope, which read:

> We desire that everything be made known to you: how with great mercy of God and His most evident support, Antioch was captured by us; how the Turks who had brought many insults on our Lord Jesus Christ, were captured and killed; how we pilgrims of Jesus Christ avenged the harm to Highest God; how we, who besieged the Turks first, were afterwards besieged by the Turks coming from Khorassan, Jerusalem, Damascus, and from many other places; and how we were liberated through the mercy of Jesus Christ. [87]

All of the Christian blood that these Muslims spilt was now avenged by these crusading warriors, who with their arms defied Islamic tyranny, upheld the Holy Cross and brought low the crescent, only to be despised by modern fools.

And after such a battle was won, the pilgrims continued on to the apple of God's eye, striving with fatigued feet and endeavoring to endure the greatest of toils to see the marvelous sight of Jerusalem. "How sweet it must be for pilgrims after the great exhaustion of their long journey," once wrote St. Bernard, "after the many perils of land and sea there at last to find rest where they know their Lord rested!"[88]

THE CONQUEST OF JERUSALEM

> Therefore, friends,
> As far as to the Sepulcher of Christ,
> (Whose soldier now, under whose blessed cross
> We are impressed and engage'd to fight)
> Forwith a power of English shall we levy;
> Whose arms were moulded in their mother's wombs
> To chase these Pagans, in those holy fields,
> Over whose acres walk'd those blessed feet
> Which, fourteen hundred years ago, were nail'd,
> For our advantage, on the bitter cross. —Shakespeare

There lied in that great city—"whose builder and maker is God" (Hebrews 11:10)—many a holy site to where simple and zealous pilgrims travelled, just to receive through the eyes the delight from the mere sight of the Tomb of the Patriarchs, from whom the world was given those prophets whose Holy Writ the Apostles taught; where laid the burial place of Abraham[89] by whose seed the world was blessed, and by whose arms and valiancy were pagan tyrants defeated, in that crusade which he took to liberate Lot and all those captured,

---

[87] The Letter of the Princes Addressed to the Roman Pontiff, in Fulcher of Chartres, chron. 1.24.2
[88] St. Bernard, *In Praise of the New Knighthood*, ch. 11, 29, trans. M. Conrad Greenia, Cictercian Fathers Series, number 19b
[89] See Alfred J. Andrea, Christendom and the Umma, in Thomas F. Madden, part 1, p. 24

after which the holy Melchizedek conferred the divine Eucharist to the saintly warrior whose body by then surely was fatigued by the shedding of despots' blood.

And now a new crusade was about to go underway, by these same zealous pilgrims, whose souls were grafted in with the same seed by which the nations were blessed, whose armies were accompanied by pious priests who, being of the order of Melchizedek, gave of that holy bread and wine, and whose valor was to quarrel with the descendants of those same tyrants who Abraham vanquished, in that same city—Jerusalem.

THE WESTERN AND EASTERN CHRISTIANS JOIN TOGETHER TO WORSHIP GOD

The pious crusaders marched to Jerusalem to take the Holy City from the Muslim heathens who stole it. A large group of Syrian and Greek Christians saw them from a far distance, but when they spotted the banners showing the crosses, they immediately knew that these men were no Muslims, but crusaders. They happily took up their crosses and banners and rushed to them with weeping and singing.

They expressed their sorrows for the immense suffering they went through under the hands of the Muslims, and feared that soon they too would be slaughtered. But they still sang their hymns of praise; for they saw the crusaders not as tyrants, as people today describe them, but as liberators who were to crush their oppressors and raise Christianity back to what it once was. These two peoples, from both West and East, were brought together under Christ and celebrated a public thanksgiving to God in the Church of the Blessed Mary.

THE CRUSADERS VISIT BETHLEHEM

Before reaching their destination, one hundred knights under the command of Tancred stopped in Bethlehem with the help of the local Christians, to give reverence to their Redeemer. One contemporary account gives a beautiful description of this visit:

> In procession did they [the Christians of Bethlehem] lead them to the Church built on the place where the Glorious Mother brought forth the Saviour of the world: there did they set eyes on that cradle where lay the Beloved Child who was also the Maker of Heaven and the Earth; and the people of the town for joy and for proof that God and their leader would give our people victory, took Tancred's banner and set it high over the Church before the Mother of God.[90]

THE CRUSADERS VISIT THE LAND WHERE JOSHUA DEFEATED THE CANAANITES

After they visited the place where Christ was born—Bethlehem, the land of my ancestors—the crusaders gave the kiss of peace to the native Christians and resumed their journey to Jerusalem. As they sojourned, they passed by the ancient city of Gibeon, and it was sublimely remembered that this was the place where Joshua defeated the five Canaanite kings to save

---

90 See Belloc, *The Crusades*, ch. vi, p. 107, brackets mine

the lives of the Hivites, and where God, through Joshua, commanded the sun and moon to stand still.[91] These warrior saints compared themselves to the Hebrews who liberated the Holy Land from the despotic Canaanites, now the Muslims.

THE CHRISTIANS DEFEAT THE MUSLIMS IN RAMLAH

Prior to taking Jerusalem, an acute battle was fought in the city of Ramlah in which two hundred Turks were overpowering seventy crusaders. Oppressed by wounds and death, these men endured the fatigue of battle regardless of them being outnumbered. Weariness soon came to their bodies, and before the crusaders were about to retreat, a storm of dust abruptly came about clouding the vision of both Christian and Turk.

The sand disturbed the vision of the enemy, and the attacking crusaders now appeared to be more in number. The aggression of the Turks turned into fret, and all two hundred of them were killed by their Christian enemies.[92]

12,000 CHRISTIAN ENTER JERUSALEM AND FIGHT 60,000 MUSLIMS

The warriors arrived in Jerusalem with the most innocent of piety; they beheld with the purest reverence the Temple of the Holy Sepulcher. They bowed in supplication and adored their Saviour as rivers of tears poured down from their surrendering eyes. Their bodies trembled before the presence of holiness, and even their feet were without shoes, for they were on holy ground.[93]

Sometime after this, the siege of Jerusalem began. The number of Muslim warriors within the city was sixty thousand, while the crusaders were only twelve thousand. As they were striving to break open the walls, two Muslim witches tried to put a spell on one of the catapults, but the machine quickly launched a boulder which immediately crushed the two wretches. The Turks sharply fought back against the catapults, burning many of them.

THE UNKNOWN KNIGHT

As the crusaders were debating whether or not they should withdraw these machines, an unknown knight was seen on top of the Mount of Olives waving his shield, giving the signal to advance into Jerusalem. The men took heart; many of them started to batter the walls while others began to ascend into the city by scaling ladders and ropes.[94] Numerous of them reached the top and fought with indomitable spirit.

When the crusaders were in the middle of taking Jerusalem from the Muslims, Count Raymond, one of the topmost leaders of the First Crusade, saw Mount Zion, remembered the miracles which God had done there, and said: "If we neglect to take this sacred offering,

---

91 Fulcher of Chartres, chron. 1.25.15–17
92 See Edward Peters, *The First Crusade*, ch. iv, pp. 204–205, The Fall of Jerusalem: The Version of Raymond d'Aguiliers
93 Robert the Monk, 9.1; Mills, Hist. Crus. ch. 6, p. 83
94 See Edward Peters, *The First Crusade*, ch. iv, pp. 211, 213, The Frankish Victory: The Version of Raymond d'Aguiliers

✝ CHRISTIANITY IS AT WAR: THE MANIFESTO FOR CHRISTIAN MILITANCY

which the Lord has so graciously offered us, and the Saracens there occupy this place, what will become of us? What if through hatred of us they [the Muslims] should destroy and pollute these sacred things? Who knows that God may not be giving us this opportunity to test our regard for Him? I know this one thing for certain: unless we carefully protect this sacred spot, the Lord will not give us the others within the city."[95]

The Temple of the Lord in Jerusalem at this time was tainted by Islamic idolatry, being filled with Muslim images and paraphernalia, and no Christian was allowed to enter.[96] But this was going to change for the better. The Crusaders held a fast and walked barefoot around the walls of Jerusalem, as Joshua and the Hebrews did in Jericho. Never did those memories escape from their minds, of how the Seljuks just twenty years before massacred thousands of the Christian inhabitants.

They chanted holy songs while making a procession from the Mount of Olives to Zion Hill before the eyes of mocking Muslims who laughed at them and presented crosses upon which they spat and defiled.[97] As the devils laughed, the air was filled with the yells of "God wills it!"

Battering-rams were set into motion, and a wave of arrows shot through the air into enemy territory. At about noon, when the very object of the warrior—Jerusalem—set western civilization tottering, the unknown knight holding a glittering shield was on top of the Mount of Olives, crying out that they should move forward in their siege and take the Holy City. Every wounded man rose up to combat, and there was no distinction seen between the healthy and injured.[98] In the final Crusade, led by Christ and His armies of saints, both the weak and the strong, the healthy and the injured, will fight for the glory of Heaven. For as the prophet Zechariah tells us,

> In that day the Lord will defend the inhabitants of Jerusalem; the one who is feeble among them in that day shall be like David, and the house of David shall be like God, like the Angel of the Lord before them. It shall be in that day that I will seek to destroy all the nations that come against Jerusalem. (Zechariah 12:8–9)

THE CHRISTIANS BREAK INTO THE CITY

On July 15th, 1099, the Crusaders were stirred to righteous anger at the Muslims' scoffing of the Holy Cross,[99] magnificently entered the city with roaring trumpets and exclaiming, "Help, God!" They pushed without stopping and posted their banner on top of the city's wall.

The heathen, stricken with fear, shifted from being bold and brave to completely terrified. They fled with desperation; many of them jumped from the top of the walls. A great

---

95 See Edward Peters, *The First Crusade*, ch. iv, p. 202, The Fall of Jerusalem: The Version of Raymond d'Aguiliers, brackets mine
96 Fulcher of Chartres, chron. 1.26.9
97 Belloc, *The Crusades*, ch. vi, p. 109
98 Mills, Hist. Crus. ch. 6, p. 86
99 See Moczar, *Seven Lies about Catholic History*, ch. iii, p. 63; Mills, Hist. Crus. ch. 6, p. 85

slaughter took place, with the Crusaders utterly defeating the Muslim tyrants; so great was their loss that a large body of them ran into the Temple of Solomon.

But this did not stop the knights. They entered the temple and killed ten thousand of the enemy. Nowhere was there a place for the Muslim to escape. Five hundred Muslims then requested that they be allowed to leave provided that their belonging be kept safe, which the count Raymond fulfilled.[100] In all, the Crusaders killed seventy thousand Muslims in their taking of Jerusalem.[101]

Muslim prisoners were allowed to go if adequate ransom was paid, and some crusader commanders even provided them with protection.[102] Subsequent to this victory, all of these knightly pilgrims came to the Temple of the Holy Sepulcher, singing with sublime highsounding voices exalting hymns to the Lord.[103] One crusader wrote on the significance of Jerusalem and the taking of it from the jihadists:

> Here He [Christ] was born, died, and rose. Cleansed from the contagion of the heathen inhabiting it at a time or another, so long contaminated by their superstition, it was restored to its former rank by those believing and trusting in Him. [104]

The warriors laid down their arms, put on vestments of holiness, washed their hands, and in the spirit of humility, wept and groaned as they walked to all the places where our Lord was present.[105] The men threw a grand celebration. "On this day we chanted the Office of the Resurrection," writes the crusader Raymond d'Aguiliers, "since on that day He, who by His virtue arose from the dead, revived us through His grace."[106]

But despite this great achievement, the reconquest of Jerusalem by the crusaders is actually condemned by a great deal of modern Christians because it involved killing Muslims. While that did happen, we cannot forget that they were purging the land from idolatry, and were fighting to put an end to the ongoing oppression and killing which the Muslims for hundreds of years were inflicting upon the Christians. Christians who affirm that this was wrong, have completely neglected the Hebrew conquest of Canaan in which they "utterly destroyed all that [was] in the city, both man and woman, young and old, and ox, and sheep, and ass, with the edge of the sword." (Joshua 6:21) As Joshua liberated Canaan from heathen despotism, so did the crusaders free the Holy Land from the Muslim yoke.

Furthermore, after the victory the natives of Nablus approached Godfrey and requested that he rule over them, for they preferred the government of Christians than that of others.[107]

---

100 Fulcher of Chartres, 1.29.2
101 Butcher, *The Story of the Church of Egypt*, ch. xviii, p. 71
102 Moczar, *Seven Lies about Catholic History*, ch. iii, p. 65
103 Fulcher of Chartres, 1.29.2; 1.30.3
104 Fulcher of Chartres, chron. 1.29.3
105 Mills, Hist. Crus. ch. 6, p. 87
106 Edward Peters, *The First Crusade*, ch. iv, p. 215, The Frankish Victory: The Version of Raymond d'Aguiliers
107 Robert the Monk, 9.12

✝ CHRISTIANITY IS AT WAR: THE MANIFESTO FOR CHRISTIAN MILITANCY

A TRUE CHRISTIAN WOULD HAVE WANTED JERUSALEM CONQUERED

It is difficult to refer to the First Crusade as being contrary to Christianity when they were fighting to preserve and purify the holy city of Jerusalem from people who were enemies to God. The crusades are condemned for believing that to fight for Jerusalem would bring salvation.

But what true believer in the Scriptures would affirm that one can truly be a Christian and stand negligent as the Holy Land is being pillaged, and his brethren are put to the slaughter? It was in the land of Israel where Christ, God in the flesh, died, His divine body buried and resurrected. By this fact alone, to not do anything to help God's people and to liberate His land, more holy than any place in the universe, would be blasphemous. The reverence which the Crusaders had for Jerusalem is expressed in the letter of Manasses II, archbishop of Reims, to his brother Lambert:

> Jerusalem, the city of our redemption and glory, delights with inconceivable joy, because through the effort and incomparable might of the sons of God it has been liberated from most cruel pagan servitude. [108]

And who could not admire the words of Godfrey de Bouillion, when he was asked to take up the crown of kingship after he was established as king of Jerusalem:

> I will not wear a crown of gold where my Master wore a crown of thorns. [109]

THE MUSLIMS TRY TO RETAKE JERUSALEM

In time, a multitude of Turks, Arabs, and Ethiopians, made this declaration:

> Let us go and seize Jerusalem with the Franks enclosed therein! After all of them have been killed, let us wipe out that Sepulcher so precious to them and hurl the very stones of the building outside the city, so that no further deceit can ever come from that place! [110]

Before this event of arms and valor commenced, the Christian men observed piety and observed Mass. The holy rite is described by a monk who made an account of this glorious event:

> When dawn first showed its head in the morning,
> the sound of the bell called all to Mass.
> Mass was said and the people joined with God.
> Receiving a blessing and the sacred gifts,
> the people left the church and ran to take up arms,
> and marched despite their fasting against their enemy.
> Once the king left the city the trumpets, brass instruments and horns
> All sounded at once; their sound

---

[108] The Letter of Manasses II, Archbishop of Reims, in Edward Peters, *The First Crusade*, ch. iv, p. 218
[109] Chesterton, *The New Jerusalem*, ch. xi, in James V. Schall, The Complete Works of G.K. Chesterton, pp. 367
[110] Fulcher of Chatres, chron. 1.32.12

Made all the mountains and valleys around echo
and struck terror into their enemies. [111]

Such is how the old Christians saw the Holy Communion: taking of the Lord's Body before warring with the devil's soldiers, as the Disciples partook in the Last Supper before Christ crushed the head of Lucifer. Then arose the next morning, on the dawning of the day when the sun showed its brilliance and awoke the warriors from their slumber. It was on a Friday, the day in which Christ vanquished the prince of Darkness when He defeated death after suffering the cross. It is said that the emir of Babylon went before his men and declared:

> "O Kingdom of Babylon, pre-eminent over all other kingdoms, how you are shamed today with such a mean people daring to march against you! I had not expected to find them even skulking within the ramparts of a city: now here they are daring to march out against me by the equivalent of a day's march! Either they have lost their senses, or they love death as much as life. So I order you, warriors of Babylon, to exterminate them from the Earth, to let your eye spare none and pity none." As the Crusaders fought the prince of Babylon, so will Christ fight the Antichrist, the king of Babylon, as we read in Isaiah: 'It shall come to pass in the day the Lord gives you rest from your sorrow, and from your fear and the hard bondage in which you were made to serve, 4 that you will take up this proverb against the king of Babylon, and say: 'How the oppressor has ceased, the golden city ceased!' (Isaiah 14:3–4)

And so the battle began.[112]

Arrows flew and lances lunged right through men. The Count of Normandy scolded the Muslim banner held within the enemy ranks, with all of its dark symbols of Islam. He slashed through the Muslim soldiers, and when he reached the standard he slew its holder and took it, as Gideon took down the idols of Zebah and Zalmunna. The Christians rushed the enemy and so vigorous were they that the Muslim archers were almost completely impotent.

The Muslims made a crescent shape formation in the attempt to surround the knights, but this did not turn out to their favor since they were quickly annihilated, and their leader Lavedal immediately turned his back and fled. The remaining Muslims took flight without help from Allah, while the crusaders made yet again a song to God in victory. The cries of valor, the proving of their gallantry, prevailed over the sons of Cain, as the waves of the Red Sea overtook the warriors of Pharaoh.

The land of Jerusalem was so holy to these Catholic fighters, that they could not bear the very idea of heretics ruling over her. So immense, passionate, and rich was this love for Jerusalem, that St. Bernard wrote of her in this way:

> Hail then, holy city, which the Most High has sanctified to himself as his tabernacle, by which in you and through you this generation might be saved! Hail, city of the great King, source of new and joyous and unheard of marvels! Hail mistress of nations and princes of provinces, province of patriarchs, mother of apostles and prophets, cradle of the faith and

---

111 Robert the Monk, 9.15
112 Robert the Monk, 9.18

glory of the Christian people! From earliest times God has permitted you to be continually besieged, so that to persons brave and virtuous you might provide the opportunity for salvation. Hail promised land, flowing once upon a time with milk and honey for your ancient inhabitants, and now with healing grace and vital sustenance for the whole earth! A good land, I say, the best, which, receiving in your ever fruitful womb the heavenly grain from the heart of the eternal Father has from that supernal seed brought forth a rich harvest of martyrs. And from among the rest of the faithful throughout the world, your fertile soil has produced no less fruit—some thirtyfold, some sixty, and some a hundredfold. Happily filled and lavishly fattened on the great abundance of your sweetness, those who have seen you are replete with your munificent bounty. Everywhere they go, even to the ends of the earth, they burble over with the memory of your glory to those who have never seen you, telling of the marvels which are being accomplished in you. Glorious things are spoken of you, city of God! [113]

THE CRUSADE OF 1101

In 1101, when the Holy City which stands on a hill was again under the piercing claws of the Muslim infidel, the Christian knights under Baldwin I arrived to wrest it away for the glory of the Cross. They had travelled for many miles devastated by the ruthlessness of nature, with only a few hundred arriving out of the many thousands who did not survive. The Muslim at this time felt so confident that victory was inevitable for their idolatrous god; he not only deemed that the crusaders could be beaten, but annihilated.

Eleven hundred and sixty Christian warriors, with sword in hand and the Law of God engraved in their hearts, stood before an Egyptian army of thirty two thousand in the city of Ramleh. The sun was about to make its appearance, and Baldwin looked to God and made his confession, his soul prepared for eternity and his arms ready to strike hard upon the heretics of the East.

The dawn had arrived with its rays glimmering upon the armor of those men, under the knight Bervold, who were called to make the first strike. They charged with fullness of heart, the hooves of their horses beating upon the earth, and with utter valiancy did most of them die, even their leader did not escape death. The second company executed an assault, and they too met the same fate, and so did the third garrison meet the ends of this life.

Under the sky, beaten by the merciless sun of the desert, where the wiles of Satan first arose in this world, Baldwin assailed the infidel alongside his men, all with waving banners and lances aimed at men whose intention was to see nothing but the blood of the Saints. The eyes of the Muslim could not bear such a sight: the imposing cavilers riding their beasts of war, their shields bearing the Cross—the most hated symbol to Muhammad—their flags displaying the holy emblems of Christendom without apology. Such a presence compelled the

---

113 St. Bernard, *In Praise of a New Knighthood*, ch. 5, 11

armies of the Saracen to fragment as a pack of wolves which flee once their leader is struck. They retreated to their costal fortress of Ascalon, and Jerusalem was saved.[114]

ONE KNIGHT DEDICATES HIS WHOLE LIFE TO THE HOLY

There was a knight named Raymond of Toulouse, and he once vowed that he would never return to Europe, to fight until his last breath left his body the holy war against the Muslim invaders. He kept his word, he fought the good fight, he finished his course, he kept the Faith, in Lebanon where he fought to take the city of Tripoli. Twenty times did the Muslims come to crush him, and twenty times did they never see victory. The siege lasted for years, and in 1105 the old warrior met his Maker. It is said that he never made too many friends; but, he kept his word, and strived to bring the Cross to Jerusalem. Baldwin I resumed what this old knight struggled to accomplish, and took Tripoli in 1109.[115]

THE CHRISTIANS INVADE EGYPT

Earlier in the year 1118 Baldwin I invaded the land where Pharaoh once reigned, and with only six hundred and sixteen men stormed Egypt which consisted of millions of Muslims. They advanced all the way to the Nile, where Baldwin fell terribly ill, but as life still moved within him he made his way to Jerusalem, where he died.[116]

A MONK HELPS FORM THE TEMPLARS

St. Bernard of Clairvaux, a monk, and the greatest spiritual authority of his age, believed in a monastic life dedicated to strict self-discipline and physically warring against wicked and evil institutions. He recalled how Christ purged the Temple of its thievery, and so taught that the saints must rid the world of sinister powers. He, without ceasing, preached crusades and even wrote a book in praise of an order of warrior monks.[117]

These spiritual teachings ended up forming the Templars, whose duty it was to protect Christian pilgrims in the Holy Land. They were originally called "Milites Christi," or Soldiers of Christ. They were founded in 1120 by a French knight named Hugh of Payens and some other companions, to establish a brotherhood to protect pilgrims entering Jerusalem from Muslims.[118]

St. Bernard wrote a praise of this body of militant monks, in which he described how these warriors read the story of their King Christ—"the Leader of knighthood"—casting out the thieves from His temple, and saw it as their obligation to cleanse the Temple of Jerusalem from the heretic Muslims who tainted it with their falsehoods, and to drive out the Muslims

---

[114] Warren H. Carroll, *A History of Christendom*, vol. 3, ch. i, p. 8
[115] Warren H. Carroll, *A History of Christendom*, vol. 3, ch. i, p. 9
[116] Warren H. Carroll, *A History of Christendom*, vol.3, ch. i, p. 24
[117] See Warren H. Carroll, *A History of Christendom*, vol. iii, ch. ii, p. 32; Moczar, *Islam at the Gates*, ch. i, p. 33; John France, War Cruel and Unremitting, in Thomas F. Madden's Crusades, part 3, p. 60
[118] Mills, Hist. Crus. ch. 8, p. 117; John France, "Impelled by the Love of God," in Thomas F. Madden's Crusades, part 2, p. 52

who oppressed the Christians in the Holy Land with tyranny. Bernard wrote of this sublime and fiery sentiment:

> Moved therefore by their King's example, his devoted soldiery, considering it far more unfitting and infinitely more intolerable for a holy place to be polluted by unbelievers than to be crowded with merchants, have installed themselves in this holy house with their horses and their armour. Having expunged it and the other holy places of every infidel stain and the tyrannical horde, they occupy themselves day and night with work as distinguished as it is practical. They honor the temple of God earnestly with fervent and sincere worship, in their devotion offering up, not the flesh of animals according to the ancient rites, but true peace offerings, brotherly love, devoted obedience, and voluntary poverty.[119]

The Templars observed the strictest discipline. No arrogant word, no unrestrained laughter, no idle deed, not even the slightest whisper or murmur, was left uncorrected. Wizards they rejected, they were repulsed by bards, they despised clowns and jokers, and they avoided poets and jousters. They had written on their minds and on their hearts, the words of Judas Maccabees when he said: "It is an easy matter for many to be shut up in the hands of a few: and there is no difference in the sight of the God of heaven to deliver with a great multitude, or with a small company: for the success of war is not in the multitude of the army, but strength cometh from heaven."[120]

They appeared gentler than lambs, but in the thick of battle they were fiercer than lions, and followed that Psalm that proclaimed: "Do I not hate those who hate you, O Lord; am I not disgusted with your enemies?"[121]

THE MUSLIMS SLAUGHTER THE CHRISTIANS IN EDESSA

The crusaders, in the First Crusade, managed to take the city of Edessa; but they were besieged in November of 1144 by the Mesopotamian Muslim Imad ad-Din Zengi. The Christians were unable to withstand the attack, and on Christmas Eve all of the city's French defenders were slaughtered, leaving the entire Christian position in the East, from Antioch to Jerusalem, in grave jeopardy.[122] Who could forget of that massacre which took place in the year 1119? Soldiers were hung by their feet and, to the sport of heretics, struck by arrows; others were buried up to their groins, some up to their navels, and some up to their chins, and bore the test of Christ and were afflicted with spears. Several were thrown onto the ground before the populace with every limb of their bodies severed.[123]

---

[119] St Bernard, *In Praise of the New Knighthood*, ch. 5, 9
[120] I Macc. 3:19, see St. Bernard, *In Praise of the New Knighthood*, ch. 4, 8
[121] Psalm 139:21, see St. Bernard, *In Praise of the New Knighthood*, ch. 4, 8
[122] Warren H. Carroll, *A History of Christendom*, vol. iii, ch. ii, p. 61
[123] Walter in John France, "Impelled by the Love of God," in Thomas F. Madden's *The Crusades*, part 2, p. 47

ST. BERNARD CALLS FOR A CRUSADE

In 1146 the preacher St. Bernard fervently began to call his brothers in France to carry their cross and march against the Muslim heretics in Jerusalem, which by now was back under Islamic control. He was much vexed by the Muslims' killing of Christians, their desecration of the sacraments and holy places. In one of his writings, being one of the best examples of Christian militancy, St. Bernard composed his praise of the knights who protected the pilgrims in Jerusalem and who combatted with the jihadists, and declared their slaying of the Muslim fighters as both biblical and just:

> Yet this is not to say that the pagans are to be slaughtered when there is any other way of preventing them from harassing and persecuting the faithful; but only that now it seems better to destroy them than to allow the rod of sinners to continue to be raised over the lot of the righteous, lest perchance the righteous set their hand to iniquity. What then? If it is never legitimate for a Christian to strike with the sword, why then did the Saviour's precursor [John the Baptist] bid soldiers be content with their pay, and not rather ban military service to them? But if, as is the case, it is legitimate for all those ordained to it by the Almighty—provided they have not embraced a higher calling—then to whom, I ask, may it more rightly be allowed than to those into whose hands and hearts is committed on behalf of all of us Sion, the city of our strength? So that once the transgressors of divine law have been expelled, the righteous nation that preserves the truth enter in surety. Surely then the nations who choose warfare should be scattered, those who molest us should be cut away, and all the workers of iniquity should be dispersed from the city of the Lord—those who busy themselves carrying off the incalculable riches placed in Jerusalem by Christian people, profaning holy things and possessing the sanctuary of God as their heritage. Let both swords of the faithful fall upon the necks of the foe to the destruction of which is the Christian faith, lest the Gentiles should say, 'Where is their God.' [124]

The words of St. Bernard, when he says, "us Sion, the city of our strength," are in accordance to the writings of the Apostle, when he wrote that we "have come to Mount Zion and to the city of the living God, the heavenly Jerusalem, to an innumerable company of angels, to the general assembly and church of the firstborn who are registered in heaven, to God the Judge of all, to the spirits of just men made perfect, to Jesus the Mediator of the new covenant, and to the blood of sprinkling that speaks better things than that of Abel." (Hebrews 12:22–24) And who will deny that those amongst the "spirits of just men" who live on the Heavenly Mount Zion are warriors? Let the modernist heretics, who want to throw away all militancy, deny that amongst those who live on the holy mountain are "Gideon and Barak and Samson and Jephthah, also of David and Samuel and the prophets: who through faith subdued kingdoms, worked righteousness, obtained promises, stopped the mouths of lions, quenched the violence of fire, escaped the edge of the sword, out of weakness were made strong, became valiant in battle, turned to flight the armies of the aliens." (Hebrews 11:32–34)

---

124 St. Bernard, *In Praise of the New Knighthood*, ch. 3, 5

CHRISTIANITY IS AT WAR: THE MANIFESTO FOR CHRISTIAN MILITANCY

The militancy of St. Bernard can also be sensed, with religious fervor, in the words of his epistle to his uncle Andrew:

> Under the sun you fight as a soldier, but for the sake of Him who is above the sun. Let us who fight upon earth look to Him for largess. Our reward for fighting comes not from the earth, not from below, but is a 'rare treasure from distant shores.'[125]

St. Bernard preached the significance of the crusade, pouring forth the dew of the divine word, and with loud outcry people from all sides rushed to demand crosses. In one speech he also preached against the dangers of the teachings of a Cistercian monk named Raoul who called for the slaughters of the Jews:[126]

> Is it not a far better triumph for the Church to convince and convert the Jews than to put them all to the sword? Has that prayer which the Church offers for the Jews, from the rising up of the sun to the going down thereof, that the veil may be taken from their hearts so that they may be led from the darkness of error into the light of truth, been instituted in vain? If she did not hope that they would believe and be converted, it would seem useless and vain for her to pray for them. But with the eye of mercy she considers how the Lord regards with favour him who renders good for evil and love for hatred. ... Who is this man [Raoul] that he should make out the Prophet to be a liar and render void the treasures of Christ's love and pity?[127]

The emperor Conrad III was approached by St. Bernard who implored him to lead the Second Crusade, an urgent request flatly refused. But the saint was gifted with persistence, and for such a noble mission he stopped at nothing. On one December St. Bernard went before the emperor and proclaimed: "Man, what ought I to have done for you that I have not done?" The emperor, with tears streaming from sorrowful eyes, declared before an audience and St. Bernard: "I do indeed acknowledge the benefactions of His divine grace; henceforth with His aid I will not be found ungrateful; seeing that you call upon me, I am ready to serve Him."[128]

Many a saintly warrior arose to follow the cause of the great war with the powers of darkness; all of Christendom united to fight the common enemy—the infidels and heretics who prostrated before the Lord of all Darkness—twenty thousand Germans, Czechs, and Poles went into the holy fray, and a great French army with a slightly lesser number joined in.[129]

Louis VII and his armies also partook in the crusade. They marched on eastward, and in six days, when they were near Mount Cadmus, they were suddenly attacked most forcefully by the dreaded Turks. To the sounds of war—to the sounds of violent cries and panic—did the king gallop upon his horse fit for battle. To his right and to his left rode amongst him his guarding cavilers, and in one swift moment after another these loyal fighters for God were

---

125 Quoted by John France, War Cruel and Unremitting, in Thomas F. Madden's *The Crusades*, part 3, p. 61
126 See Mills, Hist. Crus. ch. 8, p. 120; John France, War Cruel and Unremitting, in Thomas F. Madden's *The Crusades*, part 3, pp. 60–1
127 Quoted by Warren H. Carroll, *A History of Christendom*, vol. iii, ch. ii, p. 62
128 See Carroll, *A History of Christendom*, vol. iii, ch. ii, p. 63
129 See Carroll, *A History of Christendom*, vol. iii, ch. ii, p. 63

slain. Hysteria and trepidation were abound; everyman was distracted for the preserving of his life; every sword occupied in the cutting of flesh; and all blood pumped through the veins of a vigorous fighter, giving aid to mighty hands of war to only make the ground flooded in that scarlet fluid of life. The king looked before him and saw the crowd of the enemy, and behind him was the base of a cliff.

Before his life could be taken he latched himself on to a tree which stood on a ledge above the ground, and with vigorous strength swung himself to the top of a boulder, and for over an hour he stood alone with his sword flashing against the sunset. The Turks did not even know who he was; they were completely oblivious to his kingship, but they knew full well his valor and so they left as the glowing light of the sinking sun began to dissipate.[130]

Louis VII would later partake in an attempted siege of Damascus, which only ended in failure. This defeat would end the Second Crusade.[131]

Notwithstanding this, the spirit of crusading burned in the hearts of many, and to fulfill such a thirst to war against evil, St. Bernard urged for a crusade; he thundered from the pulpit, preaching to the multitudes in fields and churches throughout Germany and France.[132] He implored Pope Eugenius to commence a new crusade:

> Because God does what he wishes, it is no reason why we should not do our duty. But I as a faithful Christian hope for better things and think it great joy that we have fallen on diverse trials. Truly we have eaten the bread of grief and drunk the wine of sorrow. Why are you, the friend of the Bridegroom, fearful, as though the kind and wise Bridegroom had not, according to His custom, saved the good wine until now? 'Who knows but he will relent and be appeased, and leave behind a blessing.' Certainly the Divine Goodness is wont to act in this way, as you know better than I do. When has not great good been preceded by great evils. To mention nothing, was not that unique and unparalleled gift of our salvation preceded by the death of Our Saviour?[133]

But his pleas were done in vain, compelling the Saint to offer himself as leader of a crusade, and this too was rejected. The sultan Nureddin in Syria had the crusader Raymond of Poiters beheaded and his skull sent to the Caliph of Baghdad in a silver case; he also captured Joscelin II, former count of Edessa, blinded him and held him prisoner insisting that he convert to Islam, which he denied until his death in captivity. Who was going to strike with a warring hand against such sadisms? Baldwin III rode with the Templars to Syria and took Antioch, and in 1152 he became king of Jerusalem.[134]

SAINT LOUIS' CRUSADE
A HERETIC HELPS THE MUSLIMS AND BETRAYS THE CRUSADES

---

130 See Carroll, *A History of Christendom*, vol. iii, ch. ii, pp. 65–66
131 Carroll, *A History of Christendom*, vol. iii, ch. ii, pp. 69–70
132 Mills, Hist. Crus. ch. 8, p. 120
133 Quoted by Carroll, *A History of Christendom*, vol. iii, ch. ii, p. 71
134 Carroll, *A History of Christendom*, vol. iii, ch. ii, p. 71

✝ CHRISTIANITY IS AT WAR: THE MANIFESTO FOR CHRISTIAN MILITANCY

There was once a German heretic king named Fredrick II who was, in the words of Belloc, "one of the most intelligent and most dangerous men that ever ruled in Christendom."[135] He was excommunicated by Pope Gregory IX for not leading what would have been the Sixth Crusade as he promised. When he did partake in a crusade in the East, his actions and heresies brought nothing but disaster. He hated the Christian faith, and whenever he spoke of it he did so with scoffing. He preferred Islam over Christianity. When conversing on the blood relationship of the caliphs with Muhammad with the ambassador of the Sultan al-Kamil, Fakhr-ad-Din, he stated:

> That is excellent, far superior to the arrangement of those fools, the Christians. They choose as their spiritual head any fellow they will, without the smallest relationship to the Messiah, and they make him the Messiah's representative. That Pope there has not claim to such a position, whereas your Khalif is the descendent of Muhammad's uncle.[136]

The Germans have always been rebellious. Let's not forget their history; they did not convert from paganism to Christianity, but from paganism to the revolting heresy of Arianism, which was a protest against the Catholic Church. Christendom crushed the German Arians and forced them into the Catholic Church, and from then on the seed of resentment continued to germinate, and fully manifested its ugly weeds when Martin Luther, a German, helped commence the Protestant Reformation in which he, like Fredrick, expressed his favor for Islam over Christendom:

> They say that there is no better temporal government than among the Turks, though they have no canon nor civil law, but only their Koran; we must at least own that there is no worse government than ours, with its canon and civil law, for no estate lives according to the Scriptures, or even according to natural reason.

Hitler, like Luther and Fredrick before him, also preferred Islam over Catholic Christendom, saying:

> You see, it's been our misfortune to have the wrong religion. Why didn't we have the religion of the Japanese, who regard sacrifice for the fatherland as the highest good? The Mohammedan religion too would have been much more compatible to us than Christianity. Why did it have to be Christianity with its meekness and flabbiness?[137]

Hitler was the perfect Lutheran (he was indeed inspired by Luther), Nazism was the purest manifestation of Luther's teachings, the Third Reich the purest utopia of Luther, and Lutheranism was the first Skin Head movement of Germany.

Fredrick would soon do the unthinkable: he signed a treaty with the Muslims that allowed Christian control over Jerusalem for only ten years, and gave them the site where

---

135 Belloc, *The Great Heresies*, What was the Reformation, p. 87
136 See Carroll, *A History of Christendom*, vol. iii, ch. vi, p. 214
137 Speer, Albert (1971). *Inside the Third Reich*. Trans. Richard Winston, Clara Winston, Eugene Davidson. New York: Macmillan, p. 143; Reprinted in 1997. *Inside the Third Reich*: Memoirs. New York: Simon and Schuster. p. 96

Solomon built his temple. Furthermore, the same heretic agreed that he would never again support a war against Muslims in the Middle East. During the ten year treaty, Christians were to build "neither war nor dwellings" in Jerusalem. The treaty was only to the favor of the Muslims; for when it was over they simply took Jerusalem again.

So wicked was this man that he entered the Church of the Holy Sepulcher and applied the messianic prophecies found in the Psalms to himself. He threatened to murder a priest who followed him when he was walking to the Dome of the Rock, and when he arrived he evilly declared to the Muslims present: "God has now sent you to the pigs," referring to the Christians. He then ordered that the Call to Prayer be sung in Jerusalem, a ritual priory, and rightfully, prohibited by the Crusaders. It is no wonder as to why this heretic was buried not with Christian clothing, but with Muslim garb.[138]

It was this same Frederick who, in 1240, brought an army of Muslims, alongside Europeans, into Central Italy. The Muslims did not hesitate to fight and kill the Pope's troops. They ascended the walls of the church of San Damiano, saw a multitude of women and charged with the intention of ravishing them. A pious woman, St. Clare, was present, and before the heretics could seize their victims she cried out to God:

> Lord Jesus, do not permit these defenseless virgins to fall into the hands of these heathen. Protect them; for I, who have nourished them with Your love, can do nothing for them.

All of a sudden the spirit of fear seized the barbarians; their boldness turned to panic, they clambered over the walls and fled with fright,[139] and the heretics emulated the demons whom they worshipped, and fled from the ever glorious church.

THE MUSLIMS CONQUER JERUSALEM AND MAKE A DIABOLICAL SLAUGHTER OF CHRISTIANS THANKS TO THE HERETIC KING

Because of this despicable compromise a horrifying event occurred in Jerusalem. Muslims from Khwarizm, a land of Central Asia, stampeded into Jerusalem. Many of the Crusaders left the city in fatigue from the unbearable attacks of the barbarian, and soon it was wrested by these Tatar hordes.

So bloody and sanguinary was the unceasing killing that went on, that out of the six thousand Christians who lived in Jerusalem, only three hundred managed to escape. Jerusalem was sacked, all of its remaining priests were murdered, the Church of the Holy Sepulcher and the rest of its churches burnt, and the earth was engulfed by the blood of the saints as the wiles of Allah flooded that City on a Hill.

In 1244 the Khwarizmians and the Egyptians vanquished a Christian army in Gaza, massacring five thousand, including the Master of the Templars and the Archbishop of Tyre. They seized priests and as they stabbed them to death around the altars, they screamed with demonic madness and blasphemy, "let us pour their blood on the place where they

---

138 See Carroll, *A History of Christendom*, vol. iii, ch. vi, pp. 214–215, 245
139 Englebert, *St. Francis of Assisi*, ch. viii, p. 119

poured out wine in commemoration of their crucified God." The Master of the Hospitallers and Count Walter of Jaffa were both captured. All of this was a result of Fredrick—all was a consequence of allowing a heretic to rule. Pope Innocent IV wrote on these very massacres:

> Ah, who of the faithful is not cast down at the terrible oppression of that land? Ah, what Christian is not also moved by so many appalling injuries to Christ? Is the wickedness of that people to go unpunished, and are they to be allowed freely to run amok with the sword? Is not the mind of every Christian kindled against them by the zeal of devotion, the heart strengthened by the shield of steadfastness and the right hand armed with the sword of vengeance! [140]

AFTER THE SLAUGHTER, A RIGHTEOUS CHRISTIAN KING TAKES UP THE CROSS AND DECLARES A CRUSADE AGAINST THE MUSLIMS

Bishop Galeran of Beirut sojourned to Europe and affirmed the western Christians that a new crusade must be done. He received the support of Pope Innocent IV who commissioned Cardinal Otto to preach the importance of the crusade in France. The imploring words came to the ears of a thirty year old Frenchman, ambitious to prevail over the violent heretics: this was king St. Louis IX, and he would lead the last great crusade against the Muslims.[141]

It was said that he was so zealous for the cause of the crusade, that when he decided to lead an army into the East, de declared:

> Fair brother, sweet friend, where is the Bishop of Paris? Quickly now! He will give me the Cross. For my spirit has long been oversees; and my body will go there, if it is God's will, and will wrest the land of the Saracens. Blessed is he who aids me in that. [142]

He received the support of Pope Innocent IV, and funds from the Catholic Church. In one letter the Pope wrote:

> The Holy Land, bespattered with Christ's blood, in the wake of the grave disasters of frequent devastation and following her continuous laments for the frequent slaughter of her people, now experiences the lash at enemy hands even more harshly; now mourns more bitterly and expresses the sharpness of inward pain with cries of still deeper lamentation; and we, stung by her bitter tears, and spurred on by her powerful cries, are with her worn down by the hammer-blows of a persecution that is hers and ours, and with her mourn equally her and our own wretched fate. [143]

The excitement of the king's call to action was felt throughout France, and troubadours sang with pious and rustic prose:

---

140 Pope Innocent IV to Henry III, King of England, 23 January 1245, in Peter Jackson's *The Seventh Crusade*, ch. 2, document 4, p. 25
141 Carroll, *A History of Christendom*, vol. iii, ch. vi, pp. 238–239; Mills, Hist. Crus. ch. 14, p. 208
142 Troubadour's song, in Peter Jackson's *The Seventh Crusade*, documents 1–3, no. 1, p. 18
143 Pope Innocent IV to Henry III, King of England, 23 January 1245, in Peter Jackson's *The Seventh Crusade*, ch. 2, document 4, p. 25

Let us all go forth, and without delay, together with Him who summons and entreats us, ready to join Him at the point of assembly. As our reward He grants us Paradise eternally for our salvation. …Jerusalem, how great is your suffering! It is on you that disaster has fallen, Christendom has too long abandon you. The Sepulcher and the Temple, once so greatly cherished, are lost. It was surely right that you received service and honour, for in you did God hang on the Cross. And now the pagans have destroyed and ruined you. But they shall have their reward![144]

ST. LOUISE GOES TO EGYPT AND THE HERETIC CONSPIRES AGAINST HIM

On 1248, St. Louise set sail for Egypt, specifically for the city of Damietta, with warriors from England, Spain, France, Germany, Scotland, Denmark, and Brabent.[145]

Before he arrived in Egypt, the heretic Friedrich, because of his hatred for Christianity, tried to persuade St. Louis to not attack the Muslims. The heretic said: "Do not go to Egypt, but reconsider, along with your barons. …I had realized the impossibility of fighting the princes, the amirs and all the troops in the country, and my powerlessness before them. And so how do you hope to take Damietta, Jerusalem and Egypt?" But St. Louis wanted nothing to do with such words, and he sharply responded: "Say no more. Nothing, by God and by the truth of my faith—nothing shall prevent me from attacking Damietta, Jerusalem and Egypt, and nothing shall deflect me from it except my death and that of my people."

Friedrich realized that St. Louis was not falling for his trap, and so he sent a letter to a number of Muslim leaders, in which he informed them on how many numbers the Crusaders were, and how Louis' drive was based on his Christian faith. He wrote to the Sultan al-Salih Ayub: "…the King of the French has arrived in my country accompanied by a vast host." He also wrote to the religious leader Naim al-Din: "The King of the French is convinced he will conquer Egypt in a few hours…this prince is the most powerful of the princes of the West—animated by a jealous faith, the importance of his actions as a Christian and his attachment to his religion set him against everyone else. …The Frenchman has not fallen in with my views. The number of those who follow him is constantly on the increase: they total more than 60,000, and in the course of this they will land in Cyprus."[146]

It is no wonder as to why Pope Innocent IV wrote that Frederik "aspires to destroy the faith."[147]

---

144 Troubadour's song, in Peter Jackson's *The Seventh Crusade*, ch. 1, document 3, pp. 19–20
145 Carroll, *A History of Christendom*, vol. iii, ch. vi, p. 251; Pope Innocent IV to [Eudes,] Bishop of Tusculum, papal legate, 6 November 1246, in Peter Jackson's *The Seventh Crusade*, ch. 2, document 5, p. 28
146 Qaratay al Izzi al-Khazandari, Ta'rikh Majmu' al-nawadir (c. 1330), in Peter Jackson's *The Seventh Crusade*, ch. 3, document 32, pp. 46–47
147 Pope Innocent IV to P[eter], Cardinal-deacon of San Giorgio in Velabro, papal legate, 19 November 1247, in Peter Jackson's *The Seventh Crusade*, ch. iv, document 44, p. 56

CHRISTIANITY IS AT WAR: THE MANIFESTO FOR CHRISTIAN MILITANCY

THE CHRISTIANS ARRIVE IN EGYPT AND TAKE DAMIETTA

When the men were sailing and Damietta was very near their position, a lookout on Louis' ship was crying: "God help us! God help us now, for only He can. Here we are before Damietta!" The king went before his troops to bring strength to their hearts and declared:

> My friends and vassals, if we remain undivided in love, we shall be unconquered. It is not contrary to God's will that we have been so unexpectedly conveyed here. Let us disembark on these shores, however strongly they are guarded. I am not the King of France; I am not the Holy Church: it is surely you who are the king, and you who are the Holy Church. I am only one individual whose life, when God wills it, will be snuffed out like any other man's. For us, every outcome means deliverance: if we are defeated, we fly forth as martyrs; if we are victorious, the glory of the Lord will be proclaimed and that of all France—indeed of Christendom—will be enhanced. Surely it is madness to believe that the Lord has roused me up to no purpose. He Who provides everything has through this designed a mighty business. Let us fight on Christ's behalf, and He shall triumph in us, giving the glory, honour and blessing not to us but to His Own Name. [148]

The Turks began to fire arrows toward their ships. The vessels grew close enough to the enemy's territory, and the men leaped into the water to where it touched their chests and with their hands armed with swords and cross-bows, walked to the shore where they were met by a great mass of Muslims from Alexandria, Cairo, Babylon, and Damietta. A quarrel ensued and the Muslims put a very strong resistance, lunging at the men with their lances and shooting at them with arrows. It ended with the slaughter being inflicted upon the Muslims. Within a very short time the Christians approached Damietta, the Turks fled, and the city was theirs without a single sword-fight.

"In this fashion Jesus Christ made over to the Christians an impregnable city," wrote one chronicler, "to the honour of His Holy Name and the exaltation of the Catholic faith."[149]

The majority of Muslim knights in Egypt were in fact foreigners. When Islamic kings would conquer a land they would take the poor people and sell them to the sultan of Egypt, who in turn would take the Christian boys, have them convert to Islam and trained to use weak bows, and as soon as hair grew from their chins, they were given the most powerful bows and made warriors against the Crusaders. The ones who were appointed to be the sultan's personal bodyguards and to sleep in his tent were called the halqa, while the rest, who slept in separate tents, were called bahariz.[150] This is reminiscent to the Janissaries who were Christian children stolen from their parents by Ottoman Turks and made into cold and cruel jihadist fighters.

---

148 Gui, a household knight of the Viscount of Melun [late in 1249], to Master B. de Chartres, in Matthew Paris, Chronica Majora, in Peter Jackson's *Seventh Crusade*, ch. 5, document 59, p. 87
149 Robert, Count of Artois, to Queen Blanche, 23 June 1249, in Matthew Paris, Chronica Majoria in Peter Jackson's *Seventh Crusade*, ch. 5, document 57, p. 84; document 58: Jean de Beamont, royal chamberlain, to Geoffrey de la Chapelle, Damietta 25 June 1249, pp. 85–6
150 John of Joinville, *Life of Saint Louis*, 280–282

ST. FRANCIS WARNS THE CHRISTIANS OF THEIR DEFEAT

The Christian soldiers were about to make a decisive assault against the Muslims, and amongst their ranks was an ascetic named St. Francis of Assisi. He turned to a companion of his and said, "The Lord has revealed to me that the Christians are running into a new defeat. Should I warn them? If I speak, they will call me crazy. If I keep still, my conscience will reproach me. What do you think, Brother?" "The judgment of men matters little!" said the companion, "After all, this will not be the first time you have been taken for a madman! Unburden your conscience then, and tell them the truth!" He approached the men, told them of his vision, and received nothing but mockery. The troops marched forth to the place of battle, and four thousand of them were either slaughtered or captured—a devastating blow to the upholders of the Cross. When the news was brought to Francis, his eyes poured out with tears, and he wept especially for the Spanish knights, whose valor brought almost all of them martyrdom.[151]

ST. FRANCIS CONFRONTS THE SULTAN

During the crusade in Egypt, the nation's sultan, Al-Malik al-Kamil,[152] payed his troops to decapitate Christians. When the Crusaders were trying to take the city of Damietta in Egypt, jihadist warriors would enter their camps at night to behead them as they slept. The lord of Courtenay's sentry was butchered and his body found lying on a table without a head.[153] The Muslims, after beheading so many Christians, hung the heads around the walls of Cairo. When the Egyptian emirs wished to make a truce with the Crusaders, king Louis told them that he would not make any terms of peace unless they first took down all of the hanging heads of the Christians, and give back all of the Christian boys whom they kidnapped and forced to convert to Islam; the demand was fulfilled.[154]

It was this ruthless sultan who a short, scruffy and zealous Italian named Francis of Assisi confronted. Some of the crusaders thought him mad, while many looked upon him with admiration. He came to al-Kamil with the intention of converting him to Christianity and thus ending the war. He walked toward the sultan with his companion Illuminato, singing, "Though I walk in the midst of the shadow of death, I will fear no evil, for Thou art with me." This is so unlike how modern evangelicals apply this verse, to their own personal and superficial problems. As opposed to this rubbish, St. Francis applied this verse to actually walking amongst evil people who could have easily killed him. Illuminato's mind was unsettled, and to comfort him Francis cried out joyously, "Courage, brother! …Put your trust in Him who sends us forth like sheep in the midst of wolves."

The Muslim soldiers seized the saint and Illuminato and beat them. As St. Francis received the blows he cried out with the best of his ability to the sultan, "Soldan! Soldan!"

---

[151] Englebert, *St. Francis of Assisi*, ch. xiii, p. 175
[152] Name is learned from Englebert, *St. Francis of Assisi*, ch. xiii, p. 176
[153] John of Joinville, The *Life of Saint Louis*, 177; Gui, a household knight of the Viscount of Melun [late in 1249], to Master B. de Chartres, in Matthew Paris, Chronica Majora, in Peter Jackson's *Seventh Crusade*, ch. 5, document 59, p. 87
[154] John of Joinville, *Life of Saint Louis*, 469, 518

They were then chained and brought before the sultan. St. Francis implored al-Kamil to turn to Christ, an act punished by death under Sharia, asking him to "consent to become converted to Christ together with your people." St. Francis too was committing a capital offense; for just five months after this meeting five Franciscan friars were put to death in Morocco for proselytizing.

St. Francis asked the sultan to bring a sheikh and light up a furnace; whoever survived the flames had the true God. It was a test reminiscent to what occurred to the three Jews in Nebuchadnezzar's furnace. "Let a great furnace be lit," proclaimed the monk, "Your priests and I will enter it; and you shall judge by what you see which of our two religions is the holiest and truest." The sheikh fled, and the sultan replied: "I greatly fear that my priest will refuse to accompany you into the furnace." "Since that is the way things are," replied Francis, "I will enter the fire alone. If I perish, you must lay it to my sins. But if God's power protects me, do you promise to acknowledge Christ as the true God and Savior?"

The sultan affirmed that no matter the result he would never leave Islam. But he greatly admired the friar's courage and offered him gifts before his leaving, but he refused to receive them. "Take them at least to give to the poor!" urged the saint. As he left, with grief in his heart, seeing that his aspiration was not accomplished, the sultan begged him with these words: "Remember me in your prayers, and may God, by your intercession, reveal to me which belief is more pleasing to Him."[155]

We never mention Saint Frances of Assisi when he confronted the Muslims and challenged them, that they should both leap into fire, and the one who holds the true faith would survive the flames.[156] Who today has such zeal? Instead, we snicker and slander, criticize and condemn, without ever comprehending the true evils that Islam wrought over the Christian world.

THE CHRISTIANS ENTER A MOSQUE THAT WAS ONCE A CHURCH, AND CLEANSE IT

In a short time after the taking of Damietta, Louis entered a church. It was corrupted by the hands of the heretics and made into a mosque, but now that the Christians triumphed, it was restored to its original and sacred purpose. It was an ancient sanctuary wherein the Egyptian Christians prayed prior to the taking of their country by the Arabs.

The Christian Egyptians were conquered once they believed that the Arabs were not heretics. By heresy was it conquered and by the sword of orthodoxy was it retaken. The king and his men stood in the sanctuary of old, and before the priest they sung with rejoicing tears the Te Deum Laudamus. Before observing Mass holy water was taken and sprinkled throughout the church to purify it from the corruption which the heretics brought.[157]

---

155 Englebert, *St. Francis of Assisi*, ch. xiii, pp. 176–178; Carroll, *A History of Christendom*, vol. iii, ch. v, p. 197
156 See Chesterton, *St. Thomas Aquinas, St. Francis of Assisi*, ed. Ignatius, p. 19
157 Gui, a household knight of the Viscount of Melun [late in 1249], to Master B. de Chartres, in Matthew Paris, Chronica Majora, in Peter Jackson's *Seventh Crusade*, ch. 5, document 59, p. 89

A PRIEST TAKES UP ARMS AND FIGHTS THE MUSLIMS

An astonishing event which illustrates great Christian valiancy took place in Egypt: on January 9th, 1250, a priest named John of Voisey, without letting any of the knights know, put on his gambeson and iron cap and held a spear under his armpit with the tip of it being covered.

He approached a Turkish blockade without any trouble, since the eight Muslim soldiers guarding it saw no threat in a lone priest. John took up his spear and lunged right at them, and none of the eight men put up of a fight, but instead turned and fled. A number of Muslims came to their defense, but were prevented from attacking the audacious priest by fifty Christian sergeants who speedily arrived. The Muslims engaged in a fight, but dared not to combat with the foot-soldiers; instead they elusively changed direction. They continued to do this, and when one crusader had enough, he took his spear and tossed it directly at the enemy; it went right through the rib cage of a Turk who broke it off but left the spearhead inside.

When the Turks saw this accuracy they gave up on their changing directions, and were so struck with fear that they stopped moving, and the Christian soldiers were able to crush the blockade. From that moment on, this priest was known as the one "who routed eight Saracens [Muslims]."[158]

If John of Voisey was alive today he would be viewed as an extremist too radical for the minds of "baby Christians" and gentle congregants. No church would accept him to give a sermon, and if he ever decided to write a book, major publishers would deem him as conspiratorial, mock his work and would want nothing to do with his writings for fear of criticism from snobbish seminarians and their professors.

THE SULTAN DECLARES WAR ON THE CHRISTIANS

The Sultan made a declaration of war against the knights, and sent them a message letting them know that the next day they were to fight, and that the place of the battle needed to be agreed upon. Louis replied: "I do not offer this enemy of Christ my defiance on this or that day; nor do I appoint any date for peace. I defy him tomorrow and all the days of my life, from now for evermore, until he has pity on his soul and is converted to the Lord, Who desires all men to be saved and unfolds the bosom of His mercy to all those who are converted to Him."[159]

THE CHRISTIANS AND THE MUSLIMS FIGHT

The two armies eventually gathered at the fortress of Cairo, with the Sultan leading one hundred thousand men. They met in the field of carnage as the sun was rising; they clashed and fought from the morning to the evening, and one thousand Christians were slain, while many more Muslims were killed.[160]

---

158 John of Joinville, The *Life of Saint Louis*, 258–260, date is from Caroline Smith's notes on this book
159 Gui, a household knight of the Viscount of Melun [late in 1249], to Master B. de Chartres, in Matthew Paris, Chronica Majora, in Peter Jackson's *Seventh Crusade*, ch. 5, document 59, pp. 90–1
160 B[enedict of Alignano], Bishop of Marseilles, to Pope Innocent IV, 20 May [1250], in Spicilegium, in Peter Jackson's *Seventh Crusade*, ch. 5, document 66, p. 97

THE BATTLE OF MANSORA

There was a great determining battle in the town of Mansora, where the whole of the Muslim army was posted. A great knight, William Longspee, was killed in the heat of combat, and almost all of the barons, knights, and Templars, were slain in this rugged and ruthless battle. The king, St. Louis, and his men were holding off the enemy and even he was afflicted with wounds because of the exertion and pressing vigorousness of the enemy.

The following day, the Muslim came back with an even greater ferociousness. The Christians saw before them countless lances plunging their sharp ends toward their bodies, and from every direction came spiraling arrows shooting forth from the most skillful of Muslim archers. From the time when the sun was young to its very dissension into darkness, this assault did not cease in viciousness nor in fierceness.

The warriors of the crescent pounced on them with their crooked swords and not a few saw eternity on that day. Lurking about the Nile Valley were watchers who, if they ever saw a fleeing Christian, would fire upon him with arrows tipped with Greek fire that combusted men as fast as comets disappear before the naked eye.

The Christians thirsted and there was no relief to be found, for their enemies cut off all access to water. It was as though they were in a desert island in the middle of a vast ocean of heretics. Four months passed, every warrior bore grueling wounds and lived on enough water and food just to sustain life, and still they were able to lift themselves up and endure all sourness of the body, the pains and travails of an army on the verge of defeat.

Armed with their slaughter weapons, they relied upon that two edged knowledge of war, or death. They reached the banks of the Nile and there came the arrows alighted by that fire that never hungers but is always aflame. They struck and within the fastest moment men were completely engulfed into flames, and to them could no relief come.

Muslims leaped upon the others and cut them off in hand to hand combat, while other Christians jumped into the water and drowned. They attempted with all their endurance, all their training and mastery of the sword. Nightmarish can be the only word used to describe all of the blood spilt, the deaths, mutilations, the decapitations, the screams, the cries, the shrills of fighting men, the growls of assaulting warriors, and the tears which flowed from those maimed and lying on the earth.

And then, in one sudden moment, some of those living ceased to fight, offered up their sword hilts, and surrendered. The rest continued on in the assault, utilizing every ounce of energy to exert a mortal blow, until they breathed their last breath. The remaining men were soon seized by the Muslims, who as they dragged them into the prison grinned and laughed at their treaded enemies. Their standard was taken and teared to pieces, and their captors continuously mocked Christ, as He Himself was mocked.[161]

---

161 A Templar [1250; probably in fact a Hospitaller], in Matthew Paris, Chronica Majora, in Peter Jackson's *Seventh Crusade*, ch. 5, document 57, p. 99

One can only imagine what they did at that moment; many must have been pondering on Heaven, and thinking on that realm which is unseen by the eye, but hoped for by the soul; incompatible with time, incomprehensible to the darkness, unknown to all human reason, but aspired to by all touched by that divine light that enlightens us with that vigilance against all evil in the highest and lowest of places.

Others may have been wailing within themselves, unwilling to leave this world just yet, not wanting to be separated forevermore from those they loved with all fragile desperation, with all angst and despair when binded through amorous and filial love, and not desiring to see what truly was after life outside of this dark, dismal and capricious world filled with benumbed men and ruthless mortals.

And others may have turned back—just slightly—to only see the field of carnage that was once a body of men each of whom was indwelled with that breath that gives all life. In that quick moment, they would have seen their brothers, some without arms and legs, some without heads, some cut asunder, some scorched by unquenchable fire—they would have seen all of this in that flash of time.

Thirty-six thousand Christians,[162] were slain by the slaves of the crescent, to only be given that liberation with that One Who too suffered an ignominious death, and was mocked and ridiculed with arms outstretched upon on the cross, Who shall return again to avenge the deaths of His glorious saints and place the crescent idols forevermore in the state of destruction.

THE CHRISTIANS OF FRANCE WEEP

All that could be heard in France were the mournings of the people and the wailings of utter sadness. No one could console another, since all were in need of comfort, and when one was with another, the only thing they could offer to each other were their tears and the stories of death absent of all hope. The Pope, filled with sorrows, wrote:

> How great is the Church's grief, how loud its groans, and how great its cries! It bemoans, indeed, the grievous death of so many great warriors for the Faith [163]

The French theologian, Eudes de Chateauroux, did a sermon to instill hope and morale into the people. He connected the massacre of the Christians in Egypt to "Abel, a righteous man," being "killed by his godless brother."[164] For indeed, these grave wars are but a reoccurrence of what took place in that ancient valley when two brothers conversed amongst themselves, one truthfully, the other deceitfully, and the latter killed the former for his faith in redeeming blood. It is not only the Muslims who possessed the spirit of Cain, but that heretic

---

[162] This number comes from Annales Erphodenses, in Peter Jackson's *Seventh Crusade*, ch. 7, document 80, p. 175. Arab sources sighted in the same book, such as Ibn Wasil, ch. 6, document 73, pp. 146, 148, and Sibt Ibn al-Jawzi, document 74(f), p. 159, put the number as 30,000

[163] Pope Innocent IV to Queen Blanche, [August 1250], in Hans Martin Schaller, in Peter Jackson's *Seventh Crusade*, ch. 7, document 75, pp. 168–9

[164] Eudes de Chateauroux, in Peter Jackson's *Seventh Crusade*, ch. 7, p. 170

Frederick; for it was he who told the Muslims of the Christians' arrival, before Louise ever set foot on that shore of Damietta.

ST. LOUISE IS TAKEN PRISONER

On April 6 of the same year St. Louise and his men fought the Muslims at Fanskur, and after much grueling fighting, it was realized that their labors were to no avail. They were all taken prisoners by the Turks who would cruelly and mercilessly treat them, cutting the heads of three hundred Crusaders per day.[165]

Like their Cathar allies, the Muslims would take the crosses of the Christians, spit upon them and trample them under their feet.[166] The king was in fact given the opportunity to save himself, and when his brother, the Count of Anjou, urged him to save himself, Louise replied: "Count of Anjou, Count of Anjou! If you find me a burden, leave me behind, since I will not desert my people."[167]

One by one they were violently seized, and with a knife to their throats, asked the question: "Do you want to renounce your faith?" Those who rejected Islam were taken aside and beheaded, while four thousand of them[168] who accepted the false doctrine, were moved to another side and spared.

In another building young Muslims armed with scimitars approached a body of helpless knights. Amongst them was an old man who asked the Christians whether or not they believed in a God who had been imprisoned and killed for our sins; a firm "Yes" was the response. The old man replied that they should then not be disheartened by the persecutions they were enduring. "Because," he said, "you have not yet died for him [Christ] as he for you. And if he had the power to bring himself back to life, you can be certain that he will free you when he pleases."

They left the room, and to the Christians' relief, St. Louise negotiated for their release. Prior to this, they threatened Louie with a torture device called "the barnacles," in which a man was laid on two flexible planks with their ankles on intersecting teeth at the ends; their feet bones get broken, and then after three days, they are crushed again. When the Muslims saw that the king was stubborn, they relented and were willing to compromise, hence the release of his men.

The crusaders agreed that they would surrender the Egyptian city of Damietta as long as the Christian pilgrim population and their salted meats were protected, and the king's war machines secured. After the city was given to Muslim hands, the oath was not honored: the

---

165 See Carroll, *A History of Christendom*, vol. iii, ch. vi, p. 252
166 Eudes de Chateauroux, in Peter Jackson's *Seventh Crusade*, ch. 7, p. 173
167 Fragments of the deposition made by Charles I of Anjou [1282], King of Sicily, in Peter Jackson's *Seventh Crusade*, ch. 5, document 71, p. 115
168 This number comes from the Annales Erphodenses, in Peter Jackson's *Seventh Crusade*, ch. 7, document 80, p. 175

pilgrims were annihilated and the machines were hacked to pieces. They then made a tower of dead bodies and another of the salted meats and set them on fire.[169]

It was this tyranny which the crusaders, if they had succeeded, would have indefinitely crushed, and prevented from spreading all the way into our times. Our lack of appreciation for, and our willful ignorance of, the Crusades, is a product of our current indifference to the Christian Faith and to the jihadist threat before us. If all men comprehended the significance behind the Crusades, and understood their importance, then we would not, nor would we ever, be worrying about Islamic terrorist attacks and the infiltration of Islamism in our culture and government.

Our society has allowed the virus of Islam to penetrate us, on account of extreme apathy to what is important—the Kingdom of Heaven—and to extreme focus to what is useless and trivial. We care more about sports, celebrity gossip and vague tabloids than the seriousness of true history, and because of this we are suffering.

ST. LOUIS IS RELEASED AND THE CRUSADERS MASSACRED

St. Louis compromised with the Muslims and promised them eight hundred thousand bezants, but when pressed to convert to Islam he sternly refused. The Muslims let him go, but the remaining wounded crusaders they massacred without mercy. Later on he won the release of the surviving men who had been captured. The Saint would die in Tunis amongst his men, and with these words he gave his last breath:

> Gracious good God, have mercy on this people who stay here and lead them [back] to their country, that they do not fall into the hands of their enemies and are not constrained to deny Thy holy name."

Sadness was expressed by his accompanying soldiers with the words, "Jerusalem! Jerusalem!" St. Louis' brother Charles took the mantel, and after making a deal with the emir of Tunis, guaranteed the release of Christian captives and the freedom for Christians to do business and observe their Faith in that country.[170]

THE LAST OF THE CRUSADES

A LEPER DEFEATS THE MUSLIM KING AND RETAKEs JERUSALEM

Saladin, who became an idol for the Muslim pantheon, ravished Egypt in 1177 with twenty five thousand men, and as they brought destruction on lands before them and decapitated many, they made their way to Jerusalem—that City on a Hill. What man would raise his sword to scatter such a mob of ruffians? A leper named Baldwin IV, with only six hundred knights rushed their fortress in Ascalon and came before Saladin who now stood stricken with surprise that a man so inexperienced in the ways of war executed such a bold move.

---

169 John of Joinville, *Life of Saint Louise*, 334, 337–338, 340–341, 369–370, brackets mine
170 Carroll, *A History of Christendom*, vol. iii, ch. vi, p. 253; ch. vii, pp. 293–294

The men stood ready in Montigisard, and with eyes locked upon the enemy made their charge, led by St. George himself as the warriors themselves attested. A thousand Mameluke fighters, brave and viscous, surrounded Saladin to protect him, but before their faces were seen descending swords manned by fearless soldiers, striking down hard upon their armour, leaving most of them dead and Saladin vulnerable. He fled, and Jerusalem—that City of God—was saved.[171]

THE BATTLE OF KERAK

Saladin tried to lay siege to the Crusader castle of Kerak. The eyes of the Christians could not turn without seeing sharp arrows moving to and fro, being propelled at them by the warriors of Islam. So many were these devastating rocks that the men dared not to raise a hand, nor lift up their heads in utter fear of being struck dead. Some Christian soldiers attempted to setup a war machine, and as they were assembling the device a wave of stones were hurled at them. They fled with the fear of death in that somber moment. The unceasing barrage of these stones compelled the men to shake in fear, and even those who retired to the innermost parts of the citadel, under the deepest seclusion, were seized by the harrowing sound of the torrent of stones and taken by horror. But the Muslims were again repulsed by the same leper, Baldwin IV.[172]

JERUSALEM IS LOST TO A FORERUNNER OF THE ANTICHRIST

The success of the Christians would soon turn to their misery; Jerusalem, which was under the hands of the Saints, was now taken by the followers of Muhammad, with Saladin at their head. Saladin was a forerunner of the Muslim Antichrist, since he called himself the "Saviour," and "the corrector of the world and of the law."[173] Saladin was not just a mere conquerer, but a foreshadower of the Antichrist; for like Antiochus Epiphanies and Umar, he went to the place where Solomon's temple once stood, entered the mosque of Umar (today's al-Aqsa mosque), and gave his demonic thanks to Allah.[174]

The Christians attempted to repulse them, in what is called the Third Crusade, but when they had lost the Battle of Hattin in 1187, the power of the Crusades began to crumble and their fall became inevitable.[175]

The spirit of those men who endured that struggle which they all sought to partake in, was of the highest merit within Christendom. So pertinent was the war with the infidels to these holy warriors, that Friedrich von Hausen, who was amongst the slain in these battles, wrote this concerning those who did not attend the crusade:

---

171 Carroll, *A History of Christendom*, vol. iii, ch. iii, p. 121; see also John France, War Cruel and Unremitting, in Thomas F. Madden's Crusades, part 3, p. 68
172 Carroll, *A History of Christendom*, vol. iii, ch. iv, p. 123; William in John France, War Cruel and Unremitting, in Thomas F. Madden's Crusades, part 3, p. 70
173 Butcher, *The Story of the Church of Egypt*, vol. ii, part ii, ch. xxii, p. 107
174 See Carroll, *A History of Christendom*, vol. iii, ch. iv, p. 127
175 Hilaire Belloc, *The Crusades*, ch. i, p. pp. 3–4

They think that they've avoided death who cheat God of their journey. But it is my belief that they are acting against their own interests. Whoever takes the cross and does not set out, will see God appear to him at last when to him the door [of Heaven] is closed, which He opens to His chosen ones.[176]

But now these zealot fighters were defeated. Jerusalem was lost; almost all of the Christian foot soldiers were butchered; nearly all of the knights whose lives were dedicated to the Holy City were captured.[177]

THE MARTYRDOM OF RAYNALD DE CHATILLON AND THE RUBBISH OF HOLLYWOOD FILMS

In the film, Kingdom of Heaven, directed by Ridley Scott, after the Battle of Hattin Saladin meets with Guy, the king of Jerusalem, and the knight Reynald. Saladin then offers Guy a cup of melting ice, but the king gives it to Reynald who gluttonously accepts and drinks it. Saladin subtly says that he did not give the cup to Reynold who he then punishes by decapitation. After this murder, the Muslim conquerer tells Guy, "A king does not kill another king." The scene is rubbish. This is what really took place: Saladin told Reynald to convert to Islam, and when he refused, Saladin shouted "swine," cut the man down at his shoulder and had his men behead the knight. It was after this that Saladin told Guy, "Kings do not kill kings."[178]

SALADIN OVERRUNS CHRISTIAN AFRICA

Now with the crusader power diminished in the East, the Muslims overran not just the Holy Land, but other Christian territories.

Saladin sent his brother Shamse-ed-doula to enter Christian Nubia (now in today's Sudan). He devastated the land; surviving Christians were sold into slavery, the treasury of the church was sacked, its main cross pulled down and burnt, and all of this havoc and destruction was done to the sound of the Call to Prayer from a distant dome.[179] Saladin broke down the old churches in Egypt and used their parts to build a mosque,[180] since he was oblivious to the beauties of art and sublime architecture, and so had to steal from those who understood creativity and ornamentation.

THE CHRISTIANS TRY TO FIGHT IN A NEW CRUSADE

After the fall of Jerusalem, all of Syria—save Antioch, Tripoli, and Tyre—submitted to Saladin. The conquests were to the horror of the Christians in Europe, and thus a new crusade began. Saladin sent a letter to Frederic Barbarossa, one of the leaders of this crusade, in which he wrote words proving the need of the Crusades to crush the Islamist power: he assured him that the Muslims were not satisfied with only the Christian East, but desired the West, and

---

176 In John France, War Cruel and Unremitting, in Thomas F. Madden's Crusades, part 4, p. 97
177 Carroll, *A History of Christendom*, vol. iii, ch. iv, p. 127
178 Belloc, *The Crusades*, ch. xii, p. 232
179 Butcher, *The Story of the Church of Egypt*, vol. ii, part ii, ch. xxii, p. 104
180 G.K. Chesterton, *The New Jerusalem*, ch. ii, in James V. Schall, The Collected Works of G.K. Chesterton, p. 209

that he would cross into Europe, "and will take from you all your lands, in the strength of the Lord [Allah]. ...For the union of the Christian faith had twice come against us in Babylon [Egypt]; once at Damietta and again at Alexandria. ...You know how the Christians each time returned, and to what an issue they came."[181]

Barbarossa drowned on his march to the Holy Land, and the Crusaders would be afflicted by a severe blow. But this did not prevent the knights from continuing.

RICHARD THE LIONHEART ARISES

The Christians were soon joined by Richard the Lionheart, the great warrior for the Cross who is much hated today for his zealotry and fundamental belief in the use of the sword against evil doers. He fought valiantly with Saladin over Acre; the crescent and the Cross strived, the Holy Scriptures and the Koran warred, and the Christian zealot was the victor.

Terms of peace were issued in which the Crusaders were given the city and the Muslims were made to let two thousand five hundred Christian captives go free. Saladin lied, utilizing muruna or the art of Islamic deception, and all of the said captives were hung publicly outside of the city. The Lionheart, in righteous indignation to such wickedness, brought out three thousand Muslim prisoners and before the eyes of Saladin's men, had them executed. Saladin then ordered the massacre of all of the Templars and Hospitallers captured after the Battle of Hattin, except for the Grand Masters.

Twelve thousand more Christians were being sent as a convoy to Egypt to live as slaves to the Muslims; but as they journeyed to a life of servitude, there came the knights and the Lionheart with them, and they smashed right into the convoy. Richard slew some of the Muslims and took twenty of the officers alive, crushing the jihadists and freed the Christians from bondage.

The Lionheart should be being praised today by civil rights activists as a great liberator of slaves and as a fighter against the slave trade. Harriet Tubman never rescued twelve thousand people from slavery, and yet she is such a major focus, while the Lionheart receives nothing but scorn by our snobbish modern intellects.

In the heat of battle, with the rage of fighting tainting the dry eastern air, the Lionheart ordered his men to refrain from attacking until the Muslims were fully committed. His men, overly excited and not wanting to wait, made a hasty charge regardless, but the Lionheart adapted and victory was taken, with the Crusaders taking Jaffa, Ascalon, and the whole coast of Palestine. He pursued his fight with Saladin, and in the end, sadly, lost Jerusalem in 1192. But this was not a defeat in battle, but a defeat from within; the French had abandoned him, and left for Europe where they would try to steal the Lionheart's kingdom, leaving him no choice but to return to defend his estates. Before returning back to Europe, many of the Crusaders sojourned to the Church of the Holy Sepulcher, and when they asked the Lionheart if

---

181 Butcher, *The Story of the Church of Egypt*, vol. ii, part ii, ch. xxii, p. 107, brackets mine

he wished to join them, he responded that he was unworthy of visiting that most holy sight, since he was unable to win it from the hands of idolaters. He never saw Jerusalem again.[182]

THE MUSLIMS CONQUER THE HOLY LAND AND ANTIOCH, AND SLAUGHTER 100,000 CHRISTIANS

Like locusts consuming the green fields of the farmer, the Muslims had invaded the Holy Land, with but a portion of grass left to those planters of the Gospel; for the port of Acre was still under the control of the Crusaders. In 1268 the Sultan Al-Dhaher Baybars of Egypt captured Jaffa in Palestine, slaughtering much of its residents and obliterating its castle. He then took the Templar castle at Beaufort near Sidon, and enslaved all of the men he seized. He besieged Antioch, and after penetrating it, he destroyed the metropolis[183] which was so glorious in Christian history that "the disciples were called Christians first in Antioch."[184] As soon as the priests and the monks entered the city the Muslims overcame it. The Christians fiercely fought but as soon as the heretics scaled the walls and arrived within, they made such a great slaughter that they killed over one hundred thousand Christians.[185]

THE SPIRIT OF THE CRUSADE DIMINISHES

Soon the crusader spirit in most of Europe perished, like a ferocious storm dissipating after its strongest wind. In the late thirteenth century, there was a man named Rabban Sauma who travelled to Europe from China, and when he went to Naples he expected to find a unified Christendom ready to fight against the Muslims. To his dismay he saw the Christians quarreling not with the followers of the crescent, but with each other, with Spaniard killing Italian.

He went to Rome and saw the sublime churches, but was told by the cardinals that there was little hope for a crusade to be done. In France he was shown the beautiful shrine of Staine-Chapelle, built by the valiant Crusader king St. Louis, but before his eyes there were no crusaders, no calls to purify the Holy Land, no urging to advance the Holy Cross over the enemies of Christ. He went to England and was coldly told by the king Edward I that "no promises" could be made for the beginning of a new crusade. Sauma returned to Rome and told Cardinal John of Tusculum that he gravely doubted whether the West was serious about combating the Islamic threat.[186]

All of this was a sign that the crusader spirit was diminishing in Europe, and this lack of zeal was reflected by what happened in 1289 in which Venetian and Genoese ships left Tripoli and left the Christians living there abandoned and helpless, and after this the city was captured and sacked by the Turkish sultan Al Mansur Qalawun. The next year, 1290, the same sultan set his preying eyes upon the last of the crusader strongholds in the Middle East, Acre.

---

182 See Butcher, *The Story of the Church of Egypt*, vol. ii, part ii, ch. xxii, pp. 107–109; Carroll, *A History of Christendom*, vol. iii, ch. iv, pp. 136–139
183 See Carroll, *A History of Christendom*, vol. iii, ch. vii, p. 289
184 Acts 11:26
185 James M. Powell, The Loss of the Holy Land, in Thomas F. Madden's Crusades, part 7, p. 165
186 Carroll, *A History of Christendom*, vol. iii, ch. viii, pp. 320–321

CHRISTIANITY IS AT WAR: THE MANIFESTO FOR CHRISTIAN MILITANCY

THE BATTLE OF ACRE

The city had sturdy walls; few did come to her aid: Philip IV saw the hunted Acre with a cold heart, and Edward Longshanks, with a benumbed soul, deemed Acre as not as important as invading Christian Scotland. So few warriors had come, but many a saint arrived with ready hands to defend the last city which stood as the light in a dark land, as a small flame in a region plunged in the gloomy confusion of heresy. Many a saint came with sword and spear to prevent the lips of the heathen from blowing out this last candle of piety.[187]

In Acre, the year 1291, one may have beheld the assembly of the Christians from Cyprus, Naples and Sicily, Athens, Tarento, and Armenia; those valiant knights of the Order of St Lazarus, of the Venetians, the Pisans, the Genoese, the Florentines, all gathered together to defend their last portion of the Holy Land against the heretics—the Muslims—who had warred to destroy the Holy Trinity, and replace the Cross with the crescent. One can just sense the energy of divine fervor emanating from such a body of troops who strived with fiery zeal to preserve God's nation from the corruption of His enemies. You can only imagine what zealous ideas were instilled within these mens' hearts, and we are greatly reminded, with this ardent love of the Holy Land, of the words of a preacher named Martin who proclaimed in a sermon decades before this military assembly:

> Christ has been expelled from his holy place—his seat of power. He has been exiled from that city which he consecrated to himself with his own blood. Oh, the pain! … The Holy Land, which Christ impressed with his footprints, in which he cured the lame, caused the blind to see, cleansed lepers, raised the dead—the land, I say—has been given over in the hands of the impious. Its churches have been destroyed, its shrine polluted, its royal throne and dignity transferred to the gentiles. That most sacred and venerable Cross of wood, which was drenched with the blood of Christ, is locked and hidden away by persons to whom the word of the Cross is foolishness, so that no Christian might know what was done with it or where to look for it. Virtually all of our people who used to inhabit that frontier have been eliminated, either by the enemy's sword or an already prolonged activity. And so now, true warriors, hasten to help Christ. Enlist in his Christian army. Rush to join the happy ranks. [188]

But within such a gathering came a most damning contention between Charles of Anjou and Hugh III, the king of Cyprus, who both wanted to take the throne of Jerusalem for themselves. This friction, arising from the pride of men's hearts and not of pious aspiration, was to the advantage of Qalawun, who charged into Acre with a mighty army, with the goal of taking the last retreat of the Crusades; but he had died before he could fulfill his want, and his mission was resumed by his son Al-Ashraf Khalil.

The walls of the city were breached by a torrent of Muslims and flooded the streets. Melee after melee was done, with men fighting one another on the streets. The master of the Templars was struck with a wound so deep that it killed him, and the master of the Hospi-

---

187 Carroll, *A History of Christendom*, vol. iii, ch. viii, p. 324
188 In Thomas F. Madden, in his Crusades, part 5, p. 101

tallers was given a grave gash. The patriarch of Acre tried to make an escape on a boat, and after allowing many to get on with him, the boat could not withstand the weight and the patriarch drowned.

Women and maidens ran aghast and consumed with terror as they fled with children tightly embraced in their arms. The Muslims caught them and violently pried the young ones from their mothers' hands, and cruel slaughter under the hands of sinister heretics commenced. One building of the city was not yet taken by the Muslims, and the Crusaders put up a fight to keep it; but in ten days Muslim miners broke down its foundation and forced it to collapse. Khalil, with his armies of Muslims who were pervertedly desirous of the young Christian boys, successfully besieged and vanquished Acre on May of 1291.[189] All of the inhabitants of the city were slaughtered, and the entrance of the principle church was taken and became the portal to the mosque of Nasr bin Kalaoun.[190] The nuns remaining in Acre were looked upon with contempt by the Islamic warriors of the crescent, who would put all these chaste women to the sword. The last crusader kingdom in the Middle East was now gone.

Grief, despair, and carelessness was now the sentiments of the West. Pope Nicholas IV attempted to revive the crusading spirit, sending letters to kings and bishops to rile their souls, but all was done without success. Pope Nicholas IV saw no new crusade before he died in 1292. It was the end of the first heroic age of Christendom,[191] but surely was it not the last.

THE RISE OF THE OTTOMANS

Amongst the Turks who settled in western Asia Minor was a small, violent, and obscure group of four hundred ruffians with their wives and children, all converts to Islam and all under chief Osman, from whose name we get the title of Ottoman. In the last decade of the thirteenth century these bandits began capturing castles in the small area around the reaches of the Kara Su River. They began small and gradually in their career of conquest and empire, and soon their numbers swelled from four hundred to four thousand.

They made frequent attacks on Byzantine territory, defeating the Byzantine army in the battle of Baphaeon in 1301. As Osman awaited death in old age, his son Orkhan in 1326 conquered the Greek city of Brusas, a foreshadower of the coming Ottoman Empire. Just four years later, these Turks, with swords, arrows, and horse defeated the much more advanced armies of the pleasure-loving Byzantine emperor Andronicus III in the Battle of Pelekanon. In less than two years the Ottomans took Nicaea, that city where Arianism was anathematized and where the Church was marked as the leading institution in Western civilization.

To the lamentation of Nicaea's bishop, the inhabitants were so anguished that they converted to Islam in masse. The savage Turks unleashed havoc throughout Asia Minor. People

---

189 Chateaubriand, *The Genius of Christianity*, part iii, 5.1; Carroll, *A History of Christendom*, vol. iii, ch. viii, p. 324; James M. Powell, The Loss of the Holy Land, in Thomas F. Madden's Crusades, part 7, p. 171
190 See Butcher, *The Story of the Church of Egypt*, vol. ii, part ii, ch. xxiv, p. 177
191 Carroll, *A History of Christendom*, vol. iii, ch. viii, pp. 324–325

were uprooted, cities abandoned, and property stolen. Was not this the land evangelized by St. Paul, who warned against the wiles of heresy? And now heresy prevailed. Nicomedia soon went into Ottoman hands, with Andronicus III yoked as a tributary to the invaders.[192]

The earliest Turkish attacks upon Europe was in fact first supported by the traitorous Byzantine emperor John VI Kantakouzenos. He was fighting with the Serbs and asked the Turks under Orkhan to assist him, and they happily joined him and defeated the Serbian Christians who, upon that moment of a most painful defeat and betrayal by fellow Christians, realized that the Ottomans were a major threat to Eastern Europe.[193] The Byzantines were traitors to the Church, but now they too would see the Ottoman expand into their turf

A great earthquake had brought down the walls of the Greek city of Gallipolli, leaving it open to the expanding Turks, who never turned away from an opportunity to conquer, and giving them unrestricted entry into Europe. By 1363, they seized Philippopolis, a major city in northern Asia Minor.

In the same year Pope Urban V, attempted what his predecessor Urban II in the First Crusade did. He tried to keep in check the rising power of the Ottomans—which was now in Greece, Thrace, and Macedonia—by commencing a new crusade. A few were with him, such as king Peter de Lusignan of Cyprus and John II of France, but most, while they heard with their ears, were occupied with their own priorities.

WESTERN CHRISTENDOM TRIES TO FIGHT THE OTTOMANS

An army of Serbs and Hungarians, inflamed with noble fury, marched toward the Turks; they fought with endurance and valor, but in the end they were annihilated. Their deaths startled the hearts and rang an unendurable sound to the ears of Europe. The Holy Roman Emperor, John V. Charles, gave his anguished pleas to the leaders of Europe. One mighty ruler, Count Amadeus VI of Savoy, rose to the call and with a thick army took away the city of Gallipolli. But, too much time had already been wasted, and the disease of Islam was so numerous in Europe, that this victory was unseen for its merit. How great were the travails, the butchering, the massacres; and out all of those who suffered, the ones who deserve the greatest pity were the young boys of Christendom.

One fifth of Central and Eastern Europe's children were stolen by the Turks and made to conform to the unitarianism of the Arab; and it has been estimated that between half a million and a million Christian boys were kidnapped. Many of them were hardened to become some of the cruelest warriors in history, while others ended up slaves to the heartless homosexual lusts of sultans and Turkish demagogues. The one who managed to escape and endure the hard road home, just to be grasped by mother and father, would arrive only to see his parents punished with the utmost sadism. In 1446, after the Ottomans devastated the northwest part of the Morea alone, they took sixty-thousand people for slaves.[194] A letter

---

192 Carroll, *A History of Christendom*, vol. iii, ch. ix, pp. 374–375; Moczar, *Islam at the Gates*, ch. i, p. 24
193 Moczar, *Islam at the Gates*, ch. i, p. 27
194 See Moczar, *Islam at the Gates*, ch. i, pp. 36–8; ch. iii, p. 85

which provokes the mind to anguish and the eyes to tears, was written by Greek Christians to the Knights of Rhodes, and it reads:

> We inform your lordship that we are heavily vexed by the Turk, and that they take away our children and make Muslims of them. For this reason we beseech your lordship to take council that the most holy pope might send his ships to take us and our wives and children away from here, for we are suffering greatly from the Turk. [Do this] lest we lose our children, and let us come to your domains to live and die there as your subjects. But if you leave us here we shall lose our children and you shall answer to God for it. [195]

In 1369 the Turks continued to advance, taking Adrianople, the principle city in Thrace, after Constantinople. There truly was nothing in Greece or the Balkans to hinder the Turks from continuing their rapine and conquering—it was only the West that had the ability to do so, and sadly no serious effort was done by it.[196]

As a virus spreads to break down the immune system of the body, the Turks would gradually expand from Thrace into Bulgaria and the other parts of the Balkans. The armies of Satan marched forth into these lands—once blessed by the Cross—leaving the Christians no choice but to flee from the crescent; those saints who remained and refused to leave their homes, suffered the arrival of the Muslims with crooked swords and their crooked book the Koran, which brings men to crooked paths, and many martyrs were made and they walked the straight path to eternal life.[197]

At times they did not use the sword to enforce conversion, but deception. Since Islam is a Christian heresy, the Muslims used concepts and holy sites which they shared with Christians, to convince them to accept Islam as an inspired religion.[198]

THE WESTERNERS REFUSE TO HELP THEIR EASTERN BRETHREN

The Byzantine emperor John V Palaeologus rushed to Hungary and from 1365–1366 he pleaded with the Hungarian king Lajos—called "Christ's shield; the Lord's athlete"—for help in repulsing the viral Turks. Lajos, a Roman Catholic, although greatly esteemed as a most pious man, refused to help him. Some have assumed that his callousness was on account of the Eastern Orthodox position of John V, for their indeed was hatred between Eastern and Western Christians. Even Petrarch, one of the most renowned scholars in Europe's history, wrote: "the Turks are enemies, but the Greeks are schismatics and worse than enemies."[199] How foreign this is from the spirit of Urban II, who cared not that the Christians of the East were Eastern Orthodox, when he sent the crusaders to liberate them from the Muslims.

The Turks took a devastating victory in 1371 over the Serbs in the Battle of Marcia River, and then subsequently conquered Macedonia. Regardless of all this, politicians in the West

---

195 Quoted by Moczar, *Islam at the Gates*, ch. i, p. 40
196 See Carroll, *A History of Christendom*, vol. iii, ch. x, pp. 406–408; Moczar, *Islam at the Gates*, ch. i, p. 33, 36
197 Moczar, *Islam at the Gates*, ch. i, pp. 28, 30
198 Moczar, *Islam at the Gates*, ch. i, p. 29
199 Quoted by Moczar, *Islam at the Gates*, ch. i, p. 32

CHRISTIANITY IS AT WAR: THE MANIFESTO FOR CHRISTIAN MILITANCY

still, for the most part, remained careless. Prince Edward firmly rejected the pope's urging for a crusade tax to support a war to put an end to Ottoman expansion. With such indifference the only thing left for the Byzantine Empire was a tribute they had to pay to the Turks.[200]

The western Christians were more concerned about warring amongst themselves than with the coming enemy. Joan of Arc urged that the French stop fighting with the English and to instead fight the Muslims:

> I tell you, on behalf of Christ crucified, to delay no longer to make his peace. Make peace, and direct all your warfare to the infidels. Help to encourage and uplift the standard of the most holy Cross, which God shall demand from you and others to the point of death—demanding also from you an account for such ignorance and negligence as has been committed and is committed every day.[201]

ST. PETER THOMAS STRIVES TO HELP THE EASTERN CHRISTIANS

But there lived one man who strived with both soul and strength to unite the Eastern and Western Christians, and have the Church triumph over the mosque; his name was St. Peter Thomas, and he was most militant in his approach in warfare against the Muslim heretics. His name is covered with obscurity, but we must pay no attention to modern ignorance, which gives fame to lowlifes and mocks and scoffs the heroes of old. He led a great assault against the Turks on the Dardanelles, and defeated them there. This was the first time since 1261 that Western Christians brought military help for the Eastern Church. In 1366, at the age of sixty-one, Thomas led an incursion upon the Muslims in Alexandria; he received a deep wound and gave up the ghost three months later.[202]

CHRISTENDOM FIGHTS THE TURKISH SULTAN BAYAZID

A most ferocious battle took place near Kosovo in which the Turks, under Murad slew many Serbian Christians. One Serb took upon a great endeavor and assassinated the Ottoman sultan Murad; but the fruit of a wicked tree continues to grow rotten, and his son, Bayazid, resumed the battle and crushed his Christian enemies, his Muslim soldiers killing prince Lazar of Serbia.

The widow of Lazar, Milcha, agreed to submit to Ottoman rule and sent her sister to become another slave in Bayazid's harem. A last stand was made for Serbia's freedom by Vuk Brankovich in 1392, and he too ultimately gave his submission. The next year Bulgaria became another subjugated province. So volatile was the nature of Bayazid that when he conveyed all Christian rulers under his lordship to a meeting, he first threatened them, then ordered them all to be executed, and then changed his mind and spared them. But the insanity of this sultan was not to be fully tolerated under the watch of the Papacy, and in 1394 Pope Boniface IX declared a crusade to liberate Eastern Europe. Two years had passed

---

200 Carroll, *A History of Christendom*, vol. iii, ch. x, p. 415
201 Quoted by Carroll, *A History of Christendom*, vol. iii, ch. x, p. 421
202 Moczar, *Islam at the Gates*, ch. i, p. 33

when crusaders arrived in Bulgaria amidst a land ruled by wizards and cruel men whose origin is found in a soulless country; amidst wolves who never hesitated to tear the flesh from the bones of piety and holiness. This entering into Bulgaria would lead to the Crusade of Nicopolis of 1396.

THE CRUSADE OF NICOPOLIS

Commanding the Turks was Bayazid—a warlord whose mind was hardened by the intensity of war, whose sinews were conditioned to the harshness of combat, and whose heart was as dead as the men he cruelly slaughtered. The ravening Turks saw with their eyes, like predators in the night, the crusader leader John of Burgundy: he was at the young age of twenty five, this was his first time leading a large army into battle, and he was as a young and agile falcon trying to hunt his prey in the presence of a multitude of horned owls.

In the cold silence of the day, there stood the warriors of Germany, the fighting men of Hungary, the valiant troops of Poland, the militants of Germany and England, soldiers of Italy and France, and Hospitallers—all men tried and hardened by ruthless combats. They awaited for the Turks near Nicopolis, but yet the enemy did not appear, as the lion cloaks itself behind the tall grass before the gazelle.

Patience grew to fatigue, discipline to disorder, and soon did the French troops charge into enemy territory to quench the thirsts of their frenzy. The Christians began to besiege Nicopolis, whose walls were impenetrable and whose Turkish guards were strong. Those poor Crusaders continued on with the hope of success, not knowing that awaiting for them was a hidden force of forty thousand Turks. They were told prior that Bayazid and his men were approaching, but hearing with their ears they chose blindness and took no heed to the warning.

The French raised their eyes upon a nearby hill, and within that short moment they saw with trembling fear a horde of Turks screaming mad with war cries, wildly riding down with chariots and cavalry like waves crashing into a frail cottage built by a fool who built it upon the sand. The ambush was executed and in seconds the shocked Crusaders saw before their fearful eyes the countenances of viscous men adorned with turbans and their hands gripped on their disastrous scimitars.

The Christian cavalry tried to charge upon the Muslims only to have their rugged horses caught on sharp stakes planted by Bayazid before the battle even took place. He awaited them as the wolf spider waits for its victim from underground, and surely did they fall for the trap. The horsemen dismounted their robust beasts and began to fight on foot with their hardy bodies. Their armor made it all the more difficult, since now they moved explosively under the merciless summer sun against men adapted to such cruel climate. Four French leaders never saw life again, and John of Burgundy found himself captured by the violent horned owls of the Orient, and was made prisoner without ransom. Most of the prisoners were compelled to bend their necks and receive the edge of the sword. The result of this loss was that for the next five hundred years Greece and the Balkans would remain under the talons of the Ottomans.

THE TURKS CONQUER THESSALONICA AND THE POPE DECLARES A CRUSADE

The city of Constantinople—that most pristine flower of Christendom—saw the marching waves of Turks before its gates in 1425. They were repulsed, and turned to Thessalonica in 1430, where they massacred and looted the descendants of those saints whose deeds St. Paul unceasingly remembered. Their wonderful churches, built upon the foundation of the Apostles, were seized, their icons obliterated, and turned into mosques.[203]

But soon a ray of hope beamed through the cracked door of desperation. In the Council of Florence Pope Eugenius IV promised that he would rouse Christendom to commit to another crusade to liberate the Byzantine Empire. In 1442 he called for a crusading tithe and took it upon himself to volunteer a fifth of the Catholic Church's income to fund a crusade against the Turks. Because of his efforts a crusading fleet was formed, and an army of almost forty thousand men sojourned from Hungary into Turkish territory.

Amongst them was John Hunyadi, considered to be the greatest of all generals at the time. They travelled with unity, they bore a passion that surpassed national jealousies, and all were determined to inflict blows upon the evil empire of the Turk. In the middle of enemy territory they succeeded in taking the cities of Nish and Sofia in Serbia and Bulgaria. They vanquished the Ottomans near Mount Kunovica, took many prisoners and pursued fleeing enemy troops. In town after town—between the Danube and Sofija in Bulgaria—they drove out the Muslims and made the mosques into churches, which was their original state before the Turks stole them.

But soon the murderous frost of winter compelled them to leave back to their bases. The crusader leadership were offered a ten-year peace agreement, in which the liberation of Serbia was agreed upon. Cardinal Cesarini, a papal legate, strictly opposed the treaty. The Turks marched toward Asia Minor in 1444, and so did the prudent crusaders go out to meet them.

The Turks turned around and rushed back into Eastern Europe, but soon under Murad II they came face to face with the crusading army at Varna on the Black Sea. Fiercely did the superb general Hunyadi fight the Turks, and slew so many of them that only the brawny Janissaries withstood to continue on the eternal fray against the believers. Amidst the chaos, the frenzied violence of induced ferociousness, the young and ambitious king of Poland, Wladyslaw III, charged into the storm of combat with five hundred horsemen. They engaged the Janissaries, the toughest of the Muslims, fighting without worry nor fright. In his rigorous charge Wladysaw forcefully fell off his horse, only to be met with the blade of a Janissary who struck off his head, and with martyrdom. The Poles fled as sheep scatter once their shepherd

---

203 Moczar, *Islam at the Gates*, ch. ii, p. 53

is slain; Hunyadi escaped, and the militant Cardinal Cesarini met his death under the hands of the Turks.[204]

THE POPE WHO NOBODY WANTED TO LISTEN TO

A righteous pope arose named Pius II, who once wrote in his diary of his grave worries that the great sovereignties of the West were becoming too secularized, losing their faith in that Light that dispels the darkness, that they could not unite against the greater evil before them.[205] We are in a much dire situation today; in our time the masses see the waves of darkness coming toward them, and do not fight nor even run, but embrace it.

We have thrown away the armor of light for the soft and tender coat of apathy. The shepherd has become a wolf, the sheep wolverines, who both surround the now infinitesimal flock. In the year 1458 Pope Pius II analyzed the afflictions that the Turks caused upon the Christians and demonstrated how it was the mission of the Ottomans to destroy all of Christendom. He implored that an immediate attack was requisite, and conveyed a meeting in Mantua in Italy to organize it. But to his grief, not a single prince arrived to the meeting, and all they did was send a few mere observers to attend. Before the congress he stood and proclaimed with the greatest anguish a call to arms, remembering the glory days of the first crusades:

> People say that now we shall have peace; but can we expect peace from a nation which thirsts for our blood, which has already planted itself in Hungary after having subjected Greece? Lay aside these infatuated hopes. Mahomet will never lay down his arms until he is either wholly victorious or completely vanquished. Each success will be only a stepping-stone to the next until he has mastered all the Western Monarchs, overthrown the Christian Faith, and imposed the law of his false prophet on the whole world. Oh, that Godfrey, Baldwin, Eusatace, Hugh, Boemund, Tancred, and those other brave men who re-conquered Jerusalem were here! Truly they would not need so many words to persuade them. They would stand up and shout as they did of old before our predecessor Urban II: 'God wills it! God wills it!' You wait in silence and unmoved for the end of our discourse. [206]

Thus are the words of a dying old man, whose heart is close to death but yet is strong as it still beats; whose mind is ever so focused on a war, not just between men but between eternal ideas—one of darkness the other of light. These words of sublime fervor are not vague terms used for empty secular discussions on equally, jejune fabrications such as "Islamic extremism" or "Muslim radicalization," but on that most detrimental war between those who uphold the Cross and those who wish to destroy it. The victor of the war determines whether or not Christianity is triumphant or utterly uprooted. This horrid conclusion is less cared about today than it was in Pius II's time, but what the superficial populace of now does not think upon is how these same historic events repeat themselves, and with such arisings

---

204 Carroll, A History Christendom, vol. iii, ch. xiii, pp. 552, 554; Moczar, *Islam at the Gates*, ch. ii, 52
205 See Moczar, *Islam at the Gates*, ch. ii, 55
206 Quoted in Moczar, *Islam at the Gates*, ch. iv, p. 90

of evil, come both saints and hirelings. This is why we need Islam, to sieve between the shepherds who hold swords, and the thieves. Islam in the inoculation to the Body of Christ that makes sure that the immune system keeps vigilance. The one fights the wolves while the other cares not for the sheep and allows the wolves to consume the flock. St. Pius II was trying to war with the wolves as the hirelings laughed him off. He warned Christendom that the Muslims, as soon as they take all of the East, will take the West:

> Take pity on your brethren, or, in any case, take pity on yourselves; for the like fate is hanging over you, and if you will not assist those who live between you and the enemy, those who live further away will forsake you also when your turn comes. The ruin of the emperors of Constantinople and Trebizond, of the kings of Bosnia and Rascia, and other princes who have been overpowered, one after another, proves how disastrous it is to stand still and do nothing. As soon as Mahomet has subdued the East, he will quickly master the West. [207]

All the pope could obtain was a promise from the Germans of ten thousand horsemen and thirty two thousand foot soldiers. But a guarantee was never given. The pope sent a letter to Mehmet II urging him to convert to Christianity, but this too never occurred. With so much frustration in his mind and soul, Pius II declared that he would lead a crusade himself against the Ottomans, a decision approved by the cardinals. Venice then finally agreed to join the fight, but all of the other Italian cities refrained. Hunyandi of Hungary and the convert from Islam to Christianity, Skanderberg, pledged their allegiance to the crusade. Pius II, with great zealotry, made this grand statement before the College of Cardinals:

> Our cry, Go forth! Has resounded in vain. Perhaps if the word is "Come with me!" it will have more effect. That is why we have determined to proceed in person against the Turks, and by word and deed to stir up all Christian princes to follow our example. It may be that, seeing their teacher and father, the Bishop of Rome, the Vicar of Christ, a weak and silky old man, going to the war, they will be ashamed to stay at home. Should this effort fail, we know of no other means to try. We are well aware that at our age we are going to meet an almost certain death. But let us leave all to God, His holy will be done! Nevertheless, we are too weak to fight sword in hand, and this is not the priest's office. But we will imitate Moses, who preyed upon a height while the people of Israel were doing battle with the Amalekites.

How different are these words to the superficial heretics and theologians of today! They do not reject and ignore Moses, but are bent on emulating Moses and Joshua. The priest imitates Moses in his intercession, and the warriors Joshua in their doing in the Faith. They had "faith working through love" (Galatians 5:6), as the Apostle tells us, striving in the fray and extending the love of God by emulating Christ, and striking the enemies of love with strength and sacrifice. On October 22, 1463, Pope Pius II released his last bull calling for a crusade against the Turks, but to no avail. The absence of reactions to his imploring moved him to cry out:

---

[207] Quoted in Moczar, *Islam at the Gates*, ch. iv, p. 91

O stony-hearted and thankless Christians, who can hear of all these things, and yet no wish to die for Him Who died for you!

The hirelings remained careless, even after such holy exhortations. Pius II angrily chastised the Cardinals of Rome for their lack of zeal and for their opposition against his cause:

On every single thing we do, the people put the worst interpretation... the priesthood is an object of scorn and, if we are willing to tell the truth, luxury and pride of our Curia is excessive. This makes us so hateful to the people that we are not listened to even when we well tell the truth. What do you think we ought to do in such circumstances? ...We must change to paths long disused. We must ask by what means our elders won for us this far-flung rule of the Church and employ those. ...Abstinence, purity, innocence, zeal for the Faith, religious fervor, scorn of death, eagerness of martyrdom. [208]

In our own times the cardinals are much worse than in the fifteenth century, being riddled with homosexuality, the open support for sodomites, and all other sorts of devil worship. Surely has the smoke of Satan entered the Church, and it will truly take a miracle for the Vatican to restore its Christian spirit from the pagan bondage it has so enslaved itself to.

The next year Pius II declared that the crusade would happen regardless of who attended or who did not attend. He left the Vatican and sojourned all the way to Acona where the crusading fleet and army were to assemble. To his dismay only six ships of war were present; some Spaniards and French were present, but these soon left for lack of weapons and money. A few Venetian galleys arrived, and the man who was supposed to accompany them—Doge Cristoforo Moro—never showed up. No man could call this crusade a failure, since it never happened. On August 14 he laid on his deathbed and with a broken heart, looked to the cardinals around him, and said:

My hour is drawing near. God call me. I die in the Catholic Faith in which I have lived. Up to this day I have taken care of the sheep committed to me, and have shrunk from no danger or toil. You must now complete what I have begun but am not able to finish. Labor therefore in God's work, and do not cease to care for the cause of the Christian Faith, for this is your vocation in the Church. Be mindful of your duty, be mindful of your Redeemer, who sees all, and rewards every one according to his deserts. [209]

Warriors upon ships, captained by Charles V, would do an attack upon the Muslims of North Africa, those same descendants of Hannibal. The Christian forces were given the blessing, and the assistance, of Pope Paul III, who lent them ships to join this mighty imperial force. Before Charles left off from Spain, he gave his prayers and praises to God in a pilgrimage to Our Lady of Montserrat, and had a crucifix hung on the flagship of the fleet. "The Crucified Savior," he declared before his men, "shall be our captain." They reached the place of battle and naval violence between the two armies commenced. The ships of the Muslims

---

208 Quoted in Moczar, *Islam at the Gates*, ch. iv, p. 91
209 Carroll, *A History of Christendom*, vol. iii, ch. xiii, pp. 579–584

were captured, and the Christians overran Tunis. Twenty thousand Christian slaves within the Muslim stronghold revolted and joined their brethren in the fray.[210]

As careless as many of the Christians in those days may have been, it still does not eclipse the extreme indifferentism that we are now facing today. The plague of devil worship, debauchery, blasphemy, mockery of the holy, and homosexually, has riddled the Church so much, that it will require something very supernatural for it to break the prison of the diabolical and live in the liberty of Christ, and that is, the Church Militant. Soon, the spirit of Christendom will restore itself, and our Eternal General, Jesus Christ, will lead His holy armies into victory against the Antichrist, and all heresy will be obliterated.

---

[210] Moczar, *Islam at the Gates*, ch. vii, p. 149

PART 15 – THE REMNANT OF HOLY WARRIORS AND THEIR PROFOUND VICTORIES

THE BIRTH OF THE HOSPITALLERS

When the Crusaders took Jerusalem in the eleventh century an order called the Hospitallers were given by Godfrey de Bouillon certain lands of the Holy City.[1] They organized guest houses and hospitals for the wounded and sick—regardless if they were Muslim, Jew or Christian—dressed in monkish garbs over their armor, took oaths of chastity, poverty, and obedience, and earned no profit since they gave all that they received to both Christian pilgrims and their enemies—the Muslim lay people who were infirm—; for security to rid the land of robbers, and to help in the fighting side by side with the foot soldiers and mounted nobility.[2]

So every time you go to the hospital, think of these pious, devoted, caring and crusading Hospitallers. This group of saintly medics would in time be under their grandmaster Raymond Dupuy, who would divide them into three groups: knights, who were to protect the Christian pilgrims in Jerusalem and to combat the hordes of Islamic savages; chaplains, whose duties were ecclesiastical and devoted to ministering the congregation; and servitors, who were, like the knights, required to bear arms. So immense was the devotion of the Hospitallers to their duties, that in Syria they had cared for the Christians of Italy, France, England, Germany, and Greece.

THE HOSPITALLERS TAKE RHODES FROM THE TURKS

When the Muslims conquered Acre in 1291, it compelled the Hospitallers to retire into Cyprus where they would reside for eighteen years; but their stay was put to a halt when the Turks invaded the island of Rhodes. Andronicus, the Greek emperor of the East, had given

---

1 Chateaubriand, *The Genius of Christianity*, part iii, 5.1
2 See Belloc, The Crusades, ch. vii, p. 124

the grandmaster of the Hospitallers, Villaret, a grant of the island in the case that they retake Rhodes from the Muslim yoke.

Villaret utilized a skillful plan, and together with his men had disguised themselves literally as sheep and crawled in the midst of a flock, stealthily entered the town of the island, took possession of the gates, slew the guards, successfully allowed access into the place for the rest of the Christian army, and retook the whole island. The Turks had come in 1480 to fight the celibate warrior monks and take Rhodes. It was seventy thousand Ottomans, alongside a number of Greek traitors and a German engineer who assisted the enemy in siege warfare, versus six hundred monks under the grandmaster Pierre d'Aubusson, alongside about fifteen hundred mercenaries and local militia. Before the battle Pierre released a profound message to all the knights of his order in Europe:

> We resist with all power and energy and with courage sustained by our faith in the mercy of God who never abandons them whose hope is in Him and fight for the Catholic Faith. We will continue to confront the enemy while we await the aid of our brethren. Above all we are sustained by our loyalty to the Holy Religion. What is more than the defense of the Faith? What is happier than to fight for Christ? What is nobler than to redeem the promises which we made when we put on the habit of our order?

The cannons of the Turks roared with great noise and shook the city with its firepower. The Turks raised the black flag, which meant that if they succeeded every man in the city would be killed, and every women and child enslaved. The knights placed their holy standards bearing the icons of St. Mary.

The Ottomans charged to the sounds of their savage music, composed to enrage the heart and make the mind wanting death to the harrowing screams of dancing dervishes who uplifted the spirit of jihad unlike any other. The Turks ascended their siege towers, and as they climbed their way up, the knights were awaiting them. They clashed, and with that came the fear instilling sounds of bloodshed: swords clashing and men screaming; Muslims thought upon Muhammad and the Christians upon God. A knight is struck dead; a Greek traitor immediately is killed. The German engineer requested to enter the fort and declared that he had useful information for the knights. They allowed him entry, but no advise came forth from his lying lips, and his only reward was death at the hands of the knights.

A woman amongst the Christians even took part in the combat, fighting like the Amazons of antiquity. They fought the besieging Turks chest to chest, blocking the swarms of Muslims from fully overrunning the walls. Planted upon the fortress were standards of the Holy Cross, the Virgin Mary, and St. John the Baptist, images which are but pains to the eyes of the heretics.

A stone flew and hit the Grand Master d'Ambusson and knocked his helmet off; a fellow knight came and with the purest chivalry gave his helmet to his master. They were not just armed with sword, cannon, and musket, but with Greek fire, and with this terrifying weapon, they ignited the Turkish ships and made them brighter than the dawning sun.

D'Ambusson went before the Janissaries, taking the lead in the fight, and as he cut through his enemies he received five wounds. His men, beholding this man—just sixty years of age—were reminded of the five wounds of Christ and continued to combat the Muslims. They saw in this warrior Christ, for in emulating Christ, became in union with the Crucified One. Fatigue came upon the Grand Master, but rest he would have none; only victory for the Holy Cross was his objective.

In the midst of the fray the knights swore that they saw in the sky "a refulgent cross of gold, by the side of which stood a beautiful woman clothed in garments of dazzling white, a lance in her hand and a buckler on her arm, accompanied by a man dressed in goatskin and followed by a band of heavenly warriors armed with flaming swords."

A Turk lunged a spear which pierced the armor of Pierre and went into his lung. The wound was deemed fatal, but Pierre endured and persevered—a supreme soldier of God surely he was. The Turks fired their cannons; the knights—men who smiled at death and unsheathed their swords to the most formidable enemy—responded by firing their own cannons. The Turks dug trenches to sap the walls of the moat; but they looked up and saw descending stones and clay pots filled with combustibles ready to consume a man with flames, tossed down by the defending Christians. Regardless of their large numbers, the Turks suffered a most humiliating defeat, being utterly vanquished.[3]

And just to think that this zealous group for the Faith, was outlawed by the Protestants in England, since the Reformation[4] rebelliously and wickedly taught that the Catholics were a part of the Harlot of Babylon.

THE HOSPITALLERS MOVE TO MALTA AND PREPARE FOR WAR, WHILE CHRISTENDOM DECAYS

But soon the darkness would rise to insurmountable levels, and the Turks again flooded the island. When the Hospitallers were under the grandmaster Villiers-de-l'Ile-Adam, they had left Rhodes after it was taken by Suleiman, and one-hundred thousand Muslims lost their lives.[5] Suleiman allowed the remaining warrior knights to leave, out of respect for their valor.

Such a loss to the knights compelled them to find a new home, and they went about from place to place, like wandering pilgrims in a world incompatible with their spirits. As they searched for a new abode like prophets rejected by their countrymen, the greedy men of Venice displayed a most reprehensible sycophancy. The Venetian ambassador, in 1525, had this to say about the Ottoman Empire and Suleiman:

> I know of no state which is happier than this one; it is furnished with all God's gifts… no state just can be compared with it. May God long preserve the most just of all emperors.[6]

---

3 Carroll, *A History of Christendom*, vol. iii, ch. xix, pp. 605–6; Moczar, *Islam at the Gates*, ch. v, pp. 115–8
4 Mills, Hist. Crus. ch. 8, p. 116
5 Chateaubriand, *The Genius of Christianity*, part iii, 5.1, 5.2, trans. Charles I. White.
6 Quoted in Moczar, *Islam at the Gates*, ch. v, p. 132

CHRISTIANITY IS AT WAR: THE MANIFESTO FOR CHRISTIAN MILITANCY

The occurrence in Europe at the time fomented a perfect storm for a weak Christendom. The Italians were at arms against each other; Henry VIII of England—as Herod lusted for Salome—was on the verge of falling for Anne Boleyn; Venice was pathetically friendly with the Turks, and a German monk named Martin Luther was objecting to any fighting against the Muslims when they were attacking Catholic lands.

The Protestant revolutionaries proved to be quite the hindrance in fighting jihad. When the Turks were heading for Belgrade in 1521, Pope Leo X sent money to Hungary to assist their defenses. Charles V of Spain was urged to help the cause, but he was prevented by the insurrection caused by the followers of Luther. Luther himself said that "to fight against the Turks is to resist the Lord, who visits our sins with such rods." The Lutheran members of the Diet of Worms in 1521, refused to give any help to Hungary. Because of this lack of unity, Belgrade fell that same year. To the Protestants, the word "crusade" was associated with "Catholic," and therefore deserved nothing but contempt. The Peasants' War—which was ignited by Luther's teachings—prevented Charles V from sending troops, and when they finally did arrive they were two days late because the Protestant members of the Diet of Speyer would not dispatch them in time.[7] Surely were these Protestants the hirelings, who cares not for the sheep and lets the wolf tear to pieces the poor flock.

As all of this decay was occurring, the Hospitallers established themselves in the island of Malta, where they would be called the Knights of St. John, and where they would prepare for war and eventually conduct one of the greatest battles in Christendom's history.

THE SONG OF MALTA

MALTA—A HOLY LAND

A ship sailed through a torrent of vicious winds and was battered by violent waves, and as it fell into place where two seas met, the front of it went aground, and became impossible to move. Their eyes were not going to soon behold Rome, their destination, and as the storm remained unabated, the rear of the great machine was shattered into pieces by the ferocious waters. Hope was absent, and mercy bereft, amongst the ship's soldiers who decided that it was best to slaughter the prisoners present to prevent their escape.

But their commander, willing to protect a very distinct prisoner, ordered them to refrain from their ruthless plan. Instead, he told those who could swim to leap into the sea and reach the nearest coast. They surpassed their fear for the prospect of survival, and jumped into the merciless sea, under the mercy of the storm which so tormented them. Some latched onto boards and others onto pieces of the devastated ship, swam for dear life, and in the end, emerged from the depths of the watery void,[8] they reached a land unbeknownst to them, and all were saved.

Within little time, they realized they had reached Malta. They were greeted by the natives who showed not a little kindness, and illustrated that great hospitality only known in the

---

7   Moczar, *Islam at the Gates*, ch. v, p. 133; ch. viii, pp. 164–6
8   Inspired by Paulinus: "So they emerged from the sea's depths" (Poem 26, 384)

Mediterranean. The rain continued and the air was cold, and so the locals kindled a fire for their unexpected guests. The distinct prisoner, because of whom the other inmates were spared, began to gather wood to satisfy the flames, and out came the most cunning of creatures: a snake, slithering its way toward him to steal the fire's heat.

When it got close enough, it suddenly made its attack and sunk its fangs into the prisoner, and leaked its poison. The locals saw this venomous beast hang on his hand, they immediately observed their superstition. "No doubt this man is a murderer," they said, "whom, though he hath escaped the sea, yet vengeance suffereth not to live." But the man was not unsettled by this, nor was his soul tainted by fear. He simply shook the serpent off and it fell into the fire. (Acts 27:41–28:5) The viper, finding no sin in this man, could not hang any longer.[9] This man was St. Paul, and after he slew this clever beast, he broke the pagan darkness which permeated the island, and brought forth the Light of the Gospel to the humble people of Malta. Because of him the prisoners on the ship were saved, and for that does he resemble the Savior of the world; and because he cast the snake into the fire, does he foreshadow the coming day in which the old serpent will be thrown into the lake of fire.

Now, over a millennium and a half later after that seemingly minuscule but glorious moment, in the year 1565, the followers of the serpent arrived to Malta to take back what once belonged to the cunning and subtle creature who from the beginning has deceived the world to worship him, to bring back the poison of deception which he tried to inject into the hand of the apostle, and destroy that beacon of illuminating truth which St. Paul brought. These were the Ottoman Muslims, and this is how the war between God and the devil, over this little island, came to pass.

THE BATTLE BEGINS WITH A WICKED WOMAN
It began with a woman, as these types of events usually do, named Roxellane, the most favored harlot of the Sultan Suleiman. Jezebel, by the arousing power that lustful sway has over the sons of Adam, desired the death of Elijah, and shed the blood of thunderous saints who cared more for glorious eternity than guileful life. And Salome, through cruel beauty's wiles and luscious dance, gained the head of John the Baptist.

And so too did this harlot demand the blood of the saints, as she rode the beast of Turkey, and comfortably reposed with luxury upon the ottomans within palaces that once belonged to the bearers of the Cross. The Knights of St. John, the warrior monks who ruled Malta, were preventing Muslim ships carrying pilgrims from traveling to Mecca to visit the tomb of Muhammad. The harlot, most vexed by this, unceasingly urged the Sultan to destroy Malta, and through her feminine delights and cruel beauty, and the imams who she had pushed to convince her husband, he agreed to commence the attack.[10]

---

9   Chrysostom, *Eight Sermons on the Book of Genesis*, sermon 5, p. 88
10 See Correggio, *The Siege of Malta*, ch. i, p, 29, trans. from the Spanish edition of 1568, The Folio Society London, 1965

CHRISTIANITY IS AT WAR: THE MANIFESTO FOR CHRISTIAN MILITANCY

A COUNCIL OF THE WICKED

A council was conveyed with all of the ministers and pashas of the evil empire, and they connived as to how they were going to prevail over the Christian island. Speeches were made which aroused the deepest emotion in the hearts of all the officials; they were moved to that frenzy so common in the Orient, and the Chief Aga was so compelled by his passions that he madly proclaimed to the Sultan with the greatest devotion:

> Invincible and mighty Lord, if I thought it necessary to arouse Your Majesty by words, I would give you eloquent and weighty arguments. But I know well that nothing can turn you from your intention, or revoke the order that you have given in your wisdom, that we should utterly destroy this little island—which I am reluctant even to name. The thing that I regret deeply is that it should be at all necessary to send your invincible fleet and your mighty army against this accursed and insignificant island—just because nobody has bothered to take it for himself. It seems to me that we Turks who live under the invincible rule of the Ottoman dynasty are not like our fathers who served your fathers in the past, for they captured the whole of Syria from the Christians—and, one must admit, they are a warlike people. ... I conclude by most humbly begging Your Majesty to show pity upon your people, and to punish these knights without mercy, for they have shown no gratitude at all for the clemency with which Your Majesty has treated them on so many occasions. So that you may be confident of victory, let your army and your preparations be such that the pride of these men, who resisted for six months the great attack which you in person led against them in the island of Rhodes, will be abased.[11]

The heretics who desired to take the Christian land, enslave and slaughter the people of God, and destroy the sanctuaries of the Lord, made ready for their assault. Their artillery, none could compete with; they had a cannon so heavy that it weighed eighteen thousand pounds, and fired a cast iron ball weighing one hundred pounds. Six thousand Janissary troops were selected for the expedition, and so vicious were these that they seeped fear into the very beings of their enemies, and were esteemed as invincible men whose reputation for ruthlessness and sadism spread like a flood.[12]

The sultan ordered one Ali Pasha to summon before him the two commanders Mustapha and Piali, and declared to them:

> I have no fear of any of the Christian powers, but since you will be so near Sicily and Naples, which belong to the King of Spain, he may try to interfere with my plans by attacking you while you are engaged on the siege. ... There would come a time when we should take that fertile land, Sicily, the granary of the Romans who once ruled where now—praise be to Allah and to His prophet!—it is we who rule. Thus we should be able to make war upon Italy and upon Hungary, and the great German Empire would become ours. We should extend our sway to the limits of the known world, and your names would become immortal.[13]

---

11 In Correggio, *The Siege of Malta*, ch. i, p. 31, ellipses mine
12 In Correggio, *The Siege of Malta*, ch. i, p. 31
13 In Correggio, *The Siege of Malta*, ch. i, pp. 32–33, ellipses mine

THE TURKS BOARD THEIR SHIPS OF WAR AND HEAD FOR MALTA

The multitude of Muslim warriors gathered into their one hundred and thirty ships, and in an atmosphere of triumph and pompous pride, they departed to the war music of trumpets and the thunder of cannons. Outlawed men from the Levant, and troops from Greece, Anatolia, Caramania, the Morea, and other parts of the universal empire of the crescent, all joined this grand jihad.[14]

One could only imagine such a force: vicious fighters with cruel countenances, crooked and sadistic smiles, armed with crooked swords for hacking, and small blades to fulfill their cutthroat desires. Four thousand of them were named "Adventurers," these were some of the most fanatic of the warriors, dressed in white and adorned with green turbans to show that they fulfilled their duties to Allah and went on pilgrimage to Mecca, to adore the Blackstone for which they now wished to kill those saints who refused to kiss and bend the knee to that idol.

They spent their days in the mosques, wasting all of their leisure hours to proclaim the mystical verses of the Koran, and dance the dance of wizards until they attained the state of madness. And when they heard that their brothers were on their way to war with Malta, they rushed with the utmost of hysteria, and begged the sultan to allow them to go and fight for the heresy which they so loved. There were many Jewish merchants who accompanied the Muslims; they, with immense hatred for Christ, came with the hope that when the Turks would be victorious, they would be free to purchase Christian slaves.[15]

For the artillery of the Turks, there were five engineers, and surprisingly only one of these was a Turk, with the rest being a Greek, a Slav, a Venetian, and an Italian renegade.[16] The Muslims could not conquer Christian lands without the help of Christian traitors.

THE CHRISTIANS ARE ON THE WATCH FOR THE COMING ENEMY

This brood of vipers was not ignored by the watchmen of Malta, and the prudent believers of Christendom. The Grandmaster of the Knights of St. John, Jean Parisot de Valette, was not asleep, but awake as a bird before its nest. With the inexorable coming of the Turks, Valette kept in constant contact with the king of Spain, Don Philip, and the Pope, Pius IV. Immediately he looked to the defense of the island, augmented the fortifications as much as was possible.[17]

The warriors of God were ready for the wolves, and the only British member of the Knights, Oliver Starkey, was commissioned to command a force of Greeks and Maltese.[18] On Friday, May 18th, 1565, watchers on the forts of St. Angelo and St. Elmo, spotted the Turkish hoard of ships thirty miles away. The situation now intensified, and within seconds the signal was given for the locals to flee into the island's bastions; they rushed into the citadel of Birgu,

---

14 Correggio, *The Siege of Malta*, ch. i, pp. 34–35
15 Correggio, *The Siege of Malta*, ch. i, p. 36
16 Correggio, *The Siege of Malta*, ch. i, p. 36
17 Correggio, *The Siege of Malta*, ch. ii, pp. 38–40, trans. Bradford
18 Correggio, *The Siege of Malta*, ch. i, p. 42, note by Bradford

CHRISTIANITY IS AT WAR: THE MANIFESTO FOR CHRISTIAN MILITANCY

with their children, cattle, and possessions.[19] All that they had, all that they worked for, was now dependent on whether or not Christianity would prevail over those who fought so desperately for their heresy to become victorious. If the Christians lost, then their lives would be compelled into slavery and death.

THE ENEMY LANDS, THE CHRISTIANS STAND THEIR GROUND

The Muslims were now on the island, and the Christians were already posted, waiting prudently for the moment to strike. A French knight, La Riviere, alongside twelve horsemen, quietly waited for the opportunity to capture a Turk to interrogate him. Amongst another body of soldiers was a valiant man named Vendo de Mezquitus, he charged without orders and galloped to La Riviere. The Turks spotted them, and La Riviere, with the greatest ardency, charged after them. They opened fire with their muskets, his horse was struck and went down to its death. La Riviere continued to fight, but was afflicted and captured. Vendo, with a mortal wound, hid behind a wall, took off his armour, and breathed his last breath.[20]

Great sorrow came upon Valette, he remembered him as an exceptional knight, but not only that, he knew that the Muslims would inflict him with a thousand tortures. When the Turks brought La Riviere for interrogation, the only thing he had for them were the words of Christian militancy and the repulsion of tyranny:

> What good will it do you to torture me? You will learn nothing from me, except that you will never take Malta. It is both strong and well provisioned. More than that, it is defended by a commander, knights, and soldiers so valiant that they would rather die for their Order (as is their duty) than show the slightest weakness.[21]

THE PEOPLE OF MALTA WORK FOR THE GLORY OF CHRISTENDOM

All of the people worked the sweat of their brow, toiling away for a cause greater than themselves, with soul and body to defend the island. Not just soldiers, but local men, women, and children, brought earth into the citadel of Birgu and heaped it in piles for repairing the fortifications when the time came. The Turks by now were in the village of St. John, and they placed as their main base for stores and provisions in the Marsa.

The sight must have been most concerning, and looking to the heights of Santa Margarita one could see the bright flags and banners of the Turks, bearing their insignias and crescents which they had so strived to make prevail over the Cross. The whole moment was a wonder even to the knights, and they marveled at the music of the Turks, used to instill courage into the hearts of the mujahid, with its trumpets, drums and bagpipes.

---

19 Correggio, *The Siege of Malta*, ch. iii, p. 45
20 Correggio, *The Siege of Malta*, ch. iii, pp. 46–47
21 Correggio, *The Siege of Malta*, ch. iii, p. 48

PART 15

THE CHRISTIANS MAKE CHARGE TO BATTLE
The Turks were more than forty thousand, and wanted to bring fear to the knights with their imposing numbers. Valette repulsed the spirit of fright, and ordered his men to beat their drums and ascend all of their flags, and when the moment was ripe, he sent out six or seven hundred gunmen and many knights to charge the enemy. While the Turks were greater in number, the Christians overpowered them with the swiftness of their guns, which fired bullets much faster than those of the Muslims.

As the fighting went on, there stood another mass of Christian fighters, waiting with great desperation for their chance to war with the infidels, but standing in front of them was Valette, sword in hand, and if he was not there, all of the men would have charged into the fray. In the midst of violence, a Spaniard named Sese was giving gunpowder to his men, and to the surprise of all barrel exploded, killing him and ten or twelve others. After five hours of fighting the Christians managed to slay one hundred Muslims, and they brought their heads back with them.[22]

The Turks began to fire their immense cannons on St. Elmo, and the heavy cannonballs were seen ripping through windmills, homes, and boats. One wall, being very old, collapsed; the air was clouded with debris and earth covered with rubble. And there stood the Grand Master Valette, never slumbering nor reposing, but always pressing ahead, unceasingly watching his men as they operated, and he never hesitated to give advice when it was asked for. It was as though he had a hundred eyes. He discovered that the Turks were posting a colossal cannon, and so he ordered his men to make ready and set up four cannons.[23]

THE TURKS BOMBARD THE CHRISTIANS WITH CANON FIRE
Twenty four Turkish cannons now surrounded Fort St. Elmo, and never did they cease to bombard the knights. So unceasing was the firing from the cannons that the Turks never even bothered to clean them out. The Christians moved forward in their work: some were raising walls, others raising heaps of earth, while others organized fighting positions.[24] Amongst the Turks stood one of the most terrifying enemies to the Christians: Dragut, the Ottoman warrior who had such a ubiquitous reputation that he was called "The Drawn Sword of Islam." His past feats of horror and persecution was still remembered amongst the Christians, they reminisced on how he had captured Bastia in Corsica, where he kidnapped seven thousand Christians, and on how he had taken Reggio in Italia where he enslaved the entire population.[25]

From the time they arose, till it descended into its abyss, the thundering of the cannons went on and on, rupturing the fort, reaping destruction on every part where the shots fell, with the noise of their chaos resonating throughout the island. A number of Turkish engineers approached the fortifications, and to their surprise, without being spotted by the Christians. They gave the signal, and a rush of Janissaries attacked abruptly the fort; the Christian guard

---
22 Correggio, *The Siege of Malta*, ch. iii, pp. 49–50
23 Correggio, *The Siege of Malta*, ch. iv, pp. 60–61
24 Correggio, *The Siege of Malta*, ch. iv, pp. 62–63
25 Correggio, *The Siege of Malta*, ch. iv, p. 64, Bradford's note

fled to a nearby ditch in which lied fifty other soldiers who were there to defend the island. But, they were now surrounded, and so ferocious was the assault of the Muslims, that they could not stand their ground with courage, but were forced by the sense of horror to retreat.

Within a moment the Turks, like a forceful river piercing a lonely rock, stormed one of the bastions, and the defenders ran into the fort. The ravelin in front of the fort was now taken, and the Christians charged in to drive them out. For five hours they exemplified the bitterest melee; hand to hand fighting carried throughout this time. Five hundred Turks were slaughtered, while sixty soldiers and twenty knights lost their lives. The whole of the Turkish army was gradually flooding the area as the struggle continued, and in the end, the Christians had no other choice but to retire. The Muslims, with disorder and confusion, moved into the ditch behind the ravelin, and the Christians, seeing the opportunity, opened fire on them.[26]

THE CHRISTIANS DEFEND THE FORT

As all of this fighting occurred, the roaring explosions from the cannons proceeded without disruption. The Turks, like a spider looking for the tender areas of a scorpion's armour, probed for any weaknesses on the fortifications.

Yet this incessant bombardment from Turkish artillery brought no trepidation to the knights, despite the fact that on St. Elmo there was no place that was secure, no area safe for the warriors of the Cross, no position guaranteeing safety. Turks were not going to end their assault, not until the entire island was fully vanquished and the Knights of St. John destroyed. The troops defending Fort St. Elmo saw their dreadful position and sent captain Medrano to tell Valette that the fortification could not be safeguarded against the relentless attacks of the ruthless Turk. Valette, upon hearing of this sentiment, affirmed that as long as the fort's defenders withstood the Muslims, greater would it be for the whole of the island. Medrano returned to the troops, and told them to stand their ground. Fifty of the men wrote to Valette, begging him for permission to leave the fort and fight the enemy in the open. If they won, they would drive out the enemy from the ravelin; if they lost, they would poison the fort's water, destroy the guns, die with happiness and go to Heaven. Valette wrote back to them, and ordered them to remain in the fort lest the salvation of the entire Order of the knights be extinguished.[27]

The men accepted the commandment of their Grand Master, and now prepared to defend the citadel with all their might, and with the uttermost effort. From every direction there was a horde of hysterical Turks charging the fort; with the greatest madness and the most violent frenzy they rushed toward the Christians. They appeared so wild that it was as though they had consumed drugs and were suffering from their violent effects.

The bridge connecting to the fort was flooded, and a bloody fight commenced between the two eternal enemies. The shields of the Turk, bearing the mark of the beast—the crescent—collided with the shields of the saints which bore the mark of God. As the Christians utilized all of their skill to combat the Turk, bullets zipped through the air from the Turkish

---

26 Correggio, *The Siege of Malta*, ch. iv, pp. 65–66
27 Correggio, *The Siege of Malta*, ch. v, pp. 70–72

gunmen. Fanatic Muslims who wore their green turbans, showing off proudly their piety, were amongst the slaughtered, and not even the invincible Janissaries were exempt from the Christian sword. The Muslims fled the trench, and as they retreated, a Spanish traitor screamed at the Christians: "You have done well today, knights! But soon you will have to face what you seem to want so much—a general assault!"[28]

They knew that the Turks' return was inevitable, and imminent. Valette, knowing that the fort could not be abandoned, asked one Monserrat to govern it, and his response was that he was always willing and ready to fulfill his obligations "to God and the Order."

THE WORDS OF A FRIAR SET AFLAME THE ZEAL OF THE CHRISTIANS

The men gathered together, more than ready to engage the haters of Christ, and were completely absent of hesitation to kill and to be killed for the advancement of the Cross. A friar came before them, and preached with holy vigor and burning zeal; the men were so moved and struck with his words, that they showed themselves ready to withstand whatever may come against them.

The Turks returned, and a vicious struggle began. It was evening time, and in the midst of the fighting, both the Muslims and the Christians used incendiary weapons which ignited such bright flames, such eye-piercing fires, that it was as though the sun never fully descended. The only abyss that was manifested was what the men witnessed before their pious eyes. They took hoops consisting of boiling pitch, razed them, and rolled them down toward the charging enemy. They collided with the Muslims, and everywhere they looked, there was seen a Muslim engulfed in flames, extinguishing the darkness of the night, bringing them into that abyss which even the demons were terrified to go, while they hoped they were going to the eternal harem of Allah. The dawning of the day arrived, and though the glimmering light of the sun came, it did not bring peace, for the fighting remained even at this time. But the Christians had Christ's illumination with a brightness of unquenchable light.

THE SUCCESSORS OF ST. JOHN THE BAPTIST

St. John the Baptist was one crying in the wilderness, fighting against the devil, and so the Knights of St. John fought in few numbers against the followers of darkness. The next day, June 12th, a bullet fired by a Christian gunman, ripped through Curtogli, a Turkish leader. The pashas reproached the Janissaries, and chastised them for esteeming themselves "The Sons of the Sultan" and not having the strength nor the ability to prevail over the Christians. Every hour the cannons roared and the bombardment did not stop; at every moment a call-to-arms, at every time the Christians were compelled to endure continuous assaults by the enemy.[29]

---

28 Correggio, *The Siege of Malta*, ch. v, pp. 72–73
29 Correggio, *The Siege of Malta*, ch. v, pp. 79–80

THE CRY OF WOLVES IN THE NIGHT

The silence of the night was broken by the zeal of the Muslims when they awoke from their slumber, went up to high ground, and at the top of their voices screamed their praises to Allah. The imams approached them, and encouraged them to continue on in their fight, and exhorted them not to fear death. The Christians, being hidden by the nighttime's darkness, heard one Muslim singing, and then an entire multitude repeating the verse in complete unison and with the fieriest ardency. The impious singing went on until the sun arose, and as it warmed the earth, all that could be heard were the shoutings of war, the beating drums of the Muslims, and the confusing noise of the Turkish instruments; and so clamorous was all of this, that it seemed as though the world was coming to an end.

A SEVEN HOUR BATTLE

Within hours a concentrated, determined, and yet ferocious battle took place. The courage of the Turks was great, but the valiancy of the Christians was greater. The knights and the Muslims used their incendiaries against one another, but the smoke from each clouded and covered the eyes of the Christians, and they were hindered from seeing. Then, most abruptly, the fireworks of the Christians exploded, and the flames from these great weapons consumed and killed many of them. Thirty Turks came with scaling ladders and instantly ascended the tower of Colonel Mas. Valette, seeing what was happening, ordered a gunner to open fire upon the besiegers, but they aimed wrongly and ended up slaughtering eight Christians.

The gunner corrected his aim, fired his shot, and the cannon landed right in the middle of the Turkish ranks, killing twenty of the enemy. The remaining Turks were pounced on by the knights who did not let them escape, and killed them with fire and the cold steel of their swords. A Turk tried to raise a flag on a certain position, captain Medrano chased him away but a bullet pierced his head and he perished. The local Maltese fought so well that it was as if they were trained knights. The battle lasted seven hours, and over a thousand of the best Muslim warriors were slain, with one hundred and fifty Christians dead.[30] The rupturing sound of war still battered their ears, the debris of destruction tainted the air, the dark rubble from the explosions stained their faces, blood was on their grimy but determined countenances, and the aspiration of victory within their hearts. Their bodies were so worn out, their muscles so sore, and their legs so fatigued that they could not even stand.[31]

THE DEATH OF DRAGUT

The cannons went on, the thundering shots striking the fort. The Turkish commander Dragut noticed that the gunners were aiming too high, and so ordered them to be lowered. Still their aim was lofty, and he again told them to lower their aim. Now they were too high, and when Dragut put his back in front of them, they fired and a cannonball landed on a trench behind him. A rock from the explosion flew and landed on his head, his brains splattered from his

---

30 Correggio, *The Siege of Malta*, ch. vi, pp. 81–82
31 Correggio, *The Siege of Malta*, ch. vi, p. 82

mouth, nostrils, and ears. Valette was pleased with the news. But, the Turks did not flee with Dragut now dead, instead they simply continued their cannon attacks. The Christians went out to get water only to be slaughtered by the cannons; so many were killed that there was little hope of obtaining any more water. On top of this, a gun powder mill suddenly exploded and killed eight men, this was to the joy of the Turks who shouted with ecstasy upon seeing the destruction. Valette fired six cannonballs at them, and their bestial shouts came to an end.[32]

THE CHRISTIANS WORSHIP GOD AS THE MUSLIMS ATTACK
As the Turks fired their canons, the Christians gathered together and sung holy hymns; as the Turks connived new ways of destruction, the Christians adored the Cross, and took of the Bread of Life. They understood that their war was not just physical, but transcended this world into the immaterial. They ate of the table of the Lord and drunk His cup, to combat those who feasted and wildly drunk in cruel luxury at the palace of demons. They prepared their souls for eternal life, with ascending songs and the kindest charity, while the Turks prepared themselves for perdition.[33, 34]

THE INFINITE MERCY OF GOD
Outside of the fort, twenty Maltese horsemen ran into a horde of Turkish warriors. As they struggled for victory, the gallant knight Tomas Coronel, and the fierce Vincenzo Anastasi, led a garrison right into the heat of the fighting, killed many of the Turks and saved the Maltese troops.[35]

The hope for Fort St. Elmo was dwindling, and Valette was unable to even send supplies nor reinforcements into the weakened fortification. All he could do was beg God to "show mercy to our brothers out of His infinite compassion," and to stop the enemies of His Faith from prevailing.[36]

THE BLOODIEST ASSAULT SO FAR
At the dawn of June 22nd, waves of Turks came charging toward the Fort and all the noise of misery could be heard, and all the sight of cruelty seen. Melancholic groans, plaintive whispers, and the profound cries of warring men, filled the air as the scorching sun dispirits the beautiful image of a pristine winter. Cold steel severed through flesh; soldiers—putting away all knightly pride and all temporal desires, and placing their minds solely on the triumph of truth—strived through the ruthless fray as bullets fired from all directions.

They pushed forward, and the sounds of death and mayhem brought a sense truly terrifying to the Christians. This was by far the bloodiest assault the Turks ever brought so far. The enemy attempted to ascend the walls with ladders only to be stopped by cannons fired

---

32 Correggio, *The Siege of Malta*, ch. vi, pp. 84–85
33 This description is referring to the feast of Corpus Christi which the knights observed on June 21.
34 Correggio, *The Siege of Malta*, ch. vi, p. 86
35 Correggio, *The Siege of Malta*, ch. vi, p. 86
36 Correggio, *The Siege of Malta*, ch. vi, p. 87

by the Christians. They tried to cross the bridge but out came against them immense rocks thrown by the defenders who used their sword and their fire to slay the invaders.[37]

Muslim snipers took their positions in a certain ditch, took aim and fired upon the leaders of the fort, picking them off one by one. As they dropped lifelessly, the other defenders ran to their bodies, picked up their rifles, and opened fire on the Turks. About two thousand Muslims were killed, and five hundred Christians laid dead.

FORT ST. ELMO SURROUNDED BY WOLVES BUT GUARDED BY LIONS

All that were left to defend St. Elmo were only about one hundred men, and nearly every one of them was wounded, without ammunition, and without any hope of relief. Not a man who stood in that long forgotten bastion, was not covered in both his own blood and the blood of his enemy. A messenger rushed to the Grand Master, and he, hearing the benumbing news, and not desiring to depress the men around him, said with good heart: "The garrison of St. Elmo have taught the Turks a lesson. I trust in God that they will never take the fort." He sent reliefs to the fort, but these were unable to get passed the Turkish assaults.

The men of St. Elmo could not be helped. Their spirits were seized with anguish, and they exhorted one another to courage, accepted their fate, and gave themselves up to Jesus Christ. Their mouths were as dry deserts, their tongues never touched not even the slightest drop of water to cool down their hot beating hearts, pushed by zeal and exertion. Their bodies were ever so close to death on account of exhaustion, and suffering through this, they had to endure the unceasing bombardments of the Turkish cannons. What never was wounded nor afflicted, was their faith. They confessed to one another,[38] and looking passed the world before them, they saw Heaven.

FORT ST. ELMO IS ASSAILED BY THE TURKS

The twinkling light of the sun broke forth when the men were awaiting for the sons of the devil to approach them at the eve of the Feast of John the Baptist, who was slain through the gentle and vicious wants of a woman toward a tyrant. And now these battling monks, who placed this same John as their patron saint, were on the verge of fighting off the troops who, reminiscent to John, by the demands of the sultan's lady, came to take their heads.

The Turks trampled through the dry earth of Malta, before the eyes of the men within that forlorn moment, they sprinted like wild demons in the midst of the dimness of daybreak, shouting their wild and savage cries to their dismal god, and making more turbulent the day, with its scorching summer heat which now beat upon the injured Christians. Medrano, the warrior who was captured and was now a captive, asked the Turkish commander Mustapha to show mercy upon the men, for there was only a small number of them.

He asked a man who worships a god of death to refrain from killing men who worship the God of life, and the reaction of the Turks was only to push harder their attack on the fort.

---

37 Correggio, *The Siege of Malta*, ch. vi, p. 87
38 Correggio, *The Siege of Malta*, ch. vi, pp. 88–89

PART 15

The Christians rushed to the bridge; they lacked ammunition, but they strived with all their might to preserve the citadel.

The Janissaries swept right into the fort, took the high tower and cast down boulders on the fighting Christians below, crushing them. The Muslims charged passed the bridge, and ripped through the defending Christians as a sickle rips through wheat. The killers of Muhammad were now in the fort, going to and fro with every bit of the wickedest intentions.

The Christians were all inflicted with wounds; they could not fight, they could not resist—they were like John the Baptist on the block before receiving the blade on his neck. They did all they could do, they ran, they sprinted to the only place they thought would compel the enemy to mercy: a church. They hoped the sacred presence of the sanctuary would spark even the smallest bit of humanity, and spare their lives.

Men who were warriors of God now surrendered, they hoped for peace, but peace there was none, and sudden destruction did come. The Turks butchered and cut pleading fighters to pieces. They offered themselves as a living sacrifice, and their blood was spilt on the altar of a holy church.

Some of the Maltese leaped into the water and swam to safety. Nine warriors fled to some pirates, and when Mustapha demanded that the hostages be given to him, they refused to hand them over without money. Amidst the slaughter of the saints, the destruction of the fort, and the chaotic cries of the Muslims, the Turks took down the banner of John the Baptist, and hoisted up the standard of the sultan.[39] The desire of the sultan's woman was fulfilled, just like Herod's harlot. But John's mission was to bring light to the darkness, and so these bearers of the Cross would not cease until the crescent of Islam was stomped.

THE SAINTS ARE CRUCIFIED LIKE CHRIST

Anguish and grief took Valette, but he accepted their fate, and bowed himself before the will of God. During the next day the remnant of the men, who were now in the Maltese city of Birgu, saw four Christian heads skewered on lances. The Turks seized upon the dead Christians from Fort St. Elmo, hacked their heads off, ripped their bellies open, mutilated their bodies, and crucified them like Christ onto a mass of wood and planks, and threw the gory chaos over to the sea. The heap washed over to Birgu where the men beheld the horrifying site. Mustapha then paid off the pirates and bought the soldiers who surrendered, and had them beheaded in front of the Christian army.[40]

A CHRISTIAN GIRL IS BEHEADED AND THE CHRISTIANS UNLEASH HOLY VENGEANCE

The Turks, keeping their thirsty eyes out for any innocent sheep, spotted sixty Maltese men and women taking refuge in a cave, for they were fleeing from their village. A high ranking Turkish officer (or sanjak-bey) went into the cave and took for himself a young woman who

---

39 Correggio, *The Siege of Malta*, ch. vii, pp. 90–91
40 Correggio, *The Siege of Malta*, ch. vii, pp. 92–93

aroused his concupiscence, and the other Turkish soldiers remained with the rest of the Maltese. Christian soldiers led by the knights ambushed the Muslims, slaughtered thirty of them, and charged after the sanjak-bey who, after hearing of their pursuit, scurried away with freight. As they got nearer, the Turk took the girl, unsheathed his sword, and decapitated her. They attacked, and all that the sanjak-bey gained was a bullet to the head.[41]

THE TURKS WILL NEVER TAKE BIRGU

There came before the knights in Birgu an old Spanish slave with a Turkish envoy holding a white flag, who requested that he be let into the city to convey a message from the Turks to Valette. The Grand Master permitted him, but only with the exception that he be blind folded. The Spaniard said that the pashas were asking that the envoy be given an audience. "If you know what the envoy has to say," said Valette, "it is your duty as a Christian to tell me."

The slave, after much persuasion and inducing, answered: "The envoy comes from Mustapha Pasha and Piali Pasha to demand the surrender of the island to the sultan. He suggests that you do not display the same obstinacy as at St. Elmo, or he will be forced to mete out the same treatment to you. While there is still time accept his clemency. All they want is this barren island. They will grant you, and all your people, your property and your artillery, a free passage to Sicily." "Take him out and hang him!" was the response of Valette, and the old Spaniard pleaded for the love of God. But the Grand Master only said this to scare him, since he knew that it wasn't his fault, and that he was only doing what he was forced to do.

He pardoned him, and told him to return back to his masters. "For," he said, "let this be known among the Turkish army: if any other man comes here with such proposals, I will hang him without mercy!" Valette then told him to go back to the Turks and tell them that they would receive no audience, for barbarians do not deserve a hearing. "Do your worst," declared Valette, "I do not care! My trust is reposed in Our Lord Jesus Christ, He will deliver us from your hands. More than that, He will give us victory over you!"

They took down the blindfold from the slave's eyes, and let him look with dumbfounded sense the lofty and imposing walls of Birgu. On seeing such great fortifications, he could only mutter these words, "They will never take Birgu."[42]

A TURK COMES FOR HIS SALVATION

On the following day, a Turk was seen across the promontory of Birgu, which had connected to the sea. "Send a boat!" he cried, "I want to join you!" But there was no boat, so they told him to swim across. This did not stop him, something within him desired fulfillment, and he leaped into the waters, and swam with much endurance and effort just to reach the land where the Christians stood, just to reach that realm where the Cross was exalted. He swam with all exertion and effort, as St. Paul did to reach Malta after his ship was ruined by the sharp torrent. He reached the land and they helped him up, and he was so exhausted that

---

41 Correggio, *The Siege of Malta*, ch. vii, p. 96
42 Correggio, *The Siege of Malta*, ch. vii, pp. 97–98

he could hardly breathe. He arrived to where Valette was, he was offered food but turned it down, and said, "I wish to be a Christian, as were my ancestors." His request was responded to by Valette with acceptance: "You are welcome indeed!" He paddled with all his might, just to accept the Faith which Paul brought to Malta, and to assist the saints in combating the followers of the serpent which the Apostle defeated. He informed Valette on the coming Turkish force, and told him that they were approaching with great ferocity.[43]

THE SPANIARDS ARRIVE

On July 2nd it was told to Valette that the relief force from Spain landed on the island, and it was brought by the formidable and valiant Don Juan de Cardona. The next day the Turks made ready their artillery, and out came the cannonballs landing throughout the fort and causing destruction wherever they landed. The Grand Master ordered a group of his men, under Marshal de Robles, to find the relief team. They left to their mission just an hour before the sun had set, and under the cover of the dimming light, the heavy mist which went through the warm air, and through the silence of discipline, they made their way to the men.[44]

The locals were helping build up the defenses for the city, poor pious people trying with both the richest faith and purest of love for Christendom, worked without tiring nor slacking. These were the descendants of those who treated the Apostle with the utmost of hospitality, and surely were they not going to welcome the heretics with the same kindness, but instead work their hardest to repulse them. The Turks aimed their cannons at these humble rustics, fired and slaughtered them. Valette, much grieved by these deaths, ordered that the people should not do this work, and instead commanded slaves to replace them in the labour, and still the Turks fired upon these helpless people.

THE TURKS RUSH FORT ST. MICHAEL

The Turks attempted to capture Fort St. Michael, and as the enemy cannons roared unceasingly, they rushed the fort's ditch and fighting within it took place. The Christians desired to leave, so they escaped through a small opening on the Post of Marshal Robles and Don Carlo Rufo, although Don Carlo remained in the fight until death. On and on went the fire of the cannons; it pierced the ears and hindered the hearing; in one moment the eye beheld a gun exploding for some unknown reason, and in the next it witnessed forty Turks consumed by the flames. Four Turks paddled their way to the water, armed with axes, and began cutting down a chain blockade, but there stood the knights six hundred paces away, taking quick aim and killing each one with precision. In the next instance the eyes gazed upon a number of Maltese men slashing away at Turkish troops with the most intense strikes, and so fierce was this assault, that the enemy fled. But the Maltese pursued them, killed a Turk and wounded the others.

---

43 Correggio, *The Siege of Malta*, ch. vii, pp. 99–102
44 Correggio, *The Siege of Malta*, ch. vii, pp. 102–104

✝ CHRISTIANITY IS AT WAR: THE MANIFESTO FOR CHRISTIAN MILITANCY

THE CHRISTIANS ATTACK BY NIGHT

During the evening, Marshal Robles, with sword and shield, went out with the two hundred men and attacked the Turks who had taken some land near the ditch of Fort. St. Michael, killing thirty of them and driving out the remaining three hundred Muslims.

REPAID WITH TURKISH BLOOD

From a distance there were two old men—natives of the island—named Paulo Micho and Paulo Daula. There were approached by another Maltese man, but this one was quite nefarious, and he tried to beguile his two countrymen into joining the side of the Turks, telling them that the Muslims were more just than the Christian knights who ruled the island, and that the pashas would grant freedom to them, and rule with more equity. "You are lower than a dog!" angrily responded the two men, "We want no advice from a man so damned as you. We would rather be slaves of St. John than companions of the sultan!" The traitor looked to Micho and warned him that he would never enjoy his vineyard when the Turks arrive, they would seize it as Jezebel stole Neboth's vineyard. But the righteous rustic responded with the greatest sincerity and intensity:

> I have been repaid for my vineyard in Turkish blood, I have trust in God that, even if you Turks destroy it, I will plant and water it with the same blood—and that will make it a good deal richer! For my money, I have enough trust in God to know that it will never be allowed to fall into the hands of a scoundrel like you. As for wishing to find me, whenever you think you are going to find me, look where the battle is fiercest. There you will find me, old as I am with my sword and my shield, defending my God, my country, my wife, and my children. [45]

HOLY CHANTS OF MONKS HEARD IN THE NIGHT

In the evening time the spirits of the men were as blackened as the night sky, covered with the darkness of distress and yet glimmered with fragments of small but intensely bright remnants of hope. As they waited in this unsettling state, they heard from a close distance a number of priests, proclaiming their sublime chants of angst to the highest Heaven, without stopping nor ceasing, but in the deepest meditation, their mouths murmuring while their hearts so intently aspiring to victory, to the greatest of peace, when the wicked are fully defeated and the righteous left to the utmost of security. The soldiers heard these prayers, and all the while their existed the bitter taste of despair cut deep into their souls. When they heard these men proclaim the chants so relentlessly, they knew within themselves that the most dreadful coming of the Turkish beasts was near.

THE COLORS OF THE ANTICHRIST

Up came the dawn, the time when the Muslim prays to his devil who, as a dry skull looks with empty eyes on the most dispiriting of cruelty without being moved to pity, does not care for the sufferings of man, not even for his own worshippers, who by now were marching toward

---

45 Correggio, *The Siege of Malta*, ch. viii, pp. 105–110

the Christians. The Turks struck the eye with their organization, and well-structured lines, coming forth like the slithering serpent. They pierced the vision with the most striking colors, like the scales of the enticing snake which deceives the one not experienced in its ways, or the adornments of Salome who with titillating sway moved the hollow tyrant to behead the saint. Scarlet red adorned their ranks, the finest cloths bearing the colors of gold and silver were adorned by many of their warriors, and crimson damask embellished their troops. They were armed with muskets from Morocco, scimitars of Alexandria and Damascus; they all carried their strong bows, and upon each of their heads was a splendid turban.[46]

With such a presentation one cannot help but be reminded of what John saw, in his vision of the armies of the Antichrist:

> And thus I saw the horses in the vision: those who sat on them had breastplates of fiery red, hyacinth blue, and sulfur yellow; and the heads of the horses were like the heads of lions; and out of their mouths came fire, smoke, and brimstone. [47]

As their armies drew nearer, the Christians noticed that within the frontline of the Turkish ranks were a number of imams with long hair crowned with very large hats. In each of their hands was a Koran from which they read and cried out omens to their savage god, exhorting the warriors with verses such as "O you who believe, when you meet those who disbelieve marching to battle, do not turn your backs to them. Whoever turns his back on that day incurs the wrath of Allah, his destination is hell and en evil end."[48]

THE BRIDE OF CHRIST VERSES THE HARLOTS OF THE DEVIL

The battle was now about to begin, the Bride of Christ was now to war with the harlot of the devil. The fiery shots from the guns, the fierce cries and wailings of the Muslims with their malicious faces, would have undoubtedly put fear in the hearts of those unaccustomed to war. Captain Don Francisco was ready for them; they attacked his post, and it was only defended with swords, pikes, shields, and stones. Don Jaime de Sanoguera rushed into the heat of the fighting with his sword and shield, striking with the hottest of ferocity, and encouraging his men to have heart. A gun fired and gunpowder besprinkled his face and burnt his flesh, but his valiancy did not subside, and he remained in the struggle. One Piron bravely defended his position; a bullet struck him, and he fell dead to the ground. In the midst of all this gore and bloodshed, of all the stabbing and slicing, of all the cutting off of limbs, of all the severing away of lives from this miserable earth, one man lit an incendiary and its flames erupted and consumed the others around them, burning their bodies as leaves quiver under the scorching sun.

The fireworks and the incendiaries were now all gone, all that the men could use to throw at their enemies were stones. These were everywhere, and they picked them up and

---

46 Correggio, *The Siege of Malta*, ch. viii, p. 111
47 Revelation 9:17, NKJV
48 Correggio, *The Siege of Malta*, ch. viii, pp. 111–112, see the note by the editor and translator Bradford

threw them as hard as they could, and when they struck, they were more devastating than their weapons of fire.⁴⁹

Don Francisco rushed toward the oncoming Turks, alongside him was Nicolo Rodio, and protecting their charge were the rest of the men firing on the enemy with their guns. The Turks' greater numbers made them hesitate, and instead the fighting men decided to hurl rocks at them, launching them like a machine, a storm of stones. A bullet struck Don Francisco but it only dented his breastplate.

A janissary aimed and fired, and the bullet pierced the steal and Francisco fell dead to the Muslim cries to Allah. The Muslims seized the body by the legs, the Christians held onto its other side, and they struggled on who was going to own the body of a saint. The Christians took possession, but not before the enemy took Francisco's shoes. Captain Medrano, afflicted with a head wound, strove through the fighting, and ten Turkish ships were about to land on the island and release their most elite warriors. Francisco de Guiral ordered for his men to aim their cannons on the ships, and when the right moment came, they fired bags full of stones, pieces of chain and iron, sunk nine of them, and not one soul was saved.⁵⁰

Marshal Melchior de Robles and all of his knights were right in the thick of the battle, defending Fort St. Michael. Before their eyes was a horde of over eight hundred Turks, and these met a resistance that they never expected. They tried to ascend the walls of the fort, down came the piercing bullets like hail crashing onto the soft soils of earth, and not one made it up alive.

Christian reinforcements, a part of which was led by Captain Romegas, was approaching near to the Turks; they were filled with freight and fled, but they did not suffer them to escape, and the fight lasted for five hours. A friar, Roberto, fought in various positions like a swift-footed leopard, with a crucifix in one hand, and a sword in the other, calling to the men to fight for the Faith and for Jesus Christ. Don Jamie, and Don Fadrique de Toledo, talked amongst themselves when a cannonball struck and killed them. The Christians pursued the Muslims to the shore and cut them to pieces with bullets. Turkish gunners, seeing from a distance their brethren being butchered, opened fire and killed a number of the Christians. The Turks withdrew, the assault was over. The men gave thanks to God; their friar, Roberto, led them into their solemn prayers, and they sung with great rejoicing the Te Deum.⁵¹

They fought for Fort St. Michael, defending that bastion against those who were now possessed by the very demons who Michael and his army drove out of Heaven. That great war within eternity continues here on earth, between those who are watched over by God and His angels, and those who are enslaved by the devils. The servants of Satan, armed with earth-born weapons, could not prevail over the divine arrows of the Almighty with deceptions ornamented with the delicate beauty of pleasing words and verses, and nor could they defeat those whose minds were on the Sacred Scripture, who feared neither death nor exalted earthly life, and whose destination was either victory in battle or glory in Heaven.

---

49 Correggio, *The Siege of Malta*, ch. viii, pp. 112–113
50 Correggio, *The Siege of Malta*, ch. viii, pp. 114–115
51 Correggio, *The Siege of Malta*, ch. viii, pp. 116–117

PART 15

EXPLOSIONS THAT SHOOK THE SOUL
On the dawn of July 22nd, sixty four guns, manned by the Turks, fired upon the Christians. Six guns fired upon Fort St. Michael from a hill, another six from a different position, and two more manned from Paulo Micho's vineyard. Six Turkish guns incessantly fired on both the fort and the Post of Marshal Robles. They landed and killed many, and when they landed they penetrated down twenty-six feet into the earth. Their explosions and ruptures rattled the ears, shook the soul, and brought both terror and awe to the men, and like ripples on water, their noise could be heard all the way to Sicily.

THE LIBERATION OF SLAVES
It was heard that when the Turks went out to fetch water they sent a body of six hundred Christian slaves to do so, and these were guarded by two hundred Muslim warriors. When the men knew of this they endeavored to attack this coming guard to rescue their fellow Christians from the Turkish yoke. They awaited for the water carriers to come, with great patience, and spotted the approaching force, but once they realized that they would be inevitably spotted by the enemy, they swiftly assaulted the Turkish line. They furiously charged the Muslims and slaughtered forty of them. The heretics quickly formed their battle positions, the injured Christian troops were ordered to retire, and those able to fight established their stance for the battle. Only one of the saintly soldiers was slain in their killing of sixty Turks in the engagement.[52]

ORLANDO THE PARROT
Relief ships, coming from Sicily, were sailing toward Malta to defend the remnant of knights, but the Turks managed to take one of the galleys. The captain of the stolen vessel, Orlando, was taken to Malta by the Muslims, chained, and forced to act as a negotiator for the taking of the island. The Turks said that Orlando wished to speak with Valette, but the bailiff in charge called out: "Say what you what have to say to me, for the Grand Master will not come." Orlando then began to exalt the might of the Turks, and to belittle the strength of the knights; he also affirmed that the relief coming from Sicily was laughable, consisting of only fifty poorly armed ships. "They will never dare," he said, "face a fleet as powerful as the Turks, which is strong enough to attack Sicily itself, let alone to take a little place like Malta, weak and undefended as it is." Valette fully comprehended that Orlando was parroting what the Turks made him say, and so replied: "Orlando, you have risen a long way from a simple sailor, that you are now an ambassador! However, if the Turks are prepared, I will ransom you." Orlando asserted that the Turks would never let him go for money, to which Valette said that the Muslims should withdraw, and then ordered for his men to open fire upon the enemy. This was the only response of this Christian warrior.

---

52 Correggio, *The Siege of Malta*, ch. ix, pp. 125–127

✝ CHRISTIANITY IS AT WAR: THE MANIFESTO FOR CHRISTIAN MILITANCY

THE ABSENT RESCUE TEAM

The relief force was expected to come, but night and day had passed, and no rescue team arrived. Valette, realizing that help was not arriving on the day which he predicted, made a proclamation to instill hope into the hearts of his men. He declared that only God was their true relief; for since He had preserved them to this point, He would most definitely bring them to victory, and deliver them from the enemies of His Holy Faith. It was in God alone, said Valette, that we should put our trust, and not man. He asked all of his men to keep it within their minds that they were Christians, that they were ultimately fighting a war for Christianity—not for temporal purposes—for Jesus Christ, for their lives, and for their liberty. The men listened attentively, and remembered that when the Turk would show no mercy in his arrival. Not one man stood who did not resolve to die rather than be in the hands of the Muslim.[53]

A CHANGE OF PROCEDURE

Valette beheld the damage and devastation which the Turkish guns wrought, left his home and made his headquarters in a local merchant shop. Absolute discipline needed to be ingrained in each and every one of the troops, and so he ordered that the church bells be wrung two hours before daybreak, and for the drums to be beaten in every post, to signal the men to be ready, and afterwords, to ring the main bell in the main square to sound the alarm. He did this without failure, to see to it that all the men would be in their positions regardless of the situation, as opposed to them being called to fight when they are not ready. The Turks observed this and were only astonished and dispirited by the efficiency of their Christian enemies.

The knights sent out a number of scouts to analyze the Turks, and one of these watchers, a Maltese man, was captured and coldly decapitated before the bells could be rung and the drums beaten. Now the Christians were off guard, and when they saw the multitude of devils, with scimitars in their hands and turbans upon their sweaty heads, they made ready what they could and repulsed them. Four times did the Turks return, and four did they flee. In the evening, in the time when every star shines down on us,[54] suspense filled the night air, and the men were stricken with that most horrible feeling of not knowing what to expect.[55]

THE TURKS MEET THE CHRISTIAN

Some time had passed when the Aga, or captain, of the Turks approached Marshal Robles and requested an interview. Robles sharply ordered that he speak quickly on the spot, but the conniving Muslim said that the interview would take two hours, to which the Christian responded that he did not have that time, and that he must leave or be shot. As the Aga was leaving, the other troops threw incendiaries at his direction to force him to flee. The shrewd-

---

53 Correggio, *The Siege of Malta*, ch. ix, pp. 127–129
54 This line is taken from Dante, *Vita Nuova*, iii, trans. Mark Musa
55 Correggio, *The Siege of Malta*, ch. ix, pp. 130–131

ness of the knights was most prudent, they apparently knew the cunningness of the Muslim, who is like the serpent in the garden.

Robles was no Eve, more than ready to sink her young teeth into the forbidden fruit, nor was he an Adam, quickly heeding to the desires of the deceived, and nor was he an Abel, trusting Cain before receiving the blow of death. The Turks planned that while Robles conversed with the Aga, they would be able to infiltrate a certain tunnel. They would assault the fort, and while the knights would be distracted, the Turks would blow up a mine, and use the tunnel to burst into the fortification.

THE WARRIOR AND HIS HERMITAGE

An enduring state of mind was within Valette, at any moment to spare he never neglected to make his way to the Church of St. Lawrence, and in the serenity of seclusion, say his prayers to God. He did this always, even in the direst of situations, when the Turks continued to launch their assaults. The next day the bombardments went on, with waves of Muslims repeatedly charging into the fort. Against this horde of vicious devils, the Christians fought for four long hours. After such a time twenty Turks were seen on top of Marshal Robles' post, but within moments they were beheld being consumed by flames which erupted from the firebombs of the defenders, and the rest of them were chased away by three ferocious gunmen. Marshal Robles, being so relieved by such a gruesomely gained triumph, fell on his knees in the serenity of victory, and in the deepest humility gave his praise to God from Whom he received his success.

Valette's spirit was distraught, and the troubling sense of uncertainty troubled him, and yet he still kept it within himself. There was no news coming from the relief team, and no one could guess as to what the Turks were about to do. He could not send out letters, neither by land or by sea; he was completely cut off, Malta appeared as a beacon of light in the midst of an ocean of evil, without any prospect of outside help, all that was left was them and the mighty arm of God which "scattered the proud in the conceit of their heart."[56] (Luke 1:51)

WHEELS OF FIRE

As soon as the sun's light appeared before the weary eyes of exhausted warriors, on August 7, eight thousand Turks, all rushed into one body like the minions of Shinar, and went forward against the fort and the Post of Castile. They could not merely overrun the island and build with black slime their tower of Babel; instead they were met with rolling hoops blazing in flames and dipped in the same boiling pitch as was found when the Lord descended and confounded the tongues of tyrants. The wails of the afflicted were heard throughout, and war's cruel touch was seen to and fro, here and there, in every place on the site of battle. The Turks at the beginning marched to the greatest pomp, with their organized ranks and music played so that every ear could hear in awe the glory of their empire, but now they endured travails with the highest bitterness, with many a man engulfed in fire, and screaming to a god

---

56 See Correggio, *The Siege of Malta*, ch. x, pp. 133–136

who takes no heed to the sufferings of humanity, while coldly imploring his worshippers to move with pried to the fangs of death.[57]

THE DAUNTLESS KNIGHT

A knight ran to Valette, and cried out, "My Lord, come to the aid of Castile! The Turks are breaking in!" "Come, my knights," said Valette, "let us all go and die there! This is the day!" He took a helmet from a page, a pike from another, and with the greatest illustration of fortitude led his men toward the post. Some men tried to stop him, but he went forward, and his tenacity was so immense that he even headed toward a position where the ranks of the Turks were already established.

The worried men succeeded in preventing him from reaching this point, upon which time he seized a rifle from a nearby officer, aimed, and opened fire on the enemy, he then declared in the most rallying way: "This way, boys, this way!" They took aim and opened fire with rapid and successive shots; Valette's leg was wounded, but like a relentless storm his fierceness did not subside.

All the while, those above tossed rocks and firebombs. The Christians took ahold of the sultan's standard, they grasped upon its golden tassels and silk and burnt them, but in the end the Turks managed to wrest it. The battle was thick and overpowering, and as the Christians refreshed themselves with wine and bread, the Turks constantly refreshed themselves with newer troops. The intensity of the attack was too much to withstand, and the Turks retreated. Valette's wound did not unsettle him, he was still seen with the greatest energy moving out and about, assisting the men in any way he could, and making sure everything was well and in order.

SURROUNDED BY WOLVES

All of Birgu was surrounded by the ravening wolves who, foaming at the mouth while growling and barking their blasphemies, were adorned by the bright colors of their pride, and placed around the land their piercing claws with which they desired to sink into the body of every Christian. Valette ordered that Birgu's bridge be removed to erase any doubt of his intentions, which were either to win or to die.[58]

Over a thousand Turks came upon them, on August 10th, and after two hours of warring, the Muslims were stung by the sharp point of defeat. The anguishing desire for victory, and the desperate spirit of angst, possessed all of them, and so they resolved to attack again on the same day, but their exertions were to no avail, and they had to succumb with another loss. On the night of August 11th, the bombardments did not cease, it was impossible not to hear the roaring noise of cannon fire, and as the valiant Marshal de Robles gazed down from a lofty wall, a bullet struck his head, and like a sheep before the slaughter, fell to the floor without a single cry of pain. He lied down and endured the agony of his wound, and the next day he gave up the ghost. The men who surrounded his body were pressed with the most

---

57 Correggio, *The Siege of Malta*, ch. xi, p. 143
58 Correggio, *The Siege of Malta*, ch. x, pp. 143–148

overpowering grief, and before tears could flow from their eyes, they held back their passions and prepared themselves for the next assault.[59]

A LIVING HELL

On August 20th the Turks made themselves ready for another assault. Mustapha Pasha even had his servants dress up as Janissaries to inspire them with courage. The battle commenced and a bullet knocked his turban right off his head; he fell to the ground stunned. Some time passed, he got on all fours, crawled to the ditch of Fort St. Michael, and remained there until dark. Bullets and cannons ripped through the thick summer air and brought immense damage to the Christians, and in the midst of the battle, Master Marco, a loyal Maltese, was seen covered in flames, his body burning, his flesh cooking, his soul leaving into eternity. One Turk was armed with a gun which unleashed bullets as big as dove's eggs, and when they landed, the results could not be more devastating. He fired shots, the incendiaries burst, and numerous Christians were engulfed in flames; as they burned, fire spread to their supplies of flammable weapons, these exploded, and many more Christians were slaughtered. One Christian soldier shot his flame thrower at the Turks' gunpowder, and a great many of the enemy were consumed by the hot flames which now brought terror to the eyes by its brightness and imposing heat, with the little island becoming a living hell to all who were present.

A Turk stood in front of the Post of Don Bernardo de Cabrera and a bullet shot him dead. The Turks were too afraid to retrieve the body, and so to shame them, Don Bernardo took the carcass, cut off its dead head and stuck it on a pike, just to bring humiliation and fear to the hearts of his enemies. The next day, at the dawning of the day, the Turks executed an attack and the two sides tossed grenades at one another. Valette ordered for a mine to be built, designed in a way that when it exploded the Christian defenses would not be damaged. They completed it, the charges were detonated, and the roaring blast erupted with sharp debris zipping through the air, thick smoke clouding the sky, and forty Turks losing their lives in the explosion, making a most hellish sight.

EACH MAN PRAYED TO HIS GOD

On August 29th, the Turks sprinted toward the fort in a mass assault, and behind them were the officers, using their swords and sticks to compel them to move on forward. The fighting ensued, cannon balls flew across the air, ripped and shattered earth, stone, and men, with carnage, flesh and blood, pouring and splattering on the land. Each man fought for the beliefs which they had held so dearly within their throbbing hearts; every man prayed to his god, one side implored the Eternal Judge from Who life springs, and the other begged the devil who deemed them as mere slaves. During the most intense part of the battle, a rainstorm came from nowhere; drops of rain came down, one by one, when ultimately its full force came about, and drove the heretics away.[60]

---

59 Correggio, *The Siege of Malta*, ch. xi, pp. 143–145, 148; ch. xii, pp. 151, 153
60 Correggio, *The Siege of Malta*, ch. xii, pp. 157–162

The torrents of nature did not sever away the courage of the Turks who pushed forward with their hopes for conquest. Janissaries took a high tower, and with their rifles terrifyingly and accurately sniped the Christians, picking them off with absolute precision. The Christians kept a cannon hidden under a bunch of stones, quietly loaded it, and when the time came, removed the rubble and fired it. An explosion erupted from the lofty edifice, the Janissaries left like those who built the Tower of Babel, and fell to the ground where they were met with fierce Christians and slaughtered.

A Turkish officer loaded his gun, and when he put in the second charge, all that could be seen was the man obliterated by a sudden explosion that spread and brought death to all around him.

THE SHIPS OF SPAIN ARRIVE, HOPE ARISES

On September 7th, hope sprung from the souls of the fighters, when they saw ships forming up at the mouth of the harbour. It was the relief team, sent by the king of Spain, Philip II. Now were they certain that their liberty from the turbulent siege was at hand. As the Turks, with trembling and panic, were bringing their baggage into their ships, the Christians leaped in bliss and joy at the coming of the ships. Each galley fired three shots, but the men did not fire in response, for they were in no place to waste more gun powder.

THE SOUND OF HEAVEN

The next day, the Turkish trenches were like a ghost town, with the only feeling being the utter terror of the enemy's silence, and the quiet joy of the warrior monks. The soundless horror was suddenly broken, like a wave disrupting the calmest waters, when the church bells rang. At the sound of such beautiful instruments, a sudden serenity entered their minds, and stillness came to the spirits of the warrior monastics.

Never did the simplest music sound so sweet to the indomitable ears of so rugged a group of warriors. Never was the most piously rustic sound of those sacred bells so sublime, so serene, to their spirits; their sound was the most moving and softest harmony, purging the deepest melancholy, and ascending to the apex of bliss. The cries of torment, the awe-inspiring noise of cannons and explosions, had inflicted their ears, and now whatever travails they endured, was healed by the most natural and surreal cure to the mind—music, not to the pleasure of the flesh, but to the delight of the soul.

Such bells were used to make ready the men for the fray, and to instill the highest form of discipline to the most sluggish soldier; but now they were used for the praising of Heaven, the extolling of God, and the reverence to that most blessed of women—Mary—whose Seed was destined by Providence to crush the head of the serpent whose slaves were now planning their final stand.[61]

---

61 See Correggio, *The Siege of Malta*, ch. xiii, pp. 165–168

PART 15

THE SERPENT RETURNS, AND THE SUCCESSORS OF ST. PAUL BRING IT BACK TO THE FIRE

The relief force sailed through the waters to reach Malta and vanquish the heathen and drive out their violence, like the Apostle, who reached the same isle and repulsed the influence of devils. They came to the city of Mdina, settled in a suburb and positioned themselves where there was the church, dedicated to the patron saint of the island—St. Paul. It stood right near the bay upon which the holy Apostle sailed, where his ship crashed on the place where two seas met. Here was where the final stand was to happen, right there on the Bay of St. Paul, where that profound event occurred, when Paul crashed, resisted the venom of the most cunning of creatures, and shook it into the fire; here was to be the place, where the slaves to the serpent would raise their assault to take back the island for their slithering master, and where the servants of God—the citizens of Heaven—would raise the Cross and ascend their swords to shake the devils and cast them into the flames.

Mustapha who, like Herod, hearkened unto the voice of a Salome, and who with confidence sojourned to the island to behead the Knights of St. John, was now eager to leave Malta. His companion Piali rejected the idea, and told Mustapha: "What excuse will you give, O Mustapha, to the sultan? If you leave without seeing the enemy, you cannot even tell him from whose forces you fled. This is why I tell you that you ought to stay with your troops on shore and try and bring this relief force to battle. If they are as few in number as it is said they are, you will easily defeat them, and there will still be time to capture Malta. But if this relief should be too powerful, then you can retire in good order at St. Paul's Bay, where I shall be with the fleet to embark you. In this way you will be able to make excuses to the sultan, since you will have seen the enemy and will be able to give an account of them."[62]

SEPTEMBER THE 11TH—THE FINAL BATTLE

The aurora of the sun began to slightly break the hellish and murky sky, during the end of the night, with one ray of pristine light coming from another, and then rescinding, like a pilgrim who seeks his home again,[63] like Paul who, while sailing to Rome, was compelled by the violent storm to crash into the ruthless waves, and swim to the very land which this eternal battle took place.

It was on September the 11th when the last struggle commenced, not solely between two armies, but between two cosmos.[64] The alarms were sounded, the banners bearing sacred images and holy figures were unfurled, and the men formed up into their squadrons. Confusion and disorder swept the Turkish ranks, their troops were in much freight as they saw the Christians before them, as the serpent quivers in fear as it falls into the crackling flames of a fire in the midst of a storm. The two forces—one for the Cross, the other for the crooked snake—rushed toward a hill to take a dominant position.

---

62 See Correggio, *The Siege of Malta*, ch. xiv, pp. 179–182
63 This line was inspired by Dante, Paradisio, Canto 1.49–52
64 Learned from Chesterton

✝ CHRISTIANITY IS AT WAR: THE MANIFESTO FOR CHRISTIAN MILITANCY

A leader of the battle, Chiappino Vitelli, called out to the men with him, "Saint Iago, and at them!" The banners of God's soldiers were raised, and the men charged at the Turks with such tenaciousness and ferocity, that the Muslims fled. The Christians stopped, took a few breathes, and resumed their pursuit. The Muslims were now surrounded. A number of Spaniards opened fire and killed many of them. The engagement was grim and hellish, swords were dipped in blood, chaos was all around, the sun was at its highest point, and no man was free from its merciless heat.

Christians and Muslims fought on, regardless of the fact that not a man could barely stand because of exhaustion. The defenders of the Cross were tired and small in number, and the slaves to the serpent bold and fresh. They drove the saints to higher ground near St. Paul's Bay, they saw before them the rising waves approaching the coast, the same waters where the Apostle crashed.

Two or three of the men were slain, and more would have been slaughtered if it wasn't for a righteous Englishman and Captain Marcos de Toledo, who withstood the devil's army with sword and shield. As their very presence deterred the enemy, there came a reinforcing body of men led by Captain Salinas, Captain Don Alonzo de Vargas, and Captain Antonio de la Pena, whose forces crashed right into the Turks.

Mustapha jumped off his horse and killed it, and then to instill courage in his men, he stood in front of them and did all he could to keep them in order. He ordered his fleets to cover the shore and open fire on the Christians. The warrior monks were dreadfully fatigued, but they nonetheless sprinted into the fray. Not even the highest level Turk could stop this assault, and they all ran into the water to get to their ships, but unlike Paul and his fellow prisoners, many of them drowned.

The waters were covered in carnage, and so great and repulsive was the stench of gore in the air. It was right there, on the land where St. Paul cast the serpent into the flames, where the children of the serpent burned under the fires of Christian victory, and the flames of zealous love licked their flesh and consumed their bodies. Right there, where the Apostle brought the light of truth into the darkness, the devils of Muhammad were repulsed and wicked violence eschewed the consecrated land. Don Bernadino de Cardenas said to Chiappino in front of all the men, "How were thing with you today?" Chiappino responded: "There was little that I could do wherever you had been." Captain Salinas then said: "May it please God that I may always serve my king under such a man as you. I should never weary of it." Chiappino then made this answer: "Let us call it a day, Captain Salinas, for you have given ample proof of your valour."

Don Bernadino was offered some water in a helmet, he took it and gave it to some soldiers whose need he thought greater than his. After thirty-five thousand Muslims were killed, two thousand five hundred Christians warriors were slain, and seven thousand local Maltese men, women, girls and boys, lost their lives,[65] the venom of the devil was made null, the serpent was shaken off into the flames, and the light of truth which St. Paul preached was preserved.

---

65 See Correggio, *The Siege of Malta*, ch. xiv, pp. 183–186, 189

The Turks would try to invade this island, but were repulsed by the same Hospitallers, who for over a century were the only guards who prevented the Ottomans from conquering Italy.[66] And this very fact compels one to wonder, that truly it was Providence which moved the ship to crash in that ancient tempest, so that the Truth would arrive in the island, and bring zealots by whom the sunset of Christendom would never suffer to be eclipsed by the waning moon of the serpent whose destiny is the flames of the abyss under the hands of the Eternal Knight.

THE SONG OF LEPANTO
A MAN IN CONTEMPLATION
An old man sat on a beautifully carved chair, no doubt built by the finest carpenter; he wore the garbs of a pious ascetic, one who esteems his Faith as not something to question, but to behold, as a tender child looks up with awe to the clear and transcendent heavens. The place is dim in color and lacking much luster, with the only light coming off from the rays of the sun beaming through a nearby window and lightly illuminating the room, with brightness intermingling with darkness, as though hope itself was getting swallowed by a shadow, not knowing whether or not it would survive or simply die off into the realm of quiet memory.

His countenance appeared frail, but when one looked to his eyes, it was as though you could see his soul, and the troubling spirit that desperately desired to extinguish something sinister. His lips moved, and from them one heard what would sound to us as the mere murmurings of a senile old man, but this was no mumbling, but prayers which could not be heard; they were not for man to hear, but for God; they were not said to impress, but to exhort for the help of the Eternal Warrior, to end the great evil which now stood before them. He was staying in Rome, and he knew that a great horde of Muslims were on their way to take this great city which the Apostles Paul and Peter, with their sacred blood, consecrated it for the crown of Christendom and made a city of the Cross. But now the barbarians desired to force it into a slave of the Caliphate and a land of the crescent, and from them there came the blood-flecked scourge of war. The Turks had just raided Crete, and they placed in jeopardy Venice, the Kingdom of Naples, and the city of destined saints, Rome.

A SINISTER SMILE AND AN ABSENCE OF CHRISTIAN ZEAL
One can only imagine the sultan, Selim II, reposing in his palace on Turkish land stolen through the shedding of Christian blood, with hallow eyes and a smile as crooked as a young moon, knowing that Christendom is not unified, that England had no interest in fighting the Muslims because it hated the Catholic; that France had more interest in their relations with heretics than in zeal, and that Venice was more determined to fulfill their avarice than their religion. The Turkish Grand Vizier, Sokolli, discouraged the Venetians from ever confronting the rising Islamic power, telling them: "Peace is better for you than war ... You cannot cope with the Sultan, who will take from you not only Cyprus alone, but other dependencies. As for your Christian League, we know full well how little love the Christian princes bear you. If

---
66 Chateaubriand, *The Genius of Christianity*, part iii, 5.1, 5.2, trans. Charles I. White.

you would but hold by the Sultan's robe, you might do what you want in Europe, and enjoy perpetual peace."

Such was the bribery of the devil. It is the temptation that was given to Christ: bow down before me and these things will be given to you; and it is the same temptation given to His body. The survival of Christendom is dependent upon whether or not the Body bows or fights.

GOD WILL GIVE US VICTORY

It was October 5th, 1571, and under the grey sky and in the midst of the thick fog, two-hundred and eight ships were throughout the dark blue Mediterranean Sea with their sails resisting the sharp winds, appearing to the inspired eye as terrifying beasts floating over a dark and bottomless void, vested with the brightest textures, bearing their Christian standards, with each one illustrating ingenious engineering, and yet giving a most rustic site. On each one was a body of warriors tirelessly laboring in their duties, some from Italy and others from Spain, since Germany and England refused to help the Catholics, and thought it better to allow the Muslims to conquer papist lands rather than protect them. Amidst all of this working there stood Don Juan: he was twenty-four years old, his face fierce, his body lean, agile, and swift of foot, formidable in fighting and covered in the finest armor. His hand was fit for war, and his mind and soul driven by the inspiration of Providence. He once said: "I take it for certain that the Turks, swollen by their victories, will wish to take on our fleet, and God—have the pious presentiment—will give us victory."

Under his command, discipline was instilled, and blasphemy, or even the slightest religious doubt, was deemed as sedition, for if the approaching battle was to be won against the advancers of falsehood, it had to be done by men unified in truth.

THE PRAYERS OF PRIESTS IN PURE LIFE

On October 7th, Don Juan ordered the Christian fleet to weigh anchor and sail foreword to the galleys of the enemy. The admirable leader had once said, "I am taking up arms against the Turks, but the only thing that can help me is the prayers of priests of pure life," and so did the priests on board proclaim their prayers to mighty Heaven, observed Mass and conferred from their pious hands the Eucharist to the hardy fighters of the Cross, all under the night sky just moments before the ascension of the sun.

COLOSSAL DEMONS

The rowers worked the heavy oars and exerted all of their ligaments to push through the strong winds which blew passed the coast of Greece, only to approach the Gulf of Patras. The ships moved forward into the gulf, surrounded by lofty mountains caressed by the sharp breeze, overshadowing the waters as though they were nightmarish citadels from the depths of hell. As they continued to sojourn, they saw what appeared to be a body of colossus demons lurking about the murky blue abyss, arising out of the twilight and robed in the purple of the sky,[67] all formed into one single symbol most devilish and diabolic, the crescent, giving out the sight of the gaping sharp jaws of a beast ready to devour and swallow poor souls not familiar with its ways. They were Turkish ships under the command of Ali Pasha, and to utilize an efficient strategy, and for the sake of their luciferian god, each one was positioned so that all together they took the shape of a crescent moon with a ship at the center symbolizing a star, as though they were commemorating Zebah and Zalmunna and expressing their rage toward Gideon.

Ornaments they had none, showing their iconoclast spirit, and in numbers they seemed endless. They represented the spirits of the bottomless pit, and they saw before them soldiers of Light, beaming from the sunset of Christendom.[68] The Christians beheld their enemies, and they could see that the center ship bore a very large green flag, upon which was embroidered in gold the name of Allah 28,900 times—all names of blasphemy; it was taken from Mecca, and it was all but an honoring of that harlot who John saw. Don Juan, being filled with fiery zeal, ordered for the banner of Christ to be raised, and when it reached it summit, one could only behold in awe its bearing of the image of the Cross. The Muslims were fighting for the whore of the devil, and the Christians the Bride of Christ. The Muslims were about to go face to face with the ships of Chittim (Daniel 11:30), foreshadowing what is to come before the end of the age: the restoration of Christendom in the West, and the navies of Spain and Italy fighting against the armies of the Antichrist.

THE CROSS VERSUS THE CRESCENT

The acolytes of Antichrist fired their guns in the air and made their savage ululations, their uncouth war cries, and beat their drums to make a harrowing noise, as the Canaanites did to prevent women from hearing the weeping of their infants as their helpless bodies burnt in the flames of Molech. As this tempest of barbarity went on, priests went up to the decks of the ships and with crucifix in hand made blessings to the warriors of God who, with the most fervent and sweetest sentiments, held tightly on their rosaries and made prayers to the lady who the old dragon hates, and who St. John witnessed standing upon the crescent moon, the very image which the Muslims venerated and now formed. As they strived for the kingdom of the devil, the Muslims' souls were rooted in the forests of the abyss, they were haters of the Faith and enemies to Christ. They were met with a battle position completely incompatible with the diabolical: the Christians formed their armada into the shape of the Cross. The formation of the ships was that of the Holy Cross. Now was this the purest moment in which the salt of the earth was prepared to burn the repugnant and rotting flesh of Satan's seed. It was literally the Cross versus the crescent.

---

67 This line was inspired by Chesterton, The True Romance
68 The line, "the sunset of Christendom, is from Chesterton, The True Romance

THE BATTLE OF THE CROSS

Don Juan climbed into a small ship and rowed across the ranks of the moving armada, crucifix in hand, declaring to his men, "You have come to fight the battle of the Cross—to conquer or to die. But whether you die or conquer, do your duty this day, and you will secure a glorious immortality." He returned to the commanding ship, got down to his knees, looked up to the banner of the Cross, and made his supplications to God, and those around him did the same, all in unison urging the Lord for His deliverance. The rowers continued to push hard against the waters, but soon Providence intervened, the God of nature's harmony turned the winds to press upon their sails, while the Muslim galleys lost this support, and were now compelled to whip their slaves to work with the oars. The Christians, on the other hand, no longer needed the labor of slaves, and so liberated them and gave each and every one of them a weapon for the impending fight. All were to fight for God, regardless if one were a freeman or a slave, they were all to combat the wicked for Christ, under Whom all are free.

Before the crescent could even reach the Cross, the Turks were confronted with six advancing ships, and when they tried to pass these, bullets firing from one hundred guns cut open the Janissaries on the decks. The same Christian ships then launched a volley of cannonballs, they pierced some of the Turkish boats within which lied the helpless enemy Muslims who, lodged inside the wounded beasts, sunk into the ocean's abyss. Their crescent formation was made more crooked before it could even touch the Crucifix of saintly galleys.

A DUAL BETWEEN THE COSMOS

Ali Pasha, commanding the ship upholding the blasphemous green flag, set his eyes upon Don Juan, and advanced directly toward him. Don Juan, being on the galley with the banner of the Cross, did the same. The ship of Antichrist pierced through the Christian flagship with its much longer prow, the Janissaries leaped onto the galley and tried to get on deck, but were blocked by nets prudently stretched from stern to stern. Like spiders they held on with much agility and endurance onto the nets, and even though the flesh of their hands was being cooked by fires put in place by Spanish troops, they still refused to loosen their grips. They ascended the nets and were met by fierce defenders who cut them to shreds with their muskets. The two decks of the ships collided, and now more than eight hundred men were shoulder to shoulder, staring into each other with the most rugged of countenances, the fiercest of eyes, and the thickest of rage. They pulled out their guns, and looking into the whites of their eyes, opened fire at such close range. Flesh was teared apart, blood splatter and stained their hardened faces, only to hear the profound groans of the wounded on the verge of seeing the afterlife, and to see the scores of countless dead.

Turkish archers tried to use their arrows, but these sharp missiles were unable to penetrate the armor of the Christian—these were not the Crusaders of the days of Godfrey and Bohemond, but ones more advanced in the arts of war. Christians and Muslims leaped onto each other's boats, and a collision of warriors commenced. The waves of the deep sea heaved and crashed onto lonely rocks arising near the shores of the gulf's imposing mountains, and the fast moving autumn winds flowed through their dark and grimacing caves, when the cries of the dying, the raging shouts of the warriors, and the sounds of clashing weapons and exploding cannons, could be heard from the nearby coasts and by every holy hermit who made his incessant prayers on that forlorn moment, when the smell of death and burning gunpowder filled the air.

Within the commanding ship of the Muslims, Christian warriors fought with their enemies in a struggle to the death, in not just a physical war, but in one which surpassed the temporal, and transcended all together into eternity, in a dual between cosmos, in a dual between souls. Ali Pasha was on the ship when a bullet struck his head and dropped him dead. A criminal who was liberated by Don Juan decapitated him and placed it on a pike. The green flag of Lucifer, bearing his masquerading name of Allah, was brought low and replaced by the banner of the Cross, as the Hebrews shattered the lofty idols of the Canaanites.

On other ships, priests, vested with all the luster of holiness and the ardency of faith, led the warriors with their hands raised gripping onto the crucifix. On every galley there lied men without life, and on the ground there were Christians and Muslims lying together in the embrace of death. In due time, many of the Muslims were overtaken and subdued, and the Turkish commander, Muhammad Sirrocco, was slain amidst the fighting. An arrow pierced the eye of the Admiral Barbarigo, and as he lay wounded, he was told that the battle was won, and before he gave his last breath, he said, "I die contented." It was a war between those who believed in free will, and those who believed in the tyrannical tenet of "kismet," or predestination. It was not just a great war of arms, but a war of ideas, between the Christian who did his part until his coming death arose above the melancholic road of time, and the Muslim, who sought out death like a Donatist, and thirsted to kill for the hope of one day gazing upon endless gardens filled with eternal lusts, where there lies no contentment.

Almost all of the Christians Maltese ships were destroyed, and the Muslims were close to taking the victory, until the reserve ships, under the command of Santa Cruz, arrived and brought havoc to the enemy. They descended on the Muslim corsairs just as they were boarding the vanquished Maltese galleys, and made a great slaughter. Blood stained the sea, and smoke clouded the heavens and colored the sun. The battle was sustained and prolonged with that intolerant zeal which only comes when creeds collide in a battle to the end.

INSPIRATION COMES TO THE CONTEMPLATIVE MAN

The old man with whom this chapter begins was in the room, having a discussion with some other men dressed similarly to him.

He was in the conversation, yet his mind was in a world outside of his own, his eyes looked to nowhere, but they were fixated on that Spirit that is everywhere. Something struck him, his eyes widened, he abruptly arose from his seat and opened the window, and gazed heavenward. To those around him it appeared as though he was merely looking to the sky, but there was something quite profound taking place as his eyes beamed into the empyrean, as though hope, in the end, withstood the glutinous jaws of darkness. Some moments passed, he shut the window, walked back to the other men and said: "This is not a moment in which to talk business: let us give thanks to God for the victory He has granted to the arms of the Christians." He arose from the chair carved by the finest carpenter, to only praise the Eternal Carpenter in Heaven; he opened the window from which the room received its light, only to glorify the One by Whom the world receives true enlightenment and illumination. He gazed up, like a child, at the clear and transcendent heavens, only to praise God for victory over the oriental heathens, just as his predecessor Melchizedek blessed the God of Abraham for triumph over the tyrants of the east. This old man was Pope Pius V, and it was he who, "for the destruction of the Turk," formed this league of warriors, who now cried out "Domino Gloria!" "Glory to the Lord!"[69]

THE CRUSADER SPIRIT IS PUT TO SLEEP

As the Ottomans made apparent their goal to conquer the world, Protestant England, France, and Venice, were trading with them, and selling them ships, raw materials, and any supplies which they could utilize.[70] A gradual decay was occurring in the Christian world; the light which so terrified the heretic and the heathen dimmed, and so disturbing was it that years prior to this time, in the 148 , a German monk named Felix Fabri of Ulm, lamentably wrote:

> The Holy Land has been so utterly lost to us that now no one so much as thinks about recovering it, and there is no longer any way to recover it, unless it shall please God to work some miracle.[71]

What helped strike down the sublime spirit of crusading was Protestantism. The wonderful and beautiful concept of taking up the glorious Cross and raising up arms against the wicked was attacked by that vociferous heretic Martin Luther, who slanderously deemed the Church of Rome as an institution of the Devil, and the idea of crusading as false doctrine. "How shamefully," said this ravening dog, "the pope has this long time baited us with the war against the Turks, taken our money, destroyed so many Christians, and made so much mischief!" He believed most wickedly that the Christians should not make war upon the charging Turk, but simply allow them to make their attacks upon Catholic Europe, since, according to his maddening mind, the Muslims were a tool used by God to punish Catholic Europe for its sins. The fighting stance which the popes had taken for centuries against the jihad, would never be adopted in Protestant nations, where sick men—calling themselves men of God—sought out to undermine the Crusades and uplift the Turk. One of these, an English divine named John Foxe claimed to be uncertain on whether the sultan or the pope "hath been the more bloody and pernicious adversary to Christ."[72]

---

69 This whole description of the Battle of Lepanto is based on the American Chesterton Society's 2003 edition of Chesterton's Lepanto, with the poem itself alongside the notes of Dale Ahlquist and Peter Floriani, and the essay, *The Battle*, by Melvin (Buzz) Kriesel
70 Moczar, *Seven Lies about Catholic History*, ch. iii, p. 70
71 In Jonathan Harris, The Ottoman Threat, in Thomas F. Madden's Crusades, part 8, p. 175
72 Jonathan Harris, The Ottoman Threat, in Thomas F. Madden's Crusades, part 8, pp. 192–3

The Turks wanted to cross right into Italy[73] not only to invade the nation, but to fulfill the wish of Muhammad, that the Muslims conquer Rome and destroy the Vatican. Of course the Reformers were more concerned about their schism than Catholics being killed. The Protestant bishop of Salisbury, John Jewel, sinisterly and sickly wrote:

> The Turk, they say, is now hovering upon Italy. He will at least bridle the ferocity of antichrist [the pope]. [74]

Because these wretches believed that the Roman Church was the Harlot of Babylon, they saw no evil done in helping the Turks. England provided the Turks with war materials, specifically tin which was an essential material for the Turkish war cannon, and thus assisted them in their war upon Catholic Europe. What wicked men these were! They were the ones who warred upon that most important part of our Faith: Christian militancy against the forces of darkness. It was only until the Turks were close to soon enough reach Luther's hind, that the German heretic decided that it was permissible to fight the Turk, just as long as the Pope was not involved.[75] But for Luther to say this means that he himself was intervening in the war by dictating who was and who was not getting involved. Luther was simply grabbing power for himself and making himself the new pope, shattering the common Protestant lauding that they have "no pope."

This is why the Apostles, and their successors, always condemned schism and disunity within the Church. St. Paul, writing to the Corinthians, referred to schisms as indicative of heresies being present:

> For first of all, when ye come together in the church, I hear that there be divisions among you; and I partly believe it. For there must be also heresies among you, that they which are approved may be made manifest among you. (I Corinthians 11:18–19)

St. Paul later wrote, to the same people, that unity of the Church must be maintained in its formation as the Body of Christ:

> For as the body is one, and hath many members, and all the members of that one body, being many, are one body: so also is Christ. For by one Spirit are we all baptized into one body, whether we be Jews or Gentiles, whether we be bond or free; and have been all made to drink into on Spirit. For the body is not one member, but many. (I Corinthians 12:12–12)

St. Clement, a pupil of the Apostles who was commissioned by St. Peter to be the bishop of Rome, wrote in his epistle to the Corinthians a chastisement of ecclesiastical schisms and seditions:

> All sedition and schism was an abomination unto you. …Emulation sent Dathan and Abiram quick into the grave, because they raised up a sedition against Moses, the servant of God. [76]

---

73 See Belloc, *The Great Heresies*, The Great and Enduring Heresy of Muhammad, p. 60
74 Bishop Jewel to H. Bullinger, in Hastings Robinson, *The Zurich Letters*; Jonathan Harris, The Ottoman Threat, in Thomas F. Madden's Crusades, part 8, pp. 192–3
75 Jonathan Harris, The Ottoman Threat, in Thomas F. Madden's Crusades, part 8, pp. 192–3
76 St. Clement, Epistle to the Corinthians, 2, 4, trans. Archbishop Wake, ellipses mine

CHRISTIANITY IS AT WAR: THE MANIFESTO FOR CHRISTIAN MILITANCY

Disunity leaves us open to the wiles of Satan, as in the case of the Protestant schism, it made Christendom vulnerable to the attacks of the Muslims. That unity hinders the advances of Lucifer, was affirmed by St. Ignatius when he wrote:

> For when ye meet fully together in the same place, the powers of the devil are destroyed, and his mischief is dissolved by the unity of your faith. 77

The Catholics and the Protestants should have never provoked such violent contentions toward each other, but should have united in peace, as Christ wanted concord between the Jews and the Samaritans. The Protestant should have never united with the Muslim, but with the Catholic, in brotherhood and in zeal against the antichrist cult of Islam.

THE ENLIGHTENMENT—ENEMY OF THE FAITH

In years bygone, what kicked the already downed spirit of crusading were the violent and tyrannical minds of the Enlightenment movement in the 18th century. For hindrances to Christian warfare such as Enlightenment leader John Hume, the crusades were "the most signal and durable monument of human folly that has yet appeared in any age or nation."78 The violence afflicted by the Muslims was not the most wicked to these sycophants, but rather it was the defense against the jihad by the Catholic Church. In fact, all talk against the Crusades is essentially anti-Christian, since to say that the crusades should have never happened means that the Christians of the East, and ultimately the West, should have been killed by the heretics without fighting. When Christians are massacred, the world stays silent and does not lift a finger to their help; when Christians fight back, the world cries to every nation on the atrocities committed, with every impotent and flattering intellect writing books against the Church. The world witnessed this during the Kosovo War. No one really cared when the Albanian Muslims were killing Christian Serbs. But as soon as the Serbs fought back, the cries of "genocide" were heard throughout the West.

The other useless philosopher, Voltaire, argued that religion was merely a matter of personal conscience and has nothing to do with government.79 Look at religion as merely personal, and you will be crushed by those who see religion as universal; limit religion as only encompassing the individual, and you will be conquered by those who esteem religion as covering the entire cosmos. This war between the orthodox and the heterodox will be partaken not by those who see faith as a "personal decision," but by those who are ignited by an inward conviction that this is a universal struggle between two cities—two eternal realms—the one of heaven and the other of darkness, that will be fought between those who are for God and those who are for tyranny; those who are for truth and those who are for error; those who are for Jerusalem and those who are for Mecca; those who are for the Cross and those who are for crescent.

---

77 St. Ignatius, Epistle to the Ephesians, 12
78 In Jonathan Harris, The Ottoman Threat, in Madden's Crusades, part 8, p. 198
79 Jonathan Harris, The Ottoman Threat, in Madden's Crusades, part 8, p. 198

"The crusades were not only about the deliverance of the Holy Sepulcher," writes Chateaubriand, "but more about knowing which would win on earth: a religion [Islam] that was the enemy of civilization, systematically favorable to ignorance, to despotism, to slavery; or a religion that had caused to reawaken in modern people the genius of a sage antiquity, and had abolished base servitude."[80]

In both the sixteenth and seventeenth centuries, it was the popes and the Catholic Church that made great efforts to penetrate the static and apathetic minds of the West.

In the Battle of Lepanto in 1571 it only required a few ships for the Christians to defeat the Turks. This same enemy made its way toward Vienna in 1683, and as the horned owls of Turkey preyed upon that majestic falcon, the Holy Roman Empire, the Christians were much divided amongst themselves. Protestants living in Hungary had even declared their support for the Ottomans. In a previous century, Luther would do the same when he welcomed the advancement of the Turks; but he quickly changed his mind when they got nearer. Vienna, in the end, was defended and kept safe. After this the Christian armies that arose chased the predator which has forever hunted the saints, pursuing them into Hungary and the Balkans.[81]

But to those who choose to remain ignorant on the truth behind the Crusades, here are the words of Chateaubriand:

> Some have censured the knights for pursuing infidels [Muslims] even into their own countries; but such are not aware that, after all, this was but make just reprisals upon nations who had been the first aggressors. The Moors exterminated by Charles Martel justify the Crusades. Did the disciples of the Koran remain quiet in the deserts of Arabia? Did they not, on the contrary, extend their doctrines and their ravages to the walls of Delhi and the ramparts of Vienna? But perhaps a Christian people should have waited until the haunts of these ferocious beasts had been again replenished! Because our forefathers marched against them under the banner of religion, the enterprise, forsooth, was neither just nor necessary! Had the cause been that of Theutates, Odin, Allah, or any other than that of Jesus Christ, it would all be considered right enough. [82]

Sadly, the Crusades did not succeed in the long run, having lasted eighty-eight years and fully declined in the year 1192. The reason for this decline, was the decline of Christian zeal and increase of indifference towards Christian supremacy and Christendom. If the Crusades actually succeeded in the long run, and kept control of Syria, specifically the city of Damascus, Islam as a religion would have fully declined into the annals of history, and Muslims today would be an insignificant obscure sect, like the Zoroastrians.[83] Zoroastrianism, the religion of the ancient Persians, was at one point the most powerful religious system in the world, on account of the might of the Persian empire. In the time of Daniel it was supreme over the Middle East, and even going on into the fourth, fifth, sixth, and even seventh centuries, it was extremely powerful until

---

80 In James A. Powell, The Ottoman Threat, in Madden's Crusades, part 8, p. 203
81 Moczar, *Seven Lies about Catholic History*, ch. iii, p. 71, 73
82 Chateaubriand, *The Genius of Christianity*, part iii, 5.3, trans. Charles I. White.
83 See Hilaire Belloc, The Crusades, ch. i, p. 5

☦ CHRISTIANITY IS AT WAR: THE MANIFESTO FOR CHRISTIAN MILITANCY

the rise of the Islamic empire. Now what influence and prestige does Zoroastrianism have today? Nothing. The same would have been for Islam if the crusaders had destroyed it completely.

THE CRUSADES—THE ENEMY OF THE USELESS CHRISTIAN

The Crusades are one major event, made up of smaller events, only to make a whole, very significant, concatenation. Each occurrence is attributed to another event, which soon becomes a series of incidences that ultimately form a part of the great cause we call the Crusades. It is impossible to talk about Islamic expansion and tyranny, and Muhammad's utopian ideology, without describing the Crusades, since it was they who posed the greatest threat from the eleventh century all the way to the thirteenth century, to Islam. You cannot discuss the Crusades without knowing about the conquest of Jerusalem by Umar, nor is there room for efficient dialogue without making mention of the Turkish empowering of the Islamic empire. It is also inadequate to mention Islam's war with Christianity without giving much attention to the Crusades. It was the Crusades that hindered the Muslims from accomplishing the world empire they desired in the Middle Ages, and it was in this great struggle, between Christian knights and Muslim cavaliers, that illustrated just how deep, profound, and eternal, this war between the Umma and Christendom clearly is. If Islam arose in the fourteenth century, this is only because the crusading spirit died down.[84]

But yet, in our frivolous times many people wish to belittle and downplay the Crusades, seeing it only as a mere dark smudge on the annals of Christian history only to be wiped away by the murky waters of modern insanity, and some even harbor this vague hatred for the old knights and the Catholic church to the point that they will introduce all kinds of dangerous heresies.

Well known church planter enthusiast and contemporary thinking Christian Darrel Whiteman, writes that "one can enter the kingdom of God and confess Jesus as Lord and Savior without necessarily changing one's religion. At first blush this may sound scandalous to conservative Evangelical Christians. Nevertheless, many Muslims today are attracted to Jesus but turned off to Christianity, which for them conjures up negative images of the Crusades, colonialism, a foreign religion, and the 'Christian' West where we eat pork, drink alcohol, and watch R-rated movies."[85]

This deception on the Crusades and favoring to Islam can go back to Protestant propaganda against the Catholic Church. The seventeenth century Protestant historian Thomas Fuller went so far as to write that perhaps God granted the Muslims with the right to hold the Holy Land, since they had lived there for so long a time.[86]

---

84 See Moczar, *Seven Lies about Catholic History*, ch. iii, p. 70
85 Darrell L. Whiteman, Response to Paul G. Hierbert, in *MissionShift: Global Mission Issues in the Third Millennium*, ed. David John Hesselgrave and Ed Stetzer ch. 10, p. 123 (2010)
86 Moczar, *Seven Lies about Catholic History*, ch. iii, p. 55

Famous pastor (and I don't write this as a compliment) Andy Stanley, whose jejune, vague, and empty books and sermons have overran the souls of the nation, has also given his wisdom on the Crusades, as though he has exhaustively studied the immensely deep historical episode:

> Religious authorities have been misusing the name of God to serve their own ends for centuries, often resulting in the most appalling atrocities in history. The crusades. The Inquisition. Ethnic Cleansing. Terrorism. Abortion clinic bombings. [87]

If Stanley had done any in depth study on the subject, he would of at least mentioned the massacres done by the Turks, be they Seljuk or Ottoman, if he wanted to really list an example of "the most appalling atrocities in history." It does not surprise me that the name of the book in which these ridiculous words are written is called "The Grace of God," since so many today have isolated "grace" to mean tolerance, and that's exactly what the modern church elite is using to create a useless and compliant church which will recline as the world gets inundated by evil, and sit comfortably to talk trivially about "love" and focus ever so much on that word which they have made into an idol: grace. This obsession on grace, and I will affirm this without apology, is the most pernicious thing that has seeped into the civilization. They have made grace from meaning God's salvation, into loving all, never showing anger before wickedness, discernment before deception. The modern church tells us to spurn affronting the dark and sinister forces which have so creeped into our sanctuaries, and like pestiferous germs in the fresh fruit of a well rooted tree, it has beguiled men into believing that decay is better than preservation. Islam is at our gates, the modern Christian says "do not mention this since it will make Christianity look intolerant." Heretics abound saying that Islam can be adapted with Christianity, the modern Christian responds, "say nothing of it, those heretics are men of God, how dare you question a brother in Christ."

Another example of this current fragile church is Philip Yancey, the perfect prophet for today's cult of tolerance and worship of grace. He writes that "to our everlasting shame, the watching world judges God by a church whose history also includes the Crusades, the Inquisition, anti-Semitism, suppression of women, and support of the slave trade."[88]

It is not a coincidence that the book which carries this pathetic statement is similar to that of Andy Stanley: "Grace Notes." Again, this is all for the goal of neutralizing the Church, enabling Islam (whether directly or indirectly, it does not matter) to rise. The power of Islam grows stronger as the Church grows weaker.

The Church was not weak in the time of the Crusades, but strong and influential. And some today may bring the common objection that it is not the purpose of the Church to start wars, that the secular monarchs of Europe should have been the ones behind the wars against the Muslims, and that the Emperor Alexius should not have appealed to Pope Urban II, but the kings of the West. But such a protest is lunacy. Alexius had no other choice but to appeal

---

87 Andy Stanley, *The Grace of God*, ch. 4, p. 61 (2010)
88 Philip Yancey, *Grace Notes*: Daily Readings with a Fellow Pilgrim, May 6, p. 158, Someone Cares Charitable Trust (2009)

to the Pope, since the ones who cared and still care the least are politicians. When Nicholas V urged a crusade long before the fall of Constantinople, the Christian princes ignored him. After Constantinople was conquered, it was Pope Calixtus III who raised an army and commenced the crusade against Mehmet II. Pius II too tried to start a crusade only to receive the apathy of kings. When it comes to fighting evil, the biggest hindrances are politicians, and so truly the failure to war with Islam came from the monarchs and the heretics, not the popes.[89] Certainly there were monarchs who attempted crusades, and just look how they turned out. King Philip IV of France attempted a crusade in 1313, but died before it could occur. Henry V of England expressed his desire for a crusade but wasted all of his time fighting fellow Christians, the French. Philip VI of France endeavored to do a crusade, but it never happened.[90] The Church, being the light of the world, was the greatest enemy to Islam; no institution has fought against the Muslims more than the Catholic Church. Therefore, if we had the modern Christian mindset alive and well in the old days of Christendom, and affirmed that it wasn't the Church's part to start wars against heretics, then we would have allowed Islam to overrun much of the Christian world, and there would have been no war until the last moment when the barbarians would be at are doors. This is what we see today with the modern church never mentioning fighting Islam until the September 11th attacks, the pastors having the mind of Luther. But even after this, many church leaders are acquiescing to Islam.

This new worship of uselessness is much more appealing than direct and open blasphemy; it looks delightful to the eyes of most men, and obviously evil to the eyes of a few. It does not say, "worship Satan," but that "we should not focus on Satan." It does not say, "Christ is not God," but, "the Trinity is a non-issue." It does not unmask its ugly face and reveal its true intentions, and says, "the church should be useless," but that "the church should stop criticizing other cultures, and being judgmental on others of different faiths." The Church, to today's contemporary heretics, should just focus on "love" and turn away from the command of Saint Paul to "have no fellowship with the unfruitful works of darkness, but rather reprove them." (Ephesians 5:11) The Church, to the modern Christian, should stop being the Church. You cannot talk about Christianity without talking about the Crusades. In every debate, every discourse, every discussion, on Christianity, the Crusades are brought up. It is time for Christians to stop being ashamed of the Crusades, and to start exclaiming with pride and confidence, that they are a part of the Christian spirit. The Crusades are of the Christian Faith, and if one does not want to accept this, then he should simply leave the Christian Faith.

---

89 See Belloc, *How the Reformation Happened*, info, p. 57
90 Jonathan Harris, The Ottoman Threat, in Thomas F. Madden's Crusades, part 8, p. 175

PART 16 – THE RECONQUISTA, OR THE CONQUEST OF SPAIN

HOW THE CONQUEST OF SPAIN HAPPENED
The nation of Spain is a holy land, sanctified by the presence of the Apostles; consecrated by the blood of martyrs; glorified through the exertions of many Christian warriors, by whose hands God did many wondrous works. Spain is truly one of the flowers of Christendom, and when its seed was nurtured by the watering of the Apostles, it began to sprout, and slowly did it grow, and by the labors of many righteous saints, and through so many martyrdoms, soon did it bloom with its pedals outspread, and shine with its bright colors before a dismal and dark world. St. Paul was the first to have brought Christianity to this land, and we learn this from Holy Scripture. He wrote to the Romans, "whenever I journey to Spain, I shall come to you." (Romans 15:24) And in the same epistle he wrote: "Therefore, when I have performed this and have sealed to them this fruit, I shall go by way of you to Spain." (Romans 15:28) St. Paul, a pillar of the Church, reached the land when it was plunged into the darkness of paganism, and he arrived as a light to a darkened world. After his visit, both Peter and Paul sent seven bishops to Spain, as we learn from St. Gregory, and from there the country had its first church.[1]

The Islamic conquest of Spain happened not solely because the Muslims were powerful militarily and the Spaniards were weak—it happened because of treachery. As heretical Jews conspired with Antiochus Epiphanies in allowing him to invade Israel, there was treasonous activity within Spain which enabled the Muslims to break right into the great nation of Christendom. The Spanish king Roderic sent the count Julian on an embassy to the Muslim king Haboalim in North Africa.

As he was gone, Roderic had an illicit affair with, according to some, his wife, and according to others, his sister. Either way, Julian was so exasperated by this that he worked

---
[1] See St. Gregory VII, b. 1, 64, p. 93

CHRISTIANITY IS AT WAR: THE MANIFESTO FOR CHRISTIAN MILITANCY

with the king of Morocco, Abocubra, Haboalim, Ezarich, and twenty-five other Muslim kings, to invade Spain. And so it was done, and on 711 Roderic was met by these strongly united forces, intermixed with the Muslim descendants of the Canaanites—the Moors[2]—and traitors. The Spaniards tried desperately to defend their nation from invading forces, but in fourteen months they lost, and all of Spain up to Arles in Provence was now occupied by Muslims. The Christians scattered about fleeing to the wilderness and mountains, hiding in caves just like the Hebrews when they were conquered by the Midianites.[3] Spain would soon be under a variety of Muslim kings, many of whom would uphold banners upon which were grafted the symbol of a blue key on a silver ground above certain versus of the Koran, symbolizing that with a sword the Muslims had unlocked the borders of the Gibraltar, which is the key to the conquest of the West, hence why it was called "the Mountain of the Key."[4] In later times, during this great struggle to retake Spain, the Archbishop of Braga had this to say to the Muslim occupiers:

> You have held our cities and lands already for 358 years …Return to the homeland of the Moors whence you came, leaving us what is ours![5]

But the Muslims were not just going to leave, they needed to be driven out, not by some secular laws, but by Christendom.

THE RECONQUISTA BEGINS

When Spain was conquered, the Spaniards did not just stand helpless and docile. The reconquest (or the Reconquista) did not begin at a later point, but in the same year of the Islamic takeover. Their revolt began in a meeting held by Spanish chiefs in the cave of Covadonga. A new war between the slaves of Satan and the Citizens of Heaven ensued into a seven hundred and eighty one year struggle, an event unparalleled in history. Spaniards fought for their liberties and their religion, the Muslims for their annihilation, the superiority of Islam, and the desecration of the Church.[6]

In 722, without any help from foreign aid, the Spanish warrior Pelayo led a small band into victory in the Battle of Covadonga. After this, the Christians would continue to gain ground, acre by acre and city by city.[7]

The Spaniards made their way to the mountains of Sobrarbe, Ribagorza, Aragon, Berroza, Artieda, Ordona, Vizcaya, Alava, and Asturias, where they were able to establish sturdy defenses against the jihadist invaders. When the Muslims heard about this, they understood that if they allowed the Christians to build strongholds, they would in the end suffer the con-

---

2   See Procopius, *Wars*, 4.10
3   Chron. Juan de la Pena, ch. 3, 4, trans. Lynn H. Nelson
4   Mendoza, 2.12
5   See Carroll, *A History of Christendom*, vol. iii, ch. ii, pp. 63–64, see also n. 116
6   P.F., *The Spanish Inquisition*, USCM, vol. ii, p. 456
7   See Warren H. Carroll, *A History of Christendom*, vol. 3: The Glory of Christendom, ch. i, p. 5

sequence of losing what they conquered.[8] Notice what made these Muslims fear the most: Christians fighting back. Today the western church looks down upon counterattacking evil as "ungraceful" or "not being Christ like"; they seem to neglect that part of having grace is to fight against those who want to destroy grace. They never think about what would happen if every Christian on earth was killed: grace would be nonexistent. The Christian, then, must confront and war with those who wish to capture Christendom to preserve grace; if not, grace will disappear and Islamic brutality persevere.

The emir of Cordoba sent the warlord Abd al-Malik bin Khatan to suppress this great Christian affront and popular revolt to their Islamic empire. This terrorist joined a large force of cavalry and infantry toward Aragon, and they burned and pillaged all Christian places in their path, razing fortifications, capturing and killing Christians without the slightest bit of mercy. When they arrived at the fortress of Pano, not a single Christian, except for the dead and the prisoners, fled in fear, but they kept their post and fought audaciously. Abd al-Malik completely destroyed the fortifications; and regardless of the fact that the Christians lost, the spirit of liberty thrived in the Spaniards more than ever.

In 820 the Spanish king of Asturias Ordono led an assault upon the Muslims, only to lose, empowering the enemy to conquer more Spanish lands up to the city of Toulouse. Fear increased amongst the people and many of them gathered in the cave of San Juan de la Pena where a church of Saint John the Baptist was built and where they observed the saintly rites of their fathers.[9] The cave was a symbol of the fight between the Spaniard and the Muslim; it represented a time when Christendom was on the verge of losing itself, but kept striving for the light of the saint to shine on the hopelessness of Islam; for the salt of the earth to preserve the beacon of enlightenment we call the Church. Soon did these huddled believers decide to walk out of the cave and the mountains, and reclaim their lands, never forgetting the cave and its symbolic meaning which resonated in their conscience.[10]

The reconquest of Spain was essential not only for Spaniards, but for the whole of Europe. The Muslim commander who helped take the country, Musa, proclaimed his plan to, like Hannibal, conquer France and Italy, to overthrow the Roman empire of Constantinople, and enter the Vatican and preach against the Trinity.[11]

THE OLD SPANIARD VERSUS THE MODERN SPANIARD

In 2004 Muslim terrorists orchestrated the Madrid train bombings, which took one hundred and ninety one lives and injured one thousand eight hundred people. How did the modern Spaniards deal with such attack? Did they peruse the annals of Spanish history to find what their ancestors did to the Muslims who invaded their nation? No. The present day Spaniards did what any modern minded person of the twenty first century would have done: tolerance.

---

8   See *The Chronicle of San Juan de la Pena*, ch. 3, 4, trans. Lynn H. Nelson
9   *Chronicle of San Juan de la Pena*, ch. 9
10 *Chronicle of San Juan de la Pena*, ch. xi
11 See Gibbon, *Decline and Fall*, vol. v, ch. li, p. 954

CHRISTIANITY IS AT WAR: THE MANIFESTO FOR CHRISTIAN MILITANCY

How did the old Spaniards deal with Islamic terrorism?

In 1275 there was a terrorist group led by the jihadist leader al-Azraq which organized a series of attacks on the Spanish government of Valencia, in which they would kidnap and murder Christians in large numbers. Pedro of Moncayo, Master of the Order of the Knights of the Temple in Spain, was captured in an engagement with this thuggish group; though he escaped, many of his fellow knights were killed. What did the king of Spain, Pedro, do? He didn't force the knights to sensitivity courses; he didn't punish soldiers for discrimination; and he surely did not start a press conference to speak about how beautiful of a religion Islam is. In 1276, Pedro hunted down al-Azraq and his followers and killed them all; he then wrested many of the Islamic fortresses and ousted the Muslims out of Valencia, ending their reign of terror.[12] While many will say that this is "intolerant," the facts of history (which are the greatest enemies to tolerance) testify that Pedro's policies prevented terrorism—as the Laws of Moses prevent pagan tyranny—and established social order in which the native Spaniards could live without fear. As a Spanish chronicler describes it:

> Because of King Pedro's energetic forcefulness, the kingdom thus stood in tranquility and serenity, and the storm of war was transformed into the calm of peace. [13]

The Spanish king of Castile, Alfonso el Sabio, was invited by the Muslim ruler of Rueda Almofalez for a feast. Alfonso, having a knowledge of Muslim perfidy, declined the invitation, but eighteen knights did not, and when they arrived to the gates of Rueda, a body of Muslims dropped boulders upon them, killing all of them.[14] It was an act of terrorism, and it needed to be swiftly responded to. Alfonso called for El Cid to come with him to Castile, but the knight refused, and said that he would not return to Castile until he had "won that of Rueda, and delivered the villainous Moors thereof into his hands, that he might do justice upon them." He cut the food supply coming into the castle, and starved the Muslims till they had no strength to defend themselves. They gave up, alongside Almofalez, and came before Cid and willingly gave themselves as prisoners.[15]

SANCHO GARCES

There was a widowed and pregnant princess named Onenga walking with family through the valley Aibar. Suddenly a mob of Muslims attacked them, killed all the members of her family, and murdered her by thrusting a lance through her belly. A nobleman of the mountains of Aragon was walking pass the valley, contemplating the evils which the Muslims were committing in his country, and of all the suffering which his countrymen were going though, and then he found his weary self face-to-face with the bodies of the butchered royal family. Seeing that the slain princes was with child, he quickly opened her womb and carefully drew out the child, who was miraculously still alive.

---

12 *Chronicle of San Juan de la Pena*, 36
13 *Chronicle of San Juan de la Pena*, 36
14 Chron. Sid. 4.19
15 Chron. Cid. 4.20

PART 16

He dressed the child with shepherd clothing and peasant sandals and brought him before the knights, barons, and people, in the palace of Pamplona. "Barons!" he cried with the child in his hands, "Take this child, take off the clothes he wears, and take him as your king, for he is in truth your lord. You all know that his mother, the queen, was pregnant when she died on that unfortunate occasion. I am the one who passed through the valley where she lay slain and saw a baby's hand reaching out through the wound in its mother's belly. And God be praised! I drew the child out alive and without injury from her womb. My kinsmen and vassals who were then present, stand in witness thereof, and if anyone claims to the contrary, let him enter the field of battle, and I will come to do trial by combat with him."

The challenge was never taken, and all present screamed "Viva, viva!" This child, who was now entering kingship, was Sancho Garces, and he would end up being one of the greatest enemies of the Muslims, and a hero for Spain. He vigorously warred with the occupiers and reconquered Spanish territory from Cantabria to Najera, to the Montes de Oca and Tudela. He erected many castles and fortresses to act as barricades against the Islamic thugs. The area of Pamplona was at this time under Muslim control, but such an occupation would not be tolerated by Garces. He arrived to the city at dawn, gave himself up to God and carried his cross; armed with short spears, and endurably walking solely on foot, he and his men charged with great ferociousness toward the enemy and struck with such intensity that none of the Muslims escaped. He later built many churches and monasteries, and still even at this time, the memory of the Cave of San Juan de la Pena remained in his memory, endowing its monastery with numerous goods.[16]

THE SPANIARDS VERSUS THE KING OF ZARAGOZA

We see before us tens of thousands of Muslim ghazis occupying a lofty hill, and from the distance lies a multitude of Christian knights—fierce, sturdy and hardy—peering beyond a wide valley to their foreign enemies. Their leader, Pedro, watches with a prudent eye across the field; and on a sudden moment another large group of Spaniards and their captain Alfonso fall violently upon the Muslim warriors. The enemy is being crushed, giving the sign to Pedro and his men to advance on the trepidatious jihadists. The two armies kill every Moor they spot—victory is now inevitable. They fight all day, then the sun comes down, evening falling upon both the joy of the Spaniards and the misery of the Muslims. The bodies of the Christians are weary, their muscles are fatigued, but these conditions they neither express nor reveal to the enemy who desperately looks for any sign of weakness. They find no cracks in the ranks of the Spaniards, thirty thousand Muslims lie dead, and so they have no choice: they flee.[17]

---

16 *Chronicle of San Juan de la Pena*, ch. 12
17 *Chronicle of San Juan de la Pena* ch. 18

ALFONSO THE BATTLER

If the crescent was to ever stoop, if the lofty minarets were to ever be forced to bow to Christian power in Spain, the Spaniards were obligated to take the city of Zaragosa, which was then ruled by Almetzalem. As the fighters were besieging the city, Muslims from Tudela launched many attacks upon them as a hindrance to the siege. In the fray came Alfonso the Battler, then king of Aragon.[18] War was his life, and no interest in political or financial gain crept into his mind in this battle.[19]

He ordered three hundred of his cavalry to put an end to the assaults. They were very strategic in their attack: they first began to raid all of the Muslim property near Tudela. The soldiers of Tudela saw this and quickly charged at the three hundred soldiers, leaving all of the people in the city defenseless. It was the same strategy the Hebrews used when they conquered Ai in Canaan. The Christians then entered right into the gates of Tudela without difficulty and established a garrison. When the Muslims returned they were either killed or captured by the waiting Christians. Now with this problem out of the way, the siege of Zaragoza was able to continue without fear of further attacks. A major battle then took place between Almetzalem and the Battler; the victor was the follower of the Cross, and the city was finally surrendered. Alfonso the Battler gathered his men, which included a bishop named Pedro, and continued to reconquer more lands. He wasted Islamic territory all the way to Valencia, destroyed the city of Denia, advanced over Murcia and Almeria, Granada and then to Cordoba, which was the major metropolis for all Muslims in Spain. The king of the city marched out to defend it, but was defeated leaving a multitude of Muslims killed.[20]

RODRIGO VERSUS THE FIVE KINGS

Five Muslim kings plundered Carrion, Vilforado, Saint Domingo de la Calzada, Logrono, and Najara. They killed, pillaged, and kidnapped men and women for slaves. As they were returning back to Africa, the Spanish warrior Rodrigo of Bivar, or El Cid, confronted them with his mastery in arms, and in the name of the Holy Cross, took the five kings, released the captives and returned their stolen belongings as Abraham did when he rescued Lot. After giving his thanks to God, he told his mother that it was not good to keep the five kings, and so with much grace let them go. The Muslim kings were so thankful that they gave Rodrigo tribute and acknowledged themselves to be his subjects.[21] Rodrigo illustrated this same valor when he repulsed the Muslims who were invading Estremadura, taking from it much booty and many prisoners.[22] It is said that this Cid was so just that the Muslims who were governed under him in the city of Zaragoza, "rejoiced in his good speed, liking him well, because he protected them so well that they were safe from all harm."[23]

---

18 *Chronicle of San Juan de la Pena*, ch. 19
19 Warren H. Carroll, *A History of Christendom*, vol. iii, ch. i, p. 18
20 *Chronicle of San Juan de la Pena*, ch. 19
21 Chron. Sid. 1.4, trans. Robert Southey
22 Chron. Sid. 1.4, 1.12, trans. Robert Southey
23 Chron. Cid. 4.17

PART 16

THE MONKS WHO WENT AGAINST THE ISLAMISTS

In the city of Coimbra, monks were so oppressed that they implored King Don Ferrando to liberate and purge off the heretics. For months did the Spaniards fight to besiege the city, but to no avail. The men were quite low on food and on the verge of starvation. Fatigue and weakness came to them, and so the monks conveyed a meeting wherein they said: "Let us now go to the King and give him all the food which we have, both oxen and cows, and sheep and goats and swine, wheat and barley and maize, bread and wine, fish and fowl, even all that we have; for if the city, which God forbid, should not be won by the Christians, we may no longer abide there." The pious monks gave all of their sustenance to the weary troops and thus revived their spirits, enabling them to prevail over the Muslims and reconquer the city back into Christian hands. Ferrando, in gratefulness, offered the monks as much of the city of Coimbra as they desired; the pious men replied that they only wished to have a church. "Of a truth," said the king, "by our Creator, these who desire so little are men of God." The monks gave to him a gift of a crown ornamented with the finest stones, but the king rejected such a present. "Far be it from me that I should take from your Monastery what the good men before me have given to it! Take ye back the crown, and take also ten marks of silver, and make with the money a good cross, to remain with you forever."[24]

THE TRAGEDY OF LOS ARCOS

For the sake of remembrance for all of those saints who have died for the advancement of the Cross, and the toppling of pagan tyranny, this story was written for the dear reader. The Spaniards, in 1195, lost the Battle of Los Arcos in which forty thousand Christians lost their lives.[25] I write this only to show what sacrificial fervor these men had. To fight for something may seem silly to us, but in the long run is the most important (and the only) foundation of our civilization: the prevailing of Christianity over heathenism.

THE RESTORING OF CHURCHES

The restoration of the churches from, or the building of them in, Muslim hands in Spain was most pertinent; for without them they would be no Christendom, there would be a spiritual vacuum which Islam would have loved to fill. The mosque was the monument of Islamic power, and the Muslims built them frequently to fully illustrate this. Shortly after they took Spain, just in the city of Cordoba alone they built six hundred mosques.[26] The only place of worship left for the Christians of Cordoba was half of their principle church, the other half being a mosque.

The Muslims eventually made it fully into a famous mosque, and an addition was made to it by Al-Mansur, "which was entirely built with the materials of demolished churches brought to Cordova on the heads of Christian captives."[27]

---

24 Chron. Sid. 1.15–17
25 *Chronicle of San Juan de la Pena*, ch. 34, see n. 226 of the editor Lynn H. Nelson
26 Gibbon, *Decline and Fall*, vol. v, ch. li, p. 955
27 See Amad Ibn Muhammad al-Maqqari, *History of the Muhammadan Dynasties In Spain*, vol. i, b. i, ch. ii, p. 41, trans. Pascual de Gayangos

CHRISTIANITY IS AT WAR: THE MANIFESTO FOR CHRISTIAN MILITANCY

When the city of Tauste was ruled by the jihadist, King Alfonso the Battler charged right into the metropolis and ousted the Muslims out. Upon victory, he restored the city's church, and in reverence to the place which served as a refuge for his people when Spain was first conquered, he gave the church to the Cave of San Juan de la Pena.[28]

The Christians of Mallorca were oppressed by their Muslim rulers, and the king that wanted to put an end to this was Jaime. He was so fervent about Christianity that he announced his intention of "destroying the Saracen [Muslim] nation and converting it to the faith of the Cross." He prepared without delay his army, marched right into the city, found the Muslim king and seized him by the beard. He then made Mallorca a tributary to the Christian Spanish kingdom of Aragon and established a cathedral there.[29] The cathedral acted as a symbol, that the Muslim was no longer in power in Mallorca. This symbolism is the reason why Muslims destroy churches in the first place. Jaime retook the city of Valencia in 1238, there too did he build many other churches and a cathedral with uncompromising praise to God. He was tenacious in driving the Muslims out with so much conviction that one Spanish chronicler wrote that "he proposed with all his will to persist diligently in the destruction of the lands and kingdoms of Saracens."[30] If King Jaime was alive today, there is no doubt that journalists, troublesome reporters, and psychologists, would smear him as a Christian supremacist. These people do not take into account that in every era of human history, there is always a religion which has supremacy in a land, the question should be not whether a religion has a supremacy, but which religion. The world is better off with Christian supremacy than Islamic supremacy or Buddhist supremacy, and who doesn't agree should leave to Somalia or Bhutan and see how much human life is honored. If Jaime ruled Spain today the country would not be dealing with the Muslim problem it presently has on its hands. Jamie preserved this superiority over the Muslims so well, that the enemy waited for him to be on the verge of death and then attacked. Countless Muslims rushed into Spain and made a massacre. They killed the bishop Sancho, the noble Nuno, and many other barons and nobles. They occupied castles and "caused so much destruction that it is impossible to recount it."[31] The story goes to show that without a king who is intolerant toward evil, and zealous for piety and justice, Spain was unable to defend its nation.

The Muslims conquered Barcelona in 965, reducing the city to complete servility with the common cruelty of Muslims. The Spaniard Borrel immediately gathered an army of nobles, barons, knights, and infantry, in colossal numbers, and with the aid of God, fiercely expelled the wicked Muslims from Barcelona. Borrel rebuilt the monastery of Ripoll in the year 990, it being formerly ruined by the invaders.[32]

The Muslim ruler Zadan Aben Huim was ruling over the Spanish city of Lamego where the Islamists destroyed various churches. King Don Ferrando, with the help of Rodrigo, took

---

28 *Chronicle of San Juan de la Pena*, ch. 19
29 *Chronicle of San Juan de la Pena*, ch. 35
30 *Chronicle of San Juan de la Pena*, ch. 35
31 *Chronicle of San Juan de la Pena*, 35
32 *Chronicle of San Juan de la Pena*, ch. 25

up his cross and marched into the city where he besieged the walls of the heretics, slew many Muslims, and forced the rest to rebuild the churches which Muhammad's followers had brought to ruins.[33] This Rodrigo, would soon be known as El Cid, the infamous knight of Spanish history, who helped a great deal to take back what the Muslims had stolen: the land of Spain. With sword, lance, and horse, Cid and his loyal knights would crush those whom he called "the enemies of God and of the faith."[34]

MUHAMMAD VS ST. JAMES

In the battle for the city Alcocer, the valiant El Cid dispatched three hundred Muslim warriors after a great display of military strategy and endurance. "Blessed be God and all his Saints," cried out Cid, "we have bettered our quarters for both horses and men."[35] With the tumultuous sounds of tambours did the Muslims arrive by the thousands in Alcocer before the stern eyes of the Spanish warriors. The bodies, minds and spirits of these fighters itched for the heat of battle. Pero Bermudez, a companion of Cid, could no longer wait and had such a dire thirst to fight that he took the banner of the Christians, and before charging on his horse, called out to his grand master: "God help you, Cid Campeador [the champion]; I shall put your banner in the middle of that main body; and you who are bound to stand by it—I shall see how you succour it."

Cid beseeched him to come back, but Berumudez simply replied that he would "stop for nothing," and away he spurred to the ranks of the Muslims. The enemy attacked him from all sides; many blows struck him, but none that was able to take his life away. The blades of their weapons could not pierce him, nor could they pull him off his horse—he was a knight, strong in body, fierce in spirit, and zealous in his faith. No longer could the others remain witness, and so did Cid command his three hundred knights to charge; for it is written "there is no greater love, then when a man lays his life for his friends." Their shields went up and their lances were lowered, and off they went, into the fray, riding on robust horses. "Smite them, knights," declared Cid to his men, "I am Ruydiez, the Cid of Bivar!" Shields were pierced and many a horse was seen without a rider in this battle. Their spears ceased not to strike against the tablets of men's breasts, neither did the swords stop when they cut off lives from the earth, and formed puddles of human gore. The intensity was relentless, daggers and spearheads cut through men one after the other. The Muslims cried, "Mohammad!" The Christians, "Saint James!"[36]

We are told by James that "faith, if it hath not works, is dead," (James 2:17) and indeed were these men illustrating the strongest foundation of faith by their bold and valorous actions. They slew many, and in one moment thirteen hundred Muslims lied dead. One jihadist killed the horse of Alvar Fanez, a Spanish knight, and without hesitation Cid killed an enemy horseman, took his horse and gave it to his companion as he said, "Mount, Minaya

---

33 Chron. Sid. 1.14
34 Chron. Cid. 4.15
35 Chron. Sid. 4.4
36 Chron. Cid. 4.7–8; *Song of the Cid*, 1.36, trans. Burton Raffel

CHRISTIANITY IS AT WAR: THE MANIFESTO FOR CHRISTIAN MILITANCY

[brother], for you are my right hand." The will of the Muslims had become disheartened, and they began to make a speedy retreat. From a distance did Cid see Fariz, the despotic Moorish king, and without losing a breath he charged directly at him, mowing down any Muslims who tried to prevent him, struck the tyrant with two blows, and with a third and last blow wounded him so severely that he ran away. Another knight, Martin Antolinez, sunk his sword into the second Islamic king there, Galve, breaking through the metal and piercing the flesh. But it wasn't enough to eliminate him, and he too ran off alongside his weary men. The battle was over, and to God did they give their gratitude. Fifteen Spaniards lost their lives and went into Heaven, a small number compared to the great causalities of the enemy. The spoils of war were taken; the Spaniards even shared much of the goods to the Muslim inhabitants of the city,[37] to express love to their enemies. Cid was seen in a most knightly way: riding on his splendid horse, his chain mail rested on his shoulders, his sword still in hand,[38] and in such a chivalrous disposition he said to his returning men: "We thank our God, high in heaven, that we have conquered, won in such a battle."[39]

TWENTY FIVE CHRISTIANS FACE FIFTEEN THOUSAND MUSLIMS

The Islamists under Abenalfange gathered together the greatest amount of men that they could muster, entered the land of the Christians and stopped in Medinal del Campo where the liaison of Cid, Alvar Fanez, met him. Fanez came with only an infinitesimal number of twenty five horsemen, while Abenalfange was fifteen thousand strong. The odds were against them, they were a few short, but with that faith in God that no man can undermine, did they prevail, forcing Abenalfange to flee with a most ignominious defeat.[40]

THE CRUSHING OF THE CRESCENT

El Cid would go on to take the suburb of Villa Nueva, to conquer Alcantara, and to enter Alcudia where he attacked the Muslims with such relentless strikes that they screamed to Cid, "Peace! Peace!"[41] They begged for quarter at that moment, without thinking that it was they who began the war; it was their people who entered Spain and devastated the land, destroyed many churches, and made great slaughter.

When the Christians fight back, when they bear arms to do away with their enemies, they receive unswerving chastisement from moderns who come in the name of tolerance and free-thinking, when in reality they are but devils who masquerade as doves.

If the Christians never attempted a retake Spain, then we would have never heard of the massacres done by them, and we would be told of how civil the Muslim was.

But since the Christian did counterattack, then all we hear about is how savage he was, and still how wonderful the Muslim conducted himself.

---

37 *Song of the Cid*, 1.40
38 Chron. Cid. 4.8–10; *Song of the Cid*, 1.40
39 Song of Cid, 1.40
40 Chron. Cid. 5.2
41 Chron. Cid. 6.7

PART 16

Academia today is a never ending river of quagmire which comes forth from minds who will forever hate the Church, and will do anything, be it hide or manipulate evidence, or even ally with the Devil himself, to destroy it.

They claim to be for objectivity, call themselves proclaimers of truth, and affirm that one must always analyze history without religious biases.

But they always favor a religion: in the case for Spanish history they have become the eternal friends of Allah, praisers of the Koran, and flatterers of Islamic civilization. While they at the same time unceasingly portray Christendom as the persecutor of Muslims and the enemy to all reason and enlightenment, and the Bible as a violent book. Those who believe them do not have foresight; they refuse to see consequences and end results. Did the Spaniards kill Muslims? Yes, in war to prevent the further expansion of Islam in Spain. If they simply had bent the knee to the Ka'ba, Spain as we know it would have been in the annals of forgotten history—that would have been the consequence of such pacifism. Because they had fought, and continued to strive for a reconquest of their nation, the end result—the consequence—was eventually a liberated Spain.

It is true that when Cid was taking the city of Valencia back to Christian hands he massacred many Muslims,[42] but several facts must first be put into perspective before screaming racism. Valencia was originally a Spanish Christian city which was then stolen by Islamist conquerors; Cid had every moral right to reconquer it. Cid himself said that he wished to take Valencia "to make it Christian once more!"[43] After he took the city, Alvar Fanez said that Cid was now able "to restore the bishopric there,"[44] meaning that the Church was now to be reestablished since the Muslims were now defeated. Furthermore, when the city was finally surrendered, Cid, in the words of one Spanish Chronicler, "did great honor unto them [the Muslims]. ...And he commanded and requested the Christians that they should show great honour to the Moors, and respect them, and greet them when they met: and the Moors thanked the Cid greatly for the honour which the Christians did them, saying that they had never seen so good a man, not one so honourable, nor one who had his people under such obedience."[45] The Muslims, then, lived a peaceful life under the Christian, being of more felicity as opposed to residing under a Muslim ruler. We should have no problem with Muslims living peacefully in society amongst Christians, it is when they rise up to seize Christendom that we should be angered and engage them. Sadly, peaceful existence between Christian and Muslim, at the end of the day, is impossible, since Islam inherently is violently anti-Christian. The Muslims themselves have no problem with butchering believers, and were about to conduct a massacre in Valencia after Cid took the city.

---

42 Chron. Sid. 6.27
43 *Song of the Cid*, 2.72
44 *Song of the Cid*, 2.82
45 Chron. Sid. 7.2, brackets mine

CHRISTIANITY IS AT WAR: THE MANIFESTO FOR CHRISTIAN MILITANCY

EL CID'S SPEECH BEFORE FIGHTING THE MOROCCANS

The Moroccan king Yucef journeyed to Valencia with fifty thousand men to retake the city. "He swept like a storm over my lands," said Yucef of Cid, "believing Jesus Christ puts strength in his hands!"[46] As soon as Cid heard of this coming horde, did he sound the alarm for the walls to be prepared and the castles retired. He gathered together his Christian troops, as well as Muslims who lived under him, and before a multitude of believers he delivered a speech to rally them for battle. Just by reading the words does one sense the vibration of the speaker's soul:

> Friends and kinsmen and vassals, praised be God and holy Mary Mother, all the good which I have in the world I have here in Valencia; with hard labour I won the city, and hold it for my heritage, and for nothing less than death will I leave it. My daughters and my wife shall see me fight, they shall see with their own eyes our manner of living in this land, and how we get our bread. We will go out against the Moors and give them battle, and God who hath thus far shown favour unto us will still continue to be our helper. [47]

The next day Cid took his love Dona by the hand, alongside their daughters, and brought them to a nearby tower from where they saw the marching Moors beating ever so loudly on their drums. His wife was stricken by fear and could hardly contain her emotions. "Fear not," said her husband, "all this is for your good. Before fifteen days are over, if it please God, those tambours shall be laid before you, and shall be sounded for your pleasure, and then they shall be given to the Bishop Don Hieronymo, that he may hang them up in the Church of St. Mary, Mother of God."[48]

The bell for battle was rung, and the sound struck the ears of two hundred knights, signaling to them the time to fight the worshippers of the crescent. "What a great day this is!"[49] exclaimed the jovial Cid, happy to plunge himself into the fray. At the commencement of the battle they all fell fiercely upon the Muslims, smiting and slaying. The followers of the Holy Cross took the victory, cutting down two hundred and fifty of the enemy. This battle was over, but it was not the last. The Muslims were planning on a second incursion, and the Spaniards were ready, with their leader El Cid proclaiming that they would "smite them in the name of the Creator and of the Apostle Santiago."

A BATTLE FOR THE HOLY TRINITY

Three hundred well trained horsemen were to be conveyed for the next fight, and the plan was already established. They were to awaken and eat in the early morning at the cock's crow, come to the Church of Saint Pedro, hear mass, talk amongst themselves, and lastly to take up their horses and fight in the name of the Holy Trinity.[50] It was not a preparation for the body, but the soul. They fought for the Godhead: the union of the Father, Son, and Holy Spirit; it

---

46 The Song of Cid, 2.88
47 Chron. Sid. 7.17
48 Chron. Cid. 18
49 *Song of the Cid*, 2.91
50 Chron. Sid. 7.19

was a theological strike upon the Islamic heresy which wished to stomp upon that sublime belief. Truly this is why the Islamists expanded into Christendom: to convert the world into a universal unitarian kingdom. But their plan failed in the land of Spain—that beacon of Christendom—for men stouthearted in mind and body arose and charged head on upon these expanding apostates. Swords pierced through men's bodies, arrows propelled through flesh, and Cid and his knights in short time eliminated many Moors. "God and Santiago!" he screamed, to uplift the hearts of his men. The enemy ran off, and the knights simply pursued with great endurance. Cid routed the king, Yucef, and struck him three times; but the horse of the tyrant was faster than the blade of the saintly caballero. Fifty thousand Muslims arrived at the beginning of this battle, and only one hundred and four escaped. "Look," said Cid to his wife, "with a bloody sword, and a horse all sweat, this is the way that we conquer the Moors! Pray God that I may live yet awhile for your sakes, and you shall enter into great honour, and they shall kiss your hands."[51]

CHRISTENDOM VS PAGANDOM

The fire of revenge was not extinguished after the Muslims lost this battle, but it expanded to Yucef's brother Bucar, who swore upon the Koran that he would crush Cid and take back Valencia.[52] With tens of thousands of Muslim warriors, hungry for plunder and Christian blood, and twenty nine Muslim kings, Bucar sailed from Morocco to Spain to face his Spanish enemy. A messenger from the Moorish side approached El Cid and told him the options which Bucar presented: peacefully leave Valencia to Islamic hands, or remain and be vanquished by my military strength, and your daughters, your wife, and your self will be captured and tortured. Cid replied with these doughty words filled with faith, Christian valor, and a reference to the Muslims as pagans:

> Go tell their Lord King Bucar I will not give up Valencia to him: great labour did I endure in winning it, and to no man am I beholding for it in the world, save only to my Lord Jesus Christ, and to my kinsmen and friends and vassals who aided me to win it. Tell him that I am not a man to be besieged, and when he does not expect it I will give him battle in the field; and would that even as he has brought with him twenty nine Kings, so he had brought all the Moors of all Pagandom, for with the mercy of God in which I trust, I should conquer them all.[53]

What a blow to the idolaters; for certainly are Muslims a part of the heathen world, and because of this do they subscribe to a tyranny that must be brought to an end. The only entity that will stop such a force for evil, is the greatest force for good: Christendom, and so thus must zealots arise. These Spaniards who fought the Moroccan invaders were filled with holy zealotry, and just look at the difference they had made for Christianity by stopping the Muslims dead in their tracks when they were trying to conquer the earth. They are still striving

---

51 Chron. Sid. 7.20–21; *Song of the Cid*, 2.95
52 Chron. Sid. 7.23
53 Chron. Cid. 8.6

to invade all of humanity, and instead of responding with a crusade, the modern church is responding with nothing but a betrayal to the Cross for an adulterous affair with the Devil, the crescent, and the fickle wants of the masses. Never has a sermon on church diplomacy, grace for all, and building bridges with false religions stopped tyranny; what scares all tyrants is a people who know the Faith, and are willing to die and kill for it.

THE BATTLE COMMENCES AND THE BISHOP KILLS THE HERETICS

The bell was rung in the Spanish camp, and the men were told to be ready; but they were not affrighted, for they had trusted in God and His good fortune, as David did when facing Goliath. The next morning the men approached the enemy camp, even the bishop Hieronymo desired strongly to be involved in the crusade.

He came to Cid and spoke:

> I have said the mass of the Holy Trinity before you. I left my own country and came to seek you, for the desire I had to kill some Moors, and to do honour to my order and to my hands. 54

Imagine to yourself if this bishop lived in our times with such a mindset; mainstream pastors would reject him as an extremist, and many modern Christians would complain that he is "too over the top." When the Muslims saw the Spanish army, numbered over a few thousand, they rushed out of their tents and engaged them. Great skill in hand to hand combat was exemplified by the bishop; he with his lance dispatched two Muslims. The lance broke, but he swiftly unsheathed his sword and slew five more of the enemy. This bishop was like the Levites who were both priests and warriors.

The jihadists tried to kill him, but their blades could not penetrate his armor. This man was truly a warrior priest. El Cid came to the saint's defense and took out seven Moors. So loud and hallowing was the sound of the Muslim drums that no soldier could hear another speak. An African fighter in the midst of the fray, tall and robust, fiercely approached the men, only to be killed by the lance of the knight Felez Munos. Cid pursued one Moor, and when he reached him close enough, he plunged his sword upon him and split his head in two.

Blood inundated the earth, and so many dead lied on the floor that the horses could not walk without stepping on them. The Spaniards eventually smote the Moors with so efficient and viscous an attack that they began to flee. Cid peered on Bucar who now was riding on his horse. He made his pursuit, aimed, and threw his sword, landing it on the tyrant's shoulders, wounding him severally, but not fatally. Though Bucar was not killed, nevertheless the Christians won, having killed seventeen thousand Muslim troops, and seventeen of the twenty nine kings who came. "God be praised!" proclaimed Cid, "once I was poor, but now am I rich in lands and in possessions, and in gold and in honour. And Moors and Christians both fear me. Even in Morocco, among their Mosques, do they fear lest I should set upon

---

54 Chron. Cid. 8.7

them some night. Let them fear it! I shall not go to seek them, but here will I be in Valencia, and by God's help they shall pay me tribute."[55]

The victory was an affront to, and prevention of, the further expansion of Islam's militant unitarianism. It was a triumph for the Cross, a victory for Christian Orthodoxy, and a great example that truly the end of Islam will be at the hands of the Church Militant.

A MUSLIM REALIZES THE TRUTH OF THE TRINITY AND REJECTS ISLAM

There is a story which illustrates this war between the Spanish Christians and those who hated the Trinity. There was a Muslim named Alfaraxi, who worked for Cid in Valencia. One day he approached the great knight and expressed his realization that the Trinity was true, and that the teachings of Muhammad were most deceptive. "And now," he said to Cid, "Sir, thinking in my heart concerning the law in which I have lived, I find that I have led a life of great error, and that all which Mahommed the great deceiver gave to the Moors for their law, is deceit: and therefore, Sir, I turn me to the faith of Jesus Christ, and will be a Christian and believe in the Catholic faith." There was great rejoicing at the sight of seeing a lost sheep be found by his Redeemer. The next day the warring bishop baptized him, and he was then given the name Dil Diaz.[56]

It was this convert to Islam who would partake in the burial and funeral of Cid, and after this, he for years took care of his family.[57]

When Cid lay on his death bed, he sat up and declared this short and pious prayer: "Lord Jesus Christ, thine is the power and the kingdom, and thou art above all Kings and all nations, and all Kings are at thy command. I beseech thee therefore pardon me my sins, and let my soul enter into the light which hath no end."[58] To esteem God as above all kings is an utter assault on all tyrants; and indeed do the words fit those devout knights—they took up their Cross, crushed the slaves of the Old Serpent, and advanced Christendom over the cruel wiles of heathen oppression.

He died as all men do, but his legacy, and his desire for a Christian Spain, lived on. His companion Alvar Fanez would war with an army of tens of thousands of African Muslims, led by the same Bucar, who sailed to Spain to retake Valencia. With their great archers and warriors, they came with their bent on tyranny and bloodshed, superstition and heresy. They battled for idolatry, and the Christians for freedom from the despotism which comes with paganism. In the midst of all the fighting, it is said that the Muslims perceived before them a multitude of seventy thousand heavenly knights, glowing with white light; and leading them was a knight riding a horse with a bloody cross, who bore in one hand a white banner, and in the other a sword seemed to be of fire. And such a force, we are told, made a great

---

55 Chron. Cid. 8.7–9
56 Chron. Sid. 10.16
57 Chron. Cid. 11.8–9, 11.15
58 Chron. Cid. 11.6

amount of slaughter on the Islamic hordes, winning the victory for Spain.[59] and ultimately, for Christendom itself.

THE MUSLIMS OVERRUN SPAIN, AND A CRUSADE IS COMMENCED

In 1109, a great disaster struck upon Spain like a nightmare which continues in the mind, even after one wakes up. The Moorish warlord Ali ben Yusef marched in person right into the Spanish city of Talvera, ravaged the countryside around Toledo and then directly attacked the city itself. The Spaniards, under the command of Alvar Fanez, battled vigorously against the heretics as the aged Archbishop Bernard and the clergy, alongside the women and children, prayed for triumph. The heathens did not flee, but brought a formidable force armed with battering rams, siege engines, and ladders. Fanez made a sudden charge and put such contrivances to the flames, and the Muslims finally fled, but not empty-handed; they took multiple towns and even the city of Madrid.[60]

The jihadist advance, like a disease unable to be purged, continued on indefatigably, and in 1115 the areas of Lisbon, Santarem and Porto, had fallen into their hands. Muslim warships executed frequent attacks upon the coast of Galicia, and in this same year of 1115, they had been almost deserted.[61]

Again did the Moors gather, as flies upon honey, around Barcelona, where they assaulted the Catalan capitol. The Spaniards arrived—they did not come with grace or with messages of reconciliation and "building bridges," as modern pastors would do, but with the sword, and with unfailing souls did they defeat the warring heretics. Alfonso the Battler called for help from France, and many a French knight answered the call. They commenced a mighty offensive against the city of Zaragosa, the northernmost outpost of Islam in Europe and the principle base of the Moors in Spain since their conquest of the country.

In 1118 the Battler, along with his French knights, laid siege on Zaragosa, and when the Muslims were in a state of desperation, Islamic aid came for their support. But when these had arrived they saw around them a number of Christians exceeding their own. It only took ten days for the Muslims to give up the city. This was the greatest victory for the Reconquest since Alfonso VI retook Toledo in 1085. Thanks to these significant advancements, the Battler established the Spanish region of Aragon as a major kingdom in Spain, though there were some parts of it where the green flags of Islam which bore the crescents of Allah still stood.[62]

Amongst those who fought was the French warrior Viscount Gaston V, who was a veteran of the First Crusade. This brings another fact to our attention: the Reconquest of Spain was a crusade unto itself, very similar to the crusades for the Holy Land. In fact, after the Battle of Zaragosa, Pope Gelasius II blessed the war of Spain as a crusade; and in the Council

---

59 Chron. Sid. 11.7–9
60 Warren H. Carroll, *A History of Christendom*, vol. iii, ch. i, p. 19
61 Warren H. Carroll, *A History of Christendom*, vol. iii, ch. i, p. 19
62 Warren H. Carroll, *A History of Christendom*, vol. iii, ch. i, pp. 23–24; ch. ii, p. 47

of Reims, Alfonso the Battler and Alfonso VII of Castile requested from the Pope aid for the Spanish Crusade.[63]

The Battler would in the next two years efficiently secure control over the Ebro River valley, the heartland of northeastern Spain; he restored the city and the archdiocese of Tarragona, and vanquished the Muslim warlord Ibrahim in Calatayud, with the help of the French cavilers.[64]

THE CHRISTIANS OF GRANADA CALL FOR LIBERATION

The persecuted Christians who lived in Granada called for liberation, and in answering to this plea Alfonso the Battler came ready to free the enslaved saints. He marched with four thousand horsemen and fifteen thousand foot soldiers through Muslim territory that no Spanish soldiers had trod upon for more than four hundred years. He stopped in Valencia, now Muslim controlled, and conveyed the call to join him in the war to liberate Granada from the heretics.

Many joined him in his army, in which all men vowed never to abandon one another. They secured the Pena Cadiella Pass south of Valencia, and from there they pushed forward fighting through Murcia and then Baza. As they marched their ranks swelled with men who aspired to see the Cross replace every crescent idol, as Gideon did to the lunar idols of the Midianite invaders of Israel. With an army now of fifty thousand he charged into Granada; but lamentably no Christian banner flew over the city. Granada would not be taken until the fifteenth century by Ferdinand and Isabel. Though this does not mean that the Battler ceased to try to rescue his fellow Christians. Before he retreated he rescued ten thousand Christians of all ages out of the tyrannical Muslim Granada region of Spain.[65] We must ponder to ourselves as to why the Battler has not been given the credit of being a freer of slaves when he rescued more subjugated people than any American abolitionist.

"FOR THE HONOR OF ALL CHRISTENDOM"

The Battler would later make his way to Muslim controlled Fraga and conducted a siege, though it was very well fortified. In the heat of summer Ibn Ghaniya came to the Battler with a great army of Moors and a blood battle ensued. The Christians were overpowered; a bishop named Guido of Lescar was captured and forced by torture to convert to Islam, but he never capitulated. The Battler, alongside sixty one loyal men, continued to fight as he lost ground and soon he saw all around him scimitars and turbans—he was outnumbered and trapped. Desperation came upon the Christians, and with great incandescence and fury they raised their swords and struck with mighty hands, tearing through their enemies' flesh to free themselves from their crescent blades.

---

63 Warren H. Carroll, *A History of Christendom*, vol. iii, ch. i, p. 23; ch. ii, p. 40
64 Warren H. Carroll, *A History of Christendom*, vol. iii, ch. i, p. 24
65 See Warren H. Carroll, vol. iii, ch. ii, pp. 47–48

✝ CHRISTIANITY IS AT WAR: THE MANIFESTO FOR CHRISTIAN MILITANCY

Only twelve of the Christian warriors survived, including the Battler, who grew so ferocious with rage on what took place that he was found attacking Muslims loading ships on the Ebro River with the heads of his slain men. Before he died he left in a will his last command that the Spanish Crusade should never end until it was fully accomplished, regardless of its difficulties and hardships. His body was buried in the monastery-castle of Montearagon, which he had previously built "for the honor of all Christendom."[66]

It is remarkable to read how central the war over Spain was to the crusaders who were fighting with the heretics in the Middle East. In 1146, thirteen thousand Christian warriors from Germany, England, France and Flemings, came to Portugal to help the king Alfonso Henriques fight off the Moors out of the city of Lisbon. The Crusaders not only believed that the retaking of Spain would enforce the kingdom of Jerusalem, but that it would also advance Christian power over Islamic expansion. The Crusades are thus inseparable from the war over Spain.

Alfonso VII of Castile, in 1147, recaptured Almeria from the Muslims with the help of both French and Italian warriors, and after a seventeen week siege the Portuguese, with the assistance of French, German, Flemish, and English knights, took Lisbon.[67]

The north of Spain was purged of Moorish power later in 1148, when Count Ramon Berenguer IV of Barcelona, with the help of the Templars and Genoese warriors, took Tortosa at the mouth of the Ebro River after six months of fighting and besieging.[68]

In 1157, a new sect of Islam arose called the Almohads; they inspired a fiery zeal to conquer all of Spain and left to that country by the droves from North Africa. They entered Andalusia and prevailed over a garrison which the Spanish established on a pathway which they had named Despenaperros, "the Pass of the Overthrow of the Infidel Dogs."

THE KNIGHTS OF CALATRAVA

Alphonso the Fighter, king of Castile, in about the year 1147, took the fortress of Calatrava from the Moors, with the help of Templars.

In 1157, when the Spanish Crusade had so far been four hundred and thirty five years old, the Moors began their preparation for seizing the fortress from Don Sanchez, the successor of Alphonso. This king, being fearful of the coming Muslim horde, made a proclamation that whoever would defend the fortress of Calatrava, would be given it. No man accepted the offer, but one humble Cistercian monk named Don Diego Velasquez, one Raimundo, his abbot who knew nothing of warfare, and the dependents of their monastery of Fitero, valiant peasants and lay brothers who consisted of hundreds of men from Toledo, took up arms for the fortress' defense.

Many others offered money, horses and arms to the militia. Raimundo established the fighting men into a religious confraternity under the Cistercian order. It was now a monastic

---

66 See Warren H. Carroll, *A History of Christendom*, vol. iii, ch. ii, p. 49
67 Carroll, *A History of Christendom*, vol. iii, ch. ii, p. 65
68 Carroll, *A History of Christendom*, vol. iii, ch. ii, p. 70

military order. This army of saints, whose names have been forgotten in the realms of whispered history, had within their souls that valiancy and intrepidity granted by God to His warriors of the Cross. Though they were no knights, the king accepted their willingness. Their fearlessness was to the worry of the Muslims, who had, in fear of the humble Christians, abandoned their mission. The saints who defended the fortress would, because of this victory, be given the title of the Knights of Calatrava, the core of which was the religious group made by Raimundo, and they would retake various lands from the Muslims which were previously inhabited by the Spaniards, such as Favera, Maella, Macalon, Valdetormo, La Fresueda, Valderobbes, Calenda, Aquaviva, and Ozpipa.

But this precious order of civilization, this holy group of Christendom, nearly met its end in the battle of Alarcos in 1159, in which the Moors of Africa almost annihilated the Knights of Calatrava, alongside those of Alcantara and St. Jago-of-the-Sword.[69]

THE HUNCHBACK WHO DEFEATED THE MUSLIMS

In Avila to the north of Spain, a fascinating character arose to lead a penetrating attack upon the Moors: the hunchback Sancho Jimenez, whose body did not prevent him from riding upon the horse as swift as the piercing sound of a sword being unsheathed in the midst of a quarrel. He became commander of the Avila militia and led a raid all the way to Sevilla, right in the heart of Andalusia amongst the wolves of the crescent. Raid after raid, fight after fight did this man, whose body was deemed defected but his heart was of steal, lead and win, until he was finally slain in battle, after leading twenty five raids against the Muslims.[70]

ST. PETER PASCAL, A MAN WHO GAVE EVERYTHING, BUT GAINED ETERNITY

How wonderful is it, to peruse the annals of Christendom's history and behold those events which transcend the modern mind; how delighted is the man who comprehends the love of the saints, who suffered and endured the torments of the Muslim despots. What atheist or progressive of our time, would be willing to commit to the sacrifices of Saint Peter Pascal, Bishop of Jaen? After giving away all that he had for the redemption of captives and for the care of the impoverished, he was himself taken prisoner by the Turks.

To pay for his ransom, the clergy and people of his diocese sent to him a sum of money. But he did not use it for his own liberation, he instead gave it to the suffering women and children around him, in fear that they would lose their faith on account of the oppression they had been enduring under their Muslim tormentors. He remained a captive of the Turks until he was called home by his Father in Heaven, and made a martyr by his captors in the year 1300.[71] Some may say that their end was not victorious, since they were killed by their enemies. But this thinking only works for the earthly, and not the heavenly, mind. For any-

---

69 Chateaubriand, *The Genius of Christianity*, part iii, 5.2, trans. Charles I. White; see also Carroll, *A History of Christendom*, vol. iii, ch. ii, p. 63; ch. iii, p. 117
70 Carroll, *A History of Christendom*, vol. iii, ch. iii, p. 117
71 Chateaubriand, *The Genius of Christianity*, part iii, 6.2, trans. Charles I. White.

thing we say, death is the ultimate test. St. Peter Pascal gave everything, but gained eternity. For he had within him the perfect expression of love. "Greater love has no one than this, than to lay down ones life for his friends." (John 15:13)

GERALD THE FEARLESS

In 1165 one arose who exemplified the warrior spirit of Christianity: Gerald, called Sempavaor, the Fearless. From 1165 to 1166, the Fearless took back the lands of Trujillo in Extremadura, Evora in Portugal, then Montanchez and Serpa. In the spring of 1169, Gerald the Fearless captured Budajoz, the capital of Extremadura, but he could not take the city's citadel and so called on his lord Afonso Henriques for help. Afonso came himself for such a cause, and with the Fearless, took the citadel and eliminated all Islamic resistance.

Lamentably, the work of Gerald the Fearless received the kiss of betrayal when Fernando II made a treaty with the Almohad caliph which, while recognizing Christian possession of the cities of Extremadura, guaranteed Muslim control of Badajoz. This wicked treason unsettled the soul of Gerald so painfully that he would eventually abandon his allegiance from Spain and join the Muslims, who would later murder him. Afonso Henriques, in 1179, became Portugal's first king, being called by the Pope, "the intrepid destroyer of the enemies of the Christian name and the energetic defender of the Christian faith."[72]

THE MUSLIMS WANT TO CONQUER ROME, AND CRUSADES ARE CALLED

In 1211 the Almohad mujahideen left Morocco and went into Spain where they ensued a siege to the castle of Salvatierra, succeeding after fifty one days by executing constant attacks by siege weapon, and forcing the Spanish to starve and thirst. So filled with lamentations were the Spaniards that the archbishop Rodrigo de Rada of Toledo said:

> That castle is the castle of salvation, and its loss is the gaining of glory. Our people weep for it, and burst the chains binding their arms. Their zeal inspires us all. [73]

The archbishop de Rada left immediately to France to rally the people there to come and fight in the Spanish Crusade. They marched to a land called the Pass of the Overthrow of the Infidel, and then Alfonso VII with a small force hit hard the Muslims and took three Moorish castles. The Pope, Innocent III, also gave aid to the Spanish Crusade, rallying all those in France and Spain to support the war with the Moors. But most of the French, complaining of the shortage of food and cruel heat, would soon return back to their homes, leaving the Spaniards to fight for themselves.[74]

The Moorish chieftain, En-Nazir, was the master of Morocco and ruler over a part of Spain, and so filled with pride was he, that he cruelly said that he would soon charge into Rome—and to use his own words—"to purify the Church in a blood bath." The Pope, Innocent III, ordered for prayers to be said throughout Christendom, and for all Christians to take

---

72 Carroll, *A History of Christendom*, vol. iii, ch. iii, pp. 117–119
73 Carroll, *A History of Christendom*, vol. iii, ch. v, pp. 176–177
74 See Carroll, *A History of Christendom*, vol. iii, ch. v, pp. 177–179

up arms for a crusade in Spain. But many Christians were too occupied fighting amongst themselves, and the Spaniards were left to fend for themselves at Las Navas.

THE BISHOP WHO SAVED THE KING

In the year 1212, at Las Navas, the Christians crushed the Moors, preventing them from further advancing north of Andalusia and Granada and taking what they had lost to the Spaniards up to that point. The victory caused such a stir of enthusiasm across Europe that many men imagined that the Moorish threat had been given a permanent wound. When the Spanish Christians were blocked from entering the Pass by Moorish defenses, it is said that they were guided around them by a certain shepherd who was never seen again afterward.

Under a starry midnight sky these men of Spain congregated, accepted the holy Eucharist—of which Christ declared, "Except ye eat the flesh of the Son of man, and drink his blood, ye have no life in you" (John 6:53)—they observed Mass and heard a sermon from Archbishop de Rada, and then with arms fit for war and hands callous for the most brutal of combat, they took hold of their weapons. Before the Moors they appeared, face to face; for all the day the holy fray went on, with bodies pierced by lances, limbs and flesh lacerated by swords, and skulls crushed by maces. Few arrows were shot for the men quarreled so close, but scores of Spaniards were amongst the slain. So many Christians had fallen; the king, Alfonso VIII, looked around and his eyes were made sore by the sight of how much blood was swallowed by the earth. Hope was sapped from his soul, and at that moment he knew within himself that his finite life was soon to enter eternity. He did not do what Saul did, but prepared to fight to the death; his sword was ready, his mind stoic, his soul prepared. But lo, suddenly an army charged upon the Muslims, led by Archbishop de Rada. With glory they bore a painting of the Blessed Virgin Mary as they overpowered the followers of the Serpent; the archbishop prevailed over the Moors as the Shepherd defends His flock with mighty staff from ravening wolves.[75]

FIVE COURAGEOUS MONKS

In 1220, there came five Franciscan friars to Spain, not to protest against the Spaniards but to combat with the truth and the armor of Light the heresy of Islam. They arrived at Seville, entered the mosque and began to preach against the Koran. They were attacked and sent to the royal palace. "Who are you?" asked the Muslim king. "We belong to the regions of Rome." "And what are you doing here?" "We have come to preach faith in Jesus Christ to you, so that you will renounce Muhammad, that wicked slave of the devil, and obtain everlasting life like us."

The king was ignited with great fury and quickly ordered the monks to be beheaded. The Franciscans rejoiced and were glad, for great was to be their reward in Heaven. The Muslim then took pity on them, and tried to persuade them through gifts to renounce their statement. "May your money go to perdition with you!" was their reply. They were chained and thrown into the top story of a tower, but still their spirit was not wounded. They cried

---

75 See Carroll, *A History of Christendom*, vol. iii, ch. v, pp. 177–179; Englebert, *St. Francis of Assisi*, ch. ix, p. 125

out from the top of their prison to those down below that "Mohammad was an impostor." They were then placed inside of the public prison where they began to preach to the jailers and fellow prisoners.

They were brought before the king again, and were given the choice between Italy or Morocco. "Do what pleases you," they said, "and may God's will be done!" They were shipped off to Morocco where they were made to go before Amir al-Muminin Yusuf ruled in Africa in the king's name. "Who are you?" he asked the friars. "We are disciples of Brother Francis, who has sent his friars throughout the world to teach all men the way of truth." "And what is this way?" With such words are we greatly reminded of Pontius Pilate asking Jesus, "What is truth?" One of the friars, Brother Otho, began to proclaim the Nicene Creed, declaring the Trinity in a land ruled under the Arian heresy.

"It is surely the devil who speaks by your mouth," vociferously said Yusuf. They were tortured for the entire evening. Their flesh was cut open by whips, they were dragged by the throat across sharp pebbles, and had boiling oil and vinegar poured on their lacerated bodies. As they suffered such pain, one told the other to endure for Christ. When morning came, they were asked by Yusuf if they still hated the Koran, and they proclaimed that "there is no other truth than the holy Gospels." They were threatened with death, but still the poor friars persisted. "Our bodies are in your power," they declared, "but our souls are in the power of God." The executioner came with the sword, and they bent their necks to receive their crowns of glory. Their heads were then brought like trophies to be seen by the women present.[76]

JAMES THE CONQUERER

There arose a man of great strength and charisma named James, who would advance the Cross over the crescent so greatly that he would receive the appellation, "the Conquerer." He declared his intention to recapture the Spanish Balearic islands, which had been dictated under the cruel hands of Muslims for centuries. With a hundred and fifty-five ships, one thousand five hundred crusading knights and fifteen thousand foot soldiers, James sailed to the island of Majorca.

Armed with a sturdy body and strategic abilities, he went swiftly into the fight. His best general was slain in the heat of battle, but with his ferociousness he led many attacks which broke down the Moorish defenses. They set their eyes on the island's principle city, Palma, and with admirable allegiance vowed that none of them would leave the mission unless for severe injury. In 1229 a storm of Spanish warriors swept through the city, and the entire island was now finally in Christian hands.

In 1233, with the approval of the Pope, James the Conquerer broke right into Valencia, which had been taken by the Muslims after the time of El Cid, with only one hundred and twenty knights. He was driven back by the Muslims and then got amorously distracted by the softer gender—his wife Violante.

---

76 Englebert, *St. Francis of Assisi*, ch. xiii, pp. 178–180

But in 1236 James resisted the desires of the marriage bed for the heat of battle, and departed from the loving arms of Violante for Valencia. James rode with one hundred and thirty knights and two thousand foot soldiers. He seized from the Muslims the area of Puig de Cebolla (Onion Hill) and upon it built fortifications. He made his way to Aragon and left behind him a small garrison under the command of a knight named Entenza.

Then came the swarms of Muslims ready for battle, their ranks consisting of six hundred cavalry and forty thousand foot. Entenza went up against them with fifty knights and a thousand infantry, and miraculously prevailed over the mighty army. James returned and an incursion upon Valencia was finally going to begin. The Muslims arrived with an attempted offer of all the province of Valencia north of the city, much tribute and a palace. But such a proposition was firmly rejected. James declared that he would "have both the hen and the chickens."

He conveyed the siege weapons and was joined by valiant knights from England and France who swelled his forces to sixty thousand warriors. The vigorous men made a full scale attack. Melee and scuffle was all one could see, cries of anguish and rage all clouded the senses as the sounds of striking blades pierced the ears. Muslim archers shot their missiles which ripped apart many a man. A Muslim skilled in the art of the bow landed an arrow into James' face, and as one would think that victory for Islam would be made by such good aim, the Spaniards and their leader the Conquerer never capitulated. Rigorous was their assault and with untiring hands they continued their strikes, blow after blow, with their heavy hands and sharp weapons—with their undying Faith and strong conviction. The Muslims could bear no more—Valencia belonged to the Christians.[77]

SAN FERNANDO AND THE FIGHT FOR CORDOBA

In that same year, a group of Spanish Christians independently took control of one of the two fortified parts of the city of Cordoba, and knowing they needed reinforcements, called for the assistance of one San Fernando III, the Christian king of Castile and Leon. As a bird of prey vigorously strikes a serpent, Fernando journeyed to the city, enduring all of its flooding rivers and mud-bound roads. It was in this great city that so many martyrs were executed for refusing the Muslim religion; it was in Cordoba where the Muslims built the largest mosque in Spain, and it was this same place where the Moors made their capital after they conquered Spain in 711. Now was the infamous city going to be taken, now were its churches going to be allowed to thrive, now was the sword of the Christian about to descend upon the armor of the Moor who for so long had shed the blood of the saints! The Muslims, under the command of Ibn Hud, swarmed against the Spaniards but soon they withdrew after enough combat. A wave of Spaniards reinforced the siege and in time the Moors gave up the city. The Christians triumphantly entered, went to the great mosque of Cordoba—built upon the skulls of the saints and made powerful by the despotism of the Koran—took off its adorning crescent and replaced the idol with the Holy Cross as Gideon threw down the crescents of the Midian-

---

77 Carroll, *A History of Christendom*, vol. iii, ch. vi, pp. 219–221

ites. San Fernando proclaimed the victory by declaring Christ "the conquerer of Cordoba."[78] Those past martyrs of Cordoba could now rest in their city, purged of the heretics.

San Fernando III commanded a siege against Jaen, a city made of stone and well-fortified with mighty fortresses. At his side stood the valiant Pelayo Perez Correa, adorned with the flowing white robe bearing the red cross of the Order of Saint James. They pressed the Muslims hard and their leader, Muhammad "the Red" of Granada, gave up the city under the condition that the Moors would keep Granada. Fernando agreed, allowing the Muslims to form the Kingdom of Granada, a principality which would be to the misery of the Spaniards in later years.[79]

San Fernando III accomplished one of the greatest feats made in the Reconquista: he regained the rich and populous metropolis of Seville. As a result, the fighting was brought back to the southern coast of Spain to where the Muslims entered when they began their initial conquest five hundred years before. In 1246 he came with three hundred knights led by the Masters of Santiago and Calatrava, alongside five hundred Moorish warriors.

But his councilors advised that he first take the towns surrounding the city and the Moorish strong points. He consented while ordering a naval fleet to block Moorish ships from entering the city from Seville. It was in this event that Fernando founded the Castilian navy, which would in time become the world's most powerful. It was here that the ships of Khittim spoken of by Daniel the prophet, began to arise. He invaded and took Alcala de Rio, forcing its three hundred defending Muslim ghazis to flee. Twenty six Spanish ships, with their admiral Bonifaz holding up an image of the Blessed Virgin Mary, sailed down the river Guadalquivir, and crushed thirty Moorish Ships. San Fernando declared a vow that he would never give up the siege on Seville, until the city was made absent of Muslim power, a hope which he believed would be fulfilled by the will of the Almighty.

In his camp he erected three small chapels all dedicated to Mary the Mother of God. With such piety flourishing through these mens' hearts, with such wills unable to be overpowered, they made their defenses great and their coming offense as sharp as the seas which broke down Pharaoh's armies. Ships protected the catapults which Pelayo Perez Correa planned to utilize. They soon attacked the suburbs of Gelves and Triana. Ten thousand men, soldiers for Allah, made a sudden charge to counterattack the Spaniards—the rightful owners of the city. San Fernando with his band of warring saints rushed to a bridge which hovered over the Guadaira River, and ordered two knights—Lorenzo Suarez and Garci Perez de Vargas—to most firmly hold the bridge with their men. These Christians did not stand and wait to be lambs sent to the slaughter; they executed a tenacious charge upon the Muslims who were now advancing to the bridge. They slew three thousand Moors and drove them back into the city.

---

78 See Carroll, *A History of Christendom*, vol. iii, ch. vi, pp. 222–223
79 See Carroll, *A History of Christendom*, vol. iii, ch. vi, p. 246

Many months passed and many battles were fought. San Fernando stood in one of his small chapels, and as he prayed to God, Admiral Bonifaz manned a great ship of war upon the strong waters of the river amidst a clamorous battle where Muslim catapults shot up missiles which came crashing down upon Spanish garrisons fighting on land. With oars pushing through the flowing waters and sails guiding the ship through the sharp winds, Bonifaz rammed the pontoon bridge connecting Seville and Triana with two terrifying ships. The bridge snapped and became useless, and there was heard on that sudden moment a great cry of victory amongst the Spaniards.

In 1248 the cruel sun's heat inflicted all men in the struggle, both Spanish and Moorish, and so troubling was it that Muslims left the field to find comfort as opposed to dealing with the sword of the Spanish warrior, Garci Perez de Vargas. The Moors approached Fernando with negotiations, but were received with these scorning words: "Toda la ciudad, libre y quita." "The whole of the city liberated, and you gone." The Moors agreed to leave the city of Seville within a month, and the phrase of Fernando became the standard terms of victorious Spaniards to surrendering Muslims. Over one hundred thousand Muslims left Seville, and when the Spaniards entered they took the chief mosque, teared down its crescent idols, made it into a cathedral, and within it observed Mass with the Virgin Mary's triumphal carriage as the altar. On the accomplishment of the Christians we are given the words of one Spanish Chronicler:

> O grand and noble city, so strong and well-populated and defended with such heroism and valor, only a saint could have taken and conquered you! [80]

All of the fighting which the Christians had done were realized to have bore much fruit, for by the mid-thirteenth century the Muslims' power was only over the region of Granada.[81]

On June 25, 1250, San Fernando declared publicly his gratitude to God and to his loyal men:

> Remember the great benefits, the great favors, the great gifts, the great honors, and the great successes that He Who is the origin and fountainhead of all good, has done and shown to all Christendom and especially to us of Castile and Leon, in our days and the time of Don Fernando King of Castile and Leon. ...Understand and know how these benefits were manifested and accomplished, against Christians and against Moors, and not because of our merits, but out of His great goodness and mercy, and because of the merits and prayers of Holy Mary whom we all serve, and the aid she gave us with her blessed Son, and because of the merits of St. James, whose standard and insignia we bear, who always helps us to victory and through our efforts with the aid and counsel of Don Alfonso our first-born son, and Don Alfonso our brother, and our other sons, and with the aid and counsel of other nobles and our loyal vassals both Castilian and Leonese, we have conquered all Andalusia, in service to

---

80 See Carroll, *A History of Christendom*, vol. iii, ch. vi, pp. 246–249
81 Kamen, *The Spanish Inquisition*, ch. i, p. 3

God and the expansion of Christendom, more fully and decisively than the conquest of any other king.

On the next year, the Christians managed to retake Portugal from Moorish power, leaving the Muslims with only Granada and the land around the Rock and Straits of Gibraltar. Fernando aspired to bring the fight into the Muslims' own territory in North Africa; but by now he was past fifty, his body not as hardy and tenacious as it used to be. In May of 1252 he put on his finest clothes, confessed his sins before God and implored his son Alfonso to solidly continue the reconquest of his country. As he lay on his death bed, it is said that he saw Heaven before his eyes; he ordered a candle to be lit and when the midnight hour came, his last breath departed.

PRINCE SANCHO AND HIS TRAITOROUS FATHER

A most gloomy event took place in Spain, in 1275: an army from Morocco landed at Tarifa near Gibraltar. Fernando de Cerda died as he marched to his nation's defense. The Moroccan sultan Abu Yusuf met in person the Moor Muhammad II, ruler of Granada, and made an allegiance with him. A Castilian army led by Nuno Gonzalez de Lara came head to head with the invaders, but they soon tasted the bitter herb of defeat, with Lara being amongst the slain.

The Muslims overran and captured Algeciras and Gibraltar, and sent a numerous number of jihadists toward Castile. The seventeen year old prince Sancho, son of King Alfonso X of Castile, with memories of how the Spanish heroes of old broke down the heathen, appealed to the older and experienced Crusader James of Aragon for his help. The veteran did not hesitate, and sent a thousand cavalry and five thousand infantry to the aid of Sancho.

The young princely warrior managed to cut off Abu Yusuf's communications with Morocco, and after numerous months passed, the sultan agreed to surrender and go off to Morocco. It is no wonder that James gained the name "the Fierce." Sadly his father, Alfonso X, was not as zealous, for he would actually make an alliance with Abu Yusuf of Morocco. And when this Muslim arrived in Spain Alfonso X deplorably pawned his crown to him for extra funds to maintain his armies in Andalusia. Sancho repulsed Abu Yusuf from Cordoba, and for his patriotism he was rewarded with the cursing of his father who call called him and his brothers: "traitors to God and Us and Spain." When Sancho laid dying of tuberculosis in 1295, he deemed his illness a curse from God for breaking the Fourth Commandment.[82]

SANCHO AND HIS TRAITOROUS BROTHER

In 1292, Sancho the Fierce, with his wife Maria de Molina, designed a plan to invade Tarifa, a city facing Morocco. Battle ensued with the Christians coming out as the victors. Treachery came in, and the brother of Sancho, Juan, committed the sin of his father Alfonso and joined the Muslims in besieging Tarifa. Juan took the son of his brother Guzman and threatened that if he did not give up Tarifa to the Muslims he would murder the young boy. Guzman

---

82 Carroll, *A History of Christendom*, vol. iii, ch. vii, pp. 301–302; ch. viii, p. 318

looked upon the enemy and threw hard his sword at them and continued the battle to defend Tarifa. The Moors and the treasonous Juan left, but before they did they martyred Guzman's son. The next year, after Sancho died, Guzman was told by his Regent to surrender Tarifa to the Moors, only to refuse and stay loyal to the Reconquest, keeping Tarifa in Christian hands.[83]

ROBERT THE BRUCE AND DOUGLAS THE BLACK GO ON CRUSADE

Robert the Bruce had a longing for crusading against the Muslims, but he was prevented from going to the Holy Land by the rapacious Edward Longshanks. And as he lay dying on his bed, he told his companion James "the Black" Douglas, to take his heart after his death and carry it into battle against the Muslims, and then to the Church of the Holy Sepulcher. Douglas remained obedient to his wish.[84]

In 1330 Douglas sojourned to Spain with Robert's heart in a silver case around his neck, to assist the Spanish Crusade and fulfill his promise. He marched to Teba de Ardales alongside the ranks of five hundred Portuguese knights and besieged it. The Moorish commander Osmis rushed in to strike; Alfonso XI pursued him, leaving the knights and Douglas to defend the crossing of the Guada Teba River. Douglas did not wait on the Moors to arrive; he instead aggressed against them, advancing himself deep inside Moorish ranks. He saw the knight, William Sinclair of Roslin, a fellow Scot, surrounded by the enemy, and to him did Robert rush, carrying his king's heart and crying out, "A Douglas! A Douglas! I follow or die!" Slash after slash did his body receive, until he was martyred by five deep wounds. But the battle was won and the Muslims retreated.[85]

THE CHRISTIANS RETAKE THE FORTRESS OF ALGECIRAS

Ten years had passed when Spanish and Portuguese warriors pitched their tents at the Rio Salado near Tarifa, where they now faced Moors whose numbers were greater than theirs. The archbishop Gil Alnornoz of Toledo proclaimed a sermon which penetrated the souls of the knights, gave unto the pious fighters' communion and heard their confessions; and then after the rites were done did the Christian soldiers arose and rode into battle under the banner of the Church. The Muslims came, they were an army from Morocco, and after quarreling they fled back to Africa. This was the last time a formidable Islamic force came to Spain from Morocco. Two years later, with moral and material support from Pope Clement VI, Spanish soldiers alongside Crusaders from England, Catalonia, Genoa, and France, executed a siege on the great Moorish fortress of Algeciras, and after two years fighting succeeded in capturing it.[86]

---

83 Carroll, *A History of Christendom*, vol. iii, ch. viii, pp. 330–331
84 Carroll, *A History of Christendom*, vol. iii, ch. ix, pp. 369–370
85 Carroll, *A History of Christendom*, vol. iii, ch. ix, p. 370
86 Carroll, *A History of Christendom*, vol. iii, ch. ix, pp. 379–380

PEDRO THE CRUEL AND HIS HELP TO THE MUSLIMS

The cause of the Christian in Spain was hindered by the cause of a heretic, named Pedro. He murdered at least ten of his own relatives and was a rapist. The Church saw him as an enemy to God and so excommunicated him. So wicked was this man that he was deemed "Pedro the Cruel." When his brother Henry of Trastamara was fighting to take Toledo away from the Muslims, Pedro came not to help him, but to war with him. He brought an army of Muslim Moors with him as well, since he had more love for Muslims and Jews than Christians. Henry anticipated the coming of his brother and battled against him at Montiel. The heretic Pedro was overpowered, took refuge in a castle, made a false surrender, and would later receive the dagger of his brother in a hand to hand fight.[87]

RECONQUISTA IS COMPLETED

The longest war in history would continue regardless of the treachery which Pedro brought. In 1410, the Spaniards came to Antequera to recover it from Moorish rule, with ten thousand infantry and two thousand five hundred knights. They fought all summer long with the Muslims refusing to give up the city. The Spaniards, under Fernando, ascended the walls with scaling ladders and in time managed to reconquer it.[88]

In the year 1415 prince Henry of Spain accomplished what no Spaniard had done before: he conquered Ceuta, a city of North Africa. Now was this place in the hands of Christians after being, since the seventh century, for so long under Muslim hands. Henry never saw the war against Islam as "geopolitical," but as a problem which deserved the attention and efforts of all of Christendom. Henry would continue to journey to other lands, and amongst his reasons for this was that, in the words of Zurara, in "the 31 years that he had warred against the Moors, he had never found a Christian king, nor a lord outside his land, who for the love of Our Lord Jesus Christ would aid him in the said war. Therefore he sought to know if there were in those parts any Christian princes, in whom the charity and the love of Christ was so ingrained that they would aid him against those enemies of the faith."[89]

The Portuguese continued to try to advance in North Africa. Ten thousand of their warriors came to Tangiers and besieged the city; the Moorish commander Sala ben Sala withstood the attacks. In time the Portuguese were surrounded and forced to sign a truce. As they were departing droves of Moors who disagreed with the treaty ambushed them, killing many.[90]

By 1481 Muslims from Granada ambushed and captured the fortress of Zahara. Queen Isabel took immediate measures to put an end to the war with the Moors by fully completing the Reconquest. The Marques de Cadiz was more than willing to lead a victory for his country; he led five thousand men in 1482 and took Alhama, a town just twenty five

---

87 Carroll, *A History of Christendom*, vol. iii, ch. x, p. 411
88 Carroll, *A History of Christendom*, vol. iii, ch. xi, p. 467
89 See Carroll, *A History of Christendom*, vol. iii, ch. xii, p. 495, 497
90 Carroll, *A History of Christendom*, vol. iii, ch. xiii, pp. 555–556

miles from Granada. King Fernando himself went into battle, while his wife Isabel provided financial support. In a battle at the Moorish fortress of Loja, Fernando was overwhelmed and driven back. In 1483, eight hundred Spanish nobles were slain, and fifteen hundred Spanish soldiers were killed by Moors in the Ajarquia Mountains. Isabel expressed her sentiments:

> I know all about what happened with the Moors, which has greatly distressed me. But this is nothing new in war. In such matters we are in the hands of Our Lord. We may not and ought not to do otherwise than give thanks to Him for everything. Truly, since this was done in service to Our Lord and for the exaltation of our Holy Faith, that is consolation for whatever death or loss may result from it.

Fernando desired to campaign against the French, but his wife convinced him to say the course and combat the threat right in their own country. French artillery experts were hired to help engineer a very efficient cannon, known as a Lombard. It proved to be very effective, with Moorish strongholds continuously being taken, and with the climatic recapture of Ronda. For seven centuries this city was held by the Muslims, and now the Spaniards held it, celebrating their victory with song and dance. In 1486 the Spaniards successfully reconquered Loja, and in the next year Fernando and Isabel laid a victorious siege upon Malaga. In 1491 the final battle of the Reconquest—the final battle of the longest war in history—took place over Granada in which the Spanish were triumphant and Boabdil, the Muslim king of Granda, surrendered.[91]

Spain was now won for the glory of Christ. The Cross ruled and the crescent idols were driven out. After nearly eight hundred years of fighting Islamic domination in Spain, the Spanish Christians wanted Spain to remain Christian forever. But, Christian supremacy could not be maintained by itself; it required a system that would prevent Islam, or any other heresy, from taking over the country, and keep Spain Christian. This system would be the Spanish Inquisition.

---

91 Carroll, *A History of Christendom*, vol. iii, ch. xiv, pp. 610–612; 627–628

PART 17 – IN DEFENSE OF THE SPANISH INQUISITION

I will now compose a defense and vindication for the Spanish Inquisition. But before you burn me at the stake for doing so, there is some things you must know about the Spanish Inquisition before you can talk about it. First, you must know what Spain was, and second, you must know what an inquisition is. Spain was the crown of Christendom, it had just reclaimed its nation from seven hundred and eighty one years of Islamic subjugation.[1] and to make sure that their nation would never be taken again, the Spaniards established an inquisition, or an investigative court that inquires any entity that poses a threat to the state and (in this case) to the Church.[2] The threat was Islam, and if it had been tolerated to thrive after the Spaniards took their nation back, then jihadism would have prevailed, taking the most dominant nation of the continent and thus jeopardizing all of Europe. The Spanish Inquisition was a strike against Jihad.

After the Catholic Kings Ferdinand and Isabella took the city of Granada in 1491 they expelled the last Muslim king in Spain, Boabdil, and established their nation as a fully Christian power. The Reconquest of Spain was the longest war in human history[3]—of course something had to be done to prevent such a bloodbath from ever taking place. Yet people today, who claim to hate war so much, never consider this fact, but reject it. The same can be said of nationalists. If America was under Islamic power for almost eight hundred years, and then retook its country, there is no doubt that Americans would create an inquisition to prevent the Muslims from gaining any power. After the Japanese attacked Pearl Harbor, the US government considered Buddhist monks to be "dangerous enemy aliens," and their arrests were esteemed as a priority.[4] All nations have inquisitions. Without inquisitions, no nation could survive.

---

1 See P.F., *The Spanish Inquisition*, USCM, vol. ii, p. 456
2 See Moczar, *Seven Lies about Catholic History*, ch. iv, p. 83
3 See Warren H. Carrol, *A History of Christendom*, vol. 3: The Glory of Christendom, ch. i, p. 5, (1993)
4 Peter Manseau, When Buddhists were Public Enemy No. 1

THE INQUISITION WAS A REACTION TO THE OTTOMAN EMPIRE AND TO ISLAMIC INFILTRATION

It is amazing to see what Christian love was done for the Muslims in Al-Andalus even after the fact that they were once the masters of Spain. The government allowed them the free exercise of their religion, but after much sedition, and after intercepted letters proved that Spanish Moors corresponded with Muslims in Africa, the state was left with no other choice but to give them two options: convert to Christianity or leave the country.[5] No sane man could blame them; they granted freedom to the Moors even after they suppressed their culture, and still this was not good enough to the followers of Muhammad.

Any just statesman would identify Islam as a public enemy—an enemy to all liberty that must be expunged from Christendom. Ministers were commissioned to preach Christianity unto the Muslims,[6] comprehending that Islam was a danger to Spanish sovereignty, much like Marxism is for us today. Modern intellects may snidely mock this policy, but such people follow fragmented history, never or rarely connecting other historical events together to clearly understand why the Inquisition took place.

The expulsion of the Moorish menace in 1492 purged the land, and relieved the minds of Western Europe, but still upon that time, and before then, a darkness was spreading upon the land, the roots of which were planted in the lowest depths of the underworld, growing ever so deeper as long as the arms of Christendom turned their valiancy away from it: the Ottoman Empire, which by now had flooded itself into Eastern Europe and across North Africa where it stole the crown of the Arab and the Berber.[7] The Ottomans would become the superior of Europe, in troops, weaponry, siege warfare, and artillery—in fact, they even introduced the shell.[8]

Before we can comprehend the Inquisition—which was established officially in 1480—we must first know about a certain event that occurred just twenty seven years before it: the conquest of Constantinople by the Ottoman Turks in 1453. In a word, the Spanish established the Inquisition to prevent their country from becoming another Constantinople. If we do not grasp this prior conquest, then we will never comprehend the purpose of the Spanish Inquisition.

THE TAKING OF CONSTANTINOPLE

THE MUSLIMS ARRIVE WITH A MESSAGE

It was the year 1453, Mehmet II was now the sultan of the Ottoman Empire, and he believed that with the aid of Allah "and the prayers of the prophet, we shall speedily become the masters of Constantinople."[9]

---

5 P.F., *The Spanish Inquisition*, USCM, vol. ii, pp. 456–457. See also Mendoza, 1.3
6 See Hurtado de Mendoza, *The War in Granada*, 1.3, trans. Martin Shuttleworth
7 See Moczar, *Islam at the Gates*, prologue, p. 12
8 Belloc, *How the Reformation Happened*, ch. i, p. 85
9 In Gibbon, *Decline and Fall*, vol. v, ch. lxviii, p. 1202

CHRISTIANITY IS AT WAR: THE MANIFESTO FOR CHRISTIAN MILITANCY

We are now in the city of Constantinople. The emperor Constantine XI is within the senate house; the faces of all present express nothing but weariness. Constantine XI is adorned with imperial garb, his hair is braided and ornamented, and his head is adorned with the dome shaped crown of Byzantium. A man rushes into the room, he is an envoy who comes with a message from Mehmet II:

> The preparations for the assault have been concluded. It is now time to consummate what we planned long ago. Let us leave the outcome of this undertaking to God. What say you? Do you wish to quit the City and go wherever you like together with your officials and their possessions, leaving behind the populace unharmed by us and by you? Or do you choose to resist and to lose your life and belongings, and to have the Turks take the populace captive and scatter them throughout the earth?

The emperor and the senators arose, and Constantine XI told the envoy to return to the Turkish tyrant with these words:

> If you so wish, as your fathers did before you, you too, by the grace of God, can live peacefully with us. Keep the fortress and the lands which have been unjustly seized from us as justly yours. Extract as much tribute annually as we are able to pay you, and depart in peace. Can you be certain that victory instead of defeat awaits you? The right to surrender the City to you belongs neither to me nor to anyone who dwells therein. Rather than to have our lives spared, it is our common resolve willing to die.

The herald left to give the message, leaving the Christians with no time to prepare, giving them nothing but anguishing suspense and the fear of not knowing what is to come.

THE DANCE OF THE DERVISHES

As the Christians stood in fear, a crowd of dervishes—those Sufis who kept up the spirit of Jihad—[10] visited the tents of the Muslims and danced to the sound of the mystical and wild music of the Orient, and with the harmony of lute, kaval, drum and voice, they instilled in the warriors the fearlessness of death and the hope of the gardens of paradise where flowed rivers of wine and where reposed the black eyed and voluptuous virgins.[11]

Mehmet II stood before his ruthless troops and told them that when they take the city, Constantinople's walls and buildings will be in his possession. He looked to his warriors, rapacious and urging booty, and remarked that as for captives and treasures, "Let those be your reward." The whole body of soldiers, with their fickle and volatile minds, screamed that there is no god but Allah and Muhammad is his messenger.[12]

BETWEEN SAINTS AND WIZARDS

The sun now descended to its slumber while the souls of the city were kept awake by the plague of trepidation and angst. The sea, from a pristine body of water, appeared now to be

---
10 Moczar, *Islam at the Gates*, ch. i, p. 29
11 See Gibbon, *Decline and Fall*, lxviii, pp. 1208–1209
12 See Gibbon, *Decline and Fall*, vol. v, ch. lxviii, p. 1209

an endless void as black as the abyss and as hopeless as the desert from where Muhammad came with his heresy. Bright lights began to be seen from a distance; within a moment all of the sea appeared as though the fires of hades had bulged out from beneath the ocean floor, while piercing lights were seen above the lands outside of the city, illuminating Constantinople with radiating brilliance as bright as the sun.

It appeared as though the surface of the water was transformed into lightening. Out ran the Romans who thought that a fire had fallen on their military camp, only to see that no arson was done. Torches were lit all about the land, and in all the hundreds of Turkish ships on the sea. Their lights broke the evening darkness and when they looked out the city walls all they could see before their weary eyes were hundreds of thousands of Turks dancing like wild men, screaming, roaring and shouting their cries of battle. "Spare us, O Lord," prayed the watchmen, "from Thy just wrath and deliver us from the hands of the enemy." This was a plea to Heaven of the purest sincerity, and it was unlike any frivolous prayer that is done so frequently today.

They rushed back and alarmed the inhabitants, and now the city was so worried that the air itself was plagued with the virus of fear. It spread throughout, afflicting terror to all those hearts residing in this once great beacon of Christendom. The Christian fighters joined together and there arose an impetus of zealous unity to the highest degree: they wailed and wept, embraced one another, devoted their lives to Christ, and took their stations. The emperor, with some faithful companions, entered the Church of St. Sofia and with fervent tears running down their faces received the sacraments of the Holy Communion. Constantine XI at times reclined in his palace, which was now surrounded with cries and lamentations, pled for forgiveness from anyone who he may have injured in the past, and rode off on his horse to his men.

As this was occurring Mehmet II relied on astrology for wisdom, and concluded that the attack must be commenced at dawn.[13] He was a seeker after stars, auspices, and the harbingers of dreamers, and thus was this a war between wizards and saints.

A POORLY DEFENDED CITY

The break of dawn arrived, and by this time small skirmishes between Turk and Christian commenced, but nothing too grave—nothing major occurred until the ninth hour of the day. An army of Muslims came in front of the Golden Gate, and upon the waters did one see eighty ships fit for war lurking about like infernal leviathans ready to devour, stationed from the Xyloporta Gate to the Plataea Gate, all entrances into the city. Other ships encircled the city, covering numerous areas. Just at the moment when the sun set, the call to battle arose and the souls of the fighters vibrated with an impenetrable motivation. Mehmet gave battle with his ten thousand slaves—all men with great muscular physic and robust statures, who fought so viciously that they were compared to combating lions. To the rear and on both sides of the city more than one hundred thousand Muslims were making their assault.

To the south of these and as far as the Golden Gate there were another one hundred thousand heretics and more. From where Mehmet stood there was stationed fifty thousand

---

13 See Gibbon, *Decline and Fall*, vol. v, ch. lxviii, p. 1209–1210

warriors of Allah's crescent. A small number of three thousand Italian fighters made a stand, alongside hundreds of crossbowmen, archers, and gunmen, all under the command of their Genoese general Giovanni Giustiniani. To the eternal shame of Christendom almost no help came to the aid of the city, and only three ships were given by the pope.[14] Throughout the evening these were watchmen on the wall, neither resting nor slumbering. The Christians were kept awake by fear, the Muslims by the hope that the rising crescent of Islam was soon to ascend above the world.

NOT THE FIRST TIME THE MUSLIMS TRIED TO CONQUER CONSTANTINOPLE

The Muslims always wanted to take Constantinople; for it was the city of eastern Christendom, built by Constantine, the pious emperor who orchestrated the Council of Nicaea which first confronted the evil of Arianism, the heresy that would influence Muhammad who would in turn begin his cult. Not only that, but Constantine built Constantinople to be a city without the blemish of heathenism and idolatry, without the worship of demons and pagan temples.[15] The desire to take this metropolis was rooted into their bowls: the very thought of capturing the renown metropolis excited the god of their bellies; it rallied their hearts and ascended their spirits to the call of the prophet who declared that the first Muslim army who could take Constantinople would have their souls cleansed and their sins forgiven.[16]

Let us imagine to ourselves the first time the Muslims attempted to take the city in 654 under Muawiyah. They were preparing for this conquest in Tripoli (located in Phoenicia), and two zealots, noticing their plan, rushed to the commander of the city and killed him and his men, burned all of their gear, and ran off to Romania.[17] But now we are in the fifteenth century, and the Muslims have arrived with a force far more organized and far more ruthless than the Romans could have ever imagined.

THE TURKS OVERRUN THE CITY

The Turks had come and in their midst was a weapon never before seen nor used in Christian lands: a prodigiously colossus cannon, built by a heretic from Hungary named Urban who engineered the contrivance for the enemies of God the Turks. The monstrous machine was twenty seven feet long, a muzzle eight inches wide, and so heavy was it that when it was seen by the terrified Christians it came toward them being carried by sixty oxen and seven hundred men. No wall in the world was strong enough to withstand it, no man of war to prevail over it. As the rays of the sun dissipated in darkness of eve, a shot was fired which struck the soul with a harrowing sound, and a one thousand two hundred pound ball crashed into the city walls. But still there stood the emperor Constantine with sword in hand, ready to lead his men.[18]

---

14   See Carroll, *A History of Christendom*, vol. iii, ch. xiii, p. 565
15   Augustine writes that Constantine built the city "without any temple of image of the demons." (*City of God*, 5.25)
16   See Gibbon, *Decline and Fall*, vol. v, ch. lii, p. 962
17   Chron. Theophan. Annus Mundi 6146
18   See Carroll, *A History of Christendom*, vol. iii, ch. xiii, pp. 565–7

The Turks rushed the walls and from the ground did numberless scaling ladders ascend against the city. The sounds of battle and death was drowned by the Turkish bands who pounded their drums and blew their trumpets.[19] Mehmet was amongst his troops with a sadistic dispossession as he brandished an iron mace and vociferously forced his archers to attack the walls. As the wicked growled in fury, the Christians held their holy icons around the walls and through the city in procession.[20] Giovanni and his Italians, and the emperor and his troops fought with all the strength any supreme warrior could muster. A Turk fired a musket and the ball pierced through Giovanni's arm and broke through his Roman breastplate. The bullet is in his chest; the wound is dismaying. "Stand your ground bravely," he cried, "and I will retire to the ship to attend to my wound. Then I will quickly return."

The general retreated and so did the morale of the fighters. The emperor lost heart, but his mind prevailed over his emotions and he continued to fight, leading the men with great intensity. A swarm of Turks was seen gradually making their way toward the walls with shields hovering above their bodies; the reflection of the sun's light from the metal was a sight for soar eyes. Then suddenly their arose from this hoard multiple scaling ladders whose tops now rested on the walls. As they were trying to ascend the ladders down came boulders from the watchmen which crushed the Turks and repulsed their assault. But lo, there was a sally port left open, to which fifty of Mehmet's slaves leaped. They climbed to the top of the walls filled with rage and thirst for blood. They killed anyone they found and cut to pieces the warriors who defended the city from scaling Turks. Other soldiers could not bear such a sight and leaped out of the walls to land to their deaths. Many fled as soon as they spotted the flag of the Turk waving within their sights.[21]

Now were the walls finally defenseless; the Turks threw up their scaling ladders and ascended like crawling spiders. In another part of the city Constantine XI and his troops still kept fighting without knowledge that much of the enemy were already within the walls and were now within Constantinople. The emperor and his garrison were outnumbered twenty to one, and were nowhere near as conditioned and battle hardened for war as these Mongol barbarians and their Slavic auxiliaries. As they were fighting, with Roman sword hitting against Muslim scimitar, arrows darkened the sky and came from above like demons descending from heaven, tearing right through the flesh of the Christians as lightning bolts crack the peaks of mountains.

The arrows rushed down like a storm and their landing made a flood of human blood. They tried to run back through a major gate, but were unable to on account of their numbers. They were confounded and in chaos; the stronger soldiers trampled over the weak, and as Mehmet's men saw this disorderly bunch, they screamed their war cry—their praise to Allah—and sharply commenced a charge. They stampeded the retreaters, crushing many with their feet, and hacking to death bodies of men with those thin but agonizing blades so popular in Muslim

---

19 See Gibbon, Decline, and Fall, vol. v, ch. lxviii, p. 1211
20 See Carroll, A History of Christendom, vol. iii, ch. xiii, p. 566
21 See Carroll, A History of Christendom, vol. iii, ch. xiii, p. 567

warfare. By the time they reached the gate their entering was hindered on account of the lofty pile of bodies which blocked the entrance. They came into the city through the breaches on the walls and they cut down all those they met. "The city is ours!" cried out Mehmet.[22]

THE EMPEROR FIGHTS

There lied the emperor, alone and dismayed; despair and hopelessness are all one feels when setting sight on him. Imagine to yourself such a disquieting image: here lied the emperor of the most glorious Roman Empire, the history of which never ceases to be spoken of. And now it was all crumbling down into the ashes of history to the prevailing force of the Muslim. Constantine XI stood with his sword, no doubt especially made for an emperor, with its narrow blade, and handle shaped into the form of a cross, the symbol of his religion, the symbol of everything he fought for, and it was the symbol which the Muslims most hated, for it was on that Cross on Calgary where the greatest enemy to tyranny died to destroy the works of the Devil—the works of Allah.

His heart was plunged into sorrow and he cried out, "Is there no one among the Christians who will take my head from me?" A Turk came about and wounded him, but the emperor swiftly struck him. Another appeared and hit him from behind. The emperor quivered to the earth, and received the swords from his mocking enemy, only to die not with the honor of an emperor, but only as a mere civilian. Here lied the last of the Caesars, who did not leave this world to the sounds of funeral music, but to the cruel laughs of the conquering Muslim. The last remnant of soldiers were scattered about, some fleeing and some resisting to no avail, since two thousand of them were quickly slaughtered. The Janissaries—sinewy men from the Balkans who were stolen as Christian children by the Turks and made into Muslim killers—stormed the city's palace, the Petra Monastery and the Monastery of Chora where they spotted a statue of Mary the mother of Christ, God in the flesh. One of them took it, and with an axe and demonic hatred hacked it to pieces. Like the Romans did with Christ's garments, they casted lots for the fragments of the image before riding away.

A SURREAL SIGHT OF HUMAN SUFFERING

Romans ran as fast as they could to their homes to save their wives and children from the Turks who now lurked everywhere as Satan prows like "a roaring lion" "seeking whom he may devour." (I Peter 5:8) Families were seen treading down a certain road, their bodies covered in blood and their demeanor appearing as soulless corpses. They passed by the Column of the Cross in the Forum of Constantine which was a symbol of Rome's innovation; but now they were to be images to evoke the memories of past glory now at the edge of the cliff of destiny.

The women in most lamenting voices cried out to heaven, "What is to become of us?" A man arrived to the disquieted multitude of families and exclaimed with a fearful voice, "The Turks are slaughtering Romans within the City's walls," and they did not believe him, and in fact cursed the messenger for bringing such a terrifying message. But from behind him came

---

22 See Carroll, *A History of Christendom*, vol. iii, ch. xiii, p. 567

a man, his clothes covered in blood, and then another arrived, he too stained with gore. It was almost a surreal thing to behold; a nightmare only existing in a slumbering mind came to past as sheer horror tainted the air of that once beautiful city. Monks and nuns, men and women, grasping onto their little ones with trembling hands, all ran as one into the Great Church of Constantinople. They burst into the sanctuary, bolted the doors, and sat and waited for an anonymous savior. From a distance were the Turks, killing and taking captives as they walked down that road which led to the church. The gates to the church were barred, but they hacked them apart with their axes and entered with swords unsheathed, beholding the defenseless people whom they saw as nothing more than open game. They were but sheep being taken to the slaughter. No man could describe the wailings and the cries of the babes, no chronicler the tearful screams of the mothers, no historian the lamentations of the fathers.

The loveliest maiden was sought out by the most degenerate Turk, and not even the nuns were spared by the rapacious Muslims who indulged themselves in the wickedest acts of rape and kidnapping. The braids of women were tugged and pulled by Turks who competed for them; they ripped through their garments and exposed their breasts and bosoms. People were driven out of the church and flogged, and within one hour all of the men where bounded together by a cord like the Hebrew slaves in ancient Egypt. They were chained together and were treated as though they were not human, but a herd of beasts. Over sixty thousand people were transported to the Muslim camps and ships, exchanged and sold, and dispersed throughout the provinces of the Ottoman Empire.[23]

The Janissaries tore down the crucifix in the Hagia Sofia, placed a Turkish turbin on the thorn-pierced head and mockingly paraded through the streets as they scoffingly said, "Behold the God of the Christians." Ever since then the Hagia Sofia has never been touched by Christian hands; it still remains in Turkey as a great bare slab in iconoclastic fury.[24]

In another part of the city the citizens did not even expect the Turks to reach them. It was the Feast Day of the Holy Martyr Theodosia, and as their countrymen were reduced to the lowest of servility, women and men weeped all night in a vigil at the saint's sepulchre. In the morning, these Christians set out to revere the saint in her church with their candle sticks and incense, and suddenly the Turks ambushed them mercilessly. Surely was this the hour of the City of Satan, surely was this the times of "the power of darkness."[25]

They took up torches and burned the city from the Gates of Charisios and St. Romanos to the surroundings of the palace. Roman naval ships prevented further Turkish ranks from entering the city by launching boulders and arrows at them. When Romans, who were upon some of the walls, realized that the Turks were by then within the city and destroying her, they proclaimed an anguished cry of woe and threw themselves to their deaths. Upon this, Turks put up more scaling ladders and climbed over the wall. Once inside they pulled down the city's gates and all the rest of them rushed inside. The grand duke, when seeing the enemy

---

23 Gibbon, *Decline and Fall*, vol. v, ch. lviii
24 Carroll, *A History of Christendom*, vol. iii, ch. xiii, p. 568
25 Luke 53

stampeding toward his post, fled with a few companions. Romans ran to their homes to save their families; others, when they came home saw no wife nor children—all was hopeless, all was despair. Before these fathers had time to groan and wail their hands were already bound behind them. Old men and elderly women who were too frail to move were slaughtered without pity for their infirmities. New born infants were found being tossed into the air and crushed. General Giovanni, after recovering from his gunshot wound, ordered that his inferiors and marines leave the ravished city.

The soldiers went into their ships, and saw before them men, women, monks, and nuns crying with the most horrid sound of agony, screaming with the highest tone of torment piteously pleading to them for rescue. The soldiers declined, they could not take them. Once they found their passage cleared, the ships sailed away out of the harbour, and still not even the sounds of the roaring waves could prevail over the blood chilling shrieks which resounded through the sky. Though their wailings dwindled away, with the axes of their pitiful cries they carved out an egress into the weary caves of the hearts of their listeners. The place once esteemed as "the highest glory of the Christian world,"[26] was now a place of desolation. So great was this city, that before the time of its capture, one monk wrote of it thus:

> For if such a city had not been founded, where would the Christianity of the East have found a refuge?[27]

That city built by Constantine, who fought against the wiles of Arius, was now being vanquished by men who were mere products of Arianism.

THE ABOMINATION OF DESOLATION
Mehmet came to the Great Church, or the Hagia Sophia, and saw a Turk smashing a piece of marble pavement and asked why he was doing this. "For the faith," replied the barbarian. He struck the Turk with his sword so forcefully that he fell to the floor half-dead. The tyrant then declared: "You have enough treasures and captives. The City's buildings are mine." The crosses were ordered to be thrown down, and the beautiful statues and mosaics were all gotten rid of, leaving the place from being a magnificent church to a white washed tomb.[28] He summoned a vile sheikh to ascend the church's pulpit, and when he did, he cried the Call to Prayer declaring that Allah is greater and thus expressing the superiority of Islam over Christianity. He then went on top of the great altar and preformed an Islamic prayer. The bringing of this prayer—the enemy of Orthodoxy—into the Hagia Sophia, was an abomination of desolation.

The Muslims in Constantinople then broke into the Temple of the Holy Trinity and transformed it into a mosque. The name of the church itself reflects what was done in the Council of Nicaea against Arianism, and now the new Arianism—Islam—has taken and made it into a church of Satan intentionally to obliterate the concept of the Holy Godhead. The libraries of the city were destroyed, with one hundred and twenty thousand volumes

---

26 Impiglia, *The Song of the Fall*, p. 19
27 Robert the Monk, *History of the First Crusade*, 2.20
28 See Gibbon, *Decline and Fall*, vol. v, ch. lxviii, p. 1216

disappearing,[29] since the Devil hates more than anything a knowledgeable people and thrives on vaguely thinking societies.

A few years later, after the destruction of Constantinople was done, after all of this torment and suffering occurred, a Greek historian named Doukas, wrote an account of it so that men in the future could never forget what took place (sadly most have). In this account he describes the sheikh who made the Call to Prayer in the Great Church as "The son of iniquity, the forerunner of Antichrist," and at the end we read his awe-inspiring yet saddening words:

> O City, City, head of all cities! O City, City, the center of the four corners of the earth! O City, City, the boast of Christians and the ruin of barbarians! O City, City, a second Paradise planted in the West and containing within many plants, laden with spiritual fruits. Where is your beauty, O Paradise? [30]

The darkness of heresy overran the majestic metropolis, and only guile and fearful diplomacy sunk the churches into the grasps of Islam. The sultan approved of the election of Gennadius as patriarch of Constantinople and the two would have warm discussions on the comparisons between Islam and Christianity.[31] Thus are the conversations between the master and his slave, and yet we—supposedly an enlightened and free people—have stooped into the same level, bestowing to Islam that fabricated and empty term, "Abrahamic."

THE HEAD OF THE EMPEROR

Mehmet had the grand duke brought forth. He timidly approached the tyrant and bowed down to him, not in reverence, but in fear. "Did you do well not to surrender the City?" asked the Islamic despot, "Behold the damage and ruin! Behold the captivity of so many!" The duke replied: "Lord, we did not have the authority. Moreover, some of your own officials urged the emperor to do otherwise by writing such words as: Fear not. He will not prevail against you." The very word "emperor" provoked Mehmet to ask concerning the fate of Constantine XI. The duke stated that he did not know, then two young Turks, the same soldiers who slew the emperor, stepped forward, and one proudly stated: "Lord, I slew him. I was in a hurry to enter the City with my companions to search for plunder, so I left him behind dead." The second sadistic youth pompously said: "I struck him the first blow." Mehmet commanded them to bring him the body as proof of their claim. They returned back with the emperor's head. "Tell me truthfully," said Mehmet to the duke, "if this is the head of your emperor." "It is his, Lord."

They attached the head to a column and let it remain there until evening, they then flayed its skin off and stuffed it with straw. Mehmet sent it around for the Arabs, Persians, and Turks to behold as a symbol of triumph for the Islamic empire. It is deplorable, after hearing of this story, to read the words of the pro-Islamic and deistic historian Edward Gibbon where he writes that Mehmet gave Constantine XI "the honors of a decent funeral."[32]

---

29 Gibbon, *Decline and Fall*, vol. v, ch. lxviii, p. 1215
30 Doukas, *The Fall of Constantinople*, in McCullough, *Chronicles of the Barbarians*, ch. xv, pp. 373–374
31 Moczar, *Islam at the Gates*, ch. iii, p. 72
32 Gibbon, *Decline and Fall*, vol. v, ch. lxviii, p. 1216

THE CRUEL SODOMITE SULTAN

The city was in complete anarchy, with Turk killing Turk—surely were they possessed by a dark spirit. As chaos took hold of Constantinople, Mehmet reposed in a banquet. Full of wine and drunk off cruelty he sent a message to the duke: "send your younger son to the banquet." The father fully comprehended what this meant: the tyrant wanted his son for the vilest purpose of pederasty. Mehmet was truly demoniacal. The duke gave a stern response: "It is not our custom to hand over my own child to be despoiled by him. It would be far better for me if the executioner were sent to take my head." But this would not suffice; the messenger persisted that the son must go. "If you want him," said the duke, "you will have to seize him." The messenger returned these words to Mehmet who then ordered him, "Take the executioner with you, and bring me back the boy. Let the executioner bring the duke and his sons."

When they arrived the duke bade his wife farewell, and left with the executioner alongside his son and son-in-law, Kantakouzenos. Mehmet ordered that their heads be cut off. The young boy wept, but his courageous father told him to be of good cheer and be ready to die. Their souls were prepared for eternal glory, and their heads adorned with the crowns of righteousness. As the father watched his son's head being severed off and his son-in-law being decapitated, he expressed the most sublime level of faith by murmuring, "I thank Thee Lord," and "Thou art just, Lord." What modern Christian today, who preaches nothing but watered down doctrine, empty love and vague faith, would be able to endure such torment and still exemplify this great degree of loyalty to God? This was Christianity in its purest form.

It was now the father's turn to be beheaded. "Brother," he told the executioner, "grant me a little time to pray." The request was granted and he entered a small chapel that was within the palace. He made his prayer, exited the chapel, and as he was walking he looked and saw the two bodies of his sons and noticed that they were still twitching. He bowed, praised God, and down came the sword and took his head. The killer picked up the heads and presented them to Mehmet, who later ordered for the chief nobles of the city and palace officials to be slaughtered. From among their wives and boys he selected a multitude for his sadistic pleasure.[33] The historian Phranza was amongst the Christians who were sold into slavery, and after four months of being yoked he escaped and ransomed his wife. His daughter murdered, and his two sons were forced to become the victims of Mehmet's pedophilia. One of them, aged fifteen, refused to be raped and so was stabbed to death by the possessed sultan.[34]

THE MARTYRS IN HEAVEN

The city was now empty, with nothing but bodies lying dead, soundless, and having neither form nor beauty. Quiet horror was all that could be felt, hope could have never been so absent. The souls of the dead transcended into the eternal realm, and now they sit amongst those saints who were seen by John who wrote of them in his Revelation:

---

33 This entire recounting of the Fall of Constantinople is based on the work of the historian Doukas, *The Fall of Constantinople*, in McCullough, *Chronicles of the Barbarians*, ch. xv, pp. 363–373
34 Gibbon, *Decline and Fall*, vol. v, ch. lxviii, p. 1213

I saw the souls of them that were beheaded for the witness of Jesus; and for the word of God, and which had not worshipped the beast, neither his image, neither had received his mark upon their foreheads, or in their hands; and they lived and reigned with Christ a thousand years. [35]

The image is the Blackstone in the Kaaba, which the Muslims force Christians under penalty of death to bow down to. The mark is the words of the Call to Prayer, that there is no god but Allah and Muhammad is his messenger. It is the same remark that the sheikh cried in the Great Church of Constantinople. It is amazing to ponder on the fact that some of the greatest pagan kingdoms wanted to take either Rome, Constantinople, Jerusalem, or all three. Hannibal almost succeeded in taking Rome, the Sassanid Persians almost captured Constantinople and succeeded in stealing Jerusalem, but failed to take the Italian city. Islam, the ultimate Satanic religion, and the last of the two horns of the Beast, was able to capture the lands of the former powers of the East, such as Carthage and the rest of North Africa, Persia, Babylon, Assyria, Jerusalem, and all the Roman empire of Constantinople. When they tried to take Rome in Italy in 846, they plundered the churches of St. Paul and St. Peter,[36] but they could never triumph over the city.

The terrified Constantinople was now to be ruled by cruel luxury, where the floating waters of the Bosporus are overshadowed by the silken tents of tyrants drunk off lusciousness, where sultans are unceasingly spoiled by the passions of the palaces of pleasure, and their eyes forevermore thirsting for the lustrous sight of gold, silver, and precious stones[37] wrested from the hands of Christians now forced from a life of liberty to slavery. In time, the city, from the jewel of Christendom, would be a land where Christians were presented gasping for breath as they were impaled or hanging by their chins upon a sharp hook as sultans listened with ease in their palaces to the poet who sang, "Let us laugh, let us play, let us enjoy the delights of the world to the full."[38]

ROME RESPONDS WITH A CALL TO A CRUSADE

The invasion of Constantinople sent a shaking fear into the spines of Rome; no one expected such a tragedy to occur. The trembling Pope, Nicholas V, appealed to so many kings of Christendom, but none cared; none were unsettled on the blood which was shed by the greatest of heretics. Cardinal Bessarion, Bishop of Nicaea, awaited for help in Asia Minor where the devils had ravished the great city, but no one came. He wrote desperately and passionately to Doge Francisco Foscari of Venice who told the cardinal that he promised "war against the Turks." The promise was not fulfilled and the Ottomans saw no obstacle. The pope persistently urged crusade, and he received nothing but pathetic excuses and cruel silence. England did

---

35 Revelation 20:4
36 See Schmidt, *The Great Divide*, ch. vi, p. 143
37 This description of luxury was partially inspired by a description of the Ottomans in the work of Alan Palmer, *The Decline and Fall of the Ottoman Empire*, ch. iii, p. 38
38 See Alan Palmer, *The Decline and Fall of the Ottoman Empire*, ch. iii, p. 39

not respond, Alfonso V of Aragon and Naples complained of an ulcer, Charles VII was indifferent, and the emperor Fredrick III did not even attend the Imperial Diet at Regensburg done to support the crusade. So far the only one who seriously cared was Hungary, and for good reason, since Mehmet II was targeting that country as his next victim. Pope Nicholas V, on 1454, died, and a new pontificate needed to arise—one who would comprehend the threat without politics nor diplomacy. This was the Spaniard Alfonso Borja, mostly known as Pope Calixtus III. He was a product of the Reconquest, who fully understand, on account of experience, the cruelty and expansionism of the Muslim. Because of his religious fervor and his grasp on the Islamic threat, Calixtus III was the only one at this time in Western Christendom to initiate a crusade with the uttermost of concern. At his papal consecration he declared:

> I, Pope Calixtus III, promise and vow to the Holy Trinity, Father, Son and Holy Spirit, to the Ever-Virgin Mother of God, to the Holy Apostles Peter and Paul, and to all the heavenly host, that I will do everything in my power, even if need be with the sacrifice of my life, aided by the counsel of my worthy brethren, to reconquer Constantinople, which in punishment for the sin of man has been taken and ruined by Mahomet II, the son of the devil and the enemy of our Crucified Redeemer. Further, I vow to deliver the Christians languishing in slavery, to exalt the true Faith, and to extirpate the diabolical sect of the reprobate and faithless Mahomet of the East. For there the light of faith is almost completely extinguished. If I forget thee, O Jerusalem, let my right hand be forgotten. Let my tongue cleave to my jaws, if I do not remember thee. If I make not Jerusalem the beginning of my joy, God and His holy Gospel help me. Amen. 39

THE CHRISTIANS FIGHT AGAINST THE TURKS FOR THE DEFENSE OF BELGRADE

The Pope sent cardinals to France, Germany, and Poland to preach the crusade against the Ottomans. Alfonso V of Aragon and Naples joined the cause and agreed to supply fifteen galleys for the crusading fleet. Afonso V of Portugal vowed to give twelve thousand men; and St. John Capistrano, a Franciscan preacher filled with fervor, raised many a man in Hungary and Transylvania to enter the crusade. He pulled men into the righteous cause with his words filled with zeal; men more concerned about image rather than our eternal war with evil discouraged him from preaching. But one day, during the Mass, he saw, in a vision, an arrow with the words, "Fear not, John. Go down quickly. In the power of my name and of the Holy Cross thou wilt conquer the Turks."

And so he continued his mission. The Germans, on the other hand, did nothing to assist the cause of the Cross, and its bishops grumbled most impiously because of the crusading tax. The crusaders marched on to Belgrade, for if Belgrade fell the whole of southeastern Europe would be open to the Turks. Capistrano brought eight thousand men, while Hunyadi led about sixteen thousand. Such numbers were inferior to the eighty thousand jihadists Mehmet had under his grasp. Pope Calixtus III called on all archbishops, abbots and priests

---

39 Carroll, *A History of Christendom*, vol. iii, ch. xiii, pp. 569–571

to pray, fast and give penance for deliverance from the Turks. The warriors arrived in Belgrade, Capistrano said Mass, and commanded the other priests present to not participate in the fighting, but to tend the wounded. Shells struck the walls of the city, and such a terrifying bombardment continued on for two weeks. But still the saints remained steadfast. It came to their knowledge that the Turks were planning on cutting off the city from all outside support, but to such a worry Capistrano left the city with a promise that he would return with another army. On his arrival he brought with him a rustic bunch; the Ottomans were already there, and their numbers caused so much fear that Hunyandi, looking upon the lowly army of Capistrano, even proposed retreating. Capistrano would not allow it, and he sharply told Hunyandi that they would never leave, but would go down fighting.

The Crusaders under Hunyandi advanced with two hundred boats, and as they fought a naval battle, Capistrano stood on the shore holding up high a crucifix which the pope had given him, declaring "Jesus, Jesus, Jesus!" The Christian prevailed on the waters, and the fighting continued in Belgrade itself. The Turks beat the walls with their canons, and at that time all seemed hopeless. Hunyandi again suggested retreat, and again Capistrano turned it down. The Turks penetrated the walls at certain parts of the city and were in the midst of the Christians. Turk and Christian fought hand to hand in the streets as Hunyandi directed them, and Capistrano held high the Holy Cross. As the crucifix remained ascended, the Christians advanced. On Every street and in almost every building fighting took place. Turkish artillery was now of little help; the gunners could not see the enemy. It was at this moment that the preying horned owls were blinded, and the strong falcons prevailed. By the next morning the Turks began their retreat from the streets which were now engulfed in blood. The Christians followed through and relentlessly pursued them to finish them off. Hunyandi was able to seize some of the Turks' guns and use them on his enemy, and an arrow struck the body of Mehmet, the wound compelling the sound for the retreat. And as all of this took place, there stood the saintly fighter, Capistrano, with arms stretched above his head toward Heaven, and his hands gripped on the crucifix.[40] By this we are so reminded of that holy day in which the Hebrew saints defeated the heathen Amalekites as Moses stood holding his staff up to the air:

> And it came to pass, when Moses held up his hand, that Israel prevailed: and when he let down his hand, Amalek prevailed. But Moses' hands were heavy; and they took a stone, and put it under him, and he sat thereon; and Aaron and Hur stayed up his hands, the one on the one side, and the other on the other side; and his hands were steady until the going down of the sun. And Joshua discomfited Amalek, and his people with the edge of the sword.[41]

The Holy Spirit never ceased to work through His saints, from Israel onwards, it continued, from Moses to Capistrano, from Hunyandi to Joshua. The warpath of the infidel Turk had been hindered by this great victory, which moved Pope Calixtus III so much that he called it, "the happiest event of my life." They massacred fifty-thousand Turks in that battle. Calixtus III would

---

40 Carroll, *A History of Christendom*, vol. iii, ch. xiii, pp. 571–572; Moczar, *Islam at the Gates*, ch. iii, pp. 76–9
41 Exodus 17:11–13

also appoint an ex-Muslim from Albania who converted to Christianity, named Skanderbeg, as "Captain-General for the Turkish war," and he would lead successful attacks on the Turks until his death in 1468.[42] Now was the time to set the final blow upon the Turk, if only Christendom arose at that moment the crescent would have been driven fully out of Europe.[43]

Now, it must be remembered that Calixtus III was the only one amongst the Westerners to commence a holy war, partially because he was a Spaniard, and came from a nation which suffered under the Moorish conquests, which brought to him a knowledge on Islam, based on experience, better than that of any western European country, which helps us understand the purpose of the Spanish Inquisition.

THE MASSACRE OF OTRANTO AND THE SPANISH INQUISITION

After witnessing the horrid conquest of Constantinople, and after taking Spain back, it should not be a surprise as to why the Spaniards repressed Islam. The Spaniards who picked up their weapons and defeated the Muslims in Granada in 1492, would have most definitely remembered the conquest of Constantinople in 1453.[44]

The Spaniards would have also known about the massacre of Otranto, in which the Turks stormed the southern Italian city of Otranto, and captured twenty two thousand people, twelve thousand of which were butchered, most of them for refusing to become Muslim, and the rest were sold into slavery. Eight hundred men were each given the chance to bend the knee to Allah, and each refused, and like the prophets of Israel they were all put to death, and their bodies fed to dogs. The Turks murdered every cleric in the city. The Archbishop of Otranto remained in his cathedral, standing before the altar, his hands holding onto the Blessed Sacraments; the Turks seized him and cut his body in half. Isabel, the queen of Spain and main instituter of the Inquisition, reacted at once to the massacre by sending a Castilian fleet to Italy to fight the Turks. Fear took hold of Pope Sixtus IV, who considered fleeing; for no doubt the Muslims would have wanted nothing more than to conquer the Vatican. But in short time he decided to remain, and sent out warriors throughout Italy and Europe or protect the peninsula from the raging Turks. The king of England, on the other hand, did nothing; neither did the French nor the Germans decide to help their Christian brethren.

It was in this very intense predicament that the Inquisition was made.[45]

So crucial was this Tribunal that in 1812 the convention of the Spanish Cortes for drafting a new constitution, appointed a special committee to compose a report on the Spanish Inquisition, and though they hated the organization, they concluded that "it was an institution demanded and established by the monarchs of Spain in difficult and extraordinary circum-

---

42 Carroll, *A History of Christendom*, vol. iii, ch. xiii, pp. 372–373
43 Moczar, *Islam at the Gates*, ch. iii, p. 81
44 Belloc, *The Great Heresies*, The Great and Enduring Heresy of Muhammad, p. 60
45 See Carroll, *A History of Christendom*, vol. iii, ch. xix, pp. 606–607; Moczar, *Islam at the Gates*, ch. v, pp. 120–1

stances."⁴⁶ These extraordinary circumstances were the hordes of warlike Muslims from North Africa and Turkey.

THE KORAN IS BANNED

The Spanish Christians would have known full well the fate of Constantinople, and thus would establish an institution within the same century, made to prevent Spain from suffering under the hands of the Ottoman Turks and the Berbers, or North African Muslims. If we could only understand that this was the purpose of the Inquisition, then we could realize what we need to do now to rid ourselves of the current Islamic problem. Those who think that the Inquisition was unnecessary, and that Islam should have been allowed to be freely observed, does not understand Islam.

The Spaniards had already planned on configuring the institution before 1474, when parts of Spain were still under Muslim control, and they established it officially in 1480, before even the Battle of Granada of 1492 when Spain became fully independent from the Islamists. Thus it was founded at a time when Jihadism was right in the midst of the nation.⁴⁷

After nearly eight hundred years of fighting against, and being butchered by the Muslims, the Spaniards wanted to prevent Spain from ever being conquered again by establishing an institution which did not tolerate jihadists, nor their sympathizers. The Spanish government would soon take measures to cut off the hands of Islam before they could further sink their claws into the now Christian society. At the beginning they were given toleration—that ruiner of nations—and allowed to observe their religion, language, and culture. In 1499, wisdom stepped in and a prudent inquisitor named Cisneros requested from Ferdinand and Isabella for permission to take more aggressive measures on the Muslims.

A vast number of baptisms of Muslims occurred and a mosque was made into a church. This ignited the Muslims into anger and revolt ensued. Cisneros prudently affirmed that the rebellions indicated that the Muslims forfeited their rights, and that they should be presented with the options of converting to Christianity or expulsion. Ferdinand preferred toleration rather than expulsion. "If your horse trips up," the king said, "you don't seize your sword to kill him, instead you give him a smack on his flanks. So my view and that of the queen is that these Moors be baptized. And if they don't become Christians, their children and grandchildren will."⁴⁸ Muslims were prohibited to speak Arabic and use their bath houses to bathe themselves for their daily prayers; they were forbidden to dress in Islamic clothing and compelled to attire themselves in the Castilian manner. A huge pyre was made for the burning of Arabic books in Granada in 1501. Islamic religious festivals were outlawed and no longer were they allowed to play their music.

---

46 Quoted by P.F., *The Spanish Inquisition*. USCM, vol. ii, p. 458
47 See J. Balmes, *Protestantism and Catholicity Compared*, ch. xxxvi, p. 206
48 Kamen, *The Spanish Inquisition*, ch. 10, pp. 214–215

CHRISTIANITY IS AT WAR: THE MANIFESTO FOR CHRISTIAN MILITANCY

The Koran would eventually be prohibited unless in the confines of a public library in 1558.[49] By 1501, it was presumed that most of Granada's populace had converted to Christianity, and in 1502 all Muslims were told to convert or leave Spain. Similar orders were made in 1525 for the Muslims in Valencia and in 1526 for the ones in Aragon. Before this time, in 1504, a mufti living in North Africa issued a fatwa declaring that Muslims were allowed to observe the rules of Christianity, just as long as they had no inward convictions of Christian theology. This meant that Moriscos were secretly denying the Trinity and the sacraments of the Eucharist and baptism. When they would go home they would observe Islamic ritual washing to deter the effects of the baptism. This may sound as not a major concern to the modern mind, but as we will find out, this heresy led to tremendous amounts of violence.

Muslim converts—or Moriscos—generally refused to assimilate, and these made up the majority in Granada. From 1525 Islam officially was nonexistent in Spain, or so they thought.[50]

ISLAMIC INFILTRATION WAS DONE IN SPAIN AND THIS WARRANTED THE SPANISH INQUISITION

When the Battle of Granada was completed, the Muslims lost a very strategic position since the city is so close to Africa. Ferdinand and Isabella had declared that the city was to be Spain's "chief bastion against the Moors who in times gone by had conquered."[51] Regardless of the victory, the war with Islam was not over, and neither was the persistence of the Muslims to infiltrate Spain. A common attack on the Inquisition is that it investigated Muslims who said they converted to Christianity—called Moriscos. What is not taken into perspective is that many Moriscos feigned their faith to undermined the country and continue their jihadism.

The Moriscoes had a substantial population in Spain: in Granada they constituted fifty-four percent of the populace; in the Alpujarra Mountains they were the entire population; in Valencia a third, in Aragon about a fifth. There were some twenty-thousand Moriscoes living in Castile in 1502.[52] As we shall see, it was enough people to start a war.

They were very stealth in their jihad against Spain, and they would utilize methods which made it very difficult for the Inquisition to recognize their cunning. They wrote in a form of Spanish called aljamia; it was written in an Arabic script incomprehensible to the inquisitors. Evangelism toward Muslims was taken up by Catholics. In the 1540s a Franciscan named Fray Bartolome de los Angeles witnessed to them in Valencia, and further evangelism was done in the 1560s. In 1566 there was actually a manual published for witnessing to Muslims by the archbishop of Valencia, entitled Christian Doctrine in Arab and Castilian. Juan de

---

49 Hurtado de Mendoza, *The War in Granada*, 1.5; Consultation of Master Sancho about the books, 1558, in Homza, *The Spanish Inquisition*, document 19, p. 217; Kamen, *The Spanish Inquisition*, ch. 10, p. 215
50 See Homza's introduction to document 22 of her Spanish Inquisition, pp. 238–239; Kamen, *The Spanish Inquisition*, ch. 10, pp. 215, 217
51 Hurtado de Mendoza, War in Granada, 1.3
52 Kaman, *The Spanish Inquisition*, ch. 10, p. 217

Ribera, who became archbishop of Valencia in 1568, started a fund for Muslim evangelism and even founded a seminary for Morisco boys and girls.[53]

But still, as much as these were loving acts on the part of the Church, this did not extinguish the fires of hatred amongst the secret Muslims. As the Cathars were protected and tolerated by the wealthy counts of southern France, so were the Moriscoes watched out for by powerful counts, to the dismay of the Inquisition. In 1541 the Spanish nobleman of Valencia and Admiral of Aragon, Sancho de Moncada, was reprimanded by the Inquisition for constructing a mosque for the Muslims of his area and telling them "that they should pretend to be Christians externally but remain Muslim internally." The nobleman was placed under house arrest in 1569 for protecting his Moriscoes. When Jaime Palafox, the Lord of Ariza, heard that the Inquisition had arrested three of his Moriscoes, he and his men broke into the home of a worker for the Inquisition, and beat and stabbed him to death. He was arrested and sent to life in the North African prison of Oran.[54]

A number of Morisco leaders (who were really Muslims in disguise) conducted a secret meeting in Cadiar in which they planned a full scale assault on Christians which was to take place at Christmas Eve because they knew that all of the towns would be open to attack since all of the people would be in church observing the Mass. They planned that four thousand jihadists would descend from the Alpujarras area and join their companions in the Albaicin district from where they were to invade Granada and slaughter the Christian inhabitants with fire and scimitar.

This full scale incursion was not to be done solely by the Spanish Muslim populace, but by foreign assistance from Turkey and North Africa. In fact, years prior to this attack was even planned, the Muslims in Spain were sending emissaries to the kings of Barbary and the Turkish sultan to request assistance for an attempted reconquest of the nation. Closer to the time of the conspiracy, the Moors requested help from the king of Algeria, telling him that they lacked formidable commanders to lead them in their jihad, trained soldiers, and arms and ammunition. They continued to send for foreign support as they themselves developed their own armory and weapons. Some four thousand Turks and Berbers would enter Spain to support their fellow jihadis.[55]

THE MUSLIMS OPEN A HOSPITAL AND USE IT TO CONSPIRE AN ISLAMIC REVOLUTION IN SPAIN

While many label the Inquisition as bigoted and xenophobic, what aided this stealth jihad was in fact the tolerance of Spain. The Spanish church had allowed the Muslims who supposedly converted to Christianity to start their own religious order. This new brotherhood had opened a hospital,[56] which to the eyes of the state seemed like a harmless and innocent

---

53 Kamen, *The Spanish Inquisition*, ch. 10, pp. 218, 222
54 Kamen, *The Spanish Inquisition*, ch. 10, pp. 222–223
55 Hurtado de Mendoza, *The War in Granada*, 1.6; Kamen, *The Spanish Inquisition*, ch. 10, p. 224
56 Hurtado de Mendoza, *The War in Granada*, 1.7

enterprise. What the Spaniards didn't know was that it was in this hospital where the Muslims held secret meetings on how they were going to take the country. In order to determine their manpower and receive funds for their plan, these terrorists would send men disguised as beggars who went throughout Andalusia and made the Muslim men, between the ages of twenty and forty-five, to give money. This not only provided funds, but gave them the estimate as to how many men they had who were fit for war, who could bear arms and who already owned weapons.[57] These Islamists were so elusive that of course an inquisition was incumbent for the welfare of Spain. In truth, the fact that they were allowed to build this hospital shows the tolerance of the country and the lack of intolerance which was needed at such a detrimental time.

But, this did not go under the radar of the Inquisition nor of the government as a whole. What was being done in the hospital alerted the Marquess of Mondejar and his son, the Count of Tendilla, who was in charge of the armed forces.

Pedro de Deza, president of the Inquisition's Supreme Council, held his own intelligence on the scandal, and both the archbishop and judges of the Inquisition knew what was happening. All of these had sent letters to the king requesting him to help them punish the Moors. As usually happens, the truth was taken lightly; for when the evidence of the plot was presented to officials in Madrid, it was considered an exaggeration and they were not convinced. They in fact blamed those who reported on the plot of asking for troops merely to "bolster their own position." While these politicians wasted time, the Muslims took notice of this weakness and decided to commence their violence immediately. They sent a message to the North African kings of Tetuan in Morocco and of Algeria asking for arms and men and that when they sent their ships to Spain their flags should be colored so as to signal their arrival.[58] The ships were to be sent to the Marbella shore, and Cabo Gato where they were to make their way inland to the Alpujarras and the valleys of the Almonzora and Almeria rivers. They had also hoped that the Muslims of Valencia would arise too.

THE MUSLIMS SPARK A REVOLUTION

A very influential Muslim named Aben Xahuar provoked a fervent rally amongst his fellow warriors for Allah. As typical of Islamic rebel rousers, Xahuar began his speech with words of self-pity and the striving for tolerance: "We Moriscoes suffer this misery and poverty because the Christians will not accept us or let us live amongst them as their neighbors and equals."[59] Where was equality when the Muslim invaders defiled countless churches by making them into mosques? Where was equality when Tariq ibn Ziyad, one of the major invaders of Spain, had Christian males be cut to pieces and their flesh boiled in cauldrons?[60] He used the term equality for the same reason the communists of today use it: to advance tyranny. He then

---

57 See Hurtado de Mendoza, *The War in Granada*, 1.7
58 See Hurtado de Mendoza, *The War in Granada*, 1.8
59 In Hurtado de Mendoza, 1.9
60 See Schmidt, *The Great Divide*, ch. 2, p. 45

proceeded to his true intention, mixing both a call to violence and then justifying it by exaggerated oppression:

> If we rise up surprise them, not only the kingdom of Granada but that part of Andalusia that used to belong to us in the past and is now in enemy hands can be regained in the first rush, or else, if you so decide, we can restrict the revolt to our own Granada. ... For years now, we have all been companions in persecution and adversity, so let us now resolve to bring things forward and to work together for victory, for there is no way in which the crimes against us can be avenged, nor the evil that has been done to us undone, nor to hold on to anything that we possess—even our very lives—unless we rid ourselves of this slavery by the sword![61]

This same ruffian encouraged his people to elect a leader to rule them, and so they ascended Muhammad ibn Humeya, a man who just prior to this professed the Christian faith.[62] This explains why the Spanish Inquisition investigated Muslims who claimed to have converted to Christianity. Many of them were stealth jihadists who slyly professed the Faith only to plan attacks on Christendom without the assiduous watch of zealous inquisitors. Ibn Humeya, upon his election, faced east toward that center for Mecca, and proclaimed that he swore "to live and die by the Law [Sharia] of the Prophet within his kingdom and to defend the Law, and his kingdom, and all his subjects, and all his vassals." The people congregated around him, carried him up and paraded him as they fervently declared him "King of Granada and Cordoba."[63]

They esteemed him as king over cities which never belonged to him, because they saw themselves as now the future rulers of Spain who were going to enforce the land under the Sharia code of Muhammad. Luckily, this rebellious and seditious appointing of a Islamist dictator was being closely watched by agents of the Inquisition[64]—yes, that system which so many in today's church chastise and scorn as evil or antichrist; that system which was the blockade that kept these mobsters from further enslaving another multitude of saints, burning down another numberless amount of churches, and tainting with their heathenism a nation dedicated to God. It kept the Muslims—those modern Zebahs and Zalmunnas—from charging against and invading the land of the Spanish cavaliers declaring to take the sanctuaries of God.

THE MOROCCAN GOVERNMENT WAS SUPPORTING THE ISLAMIC REVOLUTION

As they were preparing for their attack upon Spain, the Moroccan king of Fez sent his promises to the Moors that he would lend them all the help they needed, since he was a very fundamentalist believer in the Koran[65] and affirmed their cause against Christendom. The kings of Algeria and Fez both permitted their mercenaries to fight the jihad in Granada, and

---

61 In Hurtado de Mendoza, *The War in Granada*, 1.9, ellipses mine
62 Hurtado de Mendoza, *The War in Granada*, 1.10
63 Mendoza, 1.10, brackets mine
64 Mendoza, 1.10
65 See Mendoza, 1.11

sold arms to the rebels.⁶⁶ All of this shows the constant involvement which the Muslims had done to recapture Spain, further making clear the necessity for the Inquisition.

In September of 1568 the Moors in Spain were corresponding with the Algerian Aluch Ali who arrived with a fleet of warriors; but when he realized that the Spaniards knew of his coming and were already waiting for him, he turned his ship and fled back to Africa.⁶⁷ This Berber being already expected to come would have never happened if it wasn't for inquisitors who took the time to investigate the arrival of this foreign enemy.

THE MUSLIMS BEGIN TO MURDER SPANIARDS

The Muslim threat was very real in Spain, it was not a mere imagined fear fabricated by bigoted priests as a scare-mongering tactic; and it was close, right in the front doors of the people. The Muslims always had, and still have, the amazing ability to smell fear, and they surely did when they were in the Albaicin where they murdered a Spanish soldier, wounded another, and sacked a shop. So close to home was the enemy that no one felt safe anymore, laughter left and worry, trepidation, and turmoil prevailed. Houses were deserted and stores closed, men went to work at irregular hours and women filled the churches praying forevermore, and pressingly asked questions as to what was happening.⁶⁸ They had thought the Muslim problem was already long and gone, but now they were yet again confronted with it. If only they had erased the existence of Islam in Spain they would have never suffered through this.

The Muslims then surrounded the town of Orgiva and pounded its walls with a battering ram; and as all of this chaos went on the poor people within the walls heard the savage screams of a mullah to surrender the city and convert to Islam. The siege proceeded all to the sounds of battering rams and the maniacal sermons of a preaching tyrant.⁶⁹ All throughout the lands of the Alpujarras, the valley of the Almeira River, the Bolodui, and the surrounding places, the Muslims lurked about searching for victims. As Satan showed Christ "all the kingdoms of the world, and the glory of them," and said to Him, "All these things will I give thee, if thou wilt fall down and worship me," (Matthew 4:8) so did the Muslims offer freedom, riches and good jobs if the Christians there bowed down and worshipped Allah. All refused.

THE MUSLIMS ATTACK CHURCHES

In response, the Islamists burnt churches and profaned sacraments. They took priests and Christians and those Muslims who converted to Christianity, and slaughtered them for defying Sharia. In Guecija they agreed to burn down a monastery of Augustinian friars. The friars fled to a monastery tower, climbed to the roof, looked down upon the barbarians and poured on them boiling olive oil. The Muslims seized the curate of Mairena, covered him in gunpowder and set him on fire. They buried the vicar just up to the waist so as to use his body for target practice. They did the same to numerous others, but instead of killing them

---

66 Mendoza, 1.11
67 Mendoza, 1.12
68 Mendoza, 1.16
69 Mendoza, 1.17

instantly, they wounded them and let them bleed and starve to death. They took many a saint and mutilated their bodies, and then handed them over to their women to finish them off.[70] Even the women did not refrain from such sadism, and thus why even the softer gender did Joshua not spare when he utterly destroyed "both man and woman" in Canaan.[71] Others were stoned to death; some were beaten till they perished; numerous of them were skinned alive or thrown off the tops of cliffs. They took the two sons of a prominent man named Arze and beheaded one of them. The other they crucified; but he very happily accepted his fate to die as his Redeemer did. Out of all the martyrs who died in this great but ignored massacre, not one denied Christ to save his life.[72]

After such a slaughter any attack upon the Moors by the Spaniards would have been justified as a means to protect Spain and Christendom. On top of all this, the Spanish Muslims were still corresponding with the Turks and Berbers, foreign enemies. They sent a young messenger named Abdala to bring to the king of Algeria a body of Christian captives as a gift to persuade him to help their cause in Spain and to swear fealty to Turkey.

THE OTTOMAN INFILTRATION OF SPAIN

Another Moorish traitor named Hernando el Habaqui recruited Turkish warriors and returned to Spain with a ship filled with weapons and a Turk named Dali who was to help in this grand jihad.[73] The Turks had just recently conquered Constantinople, and now they were trying to wrest Spain back into Islamic control. The Marquess of Mondejar understood this; for he knew that if the Spaniards did not move quickly and squash the rebellion, the greater likelihood it was for the Turks and Barbary Moors to gain a foothold into Spain, build fortifications there and reestablish Muslim power in this Christian land.[74]

A number of Turkish and Berber contingents were spotted in Spain. The Moor Gil de Andrada was found coming to Spain from a ship filled with North Africans and at least thirty Turks. Aben Humeya would eventually have five hundred Turks and Berbers as members of his army. From captured documents the Spaniards discovered that the ambassadors of Aben Humeya were going to and fro to the princes of Barbary, providing them with Christian captives, money, and booty. Barbary help was so prevalent that the Marquess of Velez was compelled to disrupt any further arrivals.

The Spanish also learned of a number of Turkish captains, named Caracax and Hosceni, assisting the Moors. The Moorish leader Aben Aboo also selected Dali, a Muslim from Turkey, to be his captain and a part of his military council. The Ottoman warlord Barbarossa, in extending his power, invaded the Spanish island fortress of Penon. After the Moriscoes failed to conquer the town of Salobrena, the Grand Turk, or sultan of Turkey, sent orders that "they should be given whatever help was possible." Spanish forces would later capture a

---

70 Mendoza, 1.18
71 Joshua 6:21
72 Mendoza, 1.18
73 See Mendoza, 1.18
74 Mendoza, 1.20

number of Muslim spies and discover that the Turkish government was already determined to land reinforcements for the jihadists in Spain. As the Spaniards were retaking the Castil de Ferro from the Moors, fourteen Turkish ships arrived to give aid to the enemy; but as soon as they heard Spanish artillery fire, they fled.[75]

The Inquisition was not just battling with local Moors, but with entire Islamic nations working together to just not overrun Spain but all of Christendom. The sooner this is understood, the sooner the Inquisition will make sense. The Muslims, who were really counterfeit Christians, owed their loyalty not to Spain but to Algeria. After Aben Humeya was murdered by his own soldiers, the Moriscoes nominated Aben Aboo as their new king, but this was not approved officially until he was accepted by the crown of Algeria.[76] The revolt of the Muslims, then, was no grassroots movement—it was an internal invasion supported by powers from without.

There were even numerous Moorish spies pretending to be Spaniards who would masquerade as soldiers to hear the plans of their enemy armies. Spanish Christians would even sympathize with these spies, knowing who they were, reveal to them the intentions of the Spaniards, and sell them ammunition and arms.[77]

THE MUSLIMS MASSACRE THE CHRISTIANS IN ORCE

The distrust which the Spaniard felt for the Muslim who professed Christianity is further justified when one reads what took place in the town of Orce.

The Moriscoes there began an uprising, and when the Spanish citizens were determined to repulse it, the charlatan Christians sent word to their fellow jihadists, who then planned to ambush the true Christians of the town. But these saints were no fools, and when they realized the coming attack they anticipated the enemy and unleashed an effective assault which killed six hundred Muslim fighters. If it wasn't for the more trained Turks and Moors these Muslims would have been able to efficiently retreat.[78]

But if it wasn't for the fake Christians, this attempted ambush would have never occurred. The Moriscoes of Sierra de Ronda, while hiding their true sentiments, had always aspired to rise up for the cause of Allah, as we learn from the Historian Mendoza.[79] The very existence of this treachery gave ample reason for an investigation on the Moriscoes. This is not to say that they were no true converts—they were—and these were in fact persecuted by the impostors.

The Moorish warlord El Alarabi made a most viscous attack on a body of Spanish troops, trapping them, and while his men slaughtered a thousand of these poor soldiers, they also

---

75 Mendoza, 2.14; 2.20; 2.21; 2.25; 3.3; 3.7; 3.10; 3.14; 3.23; 4.9. See also 3.15; 4.19. That the sultan encouraged the revolution, see Dale Ahlquist's and Peter Floriani's notes on Chesterton's Lepanto, n. 15
76 Mendoza, 3.14
77 Mendoza, 3.9; see also Kamen, *The Spanish Inquisition*, ch. i, p. 6
78 Mendoza, 3.18
79 Mendoza, 4.11

took the pleasure in massacring the authentic Moriscoes who were loyal to Spain.[80] An inquisition on false Christians, therefore, was a favor to the true converts.

ISLAMIC HUMAN SACRIFICE IN SPAIN

The surprise assaults by Muslims toward Spanish soldiers continued to be relentless. They attacked a group of warriors at a bridge in Tablate, cutting them all down without mercy. The poor men fled to a church to which the pursuing enemy, their scimitars still wet in blood, set ablaze and burned all who were inside alive.[81] There were a number of acts done by the Muslims in Ohanez which not only exemplified utter cruelty, but exposed the truly diabolical side to this war between the crescent and the Cross. The savages were greatly worried on how they were to win over the Spanish, and so to guarantee a victory they conducted a human sacrifice and took twenty Christian girls, beheaded them and lined up their heads on the steps of the local church, and then seized twenty friars, and after some resisting, managed to fry them in olive oil, all in the belief that their blood would propitiate Allah to grant them victory. A similar situation took place in Carthage, in which the Muslims, in fear of a coming Spanish army under the emperor Charles, ritually sacrificed five Christians to gain the protection of Allah. They chose five because, according to Mendoza, "there are five places in the Koran that call for human sacrifice."[82]

Moriscoes from the Sierra de Baza and the Almonzora Valley formed themselves into raiding parties and would put entire rural areas to the flame and to the sword. Aben Humeya, with seven thousand men, stormed much of the Spanish countryside and burned gardens and irrigation centers by which the farmers cared for their crops. Like rodents in a an abundant field, Aben Aboo captured Almanzora, the Sierra de Filabres, the major towns and villages of the Baza country, Seron, Tijola, and Guejar.[83]

A vicious incursion was done by the Moors in which they destroyed the headquarters of a Spanish official, murdered a captain Leon and twenty of his men, who were all beheaded; their heads were taken as trophies and stuck upon pikes and hung on walls.[84] When the Muslims took Tarifa, they kidnapped the son of Guzman, the town's garrison leader, and held the boy at knife point. The father implored them to throw down the knife, but instead the savage Moors slit the boy's throat.[85]

THE WAR AGAINST THE MOORS BEGINS

The government could no longer take the violence and military expansion that was done by the Moriscoes, and so he commissioned Don Alonso de Guzman and Don Luis Ponce de Leon to purge the country from the Moriscoes by finding "them wherever they might be hiding" and "to gather them into camps with their women, their children and household

---

80 Mendoza, 3.6
81 Mendoza, 2.1
82 Mendoza, 2.9
83 Mendoza, 3.11; 3.12; 3.19
84 Mendoza, 3.23
85 Mendoza, 4.12

goods and drive them out of Spain into Africa."[86] While this may terrify the modern mind, the consequences of not carrying out this plan quickly enough were detrimental.

The Islamic rebel leader El Melqui, who made trips back and forth from Spain to Morocco, stirred in the hearts of the Moriscoes a new spirt of revolt. He was arrested by the Inquisition for heresy, and while many today would deem this bigoted and racist, there was an obvious lack of foresight by that same institution, and El Melqui was released.[87] This would receive adulation by our press, but because of this imprudent tolerance, El Melqui took the opportunity to become a dominate force and a tyrant amongst his own people. He had Moriscoes who were loyal to Spain arrested by his henchmen and forced to conform to the jihad. The Spaniards did not wish initially to get rid of all of the Moriscoes, just the ones who were involved in sedition and who refused to integrate in Spanish culture. For when the Moriscos of Benahabiz wished to agree to the terms of peace of the king of Spain, one Barcoqui, also a friendly Morisco, came forth and journeyed to report this. When he arrived to the fort of Montemayor the Spanish attempted to lead him to a safe house, but he was seized by the local Muslims, followers of El Melqui, and murdered.[88]

A CONSPIRACY TO INVADE SPAIN IS DISCOVERED

In 1580 there was a discovered conspiracy to invade Spain from Morocco. When king Philip II—staggered by the massacres of priest by the Muslim rebels[89]—published an order "to root out all of the Moors and resettle them in Castile," it was also commanded by the Duke, who was in charge of this expulsion, "that all of the Moors who had nothing to do with the rebellion should be gathered together at the castle at Ronda with all their household goods and clothes that they could carry and their women and children."[90] This just policy illustrates the civility and equity of the Christian Spaniard, which was, and still is, far more superior to the values of Muhammad and his barbaric followers of the Orient. But this did not stop the brutal spirit of El Melqui and his followers, who led many massacres, as Mendoza describes:

> They [the Moors] began to appear here, there and everywhere, from Rona to Marbella, at all hours of the day and night, kidnapping farmworkers, stealing herds, robbing travelers on the roads even under the walls of Ronda. ...[A]lmost every day people were being killed in the Valley of Rioverde and the Sierra de Alborno.[91]

With the jihad gaining great momentum, and with the Islamic threat from North Africa so close, the Spaniards concluded that they had to finish off the vicious Moors before their power could reach its highest impetus.[92]

---

86 Mendoza, 4.13
87 Mendoza, 4.15
88 Mendoza, 4.15
89 See Kamen, *The Spanish Inquisition*, ch. 10, p. 224
90 Mendoza, 4.18
91 Mendoza, 4.19, brackets mine
92 See Mendoza, 4.19

THE SPANISH GOVERNMENT DECLARES THAT THE MUSLIMS MUST BE DRIVEN OUT

After many battles, and many deaths,[93] the Moorish rebellion (or what is called the Morisco Revolt) was crushed. The idea of expulsion was approved by both Inquisition and Church. At the beginning, wealthy landowners opposed the expulsion, since so many of their vassals were Moors, but as soon as the Muslim population increased to a terrifying level, much violence arose, the pompous counts saw their own lives at stake and they changed their position and agreed to expulsion.[94] The Spanish government set out to arrest Moors and oust them out, and their chiefs, elders, and captains, were all hung like Haman and his sons.

A praise should be made to the Spaniard Francisco Barredo, for he was awarded by the state for his help to purge Spain of Moorish danger, and made a number of trips to Barbary to rescue Spanish Christians who were kidnapped. During one of his missions he received the crown of martyrdom and was killed. Many of the Moors in Spain fled to North Africa, while others of them became what was called Moros de paz, or "peaceful Moors."[95] Unapologetic inquisition and military force, then, were the only ways to make these renegades tranquil. The expulsion of the Moors was eventually decreed in 1609, and was finally carried out in 1614.[96] It was done with complete justification within Orthodoxy and the authority of the Church using the temporal arm to expel them. Vitoria, one of the most respected of the Church's theologians, approved of the expulsion of heretics for the sake of preventing their sedition and rebellion:

> The king may order the expulsion of unbelievers from the kingdom to prevent civil seditions among the populace; this is lawful, so long as it does not bring the worship of God into contempt. [97]

THE SPANISH INQUISITION PUNISHES THE MUSLIMS

In the process of this squashing of covert jihad, many Moriscos were arrested and punished, sometimes by whipping, at other times by renunciation, and at occasions by execution. From the 1570s in Aragon and Valencia, Moriscoes made the majority of Inquisition prosecutions, and not Jews as is so commonly presented in anti-Catholic propaganda. Over the years 1540–59 two hundred and sixty-six Moriscoes were tried in Saragossa alone, and in between 1560 and 1614 the amount of Moriscoes prosecuted shot up to 2,371. In Valencia, in the later period of the Inquisition, there were 2,465 Moriscoes tried.[98] Heresy abounded in the Morisco areas so much that the bishop of Tortosa wrote in 1568:

> These people have me fed up and exasperated. …they have a damnable attitude and make

---

93 For descriptions and details on these battles, see Mendoza, 1.14; 1.15; 1.19; 1.21; 1.22; 1.24; 2.1; 2.4; 2.7; 2.14; 3.4; 3.6; 3.20; 4.3; 4.7; 4.14; 4.15; 4.16; 4.17; 4.19
94 Kamen, *The Spanish Inquisition*, ch. 10, pp. 226–227
95 Mendoza, 4.24
96 Kaman, *The Spanish Inquisition*, ch. 10, p. 227
97 Vitoria, *On Law*, ST I–II. 99. 4–5, 135
98 Kamen, *The Spanish Inquisition*, ch. 10, p. 224

me despair of any good in them. I have been through these mountains for eight days now and find them more Muslim than ever and very set in their bad ways. I repeat my advice that they should be given a general pardon without insisting on confessions, for there is no other way (unless it be to burn them all). [99]

Ramiro de Palencia, a Moor who resided in Granada, professed Christianity but was soon fined and renounced as a heretic because he was caught observing Islamic prayers and was heard saying, while yawning, "May Muhammad close my eyes."

Sebastian de Alcaraz was declared a heretic, whipped and fined for owning several Islamic books. Yasbel Xaquiza was renounced and made to pay thirty ducats for owning koranic commentary. Mayor Garcia, a Moorish woman, was renounced as a heretic because she said, in regard to Mary, "How could a married woman remain a virgin after giving birth?"

"This is so intolerant!" cries the modern, but he never realized what consequences would come about if the Spaniards never reprimanded the Moors for following Islam. Let us look at other cases of arrests which indicated that the false Moriscos were indeed a threat that needed to be suppressed.

Lucia de Huete was punished by abjuration and whipping after it was proven that she joined the Moors in the Morisco Revolt and prayed to Muhammad "to favor the rebels against the Christians." Another Moor, named Juan Martin Azara, a brother of an Islamic rebel leader in Spain, was found to have joined the jihad, declared that Sharia was the superior law over all others, and proclaimed reverence to Muhammad. He was convicted of observing Sharia and not just promoting it in Spain. He was sentenced to prison and to labor in the ships.[100]

Garcia de Luna el Guarguali was discovered to have been involved in raids to murder Spanish Christians, but the Christians fended them off. He was also found guilty of partaking in Islamic rituals. It was agreed that he be sent to a secular court to be tried and executed, but after confessing all of his crimes he was given the much lighter punishment of working in ships. Luis Abenjafar was tried by the Inquisition for observing Ramadan. "How bigoted!" would be our first reaction because of our modern mindsets, but if we just continue on we will find that he also purchased weapons to kill Spaniards. But, with the Inquisition and all of its mercy for anyone who confessed, this terrorist was compelled to work in the galleys.[101]

Quite an illustrative case for how dangerous the Moriscos were is that of Alonso Rufian. He was born and raised in Granada, and travelled back to North Africa to live amongst his own, attend mosque services and observe his Muslim rituals. This would sound all quite pious if you are an orientalist, but anyone with foresight would see the perilous potential of this behavior. As soon as he heard of the uprising of the Moors against Christianity, he returned to Spain and took up arms against the saints. He was arrested, found guilty, and swiftly executed.[102]

99 Quoted in Kamen, *The Spanish Inquisition*, ch. 10, p. 225
100 Auto de Fe Celebrated in Granada, March 18, 1571, in Homza, *The Spanish Inquisition*, document 22, p. 241
101 Auto de Fe Celebrated in Granada, March 18, 1571, in Homza, *The Spanish Inquisition*, document 22, pp. 243–244
102 Auto de Fe Celebrated in Granada, March 18, 1571, in Homza, *The Spanish Inquisition*, document 22, p. 244

Juan de Luna partook in the violent opposition, and because he confessed to this he was not severely punished, but only had to wear the sanbenito—an outfit worn by heretics—for a short moment. Hernan Perez Alcaraz did away with his Spanish name, took up a Muslim name and joined the revolution. He too was not punished and merely made to wear the sanbenito.[103] These particular cases further reveal the threat of the Muslim and the mercy of the Inquisition.

The Spaniards did all of this for the sake of self-preservation, and not for the pleasure of causing bloodshed against people simply because they were Moors. When a group of Moors were found guilty of falsely accusing another one of their fellow Moors, Juan Fernandez de Quadros, and of desecrating a cross, they were each punished with four hundred lashes and sentenced to eight years in the galleys.[104]

Beatriz el Tez, though she said she was a Catholic, soon took off her false mask and proclaimed that there was no god but Allah and Muhammad was his messenger; she also expressed her wish to die so that "Muhammad would take her."[105] These suicidal and bizarre convictions were signs of a dangerous person. She believed that a belief in Sharia was required for salvation, and the response to this seditious behavior was the sanbenito and one hundred lashes.[106] Lady Constanca Lopez was a more serious case. She expressed her happiness for the Morisco uprising by stealing a cross from a church, placing it in her basement, and using it for firewood. She would go before Christians and pompously say, "What do you think? That the world is always going to be yours? And because you dress us in a certain way, we have to be Christian? Underneath it all, we have done and will do what we want, because we were Moors, and Moors we shall remain." She gave a fervent sermon which lasted from morning to midday calling for the support of the great Muslim warlord Aben Humeya, who as we have already read, orchestrated numerous massacres on innocent Spaniards. She exalted Sharia, invoked Muhammad and preformed her prayers. For all of this she was sentenced to prison.[107]

There was one Spaniard, though said to be a Christian, who was tried for saying that "he was a Muslim, and for praying in the mosque like a Muslim."[108]

The expulsion of the Moors in 1571, after reading about all of these mutinies, was thus justified.

The conversion of the Moors to Christianity still receives the outcry and mocking of the moderns. But here is the reality: when Muslims ruled Spain they enacted edicts for the obliteration of Christianity and for the enslavement and extermination of Christians, while the Inquisition strived for the redemption of the Muslim's soul.[109] The expulsion of those who

---

103 Auto de Fe Celebrated in Granada, March 18, 1571, in Homza, *The Spanish Inquisition*, document 22, pp. 244–245
104 Auto de Fe Celebrated in Granada, March 18, 1571, in Homza, *The Spanish Inquisition*, document 22, p. 240
105 Auto de Fe Celebrated in Granada, March 18, 1571, in Homza, *The Spanish Inquisition*, document 22, p. 245
106 Auto de Fe Celebrated in Granada, March 18, 1571, in Homza, *The Spanish Inquisition*, document 22, p. 245
107 Auto de Fe Celebrated in Granada, March 18, 1571, in Homza, *The Spanish Inquisition*, document 22, pp. 245-246
108 Kamen, *The Spanish Inquisition*, ch. i, p. 6
109 P.F., *The Spanish Inquisition*, USCM, vol. ii, p. 456

remained Muslim was a necessity for the preservation of Spain; any further tolerance would have led to another Morisco revolt, and another multitude of dead people. If the uprising actually succeeded, it could have led to the collapse of the Spanish kingdom, and to the end of a major military support to the rest of a Catholic Christendom which was trying to fight invading Muslims.[110]

AMERICA HAD AN INQUISITION AGAINST THE NATIVE INDIANS

One can even say that the American president Andrew Jackson was implementing an inquisition when he signed the Indian Removal Act of 1830, in which all Indians who did not fully assimilate to American society were to be removed west of the Mississippi. The Creeks and the Chickasaws complied while eight million Cherokees were forced to journey two thousand miles from Georgia to what is today Oklahoma. Twenty percent of them died of starvation, or from rain, sleet, and snow.[111] But I will not reiterate the common jargon and say that I am ashamed of such history. I will not ignore the fact that the Americans were suffering from attacks by the Indians similar to those which the Moors afflicted upon the Spaniards. I will not ignore that in 1813, just sixteen years prior to the signing of the Act, the Creek Indians executed a gory raid on Fort Mims in Alabama where they butchered two hundred soldiers, massacred two hundred and fifty old men, women and children by fire and tomahawk, and murdered another one hundred friendly Indians.[112] I will not ignore the words of an eyewitness to this horror, who stated that "blood and brains bespattered the whole earth. The children were seized by the legs, and killed by batting their heads against the stockading. The women were scalped and those who were pregnant were opened, while they were alive, and the embryo infants let out of the womb."[113]

Did America, after such an atrocity, strive for a policy of toleration? Did America throw the event under the rug to preserve relations with the Indians? No—America conducted a stern inquisition on the Creeks and commissioned the then Major General Andrew Jackson to crush the threat. When he arrived at a Creek Indian village suspected of having violent intentions toward America, he burnt it to the ground, and if anybody resisted, he ordered them to be seized and executed.[114] But again, I will not condemn Jackson for taking this measure due to the violence and savage raids of the Indians, just as I will not chastise the Spaniards for their expulsion of the Moors for their continuous terror attacks. The infamous Davy Crocket fought under Jackson and when describing the killing of the Creeks, he writes that "we shot them like dogs." When a Creek squaw, who was guarding a hut hiding many Indians including several dozen warriors, killed an American lieutenant, Jackson's men shot

---

110 See Dale Ahlquist's and Peter Floriani's notes on Chesterton's Lepanto, n. 15
111 See Winston Groom, *Patriotic Fire*, ch. iv, p. 55, note; ch. xviii, p. 255, Alfred A. Knopf, New York, 2006
112 See William Burdick, Political and Historical Register, vol. i, p. 191; A Copy of a letter from Captain Kennedy Brigadier-General Claiborne, dated Mount Vernon, September 26th, 1813, in T.H. Palmer, The Historical Register, vol. ii, p. 332
113 In Winston Groom, *Patriotic Fire*, ch. iii, pp. 46–47
114 In Winston Groom, *Patriotic Fire*, ch. iii, p. 47; ch. iv, p. 48

her down and then burned the entire hut, killing one hundred and eighty Indians.[115] Sixteen years later, after the Creek War, Jackson passed and advocated the Indian Removal Act which, in a way, could be compared to the sentiments of the Spanish inquisitors. The Inquisition in Spain was done for the establishment of Christian supremacy, in that it wanted the people to integrate into Spanish culture and become Christian, and in comparison, Jackson himself said that one of the purposes of the Indian Removal Act was to have the Indians who refused to assimilate into American society convert to Christianity. In his own words on the Act:

> It will separate the Indians from immediate contact with settlements of whites; free them from the power of the States; enable them to pursue happiness in their own way and under their own rude institutions; will retard the progress of decay, which is lessening their numbers, and perhaps cause them gradually, under the protection of the Government and through the influence of good counsels, to cast off their savage habits and become an interesting, civilized, and Christian community. ...He [the Indian] is unwilling to submit to the laws of the States and mingle with their population. To save him from this alternative, or perhaps utter annihilation, the General Government kindly offers him a new home, and proposes to pay the whole expense of his removal and settlement.[116]

No one can deny that the expulsion of the Indians made a more peaceful society for the Americans, and that this security still exists today: no one worries anymore about Indians raiding one's town. This freedom from the capricious hand armed with the tomahawk could only be attributed to the expulsion of the Indians—and as harsh as it sounds, this is only the honest truth that most are too afraid to confront: American civilization would have been impossible to build if Christian Europeans never settled on the land in the first place. Is it Christian supremacy over Indian religion and culture?

Yes, it would be dishonest to deny this, but since when were we ever obligated to lament over this very fact? Those who point the finger and look down upon any part of Western history which illustrates Christian supremacy should realize that there is no nation on earth that does not have supremacy. If Christian dominance was never made in America, then this nation would be ruled under the supremacy of the savage religion of the Indian. Whether or not a nation has within its society religious supremacy is insignificant, what matters is what type of supremacy. What man, living a civilized life in America, would decide to leave his homeland for a country ruled under Islamic supremacy? If the people who complain about Christian supremacy have their way and the major influence of the Bible was gotten rid of, they would never bicker about a nation adopting atheist supremacy.

Just look at America in the present day: we have torn down the Christian supremacy of Jackson and have now allowed ourselves to be yoked by a socialist supremacy, where children can be murdered in the womb, where financial success is punished by taxes worse than those imposed on the Colonies by the British Empire, and where the Bible cannot be brought in

---

115 Winston Groom, *Patriotic Fire*, ch. iv, p. 49
116 Transcript of President Andrew Jackson's Message to Congress 'On Indian Removal' (1830), found in ourdocument.gov

public without offending someone. The same can be applied to the Spanish Inquisition. Was it Christian supremacist? Yes. But what would have happened if it was never established, and the Moor was permitted the free exorcise of Islam? Eventually the Muslims, because of the liberal toleration for their religion, would have easily retaken Spain, and that beautiful crown of Christendom would have wilted away like a flower before the scorching sun. Islamic supremacy would then take power, and today's historians would not care to write a paragraph in protest. In the place of the Indians put the Moors; in the place of the Americans put the Spaniards, and the Spanish Inquisition makes a lot more sense.

ISLAMIC VIOLENCE WOULD BE IMPOSSIBLE WITHOUT MUSLIM SYMPATHIZERS

Islamic violence and revolt was impossible without sympathizers to the Islamic cause who would help direct Muslim warriors inside the now fully Christian nation. King Philip II, who is continuously portrayed by today's historians as a bigoted tyrant of the Inquisition, gave actual details in 1567 on how the Muslims used sympathizers within Spain to help them penetrate the borders:

> Having been informed that, notwithstanding what has been ordained by us, as well by sea and by land, particularly for the kingdom of Granada, for the purpose of insuring the defense and security of our kingdoms, the Turks, Moors, and corsairs have already committed, and still commit, in the ports of this kingdom, on the coasts, in maritime places, and those bordering on the sea, robberies, misdeeds, injuries, and seizures of Christians; evils which are notorious, and which, it is said, have been, and are, committed with ease and security, by favor of the intercourse and understanding who the ravishers have had, and still have, with some of the inhabitants of the country, who give them intelligence, guide them, receive them, hide them, and lend them favor and assistance; some of them even going away with the Moors and Turks, leading away and carrying with them their wives, their children, their goods, Christian captives, and the things which they are able to ravish from the Christians; while other inhabitants of the same kingdom, who have participated in these projects, or have been acquainted with them, remain in the country, without having been or being punished; for it appears that measures are not executed with due severity, nor as completely, or with as much care as they ought to be: as, moreover, it seems very difficult to get accurate information, as it appears that even the justices and the judges, to whom it belongs to make inquiries and to punish, have displayed remissness and negligence in their deployment."[117]

---

117 The new Recopilacion, b. 8, ch. 2, Law xx, in J. Balmes, *Protestantism and Catholicity* Compared, p. 452, Notes, n. 26

THE WEAKNESS OF THE SPANISH GOVERNMENT BEFORE THE EXPULSION OF THE MUSLIMS COULD BE COMPARED TO THE HESITANCY OF THE FOUNDING FATHERS BEFORE FIGHTING AGAINST THE BARBARY PIRATES

The Muslims did not want peace, nor would they have ever asked for it. Their violent inveteracy of trying to recapture Spain was aided by traitors within the country, and so crucial was it to keep Spain forever independent that such treasonous fellows needed to be punished.

No American would ever disagree with conducting an inquisition in his own country if it was ever in the same predicament as Spain. If Turks and Algerians ever invaded America, and the citizens recaptured their nation back into independence, surely they would set a government system to combat any attempts by the Muslims to conquer it again. No American would disagree with this. Those Muslims who were committing piracy on American ships in the eighteenth century were of the same race as those who were continuously trying to steal Spain during her Inquisition: Turks and North Africans. When Jefferson and John Adams asked the ambassador of Tripoli as to why the Muslims were attacking American ships, seeing that the United States never started a war with them, the Jihadist simply responded that "it was founded on the Laws of their Prophet, that it was written in their Koran, that all nations who should not have acknowledged their authority were sinners, that it was their right and duty to make war upon them wherever they could be found, and to make slaves of all they could take as Prisoners, and that every Musselman [Muslim] who should be slain in battle was sure to go to Paradise."[118]

It would be impossible to make any solid peace agreement with such criminals; the only solution for Spain was a strict intolerance toward Islamism, and any aiders to its expansionist cause. Even the two Founders affirmed that if tribute could not be obtained to pay the pirates, "our best endeavours shall be used to remove this formidable obstacle out of the way of the prosperity of the United States."[119] It is a shame that Jefferson and Adams wasted precious time in trying to reason with the Turks and Moors through money, instead of making an immediate attack on the enemy, which they eventually had to do. The Spaniard, on the other hand—because he suffered so much under Islamic tyranny—took swift measures to stop any Muslim advances. The Americans made war upon the jihadists, and no American today would condemn this, so why do so many today express their hatred for the Spanish Inquisition when it was done for the same purpose of crushing Jihadism?

If the Americans did nothing, the Moorish pirates would have landed right on the shores of New York and Philadelphia, pleasurably taken a sip from the Mississippi River, happily seized fair maidens for concubines, and with no mercy burned down churches. The Spaniards were in a similar, but worse situation, since they were so close to the Middle East. If they took no action, and accepted fully the lies of tolerance, the beautiful cities of Valencia and Barcelona would have become the subject of the Ottoman Turks and their Moroccan

---

118 J.A. & T.J., American Commissioners to John Jay, in Thomas Jefferson, Travels, ed. Anthony Brandt, p. 105
119 J.A. & T.J., American Commissioners to John Jay, in Thomas Jefferson, Travels, ed. Anthony Brandt, p. 105

pirates. Philip described a time of toleration toward Moors, or Moriscos, allowing them time to convert to Christianity. Now, before one brings the accusation of racism and bigotry, it must be understood ones religion in that time was not a mere preference, as we do today, but a political identity. Spain was a Christian nation, and so to embrace Christianity implied that one was patriotic for the country. To be Muslim, then, meant that one believed in Sharia, and not Spanish law; it meant that one desired a universal Islamic nation and not in independent Spanish sovereignty. This did not just apply to Muslims, but anyone not Christian. Religion and politics, unlike in our day, were not separated. Muslims, therefore, were identified as an enemy to the state. This fear was not some fabricated paranoia made by dogmatic priests; it was a real existing threat. Hesitation in squashing this problem would lead to a quick, and second, invasion of Spain.

King Philip's liberal giving of chances and leniency was not working, and the local Moorish communities never ceased to communicate with Muslims in North Africa to aid them in having the lawlessness of Muhammad abound in Spain. "On the contrary," writes Philip on the Moors, "their obstinacy has increased; the peril which threatens our kingdoms, if we keep the Moriscoes [Moors], has been represented to us by persons very well informed and full of the fear of God, who, thinking it proper that a prompt remedy should be applied to this evil, have represented to us that the delay might be charged upon our royal conscience, considering the grave offenses which our Lord receives from that people. We have been assured that we might, without scruple, punish them in their lives and properties, since they were convicted by their continued offenses of being heretics, apostates, and traitors of lese-majeste [treason] divine and human. Although it would have been allowable to proceed against them with the rigor which their offenses deserve, nevertheless, desiring to bring them back by means of mildness and mercy, I ordained, in the city and kingdom of Valencia, an assembly of the patriarchs, and other prelates and wise men, in order to ascertain what could be resolved upon and settled; but having learned that, at the very time they were engaged in remedying the evil, the Moriscoes of the said kingdom of Valencia, and of our other domains, continued to urge forward their pernicious projects; knowing, moreover, from correct and certain intelligence, that they had sent to treat at Constantinople with the Turks, and at Morocco with the king, Muley Fidon, in order that there might be sent into the kingdom of Spain the greatest number of forces possible to aid and assist them; being sure that there would be found in our kingdom more than 150,000 men, as good Moors as those from the coasts of Barbary, all ready to assist them with their lives and fortunes."[120]

Nations cannot survive without inquisitions. France was overran by deist heretics in the eighteenth century, in what is called the French Revolution, in which hundreds of thousands of people were massacred. This could have been prevented if there were measures taken against the deist heresy. As Maistre, a survivor and critique of the Revolution and its deistic foundation, writes, "It is true, there is no longer, now, any reason for entertaining the same alarms. And yet,

---

[120] The new Recopilacion, b. viii, ch. 2, Law xxv, in J. Balmes, *Protestantism and Catholicity* Compared, p. 454, Notes, n. 26, p. 219

when we reflect, that the Inquisition, by its restrictions, and authority, would have prevented the French Revolution,—it is hard to say, whether the Sovereign, who, wholly, and without reserve, gave up this instrument, would not, in reality, be doing an injury to humanity."[121]

If anybody still believes that the Spanish Inquisition was evil and bigoted, they should ask themselves how many inquisitions America has done. What would you call what the U.S. government did to the Japanese because of Pearl Harbor, the Germans because of Hitler, and the Italians because of Mussolini? And what of the arrests of communists in the fifties? These were all inquisitions, done for good reasons, since the state was inquiring to see if any traitors were in the nation. I remember one night when I was with my father in an old dented pickup truck hauling our hot dog cart. It was only about a month after 9/11 and we were picking up a new employee who was from Afghanistan; during the ride he was complaining of how he was arrested and investigated by the authorities. I was shocked, not because I thought it was wrong, but because I never knew this was happening. He then told us of how the police were literally picking Muslims off the street to be interrogated. This was inquisition: the Muslims being arrested were being inquired, and means were being taken to see to it that the nation does not get overran by jihadists. Yet many conservatives will praise this while hypocritically condemning the Inquisition. They seem to forget that a nation that never has inquisitions, is a nation that will never survive. As expected, this nation does not exist, and will never exist.

THE BIRTH OF THE CONVERSO
If you are one who is outspoken about Christianity, there is one thing that will definitely happen: somebody will tell you that he is offended, and if you ask why, he will respond that your religion caused the Inquisition, and he will make it as though the Inquisition was no different than Hitler's Germany or Stalin's Russia. Talk of dungeons, secret interrogation meetings, horrific torture chambers, unbearable prison cells, ruthless priests, and worst of all, a maniacal and sadistic pope. But with some research and perusing of the annals of the Inquisition, you will find that such claims are not based on fact, but fragmented history, in that pieces of propaganda from either the hijacked History Channel, maddening websites, mind numbing movies, or all of the above, are pieced together to make a hastily conclusion. A lie frequently repeated becomes true to the eyes of the masses, and today if anybody expresses outrage for the Inquisition, he is generally accepted, while the few who wish to unbiasedly describe the Inquisition are unfairly painted as bigoted and anti-Semitic.

There are certain points which have to be made in order to comprehend the true Inquisition and the rubbish claims of conspiracy theorists.

Firstly, there were massacres done against Jews in Spain, nobody can deny this, but this is almost all we hear about when reading Spanish history. In the Middle Ages, Spain practiced a fair degree of toleration rare to Medieval Europe, called Convivencia. It was in fact the most diverse and tolerant country in Medieval Europe; England expelled its Jews in 1290, so did France in 1306. Pope Clement IV, in his 1268 Bull, scolded the French king Louis IX for

[121] Maistre, *Letters on the Spanish Inquisition*, letter 2

CHRISTIANITY IS AT WAR: THE MANIFESTO FOR CHRISTIAN MILITANCY

his harsh laws against blasphemers. Yet Spanish Jews were given the liberty to succeed and prosper at every level of society. In the kingdom of Aragon "there was not a noble or prelate in the land who did not keep a Jewish physician," and this was a similar situation in Castile. In Madrid Jewish doctors were even exempted from certain laws and taxes.[122] A most hidden historical fact is that in 1272 the Pope Gregory X issued "an encyclical to all Christians forbidding them to baptize Jews by force or to injure their persons, or to take away their money, or to disturb them during the celebration of their religious festivals."[123] Similarly Pope Clement IV, in his Bull to the king of Navarre in Spain, warned against "rigourous laws" against blasphemers.[124] In 1348, Pope Clement VI warned that anybody who attacked Jews on the suspicion that they caused the Black Death, would be excommunicated. He also opened the doors of Avignon in France, the city in which he lived, for fleeing Jews.[125] Where forced conversion occurred, they were always condemned by the Catholic Church.[126]

In time, bigotry fomented in Spain, and in 1391 a mob from Barcelona attacked the rich and overran Jewish quarters, they were also attacked in Sevile with hundreds killed. The mob gave Jews the choice between baptism or death. Most chose baptism; but how was this responded to? While we hear much about violence toward Jews in Spain, who we are never told about is John I, king of Aragon, who at this time declared that coerced conversion was not sincere as the voluntary conviction of the soul, and decreed that the Jews who were wrested into baptism could return to their religion.

However, the Jews of Castile also endured the same mob violence in 1390, many being put to the sword and forced to be baptized. It was a horrific act, shameful and cruel, but it was not condoned nor encouraged by the government of Castile, nor was it instigated by the Church. We are never told about how the royal authorities of both Castile and Aragon denounced the violence and worked, in the major cities, to protect the Jews. Reuben ben Nissim, a Jew who lived in this time, wrote: "many of the governors of the cities, and the ministers and nobles, defended us, and many of our brethren took refuge in castles, where they provided us with food."[127] When have we heard of this righteousness, coming from Catholic rulers partaking in Christian love? There was even some sectarian violence between Jews and Jewish converts to Christianity. The Jews of Burgos in 1392 gave their remonstrance on how "the Jews who recently turned Christian oppress them and do them much harm." The Jews even saw the voluntary converts as "meshumadim" (renegades). In 1492 Jews were asked to spy on the conversos, and at Toledo in 1485 rabbis were required to condemn, in their synagogues, Jews who did not denounce Judaizers.[128]

---

122 See Thomas F. Madden. "The Truth about the Spanish Inquisition." Crisis (October 2003); Kamen, The Spanish Inquisition, ch. 2, p. 10–11; Maistre, Letters on the Spanish Inquisition, letter 1
123 See Carroll, A History of Christendom, vol. iii, ch. vii, p. 295
124 Maistre, Letters on the Spanish Inquisition, letter 1
125 Carroll, A History of Christendom, vol. iii, ch. x, pp. 392–393
126 Moczar, Seven Lies about Catholic History, ch. iv, p. 78
127 See Thomas F. Madden, The Truth About the Inquisition; Kamen, The Spanish Inquisition, ch.2, p. 10
128 Kamen, The Spanish Inquisition, Ch. 2, pp. 17–18; ch. 4, p. 71

Andres Bernaldez, a contemporary writer and supporter of the Inquisition, complained that Judaism was "allowed to exist through the negligence of the prelates—namely, the archbishops and bishops of Spain—who never acknowledge or denounced it to the popes as they were obliged to do." Even in the heat of hatred toward Judaism, the same primary source writes that many "unbaptized Jews and synagogues still remained in Castile, and the lords and kings always protected them because of their great utility."[129] We cannot ignore the violence of the people, and that also implies that we cannot neglect the civility of many of the Church officials and the government.

Many Jews remained Catholic, some from the fear that it would be heresy if they reverted back to Judaism, others from the fear of future persecution. But in many places, such as Barcelona and Mallorca, the converts felt safer to remain as Christians, their adherence was voluntary. As time went on, their souls rooted in the Gospel, these converts (called Conversos) settled into Christianity, observing the Faith, in many cases, more fervently and admirably than the Spaniards. Their dress, dialect, and cuisine were still Jewish, but their faith was upon the Nazarene. Continuing on into the fifteenth century, religious debate was alive and done in freedom. In 1414 a discourse was held in Tortosa between Jeronimo de Santa Fe, a Catholic who converted from Judaism, and Jewish leaders. Even the Pope, Benedict XIII, was present. When the event was done, three thousand Jews electively accepted Christ as their Messiah.[130]

It is true that in 1412 a law was passed in Castile which prevented the Jews from running for office, possessing titles, and other rights such as bearing arms. But, while this law was written, in practice it was not enforced. The King of Aragon, Alfonso V, reversed anti-Jewish legislation in 1416, and Jews under his power were protected, all of the attacks against them rejected, and all requests for Jewish ghettos denied.[131]

Conversos took pride that they and Christ shared the same blood, and when the Converso bishop of Burgos, Alonso de Cartagena, prayed the Hail Mary, he proclaimed with dignity, "Holy Mary, Mother of God and my blood relative, pray for us sinners." To combat antisemitism in Spain, Pope Nicholas wrote his Papal Bull Humani Generis Enemicus (Enemy of the human race), in which he wrote: "We decree and declare that all Catholics are one body in Christ according to the teaching of our faith." In 1468, Alonso Carrillo, archbishop of Toledo, condemned the guilds organized on racial lineages:

> What is evil is that in the city of Toledo, as in the other cities, towns and places of our see, there are many guilds and brotherhoods of which some under pretense of piety do not receive conversos and others do not receive Old Christians.

Though the Conversos were sincere practicing Christians, their financial success and political accomplishments were to the jealousies of many, and the call to inquire their con-

---

[129] Andres Bernaldez, Recollections of the Reign of the Catholic Kings, in Homza, *The Spanish Inquisition*, document 1, p. 1, Hacket Publishing Company (2006)
[130] Thomas F. Madden. *"The Truth about the Spanish Inquisition."* Crisis (October 2003); Kamen, *The Spanish Inquisition*, ch. 2, pp. 10–11; Kamen, *The Spanish Inquisition*, ch. 2, p. 14
[131] Kamen, *The Spanish Inquisition*, ch. 2, p. 14–15

CHRISTIANITY IS AT WAR: THE MANIFESTO FOR CHRISTIAN MILITANCY

viction was made to the king Ferdinand. Believe it or not, accusations against the Conversos were made not only by Christians, but by Jews as well. In Ucles, in 1491, Jewish citizens voluntarily gave testimony against Christians of Jewish origin. The Jewish poet Selomoh Bonafed complained of how so many Jews turned to Christianity, he lamented how "many of the most respected leaders of our aljamas [communities] abandoned them." Because there were a high number of Conversos working in his court, Ferdinand was reluctant and did not heed to the demands of the mob, but because the clamor of the masses was frequent and intense, he acquiesced.[132]

Those who were always Jewish and never professed Christianity had nothing to fear from the Inquisition: the institution was made, in the words of historian Thomas F. Madden, "to find and correct the lost sheep of Christ's flock."[133] Throughout the first decade of the Inquisition, Ferdinand and Isabella protected the Jews, as they at the same time tried to extinguish Judaizing. The movement against Judaizing was a result of social and political pressures against the conversos,[134] not a conspiracy done by the Catholic Church.

THE ABUSES OF THE INQUISITION WERE COMBATED BY THE CHURCH

It is most repeated that the Catholic Church was the orchestrator behind this coercion, and to this must be said another point which illustrates the true nature of the Inquisition: the Catholic Church was not involved.[135]

While most accused Conversos were acquitted, some were executed—not on account of Christianity, but the antithesis of this beautiful Faith: false testimony. For those who want to ascribe all of this to the popes or the Vatican, I must say that the excesses of the Inquisition, though they weren't many, were condemned by the Church. Ferdinand issued certain orders for investigation on the Conversos and had them sent throughout the city of Seville and its archbishopric. After this was done, two years had passed and nothing happened against the Conversos. The inquisitors and the archbishops cared not to investigate them, and allowed the Catholic Jews to wander freely. Finally, on the instigation of certain officials[136] the king now truly affirmed the rampant conspiracies and suspicions, and believed in the danger of false Conversos.[137]

Ferdinand and Isabella requested from Pope Sixtus IV permission to appoint their own inquisitors, the Pope issued the papal bulls demanded in 1478. On the appeal of the Conversos

---

132 Thomas F. Madden. "The Truth about the Spanish Inquisition." Crisis (October 2003); Kamen, The Spanish Inquisition, ch. i, p. 5; ch. ii, p. 17; ch. 3, p. 34–5
133 Thomas F. Madden, The Truth About the Inquisition. See also Carroll, A History of Inquisition, vol. iii, ch. xiv, p. 608; Moczar, Seven Lies about Catholic History, ch. iv, p. 87, 95
134 Kamen, The Spanish Inquisition, ch. 3, p. 61
135 P.F., The Spanish Inquisition, published in the United States Catholic Magazine (USCM), vol. ii, p. 456 (1843)
136 For those who want to know the names: Pedro Fernandez de Solis, Chief Officer of Justice and Bishop of Cadiz; Diego de Merlo, Chief Officer of Justice; and Friar Alonso (Andres Beraldez, Recollections of the Reign of the Catholic Kings, ch. 43, in Homza, The Spanish Inquisition, document 1, p. 5)
137 Andres Beraldez, Recollections of the Reign of the Catholic Kings, ch. 43, in Homza, The Spanish Inquisition, document 1, p. 5

against excessive harshness, the Pope issued another bull in 1481 in which "he rebuked their intemperate zeal, and even threatened them with deprivation."[138] Spanish clergy complained of the abuses done by the Inquisition in Seville. The Pope, in realizing his mistake of granting independence to the Inquisition, responded in 1482 by revoking the powers granted by the bull, and allowed the Seville inquisitors to continue their work unless they were stopped by their bishop. Ferdinand protested bitterly to Rome. The Inquisition became effectively more dependent on the crown rather than on the papacy. This contention between the Spanish monarchy and the Pope, and pressure on Rome from Conversos, brought the Inquisition to a temporary halt.[139]

All of those who blame the Papacy for the Inquisition, should care to read these words of Pope Sixtus IV, who reigned at the beginning of the Inquisition:

> In Aragon, Valencia, Mallorca, and Catalonia the Inquisition has for some time been moved not by zeal for the faith and salvation of souls but by lust for wealth. Many true and faithful Christians, on the testimony of enemies, rivals, slaves, and other lower and even less proper persons, have without any legitimate proof been thrust into secular prisons, tortured and condemned as relapsed heretics, deprived of their goals and property and handed over to the secular arm to be executed, to the peril of souls, setting a pernicious example, and causing disaster to many.[140]

Sixtus now ordered his bishops to take charge and play a significant role in the Inquisition. The accused were to be granted legal council and the liberty to make their case to Rome.[141] Ferdinand was furious at hearing this, and made it clear that the Catholic Church was to no longer have any say so in the Inquisition, disconnecting any influence from Rome. He sent this stern letter to the Pope:

> Things have been told me, Holy Father, which if true, would seem to merit the greatest astonishment…To these rumors however, we have given no credence because they seem to be things which would in no way have been conceded by your Holiness who has a duty to the Inquisition. But if by chance concessions have been made through the persistence and cunning persuasion of the Conversos, I intend never to let them take effect. Take care therefore not to let the matter go further, and to revoke any concessions and entrust us with the care of this question.[142]

The king had severed ties from the Church, and the Inquisition was under the control of Spanish monarchs, since the institution was a Spanish affair, not under the jurisdiction of the papacy. While the authority of the inquisitors came directly or indirectly from Rome, the fact still remains that from its very inception the Inquisition was established to be under the control of the monarchs. "Although you and the others enjoy the title of inquisitor," Fer-

---

138 Quoted in P.F., *The Spanish Inquisition*, USCM, vol. ii, p. 462
139 Kamen, *The Spanish Inquisition*, ch. 3, p. 49; ch. 7, p. 137
140 Quoted in Thomas F. Madden, *The Truth About the Inquisition*
141 Kamen, *The Spanish Inquisition*, ch. 3, p. 49
142 Quoted in Thomas F. Madden, *The Truth About the Inquisition*

dinand said to his inquisitors of Aragon in 1486, "it is I and the queen who have appointed you, and without our support you can do very little." Ferdinand actually once claimed that confiscations of property imposed upon heretics were by the order of the pope, making it seem as though it was the Church that was responsible for the punishment. But in fact it was the secular authorities who carried out the taking of property, not the Church. Ferdinand, in 1501, actually issued a decree prohibiting anyone from asserting that the Inquisition was under papal authority, "because," he said, "in fact it is all ours."[143]

The constitutional rules for the Inquisition, written by Cardinal Torquemada, were made "in concert with the King." The lower inquisitors answered to the Grand Inquisitor who could not act without the authorization of the Supreme Council, which was not established by the Catholic Church. Thus when the Inquisition acted, they did so as royal judges, not ecclesiastical judges.[144]

From a report of the Spanish Committee we find that "in no Papal Bull, can it be found, that the Supreme Council has the right to decide any cause, in the absence of the Grand Inquisitor,—but which, however, is constantly done, without the slenderest difficulty." The report concludes to say that "in these cases, the Councilors act, not as Ecclesiastical, but as Royal judges." Moreover, in showing its secular status, the Committee states that "neither at present, nor formerly, could any order of the Inquisition be, I do not say, executed, but so much as published, without the previous consent of the King."[145] The historian Garnier affirms that "the Religious Inquisition was nothing more nor less than a Political Institution."[146]

So furious was Ferdinand against the Pope that he pretended to disbelieve in the legitimacy of the papal bull.

For the next half-century the Papacy attempted to intervene in the Inquisition in order to stop abuses. For example, there were bulls by Pope Innocent VIII issued on February 11 and July 15, 1485, which asked for more mercy and leniency, and for greater use of secret conversions of heretics, on the part of the Inquisition. Papal intervention would lead to several quarrels between the crown and the Catholic Church.[147] Whether or not the crown would listen to the Pope completely depended on the monarchy. When Innocent VIII strived to have a policy of sending papal letters to accused people appealing to Rome, Ferdinand hindered the Pope and decreed that anyone who used papal letters of appeal without royal permission would be put to death and their property confiscated by the state. In 1584 the Inquisition made the false claim that the Pope gave exclusive power over heresy to them.[148] Bartolome de Carranza y Miranda was arrested for Lutheranism, but it was Pope Pius V who bailed him out by negotiating his release having him stay in Rome in the castle of Sant' Angelo.[149]

---

143 Kamen, *The Spanish Inquisition*, ch. 7, p. 165
144 Maistre, *Letters on the Spanish Inquisition*, letter i
145 Maistre, *Letters on the Spanish Inquisition*, letter 1
146 In Maistre, *Letters on the Spanish Inquisition*, letter 1
147 Thomas F. Madden, *The Truth About the Inquisition*; Kamen, *The Spanish Inquisition*, ch. 3, p. 49–50; ch. 4, p. 71; ch. 7, pp. 137–8, 149
148 Kamen, *The Spanish Inquisition*, ch. 7, p. 157
149 Kamen, *The Spanish Inquisition*, ch. 7, pp. 160–163

THE DARKEST POINT OF THE INQUISITION, AND THE CATHOLIC CHURCH'S HELP OF THE JEWS

It was at the beginning of the Inquisition that would be its darkest point. People began to be sentenced to death by fire, the first victims being six men and women in Seville. Within a few days four very prominent Conversos, two of whom were actually the chief keeper of Seville's cathedral and a great rabbi, were unjustly put to the flame. Some of the Conversos tried to escape Seville, but were prevented by an edict which ordered that they be kept in the city. Many of them managed to flee to the lands of Spanish nobles, to Portugal, and even to Moorish lands. A plague came to Spain which took tens of thousands of lives, but this did not stop the persecutions. The inquisitors transferred to Aracena where they had put twenty-three people to the flames. Over the next eight years, until 1488, the Inquisition was responsible for the deaths of six hundred people, and had five thousand people reconciled into the Church. There were even ordained clerics and monks amongst those killed.[150] In 1488 alone there were only seven executions, and in 1489 only three.[151]

Now it must be admitted that such a small number indicates that the Inquisition was not interested in bloodshed, and thus cannot be considered to be a holocaust institution. In the first fifteen years of the Inquisition's existence two thousand Jews were slaughtered. While this cannot be undermined, this was not because of the Catholic Church, but on account of the rejection of its authority and influence. In fact, when Conversos fled Spain the nation that opened their borders for them more than any other was Rome. There was even a saying within the Catholic Church, that "Rome is the paradise of the Jews." Most of the Spanish clergy in Rome were of Jewish origin.[152]

And regardless of the common assertion, no Jews are known to have fled to Turkey until a long time later. It is thus unjust to attribute the abuses of the Inquisition to the popes or to the Church, since they did all they could to restrain them. The cruelties committed were not done by the Catholic Church, but by the Spanish government.[153] Rome was known for its equity, and one contemporary writer, Count Pollnitz, recounts his stay in the great city as such: "I was formerly sixteen months in Rome: and during all that time, never did I, so much as once, hear of a single individual being arrested by the Inquisition. On the contrary, I was witness to acts of clemency in the Holy Office, such as would, by no means be shown in the consistory of Geneva."[154]

In 1484, in Burgos, Jews were not allowed to sell food; they were ordered to shut down their community on all Christian feast-days. There was an edict of total expulsion of the Jews in the late fifteenth century, but this was not because of their race, but their religion. It gave them a choice between conversion or emigration, and for this there was a great effort on the

---
150 Andres Bernaldez, Recollections of the Reign of the Catholic Kings, ch. 44, in Homza, *The Spanish Inquisition*, document 1, pp. 6–8
151 Kamen, *The Spanish Inquisition*, ch. iv, p. 53
152 Quoted in P.F., *The Spanish Inquisition*, USCM, vol. ii, p. 462. See also Kamen, *The Spanish Inquisition*, ch. 2, p. 24; ch. 3, p. 32; Maistre, *Letters on the Spanish Inquisition*, letter 1
153 P.F., *The Spanish Inquisition*, USCM, vol. ii, p. 462; Kamen, *The Spanish Inquisition*, ch. 2, p. 24
154 See Fletcher's notes on Maistre's second letter on the Spanish Inquisition, C

part of the clergy to witness to them. Ferdinand himself told the grand inquisitor Torquemada two months after issuing the edict, "many wish to become Christians, but are afraid to do so because of the Inquisition," and ordered that "you will write to the inquisitors, ordering them that even if something is proved against those persons who become Christians after the decree of expulsion, no steps be taken against them, at least for small matters." In 1494 the Spanish government prosecuted an official of Ciudad Real for extorting Jews crossing to Portugal. Those who had returned converted to Christianity and were protected by the state against antisemitism, and in 1493 the king and queen ordered people in the dioceses of Cuenca and Osma not to refer to Jews as tornadizos (turncoats). The number of Jews who left, and never returned (since they were those who returned) were no more than forty thousand. This is the equivalent to the population of Bethlehem, one out of a thousand or so villages in Israel. Yet they are making this expulsion to be as though it was the Exodus of the Jews from Egypt, which some estimate to have been around million people, and that was a thousand years ago.

MANY SPANIARDS DISAGREED WITH THE PERSECUTION OF THE JEWS

It was not as though every Spaniard gave his support and his defense to the expulsion. Luis de Paramo, the first historian on the Inquisition, wrote a century after the expulsion: "I cannot omit to mention that there were learned men who did not feel that the edict was justified."[155]

Nor were there many Spaniards who supported the executions done on account of the Inquisition's investigations. "We are all aghast," said the Consellars of Barcelona to Ferdinand in 1484, "at the news we receive of the executions and proceedings that they say are taking place in Castile."[156] Hernando del Pulgar, a very prestigious Spanish writer at the time, wrote to the archbishop of Seville that thousands of young conversos in Andalusia "had never been out of their homes or heard and learned any other doctrine but that which they had seen their parents practice at home. To burn all these would be not only cruel but difficult to carry out. I do not say this, my lord, in favour of the evildoers, but to find a solution, which it seems to me would be to put in that province outstanding persons who by their exemplary life and teaching of doctrine would convert some and bring back others. Of course [the inquisitors] Diego de Merlo and doctor Medina are good men; but I know very well that they will not produce such good Christians with their fire as the bishops Pablo [de Santa Maria] and Alonso [de Cartagena] did with water."[157]

Many educated Spaniards, according to inquisitor Luis de Paramo, deemed the explosion of the Jews to be unjust and hurtful to the Church. Firstly, because those who were forced to convert did not receive the sacraments adequately; and secondly, because the expulsion of the Jews was an indirect way of annihilating them, and such a cruel action was contrary to Scripture.[158] The Inquisition, therefore, was unjust because the government rejected the

---

155 Kamen, *The Spanish Inquisition*, ch. 2, p. 22, 25–7
156 In Kamen, *The Spanish Inquisition*, ch. 4, p. 69
157 Kamen, ch. 4, p. 69
158 Kamen, *The Spanish Inquisition*, ch. 4, p. 70

teachings of the Church and those of Scripture. In fact, the Church official, archbishop of Granada Hernando de Talavera, according to sixteenth historian Jose de Siguenza, "would not allow anyone to harm them [the conversos] in word or deed, or burden them with new taxes and impositions, for he detested the evil custom prevalent in Spain of treating members of the sects worse after their conversion than before it …so that many refused to accept a Faith in whose believers they saw so little charity and so much arrogance."[159]

Talavera was later arrested by the Inquisition after falsely being accused by the inquisitor Lucero of owning a synagogue. The papacy intervened and he and his family were set free. He soon died, and on his death bed he condemned Lucero for his persecution against the conversos, 'which', he said, "is clearly against the Holy Catholic Faith, which requires that there be no distinction between Jew and Greek."[160] The abusive inquisitor Lucero was eventually arrested by the Inquisition and all of his victims were released and received no punishment.[161]

THE BRUTALITY OF THE INQUISITION IS OVERLY EXAGGERATED

The Spanish government was not as brutal as much as the clamor of anti-Catholics make it out to be. A foreign traveler wrote concerning Isabella that "her subjects say publicly that the queen is a protector of Jews." The Jews were enabled to own great amounts of land. In Toledo there lived two hundred and eighty one Jewish families, and only fifty one Christian families. In Buitrago the Jews owned one hundred and sixty five fields of flax, one hundred and two meadows, eighteen market gardens, and a large amount of pasture. In Hita there existed two synagogues and nine rabbis. The major investment in Hita was wine, and there were three hundred and ninety six vineyards and sixty six thousand four hundred vines all owned by Jews. In Sos, the birthplace of King Ferdinand himself, the Jews were "cultivators of vines, flax and cereals, and their business relations with Christians contributed to fraternal amity." In Avila, where the population was seven thousand, the Jews consisted of half the people there. It has even been argued that "relations between Jews and Christians remained extremely cordial throughout the century" in many parts of Castile. In 1479, Ferdinand officiated the autonomy of the Jewish community in Saragossa.[162]

In 1480, the government agreed to decree that in Castile Jews were to be separated from the rest of society. We should acknowledge that a law such as this was done sometimes in the interest of the Jews, in order to protect them from harassment. Nonetheless, the law was not entirely enforced. In Soria, in 1489, richer Jews still lived outside the ghettos, and in 1484 the authorities went into the synagogue and ordered the Jewish community to "observe the laws of Toledo," giving them three days to comply.[163] The fact that they did this indicates that the decree was not sufficiently followed. In 1493, Ferdinand

---

159 In Kamen, *The Spanish Inquisition*, ch. 4, p. 70
160 Kamen, *The Spanish Inquisition*, ch. 4, p. 73
161 Kamen, *The Spanish Inquisition*, ch. 4, p. 74
162 Kamen, *The Spanish Inquisition*, ch. 2, p. 12–14
163 Kamen, *The Spanish Inquisition*, ch. 2, p. 15

commanded that Jews in Saragossa wear a red patch to distinguish them, but there is no evidence that this was observed. In 1488, five years later, there were still vain efforts made to enforce separation in Orense, and in Aragon Isabella and Ferdinand firmly went against any measures at separating the Jews.

Both Jews and former Jews were favored under the crown, and it is worth remembering that under this monarchy the Jewish financiers Seneor and Abravnel prospered greatly, and the Caballeria family dominated politics in Saragossa. As early as 1468, the Jewish doctor David Abenasaya served Ferdinand as his physician, and both the king and Isabella continued to have Jewish doctors as their closest collaborators. "All the Jews in my realms," said Isabella declaring protection to the Jews of Trujillo in 1477, "are mine and under my care and protection and it belongs to me to defend and aid them and keep justice." She as well lent protection to the Jewish community in Caceres. The city of Bilbao was ordered to make null the commercial restrictions it had placed upon Jews in the town of Medina de Pomar. The town of Olmedo was ordered to erect a wall of a Jewish community to give Jews access to the town square. Furthermore, the king and queen repeatedly got involved against municipalities trying to hinder the business activities of Jews. In 1486 a limit was placed on the number of Jews in the Jewish ghetto of Burgos, but this quickly was annulled by the monarchy. In the same year the Consellers of Barcelona forcefully said: "We do not believe that all conversos are heretics, or that to be a converso makes one a heretic."[164]

If the Inquisition was all about cruelty and sadism, then the instruction book for the institution, written by Jean le Sauvage, would have never pointed out and condemned that "accused people have not been able to defend themselves fully, many innocent and guiltless have suffered death, harm, oppression, injury and infamy… and many of our vassals have absented themselves from these realms: and (as events have shown) in general these our realms have received and receive great ill and harm: and have been and are notorious for this throughout the world."[165]

REFORMS OF THE INQUISITION PURGE IT OF CORRUPTION

By 1500, the cardinal archbishop of Toledo, Francisco Jimenez Cisneros, took control of the Inquisition and began purging it from any corrupt persons in order to make it equitable and just. Every tribunal was provided two Dominican inquisitors, a legal advisor, a constable, a prosecutor, and a large body of assistants. After the reforms of Cisneros, the Inquisition became one of the most merciful and orderly institutions in Europe.[166]

Clerical inquisitors were bounded by the maxim, "The Church abhors bloodshed,"[167] and so there was no intention or incentive for sadism on the part of the inquisitors. "We have always had these people," said Ferdinand in 1507 on the Conversos, "and they have served us

---

164 Kamen, *The Spanish Inquisition*, ch. 2, pp. 15–16; ch. 3, p. 41
165 In Kamen, *The Spanish Inquisition*, ch. 4, pp. 76–7
166 Thomas F. Madden. "*The Truth about the Spanish Inquisition*." Crisis (October 2003)
167 P.F., *The Spanish Inquisition*, USCM, vol. ii, p. 460

well. My intention always has been and still is that the good among them be rewarded and the bad punished, though charitably and not harshly."[168]

THE PROCEDURES OF THE INQUISITION IS PROOF OF ITS CIVILITY

The Inquisition was not fit to implement a full-on despotism upon the masses, and nor was that even its intention.[169] If this was so, then why did the Inquisition establish the following procedures?

The Inquisition established a "period of grace" which was a thirty or forty day chance for all people to confess their crimes. The instructions of the Inquisition state quite clearly that "reconciled heretics and apostates should be treated with much mercy and kindness. They should be pardoned from fire and perpetual prison and left with all their goods if, as noted, they come and confess their errors within the time period established by the edict of grace." However, depending on the gravity of the crime, and the quality of the confessing person, some belongings were confiscated and donated to Spain's war against the Moors.[170] In Toledo, the overwhelming majority of the eight-thousand cases which the tribunal may have dealt with, were never even brought to trial thanks to the edicts of grace.[171]

Differences in age were also taken into account under the tribunals. If a person was under twenty, the inquisitors were required to "receive them kindly and with light penances, even if they come after the period of grace."[172]

If the person was under twenty-five he was provided with a guardian to accompany him before he responded to any accusations.[173]

Even after the period of grace, if a person confessed and did penance after his arrest, the inquisitors were obligated to reconcile him back into the Church, with the required punishment of not death, but some prison time. This also applied to accused persons who were tried and had legitimate witnesses attesting to his crimes.[174] Was this coercion? Absolutely. But was this a part of a system that wanted to butcher people mercilessly? Absolutely not.

Another proof to this is the fact that even if a person continually denied his crimes in spite of multiple testimonies, the inquisitors were still under obligation to conduct another assiduous investigation upon the witnesses before making any conclusion on the defendant. As the instructions of the Inquisition demands:

---

168 In Kamen, *The Spanish Inquisition*, ch. 3, p. 61
169 Kamen, *The Spanish Inquisition*, ch. 4, p. 66
170 Gaspar Isidro de Arguello, *Instructions of the Holy Office of the Inquisition*, Handled Summarily, Both Old and New, part i, document 7, pp. 65–66
171 Kamen, *The Spanish Inquisition*, ch. 3, p. 59
172 Gaspar Isidro de Arguello, *Instructions of the Holy Office of the Inquisition*, Handled Summarily, Both Old and New, part i, document 7, p. 66
173 Compilation of Instructions for the Office of the Holy Inquisition, Toledo 1561, in Homza, *The Spanish Inquisition*, document 20
174 Gaspar Isidro de Arguello, *Instructions of the Holy Office of the Inquisition*, Handled Summarily, Both Old and New, part i, document 7, pp. 66–67

But inquisitors must thoroughly investigate such cases, and examine the witnesses and endeavor to know what kind of persons they are, and whether they deposed out of hatred, ill will, or some other depravity. The inquisitors shall diligently interrogate the witnesses again. The inquisitors shall also collect information from other witnesses about the conversation, reputation, and conscience of the witnesses who deposed against the accused. [175]

The names of witnesses had to be hidden and kept from the accused so as to protect them. It was in fact documented that there were several cases in which witnesses were murdered, assaulted and maltreated by guilty heretics. An example of this was in Talavera de la Reina where an accused converso murdered his denouncer after he found out his name.[176]

Before an accused person was arrested it was required to have evidence from three witnesses, each of whom was liable to excommunication if they were found motivated by malice. The testimonies of the three witnesses were assiduously analyzed, and if but one contradiction was found in a testimony, the witness was rejected, not accepted as a true bearer of evidence, and liable to imprisonment or other severe punishments.[177] This was in accordance with the commandment of God of "Thou shalt not bear false witness against thy neighbour." (Exodus 20:16)

The defendants were given the liberty to choose their witnesses to support their case.[178]

If notaries and scribes were caught examining witnesses without the presence of an inquisitor, they were punished with excommunication, deprivation of their offices, and a fine of ten thousand maravedis. A witness examined not by trained authorities would have possibly placed the accused in uncertain troubles, and thus is this order one of equity and justice, not murderous havoc.[179]

The Ecclesiastical branch of the Inquisition always offered mercy, and if mercy was refused then the accused was sent to the secular court, and always with a recommendation to "mercy."[180]

If somebody was executed and their children were made orphans, the Inquisition saw to it that they were placed under the care of pious families or religious orders, and the kings were even required to give money to them.[181] As much as one may disagree with this, the

---

[175] Gaspar Isidro de Arguello, *Instructions of the Holy Office of the Inquisition*, Handled Summarily, Both Old and New, part i, document 7, p. 67

[176] Gaspar Isidro de Arguello, *Instructions of the Holy Office of the Inquisition*, Handled Summarily, Both Old and New, part i, document 7, p. 68. See also Carroll, *A History of Christendom*, vol. iii, ch. xiv, pp. 608–609; Kamen, *The Spanish Inquisition*, ch. 4, p. 76

[177] P.F. USCM, vol. ii, p. 459; see also Excerpts from the Trial of Maria de Cazalla, in Homza, *The Spanish Inquisition*, document 12, pp. 120–121; Carroll, *A History of Christendom*, vol. iii, ch. xiv, p. 609; Moczar, *Seven Lies about Catholic History*, ch. iv, p. 94

[178] See the Inquisition Trial of Pedro de Villegas, in Homza, *The Spanish Inquisition*, document 4, pp. 17, 25; document 5, p. 27

[179] Gaspar Isidro de Arguello, *Instructions of the Holy Office of the Inquisition*, Handled Summarily, Both Old and New, part i, in Homza, *The Spanish Inquisition*, document 7, p. 75

[180] P.F., *The Spanish Inquisition*, USCM, vol. ii, p. 459; Moczar, *Seven Lies about Catholic History*, ch. iv, p. 89

[181] Gaspar Isidro de Arguello, *Instructions of the Holy Office of the Inquisition*, Handled Summarily, Both Old and New, part i, in Homza, *The Spanish Inquisition*, document 7, p. 69

accusation that the Inquisition was established with the intention of butchering is proven emphatically wrong by this very law of mercy toward children.

Bribery was proscribed by punishments of excommunication and loss of office for a lawyer, prosecutor, warden, notary, or quartermaster of a prison for accepting any donations in a case. They were also made to return double the money they received.[182]

If inquisitors were dealing with a case in one part of the country, other inquisitors from another part were forbidden from intervening until they fully understood the nature of the situation. This was decreed in order to pacify the investigators and keep a system of order.[183]

When prisons did not have sufficient room to incarcerate a suspect, the accused were allowed to remain in their homes.[184] Before any imprisonments were made, the inquisitors could do so only with concrete evidence against the person. Delays during a case were not allowed since they required that the person continue to stay in his cell, which was tormenting for the person. When fining somebody, it was prohibited that the money demanded be increased for financial gain.[185]

If the person was ever fined and was unable to pay, it was unacceptable to the instructions of the Inquisition that the person be whipped, or sent to the galleys to labor in a ship as a punishment, or suffer any other form of humiliation.[186]

In respect to genders, women were placed in a prison separate from men.[187]

To keep prisons orderly and coherent, prison wardens were commissioned to make sure that letters were never communicated between prisoners.[188] Just look at today's prison system and you will see the destructive results of prisoners sending secret messages to one another.

When the prisoner was interviewed by a tribunal he was never to be aggressively pushed by the inquisitors.[189]

If the accused requested a lawyer it was required by law that he was given one. And if the lawyer saw that his client was truly wrong and guilty, he had the legal right to leave the

---

182 Gaspar Isidro de Arguello, *Instructions of the Holy Office of the Inquisition*, Handled Summarily, Both Old and New, part i, in Homza, *The Spanish Inquisition*, document 7, p. 69
183 Gaspar Isidro de Arguello, *Instructions of the Holy Office of the Inquisition*, Handled Summarily, Both Old and New, part i, in Homza, *The Spanish Inquisition*, document 7, p. 72
184 Gaspar Isidro de Arguello, *Instructions of the Holy Office of the Inquisition*, Handled Summarily, Both Old and New, part i, in Homza, *The Spanish Inquisition*, document 7, p. 72
185 Gaspar Isidro de Arguello, *Instructions of the Holy Office of the Inquisition*, Handled Summarily, Both Old and New, part i, in Homza, *The Spanish Inquisition*, document 7, p. 74
186 Compilation of Instructions for the Office of the Holy Inquisition, Toledo, 1561, in Homza, *The Spanish Inquisition*, document 20, p. 230
187 Gaspar Isidro de Arguello, *Instructions of the Holy Office of the Inquisition*, Handled Summarily, Both Old and New, part i, in Homza, *The Spanish Inquisition*, document 7, pp. 74–75
188 Gaspar Isidro de Arguello, *Instructions of the Holy Office of the Inquisition*, Handled Summarily, Both Old and New, part i, in Homza, *The Spanish Inquisition*, document 7, p. 76
189 Compilation of Instructions for the Office of the Holy Inquisition, Toledo, 1561, in Homza, *The Spanish Inquisition*, document 20, pp. 224–225

case, and a legal obligation to report the truth to the inquisitors.[190] The lawyer had freedom to represent or not represent the accused, and no modern should have issue with this.

If there is one thing you could say good about the Inquisition, it would be that it documented records in a very organized and intricate manner. Documents of cases were carefully protected, being kept in a chest with three locks which could only be opened by three different officials—two notaries and the prosecutor—who each were the sole possessors of one of the three keys. The chest could not be unlocked unless all three were present, and if one of the notaries was found guilty of falsifying documents he was heavily fined or exiled.[191]

TORTURE

Torture was very restricted, and was to be done within very narrow limits. Torture was allowed only when an inquisitor and an ordinario—a bishop's representative—was present, or at least one of them. If they were unable to come they had to appoint a substitute who had to be "a wise, faithful man, of good reputation and conscience; a man who would not be expected to do something he shouldn't out of hatred, affection, or self-interest."[192]

Torture was never used as a punishment, but only as a tool for interrogation. This is important to know because it shows that the Inquisition was not done for the sake of taking pleasure in pain, but of preserving Christianity. Research has shown that in all of its three hundred and fifty six years of existence, the Inquisition used torture in only two percent of its cases; it was limited to a maximum of fifteen minutes, and in only one percent of the cases it was utilized twice and never a third time. Out of the seven thousand who came before the Inquisition in Valencia, for example, only two percent were tortured, and for no more than fifteen minutes.[193] The prevalent form of torture was waterboarding, which is the same utilized by the US. Now compare this orderly procedure to what took place in England, where traitors were hung until on the verge of death, then they were made to watch their own intestines get ripped out and boiled before perishing. Such a cruelty was never implemented by the Spanish Inquisition.[194]

PRISONS IN THE SPANISH INQUISITION

Descriptions of Spanish prisons sound more like vacation resorts than dungeons. Prisons were so comfortable that there were cases of people who were being tried in the secular

---

190 Gaspar Isidro de Arguello, *Instructions of the Holy Office of the Inquisition*, Handled Summarily, Both Old and New, part i, document 7, p. 68
191 Gaspar Isidro de Arguello, *Instructions of the Holy Office of the Inquisition*, Handled Summarily, Both Old and New, part i, in Homza, *The Spanish Inquisition*, document 7, p. 75
192 Gaspar Isidro de Arguello, *Instructions of the Holy Office of the Inquisition*, Handled Summarily, Both Old and New, part i, document 7, p. 68
193 Thomas F. Madden. "*The Truth about the Spanish Inquisition*, Crisis (October 2003); see also Gaspar Isidro de Arguello, *Instructions of the Holy Office of the Inquisition*, Handled Summarily, Both Old and New, part i, document 7, p. 67; Moczar, *Seven Lies about Catholic History*, ch. iv, p. 88, 94
194 Carroll, *A History of Christendom*, vol. iii, ch. xiv, p. 609

courts who would deliberately do something that would get them to the Inquisition prisons. Prisoners were permitted to have servants and were even served wine.[195]

They were granted the liberty to make requests which were frequently granted. One prison record gives this illustration:

> Francisco de Cordoba, who requested a hearing… Andres Lopez, who requested a blanket… Hernando de Aguilar had swollen hands, and requested that he be provided with a bed… Catalina Armijo, who requested some shoes… Juan de Avila requested a shirt and some undershirts and some short socks, and said they [sic] may go to his house to get them… Florian Rodriguez asked that the food ration be increased, as they have reduced it… Henoc asked that they finish his case… Antonio de Villena asked for more company… Friar Alonso de Vergara said that he is ill, asked that they give him more company, and asked that the quartermaster take better care of him. …Andres de Vaenas asked that they give him company because he is melancholy, and a candle for nighttime… Hernan Dominguez, Hernando de Leyva, and Diego de Mesa asked to be given the Cordoban bread at ten. They say the villager comes by at ten, and its better that the villager give the bread to them. They asked to be given more oil, as stipulated. …Friar Andres Cepero, who said the food rations arrive late. …Francisco de Avila asked that they buy him some shoes… Andres de Vaenas asked that they give him the handkerchiefs that he requested [196]

Remind me how this is brutal again?

A prisoner named Forian Rodriquez "requested that straw be put in the mattress and that the doctor visit him. He also asked for a pigeon because the cow's meat made him sick, and consequently, he had eaten no meat that day. Thursday, at one o'clock, the quartermaster brought him two pies, and he and the other prisoners did not see [the quartermaster and his servant] weigh the food rations."

The Inquisition made a note that the straw requested will be granted, the belt which Florian asked for will be given, and the "fig tree" in the prison "shall be removed, so that the boys shall not throw things."[197]

What type of a brutal and ruthless institution puts a fig tree in a prison cell? This does not add up to how today's conspiracy theorists describe the Inquisition. The quartermaster, as was demanded, was made to ration the food before the eyes of the prisoners, and if he failed to do so, "he would be punished." And when Senor Florian asked for more coal, a pound extra was granted to him.[198] One prisoner became ill and was allowed to go home and come back when he got better; another prisoner was given leave to attend a funeral of a relative,

---

195 See Excerpts from the Trial of Maria de Cazalla, in Homza, *The Spanish Inquisition*, document 12, pp. 147–149; Moczar, *Seven Lies about Catholic History*, ch. iv, p. 94

196 Excerpts from the visitation to the inquisition prison of the tribunal of Cordoba, 1569, in Homza, *The Spanish Inquisition*, document 21, pp. 233–236

197 Excerpts from the visitation to the inquisition prison of the tribunal of Cordoba, 1569, in Homza, *The Spanish Inquisition*, document 21, p. 236

198 Excerpts from the visitation to the inquisition prison of the tribunal of Cordoba, 1569, in Homza, *The Spanish Inquisition*, document 21, p. 237

and was asked to return "when he could."199 Prisoners were fed with the delicacies of bread, meat, and even wine. In the cells in Madrid, in 1676, prisoners were spoiled with sardines, oil, vinegar, lettuce, soups, and figs. One prisoner in 1709 managed to get himself a supply of bacon and chocolate. There is no greater evidence for the superiority of the Inquisition's prisons than what took place in Cordoba in 1820, when the prison authorities said that the state of city prisons was dismal and unhealthy, and that the prisoners should be transferred to the Inquisition prison which was "safe, clean, and spacious. At present it has twenty-six cells, rooms which can hold two hundred prisoners at a time, a completely separate prison for women, and places for work."200 The historian Charles Lea—a sharp critique of the Inquisition—writes "that the secret prisons of the Inquisition were less intolerable places of abode than the episcopal and public goals. The general policy respecting them was more humane and enlightened than that of other jurisdictions, whether in Spain or elsewhere."201

SECRET TRIALS

A common statement is that the Inquisition conducted secret trials, and that this covertness was utilized to instill terror. An example of this comes from military historian Victor Davis Hanson, who writes that "secret tribunals terrorized the countryside."202 This claim, though popular, is unfounded. Secret tribunals were not done for the sake of terror, but judiciousness. The inquisitors had their proceedings in secret so that the civil court gained no knowledge on the case until the facts were exhaustedly obtained—this prevented bias and rumors from seeping into the ears of the secular judges.203

When the Inquisition wanted people to renounce their heresies, it was prohibited from doing so in secret, unless the sin was so great that it could not be known by anyone else. In such a case, the inquisitors would absolve the person privately without the public knowing.204

CONCLUSION ON THE INQUISITION

The cruelties of the Inquisition are greatly exaggerated, and Monsieur Bourgoing, an opponent of the Inquisition who was sent by the French republic in 1789 to Spain as diplomat, admitted: "I will acknowledge, in order to give homage to truth, that the Inquisition might be cited in our days, as a model of equity."205

While dungeons, sinister priests and despotic popes cloud many minds just at the very hearing of the word Inquisition, the description of this institution by the German adventurer Karl Ludwig Pollnitz is a remedy to this dark confusion:

---

199 Moczar, *Seven Lies about Catholic History*, ch. iv, p. 88
200 Kamen, *The Spanish Inquisition*, ch. 8, pp. 185–186
201 Quoted by Kamen, *The Spanish Inquisition*, ch. 8, p. 187
202 Victor Hanson, Carnage and Culture, part ii, ch. vi, p. 198, First Anchor Books edition, September 2002
203 See P.F., *The Spanish Inquisition*, USCM, vol. ii, pp. 459–460
204 Gaspar Isidro de Arguello, *Instructions of the Holy Office of the Inquisition*, Handled Summarily Both Old and New, part i, in Homza, *The Spanish Inquisition*, document 7, p. 65
205 P.F., *The Spanish Inquisition*, USCM, vol. ii, pp. 456, 459

I own, for my part, that I don't see wherein that barbarity and that inhumanity consists which the Holy Office is charged with in Protestant countries; on the contrary, it seems to me to be the mildest tribunal in the world. [206]

And this is coming from a German, someone from an anti-Catholic Protestant country. In the three hundred and fifty or so years of its existence, the Inquisition executed only four thousand people,[207] and many of these were not innocent, but guilty of evil crimes. That's about eleven people a year. It took them this amount of time to execute four thousand lives, whereas the Moors, in the one year of 1066, managed to slaughter three thousand Jews in Granada.[208] And why don't these modern liberals speak of this sudden massacre instead of having nothing better to do than cry out on the Inquisition? It is not objective journalism that they care about, nor is it accurate history, it is a direct aspiration to undermine Christianity and uproot the Faith of all of its influence. The end result of this recklessness will only be the enabling of Islam to rise again and execute its past violence. Those who complain of Christian intolerance, will have to endure the consequences of removing the Cross to suffer the cruelty of the crescent, and by that time only a crusade will be the solution to the problem these destructive writers are creating.

The Inquisition in Italy also had another very low rate of capital punishment. In the Venetian Republic, from the mid-sixteenth to the mid-seventeenth century, there were only four executions. One historian has estimated that in the two hundred year existence of the Italian Inquisition, only two percent of its cases ended with the death penalty.[209]

Though there were injustices done in the Spanish Inquisition, such as the execution of Marina Gonzalez,[210] we cannot say that the Inquisition was established to orchestrate a holocaust. To compare it with Hitler or Stalin is unreasonable; for these two had the intention of massacring, while the Inquisition did not.

Those who are in the habit of continuously condemning the Inquisition as the epitome of antisemitism should look to the massacres committed by pagans. It took the Spaniards three hundred and fifty or so years to kill four thousand people—but in a short moment the Roman governor Catullus rounded up three thousand Jews in Libya and massacred them.[211]

The slanderers of the Church will forever more cry to the tops of their lungs on the deaths caused by the Inquisition, but they will never admit that the Roman emperor Titus killed more Jews in one birthday party than the Spaniards did in fifteen years. To merely enjoy the passions of sadism in his father's and brother's birthday celebration, and to please the fiendish demands of the ruthless masses, Titus had two thousand five hundred Jews gruesomely

---

206 Pollnitz, Memoirs, Letter xxxiv, Rome, October 10, 1731, p. 125
207 Thomas F. Madden. *"The Truth about the Spanish Inquisition."* Crisis (October 2003)
208 See Moczar, *Islam at the Gates*, prologue, act 2, p. 17
209 See Moczar, *Seven Lies about Catholic History*, ch. iv, p. 97
210 See the Inquisition Trial of Marina Gonzalez, in Homza, *The Spanish Inquisition*, document 5, pp. 27–49; document 6, pp. 50–60
211 Josephus, *Wars of the Jews*, 7.11.2, trans. William Whiston

butchered in the arena, by having them burned alive, fed to beasts, and take part in the devilish games of the gladiators—all as a mere entertainment. He organized more of these sinister spectacles in every city in Syria, in which Jews were murdered to win the crowd.[212]

The ancient Syrians, when they were still plunged into paganism, killed more Jews in one hour than the Inquisition did in all of its three hundred and fifty six years. In the time of the emperor Nero they ambushed the Jews in Damascus and cut their throats, murdering ten thousand. At another time, the Syrians took eighteen thousand Jewish women, men, and children, and mercilessly butchered all of them. The pagans of Caesarea, within one day, massacred their local Jewish population by slitting their throats. And who with a reasonable mind could even compare the Inquisition to what the pagans of Egypt did in 70 A.D. when they slaughtered sixty thousand Jews?[213]

Let's compare the Inquisition to massacres orchestrated by other pagans. People lament on how the Spaniards killed Muslims, but whoever has denounced the Mongol Khan Mangu who sacked Baghdad and butchered eighty thousand people?[214]

It is said that the Jews were tolerated under the Muslim caliphate of Cordoba, but as soon as the Almoravid Muslims took control in the twelfth-century, the Muslims persecuted them. And where did these Jews go? To Christian parts of Spain where they were tolerated.[215] But would any of these anti-Catholics admit this? Would any liberal Jew confess this if he was informed of it?

MASSACRES OF CHRISTIANS DONE BY JEWS

Anti-Christian sentiments amongst the Jews were prevalent. They aided the Sassanid Persians in their conquest of Jerusalem and in their massacre of ninety thousand Christians in the city. They supported the Muslims under Omar when they conquered Jerusalem and killed the Christians there. They assisted the Arab Mundhir when he was butchering the Christians in Hadramaut in Arabia, where they slaughtered twenty thousand Christians.

St. Ambrose wrote of "how many of the Church's basilicas the Jews burnt in the time of the Emperor Julian: two at Damascus, one of which is scarcely now repaired, and this at the cost of the Church, not of the Synagogue; the other basilica still is a rough mass of shapeless ruins. Basilicas were burnt at Gaza, Ascalon, Berytus, and in almost every place, in those parts, and no one demanded punishment. And at Alexandria a basilica was burnt by heathens and Jews, which surpassed all the rest."[216]

Their hatred toward the Christians was the same as it was when they implored Pontus Pilot to kill Christ, or when they murdered James and Stephan. A number of years before the Persians took Jerusalem, the Jewish people in Antioch commenced a collective attack upon the Christians in which they castrated the patriarch Anastasios and hurled his genitals into

---

212 Josephus, *Wars of the Jews*, 7.3.1; 7.5.2
213 Josephus, *Wars of the Jews*, 2.20.2; 7.8.7
214 See Carroll, *A History of Christendom*, vol. iii, ch. vii, p. 274
215 Kamen, *The Spanish Inquisition*, ch. 2, p. 9
216 St. Ambrose, letter 40, 15

his face before murdering him and many landowners and burning their bodies. The Jews of Syria and Mesopotamia executed a full on attack on the Christians, slaughtering them and destroying their churches wherever they could find them. The Christians counterattacked and killed a great number of them in self-defense.[217]

In the late fifth century, the Jews conspired to massacre the Christians in Alexandria. They sent several people into the street to cry out that the Church of Alexander was on fire. The Christians, believing these successors of Cain, went out to extinguish the fire. But there was no fire, only armed Jews who ambushed them and made great slaughter of the Christians.[218] In a place called Inmestar, which lies between Chalcis and Antioch in Syria, the Jews took a Christian boy, and in sadistic mockery of Christ, nailed him to a cross. In the words of Socrates:

> ...and in derision of the cross and those who put their trust in the Crucified One, they seized a Christian boy, and having bound him to a cross, began to laugh and sneer at him. But in a little while becoming so transported with fury, they scourged the child until he died under their hands. This conduct occasioned a sharp conflict between them and the Christians; and as soon as the emperors were informed of the circumstances, they issued orders to the governor of the province to find out and punish the delinquents. And thus the Jewish inhabitants of this place paid the penalty for the wickedness they had committed in their impious sport.[219]

There was a Jewish physician from Laodicea at around the eighth century who told the Caliph Yazid, that he would rule over the Arabs for forty years if he "destroyed the holy icons that were venerated in Christian churches throughout his dominions." Yazid believed him and signed an edict ordering for the destruction of all Christian icons. But Providence did not allow for such an evil, and Yazid died before it could be carried out.[220]

At the peak of the Ottoman Empire, when the Ottoman Muslims were trying to exterminate the Armenians, the valiant and brave Armenian Christians put up a resistance against the Islamic enemy, fighting for their Faith and their survival. The Sultan of the Ottoman Empire, Abdul Hamid II, went to a very famous Jewish activist named Theodor Herzl, and requested that he try to convince the Armenians to stop the resistance. Initially, Herzl at first offered money to pay for the Ottoman Empire's huge debt, in exchange for land in Palestine. But this proposition was rejected by the Sultan. Herzl's diplomatic agent Philip Michael Nevlinski (who was also an advisor to the Sultan), advised Herzl: "Instead of offering the Sultan money... give him political support on the Armenian issue, and he'll be grateful and accept your proposal, in part at least." Herzl backed the Ottoman Empire in their cause in vanquishing the Armenians, and had meetings with Armenian resistance fighters to convince them to cease fighting, telling them that the Sultan promised them peace if they would comply. The Armenians were not convinced, knowing full well the intentions of a Cain. There

---

217 Chron. Theophan. 296, p. 7; Theophil. Edess. Chron. sect. 1, Agapius, trans. Robert G. Hoyland, Liverpool University Press
218 Socrates, 7.13
219 Socrates, 7.16
220 Theophilus of Edessa's *Chronicle*, section 2, Theophanes, pp. 221–222

were numerous Zionists who were completely against Herzl for this evil. When Herzl tried to recruit Max Nordau, a major figure in the Zionist movement, to join him in trying to convince the Armenians, Nordau sent him a simple reply in a one-word telegram: "No." Bernard Lazare, a French Jewish leftist who supported a Jewish state, was so enraged over what Herzl was doing, that he cut off all ties with him.[221] These Jewish men were righteous for going against Herzl, and the actions of Herzl show that the Jews are not exempt from criticism, and that they as well have committed evils against the Church.

But most importantly, in regards to the Spanish people, the Spanish Jews gave aid to the Muslim invader Tariq ibn Zaid, who took part in the invasion of Spain in the year 711.[222]

After the complete reconquest of Spain, it was greatly feared that Conversos would make another league with the Muslim enemy against the Christians,[223] causing another Otranto massacre, or worse, another conquest of Spain. Hiliare Belloc adequately defined the Inquisition in light of the problem which Spain faced with the Jews and the Muslims:

> The Spanish Inquisition was devised against Jews and Mohammedans by a State which had only lately triumphantly freed itself from Mohammedan pressure backed by Jewish guidance.[224]

---

221 See Rachel Elboim-Dror (professor emeritus of history of education and culture at Hebrew University), *How Herzl sold out the Armenians*
222 See Gibbon, *Decline and Fall*, vol. v, ch. li, p. 953. See also Moczar, *Seven Lies about Catholic History*, ch. iv, p. 94
223 J. Balmes, *Protestantism and Catholicity* Compared, ch. xxxvi, p. 205; Belloc, *How the Reformation Happened*, ch. iii, p. 128 Moczar, *Seven Lies about Catholic History*, ch. iv, p. 94
224 Belloc, *How the Reformation Happened*, ch. v, p. 200

PART 18 – THE SONG OF KULIKOVO – THE PURE IMAGE OF CHRISTIAN MILITANCY

As St. Paul made his refuge in the land of Corinth, he wrote his letter to the Church of Rome, and in it are inscribed these words:

> Greet Andronicus and Junia, my countrymen and my fellow prisoners, who are of note among the apostles, who also were in Christ before me. (Romans 16:7)

We ask ourselves, what came from this Andronicus? Such a short line, composed by the Apostle, dedicated to this man, and yet a boundless labor shines as a light before the world, and emanates from the work that this one person did. The lands of Eastern Europe were absent of all the fruit of the Gospel, and lied barren with the malnourished dirt of heathenism. Andronicus would travel to Eastern Europe where he would bring the light of truth to the hearts of the Moravians, who live in today's Czechoslovakia, and the Apostle Paul, too, journeyed to this nation,[1] to introduce the eternal flame to a people who knew not light and stood blind within dried up souls thirsty for the water that ceases all thirst. These two pious men planted the seeds of holy doctrine, and from there did the light of God spread, setting the murky clouds of deception into disarray with ineffable rays that transcended the illuminating hands of the sun. What was rejected by the Jew was now embraced by the pagan, "That he may be enlightened with the light of life." (Job 33:30)

The light that no man fully comprehends warred with the darkness that reigned over the people for countless ages, and after much combat, the sinister met their end. The roots of heavenly inspiration broke forth from the seeds of the Apostles that lied so delicately on the bitter cold earth, ignored and forsaken. Birds did not devour them, for they heard the truth and understood, and were never snatched up by the wicked; they did not land on

---

[1] See The *Russian Primary Chronicle*, Laurentian Text, 28

rocky ground and heartless stones, for they endured persecution and triumphed; they were not scorched by the flaming sun; nor were they strangled by thorns and thistles, for they detached themselves from the capricious moods of humanity. No, these seeds, planted by good sowers, "yielded a crop" (Matthew 13:8) and heard the word and understood it, bearing much fruit, "some a hundredfold, some sixty, some thirty." (Matthew 13:23) Their roots sunk into the souls of the Slavic nations and expanded throughout, and from them, the tree of Orthodoxy sprung, and the shade of Christendom overshadowed the holy land of Russia.

Here lies the battleground, where many crosses were carried, where many heads were adorned by crowns of glory, where the flames of valiancy brought blindness to the heathen, where victory was won, where death was mocked, where martyrs remained unconquered; here lies majesty's field, here is the Kulikovo Field, and from its soils we can still hear the eternal song of triumphant spirits.

THE BOY WHO COULD NOT READ

A young boy stood behind an old wooden desk in a rustic cottage, staring with frustration into an open book; he tried to peruse through the words but he couldn't—he had no interest, no concern for things written on earthly matters. Next to him were two other boys—his brothers—and they appeared to be reading without much effort. They discussed mathematics and reading with a tutor, but the other boy stood by and watched, not at the work before him, but instead he was lost in his mind, in a world known only to the imagination. The boy's parents berated him for his inattentiveness; he could not read, he could not spell, he knew nothing of mathematics. 'What good was he?' his parents thought. As he stood in that modest cottage, he must have looked out the window, staring into eternity and escaping this temporal world.

THE SWEET TASTE OF ORTHODOXY

A horse that belonged to the family escaped the barn, and went out into the rugged fields. The boy's father sent him out to find it, and into the cold wilderness he walked, looking for the runaway foal. As he searched here and there, and wandered about, he saw an old man—a monk, standing beneath an oak tree; he was lost in deep prayer, and his cheeks were wet with bitter tears. The child made a bow in respect toward the venerable man, and waited patiently for him to finish his prayers. The monk called the boy over, kissed him in the name of Christ, and asked:

What are you seeking, or what do you want, child? [2]

The child, sad and irritated, said:

My soul desires above all things to understand the Holy Scriptures. I have to study reading and writing, and I am sorely vexed that I cannot learn these things. Will you, Holy Father, pray to God for me, that he will give me understanding of book learning?

---

[2] Epiphanius the Wise, Life of Sergius, ch. 1, in Serge A. Zenkovsky, Medieval Russia's Epics, Chronicles, and Tales. The original line of this story has Shakespearian English, and amended it

The monk went into a contemplative state, raised up his hands, and spoke to God in his heart, and after a moment, he said: "Amen." He then took up his bag and, as though he were pulling out some treasure, took out a Eucharist host, and said:

> Take this in your mouth, child, and eat; this is given to you as a sign of God's Grace and for the understanding of Holy Scriptures. Though the gift appears but small, the taste thereof is very sweet.

The boy opened his mouth, and the monk fed him the host. The boy was then taken by the rich flavor, and said: "Is it not written, How sweet are thy words to my palate, more than honey to my lips, and my soul doth cherish them exceedingly?"

"If you believe," said the monk, "more than this will be revealed to thee; and do not vex yourself about reading and writing; you will find that from this day forth the Lord will give you learning above that of your brothers and others of your own age."

The monk turned away and was about to leave, when the boy frantically flung himself onto his feet, and begged him to visit his home. The boy and the monk journeyed back to the cottage, and before they entered his parents came out to meet him, and prostrated before him. They invited him inside for supper, but he said that before he could eat he had to take them into the chapel. They entered the church and the monk opened a book of Psalms and told the boy to recite them. "I do not know them, Father." "I told you," replied the monk, "that from today the Lord would give you knowledge of reading and writing; read the Word of God, nothing doubting."

The boy looked at the holy words, and at the opening of his mouth, began to read the Psalms, not with plain pronunciation, but in a beautiful rhythm. His parents were astonished, and enchanted by the beautiful harmony of the boy's voice. They took the monk into the house and fed him supper, celebrating the miracle they brought to their son. After he was done eating he was about to leave, but the parents of the boy anxiously stopped him. "Reverend Father," they said, "hurry not away, but stay and comfort us and calm our fears. Our humble son, whom you bless and praise, is to us an object of marvel. While he was yet in his mother's womb three times he uttered a cry in church during the holy Mass. Wherefore we fear and doubt of what is to be, and what he is to do." The monk gently explained to them:

> Why do you fear where there is no place for fear? Rather rejoice and be glad, for the boy will be great before God and man, thanks to his life of godliness.

He headed for the door, they opened it, and he departed, and as he was walking away, he suddenly disappeared, and was never to be seen again.

THE BUILDING OF THE MONASTERY OF THE HOLY TRINITY

In the wilderness, rugged and desolate, lonely and isolated, one could see two young men, one of whom was the young boy, but now older. This was Sergius, and the other young man next to him was his brother, Bartholomew. They were both working very hard: cutting wood and building a small hut that was to be their monastery. Once its construction was completed, they both stood before it and marveled at the house of hermitage. "Now," said Bartholomew, "my lord and eldest brother by birth and by blood, tell me, in honor of whose feast shall this chapel be, and to which saint shall we dedicate it?" Sergius looked to his brother and said:

"It behooves you to dedicate a chapel above all others to the Blessed Trinity."[3]

THE TATARS COME

The winds were quite above the cold swaying grass, as they moved and zipped through the crisp air under the lofty skies which appeared almost like a mirror as they blended with the colors of the autumn trees, with the hues of yellow, red and orange leaves waving to the rhythm of the winds as they hung from the branches of the trees. One could liken them to the tree of Christendom, shaken by the harsh winds of hell's onslaught, yet never being uprooted. The sun was almost lost in the hazy clouds as it crept behind the sapphire curtain of the fall sky, and the colors of its translucent waves harmonized with the multiple shades of the season, which could be seen upon the mirror of a nearby river. The tranquil sound of the stream, and the symphony of nature's song, was suddenly disrupted by the sound of a tenacious march. Oh, how the earth trembled when they arrived on that day in 1379.

These were the Muslim Mongol hoard, headed by Mamai, and all that he strived for was the destruction of Russia, that crown of Christendom. They were attired by the thickest chain metal, which covered their silk clothing; their helmets, like those of their Turkish brethren, were conical in shape; and their swords were curved like the lunar crescent they worshiped. They rode upon short horses, and these beasts were covered with armor made of leather as they galloped upon the earth and made thick clouds of dust behind them. They held up shields as circular as the lightening white moon, and howled like wolves in the night.

The land was blackened by their presence, and their eyes were as red as how they desired the earth to be, crimsoned by the rivers of Christian blood that they so wanted to spill.

THE TATARS RAZE RYAZAN

The Mongols charged right into the city of Ryazan. The prince of the city, Oleg Ivanovich, looked about and beheld the massive horde of Muslim Mongols, thirsty for saintly blood and bent on the desecration of churches; he knew not what to do, whether to run or to fight. He fled the city, for he was not prepared, and left his people to the unrestrained furies of the heathen. The Muslims overran the metropolis with all of its towns, shires and villages and set them all ablaze. They seized so many people, with only a few escaping captivity, and so many souls were left bitter and filled with grief.

As the fall season reached its end, and the yellow, red and orange leaves were torn out by the rushing winds, the winter season came, the season when the stars are no longer bidden to stay their course, when their light swiftly passes, and the evening's darkness slowly lingers. On that dismal December, the moon turned red like the blood that was so ruthlessly shed;

---

[3] Epiphanius the Wise, *Life of Father Sergius*, ch. 2, ellipses mine

but then, eventually, it regained its brightness and lost the forlorn red hue. One can say that a message was being taught through the moon: Much slaughter is to come, but after a great clash of arms, glory shall arise like the glistening light of the night sky. A test of valor is soon to come, and all that is needed is the striving of the will and the passion of the zealous.

THE PRINCE TAKES REFUGE IN THE MOTHER OF GOD

The Muslim hoard of Mongol barbarians set their sights from the now ravished Ryazan, to the great city of Moscow. Prince Dmitry Ivanovich was informed of the enemy's charge into his city, and as the spear strikes the shield, agony pierced his heart and filled him up with grief. He did the only thing he could have done to quell the storms of fear: he entered the great Cathedral of the Dormition, and before the icon of Mary the Mother of God that was painted by St. Luke, and the tomb of St. Peter of Moscow, and with bitter tears and cries, and asked a blessing from the metropolitan of the nation, Cyprian, and told him of the coming of the invaders. "The effective, fervent prayer of a righteous man avails much." (James 5:16) And surely was this time for the intercession of the saints. As Jeremiah prayed for the Maccabees in Heaven, the prayers of saints both in Heaven and on earth were much needed.

THE MUSLIMS HEAD TOWARD THE CHILDREN OF CHRIST

On March, the year 1380, Prince Ivanovich, with all of his family, his nobles, and all of the people of Moscow, gathered together to celebrate the Feast of the Ascension of Christ in which our Lord declared:

> Go ye into all the world, and preach the gospel to the whole creation. He that believeth and is baptized shall be saved; but he that disbelieveth shall be condemned. And these signs shall accompany them that believe: in my name shall they cast out demons; they shall speak with new tongues; they shall take up serpents, and if they drink any deadly thing, it shall in no wise hurt them; they shall lay hands on the sick, and they shall recover. (Mark 16:15–18)

Suddenly, the news arrived: those that rejected baptism, those that were condemned, those who did not cast out demons but embraced them, were close to the city. Cyprian immediately looked to Prince Ivanovich and said: "Find out whether this is really so, and gather your force, so as not to be taken unawares." The prince was swift to act and quick to prudence: he gathered multitudes of warriors, not just from Moscow but from numerous other principalities of Russia. As the men of valor were rallied, fresh reports of the looming heathens were constantly coming, and thus, the invasion was confirmed.

Prince Dimitry Ivanovich stood strong and tenacious amongst his men, but within himself grief cried out like a wounded lion, and he went into his only bastion of comfort, "A refuge in times of trouble" (Psalm 9:9). He secluded himself into his bedchamber, and before an icon of Jesus Christ that lied at the head of his bed, he exclaimed:

> Our Lord and Master, Jesus Christ, Thou art God merciful and man-loving! I, Thy servant and miserable sinner, dare to call upon Thee in my affliction; for upon Thee, O merciful

CHRISTIANITY IS AT WAR: THE MANIFESTO FOR CHRISTIAN MILITANCY

> Lord our God, do I cast my burden! Do not unto us as Thou didst unto our forefathers when Thou broughtest upon them the evil Batyi; the dread and horror of those days are still great in our hearts; and now, O Lord, do not stir up all Thy wrath against us. For I know, O Lord, that because of me Thou wishest to destroy the whole land: truly I have sinned against Thee more than all men; but show mercy to me, O Lord, for the sake of my tears!

After the prayer of a pious prince was made, he visited the holy man of Russia, Cyprian, and said: "In very truth, good father, the infidel Mamai does march against us in great strength, and full of wrath." "Let it not trouble you," said Cyprian, "my lord and beloved son! for 'Many are the afflictions of the righteous, but the Lord delivers him out of them all'; and 'The Lord has chastened me sorely, but He has not given me over to death.' 'God is our refuge and strength, a well-proved help in trouble.' Tell me the truth, my son: in what have you failed him [Mamai]?" "I have examined myself in all strictness, good father," replied Prince Ivanovich, "and I am without guilt toward him; as we have settled with him, so do I pay him, according to our treaty; and so I am without fault before him."

As their conversation went on, there unexpectedly appeared several men, slanted eyed and no doubt Mongols—these were envoys from Mamai. Prince Ivanovich departed from Cyprian and joined with the envoys in a meeting. They demanded the tribute that the Russians used to pay to the Mongolian rulers of old. Prince Ivanovich expressed his willingness to pay the same tribute that he was already paying the Muslims, but this was not enough. The Muslims were insatiable for greed, and they were determined to slaughter and pillage to obtain what they sought. The envoys insulted and scoffed the dear prince, and announced that Mamai and his great army of Mongol hordes was on their way.

THE WARRIORS ARE ASSEMBLED

And so Prince Ivanovich, not wasting any time in sloth or trepidation, sent out a message to all Russian lands, and ordered them to gather together all of their men of war. He then assembled with a host of warriors and poured out all of his worries and fears, all of the grief and agony that consumed his very being, into the hands of Christ and His Mother Mary, and St. Peter and all of the saints in glorious Heaven. He then made generous donations to monasteries and churches, and gave many alms to the poor and to traveling pilgrims. And when he did this, suddenly the spirit of peace spread itself across the land, and serenity made its home in the hearts of the people.

Prince Ivanovich attended a feast, alongside his brother Vladmir Andreyevich, and during the festivity, he rose up and declared:

> Brethren and princes of the Russian land, we are all descendants of Prince Vladmir of Kiev. Since our birth we have never permitted ourselves to be offended, neither by the falcon nor the gyrfalcon, nor by the black raven nor by the infidel Mamai.

IN THE FLAMES OF SELFLESS LOVE

The arrival of the Mongols was nigh, and the faith and zeal of the warriors was already engulfed in the flames of selfless love. Already the sounds of the galloping horses seized the ears; already the cries of the knights of Christ could be heard from modest fields, roaring through the sky and ascending up to the stars. They shouted with all might: "We are ready to labour in the name of Christ and for the Christian faith and to fight in your quarrel." This was the cry of the men when they saw the grand Prince Ivanovich. Surely was this a war, not between flesh and blood, but between eternities, between angels and demons, between cosmos, between principles, between the holders of holy icons and iconoclasts, between the sword and the scimitar, between the Holy Trinity and a unitarian demon, between God and Satan.

THE PRINCE VISITS THE MONASTERY OF THE HOLY TRINITY

Before the riders could brace upon the stirrups of their horses, and before the knights could raise the banner that bore their Hope, the humble Prince Ivanovich journeyed from the confounding crowed of the city, and journeyed into the wilderness where the lofty tree reigned over the eye, where the bear and the deer made their home amongst pensive hermits, and the elegant lady of silence brushed our hearts with her graceful locks of tranquility. Here, in the midst of desolate wood, in the midst of nothingness, one could find everything, for here was the mind free from the vicissitudes of city life, and journeyed to the meadows of contemplation on all things eternal. As the prince continued on his horse, passing by the multitudes of trees and pristinely hearing the singing of birds, he eventually came by a little hut. But this cottage did not appear to be a mere home, for it was adorned with the Holy Cross. This was the Monastery of the Life-Giving Trinity, and belonged to Sergius, the man who we saw as a young boy who was now a monk. Prince Ivanovich was so in need of his gift of prophecy, and asked him whether it was wise to go to battle against the Mongols. The prince was shaken by angst, but the monk was filled with stillness of mind, and told him to break bread with him at a meal.

As they ate their supper, the monk looked upon the prince with his eyes, in which one could see the deepness of his soul, and said with humble voice: "May the Lord our God and the Holy Mother of God give you help; the time has not yet come for you to wear a crown of victory in eternal rest; but for untold multitudes of others are the crowns of eternal memory being prepared."

He then ordered holy water to be brought, and he took up a crucifix and blessed him with it, and then sprinkled the holy water upon his face. Prior to the prince's departure, it is said that the monk Sergius told him:

> It behooveth you, lord, to have a care for the lives of the flock committed to you by God, conquer; and return to your country sound in health, and glorify God with loud praise.

Before Prince Ivanovich would make his leave, he knew that this army would be lacking without the help of warring monks, monastic men who did not just fight devils with prayers, but with swords. These were like "Zadok, a young man, a valiant warrior," (1 Chronicles

12:28) efficient in the office of the priesthood, and with spiritual strength took up the cause of knighthood with great prowess. These were warrior monks, and they were needed for the battle, for with their selfless spirits they could commit to the most daring feats, without fear of death nor concern for living. "Good father," said Prince Ivanovich to Sergius, "give me two warriors of your monastic troop, two brethren, Peresvet and Osliabia. For they are universally acclaimed as mighty warriors and valorous knights, highly expert in the art and practice of warfare." He called the two knightly monks and ordered them to attend the prince in the battle, and without any wavering or complaint, they obeyed. They each took up a helmet, on which was engraved an icon of the Holy Cross, and as they placed them on their heads, one could hear Sergius exhorting them to fight for Christ "against his enemies." The two valorous monks joined the prince who was taken by the heartfelt eyes of Sergius who declared to him:

> Here, Prince, are my warriors, desirable in your eyes, whom you wish to have with you amidst the disasters of this our time, full of troubles and trials.

The monk, with piercing eyes and grave countenance, looked to Prince Ivanovich and cried out: "Peace be with you, my beloved brothers in Christ Peresvet and Osliabia! Labour for Christ as His brave warriors: for the time of your service has come."

Upon the two monks and the prince he sprinkled holy water and blessed them with the Crucifix, and then took aside Ivanovich and quietly told him: "The Lord our God will be your help and shield, and He will vanquish and bring low your enemies, and exalt you." Prince Ivanovich embraced these reverent words and took them into his heart, cherished them, and they brought him peace, and a stillness of mind only God could bring.

THE WARRIORS GATHER BEFORE THE CHURCH

The warriors of God were all assembled together, and from a distance one could see what labors they were conducting: they prepared their horses, attired themselves in their armor; the sounds of clinging metal was heard, and one could witness the multitude of blacksmiths forging the metal that would become blades, the blades that would be attached to hilts shaped as crosses, and one could be brought to wonder of all the men who were about to carry their own crosses.

Prince Ivanovich rode up to the cathedral, entered its doors, and fell before the icon of the Holy Mother of God, and urged her intercession for the battle that was soon to occur. She was the woman who told her Son, "They have no wine (John 2:3), and by her words the Savior of humanity brought "water that was made wine" (John 2:9). She will be the saint in Heaven, who has gathered for herself so many eternal treasures, who will tell her Son to make the waters of the nations blood red like wine, and He shall "trodden the winepress alone; and of the people there was none with me: for I will tread them in mine anger, and trample them in my fury; and their blood shall be sprinkled upon my garments, and I will stain all my raiment." (Isaiah 63:3) And now, in this time, the Prince of Moscow was soon going to make the hordes of barbarians, which charged like a mighty river, red like the nectar of the grape.

PART 18

After he made his prayers, Prince Ivanovich went to his spiritual father, Cyprian, and confessed his sins to the man who upheld the authority of the Apostles to whom Christ said: "If you forgive the sins of any, they are forgiven them; if you retain the sins of any, they are retained. (John 20:23) Cyprian absolved him from his sins, blessed him with the Holy Cross and sprinkled him with holy water.

Before a beautiful cathedral there stood the Gates of St. Nicholas, St. Florus, the Saints Constantine and his mother Helena, the two rulers who crushed paganism, and in their presence one could see—even from a far distance—an almost endless multitude of warriors: knights and cavalry, archers and mighty combatants, some thin, some robust, some tall and some stocky, but all united under one timeless zeal, one baptism, one Church, one Holy Faith, their unshakable hope descending from the Apostles, Paul and Andronicus, "my kinsmen, and my fellow prisoners" (Romans 16:7). And now you had the inheritors of these apostles, all kinsmen in one Spirit, all fellow prisoners in the world ruled by the Wicked One, and all warriors willing to break free from the persecutors, and triumph with unconquerable destiny.

An army of priests and deacons, all holding crosses, assembled before this colossal army, and gave each warrior blessings with holy water and with crosses. Prince Ivanovich went before the Church of St. Michael the Archangel, the heavenly captain who led the army of angels to victory against the devil and his demons, and he knew all too well that soon he, like the angels, was going to lead a battle against demons, against the spirits of the abyss, for the glory of the Kingdom of Heaven. He stood before holy icons, and made the sign of the Cross, he prayed before the tombs of saints, and asked with all contrition for divine intercession.

He had his brother, Vladmir, lead his army to the Brashkov road, and the princes of Belozersk, with their armies, into the Bolvanovka road. Prince Ivanovich, after all this, joined his own warriors, and with strength and majesty, they marched down the road that lead to Kotiol. The sun of the August season brought about its warm light on the goodly soldiers, and suddenly a soft breeze glided past them, as they traveled toward the sight of battle.

HERMITAGE

It was August 28th, 1380. Prince Ivanovich and his body of troops reached the land of Kolomna where a great many soldiers and commanders were awaiting their arrival. The local bishop welcomed the men with an awe inspiring procession with crosses and hymns. Prince Ivanovich found peace in the nearby church, where he took refuge in hermitage, asking from Christ and His Mother victory over the enemy. The local bishop came to him, and the prince, looked up with widened eyes. One could see in his countenance fear and yet determination, as he said: "Bless me, good father, to go against the Tatars."

"AN INCALCULABLE MULTITUDE"

September, 1380: Prince Ivanovich and the entire sea of warriors were settled in a land called Berezuy, all awaiting for his scouts to return for information on the enemy. They returned with a captive Tatar and brought the captive before Ivanovich who asked him how great the strength of Mamai's army was. That Tatar looked up the prince, and all the men around him, and with fearful face, said: "It is an incalculable multitude of forces."

At such words the plague of fright latched itself onto their hearts, and ate away, bit by bit, at their fortitude.

THE ARRIVAL OF THE LITHUANIANS

"What shall we do?" asked Prince Ivanovich to his brother, and to his military council, "How shall we give battle to these infidel Tatars; on this side of the Don, or having passed over to its other bank? For to each of us the day and hour of choice has come."

Terror and dread possessed their souls and clouded the air; they breathed the breath of fear, and its potent scent was inhaled by the nostrils of the Mongols who were quite close to the Christian camp. Then suddenly something occurred that brought the mind to admiration: a massive body of warriors, led by Christian princes from Lithuania, arrived to the camp, filled with soldiers from all across Russia. The Lithuanian princes arrived to the council and declared to the fearful men:

> If we stay where we are, this Russian host will be weak, if we pass over to the other bank of the Don, it will be strong and valiant. For all will renounce life, expecting death at any moment; and should we vanquish the Tartars, we shall die together, sharing a common fate. And let none fear their great might: for God is not on the side of force, but of truth and justice; and He bestows His mercy, and His assistance, on whomsoever He wills.

All of a sudden, a great many messengers arrived shouting out the news: The Tatars were now approaching.

A BATTLE FOR CHRISTENDOM AND FOR THE HOLY TRINITY

An innumerable array of warriors, all attired in their armor, all sheathes filled with the well forged blade, all bearing the sign of the Cross, stood by the great River Don, the site not of death, but of glory. The Grand Prince Ivanovich went before his army; he fortified his heart in the name of Christ, and like David, "strengthened himself in the Lord his God (1 Samuel 30:6), and roared with a thundering voice to his men at arms:

> Brethren, better an honourable death than a life purchased by shame; and it were better not to stir against the infidel Tatars at all than, having come, achieve nothing and go back. Let us now cross the Don and there lay our lives for the holy church and the Orthodox faith, for our brotherhood, for Christendom!

The cries of zeal reached the clouds and shook the earth, and the roaring thunder gathered into the raging storms that broke out in their hearts. All together they built a bridge across the Don River, and passed it.

THE FLESH OF KINGS

The night sky eclipsed the morning light, and as twilight still maintained her remaining lamp, the shadows of darkness casted gloom over the wilderness they were now in. In the silence of the night, all that could be heard was the creaking of the trees, and then, as they eagerly waited for the day to come, the howl of the night wolf was heard. With such a harrowing sound one is reminded that the Mongols revered this beast, and howled when facing their enemies. Suddenly a bone chilling screech clashed with the howls, and when one looked up, one could behold a countless army of ravens on the trees, just waiting. It is almost as though they knew that this earth was to be covered with the flesh of kings and soldiers. Those who were brave gained strength, as wild fires consume entire fields; and those who were weak, gained more fear, as ice melts before the flames.

A PACK OF WOLVES AND A MULTITUDE OF LIGHTS

The last evening light faded away as twilight finally put out the last glimmering flame of her candles. Prince Ivanovich rode on his robust horse, and stood between two armies, as a ship stands before two great waves on the brink of cutting it asunder. On one side were the Russians, determined yet frightful, with their crosses aloft, shields clasped and swords still in their sheathes. On the other side were the Mongols, and so high were their savage cries as they shrieked and howled. Prince Ivanovich saw behind them grey wolves, howling, adding to the symphony of chaos. "Behold, I send you forth as sheep in the midst of wolves: be ye therefore wise as serpents, and harmless as doves." (Matthew 10:16) And surely were the Christians sheep amongst wolves, harmless yes, but once threatened, as vicious as vipers. Prince Ivanovich looked to the right side of the Mongol horde, and saw the army of black ravens shrieking with their tumultuous sounds of death. Then suddenly, the wolves disappeared, their howls ceased; the ravens dissipated and their shrieks were put to an end, as though a nightmare appeared before his eyes and vanished. The man who was next to Ivanovich, Dimitry Bobrok, noticed that he was seeing something, although his own eyes could not behold it.

"What did you hear?" asked Bobrok.

"Sounds awful and most ominous."

"And now, Prince," said Bobrok, "turn your face to the Russian host."

He looked, and beheld something that brought wonder to his eyes. "What did you hear, my lord Prince?" asked Bobrok. "Nothing; I only saw a dawn gleam from a multitude of lights."

Bobrok was astonished at this, and said: "My lord Prince, thank God and the Holy Mother of God and the great wonderworker St. Peter, and all the saints: for lights are a good omen."

HEAVEN'S FIELDS

The dawn broke forth from its shadowy fetters, after a moment upon which one could have witnessed the dreamy glance of daybreak's gleaming, and the sun soon arose from its slumber. The men arose from their sleep, on that 8th of September, the day in which the

Christians celebrated the birth of Mary, the Mother of our Hope, for Whom the knights of Christ struggle "until the day dawns and the morning star rises in your hearts" (2 Peter 1:19). A thick fog clouded the morning air, and when the third hour after daybreak came to be, the hazy mist faded away. All of the warriors assembled themselves together—the battle was now about to begin. In their minds the will to fight lingered; in their hearts the pulsing determination for the fray boiled their blood; in their spirits were Heaven's fields, and before their eyes lied the Kulikovo Field.

A LETTER FROM THE MONK WHO ONCE COULD NOT READ

Prince Ivanovich rode about the ranks of his men, and cried out with cheeks tinged with the tears of passion and zeal:

> My beloved fathers and brethren, for the sake of the Lord and the Holy Mother of God, and for your own salvation, stand firm for the Orthodox faith and for our brotherhood! For we are all brothers, and from the least to the greatest; grandsons of Adam, one house, and one tribe; one baptism is ours, one Christian faith; we have one God, our Lord Jesus Christ, glorified in the Trinity; so let us now lay down our lives for His holy name, and for the Orthodox faith, for the holy church, and all our brotherhood, the whole Orthodox Christendom!

His words pierced into the souls of the men, and so stirred were their spirits, that tears came down their eyes and ran down their faces. He raised up an image of the Holy Cross, and shedding many tears, cried out:

> In Thee do I put all my trust, O Christ our God! Give me a victory over mine enemies by the power of Thy cross, as Thou gavest it to Constantine in the days of old.

Suddenly there appeared messengers who approached him with a small letter from Sergius, the monk, and handed it to the prince. In it were the words of a man who at one point could not read and write, and through a miracle received these abilities, and through such talents he was now praying for a miracle. Ivanovich opened the letter and read it thus:

> May the Lord our God be your helper, and the Holy Mother of God, and the holy wonder-worker St. Peter.

They also brought from Sergius a Eucharist, and he ate the host, as the Disciples ate the consecrated bread before Christ's war with the devil. And after he consumed the Eucharist, he cried out to his men:

> Great is the name of the Holy Trinity! Our Lady, Holy Mother of God, succour us! Christ our God, hearken unto Her prayers, and those of the holy wonderworker St. Peter, and the great and holy Metropolitan Cyprian, and the venerable hegoumenon Sergius; and have mercy upon us, and deliver us from those infidels who have risen against us!

THE WARRIOR MONK WHO BORE THE CROSS OF CHRIST

Prince Ivanovich ordered the men to go forward, and slowly did they advance toward the enemy. Suddenly there came down upon them a massive wave of Mongol warriors from a nearby hill. The two armies looked upon each other, each one formed like a wall, with the Christians assembled into the phalanx formation: each man rested his spear on the shoulder of the man before him. The two forces were getting closer, bent upon the making the earth beneath their feet into a crimson hued ocean. The Mongols raged and were in a frenzy, as they approached the Christians with ominous movement, while the army of God flowed smoothly like a river, with organization and order, shining bright with the illuminating rays of the sun. They appeared from a distance like burning lamps, and the Mongols were like a pack of wolves charging at what they thought to be a maimed animal.

Mamai took a position upon a high hill with a number of his men, and watched with anticipation to see the bloodshed and misery he so craved with insatiable fury.

The two forces were on the brink of clashing, when suddenly a fierce warrior from the Mongol horde rode ahead of all the ranks. His name was Temir-Murza: he was tall and distinguished, and his prowess could be seen in the sternness of his features and the vigor of his hardy body. The Christian warriors were instilled with fear at the sight of so great a fighter; every man told his neighbor to fight him, and each one refused. Then suddenly a monk, who was truly a monastic knight, came forward and accepted the challenge. This was Peresvet, the warrior monk who came from Sergius' monastery. He rose up above all men in courage, and declared:

> Be not alarmed: for great is our God, and great is His power. With God's aid, and that of His Holy Mother, and all the saints, and the prayers, of the venerable hegoumenon Sergius, will I encounter him.

He put on his helmet which bore the image of the Holy Cross, and covered himself with his monastic habit, made the sign of the cross and sprinkled holy water upon himself, asked for forgiveness from his spiritual father, and also of all the princes present. "Succour him, O God," cried Ivanovich, "for the sake of Thy Holy Mother's prayers, and of all the saints', as Thou didst succour David against Goliath in the days of old."

The monk rode upon his horse, bracing tightly upon the stirrups as he charged with the fullest of exertion against Temir-Murza who also charged on his horse at the uttermost speed. They continued on, riding as fast as hawks looming down to clench their prey; their eyes locked, the fear of death dissipated. In the Muslim, temporal triumph ruled over him; in the monk, unconquerable salvation penetrated all temporal desires. They collided, and so loud was the crash that all could hear it. They each fell down to the ground, and landed upon the hard earth, and both of them perished, one seeing Heaven and the other seeing hell. The monk, Peresvet, sacrificed himself to slay the elite warrior of the Mongols. Now was the time to commence the charge and do battle. Prince Ivanovich exclaimed to his men:

> Brothers, the hour is at hand for us to drink our cup. Here let us fight unto death in the name of Christ, for the Christian faith, and for all Orthodox Christendom.

CHRISTIANITY IS AT WAR: THE MANIFESTO FOR CHRISTIAN MILITANCY

THE ARMIES COLLIDE AND THE FRAY COMMENCES

They unsheathed their swords, spears no longer rested, the cross was laid, and they were all now lifting it up with their Savior, like Simon of Cyrene, partaking in the eternal struggle, and in the Holy War of humanity's salvation. The two forces clashed, and cruel slaughter commenced immediately. Swords struck off limbs, spears pierced through men and impaled them from the back, blades severed heads right off. The earth was soon wet by the overflowing rivers of blood that flooded the ground. So many times was it seen, a Christian man wrestled and struggling with a Muslim on the ground; a Muslim on top of a Christian, hands violently grasping his body, trying to kill him. They slipped and skidded over the wet warm blood that flowed beneath them. Christian blood and Muslim blood came together, and became a single swamp of gore and carnage; so much flesh and butchery lied before the eyes, such a horrifying sight, such a dismal thing to look upon. So many bodies lied stacked up on one another, so many lied next to each other, so many cries and so many screams; so many widows would be forged, so many orphans created, so many martyrs ascended to their homeland, where neither tears nor wails exist, to be adorned with victorious crowns above the earth where misery reigns and agony rules. Horses could not walk the ground with so great a number of corpses, they fell and slipped on the fresh blood as they bellowed and hollered. The horses frantically galloped about in wild fright, and men who lied on the ground wounded or struck down, were crushed to death by their heavy hooves.

Dimitry Ivanovich continued to fight, but then the enemy slew his horse and he fell to the ground. He stood back up, a prince without a horse, and fought on like so many of his men had done. He strived and endured, struck and killed, although he saw his soldiers, even princes and nobles, get cut down like trees. He saw a horse without a rider and quickly mounted it, but a number of Tatars again slew his horse; he fell back down, and a Muslim wounded him with a sharp blade. He looked about only to see the barbarians overpowering the Christians: they slew and slaughtered countless of the saintly knights. He too was about to be amongst the dead, but he could not die now, he could not perish just yet. He fled with all exertion, sprinting all the way to a nearby wood and taking refuge.

THE MIGHT OF THE HOLY SPIRIT

The Muslims took many a noble and prince, and slaughtered all of them; they took the banner of Prince Ivanovich and brought it down, and slew an incalculable number of Christian commanders. The whole field was covered with the bodies of Christendom's loyal soldiers, the whole land was covered with bright red blood; and one could imagine the corpses, with eyes still open, wide and frightened, lifeless and without spirit, looking up to the endless sky.

Some Christians walked here and there throughout the field of blood, perhaps searching for a brother, perhaps looking for a friend, who they could not find alive in their midst.

The remaining troops who survived the slaughter were now in the woods with Prince Ivanovich. They cried and wept with bitter tears. Andreyevich was with them, with face wet with streams of forlorn tears, and he said to Bobrok: "Brother, what is the good of our staying where we are, how can it help them? And whomever shall we help now that all the Christian troops are lying dead?"

"Great is the disaster, Prince!" cried Bobrok, "The wrath of God has fallen upon us for our sins. But the time has not yet come for us to strike at our foes. Let us wait awhile with patience, praying to God with contrite hearts, and He will bring our enemies low."

They continued to grieve, and their lamentations soared up to the highest heaven like incense. They made their petitions to God, to Christ and His Mother Mary. Suddenly, as pain and sorrow barred around them like a prison, a cool wind came upon them, and the hand of inspiration touched their souls, and they were inspired to rise up again from the graves of anguish. "My lord Prince," said Andreyevich, "the hour has come, the time is at hand." He looked to all the warriors—his sorrows were now gone—and said:

> My lords, my fathers, my brothers, my children, and my friends! Fall on the enemy, our good hour has come! For the might of the Holy Spirit is with us!

THE SAINTS ARISE FROM THEIR AGONY

Filled with God-inspired fury and divine zeal, they, with their Prince Ivanovich, now found refuge in the divine union, sallied forth to fight against the pagans. The Mongols were on the field, and all they could hear were the cries of the Christians—not of sorrow but of valor—all they could see were the endless armies of the warriors of Christ, not willing to accept defeat, but only bent upon victory. The Christians crashed right into their ranks. They slew the enemy with an impenetrable fury; no longer did the heathen rage, but panic, and now it was the meek Christians, stirred by insult made to the Faith, who were unleashing the onslaught of pristine ferocity. A Christian struck the edge of his blade into the side of a Muslim, and pushed it deep into his body; another saintly fighter drove his sword into the scalp of an enemy and split his head in two. A Christian spearman propelled his spear into one Mongol and impaled him; here a head was cut off, there a leg was cut asunder; in one place a man is cut in half; in another a Christian fighter thrusts his sword right through the chest of a Mongol and the point of the blade comes out from the back. A Muslim rushes toward a Christian trying to strike him with his scimitar; the Christian ducks and severs off a leg with one blow.

A whole crowd of Muslim Mongols surrounded Prince Ivanovich, from right to left; they thrusted their spears at him and viciously struck at him with swords. He was like a sharp tempest, a tornado, cutting and attacking whoever was around him. The Muslims struck him in the head, hit him in the belly with their swords, and thrashed him in the chest. Blood seeped out of all the wounds that covered his body, but he still endured, he still fought on with an ineffable tenacity. One could see Christ within his heart, carrying his cross with his flesh so lacerated and his bleeding, yet continuing on, drinking the cup of his passion, uplifting the Holy Wood with his Savior, as Simon of Cyrene did with the suffering Messiah. He fought against multiple enemy troops all at once. He thrusted, he struck, he slaughtered, he killed. The roaring cries of terrifying rage overflowed from the Christian ranks, and the cries of helplessness was heard from the Muslim side as they were mowed down by the armies of holy Russia. As they killed and slew, both the Christians and the Muslims saw amongst them men with glorified bodies: St. Demetrius and St. Michael the Archangel, and numerous other saints from the Church Triumphant who came from Heaven to aid the Church Militant. They glowed with sublime light, and scattered the darkness that so possessed the enemy horde. "Woe is us!" cried the frightful Muslims, "Woe is us! The Christians have outwitted us: their best and bravest princes and commanders have they kept concealed, and now have fresh reserves against us."

The Muslims fled, and no longer did Mamai smile at the sight of Christian blood; his face turned somber, and his lips no longer curved like the upright crescent moon, and arched down, for now the crescent idol that he so worshipped was brought low by the warriors of the Trinity, the inheritors of Gideon who took down the crescents of the Midianites. The ones who wanted to destroy the Blessed Trinity were taken by horrid destruction's fierce grip, and the ones who upheld the beautiful Creed that was said in Nicaea, to combat the horrid Arius, were lifted up in the bliss of wonderful Orthodoxy.

THE DAY WHICH THE LORD HAS MADE

The men went about, looking for Prince Ivanovich, the fighter of Orthodoxy and the protector of Christianity. They scurried through the battlefield, passed the ocean of dead bodies that covered every inch of the earth in that Field of Kulikovo, where vultures gathered on all the corpses, filling their bellies with the flesh of princes, of nobles, of generals, of knights and soldiers, of husbands and fathers, brothers and sons. They finally spotted Ivanovich, lying on the earth covered in tree branches. They removed the branches and saw him there: he appeared lifeless, his eyes fully shut; his armor dented throughout, and one could see on his flesh a multitude of wounds and seeping blood. His loyal men, including Andreyevich, encompassed him. They saw that there was still life in him, and they rejoiced, and through their praises and cries of joy, the prince gained strength and said:

> Let us rejoice and be glad in this day which the Lord has made!

They helped him up and supported him up to his horse, and all the Christian warriors who stood alive on the battlefield shook the earth with their cries of bliss and exaltation. "Do you know how great a grace was shown toward us by God and His Holy Mother?" said Andreyevich, "For even in those parts where our troops never came, even their multitudes of Tatars were slain by the invisible power of God, and His Holy Mother, and the great wonderworker St. Peter, and all the saints."

The battle was now won; the Cross triumphed, the martyrs were crowned, the Church made its victory over the enemies of Christ. Prince Ivanovich returned to Moscow, he was not going to celebrate with debauchery, but with holiness. He returned back to visit an old friend, to remember where he came from, to remember that the glory of Christendom did not come about through sword and bloodshed, but through the teachings of those very Apostles who first traveled to the Slavic lands and brought them out of heathendom, which they just defeated.

A PILGRIMAGE TO THE MONASTERY

Prince Ivanovich returned to the Monastery of the Life-giving Trinity, to give thanks to God for the victory over the enemy of the Trinity. This was the monastery that Sergius built as a young man, and now it was being visited by the prince who embraced him as his father. "Good father," said Ivanovich to Sergius, "through your holy prayers we have defeated the Ishmaelites." Prince Ivanovich provided whatever needs the monastery had, and then returned to the city of Moscow with celebration.

THE VIRGIN MARY PROMISES TO ALWAYS PROTECT RUSSIA

Years had passed since that day on Kulikovo Field. Sergius, who was now in old age, stood in his modest monastery praying before an image of the Mother of God, and he sung to himself the Magnificat of Mary:

> My soul doth magnify the Lord,
> And my spirit hath rejoiced in God my Saviour.
> For he hath regarded the low estate of his handmaiden: for, behold, from henceforth all generations shall call me blessed. For he that is mighty hath done to me great things; and holy is his name.
> And his mercy is on them that fear him from generation to generation.
> He hath shewed strength with his arm; he hath scattered the proud in the imagination of their hearts.
> He hath put down the mighty from their seats, and exalted them of low degree.
> He hath filled the hungry with good things; and the rich he hath sent empty away.
> He hath helped his servant Israel, in remembrance of his mercy;
> As he spake to our fathers, to Abraham, and to his seed forever. (Luke 1:46–55)

Surely were the proud scattered by God through the arm of His mighty warriors. And now the one who interceded for Christendom's soldiers was in prayer, in his monastery, contemplating on God. He looked to one of his spiritual sons, named Micah, and said: "Son, be calm and be bold, for a wonderful and fearful event is about to happen." Suddenly a voice came from nowhere: "The Blessed Virgin is coming." Sergius rushed into the corridor of the monastery and instantly he beheld a majestic radiance, brighter than the sun, and he beheld in the inexplicable light the Virgin Mary, and standing beside her were the Apostles John and Peter, all in ineffable glory. Sergius was incapable of bearing such a sight, and being overwhelmed in the presence of holiness, he fell down to the ground. The Blessed Virgin Mary touched Sergius with his hand, and said:

> Be not afraid, mine own elect, I have come to visit thee. Thy prayers for thy disciples for whom thou prayest, and for thy monastery, have been heard. Be not troubled; from hence-

forth it will flourish, not only during thy lifetime but when thou goest to the Lord, I will be with thy monastery, supplying its needs lavishly, providing for it, protecting it.

After she said these words, she vanished. Saint Sergius still remained in the ground in a state of pure ecstasy and bliss. He returned gradually to his own senses from such a state of ascendency, and stood up only to see his disciple Micah lying on the ground, horrified and stricken with terror. He helped his disciple up, but he quickly trembled to the floor, struck with awe and wonder. He said to Sergius: "Tell me, Father, for God's sake what miraculous vision was this? For my spirit almost loosed its bonds with the flesh from so resplendent a vision."

Sergius was so filled with heavenly elation that he could not talk with ease. "Wait a while, son," said Sergius with difficulty, "for I, too, am trembling with awe and wonder at the miraculous vision."

They stood still, adoring with silence the God Who forever watches His flock, and through His valorous shepherds slays the wolves.

THE REASON FOR ANDRONICUS

Now we know the reason for the brave Andronicus: to bring to Russia, and all the Slavic nations, the Gospel, so that their valorous warriors could be the strong guards of Christendom—to uphold the eternal truths of the Divine Law and vanquish the lawless—and to be a holy bulwark against pagandom. Now we know the reason for Church, to war against evil.

Let the story of Kulikovo, and all the battles of this book, stir within our souls the will to unsheathe the Sword of Christ once again, to divide the world, from light and dark, to restore Holy Christendom, to bring back the Christian Militant.

EPILOGUE

The song of Christendom has been heard from the very depths of the soul; the harmony of her sound emanates from the annals of her history, the cries of her martyr's blood, and hearing this sublime song compels one then to be confronted with the choice between advancing the empire of Christ or being a slave to the despotism of the devil. But how can one not choose Christendom after reading her valiant history? The inspiration of the Faith flows from an eternal spring; the enemies of truth may cut her down, but like a reed rooted onto a perpetual river, it always grows back. Eternity has no owner, time can never be possessed, and Christianity will never cease, for from the timeless realms do the words of Truth speak, and from them the soul is enflamed with the fires of love.

The fire is sparked, the heavens breath, the winds rush and the light coming forth from the coal becomes brighter. Such is the spirit of zeal. The soul is like coal, without the spark of zeal from the spirit it remains cold and callous. But once the soul is enflamed, once it has spirit, then its zeal and valor never die, because a heart burning with fire is a heart gripped by the hand of eternity. God is love, as St. John tells us, and a heart gripped by the liberating spirit of God will never cease in its battle against the enemies of love. The zeal, the enthusiasm, the valor, the will, the indomitable spirit, the thirst for justice, the aspiring to see evil vanquished, all of these virtues will never end once they are ignited in the soul.

All it takes is the flame to be ignited in our hearts, for the rising of Christendom, for the world to see our zeal, to behold Christianity and thus, to see God. Through beholding zeal, man sees the light of eternal love. "So let your light shine before men, that they may see your good works, and glorify your Father who is in heaven." (Matthew 5:16)

The modern world saw the light of the Faith in the 20th century, in that almost forsaken land of Mexico, when the government of the tyrant, Plutarco Elias Calles, imposed his despotic edicts to uproot Christianity from the land. The Episcopalian and Methodist churches sided with the government; the US government sided with the Mexican despot; Margaret Sanger and the Ku Klux Klan sided with the antichrist government. But only a small group of valorous warriors, were for Christ. These were the Cristeros, and they let their whole souls be illuminated by the light that beams from the Cross of selfless love and inspires us to sacrifice ourselves as the Holy One sacrificed Himself.

These Crusaders of Mexico were not just warriors, but intellects, who understood how their war was not one of physical desires, but of aspirations that transcended all things corporal. The Cristero general, Aurelio Acevedo, declared: "Our leader is Christ the King," and the Cristero and martyr, Noberto Lopez, declared before government soldiers executed him:

> Since I took up arms, I was determined to give up my life for Christ.

These warriors of the Cross, indeed did they took up arms for Christ, and they dauntlessly combated the evil government that ruled Mexico, which was filled with Freemasons and occultists. It is true that when the Cristeros fought in battle with government soldiers, that they cried out "Viva Cristo Rey!" (Long live Christ the King), while the enemy troops screamed, "Hail Satan!" The story of the Cristeros is the story of Christendom: a perpetual war beginning from the most ancient of times between the sons of God and the sons of Belial, between those who sit on the table of God and drink of the cup of God, and those who sit on the table of Satan and drink of the cup of the devils.

The Cristeros were Catholics who partook in the Mass and consumed the Eucharist—the Body and Blood of Christ—, and the enemy was a mixture of occultists and protestants who hated everything about the Catholic Church. The dictator of Mexico, Calles, was in fact a protestant who received support from the protestant Episcopalians (Margaret Sanger being one of them), the protestant Methodists, and the protestant Ku Klux Klan, and Calles even started his own church. While he was governor of Sonora, Calles wanted to create his own protestant church, and to drive out the Catholic priests and replace them with a new priesthood. He worked heavily on this goal with the Confederacion Regional Obrera Mexicana (Regional Confederation of Mexican Workers). This institution was headed by Luis Morones who hated all Catholic workers' unions, and who also founded the "Mexican Catholic Apostolic Church," founded as a protest against and a replacement for the Catholic Church.

Thus, when the Cristeros rose up against the shackles of occult despotism, it was a war between those of the Catholic Faith and enemies who were but mere successors of the Protestant Reformation. The Cristeros, when they fought, they held up giant crosses and strived in the struggle against evil with total trust on and submission to the will of God. The Cristeros were the last of the Crusaders.

Hope overcame their souls and the eternal rivers of love and selfless compassion flowed into their beings and ignited zeal within them, and what kept their spirits up was a fervor ascending from the very depths of an enflamed heart. A journalist once asked the Cristero veteran, Antonio Alfonso Galvez, "Were you a Cristero?" and he responded with, "Yes, from the heart!" It was from the heart that he knew himself to be a combatant for the Holy Cross.

EPILOGUE

It was from the heart that the Cristeros were aware that they were soldiers for a spiritual struggle, for the saints in Heaven—the spirits of men made perfect—; for the valorous angels who won the first sacred war which took place in Heaven; for the Son of God Who is Our Victory and our Hope and Our Inspiration, for it was He who vanquished evil on the Cross, as they combated evil while they carried their cross.

When the Cristeros rose above the enslaving ways of conformity, and ascended to a higher awareness, one that looks beyond servitude to tyranny and gazes upward to Heaven; when they vanquished armies through Faith and subdued trained soldiers with the flames of passion and avidity, the American government gave weapons to the Mexican government so that they could slaughter the Catholics. Just as the protestants helped the Ottoman Empire to kill the Catholics, the protestant forces assisted the antichrist government of Mexico to slaughter the Catholics warriors. But as the Maccabees were a small body of warriors when they strived against an empire, the Cristeros continued on in their eternal struggle, regardless of their small number and of what power their enemies had.

It was from a heart burning with ardor that they cried out, "The soldiers of Christ will not be defeated!" Galves recounted how that when they exclaimed this war cry, and when they cried out "Long live Christ the King and our Lady of Guadalupe!," that, in his words, "we felt incredible bravery ... incredible." This is because they had zeal sparked from the enflaming of the heart, and from that zeal, their enemies knew what true Christians were. They knew that true Christians are not those who comply with evil, who make deals with tyranny, who submit to despotism; they comprehended that true Christians fight evil and obey God rather than man. In the valor of the Cristeros, the world beheld true Christianity, they beheld the light of love that springs forth from mystical union between the heart of humanity and the Heart of Christ.

As the Serbian hymn says, "Lord, I am listening to you, speak to me until my heart burns." And in that day, the hearts of these Christians who sold their purses and bought swords, burned. Gregory Palamas spoke of the person united with God, that he knows that he is one with Him "from the peace which fills his mind, and the fire of love for God which burns in him."[1] The warriors of Christ thirst after righteousness and they fight for it, as Moses fought the shepherds so that the women could take water from the well. They thirst for that which they fight for: righteousness, "judgment, and mercy, and faith." (Matthew 23:23) Their faith is manifested in their actions, and through their actions the world beholds the light that enlightens.

The warriors of Christ, the Cristeros, manifested their faith by their actions of selfless compassion, and truly could they say with the Apostle, "For God, who commanded the light to shine out of darkness, hath shined in our hearts, to give the light of the knowledge of the glory of God, in the face of Christ Jesus." (2 Corinthians 4:6) These words of the Apostle,

---

1 Palamas, *The Triads*, 1.3.22

indeed they are speaking of theosis, that union with God that all of humanity was created for, and surely are the emulator's of Christ's valor one with the Divine.

The soldiers of Mexico fled, but the Cristeros pushed forward without fear nor trepidation, because their enemies fought for transient things while they fought for that which is beyond the self. Surely can we say with these Cristeros,

> The righteous will rejoice when he sees the vengeance;
> he will bathe his feet in the blood of the wicked. (Psalm 58:10)

Where are the Christians today reciting these verses? They are ashamed of them, ashamed of their own history, and thus have no identity. People who say they are Christians, but have no connection with the history of the Faith, have no connection with the martyrs of the Faith, no connection with its warriors, its selfless combatants, have no identity. The lie of the devil is that we can create our own identities, but the only true identity is one founded in Christ. Without Christ, we are nothing but dry leaves ready to be dissipated through the vicious winds, we are "clouds without water, which are carried about by winds, trees of the autumn, unfruitful, twice dead, plucked up by the roots, raging waves of the sea, foaming out their own confusion; wandering stars, to whom the storm of darkness is reserved for ever." (Jude 3:12-13) It is in Christ that humanity has its identity, and in Christ is all of His warriors and martyrs. Thus to see a holy combatant of the Cross, is to see Christ. As Juan Donoso Cortes wrote:

> The Church militant, the Church suffering, and the Church triumphant are one in our Lord Jesus Christ, through the prayers of Christians in heaven, whose petitions descend as a beneficent dew upon those who combat

The martyr and Christ are one; the warrior and Christ are one, for both sacrifice, and wherever there is sacrifice, there is Christ. Every drop of saintly blood that drips upon the earth, is a reflection of the Cross, a small image of the blood of God that dripped in the victory over the Mountain of Death. The Crucifixion is not some mere execution, the Crucifixion is the war of all wars, for it is the war of humanity. It is the war between those who love humanity and those who want to destroy humanity; it is the war between those who emulate Christ and those who emulate the devil. When the Cristeros fought the enemies of God they saw themselves as in God, as participating in His divine nature. As the Cristero colonel, Ezequiel Mendoza Barragan said:

> You and I regret in a heartfelt way the death of those men who by faith gave up their lives, families, and other earthly interests; and shed their blood for the sake of God and our beloved homeland as true Christian martyrs do. Their blood, together with that of our Lord Jesus Christ and that of all the martyrs of the Holy Spirit, will afford us from God the Father the blessings we hope for on earth and in heaven.

The Cristeros did not see their war as secular, rather they knew that their struggle was simply a continuation of that war that commenced in Heaven, between God and His Angels and Satan and his demons. The Cristero warrior, Ezequiel Mendoza, knew of this spiritual war and comprehended the sublime truth that it was in the midst of the cause against the tyrannical government of Mexico:

> All those impious men who, from Cain to those who desolate the universe now, who appear to be great and powerful, who make a great noise and demand that men worship them, are only princes of error; they are nothing but beasts come up out of the abyss, but God has always sent truly great men to fight them, ever since the Archangel Michael in Heaven, all history is the history of this war. Woe to the tyrants who persecute Christ the King! They are the beasts in human shape of whom the Apocalypse speaks! ... Now the Calleses are pressing us, they say it is because we are bad, because we are stubborn in wanting to defend the honour and glory of Him who died naked on the highest Cross between two thieves, because He was the worst of all humans because He did not wish to submit to the supreme lord of the earth.

When we read of how Don Juan de Austria fought the Turks, how the soldiers in the Battle of Lepanto, in unison, exhorted the Virgin Mary to pray for them in the fight; when we read of how El Cid pushed forward against the Moors for the retaking of Catholic Spain; when we read of how the Crusaders valiantly retook entire regions from the Muslims for the glory of Christendom; when we read of how Romanos Diogenes sacrificed everything he had, even his very life, for the empire of Christianity; when we read of how Constantine crushed the pagan tyrants through the power and valor of the Cross, we must never forget that the flame of Christendom was never extinguished. Christendom is ever ready to be awakened in our hearts.

Hernan Cortez conquered Mexico and overthrew the Aztec empire. When he entered, the indigenous saw in him a humanity unknown to their souls which were so conditioned to sinister despotism. Catholic Spain brought to the Indians a new way—the Way—to life. And when they saw the righteous actions of these warriors of the Cross, they witnessed Christianity, they beheld the light. It was through arms and warfare that Christianity entered this land where God was unknown. Cortez commenced and led a revolt against the tyrannical Aztecs, and brought the people to freedom. Once the pagan bastions were destroyed, the Virgin of Guadalupe was seen by St. Juan Diego, and by the image that she imprinted on his poncho, Mexico was converted. If you say that the image of the Virgin of Guadalupe is "idolatrous," do not forget that what you see on the icon is what John beheld with his own eyes:

> And a great sign appeared in heaven: A woman clothed with the sun, and the moon under her feet, and on her head a crown of twelve stars (Revelation 12:1)

Do you not see, how the saints of Heaven work with the warriors of God to convert nations?

God used the Conquistadors to overthrow pagan despotism, and it was the Mother of God the Son who brought the nation to the Faith. And if you think that Mary cannot bring people to Christ, read in the holy Gospel where it says, "His mother saith to the waiters:

Whatsoever he shall say to you, do ye." (John 2:5) Mary commanded people to obey her Son, and so she can have entire nations follow Christ.

Mary asked her Son to make more wine, and He did. As St. Bernard of Clairvaux wrote: "that a woman should command the Son of God is a dignity without parallel." At the word of His mother, Christ made water into wine. Christ did not arise and do this miracle, until His mother told Him to do so. When she said to her Son, "They have no wine" (John 2:3), Christ told her, "Woman, what have I to do with thee? mine hour is not yet come." (John 2:4) Christ did not say this to chide her, rather He told her that the hour of His Passion has not yet come. But what does wine have to do with Christ's passion? Wine is symbolic of blood and death, thus why Christ tells His Father, "let this cup pass from me" (Matthew 26:39), and to Peter He says, "Shall I not drink the cup the Father has given me" (John 18:11). The cup is pictorially sublime, being filled with wine, that is, suffering and anguish.

Now, In order for wine to be made, grapes must first be crushed and squeezed under a winepress, and this is symbolic of the shedding of human blood in war, and it is this very imagery that God uses when describing the victory over His enemies. For in Lamentations we read:

> The Lord hath trodden under foot all my mighty men in the midst of me: he hath called an assembly against me to crush my young men: the Lord hath trodden the virgin, the daughter of Judah, as in a winepress. (Lamentations 1:5)

Thus, we know that the wine Christ made from the water represents blood, fury and slaughter. But what of the water? Water is symbolic of nations, of peoples. Hence the angel tells John,

> The waters which thou sawest, where the whore sitteth, are peoples, and multitudes, and nations, and tongues. (Revelation 17:15)

As Mary entered Mexico to finish the conquest by the Cross, and as she told her Son to make more wine, so will she in the end participate with her Son in the Final Crusade in which the Antichrist will be defeated, all the world will be conquered under Christendom, and the flood of the enemies of the Cross made into blood as grapes crushed under the winepress. As Deborah exhorted Barak to crush the Canaanite tyranny, Mary will help lead the armies of Christendom to victory. St. Paul speaks of "the coming of our Lord Jesus Christ, with all his saints." (1 Thessalonians 3:13)

Since all of the saints will be with Christ, then Mary will as well be with Him, and because she has a position so great (the Mother of our Salvation), it is not inadequate to sat that she will have a distinct position in the army of the Lord. As Jael, Deborah, Esther and Judith all had distinct positions in the wars and defense of Israel, so shall Mary in that Final Crusade when Christ will establish His Empire throughout all the world, vanquishing and conquering all of the governments of Islam, of paganism and heresy. The warriors of the Cross will be as burning flames, filled with zeal so great that it will be as a thousand suns before the enemy. St. Louis de Montfort describes these soldiers, and their leadership under St. Mary as such:

> They shall be a burning fire of the ministers of the Lord, who shall kindle the fire of divine love everywhere, and sicut sagittce in manu potentis—like sharp arrows in the hand of the powerful Mary to pierce her enemies. ... They shall carry on their shoulders the bloody standard of the cross, the crucifix in their right hand and the rosary in their left, the sacred names of Jesus and Mary in their hearts, and the modesty and mortification of Jesus Christ in their own behavior. These are the great men who shall come. But Mary shall be there by the order of the Most High, to extend His Empire over that of the impious, the idolaters, and the Mahometans.[2]

When the Christians fought the Muslims in the Battle of Lepanto, every soldier had a rosary in his hand; when the Christians fought the Muslims in the Crusades, they held up the Cross; when the Cristeros fought Mexican troops, they held up the Crucifix. As these battles were, so shall it be in the Final Crusade, except that in that time the flames of zeal will be at their highest, greater than anything the world has seen.

The Final Crusade will be between those who love and honor the Mother of Christ, and those who hate her. Read what St. John wrote of the end times, that "the dragon was angry against the woman: and went to make war with the rest of her seed, who keep the commandments of God, and have the testimony of Jesus Christ." (Revelation 12:17) The dragon—that is, the coming Islamic empire of the Antichrist—hates Mary and wars against her seed who are the Church. What John saw was a further expounding on what God said in Genesis: "I will put enmities between thee and the woman, and thy seed and her seed" (Genesis 3:15). Notice that the Scripture does not refer to an enemy, but enmities. The Scripture was saying that there will be many enmities, many wars and struggles between the seed of Mary, that is the Church of Apostolic succession, and the seed of Satan who despise Mary. As Montfort wrote:

> God has not only set an enmity but enmities, not simply between Mary and the devil, but between the race of the holy Virgin and the race of the devil[3]

What St. John wrote in regards to the enmity between the dragon and the woman, is an image of the entire history of Christendom, wherein tyrannies and despotisms war against those who revere Mary. The pagans warred against Christians who revered Mary, and Constantine defeated them. At around 250 AD, a hymn to Mary the Theotokos (God-bearer) was written that said:

> Beneath your compassion we take refuge,
> Theotokos!
> Our prayers, do not despise in necessities,
> but from danger deliver us,
> only pure, only blessed one.

---

2 Montfort, *True Devotion to Mary*, 1.56–59, ellipses mine
3 Montford, *True Devotion to Mary*, 1.53

CHRISTIANITY IS AT WAR: THE MANIFESTO FOR CHRISTIAN MILITANCY

This prayer was written at around the year 250, before the reign of Constantine in 312, which flies in the face of all those who argue that reverence to Mary is of more recent origin. Christians were revering Mary as they were being persecuted by pagan Rome, and it was these Christians who Constantine, guided and destined by God, defended and liberated. the Muslims for a millennia have been trying to destroy both the Catholic and the Orthodox Churches, both of whom revere the Mother of God.

When the tyrant Calles attempted to destroy Christianity in Mexico, it was not just some political move of despotism, but a manifestation of the eternal war that transcends all of the physical realm, of that war between the Mother of our Salvation and the devil, fueled by the desire to uproot the whole of the Faith, to prevent the people from worshipping Christ, from receiving the Sacraments, and from revering the Virgin of Guadalupe. St. John wrote the Book of Revelation and beheld the woman clothed with the sun, with the moon under her feet and her head crowned with twelve stars, as he lived imprisoned in Patmos for defying the tyranny of Domitian; and the lowly warriors in Mexico, with humble hearts melting under the candlelight of hope, beheld the same woman John once saw, as the Virgin of Guadalupe, when they defied the tyranny of Calles.

The story of the Cristeros is the story of Christendom, a small kindling flame in which lies the whole spirit of the Cross, and the way of self-sacrifice; a shadow of the greatest glory in which humble men become self-sacrificers and ascend to be greater than empires; a small image of the greatest glory, an eternal love that saves us all.

Read the stories of Christendom, and what you will find is that her greatest warriors were either Catholic or Orthodox. What does this tell us, but that the Church Militant is of the Church that can trace itself back to the Apostles? and only the Catholic and Orthodox can do this. The Church Militant on earth is the Catholic Church, and it is this Church that can boast of being of the lineage from Christ to the Apostles to now. Throughout history the Catholic Faith—the Western and the Eastern—has fought the forces of evil, for its founder is Christ, the Holy One Who came to destroy the works of the devil.

The mission of the Church's Founder is the same aspiration of His Church, and the war never ends, it is ceaseless until the final victory of Christ and His armies of saints. And who will be these saints but those in Heaven and on earth? They will all be together, they will be one army under Christ, and the victory will transcend all corporal happiness, all sadness, all despair, all tears.

To read the history of Christendom is to read the continuation of divine history. So many believe that divine history ends at the New Testament. But the Apostles were just as historical as they were spiritual. They had successors, and their successors had successors; Christianity's history continued, and in it were martyrs, warriors, persecutions, empires, kingdoms and wars. As Israel had her miracles, martyrs, persecutions and wars, so did Christendom have the same. Christianity is not a letter on a book, but a living reality in which the beautiful and dauntless works of selfless men manifest the sublime and eternal truth that ascends our souls to the mountain of heavenly Zion.

To read the history of Christian warfare is to realize that Christianity did not go underground until the Protestant Reformation, or that it only kept going through some obscure heretical groups here and there; to read the stories of Christian wars is to realize Christianity itself, it is to realize that the Faith flowed like a river from an eternal spring, building empires and appointing great fighters and emperors, queens and monastics who upheld justice and charity; it is to realize that the Faith consists of so many peoples united by Christ for the cause of one struggle: to liberate all of mankind and bring humanity into the light of the Cross; it is to realize that the sword of St. Peter was never disposed, but always remained in the sheath of the Church; it is to realize the perpetual story of Christianity's struggle, that it was continuously done by the hands of Catholics and Orthodox, and righteous men who honored the Catholic Faith. To read the history of Christendom and her wars, is to cease to be protestant.

After the British conquered Jerusalem in 1917, the areas General Lord Allenby—who was neither Catholic nor Orthodox—treaded the holy ground of the divinely destined city as a pensive pilgrim, as the warriors of the First Crusade were in their conquest of Jerusalem. On August 5th, 1918, a Dominican lay brother guided the soldiers in a pilgrimage led by a Catholic sergeant-major, carrying up high a silver crucifix, as the Crusaders of old had done, and as the Cristeros did in their battle against the enemies of the Cross. It was a carrying on of the beautiful custom of Christendom. In this event, Englishmen, Irishmen, Scots and Australians became one under the Cross and in the sacrificial emulation of their Lord. As the English monk, Dom Bede Camm, who was present in this procession, wrote:

> Down the steep hill from the gate into the Valley of Hinnom, and thence up the Mount of Evil Counsel on the other side, on the road to Bethlehem, as far as the eye could see, stretched the long ranks of soldier pilgrims, two deep—English, Scots, Irish, Australians, New Zealanders, Canadians, South Africans, British West Indians, and even some Catholics from the Indian Army. ... It was an inspiring sight that met one's eyes. The big church was packed. The general [Weston] and the officers had seats in the nave, but the choir, sanctuary, nave, aisles, were thronged with men, some sitting on the ground, others standing pressed together so closely that the priests had the greatest difficulty in getting to the altar. I shall never forget facing that great throng of bronzed men who had been through so many dangers, endured so many hardships in order to deliver Jerusalem. ...It was wonderful to hear them sing the familiar hymns during the Mass that followed. I have never heard anything like that Faith of Our Fathers shouted from fifteen hundred lusty throats, and it was even more wonderful to kneel in the hush and the stillness that fell on that great crowd when the bell rang out and the Host was raised. I don't wonder that the celebrant burst into tears and could hardly go on with the Mass. He told us afterwards that he had never been so moved in his life, and he wrote a detailed account of the pilgrimage to Rome, which (as I found later on) had delighted the Holy Father.

CHRISTIANITY IS AT WAR: THE MANIFESTO FOR CHRISTIAN MILITANCY

The unity of races, the enflaming of hearts, the rushing of warm tears from the overwhelming presence of the General Christ in the midst of His warriors, who embraced sacrifice and became one with divinity—this is of the essence of Christianity. Though Allenby was not Catholic officially, he fully welcomed this procession with grace and a pious heart, so much so that we can say that he was Catholic in spirit, and one can go so far as to say that he was more Catholic than most who take upon that title today.

The Final Crusade will not be limited to just Christians versus Muslims, but Catholic Christendom—in which Latin and Orthodox will be united—verses those who protest Catholic truth. Muslims are protestant, for they protest the Catholic teaching of the Trinity, of the Eucharist, of baptism and of the saints. I would go so far as to say that Muslims are some of the most zealous protestants, because they tried to conquer Rome numerous times, and managed to even sack Rome, and till this day they are bent on overtaking this holy city wherein lie the people, "called to be saints." (Romans 1:7) Do not forget how the protestants assisted the Ottoman Empire; do not forget how the reformers desired to see the destruction of Catholic Christendom; do not forget how protestant America, England and Australia gave weapons to the Indonesians so that the Muslims could slaughter the Catholics of East Timor simply because they wanted independence from an Islamic government; and don't forget that it was a protestant government, allied with protestant churches, organizations and institutions, that wanted to obliterate the Catholic Faith from Mexico.

To read the history of Christian war, is to know how much the world hates the Catholic Faith, and that which is the most hated, should be the one that we turn to, and not the most popular. To read the stories of Christian war, is to read the history of the Catholic Church. The holy wars were not just wars fought by armies; they were cosmic wars, they were the wars for the souls of humanity, they were our wars. Our war continues, but now we are being conquered by the forces of modernism and disorder. What is needed is not more diplomacy, rather an entire reconquista must be commenced over the world. All that is needed for the commencement of the restoration of Christendom is the will of the Universal Church; passion, enthusiasm, emphatic affirmation, the spark of hope's flame, this is all that is needed to commence the reconquest of the earth.

Christendom never ended, but is only waiting to be reawakened in our hearts. The Cristeros, the last of the Crusaders, the remnant of Christendom, the remaining flames that survived the floods of indifferentism, and who kept the ancient virtues of their ancestors lodged in their hearts, these men refused to bow the knee before the idol of diabolical conformity, and instead were determined to war against the enemies of humanity. For to war against Christ is to war against humanity itself, for in that most sublime day, when the Holy Virgin conceived the Savior of man, God became one with Humanity, and Mary gave birth to Emanuel, God with Us. The tyrant declared war on Christ, thus he made war against us. The war of the Cristeros is the war of us, it is the cosmic struggle of humanity, for it is the war for Love, the Creator of us all. Christ is Love, and in Christ, humanity becomes one with Love.

All of the slaves of the devil, they hate humanity and are bent on destroying us, enslaving us with depravity and deceiving us to destroy ourselves in the name of some false good. Their hatred for humanity is always deeply rooted in their hatred for Christ, for in Christ we are one, and it is the unity of humanity that they so despise. A humanity that is in disarray and full of divisions and chaos, is a humanity easily controlled, but a humanity united under the Cross, under zeal, under will and the Divine Love, is a humanity that is one with God, in and in God nothing is moved.

A humanity united under Truth Himself, is a humanity filled with the flames of will to war against the imperialism of delusion.

THE END